VATICAN COUNCIL II

More Postconciliar Documents

This edition authorized for distribution in the following areas only: North America, the Carribbean, South America, the Philippines and Japan.

Other volumes of Vatican Collection in preparation:

Volume III: MAJOR PAPAL DOCUMENTS,
            (John XXIII to John Paul II)

Volume IV: MAJOR DOCUMENTS FROM PAPAL
           COMMISSIONS

Vatican Collection
Volume II

VATICAN COUNCIL II

More Postconciliar Documents

General Editor,

AUSTIN FLANNERY, O.P.

THE LITURGICAL PRESS
Collegeville, MN 56321

Vatican Collection
Volume II

VATICAN II
MORE POST CONCILIAR DOCUMENTS

First Edition

Library of Congress Catalog Number: 82-74114

International Standard Book Number: 0-918344-16-6

Typeset by Roth Advertising. Printed in the U.S.A.

Costello Publishing Company, Inc.
P.O. Box 9
Northport, New York 11768

TABLE OF CONTENTS

1. For easier reference, all Documents are numbered consecutively and are referred to subsequently as D.I, D.2, etc.
2. When referring to an official Roman Document, it is customary to indicate: (a) its provenance (e.g., The Second Council of the Vatican, here referred to as Vatican II, or the Vatican department which issued it, such as the Sacred Congregation of Rites, here abbreviated to S.C.R.); (b) the first words of the original document, usually Latin (e.g., *Sacrosanctum concilium*); and (c) the date of its publication. As a help to the reader, these details are added underneath each title in the Table of Contents and at the commencement of each Document.
3. An alphabetically arranged key to the abbreviations used for Vatican departments is given after the Table of Contents.

Section 2: ECUMENISM

Section 3: THE RELIGIOUS LIFE

Section 4: ON MINISTRY

Section 5: CURRENT PROBLEMS

Section 6: EDUCATION

Section 7: THE SYNOD OF BISHOPS

ABBREVIATIONS FOR VATICAN CONGREGATIONS AND OTHER DEPARTMENTS

C.C.P.A.	Council for the Church's Public Affairs (split off from the Secretariat of State in 1967)
C.L.	Council for the Laity
C.P.I.C.L.	Consilium for the Proper Implementation of the Constitution on the Sacred Liturgy
C.R.R.J.	Committee for Religious Relations with the Jews
P.C.I.S.C.	Pontifical Council for the Instruments of Social Communication
S.A.P.	Sacred Apostolic Penitentiary
S.C.B.	Sacred Congregation for Bishops
S.C.C.	Sacred Congregation for the Clergy
S.C.C.E.	Sacred Congregation for Catholic Education
S.C.C.S.	Sacred Congregation for the Causes of the Saints (Sacred Congregation of Rites was split in 1969 into this and S.C.D.W., q.v.)
S.C.D.F.	Sacred Congregation for the Doctrine of the Faith (had been called S.S.C.H.O. until 1965: see A. 20)
S.C.D.S.	Sacred Congregation for the Discipline of the Sacraments (merged with S.C.D.W. to form S.C.S.D.W., q.v. in 1975)
S.C.D.W.	Sacred Congregation for Divine Worship (had been part of S.C.R. [q.v.] until 1969: see A. 26): merged with S.C.D.S. to form S.C.S.D.W., q.v., in 1975)
S.C.E.P.	Sacred Congregation for the Evangelization of Peoples, or Propaganda Fide
S.C.O.C.	Sacred Congregation for the Oriental Churches
S.C.R.	Sacred Congregation of Rites (in 1969 split into S.C.D.W. and S.C.C.S. See A. 26)
S.C.Rel.	Sacred Congregation for Religious (known as S.C.R.S.I. after 1967: See A. 24)
S.C.R.S.I.	Sacred Congregation for Religious and Secular Institutes (see previous entry)
S.C.S.D.W.	Sacred Congregation for the Sacraments and Divine Worship (S.C.D.S. and S.C.D.W. merged to form this in 1975: see A 34a)
S.P.U.C.	Secretariat for the Promotion of the Unity of Christians
S.S.	Secretariat of State, or Papal Secretariat (See note on C.C.P.A.)
S.S.C.H.O.	Supreme Sacred Congregation of the Holy Office (see S.C.D.F.)
S.T.A.S.	Supreme Tribunal of the Apostolic Signature
S.U.	Secretariat for Unbelievers

OTHER ABBREVIATIONS (BIBLIOGRAPHICAL AND OF THE DOCUMENTS OF VATICAN II)

A	Appendix: used here when referring to documents listed in the appendix, "Descriptive catalogue of the more important post-conciliar documents."
A.A.	*Apostolicam actuositatem*: The Decree on the Apostolate of the Laity
A.A.S.	*Acta Apostolicae Sedis*, the Vatican gazette, published a varying number of times each year. Carries the original text (mostly Latin) of the more important Vatican documents.
A.G.D.	*Ad gentes divinitus*: The Decree on the Church's Missionary Activity
A.S.S.	*Acta Sanctae Sedis*: title of A.A.S. up to 1 January, 1909
C.C.L.	Corpus Christianorum, Series Latina (Collected Works of Christian Writers, Latin Series)
C.D.	*Christus Dominus*; The Decree on the Pastoral Office of Bishops in the Church.
C.I.C.	*Codex Juris Canonici*: The Code of Canon Law.
Const.	Constitution
C.R.M.	*Commentarium pro Religiosis et Missionariis*: Commentary for Religious and Missionaries, a quarterly review published in Rome.
C.S.E.L.	*Corpus Scriptorum Ecclesiasticorum Latinorum*. Vienna, 1866 ff. (Collected Works of Latin Church Writers)
C.T.S.	Catholic Truth Society, London
D	Document: used here when referring to the documents published in the present collection, e.g. D.*1*, D.*2*, etc.
Denz.	H. Denzinger, *Enchiridion Symbolorum*, 32nd edition, 1963 (Collection of more important Church Documents)
Denz. Schön.	New edition of Denzinger, edited by A. Schönmetzer.
D.H.	*Dignitatis humanae*; The Declaration on Religious Liberty
D.V.	*Dei verbum*: The Dogmatic Constitution on Divine Revelation
E.V.	*Enchiridion Vaticanum*, 6 volume collection of official Catholic documents in original languages plus Italian translation, Edizioni Dehoniane, Bologna, Italy.
F.	Austin Flannery, O.P., *Vatican II: Conciliar and Postconciliar Documents*, being volume I of 'Vatican Collection.'
Funk	F. X. Funk, *Patres Apostolici*, two volumes, Tubingen, 1901

G.C.S.	*Die Grieschischen Christlichen Schriftsteller der ersten drei Jahrhunderte* (Greek Christian authors of the first three centuries; in fact the series extends further. Edited in Berlin since 1897.
G.E.	*Gravissimum educationis*: The Declaration on Christian Education
G.S.	*Gaudium et spes*: The Pastoral Constitution on the Church in the Modern World
I.M.	*Inter mirifica*: The Decree on the Means of Social Communication
L.G.	*Lumen gentium*: The Dogmatic Constitution on the Church
Mansi	J. D. Mansi, *Sacrorum conciliorum nova et amplissima collectio*, thirty-one volumes, (1757-1798)
M.G.	Migne, Greek; same as P.G.
M.L.	Migne, Latin; same as P.L.
N.A.	*Nostra aetate*: The Declaration on the Church's Relations with non-Christian Religions
Notitiae	A monthly, organ of the Sacred Congregation for Divine Worship, Vatican City
O.E.	*Orientalium ecclesiarum*: The Decree on the Catholic Oriental Churches
Oss. Rom.	*Osservatore Romano*, Vatican daily, published in Italian. English version, with same title, published weekly.
O.T.	*Optatam totius*: The Decree on the Training of Priests
P.C.	*Perfectae caritatis*: The Decree on the Up-to-date Renewal of Religious Life
P.G.	J. P. Migne, *Patrologia Graeca*, 161 volumes, 1857-1865
P.L.	J. P. Migne, *Patrologia Latina*, 217 volumes, 1878-1890
P.O.	*Presbyterorum ordinis*: The Decree on the Life and Ministry of Priests
S.C.	*Sacrosanctum concilium*: The Constitution on the Sacred Liturgy.
S.Ch.	Sources Chretienne (Christian Sources), edited by H. deLubac and J. Danielou, Paris
Sess.	Session (of an ecumenical council)
Summa Theol	*Summa Theologiae*, by St. Thomas Aquinas
U.R.	*Unitatis redintegratio*: The Decree on Ecumenism.

ABBREVIATIONS OF THE BOOKS OF THE BIBLE

Acts The Acts of the Apostles
Am. Amos
Apoc. Apocalypse (Revelation)
Bar. Baruch
Cant. Canticle of Canticles
  (S. of S.)
1 Chr. 1 Chronicles (Paralip.)
2 Chr. 2 Chronicles (Paralip.)
Col. Colossians
1 Cor. 1 Corinthians
2 Cor. 2 Corinthians
Dan. Daniel
Dt. Deuteronomy
Ec. Ecclesiastes
Eccl. Ecclesiasticus (Sirach)
Eph. Ephesians
1 Esd. 1 Esdras
2 Esd. 2 Esdras
Est. Esther
Ex. Exodus
Ezel. Ezekiel
Ezra Ezra
Gal. Galatians
Gen. Genesis
Hab. Habakkuk
Hag. Haggai (Aggeus)
Heb. Hebrews
Hos. Hosea (Osee)
Is. Isaiah
Jas. James
Jdt. Judith
Jer. Jeremiah
Jg. Judges
Jl. Joel
Jn. John (Gospel)
1 Jn. 1 John (Epistle)
2 Jn. 2 John
3 Jn. 3 John
Job Job
Jon. Jonah
Jos. Joshua
Jude Jude
1 Kg. 1 Kings

2 Kg. 2 Kings
Lam. Lamentations
Lev. Leviticus
Lk. Luke
1 Macc. 1 Maccabees
2 Macc. 2 Maccabees
Mal. Malachi
Mic. Micah
Mk. Mark
Mt. Matthew
Nah. Nahum
Neh. Nehemiah
Num. Numbers
Ob. Obadiah (Abdias)
Os. Osee (Hosea)
1 Paralip. 1 Paralipomenon
  (1 Chronicles)
2 Paralip. 2 Paralipomenon
  (2 Chronicles)
1 Pet. 1 Peter
2 Pet. 2 Peter
Phil. Philippians
Philem. Philemon
Pr. Proverbs
Ps. Psalms
Rev. Revelation (Apocalypse)
Rom. Romans
Ru. Ruth
1 Sam. 1 Samuel
2 Sam. 2 Samuel
Sir. Sirach (Ecclesiasticus)
S. of S. Song of Solomon
  (Canticle of Canticles)
Soph. Sophoniah (Zephaniah)
1 Th. 1 Thessalonians
2 Th. 2 Thessalonians
1 Tim. 1 Timothy
2 Tim. 2 Timothy
Tit. Titus
Tob. Tobit (Tobias)
Wis. Wisdom of Solomon
Zech. Zechariah
Zeph. Zephaniah (Sophoniah)

INTRODUCTION

This is a companion volume to *Vatican II: Conciliar and Postconciliar Documents*. It contains fifty-seven additional documents and for ease of reference the numbering of the documents commences where the previous volume left off.

The documents are grouped under seven headings and all of those in sections one through four and in section six are further applications or elucidations of conciliar documents. Some of the documents grouped under 'Current Problems' deal with the Council's unfinished business, some relate to matters discussed in the Pastoral Constitution on the Church in the Modern World and some deal with matters which have occasioned concern in the postconciliar period.

With regard to the seventh section, on the Roman Synods, it will be recalled that the first two synods produced their own definitive documents, one of them being the important and much-quoted 'Justice in the Modern World.' A different process, however, was adopted for subsequent synods. The synods of 1974, 1977 and 1980 all produced merely interim statements, or 'messages', leaving it to the pope of the time to issue a definitive statement in the light of each synod's deliberations and findings. This process has resulted in the publication of Pope Paul VI's underestimated (until fairly recently) *Evangelii Nuntiandi* and Pope John Paul II's *Catechesi Tradendae* and *Familiaris Consortio*. These three documents are included, as are the synodal documents of the first two ordinary synods.

The 'extraordinary' synod of 1969, on collegiality, presents a special difficulty. It did not produce a statement of its own, but had read to it and approved three reports on collegiality. Being in doubt about the status of these 'reports', I did not include them. The full texts, in Latin and Italian, are available in *Enchiridion Vaticanum* (see below), volume III, pages 996 to 1069.

Mention of underestimated documents brings to mind another of Pope Paul VI's contributions, his 'Apostolic Constitution on Penance,' *Paenitemini*, which was published in 1966, but which remained untranslated into English until 1973. I had thought of holding it over until volume III (see below), but decided to include it in the section on liturgy which also carries two documents on the sacrament of penance, all of which should prove useful as we prepare for the 1983 synod on 'Reconciliation and Penance in the Mission of the Church.'

The Introductions, or *praenotanda*, to liturgical books are of particular pastoral importance. The previous volume contained the 'General Introduction to the Roman Missal' and in this volume I have added the introductions to the rites of Christian Initiation, Infant Baptism, Penance, the Anointing and Pastoral Care of the Sick, the new Eucharistic Prayers for Children and for Reconciliation and the considerably expanded Introduction to the new (1981) edition of the Lectionary.

Of special importance for ecumenism is the 1975 document on 'Ecumenical Collaboration at the Regional, National and Local Level,' while for religious and for diocesan clergy there are two documents of particular pastoral importance: 'Directives for Mutual Relations Between Bishops and Religious in the Church' and 'Norms for Cooperation Among Local Churches and for a Better Distribution of the Clergy.' These are all included.

The 'General Catechetical Directory' is fairly easily available, but is not as well known as it deserves. I have included it, in a new translation, in the section on Education, together with the 1977 documents on 'Catholic Schools' and 'Lay Catholics in Schools: Witnesses to the Faith'.

Readers may be somewhat surprised that the great problems of global injustice, the arms race, the nuclear threat, atheism, the environment do not figure in section five, 'Current Problems.' The reason is that such problems are treated extensively in documents of different provenance from those in section five (the provenance of document number 102 is the exception in this section.) Thus, they are treated in the 'Pastoral Constitution on the Church in the Modern World' in volume I and in documents numbers 119, 120 and 122 in the present volume. They will also be treated in documents scheduled to be included in the two further volumes which are in preparation: volume III, *Major Papal Documents, John XXIII to John Paul II* (in addition to those in volumes I and II) and volume IV, *Documents from Papal Commissions*, of which there have been a considerable number, on topics such as justice and peace, the family, the Bible, theology, tourism, the laity, and so forth. The series of four volumes will be known as 'Vatican Collection'.

In preparing this and succeeding volumes, I have found the six-volume *Enchiridion Vaticanum* very helpful. It is the most complete collection of Catholic Church documents since the Council that I know of. Volume I contains the sixteen Council documents and the other five volumes take one up to the end of December, 1979. Volume VII, doubtless, is in preparation. Documents are given in their original language, with an Italian version—of documents not in Italian—on each facing page.

The publishers of *Enchiridion Vaticanum* are Edizioni Dehoniane, Via Nosadella 6, 40123 Bologna, Italy. Dominican Publications, Saint Saviour's, Dublin 1, Ireland, can supply sets, given sufficient notice.

Austin Flannery, O.P.
Editor *Doctrine and Life* and
   Religious Life Review
Saint Saviour's, Dublin 1, Ireland.
7 August, 1982.

FOREWORD

The implementation of the documents and directives of the Second Vatican Council depends in great measure on the direction given to us by official, postconciliar documents.

Volume one of "Vatican Council II: The Conciliar and Post-Conciliar Documents" began that directional function by gathering together the sixteen documents of the Council and the most important documentation of the following decade. The volume now in hand continues that service with an extensive collection of official documents that carries up to the present moment.

Included in the present volume are sixteen documents on liturgy, four on ecumenism, nine on religious life, six on ministry, three on education, thirteen on current problems and six from the Synod of Bishops. The work is under the able editorship of Austin Flannery, O.P.

It is our estimation that this work and its companion volume are major reference works for our time and that they are deserving of a place in the libraries of all who labor for the Lord with fidelity and love.

Timothy Cardinal Manning
Archbishop of Los Angeles

66

APOSTOLIC CONSTITUTION ON PENANCE*

Paul VI, *Paenitemini*, 17 February, 1966

"Be converted and believe in the Gospel."[1]

It seems to us that we must repeat these words of the Lord today at a moment when—with the closing of the Second Vatican Ecumenical Council—the Church continues along its path with more vigorous steps. Among the grave and urgent problems which in fact summon our pastoral concern, it seems to us that not the least is to remind our sons—and all religious men of our times—of the significance and importance of the divine precept of penitence. We are prompted to this by the fuller and more profound vision of the Church and its relationship with the world given us recently by the supreme ecumenical assembly.

During the council, in fact, the Church, in an effort to arrive at a more profound meditation on the mystery of itself, examined its own nature in all its dimensions and scrutinized its human and divine, visible and invisible, temporal and eternal elements. By first of all examining more thoroughly the link which binds it to Christ and His salvific action, it has underlined more clearly how all its members are called upon to participate in the work of Christ and therefore to participate also in His expiation.[2]

In addition, it has gained a clearer awareness that, while it is by divine vocation holy and without blemish,[3] it is defective in its members and in continuous need of conversion and renewal,[4] a renewal which must be implemented not only interiorly and individually but also externally and socially.[5]

Lastly, the Church has considered more attentively its role in the earthly city,[6] that is to say, its mission of showing man the right way to use earthly goods and to collaborate in the "consecration of the world." But at the same time it has considered more attentively its task of prompting its sons to that salutary abstinence which will forearm them against the danger of allowing themselves to be delayed by the things of this world in their pilgrimage toward their home in heaven.[7]

For these reasons we should like today to repeat to our sons the words spoken by Peter in his first speech after Pentecost: "Repent. . .then for the forgiveness of your sins."[8] And at the same time we want to repeat once more to all the nations of the earth the invitation of Paul to the Gentiles of Lystra: "Turn. . . to the living God."[9]

CHAPTER I

The Church—which during the council examined with greater attention its relations not only with the separated brethren but also with non-Christian religions—has noted with joy that almost everywhere and at all times penitence has held a place of great importance, since it is closely linked with the intimate sense of religion which pervades the life of most ancient peoples as well as with the more advanced expressions of the great religions connected with the progress of culture.[10]

In the Old Testament the religious sense of penitence is revealed with even greater richness. Even though man generally has recourse to it in the aftermath of sin to placate the wrath of God,[11] or on the occasion of grave calamities,[12] or when special dangers are imminent,[13] or in any case to obtain benefits from the Lord,[14] we can nevertheless establish that external penitential practices are accompanied by an inner attitude of "conversion," that is to say of condemnation of and detachment from sin and of striving toward God.[15] One goes without food or gives away his property (fasting is generally accompanied not only by prayer but also by alms[16]) even after sins have been forgiven and independently of a request for graces. One fasts or applies physical discipline to "chastize one's own soul,"[17] to "humble oneself in the sight of his own God,"[18] to "turn one's face toward Jehovah,"[19] to "dispose oneself to prayer,"[20] to "understand" more intimately the things which are divine,[21] or to prepare oneself for the encounter with God.[22]

Penance therefore—already in the Old Testament—is a religious, personal act which has as its aim love and surrender to God: fasting for the sake of God, not for one's own self.[23] Such it must remain also in the various penitential rites sanctioned by law. When this is not verified, the Lord is displeased with His people: "Today you have not fasted in a way which will make your voice heard on high. . . . Rend your heart and not your garments, and return to the Lord your God."[24]

The social aspect of penitence is not lacking in the Old Testament. In fact, the penitential liturgies of the Old Covenant are not only a collective awareness of sin but constitute in reality a condition for belonging to the people of God.[25]

We can further establish that penitence was represented even before Christ as a means and a sign of perfection and sanctity. Judith,[26] Daniel,[27] the prophetess Anna and many other elect souls served God day and night with fasting and prayers,[28] and with joy and cheerfulness.[29]

Finally, we find among the just ones of the Old Testament those who offered themselves to satisfy with their own personal penitence for the sins of the community. This is what Moses did in the 40 days when he fasted to placate the Lord for the guilt of his unfaithful people.[30] This above all is how the character of the Servant Jehovah is presented, "who took on our infirmities" and in whom "the Lord hath laid on Him the iniquity of us all."[31]

All this, however, was but a foreshadowing of things to come.[32] Penitence—required by the inner life, confirmed by the religious experience of mankind and the object of a particular precept of divine revelation—assumes "in Christ and the Church" new dimensions infinitely broader and more profound.

Christ, who always practiced in His life what He preached, before beginning His ministry spent 40 days and 40 nights in prayer and fasting, and began His public mission with the joyful message: "The kingdom of God is at hand." To this He added the command: "Repent and believe in the Gospel."[33] These words constitute, in a way, a compendium of the whole Christian life.

The kingdom of God announced by Christ can be entered only by a "change of heart" ("metanoia"), that is to say through that intimate and total change and renewal of the entire man—of all his opinions, judgments and decisions—which takes place in him in the light of the sanctity and charity of God, the sanctity and charity which were manifested to us in the Son and communicated fully.[34]

The invitation of the Son to "metanoia" becomes all the more inescapable inasmuch as He not only preaches it but Himself offers an example. Christ, in fact, is the supreme model for those doing penance. He willed to suffer punishment for sins which were not His but those of others.[35]

In the presence of Christ man is illumined with a new light and consequently recognizes the holiness of God and the gravity of sin.[36] Through the word of Christ a message is transmitted to him which invites him to conversion and grants forgiveness of sins. These gifts he fully attains in baptism. This sacrament, in fact, configures him to the passion, death and resurrection of the Lord,[37] and places the whole future of the life of the baptized under the seal of this mystery.

Therefore, following the Master, every Christian must renounce himself, take up his own cross and participate in the sufferings of Christ. Thus transformed into the image of Christ's death, he is made capable of meditating on the glory of the resurrection.[38] Furthermore, following the Master, he can no longer live for himself,[39] but must live for Him who loves him and gave Himself for him.[40] He will also have to live for his brethren, completing "in his flesh that which is lacking in the sufferings of Christ . . . for the benefit of his body, which is the church."[41]

In addition, since the Church is closely linked to Christ, the penitence of the individual Christian also has an intimate relationship of its own with the whole ecclesial community. In fact, not only does he receive in the bosom of the Church through baptism the fundamental gift of "metanoia," but this gift is restored and reinvigorated, through the sacrament of penance, in those members of the Body of Christ who have fallen into sin. "Those who approach the sacrament of penance receive from the mercy of God forgiveness for offenses committed against Him and at the same time become reconciled with the Church on which they have inflicted a wound by sinning, and the Church cooperates in their conversion with charity, example and prayer."[42] And in the Church, finally, the little acts of penitence imposed each time in the sacrament become a form of participation in a special way in the infinite expiation of Christ to join to the sacramental satisfaction itself every other action he performs, his every suffering and sorrow.[43]

Thus the task of bearing in his body and soul the death of the Lord[44] affects the whole life of the baptized person at every instant and in every aspect.

CHAPTER II

The preeminently interior and religious character of penitence and the new wondrous aspects which it assumes "in Christ
and in the Church" neither excludes nor lessens in any way the
external practice of this virtue, but on the contrary reaffirms its
necessity with particular urgency[45] and prompts the Church—
always attentive to the signs of the times—to seek, beyond fast
and abstinence, new expressions more suitable for the realization, according to the character of various epochs, of the precise
goal of penitence.

True penitence, however, cannot ever prescind from physical
ascetism as well. Our whole being, in fact, body and soul, (indeed the whole of nature, even animals without reason, as Holy
Scripture often points out)[46] must participate actively in this
religious act whereby the creature recognizes divine holiness and
majesty. The necessity of the mortification of the flesh also
stands clearly revealed if we consider the fragility of our nature,
in which, since Adam's sin, flesh and spirit have contrasting
desires.[47] This exercise of bodily mortification—far removed
from any form of stoicism—does not imply a condemnation of
the flesh which sons of God deign to assume.[48] On the contrary,
mortification aims at the "liberation"[49] of man, who often finds
himself, because of concupiscence, almost chained[50] by his own
senses. Through "corporal fasting"[51] man regains strength and
the "wound inflicted on the dignity of our nature by in-
temperance is cured by the medicine of a salutary abstinence."[52]

Nevertheless, in the New Testament and in the history of the
Church—although the duty of doing penance is motivated
above all by participation in the sufferings of Christ—the
necessity of an ascetism which chastises the body and brings it
into subjection is affirmed with special insistence by the example
of Christ Himself.[53]

Against the real and ever recurring danger of formalism and
pharisaism the Divine Master in the New Covenant openly condemned—and so have the Apostles, Fathers and supreme pontiffs—any form of penitence which is purely external. The intimate relationship which exists in penitence between the external act, inner conversion, prayer and works of charity is affirmed
and widely developed in the liturgical texts and authors of every
era.[54]

CHAPTER III

Therefore the Church—while it reaffirms the primacy of the religious and supernatural values of penitence (values extremely suitable for restoring to the world today a sense of the presence of God and of His sovereignty over man and a sense of Christ and His salvation)[55]—invites everyone to accompany the inner conversion of the spirit with the voluntary exercise of external acts of penitence:

A—It insists first of all that the virtue of penitence be exercised in persevering faithfulness to the duties of one's state in life, in the acceptance of the difficulties arising from one's work and from human coexistence, in a patient bearing of the trials of earthly life and of the utter insecurity which pervades it.[56]

B—Those members of the Church who are stricken by infirmities, illnesses, poverty or misfortunes, or who are persecuted for the love of justice, are invited to unite their sorrows to the suffering of Christ in such a way that they not only satisfy more thoroughly the precept of penitence but also obtain for the brethren a life of grace and for themselves that beatitude which is promised in the Gospel to those who suffer.[57]

C—The precept of penitence must be satisfied in a more perfect way by priests, who are more closely linked to Christ through sacred character, as well as by those who in order to follow more closely the abnegation of the Lord and to find an easier and more efficacious path to the perfection of charity practice the evangelical counsels.[58]

The Church, however, invites all Christians without distinction to respond to the divine precept of penitence by some voluntary act, apart from the renunciation imposed by the burdens of everyday life.[59]

To recall and urge all the faithful to the observance of the divine precept of penitence, the Apostolic See intends to reorganize penitential discipline with practices more suited to our times. It is up to the bishops—gathered in their episcopal conferences—to establish the norms which, in their pastoral solicitude and prudence, and with the direct knowledge they have of local conditions, they consider the most opportune and efficacious. The following, however, is established:

In the first place, Holy Mother Church, although it has always observed in a special way abstinence from meat and fasting, nevertheless wants to indicate in the traditional triad of "prayer—fasting—charity" the fundamental means of complying with the divine precepts of penitence. These means were the same throughout the centuries, but in our time there are special reasons whereby, according to the demands of various localities, it is necessary to inculcate some special form of penitence in preference to others.[60] Therefore, where economic well-being is greater, so much more will the witness of asceticism have to be given in order that the sons of the Church may not be involved in the spirit of the "world,"[61] and at the same time the witness of charity will have to be given to the brethren who suffer poverty and hunger beyond any barrier of nation or continent.[62] On the other hand, in countries where the standard of living is lower, it will be more pleasing to God the Father and more useful to the members of the Body of Christ if Christians—while they seek in every way to promote better social justice—offer their suffering in prayer to the Lord in close union with the Cross of Christ.

Therefore, the Church, while preserving—where it can be more readily observed—the custom (observed for many centuries with canonical norms) of practicing penitence also through abstinence from meat and fasting, intends to ratify with its prescriptions other forms of penitence as well, provided that it seems opportune to episcopal conferences to replace the observance of fast and abstinence with exercises of prayer and works of charity.

In order that all the faithful, however, may be united in a common celebration of penitence, the Apostolic See intends to establish certain penitential days and seasons[63] chosen among those which in the course of the liturgical year are closer to the paschal mystery of Christ[64] or might be required by the special needs of the ecclesial community.[65]

Therefore, the following is declared and established:

I. 1. By divine law all the faithful are required to do penance.
   2. The prescriptions of ecclesiastical law regarding penitence are totally reorganized according to the following norms:

II. 1. The time of Lent preserves its penitential character. The days of penitence to be observed under obligation throughout the Church are all Fridays and Ash Wednesday, that is to say the first days of "Grande Quaresima" (Great Lent), according to the diversity of the rites. Their substantial observance binds gravely. (See note at end.)
   2. Apart from the faculties referred to in VI and VIII regarding the manner of fulfilling the precept of penitence on such days, abstinence is to be observed on every Friday which does not fall on a day of obligation, while abstinence and

fast are to be observed on Ash Wednesday or, according to local practice, on the first day of 'Great Lent' and on Good Friday (see note at end).

III. 1. The law of abstinence forbids the use of meat, but not of eggs, the products of milk or condiments made of animal fat.

    2. The law of fasting allows only one full meal a day, but does not prohibit taking some food in the morning and evening, observing—as far as quantity and quality are concerned—approved local custom.

IV. To the law of abstinence those are bound who have completed their 14th year of age. To the law of fast those of the faithful are bound who have completed their 21st year and up until the beginning of their 60th year.

As regards those of a lesser age, pastors of souls and parents should see to it with particular care that they are educated to a true sense of penitence.

V. All privileges and indults, whether general or particular, are abrogated with these norms, but nothing is changed either regarding the vows of any physical or moral person or regarding the constitutions and rules of any approved religious congregation or institute.

VI. 1. In accordance with the conciliar decree Christus Dominus regarding the pastoral office of bishops, number 38,4, it is the task of episcopal conferences to:

A. Transfer for just cause the days of penitence, always taking into account the Lenten season;

B. Substitute abstinence and fast wholly or in part with other forms of penitence and especially works of charity and the exercises of piety.

    2. By way of information, episcopal conferences should communicate to the Apostolic See what they have decided on the matter (See note at end.)

VII. 1. While the faculties of individual bishops of dispensing, according to the decree Christus Dominus, number 8b, remain unchanged, pastors also for just cause and in accordance with the prescriptions of the Ordinary may grant to individual faithful as well as individual families dispensation or commutation of abstinence and fast into other pious practices. The superior of a religious house or clerical institute enjoys the same faculties for his subjects.

VIII. In the Eastern rites it is the right of the patriarch, together with the synod or supreme authority of every rite, together with the council of hierarchs, to determine the days of fast and abstinence in accordance with the conciliar decree on the Eastern rites, number 23.

IX. 1. It is strongly desired that bishops and all pastors of souls, in addition to the more frequent use of the sacrament of penance, promote with zeal, particularly during the Lenten season, extraordinary practices of penitence aimed at expiation and impetration.

2. It is strongly recommended to all the faithful that they keep deeply rooted in their hearts a genuine Christian spirit of penitence to spur them to accomplish works of charity and penitence.

X. 1. These prescriptions which, by way of exception, are promulgated by means of L'Osservatore Romano, become effective on Ash Wednesday of this year, that is to say on the 23rd of the present month.

2. Where particular privileges and indults have been in force until now—whether general or particular of any kind—"vacatio legis" [suspension of the law] for six months from the day of promulgation is to be regarded as granted.

We desire that these norms and prescriptions for the present and future be established and effective notwithstanding—inasmuch as is necessary—apostolic constitutions and regulations issued by our predecessors and all other prescriptions, even if worthy of particular mention and revocation.

---

* Translation reproduced by kind permission of the Incorporated Catholic Truth Society, 38–40 Eccleston Square, London SWIV IPD.
1. Mark 1:15.
2. Cf. Dogmatic Constitution on the Nature of the Church (Second Vatican Council), no. 2, and no. 8; and Decree on the Lay Apostolate, no. 1.
3. Cf. Eph. 5:27.
4. Cf. Constitution on the Nature of the Church, no. 8 and Decree on Ecumenism, nos. 4, 7 and 8.
5. Cf. Constitution on the Liturgy, no. 110.
6. Cf. Constitution on the Church in the Modern World, throughout, but especially no. 40.
7. Cf. 1 Cor. 7:31; Rom. 12:2; Decree on Ecumenism, no. 6; Constitution on the Nature of the Church, nos. 8 and 9; Constitution on the Church in the Modern World, nos. 37, 39 and 93.
8. Acts 2:38.
9. Acts 14:14; Cf. Pope Paul VI's speech to United Nations of Oct. 4, 1965: AAS 57 (1965), p. 885.
10. Cf. Declaration on Church's Relations with Non-Christian Religions, nos. 2 and 3.

11. Cf. 1 Sam. 7:6; 1 Kings 21:20-21, 27; Jer. 3:3, 7, 9; John 1:2; 3:4-5.
12. Cf. 1 Sam. 31:13; 2 Sam. 1:12; 3:35; Baruch 1:2, 5; Judith 20:25-26.
13. Cf. Judith 4:8, 12; 8:10-16; Esther 3:15; 4:1, 16; Psalms 34:13; 2 Chron. 20:3.
14. Cf. 1 Sam. 14:24; 2 Sam. 12:16, 22; Esd. 8:21.
15. In reference cited above, need for interior penitence is clearly illustrated: Cf. 1 Sam. 7:3; Jer. 36:6-7; Baruch 1:17-18.; Judith 8:16-17; John 3:8; Zach. 8:9, 21.
16. Cf. Is. 58:6-7; Tob. 12:8-9.
17. Cf. Levit. 16:31.
18. Cf. Dan. 10: 12; Esd. 8:21.
19. Cf. Dan. 9:3.
20. Cf. *ibid.*
21. Cf. Dan. 10:12.
22. Cf. Exodus 34:28.
23. Cf. Zach. 7:5.
24. Is. 58:4; Joel 2:13. Cf. Is. 58:3-7 throughout; Cf. Amos 5 throughout; Is. 1:13-20; Jer. 14:12; Joel 2:12-18; Zach. 7:4-14; Tobias 12:8; Psalms 50:18-19; etc.
25. Cf. Lev. 23:29.
26. Cf. Judith 8:6.
27. Cf. Dan. 10:3.
28. Cf. Luke 2:37; Eccles. 31:12, 17-19; 37:32-34.
29. Cf. Dan. 1:12, 15; Judith 8:6, 7; Matt. 6:17.
30. Cf. Deut. 9:9, 18; Exod. 24:18.
31. Cf. Is. 53:4-11.
32. Cf. Heb. 10:1.
33. Mark 1:15.
34. Cf. Heb. 1:2; Col. 1:19 and throughout; Eph. 1:23 and throughout.
35. Cf. St. Thomas, Summa Theol., III, q. XV, a. 1, ad. 5.
36. Cf. Luke 5:8 and 7:36-50.
37. Cf. Rom. 6:3-11; Col. 2:11-15; 5:1-4.
38. Cf. Phil. 3:10-11; Rom. 8:17.
39. Cf. Rom. 6:10; 14:8; 2 Cor. 5:15; Phil. 1:21.
40. Gal. 2:20; Cf. Constitution on the Nature of the Church, no. 7; also Gal. 4:19; Phil. 3:21; 2 Tim. 2:11; Eph. 2:6; Col. 2:12 etc.; Rom. 8:17.
41. Cf. Col. 1:24; Decree on Church's Missionary Activity, no. 36; Decree on Seminaries, no. 2.
42. Cf. Constitution on the Nature of the Church, no. 11; James 5:14, 16; Rom. 8:17; Col. 1:24; 2 Tim. 2:11-12; 1 Peter 4:13; Decree on Priestly Life and Ministry, nos. 5 and 6.
43. Cf. St. Thomas, Quaestiones Quodlib., III, q. XIII, a. 28.
44. Cf. 2 Cor. 4:10.
45. For example: a) with regard to priests, cf. Decree on Priestly Ministry and Life, no. 16; b) regarding spouses, cf. Constitution on the Church in the Modern World, no. 49; also cf. same constitution, no. 52; cf. Pius XII, speech to cardinals, archbishops, bishops, etc., of Nov. 2, 1950: *AAS* 17 (1950), pp. 786–788; cf. Justin, Dialogue with Triphon, 141: 2-3 (MG 6: 797-799).
46. Cf. John 3:7-8.
47. Cf. Gal. 5:16-17; Rom. 7:23.
48. Cf. Roman Martyrology for the Vigil of Christmas; 1 Tim. 4:1-5; Phil. 4:8; Origen, Against Celsus 7:36 (MG 11:1472).

49. Cf. Lenten Liturgy, throughout; and footnote no. 53 of this document, part B.

50. Cf. Rom. 7:23.

51. Cf. Roman Missal, Preface for Lent: "corporali jejunio vitia comprimis, mentem elevas, virtutem largiris . . ."

52. Cf. ibid., Collect for Thursday after First Sunday of the Passion (Passion Sunday).

53. A) In the New Testament: 1) words and example of Christ: Matt. 17:20 (cf. Mark 9:28); Matt. 5:29-30; 11:21-24; 3:4; 11:7-11; and 4:2; Mark 1:13; Luke 4:12; cf. Matt. 8:18-22; 2) witness and doctrine of St. Paul: 1 Cor. 9:24-27; Gal. 5:16; 2 Cor. 6:5; ibid. 11:27; 3) in the Early Church: Acts 13:3; ibid. 14:22; etc.

B) Among the Fathers: several references arranged according to order of time: Didache 1:4 (F. X. Funk, Patres Apostolici, ed. 2, Tubingen, 1901, 1:2); Clement of Rome, 1 Cor. 7:4 and 8:5 (Funk 1:108-110); 2 Clement 16:4 (Funk 2:204); ibid. 8:1-3 (Funk 1:192-194); Aristides, Apologia 15:9 (Goodspeed, Goettingen, 1914, 21); Hermas, Pastor, Sim. 5:1, 3-5 (Funk 1:530); cf. ibid. Sim. 7:2-5 (Funk 1:554); Tertullian, DePaenitentia 9 (ML 1:1243-1244); Tertullian, De Jejunio 17 (ML 2:978); Origen, Homeliae in Lev, Hom. 10:2 (MG 12:528); St. Athanasius, De Virginitate, 6 (MG 28:257); ibid., 7, 8 (MG 28:260, 261); Basil, Homeliae, Hom. 2:5 (MG 31:192); Ambrose, De Virginitate, 3:2, 5 (ML 16:221); idem, De Elia et Jejunio 2:2, 3:4, 8:22 and 10:33 (ML 14:698, 708); Jerome, Epistola 22:17 (ML 22:404); idem, Epistola 130:10 (ML 22:1115; Augustine, Sermo 208:2 (ML 38:1045); idem, Epistola 211:8 (ML 33:960); Cassian, Collationes 21:13, 14, 17 (ML 49:1187); Nilus, De Octo Spiritibus Malitiae 1 (MG 79:1145); Diadochus Photicensis, Capita Centum de Perfectione Spirituali 47 (MG 65: 1182); Leo the Great, Sermo 12:4 (ML 54:171); idem, Sermo 86:1 (ML 54:437-438); Leonine Sacramentary, Preface for Autumn (ML 55:112).

54. A) In the New Testament: Luke 18:12; Cf. Matt. 6:16-18 and 15:11; Hebrews 13:9; Romans 14:15-23.

B) Among the Fathers: cf. footnote no. 53, B.

55. Cf. Constitution on the Church in the Modern World, nos. 10 and 41.

56. Constitution on the Nature of the Church, nos. 34, 36 and 41; cf. Constitution on the Church in the Modern World, no. 4.

57. Ibid., no. 41.

58. Cf. Decree on Priestly Ministry and Life, nos. 12, 13, 16 and 17; Constitution on the Nature of the Church, no. 41; Decree on Missionary Activity of the Church, no. 24; Constitution on the Nature of the Church, no. 42; Decree on Renovation of the Religious Life, nos. 7, 12, 13, 14 and 25; Decree on Seminaries, nos. 2, 8 and 9.

59. Cf. Constitution on the Nature of the Church, no. 42; Constitution on the Liturgy, nos. 9, 12 and 104.

60. Cf. Ibid., no. 110.

61. Cf. Romans 12:2; Mark 2:19; Matt. 9:15; Constitution on the Church in the Modern World, no. 37.

62. Cf. 1 Cor. 16:1; Romans 15:26-28; Gal. 2:10; 2 Cor. 8:9; Acts 24:17; Constitution on the Church in the Modern World, no. 88.

63. Cf. Constitution on the Liturgy, no. 105.

64. Cf. Ibid., no. 107. Regarding the Lenten season as a preparation for celebrating the Paschal Mystery, cf. ibid., no. 109. Concerning the

celebration of the Paschal Mystery each week, cf. ibid., no. 102 and
106; Eusebius, De Solemnitate Paschali, 12 (MG 24:705); idem, ibid.,
no. 7 (MG 24:701); John Chrysostom, In Epistola I ad Tim. 5:3 (MG
62:529-530). Epistola I ad Tim. 5:3 (MG 62:529-530).
65. Cf. vg. in Acts 13:1-4 (on fasting of the Antioch Church, when Paul
and Barnabas were sent to announce the Gospel to the Gentiles).

The Lenten Fast:
Editor's Note

Since the promulgation of *Caenitemini*, national episcopal conferences
have changed the regulations on fast and abstinence during Lent and on
Fridays, in accordance with rule number VI on p. 8. Such local regulations will be familiar to readers of this volume, or can be easily ascertained.   A.F.

67

APOSTOLIC CONSTITUTION ON THE SACRAMENT OF THE ANOINTING OF THE SICK*

Paul VI, *Sacram unctionem infirmorum*,
30 November, 1972

According to the teaching of the Catholic Church, the anointing of the sick is one of the seven New Testament sacraments instituted by Christ. There is reference to it in Mark (6:13) and the apostle James, the brother of the Lord, recommends it to the faithful. He says:'Is there anyone sick among you? He should ask for the presbyters of the Church. They in turn are to pray over him, anointing him with oil in the Name of the Lord. This prayer uttered in faith will reclaim the one who is ill, and the Lord will restore him to health. If he has committed any sins, forgiveness will be his.' (James 5:14-15)[1]

From earliest times the Church's tradition, especially its liturgical tradition, in East and West, testifies to the existence of the rite of anointing. Especially noteworthy is the letter of our predecessor, Innocent I, to Decentius bishop of Gubbio and the prayer used for blessing the oil of the sick: 'Send forth, Lord, your holy Spirit, the Paraclete,' which is inserted into the canon of the Mass and is still preserved in the Roman pontifical. . . .

The Council of Florence listed the essential elements of the anointing of the sick, the Council of Trent affirmed that it was of divine institution. It expounded Saint James's teaching concerning holy anointing, especially with regard to the central reality of the sacrament and its effects: 'The central reality is the grace of the Holy Spirit. The anointing removes any remaining sin and its remnants. It brings relief and strength to the soul of sick persons, making them greatly confident in the divine mercy. Thus sustained, they can more easily bear their illness, be better able to withstand the temptations of the devil in ambush (Genesis 3:15) and sometimes they regain bodily strength, if this will contribute to the health of the soul.' (Decree for the Armenians). The Council also declared that Saint James's words make it quite clear that 'this anointing is to be administered to

13

the sick, especially to those who appear to be dying, for which reason it is also called the sacrament of the dying.' Lastly, it declared that the appropriate minister of the sacrament is a priest.

The Second Vatican Council says: 'Extreme Unction,' which may also and more fittingly be called 'Anointing of the Sick,' is not a sacrament for those only who are at the point of death. Hence, as soon as anyone of the faithful begins to be in danger of death from sickness or old age, the fitting time for him to receive the sacrament has certainly arrived already. (Const. on the Liturgy, 73)

The sacrament is of concern to the whole Church: 'By the sacred anointing of the sick and the prayer of the priests the whole Church commends those who are ill to the suffering and glorified Lord that he may raise them up and save them. And indeed she exhorts them to contribute to the good of the People of God by freely uniting themselves to the passion and death of Christ.' (Const. on the Church, 11). . . .

The sacrament of anointing of the sick is administered to those who are dangerously ill. They are to be anointed on the forehead and hands with blessed olive oil or, as circumstances suggest, with another oil extracted from plants. . . .

In case of necessity, a single anointing on the forehead, or on some other part of the body as circumstances suggest, will suffice. The entire formula is to be pronounced.

The sacrament may be repeated if the sick person recovers subsequently only to become ill again, or if the danger becomes more acute during the same illness. . . .

*The translation, by A. F., is of the main portion of the text. Latin original in *AAS* 65 (1973), 5-9.
1. Council of Trent, Session XIV, Extreme Unction, chapter 1.

68

INTRODUCTION TO THE RITE OF ANOINTING AND TO THE PASTORAL CARE OF THE SICK*

S.C.D.W., *Hominum dolores*, 7 December, 1972

THE MEANING OF HUMAN SICKNESS IN THE MYSTERY OF SALVATION

1. People have always had to bear the heavy and paradoxical burden of illness and pain. Christians, like other people, suffer illness and pain, but their faith helps them to achieve a better understanding of the mystery of suffering and to bear their pain with greater fortitude. Christ's words show them that illness has a meaning and a value for their own salvation and that of the world. They are also aware that during his life Christ loved the sick and that he often healed them.

2. While sickness is closely connected with man's sinful state, it would be wrong to see it as punishment on man for his sins (see John 9:3). Christ was himself without sin, yet, in fulfillment of the prophecy of Isaiah he underwent his own passion and came to know human sorrow (see Isaiah 53:4-5). Christ still suffers and undergoes torments whenever we his followers suffer. If we realize that the sufferings that come our way are a preparation for an eternal life in glory they will seem short-lived and even more bearable (see 2 Cor., 4:17).

3. It is part of God's plan that we should combat all illness and should prudently seek the blessings of good health. We will thus be able to play our part in secular society and in the Church. However, we should always be willing to complete what is lacking in the sufferings of Christ for the salvation of the world, as we look towards the liberation of all creation in the glory of the sons of God (see Col. 1:24; Rom. 8:19-21).

Further, sick people have this role in the Church: to put others in mind of the essential, the higher things, reminding them that through the mystery of Christ's death and resurrection our mortal life is given back to us.

4. Sick people are not left to combat their illness alone. It is the duty of doctors and all who have taken it on themselves to succour the sick to do whatever they deem necessary to help them both physically and spiritually. When they do this they are fulfilling Christ's command to visit the sick, for it was Christ's intention that the whole person should be their concern and that they should offer both physical relief and spiritual comfort.

THE CELEBRATION OF THE SACRAMENTS OF THE SICK

A. The Anointing of the Sick

5. The sacrament of anointing is the prolongation of the concern which, as the gospels tell us, our Lord himself showed for the bodily and spiritual welfare of the sick and which he commended to his followers. Christ is the source of the sacrament and it is mentioned in the Epistle of James. He relates how the Church by the anointing of the sick and the prayer of the priests commends the sick to the suffering and glorified Lord, that he might raise them up and save them (see James 5:14-16). The Church, further, urges the sick to help improve the lot of God's People by associating themselves freely with the passion and death of Christ (see Rom. 8:17).

People who are seriously ill have special need of the help of divine grace in what is an anxious time, lest they become dispirited, beset by temptations and prone to a diminution of their faith.

This is why Christ strengthens and supports with the sacrament of anointing those who are ill.

The essentials of the sacrament are the laying on of hands by the priests of the Church, the prayer of faith and the anointing of the sick person with oil sanctified by God's blessing. The rite signifies and imparts the grace of the sacrament.

6. The sacrament gives to the sick person the grace of the Holy Spirit by which the whole person is made healthy, is encouraged to trust in God and is given the strength to resist the temptations of the Evil One and avoid succumbing to anxiety about death. The sick are thus able not only to bear their affliction with courage but also to struggle to overcome it. Restoration to health may follow the reception of the sacrament if this will be in the interests of the sick person's salvation. If such be needed, the sacrament also offers the sick person the forgiveness of sin and the completion of Christian penance.

7. The anointing of the sick includes the prayer of faith (see

James 5:15). This is important for both minister, and especially, recipient of the sacrament. It is their faith and the faith of the Church which will save those who are ill, a faith which looks back to the death and resurrection of Christ, the source of the efficacy of the sacrament (see James 5:15) and which looks forward to the future kingdom which the sacraments promise.

THE PEOPLE TO BE ANOINTED

8. The Letter of Saint James states that the sick should be anointed in order to raise them up and to save them. It is a matter for special concern that those who are dangerously ill through sickness or old age should receive this sacrament.

A prudent or probable judgment about the seriousness of the illness is all that is required. There is no reason to be scrupulous in the matter, but if necessary a doctor may be consulted.

9. The sacrament may be imparted again if the sick person recovers subsequently or if the danger becomes greater in the course of the same illness.

10. A sick person should be anointed before surgery whenever the surgery is necessitated by a dangerous illness.

11. Elderly people may be anointed if they are weak, though not dangerously ill.

12. Sick children may be anointed if they are sufficiently mature to be comforted by the sacrament.

13. The faithful should be taught in public and in private to ask for anointing and, when the time for anointing comes, to accept it with total faith and devotion, not misusing the sacrament by postponing its reception. All who have the care of the sick should be taught the meaning and purpose of anointing.

14. Sick people who have lost consciousness or have lost the use of reason may be anointed if, as befits Christians, they would have requested it if they had been in possession of their faculties.

15. When a priest is called to minister to a person who is already dead, he should pray for the dead person, asking God to forgive him or her and to receive him or her into his kingdom. The priest must not in such circumstances administer the sacrament of anointing. But if the priest is not sure if the person is dead, he may administer the sacrament conditionally.

. . . .

B. Viaticum

26. Christians who are strengthened by the body and blood of Christ as they depart from this life have the Lord's promise

that they will rise from the dead: "He who feeds on my flesh and drinks my blood has life eternal, and I will raise him up on the last day." (John 6:54)

Viaticum should be received during Mass whenever possible, so that the sick person may communicate under both kinds. Communion received as viaticum should be seen as a special sign that a person shares in the mystery of the death of the Lord and of his passage to the Father, the mystery which is celebrated in the eucharist.

27. All baptized Christians who can receive communion are obliged to receive viaticum, if in danger of death from any cause. Pastors must ensure that the administration of this sacrament is not delayed, but that it is made available to the faithful while they are still in possession of their faculties.

28. It is also desirable that during the celebration of viaticum Christians should renew their baptismal profession of the faith which made them adopted children of God and co-heirs of the promise of eternal life.

29. The ordinary ministers of viaticum are the pastor and his assistants. . . . If no priest is available, viaticum may be taken to the sick by a deacon or by a layman or laywoman appointed by the bishop, through the authority of the Holy See, to distribute the eucharist to the faithful. . . .

OFFICES AND MINISTRIES FOR THE SICK

32. If one member of Christ's body, the Church, suffers, all members suffer with that member. Consequently, kindness towards the sick, works of charity and help given for the relief of human want should be held in high esteem. Every scientific effort to prolong life and every act of love shown the sick is a preparation for the gospel and a sharing in Christ's healing ministry.

33. It is therefore fitting that all Christians share in this ministry of charity within the body of Christ, combatting disease, caring for the sick and celebrating the sacrament of the sick. Like the other sacraments, these have a communal aspect, which should be brought into play as much as possible.

34. The family and friends of the sick person and those who have care of them have a special share in this ministry of comfort. It is for them to strengthen the sick with words of faith, to pray with them, commending them to the Lord who suffered and was glorified, to urge the sick to associate themselves with the passion and death of Christ for the sake of God's people. If a

sick person's condition deteriorates, the family and friends and those looking after them are to inform the pastor. They ought also to prepare the sick person, kindly and prudently, for the reception of the sacraments. . . .

36. The faithful should have a clear understanding of the anointing of the sick so that the sacraments will nourish, strengthen and express their faith. Instruction is of the greatest importance in this connection, for the faithful in general and above all for the sick, especially if the celebration is to be communal. The prayer of faith which is part of the celebration of the sacrament is given support by this profession of faith.

37. When the priest is preparing to celebrate the sacrament, he should ascertain the condition of the sick person and should take this into account when arranging the celebration, in the choice of readings and prayers and in determining whether he will celebrate Mass for the celebration, etc. If possible, all this should be arranged beforehand with the sick person of the family while the priest explains the meanings of the sacraments.

*Excerpts from the introduction chosen and translated by A.F. The selection was made with the needs of the non-ordained mostly in mind. Priests have easier access to the entire instruction and to the parts that concern them. Latin original in *Notitiae*, 1973, 56–65.

69

DECREE PROMULGATING THE NEW ORDER OF PENANCE*

Paul VI, *Reconciliationem*, 2 December, 1973

Our Lord Jesus Christ reconciled God and men through the mystery of his death and resurrection (see Rom. 5:10). This ministry of reconciliation was committed to the Church through the apostles by our Lord (2 Cor. 5:18) and the Church has executed the commission by bearing the glad tidings of salvation to men and by baptizing them in water and the Holy Spirit (see Matt. 28:19).

Because of human weakness, however, it happens that Christians 'abandon the love they had at first' (see Apoc. 2:4) and by sinning break the links of friendship that bind them to God. For this reason, the Lord instituted a special sacrament for the remission of sins committed after Baptism (see John 20:21-23). The Church has celebrated this sacrament through the ages, in various ways indeed, but always retaining its essential elements.

The Second Council of the Vatican decreed: 'The rites and formulae of penance are to be revised in such a way that they will express more clearly the nature and effects of the sacrament.'[1] With this in view, the Sacred Congregation for Divine Worship has carefully prepared a new 'Order of Penance', so that the administration of the sacrament would be more fully understood by the faithful.

This new Order contains, over and above the 'Order for the reconciliation of individual penitents', an 'Order for reconciling several penitents'—so as to emphasize the communal aspect of the sacrament—the confession and absolution of individuals being inserted into a celebration of the word of God. But there has also been composed, for certain cases, an 'Order for the reconciliation of several penitents, with communal confession and absolution', in accordance with the norms given by the sacred Congregation for the Doctrine of the Faith on 16 June 1972, for imparting general absolution.

The Church has it at heart to call the faithful to continual conversion and renewal. It wishes that when the baptized should fall from grace they should acknowledge the sins they have committed against God and their brethren and should be truly penitent in their hearts. Anxious to prepare them for the celebration of the sacrament of Penance, it urges them to take part in penitential services from time to time. For this reason the Sacred Congregation has drawn up norms for the celebration of such services and has composed a number of sample services which episcopal conferences can adapt to the needs of their own regions.

The Supreme Pontiff Paul VI has approved the 'Order of Penance', prepared by the Sacred Congregation, and has ordered its publication and its substitution for the section on penance in the Roman Ritual. The Order comes into force in Latin on the day of its publication. It will be for episcopal conferences to appoint the day that the vernacular rendering comes into use, after they shall have approved the translation and secured its confirmation by the Holy See.

---

* Translation by A.F. Latin original in *AAS* 66 (1974), 172–173.
1. Constitution on the Sacred Liturgy, n. 72.

70

GENERAL INTRODUCTION
TO CHRISTIAN INITIATION* (Second edition)

S.C.D.W., *Per initiationis Christianae*, 24 June, 1973

1. Men and women are delivered from the power of darkness through the sacraments of Christian initiation. They die with Christ, are buried with him and rise again with him. They receive the Spirit which makes them God's adopted sons and daughters and, with all God's people, they celebrate the memorial of the Lord's death and resurrection.[1]

2. They are incorporated into Christ and are made God's people; with all their sins forgiven, they are delivered from the power of darkness[1a] and are made adopted sons and daughters.[2] They are made a new creation through water and the Holy Spirit: they are called, and are, God's children.[3]

Signed by the giving of the same Spirit in Confirmation, they become more like Our Lord and filled with the Holy Spirit. They are thus able to bear witness to him before the world and to help bring as close as possible the achievement of the fullness of the Body of Christ.[4]

Finally, as part of the eucharistic assembly, they eat the flesh of the Son of Man and drink his Blood so that they may have eternal life[5] and manifest the unity of God's people. Offering themselves with Christ, they share in the universal sacrifice which is all of redeemed humanity offered to God by the high priest.[6] They pray that, with a great outpouring of the Holy Spirit, the entire human race would achieve the unity of God's family.[7]

The three sacraments of Christian initiation are thus closely intertwined that they may bring Christians to their full stature, enabling them to carry out their mission in the Church and in the world.[8]

I THE DIGNITY OF BAPTISM

3. Baptism, entrance to life and to the kingdom, is the first

22

sacrament of the new law, offered by Christ to all, that they might have eternal life[9] and afterwards entrusted, with the Gospel, to his Church, when he commanded his apostles: 'Go forth, therefore, and make all nations my disciples; baptise people everywhere in the name of the Father and the Son and the Holy Spirit.'[10] Baptism is, therefore, first of all the sacrament of that faith by which men and women, enlightened by the grace of the Holy Spirit, respond to the gospel of Christ. For the Church, therefore, there is nothing more important, nothing more in character than to awaken in all—catechumens, parents of children awaiting baptism, godparents—that true and active faith by which they give their allegiance to Christ and enter into the new covenant, or re-affirm their acceptance of it. It is this, in fact, that the pastoral formation of the catechumenate, the preparation of the parents, the celebration of God's word and the profession of baptismal faith are intended to achieve.

4. Baptism, further, is the sacrament by which men and women are incorporated into the Church, assembled together into the house of God in the Spirit,[11] into a royal priesthood and a holy nation.[12] It is the sacramental bond of unity between all those who have received it. This unalterable effect is symbolised in the Latin liturgy by the anointing of the baptised persons with chrism in the presence of God's people and because of it the rite of Baptism is held in the highest esteem by all Christians. It is never lawful to repeat it if it has been validly celebrated, even by our separated fellow Christians.

5. Baptism, which is washing with water accompanied by the living word,[14] cleanses men and women of all stain of sin, original and personal,[14a] makes them sharers in God's life[15] and his adopted children.[16] As the prayers for the blessing of the water attest, baptism is water of heaven-sent regeneration[17] of God's children and of their re-birth. Readings from the scriptures, the prayer of the community and a triple profession of faith prepare for and lead up to the culmination of the rite: the invocation of the blessed Trinity over those to be baptised. Signed with this name, they are consecrated to the blessed Trinity and enter into fellowship with the Father, the Son and the Holy Spirit.

6. Baptism, much more effective than the purifications of the old law, produces these effects by the power of the mystery of the Passion and Resurrection of the Lord. When people are baptised, they share sacramentally in Christ's death,[17a] they are buried with him and lie dead,[18] they are brought back to life with him and rise with him.[19] For baptism recalls and actualises the

very paschal mystery itself, since by its means men and women pass from the death of sin to life. For this reason it is fitting that the joy of the resurrection should be reflected when it is celebrated, especially during the Easter Vigil and on Sundays.

II   OFFICES AND MINISTRIES OF BAPTISM

7. Preparation for baptism and Christian formation are very much the responsibility of God's people, that is, the Church, which transmits and nourishes the faith received from the apostles. Adults are called to the Gospel by the Holy Spirit through the ministry of the Church and infants are baptised and educated in its faith. It is of great importance, therefore, that catechists and other lay people should collaborate with priests and deacons in the preparations for baptism. Further, representatives of God's people should take an active part in the actual celebration—not just the godparents, parents and relatives, but also friends, acquaintances, neighbours and members of the local Church—thus manifesting their common faith and expressing the joy they share that the newly baptised have been received into the Church.

8. By very ancient Church custom, an adult is not admitted to baptism without a godparent, a member of the Christian community, who will assist him or her in the final preparations at least and afterwards will help the newly baptised to persevere in the faith and in Christian living.

There should be a godparent at the baptism of a child, also, to represent both the spiritually augmented family and Mother Church and to help the parents, as occasion offers, ensure that the child learns to profess the faith and to express it in its life.

9. The godparent takes part in the final rites of the catechumenate, at least, and in the actual celebration of baptism, to testify to the faith of the adult candidate or, together with the parents, to profess the faith of the Church, in which the child is baptised.

10. The godparent is chosen by the catechumen or by the child's family. Godparents—and this is a matter for the pastor of souls to judge—should have the following qualities if they are to perform the liturgical functions described in number 9. They should:

(1) be mature enough to undertake the responsibility;
(2) have received the three sacraments of initiation: baptism, confirmation and the eucharist;

(3) be members of the Catholic Church, legally free to take on this duty.

If the parents so choose, a baptised and believing member of another Christian Church or Communion may act, with a Catholic godparent, as godparent or Christian witness, taking into account the norms for various ecumenical situations.[19a]

11. The ordinary ministers of baptism are bishops, priests and deacons. They should bear in mind that in every celebration of this sacrament they act in the Church in the name of Christ and by the power of the Holy Spirit. They should therefore take great care in proclaiming the word of God and administering the sacrament. They should avoid doing anything which the faithful might justifiably condemn as favouritism.[20]

12. Bishops are the principal dispensers of God's mysteries and are responsible for the regulation of the entire liturgical life of the Church entrusted to them. They are in charge therefore of the administration of baptism, which gives a share in Christ's royal priesthood, and they should not themselves neglect to administer this sacrament, especially at the Easter Vigil. The baptism of adults and their preparation for it is especially commended to them.

13. It is for parish priests to assist the bishop in the instruction and baptism of the adults in his care, unless the bishop makes other arrangements. It is for them also, employing suitable pastoral means and with the help of catechists and other qualified lay people, to prepare and assist parents and godparents of child candidates for baptism and to baptise the children.

14. Other priests and deacons, as cooperators in the ministry of bishops and of parish priests, also prepare candidates for baptism and, at the invitation or with the consent of the bishop or parish priest, administer it.

15. The celebrant, especially if there is a large number to be baptised, may be assisted by other priests and deacons and by the laity in those parts which pertain to them, as is set out in the rite.

16. If no priest or deacon is available, any member of the faithful and indeed any person at all with the intention of doing what is right may and sometimes must administer baptism when there is imminent danger of death or, especially, if the actual moment of death has come. If the danger of death is not yet imminent, the sacrament ought if possible to be administered by a member of the faithful, using the shorter form . . . It is desirable that even in this case a small community be collected, or that at

least there be, if possible, one or more witnesses.

17. All the laity, as members of the priestly people, should take care to know as well as possible the exact method of administering baptism in case of necessity. This is especially true of parents and, in view of their office, catechists, obstetricians, women social workers and nurses, physicians and surgeons. They should be taught by parish priests, deacons or catechists and bishops should provide such instruction within their dioceses.

III   WHAT IS NEEDED FOR THE CELEBRATION OF BAPTISM

18. The water for baptism should be natural and clean to ensure the authenticity of the symbolism and in the interest of hygiene.

19. The baptismal font, or, if such it be, the vessel in which the water is placed for the celebration of the sacrament in the sanctuary, should be scrupulously clean and decorative.

20. Provision should be made for heating the water beforehand in cold weather.

21. Except in a case of necessity, the priest or deacon should not baptise with unblessed water. Water consecrated at the Easter Vigil should if possible be kept and used during the whole of the Easter season, thus emphasising the relationship between the sacrament of baptism and the paschal mystery. It is preferable that outside of the Easter season the water be blessed each time the sacrament is administered, so that the mystery of salvation which the Church recalls and proclaims may be clearly signified by the very words of the blessing. If the baptismal font incorporates running water, the water should be blessed as it flows.

22. It is permissible to use either the rite of immersion, which is a clearer symbol of sharing in the death and resurrection of Christ, or the rite of pouring.

23. The words with which baptism is conferred in the Latin Church are: 'I baptise you in the name of the Father, and of the Son and of the Holy Spirit.'

24. A suitable place for the celebration of the word of God should be provided in the baptistery or in the church.

25. The baptistery is the place where the font, with or without flowing water, is located. It must be reserved for the sacrament of baptism and should be entirely worthy, as befits the place where Christians are reborn from water and the Holy Spirit. Whether it be in a chapel inside or outside the church, or in some

part of the church in clear view of the faithful, it should be capable of accommodating a large number of people. After the Easter season, the paschal candle should be given a place of honour in the baptistery: thus it can be lit during the celebration of baptism and the candles of the candidates for baptism may be easily lit from it.

26. The portions of the baptismal rite which are to be celebrated outside the baptistery should be performed in whatever parts of the church best facilitate the numbers taking part and best suit the stages of the celebration. If the baptistery is not able to accommodate all the catechumens and the congregation, the parts of the rite which ordinarily take place there can be moved to some other suitable area in the church.

27. If possible, there should be a common celebration of baptism, on the same day, for all recently born babies. The sacrament should not be celebrated twice on the same day in the same church, except for a just cause.

28. . . . . . The celebration of the sacrament should always manifest its paschal character.

29. Parish priests should carefully and without delay enter in the baptismal register the names of the baptised, of the minister, the parents and godparents and the place and date of the ceremony.

[There follow directives for conferences of bishops about adapting the general rite to their local situation, and for the minister about taking advantage of the choices offered in the rite.]

---

*Translated by Austin Flannery, O.P., from the second *editio typica* (24 June, 1973), as given in Enchiridion Vaticanum, vol. 3, nn 1092 ff. The second *editio typica* made a number of changes, none of them major, from the original version, published on 15 May, 1969. These are noted in a declaration by Congregation for Divine Worship, *Cum necesse sit*, published in Notitiae, 1973, p. 268 and in E.V., vol 3, pp. 644-645, footnote. The translator has indicated two of these changes in footnotes using numerals and letters, e.g. 1a. He has done the same with other footnotes not in the original. The original *De Initiatione Christiana: Ordo Baptismi parvulorum* was published by the Vatican Polyglot Press, 1969

1. A.G.D., 14,
1a. The earlier version had 'from their natural human condition: *a nativa hominum condicione*' instead of 'delivered from the power of darkness: *de potestate tenebrarum erepti*'.
2. See Col. 1:13 (added in second *editio typica*), Rom. 8:15; Gal 4:5; Council of Trent, Sixth session, Decree on Justification, ch. 4, Denz. 1524.

3. See 1 John 3:1
4. See A.G.D., 36
5. See John 6:55.
6. Saint Augustine, *The City of God*, X, 6: PL 41, 284; LG 11
7. See LG 28
8. See LG 31
9. See John 3:5
10. Matt., 28:19
11. Eph. 2:22
12. 1 Pet., 2:9
13. U.R., 22
14. Eph. 5:26
14a. The earlier version did not have the phrase 'cleanses [men and women] of all stain of sin, original and personal, and: *ab omni culpae labe, tum originali tum personali, abluit eosque'*
15. 2 Pet 1:4
16. See Rom 8:15; Gal 4:5.
17. See Tit. 3:5.
17a. The Latin is *'complantati similitudini mortis Christi*; ICEL version is quite literal: 'engrafted in the likeness of Christ's death.' Italian version in E.V. has *'coloro che ricevono il battesimo, segno sacramentale della morte di Cristo'*
18. Rom 6:4–5.
19. See Eph 2:6.
19a. See 'Directory Concerning Ecumenical Matters, Part 1,' nos. 48, 57, apud F., I pp. 497-498, 500, where it is stated that a member of 'the separated Eastern Churches' may be a godparent, in such a case 'because of the close communion' between these churches and the Catholic Church (no. 2 & 8), a member of another Christian Church may not be a godparent 'in the liturgical and canonical sense,' but may be a 'Christian witness.' (no. 50)
20. See SC 32; GS 29
21. CD 15
22. LG 26

71

**INTRODUCTION TO THE RITE
OF INFANT BAPTISM* (Second edition)**

S.C.D.W., *Nomine parvulorum*, 24 June, 1973

I THE IMPORTANCE OF BAPTISING CHILDREN

1. The words 'children' or 'infants' are to be taken to mean those who have not yet attained the use of reason and consequently cannot profess personal faith.[a]

2. The Church, which was given the mission of evangelizing and baptising, has baptised not only adults but children as well from the earliest times. It has always understood the words of our Lord: 'No one can enter the kingdom of God without being born from water and spirit'[1] to mean that children are not to be deprived of baptism, for they are baptised in the faith of the Church, proclaimed by their parents, godparents and the others present. All these represent both the local Church and the whole society of saints and of the faithful: 'Mother Church: for the entire Church gives birth to all and to each one.'[2]

3. To complete the true meaning of the sacrament, the children must subsequently be formed in the faith in which they have been baptised, the foundation for the process being the sacrament they have received. The object of the Christian formation to which the children are entitled is to lead them gradually to discern God's plan in Christ. They will thus be able personally to ratify the faith in which they have been baptised.

II MINISTRIES AND ROLES IN THE CELEBRATION
OF BAPTISM

4. God's people, that is the Church, present in the local community, have an important role in the baptism of children no less than of adults. The child has a right to the love and the help of the community, before and after the celebration of the sacrament. During the celebration and apart from what are assigned to the congregation in number 7 of the General Introduction,

the community fulfils its role when, after the profession of faith by parents and godparents, it expresses its assent, with the celebrant. It is thus made clear that the faith in which the children are baptised is not just that of its family, but is a treasure common to the entire Church.

5. It is of the very order of creation that the parents have a more important ministry and role in the baptism of children than have godparents.

(1) It is of great importance that, beforehand, parents should set about acquiring greater understanding of the rite in which they are to take part, relying on the guidance of their own faith, or on the help of friends or other members of the community and employing suitable means, like books, instructions, family catechisms. The parish priest should make a point of visiting them, or having them visited. Indeed, he should arrange to have several families come together and should prepare them for the coming celebration by pastoral counsel and prayer in common.

(2) It is very important that parents be present at the baptismal celebration in which their own child is born again of water and the Holy Spirit.

(3) The parents of children have their own parts in the celebration of baptism. Apart from listening to the words addressed to them by the celebrant, taking part in the prayer in common, with the rest of the faithful, they exercise a true ministry when:

    (a) they publicly ask to have their child baptised;
    (b) they sign their child with the sign of the cross on the forehead, after the celebrant;
    (c) they renounce Satan and make their profession of faith;
    (d) they (and especially the mother) take their child to the font;
    (e) they hold the lighted candle;
    (f) they are blessed with special prayers for mothers and fathers.

(4) If one of the parents is unable to make the profession of faith—if, for example, he or she is not a Catholic—he or she may remain silent. All that is asked of such parents is that having requested baptism for their child, they provide for, or at least permit, its instruction in the faith.

(5) When the baptism has been administered, the parents are obliged, in gratitude to God and in fidelity to their undertaking, to lead the child to knowledge of God, whose adopted child it has become, and to prepare it for the reception of con-

firmation and for sharing in the holy eucharist. The parish priest should give them whatever help is appropriate for this task.

6. Each child may have a godfather and a godmother. The word 'godparents' in the rite refers to both.

7. In addition to what is set out in the General Introduction, (numbers 11-15) about the ordinary minister of baptism, the following should be noted:

(1) It is for parish priests to prepare families for the baptism of their children and to help them to carry out the task of education which they have undertaken. It is for the bishop to coordinate such pastoral initiatives in his diocese, with the help of deacons and also of lay people.

(2) It is for the parish priest to see to it that every baptismal celebration is dignified and, as far as possible, in keeping with the circumstances and the wishes of the family. Whoever performs the baptism should do it carefully and devoutly and he should be friendly and courteous towards everyone.

III TIME AND PLACE FOR THE BAPTISM OF CHILDREN

8. In deciding when a baptism is to take place, the first consideration should be the spiritual welfare of the child, lest it be deprived of the benefit of the sacrament. Then the mother's health must be taken into account, ensuring that she be present, if possible. Lastly, there are pastoral considerations, such as allowing time to prepare the parents and to plan for a celebration calculated to make the rite's meaning clear, provided this is not allowed to jeopardise the child's well-being, which is more important.

Thus, (1) if the child is in danger of death, it is to be baptised at once in the manner described in number 21. (2) Otherwise, the parents should contact the parish priest as soon as possible after the birth of their child, or even before it, to arrange for the celebration of the sacrament. (3) The baptism should be celebrated in the first weeks after the birth of the child. The episcopal conference may decide on a longer interval, for grave pastoral reasons. (4) If the parents of a child are not yet prepared to profess the faith and take on the obligation of bringing it up in the Christian faith, the parish priest is to decide when the baptism is to take place, bearing in mind any regulations made by the conference of bishops.

9. It is recommended, in order to set in relief its paschal character that baptism be celebrated at the Easter vigil or on a Sunday, when the Church commemorates the Lord's resurrection. On Sundays, baptism may be celebrated even during Mass, so that the entire community may be able to attend and so that the link between baptism and eucharist may be seen more clearly. However, this should not be done too often . . . .

10. Baptism is normally celebrated in the parish church, which ought to have a baptismal font. In this way it is more clearly seen that baptism is the sacrament of the faith of the Church and of incorporation in God's people.

11. The bishop, having consulted the parish priest, may permit or direct that a baptismal font be placed also in another church or public oratory in the parish. Normally, it is for the parish priest to celebrate the sacrament in those places too.

12. Baptism must not be celebrated in a private house, except in danger of death.

13. Unless the bishop should have decided otherwise (see no. 11), baptism should not be celebrated in a hospital except in case of necessity or for some other impelling pastoral reason. The parish priest should always be informed and there should be adequate preparation of the parents.

14. While the liturgy of the word is being celebrated, it is advisable to remove the children to another place, leaving the mothers and godmothers free to take part in the liturgy of the word, the children being left in the care of other women.

IV STRUCTURE OF THE RITE

A. Order of Baptism Celebrated by the Ordinary Minister

15. The celebrant of baptism, whether of one child or several, or of a large number, should perform the rite in its entirety, unless there is an immediate danger of death.

16. The ceremony begins with the reception of the children, during which the desire of the parents and godparents and the intention of the Church to celebrate the sacrament of baptism are expressed; parents and celebrant then symbolise this by tracing the sign of the cross on the children's foreheads.

17. The liturgy of the word, which precedes the administration of the sacrament, is intended to evoke the faith of the parents, godparents and congregation and it includes prayer in common for the fruits of the sacrament. It consists of one or more passages of scripture, a homily, followed by a period of

silence; the prayer of the faithful, concluding with a prayer drawn up after the manner of an exorcism and introducing the anointing with the oil of catechumens or the laying on of hands.

18. (1) The celebration of the sacrament is immediately preceded by:

> (a) The solemn prayer in which the celebrant, invoking God and recalling his plan of salvation, blesses the baptismal water or commemorates the blessing already imparted.
>
> (b) The renunciation of Satan by parents and godparents, their profession of faith, to which the celebrant and the congregation add their assent; and the final interrogation of the parents and godparents.

(2) The sacrament is administered by washing with water—either by immersion or by pouring, according to local custom—and invoking the blessed Trinity.

(3) The ceremony concludes with the anointing with chrism, symbolising the royal priesthood of the baptised and its reception into the fellowship of God's people; this is followed by the rites of the white garment, the lighted candle and the *Ephphetha*, which last is optional.

19. Lastly, at the altar, thereby pointing ahead to the children's future participation in the eucharist, after an address by the celebrant, the Lord's Prayer is said—God's family invoking their Father in Heaven. Then the celebrant blesses the mothers and fathers present, that God's grace may abound in all.

B. The Shorter Rite of Baptism

20. In the shorter form of baptism for the use of catechists,[3] there are the rites of the reception of the children, the celebration of the word of God, or the instruction by the minister, and the prayer of the faithful. Before the font, he recites a prayer invoking God and recalling the history of salvation in relation to baptism. After the baptismal washing, the anointing with chrism is omitted and a specially adapted prayer is said in its place, the ceremony being concluded in the ordinary way. The rites omitted, therefore, are the exorcism, the anointing with oil of catechumens and with chrism, and the *Ephphetha*.

21. The shorter form for baptising children in danger of death, when the ordinary minister is not available, is of two different kinds:

(1) At the moment of death, or when the matter is urgent

because death is imminent, the minister,[4] omitting all else, pours water, blessed or not, but real water, on the child's head, reciting the usual formula.[5]

(2) If it be prudently judged that there is sufficient time, a group of the faithful should be collected and if one of them is able to lead the others in a short prayer, the following rite may be used: an instruction by the minister of the sacrament, a short prayer of the faithful, profession of faith by the parents or one godparent, the pouring of the water with the normal formula. If those assembled are incapable of participating in this rite, the minister should recite the creed aloud and should pour the water in the manner prescribed for the moment of death.

22. A priest and deacon may also use the shorter form when necessary when there is danger of death. A parish priest or any priest possessing the same faculties should administer the sacrament of confirmation in such a situation if there is time and if he has the sacred chrism. In which case he should omit the postbaptismal anointing with chrism.

[There follows a section of changes which episcopal conferences and individual ministers can make in the rite.]

---

*Translated by Austin Flannery, O.P., from the second *editio typica* (24 June, 1973), as given in *Enchiridion Vaticanum*, 3, nn 1127 ff. As stated in the editor's footnote at the beginning of the 'General Introduction to Christian Initiation,' the second *editio typica* changed the earlier (1969) version in a few places. There is one such change in this document, indicated in footnote (a).

a. The earlier version had 'cannot have and profess personal faith: *fidem propriam habere et profiteri nequeunt'*.

1. John 3:5.

2. Saint Augustine, Letter 98, 5: PL 33, 362.

2a. Following the Italian version in *Enchiridion Vaticanum: Infine, si va all'altare, per indicare la futura participazione all'eucaristia, e dopo una monizione del celebrante, si dice la preghiera del Signore. . . .* The ICEL version is 'After the celebrant speaks of the future reception of the eucharist by the baptised children, the Lord's prayer . . . is recited. . . .' The Latin is: *Post celebrantis monitionem, ad praesignandam futuram Eucharistiae participationem, ante altare dicitur oratio dominica. . . .*

3. See SC 68

4. See *General Introduction to Christian Initiation*, number 16

5. See ibid., number 23.

72

INTRODUCTION TO THE NEW ORDER OF PENANCE*

S.C.D.W., *Misericordiam suam*, 7 February, 1974

I. THE MYSTERY OF RECONCILIATION IN THE HISTORY OF SALVATION

1. The Father manifested his mercy by reconciling the world to himself in Christ, making peace by the blood of his cross with all who are in heaven and on earth.[1] The Son of God became man and lived among men so that he might liberate them from slavery to sin[2] and call them out of darkness into his wonderful light.[3] Thus he commenced his task on earth by preaching penance and saying: 'Repent and believe the Gospel' (Mark 1:15).

This invitation to penitence, which had often been issued by the prophets, prepared the hearts of men for the coming of the kingdom through the voice of John the Baptist, who came preaching 'a baptism of repentance for the forgiveness of sins' (Mark 1:4).

But not only did Jesus exhort men to do penance, to give up their sins and be converted to God with all their hearts.[4] He also received sinners and reconciled them to the Father.[5] He cured the sick as a sign of his power to forgive sins.[6] He himself even died for our sins and rose from the dead for our justification.[7] On the night he was betrayed, as he commenced his saving passion,[8] he instituted the sacrifice of the new covenant in his blood for the remission of sins,[9] and after his resurrection he sent his Spirit to the apostles that they might have the power to forgive sins or to retain them,[10] and that they might accept the task of preaching penance and the remission of sins to all nations in his name.[11]

It was to Peter that the Lord said 'I will give you the keys of the kingdom of heaven, and whatever you bind on earth shall be bound in heaven, and whatever you loose on earth shall be loosed in heaven' (Matt. 16:19). In obedience to the Lord's command, Peter preached the remission of sins by baptism on the day of Pentecost: 'Repent and be baptized, every one of you, in the name of Jesus Christ for the forgiveness of your sins' (Acts 2:38).[12] From then on the Church has never ceased to call sinners to conversion and to exhibit the victory of Christ over sin in the celebration of penance.

2. This victory of Christ over sin is shown first in baptism, by which the old man is crucified with Christ so that the body of sin may be destroyed and we might no more serve sin, but rise with Christ and live thenceforth.[13] Thus the Church confesses its faith 'in one baptism for the remission of sins'.

In the sacrifice of the Mass, the passion of Christ is represented. The body which is given for us and the blood which is shed for the remission of sins are offered to God by the Church for the salvation of the whole world. In the Eucharist Christ is present and is offered as 'the sacrifice which had made our peace'[14] and so that we might 'be brought together in unity' by his Holy Spirit.[15]

Further, when our Saviour Jesus Christ gave the power to forgive sins to the apostles and their successors, he instituted the sacrament of penance, so that the faithful who had committed sin after baptism could be restored to grace and reconciled to God.[16] For the Church has both water and tears: the water of baptism, the tears of penitence.'[17]

II. THE RECONCILIATION OF SINNERS IN THE LIFE OF THE CHURCH

The Church Holy and Yet Always in Need of Purification

3. Christ 'loved the Church and gave himself up for her, that he might sanctify her' (Eph. 5:25-26). He united her to himself as a spouse.[19] He fills her, his Body and completion, with his divine gifts and through her he distributes truth and grace to all.

The members of the Church are exposed to temptation, however, and it often happens that, unhappily, they fall into sin. Thus it is that 'while Christ, "holy, innocent and undefiled" (Heb. 7:26) knew nothing of sin (2 Cor. 5:21), but came to expiate only the sins of the people (see Heb. 2:17), the Church, at the same time holy and always in need of purification, clasping sinners to her bosom, follows continuously the way of penance and renewal.'[20]

Penance in the Life and Liturgy of the Church

4. The people of God do penance continually in many and

various ways. Sharing in the sufferings of Christ by their own
suffering,[21] performing works of mercy and charity,[22] undergoing a constant conversion to the Gospel of Christ, they become
to the world a symbol of conversion to God. This the Church expresses in its life and celebrates in its liturgy, when the faithful
profess themselves sinners and ask pardon of God and their
brothers—as happens in penitential services, in the proclamation of the word of God, in prayer, in the penitential elements of
the Mass.[23]

And in the sacrament of Penance, the faithful 'obtain pardon
from God's mercy for the offence committed against him and
are, at the same time, reconciled with the Church, which they
have wounded by their sins and which by charity, example and
prayer labours for their conversion.'[24]

Reconciliation With God and With the Church

5. Since sin is an offence against God and breaks our friendship with him, penance 'has for its ultimate objective that we
should love God and commit ourselves wholly to him.'[25] When
the sinner, therefore, by God's mercy takes the road of penance,
he returns to the Father who 'loved us first' (1 John 4:19), to
Christ who gave himself up for us,[26] and to the Holy Spirit who is
poured out on us abundantly.[27]

But, 'because of a secret and loving mystery of dispensation,
men are joined together by a supernatural necessity, in such wise
that the sin of one injures the others, and the holiness of one
benefits the others'.[28] In the same way, penance affords reconciliation with a man's brothers, who likewise are injured by sin.

Further, men often act together in committing sin. In the same
way, they help one another when doing penance, so that, freed
from sin by the grace of Christ, they might, with all men of good
will, make peace and achieve justice in the world.

The Sacrament of Penance and Its Parts

6. When the follower of Christ, moved by the Holy Spirit,
approaches the sacrament of penance after sin, he ought before
all else to turn to God with his whole heart. This profound conversion of heart, which comprises sorrow for sin and a firm purpose of starting a new life, finds expression in confession to the
Church, satisfaction and improvement of life. God forgives sins
through the Church, which operates by means of the ministry of
the priest.[29]

(a) *Contrition:* Contrition holds first place among the acts of the penitent. It is a 'heart-felt sorrow and detestation of sin, with a firm purpose not to sin again.'[30] For 'the only right way for us to approach the Kingdom of God is with "metanoia": that is, with a profound change of the whole man, by which he begins to think, judge and regulate his life by that sanctity and charity of God which in these last days have been manifested in his Son and have been given to us in abundance (see Heb. 1:2; Col. 1:19, and passim; Eph. 1:23 and passim).'[31] Penance cannot be true penance without this heart-felt sorrow. Conversion must affect a man interiorly, permeating him more and more deeply and bringing him more and more into conformity with Christ.

(b) *Confession:* Confession of sins is part of the sacrament of penance. It issues from true self-knowledge and sorrow for sin. Such interior heart-searching and external accusation ought to be done in the awareness of God's mercy. Confession presupposes in the penitent the willingness to open his heart to God's minister. It presupposes in the minister spiritual judgement, for it is he who, acting for Christ and having the power of the keys, the power to forgive and to retain sins, pronounces judgment.[32]

(c) *Satisfaction:* True conversion is completed by satisfaction for sin, by improvement of life and repair of the damage done.[33] The work of satisfaction and its measure should be suited to the penitent, so that he should restore the order he had damaged and take suitable medicine for the malady which afflicted him. The penance imposed therefore should be a real remedy for sin and should contribute to renewal of life. Thus the penitent, 'forgetting what is in the past' (Phil. 3:13) enters once more into the mystery of salvation and sets out for what lies ahead.

(d) *Absolution:* When a sinner discloses his conversion to the Church's minister in sacramental confession, God grants him pardon through the sign of absolution and thus the sacrament of penance is completed. In keeping with the divine economy, by which the humanity and kindness of God our Saviour appeared to men[34], God wishes to bestow salvation on us through visible signs and to renew again the broken covenant.

In the sacrament of penance, therefore, the Father receives the home-coming son, Christ puts the lost sheep on his shoulder and returns it to the sheep-fold, and the Holy Spirit sanctifies his temple again or dwells in it more fully. All this is manifested by a renewed and more fervent sharing in the table of the Lord where there is great joy in the banquet given by the Church of God for the son returned from afar.[35]

On the Necessity and Usefulness of This Sacrament

(7) The wounds inflicted by sin on the individual and on the community are many and varied. In the same way, the remedies offered by penance are varied. Those who depart from the fellowship of the love of God through grave sin are recalled through the sacrament of Penance to the life which they had lost. Those who fall into venial sin, however, experiencing their weakness daily, receive through frequent confession the strength to arrive at the full freedom of the children of God.

(a) The God of mercy laid down that, in order to receive the saving remedy of the sacrament of Penance, the Christian should confess to a priest all and every grave sin which he can recall after an examination of his conscience.[36]

(b) Further, frequent and reverent recourse to this sacrament, even when only venial sins are in question, is of great value. Frequent confession is not mere ritual repetition, nor is it merely a psychological exercise. Rather is it a constant effort to bring to perfection the grace of our baptism, so that, as we carry about in our bodies the death that Jesus Christ died, the life that Jesus Christ lives may be more and more manifested in us.[37] In such confessions, penitents, while indeed confessing venial sins, should be mainly concerned with becoming more deeply conformed to Christ and more submissive to the voice of the Spirit.

If this saving sacrament is really to be effective in the faithful, it is necessary that it should take root in their entire lives and should inspire them to more zealous service of God and their brothers.

The celebration of this sacrament is, therefore, always an action by which the Church proclaims her faith, thanks God for the liberty which Christ won for us[38] and offers her life as a spiritual sacrifice in praise of the glory of God, as she hastens to meet Christ.

III. OFFICES AND MINISTRIES IN THE RECONCILIATION OF PENITENTS

The Role of the Community in the Celebration of Penance

(8) The Lord has entrusted to the whole Church, as to a priestly people, the task of effecting reconciliation and the Church performs this task in a number of ways. Not merely does she call sinners to penance by the preaching of the word of God, she also intercedes for them and in her maternal solicitude

she goes to the aid of penitents so that they will acknowledge their sins and confess them and will obtain mercy from God, who alone has the power to forgive sin. Further, the Church herself becomes the instrument of conversion and absolution of the penitent through the ministry entrusted to the apostles and their successors by Christ.[39]

The Minister of the Sacrament of Penance

(a) The Church exercises the ministry of the sacrament of penance through bishops and priests, who call the faithful to conversion by preaching the word of God and who testify to the forgiveness of their sins and impart it to them in the name of Christ and by the power of the Holy Spirit.

In exercising this ministry priests act in communion with the bishop and share in his power and role, for he is the moderator of the discipline of penance.[40]

(b) The competent minister of the sacrament of penance is a priest who has the faculty of absolving, in accordance with canon law. All priests, however, even if not authorised to hear confessions, act validly and licitly if they absolve any penitents who are in danger of death.

The Pastoral Exercise of This Ministry

(a) If a confessor is to fulfill his task well and faithfully, if he is to diagnose sicknesses of souls, and if he is to be a wise judge, he must acquire the requisite knowledge and prudence by assiduous study under the guidance of the Church's magisterium, and especially in prayer to God. For the discernment of spirits demands an intimate knowledge of the working of God in the hearts of men, it is the gift of the Holy Spirit and the fruit of charity.[41]

(b) A confessor should always be ready to hear the confessions of the faithful, in response to every reasonable request.[42]

(c) When he receives a repentent sinner and leads him to the light of truth the confessor fills a fatherly role, revealing the heart of the Father to men and bearing the likeness of Christ the Pastor. Let him remember that it is Christ's task which has been entrusted to him, Christ who, to save men, mercifully completed the work of redemption, and who is present by his power in the sacraments.[43]

(d) The confessor, realizing that, as God's minister, he knows the secret conscience of his brother, is under a most sacred obligation to maintain the sacramental seal.

The Penitent Himself

(11) The role of the penitent himself is of the greatest importance in this sacrament.

When, properly disposed, he approaches this saving remedy which Christ instituted, and confesses his sins, his actions form part of the sacrament itself. The words of absolution, pronounced by the minister in the name of Christ, complete the sacrament.

Thus the penitent, while experiencing the mercy of God in his life and proclaiming it, joins the priest in celebrating the liturgy of a Church engaged in the holy task of self-renewal.

IV. THE CELEBRATION OF THE SACRAMENT OF PENANCE

The Place of the Celebration

(12) The sacrament of penance is to be administered in a confessional located as prescribed by law.[44]

The Time of the Celebration

(13) The reconciliation of penitents may take place on any day and at any season. A suitable arrangement, however, is for the priest to be in attendance for the exercise of this ministry at a set time on a set day, previously advertised to the faithful. The faithful should be encouraged to develop the habit of approaching this sacrament outside of the celebration of Mass, especially at set times.[45]

The season of Lent is especially suitable for the celebration of the sacrament of penance, for on Ash Wednesday the faithful are admonished: 'Repent and believe the Gospel.' It is appropriate, therefor, to arrange for frequent penitential services during Lent, so that all the faithful might be offered the opportunity of being reconciled to God and their brothers and of celebrating the Paschal mystery with renewed heart during the holy triduum.

Liturgical Vestments

(14) With regard to the liturgical vestments for the celebration of penance, the regulations of local ordinaries are to be obeyed.

a. Order for the Reconciliation of Individual Penitents

The Preparation of the Priest and of the Penitent

(15) Both priest and penitent should in the first place prepare for the celebration of this sacrament by prayer. The priest should invoke the Holy Spirit, asking for light and charity from him. The penitent should compare his life with the example and commandments of Christ and should ask God to forgive his sins.

The Reception of the Penitent

(16) The priest receives the penitent with fraternal charity and if needs be, speaks to him in an informal, friendly way. The penitent then makes the sign of the cross, saying: *In the name of the Father, and of the Son and of the Holy Spirit. Amen.* The priest may join him in this. The priest then invites the penitent, in a short formula, to have confidence in God. If the penitent is not known to the confessor, it will be helpful if he discloses his condition to him, the time of his last confession, the difficulties he encounters in leading a Christian life, and anything else which it might help the confessor to know in exercising his ministry.

The Reading of the Word of God

(17) Then the priest, or the penitent himself, reads some text from the sacred scripture, when appropriate. This can also be done in the course of the preparation for the sacrament. The word of God enlightens the penitent for the discovery of his sins and he is called to conversion and to trust in God's mercy.

The Confession of Sins and Satisfaction

(18) The penitent confesses his sins, commencing where this is customary with the general formula, *I confess.* If there is need of it, the priest helps him to make a complete confession; he subsequently urges him to repent sincerely of his offences against God; he offers him suitable advice to help him begin a new life and if necessary instructs him on the duties of the Christian life.

If the penitent has been the cause of loss or a source of scandal, the confessor should persuade him to make suitable reparation.

The priest then imposes a penance[46] on the penitent. This should be not merely an expiation for past actions, but also a help towards a new life and medicine for his malady. For this reason it should correspond, as far as possible, to the gravity and the nature of the sins. The penance imposed may fittingly take the form of prayer, or self-denial, but especially of service of the neighbour and works of mercy. By these latter the social aspect of sin and of its forgiveness are set in relief.

The Prayer of the Penitent and Absolution of the Priest

(19) After this the penitent, in a prayer for pardon from God the Father, manifests his sorrow and his resolve to lead a new life. It will be found advantageous to use a prayer composed of the words of sacred scripture.

After the penitent's prayer, the priest, extending both hands, or at least his right hand, over the penitent's head, pronounces the formula of absolution. The essential words of the formula are: *I absolve you from your sins, in the name of the Father, and of the Son, and of the Holy Spirit.* As he says these last words, the priest makes the sign of the cross over the penitent. The formula of absolution (see no. 46) indicates that the reconciliation of the penitent proceeds from the mercy of the Father. It shows the connection between the reconciliation of the sinner and the paschal mystery of Christ. It highlights the role of the Holy Spirit in the forgiveness of sins. Lastly, it emphasizes the ecclesial aspect of the sacrament, in that reconciliation with God is asked for and is granted by the ministry of the Church.

Proclamation of Praise and Dismissal of Penitent

(20) When he has been given absolution, the penitent proclaims the mercy of God and offers thanks to God in a short invocation taken from scripture. Then the priest bids him go in peace.

The penitent continues his conversion and gives it expression in a life reformed in the spirit of the Gospel of Christ and increasingly pervaded by charity, 'for charity covers a multitude of sins' (1 Peter 4:8).

The Shorter Rite

(21) When pastoral necessity demands it, the priest may omit or shorten certain parts of the rite. The following must, however, always be retained in their entirety: confession of sins and acceptance of the penance, the invitation to sorrow (n. 44), the formula of absolution and the formula of dismissal. If there is danger of death, however, it is sufficient for the priest to say

the essential words of the formula of absolution: *I absolve you from your sins, in the name of the Father, and of the Son, and of the Holy Spirit.*

b. Order for the Reconciliation of a Number of Penitents, but With Individual Confession and Absolution

(22) When a number of penitents are gathered together to receive sacramental reconciliation, it will be helpful to prepare them for this by the celebration of the word of God.

Others, however, who intend approaching the sacrament at another time, may share in the celebration.

A common celebration manifests more clearly the ecclesial nature of penance. For the faithful together listen to the word of God which proclaims God's mercy and invites them to conversion. Together, they compare their own lives with God's word and they help one another by mutual prayer. After each one has confessed his sins and has been absolved, all together praise God because of the wonderful things he has done for the good of the people whom he acquired by the blood of his Son.

There should be enough priests present who, if necessary, can hear and reconcile individual penitents in appropriate locations.

Opening Rites

(23) When the congregation has assembled, a suitable hymn may be sung. The priest then greets the congregation and he or another minister introduces the ceremony, if this is necessary, explaining the order of the service. After that he invites all to prayer and after an interval of silence he recites a prayer.

The Celebration of the Word of God

(24) It is right that the sacrament of penance should begin with the hearing of the word of God: through his word God calls men to repentance and leads them to true change of heart. If there is only one reading, it ought to be from the Gospel.

Readings are to be chosen in which, especially:

(a) God's voice calls men to conversion and increasingly greater conformity to Christ;

(b) the mystery of reconciliation through the death and resurrection of Christ and by the gift of the Holy Spirit is described;

(c) God's judgement on good and evil in the lives of men is recorded for enlightenment and examination of conscience.

(25) The homily, based on a text of scripture, will lead the penitents to examine their consciences, to turn away from sin and towards God. It will remind the congregation that sin acts against the community, against the neighbour and the sinner himself. It is also helpful to recall:

(a) God's infinite mercy, which is greater than all our iniquities and by which he recalls us to himself again and again;

(b) the necessity of interior repentance, involving a genuine preparedness to repair the damage caused by sin;

(c) the social aspects of grace and sin, whereby the actions of individuals somehow affect the entire body of the Church;

(d) our satisfaction, which derives its efficacy from the satisfaction of Christ, and which involves first of all, apart from works of penance, the exercise of true charity towards God and our neighbour.

(26)   When the homily is finished, there follows a suitable silent interval for the examination of conscience and the arousal of genuine sorrow for sin. The priest, or deacon, or another minister, may help the congregation with short ejaculations or a litany-type prayer, taking their condition and age, etc., into account.

If it is deemed appropriate, this common examination of conscience may substitute for a homily. In this case, however, it must clearly be derived from the text of scripture which was read beforehand.

The Rite of Reconciliation

(27) Then, at the invitation of the deacon or another minister, all kneel down, or bow, and recite a formula of general confession—the *Confiteor,* for example. They then stand and recite a litany-type prayer or sing a suitable hymn, both however expressing the confession of sins, sorrow, prayer for forgiveness and trust in God's mercy. The Lord's prayer is said at the end and is never omitted.

(28) At the end of the Lord's prayer the priests go to the confessionals. Penitents who wish to confess go to the confessors of their choice and when they have been given their penances they are absolved with the formula for reconciling individual penitents.

(29) When the confessions have ceased, the priests return to the sanctuary. The person in charge of the celebration invites all

to give thanks and to profess God's mercy. This can be done by a psalm, a hymn or a litany-type prayer. Then the priest concludes the celebration with a prayer, praising God for his great love for us.

Dismissal of the Congregation

(30) When the thanksgiving has ceased, the priest blesses the faithful. Then the deacon or the priest dismisses them.

c. The Order for Reconciliation of Penitents with Communal Confession and Absolution

The Discipline of Communal Absolution

(31) Individual and integral confession and absolution remains the only ordinary way by which the faithful may be reconciled with God and with the Church, except when this is physically or morally impossible.

It can happen that, because of a particular combination of circumstances, absolution may be, or even ought to be, given to a number of people together, without individual confession of sins.

Aside from danger of death, it is permissible, in a case of grave necessity, to absolve a number of people together, even though they have confessed only in general terms, if they are truly repentant. This can happen when the number of penitents is too great for the number of confessors present to hear their confessions properly, individually, in the time available, with the result that the penitents through no fault of their own would be compelled to remain without sacramental grace or holy communion for a long time. This can happen on the missions especially, but also in other places, in any gathering where the need arises.

If enough confessors are available, the mere presence of a large crowd of penitents—as on a great festival or at a pilgrimage—does not justify communal confession and absolution.[47]

(32) It is for the bishop of the diocese to judge whether the conditions are such as to justify communal sacramental absolution, after he has taken counsel with the other members of the episcopal conference.

Apart from the instances laid down by the bishop of the diocese, if on other occasions there should arise grave need for communal sacramental absolution, the priest should, for legality, apply to the local ordinary beforehand, if this is possible. But if it is not possible to approach the bishop beforehand, he should at the earliest opportunity inform him of the necessity which arose and that he had administered communal absolution.[48]

(33) In order that penitents may avail of communal sacramental absolution, it is absolutely necessary that they be suitably disposed. Each, that is to say, should repent of his sins, should resolve to refrain from sinning, should be determined to make good any losses inflicted and should intend, in due course, to confess singly the grave sins he was unable to confess then. Priests ought carefully to instruct the faithful about these dispositions and conditions: they are required for the validity of the sacrament.[49]

(34) Those whose grave sins are forgiven by communal absolution ought to make an auricular confession before they receive another such absolution, unless a just cause prevent them. They should certainly, unless it be morally impossible, go to confession within the year. They too are subject to the precept which obliges all the faithful to confess, individually, to a priest, at least once a year all the sins, certainly their grave sins, which they have not hitherto confessed singly.[50]

The Rite of Communal Absolution

(35) In reconciling penitents through communal confession and absolution, in the instances defined by law, everything is to be done as outlined above for the reconciliation of a number of penitents, but with individual confession and absolution, apart from the following:

(a) After the homily, or in the course of the homily, the faithful who wish to avail of communal absolution are to be instructed to dispose themselves properly: each should repent of his sins, should resolve to refrain from sinning, should be determined to make good any losses inflicted and should intend, in due course, to confess singly the grave sins he was unable to confess then.[51] A penance should then be imposed on all, individuals adding to it if they wish.

(b) Then the deacon, or another minister, or the priest himself, asks the penitents who wish to be absolved to signify their request in some way (by inclining their heads, for example, by kneeling, or by some other sign determined by the episcopal conference), reciting together a formula of general confession (such as the *Confiteor*). A litany-type prayer or a penitential chant may then follow and the Lord's Prayer is said or sung by all, as in no. 27 above.

(c) The priest then pronounces an invocation, asking for the grace of the Holy Spirit for the forgiveness of sins, proclaiming victory over sin through the death and resurrection of Christ and granting sacramental absolution to the penitents.

(d) Lastly, the priest invites the faithful to give thanks, as in no. 29 above. The concluding prayer is omitted and he immediately blesses the people and dismisses them.

V. PENITENTIAL SERVICES

Nature and Structure

(36) Penitential services are gatherings of God's people to hear God's word through which they are invited to conversion and renewal of life and through which our liberation from sin by the death and resurrection of Christ is announced. They are structured after the fashion of bible services,[52] as outlined in the *Order for the reconciliation of a number of penitents*.

A suitable formula, therefore, is as follows: after the opening rites (hymn, greeting, prayer) there should be one or more readings from the scriptures, interspersed with chants or psalms or moments of silence. The readings are then explained and applied in the homily. There is no reason why, before or after the scripture readings, there should not be readings from the Fathers or from other sources which may help the congregation or individuals to arrive at a true awareness of sin and a true contrition—which, in other words, may convert them.

After the homily and the meditation on the word of God, it is fitting that the congregation should pray with one heart and one voice, using a litany-type prayer, or any other form which will help them to pray together. Lastly, the Lord's Prayer is said, so that God our Father will 'forgive us our trespasses, as we forgive those who trespass against us. . .and deliver us from evil.' The priest or minister who presides concludes with a prayer and the dismissal of the people.

Usefulness and Importance

(37) One must be careful lest the faithful should confuse such services with the celebration of the sacrament of penance.[53] However, penitential services are very helpful in promoting conversion and purification of heart.[54]

Penitential services may usefully be arranged for the following purposes especially:

to foster the spirit of penitence in the Christian community;

to help the faithful to prepare for the confessions which they will subsequently make individually, when opportunity offers;

to train children gradually to inform their consciences with regard to sin in human life and with regard to liberation from sin through Christ;

to help catechumens in their conversion.

Further, where there is no priest to impart sacramental absolution, penitential services are most helpful. They are a help to the attainment of perfect contrition, through which the faithful can obtain God's grace, with the intention of future sacramental confession.[55]

VI. ON ADAPTING THE RITE TO VARIOUS REGIONS AND CIRCUMSTANCES

Adaptations Which the Episcopal Conferences May Make

(38) It will be for episcopal conferences, in preparing particular rituals, to adapt this Order of Penance to the needs of their regions. These will then be employed in their regions, after they shall have been approved by the Holy See. It will be for episcopal conferences:

(a) To frame the regulations for the discipline of the sacrament of penance, especially with regard to the ministry of priests and the reservation of sins;

(b) To frame more precise regulations with regard to a suitable location for the ordinary celebration of penance and with regard to the way in which the faithful are to signify repentance in the administration of communal absolution (see no. 35 above);

(c) To prepare translations of the texts which are truly suited to the character and speech of the people; also to compose new texts for the prayers of faithful and ministers, maintaining the sacramental formula intact.

What Pertains to the Bishop

(39) It will be for the diocesan bishop:

(a) To regulate the discipline of penance in his diocese,[56] even to make changes in the rite in keeping with the norms laid down by the episcopal conference.

(b) To determine, having taken counsel with the other members of the episcopal conference, when communal sacramental absolution may be administered, within the terms prescribed by the Holy See.[57]

The Changes Which the Minister Can Make

(40) It will be for priests, especially parish priests:

(a) To adapt the communal or individual celebration of reconciliation to the concrete circumstances of the penitents, provided the essential structure and the integrity of the formula of absolution be retained. The priest may omit certain parts, if pastoral reasons demand this, or he may enlarge them; he may choose the texts of readings or of prayers; he may select the place best suited to the celebration, in accordance with the regulations laid down by the episcopal conference, so that the entire celebration will be rich and fruitful.

(b) To arrange penitential services a few times a year, especially during Lent, and to prepare them with the help of others, including layfolk, so that the texts chosen and the order of the celebration will be properly suited to the character and circumstances of the community or congregation (children, for example, or invalids, etc.).

(c) In a case of grave necessity not foreseen by the bishop of the diocese, and when recourse to him is not possible, to decide to administer communal absolution, preceded by only a general confession. He must, however, inform the ordinary at the earliest opportunity about the necessity which arose and that he had given the communal absolution.

* Translated by A.F. from Latin text in *Notitiae*, 10 (1974), 44–62.
1. See 2 Cor. 5:18 ff; Col. 1:20.
2. See John 8:34-36.
3. See 1 Peter 2:9.
4. See Luke 15.
5. Luke 5:20, 27-32; 7:48.
6. See Matt. 9:2-8.
7. See Rom. 4:25.
8. See Roman Missal, Third Eucharistic Prayer.
9. See Matt. 26:28.
10. See John 20:19-23.
11. See Luke 24:47.
12. See Acts 3:19, 26; 17:30.
13. See Rom. 6:4-10.
14. Roman Missal, Third Eucharistic Prayer.
15. Roman Missal, Second Eucharistic Prayer.
16. See Council of Trent, Session XIV, *De Sacramento Paenitentiae*, ch.1. Denz.-Schön., 1668, 1670, 1701.

17. Saint Ambrose, Letter 41, 12.
18. See Apoc. 19:7.
19. See Eph. 1:22-23; Second Vatican Council, Const. *Lumen Gentium,* n. 7.
20. Second Vatican Council, Const. *Lumen Gentium,* n. 8.
21. See 1 Peter 4:13.
22. See 1 Peter 4:8.
23. See Council of Trent, Session XIV, *De Sacramento Paenitentiae:* Denz.-Schön., 1638, 1740, 1743; Congr. of Rites, *Eucharisticum Mysterium,* n. 35; General Introduction to the Roman Missal, nn. 29, 30, 56 a, b, g.
24. Second Vatican Council, Const. *Lumen Gentium,* n. 11.
25. Paul VI, Apost. Const., Paenitemini; Second Vatican Council, Const. *Lumen Gentium,* n. 11.
26. See Gal., 2:20; Eph., 4:25.
27. See Tit. 3:6.
28. Paul VI, Apost. Const. *Indulgentiarum Doctrina,* n. 4; See Pius XII, *Mystici Corporis.*
29. See Council of Trent, *loc. cit,* ch. 1: Denz.-Schön., 1673-1675.
30. *Ibid.,* ch. 4: Denz.-Schön., 1676.
31. Paul VI, Apost. Const., *Paenitemini.*
32. See Council of Trent, *loc. cit.,* ch. 5: Denz.-Schön., 1679.
33. See Council of Trent, *loc. cit.,* ch. 8: Denz.-Schön., 1690-1692; Paul VI, Apost. Const., *Indulgentiarum Doctrina,* nn. 2, 3.
34. See Tit., 3:4-5.
35. See Luke 15:7, 10, 32.
36. See Council of Trent, *loc. cit.,* can. 7, 8:Denz.-Schön. 1707-1708.
37. See 2 Cor., 4:10.
38. See Gal., 4:31.
39. See Matt., 18:18; John 20:23.
40. See Second Vatican Council, Const. *Lumen Gentium,* n. 26.
41. See Phil., 1:9-10.
42. See S. Congr. for the Doctrine of the Faith, Pastoral Norms for the imparting of general absolution, n. 12. (Text in DOCTRINE AND LIFE, August, 1972, pp. 436-439.)
43. See Second Vatican Council, Const. *Sacrosanctum Concilium,* on the Liturgy, n. 7.
44. The Latin has: *Sacramentum Paenitentiae administratur in loco et sede, quae jure statuuntur.* The existing canon law speaks of the *locus,* or place, of confession in canon 908 ('a church, a public oratory, or a semi-public oratory'). It speaks of the *sedes confessionalis*—literally, 'confessional seat': our normal term is 'confessional'—in canon 909. (Translator).
45. See *Euch. Mysterium,* n. 35.
46. Here and elsewhere in this paragraph I have rendered 'satisfactio' by 'penance', which is the more usual word in English. (Translator).
47. S. Congr. for the Doctrine of the Faith, *Pastoral Norms for Imparting Communal Sacramental Absolution,* n. III.
48. *Ibid.,* n. V.

49. *Ibid.,* nn. VI and XI.
50. *Ibid.,* nn. VII and VIII.
51. See *ibid.,* n. VI.
52. S. Congr. for Rites, Instr. *Inter Oecumenici,* nn. 37-39.
53. St. Congr for the Doctrine of the Faith, *Pastoral Norms for Imparting Communal Sacramental Absolution,* n. X.
54. *Ibid.*
55. See Council of Trent, Session XIV, ch. 5. Denz-Schön, 1677.
56. See Second Council of the Vatican, Const. Lumen Gentium, n. 26.
57. S. Congr. for the Doctrine of the Faith. *Pastoral Norms for Imparting Communal Sacramental Absolution,* n. V.

73

INSTRUCTION ON
THE EUCHARISTIC PRAYERS
FOR CHILDREN'S MASSES*

S.C.D.W., *Textus precis eucharisticae*, 1 November, 1974

1. A text of the eucharistic prayer suited to children should help them to share more fruitfully in the Mass for adults.

For this reason, the Directory on Children's Masses prescribed that certain texts of the Mass should never be changed for children, 'to prevent children's Masses from becoming altogether too different from adult Masses'. Among them are 'the acclamations and responses of the faithful to the priest's greetings'.[1] Thus, in these eucharistic prayers the dialogue of the Preface is always the same as in Masses for adults. This is also true of the 'Sanctus', apart from what is said below in nn. 18 and 23.

2. Similarly, in accordance with the Apostolic Constitution, *Missale Romanum*, the words of Our Lord are the same in the formula of every Canon.[2]

3. In order to establish a clear distinction for the children between the words said over the bread and wine, on the one hand, and the command to repeat the celebration, on the other, the sentence: 'Then, he said to them' is introduced before the sentence: 'Do this in memory of me.'

4. Each of the three eucharistic prayers for children contains, with a few rare exceptions, all the elements which, according to n. 55 of the General Instruction on the Roman Missal, go to make up a eucharistic prayer.

5. Not only are all the elements present, but, in simpler language suited to children, they express those things which according to tradition are always expressed, such as in the epiclesis, or memorial prayer, for example.

6. Although the language has been simplified, the editors were all the time conscious of the need to avoid the danger of infantilism, which would jeopardise the dignity of the eucharistic

celebration, especially if the words spoken by the celebrant were affected by it.

7. The principles of active participation are especially relevant in the case of children. The number of acclamations has been increased, therefore, in the eucharistic prayers for children, without at the same time obscuring the character of the eucharistic prayer as a *presidential* prayer. The object was to increase the children's participation and make it more fervent.[3]

8. There are difficulties about having just one eucharistic prayer all over the world in Masses for children, granted the differences of culture and temperament between the various countries. For this reason it was felt that it was better to provide three texts, each of a different kind (see nn. 23-25 below).

The Translation of These Prayers in the Different Languages

9. It will be for the episcopal conference to choose one of the proposed schemes and to see to the production of a translation which will be fully in accord with pastoral, pedagogic and liturgical requirements. The text should be approved by the episcopal conference and sent to the Holy See for confirmation.

10. It is to be hoped that the work of translation would be entrusted to a group of men and women competent not merely in liturgy, but also in pedagogy, catechetics, and in literary and musical matters.

11. This group should bear in mind that the Latin text on this occasion is not destined for liturgical use and that therefore it is not simply to be translated.

The Latin text determines indeed the thrust, the substance and the general form of these prayers which must be the same in the different vernacular renderings. But there are certain characteristics of the Latin language (which never developed its own style of talking to children) which must on no account be transferred to the actual vernacular texts intended for liturgical use. These are its preference for hypotaxis[a] and its ornate and diffuse style, what is known as its 'cursus'.[b] The language of the liturgical texts must be adapted to the spirit of each language and to the way in which people using that language speak to children when matters of importance are being discussed. All this is even more true of the languages which are at a greater remove from the Latin language, especially the non-Western languages. For each eucharistic prayer a sample translation into some Western language is offered as a help to the translators.

12. The different literary *genres* in the eucharistic prayer

should be carefully distinguished in preparing these texts—the preface, the intercessions, the acclamations—in accordance with the sound principles on the translation of liturgical texts offered in the Instruction of 25 January, 1949.[4]

13. Episcopal conferences should see to the preparation of music suited to the spirit of their region for the parts to be sung by the children themselves in these prayers.

The Liturgical Use of These Prayers

14. The use of these prayers is to be limited to Masses celebrated with children, as is laid down in the Directory on Children's Masses,[5] with due respect however for the right of the bishop.

15. From the three prayers, the one which seems best suited to the children's condition is to be chosen: either the first, because it is simpler, or the second because it offers fuller scope for participation, or the third because it offers greater scope for variation.

16. The new acclamations can easily be put into liturgical use if the cantor or one of the children leads the way and then all together repeat them, singing or speaking them. In preparing the translations one should take care that the acclamations are introduced simply, for example by using some word which is easily recognised as inviting an acclamation.

17. Episcopal conferences may substitute other acclamations for those in these eucharistic prayers, provided they are similar in spirit.

18. The children must learn to sing or say the Sanctus, though in the meantime the law remains in force which prescribes that 'to make it easier for the children to participate . . . popular adaptations of these texts with appropriate musical settings can be authorised by the competent authority, even though they do not strictly adhere to the liturgical texts.'[6] Wherever the custom prevails of singing responsorially, the episcopal conference may allow the Sanctus to be sung responsorially.

19. The acclamation of the faithful after the consecration is put at a different place, for pedagogical reasons: to make clear to the children the connection between the words of our Lord, 'Do this in memory of me', and the memorial prayer recited by the priest. The acclamation, whether memorial or praise, is not made until after the memorial prayer.

20. In order to foster the participation of the children it is permissible, according to the Directory on Children's Masses, to in-

sert special reasons for giving thanks before the preface dialogue.[7] With regard to participation by gesture and bodily attitude, what has been said in n. 33 of the Directory holds good. Above all, great attention must be paid to interior participation: what is said on this score about festive, fraternal and prayerful participation in n. 23 is especially relevant to the eucharistic prayer.

21. Those who have pastoral charge of children should be convinced of the importance of this interior participation. In order to promote it, diligent catechetical instruction should precede and follow the celebration. The more important of the texts on which this catechesis throws light for the children are those prayers which are the culmination of the eucharistic celebration for children.[8]

22. The rubrics which are found in the Latin text for each eucharistic prayer are to be inserted in the translations.

The special rubrics for concelebration which are to be found in the existing four eucharistic prayers are not found in these new prayers. Taking the psychology of children into account, it would seem advisable not to have concelebration when Mass is celebrated for children.

a) *The First Eucharistic Prayer*

23. In order to familiarise the children with the singing of the Sanctus, the first prayer divides it into two parts, each of which finishes with the acclamation: 'Hosanna in the highest'. In accordance with what is said about it in n. 16, these acclamations may be sung or said, a cantor or one of the children doing so first. The third time, when 'Holy, holy, holy' is to be sung the entire chant may be sung or said by all. After the memorial prayer of this eucharistic prayer one of the acclamations provided for the four existing eucharistic prayers may be substituted for the simpler acclamation provided in the text.

b) *The Second Eucharistic Prayer*

24. With the exception of the Sanctus and the acclamation after the memorial prayer, the acclamations are optional. The acclamations inserted after the words of our Lord over the bread and wine must be regarded and must be sung as a communal meditation on the mystery of the eucharist.

c) *The Third Eucharistic Prayer*

25. In the third eucharistic prayer variations are provided for

one occasion only, that is for paschal time. The idea is that variations would be approved by the episcopal conferences for the other times and occasions and, after being duly confirmed by the Apostolic See in accordance with the circular letter on the eucharistic prayers, n. 10, would be introduced into liturgical use.[9] In preparing these texts, one should be careful to ensure that the three parts (the preface, the part after the Sanctus, the epiclesis) should be in harmony.

The same acclamation is repeated three times after the consecration, in order to instil into the children the nature of the prayer as made up of praise and thanksgiving.

---

*Translated by A.F. Latin text in *Notitiae*, 11 (1975), 7–12.
1. Directory on Children's Masses, no. 39.
2. A.A.S., 1969, 219.
3. See Directory on Children's Masses, n. 22.
(a) I.e. dependent construction: Latin construction tends to be very involved, with a lot of dependent clauses where English, for example, uses separate sentences.
(b) I.e. 'flow', what in English would be classed as rhetorical, 'high-flown'.
4. See *Notitiae*, 1969, 3-12.
5. See Directory on Children's Masses, n. 19.
6. See *ibid*, n. 31.
7. See *ibid*, n. 22.
8. See *ibid*, n. 12.
9. See F., 1, p. 237.

74

**INSTRUCTION ON
THE EUCHARISTIC PRAYERS FOR
MASSES FOR RECONCILIATION***

S.C.D.W., *Opportunum esse*, 1 November, 1974

1. The intentions for the Holy Year have been proposed again and again by the Holy Father and it seemed fitting that they should find expression in liturgical celebrations, especially in the sacrifice of the Mass, by no means excluding the eucharistic prayer itself. For this reason two eucharistic prayers have been prepared which have emphasised aspects of reconciliation in so far as they can be the object of thanksgiving.

2. An episcopal conference may choose one text for use in its territory during the Holy Year in Masses which put forward the intentions of the Holy Year. After the Holy Year, it may be used in Masses at which the mystery of reconciliation is especially emphasised for the faithful.

3. The proposed texts contain all the elements mentioned in n. 55 of the General Instruction of the Roman Missal as constituting a eucharistic prayer. The order of these elements is the same as in the second and fourth eucharistic prayers of the Roman Missal.

4. The rubrics are given in the Latin version of the prayers. As a service to the translators, a translation of each prayer is added in a Western language. The rubrics must be inserted in the translation of each of the eucharistic prayers.

The parts to be said by concelebrants are indicated and the rubrics for concelebration are given.

* Translated by A.F. from Latin text in *Notitiae*, 11 (1975), 6.

75

DECREE ON THE PUBLIC CELEBRATION OF MASS IN THE CATHOLIC CHURCH FOR OTHER DECEASED CHRISTIANS[*]

S.C.D.F., *Accidit in diversis*, 11 June, 1976

From time to time Catholic ministers in this or that region are asked to celebrate Mass for *deceased* persons who are baptized members of other Churches or ecclesial communions. This is especially likely to happen when the deceased person had a high regard and esteem for the Catholic religion, or had held public office in the service of the entire civil community.

There is no difficulty, as one knows, about the celebration of private[**] Masses for such deceased persons. Quite the contrary: it can be recommended on several grounds, such as respect, friendship, gratitude and the like, provided no prohibition stands in the way.

The current discipline forbids the celebration of public Masses for deceased persons who had not been in full communion with the Catholic Church.[1]

The religious and social conditions in which that discipline was deemed advisable have now changed and this Sacred Congregation has been asked from many quarters if public Masses may in certain cases be celebrated for such deceased persons.

The Fathers of the Sacred Congregation for the Doctrine of the Faith examined the problem in detail in the ordinary congregation on 9 June 1976 and issued the following decree:

I. The current discipline with regard to the celebration of public Masses for other deceased Christians shall remain in force as a general rule. Due consideration for the consciences of such deceased persons would itself require this, since they did not profess the Catholic faith in full.

II. Exceptions to this general rule may be allowed, until the new code shall have been promulgated, whenever both the following conditions obtain:

1. The public celebration of Masses must be expressly re-

quested by the relatives, friends or subjects of the deceased person, for a genuine religious motive.

2. There must be, in the judgment of the ordinary, no scandal to the faithful.

These two conditions can be more easily verified of our brothers of the Eastern Churches, for we have a closer, though not complete, fellowship with them in matters of faith.

III. In such cases, public Mass may be celebrated. However, the name of the deceased may not be mentioned in the eucharistic prayer, since this would presuppose full communion with the Catholic Church.

If other Christians are present as well as the Catholics who participate in the celebration of the Masses, the regulations made by the Second Vatican Council[2] and by the Holy See[3] with regard to *communicatio in sacris* must be most faithfully observed.

In an audience granted to the undersigned Cardinal Prefect of the Sacred Congregation for the Doctrine of the Faith on 11 June 1976, the Supreme Pontiff Paul VI repealed as far as was necessary canon 809 (together with canon 2262,2,2) and canon 1241. He ratified, approved and ordered the promulgation of the above-mentioned decision of the Fathers, all things to the contrary notwithstanding.

---

* Translated by A.F. from Latin of *AAS* 68 (1976), 621–622.
** The document uses the terms 'public' and 'private' rather than the terms 'Mass with a congregation' and 'Mass without a congregation' used in the 'General Instruction of the Roman Missal' nn 77 ff and 209 ff. The reason, presumably, is partly because the Code here uses the terms 'public' and 'private', partly because the meaning intended is not quite the same as that intended by the terminology of the General Instruction. The terms 'public' and 'private' in the present context would appear to have more to do with putting notices in the newspapers, and such like, than with whether or not the faithful participate (see B. H. Merkelbach, O.P., *Summa Theologiae Moralis, vol. 3,* p. 297). Thus, presumably the term 'private Mass' as used in this document could cover a Mass in which some of the faithful participated, in a private venue and without publicity.
1. See *Canon 1241*, together with *Canon 1240*, I; I.
2. *Decree on the Catholic Eastern Churches, Orientalium Ecclesiarum, 26–29,* in *Vatican Council II: The Conciliar and post-conciliar documents,* edited by Austin Flannery, O.P., pp. 450–451; *Decree on Ecumenism, Unitatis Redintegratio, 8,* in Flannery, *op cit.,* 460–461.
3. See *Directory concerning ecumenical matters,* 40–42, 55–56, in Flan-

nery, *op. cit.*, pp. 496–497; *On admitting other Christians to Eucharistic Communion in the Catholic Church,* 5–6, in Flannery, *op. cit.*, pp. 558–559.

76

A QUESTION ABOUT GENERAL ABSOLUTION[*]

S.C.D.F., *In the case*, 20 January, 1978

In the case of a certain ecclesiastical jurisdiction "X", special penitential services in preparation for Easter were planned, specifying places and times in which general absolution would be given, together with provision for preparation of the people for such services.

This pastoral plan was favorably received by the faithful, and general absolution was given in the presence of several priests, some of whom were also penitents.

Is the case described above in conformity with the norms for general absolution?

RESPONSE

The Congregation for the Doctrine of the Faith replies that the case described does not conform to the 1972 *Normae pastorales circa absolutionem sacramentalem generali modo impertiendam* because the conditions listed for the use of the extraordinary practice of general absolution are not necessarily verified.

1. Norm III requires that the faithful, too large in number for the small number of priests to hear their individual confessions properly within a suitable period of time, would have to go without sacramental grace or holy communion for a long time and through no fault of their own.

The case described does not offer any reason why the faithful could not find other opportunities for confession and holy communion, which are normally offered on a regular basis in their parishes; such a reason might be present, for example, where a priest could visit a remote mission station only infrequently.

2. Norm IV requires that bishops and priests dispose the arrangement of pastoral duties so that a sufficient number of priests will be available for the ministry of sacramental confession.

The case described does not offer any reason why the available priests could not arrange for the normal confession procedures according to nn. 15–21 and 22–30 of the *Ordo Paenitentiae*.

*English original in E.V., 6, nn. 576–577.

77

ON THE MYSTERY AND WORSHIP
OF THE EUCHARIST*

John Paul II, *Dominicae cenae*, 24 February, 1980

1. Again this year, for Holy Thursday, I am writing a letter to all of you. This letter has an immediate connection with the one which you received last year on the same occasion, together with the letter to the priests. I wish *in the first place to thank you cordially* for having accepted my previous letters with that spirit of unity which the Lord established between us, and also for having transmitted to your priests the thoughts that I desired to express at the beginning of my pontificate.

During the Eucharistic Liturgy of Holy Thursday, you renewed, together with your priests, the promises and commitments undertaken at the moment of ordination. Many of you, venerable and dear Brothers, told me about it later, also adding words of personal thanks, and indeed often sending those expressed by your priests. Furthermore, many priests expressed their joy, both because of the profound and solemn character of Holy Thursday as the annual "Feast of Priests" and also because of the importance of the subjects dealt with in the letter addressed to them.

Those replies form a rich collection which once more indicates how dear to the vast majority of priests of the Catholic Church is the path of the priestly life, the path along which this Church has been journeying for centuries: how much they love and esteem it, and how much they desire to follow it for the future.

At this point I must add that *only a certain number of matters were dealt with in the letter to priests*, as was in fact emphasized at the beginning of the document.[1] Furthermore, the main stress was laid upon the pastoral character of the priestly ministry; but this certainly does not mean that those groups of priests who are not engaged in direct pastoral activity were not also taken into consideration. In this regard I would refer once more to the teaching of the Second Vatican Council, and also to the declarations of the 1971 Synod of Bishops.

The pastoral character of the priestly ministry does not cease to mark the life of every priest, even if the daily tasks that he carries out are not explicitly directed to the pastoral administration of the Sacraments. In this sense, the letter written to the priests on Holy Thursday was addressed to them all, without any exception, even though, as I said above, it did not deal with all the aspects of the life and activity of priests. I think this clarification is useful and opportune at the beginning of the present letter.

I

THE EUCHARISTIC MYSTERY IN THE LIFE OF THE CHURCH AND OF THE PRIEST

Eucharist and Priesthood

2. The present letter that I am addressing to you, my venerable and dear Brothers in the Episcopate—and which is, as I have said, in a certain way a continuation of the previous one— is also closely linked with the mystery of Holy Thursday, and is related to the priesthood. In fact I intend to devote it to the Eucharist, and in particular *to certain aspects of the Eucharistic mystery and its impact on the lives of those who are the ministers of it*: and so those to whom this letter is directly addressed are you, the Bishops of the Church; together with you, all the priests; and, in their own rank, the deacons too.

In reality, the ministerial and hierarchical priesthood, the priesthood of the Bishops and the priests, and, at their side, the ministry of the deacons—ministries which normally begin with the proclamation of the Gospel—are in the closest relationship with the Eucharist. The Eucharist is the principal and central *raison d'être* of the Sacrament of the priesthood, which effectively came into being at the moment of the institution of the Eucharist, and together with it.[2] Not without reason the words "Do this in memory of me" are said immediately after the words of Eucharistic consecration, and we repeat them every time we celebrate the Holy Sacrifice.[3]

Through our ordination—the celebration of which is linked

to the Holy Mass from the very first liturgical evidence[4]—we are
united in a singular and exceptional way to the Eucharist. In a
certain way we derive *from* it and exist *for* it. We are also, and in
a special way, responsible for it—each priest in his own community and each Bishop by virtue of the care of all the communities entrusted to him, on the basis of the *"sollicitudo omnium ecclesiarum"* that Saint Paul speaks of.[5] Thus we Bishops
and priests are entrusted with the great "Mystery of Faith", and
while it is also given to the whole People of God, to all believers
in Christ, yet to us has been entrusted the Eucharist also "for"
others, who expect from us a particular witness of veneration
and love towards this Sacrament, so that they too may be able to
be built up and vivified "to offer spiritual sacrifices".[6]

In this way our Eucharistic worship, both in the celebration of
Mass and in our devotion to the Blessed Sacrament, is like a life-
giving current that links our ministerial or hierarchical priesthood to the common priesthood of the faithful, and presents it
in its vertical dimension and with its central value. The priest fulfils his principal mission and is manifested in all his fullness
when he celebrates the Eucharist,[7] and this manifestation is
more complete when he himself allows the depth of that mystery
to become visible, so that it alone shines forth in people's hearts
and minds, through his ministry. This is the supreme exercise of
the "kingly priesthood", "the source and summit of all Christian life".[8]

Worship of the Eucharistic Mystery

3. This worship is directed towards God the Father through
Jesus Christ in the Holy Spirit. In the first place towards the
Father, who, as Saint John's Gospel says, "loved the world so
much that he gave his only Son, so that everyone who believes in
him may not be lost but may have eternal life".[9]

It is also directed, in the Holy Spirit, to the Incarnate Son, in
the economy of salvation, especially at that moment of supreme
dedication and total abandonment of himself to which the
words uttered in the Upper Room refer: "this is my body given
up for you. . . this is the cup of my blood shed for you. . .".[10]
The liturgical acclamation: "We proclaim your death, Lord
Jesus" takes us back precisely to that moment; and with the
proclamation of his Resurrection we embrace in the same act of
veneration Christ risen and glorified "at the right hand of the
Father", as also the expectation of his "coming in glory". *Yet it
is the voluntary annihilation, accepted by the Father and*

glorified with the Resurrection, which, sacramentally celebrated together with the Resurrection, brings us to adore the Redeemer who "became obedient unto death, even death on a cross".[11]

And this adoration of ours contains yet another special characteristic. It is compenetrated by the greatness of that human death, in which the world, that is to say each one of us, has been loved "to the end".[12] Thus it is also a response that tries to repay that love immolated even to the death on the Cross: it is our "Eucharist", that is to say our giving him thanks, our praise of him for having redeemed us by his death and made us sharers in immortal life through his Resurrection.

This worship, given therefore to the Trinity of the Father and of the Son and of the Holy Spirit, above all accompanies and permeates the celebration of the Eucharistic liturgy. But it must fill our churches also outside the timetable of Masses. Indeed, since the Eucharistic mystery was instituted out of love, and makes Christ sacramentally present, it is worthy of thanksgiving and worship. And this worship must be prominent in all our encounters with the Blessed Sacrament, both when we visit our churches and when the sacred species are taken to the sick and administered to them.

Adoration of Christ in this Sacrament of love must also find expression *in various forms of Eucharistic devotion*: personal prayer before the Blessed Sacrament, hours of adoration, periods of exposition—short, prolonged and annual (Forty Hours)—Eucharistic benediction, Eucharistic processions, Eucharistic Congresses.[13] A particular mention should be made at this point of the Solemnity of the Body and Blood of Christ as an act of public worship rendered to Christ present in the Eucharist, a feast instituted by my predecessor Urban IV in memory of the institution of this great Mystery.[14] All this therefore corresponds to the general principles and particular norms already long in existence but newly formulated during or after the Second Vatican Council.[15]

The encouragement and the deepening of Eucharistic worship are *proofs of that authentic renewal* which the Council set itself as an aim and of which they are *the central point*. And this, venerable and dear Brothers, deserves separate reflection. The Church and the world have a great need of Eucharistic worship. Jesus waits for us in this Sacrament of love. Let us be generous with our time in going to meet him in adoration and in contemplation that is full of faith and ready to make reparation for the great faults and crimes of the world. May our adoration never cease.

Eucharist and Church

4. Thanks to the Council we have realized with renewed force the following truth: just as the Church "makes the Eucharist" so "the Eucharist builds up" the Church;[16] and this truth is closely bound up with the mystery of Holy Thursday. The Church was founded, as the new community of the People of God, in the apostolic community of those Twelve who, at the Last Supper, became partakers of the Body and Blood of the Lord under the species of bread and wine. Christ had said to them: "Take and eat. . . take and drink". And carrying out this command of his, they entered for the first time into sacramental communion with the Son of God, a communion that is a pledge of eternal life. From that moment until the end of time, *the Church is being built up through that same communion with the Son of God, a communion which is a pledge of the eternal Passover.*

Dear and venerable Brothers in the Episcopate, as teachers and custodians of the salvific truth of the Eucharist, we must always and everywhere preserve this meaning and this dimension of the sacramental encounter and intimacy with Christ. It is precisely these elements which constitute the very substance of Eucharistic worship. The meaning of the truth expounded above in no way diminishes—in fact it facilitates—the Eucharistic character of spiritual drawing together and union between the people who share in the Sacrifice, which then in Communion becomes for them the banquet. This drawing together and this union, the prototype of which is the union of the Apostles about Christ at the Last Supper, express the Church and bring her into being.

But the Church is not brought into being only through the union of people, through the experience of brotherhood to which the Eucharistic banquet gives rise. The Church is brought into being when, in that fraternal union and communion, we celebrate the Sacrifice of the Cross of Christ, when we proclaim "the Lord's death until he comes",[17] and later, when, being deeply compenetrated with the mystery of our salvation, we approach as a community the table of the Lord, in order to be nourished there, in a sacramental manner, by the fruits of the Holy Sacrifice of propitiation. Therefore in Eucharistic Communion we receive Christ, Christ himself; and our union with him, which is a gift and grace for each individual, brings it about that in him we are also associated in the unity of his Body which is the Church.

Only in this way, through that faith and that disposition of mind, is there brought about that building up of the Church, which in the Eucharist truly finds its "source and summit", according to the well known expression of the Second Vatican Council.[18] This truth, which as a result of the same Council has received a new and vigorous emphasis,[19] must be a frequent theme of our reflection and teaching. Let all pastoral activity be nourished by it, and may it also be food for ourselves and for all the priests who collaborate with us, and likewise for the whole of the communities entrusted to us. In this practice there should thus be revealed, almost at every step, that *close relationship between the Church's spiritual and apostolic vitality* and *the Eucharist, understood in its profound significance* and from all points of view.[20]

Eucharist and Charity

5. Before proceeding to more detailed observations on the subject of the celebration of the Holy Sacrifice, I wish briefly to reaffirm the fact that Eucharistic worship constitutes the soul of all Christian life. In fact Christian life is expressed in the fulfilling of the greatest commandment, that is to say in the love of God and neighbour, and this love finds its source in the Blessed Sacrament, which is commonly called the Sacrament of love.

The Eucharist signifies this charity, and therefore recalls it, makes it present *and at the same time brings it about*. Every time that we consciously share in it, there opens in our souls a real dimension of that unfathomable love that includes everything that God has done and continues to do for us human beings, as Christ says: "My Father goes on working, and so do I".[21] Together with this unfathomable and free gift, which is *charity* revealed in its fullest degree in the saving Sacrifice of the Son of God, the Sacrifice of which the Eucharist is the indelible sign, there also springs up within us a lively response of love. We not only know love; we ourselves *begin to love*. We enter, so to speak, upon the path of love and along this path make progress. Thanks to the Eucharist, the love that springs up within us from the Eucharist develops in us, becomes deeper and grows stronger.

Eucharistic worship is therefore precisely the expression of that love which is the authentic and deepest characteristic of the Christian vocation. This worship springs from the love and serves the love to which we are all called in Jesus Christ.[22] A living fruit of this worship is the perfecting of the image of God that we bear within us, an image that corresponds to the one that Christ has revealed to us. As we thus become adorers of the Father "in spirit and truth",[23] we mature in an ever fuller union with Christ, we are ever more united to him, and—if one may use the expression—we are ever more in harmony with him.

The doctrine of the Eucharist, sign of unity and bond of charity, taught by Saint Paul,[24] has been in subsequent times deepened by the writings of very many saints who are a living example for us of Eucharistic worship. We must always have this reality before our eyes, and at the same time we must continually try to bring it about that our own generation too may add new examples to those marvellous examples of the past, new examples no less living and eloquent, that will reflect the age to which we belong.

Eucharist and Neighbour

6. *The authentic sense of the Eucharist becomes of itself the school of active love for neighbour.* We know that this is the true and full order of love that the Lord has taught us: "By this love you have for one another, everyone will know that you are my disciples".[25] The Eucharist educates us to this love in a deeper way; it shows us, in fact, what value each person, our brother or sister, has in God's eyes, if Christ offers himself equally to each one, under the species of bread and wine. If our Eucharistic worship is authentic, it must make us grow in awareness of the dignity of each person. The awareness of that dignity becomes the *deepest motive of our relationship with our neighbour.*

We must also become particularly sensitive to all human suffering and misery, to all injustice and wrong, and seek the way to redress them effectively. Let us learn to discover with respect the truth about the inner self of people, for it is precisely this inner self that becomes the dwelling-place of God present in the Eucharist. Christ comes into the hearts of our brothers and sisters and visits their consciences. How the image of each and every one changes, when we become aware of this reality, when we make it the subject of our reflections! The sense of the Eucharistic Mystery leads us to a love for our neighbour, to a love for every human being.[26]

Eucharist and Life

7. Since therefore the Eucharist is the source of charity, it has always been at the centre of the life of Christ's disciples. It has the appearance of bread and wine, that is to say of food and

drink; it is therefore as familiar to people, as closely linked to their life, as food and drink. The veneration of God, who is Love, springs, in Eucharistic worship, from that kind of intimacy in which *he himself, by analogy with food and drink, fills our spiritual being*, ensuring its life, as food and drink do. This "Eucharistic" veneration of God therefore strictly corresponds to his saving plan. He himself, the Father, wants the "true worshippers"[27] to worship him precisely in this way, and it is Christ who expresses this desire, both with his words and likewise with this sacrament in which he makes possible worship of the Father in the way most in conformity with the Father's will.

From this concept of Eucharistic worship there then stems the whole *sacramental style of the Christian's life*. In fact, leading a life based on the sacraments and animated by the common priesthood means in the first place that Christians desire God to act in them in order to enable them to attain, in the Spirit, "the fullness of Christ himself".[28] God, on his part, does not touch them only through events and by this inner grace; he also acts in them with greater certainty and power through the sacraments. The sacraments give the lives of Christians a sacramental style.

Now, of all the sacraments it is the Holy Eucharist that brings to fullness their initiation as Christians and confers upon the exercise of the common priesthood that sacramental and ecclesial form that links it—as we mentioned before[29]—to the exercise of the ministerial priesthood. In this way Eucharistic worship is the *centre and goal of all sacramental life*.[30] In the depths of Eucharistic worship we find a continual echo of the sacraments of Christian initiation: Baptism and Confirmation. Where better is there expressed the truth that we are not only "called God's children" but "that is what we are"[31] by virtue of the Sacrament of Baptism, if not precisely in the fact that in the Eucharist we become partakers of the Body and Blood of God's only Son? And what predisposes us more to be "true witnesses of Christ"[32] before the world—as we are enabled to be by the Sacrament of Confirmation—than Eucharistic communion, in which Christ bears witness to us, and we to him?

It is impossible to analyze here in greater detail the links between the Eucharist and the other Sacraments, in particular with the Sacrament of family life and the Sacrament of the sick. In the Encyclical *Redemptor Hominis*[33] I have already drawn attention to the close link between the Sacrament of Penance and the Sacrament of the Eucharist. *It is not only that Penance leads to the Eucharist, but that the Eucharist also leads to Penance.* For when we realize who it is that we receive in Eucharistic Communion, there springs up in us almost spontaneously a sense of unworthiness, together with sorrow for our sins and an interior need for purification.

But we must always take care that this great meeting with Christ in the Eucharist does not become a mere habit, and that we do not receive him unworthily, that is to say in a state of mortal sin. The practice of the virtue of penance and the Sacrament of Penance are essential for sustaining in us and continually deepening that spirit of veneration which man owes to God himself and to his love so marvellously revealed.

The purpose of these words is to put forward some general reflections on worship of the Eucharistic mystery, and they could be developed at greater length and more fully. In particular, it would be possible to link what has been said about the effects of the Eucharist on love for others with what we have just noted about commitments undertaken towards humanity and the Church in Eucharistic communion, and then outline the picture of that "new earth"[34] that springs from the Eucharist through every "new self".[35] *In this Sacrament* of bread and wine, of food and drink, *everything that is human really undergoes a singular transformation and elevation.* Eucharistic worship is not so much worship of the inaccessible transcendence as worship of the divine condescension, and it is also the merciful and redeeming transformation of the world in the human heart.

Recalling all this only very briefly, I wish, notwithstanding this brevity, to create a wider context for the questions that I shall subsequently have to deal with: these questions are closely linked with the celebration of the Holy Sacrifice. In fact, in that celebration there is expressed in a more direct way the worship of the Eucharist. This worship comes from the heart, as a most precious homage inspired by the faith, hope and charity which were infused into us at Baptism. And it is precisely about this that I wish to write to you in this letter, venerable and dear Brothers in the Episcopate, and with you to the priests and deacons. It will be followed by detailed indications from the Sacred Congregation for the Sacraments and Divine Worship.

II

THE SACRED CHARACTER OF THE EUCHARIST AND SACRIFICE

Sacred Character

8. Beginning with the Upper Room and Holy Thursday, the celebration of the Eucharist has a long history, a history as long as that of the Church. In the course of this history the secondary elements have undergone certain changes, but *there has been no change in the essence of the "Mysterium"* instituted by the Redeemer of the world at the Last Supper. The Second Vatican Council too brought alterations, as a result of which the present liturgy of the Mass is different in some ways from the one known before the Council. We do not intend to speak of these differences: it is better that we should now concentrate on what is essential and immutable in the Eucharistic liturgy.

There is a close link between this element of the Eucharist and its sacredness, that is to say its being a holy and sacred action. Holy and sacred, because in it are the continual presence and action of Christ, "the Holy One" of God,[36] "anointed with the Holy Spirit",[37] "consecrated by the Father"[38] to lay down his life of his own accord and to take it up again,[39] and the High Priest of the new covenant.[40] For it is he who, represented by the celebrant, makes his entrance into the sanctuary and proclaims his Gospel. It is he who is "the offerer and the offered, the consecrator and the consecrated".[41] The Eucharist is a holy and sacred action, because it constitutes the sacred species, the *Sancta sanctis*, that is to say the "holy things (Christ, the Holy One) given to the holy", as all the Eastern liturgies sing at the moment when the Eucharistic bread is raised in order to invite the faithful to the Lord's Supper.

The sacredness of the Mass, therefore, is not a "sacralization", that is to say something that man adds to Christ's action in the Upper Room, for the Holy Thursday Supper was a sacred rite, a primary and constitutive liturgy, through which Christ, by pledging to give his life for us, himself celebrated sacramentally the mystery of his Passion and Resurrection, the heart of every Mass. Our Masses, being derived from this liturgy, possess of themselves a complete liturgical form, which, in spite of its variations in line with the families of rites, remains substantially the same. The sacred character of the Mass is a sacredness instituted by Christ. The words and action of every priest, answered by the conscious active participation of the whole Eucharistic assembly, echo the words and action of Holy Thursday.

The priest offers the Holy Sacrifice *in personna Christi*; this means more than offering "in the name of" or "in the place of" Christ. *In persona* means in specific sacramental identification with "the eternal High Priest"[42] who is the Author and principal Subject of this Sacrifice of his, a Sacrifice in which, in truth, nobody can take his place. Only he—only Christ—was able and is always able to be the true and effective "expiation for our sins and. . .for the sins of the whole world".[43] Only his sacrifice— and no one else's—was able and is able to have a "propitiatory power" before God, the Trinity, and the transcendent holiness. Awareness of this reality throws a certain light on the character and significance of the priest čelebrant who, *by confecting the Holy Sacrifice and acting "in persona Christi",* is sacramentally (and ineffably) brought into that most profound *sacredness,* and made part of it, spiritually linking with it in turn all those participating in the Eucharistic assembly.

This Sacred Rite, which is actuated in different liturgical forms, may lack some secondary elements, but it can in no way lack its essential sacred character and sacramentality, since these are willed by Christ and transmitted and regulated by the Church. Neither can this Sacred Rite be utilized for other ends. If separated from its distinctive sacrificial and sacramental nature, the Eucharistic mystery simply ceases to be. It admits of no "profane" imitation, an imitation that would very easily (indeed regularly) become a profanation. This must always be remembered, perhaps above all in our time, when we see a tendency to do away with the distinction between the "sacred" and "profane", given the widespread tendency, at least in some places, to desacralize everything.

In view of this fact, *the Church has a special duty to safeguard and strengthen the sacredness of the Eucharist.* In our pluralistic and often deliberately secularized society, *the living faith* of the Christian community—a faith always aware of its rights vis-à-vis those who do not share that faith—ensures respect for this sacredness. The duty to respect each person's faith is the complement of the natural and civil right to freedom of conscience and of religion.

The sacred character of the Eucharist has found and continues to find expression in the terminology of theology and the liturgy.[44] This sense of the objective sacred character of the Eucharistic Mystery is so much part of the faith of the People of God that their faith is enriched and strengthened by it.[45]

Therefore the ministers of the Eucharist must, especially today, be illumined by the fullness of this living faith, and in its light they must understand and perform all that is part, by Christ's will and the will of his Church, of their priestly ministry.

Sacrifice

9. The Eucharist is above all else a sacrifice. It is the sacrifice of the Redemption and also the sacrifice of the New Covenant,[46] as we believe and as the Eastern Churches clearly profess: "Today's sacrifice", the Greek Church stated centuries ago, "is like that offered once by the Only-begotten Incarnate Word; it is offered by him (now as then), since it is one and the same sacrifice".[47] Accordingly, precisely by making this single sacrifice of our salvation present, man and the world are restored to God through the paschal newness of Redemption. This restoration cannot cease to be: it is the foundation of the "new and eternal covenant" of God with man and of man with God. If it were missing, one would have to question both the excellence of the sacrifice of the Redemption, which in fact was perfect and definitive, and also the sacrificial value of the Mass. In fact, the Eucharist, being a true sacrifice, brings about this restoration to God.

Consequently, the celebrant, as minister of this sacrifice, is the authentic *priest*, performing—in virtue of the specific power of sacred Ordination—a true sacrificial act that brings creation back to God. Although all those who participate in the Eucharist do not confect the sacrifice as he does, they offer with him, by virtue of the common priesthood, their own *spiritual sacrifices* represented by the bread and wine from the moment of their presentation at the altar. For this liturgical action, which takes a solemn form in almost all liturgies, has a "spiritual value and meaning".[48] The bread and wine become in a sense a symbol of all that the Eucharistic assembly brings, on its own part, as an offering to God and offers spiritually.

It is important that this first moment of the Liturgy of the Eucharist in the strict sense should find expression in the attitude of the participants. There is a link between this and the offertory "procession" provided for in the recent liturgical reform[49] and accompanied, in keeping with ancient tradition, by a psalm or song. A certain length of time must be allowed, so that all can become aware of this act, which is given expression at the same time by the words of the celebrant.

Awareness of the act of presenting the offerings should be

maintained throughout the Mass. Indeed, it should be brought to fullness at the moment of the consecration and of the anamnesis offering, as is demanded by the fundamental value of the moment of the sacrifice. This is shown by the words of the Eucharistic Prayer said aloud by the priest. It seems worthwhile repeating here some expressions in the third Eucharistic Prayer that show in particular the sacrificial character of the Eucharist and link the offering of our persons with Christ's offering: "Look with favour on your Church's offering, and see the Victim whose death has reconciled us to yourself. Grant that we, who are nourished by his body and blood, may be filled with his Holy Spirit, and become one body, one spirit in Christ. May he make us an everlasting gift to you."

This sacrificial value is expressed earlier in every celebration by the words with which the priest concludes the presentation of the gifts, asking the faithful to pray "that my sacrifice and yours may be acceptable to God, the almighty Father". These words are binding, since they express the character of the entire Eucharistic liturgy and the fullness of its divine and ecclesial content.

All who participate with faith in the Eucharist become aware that it is a "Sacrifice", that is to say a "consecrated Offering". For the bread and wine presented at the altar and accompanied by the devotion and the spiritual sacrifices of the participants are finally consecrated, so as to become *truly, really and substantially* Christ's own body that is given up and his blood that is shed. Thus, by virtue of the consecration, the species of bread and wine re-present[50] in a sacramental unbloody manner the bloody propitiatory Sacrifice offered by him on the Cross to his Father for the salvation of the world. Indeed, he alone, giving himself as a propitiatory victim in an act of supreme surrender and immolation, has reconciled humanity with the Father, solely through his sacrifice, "having cancelled the bond which stood against us".[51]

To this sacrifice, which is renewed in a sacramental form on the altar, the offerings of bread and wine, united with the devotion of the faithful, nevertheless bring their unique contribution, since by means of the Consecration by the priest they become the sacred species. This is made clear by the way in which the priest acts during the Eucharistic Prayer, especially at the consecration, and when the celebration of the Holy Sacrifice and participation in it are accompanied by awareness that "the Teacher is here and is calling for you".[52] This call of the Lord to us through his Sacrifice opens our hearts, so that, purified in the mystery of our Redemption, they may be united to him in Eucharistic communion, which confers upon participation at Mass a value that is mature, complete, and binding on human life: "The Church's intention is that the faithful not only offer the spotless victim but also learn to offer themselves and daily to be drawn into ever more perfect union, through Christ the Mediator, with the Father and with each other, so that at last God may be all in all".[53]

It is therefore very opportune and necessary to continue to actuate a new and intense education, in order to discover all the richness contained in the new liturgy. Indeed, the liturgical renewal that has taken place since the Second Vatican Council has given, so to speak, greater visibility to *the Eucharistic sacrifice*. One factor contributing to this is that the words of the Eucharistic prayer are said aloud by the celebrant, particularly the words of consecration, with the acclamation by the assembly immediately after the elevation.

All this should fill us with joy, but we should also remember that *these changes demand new spiritual awareness and maturity,* both on the part of the celebrant—especially now that he celebrates "facing the people"—and by the faithful. Eucharistic worship matures and grows when the words of the Eucharistic prayer, especially the words of consecration, are spoken with great humility and simplicity, in a worthy and fitting way, which is understandable and in keeping with their holiness; when this essential act of the Eucharistic liturgy is performed unhurriedly; and when it brings about in us such recollection and devotion that the participants become aware of the greatness of the mystery being accomplished and show it by their attitude.

III

THE TWO TABLES OF THE LORD AND THE COMMON POSSESSION OF THE CHURCH

The Table of the Word of God

10. We are well aware that from the earliest times the celebration of the Eucharist has been linked not only with prayer but

also with the reading of Sacred Scripture and with singing by the whole assembly. As a result, it has long been possible to apply to the Mass the comparison, made by the Fathers, with the two tables, at which the Church prepares for her children the word of God and the Eucharist, that is, the Bread of the Lord. We must therefore go back to the first part of the Sacred Mystery, the part that at present is most often called *the liturgy of the word*, and devote some attention to it.

The reading of the passages of Sacred Scripture chosen for each day *has been subjected by the Council to new criteria and requirements*.[54] As a result of these norms of the Council a new collection of readings has been made, in which there has been applied to some extent the principle of continuity of texts and the principle of making all the Sacred Books accessible. The insertion of the psalms with responses into the liturgy makes the participants familiar with the great wealth of Old Testament prayer and poetry. The fact that these texts are read and sung in the vernacular enables everyone to participate with fuller understanding.

Nevertheless, there are also those people who, having been educated on the basis of the old liturgy in Latin, experience the lack of this "one language", which in all the world was an expression of the unity of the Church and through its dignified character elicited a profound sense of the Eucharistic Mystery. It is therefore necessary to show not only understanding but also full respect towards these sentiments and desires. As far as possible these sentiments and desires are to be accommodated, as is moreover provided for in the new dispositions.[55] The Roman Church has special obligations towards Latin, the splendid language of ancient Rome, and she must manifest them whenever the occasion presents itself.

The possibilities that the postconciliar renewal has introduced in this respect are indeed often utilized so as to make us *witnesses of and sharers in the authentic celebration of the word of God*. There is also an increase in the number of people taking an active part in this celebration. Groups of readers and cantors, and still more often choirs of men or women, are being set up and are devoting themselves with great enthusiasm to this aspect. The word of God, Sacred Scripture, is beginning to take on new life in many Christian communities. The faithful gathered for the liturgy prepare with song for listening to the Gospel, which is proclaimed with the devotion and love due to it.

All this is noted with great esteem and gratitude, but it must not be forgotten that complete renewal makes yet other demands. These demands consist in *a new sense of responsibility towards the word of God* transmitted through the liturgy in various languages, something that is certainly in keeping with the universality of the Gospel and its purposes. The same sense of responsibility also involves the performance of the corresponding liturgical actions (reading or singing), which must accord with the principles of art. To preserve these actions from all artificiality, they should express such capacity, simplicity and dignity as to highlight the special character of the sacred text, even by the very manner of reading or singing.

Accordingly, these demands, which spring from a new responsibility for the word of God in the liturgy,[56] go yet deeper and *concern the inner attitude* with which the ministers of the word perform their function in the liturgical assembly.[57] This responsibility also concerns *the choice of texts*. The choice has already been made by the competent ecclesiastical authority, which has also made provision for the cases in which readings more suited to a particular situation may be chosen.[58] Furthermore, it must always be remembered that only the word of God can be used for Mass readings. The reading of Scripture cannot be replaced by the reading of other texts, however much they may be endowed with undoubted religious and moral values. On the other hand such texts can be used very profitably in the homily. Indeed the homily is supremely suitable for the use of such texts, provided that their content corresponds to the required conditions, since it is one of the tasks that belong to the nature of the homily to show the points of convergence between revealed divine wisdom and noble human thought seeking the truth by various paths.

The Table of the Bread of the Lord

11. The other table of the Eucharistic mystery, that of the Bread of the Lord, also requires reflection from the viewpoint of the present-day liturgical renewal. This is a question of the greatest importance, since it concerns a special act of living faith, and indeed, as has been attested since the earliest centuries,[59] it is a manifestation of *worship of Christ, who in Eucharistic communion entrusts himself to each one of us*, to our hearts, our consciences, our lips and our mouths, in the form of food. Therefore there is special need, with regard to this question, for the watchfulness spoken of by the Gospel, on the

part of the pastors who have charge of Eucharistic worship and on the part of the People of God, whose "sense of the faith"[60] must be very alert and acute particularly in this area.

I therefore wish to entrust this question to the heart of each one of you, venerable and dear Brothers in the Episcopate. You must above all make it part of your care for all the Churches entrusted to you. I ask this of you in the name of the unity that we have received from the Apostles as our heritage, collegial unity. This unity came to birth, in a sense, at the table of the Bread of the Lord on Holy Thursday. With the help of your brothers in the priesthood, do all you can to *safeguard the sacred dignity of the Eucharistic ministry and that deep spirit of Eucharistic communion* which belongs in a special way to the Church as the People of God, and which is also a particular heritage transmitted to us from the Apostles, by various liturgical traditions, and by unnumbered generations of the faithful, who were often heroic witnesses to Christ, educated in "the school of the Cross" (Redemption) and of the Eucharist.

It must be remembered that the Eucharist as the table of the Bread of the Lord is a continuous invitation. This is *shown in the liturgy when the celebrant says: "This is the Lamb of God. Happy are those who are called to his supper"*;[61] it is also shown by the familiar Gospel parable about the guests invited to the marriage banquet.[62] Let us remember that in this parable there are many who excuse themselves from accepting the invitation for various reasons.

Moreover our Catholic communities certainly do not lack people who *could participate* in Eucharistic Communion *and do not*, even though they have no serious sin on their conscience as an obstacle. To tell the truth, this attitude, which in some people is linked with an exaggerated severity, has changed in the present century, though it is still to be found here and there. In fact what one finds most often is not so much a feeling of unworthiness as a certain lack of interior willingness, if one may use this expression, a lack of Eucharistic "hunger" and "thirst", which is also a sign of lack of adequate sensitivity towards the great Sacrament of love and a lack of understanding of its nature.

However, we also find in recent years another phenomenon. Sometimes, indeed quite frequently, everybody participating in the Eucharistic assembly goes to communion; and on some such occasions, as experienced pastors confirm, there has not been due care to approach the Sacrament of Penance so as to purify one's conscience. This can of course mean that those approaching the Lord's Table find nothing on their conscience, ac-

cording to the objective law of God, to keep them from this
sublime and joyful act of being sacramentally united with
Christ. But there can also be, at least at times, another idea
behind this: the idea of the Mass as *only* a banquet[63] in which
one shares by *receiving the Body of Christ in order to manifest,
above all else, fraternal communion*. It is not hard to add to
these reasons a certain human respect and mere "conformity".

This phenomenon demands from us watchful attention and a
theological and pastoral analysis guided by a sense of great
responsibility. We cannot allow the life of our communities to
lose the good quality of sensitiveness of Christian conscience,
guided solely by respect for Christ, who, when he is received in
the Eucharist, should find in the heart of each of us a worthy
abode. This question is closely linked not only with the practice
of the Sacrament of Penance but also with a correct sense of
responsibility for the whole deposit of moral teaching and for
the precise distinction between good and evil, a distinction
which then becomes for each person sharing in the Eucharist the
basis for a correct judgment of self to be made in the depths of
the personal conscience. Saint Paul's words, "Let a man examine himself",[64] are well known; this judgment is an indispensable condition for a personal decision whether to approach
Eucharistic communion or to abstain.

Celebration of the Eucharist places before us many other requirements regarding the ministry of the Eucharistic Table.
Some of these requirements concern only priests and deacons,
others concern all who participate in the Eucharistic liturgy.
Priests and deacons must remember that the service of the table
of the Bread of the Lord imposes on them special obligations
which refer in the first place to Christ himself *present in the
Eucharist* and secondly to all who actually participate in the
Eucharist or who might do so. With regard to the first, perhaps
it will not be superfluous to recall the words of the *Pontificale*
which on the day of ordination the Bishop addresses to the new
priest as he hands to him on the paten and in the chalice the
bread and wine offered by the faithful and prepared by the
deacon: *Accipe oblationem plebis sanctae Deo offerendam.
Agnosce quod agis, imitare quod tractabis, et vitam tuam
mysterio dominicae crucis conforma.*[65] This last admonition
made to him by the Bishop should remain as one of the most
precious norms of his Eucharistic ministry.

It is from this admonition that the priest's attitude in handling
the Bread and Wine which have become the Body and Blood of
the Redeemer should draw its inspiration. Thus it is necessary

for all of us who are ministers of the Eucharist to examine carefully our actions at the altar, in particular the way in which we handle that Food and Drink which are the Body and Blood of the Lord our God in our hands: the way in which we distribute Holy Communion; the way in which we perform the purification.

All these actions have a meaning of their own. Naturally, scrupulosity must be avoided, but God preserve us from behaving in a way that lacks respect, from undue hurry, from an impatience that causes scandal. Over and above our commitment to the evangelical mission, our greatest commitment consists in exercising this mysterious power over the Body of the Redeemer, and all that is within us should be decisively ordered to this. We should also always remember that to this ministerial power we have been sacramentally consecrated, that we have been chosen from among men "for the good of men".[66] We especially, the priests of the Latin Church, whose ordination rite added in the course of the centuries the custom of anointing the priest's hands, should think about this.

In some countries *the practice of receiving communion in the hand* has been introduced. This practice has been requested by individual Episcopal Conferences and has received approval from the Apostolic See. However, cases of a deplorable lack of respect towards the Eucharistic species have been reported, cases which are imputable not only to the individuals guilty of such behaviour but also to the pastors of the Church who have not been vigilant enough regarding the attitude of the faithful towards the Eucharist. It also happens, on occasion, that the free choice of those who prefer to continue the practice of receiving the Eucharist on the tongue is not taken into account in those places where the distribution of Communion in the hand has been authorized. It is therefore difficult in the context of this present letter not to mention the sad phenomena previously referred to. This is in no way meant to refer to those who, receiving the Lord Jesus in the hand, do so with profound reverence and devotion, in those countries where this practice has been authorized.

But one must not forget the primary office of priests, who have been consecrated by their ordination to represent Christ the Priest: for this reason their hands, like their words and their will, have become the direct instruments of Christ. Through this fact, that is as ministers of the Holy Eucharist, they have a primary responsibility for the sacred species, because it is a total responsibility: they offer the bread and wine, they consecrate it, and then distribute the sacred species to the participants in the assembly who wish to receive them. Deacons can only bring to the altar the offerings of the faithful and, once they have been consecrated by the priest, distribute them. How eloquent therefore, even if not of ancient custom, is the rite of the anointing of the hands in our Latin ordination, as though precisely for these hands a special grace and power of the Holy Spirit is necessary!

To touch the sacred species and *to distribute them with their own hands* is a privilege of the ordained, one which indicates an active participation *in the ministry of the Eucharist*. It is obvious that the Church can grant this faculty to those who are neither priests nor deacons, as is the case with acolytes in the exercise of their ministry, especially if they are destined for future ordination, or with other lay people who are chosen for this to meet a just need, but always after an adequate preparation.

A Common Possession of the Church

12. We cannot, even for a moment, forget that the Eucharist is a special possession belonging to the whole Church. It is the *greatest gift* in the order of grace and of sacrament that the divine Spouse has offered and unceasingly offers to his spouse. And precisely because it is such a gift, all of us should in a spirit of profound faith let ourselves be guided by a sense of truly Christian responsibility. A gift obliges us ever more profoundly because it speaks to us not so much with the force of a strict right as with the force of personal confidence, and thus—without legal obligations—it calls for *trust and gratitude*. The Eucharist is just such a gift and such a possession. We should remain faithful in every detail to what it expresses in itself and to what it asks of us, namely thanksgiving.

The Eucharist is a common possession of the whole Church as the sacrament of her unity. And thus the Church has the strict duty to specify everything which concerns participation in it and its celebration. We should therefore act according to the principles laid down by the last Council, which, in the Constitution on the Sacred Liturgy, defined the authorizations and obligations of individual Bishops in their dioceses and of the Episcopal Conferences, given the fact that both act in collegial unity with the Apostolic See.

Furthermore we should follow the directives issued by the various departments of the Holy See in this field: be it in liturgical matters, in the rules established by the liturgical books in what concerns the Eucharistic mystery, and in the Instructions devoted to this mystery,[67] be it with regard to *communicatio in sacris*, in the norms of the *Directorium de re oecumenica*[68] and in the *Instructio de peculiaribus casibus admittendi alios christianos ad communionem eucharisticam in Ecclesia catholica*.[69] And although at this stage of renewal the possibility of a certain "creative" freedom has been permitted, nevertheless this freedom must strictly respect the requirements of substantial unity. We can follow the path of this pluralism (which arises in part from the introduction itself of the various languages into the liturgy) only as long as the essential characteristics of the celebration of the Eucharist are preserved, and the norms prescribed by the recent liturgical reform are respected.

Indispensable effort is required everywhere to ensure that within the pluralism of Eucharistic worship envisioned by the Second Vatican Council the unity of which the Eucharist is the sign and cause is clearly manifested.

This task, over which in the nature of things the Apostolic See must keep careful watch, should be assumed not only by each *Episcopal Conference* but by every minister of the Eucharist, without exception. Each one should also remember that he is responsible for the common good of the whole Church. The *priest as minister*, as celebrant, as the one who presides over the Eucharistic assembly of the faithful, should have a special *sense of the common good of the Church*, which he represents through his ministry, but to which he must also be subordinate, according to a correct discipline of faith. He cannot consider himself a "proprietor" who can make free use of the liturgical text and of the sacred rite as if it were his own property, in such a way as to stamp it with his own arbitrary personal style. At times this latter might seem more effective, and it may better correspond to subjective piety; nevertheless, objectively it is always a betrayal of that union which should find its proper expression in the Sacrament of unity.

Every priest who offers the Holy Sacrifice should recall that during this Sacrifice it is not *only* he with his community that is praying but the whole Church, which is thus expressing in this Sacrament her spiritual unity, among other ways by the *use of the approved liturgical text*. To call this position "mere insistence on uniformity" would only show ignorance of the objective requirements of authentic unity, and would be a symptom of harmful individualism.

This subordination of the minister, of the celebrant, to the *Mysterium* which has been entrusted to him by the Church for the good of the whole People of God, should also find expression in the observance of the liturgical requirements concerning the celebration of the Holy Sacrifice. These refer for example to dress, and in particular to the vestments worn by the celebrant. Circumstances have of course existed and continue to exist in which the prescriptions do not oblige. We have been greatly moved when reading books written by priests who had been prisoners in extermination camps, with descriptions of Eucharistic celebrations without the above-mentioned rules, that is to say without an altar and without vestments. But although in those conditions this was a proof of heroism and deserved profound admiration, nevertheless in *normal conditions* to ignore the liturgical directives can be interpreted as a lack of respect towards the Eucharist, dictated perhaps by individualism or by an absence of a critical sense concerning current opinions, or by a certain *lack of a spirit of faith*.

Upon all of us who, through the *grace* of God, are ministers of the Eucharist, there weighs a particular responsibility for the ideas and attitudes of our brothers and sisters who have been entrusted to our pastoral care. It is our vocation to nurture, above all by personal example, every healthy manifestation of worship towards Christ present and operative in that Sacrament of love. May God preserve us from acting otherwise and weakening that worship by "becoming unaccustomed" to various manifestations and forms of Eucharistic worship which express a perhaps "traditional" but healthy piety, and which express above all that "sense of the faith" possessed by the whole People of God, as the Second Vatican Council recalled.[70]

As I bring these considerations to an end, I would like to ask forgiveness—in my own name and in the name of all of you, venerable and dear Brothers in the Episcopate—for everything which, for whatever reason, through whatever human weakness, impatience or negligence, and also through the at times partial, one-sided and erroneous application of the directives of the Second Vatican Council, may have caused scandal and disturbance concerning the interpretation of the doctrine and the veneration due to this great Sacrament. And I pray the Lord Jesus that in the future we may avoid in our manner of dealing with this sacred mystery anything which could weaken or disorient in any way the sense of reverence and love that exists in our faithful people.

May Christ himself help us to follow the path of true renewal towards that fullness of life and of Eucharistic worship whereby the Church is built up in that unity that she already possesses, and which she desires to bring to ever greater perfection for the glory of the living God and for the salvation of all humanity.

CONCLUSION

13. Permit me, venerable and dear Brothers, to end these reflections of mine, which have been restricted to a detailed examination of only a few questions. In undertaking these reflections, I have had before my eyes all the work carried out by the Second Vatican Council, and have kept in mind Paul VI's Encyclical *Mysterium Fidei* promulgated during that Council and all the documents issued after the same Council for the purpose of implementing the postconciliar liturgical renewal. A very close and organic *bond exists between the renewal of the liturgy and the renewal of the whole life of the Church*.

The Church not only acts but also expresses herself in the liturgy, lives by the liturgy and draws from the liturgy the strength for her life. For this reason liturgical renewal carried out correctly in the spirit of the Second Vatican Council is, in a certain sense, the measure and the condition for putting into effect the teaching of that Council which we wish to accept with profound faith, convinced as we are that by means of this Council the Holy Spirit "has spoken to the Church" the truths and given the indications for carrying out her mission among the people of today and tomorrow.

We shall continue in the future to take special care to promote and follow the renewal of the Church according to the teaching of the Second Vatican Council, *in the spirit of an ever living Tradition*. In fact to the substance of Tradition properly understood belongs also a correct re-reading of the "signs of the times", which require us to draw from the rich treasure of Revelation "things both new and old".[71] Acting in this spirit, in accordance with this counsel of the Gospel, the Second Vatican Council carried out a providential effort to renew the face of the Church in the sacred liturgy, most often having recourse to what is "ancient", what comes from the heritage of the Fathers and is the expression of the faith and doctrine of a Church which has remained united for so many centuries.

In order to be able to continue in the future to put into practice the directives of the Council in the field of liturgy, and in particular in the field of Eucharistic worship, *close collaboration is necessary* between the competent department of the Holy See and each Episcopal Conference, a collaboration which must be *at the same time vigilant and creative*. We must keep our sights fixed on the greatness of the most holy mystery and at the same time on spiritual movements and social changes, which are so significant for our times, since they not only sometimes create difficulties but also prepare us for a new way of participating in that great mystery of faith.

Above all I wish to emphasize that the problems of the liturgy, and in particular of the Eucharistic Liturgy, must not be *an occasion for dividing Catholics and for threatening the unity of the Church*. This is demanded by an elementary understanding of that Sacrament which Christ has left us as the source of spiritual unity. And how could the Eucharist, which in the Church is the *sacramentum pietatis, signum unitatis, vinculum caritatis,*[72] form between us at this time a point of division and a source of distortion of thought and of behaviour, instead of being the focal point and constitutive centre, which it truly is in its essence, of the unity of the Church herself?

We are all equally indebted to our Redeemer. We should all listen together to that Spirit of truth and of love whom he has promised to the Church and who is operative in her. In the name of this truth and of this love, in the name of the Crucified Christ and of his Mother, I ask you, and beg you: let us abandon all opposition and division, and let us all unite in this great mission of salvation which is the price and at the same time the fruit of our Redemption. The Apostolic See will continue to do all that is possible to provide the means of ensuring that unity of which we speak. Let everyone avoid anything in his own way of acting which could "grieve the Holy Spirit".[73]

In order that this unity and the constant and systematic collaboration which leads to it may be perseveringly continued, I beg on my knees that, through the intercession of Mary, holy Spouse of the Holy Spirit and Mother of the Church, we may all receive the light of the Holy Spirit. And blessing everyone, with all my heart I once more address myself to you, my venerable and dear Brothers in the Episcopate, with a fraternal greeting and with full trust. In this collegial unity in which we share, let us do all we can to ensure that the Eucharist may become an ever greater source of life and light for the consciences of all our brothers and sisters of all the communities in the universal unity of Christ's Church on earth.

In a spirit of fraternal charity, to you and to all our confrères in the priesthood I cordially impart the Apostolic Blessing.

* Translation by Vatican Press Office. Latin original in *Notitiae*, 1980, 125-154.

1. Cf. chapter 2: *AAS* 71 (1979), pp. 395f.

2. Cf. Ecumenical Council of Trent, Session XXII, can. 2: *Conciliorum Œcumenicorum Decreta*, ed. 3, Bologna 1973, p. 735.

3. Because of this precept of the Lord, an Ethiopian Eucharistic Liturgy recalls that the Apostles "established for us Patriarchs, Archbishops, Priests and Deacons to celebrate the ritual of your holy Church": *Anaphora Sancti Athanasii: Prex Eucharistica*, Haenggi-Pahl, Fribourg (Switzerland) 1968, p. 183.

4. C.F. *La Tradition apostolique de saint Hippolyte*, nos. 2-4, ed. Botte, Münster/Westfalen 1963, pp. 5-17.

5. *2 Cor* 11:28.

6. *1 Pt* 2:5.

7. Cf. Second Vatican Ecumenical Council, Dogmatic Constitution on the Church *Lumen Gentium*, 28: *AAS* 57 (1965), pp. 33 f.; Decree on the Ministry and Life of Priests *Presbyterorum Ordinis*, 2, 5: *AAS* 58 (1966), pp. 993, 998; Decree on the Missionary Activity of the Church *Ad Gentes*, 39: *AAS* 58 (1966), p. 986.

8. Second Vatican Ecumenical Council, Dogmatic Constitution on the Church *Lumen Gentium*, 11: *AAS* 57 (1965), p. 15.

9. *Jn* 3:16. It is interesting to note how these words are taken up by the Liturgy of Saint John Chrysostom immediately before the words of consecration and introduce the latter: cf. *La divina Liturgia del nostro Padre Giovanni Crisostomo*, Roma-Grottaferrata 1967, pp. 104 f.

10. Cf. *Mt* 26:26-28; *Mk* 14:22-25; *Lk* 22:18-20; *1 Cor* 11:23-25; cf. also the Eucharistic Prayers.

11. *Phil* 2-8

12. *Jn* 13:1.

13. Cf. John Paul II, Homily in Phoenix Park, Dublin, 7: *AAS* 71 (1979), pp. 1074 ff.; Sacred Congregation of Rites, Instruction *Eucharisticum Mysterium: AAS* 59 (1967), pp. 539-573; *Rituale Romanum. De sacra communione et de cultu Mysterii eucharistici extra Missam*, ed. typica, 1973. It should be noted that the value of the worship and the sanctifying power of these forms of devotion to the Eucharist depend not so much upon the forms themselves as upon interior attitudes.

14. Cf. Bull *Transiturus de hoc mundo* (11 August 1264): Æmilii Friedberg, Corpus Iuris Canonici, Pars II. *Decretalium Collectiones*, Leipzig 1881, pp. 1174-1177; *Studi eucaristici*, "VII Centenario della Bolla *Transiturus* 1264-1964", Orvieto 1966, pp. 302-317.

15. Cf. Paul VI, Encyclical Letter *Mysterium Fidei: AAS* 57 (1965), pp. 753-774; Sacred Congregation of Rites, Instruction *Eucharisticum Mysterium: AAS* 59 (1967), pp. 539-573; *Rituale Romanum, De sacra*

communione et de cultu Mysterii eucharistici extra Missam, ed. typica, 1973.
16. John Paul II, Encyclical Letter *Redemptor Hominis*, 20: *AAS* 71 (1979), p. 311; cf. Second Vatican Ecumenical Council, Dogmatic Constitution on the Church *Lumen Gentium*, 11: *AAS* 57 (1965), pp. 15 f.; also, note 57 to Schema II of the same Dogmatic Constitution, in *Acta Synodalia Sacrosancti Concilii Œcumenici Vaticani II*, vol. II, periodus 2ᵃ, pars I, sessio publica II, pp. 251 f.; Paul VI, Address at the General Audience of 15 September 1965: *Insegnamenti di Paolo VI*, III (1965), p. 1036; H. De Lubac, *Méditation sur l'Eglise*, 2 ed., Paris 1963, pp. 129–137.
17. *1 Cor* 11:26.
18. Cf. Second Vatican Ecumenical Council, Dogmatic Constitution on the Church *Lumen Gentium*, 11: *AAS* 57 (1965), pp. 15 f.; Constitution on the Sacred Liturgy *Sacrosanctum Concilium*, 10: *AAS* 56 (1964), p. 102; Decree on the Ministry and Life of Priests *Presbyterorum Ordinis*, 5: *AAS* 58 (1966), pp. 997 f.; Decree on the Bishops' Pastoral Office in the Church *Christus Dominus*, 30: *AAS* 58 (1966), pp. 688 f.; Decree on the Church's Missionary Activity *Ad Gentes*, 9: *AAS* 58 (1966), pp. 957 f.
19. Cf. Second Vatican Ecumenical Council, Dogmatic Constitution on the Church *Lumen Gentium*, 26: *AAS* 57 (1965), pp. 31 f.; Decree on Ecumenism *Unitatis Redintegratio*, 15: *AAS* 57 (1965), pp. 101 f.
20. This is what the Opening Prayer of Holy Thursday asks for: "We pray that in this eucharist we may find the fullness of love and life": *Missale Romanum, ed. typica altera* 1975, p. 244; also the Communion epiclesis of the Roman Missal: "May all of us who share in the body and blood of Christ be brought together in unity by the Holy Spirit. Lord, remember your Church throughout the world; make us grow in love": *Eucharistic Prayer* II: *ibid.*, pp. 458 f.; *Eucharistic Prayer* III, p. 463.
21. *Jn* 5:17.
22. Cf. Prayer after Communion of the Mass for the Twenty-second Sunday in ordinary time: "Lord, you renew us at your table with the bread of life. May this food strengthen us in love and help us to serve you in each other": *Missale Romanum, ed. cit.*, p. 361.
23. *Jn* 4:23.
24. Cf. *1 Cor* 10:17; commented upon by Saint Augustine: *In Evangelium Ioannis tract.* 31, 13: *PL* 35, 1613; also commented upon by the Ecumenical Council of Trent, Session XIII, can. 8: *Conciliorum Œcumenicorum Decreta*, ed. 3, Bologna 1973, p. 697, 7; cf. Second Vatican Ecumenical Council, Dogmatic Constitution on the Church *Lumen Gentium*, 7: *AAS* 57 (1965), p. 9.
25. *Jn* 13:35.
26. This is expressed by many prayers of the *Roman Missal*: the Prayer over the Gifts from the Common "For those who work for the under-privileged": "May we who celebrate the love of your Son also follow the example of your saints and grow in love for you and for one another": *Missale Romanum, ed. cit.*, p. 721; also the Prayer after Communion of the Mass "For Teachers": ". . . may this holy meal help us to follow the example of your saints by showing in our lives the light of truth and love for our brothers": *ibid.*, p. 723; cf. also the Prayer after Communion of the Mass for the Twenty-second Sunday in ordinary time, quoted in Note 22.
27. *Jn* 4:23.

28. *Eph* 4:13.
29. Cf. above, no. 2.
30. Cf. Second Vatican Ecumenical Council, Decree on the Missionary Activity of the Church *Ad Gentes*, 9, 13: *AAS* 58 (1966), pp. 958, 961 f.; Decree on the Ministry and Life of Priests *Presbyterorum Ordinis*, 5: *AAS* 58 (1966), p. 997.
31. *1 Jn* 3:1.
32. Second Vatican Ecumenical Council, Dogmatic Constitution on the Church *Lumen Gentium*, 11: *AAS* 57 (1965), p. 15.
33. Cf. no. 20: *AAS* 71 (1979), pp. 313 f.
34. *2 Pt* 3:13.
35. *Col* 3:10.
36. *Lk* 1:34; *Jn* 6:69; *Acts* 3:14; *Rev* 3:7.
37. *Acts* 10:38; *Lk* 4:18.
38. *Jn* 10:36.
39. Cf. *Jn* 10:17.
40. *Heb* 3:1; 4:15, etc.
41. As was stated in the ninth-century Byzantine liturgy, according to the most ancient codex, known formerly as *Barberino di San Marco* (Florence), and, now that it is kept in the Vatican Apostolic Library, as *Barberini Greco* 366 f° 8 verso, lines 17–20. This part has been published by F. E. Brightman, *Liturgies Eastern and Western*, 1. *Eastern Liturgies*, Oxford 1896, p. 318, 34–35.
42. Opening Prayer of the second votive Mass of the Holy Eucharist: *Missale Romanum, ed. cit.*, p. 858.
43. *1 Jn* 2:2; cf. *ibid.*, 4:10.
44. We speak of the *divinum Mysterium*, the *Sanctissimum*, the *Sacrosanctum*, meaning what is *Sacred* and *Holy* par excellence. For their part, the Eastern Churches call the Mass *raza* or *mysterion, hagiasmos quddasă, qedassĕ*, that is to say "consecration" par excellence. Furthermore there are the liturgical rites, which, in order to inspire a sense of the sacred, prescribe silence, and standing or kneeling, and likewise professions of faith, and the incensation of the Gospel book, the altar, the celebrant and the sacred species. They even recall the assistance of the angelic beings created to serve the Holy God, i.e. with the *Sanctus* of our Latin churches and the *Trisagion* and *Sancta Sanctis* of the Eastern Liturgies.
45. For instance, in the invitation to receive communion, this faith has been so formed as to reveal complementary aspects of the presence of Christ the Holy One: the epiphanic aspect noted by the Byzantines ("Blessed is he who comes in the name of the Lord: the Lord is God and *has appeared to us*": *La divina Liturgia del santo nostro Padre Giovanni Crisostomo*, Roma–Grottaferrata 1967, pp. 136 f.); the aspect of relation and union sung of by the Armenians (Liturgy of Saint Ignatius of Antioch: "Unus Pater sanctus *nobiscum*, unus Filius sanctus *nobiscum*, unus Spiritus sanctus *nobiscum*": *Die Anaphora des heiligen Ignatius von Antiochien*, übersetzt von A. Rücker, *Oriens Christianus*, 3ª ser., 5 [1930], p. 76); and the hidden heavenly aspect celebrated by the Chaldaeans and Malabars (cf. the antiphonal hymn sung by the priest and the assembly after communion: F. E. Brightman, *op. cit.*, p. 299).
46. Cf. Second Vatican Ecumenical Council, Constitution on the Sacred Liturgy *Sacrosanctum Concilium* 2, 47: *AAS* 56 (1964), pp. 83 f.; 113; Dogmatic Constitution on the Church *Lumen Gentium*, 3 and

28: *AAS* 57 (1965), pp. 6, 33 f.; Decree on Ecumenism *Unitatis Redintegratio*, 2: *AAS* 57 (1965), p. 91; Decree on the Ministry and Life of Priests *Presbyterorum Ordinis*, 13: *AAS* 58 (1966), pp. 1011 f.; Ecumenical Council of Trent, Session XXII, chap. I and II: *Conciliorum Œcumenicorum Decreta*, ed. 3, Bologna 1973, pp. 732 f.; especially: *una eademque est hostia, idem nunc offerens sacerdotum ministerio, qui se ipsum tunc in cruce obtulit, sola offerendi ratione diversa* (*ibid.*, p. 733).

47. Synodus Constantinopolitana adversus Sotericum (January 1156 and May 1157): Angelo Mai, *Spicilegium romanum*, t. X, Rome 1844, p. 77; *PG* 140, 190; cf. Martin Jugie, *Dict. Théol. Cath.*, t. X, 1338; *Theologia dogmatica christianorum orientalium*, Paris 1930, pp. 317-320.

48. *Institutio Generalis Missalis Romani*, 49 c: *Missale Romanum, ed. cit.*, p. 39; cf. Second Vatican Ecumenical Council, Decree on the Ministry and Life of Priests *Presbyterorum Ordinis*, 5: *AAS* 58 (1966), pp. 997 f.

49. *Ordo Missae cum populo*, 18: *Missale Romanum, ed. cit.*, p. 390.

50. Cf. Ecumenical Council of Trent, Session 22, chap. I, *Conciliorum Œcumenicorum Decreta*, ed. 3, Bologna 1973, pp. 732 f.

51. *Col* 2:14.

52. *Jn* 11:28.

53. *Institutio Generalis Missalis Romani*, 55 f.; *Missale Romanum, ed. cit.*, p. 40.

54. Cf. Constitution on the Sacred Liturgy *Sacrosanctum Concilium*, 35, 51: *AAS* 56 (1964), pp. 109, 114.

55. Cf. Sacred Congregation of Rites, Instruction *In edicendis normis*, VI, 17–18; VII, 19–20: *AAS* 57 (1965), pp. 1012f.; Instruction *Musicam Sacram*, IV, 48: *AAS* 59 (1967), p. 314; Decree *De titulo Basilicae Minoris*, II, 8: *AAS* 60 (1968), p. 538; Sacred Congregation for Divine Worship, Notif. *De Missali Romano, Liturgia Horarum et Calendario*, I, 4: *AAS* 63 (1971), p. 714.

56. Cf. Paul VI, Apostolic Constitution *Missale Romanum*: "We are fully confident that both priests and faithful will prepare their minds and hearts more devoutly for the Lord's Supper, meditating on the scriptures, nourished day by day with the words of the Lord": *AAS* 61 (1969), pp. 220 f.; *Missale Romanum, ed. cit.*, p. 15.

57. Cf. *Pontificale Romanum. De Institutione Lectorum et Acolythorum*, 4, *ed. typica*, 1972, p. 19 f.

58. Cf. *Institutio Generalis Missalis Romani*, 319–320: *Missale Romanum, ed. cit.*, p. 87.

59. Cf. Fr. J. Dölger, *Das Segnen der Sinne mit der Eucharistie. Eine altchristliche Kommunionsitte: Antike und Christentum*, t. 3 (1932), pp. 231–244; *Das Kultvergenen der Donatistin Lucilla von Karthago. Reliquienkuss vor dem Kuss der Eucharistie, ibid.*, pp. 245–252.

60. Cf. Second Vatican Ecumenical Council, Dogmatic Constitution on the Church *Lumen Gentium*, 12, 35: *AAS* 57 (1965), pp. 16, 40.

61. Cf. *Jn* 1:29; *Rev* 19:9.

62. Cf. *Lk* 14:16 ff.

63. Cf. *Institutio Generalis Missalis Romani*, 7–8: *Missale Romanum, ed. cit.*, p. 29.

64. *1 Cor* 11:28.

65. *Pontificale Romanum. De Ordinatione Diaconi, Presbyteri et Episcopi, ed. typica*, 1968, p. 93.

66. *Heb* 5:1.

67. Sacred Congregation of Rites, Instruction *Eucharisticum Mysterium: AAS* 59 (1967), pp. 539–573; *Rituale Romanum. De sacra communione et de cultu Mysterii eucharistici extra Missam, ed. typica,* 1973; Sacred Congregation for Divine Worship, *Litterae circulares ad Conferentiarum Episcopalium Praesides de precibus eucharisticis: AAS* 65 (1973), pp. 340–347.

68. Nos. 38–63: *AAS* 59 (1967), pp. 586–592.

69. *AAS* 64 (1972), pp. 518–525. Cf. also the *Communicatio* published the following year for the correct application of the above-mentioned Instruction: *AAS* 65 (1973), pp. 616–619.

70. Cf. Second Vatican Ecumenical Council, Dogmatic Constitution on the Church *Lumen Gentium,* 12: *AAS* 57 (1965), pp. 16 f.

71. *Mt* 13:52.

72. Cf. Saint Augustine, *In Evangelium Ioannis tract.* 26, 13: *PL* 35, 1612 f.

73. *Eph* 4:30.

78

INSTRUCTION ON CERTAIN NORMS CONCERNING THE WORSHIP OF THE EUCHARISTIC MYSTERY*

S.C.S.D.W., *Inaestimabile donum*, 3 April, 1980

Foreword

Following the letter that Pope John Paul II addressed on 24 February 1980 to the Bishops and, through them, to the Priests, and in which he again considered the priceless gift of the Holy Eucharist, the Sacred Congregation for the Sacraments and Divine Worship is calling to the Bishops' attention certain norms concerning worship of this great mystery.

These indications are not a summary of everything already stated by the Holy See in the documents concerning the Eucharist promulgated since the Second Vatican Council and still in force, particularly in the *Missale Romanum*,[1] the Ritual *De sacra Communione et de cultu Mysterii eucharistici extra Missam*,[2] and the Instructions *Eucharisticum Mysterium*,[3] *Memoriale Domini*,[4] *Immensae Caritatis*,[5] and *Liturgicae Instaurationes*.[6]

This Sacred Congregation notes with great joy the many positive results of the liturgical reform: a more active and conscious participation by the faithful in the liturgical mysteries, doctrinal and catechetical enrichment through the use of the vernacular and the wealth of readings from the Bible, a growth in the community sense of liturgical life, and successful efforts to close the gap between life and worship, between liturgical piety and personal piety, and between liturgy and popular piety.

But these encouraging and positive aspects cannot suppress concern at the varied and frequent abuses being reported from different parts of the Catholic world: the confusion of roles, especially regarding the priestly ministry and the role of the laity (indiscriminate shared recitation of the Eucharistic Prayer, homilies given by lay people, lay people distributing communion while the priests refrain from doing so); an increasing loss of the sense of the sacred (abandonment of liturgical vestments, the Eucharist celebrated outside church without real need, lack of reverence and respect for the Blessed Sacrament, etc); misunderstanding of the ecclesial character of the liturgy (the use of private texts, the proliferation of unapproved Eucharistic Prayers, the manipulation of the liturgical texts for social and political ends). In these cases we are face to face with a real falsification of the Catholic liturgy: "One who offers worship to God on the Church's behalf in a way contrary to that which is laid down by the Church with God-given authority and which is customary in the Church is guilty of falsification".[7]

None of these things can bring good results. The consequences are—and cannot fail to be—the impairing of the unity of faith and worship in the Church, doctrinal uncertainty, scandal and bewilderment among the People of God, and the near inevitability of violent reactions.

The faithful have a right to a true Liturgy, which means the Liturgy desired and laid down by the Church, which has in fact indicated where adaptations may be made as called for by pastoral requirements in different places, or by different groups of people. Undue experimentation, changes and creativity bewilder the faithful. The use of unauthorized texts means a loss of the necessary connection between the *lex orandi* and the *lex credendi*. The Second Vatican Council's admonition in this regard must be remembered: "No person, even if he be a priest, may add, remove or change anything in the liturgy on his own authority".[8] And Paul VI of venerable memory stated that: "Anyone who takes advantage of the reform to indulge in arbitrary experiments is wasting energy and offending the ecclesial sense".[9]

A. THE MASS

1. "The two parts which in a sense go to make up the Mass, namely the liturgy of the word and the Eucharistic liturgy, are so closely connected that they form but one single act of worship".[10] A person should not approach the table of the bread of the Lord without having first been at the table of his word.[11] Sacred Scripture is therefore of the highest importance in the celebration of Mass. Consequently there can be no disregarding what the Church has laid down in order to ensure that "in sacred celebrations there should be a more ample, more varied and more suitable reading from sacred scripture".[12] The norms laid down in the Lectionary concerning the number of readings, and the directives given for special occasions are to be observed. It would be a serious abuse to replace the word of God with the word of man, no matter who the author may be.[13]

2. The reading of the Gospel passage is reserved to the ordained minister, namely the deacon or the priest. When possible, the other readings should be entrusted to a reader who has been instituted as such or to other spiritually and technically trained lay people. The first reading is followed by a responsorial psalm, which is an integral part of the liturgy of the word.[14]

3. The purpose of the homily is to explain to the faithful the word of God proclaimed in the readings, and to apply its message to the present. Accordingly the homily is to be given by the priest or the deacon.[15]

4. It is reserved to the priest, by virtue of his ordination, to proclaim the Eucharistic Prayer, which of its nature is the high point of the whole celebration. It is therefore an abuse to have some parts of the Eucharistic Prayer said by the deacon, by a lower minister, or by the faithful.[16] On the other hand the assembly does not remain passive and inert: it unites itself to the priest in faith and silence and shows its concurrence by the various interventions provided for in the course of the Eucharistic Prayer: the responses to the Preface dialogue, the *Sanctus*, the acclamation after the consecration, and the final *Amen* after the *Per Ipsum*. The *Per Ipsum* itself is reserved to the priest. This *Amen* especially should be emphasized by being sung, since it is the most important in the whole Mass.

5. Only the Eucharistic Prayers included in the Roman Missal or those that the Apostolic See has by law admitted, in the manner and within the limits laid down by the Holy See, are to be used. To modify the Eucharistic Prayers approved by the Church or to adopt others privately composed is a most serious abuse.

6. It should be remembered that the Eucharistic Prayer must not be overlaid with other prayers or songs.[17] When proclaiming the Eucharistic Prayer, the priest is to pronounce the text clearly, so as to make it easy for the faithful to understand it, and so as to foster the formation of a true assembly entirely intent upon the celebration of the Memorial of the Lord.

7. *Concelebration*, which has been restored in the Western Liturgy, manifests in an exceptional manner the unity of the priesthood. Concelebrants must therefore pay careful attention to the signs that indicate that unity. For example, they are to be present from the beginning of the celebration, they are to wear the prescribed vestments, they are to occupy the place appropriate to their ministry as concelebrants, and they are to observe faithfully the other norms for the seemly performance of the rite.[18]

8. *Matter of the Eucharist*. Faithful to Christ's example, the Church has constantly used bread and wine mixed with water to celebrate the Lord's Supper. The bread for the celebration of the Eucharist, in accordance with the tradition of the whole Church, must be made solely of wheat, and, in accordance with the tradition proper to the Latin Church, it must be unleavened. By reason of the sign, the matter of the Eucharist celebration "should appear as actual food". This is to be understood as linked to the consistency of the bread, and not to its form, which remains the traditional one. No other ingredients are to be added to the wheaten flour and water. The preparation of the bread requires attentive care, to ensure that the product does not detract from the dignity due to the Eucharistic bread, can be broken in a dignified way, does not give rise to excessive fragments, and does not offend the sensibilities of the faithful when they eat it. The wine for the Eucharistic celebration must be of "the fruit of the vine" (Lk 22:18) and be natural and genuine, that is to say not mixed with other substances.[19]

9. *Eucharistic Communion*. Communion is a gift of the Lord, given to the faithful through the minister appointed for this purpose. It is not permitted that the faithful should themselves pick up the consecrated bread and the sacred chalice; still less that they should hand them from one to another.

10. The faithful, whether religious or lay, who are authorized as extraordinary ministers of the Eucharist can distribute Communion only when there is no priest, deacon or acolyte, when the priest is impeded by illness or advanced age, or when the number of the faithful going to communion is so large as to make the celebration of Mass excessively long.[20] Accordingly, a reprehensible attitude is shown by those priests who, though present at the celebration, refrain from distributing Communion and leave this task to the laity.

11. The Church has always required from the faithful respect and reverence for the Eucharist at the moment of receiving it.

With regard to the manner of going to Communion, the faithful can receive it either kneeling or standing, in accordance with the norms laid down by the Episcopal Conference. "When the faithful communicate kneeling, no other sign of reverence towards the Blessed Sacrament is required, since kneeling is itself a sign of adoration. When they receive Communion standing, it is strongly recommended that, coming up in procession, they should make a sign of reverence before receiving the Sacrament. This should be done at the right time and place, so that the order of people going to and from Communion is not disrupted".[21]

The *Amen* said by the faithful when receiving Communion is an act of personal faith in the presence of Christ.

12. With regard to Communion under both kinds, the norms laid down by the Church must be observed, both by reason of the reverence due to the Sacrament and for the good of those receiving the Eucharist, in accordance with variations in circumstances, times and places.[22]

Episcopal Conferences and Ordinaries also are not to go beyond what is laid down in the present discipline: the granting of permission for Communion under both kinds is not to be indiscriminate, and the celebrations in question are to be clearly defined, well disciplined, and homogeneous.[23]

13. Even after Communion the Lord remains present under the species. Accordingly, when Communion has been distributed, the sacred particles remaining are to be consumed or taken by the competent minister to the place where the Eucharist is reserved.

14. On the other hand, the consecrated wine is to be consumed immediately after Communion and may not be kept. Care must be taken to consecrate only the amount of wine needed for Communion.

15. The rules laid down for the purification of the chalice and the other sacred vessels that have contained the Eucharistic species must be observed.[24]

16. Particular respect and care are due to the sacred vessels, both the chalice and paten for the celebration of the Eucharist, and the ciboria for the Communion of the faithful. The form of the vessels must be appropriate for the liturgical use for which they are meant. The material must be noble, durable and in every case adapted to sacred use. In this sphere judgment belongs to the Episcopal Conference of the individual regions.

Use is not to be made of simple baskets or other receptacles meant for ordinary use outside the sacred celebrations, nor are the sacred vessels to be of poor quality or lacking any artistic style.

Before being used, chalices and patens must be blessed by the Bishop or by a priest.[25]

17. The faithful are to be recommended not to omit to make a proper thanksgiving after Communion. They may do this during the celebration, with a period of silence, with a hymn, psalm or other song of praise,[26] or also after the celebration, if possible by staying behind to pray for a suitable time.

18. There are of course various roles that women can perform in the liturgical assembly: these include reading the word of God and proclaiming the intentions of the prayer of the

faithful. Women are not however permitted to act as altar servers.[27]

19. Particular vigilance and special care are recommended with regard to Masses transmitted by the audiovisual media. Given their very wide diffusion, their celebration must be of exemplary quality.[28]

In the case of celebrations that are held in private houses, the norms of the Instruction *Actio Pastoralis* of 15 May 1969 are to be observed.[29]

B. EUCHARISTIC WORSHIP OUTSIDE MASS

20. Public and private devotion to the Holy Eucharist outside Mass also is highly recommended: for the presence of Christ, who is adored by the faithful in the Sacrament, derives from the Sacrifice and is directed towards sacramental and spiritual Communion.

21. When Eucharistic devotions are arranged, account should be taken of the liturgical season, so that they harmonize with the liturgy, draw inspiration from it in some way and lead the Christian people towards it.[30]

22. With regard to exposition of the Holy Eucharist, either prolonged or brief, and with regard to processions of the Blessed Sacrament, Eucharistic Congresses, and the whole ordering of Eucharistic piety, the pastoral indications and directives given in the Roman Ritual are to be observed.[31]

23. It must not be forgotten that "before the blessing with the Sacrament an appropriate time should be devoted to readings of the word of God, to songs and prayers and to some silent prayer".[32] At the end of the adoration a hymn is sung and a prayer chosen from among the many contained in the Roman Ritual is recited or sung.[33]

24. The *tabernacle* in which the Eucharist is kept can be located on an altar, or away from it, in a spot in the church which is very prominent, truly noble and duly decorated, or in a chapel suitable for private prayer and for adoration by the faithful.[34]

25. The tabernacle should be solid, unbreakable, and not transparent.[35] The presence of the Eucharist is to be indicated by a tabernacle veil or by some other suitable means laid down by the competent authority, and a lamp must perpetually burn before it, as a sign of honour paid to the Lord.[36]

26. The venerable practice of genuflecting before the Blessed Sacrament, whether enclosed in the tabernacle or publicly exposed, as a sign of adoration, is to be maintained.[37] This act re-

quires that it be performed in a recollected way. In order that the heart may bow before God in profound reverence, the genuflection must be neither hurried not careless.

27. If anything has been introduced that is at variance with these indications it is to be corrected.

Most of the difficulties encountered in putting into practice the reform of the liturgy and especially the reform of the Mass stem from the fact that neither priests nor faithful have perhaps been sufficiently aware of the theological and spiritual reasons for which the changes have been made, in accordance with the principles laid down by the Council.

Priests must acquire an ever deeper understanding of the authentic way of looking at the Church,[38] of which the celebration of the liturgy and especially of the Mass is the living expression. Without an adequate biblical training, priests will not be able to present to the faithful the meaning of the liturgy as an enactment, in signs, of the history of salvation. Knowledge of the history of the liturgy will likewise contribute to an understanding of the changes which have been introduced, and introduced not for the sake of novelty but as a revival and adaptation of authentic and genuine tradition.

The liturgy also requires great balance, for, as the Constitution *Sacrosanctum Concilium* says, it "is thus the outstanding means by which the faithful can express in their lives, and manifest to others, the mystery of Christ and the real nature of the true Church. It is of the essence of the Church that she be both human and divine, visible and yet invisibly endowed, eager to act and yet devoted to contemplation, present in this world and yet not at home in it. She is all these things in such a way that in her the human is directed and subordinated to the divine, the visible likewise to the invisible, action to contemplation, and this present world to that city yet to come, which we seek".[39] Without this balance, the true face of Christian liturgy becomes obscured.

In order to reach these ideals more easily it will be necessary to foster liturgical formation in seminaries and faculties[40] and to facilitate the participation of priests in courses, meetings, assemblies or liturgical weeks, in which study and reflection should be properly complemented by model celebrations. In this way priests will be able to devote themselves to more effective pastoral action, to liturgical catechesis of the faithful, to organizing groups of lectors, to giving altar servers spiritual and practical training, to training animators of the assembly, to enriching progressively the repertoire of songs, in a word to all the initiatives favouring an ever deeper understanding of the liturgy.

In the implementation of the liturgical reform great responsibility falls upon national and diocesan Liturgical Commissions and Liturgical Institutes and Centres, especially in the work of translating the liturgical books and training the clergy and faithful in the spirit of the reform desired by the Council.

The work of these bodies must be at the service of the ecclesiastical authority, which should be able to count upon their faithful collaboration. Such collaboration must be faithful to the Church's norms and directives, and free of arbitrary initiatives and particular ways of acting that could compromise the fruits of the liturgical renewal.

This Document will come into the hands of God's ministers in the first decade of the life of the *Missale Romanum* promulgated by Pope Paul VI following the prescriptions of the Second Vatican Council.

It seems fitting to recall a remark made by that Pope concerning fidelity to the norms governing celebration: "It is a very serious thing when division is introduced precisely where *congregavit nos in unum Christi amor*, in the Liturgy and the Eucharistic Sacrifice, by the refusing of obedience to the norms laid down in the liturgical sphere. It is in the name of Tradition that we ask all our sons and daughters, all the Catholic communities, to celebrate with dignity and fervour the renewed liturgy".[41]

The Bishops, "whose function it is to control, foster and safeguard the entire liturgical life of the Church entrusted to them",[42] will not fail to discover the most suitable means for ensuring a careful and firm application of these norms, for the glory of God and the good of the Church.

---

* Translation by Vatican Press Office. Latin text in *Notitiae*, 1980, 287–296.
1. *Ed. typica altera*, Romae 1975.
2. *Ed. typica*, Romae 1973.
3. Sacred Congregation of Rites, 25 May 1967: *AAS* 59 (1967), pp. 539–573.
4. Sacred Congregation for Divine Worship, 29 May 1969: *AAS* 61 (1969), pp. 541–545.
5. Sacred Congregation for the Discipline of the Sacraments, 29 January 1973: *AAS* 65 (1973), pp. 264–271.
6. Sacred Congregation for Divine Worship, 5 September 1970: *AAS* 62 (1970), pp. 692–704.
7. St. Thomas, *Summa Theologiae*, 2–2, q. 93, a. 1.
8. Second Vatican Council, Constitution on the Sacred Liturgy, *Sacrosanctum Concilium*, 22, 3.

9. Paul VI, *Address* of 22 August 1973: *L'Osservatore Romano*, 23 August 1973.
10. Second Vatican Council, Constitution on the Sacred Liturgy *Sacrosanctum Concilium*, 56.
11. Cf. *ibid.*, 56; cf. also Second Vatican Council, Dogmatic Constitution on Divine Revelation *Dei Verbum*, 21.
12. Second Vatican Council, Constitution on the Sacred Liturgy *Sacrosanctum Concilium*, 35.
13. Cf. Sacred Congregation for Divine Worship, Instruction *Liturgicae Instaurationes*, 2, a.
14. Cf. *Institutio generalis Missalis Romani*, 36.
15. Cf. Sacred Congregation for Divine Worship, Instruction *Liturgicae Instaurationes*, 2, a.
16. Cf. Sacred Congregation for Divine Worship, Circular Letter *Eucharistiae Participationem*, 27 April 1973: *AAS* 65 (1973), pp. 340–347, 8; Instruction *Liturgicae Instaurationes*, 4.
17. Cf. *Institutio generalis Missalis Romani*, 12.
18. Cf. *ibid.*, 156, 161–163.
19. Cf. *ibid.*, 281–284; Sacred Congregation for Divine Worship, Instruction *Liturgicae Instaurationes*, 5; *Notitiae* 6 (1970), 37.
20. Cf. Sacred Congregation for the Discipline of the Sacraments, Instruction *Immensae Caritatis*, 1.
21. Sacred Congregation of Rites, Instruction *Eucharisticum Mysterium*, 34. Cf. *Institutio generalis Missalis Romani*, 244 c, 246 b, 247 b.
22. Cf. *Institutio generalis Missalis Romani*, 241–242.
23. Cf. *ibid.*, end of 242.
24. Cf. *ibid.*, 238.
25. Cf. *Institutio generalis Missalis Romani*, nos. 288, 289, 292, 295; Sacred Congregation for Divine Worship, Instruction *Liturgicae Instaurationes*, 8; *Pontificale Romanum, Ordo Dedicationis Ecclesiae et Altaris*, p. 125, no. 3.
26. Cf. *Institutio generalis Missalis Romani*, 56 j.
27. Cf. Sacred Congregation for Divine Worship, Instruction *Liturgicae Instaurationes*, 7.
28. Cf. Second Vatican Council, Constitution on the Sacred Liturgy *Sacrosanctum Concilium*, 20; Pontifical Commission for Social Communications, Instruction *Communio et Progressio*, 23 May 1971: *AAS* 63 (1971), pp. 593–656, no. 151.
29. *AAS* 61 (1969), pp. 806–811.
30. Cf. *Rituale Romanum, De sacra Communione et de cultu Mysterii eucharistici extra Missam*, 79–80.
31. Cf. *ibid.*, 82–112.
32. *Ibid.*, 89.
33. Cf. *ibid.*, 97.
34. Cf. *Institutio generalis Missalis Romani*, 276.
35. Cf. *Rituale Romanum, De sacra Communione et de cultu Mysterii eucharistici extra Missam*, 10.
36. Cf. Sacred Congregation of Rites, Instruction *Eucharisticum mysterium*, 57.
37. Cf. *Rituale Romanum, De sacra Communione et de cultu Mysterii eucharistici extra Missam*, 84.
38. Cf. Second Vatican Council, Dogmatic Constitution on the Church *Lumen Gentium*.
39. Second Vatican Council, Constitution on the Sacred Liturgy *Sacrosanctum Concilium*, 2.

40. Cf. Sacred Congregation for Catholic Education, Instruction on Liturgical Formation in Seminaries *In ecclesiasticam futurorum sacerdotum formationem*, 3 June 1979.

41. Consistorial Address of 24 May 1976: *AAS* 68 (1976), p. 374.

42. Second Vatican Council, Decree *Christus Dominus*, 15.

79

INSTRUCTION ON INFANT BAPTISM*

S.C.D.F., *Pastoralis Actio*, 20 October, 1980

INTRODUCTION

1. Pastoral work with regard to infant baptism was greatly assisted by the promulgation of the new Ritual, prepared in accordance with the directives of the Second Vatican Council.[1] The pace of change in society, however, is making it difficult for the young to be brought up in the faith and to persevere in it, and the resulting problems encountered by Christian parents and pastors have not been completely eliminated.

2. Many parents are distressed to see their children abandoning the faith and no longer receiving the sacraments, in spite of their own efforts to give them a Christian upbringing, and some pastors are asking themselves whether they should not be stricter before admitting infants to baptism. Some think it better to delay the baptism of children until the completion of a catechumenate of greater or less duration, while others are asking for a reexamination of the teaching on the necessity of baptism, at least for infants, and wish the celebration of the sacrament to be put off until such an age when an individual can make a personal commitment, perhaps even until the beginning of adult life.

However, this questioning of traditional sacramental pastoral practice cannot fail to raise in the Church justified fears of jeopardizing so essential a doctrine as that of the necessity of baptism. In particular, many parents are scandalized at finding baptism refused or delayed when, with full awareness of their duty, they request it for their children.

3. In view of this situation and in response to the many petitions received, the Sacred Congregation for the Doctrine of the Faith, in consultation with various Episcopal Conferences, has prepared the present Instruction. The purpose of the document is to recall the principal points of doctrine in this field which justify the Church's constant practice down the centuries and demonstrate its permanent value in spite of the dif-

ficulties raised today. The document will then indicate some general guidelines for pastoral action.

Part One

TRADITIONAL DOCTRINE ON INFANT BAPTISM

Immemorial practice

4. Both in the East and in the West the practice of baptizing infants is considered a rule of immemorial tradition. Origen, and later Saint Augustine, considered it a "tradition received from the Apostles".[2] When the first direct evidence of infant baptism appears in the second century, it is never presented as an innovation. Saint Irenaeus, in particular, considers it a matter of course that the baptized should include "infants and small children" as well as adolescents, young adults and older people.[3] The oldest known ritual, describing at the start of the third century the *Apostolic Tradition*, contains the following rule: "First baptize the children. Those of them who can speak for themselves should do so. The parents or someone of their family should speak for the others".[4] At a Synod of African Bishops Saint Cyprian stated that "God's mercy and grace should not be refused to anyone born", and the Synod, recalling that "all human beings" are "equal", whatever be "their size or age", declared it lawful to baptize children "by the second or third day after their birth".[5]

5. Admittedly there was a certain decline in the practice of infant baptism during the fourth century. At that time even adults postponed their Christian initiation out of apprehension about future sins and fear of public penance, and many parents put off the baptism of their children for the same reasons. But it must also be noted that Fathers and Doctors such as Basil, Gregory of Nyssa, Ambrose, John Chrysostom, Jerome and Augustine, who were themselves baptized as adults on account of this state of affairs, vigorously reacted against such negligence and begged adults not to postpone baptism, since it is necessary for salvation.[6] Several of them insisted that baptism should be administered to infants.[7]

The teaching of the Magisterium

6. Popes and Councils also often intervened to remind Christians of their duty to have their children baptized.

At the close of the fourth century the ancient custom of baptizing children as well as adults "for the forgiveness of sins" was used against the teachings of Pelagius. As Origen and Saint Cyprian had noted, before Saint Augustine,[8] this custom confirmed the Church's belief in original sin, and this in turn showed still more clearly the necessity of infant baptism. There were interventions on these lines by Pope Siricius[9] and Pope Innocent I.[10] Later, the Council of Carthage in 418 condemned "whoever says that newborn infants should not be baptized", and it taught that, on account of the Church's "rule of faith" concerning original sin, "even babies, who are yet unable to commit any sin personally, are truly baptized for the forgiveness of sins, for the purpose of cleansing by rebirth what they have received by birth".[11]

7. This teaching was constantly reaffirmed and defended during the Middle Ages. In particular, the Council of Vienne in 1312 stressed that the sacrament of baptism has for its effect, in the case of infants, not just the forgiveness of sins but also the granting of grace and the virtues.[12] The Council of Florence in 1442 rebuked those who wanted baptism postponed and declared that infants should receive "as soon as is convenient" (*quam primum commode*) the sacrament "through which they are rescued from the devil's power and adopted as God's children".[13]

The Council of Trent repeated the Council of Carthage's condemnation,[14] and, referring to the words of Jesus to Nicodemus, it declared that "since the promulgation of the Gospel" nobody can be justified "without being washed for rebirth or wishing to be".[15] One of the errors anathematized by the Council is the Anabaptist view that "it is better that the baptism (of children) be omitted than to baptize in the faith of the Church alone those who do not believe by their own act".[16]

8. The various regional councils and synods held after the Council of Trent taught with equal firmness the necessity of baptizing children. Pope Paul VI also solemnly recalled the centuries-old teaching on this matter, declaring that "baptism should be conferred even on infants who are yet unable to commit any sin personally, in order that, having been born without supernatural grace, they may be born again of water and the Holy Spirit to divine life in Christ Jesus".[17]

9. The texts of the Magisterium quoted above were chiefly concerned with refuting errors. They are far from exhausting the riches of the doctrine on baptism expressed in the New Testament, the catechesis of the Fathers, and the teaching of the Doctors of the Church: baptism is a manifestation of the Father's

prevenient love, a sharing in the Son's Paschal Mystery, and a communication of new life in the Spirit; it brings people into the inheritance of God and joins them to the Body of Christ, the Church.

10. In view of this, Christ's warning in Saint John's Gospel, "unless one is born of water and the Spirit, he cannot enter the kingdom of God",[18] must be taken as an invitation of universal and limitless love, the words of a Father calling all his children and wishing them to have the greatest of blessings. This pressing and irrevocable call cannot leave us indifferent or neutral, since its acceptance is a condition for achieving our destiny.

The Church's mission

11. The Church must respond to the mission that Christ gave to the Apostles after his Resurrection. Saint Matthew's Gospel reports it in a particularly solemn form: "All authority in heaven and on earth has been given to me. Go therefore and make disciples of all nations, baptizing them in the name of the Father and of the Son and of the Holy Spirit".[19] Transmitting the faith and administering baptism are closely linked in this command of the Lord, and they are an integral part of the Church's mission, which is universal and cannot cease to be universal.

12. This is how the Church has understood her mission from the beginning, and not only with regard to adults. She has always understood the words of Jesus to Nicodemus to mean that "children should not be deprived of baptism".[20] Jesus' words are so universal and absolute in form that the Fathers employed them to establish the necessity of baptism, and the Magisterium applied them expressly to infants:[21] the sacrament is for them too entry into the people of God[22] and the gateway to personal salvation.

13. The Church has thus shown by her teaching and practice that she knows no other way apart from baptism for ensuring children's entry into eternal happiness. Accordingly, she takes care not to neglect the mission that the Lord has given her of providing rebirth "of water and the Spirit" for all those who can be baptized. As for children who die without baptism, the Church can only entrust them to God's mercy, as she does in the funeral rite provided for them.[23]

14. The fact that infants cannot yet profess personal faith does not prevent the Church from conferring this sacrament on them, since in reality it is in her own faith that she baptizes them. This point of doctrine was clearly defined by Saint Augustine:

"When children are presented to be given spiritual grace", he wrote, "it is not so much those holding them in their arms who present them—although, if these people are good Christians, they are included among those who present the children—as the whole company of saints and faithful Christians... It is done by the whole of Mother Church which is in the saints, since it is as a whole that she gives birth to each and every one of them".[24] This teaching is repeated by Saint Thomas Aquinas and all the theologians after him: the child who is baptized believes not on its own account, by a personal act, but through others, "through the Church's faith communicated to it".[25] This same teaching is also expressed in the new Rite of Baptism, when the celebrant asks the parents and godparents to profess the faith of the Church, the faith in which the children are baptized.[26]

15. Although the Church is truly aware of the efficacy of her faith operating in the baptism of children, and aware of the validity of the sacrament that she confers on them, she recognizes limits to her practice, since, apart from cases of danger of death, she does not admit a child to baptism without its parents' consent and a serious assurance that after baptism it will be given a Catholic upbringing.[27] This is because she is concerned both for the natural rights of the parents and for the requirements of the development of faith in the child.

Part Two
ANSWERS TO DIFFICULTIES BEING RAISED TODAY

16. It is in the light of the teaching recalled above that we must judge certain views which are expressed today about infant baptism and which question its legitimacy as a general rule.

Link between baptism and act of faith

17. Noting that in the New Testament writings baptism follows the preaching of the Gospel, presupposes conversion and goes with a profession of faith, and furthermore that the effects of grace (forgiveness of sins, justification, rebirth and sharing in divine life) are generally linked with faith rather than with the sacrament,[28] some people propose that the order "preaching, faith, sacrament" should become the rule. Apart from cases of danger of death, they would apply this rule to children, and would institute an obligatory catechumenate for them.

18. It is beyond doubt that the preaching of the Apostles was normally directed to adults, and the first to be baptized were

people converted to the Christian faith. As these facts are related in the books of the New Testament, they could give rise to
the opinion that it is only the faith of adults that is considered in
these texts. However, as was mentioned above, the practice of
baptizing children rests on an immemorial tradition originating
from the Apostles, the importance of which cannot be ignored;
besides, baptism is never administered without faith: in the case
of infants, it is the faith of the Church.

Furthermore, in accordance with the teaching of the Council
of Trent on the sacraments, baptism is not just a sign of faith but
also a cause of faith.[29] It produces in the baptized "interior enlightenment", and so the Byzantine liturgy is right to call it the
sacrament of enlightenment, or simply enlightenment, meaning
that the faith received pervades the soul and causes the veil of
blindness to fall before the brightness of Christ.[30]

Harmony between baptism and personal reception of grace

19. It is also said that, since every grace is intended for a person, it should be consciously accepted and appropriated by the
person who receives it, something that an infant is quite incapable of doing.

20. But in reality the child is a person long before it can show
it by acts of consciousness and freedom. As a person, the child is
already capable of becoming, through the sacrament of baptism, a child of God and a coheir with Christ. Later, when consciousness and freedom awake, these will have at their disposal
the powers placed in the child's soul by the grace of baptism.

Harmony between baptism and the child's freedom

21. Some people also object that baptizing infants is a restriction of their freedom. They say that it is contrary to the dignity
of the children as persons to impose on them future religious
obligations that they may perhaps later be led to reject. In this
view it would be better to confer the sacrament only at an age
when free commitment has become possible; until then parents
and teachers should restrain themselves and avoid exercising
any pressure.

22. Such an attitude is simply an illusion: there is no such
thing as pure human freedom, immune from being influenced in
any way. Even on the natural level, parents make choices for
their child that are essential for its life and for its orientation
towards true values. A so-called neutral attitude on the part of
the family with regard to the child's religious life would in fact be

a negative choice that would deprive the child of an essential good.

Above all, those who claim that the sacrament of baptism compromises a child's freedom forget that every individual, baptized or not, is, as a creature, bound by indefeasible duties to God, duties which baptism ratifies and ennobles through the adoption as a child of God. They also forget that the New Testament presents entry into the Christian life not as a form of slavery or constraint but as admittance to true freedom.[31]

It can happen that, when a child grows up, it will reject the obligations derived from its baptism. Although its parents may be hurt as a result, they should not reproach themselves for having had the child baptized and giving it a Christian upbringing, as was their right and their duty.[32] In spite of appearances, the seeds of faith sown in the child's soul may one day come to life again, and the parents will contribute to this by their patience and love, by their prayers and by the authentic witness of their own faith.

Baptism in the present sociological situation

23. In view of the link between the person and society, some people hold that infant baptism is still suitable in a homogeneous type of society, in which values, judgments and customs form a coherent system; but they hold that it is inappropriate in today's pluralistic societies, which are characterized by instability of values and conflicts of ideas. In the present situation, they say baptism should be delayed until the candidate's personality has sufficiently matured.

24. The Church is well aware that she must take the social reality into account. But the criteria of homogeneity and pluralism are merely pointers and cannot be set up as normative principles; they are inadequate for settling a strictly religious question, which by its nature is a matter for the Church and the Christian family.

While the criterion of the homogeneous society would legitimize infant baptism if the society is Christian, it would also lead one to consider it as illegitimate when Christian families are in a minority, whether within an ethnic group that is still predominantly pagan or in a militantly atheistic regime. This obviously cannot be admitted.

The criterion of the pluralistic society is no more valid than the preceding criterion, since in this type of society the family and the Church can act freely and accordingly provide a Christian education.

Besides, a study of history clearly shows that if these "sociological" criteria had been applied in the first centuries of the Church they would have paralyzed all her missionary expansion. It is worth adding that all too often pluralism is being invoked in a paradoxical way, in order to impose on the faithful behaviour patterns that in reality are an obstacle to the exercise of their Christian freedom.

In a society whose mentality, customs and laws are no longer inspired by the Gospel it is therefore of great importance that in questions connected with infant baptism the Church's own nature and mission should be taken into consideration before all else.

In spite of being intermingled with human society and in spite of being made up of different nationalities and cultures, the People of God has its own identity, characterized by unity of faith and sacraments. Animated as it is by a single spirit and a single hope, it is an organic whole, capable of producing within the various groups of humanity the structures necessary for its growth. It is in this context that the Church's sacramental pastoral practice, in particular with regard to infant baptism, must be placed; her practice must not depend only on criteria borrowed from the human sciences.

Infant baptism and sacramental pastoral practice

25. A final criticism of infant baptism would have it that the practice comes from a pastoral usage lacking missionary impetus and concerned more with administering a sacrament than with stirring up faith and fostering commitment to spreading the Gospel. It is asserted that, by retaining infant baptism, the Church is yielding to the temptation of numbers and social establishment, and that she is encouraging the maintenance of a magical concept of the sacraments, while she really ought to engage in missionary activity, bring the faith of Christians to maturity, foster their free conscious commitment, and consequently admit a number of stages in her sacramental pastoral practice.

26. Undoubtedly, the Church's apostolate should aim at stirring up lively faith and fostering a truly Christian life; but the requirements of pastoral practice with regard to administering the sacraments to adults cannot be applied unchanged to children who, as mentioned above, are baptized "in the faith of the Church". Besides, we must not treat lightly the necessity of the sacrament: it is a necessity that has lost none of its importance

and urgency, especially when what is at stake is ensuring that the child receives the infinite blessing of eternal life.

With regard to preoccupation with numbers, if this preoccupation is properly understood it is not a temptation or an evil for the Church but a duty and a blessing. The Church, described by Saint Paul as Christ's "body" and his "fullness",[33] is the visible sacrament of Christ in the world, with the mission of extending to everyone the sacramental link between her and her glorified Saviour. Accordingly, she cannot fail to wish to give to everyone, children no less than adults, the first and basic sacrament of baptism.

If it is understood in this way, the practice of infant baptism is truly evangelical, since it has the force of witness, manifesting God's initiative and the gratuitous character of the love with which he surrounds our lives: "not that we loved God but that he loved us... We love, because he first loved us".[34] Even in the case of adults, the demands that the reception of baptism involves[35] should not make us forget that "he saved us, not because of deeds done by us in righteousness, but in virtue of his own mercy, by the washing of regeneration and renewal in the Holy Spirit".[36]

Part Three

SOME PASTORAL DIRECTIVES

27. While certain suggestions being put forward today cannot be accepted—suggestions such as the definitive abandonment of infant baptism and freedom to choose, whatever the reasons, between immediate baptism and deferred baptism —one cannot deny the need for a pastoral effort pursued in greater depth and renewed in certain aspects. It is appropriate to indicate the principles and fundamental guidelines at this point.

The principles of this pastoral practice

28. In the first place it is important to recall that the baptism of infants must be considered a serious duty. The questions which it poses to pastors can be settled only by faithful attention to the teaching and constant practice of the Church.

Concretely, pastoral practice regarding infant baptism must be governed by two great principles, the second of which is subordinate to the first.

1. Baptism, which is necessary for salvation, is the sign and

the means of God's prevenient love, which frees us from original sin and communicates to us a share in divine life. Considered in itself, the gift of these blessings to infants must not be delayed.

2. Assurances must be given that the gift thus granted can grow by an authentic education in the faith and Christian life, in order to fulfill the true meaning of the sacrament.[37] As a rule, these assurances are to be given by the parents or close relatives, although various substitutions are possible within the Christian community. But if these assurances are not really serious there can be grounds for delaying the sacrament; and if they are certainly non-existent the sacrament should even be refused.

Dialogue between pastors and believing families

29. On the basis of these two principles, concrete cases will be examined in a pastoral dialogue between the priest and the family. The rules for dialogue with parents who are practising Christians are given in the Introduction to the Ritual. It is sufficient to recall here two of the more significant points.

In the first place, much importance is given to the presence and active participation of the parents in the celebration. The parents now have priority over the godparents, although the presence of the latter continues to be required, since their assistance in the child's education is valuable and can sometimes be essential.

Secondly, preparation for the baptism has an important place. The parents must give thought to the baptism; they should inform their pastors of the coming birth and prepare themselves spiritually. The pastors, for their part, will visit the families or gather them together and give them catechesis and appropriate advice. They will also urge the families to pray for the children that they are expecting.[38]

As for the time of the actual celebration, the indications in the Ritual should be followed: "The first consideration is the welfare of the child, that it may not be deprived of the benefit of the sacrament; then the health of the mother must be considered, so that, as far as possible she too may be present. Then, as long as they do not interfere with the greater good of the child, there are pastoral considerations such as allowing sufficient time to prepare the parents and for planning the actual celebration to bring out its paschal character". Accordingly, "if the child is in danger of death, it is to be baptized without delay"; otherwise, as a rule "an infant should be baptized within the first weeks after birth".[39]

Dialogue between pastors and families with little faith or non-Christian families

30. It sometimes happens that pastors are approached by parents who have little faith and practise their religion only occasionally, or even by non-Christian parents who request baptism for their children for reasons that deserve consideration.

In this case the pastor will endeavour by means of a clearsighted and understanding dialogue to arouse the parents' interest in the sacrament they are requesting and make them aware of the responsibility that they are assuming.

In fact the Church can only accede to the desire of these parents if they give an assurance that, once the child is baptized, it will be given the benefit of the Christian upbringing required by the sacrament. The Church must have a well-founded hope that the baptism will bear fruit.[40]

If the assurances given—for example, the choice of godparents who will take sincere care of the child, or the support of the community of the faithful—are sufficient, the priest cannot refuse to celebrate the sacrament without delay, as in the case of children of Christian families. If on the other hand they are insufficient, it will be prudent to delay baptism. However the pastors should keep in contact with the parents so as to secure, if possible, the conditions required on their part for the celebration of the sacrament. If even this solution fails, it can be suggested, as a last recourse, that the child be enrolled in a catechumenate to be given when the child reaches school age.

31. These rules have already been made and are already in force,[41] but they require some clarifications.

In the first place it must be clear that the refusal of baptism is not a means of exercising pressure. Nor can one speak of refusal, still less of discrimination, but rather of educational delay, according to individual cases, aimed at helping the family to grow in faith or to become more aware of its responsibilities.

With regard to the assurances, any pledge giving a wellfounded hope for the Christian upbringing of the children deserves to be considered as sufficient.

Enrollment for a future catechumenate should not be accompanied by a specially created rite which would easily be taken as an equivalent of the sacrament itself. It should also be clear that this enrollment is not admittance to the catechumenate and that the infants enrolled cannot be considered catechumens with all the prerogatives attached to being such. They must be presented later on for a catechumenate suited to their age. In this regard, it must be stated clearly that the existence in the Rite of Christian Initiation of Adults of a Rite of Initiation for Children of Catechetical Age[42] in no way means that the Church considers it preferable or normal to delay baptism until that age.

Finally, in areas where families of little faith or non-Christian families make up the majority, so as to justify the local setting up by the Bishops' Conference of a joint pastoral plan which provides for postponing baptism beyond the time fixed by the general law,[43] Christian families living in these areas retain the full right to have their children baptized earlier. The sacrament is therefore to be administered in accordance with the Church's will and as the faith and generosity of these families deserve.

The role of the family and of the parish community

32. The pastoral effort brought into play on the occasion of the baptism of infants should be part of a broader activity extending to the families and to the whole of the Christian community.

From this viewpoint it is important to intensify pastoral care of engaged couples at meetings in preparation for marriage, and likewise the pastoral care of young couples. The whole ecclesial community must be called upon as circumstances demand, especially teachers, married couples, family action movements, religious congregations and secular institutes. Priests must give this apostolate an important place in their ministry. In particular, they will remind parents of their responsibilities in awakening their children's faith and educating it. It is in fact for parents to begin the religious initiation of the child, to teach it to love Christ as a close friend and to form its conscience. This task will be all the more fruitful and easy if it builds on the grace of baptism present in the child's heart.

33. As is clearly indicated in the Ritual, the parish community, especially the group of Christians that constitute the family's human environment, should play a part in the pastoral practice regarding baptism. "Christian instruction and the preparation for baptism are a vital concern of God's people, the Church, which hands on and nourishes the faith it has received from the Apostles".[44] This active participation by the Christian people, which has already come into use in the case of adults, is also required for the baptism of infants, in which "the people of God, that is the Church, made present in the local community, has an important part to play".[45] In addition, the community itself will as a rule draw great profit, both spiritual and apostolic, from the

baptism ceremony. Finally, the community's work will continue, after the liturgical celebration, through the contribution of the adults to the education of the young in faith, both by the witness of their own Christian lives and by their participation in various catechetical activities.

CONCLUSION

34. In addressing the Bishops, the Congregation for the Doctrine of the Faith is fully confident that, as part of the mission that they have received from the Lord, they will take care to recall the Church's teaching on the necessity of infant baptism, promote an appropriate pastoral practice, and bring back to the traditional practice those who, perhaps under the pressure of comprehensible pastoral concerns, have departed from it. The Congregation also hopes that the teaching and guidelines contained in this Instruction will reach all pastors, Christian parents and the ecclesial community, so that all will become aware of their responsibilities and make their contribution, through the baptism of children and their Christian education, to the growth of the Church, the Body of Christ.

*Translation put out by Vatican Press Office. Latin text in *AAS* LXXXII (1980) 1137–1156.

1. *Ordo baptismi parvulorum,* ed. typica, Romae, 16 May 1969.

2. Origen, *In Romanis,* V, 9: PG 14, 1047; cf. Saint Augustine, *De Genesi ad litteram,* X, 23, 39: PL 34, 426; *De peccatorum meritis et remissione et de baptismo parvulorum ad Marcellinum, I, 26, 39: PL* 44, 131. In fact, three passages of the Acts of the Apostles (16:15, 16:33, 18:8) speak of the baptism of a whole household or family.

3. *Adv. Haereses* II, 22,4: PG 7, 784; *Harvey* I, 330. Many inscriptions from as early as the second century give little children the title of "children of God", a title given only to the baptized, or explicitly mention that they were baptized: cf., for example, *Corpus Inscriptionum Graecarum,* 9727, 9801, 9817,; E. Diehl, *Inscriptiones Latinae Christianae Veteres* (Berlin 1961), nn. 1523 (3), 4429 A.

4. *La Tradition apostolique de saint Hippolyte,* edited and translated by B. Botte, Munster, Aschendorff, 1963 (*Liturgiewissenschaftliche Quellen und Forschungen* 39), p. 44.

5. *Epist. LXIV, Cyprianus et coeteri collegae, qui in concilio adfuerunt numero LXVI. Fido fratri:* PL 3, 1013–1019; ed. Hartel, (CSEL 3), pp. 717–721. This practice was particularly strong in the Church in Africa,

in spite of the position taken by Tertullian, who advised that baptism of children should be delayed in view of the innocence associated with their age and the fear of possible lapses in young adulthood. Cf. *De baptismo,*XVIII, 3—XIX, 1: PL 1, 1220-1222 *De anima*, 39–41: PL 2, 719ff.

6. Cf. Saint Basil, *Homilia XIII exhortatoria ad sanctum baptisma:* PG 424-436; Saint Gregory of Nyssa, *Adversus eos qui differunt baptismum oratio:* PG 46, 424; Saint Augustine, *In Ioannem Tractatus XIII,* 7: PL 35, 1496; CCL 36, p. 134.

7. Cf. Saint Ambrose, *De Abraham, II,* 11, 81-84: PL 14, 495–497: CSEL 32, 1, pp. 632–635; Saint John Chrysostom, *Catechesis,* III, 5–6, ed. A. Wenger, SC 50, pp. 153-154; Saint Jerome, *Epist.* 107, 6: PL 22, 873, ed. J. Labourt (Budé), vol. 5, pp. 151–152. However, while Gregory of Nazianzus urged mothers to have their children baptized at the earliest possible age, he was content to fix that age as the first three years; cf. *Oratio XL in sanctum baptisma,* 17 and 28: PL 380 and 399.

8. Origen, *In Leviticum hom.* VIII, 3: PG 12, 496; *In Lucam hom.* XIV, 5: PG 13, 1835; Saint Cyprian, *Epist.* 64, 5: PL 3, 1018; ed. Hartel, CSEL, p. 720; Saint Augustine, *De peccatorum meritis et remissione et de baptismo parvulorum* I, XVII–XIX, 22–24: PL 44, 121–122; *De gratia Christi et de peccato originali,* I, XXXII, 35: *ibid.*, 377; *De praedestinatione sanctorum,* XIII, 25: *ibid.,*978; *Opus imperfectum contra Iulianum,* V, 9: PL 45, 1439.

9. *Epist. "Directa ad decessorem" ad Himerium episc. Tarraconensem, 10 febr. 385, 2: DS* (Denzinger-Schönmetzer, *Enchiridion symbolorum, definitionum et declarationum de rebus fidei et morum,* Herder 1965) 184.

10. *Epist. "Inter ceteras Ecclesiae Romanae" ad Silvanum et ceteros Synodi Milevitanae Patres,* 27 ian. 417, 5: DS 219.

11. *Canon 2:* Mansi, III, 811–814 and IV, 327 A-B: DS 223.

12. *Council of Vienne:* Mansi, XXV, 411 C-D: DS 903–904.

13. *Council of Florence, sessio* XI: DS 1349.

14. *Sessio V, can. 4:* DS 1514; cf. the 418 Council of Carthage, note 11 above.

15. *Sessio VI, cap. IV:* DS 1524.

16. *Sessio VII, can. 13:* DS 1626.

17. *Sollemnis Professio Fidei, 18: AAS* 60 (1968), p. 440.

18. Jn. 3:5.

19. Mt. 28:19; cf. Mk. 16:15–16.

20. *Ordo baptismi parvulorum, Praenotanda,* n. 2, p. 15.

21. Cf. note 8 above for the patristic texts, and notes 9 to 13 for the Councils. Another text is the Profession of Faith of Patriarch Dositheus of Jerusalem in 1672: Mansi XXXIV, 1746.

22. "What is done when children are baptized", wrote Saint Augustine, "is to incorporate them into the Church, that is to say to associate them with Christ's body and members" (*De peccatorum meritis et remissione et de baptismo parvulorum,* III, 4, 7: PL 44, 189; cf. I, 26, 39: *ibid.*, 131).

23. *Ordo exsequiarum,* ed. typica, Romae, 15 August 1969, nn. 82, 231–237.

24. *Epist.* 98, 5: PL 33, 362; cf. *Sermo* 176, 2, 2: PL 38, 950.

25. *Summa Theologica, III^a,* q. 69, a. 6, ad 3; cf. q. 68, a. 9, ad 3.

26. *Ordo baptismi parvulorum Praenotanda,* n. 2: cf. n. 56.

27. There is a long-standing tradition, appealed to by Saint Thomas Aquinas (*Summa Theologica,* II^a-II^{ae}, q. 10, a. 12, in c.) and Pope

Benedict XIV (Instruction *Postremo Mense* of 28 February 1747, 4–5: DS 2552–2553), against baptizing a child of unbelieving or Jewish parents, except in danger of death (CIC, can. 750, § 2), against the parents' wishes, that is unless the parents ask for it and give guarantees.

28. Cf. Mt. 28:19; Mk. 16:16; Ac 2:37–41, 8:35–38; Rom. 3:22, 26; Gal 3:26.

29. *Council of Trent, sessio* VII, *Decr. de sacramentis,* can. 6: DS 1606.

30. Cf. 2 Cor 3:15–16.

31. Jn 8:36; Rom 6:17–22, 8:21; Gal 4:31, 5:1, 13; 1 Pt 2:16, etc.

32. This right and duty, specified in detail by the Second Vatican Council in the Declaration *Dignitatis Humanae,* 5, has been given international recognition in the Universal Declaration of Human Rights, art. 26 (3).

33. Eph 1:23.

34. 1 Jn 4:10, 19.

35. Cf. *Council of Trent,* sessio VI, *De iustificatione*, capp. 5–6, can. 4 and 9: DS 1525–1526, 1554, 1559.

36. Tit. 3:5.

37. Cf. *Ordo baptismi parvulorum, Praenotanda,* n. 3. p. 15.

38. Cf. *ibid.*, n. 8, § 2, p. 17; n. 5, §§ 1 and 5, p. 16.

39. *Ibid.,* 8, § 1, p. 17.

40. Cf. *ibid.*, n. 3, p. 15.

41. These rules were first given in a Letter of the Congregation for the Doctrine of the Faith replying to a request by the Most Reverend Barthélemy Hanrion, Bishop of Dapango, Togo, and they were published, together with the Bishop's request, in *Notitiae* No. 61 (volume 7, year 1971), pp. 64–70.

42. Cf. *Ordo initiationis christianae adultorum,* ed. typica, Romae, 6 Jan. 1972, cap. 5, pp. 125–149.

43. Cf. *Ordo baptismi parvulorum, Praenotanda,* n. 8, §§ 3–4, p. 17.

44. *Ibid.*, de initiatione christiana, *Praenotanda generalia*, n. 7, p. 9.

45. *Ibid.*, *Praenotanda,* n. 4, p. 15.

80

PERMISSION TO USE EUCHARISTIC PRAYERS FOR CHILDREN AND FOR RECONCILIATION EXTENDED INDEFINITELY*

S.C.S.D.W., *Officium mihi*, 13 December, 1980

It is my duty to communicate to you the Holy Father's decision regarding the use of the eucharistic prayers for children and for reconciliation. As you know, the permission to use these eucharistic prayers lapsed at the end of 1980.

The Most Holy Father, John Paul II, in an audience granted on 13 December, 1980, to James R. Cardinal Knox, Prefect of the Sacred Congregation for the Sacraments and for Divine Worship, graciously extended the permission to use the eucharistic prayers for children and for reconciliation, under the same conditions as before. This applies both to those episcopal conferences who already have the Holy See's permission and to those also who, with the approval of the Holy See, wish to introduce these prayers in their own territories. The permission will remain in force until the Holy See decide otherwise.

---

* Translation by A.F. When the three eucharistic prayers for children and the two for reconciliation were promulgated at the end of 1974, they were approved 'for experiment and for three years, that is, until the end of 1977' (Cardinal Knox, in his Introduction). However, he went on: 'The texts may not be published in official editions and are not to be inserted in the Roman Missal.'
A letter sent by the S. Congregation for the Sacraments and for Divine Worship to episcopal conferences on 10 December 1977 stated that the Holy Father had granted an extension of the permission for a further three years, until the end of 1980 (*Notitiae*, Dec., 1977, pp 555-556). The above letter to presidents of episcopal conferences, dated 15 December, 1980, was published in *Notitiae* (the organ of the congregation), January, 1981, p. 23.

81

GENERAL INTRODUCTION TO THE LECTIONARY FOR MASS (Second edition)

S.C.S.D.W., *De verbi Dei*, 21 January, 1981

CHAPTER ONE: THE LITURGICAL CELEBRATION OF THE WORD: GENERAL PRINCIPLES

1 PRELIMINARY REMARKS

a. *The importance of the word of God in liturgical celebration.*

1. There have been numerous worthwhile statements before now—by the Second Vatican Council,[1] the popes[2] and, since the Council, Roman congregations[3]—about the importance of the word of God and about the restoration of the use of sacred Scripture in all liturgical celebrations. Further, a number of the more important principles have been propounded and briefly explained in the Introduction to the 1969 edition of the Order of Readings at Mass.

A number of requests have come from different quarters that for this new edition of the Order of Readings at Mass a more extended version of those principles be given. This expanded and more accessible arrangement of the Introduction was accordingly prepared. It first describes in general terms the relationship between the word of God and liturgical celebration, then, more specifically, it deals with the word of God in the celebration of Mass, going on finally to outline the actual plan of the Order of Readings.

b. *Terms used for the word of God.*

2. Granted, a case could be made here for a definition of terms, in the interests of clarity and precision. However, in this Introduction we will be content to use the terms found in the conciliar and postconciliar documents. We will also use 'Sacred Scripture' and 'word of God' interchangeably throughout to refer to the inspired books, thus avoiding confusion concerning terms or their meaning.[4]

c. *The liturgical meaning of the word of God.*

3. The multiple treasures of the one word of God are marvellously disclosed, in the various liturgical celebrations and assemblies of the faithful, as the mystery of Christ unfolds and is recalled through the year and as the Church's sacraments and sacramentals are celebrated, or as individual members of the faithful respond to the action of the Holy Spirit within them.[5] For the liturgical celebration itself, drawing sustenance and support in the first place from God's word, becomes a new event and enriches the word also with new meaning and power. Thus in the liturgy the Church remains faithful to Christ's way of reading and interpreting the sacred Scriptures. He encouraged everybody to search the Scriptures from the day of his 'event,' his 'today.'[6]

2   THE LITURGICAL CELEBRATION OF THE WORD OF GOD

a. *The characteristics of the word of God in liturgical celebration.*

4. There is not just one way of propounding the word in liturgical celebrations,[7] nor is it always equally effective in evoking a response in the hearts of listeners. Always present in his word, however, is Christ:[8] effecting the mystery of salvation, he sanctifies men and women and offers perfect worship to the Father.

The plan of salvation, unceasingly recalled and propagated by God's word, attains its full significance in liturgical celebrations, to such effect that these become the constant, total and effective proclamation of God's word.

The word of God, therefore, constantly proclaimed in the liturgy, is always living and effective through the power of the Holy Spirit and it reveals the Father's unfailingly effective love for us.

b. *The word of God in the plan of salvation.*

5. It is the one mystery of Christ which is in question whether it is the Old or the New Testament which is being proclaimed by the Church in the liturgy.

The New Testament lies hidden in the Old and in the New Testament the Old is made manifest. Christ is the centre and completion of all of Scripture[9] as of all liturgical celebration. Therefore those who seek salvation and life must drink from its fountains.

The more profound one's understanding of liturgical celebration, the higher will be one's esteem for the word of God.

What is said of one can be said also of the other and the mystery of Christ is recalled by both and each in its own way perpetuates it.

c. *The word of God in the liturgical celebration of the faithful.*

6. In liturgical celebrations, the Church utters the same *Amen* that Christ, mediator between God and humanity, uttered once for all, spilling his blood, putting the divine seal on the new covenant in the Holy Spirit.

When therefore God communicates his word, he always expects a response in the form of listening and worship 'in spirit and in truth' (John 4:23). The Holy Spirit makes the response effective, so that what is heard in the liturgical celebration is given expression in our lives, in accordance with the text: 'be doers of the word, not hearers only.' (James 1:22)

The liturgical celebration takes shape through bodily postures, actions and words and these are also the outward expression of the faithful's participation. They derive their meaning, not just from human experience, in which they are rooted, but from the word of God and the plan of salvation, to which they refer. Accordingly, as the faithful listen to the word of God proclaimed in the liturgy, their participation will increase in proportion to the depth of their commitment to the Word of God made flesh in Christ; so that what they celebrate in the liturgy they try to maintain in their lives and their day-to-day lives they try to take into the liturgy.

3   THE WORD IN THE LIVES OF THE PEOPLE OF THE COVENANT

a. *The word of God in the life of the church.*

7. The Church is built up and grows and the wonders which God did in the past in the history of salvation are truly and mystically made present again in the liturgical symbols. Further, God makes use of the worshipping assembly of the faithful to ensure that his word may spread and be honoured and his name be exalted among the nations.

Whenever therefore the Church, gathered together by the Holy Spirit in a liturgical celebration, announces and proclaims God's word, it is aware that it is a new people in which the ancient covenant is perfected and made absolute. All of the faithful have been made messengers of God's word by baptism and confirmation in the Holy Spirit. Having been given the grace of hearing, they are to proclaim that word of God in the Church and to the world, at least by the example of their lives.

The word of God which is proclaimed during the celebration of the divine mysteries is not concerned with the present, merely; it looks back also to the past and forward to the future, pointing to what should be so much the object of our hopes that in this changing world our hearts will be set on the source of true joy.

b. *The word of God as proclaimed by the church.*

8. Since by the will of Christ himself the new people of God comprise a wonderful diversity of members, the responsibilities and tasks which are assigned to individual members with regard to the word of God are varied also. The faithful listen to the word of God and meditate on it, but its exposition is confined to those who by ordination have been given the office of teaching and to those to whom the exercise of the ministry has been assigned.

Thus, in its teaching, life and worship, the Church maintains intact and transmits to successive generations all that it is, all that it believes, so that over the centuries it may never cease to advance towards the fullness of divine truth, until the word of God shall have been brought to fulfillment in it.

c. *The link between the word of God proclaimed and the action of the Holy Spirit.*

9. If the word of God which people hear with their ears is really to have its effect in their hearts, the action of the Holy Spirit is required. With the inspiration and help of the Holy Spirit, the word of God becomes the foundation of liturgical celebration and the rule and support of all of life.

Not only does the activity of the Holy Spirit anticipate, accompany and follow a liturgical celebration in its entirety, it also conveys to the heart of each individual in the assembly of the faithful what is said to all of them; and while it cements the unity of the whole assembly, it also enlivens the diversity of charisms and energises their multiple activities.

d. *The intimate link between the word of God and the eucharistic mystery.*

10. The Church has always treated the word of God and the eucharistic mystery with like reverence, though not with the same worship, and has always and everywhere decreed that they be so treated. It has never ceased, after the example of its Founder, to celebrate his paschal mystery, gathering together to read

'in all the scriptures the things concerning himself' (Luke 24:27) and to accomplish the work of salvation through the memorial of the Lord and the sacraments. For 'the preaching of the word is required for the sacramental ministry itself, since the sacraments are sacraments of faith, drawing their origin and nourishment from the word.' (Vatican II, P.O., 4)

Drawing spiritual nourishment from both tables, at the one the Church receives further instruction and at the other is more fully sanctified. In God's word is the announcement of the covenant, in the eucharist is the renewal of the new and eternal covenant itself. There the history of salvation is evoked by the sounds of words, here the same history is enacted in the liturgy's sacramental symbols.

Consequently, it must always be borne in mind that the word of God read and proclaimed in the church leads on the sacrifice of the covenant and to the banquet of grace as to its goal. The celebration of Mass, therefore, at which the word is heard and the eucharist offered and received, is one act of divine worship by which the sacrifice of praise is offered to God and the fullness of redemption is made available to men and women.

CHAPTER TWO: THE WORD OF GOD IN THE CELEBRATION OF MASS

1   THE ELEMENTS OF THE LITURGY OF THE WORD AND THEIR RITES

a. *The readings and their proclamation.*

11. 'The most important part of the Liturgy of the Word consists of the readings from sacred Scripture and the chants linking them. The homily, the profession of faith and the general intercessions, or prayers of the faithful, develop and conclude it.' (*General Instruction on the Roman Missal*, 33)

12. In the celebration of Mass, the biblical readings and the chants from sacred Scripture may be neither omitted nor shortened nor, which would be worse, replaced by non-biblical readings.[10] For 'God speaks to his people' (Vatican II, *S.C.*, 33) still in the written word of God and the daily use of the Scriptures empowers the people of God, become docile to the Holy Spirit in the light of faith, to bear witness to Christ before the world in their lives and in their behaviour.

13. The reading of the gospel is the high point of the liturgy of the word. The other readings, in the traditional sequence from

Old Testament to New, prepare the assembly of the faithful for it.

14. The first requisite for the proper communication of the word of God to the assembly by the readers is an audible, clear and intelligent delivery. The readings, taken from approved editions, may, in keeping with the characteristics of the different languages, be sung, but in such a way that the words are not thereby obscured, but rather highlighted. When the readings are sung in Latin, the method prescribed in the *Ordo cantus Missae* should be followed.

15. Short and suitable introductions may be given before the readings, especially before the first. Careful consideration should be given to the literary style of these introductions. They should be simple, faithful to the text, short, carefully prepared and should be varied to suit each text to be introduced.

16. Readings should always be delivered from the ambo at Masses for the people.

17. In the liturgy of the word, attention should be given to the reverence which should attend the reading of the gospel. Where a Book of the Gospels is used, carried in the entrance procession by the deacon or reader, it is most fitting that it be carried from the altar to the ambo by the deacon, or if there be no deacon, by a priest, preceded by ministers with candles and incense or other symbols of veneration, according to custom. The faithful stand and, acclaiming the Lord, pay honour to the Book of the Gospels. The deacon who is to proclaim the gospel bows to the presiding priest and asks for a blessing. When no deacon is present, the priest bows before the altar and prays quietly: 'Almighty God, cleanse my heart. . . .'

From the ambo, the person proclaiming the gospel salutes the congregation, announces the title of the reading, signing himself on the forehead, lips and breast. He then incenses the book, when appropriate. When he has finished reading the gospel, he kisses the book, saying the prescribed words quietly.

The salutation 'A reading from the holy gospel. . .' and the phrase 'This is the Gospel of the Lord,' with which the gospel is terminated, may be sung, thus offering the assembly the opportunity of singing the responses, even if the gospel has been read. This serves to emphasise the importance of the gospel and to foster the faith of the listeners.

18. The phrase 'This is the word of the Lord' with which the other readings are terminated may be sung by someone other than the reader, the congregation singing the response. In this way, the congregation honours the word of God which they have

accepted with faith and gratitude.

b. *The responsorial psalm.*

19. The responsorial psalm, or gradual, is 'an integral part of the liturgy of the word' (General Instruction on the Roman Missal, 36) and as such is of considerable liturgical and pastoral importance. For this reason, the faithful should be assiduously taught how to perceive the voice of God speaking in the psalms and how to make them the prayer of the Church. This will certainly 'be more easily achieved if the clergy are carefully schooled in that deeper meaning which the psalms acquire when sung in the sacred liturgy and if this knowledge is imparted to all the faithful by suitable catechesis.'[11]

A short introduction explaining the choice of psalm, and how psalm and its response harmonise with the readings, can be helpful.

20. The responsorial psalm should be sung, normally. There are two ways of singing the psalm after the first reading, responsorially or directly. In the responsorial method, which normally is the method to be preferred, the psalmist, or psalm cantor, sings the verses of the psalm, the entire congregation joining in by singing the response. In the direct method, the psalm is sung without a response from the congregation. The psalm may be sung either by the psalmist, the congregation listening, or by the entire congregation.

21. The singing of the psalm, or of only the response, is of considerable stimulus to the perception of the spiritual sense of the psalm and an aid to reflection on it.

In each culture, use should be made of all the means at hand for encouraging congregational singing. Especially helpful is recourse to the liturgical seasonal options provided with a view to this in the Order for Readings at Mass.

22. If the psalm after the reading be not sung, it is to be recited in a manner conducive to meditation on the word of God.

The responsorial psalm should be recited or sung at the ambo by the psalmist or cantor.

c. *The acclamation before the reading of the gospel.*

23. The Alleluia or, according to the liturgical season, the verse before the gospel, is also 'a rite or action on its own' (General Introduction to the Roman Missal, 39) in which the assembly of the faithful welcomes the Lord as he is about to address them, salutes him and professes its faith in song.

The Alleluia, or the verse before the gospel, should be sung, with everybody standing, the choir or the entire congregation taking up the singing after the cantor's intonation.

d. *The homily.*

24. In the homily, the mysteries of faith and the guiding principles of the Christian life are expounded from the sacred text in the course of the liturgical year. As part of the liturgy of the word it has been frequently and, since the promulgation of the Liturgy Constitution of Vatican II, most strongly, recommended; in some instances it is obligatory. Normally it should be delivered by the person presiding (General Introduction to the Roman Missal, 42). What the homily sets out to achieve is to make of the word of God proclaimed, together with the eucharistic liturgy, 'as it were the proclamation of God's wonderful works in the history of salvation, which is the mystery of Christ' (Vatican II, *S.C.*, 35, 3). For the paschal mystery of Christ, which is proclaimed in the readings and in the homily, is accomplished by the sacrifice of the Mass. Christ is always present and active in the preaching of his Church.

The homily, therefore, whether it be an exposition of the word of Scripture which has been read, or of another liturgical text, should lead the community of believers to active celebration of the eucharist, so that 'they should hold fast in their lives to what they have grasped in faith' (Vatican II, *S.C.*, 10). The word of God which is read and the Church's celebration will draw greater effectiveness from this living exposition if the homily be truly the fruit of reflection, if it be properly prepared, not too long, nor too short, and if it take everyone present into account, even children and the uneducated.

At a concelebrated Mass, the homily is usually given by the chief celebrant or by one of the concelebrants.

25. On the prescribed days, on Sundays that is and on holydays of obligation, a homily should be preached at all Masses celebrated with a congregation, even when the Sunday or holyday Mass is celebrated on the previous evening. The same holds true if the congregation comprises children or a special group.

It is strongly recommended that on the weekdays of Advent, Lent and Eastertide a homily be preached to the faithful who regularly share in the celebration of Mass, and also on other feasts and occasions when there is a large congregation in the church.

26. The priest celebrant delivers the homily, standing or sitting, or at the ambo.

27. Such brief announcements as need to be made to the people should be kept clearly separate from the homily and should be made after the post-communion prayer.

e. *Silence.*

28. The liturgy of the word should be celebrated in a way that favours meditation. Any kind of haste is to be totally avoided, for it impedes recollection. Dialogue between God and his people, with the help of the Holy Spirit, requires short periods of silence, adjusted to the assembly, during which the heart opens to the word of God and a prayerful response takes shape.

Such moments of silence can be appropriately observed just before the commencement of the liturgy of the word, for example, after the first and second readings and after the homily.

f. *The profession of faith.*

29. The creed or profession of faith is recited at Mass when the rubrics prescribe it. The creed offers the congregation the opportunity of assenting to the word of God heard in the readings and in the homily and of responding to it. It recalls to their minds, in a formula approved by the Church, the rule of faith, before they begin to celebrate in the eucharist the mystery of faith.

g. *The general intercessions or the prayers of the faithful.*

30. In the general intercessions the congregation normally prays—in the light of God's word and in a sense responding to it —for the needs of the universal Church and of the local community, for the salvation of the world, for those in difficulties and for certain categories of people.

Directed by the celebrant himself, the deacon, another minister or some of the faithful may propose simple petitions, composed with sensible flexibility, in which 'the people exercise their priestly function by praying for all mankind' (General Introduction to the Roman Missal, 45); thus drawing its full fruit from the liturgy of the word, they are better prepared to proceed to the liturgy of the eucharist.

31. The celebrant directs the general intercessions from the chair, the intentions are announced from the ambo.

The congregation, standing, share in the prayers by saying or singing the common response after each intention, or by praying silently.

2   AIDS TO THE PROPER CELEBRATION
OF THE LITURGY OF THE WORD

a. *The place for the proclamation of God's word.*

32.   There should be in the church an elevated and fixed location, suited by its design and high quality to the dignity of the
word of God, a clear reminder to the faithful that in the Mass is
the table of God's word and the table of Christ's body. Finally, it
should be of the greatest help to the faithful to listen attentively
during the liturgy of the word. Within the context of the church's
design, therefore, careful attention should be given to the structural harmony and the spatial relationship between ambo and
altar.[12]

33.   The ambo itself should be simply decorated, permanently
or at least on occasions of greater solemnity, in keeping with its
design.

Since the ambo is the place from which the word of God is
proclaimed by the ministers, in the nature of things it should be
reserved for the readings, the responsorial psalm and the Easter
hymn (the *Exultet*). The homily may be given from the ambo
and the responsorial psalm, because in the liturgy of the word
these belong with the more essential parts of the whole. It is less
fitting for other persons to use the ambo, such as the commentator, for example, or the director of singing.

34.   The ambo should be sufficiently large for its liturgical purpose, taking into account the fact that on occasion it will need to
accommodate several ministers. Further, there should be sufficient lighting to enable the ministers to read the texts and, where
needed, sound equipment should be installed to enable the congregation to hear without difficulty.

b. *The books for announcing the word of God.*

35.   The books from which the readings are taken recall to the
listeners' minds the memory of God present and speaking to his
people, just as do the ministers, the actions, the places and the
other elements. Care must be taken, therefore, that the books,
as symbols of the supernatural in the liturgical celebration, are
of high quality, tastefully and even beautifully produced.[13]

36.   The proclamation of the gospel being, as it always has
been, the high point of the liturgy of the word, the liturgical traditions of east and west have always made a distinction between
the books of readings. The Book of the Gospels was most carefully produced, was more highly embellished and was shown
greater respect than was any other book of readings. It is much

to be desired that in our own day too there be beautifully embellished Books of the Gospel in cathedrals and also at least in the more densely populated parishes and better-attended churches. This is the book that by right is handed to a deacon at his ordination and is placed on the head of a bishop-elect at his ordination for some time.

37. The dignity of the word of God demands that the books of readings which are used in the celebration should not be exchanged for other pastoral aids, such as leaflets designed to help the faithful prepare the readings, or to be used by them for their own meditation.

CHAPTER THREE: MINISTRIES AND OFFICES IN THE CELEBRATION OF THE LITURGY OF THE WORD AT MASS

1 THE ROLE OF THE PERSON PRESIDING AT THE LITURGY OF THE WORD

38. The person presiding at the liturgy of the word communicates to the faithful, especially in the homily, the hidden nourishment[14] which it contains. Although himself a listener when others are proclaiming the word, he is the one with the primary responsibility for its proclamation. Personally, or with the help of others, he ensures the proper proclamation of God's word. However, he normally reserves to himself the interjection of comments aimed at ensuring more attentive listening by the congregation and, in particular, he reserves to himself the preaching of the homily, whose object it is to help them understand the word of God more fully.

39. The first requirement in the person who is to preside over the celebration is that he be thoroughly familiar with the structure of the order of readings, so as to be able to elicit an effective response to them in the hearts of the faithful. Further, by dint of prayer and study, he should acquire a full understanding of the harmony and interconnection between the different texts of the liturgy of the word, so as to inculcate, from the order of the readings, a correct understanding of the mystery of Christ and of his saving word.

40. The person presiding should freely avail himself of the choices offered in the Lectionary with regard to readings, responses, responsorial psalms and gospel acclamations, but in agreement with all those involved and in consultation with the faithful on what pertains to them.

41. The person presiding also exercises his proper office and the ministry of the word of God when he preaches the homily. By its means he leads his brothers and sisters to the sacred Scriptures, to know and savour them, he evokes gratitude in their hearts for the wonderful works of God, he nourishes their faith in the word which in the celebration becomes a sacrament by the power of the Holy Spirit. Finally, he prepares them for the fruitful reception of communion and invites them to accept the responsibilities of the Christian life.

42. At times the person presiding has the task of introducing the readings beforehand to the faithful. These introductions can certainly help the congregation to hear the word of God better, since they are productive of faith and of good will. The person presiding may have this task done by others, such as the deacon or commentator.

43. The person presiding leads the faithful into the eucharistic liturgy as he directs the general intercessions, utilising the introduction to them and the concluding prayer to connect them, if possible, with that day's readings and homily.

2   THE ROLE OF THE FAITHFUL
IN THE LITURGY OF THE WORD

44. The people of God is gathered together, is increased in number and is nourished by the word of Christ. 'This is particularly true of the liturgy of the word within the celebration of the Mass, where there is an inseparable union of the proclamation of the Lord's death and resurrection, the response of the listening people and the offering itself by which Christ confirmed the new covenant in his blood. In this offering the faithful share both by their sacrificial sentiments and by the reception of the sacrament.' (Vatican II, *P.O.*, 4) For 'not only when things are read "which were written for our instruction" (Rom. 15:4), but also when the Church prays or sings or acts, the faith of those taking part is nourished, and their minds are raised to God so that they may offer him their spiritual homage and receive his grace more abundantly.' (Vatican II, *S.C.*, 33)

45. In the liturgy of the word the assembly of the faithful still receives today from God the announcement of his covenant through the faith that comes by hearing.

The people of God has a right to receive in abundance from the spiritual treasury of God's word. This is achieved with the aid of the order of readings at Mass, homilies and pastoral activity.

During the celebration of Mass, the faithful should listen to the word of God with that internal and external reverence which will enable them gradually to grow in the spiritual life and will involve them more fully in the mystery which they celebrate.

46. The faithful will be able to celebrate the memorial of the Lord with devotion if they are aware that it is the one presence of Christ both in the word of God 'since it is he himself who speaks when the holy scriptures are read in church' and also and 'especially in the eucharistic species.' (Vatican II, *S.C.*, 7)

47. A lively faith is needed if the word of God is to be accepted and to influence the lives of the faithful. Such faith is aroused by listening constantly to the word of God proclaimed.

The sacred Scriptures are the source of life and strength, especially when proclaimed in the liturgy. Saint Paul testifies that the gospel has the power to save everyone who believes (Rom. 1:16). Consequently, love of the Scriptures is strength and renewal for all of the people. Every one of the people of God should therefore always be prepared and be happy to hear God's word. When the word of God is announced by the church and is practised, it enlightens the faithful by the action of the Holy Spirit and draws them towards the realization of the entire mystery of the Lord. When the word of God has been faithfully understood it moves the heart and its sentiments to conversion and to a life resplendent with both individual and community faith, since it is both the food of the Christian life and the source of the prayer of the entire Church.

48. The very close connection between the liturgy of the word and the eucharistic liturgy should persuade the faithful to be present from the very beginning of the celebration, to take part in it with attention and, as far as possible, to have prepared themselves beforehand to listen, especially by acquiring a deeper knowledge of the Scriptures. It should evoke in them a desire for a liturgical understanding of the texts read and a willingness to respond with song.

Thus, when they have listened to God's word and reflected on it, the faithful are able to make an active response to it, one replete with faith, hope and charity, by prayer and self-offering, not only during the celebration, but in their Christian lives.

3   MINISTRIES IN THE LITURGY OF THE WORD

49. Liturgical tradition assigns to ministers—readers and deacons—the task of reading the lessons at Mass. The priest-

celebrant should himself read the gospel, however, if there is neither deacon nor another priest present and, if a reader too is lacking, should do all of the readings.

50. It is for the deacon to proclaim the gospel in the liturgy of the word at Mass and sometimes, when appropriate, to give the homily. It is also for him to propose to the people the intentions for the general intercessions.

51. 'The reader has his own particular functions in the Mass, and it is he who should fulfil them even though ministers of higher rank may be present.' (General Instruction on the Roman Missal, 55) The reader's ministry, conferred by a liturgical rite, is to be held in esteem. Commissioned readers should perform their task on Sundays and major feasts at least, especially at the principal Mass. They may also be given the task of helping to plan the liturgy of the word and, so far as it is necessary, of seeing to the preparation of others of the faithful who are asked to read at Mass from time to time.

52. Readers, whether commissioned or not, are required in the liturgical assembly. Arrangements should therefore be made to have qualified lay persons trained for this ministry. When there is more than one reading, it is better to assign them to different readers than to have them all read by one person.

53. At a Mass without a deacon, the task of announcing the intentions for the general intercessions is to be assigned to the cantor, especially if they are to be sung, to a reader or to another person.

54. When a second priest, a deacon and a commissioned reader go to the ambo to read the word of God at a Mass celebrated with the people they should wear the sacred vestment appropriate to their office. Those who exercise the ministry of reading occasionally or even regularly but have not been commissioned for it should wear ordinary clothes when they go to the ambo, in accordance however with local custom.

55. 'So that the faithful may derive a keen appreciation of holy scripture by listening to the readings, it is necessary that those who read it to them, whether commissioned readers or not, should be competent and carefully prepared for the task.' (General Introduction to the Roman Missal, 66)

This preparation should be primarily spiritual, but technical training is also needed. The spiritual preparation presupposes at least a biblical and liturgical formation. The biblical formation should aim at imparting an understanding of the readings in their context and a grasp, by faith, of the central point of the revealed message. The liturgical formation should give some understanding of the meaning and structure of the liturgy of the word and of the relationship between the liturgy of the word and the liturgy of the eucharist. The technical training should teach how to read in public, with and without an amplification system.

56. It is for the psalmist, or the cantor of the psalm, to sing responsorially or directly the psalm or other biblical chant, the gradual and 'Alleluia' or other chant between the readings. The psalmist may, as needed, intone the 'Alleluia' and verse.

If the psalmist's task is to be properly carried out, it will be found very helpful if in each ecclesial community there be lay persons who are able to sing and to speak and pronounce properly. What has been said above about the formation of readers applies also to cantors.

57. Commentators exercise a true liturgical ministry when they give to the assembly of the faithful, from an appropriate location, relevant explanations and introductions which are clear, simple and carefully prepared. Normally, they should be written and should be approved beforehand by the celebrant.

CHAPTER FOUR: GENERAL PLAN OF THE ORDER OF READINGS FOR MASS

1 PASTORAL PURPOSE OF THE ORDER OF READINGS FOR MASS

58. The primary objective in the preparation of the Order of Readings in the Lectionary of the Roman Missal was pastoral, after the mind of the Second Vatican Council. To achieve this aim, the principles on which the new Order is based and indeed the very collection of texts which it contains have been examined and refined again and again with the collaboration of numerous experts in exegesis, liturgy, catechetics and pastoral matters from all parts of the world. The Order is the fruit of their combined efforts.

It is to be hoped that in time the reading and exposition of the sacred Scripture to the Christian people during the celebration of the Eucharist will effectively contribute to the realization of the objective proposed repeatedly by the Second Vatican Council.

59. What was visualized in this revision was the compilation and production of a single, well-stocked and ample Order of Readings, wholly in conformity with the intention and directives of the Second Council of the Vatican and which at the same time would be suited to the requirements and usage of particular

Churches and worshipping communities. For this reason, those entrusted with the work of revision were at pains to safeguard the liturgical tradition of the Roman rite, while esteeming highly all systems of selection, arrangement and employment of biblical readings in other liturgical families and in some particular Churches. They used what experience had shown to be worthwhile and at the same time endeavoured to avoid certain defects found in the earlier tradition.

60. The present Order of Readings at Mass offers to the faithful a knowledge of the whole of God's word, appropriately arranged. The selection and arrangement of readings through the liturgical year, but especially during Paschal-time, Lent and Advent, are intended as an aid to the faithful gradually to acquire a more profound knowledge of the faith which they profess and of the history of salvation. The Order of Readings is thus seen to answer the needs and concerns of the Christian people.

61. Although a liturgical celebration is not of itself a form of catechesis, it does at the same time have a didactic element. This finds expression in the Lectionary of the Roman Missal, which can thus be justly regarded as a catechetical teaching aid.

The Order of Readings for Mass offers an appropriate scriptural presentation of the most important of all that was done and said in the history of salvation. In its many movements and events, that history is itself successfully called to mind in the liturgy of the word. And it is perceived by believers to be continued[15] here and now in the representation of the paschal mystery of Christ in the celebration of the Eucharist.

62. The pastoral advantage of having a single Order of Readings is that it enables all of the faithful who, for many reasons, might not always worship at the same assembly, to hear everywhere the same readings on certain days and at certain times and to meditate on their relevance to their own situations. This applies to places where there is no priest and where a deacon or someone else has been delegated by the bishop to conduct a celebration of God's word.

63. Pastors may wish to offer a special response from God's word to problems of concern to their own congregations. While not forgetting that they are first and foremost heralds of the totality of the mystery of Christ and of the gospel, they may quite properly avail themselves of the options on offer in the Order of Readings at Mass, especially at a ritual or votive Mass, or at a Mass in honour of the saints or for various needs and occasions. Special permissions are granted, in conformity with the

general regulations, for the readings at Masses with special groups.

2   THE PRINCIPLES GOVERNING THE COMPOSITION OF THE ORDER OF READINGS FOR MASS

64. In order to achieve the purpose of the Order of Readings for Mass the selection and arrangement of its parts was guided both by the sequence of the liturgical seasons and by the principles of present-day biblical hermeneutics.

It was therefore judged helpful to outline here the principles guiding the composition of the Order of Readings for Mass.

a. *The selection of texts.*

65. The arrangement of readings in the Proper of Seasons is as follows: the more important passages are read on Sundays and holydays, thus ensuring that the more significant sections of the word of God can be read within an appropriate time-span. Another series of biblical texts, which in a sense completes the message of salvation proclaimed on Sundays and holydays, is read on weekdays. The two series, the Sunday-holyday and the weekday, are independent of each other. Indeed, the Sunday-holyday series of readings extends over three years, the weekday over two. Thus, each series is quite separate from the other.

The arrangement of the other portions of the Order of Readings—such as that for celebrations of saints, ritual Masses, Masses for various needs and occasions, votive Masses, Masses for the dead—is governed by its own rules.

b. *Arrangement of the readings for Sundays and Holydays.*

66. The following are the characteristics of the readings for Sundays and holydays:

1. There are three readings at each Mass: the first from the Old Testament, the second from an apostle (that is, from one of the epistles, or from the Apocalypse, depending on the season) and the third from the gospels. This arrangement illustrates the unity of the two Testaments and of the history of salvation, whose centre is Christ, commemorated in his paschal mystery.

2. A more varied and a wider selection is achieved on Sundays and holydays by presenting the readings over a three-year period, thus ensuring that the passages are repeated only every four years.[16]

3. The principles guiding the arrangement of readings on Sundays and holydays are known as the principles of 'harmonious composition' and 'semicontinuous reading.' One or other principle is applied, depending on the season of the year and the particular characteristics of the liturgical season.

67. The best example of harmony between the Old and the New Testament is that suggested by Scripture itself, when, that is to say, the teaching and events narrated in New Testament passages bear a more or less explicit relationship to the teaching and events of the Old Testament. In the present Order of Readings, the Old Testament passages are chosen mainly because they harmonize with New Testament passages, with the gospel especially, which are read at the same Mass.

Another kind of harmony is found between the readings at Mass in Advent, Lent and Paschal-time, those seasons which have a particular importance and character.

On the other hand, on Sundays 'through the year', which do not have a distinctive character of their own, the apostolic and gospel passages are arranged in semicontinuous sequence, while the Old Testament passages are chosen to harmonize with the gospels.

68. It was decided not to extend to Sundays, for the sake of facilitating homiletic instruction, the thematic arrangement of readings which suits the liturgical seasons mentioned above. Such an arrangement would be at variance with the true meaning of the liturgy, which is always a celebration of the mystery of Christ and which employs the word of God in keeping with its own tradition, moved not by logical or extrinsic considerations but by the desire to proclaim the gospel and to lead believers to the fullness of truth.

c. *The arrangement of readings for weekdays.*

69. The weekday readings have been arranged as follows:

1. Every Mass has two readings: the first reading from the Old Testament or from an apostle (that is, from the epistles or from the Apocalypse and from the Acts of the Apostles during Paschaltime), the second reading from the gospels.

2. The annual Lenten cycle is arranged according to special principles, which take into account the season's baptismal and penitential character.

3. There is also an annual cycle for the weekdays of Advent, Christmastide and Paschal-time: which means that the readings are not changed from year to year.

4. There is a one-year cycle of the gospel readings on week-

days of the thirty-four weeks 'through the year' and it is repeated each year. The first readings, however, are arranged in a two-year cycle, read on alternate years, the first on odd-numbered years, the second on even-numbered.

Thus, as on Sundays and holydays, the Order of Readings for weekdays is arranged in accordance with the principles of harmony and semicontinuous reading, especially during the seasons with their own characteristics.

d. Readings for saints' celebrations.

70. Two series of readings are provided for celebrations of saints:

1. One, in the Proper, for solemnities, feasts and memorials, especially if special readings are provided for such celebrations. Sometimes a reference is given to one or other passage in the Common as being preferable.

2. The other and larger series is contained in the Common of Saints. This provides, firstly, texts suited to various categories of saints (Martyrs, Pastors, Virgins, etc.), then a number of texts on the theme of holiness in general, from which one may select freely whenever the Common is indicated as the source of readings.

71. It is to be noted that all these texts are collected together in the order in which they are read at Mass. Thus, the readings from the Old Testament are given first, then the apostolic texts, the psalms and the verses between the readings and finally the gospels. The purpose of this arrangement is to enable the celebrant to choose from them freely, unless stated otherwise, bearing in mind the pastoral needs of the assembly taking part in the celebration.

e. Readings for ritual Masses, Masses for various needs and occasions, votive Masses and Masses for the dead.

72. There is the same arrangement of readings for ritual Masses, Masses for various needs and occasions, votive Masses and Masses for the dead. A number of texts are proposed, in other words, as in the Common of Saints.

f. The main criteria employed in choosing and arranging the readings.

73. Over and above the principles governing the arrangement of readings in the different sections of the Order of Readings,

there were other principles of a more general nature, which can be described as follows:

1. The reservation of some books to particular liturgical seasons.

74. In this Order of Readings, some books of the Bible are reserved for particular liturgical seasons, and this both because of the intrinsic importance of the subject matter and because of liturgical tradition. Thus, for example, the Western (Ambrosian and Hispanic) and Eastern tradition of reading Acts during Paschal-time is observed. This illustrates how the entire life of the Church began with the paschal mystery. Likewise, the Western and Eastern tradition of reading the gospel of John in the latter weeks of Lent and in Paschal-time is also observed.

The reading of Isaiah, especially First Isaiah, is traditionally assigned to Advent. Certain texts of the same book are read at Christmas time and the first epistle of John is also assigned to the same time.

2. The length of texts.

75. A *via media* has been followed with regard to the length of texts. A distinction was made between narrative passages, which need to be of some length and are usually listened to attentively by the faithful, and passages of great doctrinal density, which should not be long.

A longer and a shorter form of some lengthy passages has been provided, a task which was done with great care.

3. More difficult texts.

76. For pastoral reasons, genuinely more difficult biblical passages have been avoided in choosing the readings for Sundays and solemnities, whether they be objectively more difficult in that they pose difficult literary, critical or exegetical problems, or because to some extent it will be hard for the faithful to follow them. However, one may not hide the spiritual riches of certain passages from the faithful on the grounds that they will find them difficult, if in fact the source of the difficulty is the lack either of that Christian formation which no Christian should be without, or of that biblical formation which every pastor of souls should have. It frequently happens that light is thrown on a difficult reading by comparing it with another reading in the same Mass.

4. The omission of verses.

77. It has been the custom in many liturgies, including the Roman liturgy, to omit some verses at times in Scripture readings. On the other hand, it must be admitted that such omissions ought not to be made lightly, lest violence be done to the mean-

ing of the text or to the mind and the style of Scripture. However, it was decided on pastoral grounds to continue the tradition in this Order of Readings, while taking care to preserve intact the essential meaning of the passages. Otherwise, some texts would have been too long; readings of considerable and sometimes of great spiritual value for the faithful would have had to be omitted because they contained one or other verse of little pastoral use or which posed really difficult problems.

3 THE PRINCIPLES TO BE OBSERVED IN USING THE ORDER OF READINGS

a. *Options in choosing texts.*

78. The Order of Readings sometimes leaves it to the celebrant to choose between alternative texts, or from a number of texts proposed for the same reading. This rarely happens on Sundays, solemnities and feasts, lest the proper characteristics of a liturgical season be obscured, or the semicontinuous reading of a particular book be unduly interrupted. This option is more freely given for celebrations of saints, for ritual Masses, Masses for various needs and occasions, votive Masses and Masses for the dead.

The aim, in allowing these options and others outlined in the General Instruction on the Roman Missal and the *Ordo Cantus Missae*, is pastoral. In planning the liturgy of the word, therefore, the priest 'ought to consider the spiritual good of the people rather than his own preferences. He should remember also that the choice of the various parts can best be made in consultation with the ministers and servers who have roles to play in the celebration, and with members of the congregation as regards the parts which directly concern them.' (General Instruction on the Roman Missal, n. 313)

1. The two readings before the gospel.

79. In Masses where three readings are assigned, all three ought to be read. However, if an episcopal conference should decide, for pastoral reasons, that the readings should be reduced to two, the choice between the first two readings should be made in a way that will not thwart the plan to instruct the faithful more fully in the mystery of salvation. Thus, unless the contrary be indicated, of the first two readings, preference should be given to the one which best harmonises with the gospel, or to the one which, in keeping with the above-mentioned plan, is better suited to imparting a coherent catechesis over a period, or to the

one which makes possible the semicontinuous reading of a particular book.[17]

2. Long and short versions of texts.

80. The selection of the longer or of the shorter version of a text should also be guided by pastoral criteria. Sometimes a longer and a shorter version of the same text is given. The question to be asked is: which of the two can the faithful listen to with profit? Or if they can listen to the full text if it is explained subsequently in the homily?

3. When two texts are provided.

81. When a choice is offered between alternative texts, fixed or optional, consideration should be given to the needs of the participants: whether it be a matter of using a text which is simpler, or one which is more relevant to the congregation, or, as pastoral advantage may suggest, of repeating or replacing a text which is assigned as proper in one celebration and as optional in another.

A problem can arise when it is feared that a particular text will create difficulties for a particular congregation, or when a text has to be repeated after a few days—when a text assigned to a Sunday has to be read again during the following week.

4. Weekday readings.

82. Texts are assigned for every day of every week of the entire year in the arrangement of readings for weekdays. For the most part, therefore, those readings are to be read on the days to which they are assigned, except on the days on which there is a solemnity, a feast or a memorial with its own proper readings.

In using the Order of Readings for weekdays one should see if one or other passage of a biblical book is due to be omitted in the course of the coming week because of the occurrence of some celebration. In that case, bearing in mind the plan of readings for the entire week, the priest should arrange to omit the less important passages or, if without them the over-all theme would not be clear, to combine them, suitably, with other readings.

5. Celebrations of the saints.

83. When they are available, proper readings are provided for saints' celebrations: readings, that is, about the saint or the mystery which the Mass celebrates. Such readings, even if provided on a memorial, must take the place of the weekday readings. Whenever such readings are provided on a memorial, this is expressly indicated in the Order of Readings.

There are also 'appropriated' readings, which illustrate a special aspect of the spiritual life or of the activities of a saint. In such cases, the use of those readings does not seem to be something to be insisted upon, except for compelling pastoral reasons. Mostly, references are given to readings in the Common in order to facilitate choice. But they are merely suggestions. Any other reading from the Common may be selected in place of an appropriated reading or a proposed reading from the Common.

The priest will have a care, in the first place, for the spiritual good of the faithful and he will be mindful not to impose his own preferences on them. He will be especially careful not to omit frequently and without sufficient reason the readings assigned in the Lectionary for weekdays. They are important in the church's plan to provide a richer table of God's word for the faithful.

Readings are also provided in the Commons for certain categories of saints (such as martyrs, virgins, pastors) or for saints in general. Since a number of readings are provided in such cases, it will be for the celebrant to select the one best suited to his congregation.

In all celebrations, readings may always be taken from the Common to which specific reference is made, but also from the Common of Holy Men and Women, whenever there is a special reason.

84. Further, the following should be borne in mind with regard to saints' celebrations:

a. Readings from the Proper or Common should always be used on solemnities and feasts. Proper readings are always assigned for solemnities and feasts of the General Roman Calendar.

b. Three readings should be assigned on solemnities of particular calendars, unless the conference of bishops has ruled that there should be only two readings. The first reading should be from the Old Testament (but from the Acts of the Apostles or the Apocalypse during Paschaltime), the second from an apostle and the third from the gospels.

c. On feasts and memorials, when there are only two readings, the first reading can be chosen from the Old Testament or from an apostle, the second from the gospels. During Paschaltime, however, following the Church's traditional custom, the first reading should be from an apostle and the second, as far as possible, from St. John's Gospel.

6. Other parts of the order of readings.

85. In the Order of Readings for ritual Masses, the references are to the texts already promulgated for individual rites, except, as is obvious, for texts assigned to celebrations outside of Mass.

86. The Order of Readings for various needs and occasions,

for votive Masses and Masses for the dead provides many texts which will be found helpful in adapting such celebrations to the situation, circumstances and problems of the various groups taking part.

87. In ritual Masses, Masses for various needs and occasions, votive Masses and Masses for the dead, several texts are provided. The choice of readings, therefore, should be made according to the criteria described above for choosing readings from the Common of Saints.

88. On a day when one of the ritual Masses is not permitted and the norms for the individual rite permit the choice of one of the readings provided for ritual Masses, consideration should be given to the common spiritual good of the participants.

b. *The responsorial psalm and the acclamation before the gospel.*

89. The psalm after the first reading is of great importance. Normally the psalm assigned to the reading is the one to be used. However, when the readings are from the Common of Saints or from ritual Masses, Masses for various needs and occasions, votive Masses and Masses for the dead, the choice is left to the celebrant who should have as his aim the pastoral benefit of those taking part.

However, in order to facilitate the people's response to the psalm when it is sung, the Order of Readings provides other texts of psalms and responses, chosen for the different liturgical seasons or for the different categories of saints. These may be used in place of the text corresponding to the reading.

90. The second chant, that between the second reading and the gospel, is either provided in each Mass and goes with the gospel, or is to be chosen from the series for the liturgical season or from one of the Commons.

91. During Lent, one of the acclamations provided[18] may be used before and after the verse before the gospel.

CHAPTER FIVE:
DESCRIPTION OF THE ORDER OF READINGS

92. To help pastors of souls to understand the structure of the Order of Readings and thus to be able to use it more effectively, for the benefit of the faithful, it seems useful to give a brief description of the Order of Readings, at least of the principal celebrations and the different liturgical seasons for which readings were chosen according to the rules described above.

1   ADVENT

a. *Sundays*

93. The gospels have their own themes: they refer to the Lord's coming at the end of time (first Sunday), to John the Baptist (second and third Sundays), to the events which immediately preceded our Lord's birth (fourth Sunday).

The Old Testament readings are prophecies of the Messiah and of Messianic times, especially from the book of Isaiah.

The apostolic readings provide exhortations and proclamations in keeping with the different Advent themes.

b. *Weekdays*

94. There are two series of readings, one from the beginning of Advent to 16 December, the other from the 17 to 24 December.

In the first part of Advent, the book of Isaiah is read, the readings following the order of the book and including some more important texts which are read also on Sundays. The gospels for those days are chosen in view of the first readings.

On the Thursday of the second week the gospel readings about John the Baptist commence. The first readings are either the continuation of Isaiah or are texts chosen in view of the gospels.

In the last week before Christmas, the Gospels of Matthew (chapter 1) and Luke (chapter 2) describe the events immediately preceding the birth of our Lord. The first readings are chosen, in view of the gospels, from several books of the Old Testament and contain important Messianic prophecies.

2   CHRISTMAS TIME

a. *Solemnities, feasts and Sundays*

95. For the vigil and for the three Masses of Christmas, both the prophetic and the other readings have been chosen from the Roman tradition.

On the Sunday within the octave of Christmas, the feast of the Holy Family, the gospel is about the infancy of Jesus, the other readings about the virtues of family life.

On the octave of Christmas, solemnity of Mary, Mother of God, the readings are about the Virgin Mother of God and the giving of the holy name of Jesus.

On the second Sunday after Christmas, the lessons are about the mystery of the Incarnation.

On the Epiphany, the Old Testament and the gospel readings follow the Roman tradition, while the apostolic reading is about the call of the gentiles to salvation.

On the feast of the Baptism of the Lord, the readings are about that mystery.

b. *On weekdays.*

96. After 29 December, there is a continuous reading of the whole of the first epistle of John, the reading of which in fact had begun on 27 December, the feast of Saint John himself and on the following day, the feast of the Holy Innocents. The gospels are about manifestations of our Lord. Events from the childhood of Jesus are read from the Gospel of Luke (29 and 30 December), the first chapter of John is read (31 December to 5 January) and the principal manifestations of Jesus from the four evangelists.

3   LENT

a. *Sundays*

97. The readings from the gospels are arranged as follows:

The accounts of the temptation and of the transfiguration of our Lord are retained (for all three years of the cycle) on the first and second Sundays respectively, using the three synoptics.

On the three subsequent Sundays, the gospel accounts of the Samaritan woman, the man born blind and the raising of Lazarus have been restored in year A. Since these gospels are of major importance in the context of Christian initiation, they may also be used in years B and C, especially where there are catechumens.

However, other texts are provided for years B and C: for year B, texts from John about the coming glorification of Christ through his cross and resurrection and for year C, texts from Luke about conversion.

On the Passion (Palm) Sunday, the texts for the procession are chosen from the synoptic gospels' accounts of our Lord's triumphal entrance into Jerusalem. The account of our Lord's Passion is read at the Mass.

The readings from the Old Testament are about the history of salvation, which is one of the themes of the Lenten catechesis. Every year a series of texts is read which present the main elements of salvation history from its beginning to the promise of the new covenant.

The readings from the apostles have been chosen to correspond with the readings from the Old Testament and the Gospel and as far as possible to establish a connection between them.

b. *Weekdays*

98. Inter-related readings from the Gospels and the Old Testament were selected. They treat of various themes of Lenten catechesis which are suited to the spiritual significance of this season. From the Monday of the fourth week there is a semi-continuous reading of the Gospel of John, with texts which correspond more closely to the Lenten themes.

Since the readings about the Samaritan woman, the man born blind and the resurrection of Lazarus are now read on Sundays, but only in year A (they are optional on the other years), provision has been made for their use on weekdays. At the beginning of the third, fourth and fifth weeks, optional Masses with these texts have been inserted and may be used in place of the readings of the day on any day of the respective week.

On the first days of Holy Week, the readings are about the mystery of Christ's Passion. In the Mass of the Chrism, the readings emphasize both the messianic role of Christ and the continuation of that role through the Church's sacraments.

4 THE EASTER TRIDUUM AND THE EASTER SEASON

a. *The Easter Triduum*

99. On Holy Thursday, the remembrance of the Last Supper at the evening Mass casts its own special light. There is the example of Christ washing the feet of the disciples and Paul's account of the institution of the Christian passover in the eucharist.

The high point of the liturgical celebration on Good Friday is John's account of the Passion of him who was foretold in Isaiah as the Servant of Yahweh and who became the unique priest by offering himself to the Father.

There are seven readings from the Old Testament on the holy night of the paschal vigil. They recall the wonderful works of God in the history of salvation. There are two readings from the New Testament: the announcement of the resurrection in one of the three synoptic gospels each year and an apostolic reading on Christian baptism as the sacrament of Christ's resurrection.

On Easter Sunday, the gospel reading is from John, on the discovery of the empty tomb. One may also, however, use the gospel texts from the Easter vigil, or at an Easter Sunday evening Mass, Luke's account of the appearance to the disciples on the road to Emmaus. The first reading is from Acts. It replaces the Old Testament readings during Paschal-time. The apostolic reading is about the living of the paschal mystery in the Church.

b. *Sundays*

100. For the first three Sundays, the gospels recall the appearances of the risen Christ. The readings about the Good Shepherd are assigned to the fourth Sunday of Paschal-time. On the fifth, sixth and seventh Sunday after Easter, passages from our Lord's discourse and prayer after the Last Supper are read.

The first reading is taken from the Acts of the Apostles, in a three-year cycle, parallel and in sequence. Thus, something of the life, witness and progress of the primitive Church is presented each year.

For the apostolic readings: 1 Peter is read in year A, 1 John is read in year B and the Apocalypse is read in year C. These are the texts which are most appropriate to the spirit of joyful faith and firm hope that belong to this season.

c. *Weekdays*

101. The first reading is a semicontinuous reading from Acts, as on Sundays. During the Easter octave, the gospel readings are accounts of our Lord's appearances. Then there is a semicontinuous reading of the Gospel of John, except that now texts with a more paschal character are chosen, in order to complement the texts read during Lent. Much of this paschal reading is made up of our Lord's discourse and prayer at the last supper.

d. *Solemnities of the Ascension and Pentecost*

102. The first reading on the solemnity of the Ascension is the account of the Ascension in Acts. This is complemented by the second, apostolic, reading on Christ exalted at the right hand of the Father. The gospel readings have their own three year cycle, with each year offering its own text.

Four Old Testament readings are provided at the evening Mass on the vigil of Pentecost, illustrating the manifold meaning of the solemnity. Any one of the readings may be chosen. The apostolic reading describes the Holy Spirit actually at work in the Church. The gospel recalls the promise of the Spirit made by Christ before his glorification.

At the Mass on the day of Pentecost, the customary account of the great event of Pentecost provides the first reading, the apostolic reading describes the effect of the action of the Holy Spirit in the life of the Church. The gospel recalls the bestowal of the Spirit on the disciples by Jesus on the evening of Easter. Other, optional, texts describe the action of the Spirit on the disciples and on the Church.

5   ORDINARY TIME

a. *The arrangement and selection of texts.*

103. Ordinary Time begins on the Monday after the Sunday following 6 January and continues until the Tuesday before Lent, inclusive. It recommences on the Monday after Pentecost Sunday and finishes before first Vespers of the first Sunday of Advent.

The Order of Readings provides readings for thirty-four Sundays and the weeks following them. Sometimes there are only thirty-three weeks of Ordinary Time. Further, some Sundays either belong in another season (such as the Sunday on which the feast of the Baptism of the Lord falls and Pentecost Sunday) or are replaced by a solemnity celebrated on a Sunday (such as Trinity Sunday and the feast of Christ the King).

104. The following are to be observed to ensure the correct use of the readings in Ordinary Time:

1. The Sunday on which the Baptism of the Lord falls replaces the first Sunday of Ordinary Time. Consequently, the readings for the first week of Ordinary Time commence on the Monday following the Sunday after 6 January. If the feast of the Baptism of the Lord is celebrated on the Monday after the Sunday on which the Epiphany has been celebrated, the readings for the first week begin on the Tuesday.

2. The Sunday which follows the feast of the Baptism of the Lord is the second Sunday of Ordinary Time. The remaining Sundays are numbered consecutively, up to the Sunday before Lent. The readings for (the week following that Sunday) the week in which Ash Wednesday falls are dropped after the Tuesday.

3. When the readings for Ordinary Time are resumed after Pentecost Sunday, this is what happens:

In a year in which there are thirty-four Sundays in Ordinary Time, the week to be used is the one which immediately follows the last week used before Lent.

In a year in which there are thirty-three Sundays in Ordinary Time, the first week which would have been resumed after Pentecost is omitted, thus ensuring that the eschatological texts assigned to weeks thirty-three and thirty-four are reserved to the last two weeks in the Church's year.

b. *Sunday Readings*.

1. Gospel readings.

105. On the second Sunday of Ordinary Time, the gospel is still about the manifestation of our Lord, which the Epiphany had celebrated: there is the traditional passage about the wedding feast at Cana and two other passages from John.

From the third Sunday, there is a semi-continuous reading of the synoptic gospels. This reading is so arranged that the teaching of each synoptic is presented in the unfolding of our Lord's life and preaching.

This arrangement also provides a certain correlation between the meaning of each gospel and the progress of the liturgical year. After Epiphany we read about the commencement of our Lord's preaching and all of this combines well with the baptism and first public appearances of Christ. At the end of the liturgical year one arrives quite naturally at the eschatological theme which is featured on the last Sundays; the chapters of the gospels which precede the account of the Passion treat of this theme quite extensively.

In year B, after the sixteenth Sunday five readings are inserted from the sixth chapter of John (from the sermon on the bread of life).[19] This insertion seems acceptable since John's account of the multiplication of the loaves takes the place of Mark's account of the same event. The prologue of the gospel (of John) has been inserted before the first text of the semicontinuous reading of Luke (which is on the third Sunday). The passage (from John) expresses the author's intention very beautifully and there seemed to be no better place for it.

2. Readings from the Old Testament.

106. These readings have been chosen to correspond with the gospels, thus avoiding too great diversity in the readings in individual Masses and, in particular, demonstrating the unity of the two Testaments. The relationship between the readings at each Mass is indicated by the carefully selected titles given to the passages.

As far as was possible, short and simple passages have been chosen. However, provision was also made for the reading of many of the more important Old Testament passages on Sundays. These readings are not arranged in logical sequence, but for their relationship to various gospels. None the less, the treasury of God's word will be opened up to such an extent that all those taking part in Sunday Mass will come to know all the principal parts of the Old Testament.

3. Apostolic Readings.

107. A semicontinuous reading of the epistles of Paul and James is provided. (The epistles of Peter and John are read during the Easter and Christmas seasons.)

Since the first epistle to the Corinthians is fairly long and deals with a variety of topics, it is distributed over three years, at the beginning of Ordinary Time each year. It was likewise deemed best to divide the epistle to the Hebrews in two parts, the first part being assigned to year B and the second to year C.

It is to be noted that the passages selected are reasonably short and within the faithful's powers of comprehension.

c. *Readings for solemnities of Our Lord in Ordinary Time.*

108. On the solemnities of the Blessed Trinity, Corpus Christi and the Sacred Heart, passages have been provided which feature the principal themes of these celebrations.

The readings for the thirty-fourth and last Sunday of the year celebrate Christ, prefigured by David, proclaimed universal king amid the humiliations of his passion and cross, reigning in the Church and destined to return at the end of time.

d. *Weekday Readings.*

109. Of the gospels, Mark is read first (weeks one to nine), then Matthew (weeks sixteen to twenty-one) and lastly Luke (weeks twenty-two to thirty-four). Chapters one to twelve of Mark are read in their entirety, except for two passages of the sixth chapter which are read on weekdays at other times. Everything not covered by Mark is read from Matthew and Luke. Passages dealing with the same matters may be read from two or even all three of the synoptics if there is something distinctive about the presentation in each gospel or if each of the passages themselves is crucial to a grasp of the sequence of the gospel in question. The eschatological discourse is contained in its entirety in Luke and is read at the end of the liturgical year.

110. The *first* reading is taken from one Testament for a number of weeks, then from the other, the length of time depending on the length of the books read.

Quite long passages are read from the New Testament, so as to give the substance of each of the epistles, as it were.

There is space for only selected passages from the Old Testament, as representative as is possible of the character of the individual books. The historical passages have been chosen so as to provide an overview of the history of salvation before the Incarnation of our Lord. Over-long narratives could scarcely be presented: sometimes verses have been selected which have comprised a reading which is not too long. Further, the religious significance of the historical events is sometimes indicated by passages taken from the Wisdom books and inserted as prologues or conclusions to a series of historical readings.

Nearly all of the books of the Old Testament have been given a place in the Order of Readings for weekdays in Ordinary Time. Only the shortest of the prophetic books (Obadiah and Zephaniah) and the poetic book (Song of Solomon) have been omitted. Of the stories written for edification and requiring a somewhat lengthy reading to be intelligible, the books of Tobit and Ruth are read, the others (Esther and Judith) being omitted. Texts from these two books are however read on Sundays and weekdays at other times of the year.

At the end of the year, the books of Daniel and of the Apocalypse, which correspond to the eschatological character of the season, are read.

(Chapter Six, the final chapter, is omitted here, since it is of less general interest. It has to do with the method of publication of the Lectionary and with its general format and presentation. Editor.)

* Translated by Austin Flannery, O.P., from the Latin text published in *Notitiae*, nn. 180–183, pp 361 & ff. A number of footnotes have been omitted and a number of others cut down in length. The entire document is divided into six chapters, which are distributed over a Prologue, coinciding with chapter one, over Part One: 'The Word of God in the celebration of Mass,' coinciding with chapters two and three, and Part Two, 'Structure of the Order of Readings for Mass,' coinciding with chapters four to six. In the text which follows, we have retained the chapter headings and all the headings within each chapter, but have not retained the larger divisions. We have also retained the consecutive numbering of the paragraphs.
1. See Vatican II, *S.C.*, nn. 7, 24, 33, 35, 48, 51, 52, 56; *D.V.*, nn. 1, 21, 25, 26; *A.G.D.*, n. 6; *P.O.*, n. 18.
2. See Paul VI, *Ministeria quaedam*, n. V; *Marialis cultus*, n. 12; *Evangelii nuntiandi*, n. 28; John Paul II, *Catechesi tradendae*, n. 23.
3. See S.C.R., 'Instruction on the Worship of the Eucharistic Mystery,' n. 10; S.C.D.W., 'Third Instruction on the Correct Implementation of the Constitution on the Sacred Liturgy,' n. 2; S.C.C., 'General Catechetical Directory,' n. 25; S.C.D.W., 'General Instruction on the Roman Missal,' nn. 9, 11, 24, 33, 60, 62, 316, 320; S.C.S.D.W., 'In-

struction on Certain Norms Concerning the Worship of the Eucharistic Mystery,' nn. 1, 2, 3.

4. For example, 'the word of God, sacred scripture, Old and New Testament, Reading(s) of the word of God, Reading(s) from sacred scripture, celebration(s) of the word of God,' etc.

5. Further, one and the same text may be read and used under different aspects, on different liturgical occasions and in different liturgical celebrations in the course of the year. This must be borne in mind for the homily, for pastoral exegesis and in catechesis. The point becomes clear when one notes that, for example, Romans chapter 6 and chapter 8 are used at different times through the liturgical year and in different celebrations of sacraments and sacramentals.

6. The Latin reads: 'Sic in Liturgia Ecclesia fideliter sequitur modum legendi et interpretandi Scripturas sacras, quo ipse Christus, qui ab "hodie" eventus sui, ad Scripturas omnes perscrutandas adhortatur, usus est.' The I.C.E.L. translation reads: 'Thus in the liturgy the Church faithfully adheres to the way Christ himself read and explained the Scriptures, beginning with the "today" of his coming forward in the synagogue and urging all to search the Scriptures.' I take it, and I hope I am not being fanciful, that the word 'eventus' above is used in the same sense as in the preceding sentence, which says that the liturgical celebration 'becomes a new event.' The footnote reference is to Luke 4:16–21; 24:25–35, 44–49. The first of these texts describes our Lord reading the famous passage from Isaiah, 'The Spirit of the Lord is upon me, because he has anointed me to preach good news to the poor, etc.' After he had handed back the book to the attendant, Jesus said, 'Today this scripture has been fulfilled in your hearing.' This, I take, was our Lord's event, the new happening, taking place before the eyes of his listeners. (Translator)

7. Thus, for example, one finds 'proclamation' or 'reading,' etc., in the celebration of Mass. See General Introduction to the Roman Missal, nn. 21, 23, 95, 131, 146, 234, 235. Thus, also, in the celebrations of the word of God in the Pontifical, the Roman Ritual and the Liturgy of the Hours, all revised by decree of the Second Vatican Council.

8. See Vatican II, S.C., nn. 7 and 33; Saint Augustine: 'The Gospel is Christ's mouth. He is in heaven, but he does not cease to speak on earth.' (Sermon 85); the Roman-Germanic Pontifical: 'The gospel is read, in which Christ addresses the people with his own lips so that . . . the gospel would resound in the Church, as if Christ himself were speaking.'

9. See Saint Jerome: 'If for the apostle Paul (1 Cor. 1:24), Christ is the power of God and the wisdom of God, then whoever is ignorant of scripture knows neither the power of God nor his wisdom. For ignorance of the scriptures is ignorance of Christ.' (Commentary on Isaiah, Prologue.)

10. See Third Instruction on the Correct Implementation of the Liturgy Constitution, Liturgiae Instaurationes, n. 2.

11. Paul VI, Apostolic Constitution, Laudis canticum.

12. The Latin reads: '. . .studendum est. . .congruentiae ac coniunctioni ambonis cum altare. The I.C.E.L. text has: '. . .pains must be taken. . .over the harmonious and close relationship of the lectern with the altar.' (Translator)

13. The Latin reads: 'vere digni, decore et pulchri.' (Translator)

14. The Latin reads 'intimum nutrimentum.' (Translator)

15. Latin: actu continuatur, I.C.E.L., 'contained here and now.'

16. The years are called A, B and C respectively. This is how one dis-

covers when A occurs, when B and when C. The letter C always designates a year which is a multiple of three. Thus, for example, 1980 was year C, 1981 year A, 1982 is year B and 1983 will be year C once more. And so on. However, each cycle coincides with the liturgical year, beginning therefore on the first Sunday of Advent of the previous civil year.

Each yearly cycle takes its character from the synoptic gospel read during it on Sundays 'through the year'. Thus, the first is the year for reading Matthew, the second the year for reading Mark and the third for reading Luke.

17. For example, during Lent the continuity of the Old Testament readings is proposed, in keeping with the development of the history of salvation. On Sundays through the year, there is the semicontinuous reading of an epistle. It is thus appropriate for the pastor of souls to select one or other reading systematically over several successive Sundays in order to establish a harmonious catechesis. It is entirely unsuitable that he should read, without any order, now from the Old Testament, now from the New Testament, without any attempt at a link between successive readings.

18. They are: 'Praise to you, Lord Jesus Christ, King of endless Glory,' 'Praise and honour to you, Lord Jesus Christ,' 'Glory and praise to you, Lord Jesus Christ!,' 'Glory to you, Word of God, Lord Jesus Christ!'.

19. Year B being the year when Saint Mark's Gospel is read in Ordinary Time. (Translator)

82

ECUMENICAL COLLABORATION AT THE REGIONAL, NATIONAL AND LOCAL LEVELS*

S.P.U.C., *Réunis à Rome*, 22 February, 1975

INTRODUCTION

The representatives of Ecumenical Commissions meeting in Rome in November, 1972, stated in their conclusion: "It is at the level of the local church that the spirit of ecumenism must find a concrete expression".[a] The present document aims at being in part a response to the expressed need of many Catholics working on local ecumenical commissions.

The first draft was prepared by a small working group of consultors and staff of the Secretariat for Promoting Christian Unity in June, 1971. It was then sent to all members and a number of consultors as part of the preliminary documentation for the forthcoming Plenary. The Plenary was held in February, 1972 and the draft document was discussed both in groups and in plenary session. Substantial approval was given, subject to important suggestions for re-writing several parts of it.

Meanwhile a study of forms of ecumenical collaboration on regional, national and local levels had been going on between the Catholic Church and the World Council of Churches under the aegis of the Joint Working Group. This was the occasion for the production of two studies, one on a factual basis by Reverend Victor Hayward of the World Council of Churches Secretariat for Relations with Christian Councils and Reverend Basil Meeking of the staff of our Secretariat, and the other prepared by a small group at the request of the Joint Working Group and composed of people named by the Catholic Church and the World Council of Churches. While the former document was published along with a number of other articles on councils of churches, the latter was not, but was made available to the Secretariat by the Joint Working Group in its 1972 meeting as a contribution to the present document. We acknowledge with gratitude this generous gesture. It has contributed greatly to the value of our document.

153

Again in November 1972 and in April 1973 a small group of members, consultors and staff, using this new documentation, worked on the draft according to the instructions of the 1972 Plenary, preparing the version which was presented finally at the Plenary in November, 1973. Here it was given unanimous approval subject to several improvements both in content and form. These changes as well as some suggestions coming from the Congregation for the Doctrine of the Faith were incorporated into the final text.

The status of the document was clearly described in the 1972 Plenary. It is not a set of directives or prescriptions endowed with authority in the juridical sense of the word. Rather it is a document that gives the kind of information which can help bishops in a certain place decide about the form to be given to the local ecumenical collaboration. But its purpose is to do more than give information. It sets out orientations which do not have the force of law but which have the weight of the experience and insights of the Secretariat.

It should also be clear that an amount of what the document contains does have the force of law when this is taken from sources of the Church's teaching and discipline such as the documents of the Second Vatican Council and the official decisions and directives of the Holy See.

With this status the document is now published. In addition to the approval of the Plenary, the Cardinal President has brought it to the notice of the Holy Father who approved of it being sent to all episcopal conferences as an aid to them in carrying out their ecumenical responsibilities. It is as such an instrument that the document must be understood and this defines both its scope and its limits.

The ecumenical dimension is a prime aspect of the life of the Catholic Church on the universal and on the local level. Catholic principles on ecumenism have been given in the conciliar Decree on Ecumenism. They maintain that ecumenical initiatives must be adapted to local needs, that the local church itself has a real and indispensable contribution to make, while always insisting that every local initiative be taken always in harmony with the bonds of communion in faith and discipline which link the Catholic Church. All of this the present document sets forth clearly.

At the same time it is not all-inclusive, nor does it aim to be so. At their meeting in 1972 the representatives of the Ecumenical Commissions raised many questions about local ecumenism. We believe our document responds to some, chiefly those touching on organised ecumenical work and its national and diocesan structures.

The Second Vatican Council stresses the responsibility of the bishops in this field. "This Sacred Synod. . .commends this work to bishops everywhere in the world for their skillful promotion and prudent guidance".[b] To this end the efforts of pastors and laity must be directed.

The Pope has proposed the theme of spiritual renewal and reconciliation with God and among Christians as one of the principal goals of the Holy Year. We trust that this present document may be a contribution to the realization of this deeply ecumenical perspective.

1.
THE ECUMENICAL TASK

In November, 1972, addressing representatives of National Ecumenical Commissions, Pope Paul VI described the primary mission of the Church as being to call men to enter into communion with God, through Christ, in the Holy Spirit, and then to help them to live in this communion which saves them and establishes among them a unity as deep and mysterious as the unity of the Father and the Son.[1]

On another occasion, in October 1967, the Holy Father in an allocution to Patriarch Athenagoras, noted that while this unity is to be a sign in the world calling forth faith, present day unbelief too can act like a summons to the churches and ecclesial communities awakening in them an urgent awareness of the need for unity and calling them to act together. "This common witness", said the Holy Father, "one yet varied, decided and persuasive, of a faith humbly self-confident, springing up in love and radiating hope, is without doubt the foremost demand that the Spirit makes of the churches today".[2]

The pre-condition of this ecumenical movement is a renewal

in the Church, according to the spirit of the truth and holiness of Jesus Christ, a renewal which must touch every member of the Church and be attested to by the quality of their lives.[3]

As the call of the Holy Spirit to unity through renewal is heard and answered by the Christian communities, the volume of study and joint action grows apace, so that one may speak of the pressure of the ecumenical movement which more and more compels Christians to dialogue, common prayer, practical collaboration and common witness.[4]

The cooperation between churches and ecclesial communities has mission and unity as its aim, not least when it is concerned with social and allied questions. For all Christian communities recognize the proclamation of the Gospel to the world, in deed as well as in word, as their first duty.[5]

The ecumenical movement is a movement of the Spirit wider than any of the particular initiatives through which it is manifested. This ecumenical impulse, which for the Catholic Church is necessarily guided by the principles set forth in the Decree on Ecumenism and the Ecumenical Directory, seeks a great variety of expressions and structural forms and the purpose of this document is to look at some of the more prominent of these. As the Catholic Church in each country becomes more aware of the manifestations of ecumenism in various parts of the world, it has to avoid both isolationism and slavish imitation of other places. Ecumenical initiatives must be adapted to local needs and will therefore differ from region to region, while always remaining in harmony with the bonds of Catholic communion. Further, the quest for a structural local unity is a challenge, but so equally is that for a qualitative unity in the confession of a sound and complete faith. Ecumenical initiatives should be true expressions of the life of the local church, and not simply the work of individuals. They should therefore be carried on under the guidance of the bishop and in close association with the ecumenical commission of the diocese or of the episcopal conference. It is important that ecumenical commissions should consider such local initiatives with discernment and sympathy and where appropriate offer encouragement and support. Ecumenism is an integral part of the renewal of the Church[6] and its promotion should be the constant concern of the local church.

A difficulty is created if ecumenical initiatives are left solely to unofficial groups.[7] Then there is an imbalance in which the full ecumenical responsibility will not be adequately and prudently met. Such difficulties will best be avoided if there is an obvious and sincere commitment to ecumenism by the local church.

2.
THE CATHOLIC UNDERSTANDING OF
LOCAL CHURCH[8] AND ITS RELATION
TO THE ECUMENICAL MOVEMENT

Ecumenism on the local level is a primary element of the ecumenical situation as a whole. It is not secondary nor merely derivative. It faces specific needs and situations and has its own resources. It has an initiative of its own and its task is a wider one than merely implementing world-wide ecumenical directives on a small scale.[9]

Not only do the local churches direct and assume responsibility for the work of local ecumenism in communion with the Holy See but in the local churches the mysteries of ecclesial communion (baptism, faith in Christ, the proclamation of the Gospel, etc.) are celebrated and thus constantly renewed, and they are the basis of ecumenical collaboration. This collaboration is served by a number of organized bodies some of which will be mentioned later. It must also be borne in mind that at the present time a good number of Christians prefer to work locally in "informal" groups of a more spontaneous nature than in institutional or "formal" groups.

The importance of local ecumenism derives from the significance of local churches in the Catholic Church as set forth in Vatican Council II:

A diocese is part of the People of God entrusted to a Bishop, to be cared for with the cooperation of his priests, so that in close union with its pastor, and by him gathered together in the Holy Spirit through the Gospel and the Eucharist, it constitutes a particular Church, in which is truly present and operative the One, Holy, Catholic and Apostolic Church of Christ (*Christus Dominus*, 11).

The same Council taught:

Individual bishops are the visible, fundamental principle of unity in their particular churches. These churches are moulded to the likeness of the universal Church; in them, and of them, consists the one, sole Catholic Church. For this reason individual bishops represent their own church; all, together with the Pope, represent the whole Church linked by peace, love and unity (*Lumen Gentium*, 23).

It further stated:

> This Church of Christ is truly present in all lawful, local congregations of the faithful. These congregations, in attachment to their pastors, themselves have the name of churches in the New Testament. They are, for their own locality, the new people called by God, in the Holy Spirit and in great fullness (cf. *1 Thess.* 1:5). In these churches the faithful are gathered together by the preaching of Christ's gospel; in them, the mystery of the Lord's Supper is celebrated 'so that the whole brotherhood is linked by the flesh and blood of the Lord's body (*ibid.*, 26).

Where the people of God, linked in belief and love with their bishop gather to manifest the unity of lived and proclaimed faith, an irreplaceable sacramental expression is given to the living unity of the Catholic Church.[10]

From this Catholic perspective ecumenical responsibilities of the local church emerge clearly. It is through the local church that the Catholic Church is present with many other Christian churches and communities in the same localities and in wider regions such as the territory of an episcopal conference or of an eastern synod. These regions have their distinctive spiritual, ethical, political and cultural characteristics. Within these regions the other Christian churches and ecclesial communities often have the highest level of their churchly authority whereby they make those decisions which direct their life and shape their future. Therefore, the local church or several local churches in the territory of an episcopal conference or a synod can be in a very favourable position to make contact and establish fraternal relations with other Christian churches and communities at these levels.

Through contacts at this point, the other Christian churches and communities may be afforded a fuller understanding of the dynamic of Catholic life as the local church makes it present both in its particularity and in its concrete universality. With the awareness that in a given place it is the vehicle of the presence and action of the Catholic Church, which is fundamentally one, the local church will be ready to take care that its free initiatives do not go beyond its competence and are always undertaken within the limits of the doctrine and the discipline of the whole

Catholic Church, particularly as this touches the sacraments. This discipline is a safeguard of the unity of faith. In this way the bonds of fraternal communion with other local churches will be manifested and the role of the Church of Rome serving the unity of all will be evident.

Thus by reason of their Catholic communion the local churches can enrich the ecumenical movement in many localities, and the local church in one region by its activity may generate an impulse that will stimulate further ecumenical developments elsewhere. Through their communion each local church may also gain ecumenical insights which would not spontaneously arise out of its particular or local situations. And in the face of new and serious ecumenical needs, the local church will rightly call upon the resources and experiences of other churches of its communion to help meet these needs and judge the possibilities. Here the work of the Secretariat for Promoting Christian Unity in stimulating an exchange of insights between the local churches may be of special value.

3.
VARIOUS FORMS OF LOCAL ECUMENISM

In addition to the sacramental expression of the unity of the Catholic Church given in the local church, the real but still imperfect communion between Christian churches and ecclesial communities finds expression in a number of forms of ecumenical action and in certain joint organizations. In this section an attempt is made by way of illustration, to describe some of these areas and forms of local ecumenical action.[11] They are not suggested as being normative, for the initiatives described remain always subjected to the pastoral authority of the diocesan bishop or the episcopal conference. The account given here is clearly not exhaustive but provides a context for later sections of this document. It has to be kept in mind that while these fields of action offer many opportunities of ecumenical collaboration, they also entail problems and difficulties which have to be solved in light of Catholic principles of ecumenism.

a. Sharing in Prayer and Worship

At the level of the local churches there are many occasions for seeking the gifts of the Holy Spirit and that "change of heart and holiness of life which, along with public and private prayer for the unity of Christians, would be regarded as the soul of the whole ecumenical movement".[12] Many forms of this "spiritual ecumenism" are emerging today in prayer groups in which members of various confessions assemble.

The Ecumenical Directory expressed the hope that "Catholics and their other brethren will join in prayer for any common concern in which they can and should cooperate—e.g., peace, social justice, mutual charity among men, the dignity of the family and so on. The same may be said of occasions when according to circumstances a nation or community wishes to make a common act of thanksgiving or petition to God, as on a national feast day, at a time of public disaster or mourning, on a day set aside for remembrance of those who have died for their country. This kind of prayer is also recommended as far as possible at times when Christians hold meetings for study or common action".[13]

The Prayer for Unity, as observed either in January or in the week preceding Pentecost, is widespread and continues to be in most places the chief occasion on which Catholics and other Christians pray together. It is promoted by special committees set up for the purpose by ministers' fraternals or associations and very often by councils of churches.

In certain places some of the great festivals of the liturgical year are marked by joint celebrations in order to express the common joy of Christians in the central events of their faith.

On the Catholic side, participation in sacramental worship is regulated by the Decree on Ecumenism (N. 8), the Directory 1 (42–44, 55), the 1972 Instruction and the Note issued in 1973.[14]

Both participation in common worship and an exact observance of the present canonical limits are a feature of normal Catholic ecumenical activity.

b. Common Bible Work

In 1968, "Guiding Principles for Interconfessional Cooperation"[15] were co-published by the United Bible Societies and the Secretariat for Promoting Christian Unity and there is official Catholic collaboration in 133 Bible translation projects in various places in accordance with these norms.

Many of the 56 national Bible societies that make up the United Bible Societies, working in agreement with a number of episcopal conferences and diocesan bishops, have developed programmes of cooperation with Catholics in Scripture distribution and promotion of Bible reading (joint national Bible Sunday, Bible Weeks, exhibitions, lectures, distribution training, seminars, etc.). In some cases Catholics have become officers of Bible Societies[16] or episcopal conferences have appointed official representatives to Bible Society Advisory Councils.[17]

Bible Societies are a meeting ground for a very wide group of Christians. Their focus is the translation and distribution of the Scripture and a great variety of Christian bodies can cooperate in this important work. Co-operation in translation, distribution and study of the Scriptures has important repercussions in missionary work, catechetics and religious education at all levels. Interconfessional cooperation in the common translation of the Scriptures has important implications for common understanding of the content of Revelation. The World Catholic Federation for the Biblical Apostolate[18] has come into existence to promote in each episcopal conference an organization that will help to coordinate Catholic cooperation with the Bible Societies and to give priests and people all the help they need for understanding and using the Scriptures.

c. Joint Pastoral Care

Where this exists, it is organized mainly in terms of some specific situation and does not compete with parish-based pastoral work. For instance, in hospitals the chaplains often adopt an ecumenical approach, both for some of their contacts with the patients and for their dealings with the hospital authorities.

In universities, industry, prisons, the armed forces, radio and television, there is increasing evidence that the work of the various churches and ecclesial communities is coordinated and, even, in a number of places is done jointly to some degree. The rapid social and economic change characteristic of the present age, is extending the fields where such special ministries, either on a city-wide or a geographical basis, are needed (e.g., to youth, drug addicts, etc.). In a few places,[19] a deliberate effort has been made to devise new pastoral approaches on an ecumenical basis in terms of sector ministries, often on a team-basis.[20]

A special area both of responsibility and difficulty concerns mixed marriages. The Motu Proprio "*Matrimonia Mixta*" encourages a joint effort on the part of the pastors of the partners in order to assist them in the best possible way before and during the marriage.

d. Shared Premises

The rule is that Catholic churches are reserved for Catholic worship. As consecrated buildings they have an important liturgical significance. Further they have a pedagogical value for inculcating the meaning and spirit of worship. Therefore sharing them with other Christians or constructing new churches jointly with other Christians can be only by way of exception.

However, the *Ecumenical Directory* (Part I) has stated:

"If the separated brethren have no place in which to carry out their religious rites properly and with dignity, the local Ordinary may allow them the use of a Catholic building, cemetery or church" (N. 61).

"Because sharing in sacred functions, objects and places with all the separated Eastern brethren is allowed for a reasonable cause (cf. *Decree on Eastern Catholic Churches*, N. 28), it is recommended that with the approval of the local Ordinary separated Eastern priests and communities be allowed the use of Catholic churches, buildings and cemeteries and other things necessary for their religious rites, if they ask for this, and have no place in which they can celebrate sacred functions properly and with dignity" (N. 52).

Because of developments in society, because of rapid growth in population and building, and for financial motives, where there is a good ecumenical relationship and understanding between the communities, the sharing of church premises can become a matter of practical interest. It does not seem possible to adduce any one model for this kind of sharing since it is a question of responding to a need or an emergency.[21]

The building of an interconfessional place of worship must be an exception and should answer real needs which cannot otherwise be met. An airport chapel or a chapel at a military camp are examples that meet this condition. An exceptional pastoral situation could also be the reason for such a building as when a government would forbid the multiplication of places of worship or in the case of the extreme poverty of a Christian community, and there the simultaneous use of a church could be allowed.

In a shared church, judicious consideration needs to be given to the question of the reservation of the Blessed Sacrament so that it is done in a way that is consonant with sound sacramental theology, as well as respectful of the sensitivities of those who use the building. In addition to strictly religious considerations, due attention ought to be paid to the practical, financial and administrative problems, as well as to the questions of civil and canon law which are involved.

Clearly, initiatives in the matter of shared premises can be undertaken only under the authority of the bishop of the diocese and on the basis of the norms for the application of those principles fixed by the competent episcopal conference. Before making plans for a shared building the authorities of the respective communities concerned ought first to reach agreement as to how their various disciplines will be observed particularly in regard to the sacraments. Arrangements should be made so that the rules of the Catholic Church concerning "communicatio in sacris" are respected.

It is important that any project for a shared church be accompanied by suitable education of the Catholic people concerned so that its significance may be grasped and any danger of indifferentism is avoided.

e. Collaboration in Education

The Second Part of the *Ecumenical Directory*, devoted to Ecumenism in Higher Education,[22] outlines many of the possibilities. The manner in which they have been realised differs greatly in different places. In this area there can be particular problems and difficulties which call for a high degree of pastoral prudence.[23]

There are now several "clusters" of theological schools and faculties.[24] In some places there is sharing of certain buildings, and especially the use of libraries, some common lectures (within the limits indicated by the Directory) and sometimes two or more confessional faculties have combined to organize a common academic degree course.

In catechetics local needs have led at times to collaboration in the teaching of religion, especially where this has to be done in non-denominational schools. But as long as Christians are not fully at one in faith, catechesis, which is formation for profession of faith, must remain necessarily the proper and inalienable task of the various churches and ecclesial communities.

The list of ecumenical institutes and study centres where there is Catholic involvement, at least by membership on governing boards and among the student bodies, is now quite considerable. Some of these offer courses in ecumenism and study certain topics on an ecumenical basis. Others which depend on a particular confession may concentrate largely on the study of another Christian confession. The experience of an ecumenical community life over a substantial period of time is an important feature of certain ecumenical institutes.

f. Joint Use of Communications Media

A concern for the better quality of religious programmes on radio and television has led to coordination and in some areas to joint planning and use of common facilities. Occasionally, there is an inter-confessional organization with full Catholic participation, with the major part of its radio, publishing and audiovisual work common to the principal churches and ecclesial communities, but giving each the facilities for enunciating its own doctrine and practice.[25] There are a few instances where religious newspapers either Catholic or of other confessions give regular space to other Christian bodies.[26]

g. Cooperation in the Health Field

New concepts of health care are increasingly supplanting earlier attitudes regarding medical work and the place of hospitals. Donor and welfare agencies prefer to supply money for those health programmes which manifest a comprehensive approach. Some governments, as they strive to develop national health services, now tend to refuse to deal with a multiplicity of religious groups. So joint secretariats for the coordination of all church-related medical and health programmes have come into being, set up with the joint approval of the Catholic episcopal conferences and the national councils of churches.[27] In several places, Catholics participate in the work of the national coordinating agencies recognized by and reporting to the national councils.[28]

In this area of health and medicine there is room for continuing study and discussion between Catholics and other Christians to deepen understanding of the theological significance of Christian involvement in this work and to elucidate common understanding as well as facing up to doctrinal divergences. Particularly where ethical norms are concerned the doctrinal stand of the Catholic Church has to be made clear and the difficulties which this can raise for ecumenical collaboration faced honestly and with loyalty to Catholic teaching.

h. National and International Emergencies

The response to emergency situations has given rise to ecumenical action in raising funds and in administering and distributing them. Although this latter is done in the main by international agencies, normally an attempt is made to work through local organizations, often a council of churches or the agency of a diocese or episcopal conference. Efficiency in the programme as well as the witness value of joint charitable concern often dictates that the work be done ecumenically.

i. Relief of Human Need

As the pressures of contemporary life, especially in great cities, become more intense, Christians are aware of their urgent responsibility to minister to the increasing number of people who become casualties of society. In many places therefore Catholics are joining with other churches and ecclesial communities to provide services for people with pressing personal problems whether of the material, moral or psychological order. There are examples of such common organizations of confessions to provide a more effective pastoral and social ministry to distressed individuals.[29]

j. Social Problems

As the Catholic Church engages its full energies in the serious effort for integral human development it works with all men of good will and especially with other Christian churches and ecclesial communities. Hence in particular situations it has been found appropriate to set up joint organizations to study and promote understanding of true human rights, to question those things which frustrate them and to promote initiatives which will secure them.[30] There are also organizations which enable Christians of various confessions to work with people of other faiths for common goals of social justice.[31]

k. Sodepax Groups

Sodepax, the international agency between the Catholic Church and the World Council of Churches for society, development and peace, is promoting several initiatives on a local scale under the direction of local ecumenical agencies.

Since collaboration in the field of development is a major feature of local ecumenical relations, the impetus given by Sodepax on the international levels has led to local groups being set up to promote education in the issues of justice and peace. Some of these also operate under the name of Sodepax while being autonomous and adapted to their own situation.

This has led in some places to the establishment of joint

secretariats for education in development, under the aegis of the Catholic Church and a national council of churches.[32]

There are also agencies for development, sponsored by all the Christian confessions of the place, which aim at promoting action for a more just and human society. In some places, this has made clear the desirability of a national or regional council of churches, with Catholic participation, in order that the Christian communities might play a significant role in the development of the region.[33]

Also notable are the considerable numbers of occasional actions in the area of local development which have not given rise to new continuing organizations but have been carried out through existing or ad hoc groups.

l. Bilateral Dialogues

Bilateral dialogues involving the Catholic Church have developed, regionally, nationally and locally since Vatican II. The structures of the Catholic Church and its theological patterns of encounter have made this kind of relationship fairly easy.[34]

A distinct progress can be noticed in the topics treated by many of the bilateral dialogues. As mutual trust and understanding grows, it becomes possible to discuss doctrinal points hitherto regarded as completely closed. In turn this has an influence on the ecumenical climate of the place. However, problems do arise when the gap in understanding of the ordinary church members and the discussions of the theologians is allowed to grow too great. It is the pastoral task of the church leaders at different levels (episcopal conferences and dioceses) with the aid of the existing organs of consultation (e.g., the national or diocesan ecumenical commission) to ensure that communication takes place in order to overcome the difficulty and to enable the work done by the theologians to be effective and this in a way that accords with the doctrine and discipline of the Church.

Most of the dialogues try to assess the common situation in which all confessions find themselves today, and to clarify existing difficulties in inter-confessional relations as well as outlining new possibilities on the way to unity. Some stick to selected topics, such as ministry, authority, etc., on which they aim at a deeper mutual understanding and possible convergence. Sometimes a specific problem, e.g., mixed marriages, religious education, proselytism, is taken up and a solution sought whether at the level of theological principle or pastoral practice. At times the task is to coordinate relations and to encourage practical cooperation and exchange on different levels.

m. Meetings of Heads of Communions

In certain places the heads of local churches or ecclesial communities meet regularly, sometimes having a permanent "continuation committee". Through their meetings they exchange information about their activities and concerns, share insights and explore areas of possible collaboration and even set on foot appropriate action. It is understood that the heads of communions have to agree on each occasion of collaboration about the extent to which they can commit the members of their particular body. The usefulness of such groups in certain circumstances has been proved beyond dispute.[35]

n. Joint Working Groups

The concept of a joint working group is that it is not itself a decision-making body, but an organ for joint exploration of possible fields of cooperation, study and action, its recommendations being submitted to the parent bodies on each side. Groups have been set up in several countries between the Catholic Church and either a council of churches or a number of churches and ecclesial communities which do not have membership in a council. In intention these groups have been often envisaged as a transitory expression of the relationship. However, their usefulness and the lack of a suitable substitute have led in most cases to their continuance in being. Since they involve a multilateral conversation they can be a handy instrument for coordinating the more local conversations and initiatives and giving them a coherent framework. They have often initiated multilateral theological studies, as well as practical cooperation in the field of social action. Indeed in some instances more theological work seems to have been achieved through these groups than when the Catholic Church has been a member of a council of churches. The implications of baptism, problems connected with mixed marriages, conscience and dissent, authority, development issues and the problem of disarmament are among the topics found on their agendas.

o. Councils of Churches and Christian Councils[36]

These organizations date in some form from the beginning of the 20th century as a means of ensuring cooperation. As they have developed they have come to promote the collaboration of various churches or groups in social projects and now see themselves as servants of the ecumenical movement in its search for a greater measure of unity.

Because of their importance we are going to consider them at greater length in the next chapter.

4.
COUNCILS OF CHURCHES AND CHRISTIAN COUNCILS

A. DESCRIPTION AND CLARIFICATIONS

a. What Councils Are

In various regions of the world, in different countries and even in areas of a particular country, the ecumenical relation between the Christian communities differs and so the structures in which it finds expression also vary. In a number of places this relationship has taken the form of Christian councils and councils of churches. While these councils have their significance from the churches which take part in them, still they are very important instruments of ecumenical collaboration.

The earliest councils in the ecumenical movement were missionary councils composed of mission agencies and were formed to stimulate thinking on missionary problems and to coordinate action for the spread of the Christian message. As service agencies and other church groups took part in them, they were described as Christian councils, and finally as councils of churches when their membership came to be composed of representatives named by the churches.

Among the principal activities of councils are joint service, the collaborative quest for a fuller unity and, to the extent possible, common witness.

Councils are multiple and diverse. Therefore theologically they must be evaluated according to their activity, and according to the self-understanding they advance in their constitutions. That is to say, councils must be considered concretely as they actually exist rather than approached through theories developed concerning them.

b. Types of Councils

We may distinguish the following principal types:

Local councils of churches, which involve the different denominations in a small area, e.g., a parish or a deanery. Such councils are not necessarily affiliated to or directed by their national council. Local councils are found in large numbers in the U.S.A. and in Great Britain.

State or area councils are "at various levels below the national and above the strictly local", and their relationship to the larger and smaller councils varies; in England some of the councils of churches in the major conurbations are of this kind; and in some of these a full time secretary acts virtually as "ecumenical officer" of the particular area.

National councils of churches are composed primarily of representatives named by the churches in a country rather than of representatives from councils at a lower level.

Regional councils or conferences of churches include churches from a number of neighbouring countries.

The World Council of Churches is a distinct category. The World Council of Churches does invite selected national councils "to enter into working relationship as associated councils", and it has set up a Committee on National Council Relationships. This does not imply any authority or control over a particular council; in fact, the decision to enter such a relationship rests always with the national council.[37] It has to be borne in mind too that Catholic membership in a local, national or regional council has implications on those levels and is therefore an independent decision, separate and distinct from any decision about relationship to the World Council of Churches.

c. The Meaning of Conciliarity

The English word "conciliarity" can convey different meanings. For this reason Catholics need to explain what they mean by it.[38]

The conciliarity which marks the life of the Catholic Church and is sometimes expressed in ecumenical and provincial councils ("conciles"),[39] is based on a full and substantial communion of local churches among themselves and with the Church of Rome which presides over the whole assembly of charity.[40] This communion finds expression in the confession of faith, the celebration of the sacraments, the exercise of the ministry and the reception of previous councils. In this sense a council is a means enabling a local church, a certain group of local churches, or all of the local churches in communion with the bishop of Rome to express the communion of the Catholic Church.

Councils of churches and Christian councils ("conseils") however are fellowships of churches and other Christian bodies which seek to work together, to engage in dialogue and to overcome the divisions and misunderstandings existing among them. Confessing Jesus Christ as Lord and Saviour according to the Scriptures, they engage in joint action, in a quest for unity, and, to the extent that it is possible, in common witness. The fellowship which they embody does not suppose at all the same degree of communion expressed by ecumenical and provincial councils ("conciles").[41]

From this understanding it is clear that councils of churches and Christian councils ("conseils") do not in and of themselves contain in embryo the beginnings of a new Church which will replace the communion now existing within the Catholic Church. They do not claim to be churches nor do they claim authority to commission a ministry of word and sacrament.

d. Points of Clarification

i. A distinction has to be made between Christian councils and councils of churches, the former including as voting members bodies and agencies other than churches.

ii. Neither Christian councils nor councils of churches are uniform in history, constitution or operation.

iii. The variety of patterns to be found in councils of churches around the world has grown up naturally; councils are autonomous bodies and no one council of churches is a sub-unit of another, nor has an attempt been made to impose uniformity. At the same time it should be noted that there are close relationships between some councils even though they are structured in different ways.

In general terms these councils at all levels of the churches' life are similar in nature, but their specific functions vary according to the possibilities and needs of each level.

iv. Although the ecumenical movement calls for fellowship and collaboration at all levels, still, given the variety and autonomy of councils of churches, the decision to join a council at one level must be taken on its own merits.

Membership in local councils does not imply that membership in national councils must then be sought, just as local or national membership does not involve membership in the World Council of Churches. The question of membership must be examined separately and afresh at each level.

v. The sole formal authority of councils is that which is accorded them by the constituent members. The degree of commitment to this fellowship of churches, which a council represents, depends entirely upon the churches themselves.

vi. Councils try to make clear that as a general rule they do not have responsibility for church union negotiations, since it is well understood that these are solely the responsibility of the churches directly involved.

vii. Councils do not claim to be the only appropriate organs of churchly cooperation.

B. THE ECUMENICAL SIGNIFICANCE OF CHRISTIAN COUNCILS AND COUNCILS OF CHURCHES

a. The Ecumenical Fact of Councils

The existence of councils of churches constitutes in numerous countries an ecumenical fact which the non-member churches cannot ignore and may well challenge the churches in countries where such councils do not exist.

In some places the trend towards collaboration is hastened when governments refuse to deal with a diversity of agencies in the fields of education, development and welfare and the churches engaged in these areas have to devise joint programmes.

b. The Limits of Ad Hoc Bodies for Council-Church Relationships

In the eyes of many councils of churches collaboration with the Catholic Church solely through ad hoc commissions is regarded as insufficient since this kind of collaboration:

i. gives the impression that the ecumenical fact represented by councils is not treated with sufficient seriousness, and

ii. it tends to remain partial and to lack the necessary continuity.

c. The Existing Relation of the Catholic Church to Councils of Churches

The Catholic Church has full membership in national councils of churches in at least 19 countries and in a very large number of state and local councils. There is membership in one regional conference of churches covering a number of countries.[42] In addition, there is considerable Catholic collaboration with councils and certain of their programmes at various levels.

Given that "no central guidelines would be found valid for the variety of councils and of particular circumstances",[43] a number of questions and ecclesial considerations may be proposed, to be taken into account in deciding the appropriate relationship with councils.

5.
CONSIDERATIONS CONCERNING
COUNCIL MEMBERSHIP[44]

a. Cooperation with Other Churches and Ecclesial Communities

The documents of the Second Vatican Council expound clearly
the conviction that the unity which is the gift of Christ already
exists in the Catholic Church,[45] although susceptible of completion and perfection,[46] and this qualifies significantly the
Catholic participation in the ecumenical movement. However,
since the Second Vatican Council's recognition of the *ecclesial*
character of other Christian communities,[47] the Church has frequently called upon Catholics to cooperate not only with other
Christians *as individuals*, but also with other churches and ecclesial communities *as such*. This cooperation is commended
both in matters of social and human concern, and even more in
support of Christian testimony in the field of mission.

> Insofar as religious conditions allow, ecumenical activity
> should be furthered in such a way that without any ap-
> pearance of indifference or of unwarranted intermingling on
> the one hand, or of unhealthy rivalry on the other, Catholics
> can cooperate in a brotherly spirit with their separated
> brethren, according to the norms of the Decree on
> Ecumenism. To the extent that their beliefs are common, they
> can make before the nations a common profession of faith in
> God and Jesus Christ. They can collaborate in social and in
> technical projects as well as in cultural and religious ones.
> This cooperation should be undertaken not only among
> private persons, but also, according to the judgement of the
> local Ordinary, among churches or ecclesial communities and
> their enterprises (*Ad Gentes*, 15).[48]

The documents published by the Secretariat for Promoting
Christian Unity have stressed that the world often poses the
same questions to all the confessions and that, in the sphere of
their internal life, most Christian communions have to face
similar problems.[49]

The nature of the Church, the normal exigencies of the
ecumenical situation, and the questions facing all Christian
communions in our own day demand that the Catholic Church
give positive consideration to the proper expression at every
level of her ecumenical relations with other churches and ec-

clesial communities.

b. Implications of Council Membership

From a theological point of view, membership in a council of churches carries certain implications:

i. the recognition of other member churches as ecclesial communities even though they may not be recognized as being churches in the full theological sense of the word;[50]

ii. recognition of the council of churches as an instrument, among others, both for expressing the unity already existing among the churches and also of advancing towards a greater unity and a more effective Christian witness.

Nevertheless, as the Central Committee of the World Council of Churches said at its Toronto meeting in 1950: ". . .membership does not imply that each church must regard the other member churches as churches in the true and full sense of the word".[51] Therefore the entry of the Catholic Church into a body in which it would find itself on an equal footing with other bodies which also claim to be churches would not diminish its faith about its uniqueness. The Second Vatican Council has clearly stated that the unique Church of Christ "constituted and organized in the world as a society subsists in the Catholic Church which is governed by the successor of Peter and the bishops in communion with that successor, although many elements of sanctification and of truth can be found outside of her visible structure".[52]

c. Councils and Christian Unity

Since councils of churches are not themselves churches, they do not assume the responsibility of acting for churches which are contemplating or have begun to engage in unity conversations. In principle their action is in the practical field. However, because of their facilities and their administrative resources, they are in a position to give important material help and can, upon request of the churches concerned, give a consultative and organisational assistance. While the study of "Faith and Order" questions, which goes on under the auspices of many councils and is authorised by member churches, has a deep importance in stimulating member churches to a deeper understanding of the demands of the unity willed by Christ, and to facing old deadlocks in a new way, nevertheless it is not the task of a council to take the initiative in promoting formal doctrinal conversa-

tions between churches. These belong properly to the immediate
and bilateral contacts between churches.

d. The Problem of Council Statements

Councils of churches, in some cases more frequently than the
member churches themselves, on occasion make public
statements on issues of common concern. These are addressed
more often to areas of social justice, human development,
general welfare, and public or private morality. They are based
on theological positions that may or may not be articulated in
the statements themselves. Unless explicitly authorized, they
cannot be considered as official utterances on behalf of the
churches, but are offered as a service to the churches. They are
often directed also to the wider public or even to specific au-
diences, such as government authorities. They vary in character
from broad statements of position or orientation in general
areas to specific stands on concrete questions. In some instances
they examine and illuminate a subject, identifying a number of
possible approaches rather than adopting a position. This practice of making statements has caused concern in some churches,
and calls especially for clarification where the Catholic Church
considers the possibility of membership in councils of churches.

i. The Decision-Making Process

In attempting to fix criteria to evaluate the deliberative process in a particular council, it will be necessary to give serious
consideration to the hesitations and objections of its members.
A common declaration which engages the moral responsibility
of its members is possible only with the consent of all.

ii. The Authority and Use of Public Statements

Important as is the process by which statements are formulated and issued, equally important is the manner in which they
are received—both by the individual members of the churches
and by the public at large. Differences in the weight of authority
given to official statements within member churches, as well as
differences in the normal mode of formulation and issuance of
statements, can result in serious difficulties. Efforts have to be
made to obviate the confusion that may arise in practice. Such
statements should clearly identify the theological principles on
which they are based so as to facilitate their acceptance by
church members as being in accord with their own Christian
commitment. Since councils cannot usurp the position of the

churches that comprise their membership, they need to study how best they can determine what matters fall within their own purpose and mandate and to be sure of the approval of member churches before publishing statements.

iii. Regard for Minority Viewpoints

Councils, being composed of separated churches, inevitably face issues on which they cannot reach a perfect consensus. A profound respect for the integrity and individuality of its member churches will lead a council to develop procedures for ensuring that a minority dissent will be adequately expressed for the mutual benefit of the council, its members, and all to whom the council speaks. Provisions have to be made within councils for such expression of minority viewpoints and in this context polarization ought to be avoided.

e. Joint Social Action—Opportunities and Problems

i. In the Apostolic Letter *Octogesima Adveniens*, the Holy Father has written:

> It is up to these Christian communities, with the help of the Holy Spirit, in communion with the bishops who hold responsibility, and in dialogue with other Christian brethren and all men of good will to discern the options and commitments which are called for in order to bring about the social, political and economic changes seen in many cases to be urgently needed (N. 4).

ii. At a number of points Christian positions permit and encourage collaboration with other spiritual and ideological families. Therefore councils and ecumenical organizations rightly pay serious attention to possible areas of collaboration (e.g., in the field of development, housing, health, and various forms of relief), which concern people of other living faiths as well as Christian churches and ecclesial communities.

iii. Christian social action to which many councils of churches and ecumenical bodies devote a large part of their endeavours also raises questions for theological reflection. In the first place there is the essential role of social action in the proclamation of the Gospel. "Action on behalf of justice and participation in the transformation of the world fully appear to us as a constitutive dimension of the preaching of the Gospel, or, in other words, of the Church's mission for the redemption of the human race and its liberation from every oppressive situation".[53] Further there are questions of morality, especially regarding family life, which more and more need to be faced seriously in all their complexity, in particular those which concern population, family life, marriage, contraception, abortion, euthanasia and others. These questions need to be studied with due regard to the moral teachings of the churches concerned and above all taking into account the objective content of Catholic ethics.[54]

6.
PASTORAL AND PRACTICAL REFLECTIONS
FOR LOCAL ECUMENICAL ACTION

a. Full account ought to be given to local needs and problems in organizing ecumenical action; models from other places cannot simply be imitated.

b. Ultimately, it is always the responsibility of the regional or national episcopal conference to decide on the acceptability and the appropriateness of all forms of local ecumenical action. They should do this in cooperation with the appropriate organ of the Holy See, viz. the Secretariat for Promoting Christian Unity.

c. What really matters is not the creation of new structures but the collaboration of Christians in prayer, reflection and action, based on common baptism and on a faith which on many essential points is also common.

d. Sometimes the best form of collaboration may be for one church and ecclesial community to participate fully in the programmes already set up by another. At other times parallel coordinated action and the joint use of the results may be more appropriate. In any event, as collaboration becomes closer, a simplification of structures should be sought and unnecessary multiplication of structures avoided.

e. Where joint actions or programmes are decided on, they ought to be undertaken fully by both sides and duly authorized by the respective authorities right from the earliest stages of planning.

f. It is necessary that where there are regional, national and local doctrinal bilateral dialogues, episcopal conferences ensure that at the right time there is contact with the Holy See.

g. Among the many forms of ecumenical cooperation councils of churches and Christian councils are not the only form but they are certainly one of the more important. Since regional, national and local councils are widespread in many parts of the world and do play an important role in ecumenical relations, the responsible contacts which the Catholic Church is having with them are welcome.

h. It is normal that councils should want to discuss and reflect upon the doctrinal bases of the practical projects they undertake. But in such cases it is important to clarify the doctrinal principles involved. It should always be clear that when Catholics take part in a council, they can enter into such discussions only in conformity with the teaching of their Church.

i. The first and immediate responsibility for a decision to join a council rests with the highest ecclesiastical authority in the area served by the council. In practical terms this responsibility is not transferable. With regard to national councils the authority would generally be the episcopal conference (where there is only one diocese for the nation, it would be the Ordinary of the diocese). In reaching a decision, there must necessarily be communication with the Secretariat for Promoting Christian Unity.

j. The degree of involvement of different confessions in the same council depends directly on their respective structures especially in those things concerning the nature and exercise of authority. However, it would seem desirable that councils be constituted in such a way that the various members can all accept the full measure of involvement possible for them.

k. Membership in a council is a serious responsibility of the Catholic bishops or their delegates. It is necessary that the Catholic representatives in councils should be personally qualified and, while representing the Church on matters within their competence, they should be clearly aware of the limits beyond which they cannot commit the Church without prior reference to higher authority.

l. It is not enough that the Church simply have delegates in a council or other ecumenical structure; unless they are taken seriously by the Catholic authorities, the Catholic participation will remain purely superficial. For the same reason all participation in ecumenical structures should be accompanied by constant ecumenical education of Catholics concerning the implications of such participation.

7.
OTHER FORMS OF ECUMENISM

A growing number of Christians in certain parts of the world seem to prefer to engage in local action which is ecumenical by means of informal groups of a spontaneous kind. These people are often motivated by renewed appreciation of the word of Christ: ". . .may they be one in us, . . .so that the world may believe it was you who sent me" (*Jn.* 17, 21).

It is the kind of activity which springs up in a common environment or in a common social condition. Or it may arise in response to a common task or need. The result is a large number of highly diverse groups: action groups, prayer groups, community-building groups, reflection and dialogue groups, and evangelizing groups.

A number of groups are made up of Christians who are rediscovering central Christian truths out of their confrontation with a surrounding world which appears de-christianized and de-personalized.

Through their varied experiences they may have new insights of importance for the future growth and direction of the ecumenical movement.[55] It is desirable that there be real communication between the more organized or formal expressions and structures of the ecumenical movement and these groups when they seek to discover new ways of meeting contemporary needs and therefore engage in experimental projects. In connection with the hierarchy of the Church, these informal groups can offer original and inspiring ideas, whereas without such a contact and apart from ecclesiastical direction they run the risk of becoming unfaithful to Catholic principles of ecumenism and even of endangering the faith. If this communication is ignored, there is not only a danger that ecumenism may become detached from the pressing concerns of people in society but these groups themselves may become unbalanced and sectarian. Communication and dialogue are basic to the success of all ecumenical endeavour.

At the same time where there are groups of this kind under Catholic responsibility, it is necessary that they function in full communion with the local bishop if they are to be authentically ecumenical.

---

* Text supplied by the Secretariat for the Promotion of the Unity of Christians. French original in *E.V.* 5, nn 1096–1198.
a. *Information Service* 20 (1973), p. 16.
b. *Unitatis Redintegratio* 4.

1. Cf. Pope Paul VI, *Allocutio* ad delegatos commissionum "pro oecumenismo" Conferentiarum Episcopalium et Catholicorum Orien-

talium Patriarchatuum Synodorum partem agentes: *AAS* 64 (1972), p. 761; cf. also *Information Service* 20 (1973), p. 23 (published by the Secretariat for Promoting Christian Unity).

2. Pope Paul VI, *Allocutio* ad Sanctitatem Suam Athenagoram, Patriarcham Oecumenicum, in Vaticana Basilica habita: *AAS* 59 (1967), p. 1051; cf. also *Information Service* 3 (1967), p. 17.

3. Cf. Ecumenical Directory I, *Ad totam Ecclesiam*, Pars Prima, § 2: *AAS* 59 (1967), p. 575; cf. also *Information Service* 2 (1967), p. 5.

4. Here we would make our own the clarification given in the Third Official Report of the Joint Working Group between the World Council of Churches and the Roman Catholic Church, Appendix II, *Common Witness and Proselytism*, in *Information Service* 14 (1971), p. 19: "Modern languages use several biblically derived terms which denote particular aspects of the announcements of the Gospel in word and deed: Witness, Apostolate, Mission, Confession, Evangelism, Kerygma, Message, etc. We have preferred here to adopt 'Witness' because it expresses more comprehensively the realities we are treating".

Worthy of note is section 10 of the *Declaration of the Synodal Fathers* (October 26th, 1974): "In carrying out these things we intend to collaborate more diligently with those of our Christian brothers with whom we are not yet in the union of a perfect communion, basing ourselves on the foundation of Baptism and on the patrimony which we hold in common. Thus we can henceforth render to the world a much broader common witness to Christ, while at the same time working to obtain full union in the Lord. Christ's command impels us to do so; the work of preaching and rendering witness to the Gospel demands it" (*L'Osservatore Romano*, English edition, Nov. 7, 1974, p. 3).

5. Cf. *Common Witness and Proselytism*, A Study Document, in *Information Service* 14 (1971), pp. 18–23.

6. Cf. *Unitatis Redintegratio*, 6.

7. Cf. Section 7 of this document: "Other forms of ecumenism".

8. In N.11 of *Christus Dominus* (cited p. 6), the "particular church" is defined very clearly and is identified with the diocese. The expression "local church" in this document is understood in a broader sense. In the first place it is what is called in the above mentioned text: "the particular church". It is the church also in territories where bishops have formed episcopal conferences or synods (cf. p. 7). Further it exists in all those legitimate gatherings of the faithful under the direction of their pastors in communion with their bishop which we call "the parish" (cf. *Sacrosanctum Concilium*, 42). The expression "local church" is more all-embracing and more easily grasped than "particular church".

9. Cf. J. Ratzinger "*Ecumenism at the local level*", in *Information Service* 20 (1973), p. 4, § 1.

10. Cf. Pope Paul VI: *Allocutio* referred to in *Note 1*.

11. In 1973, the Joint Working Group between the Catholic Church and the World Council of Churches commissioned a survey on the problems facing the various churches and ecclesial communities as they carry out their mission and an examination of the consequences for the ecumenical situation. Over twenty countries participated in the survey. The results have been published in the review *One in Christ* XI (1975), N. 1, pp. 30–88, and it is hoped will be published in French and German reviews during the year. In addition to an extensive reflection on the outcome of the survey, the publication includes appendices describing the situation in several countries.

12. *Unitatis Redintegratio*, 8.

13. *Ecumenical Directory*, 33.

14. *Instructio* de peculiaribus casibus admittendi alios christianos ad communionem eucharisticam in Ecclesia Catholica: *AAS* 64 (1972), pp. 518-525; cf. also *Information Service* 18 (1972), pp. 3-6. *Communicatio* quoad interpretationem Instructionis de peculiaribus casibus admittendi alios Christianos ad communionem eucharisticam in Ecclesia Catholica: *AAS* 65 (1973), pp. 616-619; cf. *Information Service* 23 (1974), pp. 25-26.

15. Cf. *Information Service* 5 (1968), pp. 22-25.

16. This is the case in Nigeria and Zaire.

17. For example U.S.A. and the Philippines.

18. Silberburgstrasse 121 A, D-7000 Stuttgart 1, West Germany.

19. Examples are to be found in England.

20. Local Guidelines are offered for Catholic participation in these in the booklet *The Sharing of Resources*, published by the Catholic Ecumenical Commission of England and Wales.

21. The experience of shared premises is not yet wide but in a number of places, as in some new towns in England and in "covenanted" parishes in U.S.A. it has led to a situation where certain joint social and pastoral activities are undertaken in common, while the identities of the Catholic Church and the other confessions involved are maintained and their disciplines of worship respected.

22. Cf. Ecumenical Directory II, *Spiritus Domini: AAS* 62 (1970), pp. 705-724; cf. also *Information Service* 10 (1970), pp. 3-10.

23. Cf. *Common Witness and Proselytism*, 22, 25.

24. Mainly in the U.S.A.

25. *Multimedia Zambia* is an example.

26. One such is *Moto*, the Catholic paper of the diocese of Gwelo in Rhodesia. Other examples could be given.

27. Such secretariats exist in India, Tanzania, Malawi and Ghana.

28. For example, Philippines, Uganda and Kenya.

29. One such is the Interconfessional Counselling Service of Porto Alegre, Brazil.

30. There are for instance the Latin American Ecumenical Commission for Human Rights and the Ecumenical Commission for Service in Brazil; cf. also *Message of His Eminence Cardinal Roy* on the Occasion of the Launching of the Second Development Decade, 9 November 1970, Pontifical Commission Justice and Peace, §§ 15 and 16.

31. In Indonesia there is the Committee on Community Organization.

32. Such secretariats exist in Australia and New Zealand.

33. There is the Christian Agency for Development in the Caribbean.

34. Cf. a more complete account in: Ehrenström and Gassman, *Confessions in Dialogue*, Geneva, 1975; cf. also the theological review and critique, commissioned by the Catholic Theological Society of America, *The Bilateral Consultations between the Roman Catholic Church in the U.S.A. and other Christian Communions*, July, 1972.

35. For instance in Rhodesia, Australia, New Zealand.

36. In the following pages where councils or conferences of churches are dealt with, generally the term "church" is to be understood in a sociological sense and not in a technical theological sense.

37. Cf. the *New Delhi Report* (London 1962), Appendix II, XI, p. 438.

38. The understanding not only of Catholics but of Orthodox, Anglicans and many Protestants finds expression in the description of "conciliarity" given in a paper of the Salamanca Conference (1973) of

the WCC Faith and Order Commission.

39. In some languages other than English two distinct words are used to denote the realities for which in English the single word "council" is used. In French for example there are the words "concile" and "conseil"; in Italian "concilio" and "consiglio"; in Spanish "concilio" and "consejo"; in German "Konzil" and "Rat" and in Latin "concilium" and "consilium".

40. Cf. *Lumen Gentium,* 13; *Ad Gentes,* 22; S. Ignatius M., *Ad Rom.,* Praef.

41. In the meeting of the Faith and Order Commission of the WCC held in Accra, 1974, the following comment was made: "The local, national and world councils of churches which perform such a vital role in the modern ecumenical movement do not, obviously, conform to the definition of conciliar fellowship given at Salamanca. They are federal in character and do not enjoy either the full communion or the capacity to make decisions for all their members. They might properly be described as *'pre-conciliar'* bodies".

42. The Caribbean Conference of Churches. At the present time the Catholic Church has full membership in the following 19 national councils of churches: Denmark, Sweden, The Netherlands, Swaziland, Belize (British Honduras), Samoa, Fiji, New Hebrides, Solomon Islands, Papua-New Guinea, Tonga, West Germany, Botswana, St. Vincent (British Antilles), Sudan, Uganda, Finland, Guyana, Trinidad and Tobago.

43. *Minutes: Joint Working Group between the Roman Catholic Church and the World Council of Churches* (meeting held in June, 1971, Bernhäuser Forst, Stuttgart, Germany), December 1971, p. 10 (unpublished).

44. In certain cases where Catholic membership in a national council of churches is under consideration, studies have been undertaken and later published. They are of interest as applying general principles to given situations. Examples are: *The Implications of Roman Catholic Membership of the British Council of Churches* (1972), The British Council of Churches, 10 Eaton Gate, London; *Report on Possible Roman Catholic Membership in the National Council of Churches* (1972), US Catholic Conference, 1312, Massachusetts Avenue, N. W., Washington DC 20005, USA; *Groupe mixte de travail—Comité pour de nouvelles structures œcuméniques,* Office national d'œcuménisme, 1452, rue Drummond, Montréal 107, Canada.

45. Cf. *Unitatis Redintegratio,* 1; *Lumen Gentium,* 8, 13.

46. Cf. *Unitatis Redintegratio,* 6.

47. Cf. *Lumen Gentium,* 15; *Unitatis Redintegratio,* 3 sqq.; etc.

48. Cf. also *Unitatis Redintegratio,* 4, 12; *Apostolicam Actuositatem,* 27.

49. Cf. *Ecumenical Directory,* Part II, § 1; *Reflections and Suggestions Concerning Ecumenical Dialogue,* II, 2 c and d (A working instrument at the disposal of ecclesiastical authorities for concrete application of the Decree on Ecumenism, published in *Information Service* 12 (1970), pp. 5–11).

50. Cf. *Lumen Gentium,* 15; *Unitatis Redintegratio,* 3; also *Minutes and Report of the Third Meeting of the Central Committee* (Toronto, Canada, July 9–15, 1950). The *Toronto Statement,* while it refers directly to the World Council of Churches, appears to be fully applicable to similar organizations such as a national council of churches.

51. *Ibid.* (Toronto Statement).

52. *Lumen Gentium*, 8.

53. Synod of Bishops, *Justice in the World*, Typis Polyglottis Vaticanis (1971), p. 6; *Documenta Synodi Episcoporum*, De Iustitia in Mundo: *AAS* 63 (1971), p. 924.

54. "And if in moral matters there are many Christians who do not always understand the gospel in the same way as Catholics, and do not admit the same solutions for the more difficult problems of modern society, nevertheless they share our desire to cling to Christ's word as the source of Christian virtue and to obey the apostolic command: 'Whatever you do in word or in work, do all in the name of the Lord Jesus, giving thanks to God the Father through him' (*Col.* 3:17). Hence, the ecumenical dialogue could start with discussions concerning the application of the gospel to moral questions" (*Unitatis Redintegratio*, 23, § 3).

55. Cf. *Ecumenical Directory*, Part I, § 3.

83

COMMON DECLARATION OF POPE PAUL VI
AND ARCHBISHOP DONALD COGGAN*

After Four Hundred Years, 29 April, 1977

1. After four hundred years of estrangement, it is now the third time in seventeen years that an Archbishop of Canterbury and the Pope embrace in Christian friendship in the city of Rome. Since the visit of Archbishop Ramsey eleven years have passed, and much has happened in that time to fulfil the hopes then expressed and to cause us to thank God.

2. As the Roman Catholic Church and the constituent Churches of the Anglican Communion have sought to grow in mutual understanding and Christian love, they have come to recognise, to value and to give thanks for a common faith in God our Father, in our Lord Jesus Christ, and in the Holy Spirit; our common baptism into Christ; our sharing of the Holy Scriptures, of the Apostles' and Nicene Creeds, the Chalcedonian definition, and the teaching of the Fathers; our common Christian inheritance for many centuries with its living traditions of liturgy, theology, spirituality and mission.

3. At the same time, in fulfilment of the pledge of eleven years ago to "a serious dialogue which, founded on the Gospels and on the ancient common traditions, may lead to that unity in truth, for which Christ prayed",[1] Anglican and Roman Catholic theologians have faced calmly and objectively the historical and doctrinal differences which have divided us. Without compromising their respective allegiances, they have addressed these problems together, and in the process they have discovered theological convergences often as unexpected as they were happy.

4. The Anglican/Roman Catholic International Commission has produced three documents: on the Eucharist, on Ministry and Ordination and on Church and Authority. We now recommend that the work it has begun be pursued, through procedures appropriate to our respective Communions, so that both of them may be led along the path towards unity.

The moment will shortly come when the respective Authorities must evaluate the conclusions.

5. The response of both Communions to the work and fruits of theological dialogue will be measured by the practical response of the faithful to the task of restoring unity, which, as the Second Vatican Council says, "involves the whole Church, faithful and clergy alike" and "extends to everyone according to the talents of each".[2] We rejoice that this practical response has manifested itself in so many forms of pastoral cooperation in many parts of the world; in meetings of bishops, clergy and faithful.

6. In mixed marriages between Anglicans and Roman Catholics, where the tragedy of our separation at the sacrament of union is seen most starkly, cooperation in pastoral care[3] in many places has borne fruit in increased understanding. Serious dialogue has cleared away many misconceptions and shown that we still share much that is deep-rooted in the Christian tradition and ideal of marriage, though important differences persist, particularly regarding remarriage after divorce. We are following attentively the work thus far accomplished in this dialogue by the Joint Commission on the Theology of Marriage and its Application to Mixed Marriages. It has stressed the need for fidelity and witness to the ideal of marriage, set forth in the New Testament and constantly taught in Christian tradition. We have a common duty to defend this tradition and ideal and the moral values which derive from it.

7. All such cooperation, which must continue to grow and spread, is the true setting for continued dialogue and for the general extension and appreciation of its fruits, and so for progress towards that goal which is Christ's will—the restoration of complete communion in faith and sacramental life.

8. Our call to this is one with the sublime Christian vocation itself, which is a call to communion; as St. John says: "that which we have seen and heard we proclaim also to you, so that you may have fellowship with us; and our fellowship is with the Father and His Son Jesus Christ".[4] If we are to maintain progress in doctrinal convergence and move forward resolutely to the communion of mind and heart for which Christ prayed, we must ponder still further his intentions in founding the Church and face courageously their requirements.

9. It is this communion with God in Christ through faith and through baptism and self-giving to Him that stands at the centre of our witness to the world, even while between us communion remains imperfect. Our divisions hinder this witness, hinder the

work of Christ,[5] but they do not close all roads we may travel together. In a spirit of prayer and of submission to God's will we must collaborate more earnestly in a "greater common witness to Christ before the world in the very work of evangelisation".[6] It is our desire that the means of this collaboration be sought: the increasing spiritual hunger in all parts of God's world invites us to such a common pilgrimage.

This collaboration pursued to the limit allowed by truth and loyalty will create the climate in which dialogue and doctrinal convergence can bear fruit. While this fruit is ripening, serious obstacles remain, both of the past and of recent origin. Many in both Communions are asking themselves whether they have a common faith sufficient to be translated into communion of life, worship and mission. Only the communions themselves through their pastoral authorities can give that answer. When the moment comes to do so, may the answer shine through in spirit and truth, not obscured by the enmities, the prejudices and the suspicions of the past.

10. To this we are bound to look forward and to spare no effort to bring it closer: to be baptized into Christ is to be baptized into hope — "and hope does not disappoint us because God's love has been poured into our hearts through the Holy Spirit which has been given us".[7]

11. Christian hope manifests itself in prayer and action—in prudence but also in courage. We pledge ourselves and exhort the faithful of the Roman Catholic Church and of the Anglican Communion to live and work courageously in this hope of reconciliation and unity in our common Lord.

* Text in E.V. 6, 176–187.
1. Join Declaration by Pope Paul VI and Archbishop of Canterbury.
2. UR 5.
3. Matrimonia mixta 14.
4. 1 Jn 1:3.
5. Evangelii nuntiandi 77.
6. *Ibid*.
7. Rom 5:5.

84

RECEPTION OF U.S. EPISCOPALIANS INTO THE CATHOLIC CHURCH*

S.C.D.F., *In June, 1980*, April, 1981

In June, 1980, the Holy See, through the Congregation for the Doctrine of the Faith, agreed to the request presented by the Bishops of the United States of America on behalf of some clergy and laity formerly or actually belonging to the Episcopal (Anglican) Church for full communion with the Catholic Church. The Holy See's response to the initiative of these Episcopalians includes the possibility of a "pastoral provision" which will provide, for those who desire it, a common identity reflecting certain elements of their own heritage.

The entrance of these persons into the Catholic Church should be understood as the "reconciliation of those individuals who wish for full Catholic communion" of which the "Decree on Ecumenism" (n. 4) of the Second Vatican Council speaks.

In accepting former Episcopalian clergy who are married into the Catholic priesthood, the Holy See has specified that this exception to the rule of celibacy is granted in favour of these individual persons, and should not be understood as implying any change in the Church's conviction of the value of priestly celibacy, which will remain the rule for future candidates for the priesthood from this group.

In consultation with the National Conference of Catholic Bishops, the Congregation for the Doctrine of the Faith has appointed the Most Reverend Bernard F. Law, Bishop of Springfield-Cape Girardeau, as Ecclesiastical Delegate in this matter. It will be his responsibility to develop a proposal containing elements for the pastoral provision in question to be submitted for the approval of the Holy See, to oversee its implementation, and to deal with the Congregation for the Doctrine of the Faith in questions pertaining to the admission of former Episcopalian clergy into the Catholic priesthood.

---

* Text from the *Osservatore Romano*, English edition, 6 April 1981.

85

COMMON DECLARATION BY POPE JOHN PAUL II AND THE ARCHBISHOP OF CANTERBURY, ROBERT RUNCIE*

In the Cathedral Church, 29 May, 1982

In the Cathedral Church of Christ at Canterbury the Pope and the Archbishop of Canterbury have met on the eve of Pentecost to offer thanks to God for the progress that has been made in the work of reconciliation between our communions.

Together with leaders of other Christian Churches and communities we have listened to the word of God. Together we have recalled our one baptism and renewed the promises then made. Together we have acknowledged the witness given by those whose faith has led them to surrender the precious gift of life itself in the service of others, both in the past and in modern times.

The bond of our common baptism into Christ led our predecessors to inaugurate a serious dialogue between our Churches, a dialogue founded on the gospels and the ancient common traditions, a dialogue which has as its goal the unity for which Christ prayed to his Father 'so that the world may know that Thou hast sent Me and hast loved them even as Thou has loved Me' (John 17:23).

In 1966, our predecessors Pope Paul VI and Archbishop Michael Ramsey made a common declaration announcing their intention to inaugurate a serious dialogue between the Roman Catholic Church and the Anglican Communion which would 'include not only theological matters such as scripture, tradition and liturgy, but also matters of practical difficulty felt on either side' (Common Declaration, par. 6).

After this dialogue had already produced three statements on Eucharist, Ministry and Ordination, and authority in the Church, Pope Paul VI and Archbishop Donald Coggan, in their common declaration in 1977, took the occasion to encourage the completion of the dialogue on these three important questions so that the commission's conclusions might be evaluated by the respective authorities through procedures appropriate to each communion.

The Anglican-Roman Catholic International Commission has now completed the task assigned to it with the publication of its final report, and as our two communions proceed with the necessary evaluation, we join in thanking the members of the commission for their dedication, scholarship and integrity in a long and demanding task undertaken for love of Christ and for the unity of his Church.

The completion of this commission's work bids us look to the next stage of our common pilgrimage in faith and hope towards the unity for which we long. We are agreed that it is now time to set up a new international commission. Its task will be to continue the work already begun: to examine, especially in the light of our respective judgments on the final report, the outstanding doctrinal differences which still separate us, with a view towards their eventual resolution, to study all that hinders the mutual recognition of the ministries of our communions, and to recommend what practical steps will be necessary when, on the basis of our unity in faith, we are able to proceed to the restoration of full communion.

We are well aware that this new commission's task will not be easy, but we are encouraged, by our reliance on the grace of God and by all that we have seen of the power of that grace in the ecumenical movement of our time.

While this necessary work of theological clarification continues, it must be accompanied by the zealous work and fervent prayer of Roman Catholics and Anglicans throughout the world as they seek to grow in mutual understanding, fraternal love and common witness to the Gospel.

Once more, then, we call on the bishops, clergy and faithful people of both our communions in every country, diocese and parish in which our faithful live side by side. We urge them all to pray for this work and to adopt every possible means of furthering it through their collaboration in deepening their allegiance to Christ and in witnessing to him before the world. Only by such collaboration and prayer can the memory of the past enmities be healed and our past antagonisms overcome.

Our aim is not limited to the union of our two communions alone, to the exclusion of other Christians, but rather extends to the fulfilment of God's will for the visible unity of all his people. Both in our present dialogue, and in those engaged in by other Christians among themselves and with us, we recognize in the agreements we are able to reach, as well as in the difficulties which we encounter, a renewed challenge to abandon ourselves completely to the truth of the gospel.

Hence we are happy to make this declaration today in the welcome presence of so many fellow-Christians whose Churches and communities are already partners with us in prayer and work for the unity of all.

With them we wish to serve the cause of peace, of human freedom and human dignity, so that God may, indeed, be glorified in all his creatures. With them we greet in the name of God all men of good will, both those who believe in Him and those who are still searching for Him.

This holy place reminds us of the vision of Pope Gregory in sending St. Augustine as an apostle to England, full of zeal for the preaching of the Gospel and the shepherding of the flock.

On this eve of Pentecost, we turn again in prayer to Jesus, the Good Shepherd, who promised to ask the Father to give us another advocate to be with us forever, the Spirit of Truth (Cf. John 14:16), to lead us to the full unity to which He calls us. Confident in the power of this same Holy Spirit, we commit ourselves anew to the task of working for unity with firm faith, renewed hope and ever deeper love.

* English text, Vatican Press Office.

86

INTRODUCTION TO THE RITE OF INITIATION TO THE RELIGIOUS LIFE*

S.C.D.W., *Sacris religionis vinculis*, 2 February, 1970

NATURE AND WORTH OF RELIGIOUS PROFESSION

1. Many Christians respond to God's call by dedicating themselves to his service and to the welfare of mankind in the religious life. It is their intention to follow Christ more closely in the spirit of the evangelical counsels, so that the grace of baptism may bear more fruit in them.

2. The Church has always esteemed the religious life and under the guidance of the Holy Spirit a variety of types of religious life have emerged in the course of history. The Church has given canonical status to religious life and has approved a great number of religious institutes and it protects them by wise legislation.

For it is the Church which accepts the vows of those who make religious profession, which publicly prays for God's grace to them, blesses them and unites their offering with the eucharistic sacrifice.

RITES FOR THE DIFFERENT STAGES OF RELIGIOUS LIFE

3. The steps by which religious dedicate themselves and the Church are these: novitiate, first profession (or other sacred bonds) and perpetual profession. There is also renewal of vows, in keeping with the constitutions of the different institutes.

4. Religious life begins with the novitiate, a time for testing in which both the novice and community play their parts. The novice's entry into the novitiate should be accompanied by a special rite asking God's grace for the noviceship. The rite should be simple and direct, attendance limited to the religious community. It should not take place during Mass.

5. First profession then follows. The novice vows before God and the Church to follow the evangelical counsels for a limited period. Such vows may be taken during Mass, but without special

solemnity. The rite of first profession provides for the presentation of the habit and other emblems of religious life, following the very ancient custom of giving the habit at the end of the period of probation, for the habit is a sign of consecration.

Where a promise or some other kind of bond takes the place of profession, the rite may appropriately take place during liturgical action, such as a liturgy of the word, part of the liturgy of the hours, especially morning prayer or evening prayer, or, if circumstances suggest this, at Mass.

6. After the period prescribed by law, perpetual profession is made, and the religious bind themselves permanently to the service of God and the Church. Perpetual profession is a sign of the unbreakable union between Christ and his bride the Church.

It is very fitting that the rite of perpetual profession should take place during Mass, with due solemnity and in the presence of the religious community and the people. The rite consists of these parts:

  a) the calling of those to be professed (this may be omitted if desired);

  b) the homily, which reminds the people and those to be professed of the value of religious life;

  c) the examination by which the celebrant or superior asks those who are to be professed if they are willing to be consecrated to God and to follow the way of perfect charity, according to the rule of their religious family;

  d) the litanies, in which prayer is offered to God the Father and the intercession of Our Lady and of all the saints is invoked;

  e) the profession, made in the presence of the Church, the superior of the institute, witnesses and the congregation;

  f) the solemn blessing or consecration of the professed, by which the Church accepts their vows, consecrates them to God, and asks the Father for abundant gifts of the Holy Spirit for the professed;

  g) the presentation of the emblems of profession, if this is the custom of the institute, to symbolize perpetual dedication to God.

7. In some religious communities vows are renewed at certain times in accordance with the constitutions.

This renewal of vows may take place during Mass, but without solemnity, especially if it is done frequently or annually.

A liturgical rite is appropriate only when renewal of vows has the force of law. In many religious communities the devotional renewing of vows has become established. This may be done in many ways, but the practice of performing during Mass what is a matter of private devotion is not to be commended. If it seems appropriate to renew vows publicly on special anniversaries, for example the twenty-fifth or fiftieth year of religious life, the rite for the renewal of vows may be used with the necessary adaptations.

8. Since each of these rites has its own special character, each demands its own celebration. The celebration of several rites in one liturgical action is to be avoided.

MASS FOR THE RITE OF RELIGIOUS PROFESSION

9. Whenever religious profession, and especially perpetual profession, takes place during Mass, one of the ritual Masses for the day of religious profession from the Roman Missal or approved propers should be chosen. On a solemnity or a Sunday of the Advent, Lent or Easter seasons, the Mass of the day is used with the special formulas for the eucharistic prayer and final blessing to suit the occasion.

10. Since the liturgy of the word for the rite of profession can be an important aid in expounding the meaning of religious life and its responsibilities, it is permitted to take one reading from the special lectionary on those occasions when Mass for religious profession may not be used. But this may not be done during the Paschal Triduum, on the solemnities of Christmas, Epiphany, Ascension, Pentecost or Corpus Christi, or on other solemnities of obligation.

11. White vestments are worn for the ritual Mass for the day of religious profession.

---

* Translated by A.F. Latin text in *Notitiae*, 1970, 114–116. The final section, on the changes which institutes may make in the rite, is omitted.

87

**INTRODUCTION TO THE RITE OF
CONSECRATION TO A LIFE OF VIRGINITY***

S.C.D.W., *Mos virgines consecrandi*, 31 May, 1970

NATURE AND VALUE OF CONSECRATION TO VIRGINITY

1. The custom of consecrating women to a life of virginity dates back to the early Church. It led to the institution of a solemn rite constituting the candidate a person set apart, a surpassing sign of the Church's love for Christ, and an eschatological image of the world to come and the glory of the heavenly Bride of Christ. In the rite of consecration the Church reveals its love of virginity, asks for God's grace on those who are consecrated, and prays fervently for an outpouring of the Holy Spirit.

THE MAIN DUTIES OF THOSE CONSECRATED

2. Those who consecrate themselves to chastity under the inspiration of the Holy Spirit do so for the sake of more fervent love of Christ and of greater freedom in the service of their brothers and sisters.

They are to spend their time in works of penance and of mercy, in apostolic activity and in prayer, in keeping with their state of life and spiritual gifts.

To fulfill their duty to prayer they are strongly advised to recite *The Liturgy of the Hours* each day, especially Morning Prayer and Evening Prayer. In this way, by joining their voices to those of Christ the High Priest and of his Church, they will offer ceaseless praise to their heavenly Father, and will pray for the salvation of the whole world.

THOSE WHO MAY BE CONSECRATED

3. Both nuns or women living in the world may thus consecrate themselves.

4. For nuns, it is necessary:

a) that they should always have been unmarried, and should

never have lived in open violation of chastity;

b) that they should have made their perpetual profession, either in the same ceremony or in a previous one;

c) that their religious institute should make use of this rite because of long established custom or by special permission of the competent authority.

5. For women living in the world it is necessary:

a) that they should always have been unmarried, and should never have lived in open violation of chastity;

b) that their age, prudence, and universally esteemed character should provide assurance of perseverance in a life of chastity dedicated to the service of the Church and of their neighbor;

c) that they should be admitted to this consecration by the local Ordinary.

It is for the bishop to decide on the conditions under which women living in the world are to undertake a life of perpetual virginity.

THE MINISTER OF THE RITE

6. The minister of the rite of consecration is the local Ordinary.

* An excerpt from the Introduction. Translation by A.F. Latin text in *Notitiae*, 1970, 314–315.

88

ACTS OF SPECIAL GENERAL CHAPTERS*

S.C.R.S.I., *Par une lettre*, 10 July, 1972

In a letter dated 4 December 1967 the Sacred Congregation for Religious and Secular Institutes requested institutes to send the acts of their special general chapters which were to be held according to the motu proprio, *Ecclesiae sanctae*, part II, no. 3.

In making this request the Sacred Congregation wished to be aware of the experiments in progress and also to know if the chapters remained within the limits set by the motu proprio. This permitted modifications of the constitutions 'ad experimentum' as long as the nature, end, and purpose of the institute would be preserved.

Following this letter, many institutes sent their capitular acts and this Sacred Congregation has responded to many, making the necessary observations and also permitting experiments contrary to common law.

The examination of capitular decrees up to this time shows that institutes have had to face many similar problems and, consequently, observations sent by the Sacred Congregation have also been similar. However, since six years have passed following the publication of the motu proprio and it is not possible to make as complete a study as we would like of the remaining acts of chapters from English-speaking communities, the Sacred Congregation believes it opportune to send a list of principal observations and suggestions. In this way each institute will be able to see those things which should be modified or improved.

Several comments are in order at this point. In this period of experimentation the Sacred Congregation does not approve new constitutions. This does not prevent the acts of the general chapters from becoming immediately effective provided, as mentioned above, the purpose, nature and character of the institute are preserved (*Ecclesiae sanctae*, part II, no. 6).

However, every derogation from common law must have a dispensation explicitly granted. In some cases, it might easily have happened that the Sacred Congregation omitted to call attention to some change contrary to the law in force. This would have been due to an oversight and may not be interpreted as an explicit concession.

We wish here to recall some observations which the Sacred Congregation has made most frequently about acts of chapters and which we hope will be guiding norms for you in the serious work of writing constitutions.

VOWS

In general, a clear definition of each vow is necessary.

1. Chastity or Consecrated Celibacy: 'Chastity is decisively positive. It witnesses to preferential love for the Lord and symbolizes in the most eminent and absolute way the mystery of the union of the mystical body with its head, the union of the bride with her eternal bridegroom' (*Evangelica testificatio*, no. 13).

The term, *virginity*, has a specific meaning and should not be substituted for the word, *chastity*.

2. Poverty: The matter of the vow of poverty and its practice should be accurately specified by the chapter. Several factors should be included in the explanation:

Religious must recognize the importance and dignity of work in earning their livelihood. Their life style, characterized as it should be by simplicity, will result in genuine fraternal sharing, an intrinsic part of both poverty and common life.

A correct sense of dependence must be included not only in legislation but also in actual living.

Chapter decisions which tend to dispense with any kind of dependence or accountability are not acceptable.

'The forms of poverty of each person and of each community will depend on the type of institute and on the form of obedience practiced in it. Thus will be brought to realization, in accordance with particular vocations, the character of dependence which is inherent in every form of poverty' (*Evangelica testificatio*, no. 21; also nos. 16-22).

3. Obedience: The necessity for consultation and collaboration should be included but the obligation and the right of the superior to exercise prudently the role of personal authority should be respected.

'Thus, far from being in opposition to one another, authority and individual liberty go together in the fulfilment of God's will, which is sought fraternally through a trustful dialogue between the superior and his brother in the case of a personal situation, or through a general agreement regarding what concerns the whole community.

'This labour of seeking together must end, when the time comes, with the decision of the superiors whose presence and acceptance are indispensable in every community' (*Evangelica testificatio*, no. 25).

4. 'The formula for religious profession for each congregation should be based on the ritual *Ordo professionis* and should be approved by the Sacred Congregation for Religious. This formula, pronounced by each sister, has to be the same since each member professes vows especially recognized by the Church and since obligations and privileges deriving from it are the same for all. This, however, does not prevent a sister from adding something personal before or after the formula itself' (*Ordo professionis*, Ritual, 2 February 1970, Sacred Congregation for Divine Worship).

GOVERNMENT

1. Method of election of the superior general: Although direct election has been permitted at the request of some small communities, this has been by way of exception.

2. General chapter: Provision should be made for the collaboration of the members of the institute and for adequate representation. Although some institutes give active voice to those members in temporary commitment, whether by vows or by promises, it is not considered feasible to give them passive voice since they have not yet made a permanent commitment of themselves in the particular institute. Those in temporary commitment may not hold positions of authority in the institute.

3. Enlarged councils: Powers given to enlarged councils (e.g., council members, provincials and/or local superiors) should be clearly determined. Enlarged councils are of considerable help in the task of evaluation of experiments but they should not interfere in legislative and executive functions of general councils.

4. Local councils: There is nothing to prevent the entire community from being members of the local council, especially in small communities. But, in larger communities the usual type of council would be necessary particularly when rather delicate matters must be discussed; however, in other items of general interest the consultation of the entire local community is to be favoured.

5. Smaller communities: There is no objection to these provided the 'life style' be that of a religious community with a person in authority, no matter what the title. Experience of many institutes indicates that small communities should not be com-

posed of only peer groups nor according to personal choice.

COMMON LIFE

1. Prayer: Since the eucharistic mystery is truly the centre of the liturgy and even of the entire Christian life, it is normal that it hold first place in the life of religious communities and of each consecrated person (Instruction, *Eucharisticum mysterium*, S.C. Rites, 25 May 1967).

In the light of *Perfectae caritatis* and of *Evangelica testificatio*, as well as from the experience of common life itself, chapters should not hesitate to prescribe a minimum of time for daily prayer, providing for both communal and personal prayer.

2. Apostolate: The religious, not as a private individual but as a member of her institute, engages in apostolic work which is according to the end of her institute.

'But your activities cannot derogate from the vocation of your various institutes...' (*Evangelica testificatio*, no. 20).

3. Religious dress: Chapter decisions in this matter should follow the statements in the documents.

'The religious habit, an outward mark of consecration to God, should be simple and modest, poor and at the same time becoming' (*Perfectae caritatis*, no. 17 ff.).

'While we recognize that certain situations can justify the abandonment of a religious type of dress, we cannot omit to mention that it is fitting that the dress of religious men and women should be, as the Council wishes, a sign of their consecration and that it should be in some way different from the forms that are clearly secular' (*Evangelica testificatio*, no. 22).

The letter sent from this Sacred Congregation on 25 February 1972 re-affirms the above directives.

4. Other matters: Some chapters leave to the individual the responsibility for decisions on recreation, vacations, going out, visits, correspondence.

In these matters superiors cannot totally abdicate their authority, since 'Superiors are responsible for the souls confided to their care...' (*Perfectae caritatis*, no. 14).

In view of writing future constitutions, it is well to remark here that there should be a union of spirituality and law. Above all, the *spirit of the gospel* should be the basis of constitutions, emphasizing that the essence of the consecrated life is in the total gift of self to God. The *spirit of the foundress*, that special charism given to an institute through its foundress, should permeate the constitutions which embody the spiritual heritage of her daughters.

The general legislation of the Church permits each institute to decide what will be done in some juridical matters, e.g., who will have active and passive voice, the practice of poverty within the institute, the manner of admittance to profession; therefore, these should be expressed in the constitutions.

The above observations are intended to be of assistance in answering the questions and in resolving in some degree the problems facing religious institutes today. Not all these observations will affect the present legislation of all institutes but the members of the institutes and the participants in general chapters will see those things which refer to their respective institutes.

It is hoped that these observations will serve as guidelines for the writing of constitutions which eventually must be submitted to the competent authority for approval.

It is the fervent prayer of all those privileged to assist religious institutes that the foregoing information will enable you and your sisters by means of generous efforts to bring to living reality not only the necessary external changes but also to render more fruitful that spiritual renewal which the Church asks of all of us.

---

* Translation by Vatican Press Office. French original in *E.V.*, 4, 1080–1090.

89

ON HELP TO BE GIVEN TO THOSE
WHO LEAVE RELIGIOUS INSTITUTES*

S.C.R.S.I., *Sacra congregatio*, 25 January, 1974

The Sacred Congregation for Religious and Secular Institutes, in bringing to the notice of the Superiors General certain directives of the Plenary Assembly concerning the help which should be given to those who leave their religious communities, wishes to indicate at the same time the considerations and principles on which the directives are based.

The Sacred Congregation is aware of the difficulties facing Institutes themselves both on account of the considerable increase in the numbers of those who leave and by reason of the criteria by which those who leave would justify their claims.

Every religious family has the obligation of providing for the spiritual, moral and social, as well as temporal well-being of its members while they retain their membership. This obligation extends also in some fashion, though for a different reason, and within certain limits, to those who leave the Institutes and who find themselves faced with the necessity of inserting themselves into society as lay people after having spent, perhaps, many years in religious life.

The Code of Canon Law prescribes that those who leave their religious community, because dispensed from their vows or dismissed from the Institute, cannot make any claims for the work they have done as members of it. This principle, as stated in can. 643, paragraph 1, is intrinsic to religious professions. Those who enter religious life freely and voluntarily place themselves in a situation which is entirely special. Religious profession is a fact of a spiritual nature which implies the total surrender to God of all that one can earn during one's religious life, even if this implies some uncertainty regarding the future.

It would be contrary to the nature of religious life to equate it with a business or a factory or to put the relations between institutes and members on a par with relations between employers and employees.

The above does not release the Institute from the duty, based on the principles of charity, equity, justice and social responsibility, of assisting those who leave it. Above all, the necessity for tact at the moment of departure from the religious life and the difficulty inherent in the transfer, involving the entire nature of the person concerned, require that this person should depart feeling that he or she is being treated with all the respect due to a person. For the same reasons those in whose care the Institute rests should be conscious of having acted justly, according to the principles indicated.

The Church has made its stipulations for those departing from religious life, according to can. 643, paragraph 2, originally formulated for the benefit of ex-religious women and subsequently applied to ex-religious men. But the prescriptions of this canon appear inadequate in view of the new social conditions obtaining today and in the light of the contemporary social conscience. On the other hand, considering the actual state of affairs and the complexity of the matter, it is neither possible nor advisable to formulate general norms applicable to all cases.

Above all, it is necessary to give appropriate assistance to the one leaving religious life in order to enable him to find the place in the lay state which is best suited to his capabilities. Of course, the measure of such assistance, the financial help provided, would have to be weighed according to each individual case, since no two are the same. The situation of those who have good qualifications and experience and whose placement in the world is assured in advance is far different from that of those religious who by reason of age or other circumstances are physically or morally unsuited for a remunerative position.

Moreover, the measure of the assistance depends on the possibility of the Institute itself and of its obligations of charity, equity and justice towards its members who persevere in the community, not to burden them with unjustifiable obligations caused by an ill-proportioned generosity towards those who leave the community.

Religious Institutes could undertake provision for the temporal needs of their members, a provision applicable to them even if they leave religious life, by using the means more consonant with the spirit of the times in which we live, in the context of justice and social security and at the same time respecting the nature of religious life. Among these means, one might consider, according to circumstances, the establishment of programs of social security at the Community level or with the intervention of the National Conferences, as well as enrollment of members in the already existing organizations of social security and insurance.

It is commendable that Institutes set up or support offices for the moral and economic assistance of those who leave, in order to give them advice and help them, according to their qualifications, to find as soon as possible a position and earn a salary in order to maintain themselves decently and properly.

The Plenary Assembly of this Sacred Congregation, in its session of October 23–25, 1972, after examining all the theoretical and practical aspects of the problem, formulated the following directives:

1. As a matter of principle, the norm laid down in paragraph 1 of canon 643 remains in force.

2. Every religious family is urged to provide properly for the spiritual, moral, social and economic well-being of those who leave the institute.

3. Religious Institutes should study and adopt suitable measures to provide for the future of their religious and consequently of those who return to the secular state.

---

* This document first appeared in French, when it was sent as a letter to Father Pedro Arrupe, S.J., by the Congregation for Religious and Secular Institutes, who asked Father Arrupe, as President of the Union of Superiors General, to circulate it to all major superiors, male and female. The French version was published in *Documentation Catholique*, 2 June, 1974. An English text was circulated to English-language superiors and was published in one or two periodicals. Subsequently, *Commentarium pro Religiosis*, volume 55, fasc. 1, pp. 73–75, published the document in Latin as a decree of the Congregation for Religious and Secular Institutes. Our translation is made, by A. F., from the Latin text, which differs in some minor details from the French.

90

DECREE ON THE EXPULSION OF RELIGIOUS WHO HAVE TAKEN PERPETUAL VOWS IN AN EXEMPT CLERICAL RELIGIOUS INSTITUTE*

S.C.R.S.I., *Processus judicialis*, 2 March, 1974

Experience has shown that many difficulties and harmful delays can result from the judicial process which, in accordance with canons 654-668 of the Code of Canon Law, must be established when there is question of the expulsion of a (male) religious in perpetual vows, whether solemn or simple, from an exempt religious institute.

The heads of such religious institutes have frequently requested a dispensation—already granted to some religious institutes, on an experimental basis, in accordance with the *Motu Proprio, Ecclesiae Sanctae*, II, 6—from the obligation of establishing such a process for the expulsion of religious. They have requested that, instead, they be allowed to adopt the administrative procedure laid down (canons 648-653) for the expulsion of (male) religious who have taken perpetual vows in non-exempt clerical institutes or lay institutes. That procedure is recognized as being in keeping with the demands of justice, canonical equity and respect for the person.

Having taken everything into account, the Fathers of this Sacred Congregation unanimously decided on the following, in plenary session on 23-25 October 1973:

When there is question of expelling (male) religious with solemn vows or simple perpetual vows, the religious orders and exempt clerical congregations referred to in canon 654 are to follow the procedure prescribed in canons 548-653 for the expulsion of (male) religious with perpetual vows in non-exempt clerical congregations.

The undersigned Cardinal Prefect conveyed this decision to the Supreme Pontiff, Paul VI, in an audience on 16 November, 1973. He ratified the decision of the plenary session and ordered it to be confirmed and promulgated.

The Sacred Congregation for Religious and Secular Institutes therefore publishes the decision, by means of this decree. The decree comes into force at once, nor does it need a 'formula of execution'. It will remain in force until the revised code of canon law shall have been introduced. Notwithstanding anything to the contrary.

* Translated from the Latin text in *A.A.S.* LXVI, no. 4 (30 April 1974), pp. 215–216, by Austin Flannery, O.P.

91

RELIGIOUS OBLIGED TO ASSIST AGED OR SICK PARENTS*

S.C.R.S.I., *Quitte ton pays*, 1976

'Leave your country, your family and your father's house and go...' (Gen. 12:1). Like Abraham, the religious has heard the Lord's call and, like him, has responded to it. The option for a particular form of consecrated life, involving the practice of the evangelical counsels, involves also detachment from former material and spiritual values and separation from the closest members of a person's family. The words of the Gospel then become very relevant indeed: 'He who loves father and mother more than me is not worthy of me'. (Matt. 10:37).

However, this separation does not imply the end of affection. It does not free a person from the obligations imposed on him or her by the fourth commandment of God, especially with regard to the help to be given to parents who are in great difficulties because of sickness, age or infirmity. The Church has always taken account of these filial obligations in its legislation. Canon law lays down: 'the following may not licitly enter religion: sons or daughters who are under obligation to help their relations, that is their parents or grandparents who are truly in need, or to help parents rear or educate their children.' (canon 542)

It is well to recall here that the obligations envisaged by the code refer to descendants in the direct line only.

It sometimes happens, however, that a family's situation changes after one of its members enters religion. Where previously no problem had existed, a family's situation may disimprove because of sickness, age or infirmity, or because of severe economic set-backs. More direct help from sons or daughters in religion may then become necessary. In principle, this problem concerns both men and women religious, but it must be acknowledged that, when it comes to providing nursing or home-help, sisters feel more directly involved because generally speaking they are better qualified to render such services.

Religious institutions have always been mindful of such needs and have tried to meet them in various ways. Sometimes aged or infirm relatives are accommodated in a home run by the sisters, their daughter living in the same house or nearby. Sometimes, when the family lives near one of the congregation's houses the sisters take it in turns to visit and help regularly. One must underline at this point the generosity of very many congregations of religious sisters who go out of their way to discover solutions which will ensure that a sister will not be absent from her community for too long. It might also be recalled that some of the more important institutes have built homes for the parents of their sisters.

In situations where it has not been possible to adopt any of the above measures, institutes have asked the Holy See to authorize leave of absence, which has been freely granted when needed, sometimes for a definite period, sometimes for an indefinite period: 'for as long as the need persists'.

All this shows that the problem has always been present to the pastoral solicitude of the Church and of religious institutes. Recently, the decree *Religionum laicalium*, 31 May, 1966 (1, n. 4) allowed superiors general, with the consent of their councils, to grant leave of absence to their members for one year, thus facilitating further the giving of help to families in difficulties.

PROBLEM MORE FREQUENT AND MORE ACUTE

However, in recent years the problem of aged and sick parents has become more frequent and more acute. There are several reasons for this:

First, people are living longer and consequently the number of old people has increased considerably.

Increasing urbanization and the spread of the nuclear family has meant that the average family apartment in cities is not big enough to allow a family to accommodate aged parents. This had been easier to do in the past.

The considerable reduction in the numbers of sisters and the resultant closures of houses has made it increasingly difficult to accommodate old people in homes run by religious institutes.

At the same time, since the council, religious sisters and their communities are more aware of the problem confronting them in this important domain. The cases have multiplied in which parents are in need of constant help from their daughters in religion and for longer periods. Specific requests in this regard have been made to the sacred congregation for religious and secular institutes from some superiors general. The arguments put forward have been, in general, as follows: 'Our institute is particularly consecrated to the service of the poor. Could not more latitude be given to superiors with regard to assisting the aged or sick parents of sisters? Could not these be considered, by natural law, as the first poor, for as long as such a situation lasts?'

DIRECTIVES BY THE CONGREGATION FOR RELIGIOUS

The sacred congregation studied the question with all the attention that so important a matter warranted and puts forward some consideration which should help institutes resolve the delicate problems encountered in this domain.

The congregation re-affirms, firstly that a sister cannot be unconcerned about the situation of her parents if, in consequence of infirmities, sickness or old age, they are no longer able to provide for themselves. The congregation to which she belongs should do all in its power to help her do what is demanded of her as a daughter. This is one of the reasons why the decree *Religionum laicalium* gave superiors general and their councils the power to grant sisters leave of absence from their communities for one year.

At the same time, religious are not the only ones who have obligations towards their parents. The obligation falls in equal measure and under the same title on the other members of a religious's family, whether they be married or single. When there is need for constant assistance, the family should examine the problem together to discover how each one can play his or her part in carrying out this sacred duty. In such a case, it would be an abuse and unjust if the members of the family who are not religious were, without grave reasons, to dispense themselves from their obligations in the matter, urging the fallacious reasoning that the religious and apostolic duties of a sister are of secondary importance and that therefore she alone ought to be totally and constantly available.

Of course, special circumstances may demand that a sister do more. For example, if she is an only child, or if her brothers and sisters are unable, for grave reasons, to help. In such an eventuality, it is highly desirable that the institute would set about facilitating her in giving the necessary help, safeguarding, at least partially, her community life. This can be achieved, either by sending other religious in turn to look after her parents, or by paying for a nurse or home help. For many years bodies have been in existence almost everywhere which provide such help for aged or sick people. In many instances they receive help from the state.

It can happen, at the same time, that such a solution will be impossible and that the presence of the sister herself with her parents will be essential for longer than a year. It will then be for the general council of the institute to examine the situation carefully, assessing whether the family's finances are precarious, gauging to what extent the aged and sick parents can be regarded as the 'first poor', while the situation lasts. In such a case, leave of absence for more than one year can be granted the sister for apostolic reasons.

It must be understood that apostolic reasons cannot be invoked in the case of contemplative nuns, for whom other criteria apply.

One can also, when this seems preferable, refer the matter to the sacred congregation which, having examined the request, will give the requisite permission.

It is obvious that all this demands considerable understanding on the part of superiors. Not only must they be prepared to give sisters, generously, whatever permissions are needed if they are to help their parents. They must also be prepared to listen to them and, especially, create an ambiance of sympathy and confidence in which they would be encouraged to disclose their difficulties in this domain, in all simplicity and with total freedom. Superiors will thus have a thorough understanding of every situation, will have a surer touch in solving problems as they emerge and will be very watchful lest absences from the community are improperly motivated: lest, that is to say, family problems might be used by a sister as a respectable pretext for dispensing herself from the obligations of community life.

It is for this reason that, side by side with positive action in favour of families, institutes ought to be engaged in renewing community life, making it more warm and fraternal, full of cordial sympathy, constituting a sisterly and brotherly support, surrounding with an even more attentive affection the companion whom family duties have distanced, materially, from the community for some time.

---

* Translated from INF. SCRIS, 1976, 78–82, by A.F.

92

DIRECTIVES FOR MUTUAL RELATIONS BETWEEN BISHOPS AND RELIGIOUS IN THE CHURCH*

S.C.R.S.I., *Mutuae relationes*, 23 April, 1978

INTRODUCTION

I. Mutual relations between the various members of the People of God have in recent years attracted particular attention. The conciliar teaching on the mystery of the Church, and the constant changes in modern society have deeply influenced our way of life: totally new problems have arisen, some of which, though very pressing indeed, remain delicate and complex. A problem calling for special attention is that of the mutual relations between Bishops and Religious.

Anyone will surely be filled with admiration when reflecting on the following facts—the impact of which seems to deserve better attention—that there are over one million women religious in the world, i.e. one Sister for every 250 Catholic women; that there are about 270,000 men religious—that religious priests make up 36.6 per cent of all the priests in the Church and that in some areas of Africa and South America they account for more than half of the total number of the clergy.

II. On the tenth anniversary of the promulgation of the Decrees *Christus Dominus* and *Perfectae Caritatis* (28 Oct. 1965), the Sacred Congregation for Bishops and the Sacred Congregation for Religious and Secular Institutes held a Joint Plenary Assembly (16th—18th Oct. 1975). The National Conferences of Bishops, the National Conferences of Religious and the International Unions of Superiors General, men and women, were consulted and offered their collaboration. The main questions studied in the Plenary Assembly were:—

1. What do Bishops expect from Religious?
2. What do Religious expect from Bishops?
3. What practical means should be taken for an orderly and

fruitful collaboration between Bishops and Religious at diocesan, national and international levels?

After the general criteria had been agreed upon and various additions had been made to the proposals presented to the members, the Plenary Assembly decided that a document should be drawn up giving pastoral guidelines.

The promised document, which was prepared in collaboration also with the Sacred Congregations for the Oriental Churches and for the Evangelisation of Peoples, is now published.

III. The subject is obviously treated within definite limits. It concerns relations between Bishops and Religious of all rites and territories throughout the Church with the intention of rendering these relations easier in practice. The precise matter under discussion is the relations that should exist between local Ordinaries on the one hand and Religious Institutes and Societies of Common Life on the other. Secular Institutes are not directly under consideration, except in what concerns the general principles of consecrated life (PC.11) and the insertion of these Institutes into the particular Churches (CD.33).

The text falls into two sections, one *doctrinal,* the other *normative.* The purpose is to offer guidelines for a better and more effective application of the principles of renewal set forth by the Second Ecumenical Vatican Council.

Part I
SOME DOCTRINAL ELEMENTS

Before issuing pastoral directives on some of the problems that have arisen concerning relations between Bishops and Religious, it seems necessary to offer a brief summary of the doctrinal principles on which these relations are founded. But even a short exposé of these principles presupposes an extensive survey of the doctrine contained in the conciliar documents.

Chapter I

THE CHURCH AS A 'NEW' PEOPLE

'Not According to the Flesh, but in the Spirit' (LG.9)

1.   The Council has brought into light the unique nature of

the Church, showing her as *Mystery* (LG.I).

From the day of Pentecost onwards (LG.4) there exists in the world a 'new' people, which, vivified by the Holy Spirit, is united with Christ and has access to the Father (Eph. 2, 18). The members of this People are gathered from all nations and are bound together in such an intimate unity (LG.9) that it cannot be explained solely by axioms of the sociological order: there exists between them a kind of 'newness' which transcends the human condition. It is only in this transcendent perspective that mutual relations between the various members of the Church can be correctly understood. The reality upon which this unique nature is based is the very presence of the Holy Spirit. He is, in fact, the life and strength of the People of God, the bond of its communion, the vigour of its mission, the source of its multiple gifts, the secret of its admirable unity, the radiance and beauty of its creative power, the fire of its love (LG.4,7,8,9,12). The spiritual and pastoral re-awakening of recent years—upon which some disturbing abuses have failed to cast a shadow—is due to the presence of the Holy Spirit and is clear evidence of a specially privileged moment (EN.75) for the renewal of the youth of the Church as she goes forward to the Day of her Lord (Rev. 22, 17).

'One Body: as Parts of It We Belong to Each Other' (Rom. 12, 5; I Cor. 12, 13)

2. In the mystery of the Church, unity in Christ implies a mutual communion of life among the members. For 'God has willed to make men holy and save them, not as individuals without any bond or link between them, but rather to make them into a people' (LG.9). The very life-giving presence of the Holy Spirit (LG.7) builds up, in Christ, an organic cohesion. 'He unifies the Church in communion and in the works of the ministry; he bestows upon her varied hierarchic and charismatic gifts and in this way directs her and adorns her with his fruits'. (LG.4; Eph. 4, 11-12; I Cor. 12, 4; Gal. 5,22.)

Therefore the elements which differentiate the various members of the Church—the gifts, the offices, the functions—act in a complementary manner and are truly related to the one communion and mission of the same Body (LG.7; AA.3). The fact that there are in the Church pastors, laymen or religious, does not imply inequality in the dignity common to all the members (LG.32); it rather expresses the articulation of joints and functions in a living organism.

Together Called to Make Up a 'Visible Sacrament' (LG.9).

3.   The newness of the People of God in its two aspects of a visible, living, social organism and of an invisible divine presence—intimately bound together—may be compared with the mystery of Christ: 'as the assumed nature, inseparably united to Him, serves the divine Word as a living organ of salvation, so, in a somewhat similar way, does the social structure of the Church serve the Spirit of Christ who vivifies it in the building up of the body (LG.8; Eph. 4, 16). The intimate and reciprocal connection of these two elements confers upon the Church her specific *sacramental* nature. Because of this nature the Church is not confined within the boundaries of the discipline of sociology. Thus the Council was able to affirm that the People of God is in this world 'the visible sacrament of this saving unity' (LG.9; LG.1, 8, 48; GS.42; AG.1, 5) for men of all nations.

The social evolution and the cultural changes which are being witnessed to-day oblige the Church to renew and adapt in a number of her human aspects. This in no way diminishes her specific nature as *the universal sacrament of salvation*. Those changes, which are to be encouraged, tend rather to bring her nature into clearer light.

Destined to Witness and Announce the Gospel

4.   All members, pastors, laymen and religious, each in their own manner, share in the *sacramental* nature of the Church. Likewise, each one according to his function, must be a sign and instrument both of *union with God* and of the *salvation of the world.* For any man, in fact, vocation has a twofold aspect:

(a) Vocation to holiness: 'all in the Church, whether they belong to the hierarchy or are cared for by it, are called to holiness' (LG.39).

(b) Vocation to the apostolate: the whole Church is driven by the Holy Spirit to do her part for the full realisation of the plan of God' (LG.17; AA.2; AG.1, 2, 3, 4, 5).

Therefore, before considering the diversity of gifts, ministries and duties, it is necessary to acknowledge, as a basis, the universal call to union with God for the salvation of the world. This vocation demands of every man, as a sign of his ecclesial communion, that he recognise the primacy of *life in the Spirit,* upon which depends docility to the word, interior prayer, awareness of life as a member of the whole body, desire for unity, dutiful accomplishment of one's official mission, the gift of self in service and the humility of repentance. From this common baptismal vocation to *life in the Spirit* there come to light clearer de-

mands and effective means in what concerns relations between
Bishops and Religious.

Chapter II

THE MINISTRY OF THE BISHOPS WITHIN THE
ORGANIC COMMUNION OF THE CHURCH

The Communion Proper to the People of God and Its Excellence

5. The organic communion among the members of the
Church is to such an extent the fruit of the Holy Spirit that it
necessarily presupposes the historical intervention of Jesus
Christ and his Easter passage from death to life. The Holy Spirit
is the Spirit of the Lord. Jesus Christ, exalted at God's right
hand (Acts 2, 33) 'poured out on his disciples the Spirit promised
by the Father' (LG.5). If the Spirit is what the *soul* is to the Body
(LG.7), Christ is truly its *Head* (LG.7) and the organic cohesion
of the members proceeds from both (I Cor. 12-13; Col. 2, 19), so
that there can be no real docility to the Spirit without fidelity to
the Lord who sends Him. Christ in fact, 'is the head that adds
strength and holds the whole body together, with all its joints
and sinews—and this is the only way in which it can reach its full
growth in God' (Col. 2. 19).

Moreover the organic communion of the Church is not exclusively spiritual—that is, so born of the Holy Spirit that this
spiritual birth is of its very nature prior to and responsible for all
the functions of the Church—but the Church is, at the same
time, hierarchic since, by a vital impulse, it is derived from
Christ the Head.

The very gifts that are dispensed by the Spirit are precisely
willed by Christ; by their nature they are directed towards the
fastening together of the Body, by vivifying its functions and activities: 'Now the Church is his Body; He is its head. As he is the
Beginning, He was first to be born from the dead, so that He
should be the first in every way' (Col. 1, 15-18; LG.7). Thus the
organic communion of the Church, under both its spiritual and
hierarchic aspects, traces its origin and vitality simultaneously
from Christ and his Spirit. Rightly, therefore, and most appropriately did the Apostle Paul use the words *'in Christ'* and *'in the
Spirit'* to indicate an intimate and vital convergence (Eph. 2,
21-22; and throughout his epistles).

Christ, the Head, is Present in the Episcopal Ministry

6. The Lord Himself 'set up in His Church a variety of offices which aim at the good of the whole Body' (LG.18). Among these ministries, that of the episcopate is fundamental to all the others.

The bishops in hierarchic communion with the Pope make up the College of Bishops so that together they express and give effect to the role of Christ the Head in the Church-Sacrament. 'In the person of the bishops, then, to whom the priests render assistance, the Lord Jesus Christ, supreme High Priest, is present in the midst of the faithful. . . (Bishops) in a resplendent and visible manner take the place of Christ himself, Teacher, Shepherd and Priest, and act as his representatives' (LG.21, 27, 28; PO.1, 2; CD.2).

No one in the Church other than a Bishop carries out an organic function of fecundity (LG.18, 19), unity (LG.23) and spiritual authority (LG.22), which is so basic that it influences all ecclesial activity. Although in the People of God many other gifts are granted and many initiatives are possible it is the duty of the Roman Pontiff and the Bishops—as the *Head* in the *Body*—to evaluate and harmonise these (LG.21). This implies an abundance of chosen gifts from the Holy Spirit and the special charism of regulating these diverse activities in docility of mind to the one and only vivifying Spirit (LG.12, 24, etc.).

The Indivisibility of the Ministry of Bishops

7. The Bishop, with the co-operation of his priests, renders to the community of the faithful a threefold service: that of teaching, sanctifying and ruling (LG.25-27; CD.12-20; PO.4-6). These, however, are not three separate ministries: since Christ, in the New Law, has united in Himself the three functions of Teacher, Priest and Pastor, there is only one ministry, unique in its origin. That is why the episcopal ministry in its various functions has to be exercised in an indivisible way.

If at times circumstances demand that one of these three aspects be given greater prominence, the other two must never be isolated or ignored, lest the fundamental unity of the entire ministry be endangered. The Bishop not only governs, not only sanctifies, not only teaches, but, with the help of his priests, he feeds his flock by teaching, sanctifying and ruling it in an unique and indivisible action. The Bishop, by virtue of his very ministry, is responsible in a special way for the growth in holiness of all his faithful, since he is 'the principal dispenser of the mysteries of God and the spiritual guide of his flock' according to the vocation proper to each one (cf. CD.15)—likewise, therefore, and above all according to the vocation of religious.

The Duty of the Sacred Hierarchy in Regard to Religious Life

8.   Attentive reflection on the functions and duties of the Roman Pontiff and the Bishops in regard to the practical life of Religious leads one to discover more clearly and concretely its ecclesial dimension, that is, the undeniable bond of religious life with the life and holiness of the Church (LG.44). It is God, indeed, who, through the action of the sacred Hierarchy, *consecrates* the religious for a higher service to the People of God (LG.44). Again, the Church, through the ministry of her pastors, 'besides giving legal sanction to the religious form of life and thus raising it to the dignity of a canonical state, sets it forth liturgically also as a state of consecration to God' (LG.45; SC.80, 2).

Besides, the Bishops, as members of the Episcopal College and in agreement with the will of the Supreme Pontiff, assume together the following obligations:—by wise laws they regulate the practice of the evangelical counsels (LG.45); they give authentic approval to the Rules that are presented to them (LG. 45), thus recognising and conferring on the Institutes their specific mission at the same time, encouraging them to found new churches (AG.18; 27) and, according to circumstances, entrusting them with particular tasks and duties. They see to it that 'under their vigilance and protection, religious institutes should develop and flourish in accordance with the Spirit of their Founders' (LG.45). Lastly, they define 'the exemption of certain Institutes from the jurisdiction of the local Ordinaries for the sake of the general good' (LG.45) of the universal Church so as the better 'to ensure that everything is suitably and harmoniously arranged within them and that the perfection of the religious life is promoted' (CD.35 §3).

Some Consequences

9.   The brief considerations given above, on the *hierarchic communion* in the Church throw considerable light on the relations that should be fostered between Bishops and Religious:—

(a) The *Head* of the ecclesial Body is Christ, the eternal Pastor, who chose Peter and the Apostles with their successors, namely the Roman Pontiff and the Bishops, made them sacramentally his *Vicars* (LG.18, 22, 27) and granted to them appropriate charisms. No one else has the power to exercise any function, whether of teaching, sanctifying or governing the People of God, except in participation and communion with them.

(b) The Holy Spirit is the *Soul* of the ecclesial Body. No member of the People of God, whatever his ministry may be, can personally possess in himself the totality of all the gifts, offices and duties: he must enter into communion with the other members. Differences in the People of God, whether of gifts or functions. converge and mutually complement one another for a single communion and mission.

(c) Bishops, in unison with the Roman Pontiff, receive from Christ the Head the duty (LG.21) of discerning gifts and competencies, of co-ordinating multiple energies, and of inducing the whole People of God to live in the world as a sign and instrument of salvation. To them also is entrusted the duty of caring for religious charisms; all the more so because the very indivisibility of the pastoral ministry makes them responsible for the perfection of the entire flock. Thus, in promoting religious life and protecting it in conformity with its specific character, Bishops fulfil an authentic pastoral duty.

(d) All pastors, mindful of the Apostle's exhortation never to be 'a dictator over any group that is put in their charge, but to be an example that the whole flock can follow' (I Pet. 5, 3), will be fully aware of the primacy of *life in the Spirit*. This requires that they be at the same time 'leaders' and 'members'; truly 'fathers', but also 'brothers'; teachers of the faith, but mostly 'fellow-disciples of Christ; 'masters of perfection' for the faithful, but 'witnesses' also by their personal holiness.

Chapter III

RELIGIOUS LIFE WITHIN THE ECCLESIAL COMMUNION

The 'Ecclesial' Nature of Religious Institutes

10. The religious state is not 'a kind of middle way between the clerical and lay conditions of life', but comes from both as a 'special gift' for the entire Church (LG.43).

It consists in the following of Christ by a public profession of the evangelical counsels of chastity, poverty and obedience, in community life, with a firm will to remove all obstacles 'likely to draw him away from the fervour of chastity and the perfection of divine worship' (LG.44). A religious is 'totally dedicated to

God, his supreme love, and is committed to the honour and service of God under a new and special title' (LG.44). This 'unites the religious to the Church and her mystery in a special way' and urges him to act with undivided dedication for the good of the entire Body (LG.44).

It clearly follows that religious life is a special way of sharing in the sacramental nature of the People of God. For the consecration of those who make profession of religious vows has for one of its main purposes to offer to the world a visible witness of the unfathomable mystery of Christ, in so far as, in them, Christ is shown 'contemplating on the mountain, announcing God's kingdom to the multitudes, healing the sick and the maimed, converting sinners to a good life, blessing children, doing good to all and always obeying the will of the Father who sent Him' (LG.46).

The Distinctive Character of Every Institute

11. Religious Institutes are numerous in the Church and they differ one from the other according to their own proper character (PC.7, 8, 9, 10). Each, in fact, contributes its own vocation as a gift raised by the Holy Spirit through the work of 'outstanding men and women' (LG.45; PC.1, 2) and authentically approved by the sacred Hierarchy.

The 'charism of the Founders' (ET.11) appears as 'an experience of the Spirit' transmitted to their followers to be lived by them, to be preserved, deepened and constantly developed in harmony with the Body of Christ continually in a process of growth. 'It is for this reason that the distinctive character of the various religious Institutes is preserved and fostered by the Church' (LG.44; CD.33, 35, §1, §2, etc.).

This 'distinctive character' also involves a particular style of sanctification and apostolate which creates a definite tradition so that its objective elements can be easily recognised.

In this time of cultural evolution and ecclesial renewal, it is necessary to preserve the identity of each Institute so securely as to avoid the danger of ill-defined situations arising from religious involving themselves in the life of the Church in a vague and ambiguous manner, without giving due consideration to their traditional apostolate and their distinctive character.

Some Signs of a Genuine 'Charism'

12. Every authentic charism brings an element of real originality in the spiritual life of the Church along with fresh initiatives

for action. These may appear unseasonable to many, and even cause difficulties, because it is not always easy to recognise at once that they originate from the Spirit.

The true marks of an authentic charism in any Institute demand, both in the Founder and his followers, a constant re-examination of their fidelity to the Lord, docility to His Spirit, prudent weighing of circumstances and careful reading of the signs of the times, the will to be integrated in the Church, awareness of obedience to the hierarchy, boldness in initiatives, perseverance in the gift of self, humility in the face of adversity. In a genuine charism there is always a mixture of new creativity and interior suffering. The historical fact of the connection between charism and cross, apart from other factors which may give rise to misunderstanding, is an extremely helpful sign in discerning the authenticity of a call of the Spirit.

Individual religious also possess personal gifts coming from the Spirit to enrich, develop and rejuvenate the life of the Institute, to further unite the community and to show forth its renewal. But the discernment of these gifts and their correct use can be recognised by the extent to which they harmonise with the community commitment in the Institute and with the needs of the Church, as determined by legitimate authority.

Service Proper to Religious Authority

13. *Superiors* fulfil their duty of service and leadership within the religious Institute in conformity with its distinctive character. Their authority proceeds from the Spirit of the Lord in connection with the sacred Hierarchy, which has granted canonical erection to the Institute and authentically affirmed its specific mission.

Now, from the fact that the *prophetic, priestly* and *royal* condition is common to all the People of God (LG.9, 10, 34, 35, 36), it seems useful to outline the competency of religious authority, by comparing it, analogically, with the threefold function of the pastoral ministry, namely that of teaching, sanctifying and governing, without however confusing one authority with the other, or equating them:

(a) As regards *the duty of teaching:* Religious Superiors have the competency or authority of *spiritual directors* according to the evangelical tradition of their Institute. Therefore, in this context they must impart to their Congregation as a whole or to each one of its communities, a real *'spiritual direction'*, in agreement with the authentic teaching of the Hierarchy, and fully aware of the fact that they are performing a duty of grave responsibility within the form of life laid down by the Founder.

(b) As to *the office of sanctifying:* Superiors have a special competency, as well as the responsibility, of *'perfecting',* in various ways, the life of charity, within the rule of the Institute, either in what refers to the initial and ongoing formation of their brethren, or to the communal and personal fidelity in the practice of the Evangelical Counsels according to the Rule. This duty, conscientiously performed, is considered by the Supreme Pontiff and the Bishops as a valuable help in the fulfilment of their fundamental ministry of sanctification.

(c) As to *the office of governing:* Superiors must organise the life of the community, distribute offices to its members, take care of the special mission of the Institute, develop it and work at its effective insertion into the ecclesial activity, under the direction of the Bishop.

There is, then, *an internal organisation* in religious Institutes (CD.35, §3) which has its proper field of competency and a measure of real *autonomy,* even though in the Church this autonomy can never become *independence* (CD.35, §3, §4). The right degree of this autonomy and its concrete delimitation of competency are contained in the common law and in the Rules or Constitutions of each Institute.

Some Conclusions as Guidelines

14. From the above reflections on religious life, some conclusions can be deduced:

(a) Religious and their communities are called upon in the Church to give a visible testimony of their total consecration to God. This is the fundamental option of their Christian existence and the first objective to be attained in their distinctive way of life. Whatever the specific character of their Institute, religious are, in fact, consecrated in order to proclaim publicly in the Church-Sacrament that 'the word cannot be transfigured and offered to God without the spirit of the beatitudes' (LG.31).

(b) Every Institute exists for the Church and is bound to enrich her with its distinctive characteristics according to its specific spirit and particular mission. Religious should therefore cultivate a renewed ecclesial awareness and lend their services for the building up of the Body of Christ through sustained fidelity to their Rule and obedience to their Superiors (PC.14; CD.35, §2).

(c) Religious Superiors have the grave duty—it is, in fact,

their main obligation—to pay full attention to the fidelity of their members to the charism of the Founder by promoting the renewal prescribed by the Council and required by the times. They shall make every effort to give effective orientation to their members and earnestly encourage them in the pursuit of this goal. They will consider it their privileged duty to provide them with a perfect formation, suited to the needs of the day (PC.2, d; 14, 18).

Finally, convinced of the fact that religious life, of its very nature, requires a special participation on the part of its members, Superiors shall take care to keep it alive, 'since effective renewal and right adaptation cannot be achieved save with the cooperation of all the members of the Institute' (PC.4).

Chapter IV

BISHOPS AND RELIGIOUS INTENT UPON THE ONE MISSION OF THE PEOPLE OF GOD

The Ecclesial Mission Flows from the 'Fountain of Love' (AG.2)

15. The mission of the People of God is one: it is, in a way, the heart of the whole ecclesial mystery. For the Father 'has consecrated' the Son 'and sent Him into the world' (Jn.10,36) 'as mediator between God and men' (AG.3). On the day of Pentecost, 'Christ sent the Holy Spirit from the Father to exercise inwardly his saving influence and to promote the spread of the Church' (AG.4). Thus the Church, throughout her history, 'is by her very nature missionary' (AG.2; LG.17), in Christ and in virtue of the Spirit. All, pastors, laymen and religious, each one according to his specific vocation, are called to an apostolic engagement (cf. n.4). This commitment wells from the love of the Father; then, the Holy Spirit nourishes it, 'giving life to ecclesial structures, being as it were their soul, and inspiring in the hearts of the faithful that same spirit of mission which impelled Christ himself' (AG.4). Therefore the mission of the People of God can never exist solely in the activities of the exterior life, because the apostolic engagements can never be reduced to a mere human activity—valuable as that may be—since every pastoral and missionary initiative is rooted in participation in the mystery of the Church. By its nature, the mission of the Church is none other than the mission of Christ carried on in the world's history and for that reason, it consists principally in participation in the obedience of Him who offered Himself to the

Father for the life of the world (Heb. 5, 8).

The Absolute Necessity of Union with God

16. Mission, which has its origin in the Father, requires of all who are sent that they stimulate their love in the dialogue of prayer. Therefore in these days of renewal of the apostolate—as at any time in any missionary engagement— a privileged place must be given to the contemplation of God, to meditation on His plan of salvation and to reflection on the signs of the times, in the light of the Gospel, so that prayer may be nourished and increased in quality and frequency.

The need to appreciate prayer and have recourse to it is urgent for all. Bishops and their priest-collaborators (LG.25, 27,28, 41), 'devoting themselves to prayer and to the service of the Word' (Acts 6, 4), as 'dispensers of the mysteries of God' (1 Cor. 4, 1) 'should aim to make of one mind in prayer all who are entrusted to their care, to ensure their advancement in grace through reception of the sacraments, and to take care that they become faithful witnesses to the Lord' (CD.15). Religious also in as much as they are called to be, as it were, *specialists in prayer* (Paul VI, 28 Oct. 1966), 'should seek and love above all else God. . .' and 'in all circumstances should take care to foster a life hidden with Christ in God (Col. 3, 3) which is the source and stimulus of love of neighbour' (PC.6).

Today, by disposition of divine providence, many of the faithful are led to gather in small groups to hear the Gospel, to meditate in depth and practise contemplation. Therefore, for the very efficacy of the mission, it is indispensable to make certain that all, above all pastors, give themselves to prayer, and that religious Institutes, as well, preserve intact their form of dedication to God, whether it be by proclaiming the *eminent role* held in this field by the communities of the contemplative life (PC.7; AG.18) or by seeing to it that religious who are dedicated to apostolic action preserve their intimate union with Christ and give a clear witness of it (PC.8).

Different Forms of Apostolic Commitment

17. The cultural situations in which apostolic activity is carried out vary, and so, in the reality of the mission, there will be 'differences which do not flow from the inner nature of the mission itself, but from the circumstances in which it is exercised. These circumstances depend either on the Church or on the people, classes, or men to whom her mission is directed' (AG.6).

These differences, real although contingent, have not only a considerable influence on the exercise of the pastoral ministry of Bishops and Priests, but they also affect the life-style and activities of Religious. They require delicate adaptations, especially on the part of institutes of the active life which have apostolic work at the international level.

For these reasons, in relations between Bishops and Religious, serious consideration should be given not only to the varieties of ministries (AA.2) and charisms (LG.2), but also to the concrete differences that exist between nations.

The Reciprocal Influence of Universal and Particular Values

18. The duty of inserting the mystery of the Church into the context proper to each region raises the problem of the mutual influence between universal and particular values in the People of God.

The Second Vatican Council dealt not only with the universal Church, but also with the particular and local Churches, which it presented as one of the aspects of renewal in ecclesial life (LG.13, 23, 26; CD.3, 11, 15; AG.22; PC.20). This kind of progressive decentralisation is a positive fact which obviously can affect relations between Bishops and Religious (EN.61-64).

Each particular Church is enriched with sound human elements due to the genius and nature of each nation. These elements, however, are not to be regarded as signs of division, of particularism or nationalism; they are expressions of variety in the unity and fullness of that incarnation which enriches the entire Body of Christ (UR.14-17). For the universal Church is not, in fact, the *sum total* of particular Churches, nor is it a *federation* of these (EN.62), but it makes real the full enriched presence of the unique Sacrament of Salvation (EN.54). This multiform unity, however, carries with it very concrete demands for Bishops and Religious in the performance of their duties:

(a) Bishops and their priest-collaborators are the first to be answerable for a correct discerning of local cultural values in the life of their Church and for a clear vision of universality because of their missionary duty as successors of the Apostles who were sent to the whole world (CD.6; LG.20, 23, 24; AG.5, 38).

(b) Religious, then, even if they belong to an Institute of pontifical right, should feel themselves truly a part of the *diocesan family* (CD.34) and be willing to make the necessary adaptations. They should seize every opportunity to foster local vocations both for the diocesan clergy and for religious life. Moreover, they should train the candidates for their own Institute in such a way that they actually live according to local culture but at the same time should be watchful lest any one leave aside the missionary calling inherent in the religious vocation or the unity and distinctive character of each Institute.

Missionary Duty and the Spirit of Initiative

19. A clear missionary duty, part of their very ministry and charism, is specially imposed on Bishops and Religious. This obligation becomes more pressing day by day, as modern cultural conditions evolve in two main directions, namely materialism, which is invading the masses even in countries Christian by tradition, and the expansion of international communications which effect easy contacts between all nations, including non-Christians. Again, the profound changes we witness, the increase of human values, and the many needs of the contemporary world (GS.43, 44) ask with more and more insistence for the renewal of many traditional pastoral activities and the search for new methods of apostolic presence. In such a situation, pastoral diligence is needed to devise new ecclesial experiments both apposite and courageous under the inspiration of the Holy Spirit who is by his nature *Creator*. The charismatic nature of the religious life is highly consistent with such eager search for fresh undertakings. Pope Paul VI clearly affirmed that 'thanks to their religious consecration, they (the religious) are above all free and can spontaneously leave everything and go to announce the Gospel even to the ends of the earth. They are prompt in acting and their apostolate frequently excels because of the originality and genius of their projects and undertakings, which call for the admiration of all who observe them'(EN.69).

Co-ordination in Pastoral Activity

20. The Church has not been established to be an 'organisation for activity', but rather to 'give witness as the living Body of Christ'. Nevertheless she must perform the positive task of organising and co-ordinating the manifold ministries and services, and make them converge in unified pastoral action, showing concretely the choices to be made and the priorities to be assigned among various apostolic works (CD.11; 30, §1; 35, §5; AG.22, 29). At present, it is highly desirable, in the various sections of ecclesial life, to set up a system of research and action in order to fulfil the evangelising mission of the Church in a way better adapted to the variety of situations.

For such worthy co-ordination, there are three main operative centres: the Holy See, the Diocese (CD.11) and at its own level, the Episcopal Conference (CD.38). According to ecclesial and regional needs, other organs of collaboration can be set up.

Mutual Collaboration Among Religious

21. Within the setting of religious life, the Holy See establishes Conferences of Major Superiors and Unions of Superiors General, at the local and universal level (PC.23; REU,73, 5). These, of course, differ from Episcopal Conferences in nature and authority. Their primary purpose is the promotion of religious life as it is inserted in the structures of the mission of the Church. Their activity consists in offering common services such as fraternal initiatives and proposals for collaboration, always with due respect to the distinctive character of each Institute. This also contributes to giving effective assistance for pastoral co-ordination, especially if at fixed times proper revision is made of the working statutes, and above all, 'in conformity with the directives of the Holy See, mutual relations are maintained between the Conferences of Bishops and the Conferences of Major Superiors'.

The Pastoral Meaning of Exemption

22. In view of the good of the Church (LG.45; CD.35, §3) the Supreme Pontiff grants exemption to a number of religious families so that these Institutes may more fully express their identity and devote themselves to the common good with greater generosity and on a wider scale (cf. n.8).

Of its nature, exemption is no obstacle either to pastoral co-ordination or to mutual happy relations among the People of God. In fact, 'it relates to the internal organisation of these Institutes. Its purpose is to ensure that everything is suitably and harmoniously arranged within them and the perfection of the religious life is promoted. The privilege ensures also that the Supreme Pontiff may employ these religious for the good of the universal Church, or that some other competent authority may do so for the good of the Churches under its jurisdiction'. (CD.35, §3; CD.35, §4, ES.1, 25-40; EN.69).

Therefore exempt religious Institutes, faithful to 'their own proper character and function' (PC.2, 6), should cultivate above all special docility to the Roman Pontiff and to the Bishops, placing their liberty and apostolic eagerness at their disposal with good will and in conformity with religious obedience. Similarly, they should with full awareness and zeal, apply themselves to the task of creating and manifesting in the diocesan family the specific witness and the genuine mission of their Institute. Finally, they should continually reanimate in themselves that apostolic perception and unremitting application to work which are characteristic of their consecration. The Bishops certainly acknowledge and greatly appreciate the specific help given to the particular Churches by these religious. They will see in their exemption an expression of the pastoral concern which unites them closely with the Supreme Pontiff for the universal care of all the people (cf. n.8).

If this renewed awareness of exemption is truly shared by all those who are engaged in pastoral collaboration, it will contribute immensely to an increase of apostolic creativity and missionary zeal in all the particular Churches.

Some Criteria for a Just Ordering of Pastoral Activity

23. The above considerations on the ecclesial mission suggest the following directives:—

(a) First of all, the very nature of apostolic action requires that Bishops give precedence to interior recollection and to the life of prayer (LG.26, 27, 41). It requires also that religious, in conformity with their distinctive nature, renew themselves in depth and remain assiduous in prayer.

(b) Special care should be taken to promote 'the various undertakings aimed at establishing the contemplative life' (AG.18) since it holds a very honoured place in the mission of the Church, 'no matter how pressing may be the needs of the active ministry' (PC.7). Especially today, as the danger of materialism is growing more serious, the vocation of all to the perfection of love (LG.40) is illustrated with radical evidence by Institutes entirely dedicated to contemplation, in which it is more clearly manifest that, as St. Bernard says, 'the motive for loving God is God and the measure of love is love without measure' (*De diligendo Deo,* C.1. PL.182, n.584).

(c) The activity of the People of God in the world is by its nature universal and missionary, because of the very character of the Church (LG.17) and the mandate of Christ which confers on the apostolate a universality without limitations (EN.49). Bishops and Superiors must pay attention to this apostolic dimension and take concrete initiatives to promote it.

(d) The particular Church is the frame of history in which a vocation expresses itself in concrete form and fulfils its apostolic responsibility. It is here, within the ambit of a definite culture, that the Gospel is preached and received (EN.19, 20, 29, 32, 35, 40, 62, 63). It is necessary, therefore, that this fact, which is of such importance for pastoral renewal, should be kept in mind during the work of formation.

(e) The mutual influences between the two poles, namely between active participation within a particular culture and the perspective of universality, must be founded on an unalterable esteem and constant maintenance of those values of unity which must in no way be abandoned, the unity of the Catholic Church— for all the faithful—and that of the religious Institute—for all its members. Any local community breaking away from this unity would be exposed to a twofold danger: 'on the one hand, the danger of segregation, which produces sterility; on the other, the danger of losing one's own liberty when separated from the head; isolated, it becomes subject in many ways to the forces of those who attempt to subdue and exploit it' (EN.64).

(f) Men of our times very much expect from Religious that charismatic authenticity—alive and ingenious in its initiatives— which was most eminent in their Founders—so that they may more diligently and zealously engage in the apostolic work of the Church among those who today constitute the greater part of human kind, and are specifically beloved of the Lord: the *little ones* and the *poor* (Mt. 18, 1-6; Lk. 6, 20).

Part II
DIRECTIVES AND NORMS

In the light of the above principles the experience of recent years has led to the formulation of some directives and norms concerned mostly with practical aspects of life. One effect, no doubt, will be a yet easier mutual relationship between Bishops and Religious, to the advantage of the building up of the Body of Christ.

These directives are set out under three distinct aspects which are mutually complementary:—

(a) the aspect of formation;
(b) the aspect of action;
(c) the aspect of co-ordination.

The text presupposes the juridical prescriptions already in force and at times makes reference to these. It does not in any way derogate from any rulings contained in previous documents of the Holy See which are still in force in this matter.

Chapter V

SOME POINTS CONCERNING THE ASPECT OF FORMATION

The Roman Pontiff and the Bishops exercise in the Church the supreme office of authentic *Teachers* and *Sanctifiers* of the entire flock (cf. Part I, Cap. II). For their part, Religious Superiors possess special authority to govern their own Institute and they carry the heavy burden of the formation proper to their members (PC.14, 18; cf. Part I. Cap. III).

Therefore Bishops and Superiors—each according to his respective office, but by common effort working in harmony—should give true priority to their duties regarding formation.

24. Bishops, in agreement with Religious Superiors, should promote, chiefly among the diocesan clergy, the laity and religious men and women of their territory, a vivid awareness and experience of the mystery and structure of the Church, of the vivifying in-dwelling of the Holy Spirit. To that end, they may, together, summon special meetings and seminars on spirituality. Let them, above all, make repeated efforts to promote a due appreciation and an intense practice of both public and private prayer through well-devised initiatives.

25. Religious communities for their part—contemplative Institutes, in particular, with due attention to preserving their distinctive spirit (PC.7; AG. 40)—should offer to the men of our day helpful opportunities for prayer and spiritual life, thus meeting a need for meditation and a deepening of faith which is acutely felt at present. They should also offer suitable opportunities and facilities for sharing in their own liturgical celebrations, without infringement of the laws of enclosure and other rules laid down in this regard.

26. Religious Superiors must spare no effort to ensure the perseverance in their vocation of their brothers and sisters. They should also favour the adaptations that are required by the cultural, social and economic conditions of our times, but exercise vigilance lest these adaptations go beyond just limits and conflict with a life of religious consecration. Cultural updating and specialised studies taken up by religious should deal with subjects that relate to the specific vocation of the Institute. The choice of these studies should be prompted not by a misdirected desire for self-fulfilment with a view to achieving personal ends, but with the sole intention of meeting the apostolic commit-

ments of the religious family itself, in the context of the needs of the Church.

27. In promoting ongoing formation of religious, it is important to insist on the witness of poverty and the service of the most deprived. Care should also be taken that, through a renewed spirit of obedience and chastity, communities may be clear signs of fraternal love and unity.

In Institutes of the active life, where the apostolate constitutes an essential element of their religious life (PC.8: AG.25), the apostolate must be duly emphasised in both initial and ongoing formation.

28. It is the duty of Bishops as authentic teachers and guides of perfection for all the members of the diocese (CD.12, 15, 35 §2; LG.25, 45) likewise to be the guardians of fidelity to the religious vocation in the spirit of each Institute. In the exercise of this pastoral duty, the Bishops shall take care to promote relations with Religious Superiors, to whom the religious are subject in a spirit of faith (PC.14), in open communion of doctrine and practice with the Supreme Pontiff, the Offices of the Holy See and the other Bishops and local Ordinaries.

Bishops, with their clergy, should be staunch advocates of the consecrated life, defenders of religious communities, promoters of vocations and firm guardians of the specific character of each religious family in the spiritual and in the apostolic field.

29. Bishops and Religious Superiors, each according to his specific competence, should zealously foster knowledge of the teaching of the Council and of the pontifical documents on the Episcopate, the Religious Life, the local Churches and the mutual relations that should exist among them. To achieve this, the following initiatives seem advisable:—

(a) meetings of Bishops and Religious Superiors to study these topics at greater depth;

(b) special courses for diocesan priests, for religious and for the laity engaged in apostolic activities, to discover new and more effective adaptations;

(c) studies and experiments especially adapted to the formation of lay-Brothers and Sisters;

(d) elaboration of suitable pastoral documents for the Diocese, the region or nation with a view to presenting these subjects for fruitful reflection on the part of the faithful.

Care must be taken lest this renewed formation be limited to only a few: all should have access to it and it should be an activity common to all religious.

It seems opportune, as well, to give to this deeper doctrinal study sufficient publicity through the press and other means of social communication, lectures, exhibitions, etc.

30. In the initial stages of both ecclesiastical and religious formation, there should be a systematic study of the Mystery of Christ, of the sacramental nature of the Church, of the ministry of Bishops and of religious life in the Church. Therefore:—

(a) From the novitiate onwards, religious, men and women, should be brought to a fuller awareness and concern for the local Church, while at the same time growing in fidelity to their own distinctive vocation;

(b) Bishops should see to it that the diocesan clergy have sufficient knowledge of the current problems of religious life and of the urgency of missionary needs. Some selected priests could be prepared to help religious in their spiritual progress (OT.10; AG.39), although normally that task should be preferably entrusted to prudently chosen religious priests (cf. n. 36).

31. Greater maturity of the priestly and religious vocation depends also, and to a decisive degree, on the doctrinal formation usually received in centres of study at university level or in institutes of higher studies or other institutes specially qualified for this purpose.

Bishops and Religious Superiors involved in this work should offer effective collaboration for the upkeep of these centres of study and their proper functioning. This should be particularly true when such centres are at the service of one or more dioceses and religious congregations, and can better warrant the excellence of the teaching and the presence of teachers and other personnel who, duly prepared, are able to meet the requirements of formation. It means at the same time a more effective use of personnel and resources.

In preparing, revising and implementing the statutes of these study centres, the rights and duties of each participant, the duties which by virtue of his very ministry belong to the Bishop or Bishops, the modes of action and the measure of responsibility of Religious Superiors who have a shared interest, should be clearly defined. Thus an objective and full presentation of doctrine, in harmony with the magisterium of the Church, can be put forward. Then, on the basis of the general criteria of competence and responsibility and in accordance with the statutes, the activities and undertakings of these centres should be followed up with attentive care. But in all these delicate and important matters, the directives and decisions of the Holy See must always be obeyed.

32. An adequate renewal of the pastoral methods in a diocese

requires a deep knowledge of all the factors that concretely affect the local human and religious life. These basic facts are a source of objective and appropriate theological reflection, with the possibility of establishing priorities, elaborating plans for pastoral action and assessing periodically the results achieved. This work may require that Bishops, with the help of competent persons chosen also from among religious, set up and maintain study commissions and research centres. Such undertakings appear more and more necessary not only for a better adapted formation but for a rational structure of pastoral activities.

33. Religious have a special and serious obligation to be attentive and docile to the magisterium of the hierarchy and to facilitate for the Bishops the exercise of their ministry of 'authentic leaders and witnesses of the divine and catholic truth' (LG.25) in the fulfilment of their responsibility for the doctrinal teaching of the faith, both in the centres where its study is promoted and in the use of the means of its transmission.

(a) As regards the publication of books and documents for sale in bookshops belonging to Religious or in catholic institutions or publishing houses under their care, the norms issued by the S. Congregation for the Doctrine of the Faith on 19th March 1975 are to be observed. They deal with the competent authority for the approval of texts of Holy Scripture and their translations, of liturgical books, prayer books, catechisms or any other type of works dealing with topics connected in some way with religion and morality. Disregard of these norms, often speciously and cleverly contrived, can cause serious harm to the faithful: all, but religious particularly, must make every effort to obey these rules.

(b) Even in the case of documents and publications issued by local or national religious institutions, which may not be directly intended for the public but may exercise some influence on pastoral work—such as deal, for instance, with new and grave problems on social, economic and political matters connected in some way with the faith and the religious life, there must always be mutual understanding between Religious and the competent Ordinaries.

(c) Taking into consideration the special mission of some Institutes, the Bishops should encourage and support the religious who are engaged in the important apostolate of the written word and social communications. In this matter, they should promote a wider apostolic collaboration, at the national level particularly; they should show concern about the formation of the personnel specialised in such activities, not only in regard to their technical competence but also—and primarily—in what refers to their ecclesial responsibility.

34. It would be a grave error to keep religious life and ecclesial structures independent one from the other, and still a greater mistake to oppose one to the other, as if they could subsist as two separate realities, one charismatic, the other institutional. Both elements, the spiritual gifts and the ecclesial structures, form 'one, though complex, reality' (LG.8).

Therefore religious, both men and women, while showing a definite spirit of enterprise and apostolic foresight (cf. Part I, Cap. III), should remain intensely loyal to the purpose and spirit of their Institute, in perfect submission and agreement with the authority of the hierarchy (PC.2: LG.12).

35. The Bishop, as Shepherd of the diocese, and religious Superiors, as responsible for their Institutes, should encourage the participation of men and women religious in the life of the local Church and help them to know its rules and directives. In addition, Superiors, in particular, should make every effort to foster supra-national unity within their Institute and docility to the Superiors General (cf. Part I, Cap. IV).

Chapter VI

COMMITMENTS AND RESPONSIBILITIES IN THE FIELD OF ACTION

The Church lives in the Spirit and rests upon the foundation of Peter and the Apostles and their successors, so that the episcopal ministry is really the guiding principle of the pastoral effort of the entire People of God. The Church therefore works in harmony both with the Holy Spirit who is her soul, and with the Head which operates in the Body (cf. Part I, Cap. II). This obviously entails well-defined consequences for Bishops and Religious for their undertakings and activities, although both retain their specific competence to fulfil their different roles.

The practical directives given here have reference to two kinds of needs in the field of action, namely the pastoral and the religious.

Requirements of the Pastoral Mission

36. The Council affirms that 'religious, both men and women, belong in a special sense to the diocesan family and ren-

der valuable help to the Sacred Hierarchy and, in view of the growing needs of the apostolate, they can and should constantly increase the aid they give' (CD.34).

In places where there are more than one rite, Religious who carry out activities on behalf of the faithful of rites different from their own, should respect the norms that regulate relationships between themselves and the Bishops of other rites (ES.I, 23).

It is important that such criteria should not apply only in the conclusive stages, but also in the determination and elaboration of the plans for action; the right of the Bishop to take the final decisions should always be maintained.

Religious who are priests, by the virtue of the unity inherent in the priesthood (LG.28; CD.28, 11) and because they have their share in the care of souls 'may be said, in some real sense, to belong to the diocesan clergy' (CD.34). Therefore in pastoral activities they can and should help to bring about greater union and collaboration between religious, men and women, and the diocesan clergy and local Ordinaries.

37. Between the diocesan clergy and the religious communities, efforts should be made to create new bonds of fraternity and co-ordination (CD.35, §5). Great importance should therefore be attached to such ways and means, including simple and informal ones, as may serve to increase mutual trust, apostolic solidarity and 'fraternal harmony' (ES.I, 28). This will not only bring to mind the right idea of the local Church, but it will encourage each one joyfully to render or request assistance, to look for increased cooperation and to cherish the human and ecclesial community in whose life one is inserted as the fatherland of one's vocation.

38. Major Superiors will take great care not only to have a knowledge of the talents and capabilities of their religious, but also of the apostolic needs of the dioceses in which their Institute is working. It is therefore desirable that a concrete and all-inclusive dialogue should take place between the Bishop and the Superiors of the various Institutes present in the diocese, so that, having to face some precarious situations and a persistent scarcity of vocations, religious personnel may be more evenly and advantageously distributed.

39. The pastoral duty of promoting vocations is to be considered a privileged area for cooperation between Bishops and Religious (PO.11; PC.24; OT.2). This pastoral commitment demands united action on the part of the Christian community for all vocations, so that the Church may be built up according to

the fulness of Christ and according to the variety of the charisms of His Spirit.

In the matter of vocations, the first fact to be kept in mind is that the Holy Spirit 'who breathes where He wills' (Jn.3, 8) calls the faithful, for the greater good of the Church, to various offices and states. To this divine action, it is obvious that no opposition should be made: each one should be able to answer his calling in utter freedom. History itself, for that matter, testifies to the fact that the diversity of vocations, and notably the coexistence and collaboration of secular and religious clergy are not detrimental to dioceses, but rather enrich them with new spiritual treasures and, to no small extent, increase their apostolic vitality.

It is, therefore, advisable that, under the Bishops, the various initiatives be wisely co-ordinated—that is, according to the duties proper to parents and educators, to men and women religious, to priests and to all others who work in the pastoral field. This engagement will have to be carried out in common, in harmony and with the full dedication of every one. The Bishop himself should direct the efforts of all and ensure their convergence, always conscious of the fact that it is from the action of the Holy Spirit that these movements draw their origin. This being the case, there is urgent necessity to provide frequent opportunities for praying together.

40. In renewing pastoral methods and in updating apostolic works, due consideration must be given to the profound upheavals that have affected our modern world (GS.43, 44). On that account difficult situations are met from time to time, mostly when it comes 'to help in the ministry in its various forms in dioceses or regions where the urgent needs of the Church or shortage of clergy require it' (ES.I, 36).

Bishops, in dialogue with Religious Superiors and with all who work in the diocesan sector, should try to discern the will of the Holy Spirit and should study means of providing new apostolic presences, and thus be able to face the difficulties that have arisen in the diocese. The search, however, for this renewed apostolic presence must in no way lead to a serious neglect of other genuinely traditional and still valid forms of apostolate, such as that of the school (cf. S. Congregation for Catholic Education, 'The Catholic School', 19th March 1977 CTS S.323), of the missions, of effective presence in hospitals, social services, etc. All these traditional forms, however, should without delay be carefully and wisely updated according to the norms and directives of the Council and the needs of our times.

41. Apostolic innovations to be adopted must be duly analysed and studied. On the one hand, it is the duty of the Bishops, by virtue of their office, 'not to extinguish the Spirit, but to test all things and hold fast to what is good' (1 Thess. 5, 12; 19, 21; LG.12) in such a way 'that the spontaneous zeal of those who engage in this work may be safeguarded and fostered' (AG.30). On the other hand, religious Superiors, for their own part, should cooperate actively and dialogue with the Bishops in seeking solutions, in preparing programmes relating to the choices made, in launching experiments—even totally new ones—always acting in view of the most urgent needs of the Church and in accordance with the norms and directives of the Magisterium and the distinctive character of their Institute.

42. Between Bishops and Superiors there should be at all times the possibility of mutual exchanges of help for an objective appraisal and a just evaluation of the experiments already made. This will not only forestall evasions and frustrations, but avoid also dangers of crises and deviations. Such undertakings should be reviewed periodically and if a given experiment has proved unsuccessful (EN.58), it should, with humility but due firmness, be amended, suppressed or better directed.

43. Protracted tolerance of aberrant experiments or ambiguous practice does great harm to the faithful. Therefore Bishops and Superiors, in a spirit of mutual trust in the performance of their specific duties and to the extent of their respective authority, shall endeavour, with equal charity and firmness, to make clear decisions and take the necessary measures to avoid and correct excesses of this nature.

It is above all in liturgical matters that there is an urgent need to remedy certain abuses of one trend or another. Bishops, as authentically responsible for the liturgy in the local Church (SC.22, 41; LG.26; CD.15. cf. Part I. Cap. II) and Religious Superiors for what concerns their members, should be sedulous in bringing about an appropriate renewal of worship. They should intervene when need be, to correct deviations and abuses in such a central and prominent sector (SC.10). Religious also shall not forget that they are bound to observe the laws and directives of the Holy See and the prescriptions of the local Ordinary in what refers to the exercise of public worship (ES.I, 26, 37, 38).

Requirements of Religious Life

44. In what concerns the pastoral activities of Religious, the Council expressly declares: 'All religious, whether exempt or

non-exempt, are subject to the authority of the local Ordinary in the following matters: public worship—without prejudice, however, to the diversity of rites—the care of souls, preaching to the people, the religious and moral education, catechetical instruction and liturgical formation of the faithful, especially of children. They are also subject to diocesan rules regarding the comportment proper to the clerical state and also the various activities relating to the exercise of their sacred apostolate. Catholic schools conducted by Religious are also subject to the local Ordinaries as regards their general policy and supervision, without prejudice however, to the right of the Religious to manage them. Likewise, Religious are obliged to observe all those prescriptions which episcopal councils or conferences legitimately decree as binding on all' (CD.35,§4; 35 §5; ES.I, 39).

45. In order that the relations between Bishops and Religious may day by day prove more fruitful, they should develop in an atmosphere of mutual kindness and of respect for persons and institutes, the religious being mindful of showing docility to the Magisterium and obedience to their Superiors, with the understanding that no one should trespass on the powers of another.

46. For religious who are engaged in apostolic activities outside the works of their Institute, there should be means of safeguarding their participation in community life and their fidelity to their Rules or Constitutions. 'Bishops should not fail for their part to insist on this obligation' (CD.35 §2). No apostolic engagement should become an occasion to turn away from one's vocation.

As regards the situation of some religious who wish to withdraw from the authority of their Superior and have recourse to that of the Bishop, objective consideration should be given to each case. There should be an adequate exchange of views, with an earnest desire to find a solution and the Bishop should uphold the decision made by the competent Superior, unless it be evident to him that some injustice is involved.

47. Bishops and their immediate collaborators have the duty to try and form an exact idea of the distinctive nature of each Institute; again, they should be informed about their actual situation and their criteria for renewal. For their part, Religious Superiors, through an up-to-date doctrinal vision of the local Church, shall try to be concretely informed about the actual state of pastoral activities and apostolic programmes adopted in the diocese in which they have to work.

When an Institute finds itself unable to carry on a particular apostolate, Superiors should in good time and with confidence explain the factors that prevent continuance of the work, at least in its present form, especially if this is due to shortage of personnel. The local Ordinary, for his part, should 'give the request sympathetic consideration' (ES.I, 34, §3) and, in common with the Superiors, seek an appropriate solution.

48. A need which is acutely felt and rich in promises for the actual life and apostolic dynamism of the local Church is that of promoting in earnestness, among the various religious Institutes which work in a diocese, mutual exchange of information and means of closer understanding. Superiors, therefore, shall do their best to make this dialogue a reality, in the most suitable way and at regular intervals. No doubt, contacts of this kind will make for greater trust and esteem, for services of mutual assistance, for an in-depth study of problems, for a sharing in experimental results that will express with increased evidence a profession in common of the Evangelical Counsels.

49. In the vast pastoral field of the Church, a new and most important place is given to women. In the early Church they were the devoted helpers of the Apostles (Acts 18, 26; Rom. 16, 1ff.); today they are called upon to exercise their apostolic activity in the ecclesial community, faithfully unfolding the mystery of their identity, both created and revealed (Gen. 2; Eph. 5; I Tim. 3, etc.), and aware of their growing influence in civil society.

Women religious therefore, faithful to their calling and putting to good use the inborn qualities of their womanhood, should respond to the concrete needs of the Church and the world, by seeking out and contributing new forms of apostolic service.

In imitation of Mary—who of all believers holds the highest summit of charity—animated by that burning 'spirit, so authentically human, of sensitivity and concern for others' which is so characteristic of them (Paul VI to National Congress of the Centro Italiano Femminile. Oss. Rom. 6-7 Dec. 1976)—in the light of a long history which shows outstanding examples of their initiative in apostolic work—women religious will find themselves more and more in a position to be, and to be seen to be, a very clear sign of the Church confident, inventive and fruitful in her preaching of the Kingdom (cf. *Inter Insigniores*, S.C. for the Doctrine of the Faith, 15th Oct. 1976, CTS Do493).

50. Bishops together with their collaborators in the pastoral field and Superiors, both men and women, should see to it that the apostolic service of women religious be better known, carefully studied and developed. Considering, therefore, not only the number of women religious (cf. Introduction), but above all their important role in the life of the Church, they should do

their utmost to make this greater ecclesial promotion a reality. Otherwise the People of God would be deprived of the special help which women alone can provide, owing to the gift which, as women, they have received from God. But care should be taken that women religious be held in high esteem and duly appreciated first of all because of their witness as consecrated women and not primarily because of the services they so generously render.

51. In some regions, one can notice a certain eagerness to found new religious Institutes. Those whose responsibility it is to discern the authenticity of each foundation must, humbly indeed, but objectively and steadily, appraise the prospects of the future and the signs of a possible presence of the Holy Spirit, either to receive His gifts 'with thanksgiving and consolation' (LG.12) or to avoid that 'Institutes be imprudently brought into being, which are useless or lacking in vitality' (PC.19). In fact, when the judgment relating to the birth of an Institute takes into account only the usefulness or expediency of its activity, or when it is based on the activity of a person who shows ambiguous signs of devotion, it is clear that the genuine concept of religious life in the Church is in some ways distorted (cf. Part I, Cap. III).

To pass judgment on the authenticity of a charism, the following conditions must be fulfilled:

(a) its special origin from the Spirit, distinct though not separate from personal gifts, innate or acquired, which shows itself in action and organisation;

(b) a profound desire to be conformed to Christ to give witness to some aspect of His mystery;

(c) a constructive love of the Church which shrinks from causing any discord in her.

In addition, the Founder of a genuine Religious Institute is a man or woman whose tried virtue (LG.45) reveals a sincere docility to the Hierarchy and a ready response to the gift they have received from the Spirit.

In the case, therefore, of new foundations, all who have in any way to pass judgment must speak with great prudence, with clarity, after a patient evaluation and just appraisal. This responsibility falls mostly on the Bishops, successors of the Apostles 'to whose authority the Spirit himself subjects even those who are endowed with charisms' (LG.7) and who, in communion with the Roman Pontiff have the duty 'to give a right interpretation of the evangelical counsels, to regulate their practice and to set up stable forms of living embodying them' (LG.43).

Chapter VII

THE IMPORTANCE OF SUITABLE CO-ORDINATION

The varied and fruitful vitality of the Churches necessitates some form of co-ordination to renew, create and perfect the many pastoral means of service and animation. Some of these are now considered at their diocesan, national and universal level.

At the Diocesan Level

52. In each diocese, the Bishop should try to perceive through his flock and particularly through the persons and the religious families present in his diocese what the Holy Spirit may wish to make manifest. He should, therefore, cultivate sincere and familiar relations with Superiors, in order the better to fulfil his duties of Pastor towards men and women religious (CD.15, 16). It is, in fact his specific office to uphold consecrated life, to promote and encourage the fidelity and authenticity of Religious and to help them to play their part in the communion of the Church and its evangelising action according to their distinctive character. It is clear that in such matters the Bishop should act in collaboration with the Episcopal Conference and in full agreement with the voice of the Head of the Apostolic College.

Religious, for their part, should consider the Bishop not solely as the Shepherd of the entire diocesan community, but also as the person responsible for their fidelity to vocation, whilst fulfilling their duties for the good of the local Church. 'They should comply promptly and faithfully with the requests or desires of the Bishops when asked to undertake a greater share in the ministry of salvation, due consideration being given to the character of the Institute and its Constitutions' (CD.35, §1).

53. They should always bear in mind what is set down in the Motu proprio 'Ecclesiae Sanctae':

(1) 'All religious, even exempt, are bound by the laws, decrees and ordinances laid down by the local Ordinary affecting various works, in those matters which concern the exercise of the Sacred Apostolate as well as the pastoral and social activity prescribed or recommended by the local Ordinary'.

(2) 'They are also bound by the laws, decrees and ordinances of the local Ordinary or the Episcopal Conference'—or, according to the locality, the Patriarchal Synod (CD.35, §5)—namely laws relating to various matters contained therein (ES.I, 25, §1, §2, a, b, c, d).

54. It is advisable to have the office of Vicar for Religious, men and women, set up in the diocese, as a service of collaboration with the pastoral ministry of the Bishop in this field (cf. Part I, Cap. II). This office, however, does in no way detract from the authority of Superiors. It is for each diocesan Bishop to define clearly the specific functions attaching to the office. After due consideration he should entrust it to a competent person with an in-depth knowledge of the religious life, due esteem for it and a real desire for its increase.

For the discharge of this office, it is strongly recommended that the various groups of religious—priests, brothers and women religious—who possess the necessary qualities, should have some part in it (e.g. as consultants or in some other capacity).

The role of the Episcopal Vicar for religious congregations of men and women is to help in fulfilling a task which of its nature belongs exclusively to the Bishop, namely that of watching over religious life in the diocese and of integrating it into the complex of pastoral activities. It would, therefore, seem highly advisable that the Bishop should prudently consult Religious, men and women, on the choice of a candidate.

55. To allow the presbyterium of the diocese to show clear signs of its unity, and to add greater impetus to the various sectors of the ministry, the Bishop should encourage the diocesan priests to acknowledge gratefully the fruitful contribution made to their Church by Religious, men and women, and to be glad to see them promoted to higher tasks, consonant with their vocation and their qualifications.

56. Provision should be made for religious priests to be present, in sufficient numbers, at Councils of Priests and for religious priests, brothers and sisters to be fairly represented in pastoral councils (PO.7; CD.27; ES.I, 15, 16). The local Ordinary shall formulate special directives for the selection and just proportion of these representatives.

57. To ensure stability in pastoral collaboration:

(a) A distinction must be made between works that are *proper* to an Institute and those that are *entrusted* to an Institute by the local Ordinary. The first depend on the religious Superiors, according to the Constitutions, although in actual practice they are under the jurisdiction of the local Ordinary according to Canon law (ES.I, 29).

(b) 'Whenever a work of the apostolate is entrusted to any religious Institute by a local Ordinary in accordance with the prescriptions of law, a written agreement shall be made between the local Ordinary and the competent Superior of the Institute, which will among other things, set down precisely all that concerns the work to be done, the members of the Institute assigned to it, and the finances' (ES.I, 30, §1).

(c) For works of this nature, members of the religious Institute who are really suitable should be selected by the religious Superiors after discussion with the local Ordinary and, where an ecclesiastical office is to be conferred on a member of the Institute, the religious should be nominated by the local Ordinary himself for a definite time decided upon by mutual agreement, his own Superior presenting the candidate or at least assenting to the nomination' (ES.I, 30, §2).

58. In order to safeguard the rights to modify arrangements and to seek better adaptations in view of urgent needs for renewal in Institutes, it seems opportune to determine in advance and in detail what works, and especially what offices are to be entrusted to individual religious. A written document may be deemed necessary, for instance, in the case of parish-priests (ES.I, 33), deans, episcopal vicars, assistants to groups of Catholic Action, secretaries of pastoral organisations, diocesan directors, teachers in Catholic Universities, professional catechists, directors of Catholic Colleges, etc., in view of the stability of persons in office and of the devolution of goods in case of discontinuance of the work.

If a religious is to be removed from an office entrusted to him, the following dispositions should be recalled: 'Any religious member of an Institute may for a grave cause be removed from an office entrusted to him either at the wish of the authority who entrusted him with the office, who should inform the religious Superior, or by the Superior who should inform the authority who entrusted the office; this by equal right, the consent of the other party being required in neither case. Neither party is required to reveal to the other the reasons for his action, much less to justify them. There remains the right of appeal *in devolutivo* to the Apostolic See' (ES.I, 32).

59. Associations of men and women religious, at diocesan level, have proved very useful. They should, therefore, be encouraged—with due consideration for their distinctive character and specific purpose:

(a) both as means of mutual liaison, of promotion and renewal of religious life in fidelity to the Magisterium and to the distinctive character of each Institute,

(b) and as a means for the discussion of 'mixed problems' between Bishops and Religious and for the co-ordination of the activities of religious families with the pastoral action of the diocese under the guidance of the Bishop. This, without prejudice to the relations and negotiations which can be carried on directly by the Bishop himself with any individual Institute.

At the National, Regional and Ritual Levels

60. In Episcopal Conferences of a country or region (CD.37), the Bishops 'exercise their pastoral office jointly in order to enhance the Church's beneficial influence on all men' (CD.38). In the same way, patriarchal synods exercise their ministry for their own rites (OE.9), and inter-ritual Assemblies of Ordinaries for relations among various rites take place within the sphere of their particular situation (CD.38)

61. In many nations or regions, through the kind offices of the S. Congregation for Religious and Secular Institutes—and in territories dependent on the S. Congregations for the Evangelisation of Peoples and for Oriental Churches with the consent of the respective S. Congregations—the Holy See has established Councils or Conferences of Major Superiors (men and women or both together). Such Conferences must be deeply sensitive to the diversity of Institutes, enhance their common consecration and channel the efforts of all who are engaged in apostolic work towards pastoral co-ordination by the Bishops (cf.N.21)

For Councils of Major Superiors to play an effective role, it is very desirable that their activities be periodically reviewed. In view of the fact that Institutes differ in their mission, a fair distribution should be made as to participation in various commissions or similar groups duly attached to Councils of Major Superiors.

62. Relations between the Councils of Major Superiors and the Patriarchal Synods—as also relations between the said Councils and the Episcopal Conferences and Inter-ritual Assemblies—should be determined by the same criteria as regulate relations between the individual religious Institute and the local Ordinary (ES.I, 23-25, 40); then, added norms should meet regional needs.

63. Since it is of utmost importance that the Councils of Major Superiors should earnestly and truthfully co-operate with the Episcopal Conferences (CD.35, §5; AG.33), it is desirable that questions having reference to both Bishops and Religious should be dealt with by mixed commissions consisting of Bishops and Major Religious Superiors, men or women (ES.II, 43) or by other bodies according to continental, national or regional situations.

A mixed Commission of this kind shall be so structured as to be able to fulfil its function effectively as an organism for mutual counsel, liaison, communication, study and reflection, even if the final decision is to rest on the Councils or Conferences according to their respective competencies.

Therefore, it is the duty of Pastors to promote in their diocese the co-ordination of all apostolic initiatives and activities and the duty likewise of Patriarchal Synods and Episcopal Conferences in their respective territories (CD.35, §5).

For questions concerning Religious, if need or utility require— as has happened in fact in several places—the Bishops may create a special Commission within the Episcopal Conference. The presence of such a Commission does not impede the work of the mixed Commission but rather requires it.

64. The participation of Major Superiors—or, according to the Statutes, of their delegates—in the various Commissions of the Episcopal Commission and Inter-ritual Assemblies of local Ordinaries (e.g. in the Commissions for Education, Health, Justice and Peace, Social Communications, etc.) can be of great utility for pastoral work.

65. The mutual presence, by means of delegates of Episcopal Conferences and Councils or Conferences of Major Superiors in their respective Unions or Assemblies is recommended, provided that each Conference remains free to deal alone with matters within its competence.

At the Supra-National and Universal Levels

66. At the supra-national, continental or sub-continental levels, some forms of co-ordination—for Bishops and for Major Superiors—can, with the approval of the Holy See, be devised to cover various national groups. At that level, a happy liaison among the different service centres will greatly contribute to unanimous and concerted action between Bishops and Religious. In areas where types of continental organisations are active already, their permanent Committees or Councils can profitably ensure this service.

67. At the universal level, Peter's Successor exercises a ministry specifically his own for the entire Church, but 'in exercising his supreme, full and immediate authority over the universal Church, the Roman Pontiff employs the various departments of the Roman Curia' (CD.9).

Pope Paul VI himself encouraged some forms of cooperation between Religious and the Holy See. He approved the Council of the two Unions of Superiors General (men and women) which is attached to the S. Congregation for Religious and for Secular Institutes (ES.II, 42) and he asked for the presence of Religious as representatives at the S. Congregation for the Evangelisation of Peoples (ES.III, 16).

CONCLUSION

Dialogue and collaboration are already a reality at various levels, but undoubtedly these have to be further developed and bear more abundant fruit. There is need, therefore, to recall that efforts at collaboration will be all the more efficacious if those who are first responsible for this work firmly believe that success depends mostly on their conviction and their formation. Everything will surely progress if those concerned are deeply convinced of the necessity, nature and importance of this collaboration through mutual trust, respect for each other's function, and mutual consultation in initiating and organising undertakings at every level. Then the mutual relations between Bishops and Religious, conducted with sincerity and good will, will express in clear and realistic terms the dynamism and vitality of the Church-Sacrament in its admirable mission of salvation.

The Apostle Paul, 'prisoner in the Lord', writing from Rome to the Ephesians, gave them this advice: 'I exhort you to walk in a manner worthy of the calling with which you were called, with all humility and meekness, with patience, bearing one another in love, careful to preserve the unity of the Spirit in the bond of peace' (Eph. 4, 1-3).

* Translation by Gilbert Volery, M.S.F.S., reproduced by kind permission of the Incorporated Catholic Truth Society, 38–40 Eccleston Square, London SWIV IPD.

93

THE CONTEMPLATIVE DIMENSION OF RELIGIOUS LIFE*

S.C.R.S.I., *La plenaria*, January, 1981

INTRODUCTION

On the basis of extensive research, the plenary session of the Sacred Congregation for Religious and for Secular Institutes of March 4–7, 1980, considered the contemplative dimension of religious life. The theme had been chosen at the *Plenaria* of 1978, which dealt with the specific role of religious in the Church's mission for integral human promotion, especially in its sociopolitical aspects. In highlighting at the time the fundamental importance of the spiritual in all forms of consecrated life, the Fathers of the plenary session saw the need and the urgency to stress the absolute primacy of life in the Holy Spirit.

The choice of this theme, which was approved by the Holy Father, is appropriate, in view of:

—The revival of many forms of prayer and the emergence of new forms of contemplative life among the People of God and in many religious communities, and

—the felt need to do away with the harmful dichotomy between interior life and activity in the personal and communal lives of religious in reaction to a certain period of downgrading of prayer and recollection, which has not yet completely disappeared.

The plenary session did not wish to indulge in a theoretical, theological study; but, on the basis of a sufficiently concrete and agreed doctrinal analysis, it desired to draw up some practical and formative guidelines

—to encourage the integration of the interior life and activity in Institutes of active life and

—to promote vitality and renewal in the specifically contemplative Institutes.

In presenting here the principal guidelines formulated by the *Plenaria,* account has been taken not only of the conclusions reached by the Fathers at the time of voting but also of the main ideas that emerged in other sessions (for example, in the group discussions) and which complemented the thought of the Fathers. Furthermore, appropriate headings were sought for the subject matter of the conclusions, their content was arranged in order, and subdivisions were introduced in order to clarify and make more explicit the guidelines, which were very much condensed in the final proposals.

The synthesis consists of three parts:

I. Description of the contemplative dimension.
II. Guidelines for Institutes of the active life.
III. Guidelines for specifically contemplative Institutes.

I
DESCRIPTION OF THE CONTEMPLATIVE DIMENSION

1. The contemplative dimension is basically a reality of grace, experienced by the believer as God's gift. It enables persons to know the Father (cf. Jn. 14, 8) in the mystery of trinitarian communion (cf. 1 Jn. 1-3) so that they can savour *the depths of God* (1 Cor. 2, 10).

It is not the intention here to discuss the many and delicate problems concerning the different methods of contemplation, nor to analyze contemplation in so far as it is an infused gift of the Holy Spirit.

We describe the contemplative dimension fundamentally as the theological response of faith, hope and charity, by which the believer opens up to the revelation of the living God and to communion with him through Christ in the Holy Spirit. 'The concentration of one's mind and of one's heart on God, which we define as contemplation, becomes the highest and fullest activity of the spirit, the activity which today, also, can and must order the immense pyramid of all human activities' (Paul VI, 7-XII-1965).

As the unifying act of all human movement towards God, the contemplative dimension is expressed by listening to and meditating on the Word of God; by participating in the divine life transmitted to us in the sacraments, particularly the Eucharist; by liturgical and personal prayer; by the constant desire and search for God and for his Will in events and people; by the conscious participation in his salvific mission; by self-giving to others for the coming of the Kingdom. There results, in the religious, an attitude of continuous and humble adoration of God's mysterious presence in people, events and things: an attitude which manifests the virtue of piety, an interior fount of peace and a bearer of peace to every sphere of life and apostolate.

All this is achieved in continual purification of heart under the light and guidance of the Holy Spirit, so that we can find God in all things and people and become the 'praise of his glory' (Eph. 1,6).

The very nature of consecrated life stands out in this way as the profound source which nourishes and unifies every aspect of the lives of religious.

2. 'The subject chosen for the *Plenaria* must, therefore, be considered of prime importance', the Holy Father said in his letter to the participants; 'and I am certain that from this meeting of yours there will result for all religious precious encouragement to persevere in the commitment to bear witness before the world to the primacy of the personal relationship with God. Strengthened by the directives which will issue from your meeting in Rome, they will not fail to dedicate with renewed conviction sufficiently long periods of time to prayer before the Lord to tell Him their love and, above all, to feel loved by Him'.[1]

3. In its examination of the theme, the plenary session has in mind Institutes of the active life and specifically contemplative ones (cf. PC 7–8). It is also concerned for new forms of religious life in which there is a notable desire for the contemplative life, and it hopes that their particular identity will become clearer in the ecclesial body for the service of the People of God.

II

GUIDELINES FOR INSTITUTES OF ACTIVE LIFE

A. Integration of activity and contemplation.
B. Renewed attention to life in the Holy Spirit.
C. Community animation.
D. Contemplative dimension in formation.
E. Developing the contemplative dimension in the local churches.

A. INTEGRATION OF ACTIVITY AND CONTEMPLATION

4. What Kind of 'Activity'?

For religious, it is not a question of any and every kind of activity. The Council speaks of 'apostolic and charitable activity' (PC 8), inspired and animated by the Holy Spirit. This is the only form of activity that 'is of the very nature of religious life' since a sacred ministry and a special work of charity have been consigned to the Institutes by the Church and must be performed in its name (cf. PC ibid.).

The special characteristic of this activity is that it is inspired by the love nourished in the heart of the religious, considered as the most intimate sanctuary of the person where grace unifies the interior life and activity.

It is necessary, then, to form a personal and communitarian awareness of the primary source of apostolic and charitable activity, as a lived participation in that 'mission' (of Christ and the Church) which begins with the Father (and requires that those who are sent exercise their awareness of love in the dialogue of prayer) (MR 16).

'In the case of religious of apostolic life, it will be a question of promoting integration between interiority and activity. Their first duty, in fact, is that of being with Christ. A constant danger for apostolic workers is to become so much involved in their work for the Lord, as to forget the Lord of all work' (Pope's message to the *Plenaria,* n. 2).

5. Renewal of Prayer

Prayer is the indispensable breath of every contemplative dimension. 'In these times of apostolic renewal, as always in every form of missionary engagement, a privileged place is given to contemplation of God, to meditation on his plan of salvation, and to reflection on the signs of the times in the light of the Gospel, so that prayer may be nourished and grow in quality and frequency' (MR 16). In this way, prayer, open to creation and history, becomes acknowledgement, adoration and constant praise of the presence of God in the world and its history and the echo of a life of solidarity with one's brothers and sisters, especially the poor and the suffering.

This prayer, personal and community, will come about only if the hearts of religious reach a high level of vitality and intensity in dialogue with God and in union with Christ, Redeemer of humanity (cf. PC 8;ET 10,42). Therefore, in the sometimes exhausting rhythm of apostolic commitments, there must be well-ordered and sufficiently prolonged daily and weekly periods of personal and community prayer. There must also be more intensive moments of recollection and prayer every month and throughout the year (cf. Synod of Bishops '71, AAS 63/1971, 913–914).

6. The Nature of Apostolic and Charitable Activity

The very nature of apostolic and charitable activity contains its own riches which nourish union with God. It is necessary to cultivate every day an awareness and deepening of it. Being conscious of this, religious will so sanctify their activities as to transform them into sources of union with God, to whose service they are dedicated by a new and special title (LG 44).

Moreover, a strengthening of the concrete apostolic spirituality of their own Institutes will help them still more to benefit from the sanctifying riches contained in every ecclesial ministry (cf. LG 41; PO 14; OT 9).

The Church's mission, to which the evangelical counsels unite religious in a special way (LG 44), can never, in fact, consist simply 'in the activity of the exterior life. . . The church's mission is by its very nature nothing else than the mission of Christ continued in the history of the world. It consists principally in sharing in the obedience of Him (cf. Heb. 5, 8) who offered Himself to the Father for the life of the world' (MR 15).

7. Constant Use of Appropriate Means

Constant use of the means which favour the contemplative dimension is an indispensable consequence of fidelity to the theological demands of every religious life, according to the special nature of each Institute. Among the means to be pursued there are some which are particularly suited for the achievement of a profound harmony between the active and contemplative dimensions.

This *Plenaria* indicates these in the following guidelines and appeals to the superiors of every Institute and to all religious to make careful use of them.

B. RENEWED ATTENTION TO LIFE IN THE HOLY SPIRIT

8. The Word of God

Listening to and meditating on the Word of God is a daily encounter with the 'surpassing knowledge of Jesus Christ' (PC 6; ES II, 16, 1). The Council 'warmly and insistently exhorts all the Christian faithful, especially those who live the religious life, to learn this sublime knowledge' (DV 25).

This personal and community commitment to foster the spiritual life more abundantly by giving more time to mental prayer (cf. ES II, 21) will be effective, actual and even apostolic if the

Word is heard not only in its objective richness, but also in the historical circumstances within which we live and in the light of the Church's teaching.

9. Centrality of the Eucharist

The celebration of the Eucharist and fervent participation in it, 'the source and apex of all Christian life' (LG 11), is the irreplaceable, enlivening centre of the contemplative dimension of every religious community (cf. PC 6; ET 47–48).

—Priest religious, therefore, will give a pre-eminent place to the daily celebration of the Eucharistic Sacrifice.

—Each and every religious should take an active part in it every day (SC 48) according to the concrete circumstances in which their community lives and works. 'That more perfect participation is highly recommended, by which the faithful, after the priest's communion, receive the Body of the Lord from the same Sacrifice' (SC 55; cf. ET 47; Synod of Bishops 1971).

'The commitment to take part daily in the Eucharistic Sacrifice will help religious to renew their self-offering to the Lord every day. Gathered in the Lord's name, religious communities have the Eucharist as their natural centre. It is normal, therefore, that they should be visibly assembled in their chapel, in which the presence of the Blessed Sacrament expresses and realizes what must be the principal mission of every religious family' (Pope's message to the *Plenaria,* n. 2; cf. ET 48).[2]

10. Renewal in the Celebration of the Sacrament of Reconciliation

The Sacrament of Reconciliation which 'restores and revives the fundamental gift of conversion received in Baptism' (Const. *Poenitemini,* AAS 68/1966/180) has a particularly important function for growth in the spiritual life. There can be no contemplative dimension without a personal and community experience of conversion.

This was stressed by this Sacred Congregation in its decree of December 8, 1970, in which it reminded religious and, in particular, superiors of the necessary means for a proper appreciation for this sacrament (cf. AAS 63/1971/318–319).

The Fathers of the *Plenaria* again appeal for:

—an appropriate and regular personal reception of this Sacrament;

—the ecclesial and fraternal dimension which is made more evident when this Sacrament is celebrated with a community rite (cf. LG 11;Const. *Poenitemini,* I, I, c), while the confession remains always a personal act.

11. Spiritual Direction

Spiritual direction, in the strict sense, also deserves to be restored to its rightful place in the process of the spiritual and contemplative development of religious. It cannot in any way be replaced by psychological methods. Therefore that *direction of conscience,* for which PC 14 asks *due liberty,* should be fostered by the availability of competent and qualified persons.

Such availability should come especially from priests who, by reason of their specific pastoral mission, will promote appreciation for spiritual direction and its fruitful acceptance. Superiors and directors of formation, who are dedicated to the care of the religious entrusted to them, will also contribute, although in a different way, by guiding them in discernment and in fidelity to their vocation and mission.

12. The Liturgy of the Hours

'The Divine Office, in that it is the public prayer of the Church, is a source of devotion and nourishment for personal prayer' (SC 90). It is 'designed to sanctify the whole course of the day' (SC 84).

The willingness with which religious communities have already responded to the Church's exhortation to the faithful of all walks of life to celebrate the divine praises shows how much they appreciate the importance of this more intimate participation in the Church's life (ES II, 20).

The contemplative dimension of the lives of religious will find constant inspiration and nourishment in the measure that they dedicate themselves to the Office with attention and fidelity. A greater appreciation of the spiritual riches in the Office of Readings could also help achieve this.

13. The Virgin Mary

The Virgin Mary is a model for every consecrated person and for participation in the apostolic mission of the Church (ET 56; LG 65). This is particularly evident when we consider the spiritual attitudes which characterized her:

—the Virgin Mary listening to the Word of God;
—The Virgin Mary at prayer *(Marialis Cultus,* 17–18, AAS 66/1974/128–219)—'a most excellent model of the Church in the order of faith, charity, and perfect union with Christ(LG

63), that is, of that interior disposition with which the Church, beloved spouse, is closely associated with her Lord, invokes him and through him, worships the Eternal Father' *(Marialis Cultus,* 16);

—the Virgin Mary standing courageously by the Cross of the Lord and teaching us contemplation of the Passion.

By reviving devotion to her, according to the teaching and tradition of the Church (LG 66–67; *Marialis Cultus,* 2nd and 3rd parts), religious will find the sure way to illuminate and strengthen the contemplative dimension of their lives.

'The contemplative life of religious would be incomplete if it were not directed in filial love towards her who is the Mother of the Church and of consecrated souls. This love for the Virgin will be manifested with the celebration of her feasts and, in particular, with daily prayer in her honour, especially the Rosary. The daily recitation of the Rosary is a centuries-old tradition for religious, and so it is not out of place to recall the suitability, beauty and efficacy of this prayer, which proposes for our meditation the mysteries of the Lord's life' (Pope's message to the *Plenaria,* n. 2).

14. Indispensable Personal and Community Asceticism

A generous asceticism is constantly needed for daily 'conversion to the Gospel' (cf. Const. *Poenitemini,* II–III, 1, c; Mark 1, 15). It would, therefore, seem indispensable for the contemplative dimension of every religious life also.

For this reason, religious communities must be manifestly praying and also penitential communities in the Church (cf. ES II, 22), remembering the conciliar guideline that penance 'must not be internal and personal only, but also external and social' (SC 110).

In this way, religious will also bear witness to the 'mysterious relationship between renunciation and joy, between sacrifice and opening of heart, between discipline and spiritual liberty' (ET 29). In particular, growth in the contemplative dimension certainly cannot be reconciled, for example, with indiscriminate and sometimes imprudent use of the mass-media; with an exaggerated and extroverted activism; with an atmosphere of dissipation which contradicts the deepest expectations of every religious life. 'The search for intimacy with God involves the truly vital need of silence embracing the whole being, both for those who must find God in the midst of noise and confusion and for those who are dedicated to the contemplative life' (ET 46).

'To achieve this, their entire being has need of silence, and this

requires zones of effective silence and a personal discipline to favour contact with God' (Pope's message to the *Plenaria*, n. 2).

All these means will be more effective and fruitful if they are
accompanied by the personal and communal practice of evangelical discernment; by a periodic and serious evaluation of activities; by the uninterrupted practice of an ever more profound
interpretation of the sacramental significance of everyday realities (events, persons, things), with the explicit aim of never allowing the activities of religious to be downgraded from their ecclesial level to a mere horizontal and temporal one.

C. COMMUNITY ANIMATION

15. The Religious Community

The religious community is itself a theological reality, an object
of contemplation. As 'a family united in the Lord's name' (PC
15; cf. Mt. 18:20), it is of its nature the place where the experience
of God should be able in a special way to come to fullness and be
communicated to others.

Acceptance of one another in charity helps 'to create an atmosphere favourable to the spiritual progress of each one' (ET
39).

For this very reason, religious need a 'place for prayer' in their
own houses, a place where the daily search for an encounter with
God, the source of unity in charity, finds constant reminders
and support. The real presence of the Lord Jesus in the Eucharist, devoutly reserved and adored, will be the living sign of that
communion which is daily built up in charity.

16. The Superior of the Community

According to the 'grace of unity' proper to every Institute (cf.
PC 8), the superior of the community exercises the dual role of
spiritual and pastoral animator (MR 13).

Those called to the ministry of authority should themselves
understand and then help others understand that in communities of consecrated persons, the spirit of service towards all the
members is an expression of the love with which God loves them
(PC 14).

This service of unifying animation demands, then, that superiors not be strangers to or indifferent to pastoral needs; neither
should they be absorbed merely in administrative duties. Rather
they should feel and in fact be accepted primarily as guides for
the spiritual and pastoral growth of each individual and of the
whole community.

D. THE CONTEMPLATIVE DIMENSION IN FORMATION

17. Religious Formation

The principal purpose of formation at its various stages, initial and ongoing, is to immerse religious in the experience of God and to help them perfect it gradually in their lives. With this in mind, there is need to 'duly emphasize the apostolate itself' (MR 27). The primary objective of active Institutes should be to integrate the interior life and the active life so that each religious will increasingly cultivate the primacy of life in the Spirit (MR 4), from which flows the grace of unity proper to charity.

The strongly ecclesial dimension of religious life (LG 44; ET 50; MR 10) demands that formation in every aspect be imparted in profound communion with the universal Church. This should be done in such a way that religious may be able to live their vocation in a concrete and effective way in the local church and for the local church to which they are sent, according to the mission of their Institute.

'By your vocation', the Pope said, 'you are for the universal Church; by your mission you are in a definite local church. Your vocation for the universal Church, then, is exercised within the structures of the local church. You must make every effort to carry out your vocation in the individual local churches, so as to contribute to their spiritual development, in order to be their special strength. Union with the universal Church through the local church: this is your way' (John Paul II, to Superiors General, 24–XI–1978).

18. Deepening the Knowledge of One's Institute

Knowing the special character (MR 11) of the Institute to which one belongs is an essential element in formation for the contemplative dimension.

Under this aspect also, it is important to implement that general principle of renewal which *Perfectae Caritatis* defines as 'a constant return to the sources'.

19. Solid Intellectual Formation

A solid intellectual formation, suited to the purposes of the vocation and mission of one's own Institute, is also basic for a balanced and rich life of prayer and contemplation. Therefore, study and updating are recommended as components of a healthy renewal of religious life in the Church and for society in our times (PC 2; c–d; ES II, 16). 'Studies should not be programmed with a view to achieving personal goals, as if they were a means of wrongly understood self-fulfilment, but with a view to responding to the requirements of the apostolic commitments of the religious family itself, in harmony with the needs of the Church' (MR 26).

20. The Need for Suitable Qualified Formation Personnel

Those who are responsible for formation need to have:
—the human qualities of insight and responsiveness;
—a well-developed experience of God and of prayer;
—wisdom resulting from attentive and prolonged listening to the Word of God;
—love of the liturgy and understanding of its role in spiritual and ecclesial formation;
—necessary cultural competence;
—sufficient time and goodwill to attend to the candidates individually, and not just as a group.

E. PROMOTION OF THE CONTEMPLATIVE DIMENSION IN THE LOCAL CHURCHES

21. The Bishop as 'Sanctifier of His Flock'

The pastoral ministry of the bishop, who is primarily concerned with sanctifying the church entrusted to him, highlights his mission: 'to sanctify his flock, zealously promoting the sanctity of the clergy, religious and laity, according to the vocation of each one' (CD 15; cf. MR 7).

For this reason, the pastors of the local churches will be mindful, especially in promoting the life of prayer and the contemplative dimension, that they are both 'sanctifiers' of their people (MR 7, 28) according to the vocation of each one and witnesses by their own personal sanctification (MR 9d).

Under this aspect, their pastoral care for vocations, including vocations to all forms of consecrated life, assumes greater importance (MR 32) together with their concern to ensure that already existing communities will not lack spiritual assistance.

Furthermore, there will be a more voluntary and faithful collaboration between religious and clergy if the bishop promotes an understanding and esteem for religious life as such, more than of the activities of the various Institutes (cf. MR 37). This will also better guarantee the preparation of qualified priests to support and accompany religious in their spiritual and apostolic lives according to the nature of religious life itself and the purpose of each Institute.

'On their part, women religious must be able to find in the clergy, confessors and spiritual directors capable of giving them help to understand and put into practice their consecration in a better way. The influence of priests is, moreover, very often a determinant in encouraging the discovery and subsequent development of the religious vocation' (Pope's message to the *Plenaria,* n. 4).

To achieve this, the study of the consecrated life in its various forms and under its various aspects appears necessary right from the initial stage of seminary education, so that diocesan clergy may have a complete ecclesial formation (cf. MR 30a, ibid. 49, 1).

22. Ecclesial Participation of Religious

Religious, on their part, must give witness that they effectively and willingly belong to the diocesan family (cf. CD 34). They will do this not only by being available for the needs of the local church according to the charism of their Institute (cf. CD 35; cf. MR passim), but even more so by sharing their spiritual experience with the diocesan priests and by facilitating prayer groups for the faithful.

'There is, furthermore, a particularly important matter which deserves to be mentioned today: that of the close relations between religious Institutes and the clergy regarding the contemplative dimension that every life dedicated to the Lord must have as its fundamental element. Diocesan priests need to draw from contemplation strength and support for their apostolate. As in the past, they must normally seek help from experienced religious and from monasteries that should be ready to receive them for spiritual exercises and for periods of meditation and renewal' (Pope's message to the *Plenaria,* n. 4). Besides, their participation in prayer experiences promoted by the local church could contribute to the growth and enrichment of the spiritual life of the whole Christian community (cf. MR 24, 25).

23. Co-responsibility and Harmonious Collaboration

Co-responsibility, harmonious collaboration and the spiritual growth of the local church will be greatly helped by periodic meetings between bishops and superiors of religious Institutes in the diocese, and likewise by the creation of well-ordered, appropriate structures at the level of Episcopal Conferences and Conferences of Religious (cf. CD 35, 5-6; ES II; 42-43; ET 50; MR 29, 36, 50, 54, 56, 59, 62, 65).

III

GUIDELINES FOR SPECIFICALLY CONTEMPLATIVE INSTITUTES

24. Importance of Such Institutes

The *Plenaria* recognises the fundamental importance of Institutes of men and women dedicated to the specifically contemplative life. It is very happy to express its esteem and appreciation for what they represent in the Church. Of its nature, the Church has the characteristic of being 'zealous in action and dedicated to contemplation', so that 'in it the human is directed towards and subordinated to the divine, the visible to the invisible, action to contemplation' (SC 2). Convinced of the special function of grace that these Institutes have among the People of God, the *Plenaria* exhorts them to continue faithfully to make the contribution of their specific vocation and mission to the universal Church and to the local churches to which they belong.

It exhorts them also to preserve and nourish their rich spiritual and doctrinal contemplative heritage which is a reminder and a gift to the world as well as a reply to the people of our times who are anxiously searching, even outside the Christian tradition, for contemplative methods and experiences which are not always authentic (cf. Pope's message to the *Plenaria*, n. 3).

25. Actuality of the Specifically Contemplative Life

Those called to the specifically contemplative life are acknowledged as 'one of the most precious treasures of the Church'. Thanks to a special charism, 'they have chosen the better part (cf. Lk 10, 12), that is prayer, silence, contemplation, exclusive love for God and complete dedication to his service... The Church relies a great deal on their spiritual contribution' (Pope's message to the *Plenaria*, n. 3).

For this reason, 'no matter how pressing may be the needs of the active ministry, these Institutes will always have an honoured place in the Mystical Body of Christ... For they offer to God an exceptional sacrifice of praise, they lend luster to God's people with abundant fruits of holiness, they motivate this people and by their hidden apostolic fruitfulness they make this people grow' (PC 7). Therefore, they should live in a realistic way the mystery of the desert to which their *exodus* has brought them. It is the place where, even in the struggle with temptation, heaven and earth, according to tradition, seem to meet; the world rises from its condition of arid earth and becomes paradise anew...

and humanity itself reaches its fullness' (VS, III AAAS 6 1/1969/68 1).

For this reason it could be said that 'if contemplatives are in a certain way in the heart of the world, still more so are they in the heart of the Church' (ibid.) Indeed, the decree *Ad Gentes* affirmed that the contemplative life means belonging to the fullness of the Church's presence, and it appealed for its establishment everywhere in the missions (18, 40).

26. The Apostolic Mystery of Such Institutes

The way of life of these Institutes — 'a particular way of living and expressing the paschal mystery of Christ which is death ordained towards resurrection' (VS, I) — is a special mystery of grace which manifests the Church's holiness more clearly as a 'praying community' which, with its Spouse, Jesus Christ, sacrifices itself out of love for the Father's glory and the salvation of the world.

Their contemplative life, then, is their primary and fundamental apostolate, because it is their typical and characteristic way in God's special design to be Church, to live in the Church, to achieve communion with the Church and to carry out a mission in the Church. In this perspective which fully respects the primary apostolic purpose of the cloistered life, in which contemplative religious give themselves to God alone (cf. PC 7), they offer assistance — without prejudice to enclosure and the laws that govern it — to persons in the world and share with them their prayer and spiritual life in fidelity to the spirit and traditions of their Institute (cf. MR 25).

27. Necessity for Appropriate Formation

It must be emphasized that there is need for appropriate initial and ongoing formation for their vocation and their contemplative life of seeking God 'in solitude and silence, in constant prayer and willing penance' (PC 7). There must be a serious effort to base this formation on biblical, patristic, liturgical, theological and spiritual foundations, and to prepare persons who are qualified to form others.

Special attention must be given to the developing churches and to monasteries in isolated localities and in need of the special help and means to accomplish this. In collaboration with the Sacred Congregation for Eastern Churches, ways and means should be studied to give effective help to those monasteries in the area of formation (formation teams, books, correspondence courses, tapes, records...).

28. Esteem and Sensitivity in Relationships

The relations of the bishop as pastor, guide and father with contemplative monasteries, already stressed in a previous *Plenaria,* require continuing study of the various aspects of the matter so that, with the help of the hierarchy, the presence and mission of these monasteries in the particular churches may be truly a grace which reflects the diversity of charism in the service of all the People of God.

The Fathers of the *Plenaria* also recommended that bishops seek to promote an understanding and an esteem for the specifically contemplative life among priests (even from their seminary formation, cf. OT 19; MR 30b) and among the faithful. This way of life does not make those called to it 'aloof from the rest of humanity. . . . In solitude where they are devoted to prayer, contemplatives are never forgetful of their brothers and sisters. If they have withdrawn from frequent contact with them, it is not because they are seeking their own quiet comfort, but to share more universally in the fatigue, sufferings, and hopes of all humanity' (VS III).

29. Papal Enclosure

The *Plenaria* expresses its esteem for monasteries of nuns of *papal enclosure.* If separation from the world is of the essence of the contemplative life, this enclosure is an excellent sign and means of achieving that separation according to the spirit of the different Institutes. Therefore, the *Plenaria,* fully in accord with the request of the Second Vatican Council for a suitable renewal of norms which take into account the particular circumstances of time and place (PC 16), strongly exhorts those monasteries to preserve faithfully, according to the charism and traditions of each Institute, *the special separation from the world* which is a most appropriate means for promoting the contemplative life.

CONCLUSION

30. The Contemplative Dimension

The contemplative dimension is the real secret of renewal for every religious life. It vitally renews the following of Christ because it leads to an experiential knowledge of him. This knowledge is needed for the authentic witness to him by those who have heard him, have seen him with their own eyes, have contemplated him and have touched him with their own hands (cf. 1 Jn. 1, 1; Philip. 3,8).

The more open religious are to the contemplative dimension, the more attentive they will be to the demands of the Kingdom, intensely developing their theological depth, because they will look on events with the eyes of faith. This will help them to discover the Divine Will everywhere. Only those who live this contemplative dimension will be able to see the salvific plan of God in history and to accomplish it in an effective and balanced way.

'Your houses should be especially centres of prayer, of recollection, of dialogue—personal and, above all, communitarian—with him who is, and must remain, the primary and principal Person with whom you converse in the busy round of your daily lives. If you succeed in cultivating this atmosphere of intense and loving union with God, you will be able to carry out, without traumatic tensions or dangerous aberrations, that renewal of life and discipline to which the Second Vatican Council has called you' (John Paul II, November 24, 1978).

---

* Text put out by the congregation, corrections by A.F. Italian text in INF. SCRIS, Supplemento, 32–50.
1. Cf. Osservatore Romano, March 8, 1980.
2. For a deeper understanding and evaluation of the 'mystery and cult of the Most Holy Eucharist', it will be to the advantage of all religious to reread and reflect on the Letter of John Pul II to all the bishops of the Church (Holy Thursday, 1980).
 Likewise and especially from a formative point of view, it will be necessary to consider seriously the Instruction on liturgical formation in seminaries which was issued by the Sacred Congregation for Catholic Education on June 3, 1979, and the Circular Letter of the same Congregation, dated January 6, 1980, on some 'Aspects of Spiritual Formation in Seminaries'.
Cf. also the Instruction of the Sacred Congregation for the Sacraments and Divine Worship, *Inaestimabile Donum,* on some norms concerning the cult of the Eucharistic Mystery, April 3, 1980.

94

RELIGIOUS AND HUMAN ADVANCEMENT*

S.C.R.S.I., *Le scelte evangeliche*, January, 1981

INTRODUCTION

It is a matter of importance and urgency that religious be effectively involved in the integral advancement of humankind.

The 'signs of the times' offer an incentive for the renewal of the evangelical options of the religious life. Unmistakable phenomena, the mark of modern times, they demand careful consideration by the Church in its mission in the modern world. They indicate areas for preferential treatment in evangelization and human advancement.

The teaching of the Church shows with increasing clarity the deep links between the evangelical demands of its own mission and the obligation laid on all people to foster human advancement and to build a society worthy of humans.

For the Church, to evangelize is to carry the good news to all sections of humanity and by its influence to transform humanity itself from within: the criteria of judgment, the dominant values, the sources of inspiration, the life-styles, opening them to an integral vision of humanity.[1]

The accomplishment of this mission requires of the Church the scrutiny of the signs of the times, interpreting them in the light of the gospel, thus responding to the perennial human questions.[2]

Religious are called upon to bear special witness to this prophetic dimension. The counsels of the Lord stimulate and encourage in religious the continuing conversion of heart and the freedom of the spirit which serve to remind their contemporaries that the building of the earthly city cannot but be based on the Lord and directed towards him.[3] Since the profession of the counsels establishes especially close links between religious and the Church[4] it is to them that an increasingly insistent and confident appeal is made for well-judged renewal, open to people's needs, their problems, their searchings.[5]

The Church is conscious that, aside from the social and political dramas, it was sent above all to give decisive answers to the deep questions of the human heart.[6]

Thus, the most recent documents of the magisterium endeavour effectively to integrate evangelization and human advancement and they indicate how fruitful, in the over-all mission of the Church, is the rapport between evangelization and religious life[7] and how much the work of religious has contributed in every age to people's human and spiritual advancement.[8]

A profound change of mentality and behaviour[9] is needed, however, when the object of evangelical commitment is the frequently explosive problems of human advancement in the concrete.

This path of conversion, affecting people and involving choosing between apostolic initiatives and activities, has led inevitably to moments of uncertainty and difficulty.

Besides, the renewal of theology which in different parts of the world went hand in hand with the praiseworthy effort to participate in life's complex realities revealed on the one hand positive and stimulating insights, but on the other hand shallow and questionable opinions.

The reflections of the Synod on Evangelization in the Modern World (1974) and later the apostolic exhortation *Evangelii Nuntiandi* offered valuable clarifications and guidelines.

Religious have encountered special problems and difficulties when they have attempted to intervene more decisively in areas which are more affected by injustice and oppression. The attempt to find solutions has been made more difficult still by division of opinion in the Church and in religious institutes themselves.

Further, changing social and political contexts were creating new and often unexpected situations. Religious have faced difficult challenges with regard to their traditional modes of presence and of their apostolic options. The need for greater solidarity with their contemporaries, especially with the poor and the marginalized, drew religious into more direct involvement even in the world of work and in politics.

The importance and the urgency of an effective participation by religious in work for integral human advancement persuaded the Sacred Congregation for Religious and for Secular Institutes to make a special study of the role of religious in this regard within the mission of the Church.

The intention was to encourage the generous quest for renewal and to offer, in the light of the facts and of experience, criteria for judgment drawn from the magisterium of the Church, the nature and mission of religious life and the objectives of an evangelization intimately linked with contemporary human advancement.

The Congregation's plenary session of 25–28 April was devoted to an examination of a series of questions arising from a wide-ranging international survey involving the collaboration of episcopal conferences, papal representatives, many male and female religious institutions and the conferences of male and female major superiors.

Four problems, in particular, were submitted to the consideration of the plenary session.

1. The option for the poor and for justice today.
2. The social activities and work of religious.
3. Involvement in the 'world of work'.
4. Direct involvement in politics.

The resulting guidelines are intended mainly as a contribution to the task of communication, formation and co-ordination which falls to those with responsibility for religious life in the Church.

They have the task of setting criteria and options which, while taking note of the principles and guidelines assembled here, take into account also the diversity and complexity of the different situations; in such wise that episcopal conferences and conferences of religious will be able, by whatever means they deem most suitable, to make more effective the role of religious in the common task of evangelization and human advancement.

The pastoral teaching of John Paul II, offering new matter for reflection and new stimulus, has subsequently clarified and defined the presence of the Church in the world and its involvement with the world's contemporary history. It puts in relief the present attention being given both to human problems and to that encounter with Christ and with his Gospel for which there is no substitute.

We feel encouraged to determine the direction of a path of evangelization and of human advancement which religious have taken in the Church, in virtue of their new and special consecration to God and to his design for human history.

I
FOUR MAIN PROBLEMS

1. A constant in the renewal of religious life would appear to be the impulse towards an increasing and active involvement in the contemporary development of the Church's mission:

Where religious are called upon to carry out a social mission, but one which is also profoundly religious, using the resources of their institute or of the local Church.

Where the situation demands new initiatives which are more relevant to the people's lives and problems.

In every situation, however, careful thought must be given to identifying criteria and common options.

For this reason, commencing with the four main problems disclosed by the survey, we wish to draw attention to some important points for making an evaluation and laying down guidelines.

It will then be easier to indicate the general principles of discernment.

THE OPTION FOR THE POOR AND FOR JUSTICE TODAY

2. The prophetic mission of Christ 'sent to preach the good news to the poor' (Luke 4:18) finds a strong echo in today's Church.

This is evident in numerous pontifical statements and in the clear and illuminating passages of the Pastoral Constitution on the Church in the Modern World, *Gaudium et Spes*, which urge a closer relationship between the Church and the lives of the people. The 1971 Synod of Bishops, in its document 'Justice in the World' emphasized the urgent need for awareness of this dimension of the Church's evangelizing mission.

The apostolic exhortation, 'Evangelization Today', *Evangelii Nuntiandi,* drove the point home, calling on all of the People of God to accept their own responsibility to reach out to the lives and situations of the 'peoples ... striving with all their power and energy to overcome all those circumstances which compel them to live on the border line of existence.'[10]

3. The themes of 'evangelical liberation', based on the kingdom of God,[11] ought therefore to be especially familiar to religious.

In fact, the witness of religious who have courageously taken part in the support of the lowly and in the defence of human rights, is an effective echo of the Gospel and of the voice of the Church. We have already noticed, however, that the interpretation put subsequently on such activity and the reaction to it, whether within the local Church or religious community, or from civil society, have not always shown the same sensitivity and concern.

4. It seems desirable, therefore, to look for some guiding principles to ensure that the option for the poor and concern for justice will be in harmony with the purpose and the style of the Church's mission and, within it, of religious life.

a. Religious frequently find themselves living very close indeed to the dramas which torment those to whose evangelical service they are consecrated. The very prophetic character of religious life demands of them that they be 'the living expression of the Church's aspiration to respond to the more exigent demands of the beatitudes.'[12] They are 'often to be found in the most remote mission stations where they may have to endure great dangers to health and even to life.'[13]

b. This sincere desire to serve the Gospel and to work for integral human advancement requires that at the centre of every undertaking there be communion, to be built with patience and perseverance, seeking the truth in charity.

c. Conferences of religious can, while respecting the charism of each institute, provide precious stimulus and balance in this regard, in collaboration with episcopal conferences[14] and in particular with Justice and Peace commissions and with Cor Unum. This will help to avoid the questionable stances either of a professed and not genuine neutrality or of a narrow, doctrinaire attitude.[a] It will, furthermore, provide an adequate forum for achieving mutual understanding between different cultures and temperaments, different social and political systems and for reaching a consensus, thus guaranteeing greater effectiveness.[b]

d. This presence for the defence and promotion of justice ought to be particularly alert and active in those agonising areas of 'injustice without a voice' of which the Synod of 1971 speaks.[15]

In fact, while certain categories of people are able to form their own vigorous structures for protest and support, there is also an immense amount of suffering and injustice which evokes little response in the hearts of many of our contemporaries. There is the plight of the refugees, of people persecuted because of their political ideas or for professing the faith;[16] there is the violation of the right to be born; the unjustified limitations placed on human and religious liberty; the defective social structures which increase the sufferings of the old and of the marginalized. . . .

The Church wishes to be, for these especially, voice, conscience, commitment.[17]

e. The witness of religious for justice in the world implies, especially for them, a constant review of their life-options, of their use of property, of their pattern of relationships. Anybody who has the courage to speak to others of justice must first be seen by them to be just.[18]

And it is here that we have the challenging link between evangelization and human advancement, the fruit of that 'silent witness' which is described in *Evangelii Nuntiandi* number 69 as the first and most effective challenge to the world and to the Church itself.

In this context, the 'role in evangelization of religious men and women consecrated to prayer, silence, penance and sacrifice' is particularly effective in witness and in apostolic fruitfulness.[19]

In fact, the contemplative dimension which is common to all forms of religious life assumes an especial significance in them, showing that the religious life, in all its forms, far from alienating its members from society or making them useless to it, permits them rather to welcome all, at a deeper level, in the very charity of Christ.[20]

SOCIAL WORKS AND ACTIVITIES OF RELIGIOUS[c]

5. The many works and activities which, with their various charisms, are characteristic of the apostolate of religious are among the most important vehicles for the Church's mission of evangelization and human advancement.[21]

Hence the importance of the renewal of the religious life for the renewal of the Church itself and of the world.[22]

This is why *Evangelii Nuntiandi* number 31 urges that account be taken of the deep links between evangelization and human advancement. To forget this would be to ignore 'the Gospel's teaching on love of one's suffering and needy neighbour.'

6. Attentive to the signs of the times, religious will be able to discover and put into effect a new mode of presence in keeping with their Founders' creativity and with the original purpose of their own institutes.[23]

In this context, certain lines of renewal assume a particular importance:

a. The social works and activities which have always formed part of the apostolate of religious testify to their constant commitment to full human advancement.

Schools, hospitals, relief centres, schemes for serving the poor, for people's cultural and spiritual development, all these remain relevant. Not only that, properly updated they are often revealed as privileged instruments of evangelization, of witness and of true human advancement.

In the evangelical service which they render in so many works, and these are always needed, religious offer a convincing sign of the gift of a life totally available to God, to the Church and to their brothers and sisters. [24]

b. The Spirit is constantly inspiring new forms and institutions of religious life in response to the needs of the times and he also animates existing ones, renewing their capacity for involvement, in keeping with the changing ecclesial and social contexts.

c. The Church is open to new ministries, in a constant and orderly communal growth, and in it religious are able to uncover new forms of active participation, involving the Christian community increasingly in their activities and institutions. [25]

They will thus have the opportunity of enhancing their own charism as a singular facility for promoting ministries which harmonise with the apostolic and social purpose of their own institutes.

d. The participation of the laity in the works and activities has expanded with the development of the ecclesial dimension of co-responsibility in a common mission. With adequate preparation, this could be extended to the management of works which up to now have been entrusted exclusively to religious. [26]

e. Present social conditions, on the other hand, demand new forms of solidarity and sharing. In various places a process of civil transformation is tending to develop responsibility of all those who make up society, by means of structures and organisms of participation. All citizens are thus obliged to take an active part with regard to the problems of building of the social order.

Side by side with the more direct contribution of the laity, the witness and the experience of religious can make a real contribution here towards reaching solutions in harmony with Gospel criteria and with the pastoral directives of the Church. [27]

INVOLVEMENT IN THE WORLD OF WORK

7. The pastoral concern of the Church for the world of work

has been expressed in numerous pronouncements, which the encyclical *Mater et Magistra* reaffirms, setting them in the context of modern social and economic conditions.

Faced with such a vast sector of humanity, which strongly challenges the mission of the entire Christian community, religious feel a deeper need for solidarity and sharing. They feel that their choice of evangelical poverty itself places on them the obligation to accept the authentic values of the common law of work.[28]

8. The Magisterium of the Bishops has described in detail the reasons, objectives and conditions which should guide priests when choosing more binding forms of involvement in the world of work.[29]

Obviously, these directives apply also to religious who are priests. However, because of the nature of religious life and of its special links with the mission of the Church,[30] they apply analogously to all other religious, male and female, as well.

Further, the nature of the vocation and mission of religious suggest certain criteria which could motivate and guide their involvement in the world of work:

a. Dynamic fidelity to the purposes for which the Spirit brought about their institutes in the Church.[31]

b. The investigation of the witness given by the values of the gospel which restore its dignity to work and assert its true purpose.[32]

c. A commitment to strengthening the *religious* dimension of their lives, thus demonstrating the attraction of the kingdom of God which they have experienced in all its radicality.[33]

d. Brotherly and sisterly sharing, sustained and developed by daily experience of community, showing the newness of the love of Christ in building up solidarity among people.[34]

9. There is also need for detailed guidelines with regard to choice and behaviour, in keeping with the modes of participation themselves.

In fact, there are two modes of involvement in the world of work, each of them deserving consideration.

I. Taking on a profession, subject to the same social and economic conditions as are other citizens (in schools, hospitals, etc.).

In some countries this is imposed by changed political conditions, such as nationalization and therefore the administration of the work by the state. Sometimes it is prompted by legislative renewal of the internal needs of the religious institute to opt for a presence equivalent to that of lay people in order to carry out their apostolic activity. Also, the quest for new modes of presence has led to insertion in the ordinary social structures.

In every case, concern for the achievement of the over-all objective of the religious life and of the particular objective of the individual institute demand that these new situations be faced with community needs in mind and in a spirit of obedience and religious poverty.

A civil profession commits religious more precisely as individuals, making them more dependent on external organisms and institutions and establishing a new relationship between work and salary. These are some of the aspects which the authorities in an institute should take into account when considering such options. For they demand a capacity for discernment sufficient to safeguard and enhance the religious objective for which they are undertaken.

II. Involvement in a workers' milieu presents its own problems side by side with the values which it is meant to realize. Worker religious enter a world with its own laws, tensions and, nowadays especially, its own powerful pressures from prevailing ideologies and from trade union conflicts which are sometimes tense and questionable.

Consequently, it can happen that their involvement with the workers in order to witness to the Church's pastoral concern[35] can lead religious into sharing a view of humanity, of society, of history, of the very world of work itself which is at variance with the criteria of judgment and with the directives contained in the Church's social teaching. This is why such an undertaking requires special care and guarantees.[36]

10. Further, involvement in trade union activities requires a clear understanding of pastoral objectives, but also of the limitations and of the danger of exploitation that could ensue in the lives and activities of religious.

A few clarifications, therefore, must guide reflection on this matter:

a. In principle, there would not appear to be an intrinsic incompatibility between the religious life and social involvement, even in a trade union. Sometimes, involvement in trade union activity follows necessarily, by law, on involvement in the world of work. At other times, such involvement might be prompted by solidarity in the legitimate defence of just rights.[37]

b. Political involvement, however, frequently poses difficult problems. Such situations should be evaluated in the light of the criteria given in the section entitled 'Involvement in Politics'. Particular care must be taken in the face of ideologies which promote class struggle. In such cases the teaching of *Octogesima Adveniens* would be essential.

c. From experience gleaned up to now, it is possible to deduce certain principles of behaviour to guide such enterprises towards their objective and in the manner in which they are pursued. In a group as powerful in society as the workers, religious are bearers of human and Christian values which will at times oblige them to repudiate certain kinds of trade union activity or of political manoeuvre which are not in accord with justice, which is the sole reason for their involvement.

Within their own communities, also, these religious should be able to foster the values of communion, avoiding unacceptable polarization. Such an attitude will help the community towards balanced and credible options.

d. Another essential criterion which should guide the involvement of religious is the awareness that it is to the laity by vocation and mission that the duty of promoting solidarity and justice within secular structures belongs.[38] Their role of complementarity will be expressed, above all in this area, by their witness to and contribution towards an ever more adequate formation of the laity.

INVOLVEMENT IN POLITICS

11. Religious, generally speaking, have shown themselves to be aware that their involvement in human advancement is a service of the Gospel and of humanity and that it does not imply opting for an ideology or a political party. They see, rather, that to opt for an ideology or a political party would expose them to the risk of losing their identity as religious and as Christian apostles[39] and to a dangerous tendency to absolutize ideas and means, thus becoming an easy prey to exploitation.

12. Some guiding principles, in harmony with the Magisterium, seem needed to throw light on a matter which is of itself controversial and at times confusing.

a. "Politics" can be understood in a wider and fuller sense as the dynamic organization of the whole of society. Understood in this way, it is something in which all citizens should be involved, actively and responsibly. In this regard, the work and activities of religious assume a profound significance. They serve to stimulate and to express their commitment to that cultural and social transformation which contributes to human advancement.

b. However, if "politics" means direct involvement in a political party (what is called 'party politics'), this can be assessed only in the light of the purpose of the vocation and mission of religious in the Church and in society.

> 1. Religious ought to be mindful of the worth of the contribution they make through the power of their witness and the variety of their apostolic enterprises. They should thus not permit themselves to be deluded into thinking that they will have greater influence on the development of individuals and of peoples if they change their role to a political one, in the strict sense.[40]

> 2. To establish the kingdom of God in the very structures of the world, inserting evangelical animation in human history, is certainly a theme of great interest for all Christians and therefore for religious too, but not in the sense that they themselves become directly involved in party politics. Through their schools and colleges, the communications media and their many religious and educational enterprises, they themselves can actively contribute to the formation of young people, especially, making them architects of human and social advancement. The repercussions of their apostolate will certainly be felt in the political sector too. This will not be an attempt to dominate, but rather to participate in that service of human society for which the entire Church was sent by Christ. (Lk. 22:25–27)

> 3. It is in this context that encouragement is to be given to women religious when they collaborate in the advancement of women in those areas of public life which best accord with their nature and qualities.[41]

> 4. In this way, with their witness and their activities, religious will gain credibility as 'gospel experts', contributing as such to the healing and the building of society, refraining from adopting political positions, presenting themselves not as party men or women, but as instruments of peace and of fraternal solidarity.

In fact, because the choice they have made is a forceful assertion of the primacy of the love of God,[42] religious put
themselves forward as men and women of the Absolute in the
dynamism of a Church athirst for the divine absolute.[43] They
are called to promote and signify this fundamental choice
among the people of God, a choice which stimulates and affects all other choices.

5. Active involvement in politics, then, is something to be
undertaken by way of exception, because others are not
available, and it needs to be measured according to special
criteria.[44] When extraordinary circumstances should require
such involvement, each case can be examined so that, with the
approval of the local Church and of the religious institute,
decisions can be made which benefit the ecclesial and civil
communities. But priority must be given always to the mission
and methods of the Church and of religious life.

GENERAL CRITERIA OF DISCERNMENT

13. Four great loyalties, basically, motivate the role of
religious in human advancement, in accordance with the conciliar principles for renewal[45] and taking into account the problems described to date:

Fidelity to humanity and to our times.
Fidelity to Christ and to the Gospel.
Fidelity to the Church and to its mission in the world.
Fidelity to religious life and to the charism of one's institute.

PRESENT TO HUMANITY AND TO OUR TIMES

14. The cultural, social and political changes which have affected, at times adversely, peoples and continents spur the
Church to an evangelical response to the wide range of the
aspirations and hopes of humanity.[46]
This intense pastoral concern was reinforced by the discussions and objectives of the Second Vatican Council and has re-
emerged in the Synods of Bishops and in papal exhortations.[47] It
is a clear and insistent call to the Christian community to
courageous renewal, so as to put modern men and women in
touch with the source of all authentic human and social advancement, the Gospel.[48]

15. The story of the contemporary world, given flesh in the
lives of men and women, becomes a book open for intense

meditation by the Church and by all its members, whatever their vocation, urging them to a radical renewal of lives and of commitment.[49]

Religious, because their own calling is itself radical, feel more profoundly challenged. They know that their own conversion to God's original plan for humanity, as revealed in the New Man, Jesus Christ, will be the measure of their contribution to hastening in others that conversion of mind and attitudes which will make more true and stable the reform of economic, social and political structures, ensuring a more just and peaceful society.[50]

16. All religious institutes are urged that, with a view to this, as they endeavour to renew their witness and mission, they should provide their members with 'a proper understanding of humanity, of the conditions of the times and of the needs of the Church, this to the end that, making wise judgments about the contemporary world in the light of faith, and burning with apostolic zeal, they may be able to help men and women more effectively.'[51]

BY THE TRANSFORMING POWER OF CHRIST AND THE GOSPEL

17. The Gospels bear witness to Christ and to the fidelity with which he fulfilled the mission for which he was consecrated by the Spirit.[52] It was a mission of evangelization and human redemption which led him to live among his people, sharing their lot, but illuminating and directing it, preaching and witnessing to the Gospel of conversion to the *kingdom of God*.[53]

His startling proposal of the "Beatitudes" introduced a radical change of perspective in evaluating temporal reality and human and social relations. He wished them to be centred on a justice-sanctity animated by the new law of love.[54]

His life options should be especially characteristic of religious, who make their own the "form of life which the Son of God embraced when he came into the world".[55]

18. Faithful to this *supreme norm*,[56] religious know that they are caught up daily in a path of conversion to the *kingdom of God*, which makes them in the Church and before the world a sign capable of attracting and inspiring a profound revision of life and values.[57]

This is, without doubt, the most necessary and fruitful *commitment* to which they are called,[58] even in those areas where the Christian community works for human advancement and for the development of social relations inspired by principles of solidarity and fraternal communion.

In this way, they cooperate in "safeguarding the originality of Christian liberation and the energies that it is capable of developing—liberation in its full, profound sense, as Jesus proclaimed and accomplished it."[59]

19. The power of transformation which is contained in the spirit of the Beatitudes and penetrates dynamically the life of religious, characterizes their vocation and mission.[60] For them the first beatitude and primary *liberation* is the encounter with Christ, poor among the poor, testifying that they really believe in the preeminence of the kingdom of God above all earthly things and in its highest demands.[61]

By spreading in this way the Christian and profoundly human meaning of the realities of history, which finds its origin in the Beatitudes, now become the criterion for life, religious show how close is the bond between the Gospel and human advancement in society. For this reason, the Church can point to the evangelical witness of religious as a splendid and singular proof that the way of the Beatitudes is the only one capable of "transforming the world and offering it to God".[62]

IN THE ORGANIC ECCLESIAL COMMUNION

20. The common vocation of Christians to union with God and union with each other for the salvation of the world[63] should be considered before diversity of gifts and ministries.

On this common vocation is based the communion between the ecclesial components and, especially, with those whom the Holy Spirit has chosen as Bishops to nourish the Church of God.[64]

21. Religious, united more intimately to the Church,[65] participate in their very own way in the sacramental nature of the People of God;[66] and, in the local churches, they belong in a special way to the diocesan family.[67]

The conciliar decree on the *Pastoral Office of Bishops* pays special attention to the role of religious. It places them among the cooperators with the bishop inasmuch as they attend to pastoral needs, each of them in conformity with the purposes of his or her own Institutes.[68]

22. The identity of religious life and of its specific role is further clarified by the pluriformity and complementarity of vocations and ministries in the Church.

It is necessary, therefore, to know and appreciate the duties that pertain to each of the components: the hierarchical ministry, consecrated life in its various forms, the laity.

Thus the exercise of one's own function unfolds in a constant search for fraternal convergence and mutual complementarity, which is at once an affirmation of one's own identity and of ecclesial communion.

23. This is a general criterion of discernment, more obvious when there is a clear awareness of the roles of the various groups in the Church and when their complementary aspects are taken into account.

It is the special function of the laity to seek the kingdom of God in dealing with temporal affairs and ordering them as God wishes.[69]

The *secular* nature of some Institutes, among the various forms of consecrated life, permits a more direct presence and a fuller involvement in secular realities and structures. In these Institutes, on this account called *secular*, the members individually exercise their specific apostolate in whatever context is appropriate, thus strengthening the structures of the world.[70]

On the other hand, religious, by their choice of life, limit their participation in secular structures, but do not alienate themselves from the actions of the other members of the Church in building the secular city as a place capable of receiving the kingdom of God.[71] However, they are present to it in their own special way, not by substituting for other groups in the Church either in duties or methods, but by becoming an increasingly radical sign of an evangelical way of life and of involvement through the public witness of their profession which is carried out communally in all its dimensions.

If religious participate in the ministerial priesthood, they are, by this new title, exhorted to preside over and serve the ecclesial community, thus giving a more striking witness of communion.[72]

24. *Experts in communion,* religious are, therefore, called to be an ecclesial community in the Church and in the world, witnesses and architects of the *plan for unity* which is the crowning point of human history in God's design.[73]

Above all, by the profession of the evangelical counsels, which frees one from what might be an obstacle to the fervor of charity, religious are communally a prophetic sign of intimate union with God, whom they love above all things.[74]

Furthermore, through the daily experience of communion of life, prayer and apostolate—the essential and distinctive elements of their form of consecrated life[75]—they are *a sign of fraternal fellowship*. In fact, in a world frequently very deeply divided and before their brethren in the faith, they give witness to the possibility of a community of goods, of fraternal love, of a program of life and activity which is theirs because they have accepted the call to follow more closely and more freely Christ the Lord who was sent by the Father so that, firstborn among many brothers and sisters, he might establish a new fraternal fellowship in the gift of his Spirit.[76]

25. From their communitarian way of living flows that form of presence and involvement which should characterize them in the Church's mission and which we now emphasize in view of the options concerning human advancement.

In speaking of the variety of gifts and ministries, it should be noted that the laity and members of secular Institutes can take on apostolic, social and political responsibilities as individuals in accordance with the purpose assigned them by the Spirit.

This is not the case with religious. They have freely and consciously chosen to participate completely in their mission of witness, presence and apostolic activity in obedience to the common purpose and to the superiors of their Institute. This participation expresses fraternity and support, especially when the apostolic mandate exposes religious to greater and more demanding responsibilities in the sphere of difficult social contexts.

26. The imperative need for the fundamental criterion of communion is rendered more urgent by the diversity of situations in which Christians find themselves in the world, especially in the sociopolitical field.[77]

When it is a question of choices which, in an evangelization-human advancement context, necessarily involve both one's own community and the ecclesial community, there is the need always to bear in mind the directive of OA 4.[78]

27. The characteristic of *communion* should permeate the very structures of the common life and activity of religious. In virtue of this characteristic, the profoundly ecclesial nature of religious life becomes a preeminent aspect of their mission within the Church and within secular society itself.[79]

In this light, acknowledgement of the ministry of Bishops as the center of unity in the organic ecclesial communion, and the encouragement of a similar acceptance by the other members of the People of God, is a specific requirement of the special role of religious in the Christian community.

Nor should religious fear any obstacle to the generosity and creativity of their projects[80] from the hierarchical nature of this ecclesial communion,[81] because every sacred authority is given for the purpose of harmoniously promoting charisms and ministries.[82] Indeed, on the contrary, religious are encouraged[83] to be "enterprising in their undertakings and initiatives"; this is in keeping with the charismatic and prophetic nature of religious life itself.

Through their mission which is open to the universal Church and carried out in the local churches,[84] religious are most favorably placed to strengthen those forms of *suitable coordination* which *Mutuae Relationes* presents as the path to an organic ecclesial communion.[85]

IN DYNAMIC FIDELITY TO THEIR OWN CONSECRATION ACCORDING TO THE CHARISM OF THE FOUNDER

28. A renewed presence of religious in the Church's mission of evangelization and human advancement would not be fully authentic if they were to renounce, even in part, the characteristics of religious life and the special nature of the individual Institutes.[86] This requirement, which we have noted constantly, should be a serious obligation of religious communities.

29. It is a question of a dynamic fidelity which is open to the impulse of the Spirit, who speaks through ecclesial events, the signs of the times and through the constant exhortation of the Magisterium.

Made more watchful by being better informed of the needs of humanity today, its problems, searchings and hopes,[87] religious communities are better able to discern the true signs of God's presence and designs in the happenings and expectations which they share with the other members of the Church. Communal dialogue,[88] guided by faith, by reciprocal acceptance and respect for persons and by religious obedience, is the best way of carrying on this discernment. Precisely because religious communities of their nature are built on faith, they preserve and radiate that light which helps the whole People of God to identify the intentions of the Lord regarding the integral human vocation and to discover fully human solutions to all problems.[89]

30. The *burning question,* which ET 52 makes the apex of the apostolic exhortation on the renewal of religious life, rises like a cry from the heart, in which Paul VI expressed his intense pastoral concern, his great love for humanity and today's world and the confidence he placed in religious men and women.

It throws light on the concrete choices of renewal. Their urgency appeals for a fidelity capable of restoring to the present life and mission of each Institute the ardor with which the Founders were inflamed by the original inspirations of the Spirit.[90]

31. It is a constant reference to *life* in its dynamic profundity, as Pope John Paul II with enlightening words reaffirms:[91]

> to life as it presents itself to us today, bringing with it the riches of traditions of the past, to offer us the possibility of using them today.
>
> . . . we must be very searching in our discernment of how to help the religious vocation today towards self-awareness and growth; how religious life should function in the ensemble of the Church's life at the present time. We are still seeking the answer to this question—and rightly so. We can find it in the teaching of the Second Vatican Council; in the exhortation *Evangelii Nuntiandi;* and in the many statements of the Popes, the Synods and Episcopal Conferences. This answer is fundamental and many-sided.

> The Pope reaffirms his hopes for a religious life faithful to these principles, which make it "an immense fund of generosity" without which "the Church would not be fully itself."

> In an ever renewed fidelity to the charism of the Founders, Congregations should strive to be responsive to the Church's expectations, to the commitments which the Church and its pastors consider the most urgent at this time, to implement a mission which has so much need of well-prepared workers.[92]

II

FORMATION REQUIREMENTS

32. The problems facing religious life in its renewal so that there may be a harmony between evangelization and human advancement have repercussions on the formation level.

This might require a revision of formation programs and methods at the initial period as well as during the successive phases and during ongoing formation.

In this regard, a re-reading of the conciliar criteria for renewal[93] will show that it is not a question of simple adaptations of certain external forms. It is a deep education in attitude and in life style which makes it possible to remain true to one's self even in new forms of presence. This presence will always be *as consecrated persons* who seek the full conversion of people and society to the ways of the Gospel through witness and services.[94]

33. In this regard, some aspects of formation seem to merit special attention.

a. There is need to assure an awareness of the profound nature and characteristics of religious life, both in itself and in its dynamic involvement in the mission of the ecclesial community in today's society. Fidelity to the charism of the Institute and a creative involvement in a renewal of activities and work are also among the more important elements of initial and ongoing formation.

b. The profession of the evangelical counsels, in the context of religious life-Church-modern world, may require new attitudes which are attentive to the value of prophetic sign as a power for the conversion and transformation of the world, of its mode of thinking and of its relationship.[95]

c. Life in common, seen especially as an experience and witness of *communion*, develops the capacity for adaptation[96] permitting a response to different forms of activity. These do not weaken fraternal bonds and sharing of the Institute's specific service to the Church. In fact, with this attitude, these bonds could be strengthened.

d. New forms of involvement, which have been described in examining the above problems, could possibly create unforeseen situations. This calls for a spiritual and human preparation in the formation programs of religious life which can help to achieve a mature presence on the part of consecrated persons, capable of renewed relationships, both within and outside their own communities.

Involvement in the life of the Church and in its mission, in an attitude of co-responsibility and complementarity, implies an up-to-date knowledge of its projects and the goals it hopes to attain.[97]

From the teaching of the Second Vatican Council and from the insistence with which the Synods of Bishops have referred to the matter, it is clear that there can be no dichotomy between formation for the permanent gospel commitment and human advancement according to God's plan. Therefore, a program of formation and renewal in religious Institutes would not be adequate and complete unless it took into account the Church's thinking in this matter.[98]

This is even more necessary if religious are to be capable of their apostolic duty of *reawakening consciences*,[99] of forming other Christians, particularly the laity, in such a way that they will assume their proper role in this common mission of evangelization and human advancement with competence and security.[100]

Since the *missionary* dimension of the Church depends especially on the generous availability of religious,[101] the formation of those called to this excellent form of evangelization and human promotion will need to be genuinely adaptable to the cultures, sensibilities and specific problems of the localities.[102]

34. Chapters and General Curias assume considerable importance in the programming and animation for this updating and renewal in fidelity to the Spirit and to history. It is their duty:

—to discern the options which best respond today to the original purposes of the Institute,

—to guide the religious and communities by means of appropriate initiatives of information and formation,

—to promote, in thoughtful and substantive dialogue, a rethinking of works so as to motivate those who, perhaps, have done little updating and to encourage and direct the search for new and suitable appoaches.

All this aims at encouraging a more attractive and clear discovery of the values of consecration and mission which are basic for a conscious and joyful membership and participation in one's own Institute.

35. Conferences of Religious, because of their more immediate knowledge of ecclesial and social conditions, are in a better position to identify the problems of different countries and continents. Through an exchange of experiences and study meetings, they could, in collaboration with the Episcopal Conferences and respecting the various charisms, find solutions and means more in harmony with the hopes for integral human promotion. In all of this, let them always be inspired by the Gospel and guided constantly by the Magisterium of the Church.

* Translated by Austin Flannery, O.P. The Italian original is published in a special supplement to *Informationes S.C.R.I.S.*, the bulletin published by the Sacred Congregation for Religious and for Secular Institutes. An English translation has been published by the Congregation in the English edition of the bulletin, which is called 'Consecrated Life,' and in the English-language *Osservatore Romano*. This version has been compared with the Congregation's version and with the French version published in *Documentation Catholique*, 15 February, 1981. The title given to the document in the English version uses the admittedly

almost universally used 'human promotion' as a translation of 'promo-zione umana'. The translator, however, has opted for 'human advance-ment', since surely this is what one would naturally say in English. Foot-notes indicated alphabetically have been added by the translator.

1. *Evangelii nuntiandi* (hereafter EN) 18–19.

2. *Gaudium et Spes* (hereafter GS) 4: 'It is not, then, through oppor-tunism or a desire for novelty that the Church, expert in humanity, defends human rights. It is through authentic gospel commitment which, as in Christ's case, cares for the most needy.' John Paul II, Puebla, inaugural address, III, 3.

3. *Lumen Gentium* (hereafter LG) 46.

4. LG 44; *Mutuae Relationes* (hereafter MR) 8; 10.

5. *Evangelica Testificatio* (hereafter ET) 52–53.

6. GS 10.

7. EN 69.

8. *Populorum Progressio* (hereafter PP) 12.

9. ET 17; GS 63; ET 52.

10. EN 30.

11. EN 33–34.

12. EN 69; LG 31; MR 14a.

13. EN 69.

14. MR 59–60.

a. I take it that what the document regards as questionable is the claim to be neutral between the poor and an oppressive social system, though it is not clear to me whether it also implies that no such neutrality can be genuine, or is merely criticising simulated neutrality. Many in Latin America believe that neutrality can only be theoretical in this matter: to be neutral is in fact to side with the oppressive status quo. The Italian is: 'Si favorira, in tal modo, il superamento di posizioni ambigue, sia di una pretesa e fallace neutralita, come di settarismi univoci e totalizzanti.' The Congregation's English version reads: 'It would be possible in this way to overcome positions of ambiguity taken either from a supposed and false neutrality or from group prejudices.' [Tr.]

b. The Italian is 'che dona garanzia e più sicura efficacia.' [Tr.]

15. *Justice in the World*, III

16. EN 39.

17. 'The Pope wishes to speak for you, to be the voice of those who can-not speak and of those who have been silenced, an appeal for ac-tion. . . .' (John Paul II to the peasants of Latin America, January 29, 1979).

18. *Justice in the World,* III.

19. EN 69.

20. LG 46.

c. The Italian is 'Le attività e le opere sociali dei religiosi'. I have in-verted the order, solely because it seems to sound better in English. The English word 'works', used in this connection, has a wider meaning than 'activities'. It covers institutions, such as schools and hospitals, as well as organizations and enterprises.

21. *Perfectae Caritatis,* (hereafter PC) 1; LG 46.

22. ET 52.

23. MR 19; 23f; 41.

24. EN 69; Puebla document, nn. 733–734: Apostolic openness of ministries and a preferential choice of the poor are the most evident

tendencies in religious life in Latin America. In fact, more and more, religious men and women are to be found in the difficult and under-privileged areas... This choice does not presuppose the exclusion of anyone, but it does mean a preference for and nearness to the poor. This has brought about a rethinking of traditional works so as to make a better response to the demands of evangelization....

25. LG 9–12; 34–36; CD 33–35; EN 13; 58; AA 2,6–10.

26. Cf. document of the Sacred Congregation for Catholic Education, on the Catholic school (March 19, 1977), nn. 60–61: participation of the Christian community in the educative process of the Catholic school.

27. CD 35; MR 22–23.

28. PC 13; ET 20; cf. GS 67–72 concerning the human and Christian elements of work.

29. PO 8; OA 48. The document of the Synod of Bishops which treats of the ministerial priesthood (cf. *AAS*, 1971, p. 912–913, recalling PO 8, states that the priestly ministry is to be considered a function which is valid in itself, and, indeed, in the light of faith, is more excellent than others. If, in particular circumstances, other activities accompany this ministry, the criterion of suitability is to be sought in the resulting contribution to the pastoral ministry of the Church. It is especially the Bishop and his Council of priests that must decide having consulted, when necessary, the Episcopal Conference.

30. MR 10; LG 44.

31. Cf. ET 20: "But your activities cannot derogate from the vocation of your various Institutes, nor habitually involve work such as would take the place of their specific tasks". Cf. also the doc. of the Sacred Congregation for Catholic Education on the school, n. 74–76.

32. ET 20.

33. LG 44; PC 1; ET 3.

34. PC 15; ET 21; 39.

35. OA 48.

36. OA 48 and 50.

37. Cf. Puebla doc., nn. 1162–1163 and 1244 (discourse of John Paul II to workers).

38. LG 31; 33—*AA* 7; 13—GS 67; 68; 72.

39. GS 42; 76; Synod 1971, AAS, p. 932: Puebla doc, nn. 558–559.

40. Cf. discourse of John Paul II to the Union of Superiors General, November 24, 1978, in which he asked them to "interpret in the correct gospel sense the option for the poorer classes and for all victims of human selfishness, without giving way to sociopolitical radicalism... to draw close to the people without prejudice to their religious identity, and without dimming the specific originality of their own vocation". Cf. also Puebla doc., n. 528.

41. MR 49–50.

42. ET 1; PC 6.

43. EN 69; Puebla doc., nn. 527–529.

44. Cf. Synod 1971, AAS, p. 912–913: the criterion given for priests, as already mentioned for other forms of involvement in secular structures (n. 8), guides the behavior of religious also, due to the close links of religious life with the hierarchical apostolate (CD 34) and the special relationship which binds it to the pastoral responsibility of the Church (LG 45–46). In MR (nn. 5–10–36) the theological reasons are dealt with more at length and practical conclusions are drawn for ecclesial obedience and appropriate arrangement. Cf. also the Puebla doc, n. 769,

where the Pope's words are quoted: "You are religious and priests; you are not social or political leaders or officials of a temporal power. Therefore I tell you again: let us not be under the illusion that we are serving the Gospel if we try to dilute our charism by an exaggerated interest in the wide field of temporal problems" (AAS, LXXI, p. 193).

45. Cf. PC 2.

46. GS 9.

47. Cf. especially the Synods of 1971 and 1974; the apostolic exhortation *Evangelii Nuntiandi* which is complemented under the directly social and political aspects by *Octogesima Adveniens*.

48. Cf. Redemptor Hominis 14; "The church cannot abandon man... Man in the full truth of his existence, of his personal being and also of his community and social being. This man is the primary route that the Church must travel in fulfilling her mission".

49. GS 22; RH 8.

50. GS 63.

51. PC 2,d; MR 26–32.

52. Is. 42, 1–7; 61,1–4; Luke 4,17–19; cf. Puebla doc., n. 1130: "The evangelization of the poor was for Jesus one of the messianic signs, and for us too it will be a sign of gospel authenticity".

53. Mk. 1,15.

54. Mt. 5,3–12; 5,20. 43–48.

55. LG 44; PC 1.

56. PC 2,a.

57. LG 44; EN 69.

58. MR 16; 26–28.

59. John Paul II, Puebla, inaugural dis. III, 6; EN 9; 30–39; cf. also, in the same inaugural discourse, I, 2–5 the call to a solid christology and the unique Gospel, without minimizing or deforming interpretations, as the basis for our capacity to "serve man, our people, to impregnate their culture with the Gospel, to transform hearts, to humanize systems and structures". Cf. RH 11.

60. LG 31.

61. LG 44.

62. LG 31.

63. MR 4.

64. Acts 20,28; MR 5–9.

65. LG 44.

66. MR 10.

67. CD 34; the theological principles and criteria of application are described at length in the document *Mutuae Relationes*.

68. CD 33–35.

69. LG 31.

70. Motu Proprio *Primo Feliciter* AAS, 1948, p. 285; PC 11.

71. LG 46.

72. LG 28; GS 43; MR 36.

73. GS 19; 32—cf. Puebla doc., nn. 211–219; 721: "Consecrated life is evangelizing in itself in view of communion and participation".

74. LG 44.

75. PC 15; cf. Puebla doc., nn. 730–732.

76. GS 32.

77. OA 3.

78. "Confronted with such diverse situations, we read in OA 4, it is dif-

ficult to sum it up in one word or to propose a universally valid solution. It is for the Christian communities to analyse objectively the situation in their own country, clarify it in the light of the unchanging words of the Gospel, draw principles for reflection, criteria for judging and directives for action from the Church's social teaching. It is for the Christian community to discern, with the help of the Holy Spirit, in communion with the bishops concerned and in dialogue with the other Christian brethren and all men of good will, the choices and commitments that must be made to bring about the social, political and economic changes that are obviously needed in many cases. In looking for what changes ought to be made, Christians should firstly renew their trust in the power and originality of gospel demands" - cf. Puebla doc., n. 473.

79. "Religious should not only accept, but they should loyally strive for unbreakable unity of intention and action with the Bishops. There cannot and must not be any lack of collaboration, which is at once responsible and active, but also docile and trusting, on the part of religious, whose charism makes them so much more suitable ministers in the service of the Gospel" (John Paul II, inaug. disc. Puebla, II).

80. MR 5.
81. Ibid. n. 19; 41.
82. LG 10-12; 27; PO 9; AA 2.
83. EN 69.
84. LG 45-46; CD 33-35; cf. discourse of John Paul II to Superiors General, November 24, 1978.
85. MR n. 52 and f.
86. LG ch. 6; PC 2; MR nn. 11-12.
87. GS 1-10; ET 25.
88. PC 14; ET 25.
89. GS 11.
90. MR 23, f.
91. Discourse to Superiors General, November 24, 1978.
92. Discourse to UISG, November 16, 1978.
93. PC 2; 18—ES II, 15-19; 33-38.
94. PC 18.
95. ET 13-29—cf. Puebla doc., n. 476: "Our social behaviour is an integral part of our following of Christ".
96. PC 3; 15.
97. PC 2, c.
98. "With reference to this teaching, the Church has a mission to carry out: it must preach, educate persons and groups, form public opinion, give guidance to public authorities. Draw, then, from these genuine sources. Speak with the voice of experience, of the sufferings and hopes of contemporary humanity" (John Paul II, Puebla, inaugural discourse, III, 4).
99. ET 18.
100. The document on Justice in the World (Synod, 1971, AAS pp. 935-937), together with a synthesis of the Church's principal doctrinal statements, also gives directives for a commitment to an "education for justice".

And again, John Paul II (Puebla, inaug. dis., III, 7): "Allow me then to reveal the urgency of sensitizing the faithful to this social teaching of the Church. Special attention should be given to the formation of a social conscience at all levels and in all sectors. When injustices are on the increase and the gap between poor and rich is widening painfully, social teaching, creative and open to the wide fields of the Church's presence, should be an invaluable instrument of formation and action".

101. EN 69.
102. AG 18; 25–27.

95

ENCYCLICAL LETTER ON PRIESTLY CELIBACY*

Paul VI, *Sacerdotalis caelibatus*, 24 June, 1967

INTRODUCTION

Sacred Celibacy Today

1. Priestly celibacy has been guarded by the Church for centuries as a brilliant jewel, and retains its value undiminished even in our time when mentality and structures have undergone such profound change.

Amid the modern stirrings of opinion, a tendency has also been manifested, and even a desire expressed, to ask the Church to re-examine this characteristic institution of hers. It is said that in the world of our time its observance has come to be of doubtful value and almost impossible.

2. This state of affairs is troubling consciences, perplexing some priests and young aspirants to the priesthood; it is a cause for alarm in many of the faithful and constrains Us to fulfil the promise We made to the Council Fathers. We told them that it was Our intention to give new lustre and strength to priestly celibacy in the world of today.[1] Since saying this We have over a considerable period of time earnestly implored the enlightenment and assistance of the Holy Spirit and have examined before God opinions and petitions which have come to Us from all over the world, notably from many pastors of God's Church.

3. The great question concerning the sacred celibacy of the clergy in the Church has long been before Our mind in its deep seriousness: must that grave, ennobling obligation remain today for those who have the intention of receiving major orders? Is it possible or appropriate nowadays to observe such an obligation? Has the time not come to break the bond linking celibacy with the priesthood in the Church? Could the difficult observance of it not be made optional? Would this not be a way to

help the priestly ministry and facilitate ecumenical approaches? And if the golden law of sacred celibacy is to remain, what reasons are there to show that it is holy and fitting? What means are to be taken to observe it, and how can it be changed from a burden to a help for the priestly life?

4. Our attention has rested particularly on the objections which have been and are still made in various forms against the retention of sacred celibacy. In virtue of Our apostolic office We are obliged by the importance, and indeed complexity, of the subject to give faithful consideration to the facts and the problems they involve, at the same time bringing to them, as it is Our duty and Our mission to do, the light of truth which is Christ. Our intention is to do in all things the will of him who has called Us to this office and to show what We are in the Church, the servant of the servants of God.

Celibacy in the New Testament

5. It may be said that today ecclesiastical celibacy has been examined more penetratingly than ever before and in all its aspects. It has been examined from the doctrinal, historical, sociological, psychological and pastoral point of view. The intentions prompting this examination have frequently been basically correct although reports may sometimes have distorted them.

Let us look openly at the principal objections against the law that links ecclesiastical celibacy with the priesthood.

The first seems to come from the most authoritative source, the New Testament which preserves the teaching of Christ and the Apostles. It does not demand celibacy of sacred ministers but proposes it rather as a free act of obedience to a special vocation or to a special spiritual gift.[2] Jesus himself did not make it a prerequisite in his choice of the Twelve, nor did the Apostles for those who presided over the first Christian communities.[3]

6. The close relationship that the Fathers of the Church and ecclesiastical writers made over the centuries between the ministering priesthood and celibacy has its origin in a mentality and historical situation far different from ours. In patristic texts more frequently we find exhortations to the clergy to abstain from marital relations rather than those which recommend that they observe celibacy; and the reasons justifying the perfect chastity of the Church's ministers seem often to be based on an over-pessimistic view of man's earthly condition or on a certain

notion of the purity necessary for contact with sacred things. In addition, it is said that the old arguments no longer are in harmony with the different social and cultural milieus in which the Church today, through her priests, is called upon to work.

Objections Raised Against Celibacy

7.   Many see a difficulty in the fact that in the present discipline concerning celibacy the gift of a vocation to the priesthood is identified with that of perfect chastity as a state of life for God's ministers. And so people ask whether it be right to exclude from the priesthood those who do not wish to lead a life of celibacy, but, nevertheless, feel they have a vocation to fulfil the priestly office.

8.   It is asserted, moreover, that the maintaining of priestly celibacy in the Church does great harm in those regions where the shortage of the clergy—a fact recognized with sadness and deplored by the same Council[4]— gives rise to critical situations; that it prevents the full realization of the divine plan of salvation and at times jeopardizes the very possibility of the initial proclamation of the Gospel. Thus the disquieting decline in the ranks of the clergy is attributed by some to the heavy burden of the obligation of celibacy.

9.   Then there are those who are convinced that a married priesthood would remove the occasions for infidelity, waywardness, and distressing defections which hurt and sadden the whole Church. These also maintain that a married priesthood would enable Christ's ministers to witness more fully to Christian living, by including the witness of married life, from which they are excluded by their state of life.

10.   There are also some who strongly maintain that priests by reason of their celibacy find themselves in a situation that is physically and psychologically detrimental to the development of a mature and well-balanced human personality. And so it happens, they say, that priests often become hard and lacking in human warmth; that, excluded from sharing fully the life and destiny of the rest of their brothers, they are obliged to live a life of solitude which leads to bitterness and discouragement. Is all this perhaps indicative of unwarranted violence to nature and an unjustified disparagement of human values which have their source in the divine work of creation and have been made whole through the work of the redemption accomplished by Christ?

11.   Again, in view of the way in which a candidate for the

priesthood comes to accept an obligation as momentous as this, the objection is raised that in practice this acceptance results, not from an authentically personal decision, but rather from an attitude of passivity, the fruit of a formation that is neither adequate nor one that makes sufficient allowance for human liberty. For the degree of knowledge and power of decision of a young person and his psychological and physical maturity fall far below—or at any rate are disproportionate to—the seriousness of the obligation he is assuming, its real difficulties and its permanence.

12.   We well realize that there are other objections that can be made against priestly celibacy. It is a very complex question and one which touches intimately on the ordinary view of life, to which it brings the shining light of divine revelation. A never-ending series of difficulties will present themselves to those who 'cannot receive this precept',[5] and who do not know or who forget the 'gift of God',[6] and who are unaware of the higher logic of that new concept of life, its wonderful efficacy and abundant riches.

13.   The sum of these objections would appear to drown out the solemn and age-old voice of the pastors of the Church and of the masters of the spiritual life and to nullify the living testimony of the countless ranks of saints and faithful ministers of God, for whom celibacy has been the object of the total and generous gift of themselves to the mystery of Christ, as well as its outward sign. But no, this voice, still strong and untroubled, is the voice not just of the past but of the present too. Ever intent on seeing things as they are, we cannot close our eyes to this magnificent, wonderful reality: that there are still today in God's holy Church, in every part of the world where she exercises her beneficent influence, great numbers of her ministers—subdeacons, deacons, priests and bishops—who are living their life of voluntary and consecrated celibacy in the most exemplary way. Nor can we overlook the immense ranks of religious men and women at their side, of laity and of young people too, united in the faithful observance of perfect chastity. They live in chastity, not out of disdain for the gift of life, but because of a greater love for that new life which springs from the paschal mystery. They live this life of courageous self-denial and spiritual joyfulness with exemplary fidelity and also with relative facility. This magnificent phenomenon bears testimony to an exceptional facet of the kingdom of God living in the midst of modern society, to which it renders humble and beneficial service as the 'light of the

world' and the 'salt of the earth'.[7] We cannot withhold the expression of Our admiration: the spirit of Christ is certainly breathing here.

The Law of Celibacy Confirmed

14.   Hence We consider that the present law of celibacy should today continue to be firmly linked to the ecclesiastical ministry. This law should support the minister in his exclusive, definitive and total choice of the unique and supreme love of Christ; it should uphold him in the entire dedication of himself to the public worship of God and to the service of the Church; it should characterize his state of life both among the faithful and in the world at large.

15.   The gift of the priestly vocation dedicated to the divine worship and to the religious and pastoral service of the People of God, is undoubtedly distinct from that which leads a person to choose celibacy as a state of consecrated life.[8] But the priestly vocation, although inspired by God, does not become definitive or operative without having been tested and accepted by those in the Church who hold power and bear responsibility for the ministry serving the ecclesial community. It is therefore the task of those who hold authority in the Church to determine, in accordance with the varying conditions of time and place, who in actual practice are to be considered suitable candidates for the religious and pastoral service of the Church, and what should be required of them.

16.   In a spirit of faith, therefore, We look on this occasion afforded Us by Divine Providence as a favourable opportunity for setting forth anew, and in a way more suited to the men of our time, the fundamental reasons for sacred celibacy. If difficulties against faith 'can stimulate our minds to a more accurate and deeper understanding'[9] of it, the same is true of the ecclesiastical discipline which guides and directs the life of the faithful.

We are deeply moved by the joy this occasion gives Us of contemplating this aspect of the divine riches and beauty of the Church of Christ. Her beauty may not always be immediately apparent to the human eye, because it is the fruit of the love of the divine Head of the Church and because it reveals itself in that perfection of holiness[10] which moves the human spirit to admiration, since it finds the resources of the human creature inadequate to account for it.

Part I

I. REASONS FOR CELIBACY

The Council and Celibacy

17.   Virginity undoubtedly, as the Second Vatican Council declared, 'is not, of course, required by the nature of the priesthood itself. This is clear from the practice of the early Church and the traditions of the Eastern Churches'.[11] But at the same time the Council did not hesitate to confirm solemnly the ancient, sacred and providential present law of priestly celibacy. In addition, it set forth the motives which justify this law for those who, in a spirit of faith and with generous fervour, know how to appreciate the gifts of God.

18.   Consideration of how celibacy is 'particularly suited'[12] to God's ministers is not something recent. Even if the explicit reasons have differed with different mentalities and different situations, they were always inspired by specifically Christian considerations; and from these considerations we can get an intuition of the more fundamental motives underlying them.[13] These can be brought into greater evidence only under the influence of the Holy Spirit, promised by Christ to his followers for the knowledge of things to come[14] and to enable the People of God to increase in the understanding of the mystery of Christ and of the Church. In this process of experience gained through the ages from a deeper penetration of spiritual things also has its part.

The Christological Significance of Celibacy

19.   The Christian priesthood, being of a new order, can be understood only in the light of the newness of Christ, the Supreme Pontiff and eternal Priest, who instituted the priesthood of the ministry as a real participation in his own unique priesthood.[15] The minister of Christ and dispenser of the mysteries of God,[16] therefore, looks up to him directly as his model and supreme ideal.[17] The Lord Jesus, the only Son of God, was sent by the Father into the world and he became man, in order that humanity which was subject to sin and death might be reborn, and through this new birth[18] might enter the kingdom of heaven. Being entirely consecrated to the will of the Father,[19] Jesus brought forth this new creation[20] by means of his paschal mystery; thus, he introduced into time and into the world a new form

of life which is sublime and divine and which transforms the very earthly condition of human nature.[21]

20.   Matrimony according to the will of God continues the work of the first creation;[22] and considered within the total plan of salvation, it even acquires a new meaning and a new value. Jesus, in fact, has restored its original dignity,[23] has honoured it[24] and has raised it to the dignity of a sacrament and of a mysterious symbol of his own union with the Church.[25] Thus, Christian couples walk together towards their heavenly fatherland in the exercise of mutual love, in the fulfilment of their particular obligations, and in striving for the sanctity proper to them. But Christ, mediator of a more excellent Testament,[26] has also opened a new way, in which the human creature adheres wholly and directly to the Lord, and is concerned only with him and with his affairs;[27] thus, he manifests in a clearer and more complete way the profoundly transforming reality of the New Testament.

21.   Christ, the only Son of the Father, by the power of the Incarnation itself was made mediator between heaven and earth, between the Father and the human race. Wholly in accord with this mission, Christ remained throughout his whole life in the state of celibacy, which signified his total dedication to the service of God and men. This deep connection between celibacy and the priesthood of Christ is reflected in those whose fortune it is to share in the dignity and in the mission of the Mediator and eternal Priest; this sharing will be more perfect the freer the sacred minister is from the bond of flesh and blood.[28]

22.   Jesus, who selected the first ministers of salvation, wished them to be introduced to the understanding of the mysteries of the kingdom of heaven, [29] to be co-workers with God under a very special title, and his ambassadors.[30] He called them friends and brethren,[31] for whom he consecrated himself so that they might be consecrated in truth,[32] He promised a more than abundant recompense to anyone who should leave home, family, wife and children for the sake of the kingdom of God.[33] More than this, in words filled with mystery and hope, he also commended an even more perfect consecration[34] to the kingdom of heaven by means of celibacy, as a special gift.[35] The motive of this answer to the divine call is the kingdom of heaven:[36] similarly, the ideas—of this kingdom,[37] of the gospel,[38] and of the name of Christ[39]—are what motivate those invited by Jesus to the difficult renunciations of the apostolate, by a very intimate participation in his lot.

23.   This, then, is the mystery of the newness of Christ, of all

that he is and stands for; it is the sum of the highest ideals of the gospel and of the kingdom; it is a particular manifestation of grace, which springs from the paschal mystery of the Saviour and renders the choice of celibacy desirable and worthwhile on the part of those called by our Lord Jesus. Thus, they intend not only to participate in Christ's priestly office, but also to share with him his very condition of living.

The Fulness of Love

24. The response to the divine call is an answer of love to the love which Christ has shown us so sublimely.[40] This response is included in the mystery of that special love for those souls who have accepted his most urgent appeals.[41] Grace with a divine force increases the longings of love. And love, when it is genuine, is total, exclusive, stable and lasting, an irresistible spur to all forms of heroism. And so, the free choice of sacred celibacy has always been considered by the Church 'as a badge of charity, an encouragement to charity':[42] it signifies a love without reservations, it stimulates to a charity which is open to all. Who can see in such a life so completely dedicated and motivated as shown above, the sign of a spiritual poverty, of self-seeking, and not rather see that celibacy is and ought to be a rare and very meaningful example of a life whose motivation is love, by which man expresses his own unique greatness? Who can doubt the moral and spiritual richness of such a consecrated life, consecrated not to any human ideal no matter how noble, but to Christ and to his work to bring about a new form of humanity in all places and for all generations?

25. This biblical and theological vision associates our ministerial priesthood with the priesthood of Christ; it is modelled on the total and exclusive dedication of Christ to his mission of salvation, and makes it the cause of our assimilation to the form of charity and sacrifice proper to Christ our Saviour. This vision seems to Us so profound and rich in truth, both speculative and practical, that We invite you, Venerable Brothers, and We invite you, eager students of Christian doctrine and masters of the spiritual life, and all you priests who have gained a supernatural insight into your vocation, to persevere in the study of this vision, and to go deeply into the inner recesses and wealth of its reality. In this way, the bond between the priesthood and celibacy will be seen in an ever improving union, owing to its clear logic and to the heroism of a unique and limitless love for Christ the Lord and for his Church.

The Ecclesial Significance of Celibacy

26. 'Made captive by Christ Jesus'[43] unto the complete abandonment of one's entire self to him, the priest takes on the likeness of Christ most perfectly, even in the love with which the eternal Priest has loved the Church his Body and offered himself entirely for her sake, in order to make her a glorious, holy and immaculate Spouse.[44]

The consecrated celibacy of the sacred ministers actually manifests the virginal love of Christ for the Church, and the virginal and supernatural fecundity of this marriage, by which the children of God are born,[45] but not of flesh and blood.[46]

Unity and Harmony in the Life of the Priest

27. The priest dedicates himself to the service of the Lord Jesus and of his Mystical Body with complete liberty, which is made easier by his total offering, and he realizes more fully the unity and harmony of the priestly life.[47] His ability increases for listening to the Word of God and for prayer. Indeed, the Word of God, as preserved by the Church, stirs up in the priest, who daily meditates on it, lives on it and preaches it to the faithful, echoes that are vibrant and profound.

28. Like Christ himself, his minister is wholly and solely intent on the things of God and the Church;[48] and he imitates the great High Priest who stands in the presence of God ever living to intercede in our favour.[49] So, he receives joy and encouragement unceasingly from the attentive and devout recitation of the Divine Office, by which he dedicates his voice to the Church who prays together with her Spouse,[50] and he recognizes the necessity of continuing his diligence at prayer, which is the profoundly priestly occupation.[51]

29. The rest of a priest's life acquires a greater richness of meaning and sanctifying power. In fact, his individual efforts at his own sanctification find new incentives in the ministry of grace and in the ministry of the Eucharist, in which all the riches of the Church are contained:[52] acting in the person of Christ, the priest unites himself most intimately with the offering, and places on the altar his entire life, which bears the marks of the holocaust.

30. What other considerations can We make to describe the increase of the priest's power, of his service, his love and his sacrifice for the entire People of God? Christ spoke of himself: 'Unless a grain of wheat falls into the earth and dies, it remains alone; but if it dies, it bears much fruit'.[53] And the Apostle Paul

did not hesitate to expose himself to a daily death, in order to obtain among his faithful glory in Christ Jesus.[54] In a similar way, by a daily dying to himself, and by giving up the legitimate love of a family of his own for the love of Christ and of his kingdom, the priest will find the glory of an exceedingly rich and fruitful life in Christ, because like him and in him, he loves and dedicates himself to all the children of God.

The Priest in the Community of the Faithful

31.   In the community of the faithful committed to his charge, the priest is Christ present. Thus, it is most fitting that in all things he should reproduce the image of Christ and follow in particular his example, both in his personal as well as in his apostolic life. To his children in Christ, the priest is a sign and a pledge of that sublime and new reality which is the kingdom of God, of which he is the dispenser; he possesses it on his own account and to a more perfect degree, and nourishes the faith and the hope of all Christians, who because they are such, are bound to observe chastity according to their proper state of life.

32.   The consecration to Christ, by virtue of a new and lofty title like celibacy, evidently gives to the priest, even in the practical field, the maximum efficiency and the best disposition of mind, psychologically and affectively, for the continuous exercise of a perfect charity.[55] This charity will permit him to spend himself wholly for the welfare of all, in a fuller and more concrete way.[56] It also guarantees him obviously a greater freedom and flexibility in the pastoral ministry,[57] in his active and loving presence in the world, to which Christ has invited him,[58] so that he may pay fully to all the children of God the debt due to them.[59]

The Salvific Significance of Celibacy

33.   The kingdom of God which is not of this world[60] is present here on earth in mystery, and will reach her perfection with the glorious coming of the Lord Jesus.[61] The Church here below constitutes the seed and the beginning of this kingdom. And as she continues to grow slowly but surely, she longs for the perfect kingdom and desires vehemently with all her energy to unite herself with her King in glory.[62]

The pilgrim People of God, as seen in history, is on a journey towards its true homeland,[63] where the divine sonship of the redeemed[64] will be fully revealed and where its splendour will be definitively attained by the transformed loveliness of the Spouse of the Lamb of God.[65]

34. Our Lord and Master has said that 'in the resurrection they neither marry nor are given in marriage, but are like angels in heaven'.[66] In the world of man, so deeply involved in earthly concerns and too often enslaved by the desires of the flesh,[67] the precious divine gift of perfect continence for the kingdom of heaven stands out precisely 'as a special token of the rewards of heaven,'[68] it proclaims the presence on earth of the final stages of salvation[69] with the arrival of a new world, and in a way it anticipates the fulfilment of the kingdom as it sets forth its supreme values which will one day shine forth in all the children of God. This continence, therefore, stands as a testimony to the necessary progress of the People of God towards the final goal of their earthly pilgrimage, and as a stimulus for all to raise their eyes to the things above, where Christ sits at the right hand of the Father and where our life is hidden in Christ with God until he appears in glory.[70]

II. CELIBACY IN THE LIFE OF THE CHURCH

Early Christian Testimony

35. Although it would be too long, still it would be quite instructive to study the historical documents on ecclesiastical celibacy. Let the following indication suffice. In Christian antiquity the Fathers and ecclesiastical writers testify to the spread through the East and the West of the voluntary practice of celibacy by sacred ministers[71] because of its profound suitability for their total dedication to the service of Christ and of his Church.

The Western Church

36. The Church of the West, from the beginning of the fourth century, strengthened, spread, and approved this practice by means of various provincial Councils and through the Supreme Pontiffs.[72] More than any others, the supreme pastors and teachers of the Church of God, the guardians and interpreters of the patrimony of the faith and of holy Christian practices, promoted, defended, and restored ecclesiastical celibacy in successive eras of history, even when they met opposition from the clergy itself and when the practices of a decadent society did not favour the heroic demands of virtue. The obligation of celibacy was then solemnly sanctioned by the Sacred Ecumenical Council of Trent[73] and finally included in the Code of Canon Law.[74]

37. The most recent Sovereign Pontiffs who preceded us, making use of their doctrinal knowledge, and spurred on by ar-

dent zeal, strove to enlighten the clergy on this matter, and to urge them to its observance.[75] And We do not wish to fail to pay homage to their revered memory, especially to that of Our well-beloved immediate predecessor which is still fresh in the hearts of men all over the world. During the Roman Synod, with the sincere approval of all the clergy of the city, he spoke as follows: 'It deeply hurts Us that. . .anyone can dream that the Church will deliberately or even suitably renounce what from time immemorial has been, and still remains, one of the purest and noblest glories of her priesthood. The law of ecclesiastical celibacy and the efforts necessary to preserve it always recall to mind the struggles of the heroic times when the Church of Christ had to fight for and succeeded in obtaining her threefold glory, always an emblem of victory, that is, the Church of Christ, free, chaste and catholic.'[76]

The Eastern Church

38.   If the legislation of the Eastern Church is different in the matter of discipline with regard to clerical celibacy, as was finally established by the Council of Trullo held in the year 692,[77] and which has been clearly recognized by the Second Vatican Council,[78] this is due to the different historical background of that most noble part of the Church, a situation which the Holy Spirit has providentially and supernaturally influenced.

We ourselves take this opportunity to express Our esteem and Our respect for all the clergy of the Eastern Churches, and to recognize in them examples of fidelity and zeal which makes them worthy of sincere veneration.

39.   We find further comforting reasons for continuing to adhere to the observance of the discipline of clerical celibacy in the exaltation of virginity by the Eastern Fathers. We hear within Us, for example, the voice of St Gregory of Nyssa, reminding Us that 'the life of virginity is the image of the blessedness that awaits us in the life to come.'[79] We are no less assured by the treatment of the priesthood by St John Chrysostom, which is still a fruitful subject for reflection. Intent on throwing light on the harmony which must exist between the private life of him who ministers at the altar and the dignity of the order to which his sacred duties belong, he affirmed:'. . .It is becoming that he who accepts the priesthood be as pure as if he were in heaven.'[80]

40.   Further, it is by no means futile to observe that in the East only celibate priests are ordained bishops, and the priests themselves cannot contract marriage after their ordination to the priesthood. This indicates that these venerable Churches

also possess to a certain extent the principle of a celibate priesthood. It shows too that there is a certain appropriateness for the Christian priesthood, of which the bishops possess the summit and the fullness, of the observance of celibacy.[81]

The Tradition of the Western Church

41.   In any case, the Church of the West cannot weaken her faithful observance of her own tradition. And it is unthinkable that for centuries she has followed a path which, instead of favouring the spiritual richness of individual souls and of the People of God, has in some way compromised it, or that she has with arbitrary juridical prescriptions stifled the free expansion of the most profound realities of nature and of grace.

42.   In virtue of the fundamental norm of the government of the Catholic Church, to which We alluded above,[82] while, on the one hand, the law requiring a freely chosen and perpetual celibacy of those who are admitted to Holy Orders remains unchanged, on the other hand, a study may be allowed of the particular circumstances of married sacred ministers of Churches or other Christian communities separated from the Catholic communion, and of the possibility of admitting to priestly functions those who desire to adhere to the fullnes of this communion and to continue to exercise the sacred ministry. The circumstances must be such, however, as not to prejudice the existing discipline regarding celibacy.

And that the authority of the Church may not hesitate to exercise her power in this matter can be seen from the recent Ecumenical Council which foresaw the possibility of conferring the holy diaconate on men of mature age who are already married.[83]

43.   All this, however, does not signify a relaxation of the existing law, and must not be interpreted as a prelude to its abolition. There are better things to do beside promoting this hypothesis, which tears down that vigour and love in which celibacy finds security and happiness, and which obscures the true doctrine that justifies its existence and exalts its splendour. It would be much better to promote serious studies in defence of the spiritual meaning and moral value of virginity and celibacy.[84]

44.   Holy virginity is a very special gift. Nevertheless, the whole present-day Church, solemnly and universally represented by the pastors responsible for her welfare (with due respect, as we have said, for the discipline of the Eastern Churches), manifested her absolute faith in the Spirit 'that the grace of leading a celibate life, so desirable in the priesthood of the New Testament, will be readily granted by God the Father if

those who by ordination share the priesthood of Christ humbly and earnestly ask it'.[85]

Prayer of the People of God

45. We wholeheartedly call on the entire People of God to do their duty in bringing about an increase in priestly vocations.[86] We ask them fervently to beg the Father of all, the divine Spouse of the Church, and the Holy Spirit, her principle of life, through the intercession of the Blessed Virgin Mary, Mother of Christ and of his Church, to pour out, especially at present, this divine gift, which the Father certainly does not wish to give stintingly. They should also fervently pray, in like manner, that souls may dispose themselves to receive it by a profound faith and a generous love. In this way, in our world, which needs God's glory,[87] priests, ever more perfectly conformed to the one and supreme Priest, will be a real glory to Christ,[88] and through them, 'the glory of grace' of God will be magnified in the world of today.[89]

46. Yes, venerable and well-beloved brothers in the priesthood, whom We cherish 'with the affection of Christ Jesus',[90] it is truly this world in which we live, tormented by the pains of growth and change, justly proud of its human values and human conquests, which urgently needs the witness of lives consecrated to the highest and most sacred spiritual values. This witness is necessary in order that the refined and incomparable light, radiating from the most sublime virtues of the spirit, may not be wanting to our times.

47. Our Lord Jesus Christ did not hesitate to confide the formidable task of evangelizing the world, as it was then known, to a handful of men to all appearances lacking in number and quality. He bade this 'little flock' not to lose heart,[91] for, thanks to his constant assistance,[92] through him and with him, they would overcome the world.[93] Jesus has taught us also that the kingdom of God has an intrinsic and unobservable dynamism which enables it to grow without man's awareness of it.[94] The harvest of God's kingdom is great, but the labourers, as in the beginning, are few. Actually, they have never been as numerous as human standards would have judged sufficient. But the Lord of the kingdom demands prayers, that it may be he, the Lord of the harvest, who will send out labourers into his harvest.[95] The counsels and prudence of man cannot supersede the hidden wisdom of him who, in the history of salvation, has challenged man's wisdom and power by his own foolishness and weakness.[96]

48. We appeal to the courage of faith to express the Church's

deepest conviction that a more energetic and generous answer to grace, a more explicit and substantiated hope, a more complete and open witness to the mystery of Christ, will never be the cause of her failing in her salvific mission to all mankind. It is necessary for us to learn to do all things in him who alone gives strength to souls[97] and increase to his Church.[98]

49. It is simply not possible to believe that the abolition of ecclesiastical celibacy would considerably increase the number of priestly vocations: the contemporary experience of those Churches and ecclesial communities which allow their ministers to marry seems to prove the contrary. The cause of the decrease in vocations to the priesthood is to be found elsewhere, especially, for example, in the fact that individuals and families have lost their sense of God and of all that is holy, their esteem for the Church as the institution of salvation through faith and the sacraments, the institution which must study the true roots of the problem.

III. CELIBACY AND HUMAN VALUES

Celibacy and Love

50. As We said above,[99] the Church is not unaware that the choice of consecrated celibacy, since it involves a series of hard renunciations which affect the very depths of a man, presents also grave difficulties and problems to which the men of today are particularly sensitive. In fact, it might seem that celibacy conflicts with the solemn recognition of human values by the Church in the recent Council. And yet a more careful consideration reveals that the sacrifice of human love as experienced in a family and as offered by the priest for the love of Christ, is really a singular tribute paid to that superior love. Indeed, it is universally recognized that man has always offered to God what is worthy of both the giver and the receiver.

51. On the other hand, the Church cannot and should not set aside the fact that the choice of celibacy—provided that it is made with human and Christian prudence and responsibility—is governed by grace which, far from destroying or doing violence to nature, elevates it and imparts to it supernatural powers and vigour. God, who has created and redeemed man, knows what he can ask of him and gives him everything necessary to be able to do what his Creator and Redeemer asks of him. St Augustine, who had fully and painfully experienced in himself

the nature of man, exclaimed: 'Grant what you command, and command what you will'.[100]

52. A true knowledge of the real difficulties of celibacy is very useful, even necessary, for the priest, so that he may be fully aware of what his celibacy requires in order to be genuine and beneficial. But with equal fidelity to the truth, these difficulties must not be given greater value or weight than they actually have in the human or religious sphere, or declared impossible of solution.

Celibacy Is Not Against Nature

53. After what science has now ascertained, it is not right to continue repeating[101] that celibacy is against nature because it runs counter to lawful physical, psychological and affective needs or to claim that a completely mature human personality demands fulfilment of these needs. Man, created to God's image and likeness[102] is not just flesh and blood; the sexual instinct is not all that he has; man has also, and pre-eminently, understanding, choice, freedom, and thanks to these powers he is, and must remain, superior to the rest of creation; they give him mastery over his physical, psychological and affective appetites.

54. The true, deep reason for dedicated celibacy is, as We have said, the choice of a closer and more complete relationship with the mystery of Christ and the Church for the good of all mankind: in this choice there is no doubt that those highest human values are able to find their fullest expression.

55. The choice of celibacy does not connote ignorance or the despisal of the sexual instinct and affectivity. That would certainly do damage to the physical and psychological balance. On the contrary it demands clear understanding, careful self-control and a wise sublimation of the psychological life on a higher plane. In this way celibacy sets the whole man on a higher level and makes an effective contribution to his own perfection.

56. The natural and lawful desire a man has to love a woman and to raise a family are renounced by celibacy, but marriage and the family are not said to be the only way for fully developing the human person. In the priest's heart love is by no means extinct. His charity is drawn from the purest source[103] practised in the imitation of God and Christ, and no less than any other genuine love is demanding and real.[104] It gives the priest a limitless horizon, deepens and gives breadth to his sense of responsibility —a sign of mature personality—and inculcates in him as a sign of a higher and greater fatherhood, a generosity[105] and refinement of heart which offer a superlative enrichment.

57. All of God's People must give testimony to the mystery of

Christ and his kingdom but this witnessing does not take the same form for all. The Church leaves to her married children the function of giving the necessary testimony of a genuinely and fully Christian married and family life. She entrusts to her priests the testimony of a life wholly dedicated to the ever new, absorbing realities of God's kingdom.

If this means that the priest is without a direct personal experience of married life, he will by his training, his ministry and the grace of his office, certainly not lack a knowledge, perhaps a deeper knowledge, of the human heart. This will allow him to meet those problems at their source and give solid support by his advice and assistance to married persons and Christian families.[106] The presence in the Christian family of the priest who is living his life of celibacy to the full will underscore the spiritual dimension of every love worthy of the name, and his personal sacrifice will merit for the faithful united in the holy bond of matrimony the grace of a true union.

The Solitude of the Celibate Priest

58. The priest by reason of his celibacy is a solitary: that is true, but his solitude is not emptiness because it is filled with God and the brimming riches of his kingdom. Moreover, for this solitude, which should be an internal and external plenitude of charity, he has prepared himself, if he has chosen it with full understanding, and not through any proud desire to be different from the rest of men, or to withdraw himself from common responsibilities, or to alienate himself from his brothers, or to show contempt for the world. Though set apart from the world, the priest is not separated from the People of God, because he has been appointed to act on behalf of men,[107] since he is consecrated completely to charity[108] and to the work for which the Lord has chosen him.[109]

59. At times loneliness will weigh heavily on the priest, but not for that reason will he regret having generously chosen it. Christ, too, in the most tragic hours of his life was alone—abandoned by the very ones whom he had chosen as witnesses to, and companions of, his life, and whom he had loved unto the end,[110] but he stated, 'I am not alone, for the Father is with me'.[111] He who has chosen to belong completely to Christ will find, above all, in intimacy with him and in his grace, the power of spirit necessary to banish sadness and regret and to triumph over discouragement. He will not be lacking the protection of the Virgin Mother of Jesus nor the motherly solicitude of the Church, to whom he has given himself in service. He will not be without the kindly care of his father in Christ, his bishop: nor

will the fraternal companionship of his fellow priests and the comfort of the entire People of God be lacking to him. Suspicion, hostility or the sheer lack of understanding on the part of his fellow-men may add a degree of frustration to his solitude. But he will be conscious of sharing the very experience of Christ with dramatic authenticity. He will play the role of an apostle who must not be greater than he who sent him.[112] He will play the role of a friend whose divine Friend has opened for him the most intimate secrets of his sorrows and joys. This is because he has chosen him to live a life that has the appearance of death and precisely by so doing to bring forth mysterious fruits of life.[113]

Part II

I. PRIESTLY FORMATION

Man of God

60. Our reflection on the beauty, importance and intimate fittingness of holy virginity for the ministers of Christ and his Church makes it incumbent on the Teacher and Pastor of that Church to assure and promote its positive observance, from the first moment of preparation to receive such a precious gift.

In fact, the difficulties and problems which make the observance of chastity very painful or quite impossible for some, spring, not infrequently, from a type of priestly formation which, given the great changes of these last years, is no longer completely adequate for the formation of a personality worthy of a man of God.[114]

Carrying Out the Norms of the Council

61. The Second Vatican Council has already indicated wise criteria and guidelines to this end. They are in conformity with the progress of psychology and pedagogy as well as with the changed conditions of mankind and of contemporary society.[115] It is Our will that apposite instructions be drawn up with the help of truly qualified men treating with all necessary detail the theme of chastity. They should be sent out as soon as possible to provide those who, within the Church, have the great responsibility of preparing future priests, with competent and timely assistance.

62. The priesthood is a ministry instituted by Christ for the service of his Mystical Body which is the Church. To her belongs the authority to admit to that priesthood those whom she judges qualified: that is, those to whom God has given, along with

other signs of an ecclesiastical vocation, the gift of a consecrated celibacy.[116]

In virtue of such a gift, corroborated by canon law, the individual is called to respond with free judgment and total dedication, subordinating his own ego to the will of God who calls him. Concretely, this divine calling manifests itself in a given individual with his own definite personality structure which, under normal circumstances, is not violently mastered by grace. In the candidates for the priesthood, therefore, the sense of receiving this divine gift should be cultivated; so too a sense of responsibility in their meeting with God, with the highest importance given to supernatural means.

63. It is likewise necessary that exact account be taken of the biological and psychological state of the candidate in order to guide and orient him towards the priestly ideal; so a truly adequate formation should co-ordinate harmoniously grace and nature in the man in whom one clearly sees the objective conditions and effective capability of receiving the gift of chastity. These conditions should be ascertained as soon as signs of his holy vocation are first indicated; not hastily or superficially, but carefully, with the assistance and aid of a doctor and of a competent psychologist. A serious investigation of hereditary factors should not be omitted.

Unsuitable Candidates for the Priesthood

64. Those who are discovered to be unfit—either for physical, psychological or moral reasons—should be quickly removed from the path to the priesthood. Let teachers appreciate that this is one of their very grave duties. Let them not abandon themselves to false hopes and to dangerous illusions and let them not permit the candidate to nourish these hopes in any way, with resultant damage either to himself or to the Church. The life of the celibate priest, which engages the whole man so totally and so delicately, excludes in fact those of insufficient psychophysical and moral balance. Nor should anyone pretend that grace supplies for the defects of nature in such a man.

65. After the capability of a man has been ascertained and he has been admitted to the course of studies leading to the goal of the priesthood, care should be taken for the progressive development of his personality through the means of physical, intellectual and moral education directed towards the control and personal dominion of his instincts, sentiments and passions.

66. This will be proved by the firmness of the spirit with which he accepts the personal and community type of discipline demanded by the priestly life. Such a régime, the lack or deficiency of which is to be deplored because it exposes the candidate to

grave dangers, should not be borne only as an imposition from without. It should be inculcated and implanted within the context of the spiritual life as an indispensable component.

67. The teacher should skilfully stimulate the young man to that totally evangelical virtue of sincerity[117] and to spontaneity by approving of every good personal initiative, so that he will come to know and properly evaluate himself, assume wisely his own responsibilities, and train himself to that self-control which is of such importance in the priestly education.

68. The exercise of authority, the principle of which ought to be held to firmly, will be animated by wise moderation and by a pastoral attitude. It will be used in a climate of dialogue and will be implemented in a gradual way which will afford the teacher an ever deepening understanding of the psychology of the young man, and will appeal to personal conviction.

A Free Choice

69. The complete education of the candidate to the priesthood ought to be directed to help him acquire a tranquil, convinced and free choice of the grave responsibilities which he must assume in conscience before God and the Church. Ardour and generosity are marvellous qualities of youth; illuminated and supported, they merit, along with the blessing of the Lord, the admiration and confidence of the whole Church as well as of all men. None of the real personal and social difficulties which their choice will bring in its train should remain hidden to the young men, so that their enthusiasm will not be superficial and illusory. At the same time it will be right to highlight with at least equal truth and clarity the sublimity of their choice, which on the one hand leads to a certain physical and psychic void, but on the other, brings with it an interior richness capable of elevating the person most profoundly.

70. The young candidates for the priesthood should convince themselves that they are not able to follow their difficult way without a special type of asceticism more demanding than that which is asked of all the other faithful, which is proper to themselves. It will be a demanding asceticism but not a suffocating one which consists in the deliberate and assiduous practice of those virtues which make a man a priest: self-denial in the highest degree—an essential condition if one would follow Christ;[118] humility and obedience as expressions of internal truth and of a guided liberty; prudence, justice, courage and temperance, virtues without which it is impossible for true and profound religious life to exist; a sense of responsibility, of fidelity and of loyalty in the acceptance of one's obligations; a

balance between contemplation and action; detachment and a spirit of poverty which will give tone and vigour to evangelical freedom; chastity, the result of a persevering struggle, harmonized with all the other natural and supernatural virtues; a serene and secure contact with the world for the service to which the young man will dedicate himself for Christ and for his kingdom.

In such a way the aspirant to the priesthood will acquire, with the help of divine grace, a balanced personality, strong and mature, a combination of inherited and acquired qualities, harmony of all of his powers in the light of the faith and in intimate union with Christ, whom he has chosen for himself and for the ministry of salvation to the world.

71. However, to judge with better certainty the fitness of the young man for the priesthood and to have successive proofs of his attained maturity on both the human and supernatural levels, in consideration of the fact that 'it is more difficult to conduct oneself correctly in the service of souls because of dangers coming from outside',[119] it will be advisable to have the obligation of holy celibacy observed during specified periods of experimentation before it becomes something definitive and permanent through ordination to the priesthood.[120]

72. Once moral certainty has been obtained that the maturity of the candidate is sufficiently guaranteed, he will be in a position to take on himself the heavy and sweet burden of sacerdotal chastity as a total gift of himself to the Lord and to his Church.

In this way, the obligation of celibacy which is in fact added to the order of priesthood by the will of the Church, becomes the candidate's own accepted personal obligation under the influence of divine grace and with full reflection and liberty, and evidently not without the wise and prudent advice of competent spiritual directors who are concerned not to impose the choice, but rather to dispose the candidate to become more conscious in his choice. Hence, in that solemn moment when the candidate will decide once and for all his whole life, he will not feel the weight of an imposition from outside, but rather the interior joy that accompanies a choice made for the love of Christ.

II. THE PRIESTLY LIFE

Difficulties and Risks

73. The priest must not think that ordination makes everything easy for him and screens him once for all from every temptation or danger. Chastity is not acquired all at once but results

from a laborious conquest and daily affirmation. Our world to-day stresses the positive values of love between the sexes but has also multiplied the difficulties and risks in this sphere. In order to safeguard his chastity with all care and affirm its sublime meaning, the priest must consider clearly and calmly his position as a man exposed to spiritual warfare against the seductions of the flesh in himself and in the world, continually renewing his re-solution to give an ever increasing and ever better perfection to the irrevocable offering of himself which obliges him to a fidelity that is complete, loyal and real.

74. Christ's priest will receive new strength and joy daily as he deepens in his meditation and prayer the motives for his gift and the conviction that he has chosen the better part. He will ask humbly and perseveringly for the grace of fidelity, never denied to those who ask it sincerely. At the same time he will use the natural and supernatural means at his disposal. In particular he will not disregard those ascetical norms, guaranteed by the Church's experience and no less necessary in modern cir-cumstances than in former times.[121]

75. The priest should apply himself above all else to developing with all the love grace inspires in him, his close relationship with Christ, searching the inexhaustible and enriching mystery; he should also acquire an ever deeper sense of the mystery of the Church. There would be the risk of his state of life seeming un-reasonable and unfounded if seen apart from this mystery.

Priestly piety, nourished at the table of God's Word and the Holy Eucharist, lived within the cycle of the liturgical year, in-spired by a warm and enlightened devotion to the Virgin Mother of the supreme and eternal High Priest and Queen of the Apostles,[122] will bring him to the source of a true spiritual life which alone provides a solid foundation for the observance of celibacy.

The Spirit of the Ministry

76. In this way the priest with grace and peace in his heart will face with generosity the manifold tasks of his life and ministry. If he performs these with faith and zeal he will find in them new occasions to show that he belongs entirely to Christ and his Mystical Body, for his own sanctification and the sanctification of others. The charity of Christ which urges him on[123] will help him not to renounce his higher feelings but to elevate and deepen them in a spirit of consecration in imitation of Christ the High Priest, who shared intimately in the life of mankind, loved and suffered for them,[124] and of Paul the Apostle who shared in the cares of all,[125] in order to bring the light and power of the gospel

of God's grace to shine in the world.[126]

77. Rightly jealous of his full self-giving to the Lord, the priest should know how to guard against sentimental tendencies which imperil an affectivity not sufficiently enlightened or guided by the Spirit. He should beware of looking for spiritual or apostolic pretexts for what are in fact dangerous inclinations of the heart.

78. The priestly life certainly requires an authentic spiritual intensity in order to live by the Spirit and to conform to the Spirit;[127] it requires a truly virile asceticism both interior and exterior in one who, belonging in a special way to Christ, has in him and through him crucified the flesh with its passions and desires,[128] not hesitating to face arduous and lengthy trials in order to do so.[129] In this way Christ's minister will be the better able to show to the world the fruits of the Spirit which are 'love, joy, peace, patience, kindness, goodness, faithfulness, gentleness, self-control'.[130]

Priestly Fellowship

79. Moreover, priestly chastity is increased, guarded and defended by a way of life, surroundings and activity suited to a minister of God. For this reason the 'close sacramental brotherhood'[131] which all priests enjoy in virtue of their ordination must be fostered to the utmost. Our Lord Jesus Christ has taught the urgency of the new commandment of charity. He gave a wonderful example of it when he instituted the sacrament of the Eucharist and the Catholic priesthood,[132] and prayed to his heavenly Father that the love the Father bore for him from all eternity should be in his ministers and that he too should be in them.[133]

80. So the unity of spirit among priests should be perfect and they should be active in their prayers, friendship and help of all kind for one another. One cannot sufficiently recommend to priests a life lived in common and directed entirely towards their sacred ministry, the practice of having frequent meetings with a fraternal exchange of ideas, counsel and experience with their brother priests, the movement to form associations which encourage priestly holiness.

81. Priests should reflect on the advice of the Council,[134] which reminds them of their common sharing in the priesthood so that they may feel a lively responsibility for fellow priests troubled by difficulties which gravely endanger the divine gift they have. They should have a burning charity for those who have greater need of love, understanding and prayer, who have

need of prudent but effective help, and who have a claim on their unbounded charity as those who are, and should be, their truest friends.

Renewal of Vows

82. Venerable brothers in the episcopacy, priests and ministers of the altar, by way of completing and leaving a remembrance of this written conversation with you, We should like to suggest this resolution to you: that on the anniversary of his ordination, or on Holy Thursday when all are united in spirit commemorating the mystery of the institution of the priesthood, each one should renew his total gift of himself to Christ our Lord; reviving in this way the awareness that he has chosen you for his divine service, and repeating at the same time, humbly and courageously, the promise you have of unswerving faithfulness to his love alone in your offering of perfect chastity.[135]

III. LAMENTABLE DEFECTIONS

Celibacy Not to Blame

83. Now with fatherly love and affection, Our heart turns anxiously and with deep sorrow to these unfortunate priests who always remain Our dearly beloved brothers and whose misfortune We keenly regret: those who, retaining the sacred character conferred by their priestly ordination, have been or are unfortunately unfaithful to the obligations they accepted when they were ordained.

Their sad state and its consequences to priests and to others move some to wonder if celibacy is not in some way responsible for such dramatic occurrences and for the scandals they inflict on God's People. In fact the responsibility falls not on consecrated celibacy in itself but on a judgment of the fitness of the candidate for the priesthood which was not always adequate or prudent at the proper time, or else it falls on the way in which sacred ministers live their life of total consecration.

Justice and Charity of the Church

84. The Church is very conscious of the sad state of these sons of hers and judges it necessay to make every effort to avert or to remedy the wounds she suffers by their defection. Following the example of Our immediate predecessors We also have, in cases

concerning priestly ordinations, been prepared to allow inquiry
to extend beyond the provisions of the present canon law[136] to
other very grave reasons which give ground for really solid
doubts regarding the full freedom and responsibility of the candidate for the priesthood and his fitness for the priestly state.
This has been done to free those who, on careful judicial consideration of their case, are seen to be really unsuited.

85. The dispensations which are granted after such considerations—a minimal percentage when they are compared with the
great number of good, worthy priests—provide in justice for the
spiritual salvation of the individual, and show at the same time
the Church's concern to safeguard celibacy and the complete
fidelity of all her ministers.

In granting such dispensations the Church always acts with
heartfelt regret, especially in the particularly lamentable cases in
which refusal to bear worthily this sweet yoke of Christ results
from crises in faith, or moral weakness, and is thus frequently a
failure in responsibility and a scandal.

86. If these priests knew how much sorrow, dishonour and
unrest they bring to the holy Church of God; if they reflected on
the seriousness and beauty of their obligations and on the dangers to which they are exposed in this life and in the next, there
would be greater care and reflection in their decisions, they
would pray more assiduously, and would show greater courage
and logic in forestalling the causes of their spiritual and moral
collapse.

87. The Church has particular interest in those young priests
who are on the threshold of their ministry and full of zeal and enthusiasm. Because of the tensions to which their priestly obligations are subject, is it not to be expected that they will experience
moments of diffidence, doubt, passion, folly? Hence, it is the
wish of the Church that every persuasive means available be used
to lead them from this wavering state to one of calm, trust, penance, recovery. It is only when no other solution can be found
for a priest in this unhappy condition that he should be relieved
of his office.

88. There are some whose priesthood cannot be saved, but
whose serious dispositions nevertheless give promise of their being
able to live as good Christian lay people. To these the Holy See,
having studied all the circumstances with their bishops or with
their religious superiors, sometimes grants a dispensation, thus
letting love conquer sorrow. In order, however, that her unhappy
but always dear son may have a salutary sign of her maternal
grief and a keener remembrance of the universal need of God's

mercy, in these cases she imposes some works of piety and reparation.

89. Inspiring this discipline, which is at once severe and merciful, are justice and truth, prudence and reserve. It is without doubt a discipline which will confirm good priests in their determination to live lives of purity and holiness. At the same time it will be a warning to those aspiring to the priesthood. These, guided by the wisdom of those who educate them, will approach their priesthood fully aware of its obligations, disinterested and responding generously to divine grace and the will of Christ and his Church.

90. Finally, and with deep joy, We thank our Lord because many priests who for a time had been unfaithful to their obligations, have with the grace of the High Priest found again the path and given joy to all by becoming anew exemplary pastors. With admirable good will, they used all the means which were helpful to ensure their return, especially an intense life of prayer, humility, persevering effort sustained by regular reception of the sacrament of Penance.

IV. THE BISHOP'S FATHERLINESS

The Bishop and His Priests

91. There is an irreplaceable and very effective means to ensure for our dear priests an easier and happier way of being faithful to their obligations, and it is one which they have the right and duty to find in you, venerable brother bishops. It was you who called them and destined them to be priests; it was you who placed your hands on their heads; with you they are one in sharing the honour of the priesthood by virtue of the sacrament of Orders; it is you whom they make present in the community of the faithful; with you they are united in a spirit of trust and magnanimity since, in as far as is compatible with their order, they take upon themselves your duties and care.[137] In choosing a life dedicated to celibacy they follow the ancient examples of the prelates of the East and the West; this provides a new motive for union between bishop and priest and a sound hope that they will live together more closely.

92. The love which Jesus had for his Apostles showed itself very clearly when he made them ministers of his real and Mystical Body;[138] and even you in whose person 'the Lord Jesus Christ, the High Priest, is in the midst of the faithful'[139] know

that you owe the best part of your hearts and pastoral care to your priests and to the young men preparing to be priests.[140] In no other way can you better show this conviction than in the conscious responsibility and sincere and unconquerable love with which you preside over the education of your seminarians, and help your priests in every way possible to remain faithful to their vocation and their duties.

93. It is your fraternal and kindly presence and deeds that must fill up in advance the human loneliness of the priest, which is so often the cause of his discouragement and temptations.[141] Before being the superiors and judges of your priests, be their masters, fathers, friends, their good and kind brothers, always ready to understand, to sympathize and to help. In every possible way encourage your priests to be your personal friends and to be very open with you. This will not weaken the relationship of juridical obedience; rather it will transform it into pastoral love so that they will obey more willingly, sincerely and securely. If they are your devoted friends and if they have a filial trust in you, your priests will be able in time to open up their souls and to confide in you their difficulties in the certainty that they can rely on your kindness to be protected from eventual defeat, without a servile fear of punishment, but in the filial expectation of correction, pardon and help, which will inspire them to resume their difficult journey with a new confidence.

Authority and Kindness

94. Venerable brothers, all of you are certainly convinced that to restore to the soul of a priest joy in and enthusiasm for his vocation, interior peace and salvation, is an urgent and glorious ministry which has an incalculable influence on a multitude of souls. There will be times when you must exercise your authority by showing a just severity towards those few who, after having resisted your kindness, by their conduct cause scandal to the People of God; but you will take the necessary precautions to ensure their seeing the error of their ways. Following the example of our Lord Jesus, the Pastor and Bishop of our souls,[142] do not crush the bruised reed nor quench the smoking flax;[143] like Jesus, heal their wounds,[144] save what was lost,[145] with eagerness and love go in search of the lost sheep and bring him back to the warmth of the sheepfold[146] and, like him, try until the end,[147] to call back the unfaithful friend.

95. We are certain, venerable brothers, that you will leave nothing undone to foster, by your teaching, prudence and pas-

toral zeal, the ideal of consecrated celibacy among your clergy. We are sure too that you will never neglect those priests who have strayed from the house of God, their true home, no matter where their painful odyssey has led them, since they still remain your sons.

V. THE ROLE OF THE FAITHFUL

Responsibility of All the People of God

96. Priestly virtue is a treasure that belongs to the whole Church. It is an enrichment and a splendour above the ordinary, which redounds to the building up and the profit of the entire People of God. We wish, therefore, to address to all the faithful, Our children in Christ, an affectionate and urgent exhortation. We wish that they too feel responsible for the virtue of those brothers of theirs who have undertaken the mission of serving them in the priesthood for the salvation of their souls. They should pray and work for priestly vocations; they should help priests wholeheartedly, with filial love and ready collaboration; they should have the firm intention of offering them the consolation of a joyous response to their pastoral labours. They should encourage these, their fathers in Christ, to overcome the difficulties of every sort which they encounter as they fulfil their duties with entire faithfulness, to the edification of all. They should foster in a spirit of faith and of Christian love a deep respect and a delicate reserve in their dealings with priests, on account of their condition as men entirely consecrated to Christ and to the Church.

97. Our invitation goes out specially to those lay people who seek God with greater earnestness and intensity, and strive after Christian perfection while living in the midst of their fellow-men. By their devoted and warm friendship they can be of great assistance to the Church's ministers, since it is the laity, occupied with temporal affairs while at the same time aiming at a more generous and more perfect response to their baptismal vocation, who are in a position, in many cases, to enlighten and encourage the priest. Moreover, the perfect response to a vocation that plunges him into the mystery of Christ and the Church can suffer harm from various circumstances and from contamination with a certain kind of worldliness. In this way the whole People of God will honour Christ our Lord in those who represent him and of whom he has said: 'He who receives you receives me, and

he who receives me receives him who sent me',[148] promising an assured reward to whoever in any way shows charity toward those whom he has sent.[149]

Conclusion

98. Venerable brothers, pastors of God's flock throughout the world, and dearly beloved priests, Our sons and brothers: as We come to the end of this letter which We have addressed to you, We invite you, with a soul responsive to Christ's great love, to turn your eyes and heart with renewed confidence and filial hope to the most loving Mother of Jesus and Mother of the Church, and to invoke for the Catholic priesthood her powerful and maternal intercession. In her the People of God admire and venerate the image of the Church, and model of faith, charity and perfect union with him. May Mary Virgin and Mother obtain for the Church, which also is hailed as virgin and mother,[150] to rejoice always, though with due humility, in the faithfulness of her priests to the sublime gift of holy virginity they have received, and to see it flourishing and appreciated ever more and more in every walk of life, so that the army of those who follow the divine Lamb wherever he goes[151] may increase throughout the earth.

99. The Church proclaims her hope in Christ; she is conscious of the critical shortage of priests when compared with the spiritual necessities of the world's population; but she is confident in her expectation which is founded on the infinite and mysterious power of grace, that the high spiritual quality of her ministers will bring about an increase also in their numbers, for everything is possible to God.[152]

In this faith and in this hope, may the apostolic blessing which We impart with all Our heart be for all a pledge of heavenly graces and the testimony of Our fatherly affection.

---

* Translation by Vatican Press Office. Latin text in AAS, 59 (1967), 657-697.
1. Cf. Letter to Cardinal Tisserant, 10 Oct. 1965, read the following day in general session of the Council.
2. Cf. Mt 19:11-12.
3. Cf. 1 Tim 3:2-5; Tit 1:5-6.
4. Cf. Vatican Council II, Decree on the Pastoral Office of Bishops in the Church, *Christus Dominus,* n. 35: AAS 58 (1966), p. 690; Decree on the Apostolate of the Laity, *Apostolicam Actuositatem,* n. 1:AAS 58 (1966), p.837; Decree on the Priestly Ministry and Life, *Presbyterorum*

Ordinis, nn. 10 ff.; AAS 58 (1966), pp. 1007-1008; Decree on the Missionary Activity of the Church, *Ad Gentes,* nn. 19 and 38: AAS 58 (1966), pp. 969 and 984.

5. Mt 19:11.
6. Jn 4:10.
7. Cf. Mt 5:13-14.
8. Cf. above, nn. 5 and 7.
9. Vatican Council II, Pastoral Constitution on the Church in the World of Today, *Gaudium et spes,* n. 62: AAS 58 (1966), p. 1082.
10. Cf. Eph 5:25-27.
11. Vatican Council II, Decree on the Priestly Ministry and Life, *Presbyterorum Ordinis,* n. 16: AAS 58 (1966), p. 1015.
12. *Ibid.*
13. Cf. Vatican Council II, Dogmatic Constitution on Divine Revelation, *Dei Verbum,* n. 8: AAS 58 (1966), p. 820.
14. Cf. Jn 16:13.
15. Cf. Vatican Council II, Dogmatic Constitution on the Church, *Lumen gentium,* n. 28: AAS 57 (1965), pp. 33-36; Decree on the Priestly Ministry and Life, *Presbyterorum Ordinis,* n. 2: AAS 58 (1966), pp. 991-993.
16. Cf. 1 Cor 4:1.
17. Cf. 1 Cor 11:1.
18. Cf. Jn 3:5; Tit 3:5.
19. Cf. Jn 4:34; 17:4.
20. Cf. 2 Cor 5:17; Gal 6: 15.
21. Cf. Gal 3:28.
22. Cf. Gen 2:18.
23. Cf. Mt 19:3-8.
24. Cf. Jn 2:1-11.
25. Cf. Eph 5:32.
26. Cf. Heb 8:6.
27. Cf. 1 Cor 7:33-35.
28. Cf. Vatican Council II, Decree on the Priestly Ministry and Life, *Presbyterorum Ordinis,* n. 16: AAS 58 (1966), pp. 1015-1017.
29. Cf. Mt 13:11; Mk 4:11; Lk 8:10.
30. Cf. 2 Cor 5:20.
31. Cf. Jn 15:15; 20:17.
32. Cf. *ibid.,* 17:19.
33. Cf. Lk 18: 29-30.
34. Cf. Vatican Council II, Decree on the Priestly Ministry and Life, *Presbyterorum Ordinis,* n. 16: AAS 58 (1966), pp. 1015-1017.
35. Cf. Mt 19:11.
36. Cf. Mt 19:12.
37. Cf. Lk 18:29-30.
38. Cf. Mk 10: 29-30.
39. Cf. Mt 19:29.
40. Cf. Jn 3:16; 15:13.
41. Cf. Mk 10: 21.
42. Cf. Vatican Council II, Dogmatic Constitution on the Church, *Lumen gentium,* n. 42: AAS 57 (1965), p. 48.
43. Phil 3:12.
44. Cf. Eph 5:25-27.
45. Cf. Vatican Council II, Dogmatic Constitution on the Church, *Lumen gentium,* n. 42: AAS 57 (1965), p. 48; Decree on the Priestly

Ministry and Life, *Presbyterorum Ordinis*, n. 16: AAS 58 (1966), pp. 1015-1017.

46. Cf. Jn 1:13.

47. Cf. Vatican Council II, Decree on the Priestly Ministry and Life, *Presbyterorum Ordinis*, n. 14: AAS 58 (1966), p. 1013.

48. Cf. Lk 2:49; 1 Cor 7:32-33.

49. Cf. Heb 9:24; 7:25.

50. Cf. Vatican Council II, Decree on the Priestly Ministry and Life, *Presbyterorum Ordinis*, n. 13: AAS 58 (1966), p. 1012.

51. Cf. Acts 6:4.

52. Cf. Vatican Council II, Decree on the Priestly Ministry and Life, *Presbyterorum Ordinis*, n. 5: AAS 58 (1966), p. 997.

53. Cf. Jn 12:24.

54. Cf. 1 Cor 15:31.

55. Cf. Vatican Council II, Decree on Training for the Priesthood, *Optatam totius*, n. 10: AAS 58 (1966), pp. 719-720.

56. Cf. 2 Cor 12:15.

57. Cf. Vatican Council II, Decree on the Priestly Ministry and Life, *Presbyterorum Ordinis*, n. 16: AAS 58 (1966), pp. 1015-1017.

58. Cf. Jn 17:18.

59. Cf. Rom 1:14.

60. Cf. Jn 18:36.

61. Cf. Vatican Council II, Pastoral Constitution on the Church in the World of Today, *Gaudium et spes*, n. 39: AAS 58 (1966), pp. 1056-1057.

62. Cf. Vatican Council II, Dogmatic Constitution on the Church, *Lumen gentium*, n. 5: AAS 57 (1965), pp. 7–8.

63. Cf. Phil 3:20.

64. Cf. 1 Jn 3:2.

65. Cf. Vatican Council II, Dogmatic Constitution on the Church, *Lumen gentium*, n. 48: AAS 57 (1965), pp. 53-54.

66. Mt. 22:30.

67. Cf. 1 Jn 2:16.

68. Vatican Council II, Decree on the Renewal and Adaptation to Modern Times of the Religious Life, *Perfectae caritatis*, n. 12: AAS 58 (1966), p. 107.

69. Cf. 1 Cor 7:29-31.

70. Cf. Col 3:1-4.

71. Cf. Tertullian, *De exhort. castitatis*, 13: PL 2, 930; St Epiphanius, *Adv. Haer.* II, 48, 9, and 59, 4: PG 41, 869, 1025; St Efrem, *Carmina nisibena*, XVIII, XIX, ed. G. Bickell, Leipzig, 1866, p. 122; Eusebius of Caesarea, *Demonstr. evan.*, 1, 9: PG 22, 81; St Cyril of Jerusalem, *Catechesis*, 12, 25: PG 33, 757; St Ambrose, *De officiis ministr.*, 1, 50: PL 16, 97ff.; St Augustine, *De moribus Eccl. cath.*, 1, 32: PL 32, 1339; St Jerome, *Adversus Vigilantium*, 2: PL 23, 340-41; Bishop Synesius of Ptolemais, *Epist.* 105: PG 66, 1485.

72. First done at the Council of Elvira, c. 300, can. 33: Mansi 2, 11.

73. Sess. XXIV, can. 9-10.

74. Can. 132, §1.

75. Cf. St Pius X, Apostolic Exhortation *Haerent animo:* AAS 41 (1908), pp. 555-577; Benedict XV, *Letter to Francis Kordac, Archbishop of Prague:* AAS 12 (1920), pp. 57-58; Consistorial Address, 16 Dec. 1920: AAS 12 (1920), pp. 585-588; Pius XI, Encycl. *Ad catholici sacerdotii:* AAS 28 (1936), pp. 24-30; Pius XII, Apostolic Exhortation

Menti Nostrae: AAS 42 (1950), pp. 657-702; Encycl. *Sacra virginitas:* AAS 46 (1954), pp. 161-191; John XXIII, Encycl. *Sacerdotii Nostri primordia:* AAS 51 (1959), pp. 554-556.

76. Second Address, 26 Jan. 1960: AAS 52 (1960), p. 226.

77. Can. 6, 12, 13, 48: Mansi 9, 944-948, 965.

78. Cf. Vatican Council II, Decree on the Priestly Ministry and Life, *Presbyterorum Ordinis,* n. 16: AAS 58 (1966), pp. 1015-1016.

79. *De Virginitate,* 13: PG 381-382.

80. *De Sacerdotio,* 1, III.: PG 48, 642.

81. Cf. Vatican Council II, Dogmatic Constitution on the Church, *Lumen gentium,* nn. 21, 28, 64: AAS 57 (1965), pp. 24-25; 33-36; 64.

82. Cf. above, n. 15.

83. Cf. Vatican Council II, Dogmatic Constitution on the Church, *Lumen gentium,* n. 29: AAS 57 (1965), p. 36.

84. Cf. *ibid.* pp. 47-49.

85. Vatican Council II, Decree on the Priestly Ministry and Life, *Presbyterorum Ordinis,* n. 16: AAS 58 (1966), pp.1015-1016.

86. Cf. Vatican Council II, Decree on Training for the Priesthood, *Optatam totius,* n. 2: AAS 58 (1966), pp. 714-715; Decree on the Priestly Ministry and Life, *Presbyterorum Ordinis,* n. 11: AAS 58 (1966), pp. 1008-1009.

87. Cf. Rom 3:23.

88. Cf. 2 Cor 8:23.

89. Cf. Eph 1:6.

90. Phil 1:8.

91. Cf. Lk 12:32.

92. Cf. Mt 28:20.

93. Cf. Jn 16:33.

94. Cf. Mk 4:26-29.

95. Mt 9:37-38.

96. Cf. 1 Cor 1:20-31.

97. Cf. Phil 4:13.

98. Cf. 1 Cor 3:67.

99. Cf. above, n. 10.

100. *Conf.* X, 29, 40: PL 32, 796.

101. Cf. above, no. 10.

102. Cf. Gen 1:26-27.

103. Cf. 1 Jn 4:8-16.

104. Cf. *ibid.* 3:16-18.

105. CF. 1 Thes 2:11; 1 Cor 4:15; 2 Cor 6:13; Gal 4:19; 1 Tim 5:1-2.

106. Cf. 1 Cor 2:15.

107. Cf. Heb 5:1.

108. Cf. 1 Cor 14:4 ff.

109. Cf. Vatican Council II, Decree on the Priestly Ministry and Life, *Presbyterorum Ordinis,* n. 3: AAS 58 (1966), pp. 993-995.

110. Cf. Jn 13:1.

111. *Ibid.* 16:32.

112. Cf. *ibid.* 13:16; 15:18.

113. Cf. *ibid.* 15:15-16, 20.

114. Cf. 1 Tim 6:11.

115. Cf. Vatican Council II, Decree on Training for the Priesthood, *Optatam totius,* nn. 3-11: AAS 58 (1966), pp. 715-721; Decree on the Renewal and Adaptation to Modern Times of the Religious Life, *Perfectae caritatis,* n. 12: AAS 58 (1966), p. 721.

116. Cf. above, n. 15.
117. Cf. Mt 5:37.
118. Cf. Mt 16:24; Jn 12:25.
119. St Thomas Aquinas, *Summa Theol.*, II-II, q. 184, a. 8 c.
120. Cf. Vatican Council II, Decree on Training for the Priesthood, *Optatam totius,* n. 12: AAS 58 (1966), p. 721.
121. Cf. Vatican Council II, Decree on the Priestly Ministry and Life, *Presbyterorum Ordinis,* nn. 16, 18: AAS 58 (1966), pp. 1015-1016; 1019.
122. Cf. *ibid.* n. 18.
123. Cf. 2 Cor 5:14.
124. Cf. Heb 4:15.
125. Cf. 1 Cor 9:22;2 Cor 11:29.
126. Cf. Acts 20:24.
127. Cf. Gal 5:25.
128. Cf. *Ibid.* 5:24.
129. Cf. 1 Cor 9:26-27.
130. Gal 5:22-23.
131. Cf. Vatican Council II, Decree on the Priestly Ministry and Life, *Presbyterorum Ordinis,* n. 8: AAS 58 (1966), p. 1003.
132. Cf. Jn 13:15 and 34-35.
133. Cf. *ibid.* 17:26.
134. Cf. Vatican Council II, Decree on the Priestly Ministry and Life, *Presbyterorum Ordinis,* n. 8: AAS 58 (1966), pp. 1003-1005.
135. Cf. Rom 12:1.
136. Cf. Code of Canon Law, can. 214.
137. Cf. Vatican Council II, Dogmatic Constitution on the Church, *Lumen gentium,* n. 28: AAS 57 (1965), pp. 34-35.
138. Cf. Jn cc. 13-17.
139. Vatican Council II, Dogmatic Constitution on the Church, *Lumen gentium,* n. 21: AAS 57 (1965), p. 24.
140. Cf. Vatican Council II, Decree on the Priestly Ministry and Life, *Presbyterorum Ordinis,* n. 7: AAS 58 (1966), pp. 1001-1003.
141. Cf. *ibid.*
142. Cf. 1 Pet 2:25.
143. Cf. Mt 12:20.
144. Cf. Lk 9:11.
145. Cf. Mt 18:12.
146. Cf. Lk 15:4ff.
147. Cf. *ibid.* 22:48.
148. Mt 10:40.
149. Cf. *ibid.* 10:42.
150. Cf. Vatican Council II, Dogmatic Constitution on the Church, *Lumen gentium,* nn. 63, 64: AAS 57 (1965), p. 64.
151. Cf. Apoc 14:4.
152. Cf. Mk 10:27; Lk 1:37.

96

THE ROLE OF WOMEN IN EVANGELIZATION*

Pastoral Commission of S.C.E.P., *Dans le cadre*, July, 1976

INTRODUCTION

In the context of International Women's Year and in the more general context of the universal movement towards the liberation of women, the pastoral commission decided to examine the role of women in the apostolate, whether on the foreign missions or at home. The congregation published a document on the role of the laity in the apostolate a few years ago. The present document, without ignoring the laity, will be principally concerned with people entirely given over to the apostolate.

The commission decided that what was needed was not an examination of the problem by its own members, but rather a survey of the views of a number of people. An ample questionnaire was sent to a large number of interested groups. The questionnaire elicited about three hundred pages of illuminating replies, rich and balanced, from about forty bodies.

Subsequently, the principal results of the survey were discussed at several meetings composed of members of the commission and of senior officials of institutes involved in missionary activity to non-Christians in Africa, Asia, Oceania and in the western world.

The ideas exchanged at these meetings were assembled systematically and it was thought that they might usefully be communicated to all missionary groups. Hence the present document. What we have here are not authoritative directives. They are, rather, a gesture of confidence, an exchange of views between the congregation and missionary institutes, a free exchange of views, traditional and new, on the role of women in evangelization.

Our object will have been achieved if these pages can give

more light and confidence to all men and women in that difficult and essential missionary apostolate which the institutes, the congregation and this commission endeavour to exercise, each in their own way.

Every reflection on this document, or reaction to it, whether voicing approval or expressing constructive criticism, will be gratefully received.

Every Christian, of whatever sex, age or situation, is called to be an apostle. In virtue of their baptism, all Christians are not merely called and made capable of belief, they are also called to radiate and transmit it (*Ad gentes*—hereafter AG—35a).

The apostolic role is basically equal for all, but the motivation and the form it takes will vary according to the groups and individuals involved (AG 28). One such differentiation arises from the difference between the sexes. It is therefore possible, and also important, to examine the apostolic role from that point of view.

Such an examination is suggested by the simple fact that men and women make up humanity, women being the more numerous. In the apostolate one third are men, two thirds women.

Each category has its own characteristics, which deserve to be examined. In the document which follows, we will examine the female group, appropriately enough, since this is International Women's Year.

IN THE LIGHT OF THE BIBLE, AND SIGNS OF THE TIMES

An attentive study of the Bible shows that women have an important place in the divine perspective on the world. This can be discovered in an attentive study of the Bible, a study which can nowadays be pursued more easily than in the past.

The Genesis account, at the very beginning of the Bible, in recording that God created the human race male and female, indicates briefly, but significantly, the complementarity of the two sexes: that is to say, their resemblance, their difference and their collaboration in every human activity and, therefore, in evangelization.

The Old Testament offers a whole series of female figures who played major roles in the history and the destiny of the chosen people. Examples are Judith and Esther and their role at particularly difficult and delicate times in the history of their people.

THE NEW TESTAMENT

All these figures find their highest embodiment in the Virgin Mary, Mother of God, as closely associated as was possible with the work of salvation and the spread of the revelation of Jesus Christ, from the Annunciation to the first Pentecost, when Mary, having received the gift of the Holy Spirit, became the Queen of the Apostles, a title which we give her and which is in accord with her nature.

During the life-time of the Saviour, women took a full part in the work of evangelization, not only in good times, but—in this showing greater faithfulness than the men—in the darkest hours of the passion, death and burial of the Saviour. This was but a prelude and a foretaste of many occasions when the church would appear to be dying and when women would often manifest greater faithfulness.

It was to the women that the risen Christ committed the task of announcing his resurrection to his brethren: a foretaste of their apostolic role (Luke 24:1-2, 22-24).

Saint Paul—and the same was certainly true of the other apostles—several times spoke of the help given by women, such as Priscilla, for example, in keeping with their gifts, to preachers of the gospel and in the actual preaching of the gospel.

It would take too long to record how women continued to exercise that role through the centuries, even if at times there was a reduction of involvement or there were restrictions. Coming to modern times and to the apostolate to non-Christians, one thinks with joy of the women religious who from the second half of the nineteenth century began to appear in large numbers. One thinks of Frances Cabrini, the blessed Maria Ledochowska, Mother Mary of the Passion. And there were also those laywomen who founded the first enterprises of missionary co-operation, such as Pauline Jaricot and Jeanne Bigard.

These apostles are among the first models of that female initiative and responsibility which are so widely welcomed in our time.

If the council invites us to heed 'the signs of the times', without doubt it bids us take heed of the progress of the liberation of women. If one leaves aside the excessive assertiveness of some women, on the one hand, and the conscious or unconscious blindness of some men, on the other, one notes with satisfaction that our times have seen the increasing development of the education of women, their conscientization, their growing sharing in domestic, professional and public responsibilities.

These facts and many others are an invitation to do more than merely maintain and reinforce contingents of women who form the majority of those engaged in the work of evangelization. They invite, and more importantly, those of both sexes who hold high office to ponder more deeply the role of women in the work of evangelization and the specific nature of their charism and to ask if this is utilized in roles and ministries—in brief, in enlarged responsibilities. They also invite men and women to examine the problem of the preparation of women evangelists and their collaboration with their male counterparts in the work which they have taken on together for Christ.

This investigation is in progress everywhere. It must be pursued at ground level as well as at higher levels, involving detailed research and discussions at every level.

CERTAIN HUMAN QUALITIES WHICH ARE SPECIFICALLY FEMININE

Reflecting on this point, women evangelists believe that they can affirm: 'A woman is more suited to whatever pertains to life rather than to structures, more suited to activity involving personal relationships'.

That statement is to be understood in the context of a number of principles of which the women evangelists themselves assert the priority:

> For women and for men the most profoundly important charism is the gift of faith and of baptism.

> The true witness is a life lived according to the gospel. This goes before any other consideration. 'If you would preach a sermon you must yourself be a sermon'. *(Qui veut annoncer doit être soi-même un annonce.)*

Spiritual profundity, consistency between what a person says and how a person lives, equilibrium and joy in the Spirit resulting from that consistency, these are charisms which know no limits. All can share them, men and women.

That said, women acknowledge, and men know it from observation, that there are certain human qualities which are properly feminine and which offer a precious support to evangelization.

Women are builders of life and they know the qualities demanded of them and developed in them by the long period of gestation of children.

They have a great capacity to love the child which is to be born and to live by that hope, in spite of delay, problems, trials.

Women are capable of giving themselves without counting the cost 'in order that human beings may have life'—all life and especially that of the soul, through grace, that they may have it in abundance, that is to say, in the fullness of the gospel, the sacraments and the church.

Their devotion is often more intuitive than that of men. They are better able to discern the aspirations, the distresses, even unacknowledged, of humanity and to sense what is the appropriate response. Such intuition leads spontaneously to concrete initiatives: 'It is man's nature to have ideas; it is woman's to act'. But one should not force this antithesis.

In her work, it is easier for a woman to maintain continuity and faithfulness to life as it unfolds. Her faith in life sustains her faith in grace and gives her the patience needed for the work of natural and supernatural education.

The sanctuary in which every living person grows, woman has a more alert sense and a more profound respect for the individual person and for his characteristics. She is a better judge of character. More easily than can men, she is able to bring to flower the seeds of goodness which lie hidden in every soul. In the multiple work of evangelization women demonstrate a special capacity for cementing relationships with a delicate sympathy, for implanting deeply the seeds of Christian conviction, for building up in a hundred ways the family of the children of God.

Lastly, experience shows that women have a great capacity for personal adaptation in the face of the varied and often unexpected needs of the real life of societies and churches. They are thus often in a position to ensure not merely the survival but even the progress of evangelization.

In fact, the history of the missions has for long shown the immense part played by women in the evangelization of the world.

The church could not be too grateful for this. At the present time the best form the church's gratitude could take is, without doubt, a more thorough and more open investigation of the future of women's involvement in evangelization.

WOMEN'S ROLES IN EVANGELIZATION

It must be made clear at once that the roles which are to be examined are not seen as supplying for eventual shortages of male personnel, even if this is the case and is not to be excluded. It is a question of considering women's special charisms, of which we will go on to speak, and of what women do, want to do and are able to do—while remaining themselves—in evangelization. When questioned on this subject, dozens[1] of groups of women evangelists put forward the following projects, adopting them in accordance with the measure of evangelical witness of which they are capable.

They were unanimous that the traditional tasks undertaken by women evangelists—hospital work, teaching, social work—had an important role in all developing countries, as a witness to the love of Christ. It would seem that those engaged in these tasks would be slow to relinquish them of their own initiative. At the same time it is necessary to review them, to see if they are needed in every case, if they benefit the disinherited and, if so, whom, and how and when the local people, the laity, can take over responsibility for them (AG 12).

Should the state decide to take over responsibility for these activities, it is desirable that women evangelists should continue to help, in whatever way they are allowed and in whatever way seems best. They will thus give an example of humble, disinterested service and will at the same time become more involved in the life of the country.

For the rest, in countries where women's liberation is sufficiently advanced for such progress to be possible, the part played by women in direct evangelization and in the ministry properly so called should be considerably increased.

In the light of experience and in accordance with suggestions made by women evangelists themselves, the participation of women in the proclamation of the Good News can take many forms; one can but briefly enumerate them:

Catechizing, both catechumens and Christians (see AG 26).
Visiting families, the poor, the sick, outcasts.
Involvement in retreats and spirituality sessions.
Teaching religion, to the level of theology, in every capacity.
The mass media: press, radio, television (AG 12d).

All such kinds of activity relate to the faith and presuppose a profound faith, an adequate preparation. In a woman they involve very special attributes of finesse and of heart.

WOMEN IN PARISHES

What follows is not motivated by a need to supply for a lack of priests, even if priests in fact are in increasingly short supply. It relates rather to the natural characteristics of women in society and in the church, something about which we are rapidly learning more and more.

One can divide these activities into two groups, noting that it is not a matter of activities undertaken under direction. More and more it is a question of women taking on responsibility and making decisions. This does not mean that the women evangelists wish to be isolated from the rest of the parish or independent of a priest. It is, quite simply, a matter of taking on their full role in the parish team. This ought to be a true community where all the members, irrespective of their sex, play an adult part: 'The Holy Spirit speaks to all men and to all women' (see GS 29).

The first group of parochial activities which women could perform are what can loosely be termed 'administration'. Women involved in the apostolate have a precious contribution to make in the organization of the parish and its radiation towards the non-Christian world. They contribute a sense of concrete realities, their perseverance and methodical approach, their practical ingenuity. Their help will be particularly important in involving women in the apostolate. Here there is question of what some of them call 'their gift of friendship and their maternal instinct.'

The second and more important group of activities is directly pastoral (AG 18), but one is not talking of ministries, properly so-called. Women have a specific educational role to play, one of which men are not capable, in catechumenates, especially for women, in catechetical schools, pastoral institutes and seminaries. Women who have been trained direct groups engaged in dialogue between Christians and non-Christians, groups studying spirituality, biblical groups.

A whole area of the apostolate of preparation for the sacraments is open to women, as to priests: preparation for baptism, confirmation, marriage and the anointing of the sick. It is to be hoped that priests, often over-burdened in this field, would find in women valued collaborators. They will acknowledge their responsibility and will give them the responsible autonomy which their personal qualifications deserve.

Women will be especially capable of making contact with non-Christians through other women and through families. In some cultures they alone are capable of doing this work.

WOMEN IN LITURGY AND MINISTRY

Both long experience and certain new initiatives show clearly certain ways in which women evangelists can become increasingly involved in the apostolate. These are roles which up to now had been reserved to priests but which are not in principle part of a clerical monopoly. They can be filled by women: a sort of *diaconia*,[2] a service rendered by women.

In how many parishes is it not a woman religious who, in the absence of a priest, assumes responsibility for the paraliturgical assembly, presides over it and directs it on Sundays and weekdays, preaching to the parishioners about their duties as Christians.

It is also the woman religious whose presence makes it possible to reserve the blessed eucharist, it is she who distributes it to the faithful in case of necessity.

There are cases where, with the requisite episcopal mandate, women religious in permanent charge of a parish administer baptism and preside over marriages in an official ecclesial capacity. Further reflection is needed concerning women reciting the prayers at funerals, even though it too is a matter of urgency.

It is clear that a number of women religious experience anguish when they see how abandoned are some Christian communities, threatened with anemia and with death. When they ask to be allowed to take on pastoral responsibilities it is this anguish which inspires them and not a wish to claim rights. Their requests should be examined sympathetically and as a matter of urgency.

It still has to be determined how exactly a person is to be deputed to such work. Experience has shown that a bishop can depute a person in this way, once the requisite conditions have been laid down by the competent supreme authorities.

Whether there is question of a juridical mandate, a special blessing, or whatever, women, like men, must exercise their pastoral activity in union with the hierarchy: 'Nothing without the bishop' (Ignatius of Antioch) (AG 30). But one would hope that the authorities would respond sympathetically and readily to sisters' offers to serve and would be open to the possibilities—and they are large—thereby presented.

SELECTION AND PREPARATION OF WOMEN EVANGELISTS

The role of a woman evangelist is not comfortable. One can, certainly, count on grace, but a strict selection, based on exacting criteria is required. Experience, as recounted by those who themselves have been involved, suggests the following conditions:

The work of evangelization, humanly speaking, needs well-adjusted people, of sane and robust mentality (AG 25a). It needs people free of hang-ups, but who have not succumbed to false emancipation and have achieved a human maturity which displays their joy and their influence. Such persons are best able to form and maintain harmonious and profound relationships with non-Christians whom they encounter or associate with: 'warmth and welcome' is how one witness put it.

An intense spiritual life should be established on this human foundation, a capacity for full solitude, filled with living faith, with contemplation and activity, for the redemption of the world. The woman evangelist knows, in the words of Pope Paul VI, that for women as well as for men 'it is sanctity which is the most fruitful human development'. Her most valuable 'experience' will always be to encounter God in her neighbor as in herself.

Nobody should evangelize who has not been evangelized and converted (AG 40).

The spiritual dimension is essential and primary, but normally it must be accompanied in woman evangelists by a concrete competence. This can be a competence directly in the pastoral domain. But frequently technical competence can be of the very greatest importance, granted the circumstances of the people being evangelized. Medical, educational, social and other skills are urgently needed to secure the global liberation and development of people.

Good will and unlimited devotion were all that was needed in less complicated times, but the need is now much more pressing. It is more and more necessary to take the measures needed to provide adequate formation for evangelists and it is for superiors to see to it.

In the light of these signs of the times, women evangelists themselves increasingly prescribe certain lines along which formation should proceed, not merely initial but continuing formation.

The life of prayer should be built as far as possible on the culture and on all that is good in the traditional religious customs of the people who are being evangelized. Silence and contemplation, to which women are providentially suited, should nourish that prayer so that it will issue in liturgies and paraliturgies which are truly expressive for the people concerned. It will be for women especially, guided by their faith and their hearts, to formulate that first religious language which marks for life children and 'those who assemble them' (AG 40, 18).

Further, women evangelists will deepen their Christian theological formation to the best of their ability. But they will also endeavour to understand the non-Christian religions and especially the image and the concrete role of women in each of these religions.

The manifold pastoral experiences which so many women evangelists are now having in all the continents among non-Christians deserve to be better known. Those whose horizons are too restricted, perhaps, or whose methods are somewhat old-fashioned could learn from them. It is here that continuing formation could be most beneficial. It has become a necessity.

But all these preparations will be insufficient if they do not remain constantly open to the totality of the world which is to be saved, if they are not constantly suffused by anguish and zeal in the face of the millions of souls to whom Christ has not been preached. The words of Paul, and his ardour, remain the motive force of all preparation: 'Who is made to fall, and I am not indignant...Woe to me if I do not preach the gospel' (2 Cor. 11:29, 1 Cor. 9:16). This basic, indispensable principle should not be whittled away by the undeniable urgency of the need for human development nor by specious assertions about salvation without the gospel.

FORMS AND RHYTHMS OF WOMEN'S INVOLVEMENT IN EVANGELIZATION

Givers of life, consecrated by nature to its service, it is for women to give to evangelization a living and realistic face before the world. In this respect, certain reflections are in order concerning the size and the appearance of groups of evangelists.

In recent times criticisms have been levelled against groups deemed too numerous. These can come into existence either because the work to be done needs large numbers, or because of the tendency of human beings to organize themselves into larger units, or because of a need to group together people who needed to be formed.

It is for this reason that people have been speaking a good deal about 'small communities', especially among women.

In fact, the criteria on which to judge the size and nature of the community are the objectives to be achieved and the needs of common and apostolic life. The experiences of women evangelists suggest that if a woman were to be sent on her own to evangelize she would need to be a person of exceptional qualities. Such a course could not be envisaged unless the woman being sent on her own possessed considerable resistance and human and spiritual resources and unless she had regular contact with and visits to a support group.

It is much more usual for the evangelizing group, even if in a missionary outpost, to be composed of several people, possessing a diverse range of qualities, both spiritual and professional. Considerable experience shows the possibilities (and also some difficulties) of such variety (AG 5b, *Perfectae caritatis,* 13, 8b).

With regard to the size of the groups, it would appear that no rule can be given. It is possible that, even after the situation has been re-examined, a particular work to be done will require a larger group. It is also clear that a smaller group can more easily penetrate a milieu and adopt its style and rhythm of life. But of this we shall speak later.

When they spoke of this matter, the women evangelists hoped that the groups would have different characteristics.

Whatever its dimensions—and there is a preference for more modest dimensions—a group should more and more avoid giving an impression of being powerful and distant. Since in principle they have nothing to hide, it will be to a community's advantage to abandon structures which, to no purpose, increase their separation from the people. They should present themselves as open, possessing those qualities which go so well with femininity: availability, sympathetic listening, friendly understanding, spiritual and also material hospitality for people in difficulties.

The appearance of wealth would at once be an obstacle. Secure comfort in a poor country, where women work hard, would be a counter-witness. Possessiveness, the refusal to share modest resources even in a situation of poverty (for avarice can exist at every level) would be a sign of defiance against the providence of God the Father.

There is another characteristic which communities must have nowadays if they are really to penetrate the mass of the people. This is a characteristic which runs counter to what was hitherto accepted as the ultimate ideal of a group: a well-regulated and stable way of life. It is true, of course, that strong points of silence, of prayer and of community life are needed. But, granted these, if the community really want to penetrate the lives of people they will need to be able to adapt with flexibility to the unexpected. Structures are required as much as one must, but for a living apostolate they must be adapted as much as one can.

However, the last word of witness by female communities will be pronounced by a life of which charity is the soul, whether it is exercised inside or outside. Here female delicacy and ingenuity have a role to play. It is an irreplaceable role, giving communities that touch of human and Christian sisterhood which makes them so attractive. The witness will be all the more eloquent if it is given by people of different nations, races, groups.

TOWARDS GREATER RESPONSIBILITY

We have already described the context in which women will have to take on increased practical responsibilities in evangelization, with the same rights as men and with equivalent qualities.

In central organizations, one notes with satisfaction that here and there women are given place in different consultative and deliberative councils and commissions of the church. On several occasions the Holy Father has called on women to take on greater responsibilities and activities in evangelization. A pontifical commission on women was established and was enlarged into the committee for International Women's Year. Women have been named consultors of several Roman congregations. All these developments have opened up a path which without doubt could be made wider.

One notes that in the secular sphere women who are qualified for particular positions are admitted more easily than hitherto. This ought to take place too in the field of religion and evangelization.

It must be said, however, that much remains to be done before it will be even possible for women to place their immense resources totally at the service of the kingdom of God.

May men and women, in the light of the great part played by Mary, Queen of the Apostles, come to understand what possibilities are being offered to the church for the evangelization of the world, if it knows how to utilize them, by the conscientization of women.

* Translated from the French, *Documentation Catholique*, 1 July, 1976, pp. 612 to 618, by Austin Flannery, O.P. A footnote quotes from an introduction to the text as it appeared in *Vie Consacrée* by Father Joseph Masson, S.J., professor of missiology at the Gregorian, Rome and member of the pastoral commission of the congregation for the propagation of the faith: 'Evangelization has for too long been regarded as the responsibility of men and, indeed, of the clergy. Two complementary documents issued by the congregation have set out to rectify this view. The first of these, published some years ago, outlined the role of the laity of both sexes in the missions. The present document is directly concerned with women. It is the method, even more than the content, which should be noted. The text is the fruit of a vast

consultation, its results frequently transcribed directly, of those involved in evangelization. The three hundred pages of replies were discussed subsequently by a commission composed of men and women in equal proportions'. The word *'évangélisatrices'* occurs frequently in the text. 'Women apostles' did not quite meet the case, so we rendered it 'women evangelists', even though the word 'evangelist' normally has connotations in English other than those intended here.

There are a large number of lengthy footnotes in the original. Those which gave references to council documents or to the scriptures we have put into the text, between brackets. The rest we have omitted. For the most part they refer to Pope Paul VI's address for International Women's Year, 6 Nov., 1974, address to the committee for International Women's Year, 19 April, 1975, Bishop C. T. Dozier of Memphis, U.S.A., Pastoral Letter, 1975. The remaining were added by the translator.

1. The French, in fact, is *des dizaines*, 'tens', but we would more naturally say 'dozens' in English.

2. 'Diakonia', a service; not the same as the order of the diaconate.

97

DECLARATION ON THE
ADMISSION OF WOMEN TO THE
MINISTERIAL PRIESTHOOD*

S.C.D.F., *Inter insigniores*, 15 October, 1976

INTRODUCTION

THE ROLE OF WOMEN IN MODERN SOCIETY
AND THE CHURCH

Among the characteristics that mark our present age, Pope John XXIII indicated, in his Encyclical *Pacem in Terris* of 11 April 1963, "the part that women are now taking in public life... This is a development that is perhaps of swifter growth among Christian nations, but it is also happening extensively, if more slowly, among nations that are heirs to different traditions and imbued with a different culture".[1] Along the same lines, the Second Vatican Council, enumerating in its Pastoral Constitution *Gaudium et Spes* the forms of discrimination touching upon the basic rights of the person which must be overcome and eliminated as being contrary to God's plan, gives first place to discrimination based upon sex.[2] The resulting equality will secure the building up of a world that is not levelled out and uniform but harmonious and unified, if men and women contribute to it their own resources and dynamism, as Pope Paul VI recently stated.[3]

In the life of the Church herself, as history shows us, women have played a decisive role and accomplished tasks of outstanding value. One has only to think of the foundresses of the great religious families, such as Saint Clare and Saint Teresa of Avila. The latter, moreover, and Saint Catherine of Siena, have left writings so rich in spiritual doctrine that Pope Paul VI has included them among the Doctors of the Church. Nor could one forget the great number of women who have consecrated themselves to the Lord for the exercise of charity or for the missions, and the Christian wives who have had a profound influence on their families, particularly for the passing on of the faith to their children.

But our age gives rise to increased demands: "Since in our time women have an ever more active share in the whole life of society, it is very important that they participate more widely also in the various sectors of the Church's apostolate".[4] This charge of the Second Vatican Council has already set in motion the whole process of change now taking place: these various experiences of course need to come to maturity. But as Pope Paul VI also remarked,[5] a very large number of Christian communities are already benefitting from the apostolic commitment of women. Some of these women are called to take part in councils set up for pastoral reflection, at the diocesan or parish level; and the Apostolic See has brought women into some of its working bodies.

For some years now various Christian communities stemming from the sixteenth-century Reformation or of later origin have been admitting women to the pastoral office on a par with men. This initiative has led to petitions and writings by members of these communities and similar groups, directed towards making this admission a general thing; it has also led to contrary reactions. This therefore constitutes an ecumenical problem, and the Catholic Church must make her thinking known on it, all the more because in various sectors of opinion the question has been asked whether she too could not modify her discipline and admit women to priestly ordination. A number of Catholic theologians have even posed this question publicly, evoking studies not only in the sphere of exegesis, patrology and Church history but also in the field of the history of institutions and customs, of sociology and of psychology. The various arguments capable of clarifying this important problem have been submitted to a critical examination. As we are dealing with a debate which classical theology scarcely touched upon, the current argumentation runs the risk of neglecting essential elements.

For these reasons, in execution of a mandate received from the Holy Father and echoing the declaration which he himself made in his letter of 30 November 1975,[6] the Sacred Congregation for the Doctrine of the Faith judges it necessary to recall that the Church, in fidelity to the example of the Lord, does not consider herself authorized to admit women to priestly ordination. The Sacred Congregation deems it opportune at the present juncture to explain this position of the Church. It is a position which will perhaps cause pain but whose positive value will become apparent in the long run, since it can be of help in deepening understanding of the respective roles of men and of women.

1. THE CHURCH'S CONSTANT TRADITION

The Catholic Church has never felt that priestly or episcopal ordination can be validly conferred on women. A few heretical sects in the first centuries, especially Gnostic ones, entrusted the exercise of the priestly ministry to women: this innovation was immediately noted and condemned by the Fathers, who considered it as unacceptable in the Church.[7] It is true that in the writings of the Fathers one will find the undeniable influence of prejudices unfavourable to women, but nevertheless, it should be noted that these prejudices had hardly any influence on their pastoral activity, and still less on their spiritual direction. But over and above considerations inspired by the spirit of the times, one finds expressed—especially in the canonical documents of the Antiochian and Egyptian traditions—this essential reason, namely, that by calling only men to the priestly Order and ministry in its true sense, the Church intends to remain faithful to the type of ordained ministry willed by the Lord Jesus Christ and carefully maintained by the Apostles.[8]

The same conviction animates mediaeval theology,[9] even if the Scholastic doctors, in their desire to clarify by reason the data of faith, often present arguments on this point that modern thought would have difficulty in admitting or would even rightly reject. Since that period and up to our own time, it can be said that the question has not been raised again, for the practice has enjoyed peaceful and universal acceptance.

The Church's tradition in the matter has thus been so firm in the course of the centuries that the Magisterium has not felt the need to intervene in order to formulate a principle which was not attacked, or to defend a law which was not challenged. But each time that this tradition had the occasion to manifest itself, it witnessed to the Church's desire to conform to the model left to her by the Lord.

The same tradition has been faithfully safeguarded by the Churches of the East. Their unanimity on this point is all the more remarkable since in many other questions their discipline admits of a great diversity. At the present time these same Churches refuse to associate themselves with requests directed towards securing the accession of women to priestly ordination.

2. THE ATTITUDE OF CHRIST

Jesus Christ did not call any woman to become part of the Twelve. If he acted in this way, it was not in order to conform to the customs of his time, for his attitude towards women was quite different from that of his milieu, and he deliberately and courageously broke with it.

For example, to the great astonishment of his own disciples Jesus converses publicly with the Samaritan woman (cf. Jn 4:27); he takes no notice of the state of legal impurity of the woman who had suffered from haemorrhages (cf. Mt 9:20-22); he allows a sinful woman to approach him in the house of Simon the Pharisee (cf. Lk 7:37ff.); and by pardoning the woman taken in adultery, he means to show that one must not be more severe towards the fault of a woman than towards that of a man (cf. Jn 8:11). He does not hesitate to depart from the Mosaic Law in order to affirm the equality of the rights and duties of men and women with regard to the marriage bond (cf. Mk 10:2-11; Mt 19:3-9).

In his itinerant ministry Jesus was accompanied not only by the Twelve but also by a group of women: "Mary, surnamed the Magdalene, from whom seven demons had gone out, Joanna the wife of Herod's steward Chuza, Susanna, and several others who provided for them out of their own resources" (Lk 8:2-3). Contrary to the Jewish mentality, which did not accord great value to the testimony of women, as Jewish law attests, it was nevertheless women who were the first to have the privilege of seeing the risen Lord, and it was they who were charged by Jesus to take the first paschal message to the Apostles themselves (cf. Mt 28:7-10; Lk 24:9-10; Jn 20:11-18), in order to prepare the latter to become the official witnesses to the Resurrection.

It is true that these facts do not make the matter immediately obvious. This is no surprise, for the questions that the Word of God brings before us go beyond the obvious. In order to reach the ultimate meaning of the mission of Jesus and the ultimate meaning of Scripture, a purely historical exegesis of the texts cannot suffice. But it must be recognized that we have here a number of convergent indications that make all the more remarkable the fact that Jesus did not entrust the apostolic charge[10] to women. Even his Mother, who was so closely associated with the mystery of her Son, and whose incomparable role is emphasized by the Gospels of Luke and John, was not invested with the apostolic ministry. This fact was to lead the Fathers to present her as the example of Christ's will in this domain; as Pope Innocent III repeated later, at the beginning of the thirteenth century, "Although the Blessed Virgin Mary surpassed in dignity and in excellence all the Apostles, nevertheless it was not to her but to them that the Lord entrusted the keys of the Kingdom of Heaven".[11]

3. THE PRACTICE OF THE APOSTLES

The apostolic community remained faithful to the attitude of Jesus towards women. Although Mary occupied a privileged place in the little circle of those gathered in the Upper Room after the Lord's Ascension (cf. Acts 1:14), it was not she who was called to enter the College of the Twelve at the time of the election that resulted in the choice of Matthias: those who were put forward were two disciples whom the Gospels do not even mention.

On the day of Pentecost, the Holy Spirit filled them all, men and women (cf. Acts 2:1; 1:14), yet the proclamation of the fulfilment of the prophecies in Jesus was made only by "Peter and the Eleven" (Acts 2:14).

When they and Paul went beyond the confines of the Jewish world, the preaching of the Gospel and the Christian life in the Greco-Roman civilization impelled them to break with Mosaic practices, sometimes regretfully. They could therefore have envisaged conferring ordination on women, if they had not been convinced of their duty of fidelity to the Lord on this point. In the Hellenistic world, the cult of a number of pagan divinities was entrusted to priestesses. In fact the Greeks did not share the ideas of the Jews: although their philosophers taught the inferiority of women, historians nevertheless emphasize the existence of a certain movement for the advancement of women during the Imperial period. In fact we know from the book of the Acts and from the Letters of Saint Paul that certain women worked with the Apostle for the Gospel (cf. Rom 16:3-12; Phil 4:3). Saint Paul lists their names with gratitude in the final salutations of the Letters. Some of them often exercised an important influence on conversions: Priscilla, Lydia and others; especially Priscilla, who took it on herself to complete the instruction of Apollos (cf. Acts 18:26); Phoebe, in the service of the Church of Cenchreae (cf. Rom. 16:1). All these facts manifest within the Apostolic Church a considerable evolution vis-a-vis the customs of Judaism. Nevertheless at no time was there a question of conferring ordination on these women.

In the Pauline Letters, exegetes of authority have noted a difference between two formulas used by the Apostle: he writes indiscriminately "my fellow workers" (Rom 16:3; Phil 4:2-3) when referring to men and women helping him in his apostolate in one way or another; but he reserves the title "God's fellow workers" (1 Cor 3:9; cf. 1 Thess 3:2) to Apollos, Timothy and himself, thus designated because they are directly set apart for the apostolic ministry and the preaching of the Word of God. In spite of the so important role played by women on the day of the Resurrection, their collaboration was not extended by Saint Paul to the official and public proclamation of the message, since this proclamation belongs exclusively to the apostolic mission.

4. PERMANENT VALUE OF THE ATTITUDE OF JESUS AND THE APOSTLES

Could the Church today depart from this attitude of Jesus and the Apostles, which has been considered as normative by the whole of tradition up to our own day? Various arguments have been put forward in favour of a positive reply to this question, and these must now be examined.

It has been claimed in particular that the attitude of Jesus and the Apostles is explained by the influence of their milieu and their times. It is said that, if Jesus did not entrust to women and not even to his Mother a ministry assimilating them to the Twelve, this was because historical circumstances did not permit him to do so. No one however has ever proved—and it is clearly impossible to prove—that this attitude is inspired only by social and cultural reasons. As we have seen, an examination of the Gospels shows on the contrary that Jesus broke with the prejudices of his time, by widely contravening the discriminations practised with regard to women. One therefore cannot maintain that, by not calling women to enter the group of the Apostles, Jesus was simply letting himself be guided by reasons of expediency. For all the more reason, social and cultural conditioning did not hold back the Apostles working in the Greek milieu, where the same forms of discrimination did not exist.

Another objection is based upon the transitory character that one claims to see today in some of the prescriptions of Saint Paul concerning women, and upon the difficulties that some aspects of his teaching raise in this regard. But it must be noted that these ordinances, probably inspired by the customs of the period, concern scarcely more than disciplinary practices of minor importance, such as the obligation imposed upon women to wear a veil on the head (1 Cor 11:2-6); such requirements no longer have a normative value. However, the Apostle's forbidding of women "to speak" in the assemblies (cf. 1 Cor 14:34-35; 1 Tim 2:12) is of a different nature, and exegetes define its meaning in this way: Paul in no way opposes the right, which he elsewhere recognizes as possessed by women, to prophesy in the assembly (cf. 1 Cor 11:5); the prohibition solely concerns the official function of teaching in the Christian assembly. For Saint Paul this prescription is bound up with the divine plan of creation (cf. 1 Cor 11:7; Gen 2:18-24): it would be difficult to see in it the expression of a cultural fact. Nor should it be forgotten that we owe to Saint Paul one of the most vigorous texts in the New Testament on the fundamental equality of men and women, as children of God in Christ (cf. Gal 3:28). Therefore there is no reason for accusing him of prejudices against women, when we note the trust that he shows towards them and the collaboration that he asks of them in his apostolate.

But over and above these objections taken from the history of apostolic times, those who support the legitimacy of change in the matter turn to the Church's practice in her sacramental discipline. It has been noted, in our day especially, to what extent the Church is conscious of possessing a certain power over the sacraments, even though they were instituted by Christ. She has used this power down the centuries in order to determine their signs and the conditions of their administration: recent decisions of Popes Pius XII and Paul VI are proof of this.[12] However, it must be emphasized that this power, which is a real one, has definite limits. As Pope Pius XII recalled: "The Church has no power over the substance of the sacraments, that is to say, over what Christ the Lord, as the sources of Revelation bear witness, determined should be maintained in the sacramental sign".[13] This was already the teaching of the Council of Trent, which declared: "In the Church there has always existed this power, that in the administration of the sacraments, provided that their substance remains unaltered, she can lay down or modify what she considers more fitting either for the benefit of those who receive them or for respect towards those same sacraments, according to varying circumstances, times or places".[14]

Moreover, it must not be forgotten that the sacramental signs are not conventional ones. Not only is it true that, in many respects, they are natural signs because they respond to the deep symbolism of actions and things, but they are more than this: they are principally meant to link the person of every period to the supreme Event of the history of salvation, in order to enable that person to understand, through all the Bible's wealth of pedagogy and symbolism, what grace they signify and produce. For example, the sacrament of the Eucharist is not only a fraternal meal, but at the same time the memorial which makes present and actual Christ's sacrifice and his offering by the Church. Again, the priestly ministry is not just a pastoral service; it ensures the continuity of the functions entrusted by Christ to the Apostles and the continuity of the powers related to those functions. Adaptation to civilizations and times therefore cannot abolish, on essential points, the sacramental reference to constitutive events of Christianity and to Christ himself.

In the final analysis it is the Church, through the voice of her Magisterium, that, in these various domains, decides what can change and what must remain immutable. When she judges that she cannot accept certain changes, it is because she knows that she is bound by Christ's manner of acting. Her attitude, despite appearances, is therefore not one of archaism but of fidelity: it can be truly understood only in this light. The Church makes pronouncements in virtue of the Lord's promise and the presence of the Holy Spirit, in order to proclaim better the mystery of Christ and to safeguard and manifest the whole of its rich content.

This practice of the Church therefore has a normative character: in the fact of conferring priestly ordination only on men, it is a question of an unbroken tradition throughout the history of the Church, universal in the East and in the West, and alert to repress abuses immediately. This norm, based on Christ's example, has been and is still observed because it is considered to conform to God's plan for his Church.

5. THE MINISTERIAL PRIESTHOOD IN THE LIGHT OF THE MYSTERY OF CHRIST

Having recalled the Church's norm and the basis thereof, it seems useful and opportune to illustrate this norm by showing the profound fittingness that theological reflection discovers between the proper nature of the sacrament of Order, with its specific reference to the mystery of Christ, and the fact that only men have been called to receive priestly ordination. It is not a question here of bringing forward a demonstrative argument, but of clarifying this teaching by the analogy of faith.

The Church's constant teaching, repeated and clarified by the Second Vatican Council and again recalled by the 1971 Synod of Bishops and by the Sacred Congregation for the Doctrine of the Faith in its Declaration of 24 June 1973, declares that the bishop or the priest, in the exercise of his ministry, does not act in his own name, *in persona propria:* he represents Christ, who acts through him: "the priest truly acts in the place of Christ", as Saint Cyprian already wrote in the third century.[15] It is this ability to represent Christ that Saint Paul considered as characteristic of his apostolic function (cf. 2 Cor 5:20; Gal 4:14). The supreme expression of this representation is found in the altogether special form it assumes in the celebration of the Eucharist, which is the source and centre of the Church's unity, the sacrificial meal in which the People of God are associated in the sacrifice of Christ: the priest, who alone has the power to perform it, then acts not only through the effective power conferred on him by Christ, but *in persona Christi,*[16] taking the role of Christ, to the point of being his very image, when he pronounces the words of consecration.[17]

The Christian priesthood is therefore of a sacramental nature: the priest is a sign, the supernatural effectiveness of which comes from the ordination received, but a sign that must be perceptible[18] and which the faithful must be able to recognize with ease. The whole sacramental economy is in fact based upon natural signs, on symbols imprinted upon the human psychology: "Sacramental signs", says Saint Thomas, "represent what they signify by natural resemblance".[19] The same natural resemblance is required for persons as for things: when Christ's role in the Eucharist is to be expressed sacramentally, there would not be this "natural resemblance" which must exist between Christ and his minister if the role of Christ were not taken by a man: in such a case it would be difficult to see in the minister the image of Christ. For Christ himself was and remains a man.

Christ is of course the firstborn of all humanity, of women as well as men: the unity which he re-established after sin is such that there are no more distinctions between Jew and Greek, slave and free, male and female, but all are one in Christ Jesus (cf. Gal 3:28). Nevertheless, the Incarnation of the Word took place according to the male sex: this is indeed a question of fact, and this fact, while not implying an alleged natural superiority of man over woman, cannot be disassociated from the economy of salvation: it is, indeed, in harmony with the entirety of God's plan as God himself has revealed it, and of which the mystery of the Covenant is the nucleus.

For the salvation offered by God to men and women, the union with him to which they are called—in short, the Covenant—took on, from the Old Testament Prophets onwards, the privileged form of a nuptial mystery: for God the Chosen People is seen as his ardently loved spouse. Both Jewish and Christian tradition has discovered the depth of this intimacy of love by reading and rereading the Song of Songs; the divine Bridegroom will remain faithful even when the Bride betrays his love, when Israel is unfaithful to God (cf. Hos 1-3; Jer 2). When the "fullness of time" (Gal 4:4) comes, the Word, the Son of God, takes on flesh in order to establish and seal the new and eternal Covenant in his blood, which will be shed for many so that sins may be forgiven. His death will gather together again the scattered children of God; from his pierced side will be born the Church, as Eve was born from Adam's side. At that time there is fully and eternally accomplished the nuptial mystery proclaimed and hymned in the Old Testament: Christ is the Bridegroom; the Church is his bride, whom he loves because he has gained her by his blood and made her glorious, holy and without blemish, and henceforth he is inseparable from her. This nuptial theme, which is developed from the Letters of Saint Paul onwards (cf. 2 Cor 11:2; Eph 5:22-23) to the writings of Saint John (cf. especially Jn 3:29; Rev 19:7,9), is present also in the Synoptic Gospels: the Bridegroom's friends must not fast as long as he is with them (cf. Mk 2:19); the Kingdom of Heaven is like a king who gave a feast for his son's wedding (cf. Mt 22:1-14). It is through this Scriptural language, all interwoven with symbols, and which expresses and affects man and woman in their profound identity, that there is revealed to us the mystery of God and Christ, a mystery which of itself is unfathomable.

That is why we can never ignore the fact that Christ is a man. And therefore, unless one is to disregard the importance of this symbolism for the economy of Revelation, it must be admitted that, in actions which demand the character of ordination and in which Christ himself, the author of the Covenant, the Bridegroom and Head of the Church, is represented, exercising his ministry of salvation—which is in the highest degree the case of the Eucharist—his role (this is the original sense of the word *persona*) must be taken by a man. This does not stem from any personal superiority of the latter in the order of values, but only from a difference of fact on the level of functions and service.

Could one say that, since Christ is now in the heavenly condition, from now on it is a matter of indifference whether he be represented by a man or by a woman, since "at the resurrection men and women do not marry" (Mt 22:30)? But this text does not mean that the distinction between man and woman, insofar as it determines the identity proper to the person, is suppressed in the glorified state; what holds for us holds also for Christ. It is indeed evident that in human beings the difference of sex exercises an important influence, much deeper than, for example, ethnic differences: the latter do not affect the human person as intimately as the difference of sex, which is directly ordained both for the communion of persons and for the generation of human beings. In Biblical Revelation this difference is the effect of God's will from the beginning: "male and female he created them" (Gen 1:27).

However, it will perhaps be further objected that the priest, especially when he presides at the liturgical and sacramental functions, equally represents the Church: he acts in her name with "the intention of doing what she does". In this sense, the theologians of the Middle Ages said that the minister also acts *in persona Ecclesiae,* that is to say, in the name of the whole Church and in order to represent her. And in fact, leaving aside the question of the participation of the faithful in a liturgical action, it is indeed in the name of the whole Church that the action is celebrated by the priest: he prays in the name of all, and in the Mass he offers the sacrifice of the whole Church. In the new Passover, the Church, under visible signs, immolates Christ through the ministry of the priest.[20] And so, it is asserted, since the priest also represents the Church, would it not be possible to think that this representation could be carried out by a woman, according to the symbolism already explained? It is true that the priest represents the Church, which is the Body of Christ. But if he does so, it is precisely because he first represents Christ himself, who is the Head and Shepherd of the Church. The Second Vatican Council[21] used this phrase to make more precise and to complete the expression *in persona Christi.* It is in this quality that the priest presides over the Christian assembly and celebrates the Eucharistic sacrifice "in which the whole Church offers and is herself wholly offered".[22]

If one does justice to these reflections, one will better understand how well-founded is the basis of the Church's practice; and one will conclude that the controversies raised in our days over the ordination of women are for all Christians a pressing invitation to meditate on the mystery of the Church, to study in greater detail the meaning of the episcopate and the priesthood, and to rediscover the real and pre-eminent place of the priest in the community of the baptized, of which he indeed forms part but from which he is distinguished because, in the actions that call for the character of ordination, for the community he is—with all the effectiveness proper to the sacraments—the image and symbol of Christ himself who calls, forgives, and accomplishes the sacrifice of the Covenant.

6. THE MINISTERIAL PRIESTHOOD ILLUSTRATED BY THE MYSTERY OF THE CHURCH

It is opportune to recall that problems of sacramental theology, especially when they concern the ministerial priesthood, as is the case here, cannot be solved except in the light of Revelation. The human sciences, however valuable their contribution in their own domain, cannot suffice here, for they cannot grasp the realities of faith: the properly supernatural content of these realities is beyond their competence.

Thus one must note the extent to which the Church is a society different from other societies, original in her nature and in her structures. The pastoral charge in the Church is normally linked to the sacrament of Order: it is not a simple government, comparable to the modes of authority found in States. It is not granted by people's spontaneous choice: even when it involves designation through election, it is the laying on of hands and the prayer of the successors of the Apostles which guarantee God's choice; and it is the Holy Spirit, given by ordination, who grants participation in the ruling power of the Supreme Pastor, Christ (cf. Acts 20:28). It is a charge of service and love: "If you love me, feed my sheep" (cf. Jn 21:15-17).

For this reason one cannot see how it is possible to propose the admission of women to the priesthood in virtue of the equality of rights of the human person, an equality which holds good also for Christians. To this end use is sometimes made of the text quoted above, from the Letter to the Galatians (3:28), which says that in Christ there is no longer any distinction between men and women. But this passage does not concern ministries: it only affirms the universal calling to divine filiation, which is the same for all. Moreover, and above all, to consider the ministerial priesthood as a human right would be to misjudge its nature completely: baptism does not confer any personal title to public ministry in the Church. The priesthood is not conferred for the honour or advantage of the recipient, but for the service of God and the Church; it is the object of a specific and totally gratuitous vocation: "You did not choose me, no, I chose you; and I commissioned you. . ." (Jn 15:16; cf. Heb 5:4).

It is sometimes said and written in books and periodicals that some women feel that they have a vocation to the priesthood. Such an attraction, however noble and understandable, still does not suffice for a genuine vocation. In fact a vocation cannot be reduced to a mere personal attraction, which can remain purely subjective. Since the priesthood is a particular ministry of which the Church has received the charge and the control, authentication by the Church is indispensable here and is a constitutive part of the vocation: Christ chose "those he wanted" (Mk 3:13). On the other hand, there is a universal vocation of all the baptized to the exercise of the royal priesthood by offering their lives to God and by giving witness for his praise.

Women who express a desire for the ministerial priesthood are doubtless motivated by the desire to serve Christ and the Church. And it is not surprising that, at a time when they are becoming more aware of the discriminations to which they have been subject, they should desire the ministerial priesthood itself. But it must not be forgotten that the priesthood does not form part of the rights of the individual, but stems from the economy of the mystery of Christ and the Church. The priestly office cannot become the goal of social advancement; no merely human progress of society or of the individual can of itself give access to it: it is of another order.

It therefore remains for us to meditate more deeply on the nature of the real equality of the baptized which is one of the great affirmations of Christianity: equality is in no way identity, for the Church is a differentiated body, in which each individual has his or her role. The roles are distinct, and must not be confused; they do not favour the superiority of some vis-à-vis the others, nor do they provide an excuse for jealousy; the only better gift, which can and must be desired, is love (cf. 1 Cor 12-13). The greatest in the Kingdom of Heaven are not the ministers but the saints.

The Church desires that Christian women should become fully aware of the greatness of their mission: today their role is of capital importance, both for the renewal and humanization of society and for the rediscovery by believers of the true face of the Church.

* Translation provided by Vatican Press Office. Latin original, AAS, 69 (1977), pp. 98-116.

1. *AAS* 55 (1963), pp. 267-268.
2. Cf. Second Vatican Council, Pastoral Constitution *Gaudium et Spes,* 29 (7 December 1965): AAS 58 (1966), pp. 1048-1049.
3. Cf. Pope Paul VI, Address to the members of the Study Commission on the Role of Women in Society and in the Church and to the members of the Committee for International Women's Year, 18 April 1975: AAS 67 (1975), p. 265.
4. Second Vatican Council, Decree *Apostolicam Actuositatem,* 9 (18 November 1965): AAS 58 (1966), p. 846.

5. Cf. Pope Paul VI, *Address to the members of the Study Commission on the Role of Women in Society and in the Church and to the members of the Committee for International Women's Year*, 18 April 1975: AAS 67 (1975), p. 266.

6. Cf. AAS 68 (1976), pp. 599-600; cf. *ibid.*, pp. 600-601.

7. Saint Irenaeus, *Adversus Haereses*, I, 13, 2: PG 7, 580-581; ed. Harvey, I, 114-122; Tertullian, *De Praescrip. Haeretic.* 41, 5: CCL 1, p. 221; Firmilian of Caesarea, in Saint Cyprian, *Epist.*, 75: CSEL 3, pp. 817-818; Origen, *Fragmentum in I Cor.* 74, in *Journal of Theological Studies* 10 (1909), pp. 41-42; Saint Epiphanius, *Panarion* 49, 2-3; 78, 23; 79, 2-4: vol. 2, GCS 31, pp. 243-244; vol. 3, GCS 37, pp. 473, 477-479.

8. *Didascalia Apostolorum*, ch. 15, ed. R. H. Connolly, pp. 133 and 142; *Constitutiones Apostolicae*, bk. 3, ch. 6, nos. 1-2; ch. 9, 3-4: ed. F. H. Funk, pp. 191, 201; Saint John Chrysostom, *De Sacerdotio* 2, 2: PG 48, 633.

9. Saint Bonaventure, *In IV Sent.*, Dist. 25, art. 2, q. 1, ed. Quaracchi, vol. 4, 649; Richard of Middleton, *In IV Sent.*, Dist. 25, art. 4, n. 1, ed. Venice, 1499, f° 177ᶠ; John Duns Scotus, *In IV Sent.*, Dist. 25: *Opus Oxoniense*, ed. Vives, vol. 19, p. 140; *Reportata Parisiensia*, vol. 24, pp. 369-371; Durandus of Saint-Pourçain, *In IV Sent.*, Dist. 25, q. 2, ed. Venice, 1571, f° 364ᵛ.

10. Some who also wished to explain this fact by a symbolic intention of Jesus: the Twelve were to represent the ancestors of the twelve tribes of Israel (cf. *Mt* 19:28; *Lk* 22:30). But in these texts it is only a question of their participation in the eschatological judgment. The essential meaning of the choice of the Twelve should rather be sought in the totality of their mission (cf. *Mk* 3:14): they are to represent Jesus to the people and carry on his work.

11. Pope Innocent III, *Epist.* (11 December 1210) to the Bishops of Palencia and Burgos, included in *Corpus Iuris, Decret. Lib. 5*, tit. 38, *De Paenit.*, ch. 10 *Nova*: ed. A. Friedberg, vol. 2, col. 886-887; cf. *Glossa in Decretal. Lib. 1*, tit. 33, ch. 12 *Dilecta*, vᵒ *Iurisdictioni*. Cf. Saint Thomas, *Summa Theologiae*, III, q. 27, a. 5 ad 3; Pseudo-Albert the Great, *Mariale*, quaest. 42, ed. Borgnet 37, 81.

12. Pope Pius XII, Apostolic Constitution *Sacramentum Ordinis*, 30 November 1947: AAS 40 (1948), pp. 5-7; Pope Paul VI, Apostolic Constitution *Divinae Consortium Naturae*, 15 August 1971: AAS 63 (1971), pp. 657-664; Apostolic Constitution *Sacram Unctionem*, 30 November 1972: AAS 65 (1973), pp. 5-9.

13. Pope Pius XII, Apostolic Constitution *Sacramentum Ordinis: loc. cit.*, p. 5.

14. Session 21, chap. 2: Denzinger-Schönmetzer, *Enchiridion Symbolorum* 1728.

15. Saint Cyprian, *Epist.* 63, 14: PL 4, 397 B; ed. Hartel, vol. 3, p. 713.

16. Second Vatican Council, Constitution *Sacrosanctum Concilium*, 33 (4 December 1963): "...by the priest who presides over the assembly in the person of Christ..."; Dogmatic Constitution *Lumen Gentium*, 10 (21 November 1964): "The ministerial priest, by the sacred power he enjoys, moulds and rules the priestly people. Acting in the person of Christ, he brings about the Eucharistic Sacrifice, and offers it to God in the name of all the people..." 28: "By the powers of the sacrament of Order, and in the image of Christ the eternal High Priest... they exercise this sacred function of Christ above all in the Eucharistic

liturgy or synaxis. There, acting in the person of Christ..."; Decree *Presbyterorum Ordinis,* 2 (7 December 1965): "...priests, by the anointing of the Holy Spirit, are marked with a special character and are so configured to Christ the Priest that they can act in the person of Christ the Head"; 13: "As ministers of sacred realities, especially in the Sacrifice of the Mass, priests represent the person of Christ in a special way"; cf. 1971 Synod of Bishops, *De Sacerdotio Ministeriali* I, 4; Sacred Congregation for the Doctrine of the Faith, *Declaratio circa catholicam doctrinam de Ecclesia,* 6 (24 June 1973).

17. Saint Thomas, *Summa Theologiae,* III, q. 83, art. 1, ad 3: "It is to be said that [just as the celebration of this sacrament is the representative image of Christ's Cross: *ibid.* ad 2], for the same reason the priest also enacts the image of Christ, in whose person and by whose power he pronounces the words of consecration".

18. "For since a sacrament is a sign, there is required in the things that are done in the sacraments not only the 'res' but the signification of the 'res'", recalls Saint Thomas, precisely in order to reject the ordination of women: *In IV Sent.,* dist. 25, q. 2, art. 1, quaestiuncula 1ª. corp.

19. Saint Thomas, *In IV Sent.,* dist. 25, q. 2, quaestiuncula 1ª ad 4um.

20. Cf. Council of Trent, Session 22, chap. 1: DS 1741.

21. Second Vatican Council, Dogmatic Constitution *Lumen Gentium,* 28: "Exercising within the limits of their authority the function of Christ as Shepherd and Head"; Decree *Presbyterorum Ordinis,* 2: "that they can act in the person of Christ the Head"; 6: "the office of Christ the Head and the Shepherd". Cf. Pope Pius XII, Encyclical Letter *Mediator Dei:* "the minister of the altar represents the person of Christ as the Head, offering in the name of all his members": AAS 39 (1947), p. 556; 1971 Synod of Bishops, *De Sacerdotio Ministeriali,* I, 4: "[The priestly ministry]...makes Christ, the Head of the community, present...".

22. Pope Paul VI, Encyclical Letter *Mysterium Fidei,* 3 September 1965: AAS 57 (1965), p. 761.

98

LETTER TO PRIESTS*

John Paul II, *Novo incipiente nostro*, 6 April, 1979

1. FOR YOU I AM A BISHOP, WITH YOU I AM A PRIEST

As I set about my new ministry in the Church I am deeply conscious of my need to talk to priests, to all of you, diocesan and religious, without exception. You are my brothers, through the sacrament of orders. At the outset, I want to affirm my faith in the priestly vocation. It unites you with your bishops in a special sharing of sacrament and ministry and this is how the Church, the Mystical Body of Christ, is built up. By the special grace and gift of our Saviour, you bear 'the burden of the day and the heat' (see Mt. 20:12) as you perform the many tasks of your pastoral and priestly ministry. My thoughts and my heart have turned towards all of you from the moment that Christ called me to this See where saint Peter, through life and death, had to answer the question: Do you love me? Do you love me more than these others do? (see Jn. 21:15 ff.).

I think of you constantly. I pray for you. I seek ways of spiritual union and collaboration with you, because through the sacrament of orders which I too received from the hands of my bishop (Cardinal Adam Stephen Sapieha, of unforgettable memory, Metropolitan Archbishop of Cracow), you are my brothers. Adapting the words of Saint Augustine, I want to say to you today: 'For you I am a bishop, with you I am a priest'. There is a special reason today for confiding to you the sentiments expressed in this letter: it is the proximity of Holy Thursday. This annual feast of our priesthood unites the entire presbyterium of each diocese about its bishop in the shared celebration of the Eucharist. It is on this day that every priest is invited to renew the promises made at his priestly ordination, before his own bishop and together with him. By this very fact, my brothers in the episcopate and I are enabled to be especially at one with you and above all to be at the very heart of the mystery of Jesus Christ, the mystery in which we all share.

The second Vatican Council set the collegiality of the episcopate in strong relief and it also gave a new form to the community life of priests, seeing them as joined together by a special bond of brotherhood, united to their respective local bishops. The entire life and ministry of priests deepens and strengthens that bond. Priests' Councils accept a particular responsibility for the various tasks involved in the life and ministry of priests. Every diocese should have a functioning priests' council, according to the mind of the council and Paul VI's *Motu Proprio, Ecclesiae Sanctae* (1, 15). The purpose of all this is to ensure that every bishop, in collaboration with his presbyterium, can engage more effectively in evangelization. It is through this that the Church accomplishes its mission and indeed realizes its very nature. That priests should be at one with their bishops on this matter is confirmed by Saint Ignatius of Antioch: 'Try to do all things in accordance with the divine harmony: the bishops, representing God, presiding; the presbyters representing the council of the apostles; the deacons, so dear to me, entrusted with the service of Jesus Christ'. (Letter to the Magnesians, VI, 1).

2. LOVE FOR CHRIST AND THE CHURCH UNITES US.

This letter is not meant to be a full treatment of priestly life and ministry. For this I refer to the entire tradition of the magisterium and of the Church, especially to the documents of the Second Vatican Council and in particular the constitution *Lumen Gentium* and the decrees *Presbyterorum Ordinis* and *Ad Gentes.* I also refer to the encyclical of my predecessor, Paul VI, *Sacerdotalis Caelibatus.* Lastly, I want especially to single out the document issued by the 1971 Synod of Bishops and approved by Paul VI, *De Sacerdotio Ministeriali.* I find in this document, issued, it is true, by a body with consultative status, a statement of essential importance on priestly life and ministry in the modern world.

Having listed these sources, which are familiar to you, I wish in this letter to make just a few points which seem to me to be of the greatest importance at this moment in the history of the Church and of the world. What I have to say is dictated by my love for the Church. The Church will be able to carry out its mission to the world if, in spite of human weakness, it remains faithful to Christ. I know that I am addressing men for whom only the love of Christ has made it possible to serve the Church and, in the Church, to serve mankind, addressing themselves to the most urgent problems, especially that of man's eternal salvation.

Even though I begin by listing official documents, I want however to remind you of that living source which is our common love for Christ and his Church, a love that springs from the grace of the priestly vocation, a love that is the greatest gift of the Holy Spirit (see Rom. 5:5; 1 Cor 12:31).

3. CHOSEN FROM AMONG MEN. . .APPOINTED TO ACT ON BEHALF OF MEN (Heb. 5:1)

The Second Vatican Council deepened our understanding of the priesthood and presented it consistently as the manifestation of the inner forces, the 'dynamisms' whereby the mission of the entire people of God in the Church is constituted. On this point one should consult the Constitution Lumen Gentium, in particular, and should re-read carefully the relevant paragraphs. The People of God accomplishes its mission by sharing in the office and mission of Jesus Christ himself. This, as we know, is three-fold: it is the office and mission of Prophet, Priest and King. If we examine the council texts carefully it becomes obvious that we should speak of a three-fold dimension to Christ's office and mission, rather than of three different functions. In fact, these three dimensions are closely linked to one another and they explain, condition and clarify one another. It is in its three-fold unity, therefore, that we share Christ's office and mission. The special witness that we give in the Church and before the world, as Christians, members of God's People, and then as priests, part of the hierarchical order, is rooted in our Teacher's combined mission and office as Prophet, Priest and King.

The priesthood which we share and which the sacrament of orders has permanently 'imprinted' on our souls in a special sign or 'character' is clearly related to the common priesthood of the faithful, the priesthood of all the baptized. It differs from it, however, 'essentially and not only in degree' (Lumen Gentium, 10). This is what is meant by the author of the letter to the Hebrews when he says of the priest: 'chosen from among men. . . appointed to act on behalf of men' (Heb. 5).

At this point, it will be helpful to re-read the whole of this classic conciliar text (Lumen Gentium, 10). It expresses the basic truths about our vocation in the Church:

Christ the Lord, high priest taken from among men (cf. Heb. 5:1), made the new people 'a kingdom of priests to God, his Father' (Rev. 1:6, cf. 5:9-10). The baptized, by regeneration and the anointing of the Holy Spirit, are consecrated to be a spiritual house and a holy priesthood, that through all the works of Christian men they may offer spiritual sacrifices and proclaim the perfection of him who has called them out of darkness into his marvellous light (cf. 1 Pt. 2:4-10). Therefore all the disciples of Christ, persevering in prayer and praising God together (cf. Acts 2:42-47), should present themselves as a sacrifice, living, holy and pleasing to God (cf. Rom 12:1). They should everywhere on earth bear witness to Christ and give an answer to everyone who asks a reason for the hope of an eternal life which is theirs (cf. 1 Pt. 3:15).

Though they differ essentially and not only in degree, the common priesthood of the faithful and the ministerial or hierarchical priesthood are none the less ordered one to another; each in its own proper way shares in the one priesthood of Christ. The ministerial priest, by the sacred power that he has forms and rules the priestly people; in the person of Christ he effects the Eucharistic Sacrifice and offers it to God in the name of all the people. The faithful indeed, by virtue of their royal priesthood, participate in the offering of the Eucharist. They exercise that priesthood, too, by the reception of the sacraments, prayer and thanksgiving, the witness of a holy life, abnegation and active charity.

4. THE PRIEST AS GIFT OF CHRIST TO THE COMMUNITY

We must examine in detail both the theoretical and the existential meaning of the relationship between the hierarchical priesthood and the priesthood that is common to all believers. That they differ essentially and not only in degree is due to the very richness of the priesthood of Christ, which is the source and centre of both priesthoods. The sacrament of orders, dear brothers, which only we have received, is the fruit of the special grace of vocation and is the basis of our identity. Of its nature and because of its effects on our lives and activity, it tends to make the faithful aware of their common priesthood and to activate it (see Eph. 4:11, 12). It reminds them that they are the People of God and enables them 'to offer spiritual sacrifices' (see 1 Pt. 2:5) through which Christ himself makes us an everlasting gift to the Father (1 Pt. 3:18). This happens especially when the priest 'by the sacred power that he has. . .in the person of Christ effects the Eucharistic Sacrifice and offers it to God in the name of the people', as we read in the council text quoted above.

Our sacramental priesthood, therefore, is at the same time an hierarchical and ministerial priesthood. It is a special *minister-ium,* or service, to the community of believers. It does not originate in the community, as though it was the community which called or delegated. The sacramental priesthood is in fact a gift given to the community by Christ himself from the fullness of his priesthood. This fullness enables Christ both to make everyone capable of offering spiritual sacrifice and to call some and make them capable of being ministers of his own sacramen-tal sacrifice, the eucharist, in the following of which all the faith-ful share and in which their spiritual sacrifices are assumed.

In view of this, we can see that our priesthood is hierachical, which means that it involves the power of forming and governing the priestly people (see *Lumen Gentium,* 10) and that for pre-cisely this reason it is ministerial. We perform this ministry, through which Christ himself unceasingly serves the Father in the work of our salvation. Our whole priestly existence is and must be deeply imbued with this service, if we wish adequately to celebrate the eucharistic sacrifice in the person of Christ.

The priesthood calls for a special integrity of life and service and such integrity is supremely suited to our priestly identity. Priestly identity incorporates both great dignity and the availa-bility proportionate to it. It involves humble readiness to accept the gifts of the Holy Spirit and to transmit to others the fruits of love and peace, to impart to them that sure faith from which derives a profound understanding of human existence and makes possible the application of the moral law in the lives of in-dividuals and in the human situation.

Since the priesthood is given to us so that, after the example of our Lord, we can serve others unceasingly, it may not be re-nounced because of difficulties encountered and sacrifices ex-pected of us. Like the apostles, we have left everything to follow Christ (see Mt. 19:27). We must therefore persevere at this side, accepting the cross too.

5. IN THE SERVICE OF THE GOOD SHEPHERD

As I write, I think of the vast and varied human situations to which you are sent, dear brothers, as labourers into the Lord's vineyard (see Mt. 20:1-16). But the parable of the sheep-fold (see Jn. 10:1-16) is also applicable to you. Your priesthood imparts to you a pastoral charism, a special likeness to Christ, the Good

Shepherd. This quality belongs to you in a very special way. All the laity, the great community of the People of God, our brothers and sisters, are expected to work for the salvation of others, as the Second Vatican Council stated so clearly (see *Lumen Gentium,* 11). You priests, however, are expected to have a concern and a commitment greater than and different from that of any lay person. And this is because you share in the priesthood of Jesus Christ in a way that differs 'essentially and not only in degree' (*Lumen Gentium,* 10) from the manner in which they share.

The priesthood of Jesus Christ is the primary source and expression of an unceasing and constantly effective care for our salvation. This is why we regard him as the Good Shepherd. Do not the words: 'the good shepherd is one who lays down his life for his sheep' (Jn. 10:11) refer to the sacrifice of the Cross, the definitive act of Christ's priesthood? Do they not show all of us with whom Christ our Lord has shared his priesthood, through the sacrament of orders, the road that we too must travel? Do they not tell us that it is our vocation to have a special solicitude for the salvation of our neighbour? That this solicitude is the *raison d'être* of our priestly lives? That it is this solicitude that gives them meaning and that only through it can we discover the full significance of our own lives, perfection and holiness? This theme is treated in the conciliar decree, *Optatam Totius* (see 8-11, 19-20).

The point is made even clearer by our Teacher, when he says: 'For anyone who wants to save his life will lose it; but anyone who loses his life for my sake and for the sake of the gospel, will save it' (Mk. 8:35). These are mysterious, seemingly paradoxical, words. But they cease to be mysterious if we put them into practice. Then the paradox disappears and the profound simplicity of their meaning is fully revealed. May all of us be granted this grace in our priestly lives and ministry.

6. THE SUPREME ART IS THE DIRECTION OF SOULS

The special care committed to us by Christ—for the salvation for truth, for the love and holiness of the entire people of God, for the spiritual unity of the Church—is exercised in various ways. You will fulfil your priestly vocation in various ways, dear brothers. Some of you are involved in pastoral work in parishes, others on the foreign missions, in the training and education of youth, in social and cultural activities, in the care of the sick and the deprived. Some of you are yourselves bed-ridden and in pain. It is impossible to list the many and varied apostolates demanded by the variety of patterns of human living, of social structures and of cultures and civilizations, each with its own history and tradition. Granted all these different apostolates, however, you have always and everywhere your special vocation, you bear the grace of Christ, the Eternal Priest, and you carry the charism of the Good Shepherd. This vocation you can never forget, can never renounce, but must exercise constantly, in every place and in every way. This is the 'supreme art' to which Jesus Christ has called you. 'The supreme art is the direction of souls', wrote Saint Gregory the Great (*Regula Pastoralis,* 1:1).

I say to you, therefore, using his phraseology: endeavour to be 'artists' of pastoral work. There have been many such in the history of the Church. Each of us has something to learn from, for example, Saint Vincent de Paul, Saint John of the Cross, the Curé of Ars, Saint John Bosco, Blessed Maximilian Kolbe and many, many others. They were all different, each of them was himself, and was a man of his own time. But each of them was a man of his own time in his own original response to the gospel, a response needed in his day, a response of holiness and zeal. There is no other rule for being men of our own times in our priestly life and activity. Certainly, the various attempts to 'secularize' our priestly life and activity cannot be regarded as adequate responses to the problem.

7. STEWARD AND WITNESS

The priestly life is built upon the foundation of the sacrament of orders, which imparts on our souls an indelible mark. This mark is made in the depths of our being and it has its 'personalistic' dynamism. The priestly personality must be clearly there for others to see. It must be a sign for them. This is the first requisite for our pastoral service. The people from among whom and for whom we have been chosen (see Heb. 5:1) want above all to see this sign and this is their right. It may sometimes seem to us that they do not want this, or that they wish us to be in every way like themselves. At times it even seems that they demand this. Here, however, one needs a profound sense of faith and the gift of discernment. It is easy to allow oneself to be guided by appearances and to succumb to a fundamental illusion concerning what is essential. Those who call for the secularization of the priestly life and applaud its various manifestations will undoubtedly abandon us if we succumb to temptation. We shall then cease to be needed and wanted.

Attempts to manipulate people are common today, but it does

not follow that we have to give in to them.[1] In practice, the only priest whom people will always feel they need is the priest who is conscious of the full meaning of his priesthood, the priest of deep faith, who professes his faith courageously, prays fervently, teaches with deep conviction, serves, lives the beatitudes, knows how to love disinterestedly and is close to all, especially to those who are most in need.

Our vocation demands that we be close to people in their problems, whether personal, family, or social. But it also demands that we be close to them in a priestly way. Only thus do we remain ourselves in the midst of these problems. If we are to be of assistance to people in their problems, and they can be very difficult, we must keep our identity and remain really faithful to our vocation. In collaboration with all men, we must very clear-sightedly seek truth and justice, which only in the gospel, or rather in Christ himself, are to be found in their true and definitive dimension. It is our task to serve truth and justice for men and women in this life, but always in the perspective of eternal salvation. This salvation includes the temporal achievements of the human spirit in the spheres of knowledge and morality, as the Second Vatican Council reminds us (see *Gaudium et Spes*, 38, 39, 42), but it is not identified with them. In fact, it surpasses them: 'The things that no eye has seen and no ear has heard . . . all that God has prepared for those who love him' (1 Cor. 2:9). Our fellow believers, and unbelievers too, expect us to show them this perspective, to be genuine witnesses to it, to be dispensers of grace and ministers of the word of God. They expect us to be men of prayer.

Among us there are some who live their priestly vocation in lives of intense prayer and penance in strictly contemplative religious orders. They should remember that it is their priestly ministry to share in a special way the grand solicitude of the Good Shepherd, a solicitude for the salvation of every human being.

And this we must all remember: that none of us should ever be found to deserve the name of 'hireling', one 'whose own sheep are not', who 'is not a shepherd, . . . sees the wolf coming and leaves the sheep and flees; and the wolf snatches them and scatters them. He flees because he is a hireling and cares nothing for the sheep' (Jn. 10:12, 13). It is the wish of every good shepherd that all 'may have life and have it to the full' (Jn. 10:10), that none of them may be lost (see Jn 17:12) but may have eternal life. Let us ensure that such solicitude penetrates our souls deeply. Let us try to live by it. May it characterize us and be the basis of our priestly identity.

8. THE MEANING OF CELIBACY

Allow me at this point to touch on the question of celibacy. I shall deal with it briefly, since it was treated fully and in depth at the council, in the encyclical *Sacerdotalis Caelibatus* and at the 1971 synod of bishops. Such reflection was deemed necessary in the interests of a fuller presentation of the issue and to provide a deeper understanding of the decision taken by the Latin Church so many centuries ago, a decision which it endeavoured to abide by and which it wishes to continue to abide by in the future. Because the question is so important and the language so close to that of the gospel, we cannot discuss it in categories different from those used by the Council, the synod of bishops and the great Pope Paul VI himself. We can only aim to achieve a deeper understanding of celibacy and a more mature response, setting aside the objections which have always been, and still are, levelled against it and eschewing the application of criteria alien to the Gospel, Tradition and the Church's Magisterium. It is very doubtful, one might add, if such criteria are anthropologically accurate, have a sound basis in fact and have any but relative value.

Nor must we be too surprised by the intensification of objections and criticisms since the council, although in some places they seem to be tapering off. Did not Jesus Christ, after he had spoken to the disciples about renunciation of marriage 'for the sake of the kingdom' add the significant words: 'He who is able to receive this, let him receive it' (Mt. 19:12). It has been, and continues to be, the wish of the Latin Church, appealing to the example of Christ the Lord himself, to the teaching of the apostles and to its own entire tradition, that all who receive the sacrament of orders should accept this renunciation 'for the sake of the kingdom of heaven'.

This tradition, however, is coupled with respect for the different traditions of other churches. In fact, it is a characteristic of the Latin Catholic Church, a tradition to which it owes much and in which it is resolved to persevere. This in spite of all the difficulties endangering such fidelity and in spite of the symptoms of weakness and of crisis seen in individual priests. We are all aware that 'we have this treasure in earthen vessels' (2 Cor. 4:7). But we know well that is is indeed a treasure.

In what sense is it a treasure? Does our position imply a disparagement of the value of marriage and of the vocation to family life? Or a Manichean contempt for the human body and its functions? Are we in some way devaluing love, which brings a man and woman to marriage and to the wedded unity of the body, forming 'two in one flesh'? (Gen. 2:24, see Mt. 19:6). How could we think and reason like that if we know, believe and proclaim, with St Paul, that marriage is 'a great mystery' in reference to Christ and the Church? (see Eph. 5:32).

None of the reasons are true whereby people sometimes try to convince us that celibacy is not appropriate. The truth is what the Church proclaims and endeavours to be incarnate through the commitment which priests take on before ordination. The essential, proper and adequate reason is contained in the truth which Christ proclaimed when he spoke of the renunciation of marriage for the sake of the kingdom of heaven and which Saint Paul proclaimed when he wrote that everybody in the Church has his or her own particular gifts (see 1 Cor. 7:7). Celibacy is just that, a gift of the Spirit. The vocation to faithful married love is also a gift, though a different gift, one directed towards procreation in the lofty context of the sacrament of matrimony. This gift is obviously of fundamental importance for the building up of the community of the Church, the people of God. But if the community is to respond fully to the call of Christ, the other gift, of celibacy 'for the sake of the kingdom of heaven' will have to find its place among its members, in due proportion.

Why does the Latin Catholic Church link this gift not only with the vocation to the religious life, but also with the vocation to the hierarchical and ministerial priesthood? It does so because celibacy 'for the sake of the kingdom' is not only an eschatological sign, it also has great social relevance in this life for the service of the People of God. Through his celibacy, the priest becomes the 'man for others' differently from the way that a married man becomes, as husband and father, a 'man for others', especially within his own family: for his wife and, with her, for the children whom he begets. The priest in renouncing the fatherhood proper to married men seeks another fatherhood and even another motherhood, as it were, after the words of the Apostle concerning the children with whom he is 'in travail'(see Gal. 4:19, 1 Cor. 4:15).

The priest's are spiritual children, entrusted to his solicitude by the Good Shepherd. They are numerous, more numerous than an ordinary family could contain. The pastoral vocation of priests is great and the Council teaches us that it is universal: it is for the whole Church (see *Presbyterorum Ordinis*, 3, 6, 10, 12). Therefore it is missionary by nature. Normally, it is linked to the service of a particular community of the People of God, in which each individual expects attention, love and care. If the heart of the priest is to be available for this service, it must be free. Celibacy is a symbol of availability for service. This symbol proclaims that the hierarchical or ministerial priesthood is, in keeping with the tradition of the Church, strictly for the sake of the common priesthood of the faithful.

9. TEST AND RESPONSIBILITY

The widespread view that celibacy in the Catholic Church is imposed by law on ordinands is due to a misunderstanding if not to downright bad faith. We all know that it is not so. Every Christian who receives the sacrament of orders commits himself to celibacy in full knowledge and freedom, after a number of years spent in training and after profound reflection and assiduous prayer. He decides upon a life of celibacy only after he has become firmly convinced that Christ is giving him this gift for the good of the Church and for the service of others. Only then does he commit himself to a life of celibacy. It is obvious that such a decision is binding not only because it is a matter of Church law, but also because it is something for which one is personally responsible. It is a matter of keeping one's word to Christ and to the Church. Keeping his word is for the priest a duty but also at the same time a proof of his inner maturity. It is the expression of his personal dignity. The moment of truth comes when the priest finds it difficult to keep his promise to Christ, when the commitment that he knowingly and freely made to life-long celibacy is put to the test, when he is exposed to temptation. For the priest is not spared such things, any more than is any other Christian. At such times, he must look for support in more fervent prayer. Through prayer he must foster humility and sincerity before God and his own conscience. Prayer imparts strength to faltering resolution and induces a confidence akin to that of which St Paul speaks: 'I can do all things in him who strengthens me' (Phil 4:13). Many priests can confirm this from their own experience. It is a proven fact of life.

If a man accepts these truths it will help him to remain faithful to the promise he made to Christ and to the Church. The promise itself should be seen as an indication of genuine fidelity to oneself, one's own conscience, humanity and dignity. A man should recall such matters at a time of crisis, instead of having recourse to a dispensation, as though the problem were a purely administrative matter, to be settled by the intervention of the authorities. What is in question here is a profound problem of conscience and a testing of our humanity. God has the right to test each one of us in this way, since this earthly life is for everybody a time for testing. But God also wishes us to emerge victorious from such tests and he provides adequate help.

It is well to recall at this point that the commitment to married fidelity undertaken in the sacrament of matrimony involves similar obligations. It sometimes exposes husbands and wives to similar trials and experiences, affording them the opportunity of proving the worth of their love. For love, in all its dimensions, is not only a call but also a duty.

Lastly, our brothers and sisters who are married have the right to expect good example from us priests and the witness of faithfulness to our vocation until death. We chose our vocation just as they chose theirs. In this regard, too, we should see our ministerial priesthood as being at the service of the common priesthood of the faithful, especially of those who marry and have families. In this way we serve by 'building up the body of Christ' (Eph. 4:12). Otherwise instead of helping to build the body we in fact weaken its spiritual structure. Closely linked with the building up of the human body of Christ is the authentic development of the human personality of every Christian, and hence of every priest, according to the measure of Christ's gift. The human personality could neither develop properly nor be inadequately put to the test if the spiritual structure of the Church were dismantled.

10. EVERY DAY WE NEED TO BE CONVERTED AGAIN

'What must we do then?' This seems to be your question, dear brothers, the question put so frequently to Christ by his disciples and hearers (see Lk. 3:10). What must the Church do, when it seems there is a shortage of priests, especially in certain parts of the world? How are we to respond to the immense need for evangelization and how can we satisfy the hunger for the word and for the Body of the Lord? The Church is committed to maintaining celibacy as a special gift for the Kingdom of God and proclaims its faith and hope in its Teacher, Redeemer and Spouse, who is at the same time 'Lord of the harvest' (Mt. 9:38) and the source of the gift. In fact, 'every perfect gift is from above, coming down from the Father of lights' (James 1:17). For our part, we cannot allow our human doubts or timidity to weaken this faith and confidence.

We must therefore be converted again every day. We know that this is a fundamental demand of the Gospel. Since it is expected of everyone, all the more so is it expected of us. If it is our task to help others to be converted, we must for our part be converted constantly. Being converted means returning to the grace of our vocation. It means meditating upon the infinite goodness and love of Christ, who has addressed each of us by name and has said: 'Follow me'. Being converted means constantly rendering an account before the Lord of our hearts concerning our service, our zeal and our fidelity, for we are 'servants of Christ and stewards of the mysteries of God' (1 Cor. 4:1). Being converted also means constantly rendering an account of our negligencies and sins, of our timidity, our lack of faith and hope, of thinking only as men think and not as God thinks. We should keep before our minds the warning that Christ gave to Peter himself in this regard (see Mt. 16:23). Being converted means seeking again the pardon and strength of God in the sacrament of Reconciliation, thus constantly beginning anew, making progress daily, getting the better of ourselves, making spiritual conquests, giving cheerfully, for 'God loves a cheerful giver' (2 Cor. 9:7).

Being converted means 'always to pray and not to lose heart' (Lk. 18:1). In a sense, prayer is the first and the last requisite for conversion, spiritual progress and holinesss. In recent years there has been here and there too much discussion, perhaps, about the priesthood, the priest's identity, the value of his presence in the modern world, etc., and on the other hand there has been too little praying. There has been little enough enthusiasm for revitalizing the priesthood itself through prayer, thus making priests more effective evangelizers and establishing priestly identity. Prayer fashions the essential style of the priest, which without it is deformed. Prayer helps us to find the light that has led us since the beginning of our priestly lives and which never ceases to lead us, even though at times it may seem to vanish into the darkness. Prayer makes continual conversion possible for us and enables us to reach out to God constantly. This is essential if we are to lead others to him. Prayer helps us to believe, to hope and to love, even in spite of our human weakness.

Prayer likewise makes it possible for us to rediscover constantly the dimensions of that kingdom for whose coming we pray every day, in the words that Christ taught us. Then we become aware of our own part in securing the granting of the petition, 'Thy kingdom come' and we see how necessary is our participation. And perhaps when we pray we shall see more easily those 'fields. . . already white for harvest' (Jn 4:35) and we shall understand the meaning of Christ's words as he looked at them: 'pray therefore the Lord of the harvest to send out labourers into his harvest' (Mt 9:38).

Our own continuing formation should go hand in hand with prayer. As is stated in the document on the subject issued by the Sacred Congregation for the Clergy (AAS 62, pp. 123 ff) the formation must be interior, having to do with deepening the priest's spiritual life, and pastoral and intellectual life—this latter involving philosophy and theology. Our pastoral activity, the proclamation of the word and our entire priestly ministry depend upon the intensity of our spiritual life. But they must also find sustenance in constant study. We cannot rest content with what we once learned in the seminary, even if, as the Sacred Congregation for Catholic Education strongly recommends, our studies were done at university level. Our intellectual formation must continue all our lives, especially nowadays when there is such widespread development of education and culture in many parts of the world. We must be able to give properly qualified witness to those who enjoy the benefits of this development. As teachers of truth and morality we must tell them, convincingly and effectively, of the hope that gives us life. And this also forms part of the daily conversion to love, through the truth.

Dear brothers: you who have borne 'The burden of the day and the heat' (Mt. 20:12), who have put your hand to the plough and have not turned back (see Lk. 9:62) and—perhaps more especially—those of you who are in doubt about the meaning of your vocation or the value of your service, think of the places where people anxiously await a priest and over the years of waiting have never ceased to hope for one. Sometimes they meet in an abandoned shrine and place on the altar a stole which they still keep. They recite all the prayers of the Mass until they come to the words of the consecration. Then a deep silence comes upon them, a silence sometimes broken by a sob. . .so ardently do they long to hear the words that only a priest can speak effectively. They long for holy communion, for which they depend on the ministry of a priest, just as they also long to hear the words of pardon: *Ego te absolve a peccatis tuis.* How deeply do they feel the lack of a priest. There are such places in the world. If any of you doubts the meaning of his priesthood, if he thinks it socially unfruitful and useless, let him reflect on that.

We must be converted every day. We must rediscover every day the gift given us by Christ himself in the sacrament of orders, learning to appreciate the importance of the salvific mission of the Church, reflecting on our own vocation in the context of that mission.

11. MOTHER OF PRIESTS

Dear brothers, as I begin my ministry I entrust all of you to the Mother of Christ. She is our mother in a special way, the mother of priests. In fact, the beloved disciple, who as one of the twelve had heard the words 'Do this in memory of me', in the upper room, was given by the crucified Christ to his mother with the words 'This is your son' (Jn. 19:26). The man who on Holy Thursday received the power to celebrate the eucharist was, by these words of the dying Redeemer, given to his mother as her son. All of us, therefore, who receive the same power through priestly ordination have in a sense a prior right to see her as our mother. And so I desire that all of you should, with me, find in Mary the mother of the priesthood which we have received from Christ. I also desire that you should very specially entrust your priesthood to her. Allow me to do it myself, entrusting each of you without exception to the Mother of Christ in a manner that is at once solemn, simple and humble. And as I ask each of you, dear brothers, to do for yourselves, in the manner dictated by your own weakness, which accompanies your desire to serve and to achieve holiness. I ask you to do this.

Today's church speaks of itself in the dogmatic constitution, *Lumen Gentium*. In the last chapter it asserts that it looks to Mary as to the mother of Christ, because she calls herself a mother and wishes to be a mother, begetting people for God in a new life (ch. 8). How close you are to God's cause, dear brothers. How deeply is it imprinted on your vocation, ministry and mission. Among the people of God which looks to Mary with immense love and hope, you must look to her with exceptional love and hope. Indeed, it is your task to proclaim Christ, her Son. And who can better communicate to you the truth about him than his mother? It is your task to nourish men's hearts with Christ. And who can make you more aware of what you are doing than she who nourished him? 'Hail, true Body, born of the Virgin Mary'. There is a wonderful dimension to our ministerial priesthood: it places us near the mother of Christ. Let us try to live in that dimension. If I may be permitted a personal observation: I want to tell you that in what I have written here I am referring especially to my own experience.

As I communicate all this to you, at the commencement of my service to the universal church, I do not cease to ask God to fill you, priests of Jesus Christ, with every grace and blessing. As a token of this communion in prayer, I bless you with all my heart, in the name of the Father and of the Son and of the Holy Spirit.

Accept this blessing. Accept the words of the new successor of Peter, whom the Lord commanded: 'and when you have turned again, strengthen your brethren' (Lk. 22:32). Do not cease to pray for me, with the rest of the Church, that I may respond to the demands of a primacy of love which the Lord made the basis of Peter's mission when he said to him: 'Feed my lambs' (Jn. 21:16). Amen.

---

* Translation by A.F. Latin text in *A.A.S.* 71 (1979), 393–417.
1. 'Let us not deceive ourselves by thinking that we serve the Gospel if we try to dilute our priestly charism...' Pope John Paul II, Discourse to the Clergy of Rome, 9 Nov., 1978, no. 3.

99

NORMS FOR COOPERATION AMONG LOCAL CHURCHES AND FOR A BETTER DISTRIBUTION OF THE CLERGY*

S.C.C., *Postquam apostoli*, 25 March, 1980

INTRODUCTION

Teaching of Vatican Council II

1. After the entrusting to the apostles by Christ the Lord, before his ascension into heaven, of the mission to be witnesses "til the ends of the earth" (Acts 1:8), all their labors and solicitudes had no other aim than the faithful execution of the mandate of Christ: "Go into the whole world, and preach the Gospel to every creature" (Mark 16:15).

The church, as history tells us, through the centuries never ceased to pledge herself with faithfulness and enthusiasm for the practical fulfillment of such a mandate. And even recently, the successors of the apostles gathered from all over the world in the Second Vatican Council, insisted on the same mandate with these words: "They (the pastors) should be especially concerned about those parts of the world where the word of God has not yet been proclaimed or where, chiefly because of the small number of priests, the faithful are in danger of departing from the precepts of Christian life and even of losing the faith itself." For this reason, the bishops should "strive to see to it that suitable sacred ministers as well as assistants, both Religious and lay, are prepared for the missions and other areas suffering from a lack of clergy."[1]

Institution of a Commission for the Distribution of the Clergy.

2. In order to give practical fulfillment to this intention of the council, the supreme pontiff Paul VI, in the motu proprio "Ecclesiae Sanctae" ordered that a special commission be created within the Holy See "with the task to issue general principles for a better distribution of the clergy, keeping in mind the needs of

the various churches."[2] The seat of such commission, as it was established in the apostolic constitution "Regimini Ecclesiae Universae," is to be attached to the Sacred Congregation for the Clergy.[3]

On this matter, this sacred dicastery has already consulted the episcopal conferences and has held an international congress at Malta in 1970.[4] Furthermore, after having convoked its members often and heard the opinion of the other departments of the Roman Curia many times, this very dicastery, having considered the importance and the opportunity of this action, engaged itself in the preparation of norms which now, with the approval of the supreme pontiff, promulgates through this present document.

NEED TO IMPLEMENT THE MANDATE OF CHRIST

The Whole Church Is Called to Evangelize

3. The means through which the church has to fulfill the mandate of Christ is evangelization, following the example of her founder who was the first evangelizer. She has always considered evangelization as indeed her specific and most important task. As a matter of fact, she exists only for this task, as the bishops stated in the synod of 1977: "We wish once again to confirm that the mandate to evangelize all mankind constitutes the essential mission of the church."[5]

As a consequence, no person baptized or confirmed in the church can dispense himself from this duty, following the exhortation of Vatican Council II: "Since the whole church is missionary and the work of evangelization is a basic duty of the people of God, this sacred synod summons all to a deep interior renewal, so that they will have a vivid awareness of their own responsibility for spreading the Gospel."[6]

Even though every Christian should cooperate in the mission of the church for the part that is his, considering however the diversity of the members when it comes to the tasks to be fulfilled,[7] different will be the role of the bishop, of the priest, of the Religious as well as of the lay person.

The Role of the Bishop

4. The duty of evangelization belongs, first of all, to the bishops, who—"sub Petro et cum Petro"—must not only care for the evangelization as far as the faithful of their dioceses are concerned, but they must also feel the responsibility for the salvation of the whole world.[8] In fact, "each of them as a member of

the episcopal college and a legitimate successor of the apostles, is obliged by Christ's decree and command[9] to be solicitous for the whole church. This solicitude, though it is not exercised by an act of jurisdiction, contributes immensely to the welfare of the universal church."[10]

It is the task of the bishop to use every effort so that the faithful may have since their early childhood and may keep all their lives an authentic Catholic conscience,[11] all in order to love the whole mystical body of Christ, especially in its poorest members and in those who are suffering and are being persecuted for the sake of justice.[12] Furthermore, he should promote the missionary zeal among his people, so that the laborers of the Gospel in mission lands will not be deprived of the necessary aid, spiritual and material; he has to encourage missionary vocations among youngsters, and also foster in the candidates to the priesthood the universal dimension of their mission, and consequently their disponibility to serve also outside of the diocese.[13]

The Duty of the Priests

5. The priests, who, together with their bishops, act "in the name and in the person of Christ who is the head,"[14] contribute in a very special way, to the expansion of the kingdom of God on earth, through their office of pastors of souls, their preaching of the word of God and the administration of the sacraments of the new law.[15] They, therefore, through their ministry "make visible in their communities, the universal church."[16]

On the other hand, the same Christian community by its essence needs the presence of priests, because the community cannot really be established without the sacrifice of Christ which "through the hands of the priests and in the name of the whole church, is offered in the Eucharist in an unbloody and sacramental manner";[17] and such a liturgical action represents the center of the community of the faithful.[18] Hence, the Synod of Bishops in 1971 rightly declared concerning the ministerial priesthood: "If we would lose the presence and the action of his (of the priest's) ministry . . . the church could not have the full assurance of her faithfulness and of his visible continuity."[19] However, such spiritual gift which is received by the priests in the sacred ordination "prepares them not for any limited and narrow mission, but for the widest scope of the universal mission of salvation even to the very ends of the earth; for every priestly ministry shares in the universality of the mission entrusted by Christ to his apostles."[20]

Every priest should therefore nourish such disponibility of soul in his heart, and if someone receives a special vocation from the spirit of the Lord, with the consent of his bishop, he will not refuse to move to another diocese in order to continue his ministry.

Anyhow, all the priests should be sensitive to the needs of the universal church, and therefore, they should inquire about the state of the missions, as well as about the situation of the local churches that find themselves in some particular difficulty, so that they may exhort the faithful to share the needs of the church.[21]

The Participation of the Religious

6. Men and women Religious, already because of their vows, are intimately connected with the mystery of the church, and therefore from the particular nature of their lives, stems the duty to endeavor so that "the kingdom of Christ may be rooted and consolidated in the souls and spread all over the world."[22] Consequently Vatican Council II not only exhorts them to foster the missionary spirit, but further invites the institutes, except for their specific goals, to update themselves in order to adjust to the present situations, so that the "evangelization in the missions may become more and more effective."[23]

Men and women Religious that belong to missionary institutes have been and still are models of life entirely dedicated to the cause of Christ. In them, we admire that promptness which stems from their consecration to God, the church and their brothers; in fact "thanks to their religious consecration they are first of all volunteers and free to leave everything and go to announce the Gospel to the ends of the world."[24] Finally, since the religious state is "a special gift," it is given for the whole church, whose salvific mission in no way can operate without the participation of the Religious."[25]

The Call of the Laity

7. All lay people, in virtue of their baptism and confirmation, are called by God to an effective apostolate: "The Christian vocation is by its nature also a call to the apostolate."[26] The apostolate of the laity, even though exercised mainly in the parishes, has to be extended however also to the inter-parochial, diocesan, national and international level. And more than that, they should have at heart "the needs of the people of God over all the earth"; which could be done by helping the missionary

works with material subsidies and personal services.[27]

Furthermore, lay people may be called by the hierarchy to a more direct and immediate cooperation in the apostolate. The church, as a matter of fact, in the last decades has discovered the rich possibilities and the vast resources that the cooperation of the laity can offer to her mission of salvation. The apostolic exhortation "Evangelii Nuntiandi," already on the basis of the most recent experiences, enumerates various functions, such as that of catechist, that of Christians dedicated to the service of the word of God or to the works of mercy, that of heads of small communities, etc. This cooperation of the laity, useful everywhere, is useful especially in mission lands for the founding, the life and the development of the church.[28]

All the members of the church, therefore, be they pastors, lay people or Religious, share, each in his own way, the missionary nature of the church. The diversity of the members, due to the variety of the ministries or charisms, as the apostle tells us, has to be understood in the sense that "these members do not all have the same functions," but serving each other, they form the single body of Christ (Romans 12,4) in order to fulfill better their own mandate; the whole church, in fact, is prompted by the Holy Spirit to cooperate so that the plan of God may become a reality.[29]

THE FULFILLMENT OF THE MANDATE OF CHRIST IN OUR TIME

Statistical Data of the World's Population

8. Now, if we turn our attention to the world still to be evangelized, and, more precisely, to the non-Christian population, we cannot fail to notice the insufficiency of the means at the disposal of the church today in order to meet the enormous problem. As a matter of fact, in 1977, our planet had a population of 4,094,110,000 with a Catholic population of only 739,127,000, just 18 percent of the world's population.[30] If we, then, wish to consider the number of priests reported to the number of the world's inhabitants, we will have the following picture: for every 100,000 inhabitants, we have two priests in Asia, four in Africa, 13 in Latin America, 26 in Oceania, 29 in North America and 37 in Europe.

Inequality of Forces of the Apostolate Within the Church

9. Moreover, if you examine the distribution of sacred mini-

sters among these Catholics, the statistical data show this picture: for every 100,000 Catholics in Latin America there are 16 priests; in Southern Africa, 33 priests; in the Far East, 43 priests; in Europe, 93 priests; in Oceania, 104 priests; in North America, 120 priests; and in the Asiatic Middle East, 133 priests.

From what has been said one notes this great disproportion: While in Europe and North America one finds 45 percent of the Catholics of the world, assisted by 77.2 percent of all priests of the Catholic Church, in Latin America and in the Philippines, on the other hand, where 45 percent of the world's Catholics also live, only 12.62 percent of the priests lend their spiritual assistance.

In other words, the proportion of priests for the same number of faithful is 6 to 1 in favor of Europe and North America in comparison with Latin America and the Philippines. It is worthy of note that nearly the same inequality is found in these geographical areas if one considers the number of deacons and of men and women Religious.

It is true that the problem of a better distribution of clergy is not resolved simply with the numerical method, since it is necessary to take into account historical evolution (and) the specific conditions of more developed particular churches which, naturally, require a greater number of ministers. Nevertheless, the statistical data above carry a weight which makes one reflect and which presents grave problems for those who have at heart the healthy evolution of the church and, especially, for those who have authority in the church, as was stated earlier.

The Greatest Obstacle Springs from the Shortage of Priests

10. In our time, the greatest impediment for the fulfillment of the mandate of Christ seems to be the strong diminution of priestly and religious vocations, a phenomenon which, in the last decades, troubles many, if not all, the regions of ancient Christian tradition, either for the limited number of candidates or for the sad defection of some, or for the rather high median age of priests.

We should not forget, however, that such a shortage, if one looks at the conditions of the dioceses where more urgent is the need, is very relative, as we have stated in the last paragraph. In reality, the shortage of clergy in itself should not create an obstacle to generosity. "The dioceses that suffer from shortage of clergy," as Pius XII already said, "should not refuse to listen to the imploring petitions that come from the missions begging for help. The offering of the widow, according to the word of the Lord, should be an example to follow: 'If a poor diocese comes to the aid of another poor diocese, it will not become poorer because one cannot outdo the Lord in generosity.'"[31]

Every local church should meditate on the messianic prophecy: "The poor will be evangelized" (Luke 7:28), so that a prudence, too human and earthly, may not stifle those sentiments of generosity that impel the offering of the gift of faith to all those who today may be called poor in some way. We must, therefore, convince ourselves that the mandate of Christ cannot ever be fulfilled if a local church would like to offer only the superfluous of her energies to the churches that are poorer.

The Plan of God and the Limits of Human Forces

11. If we compare the number of Catholics with the number of non-Catholics, and at the same time we reflect on the mission entrusted today to the church for the fulfilment of the mandate of Christ, we could easily get discouraged, especially since we know that such disproportion will probably get worse in the near future, and that the indifference of a large number of Catholics is increasing, also as a consequence of other evils, as secularism, naturalism, materialism, etc., which have pervaded the standard of living in countries of ancient Christian tradition.

We should not forget, however, that the church—if we consider only the human means—was never up to the greatness of her vocation in the world. Even more, this insufficiency was foreseen by her founder, who, having designated 72 disciples, said to them: "The harvest is bountiful, but the laborers are few" and added: "Pray therefore to the master of the harvest that he may send laborers in his field" (Luke 10:2), thus wishing to inculcate in the mind of his disciples that the most effective way to overcome the obstacles is prayer, since we are dealing here not with an attempt or a project on the human level, but rather with the realization of a divine plan. It is, in fact, with prayer, through which we admit our need for the help of God, that we not only assume our responsibilities in the execution of the divine plan and we thus make ourselves available to be sent, but—which is very important—we also exercise our direct influence on the very increase of vocations, because the Lord has clearly told us that the number of laborers depends on prayer.

It is true that the divine plan of salvation for all mankind has been revealed to us, but the time when the messianic kingdom will reach its fullness remains obscure and mysterious: "The exact time is not yours to know. The father has reserved that to himself" (Acts 1:7). These words seem to hint that the mandate of Christ needs time in order to be fulfilled. The history of the church tells us that, through the centuries, we have witnessed moments of grace, when multitudes of peoples received the seed of the word of God; we must admit however that there have been, and there are, moments less favorable, particularly for some populations.[32]

It is the task of those who, enlightened by the light of Christ, can ready the signs of the times, and especially of those placed by the Holy Spirit to govern his church (Acts 28:28), to discover the moments and the hour of grace and recognize the peoples that seem mature to embrace the Gospel. We would like at this point to report the example of Pope Pius XII, who, in his encyclical letter "Fidei Donum" recommended Africa to all the children of the church, as a continent already mature for evangelization.[33]

Testimony of the Early Church

12. What has been said so far is perfectly in accord with the history of the early church. The Acts of the Apostles clearly demonstrate that our ancestors in the faith followed the same line of thinking and acting.[34] Their apostolic method was exactly this: Send the messengers of the Gospel in other regions, without being preoccupied by the fact that the local community was not converted as a whole to the faith of Christ. In this way, the apostles and their co-workers were obeying the command of Christ: "Go and teach all nations" (Matthew 28:19), placing all their trust in the will of God who wishes "all men to be saved and to come to the knowledge of the truth" (1Timothy 2:4).

The Second Vatican Council recommends this method: "It is very fitting that the young churches should participate as soon as possible in the universal missionary work of the church. Let them send their own missionaries to proclaim the Gospel all over the world, even though they themselves are suffering from a shortage of clergy." And the council gives the reason for it: "Their communion with the universal church reaches a certain measure of perfection when they themselves take an active part in missionary zeal toward other nations."[35]

TASKS AND DUTIES OF THE PARTICULAR CHURCHES

The Particular Church as a Community

13. The diocese, as a particular church, is a portion of the people of God that is entrusted to the bishop, with the collaboration

of the presbyterate, to be governed, nourished by teaching, and sanctified.[36] But for a true, living diocesan community to be formed, it is necessary that basic structures, and especially parishes, cultivate a sense of the diocese and consider themselves as living cells within it, and thus insert themselves into the universal church.[37] Therefore, the council exhorts parishes to pursue their function in such a way that "the individual parishioners and the parish communities will really feel that they are members of the diocese and of the universal church."[38]

In this particular church "the one, holy, catholic and apostolic church of Christ is truly present and operative."[39] It follows that the diocese must mirror to perfection the universal church in the concrete environment; and it is necessary for it to become a sign, able to reveal Christ to all those with whom it comes in contact.[40]

The Particular Church in Relationship With the Other Churches

14. Since the particular church is fashioned "after the model of the universal church,"[41] in its heart it mirrors the hope and anguish, the joy and sorrow of the whole church. It is true that the particular church must first of all evangelize the portion of the people of God entrusted to it, that is those who have lost the faith or no longer practice it;[42] nevertheless, there is incumbent on it the sacrosanct duty "to foster every activity which is common to the whole church."[43]

It follows that the particular church cannot be closed in upon itself but, as a living part of the universal church, must be open to the needs of the other churches. Therefore, its participation in the universal mission of evangelization is not left to its own judgment, even if this is generous, but must be considered as a fundamental law of life. For its vital zeal is diminished if, concentrating only on its own problems, it does not care for the needs of the other churches. On the other hand, it takes on new vigor whenever its horizons are expanded towards the others.

This duty of the particular church is clearly emphasized by the Second Vatican Council, which affirms that the renewal, indeed the healthy reform of the particular church depends on the degree of ecclesial charity with which it works to bring the gift of faith to the other churches: "The grace of renewal cannot flourish in communities unless each of them extends the range of its charity to the ends of the earth, and devotes to those far off a concern similar to that which it bestows on those who are its own members."[44]

The Meaning of Reciprocal Collaboration

15. The universal church will realize a great profit if the diocesan communities work to develop reciprocal relations, exchanging help and goods; thus that communion and cooperation of the churches among themselves will arise which today more than ever is necessary to pursue happily the work of evangelization.[45]

In talking of this question, often expressions such as "rich dioceses" and "poor dioceses" are used. Such expressions could lead to error, as if one church were only giving help and the other only receiving it. The fact of the matter is different: for what is involved is mutual cooperation, because true reciprocity is present between the two churches, in that the poverty of the one church that receives help makes richer the church which deprives itself in giving, and it does so both by making the apostolic zeal of the richer community more vigorous and, above all, by communicating its pastoral experiences. These are often most useful and can concern simpler but more effective methods of pastoral work, lay auxiliaries in the apostolate, small communities, etc.

The artisans of this common collaboration will be the ministers themselves, chosen by the bishop, who will view themselves as messengers of their own community, acting as ambassadors of Christ to the other community.

To make this mutual exchange of pastoral experiences more alive and effective, the diocese or even a large parish community will be able to form a kind of "twin sister" link with another poor community, to which it will be able to send not only material subsidies but also some sacred ministers as collaborators. Experience shows that cooperation of this kind can benefit both communities greatly.[46]

The Need to Hear Calls for Help

16. Since this is the situation, the particular churches must become more and more aware of their common responsibility. Making themselves sensitive to cries for help, they must show themselves ready to help those who need help. Among these, the new churches which suffer a serious shortage of priests and lack of material means are especially deserving of help; but it is also necessary to help those churches which, even though they were founded a long time ago, find themselves greatly weakened today because of various circumstances.[47]

It is clear that the more needy churches can be helped greatly by priests and other collaborators sent to their aid. The purpose of such help, obviously, is not simply to fill in the gaps, but rather to send the kind of sacred ministers who, once they are inserted among the local forces of the apostolate, will become, in the manner of teachers and guides, true helpers in the faith. Once the local churches, preserving their autochthonous character, are able to become gradually stronger and more developed, they can begin to provide for their needs with their own means. This explains why bishops and other superiors are asked to send for this kind of evangelization "some of the better priests."[48]

The Need to Reform Church Structures

17. So that a particular church can more adequately carry out its task of bringing aid to other churches that are in a state of need, above all, there is required, even in the bosom of that particular church, a process aimed at revising forces and restructuring traditionally Christian regions. Social phenomena exist which themselves have already transformed the structures of society. Thus church structures also have to be adapted to the new reality. Among the new phenomena it is enough to cite here: the transmigration of the people into industrial regions, urbanization with the resulting depopulation of other zones, the general problem of migration, both for the sake of work and for political reasons,[49] the quite widespread phenomenon of tourism for longer or shorter periods (e.g. for holidays or for weekends).[50] These phenomena require a new presence of priests who, in these changed circumstances of life, have to face a specialized care of souls.

The problem, then, is whether and how to renew the structures that once satisfactorily served the spiritual needs of the people of God. Certainly this revision is not easy and requires much prudence and circumspection. The bishop, with the help of priests' senates and pastoral councils, ought to draw up an organic project for the better employment of those who share effectively in the care of souls. It doesn't seem possible for the church to put off this problem any longer without suffering damage. In fact, despite the bemoaned scarcity of priests, it is not unusual to find priests who feel frustrated over a job that does not fill up their time, with the result that they rightfully would like to work more intensely.

The bishop, in his goal of making better provision for the growing needs of the care of souls, has the responsibility to engage the interest of religious priests who, after all, "are to be considered in a certain sense as part of the diocesan clergy"; like all other men and women Religious, even those who are exempt,

who live and work among the people of God, these too "belong
to the diocesan family under a certain aspect." In both cases it is
a matter of taking into account the particular character of each
religious institute.[51] In this regard, the Sacred Congregation for
Bishops, in union with the Congregation for Religious and
Secular Institutes, recently published wise norms for cordial collaboration on the formative, operational and organizational
levels.[52]

In recent times pastors have called the laity to the service of
the church communities more and more often. These have willingly
accepted their duties and have dedicated their energies to the service of the church on a full or part-time basis. Thus in the present
day we have again taken up the practice of the early church,
when lay persons were involved in various services according to
their inclinations and charisms and according to the necessities
and practical needs of the people of God "for the growth and
vitality of the church community."[53]

THE ORGANS OF COLLABORATION AMONG
THE PARTICULAR CHURCHES

The Bishops' Conferences

18. The principal and indispensable role for more effective
collaboration among the particular churches lies with the
bishops' conferences, which have as their specific goal the over-
all coordination of pastoral work. In this regard Pope Paul VI
decreed in his motu proprio "Ecclesiae Sanctae": "It belongs to
patriarchal synods and bishops' conferences, keeping in mind
what has been prescribed by the Holy See, to achieve an appropriate distribution of the clergy both in their own territory
and in that which comes from other areas; with such a distribution, provision will be made for the needs of all the dioceses of
one's own territory, and the good of the church in mission lands
and in countries that suffer a scarcity of clergy will also be
considered."[54]

Accordingly, beyond providing for the needs of pastoral care
in their own territory, two other requirements are recommended
to the bishops' conferences, namely the first preaching of the
Gospel in mission lands and assistance to weaker churches in
general. Both tasks are incumbent on each particular church;
nevertheless, in order for the matter to be regulated well the collaboration of all the bishops of the same nation or territory is required. To provide for these necessities, each bishops' conference must establish two commissions: one for the better

distribution of the clergy, and another for the missions.[55] Since the institution of the latter is intended to promote missionary zeal and both have in a certain way, a similar scope, it seems necessary that the two commissions collaborate or ven, in some cases, it may seem more convenient to unite the two.

Solicitude for Mission Territories

19. As regards the first preaching of the Gospel, that is, the missions, the supreme direction over the pertinent questions belongs to the Sacred Congregation for the Evangelization of Peoples, which "has competency over matters regarding all the missions instituted to spread the kingdom of Christ everywhere, and therefore over the establishment and changing of the necessary ministers and the ecclesiastical circumscriptions; over the proposing of the persons who govern them; over the promotion in the most effective way of an autochthonous clergy, to which the highest posts and government are to be gradually entrusted; over the direction and coordination of all the missionary activity in every part of the land, as regards both the missionaries themselves and the missionary cooperation of the faithful."[56]

In this context, it is up to the bishops' conferences to promote the effective participation of the diocesan clergy in the apostolate in the missions; to establish a determinate monetary contribution for missionary work; to intensify more and more their relations with missionary institutes and collaborate so that seminaries which serve the missions are erected or aided.[57]

As regards missionary works, the bishops' commission established in every bishops' conference must increase missionary activity and the appropriate collaboration among the dioceses; therefore, it will have to maintain relations with other conferences and work to see to it that, as far as possible, a just proportion is maintained in giving aid to the missions.[58]

Solicitude for More Needy Particular Churches

20. As stated above, bishops' conferences must form another bishops' commission which has as its duty "to investigate the needs of the various dioceses within their territory and the possibilities of giving some of their own clergy to other churches to carry out the decisions made and approved by the conferences regarding the distribution of the clergy and to inform the bishops of the territory of these decisions."[59]

The task, therefore, of this commission is twofold. Above all it is to remove the possible inequalities in its own territory. Quite often, in fact, one can note a great disproportion in the number of priests. While there are some dioceses with an abundance of clergy, there are others in which the scarcity of priests endangers the very preservation of the faith.

The other task concerns solicitude toward those particular churches outside one's own territory, to help them in virtue of that bond of communion between particular churches which was spoken of above.

This work must be pursued with the investigation, first of all, of the needs of the dioceses, comparing the number of the faithful with the number of pastors; then proposing to the bishops' conference a study of the more urgent needs and the possibility of helping the more needy churches.

As regards this latter task of the commission, praiseworthy initiatives have already been undertaken which have produced happy results in this field.[60]

Collaboration With the Councils of Major Superiors

21. To coordinate ministerial activities and works of the apostolate in the territory of the same bishops' conference, closer collaboration between the diocesan clergy and the religious institutes is required. The promotion of this kind of collaboration is up to the bishops' conference. But since profitable cooperation depends heavily on an attitude of putting special interests in second place and looking solely for the general good of the church, it is advisable for bishops and religious superiors to hold meetings, at set times, to study what is to be done in common in their respective territories.[61] For this reason the motu proprio "Ecclesiae Sanctae" prescribes the formation of a mixed commission of the bishops' conference and the national council of major superiors to study questions that concern both parties.[62] The principal theme of the meetings of this mixed commission ought to be precisely that of a better and more fitting distribution of the forces of the apostolate, determining the priorities and options to be pursued in a common effort to promote joint pastoral action.[63] The deliberations of this commission ought then to be submitted, for reasons of competency, to the judgment of the bishops' conference and the council of religious superiors.[64]

The Animation of the Faithful

22. One cannot stress enough the first and principal task incumbent on both commissions, which is that of continually keeping the public opinion of the faithful well informed both

about the needs of the missions and about the situations of particular churches that find themselves in difficulty. They must therefore use all the means of social communications, they must assist and spread reviews and other similar publications, and engage as well in the preparation and execution of well-defined programs to publicize the problems in this field.

The aim of all this, in addition to quick, accurate information, is to make the faithful more and more aware of their responsibilities and to develop in them a sense of catholicity regarding mature and effective collaboration of the particular churches.[65]

SACRED MINISTERS SENT TO OTHER DIOCESE

The Necessity of a Special Vocation

23. Granted that all the faithful in their own way ought to participate in the work of evangelization, nevertheless one who wants to carry out his sacred ministry in another diocese needs a special vocation. Indeed the whole community, under the guidance of the bishop, is bound to petition the Holy Spirit with prayer and works of penance for the gift of vocations, so that there may be priests, Religious and laity available who will leave their homeland and go to carry out the mandate of Christ in another area.[66]

Regarding the preparation of young souls, it is necessary to inculcate in them a truly Catholic mentality right from the earliest age; then, regarding candidates for the priesthood, during their formation it is necessary to see to it that they cultivate a sense of solicitude for the whole church in addition to a love of the diocese for the service of which they are ordained.[67]

Fitness of the Ministers

24. This special vocation presupposes, however, the right kind of character and particular natural gifts. Among the qualities of the psyche, spiritual fortitude and a sincere spirit of service are considered necessary. Thus, in the direction of souls superiors will use great diligence to find fit, appropriate candidates. And since it is to be hoped that bishops will destine the best priests for this work, these ought to be not only abundantly imbued with sound sacred doctrine but also distinguished by their robust faith, steadfast hope and zeal for souls,[68] so that they will be able to truly generate in others the faith that they themselves have.

The Necessary Preparation

25. All ministers who go to another diocese need an adequate preparation in matters regarding their human formation, orthodoxy of doctrine, and the apostolic style of life. Those who are going to a diocese in another nation to announce the Gospel, moreover, must receive a special formation. That is, they must know the culture and religion of that people; they must value highly the language and customs; they must acquire practice in the language, along with understanding of the social conditions, habits and customs; finally, they must carefully study the moral order and deepest convictions which that people, according to its sacred traditions, has formed for itself about God, the world and man.[69]

The Convention Required for the Transfer

26. The transfer of ministers, especially of priests, from one diocese to another must be done with good order. The ordinary "a quo" is to furnish the ordinary "ad quem" honest and open information about those who are to be sent, especially if the reasons for them come under suspicion.

It is absolutely necessary that the rights and duties of priests who offer themselves for such a transfer of their own free will should be accurately defined in a written convention between the bishop "ad quem";[70] this convention, drawn up with the involvement of the priest as well so that it will have normative value, must be accepted and signed by the priest himself; copies of the convention are then to be kept by the priest and by the two curias.

Similar conventions are to be made with lay auxiliaries. For Religious, it is necessary to observe the constitutions of the institute of provenance. The same principle applies to the following numbers, to the degree that it fits.

The Object of the Convention

27. In this convention it is necessary to define: a) the length of the term of service; b) the duties of the priest and his place of ministry and of residence, taking into account the living conditions in the area where the priest will go; whatever subsidies of any kind he is to receive and from whom; c) his social security in case of sickness, disability or old age. If the case permits, it will also be useful to include the possibility of revisiting one's homeland after a certain period of time.

This convention cannot be changed without the consensus of

the interested parties. The right of the bishop "ad quem" remains firm to remand the priest to his own diocese whenever his ministry has become harmful, provided that he has advised the bishop "a quo" beforehand and has observed natural and canonical equity.

The Duties of the Bishops "A Quo" and "Ad Quem" Toward the Priests

28. The bishop "a quo" should have a special solicitude, as far as possible, toward his priests who exercise their sacred ministry outside their own diocese, considering them as members of his own community who work far away. He should do this whether by letter, by visiting them personally or through others, or by helping them according to the tenor of the convention. The bishop "ad quem," who enjoys the help of these priests, remains the guarantor of their material and spiritual life, again in terms of the convention.

The Priests as Members of the Other Diocese's Presbyterate

29. In regions that differ notably in language, customs or social conditions, except in urgent necessity, priests should not ordinarily be sent individually, but rather in groups so that they can help out each other.[71] Such groups nevertheless should work to insert themselves in the midst of the local clergy in such a way as to bring not the least prejudice to brotherly cooperation.

Priests who have entered another diocese are to revere the local bishop and obey him, in accord with the convention. As regards their style of life, they are to adapt to the conditions of the autochthonous priests and work to cultivate their friendship, since all form a single presbyterate under the bishop's authority.[72] Therefore, they must insert themselves into the local community as if they were native members of that particular church; this demands an uncommon spiritual disposition and deep spirit of service. As ministers joined a new family, they are to abstain from judgments and criticisms of the local church, leaving the task of following that prophetic office to the bishop, to whom belongs the full responsibility of governing the particular church.

Return of Priests to Their Homeland

30. Priests who want to return to their own diocese at the end of the time set in the convention are to be welcomed; this return requires a preparation, just as their going to the mission did.

They are to enjoy all the rights in their diocese of origin, in which they have remained incardinated, as if they had been involved in the sacred ministry there without interruption.[73] With the various experiences they have acquired, they can bring a significant spiritual contribution to their own diocese. Further, a sufficient period of time is to be given to returnees to take up new tasks, to allow them to adapt to changes that may have taken place in the meantime.

Incardination in the Host Diocese

31. The prescriptions of the Code of Canon Law remain in force concerning the incardination of priests in other dioceses. However, the motu proprio "Ecclesiae Sanctae" has set out a new norm, for obtaining incardination "ope legis" (by the power of the law), which takes into account the service rendered: "The cleric who goes legitimately from his own diocese to another, after five years, will be incardinated by law in the latter diocese if he has expressed in writing such a desire to the ordinary of the host diocese and to his own ordinary, and has not received a judgment to the contrary from either of the two within four months."[74]

CONCLUSION

The situation of the church today, especially as regards the insufficiency of clergy for the most urgent needs of evangelization, could induce many to a pessimistic vision of things and thus create a certain sense of discouragement toward the future of the church.

Such a way of thinking is not the way of Christians and even less becoming to pastors of souls.

This, in fact, is but one aspect, not all the ecclesial reality, if we look at it not in an exterior and superficial manner but in a Christian way, that is with the eyes of faith, the supernatural light of which makes us perceive, through the interreaction of human events, the living and toiling presence of the Holy Spirit which animates the church and leads it infallibly toward the direction of salvation which God conceived for man and which he realizes despite the most violent opposition from those who seek to impede the path of the Church.

Therefore, just as we know that along all the course of the history of the church the principal agent of evangelization is the Holy Spirit who moves Christians to make progress toward the kingdom of God and opens the hearts of men to the divine word, thus also we must believe that under the direction of that same Spirit is placed the future of the church. In the meantime, the duty of us all is to pray for it incessantly and to allow ourselves faithfully to be guided by him, employing all our power in order that among the faithful the conviction of the missionary nature of the church may remain alive and the awareness of responsibility which individual Christians and especially the pastors of souls have toward the universal church may increase.

May we seek to fulfill such effort and enliven it, guided and animated always by Christian hope, "which does not disappoint" (Romans 5:5) since it is founded on the words of Christ, who, about to leave his disciples among the dangers and hostile forces of this world, promised, "know that I am with you always, until the end of the world" (Matthew 29:20). "Take courage. I have overcome the world" (John 16:33).

*Translation put out by Vatican Press Office. Latin text in AAS 72 (1980), 343–364.
1. Decree "Christus Dominus," n.6
2. Motu proprio "Ecclesiae Sanctae," l,1, in AAS 58 (1966), p. 757 f.
3. N. 68, Par. 2, AAS 59, (1967), p. 885 f.
4. Atti del 1 Congresso "Pro meliori cleri distributione in mundo," il mondo e' la mia parrocchia, Rome l971.
5. "Declarationes Patrum Synodalium," n. 4. L'Osservatore Romano (27 October 1974, p. 6). Cf. Apostolic exhortation "Evangelii Nuntiandi" nn. 6-15, AAS 68 (l976), p. 5 f.
6. Decree "Ad Gentes Divinitus," n. 35.
7. Constitution "Lumen Gentium," n. 13.
8. Decree "Ad Gentes Divinitus," n. 38.
9. Cf. Encyclical letter "Fidei Donum," Pope Pius XII, AAS 49 (1957), p. 237.
10. Constitution "Lumen Gentium," n. 23.
11. Cf. "Directorium de Pastorali Ministerio Episcoporum," 1973 n. 43, Rome.
12. Constitution "Lumen Gentium," n. 23.
13. Cf. Decree "Christius Dominus," n. 6; Decree "Ad Gentes Divinitus," n. 38.
14. Decree "Presbyterorum Ordinis," n.2.
15. Ibid. nn. 4, 5, 6.
16. Constitution "Lumen Gentium," n. 28.
17. Decree "Presbyterorum Ordinis," n. 2.
18. Ibid. n. 5.
19. I. n. 4. AAS 63 (1971), p. 898 f.
20. Decree "Presbyterorum Ordinis," n. 10.
21. Cf. apostolic letter "Graves et Increscentes," AAS 58 (1966), p. 750 f.
22. Constitution "Lumen Gentium," n. 44.
23. Decree "Perfectae Caritatis," n. 20. Cf. Decree "Ad Gentes Divinitus," n. 40.

24. Apostolic exhortation "Evangelii Nuntiandi," n. 69.

25. Constitution "Lumen Gentium," n. 43 Cf. Sacred Congregations for Religious and Secular Institutes, and for Bishops: Notae Directivae Pro Mutuis Relationibus Inter Episcopos et Religiosos in Ecclesiae, AAS 70 (1978), p. 373 f.

26. Decree "Apostolicam Actuositatem," n. 2.

27. Ibid. n. 10.

28. N. 73; Cf. Constitution "Lumen Gentium," n.22.

29. Constitution "Lumen Gentium," n. 17.

30. Cf. Annuarium Statisticum Ecclesiae, 1977, p. 44.

31. Encyclical letter "Fidei Donum," AAS 49 (1957), p. 244.

32. Cf. Apostolic exhortation "Evangelii Nuntiandi," n. 50.

33. AAS 49 (1957), pp.225 f.

34. Cf. 8, 14; 11,22; 13,3 etc.

35. Decree "Ad Gentes Divinitus," n. 20.

36. Decree "Christus Dominus," n. 11.

37. Decree "Apostolicam Actuositatem," n. 10.

38. Decree "Christus Dominus," n. 30.

39. Ibid. n. 11.

40. Decree "Ad Gentes Divinitus," n. 20.

41. Constitution "Lumen Gentium," n. 23.

42. Cf. Apostolic exhortation "Evangelii Nuntiandi," nn. 55,56.

43. Constitution "Lumen Gentium," n. 23.

44. Decree "Ad Gentes Divinitus," n. 37.

45. Ibid. n. 38.

46. Cf. Instructio S. Congregationis Pro Gentium Evangelizatione, "Pro Aptius," AAS 61 (1969), p. 276 f.

47. Decree "Ad Gentes Divinitus," n. 19.

48. Ibid. n. 38.

49. Motu proprio "Pastoralis Migratorum Cura," AAS 61 (1969) p. 601; and Instructio S. Congregationis Pro Episcopis; Ibid. p. 614 f.; Commissionis de Spirituali Migratorum Atque Itinerantium Cura: Chiesa e Mobilia Umana, AAS 70 (1978), p. 357 f.

50. Cf. Directorium generale, pro ministerio quoad "turismum" Sacred Congregation for the Clergy, in AAS 61 (1969), p. 361 f.

51. Decree "Christus Dominus," nn. 34, 35; Cf. "Ecclesiae Sanctae," I, n. 36.

52. AAS 70 (1978), p. 473 f.

53. Apostolic exhortation "Evangelii Nuntiandi," n. 73.

54. Ibid. 2.

55. Motu proprio "Ecclesiae Sanctae," I, 2. III, 9.

56. Apostolic constitution "Regimini Ecclesiae Universae," n. 82 AAS, 59 (1967), p. 885 F.

57. Decree "Ad Gentes Divinitus," n. 38.

58. Motu proprio "Ecclesiae Sanctae," III, 9.

59. Motu proprio "Ecclesiae Sanctae," n. 2.

60. To promote relations with the dioceses of Latin America, the following bishops' commissions exist: COPAL in Belgium, CEFAL in France, CEIAL in Italy, CECADE-OCSHA in Spain, Adveniat in West Germany, NCCB-LAB in the United States, OCCAL in Canada, etc. All these commissions work with the Pontifical Commission for Latin America (CAL), which maintains close relations with the Latin American Bishops Council (CELAM). In addition there is the general council of the Pontifical Commission for Latin America (COGECAL), composed of CAL, CELAM, the presidents of the bishops' commis-

sions mentioned above, the president of the International Union of
Superiors General, and the president of the Confederation of Religious
of Latin America.

61. Decree "Christus Dominus," 35:5-6
62. II, 43, cf. Sacred Congregations for Religious and Secular Institutes
and for Bishops, Notae Directivae, nn. 60-65, AAS 70 (1978), p. 503 f.
63. Decree "Perfectae Caritatis," n. 23.
64. Notae Directivae, n. 63, AAS 70 (1978), p. 504.
65. Decree "Ad Gentes Divinitus," n. 36.
66. Ibid. n. 23; Cf. Decree "Optatam Totius," n. 2.
67. Decree "Optatam Totius," n. 20.
68. Decree "Ad Gentes Divinitus," n. 25.
69. Ibid. n. 26.
70. Motu proprio "Ecclesiae Sanctae," I,1, par. 2.
71. Decree "Presbyterorum Ordinis," n. 10.
72. Decree "Ad Gentes Divinitus," n. 20.
73. Motu proprio "Ecclesiae Sanctae," I, 3, par. 4.
74. Ibid. 1, 2, par. 5.

100

NORMS FOR LAICIZATION OF PRIESTS*

S.C.D.F., *Per litteras ad universos*, 14 October, 1980

1. In his 1979 Holy Thursday letter to all the priests of the Church the Supreme Pontiff, Pope John Paul II, once again placed in clear light just how great a value is to be set on priestly celibacy in the Latin Church. In this, as he himself acknowledges, he was following the carefully reasoned teaching of the second Vatican Council, of Pope Paul VI in his encyclical *Sacerdotalis Caelibatus*, and finally of the 1971 Synod of Bishops.

The Holy Father reminded us that this is a matter of great importance, one which is connected by a special link to the message of the Gospel. Following the example of Christ our Lord and in accord with the apostolic teaching and tradition which is proper to it, the Latin church wished, and even now wishes, that all who receive the sacrament of orders embrace this renunciation not only as an eschatological sign but also as "a sign of the person's freedom, a freedom which in turn is tied to ministry."

The Supreme Pontiff observed: "Any Christian about to receive the sacrament of orders binds himself to the obligation of celibacy with full awareness and freedom. He does this after having spent many years in preparation and after having given careful deliberation to and much prayer over this matter. Since he has firmly persuaded himself that Christ grants him that 'gift' for the benefit of the entire Church and for the service of others, only then does he enter upon the plan to lead a life of celibacy... And thus it is clear that this plan, so undertaken, now obliges, not only due to some law passed by the Church, but also due to the very awareness that duties are expressly undertaken by a person. It is for this reason that it is of importance that promises made to Christ and to the Church be honoured." Finally, the Christian faithful who are married have a perfect right to expect from their priests, as His Holiness adds, "good example and a witness to fidelity in their vocation even until death."

2. It is true that in recent years priests have experienced difficulties. These difficulties have resulted in a somewhat large

number of priests requesting a dispensation from the obligations which arise from their priestly ordination, especially a dispensation from celibacy. The widespread attention given to this fact has inflicted a serious wound on the Church. The Church has been deeply stricken at the very source of its life. With equal sorrow this wound affects pastors and the entire Christian community. Because of this the Supreme Pontiff, Pope John Paul II, from the very beginning of his supreme apostolic ministry came to the conclusion that it is necessary to initiate an investigation concerning suitable remedies to be employed for it.

3. But real care is to be taken so that a process of such serious importance, as is a dispensation from celibacy, not be considered as a right which the Church must recognize indiscriminately as belonging to all its priests. On the other hand, what is to be considered as being a true right is that one which a priest through his oblation has conferred upon Christ and upon all the people of God. Despite the serious difficulties which stand in his way and which can happen to him in this life, Christ and the people of God expect the priest to observe the fidelity which he had promised them. Equally to be avoided is the notion that a dispensation from celibacy in recent times can be considered to be the result of some quasi-automatic, summary administrative process (see Pope John Paul II, Letter to All the Priests of the Church, n. 9).

Exceedingly great benefits are derived from making such a distinction: particular benefit to the priest who is requesting the dispensation and who judges that this is the only solution to his existential problem, the weight of which he thinks he can no longer bear; general benefit to the Church which in an equal manner cannot bear having its priestly structure slowly eroded since it is so necessary for the accomplishment of its office; finally, particular benefit to the local churches, that is, to the bishops with their presbyterate since both groups are moved by an eagerness to maintain—as much as is possible—necessary apostolic resources, and to all groups of the Christian faithful for whom the service of the priestly ministry is to be considered as being a right and a necessity. While observing justice and charity, the multiple aspects of this question are to be given consideration: None of them can be neglected, let alone rejected.

4. Aware then of the many and likewise complex aspects of this issue which include sad personal situations and at the same time realizing the necessity to consider everything according to the spirit of Christ, the Holy Father—to whom a good number

of bishops have supplied advice along with their ideas on the issue—had decided to spend a suitable period of time in order that with the assistance of his co-workers he might arrive at a prudent conclusion, based on strong arguments, concerning the acceptance, the examination and the resolution of petitions concerning a dispensation from celibacy. The results of this mature deliberation are here briefly explained. This studied concern to weigh all the aspects raised in this matter suggests and inspires norms which will govern the future examination of petitions sent to the Apostolic See. As is obvious, it is thoroughly necessary that norms of this type in no way be separated from the pastoral spirit which animates them.

5. With the exception of cases dealing with priests who have left the priestly life for a long period of time and who hope to remedy a state of affairs which they are not able to quit, the Sacred Congregation for the Doctrine of the Faith shall in processing the examination of petitions sent to the Apostolic See accept for consideration the cases of those who should not have received priestly ordination because the necessary aspect of freedom of responsibility was lacking or because the competent superiors were not able within an appropriate time to judge in a prudent and sufficiently fitting way whether the candidate really was suited for continuously leading a life of celibacy dedicated to God.

Since it would lessen the significance of the priesthood, the sacred character of ordination and the seriousness of obligations previously undertaken, also to be avoided in this process is any levity in procedure which can reasonably afford detriment, sorrowful astonishment or scandal to a good number of the Christian faithful. Therefore a case in favour of dispensation is to be demonstrated by the force of the number of its arguments and by their preponderance. In order that the matter proceed in a serious manner and that the good of the Christian faithful be protected, provision will be made with equal care that those petitions presented in a spirit other than one reflecting humility will not be admitted.

6. In discharging this difficult duty entrusted to it by the Roman Pontiff, the Sacred Congregation for the Doctrine of the Faith is well aware that it can place its hope in the full and trusted cooperation of all the ordinaries concerned. This congregation stands ready to furnish all the assistance which the ordinaries should desire.

Since it is also well aware of their pastoral zeal, this congregation is likewise thoroughly confident that the ordinaries will give prudent observance to the proposed norms. Such zeal in this area will generate the conditions necessary to serve the good of the Church and of the priesthood and to provide for the spiritual life of both priests and Christian communities.

Finally, this dicastery knows that the ordinaries can in no way forget their duties of spiritual fatherhood toward all their priests, especially toward those who are now in a serious spiritual crisis. It knows that these ordinaries will furnish these priests with strong, straightforward and necessary assistance so that they may more easily and joyfully safeguard the duties undertaken on the day of ordination toward the Lord Jesus Christ and his holy Church. In doing this the ordinaries will make use of all those things in the Lord which can call back a wavering brother to peace of mind, to confidence, to renewal and to quick resumption of his former state. In this the ordinaries should also employ, depending on the circumstances of the individual case, the help of his priestly brothers, friends, relatives, physicians and psychologists (cf *Sacerdotalis Caelibatus*, nn. 87 and 91.)

7. Attached to this letter are procedural norms which are to be observed in preparing the documents relating to a petition for a dispensation from celibacy.

While we communicate these matters to you as part of our duty, we are at your service and confess ourselves yours in the Lord.

PROCEDURAL NORMS

1. The ordinary who is competent to accept a petition and instruct the case is the local ordinary of incardination or the major superior of a member of a clerical institute of consecrated life of pontifical right.

2. If the proper ordinary is unable to instruct the case, the ordinary of the place where the petitioner habitually resides can be asked to do so. For a proportionate reason the Sacred Congregation for the Doctrine of the Faith can delegate another ordinary.

3. The signed petition must indicate the petitioner's name, general information about him and at least in general the facts and arguments on which his petition is based.

4. After receiving the petition, the ordinary is to decide whether to proceed further. If he decides to do so, he is to prohibit the petitioner from the exercise of orders *ad cautelam* (as a precautionary measure) unless he judges that their exercise is really necessary to protect the reputation of the priest or to foster the good of the community. The ordinary is then to in-

struct the case either personally or through an especially designated priest. A notary should be employed to authenticate the acts of the case.

5. The bishop or priest-instructor is to administer an oath *de veritate dicenda* (that the truth must be spoken) and then interrogate the petitioner according to a questionnaire specifically drawn up for this situation. If possible, superiors during the petitioner's period of formation are to be questioned; or at least their written depositions are to be obtained. Other witnesses either suggested by the petitioner or called by the instructor are likewise to be heard. Finally, documents and other proofs are to be gathered and the insights of experts are to be utilized where appropriate.

6. The questionnaire for the petitioner should contain everything necessary or useful for the investigation, i.e. (a) general information on the petitioner: time and place of birth, background and family circumstances, manner of life, studies, examination before the reception of sacred orders, or before profession in the case of religious, time and place of sacred ordination, record of priestly ministry, present juridical status, both ecclesiastically and civilly and the like; (b) causes and circumstances of leaving the active ministry and factors which could have vitiated the assumption of clerical obigations.

7. After the instruction of the case, all the acts of the case are to be forwarded in triplicate to the Sacred Congregation for the Doctrine of the Faith along with any notations that might be useful in assessing the proofs. They are to be accompanied by the *votum* (vow) of the ordinary regarding the truthfulness of the petition and the absence of scandal.

8. The sacred congregation will discuss the case and decide whether to present the petition to the Pope or to ask for a more thorough instruction of the case or to reject the petition as unfounded.

*Translation courtesy of the Tablet (London). Latin text in *AAS* LXX-XII (1980) 132–137.

101

THE *CREDO* OF THE PEOPLE OF GOD*

Paul VI, *Solemni hac liturgia*, 30 June, 1968

Introduction

With this solemn Liturgy we bring to a close the celebration of the Nineteenth Centenary of the Martyrdom of the holy Apostles Peter and Paul, and the Year of Faith. This year We dedicated to the memory of the holy Apostles with the express purpose of witnessing to Our determination to guard undiminished *the deposit of faith*[1] which they delivered to us, and to endorse Our decision to relate this same faith to the historical moment in which the Church must make her pilgrim way in the world.

We feel We must thank publicly those who responded to Our invitation and ensured that the Year of Faith should be productive of the greatest good. For, in many places, the personal adherence of members of the faithful to the word of God has been deepened, and many communities have renewed their profession of faith and the faith itself has been confirmed by the explicit testimony of a Christian life. Therefore, to Our Brothers in the Episcopate and to the sons of the Catholic Church, We express Our gratitude and grant them Our Apostolic Blessing.

Furthermore, We consider it Our duty to fulfil the mandate given by Christ to Peter, whose successor We are in spite of Our unworthiness—the command *to confirm Our brethren*[2] in faith. Therefore, although We are conscious of Our inadequacy, We nonetheless will make a profession of faith with all the strength that our Spirit draws from the mandate We have received. We are going to repeat that declaration that begins with the word 'Credo' which, though it is not a strict dogmatic definition, still, rightly interpreted in accordance with the spiritual requirements of our times, recapitulates in substance the formulation of Nicaea—the formulation of the immortal tradition of the Holy Church of God.

In making this profession We are well aware of the disquiet in matters of faith which is unsettling some of the convictions of our contemporaries. These have not escaped the influence of a world in total change, a world in which many truths are either completely denied or called into doubt. We see even Catholics possessed by what is almost a passion for change and novelty. The Church certainly regards it as her duty never to relax in her efforts to penetrate more deeply the hidden mysteries of God, from which all derive the myriad fruits of salvation, and in like manner to express them to succeeding generations in a way progressively adapted to contemporary understanding. But at the same time the greatest care must be taken that the important duty of research does not involve the undermining of the truths of Christian doctrine. If this happens—and we have unfortunately seen it happen in these days—the result is perplexity and confusion in the minds of many of the faithful.

In this matter it is of greatest importance to recognize that over and above what is visible, the reality of which we discern through the sciences, God has given us an intellect which can attain to *that which is*, not merely the subjective content of the 'structures' and developments of human consciousness. It must be borne in mind that the purpose of interpretation—hermeneutics—is to understand and elicit the meaning conveyed by the text, taking into account the words used, not to invent some new sense on the basis of arbitrary conjecture.

But above all We put Our confidence resolutely in the Holy Spirit, the Soul of the Church, and the source of even the smallest advance in truth and in charity and in the theological faith on which the Mystical Body is based. We are well aware that men expect the Vicar of Christ to speak. Therefore, We respond to this expectation with norms and instructions, such as We have already given. But today We are offered the opportunity of making Our mind known with greater solemnity.

And so, on this day on which We have chosen to close the Year of Faith, on this Feast of the Blessed Apostles Peter and Paul, We wish to offer to the living God the homage of a profession of faith, and as once at Caesarea Philippi Simon Peter, rising above the opinions of men and speaking for all the Apostles, confessed Christ as the Son of the living God, so today his humble successor, the Shepherd of the Universal Church, in the name of the whole People of God, raises his voice to pronounce the strongest testimony to the divine truth which is entrusted to the Church precisely that it may be proclaimed to all nations.

We wish Our profession of faith to be sufficiently comprehensive and explicit to satisfy convincingly the need for light which is felt so strongly by so many of the faithful and by all those in the world—whatever be their religious affiliation—who search for the truth.

To the glory, therefore, of the omnipotent God and our Lord Jesus Christ, trusting in the help of the Blessed Virgin Mary and the Blessed Apostles Peter and Paul, having in mind the profit and spiritual growth of the church, We now pronounce this profession of faith, common to all the Bishops and faithful who are united with you, beloved brethren and sons, in heart and mind.

PROFESSION OF FAITH

One God Creator of All

We believe in one God, the Father, the Son and the Holy Spirit, Creator of what is visible—such as this world where we live out our lives—and of the invisible—such as the pure spirits which are also called angels[3]—and Creator in each man of his spiritual and immortal soul.

We believe in this one God, who is as completely one in his most holy essence as in the rest of his perfections; in his omnipotence, in his infinite knowledge, in his providence, in his will and his love. *He is who is*, as he himself revealed to Moses.[4] He is *love*, as John the Apostle taught us.[5] These two names, therefore, Being and Love, express the same unattainable truth concerning him who manifested himself to us and who, *inhabiting light inaccessible*,[6] is in himself above every name, above every thing and every created intelligence. God only can grant us a true and perfect knowledge of himself, revealing himself as Father, Son and Holy Spirit in whose eternal life we are called by grace to share here on earth in the obscurity of faith and after death in everlasting light. The mutual bonds which eternally constitute the three Persons, each one of whom is one and the same divine Being, are themselves the inmost and blessed life of the Most Holy God, which is infinitely beyond our possibilities of understanding.[7] Wherefore, we give thanks to the divine Goodness that so many believers can testify with us before men to the unity of God, even though they do not know the mystery of the Most Holy Trinity.

We believe, therefore, in God, who from all eternity begets the Son, we believe in the Son, the Word of God, who is eternally begotten, we believe in the Holy Spirit, the uncreated Person who proceeds from the Father and the Son as their eternal Love. And so in the three divine Persons who are *co-eternal and co-equal with one another*,[8] the life and beatitude of God, who is

uniquely One, is realized and fulfilled in overwhelming plenitude in the supreme excellence and glory which is proper to him
who is the uncreated Being, in such wise that *unity in the Trinity
and Trinity in the unity must be humbly acknowledged*.[9]

We believe in our Lord Jesus Christ, who is the Son of God.
He is the eternal Word born of the Father before time began, one
in substance with the Father, *homousios to Patri*,[10] through
whom all things were made. He was incarnate of the Virgin Mary
by the power of the Holy Spirit and was made Man. Equal,
therefore, to the Father according to his divinity, less than the
Father according to his humanity,[11] his unity deriving not from
some impossible confusion of substance but from his Person.[12]

He dwelt among us full of grace and truth. He announced and
established the Kingdom of God, enabling us to know the
Father. He gave us the commandment that we should love one
another as he loved us. He taught us the way of the Gospel Beatitudes, according to which we were to be poor in spirit and humble, bearing suffering in patience, thirsting after justice, merciful, clean of heart, peaceful, enduring persecution for justice's
sake. He suffered under Pontius Pilate, the Lamb of God taking
to himself the sins of the world, and he died for us, nailed to the
Cross, saving us by his redeeming blood. After he had been
buried he rose from the dead of his own power, lifting us by his
resurrection to that sharing in the divine life which is grace. He
ascended into heaven whence he will come again to judge the living and the dead, each according to his merits. Those who have
responded to the love and compassion of God will go into eternal life. Those who have refused them to the end will be consigned to the fire that is never extinguished.

And of his kingdom there will be no end.

We believe in the Holy Spirit, the Lord and giver of life, who
together with the Father and the Son is adored and glorified. He
it is who spoke through the prophets. He it was who was sent to
us by Christ after his resurrection and ascension to the Father.
He enlightens, vivifies, guards and rules the Church whose
members he purifies as long as they do not turn away from grace.
His action, which reaches to the inmost centre of the soul,
enables man, in the humility which he draws from Christ, to
become perfect even as the Father in heaven is perfect.

We believe that the Blessed Mary, who ever enjoys the dignity
of virginity, was the Mother of the Incarnate Word, of our God
and Saviour Jesus Christ,[13] and that in view of her Son's merits
she was redeemed in a more exalted manner[14] and preserved
from all stain of sin,[15] outstripping in excellence all other crea-

tures by reason of the grace given her.[16]

Because of her close and indissoluble connection with the mystery of the Incarnation and Redemption[17] the most Blessed Virgin Mary, the Immaculate, at the end of her earthly life was assumed body and soul into heaven,[18] and so became like her Son, who himself rose from the dead, anticipating thereby the destiny of the just. We believe that the most holy Mother of God, the new Eve, the Mother of the Church,[19] continues in heaven her maternal role towards the members of Christ, in that she cooperates with the birth and growth of divine life in the souls of the redeemed.[20]

We believe that in Adam all have sinned. From this it follows that on account of the original offence committed by him human nature, which is common to all men, is reduced to that condition in which it must suffer the consequences of that fall. This condition is not the same as that of our first parents, for they were constituted in holiness and justice, and man had no experience of either evil or death. Consequently, fallen human nature is deprived of the economy of grace which it formerly enjoyed. It is wounded in its natural powers and subjected to the dominion of death which is transmitted to all men. It is in this sense that every man is born in sin.

We hold, therefore, in accordance with the Council of Trent, that original sin is transmitted along with human nature, *not by imitation but by propagation*, and is, therefore, incurred by each individually.[21]

We believe that our Lord Jesus Christ redeemed us by the sacrifice of the Cross from original sin and from all those personal sins to which we confess, so that the truth of the Apostle's words is vindicated that *where sin abounded, grace did more abound*.[22]

We believe in one baptism instituted by our Lord Jesus Christ for the remission of sins. Baptism is also to be given to infants, who cannot as yet be guilty of any personal sin, in order that, though born deprived of supernatural grace, they may be reborn of *water and the Holy Spirit* to divine life in Christ Jesus.[23]

We believe in one holy Catholic and Apostolic Church, built by Jesus Christ on the rock which is Peter. She is the Mystical Body of Christ, a visible society, hierarchically structured, and a spiritual community—the Church on earth, the People of God on pilgrimage, the Church enriched with heavenly blessings, the germ and beginning of the Kingdom of God, through which the work and suffering of the Redemption are continued throughout human history, and which yearns for its perfect fulfilment at the end of time in the glory of heaven.[24] The Lord Jesus forms his Church through the Sacraments which derive from his own plenitude.[25] For she ensures that her members share in the mystery of the death and resurrection of Jesus Christ in the grace of the Holy Spirit who gives her activity and life.[26] She is, therefore, holy, even though she embraces sinners in her bosom, for she enjoys no other life but the life of grace. If, then, they live her life her members are sanctified. If they withdraw from her they contract the sins and impurities of the soul which prevent the radiation of her sanctity. This is why she suffers and does penance for these offences, for she has the power to free her sons from their guilt through the blood of Christ and the gift of the Holy Spirit.

Inheriting the divine promises, daughter of Abraham according to the Spirit, through that Israel whose Scriptures she lovingly cherishes, and whose patriarchs and prophets she rightly venerates, the Church is built on the foundation of the Apostles. Their ever-living word and their pastoral powers she hands on faithfully in every century to the Successor of Peter and to the Bishops in communion with him. The Holy Spirit unfailingly assists her in her charge of guarding, teaching, explaining, and spreading that truth which was foreshadowed in the prophets and which God fully and completely revealed to men in the Lord Jesus. We believe all that is contained in the word of God, whether written or handed down, and which the Church proposes for our belief as being divinely revealed either through a solemn declaration or by the ordinary and universal magisterium.[27] We believe in the infallibility enjoyed by the Successor of Peter when he speaks *ex cathedra* as shepherd and teacher of all the faithful,[28] an infallibility which the whole Episcopate also enjoys when it exercises with him the supreme magisterium.[29]

We believe that the Church which Christ founded and for which he prayed is indefectibly one in faith and in worship, and one in the communion of a single hierarchy. Within the body of this Church the rich variety of liturgical rites and legitimate diversity in theological and spiritual heritage and particular custom, far from detracting from this unity demonstrates it yet more vividly.[30]

Recognizing that outside the framework of the Church of Christ are to be found many elements of holiness and truth, which are indeed her own possession and therefore forcefully contribute towards Catholic unity,[31] believing also in the action of the Holy Spirit who inspires this desire of unity in every disciple of Christ,[32] we cherish the hope that those Christians who do not yet enjoy the full communion of the one Church will one day be united in one flock under one Shepherd.

We believe that the Church is necessary for salvation, for Christ is the one mediator and way of salvation and he becomes present to us in his Body which is the Church,[33] but the divine design of salvation embraces all men. Those indeed who are in ignorance of Christ's gospel and of his Church through no fault of their own, who search for God in sincerity of heart, and who, acting according to conscience, strive under the influence of grace to fulfil his will, belong to his people, even though in a way we cannot see, and can obtain eternal salvation. Their number is known only to God.[34]

We believe that the Mass which is celebrated by the priest in the person of Christ in virtue of the power he receives in the Sacrament of Order, and which is offered by him in the name of Christ and of the members of his Mystical Body, is indeed the Sacrifice of Calvary sacramentally realized on our altars. We believe that, as the bread and wine consecrated by the Lord at the Last Supper were changed into his Body and Blood which were to be offered for us on the Cross, so likewise are the bread and wine consecrated by the priest changed into the Body and Blood of Christ now enthroned in glory in heaven. We believe that the mysterious presence of the Lord under the appearance of those things which, as far as our senses are concerned, remain unchanged, is a true, real and substantial presence.[35]

Consequently, in this Sacrament there is no other way in which Christ can be present except through the conversion of the entire substance of bread into his Body and through the conversion of the entire substance of wine into his Blood, leaving unchanged only those properties of bread and wine which are open to our senses. This hidden conversion is appropriately and justly called by the Church *transubstantiation*. Any theological explanation intent on arriving at some understanding of this mystery, if it is to be in accordance with Catholic faith, must maintain, without ambiguity, that in the order of reality which exists independently of the human mind, the bread and wine cease to exist after the consecration. From then on, therefore, the Body and Blood of the Lord Jesus, under the sacramental appearances of bread and wine,[36] are truly presented before us for our adoration, this being the will of the Lord himself in order that he might be our food and might incorporate us into the unity of his Mystical Body.[37]

The unique and indivisible existence of Christ the Lord whereby he lives in the glory of heaven is not multiplied by the Sacrament but rendered present in every place on earth where the eucharistic Sacrifice is celebrated. Here indeed, we have that *Mystery of Faith* and eucharistic blessings to which we must unequivocally give our assent. And this same existence remains present after the Sacrifice in the Most Blessed Sacrament which is reserved in the tabernacle, the living heart of our churches. It is, then, our bounden and loving duty to honour and adore in the Blessed Bread, which we see with our eyes, the Word Incarnate himself, whom we cannot see, but who nonetheless, without leaving heaven, is made present before us.

We likewise confess that the Kingdom of God, which had its beginnings here on earth in the Church of Christ, is not of this world, whose form is passing, and that its authentic development cannot be measured by the progress of civilization, of science or of technology. The true growth of the Kingdom of God consists in an ever deepening knowledge of the unfathomable riches of Christ, in ever stronger hope in eternal blessings, in an ever more fervent response to the love of God, and in an ever more generous acceptance of grace and holiness by men. But it is this same love that induces the Church to promote persistently the true temporal welfare of men. Although she does not cease to warn her children that here they have no abiding city, she urges them to work to improve their own human conditions within the limits of their own state of life and possibilities, to foster justice, peace and brotherhood among men, and to provide the help that is needed for their poorer and less fortunate brethren.

This urgent solicitude of the Church, the Spouse of Christ, for the needs of men—for their joys and hopes, their griefs and labours—is nothing other than her intense desire to share them in full, in order to illuminate men with the light of Christ and to gather together and unite all in him who alone is the Saviour of each one of them. This solicitude must never be taken to mean that the Church conforms herself to the things of this world, or that her longing for the coming of the Lord and his eternal reign grows cold.

We believe in eternal life. We believe that the souls of all those who die in the grace of Christ—whether they must still make expiation in the fire of Purgatory, or whether from the moment they leave their bodies they are received by Jesus into Paradise like the good thief—go to form that People of God which succeeds death, death which will be totally destroyed on the day of the Resurrection when these souls are reunited with their bodies.

We believe that the multitude of those souls gathered round

Jesus and Mary in Paradise forms the Heavenly Church. There they enjoy eternal happiness, seeing God as he is.[38] There also, in different degrees and ways, they share with the holy angels in that exercise of divine power which belongs to Christ in his glory when they intercede for us and come to the aid of our weakness in brotherly care.[39]

We believe in the communion of all the faithful of Christ, whether these still make their pilgrim way on earth, whether, their life over, they undergo purification or they enjoy the happiness of heaven. One and all they go to form the one Church. We likewise believe that in this communion we are surrounded by the love of a compassionate God and his saints, who always listen to our prayers, even as Jesus told us, *Ask and you shall receive.*[40] Confessing this faith and sustained by this hope, we await the resurrection of the dead and the life of the world to come.

Blessed be the Holy and Triune God. Amen.

* Translation by Vatican Press Office. Latin text in *AAS* 60 (1968), 433-445.
1. Cf. 1 Tim. 6:20.
2. Cf. Lk. 22:32.
3. Cf. Dz-Sch. 3002.
4. Cf. Ex. 3:14.
5. Cf. 1 Jn. 4:8.
6. Cf. 1 Tim. 6:16.
7. Cf. Dz-Sch. 804.
8. Cf. Dz-Sch. 75.
9. Cf. Dz-Sch. 75.
10. Cf. Dz-Sch. 150.
11. Cf. Dz-Sch. 76.
12. Cf. Dz-Sch. 76.
13. Cf. Dz-Sch. 251–252.
14. Cf. *Lumen Gentium*, n. 53.
15. Cf. Dz-Sch. 2803.
16. Cf. *Lumen Gentium*, n. 53.
17. Cf. *Lumen Gentium*, nn. 53, 58, 61.
18. Cf. *Dz-Sch.* 3903.
19. Cf. *Lumen Gentium*, nn. 53, 56, 61, 63.
20. Cf. *Lumen Gentium*, n. 62; cf. Paul VI, Exhort. Apost. *Signum Magnum*, p. 1, n. 1.
21. Cf. Dz-Sch. 1513 *MM*.
22. Cf. Rom. 5:20.
23. Cf. Dz-Sch. 1514.
24. Cf. *Lumen Gentium*, nn. 8 and 5.
25. Cf. *Lumen Gentium*, nn. 7, 11.
26. Cf. *Sacrosanctum Concilium*, nn. 5, 6; cf. *Lumen Gentium*, nn. 7, 12, 50.
27. Cf. Dz-Sch. 3011.

28. Cf. Dz-Sch. 3074.
29. Cf. *Lumen Gentium*, n. 25.
30. Cf. *Lumen Gentium*, n. 23; cf. *Orientalium Ecclesiarum*, nn. 2, 3, 5, 6.
31. Cf. *Lumen Gentium*, n. 8.
32. Cf. *Lumen Gentium*, n. 15.
33. Cf. *Lumen Gentium*, n. 14.
34. Cf. *Lumen Gentium*, n. 16.
35. Cf. Dz-Sch. 1651.
36. Cf. Dz-Sch. 1642, 1651–1654; Paul VI, Encycl. *Mysterium Fidei*.
37. Cf. S. Th., III, 73, 3.
38. Cf. 1 Jn. 3:2; Dz-Sch. 1000.
39. Cf. *Lumen Gentium*, n. 49.
40. Cf. Lk. 10:9–10; Jn 16:24.

102

ENCYCLICAL LETTER
ON THE REGULATION OF BIRTHS*

Paul VI, *Humanae vitae*, 25 July, 1968

The Transmission of Life

1. The most serious duty of transmitting human life, in which married people collaborate freely and responsibly with God the Creator, has always been a source of great joy to them even though sometimes not without considerable difficulties and distress.

The fulfilment of this duty has always posed problems to the conscience of married people, but the recent evolution in human society has resulted in changes which have provoked new questions which the Church could not ignore, for these concern matters intimately connected with the life and happiness of men.

Part I
NEW ASPECTS OF THE PROBLEM AND
COMPETENCY OF THE MAGISTERIUM

New Formulation of the Problem

2. The changes that have taken place are in fact of considerable importance and concern different problems. In the first place there is the question of the rapid increase in population which has made many fear that world population is going to grow faster than available resources, with the consequence that many families and developing countries are being faced with greater hardships. This fact can easily induce public authorities to be tempted to take radical measures to avert this danger. There is also the fact that not only working and housing conditions, but the greater demands made both in the economic and educational field require that kind of life in which it is frequently extremely difficult these days to provide for a large family.

It is also apparent that, with the new understanding of the dignity of woman, and her place in society, there has been an appreciation of the value of love in marriage and of the meaning of intimate married life in the light of that love.

But the most remarkable development of all is to be seen in man's stupendous progress in the domination and rational organization of the forces of nature to the point that he is endeavouring to extend this control over every aspect of his own life—over his body, over his mind and emotions, over his social life, and even over the laws that regulate the transmission of life.

New Questions

3. This new state of things gives rise to new questions. Granted the conditions of life today and taking into account the relevance of married love to the harmony and mutual fidelity of husband and wife, would it not be right to review the moral norms in force till now, especially when it is felt that these can be observed, only with the gravest difficulty, sometimes only by heroic effort?

Moreover, if one were to apply here the so-called principle of totality, could it not be accepted that the intention to have a less prolific but more rationally planned family might not transform an action which renders natural processes infertile into a licit and provident control of birth? Could it not be admitted, in other words, that procreative finality applies to the totality of married life rather than to each single act? It is being asked whether, because people are more conscious today of their responsibilities, the time has not come when the transmission of life should be regulated by their intelligence and will rather than through the specific rhythms of their own bodies.

Competency of the Magisterium

4. This kind of question required from the teaching authority of the Church a new and deeper reflection on the principles of the moral teaching on marriage—a teaching which is based on the natural law as illuminated and enriched by divine Revelation.

Let no Catholic be heard to assert that the interpretation of the natural moral law is outside the competence of the Church's Magisterium. It is in fact indisputable, as Our Predecessors have many times declared,[1] that Jesus Christ, when he communicated his divine power to Peter and the other apostles and sent them to teach all nations his commandments,[2] constituted them as the authentic guardians and interpreters of the whole moral law, not only, that is, of the law of the gospel but also of the natural law, the reason being that the natural law declares the will of God, and its faithful observance is necessary for men's eternal salvation.[3]

The Church, in carrying out this mandate, has always provided consistent teaching on the nature of marriage, on the correct use of conjugal rights, and on all the duties of husband and wife. This is especially true in recent times.[4]

Special Studies

5. The consciousness of that same responsibility induced Us to confirm and expand the Commission set up by Our Predecessor, Pope John XXIII, of happy memory, in March 1963. This Commission included married couples as well as many men, expert in the various fields pertinent to these questions. Its competence, however, was to examine views and opinions concerning married life, and especially on the correct regulation of births. But it was also intended to provide the teaching authority of the Church with such evidence as would enable it to give an apt reply in this matter, which not only the faithful but also the rest of the world were waiting for.[5]

When the evidence of the experts had been received, as well as the opinions and advice of a considerable number of Our Brethren in the Episcopate, some of whom sent their views spontaneoulsy, while others were requested by Us to do so, We were in a position to weigh up with more precision all the aspects of this complex subject. Hence We are deeply grateful to all those concerned.

Reply of the Magisterium

6. Nevertheless, we could not regard as definitive and requiring unequivocal acceptance the conclusions arrived at by the Commission. They were not such as to exempt Us from the duty of examining personally this serious question, and this because, if for no other reason, there was lacking complete agreement within the Commission itself as to what moral norms to put forward. This was all the more necessary because certain approaches and criteria for a solution to this question had emerged which were at variance with the moral doctrines on marriage constantly taught by the Magisterium of the Church.

Consequently, now that We have sifted carefully the evidence sent to Us and intently studied the whole matter, as well as prayed constantly to God, We, by virtue of the mandate entrusted to Us by Christ, intend to give Our reply to this series of grave questions.

Part II
DOCTRINAL QUESTIONS

A Total Vision of Man

7. The question of the birth of children, like every other question which touches human life, is too large to be resolved by limited criteria, such as are provided by biology, psychology, demography or sociology. It is the whole man and the whole complex of his responsibilities that must be considered, not only what is natural and limited to this earth, but also what is supernatural and eternal. And since in the attempt to justify artifical methods of birth control many appeal to the demands of married love or of 'responsible parenthood', these two important realities of married life must be accurately defined and analyzed. This is what We mean to do, with special reference to what the Second Vatican Council taught with the highest authority in its Pastoral Constitution *Gaudium et spes*.

Marriage Is a Sacrament

8. Married love particularly reveals its true nature and nobility when we realize that it derives from God and finds its supreme origin in him who 'is Love', [6] the Father 'from whom every family in heaven and on earth is named'. [7]

Marriage, then, is far from being the effect of chance or the result of the blind evolution of natural forces. It is in reality the wise and provident institution of God the Creator, whose purpose was to establish in man his loving design. As a consequence, husband and wife, through that mutual gift of themselves, which is specific and exclusive to them alone, seek to develop that kind of personal union in which they complement one another in order to co-operate with God in the generation and education of new lives.

Furthermore, the marriage of those who have been baptized is invested with the dignity of a sacramental sign of grace, for it represents the union of Christ and his Church.

Married Love

9. In the light of these facts the characteristic features and exigencies of married love are clearly indicated, and it is of the highest importance to evaluate them exactly.

This love is above all fully *human*, a compound of sense and spirit. It is not, then, merely a question of natural instinct or emotional drive. It is also, and above all, an act of the free will, whose dynamism ensures that not only does it endure through the joys and sorrows of daily life, but also that it grows, so that husband and wife become in a way one heart and one soul, and together attain their human fulfilment.

Then it is a love which is *total*—that very special form of personal friendship in which husband and wife generously share everything, allowing no unreasonable exceptions or thinking just of their own interests. Whoever really loves his partner loves not only for what he receives, but loves that partner for her own sake, content to be able to enrich the other with the gift of himself.

Again, married love is *faithful* and *exclusive* of all other, and this until death. This is how husband and wife understand it on the day on which, fully aware of what they were doing, they freely vowed themselves to one another in marriage. Though this fidelity of husband and wife sometimes presents difficulties, no one can assert that it is impossible, for it is always honourable and worthy of the highest esteem. The example of so many married persons down through the centuries shows not only that fidelity is conatural to marriage but also that it is the source of profound and enduring happiness.

And finally this love is *creative of life*, for it is not exhausted by the loving interchange of husband and wife, but also contrives to go beyond this to bring new life into being. 'Marriage and married love are by their character ordained to the procreation and bringing up of children. Children are the outstanding gift of marriage, and contribute in the highest degree to the parents' welfare.'[8]

Responsible Parenthood

10. Married love, therefore, requires of husband and wife the full awareness of their obligations in the matter of responsible parenthood, which today, rightly enough, is much insisted upon, but which, at the same time, should be rightly understood. Hence, this must be studied in the light of the various

inter-related arguments which are its justification.

If first we consider it in relation to the biological processes involved, responsible parenthood is to be understood as the knowledge and observance of their specific functions. Human intelligence discovers in the faculty of procreating life, the biological laws which involve human personality.

If, on the other hand, we examine the innate drives and emotions of man, responsible parenthood expresses the domination which reason and will must exert over them.

But if we then attend to relevant physical, economic, psychological and social conditions, those are considered to exercise responsible parenthood who prudently and generously decide to have a large family, or who, for serious reasons and with due respect to the moral law, choose to have no more children for the time being or even for an indeterminate period.

Responsible parenthood, moreover, in the terms in which we use the phrase, retains a further and deeper significance of paramount importance which refers to the objective moral order instituted by God,—the order of which a right conscience is the true interpreter. As a consequence the commitment to responsible parenthood requires that husband and wife, keeping a right order of priorities, recognize their own duties towards God, themselves, their families and human society.

From this it follows that they are not free to do as they like in the service of transmitting life, on the supposition that it is lawful for them to decide independently of other considerations what is the right course to follow. On the contrary, they are bound to ensure that what they do corresponds to the will of God the Creator. The very nature of marriage and its use makes this clear, while the constant teaching of the Church affirms it.[10]

Respect for the Nature and Purpose of the Marriage Act

11. The sexual activity, in which husband and wife are intimately and chastely united with one another, through which human life is transmitted, is, as the recent Council recalled, 'honourable and good.'[11] It does not, moreover, cease to be legitimate even when, for reasons independent of their will, it is foreseen to be infertile. For its natural adaptation to the expression and strengthening of the union of husband and wife is not thereby suppressed. The facts are, as experience shows, that new life is not the result of each and every act of sexual intercourse. God has wisely ordered the laws of nature and the incidence of fertility in such a way that successive births are already naturally

spaced through the inherent operation of these laws. The Church, nevertheless, in urging men to the observance of the precepts of the natural law, which it interprets by its constant doctrine, teaches as absolutely required that *in any use whatever of marriage* there must be no impairment of its natural capacity to procreate human life.[12]

Teaching in Harmony With Human Reason

12. This particular doctrine, often expounded by the Magisterium of the Church, is based on the inseparable connection, established by God, which man on his own initiative may not break, between the unitive significance and the procreative significance which are both inherent to the marriage act.

The reason is that the marriage act, because of its fundamental structure, while it unites husband and wife in the closest intimacy, also brings into operation laws written into the actual nature of man and of woman for the generation of new life. And if each of these essential qualities, the unitive and the procreative, is preserved, the use of marriage fully retains its sense of true mutual love and its ordination to the supreme responsibility of parenthood to which man is called. We believe that our contemporaries are particularly capable of seeing that this teaching is in harmony with human reason.

Faithfulness to God's Design

13. For men rightly observe that to force the use of marriage on one's partner without regard to his or her condition or personal and reasonable wishes in that matter, is no true act of love, and therefore offends the moral order in its particular application to the intimate relationship of husband and wife. In the same way, if they reflect, they must also recognize that an act of mutual love which impairs the capacity to transmit life which God the Creator, through specific laws, has built into it, frustrates his design which constitutes the norms of marriage, and contradicts the will of the Author of life. Hence, to use this divine gift while depriving it, even if only partially, of its meaning and purpose, is equally repugnant to the nature of man and of woman, strikes at the heart of their relationship and is consequently in opposition to the plan of God and his holy will. But to experience the gift of married love while respecting the laws of conception is to acknowledge that one is not the master of the sources of life but rather the minister of the design established by

the Creator. Just as man does not have unlimited dominion over his body in general, so also, and with more particular reason, he has no such dominion over his specifically sexual faculties, for these are concerned by their very nature with the generation of life, of which God is the source. For human life is sacred—all men must recognize that fact, Our Predecessor, Pope John XXIII, recalled, 'since from its first beginnings it calls for the creative action of God.'[13]

Unlawful Ways of Regulating Birth

14. Therefore we base our words on the first principles of a human and Christian doctrine of marriage when we are obliged once more to declare that the direct interruption of the generative process already begun and, above all, direct abortion, even for therapeutic reasons, are to be absolutely excluded as lawful means of controlling the birth of children.[14]

Equally to be condemned, as the Magisterium of the Church has affirmed on various occasions, is direct sterilization, whether of the man or of the woman, whether permanent or temporary.[15]

Similarly excluded is any action, which either before, at the moment of, or after sexual intercourse, is specifically intended to prevent procreation—whether as an end or as a means.[16]

Neither is it valid to argue, as a justification for sexual intercourse which is deliberately contraceptive, that a lesser evil is to be preferred to a greater one, or that such intercourse would merge with the normal relations of past and future to form a single entity, and so be qualified by exactly the same moral goodness as these. Though it is true that sometimes it is lawful to tolerate a lesser moral evil in order to avoid a greater or in order to promote a greater good,[17] it is never lawful, even for the gravest reasons, to do evil that good may come of it[18]—in other words, to intend positively something which intrinsically contradicts the moral order, and which must therefore be judged unworthy of man, even though the intention is to protect or promote the welfare of an individual, of a family or of society in general. Consequently it is a serious error to think that a whole married life of otherwise normal relations can justify sexual intercourse which is deliberately contraceptive and so intrinsically wrong.

Lawfulness of Therapeutic Means

15. But the Church in no way regards as unlawful therapeutic

means considered necessary to cure organic diseases, even though they also have a contraceptive effect, and this is foreseen—provided that this contraceptive effect is not directly intended for any motive whatsoever.[19]

Lawfulness of Recourse to Infertile Periods

16. However, as We noted earlier (n. 3), some people today raise the objection against this particular doctrine of the Church concerning the moral laws governing marriage, that human intelligence has both the right and the responsibility to control those forces of irrational nature which come within its ambit and to direct them towards ends beneficial to man. Others ask on the same point whether it is not reasonable in so many cases to use artificial birth control if by so doing the harmony and peace of a family are better served and more suitable conditions are provided for the education of children already born. To this question we must give a clear reply. The Church is the first to praise and commend the application of human intelligence to an activity in which a rational creature such as man is so closely associated with his Creator. But she affirms that this must be done within the limits of the order of reality established by God.

If therefore there are reasonable grounds for spacing births, arising from the physical or psychological condition of husband or wife, or from external circumstances, the Church teaches that then married people may take advantage of the natural cycles immanent in the reproductive system and use their marriage at precisely those times that are infertile, and in this way control birth, a way which does not in the least offend the moral principles which we have just explained.[20]

Neither the Church nor her doctrine is inconsistent when she considers it lawful for married people to take advantage of the infertile period but condemns as always unlawful the use of means which directly exclude conception, even when the reasons given for the latter practice are neither trivial nor immoral. In reality, these two cases are completely different. In the former married couples rightly use a facility provided them by nature. In the latter they obstruct the natural development of the generative process. It cannot be denied that in each case married couples, for acceptable reasons, are both perfectly clear in their intention to avoid children and mean to make sure that none will be born. But it is equally true that it is exclusively in the former case that husband and wife are ready to abstain from intercourse during the fertile period as often as for reasonable motives the birth of another child is not desirable. And when the infertile period recurs, they use their married intimacy to express their mutual love and safeguard their fidelity towards one another. In doing this they certainly give proof of a true and authentic love.

Grave Consequences of Artificial Birth Control

17. Responsible men can become more deeply convinced of the truth of the doctrine laid down by the Church on this issue if they reflect on the consequences of methods and plans for the artificial restriction of increases in the birth-rate. Let them first consider how easily this course of action can lead to the way being wide open to marital infidelity and a general lowering of moral standards. Not much experience is needed to be fully aware of human weakness and to understand that men—and especially the young, who are so exposed to temptation—need incentives to keep the moral law, and it is an evil thing to make it easy for them to break that law. Another effect that gives cause for alarm is that a man who grows accustomed to the use of contraceptive methods may forget the reverence due to a woman, and, disregarding her physical and emotional equilibrium, reduce her to being a mere instrument for the satisfaction of his own desires, no longer considering her as his partner whom he should surround with care and affection.

Finally, grave consideration should be given to the danger of this power passing into the hands of those public authorities who care little for the precepts of the moral law. Who will blame a Government which in its attempt to resolve the problems affecting an entire country resorts to the same measures as are regarded as lawful by married people in the solution of a particular family difficulty? Who will prevent public authorities from favouring those contraceptive methods which they consider more effective? Should they regard this as necessary, they may even impose their use on everyone. It could well happen, therefore, that when people, either individually or in family or social life, experience the inherent difficulties of the divine law and are determined to avoid them, they may be giving into the hands of public authorities the power to intervene in the most personal and intimate responsibility of husband and wife.

Consequently, unless we are willing that the responsibility of procreating life should be left to the arbitrary decision of men, we must accept that there are certain limits, beyond which it is wrong to go, to the power of man over his own body and its natural functions—limits, let it be said, which no one, whether as a private individual or as a public authority, can lawfully exceed. These limits are expressly imposed because of the reverence due to the whole human organism and its natural functions, in the light of the principles, which we stated earlier, and according to a correct understanding of the so-called 'principle of totality', enunciated by Our Predecessor, Pope Pius XII.[21]

The Church, Guarantor of True Human Values

18. It is to be anticipated that not everyone perhaps will easily accept this particular teaching. There is too much clamorous outcry against the voice of the Church, and this is intensified by modern means of communication. It should cause no surprise that the Church, any less than her divine Founder, is destined to be a 'sign of contradiction'.[22] She does not, because of this, evade the duty imposed on her of proclaiming humbly but firmly the entire moral law, both natural and evangelical.

Since the Church did not make either of these laws, she cannot be their arbiter—only their guardian and interpreter. It can never be right for her to declare lawful what is in fact unlawful, because this, by its very nature, is always opposed to the true good of man.

By vindicating the integrity of the moral law of marriage, the Church is convinced that she is contributing to the creation of a truly human civilization. She urges man not to betray his personal responsibilities by putting all his faith in technical expedients. In this way she defends the dignity of husband and wife. This course of action shows that the Church, loyal to the example and teaching of the divine Saviour, is sincere and unselfish in her regard for men whom she strives to help even now during this earthly pilgrimage 'to share as sons in the life of the living God, the Father of all men'.[23]

Part III
PASTORAL DIRECTIVES

The Church, Mother and Teacher

19. Our words would ill reflect the thought and loving care of the Church, who is the Mother and Teacher of all nations, did they not also sustain men in the proper ordering of the number of their children at a time when living conditions are harsh and press heavily on families and nations. Yet it is these men and women whom we have just urged to observe and honour the law of God concerning marriage. For the Church cannot adopt towards mankind a different attitude from that of the divine

Redeemer. She knows their weakness; she has compassion on the multitudes; she welcomes sinners. But at the same time she cannot do otherwise than teach the law. For it is in fact the law of human life restored to its native truth and led by the Spirit of God.[24]

Observing the Divine Law

20. The teaching of the Church regarding the right ordering of the increase of a man's family is a promulgation of the law of God himself. And yet there is no doubt that to many it will appear not merely difficult but even impossible to observe. Now it is true that like all good things which are outstanding for their nobility and for the benefits which they confer on men, so this law demands from individual men and women, from families and from human society a resolute purpose and great endurance. Indeed it cannot be observed unless God comes to their help with that grace by which the goodwill of men is sustained and strengthened. But to those who consider this matter diligently it will indeed be evident that this endurance enhances man's dignity and confers benefits on human society.

Mastery of Self

21. But the right and lawful ordering of the births of children presupposes in husband and wife first and foremost that they fully recognize and value the true blessings of family life, and secondly, that they acquire complete mastery over themselves and their emotions. For if with the aid of reason and of free-will they are to control their natural drives, there can be no doubt at all of the need for self-denial. Only then will the expression of love, particular to married life, conform to right order. And this is especially true as regards the practice of periodic continence. But self-discipline of this kind is a shining witness to the chastity of husband and wife and, so far from being a hindrance to their love of one another, transforms it by giving it a more truly human character. And if this self-discipline does demand that they persevere in their purpose and efforts, it has at the same time the salutary effect of enabling husband and wife to develop to the full their personalities and be enriched with spiritual blessings. For it brings to family life abundant fruits of tranquillity and peace. It helps in solving difficulties of other kinds. It fosters in husband and wife thoughtfulness and loving consideration for one another. It helps them to repel the excessive self-love

which is the opposite of charity. It arouses in them a consciousness of their responsibilities. And finally it confers upon parents a deeper and more effective influence in the education of their children. For these latter both in childhood and in youth, as years go by, develop a right sense of values as regards the true blessings of life and achieve a serene and harmonious use of their mental and physical powers.

Appeal to Those Engaged in Education

22. These considerations give Us the opportunity to address those who are engaged in education and all those whose right and duty it is to provide for the common good of human society. We would call their attention to the need to create an atmosphere favourable to the growth of chastity in such a way that true liberty may prevail over licence and the norms of the moral law be fully safeguarded.

Everything therefore in the modern means of social communication which arouses men's baser passions and encourages low moral standards, likewise every obscenity in the written word and every form of indecency on the stage and screen, should be condemned publicly and unanimously by all those who have at heart the advance of civilization and the safeguarding of the outstanding values of the human spirit. It is quite absurd to defend this kind of depravity in the name of art or of culture[25] or by pleading the liberty which may be allowed in this field by the public authorities.

To Rulers of Nations

23. And so We would like to speak to Rulers of Nations, because to them most of all is committed the responsibility of safeguarding the common good, and they can contribute so much to the preservation of morals. Do not ever allow the morals of your Peoples to be undermined. Do not tolerate any legislation which would introduce into the family practices which are opposed to the natural and divine law—for the family is the primary unit in the State. For there are other ways by which a Government can and should solve the population problem— that is to say by enacting laws which will assist families and by educating the people wisely so that the moral law and the freedom of the citizens are both safeguarded.

We are fully aware of the difficulties confronting the public Authorities in this matter, especially in the developing countries.

In fact We had in mind the justifiable anxieties which weigh upon them when We published Our Encyclical Letter, *Populorum Progressio*. But now we join Our voice to that of Our Predecessor, John XXIII of venerable memory, and We make Our own his words: 'no statement of the problem and no solution to it is acceptable which does violence to man's essential dignity, and which is based on an utterly materialistic conception of man himself and his life. The only possible solution to this question is one which envisages the social and economic progress both of individuals and of the whole of human society, and which respects and promotes true human values'.[26] No one can, without grave injustice, make divine Providence responsible for what would appear to be the result of misguided governmental policies, of an insufficient sense of social justice, of a selfish accumulation of material goods, and finally of a culpable failure to undertake those initiatives and responsibilities which would raise the standard of living of peoples and their children.[27] If only all governments which were able would do what some are already doing so nobly, and bestir themselves to renew their efforts and their undertakings! There must be no relaxation in the programmes of mutual aid between all the branches of the great human family. Here We believe an almost limitless field lies open for the activities of the great international Institutions.

To Men of Science

24. Our next appeal is to men of science. These can 'greatly serve the cause of marriage and the family and peace of conscience, if by comparative studies they try to elucidate better the conditions favourable to a lawful regulation of procreation'.[28] It is supremely desirable, and this was also the mind of Pius XII, that medical science should by the study of natural rhythms succeed in determining a sufficiently secure as well as a moral basis for the regulation of birth.[29] In this way scientists, especially those who are Catholics, will by their research establish the truth of the Church's claim that 'there can be no contradiction between two divine laws—that which governs the transmitting of life and that which governs the fostering of married love'.[30]

To Christian Husbands and Wives

25. And now We turn in a special way to Our own Sons and Daughters, to those most of all whom God calls to serve him in the state of marriage. While the Church does indeed hand on to

her children the inviolable conditions laid down by God's law, she is also the herald of salvation and through the sacraments she flings wide open the channels of grace through which man is made a new creature responding in charity and true freedom to the design of his Creator and Saviour, experiencing too the sweetness of the yoke of Christ.[31]

In humble obedience then to her voice, let Christian husbands and wives be mindful of their vocation to the Christian life, a vocation which, deriving from their baptism, has been confirmed anew and made more explicit by the sacrament of matrimony. For by this sacrament they are *strengthened* and, one might almost say, *consecrated* to the faithful fulfilment of their duties, to realizing to the full their vocation, and to bearing witness, as becomes them, to Christ before the world.[32] For the Lord has entrusted to them the task of making visible to men and women the holiness, and the joy too of the law which unites inseparably their love for one another and the co-operation they give to God's love, God who is the Author of human life.

We have no wish at all to pass over in silence the difficulties, at times very great, which beset the lives of Christian married couples. For them, as indeed for every one of us, 'the gate is narrow and the way is hard, that leads to life'.[33] Nevertheless it is precisely the hope of that life which, like a brightly burning torch, lights up their journey, as, strong in spirit, they strive to live 'sober, upright, and godly lives in this world'[34] knowing for sure that 'the form of this world is passing away'.[35]

For this reason husbands and wives should take up the burden appointed to them, willingly, in the strength of faith and of that hope which 'does not disappoint us, because God's love has been poured into our hearts through the Holy Spirit who has been given to us'.[36] Then let them beg the help of God with unremitting prayer and most of all let them drink deep of grace and charity from that unfailing fount which is the Eucharist. If, however, sin still exercises its hold over them, they are not to lose heart. Rather must they, humble and persevering, have recourse to the mercy of God, abundantly bestowed in the sacrament of penance. In this way, for sure, they will be able to reach that perfection of married life which the Apostle sets out in these words: 'Husbands, love your wives, as Christ loved the Church... Even so husbands should love their wives as their own bodies. He who loves his wife loves himself. For no man ever hates his own flesh, but nourishes and cherishes it, as Christ does the Church... This is a great mystery, and I mean in reference to Christ and the Church; however, let each one of you love his wife as himself, and let the wife see that she respects her husband'.[37]

Family Apostolate

26.   Among the fruits that ripen if the law of God be resolutely obeyed the most precious is certainly this, that married couples themselves will often desire to share with others their own experience. Thus it comes about that in the fulness of the lay vocation will be included a novel and outstanding form of the apostolate by which, like ministering to like, married couples themselves by the leadership they offer will become apostles to other married couples. And surely among all the forms of the Christian apostolate it is hard to think of one more opportune for the present time.[38]

To Doctors and Nurses

27.   Likewise we hold in the highest esteem those doctors and members of the nursing profession who, in the exercise of their calling, endeavour to fulfill the demands of their Christian vocation before any merely human interest. Let them therefore continue constant in their resolution always to support those lines of action which accord with faith and with right reason. And in the Conferences of their professional colleagues let them strive to win agreement and support for these policies. Moreover they should regard it as an essential part of their skill to make themselves fully proficient in this difficult field of medical knowledge. For then, when married couples consult them, they will be able to give them proper advice and to show them a way that is lawful. This, indeed, they have every right to expect.

To Priests

28.   And now, beloved Sons, you who are priests, you who in virtue of your sacred office act as counsellors and spiritual leaders both of individual men and women and of families—We turn to you filled with great confidence. For it is your principal duty—We are speaking especially to you who teach moral theology—to expound the Church's teaching with regard to marriage in its entirety and with complete frankness. In the performance of your ministry you must be the first to give an example of that sincere obedience, inward as well as outward, which is due to the Magisterium of the Church. For, as you know, the Pastors of the Church enjoy a special light of the Holy Spirit in teaching the

truth.[39] And this, rather than the arguments they put forward, is why you are bound to such obedience. Nor will it escape you that if men's peace of soul and if the unity of the Christian people are to be preserved then it is of the utmost importance that in moral as well as in dogmatic theology all should obey the Magisterium of the Church and should speak as with one voice. Therefore We make Our own the anxious words of the great Apostle Paul and with all Our heart We renew Our appeal to you: 'I appeal to you, brethren, by the name of our Lord Jesus Christ, that all of you agree and that there be no dissensions among you, but that you be united in the same mind and the same judgment'.[40]

Compassion for Sinners

29. Moreover if on the one hand it is an outstanding manifestation of charity towards souls to omit nothing from the saving doctrine of Christ, still on the other hand this must always be joined with tolerance and charity. Of this, the Lord himself in his conversation and dealings with men has left an example. For when he came, not to judge, but to save the world,[41] was he not bitterly severe towards sin, but patient and abounding in mercy towards sinners?

Husbands and wives therefore, when deeply distressed by reason of the difficulties of their life, must find stamped in the heart and voice of their priest the likeness of the voice and the love of our Redeemer.

We are full of confidence as We speak to you, beloved Sons, because We hold it as certain that while the Holy Spirit of God is present to the Magisterium proclaiming sound doctrine, he also illumines from within the hearts of the Faithful and invites their assent. But you are to teach married couples the necessary way of prayer and prepare them to approach more often with great faith the sacraments of the Eucharist and of Penance. Nor must they ever despair because of their weakness.

To Bishops

30. And now as We come to the end of this Encyclical Letter, We turn Our mind to you, reverently and lovingly, beloved and venerable Brothers in the Episcopate, with whom We share more closely the care of the spiritual good of the People of God. For We invite you all, We implore you, to give a lead to your priests who assist you in the sacred Ministry, and to the faithful

of your dioceses, and to devote yourselves with all zeal and without delay to safeguarding the holiness of marriage, the better to guide married life to its full human and Christian perfection. Look upon this mission as the most important work and responsibility committed to you at the present time. For as you well know, it calls for concerted pastoral action in all the fields of human activity, economic, cultural and social. For if simultaneous progress is made in all these fields, then the intimate life of parents and children in the family will be rendered not only more tolerable, but easier and more joyful. And life together in human society will be enriched with fraternal charity and made more stable with true peace when God's design which he conceived for the world is faithfully followed.

Final Appeal

31. Venerable Brothers, beloved Sons, and all men of goodwill, great indeed is the work of education, of progress and of charity to which We now summon you all. And this We do relying on the unshakeable teaching of the Church, which teaching Peter's Successor together with His Brothers in the Catholic Episcopate faithfully guards and interprets. And We are convinced that this truly great work will bring blessings both on the world and on the Church. For man cannot attain that true happiness for which he yearns with all the strength of his spirit, unless he keeps the laws which the Most High God has engraved in his very nature. These laws must be wisely and lovingly observed. On this great work, on all of you and especially on married couples We implore from the God of all holiness and pity an abundance of heavenly grace as a pledge of which We gladly bestow Our Apostolic Blessing.

---

* Translation by Vatican Press Office, with some corrections. Latin text in AAS 60 (1968), 481–503.
1. Cf. PIUS XI, Encyclical *Qui pluribus: Pii IX P.M. Acta*, 1, pp. 9-10; ST PIUS X, Encycl. *Singulari quadam,* AAS 4 (1912), p. 658; PIUS XI, Encycl. *Casti Connubii,* AAS 22 (1930), pp. 579-581 (C.T.S. translation, nn. 107-109); PIUS XII, Address *Magnificate Dominum* to the Episcopate of the Catholic World, AAS 46 (1954), pp. 671-672; JOHN XXIII, Encycl. *Mater et Magistra,* AAS 53 (1961), p. 457 (C.T.S. translation, n. 239).
2. Cf. Mt 28:18-19.
3. Cf. Mt 7:21.
4. Cf. Council of Trent Roman Catechism, Part II, ch. 8; LEO XIII, Encycl. *Arcanum: Acta Leonis XIII, 2* (1880), pp. 26-29; PIUS XI, En-

cycl. *Divini Illius Magistri*, AAS 22 (1930), pp. 58–61 (C.T.S. translation, nn. 32–41; PIUS XI, Encycl. *Casti Connubii*, AAS 22 (1930), pp. 545-546 (C.T.S. translation, nn. 16-18);PIUS XII, Address to the Italian Medico-Biological Union of St. Luke, *Discorsi e Radiomessaggi*, VI, pp. 191-192; to the Italian Association of Catholic Midwives, AAS 43 (1951), pp. 835-854 (C.T.S. translation, nn. 1-71); to the Association known as the 'Family Campaign' and other Family Associations, AAS 43 (1951), pp. 857-859 (C.T.S. translation, nn. 6-15); to the seventh Congress of the International Society of Haematology, AAS 50 (1958), pp. 734-735; JOHN XXIII, Encycl. *Mater et Magistra*, AAS 53 (1961), pp. 446-447 (C.T.S. translation, nn. 188-192); VATICAN COUNCIL II, Pastoral Constitution on the Church in the World of Today *Gaudium et spes*, nn. 47-52, AAS 58 (1966), pp. 1067-1074; Code of Canon Law, Canons 1067, 1068 § 1, Canon 1076 §§ 1-2.

5. Cf. PAUL VI, Address to the Sacred College of Cardinals, AAS 56 (1964), p. 588; to the Commission for the Study of Problems of Population, Family and Birth, AAS 57 (1965), p. 388; to the National Congress of the Italian Society of Obstetrics and Gynaecology, AAS 58 (1966), p. 1168.

6. Cf. 1 Jn 4:8.

7. Eph 3:15.

8. VATICAN COUNCIL II, Pastoral Constitutions on the Church in the World of Today *Gaudium et spes*, n. 50, AAS 58 (1966), pp. 1070-1072.

9. Cf. ST THOMAS, *Summa Theologica*, I-II, q. 94, art. 2.

10. Cf. VATICAN COUNCIL II, Pastoral Constitution on the Church in the World of Today *Gaudium et spes*, nn. 50-51, AAS 58 (1968), pp. 1070-1073.

11. Cf. *ibid.,* n. 49, AAS 58 (1966), p. 1070.

12. Cf. PIUS XI, Encycl. *Casti Connubii,* AAS 22 (1930), p. 560 (C.T.S. translation, n. 56); PIUS XII, Address to Midwives, AAS 43 (1951), p. 843 (C.T.S. translation, n. 24).

13. Cf. JOHN XXIII, Encycl. *Mater et Magistra,* AAS 53 (1961), p. 447 (C.T.S. translation, n. 194).

14. Cf. Council of Trent Roman Catechism, Part II, ch. 8; PIUS XI, Encycl. *Casti Connubii,* AAS 22 (1930), pp. 562-564 (C.T.S. translation, nn. 62-66); PIUS XII, Address to the Medico-Biological Union of St Luke, *Discorsi e Radiomessaggi,* VI, pp. 191-192; Address to Midwives, AAS 43 (1951), pp. 842-843 (C.T.S. translation, nn. 20-26); Address to the 'Family Campaign' and other Family Associations, AAS 43 (1951), pp. 857-859 (C.T.S. translation, nn. 6-15); JOHN XXIII, Encycl. *Pacem in terris,* AAS 55 (1963), pp. 259-260 (C.T.S. translation, nn. 8-13); VATICAN COUNCIL II, Pastoral Constitution on the Church in the World of Today *Gaudium et spes,* n. 51, AAS 58 (1966), p. 1072.

15. Cf. PIUS XI, Encycl. *Casti Connubii,* AAS 22 (1930), p. 565 (C.T.S. translation, nn. 67-70); Decree of the Holy Office, 22 Feb. 1940, AAS 32 (1940), p. 73; PIUS XII, Address to Midwives, AAS 43 (1951), pp. 843-844 (C.T.S. translation, nn. 24-28); to the Society of Haematology, AAS 50 (1958), pp. 734-735.

16. Cf. Council of Trent Roman Catechism, Part II, ch. 8; PIUS XI, Encycl. *Casti Connubii,* AAS 22 (1930), pp. 559-561 (C.T.S. translation, nn. 53-57); PIUS XII, Address to Midwives, AAS 43 (1951), p. 843 (C.T.S. translation, n. 24); to the Society of Haematology, AAS 50 (1958), pp. 734-735; JOHN XXIII, Encycl. *Mater et Magistra,* AAS 53

(1961), p. 447 (C.T.S. translation, n. 193).

17. Cf. PIUS XII, Address to the National Congress of the Italian Society of the Union of Catholic Jurists, AAS 45 (1953), pp. 798-799.

18. Cf. Rom 3:8.

19. Cf. PIUS XII, Address to the twenty-sixth Congress of the Italian Association of Urology, AAS 45 (1953), pp. 674-675; to the Society of Haematology, AAS 50 (1958), pp. 734-735.

20. Cf. PIUS XII, Address to Midwives, AAS 43 (1951), p. 846 (C.T.S. translation, n. 36).

21. Cf. PIUS XII, Address to the Association of Urology, AAS 45 (1953), pp. 674-675; to Leaders and Members of the Italian Association of 'corneae' donors and the Italian Association of the Blind, AAS 48 (1956), pp. 461-462.

22. Lk 2:34.

23. Cf. PAUL VI, Encycl. *Populorum Progressio,* AAS 59 (1967), p. 268 (C.T.S. translation, n. 21).

24. Cf. Rom 8.

25. Cf. VATICAN COUNCIL II, Decree on the Means of Mass Communication *Inter mirifica,* nn. 6-7, AAS 56 (1964), p. 147.

26. JOHN XXIII, Encycl. *Mater et Magistra,* AAS 53 (1961), p. 447 (C.T.S. translation, nn. 191-192).

27. Cf. PAUL VI, Encycl. *Populorum Progressio,* AAS 59 (1967), pp. 281-284 (C.T.S. translation, nn. 48-55).

28. VATICAN COUNCIL II, Pastoral Constitution on the Church in the World of Today *Gaudium et spes,* n. 52 AAS 58 (1966), p. 1074.

29. Cf. PIUS XII, Address to the 'Family Campaign' and other Family Associations, AAS 43 (1951), p. 859 (C.T.S. translation, nn. 14-15).

30. VATICAN COUNCIL II, Pastoral Constitution on the Church in the World of Today *Gaudium et spes,* n. 51, AAS 58 (1966), p. 1072.

31. Cf. Mt 11:30.

32. Cf. VATICAN COUNCIL II, Pastoral Constitution on the Church in the World of Today *Gaudium et spes,* n. 48, AAS 58 (1966), pp. 1067-1069; Dogmatic Constitution on the Church *Lumen gentium,* n. 35, AAS 57 (1965), pp. 40-41.

33. Mt 7:14; cf. Heb 12:11.

34. Tit 2:12.

35. 1 Cor 7:31.

36. Rom 5:5.

37. Eph 5:25, 28-29, 32-33.

38. Cf. VATICAN COUNCIL II, Dogmatic Constitution on the Church *Lumen gentium,* nn. 35, 41, AAS 57 (1965), pp. 40-45; Pastoral Constitution on the Church in the World of Today *Gaudium et spes,* nn. 48-49, AAS 58 (1966), pp. 1067-1070; Decree on the Apostolate of the Laity *Apostolicam Actuositatem,* n. 11, AAS 58 (1966), pp. 847-849.

39. Cf. VATICAN COUNCIL II, Dogmatic Constitution on the Church *Lumen gentium,* n. 25, AAS 57 (1965), pp. 29-31.

40. 1 Cor 1:10.

41. Cf. Jn 3:17.

103

THE WASHINGTON CASE*

S.C.C., *This sacred congregation*, 26 April, 1971

I. OFFICIAL COMMUNICATION

This Sacred Congregation for the Clergy received from the Secretariat of State of His Holiness on 21 July 1970, an appeal addressed to the Holy See by the Rev. Joseph Byron, acting as spokesman for a group of Priests in the Archdiocese of Washington. These Priests had been restricted in their faculties, though in varying degrees, by their Archbishop in reaction to their public "dissent" from the teaching of the encyclical *Humanae Vitae.*

The appeal centered around the complaint that in two years the conflict arising from their dissent and the stand of their Ordinary had not received a canonical solution in the United States.

The Congregation, acting at the instance of the Holy Father, undertook to devise an acceptable procedure for the "fair and impartial hearings" which the Priests declared to be the substance of their appeal. It had been widely reported that canonical norms had not been observed prior to the imposition of individual "penalties" on the Washington Priests involved.

Official news agencies have carried detailed explanations of the procedure accepted by all the parties concerned early in January of this year. The names of the Proxies and the fact of their meeting in Rome were duly announced, together with their reactions to the two weeks of hearings conducted under the auspices of the Vatican.

Prior to these hearings evidence accumulated on both sides had been reviewed by qualified English speaking members of Vatican departments outside the Congregation for the Clergy. These authorities constituted a commission of three whose names were published and who participated as consultors in the "fair and impartial hearings" which brought together the Proxies for both sides.

The "findings" of the Congregation itself are based on these hearings and on the analysis by the commission of the accumulated evidence.

It was found that the Proxies for the Priests had not, in fact, seen the documentation which had accumulated in the proceedings in the Archdiocese as well as in the headquarters of the United States Catholic Conference. However, the Congregation made completely available to the Proxies for the Priests all the material in its possession for depth study. The final conclusion of this study by the Proxies for the Priests was that, under existing Church law, there was no canonical case against the procedures followed by Card. O'Boyle.

At this point, the Proxies for the Priests declared that they had come to Rome to secure a "fair and impartial hearing", but on the assumption that the case involved a primarily canonical problem. In the absence of such a canonical case they were willing, nonetheless, to collaborate in seeking a pastoral solution of the issue, while candidly expressing their hope that future legislation would provide improved procedures in cases of this kind, which might reduce misunderstandings.

Their agreement on this point was the more acceptable to the Congregation since its competence is not primarily doctrinal nor judicial, but is directly concerned with pastoral and catechetical problems. The Congregation concurred that a judicial or strictly theological process was not called for in this case, but that an "administrative review", following the "fair and impartial hearings", should yield the material for "findings" on the basis of which recommendations could be made.

The "findings" of the Congregation are the following:

FINDINGS

A) The Sacred Congregation for the Clergy found that the Committee of Concerned Canon Lawyers had entered the case without reference to any doctrinal preoccupation on their part or the slightest disrespect for the person and the office of the Holy Father. Their interest had been motivated by a fraternal desire as canon lawyers to discover whether, as commonly reported, the rights of brother priests had been neglected.

B) The Congregation concurred with the dismissal, by agreement, of a supposed canonical case against Card. O'Boyle, and found that he had observed the requirements of existing law. The Congregation took due note of the expressed desire of the

Proxies, recorded above, that relevant canonical procedures be improved.

C) The Congregation found that the National Conference of Catholic Bishops could not, for many reasons, accept competency in the case.

D) It was also found that the Priests' Senate of Washington, elected by the priests of the Archdiocese, had, at a meeting of 26 June 1969, unanimously appealed for the elimination of divisions in the Archdiocese arising out of the dispute. The consequent efforts of a conciliation committee to accomplish this purpose had proved insufficient, though some of the group had later responded positively to a special plea of the Holy Father that reconciliation be achieved.

E) The Congregation discovered that, despite the phrase "Washington Nineteen", none of the Proxies on either side could affirm with certainly how many priests were still actually included in the appeal to the Holy See, remained in the service of the Archdiocese, or would be open to the recommendations of this Congregation. At least two do not belong to the Archdiocese of Washington and some either already had, or have since, abandoned the exercise of their priesthood or forfeited their status in the Archdiocese on other grounds than the dispute which prompted the appeal to Rome.

F) In the course of the hearings, the Proxies for the Priests emphasized the climate of emotion and general confusion in which the so-called "Statement of Conscience" had been issued by the Priests. As a result, the Proxies for the Priests, in consultation with Fr. Byron, present in Rome, agreed to the substitution of a more considered statement which would take into account the declared original intention of the Priests and the criticisms made of the controversial "Statement of Conscience".

G) The Proxies for the Priests argued that it was at no time the intention, at least of those for whom Fr. Byron spoke, to depart from or contradict the theology of Vatican Council II, and that they did not speak for any theological group or tendency, above all with respect to the nature of the church or the Magisterium. The Congregation accepted this assurance as a fair statement of the position certainly of those Priests who had remained at their posts.

H) Having heard the arguments of the opposing sides and having in mind the authentic principles of faith and morals by which Catholics are bound, the Congregation outlined its theological and pastoral "findings" as follows:

STATEMENT OF THEOLOGICAL
AND PASTORAL PRINCIPLES

I. Magisterium

1. The Ordinary Magisterium, i.e., the Pope and the bishops in their local churches, has the duty and responsibility to teach on matters pertaining to faith and morals.

2. By virtue of the pastoral office proper to him, it is the duty and responsibility of the bishop in his local church to instruct his priests in their pastoral ministries of preaching, teaching and counselling.

3. The encyclical *Humanae vitae*, which declares without ambiguity, doubt or hesitation the objective evil of the contraceptive act, is an authentic expression of this Magisterium and is to be understood in accord with the dogmatic tradition of the Church concerning the assent due to the teachings of the Ordinary Magisterium (cf. Lumen gentium, No. 25).

4. Those who receive canonical faculties of a diocese are assumed to intend to communicate this teaching, according to the traditional norms of the Church, to those under their care.

II. Conscience

1. Conscience is the practical judgment or dictate of reason by which one judges what here and now is to be done as being good, or to be avoided as evil.

2. In the light of the above, the role of conscience is that of a practical dictate, not a teacher of doctrine.

3. Conscience is not a law unto itself and in forming one's conscience one must be guided by objective moral norms, including authentic Church teaching (cf. Gaudium et spes, No. 50).

4. Particular circumstances surrounding an objectively evil human act, while they cannot make it objectively virtuous, can make it inculpable, diminished in guilt or subjectively defensible. (For full context, confer Human Life in Our Day; Collective Pastoral of the American Hierarchy, Nov. 15, 1968, p. 12).

5. In the final analysis, conscience is inviolable and no man is to be forced to act in a manner contrary to his conscience, as the moral tradition of the Church attests (Human Life in Our Day, p. 14).

III. Pastoral practice

1. In the task of counselling married persons, either inside or

outside the confessional, the pastoral counsellor may encounter a question concerning the practice of contraception. The counsellor is obliged in conscience to follow the previously mentioned principles in accordance with the pastoral prudence and doctrinal truth required for guiding the person or persons who consult him.

2. While the counsellor has the obligation to render an objective judgment on the data presented to him, he should not too quickly presume either complete innocence, on the one hand, or, on the other, a deliberate rejection of God's loving commands in the case of a person who is honestly trying to lead a good Christian life (cf. Sex in Marriage, Love-giving, Life-giving. Archdiocese of Washington, 1968, p. 2, No. 2).

3. Sound pastoral practice is always based upon firm faith in the mercy of God and the forgiving power of Christ, but also on the necessity and availability of God's grace to enable every person who remains open to that grace and faithful to the sacraments, which are channels of God's grace, to persevere in the friendship of Christ in all moral crises. (Cf. In 15, 5; 2 Cor. 12, 9; Humanae Vitae, No. 20; St. Thomas Aquinas, Summa Theologica, I^a-II^{ae} q. 109, a. 6.2).

RECOMMENDATIONS

Given the varied kinds and degrees of the differences which have arisen among the Priests formerly or presently parties to this appeal; given the basic priestly fidelity of those who have remained at their posts despite those differences; given the long delay and painful misunderstanding endured by them and by the Cardinal Archbishop to whom they are bound in common love for the Church, priestly unity and zeal for souls; given the prayerful desire of all the Archdiocese that an unhappy crisis come to an early end; and, finally, given that the Holy Father himself has approved with prayerful hope the procedures provided in agreement with the parties seeking a "fair and impartial hearing": —

Therefore, this Sacred Congregation for the Clergy urgently recommends that, without further delay, formality or necessity for written or oral explanations, each priest who accepts the "findings" set forth above present himself individually, at his earliest convenience, to his Ordinary and declare his desire to enjoy the full faculties of the Archdiocese.

This Congregation is confident that the Cardinal Archbishop of Washington will respond promptly and gladly to each request so made, just as we are confident that those, who with generous openness toward this Congregation agreed to our procedure, will, not less generously, accept the recommendations and "findings" which the Congregation has felt bound to make.

The so-called "Washington Case" has been a source of grave concern to all persons in the Archdiocese. It is the hope of this Congregation that the Catholics of Washington will not falsely conclude, because of the publicity tag "Washington Case", that their local crisis is either unique or a reflexion of the holy traditions, the spiritual stability, and the high prestige of the Archdiocese of Washington. The members of the Archdiocese should be grateful for the sensitive, forthright leadership of their Cardinal and for the persevering commitment, on the deepest sacerdotal levels, of those priests who patiently awaited the hearing that is now concluded.

* Original English text in *E.V.* 4, nn. 678–706.

104

ERRORS CONCERNING THE MYSTERIES OF THE INCARNATION AND THE TRINITY*

S.C.D.F., *Mysterium filii Dei*, 21 February, 1972

The mystery of the Son of God made man, and the mystery of the Most Holy Trinity, both pertaining to the Most Holy Trinity, both pertaining to the inner-most substance of Revelation, must be, in their authentic truth, the source of light for the lives of Christians. But because some recent errors undermine these mysteries, the Sacred Congregation for the Doctrine of the Faith has determined to reaffirm and safeguard the belief in them that has been handed down to us.

Jesus Christ, while dwelling on this earth, manifested in various ways, by word and deed the adorable mystery of His person. After being made "obedient to death,"[1] He was divinely exalted in His glorious resurrection, as was fitting for the Son "through whom all things"[2] were made by the Father. Of Him St. John solemnly proclaimed: "in the beginning was the Word, and the Word was with God; and the Word was God...And the Word was made flesh."[3]

The Church has reverently preserved the mystery of the Son of God made man, and "in the course of the ages and centuries"[4] has propounded it for belief in a more explicit way. In the Creed of Constantinople, which is still recited today during the Eucharistic celebration, the Church proclaims her faith in "Jesus Christ, the only begotten Son of God, born of the Father before all ages,...who for us men and for our salvation, ...was made man."[5] The Council of Chalcedon decreed for belief that the Son of God according to His divinity was begotten of the Father before all ages, and according to His humanity was born in time of the Virgin Mary.[6] Moreover, this Council spoke of one and the same Christ the Son of God as a "person" or *hypostatis*, but used the term "nature" to denote His divinity and His humanity. Using these terms, it taught that both His natures, divine and human, together belong—without confu-

423

sion, unalterably, indivisibly and inseparable—to the one person of our Redeemer.[7]

In the same way, the Fourth Lateran Council taught for belief and profession that the Son of God, coeternal with the Father, was made true man and is one person in two natures.[8] This is the truth, a constant in the tradition of the whole Church, clearly expressed in many passages of the Second Vatican Council.[9]

Opinions which hold that it has not been revealed and made known to us that the Son of God subsists from all eternity in the mystery of the Godhead, distinct from the Father and the Holy Spirit, are in open conflict with this belief. The same is true of opinions which should abandon the notion of the one person of Jesus Christ begotten in His divinity of the Father before all ages, and born in His humanity of the Virgin Mary in time; and, lastly, of the assertion that the humanity of Christ existed not as being assumed into the external person of the Son of God, but existed rather of itself as a person, and therefore that the mystery of Jesus Christ consists only in the fact that God, in revealing Himself, was present in the highest degree in the human person Jesus.

Those who think in this way are far removed from true belief in Christ, even when they maintain that the special presence of God in Jesus results in His being the supreme and final expression of Divine Revelation; nor do they come back to true belief in Christ's divinity by adding that Jesus can be called God because God is supremely present in what they call His human person.

Once the mystery of the divine and eternal person of Christ the Son of God is abandoned, the truth respecting the Most Holy Trinity is also undermined, and with it the truth regarding the Holy Spirit who proceeds eternally from the Father and the Son, or from the Father through the Son.[10] Therefore, in view of recent errors, some points concerning the belief in the Most Holy Trinity, and especially in the Holy Spirit, should be recalled to mind.

The Second Epistle to the Corinthians concludes with this admirable expression: "The grace of our Lord Jesus Christ, and the charity of God, and the fellowship of the Holy Spirit be with you all."[11] The commission to baptize, recorded in St. Matthew's Gospel, names the Father, the Son and the Holy Spirit as the three pertaining to the mystery of God, and it is in their name that the new faithful must be reborn.[12] Lastly, in St. John's Gospel, Jesus speaks of the coming of the Holy Spirit: "When the Advocate has come, whom I will send you from the Father, the Spirit of truth who proceeds from the Father, he will bear witness concerning me."[13]

Following Divine Revelation, the magisterium of the Church, to which alone is entrusted "the task of authentically interpreting the word of God, whether written or handed down,"[14] acknowledges in the Creed of Constantinople "the Holy Spirit, the Lord and giver of life, . . . who together with the Father and the Son is adored and glorified."[15] In like manner, the Fourth Lateran Council taught that it is to be believed and professed "that there is but one true God, . . . Father and Son and Holy Spirit: three persons indeed, but one essence . . . : the Father proceeding from none, the Son from the Father alone, and the Holy Spirit equally from both, without beginning, always and without end."[16]

The opinion that Revelation has left us uncertain about the eternity of the Trinity, and in particular about the eternal existence of the Holy Spirit as a person in God distinct from the Father and the Son, deviates from the faith. It is true that the mystery of the Most Holy Trinity was revealed to us in the economy of salvation, and most of all in Christ Himself, who was sent into the world by the Father and together with the Father sends the life-giving Spirit to the People of God. But by this Revelation there is also given to believers some knowledge of God's intimate life, in which "the Father who generated, the Son who is generated, and the Holy Spirit who proceeds" are "consubstantial and co-equal, alike omnipotent and co-eternal."[17]

What is expressed in the above-mentioned conciliar documents concerning the one and same Christ the Son of God, begotten before the ages in His divine nature, and also concerning the eternal persons of the Most Holy Trinity, belongs to the immutable truth of the Catholic faith.

This certainly does not prevent the Church, in her awareness of the progress of human thought, from considering it her duty to have these mysteries continually examined by contemplation of the faith and theological examination, and to have them fully expounded in up-to-date terminology. But while the necessary duty of investigation is being pursued, diligent care must be taken that these profound mysteries are not interpreted in a sense other than that in which "the Church has understood and understands them."[18]

The unimpaired truth of these mysteries is of the greatest moment for the whole Revelation of Christ because they pertain to its very core in such a way that, if they are undermined, the rest of the treasure of Revelation is adulterated. The truth of these same mysteries is of no less concern to the Christian way of life because nothing so effectively manifests the charity of God, to which the whole of Christian life should be a response, as does the Incarnation of the Son of God, our Redeemer,[19] and also because "through Christ, the Word made flesh, man might have access in the Holy Spirit to the Father and come to share in the divine nature."[20]

With regard to the truths which the present declaration is safeguarding, it is up to the pastors of the Church to see that there is unity on the part of their people in professing the faith, especially on the part of those who, by the magisterium's mandate, teach the sacred sciences or preach the Word of God. This function of the bishops belongs to the office divinely committed to them "of keeping pure and entire" "the deposit of faith" in communion with Peter's successor, and "of proclaiming the Gospel unceasingly."[21] By reason of this same office they are bound not to permit ministers of the Word of God, deviating from the way of sound doctrine, to transmit it corrupt or incomplete.[22] The people entrusted to the care of the bishops, who "are responsible for them before God,"[23] enjoy the "inalienable and sacred right to receive the word of God, the whole word of God, which the Church has unfailingly studied more and more deeply."[24]

Christians, then—and theologians above all, because of their important office and necessary function in the Church—must make faithful profession of the mysteries which this declaration reaffirms. In like manner, by the movement and illumination of the Holy Spirit, the Church's sons must hold fast to the whole doctrine of the faith under the leadership of their pastors and of the pastor of the universal Church.[25]

"Thus there is a single common effort by the bishops and the faithful to hold onto the heritage of faith and to practice and profess it."[26]

---

* Translation by Vatican Press Office. Latin text in *AAS* 64 (1972), 237–241.

1. See Phil. 2:6–8.
2. 1 Cor. 8:6.
3. Jn. 1:1, 14 (*see* 1:18).
4. See Vatican Council I, Dogmatic constitution *Dei Filius*, chap. 4; *Conc. Oec. Decr.*, Herder (1962), p. 785; Dz-Sch. 3020.
5. *Missale Romanum*, Vatican Polyglot Press (1970), p. 389.
6. See Council of Chalcedon, *Definitio; Conc. Oec. Decr.*, p. 62; Dz-Sch. 301.
7. See *ibid*. Dz-Sch. 302.
8. See 4th Lateran Council, Constitution *Firmiter credimus; Conc. Oec. Decr.*, p. 206; Dz-Sch. 800 f.

9. See Vatican Council II, *Dogmatic Constitution on the Church*, nn. 3, 7, 52, 53.

10. See Council of Florence, Bull *Laetentur caeli; Conc. Oec. Decr.*, p. 501 f.; Dz-Sch. 1300.

11. 2 Cor. 13:13.

12. See Mt. 28:19.

13. Jn. 15:26.

14. Vatican Council II, *Dogmatic Constitution on Divine Revelation*, n. 10.

15. *Missale Romanum*, loc. cit.; Dz-Sch. 150.

16. See 4th Lateran Council, Constitution *Firmiter credimus; Conc. Oec. Decr.*, p. 206; Dz-Sch. 800.

17. *Ibid.*

18. Vatican Council I, Dogmatic Constitution *Dei Filius*, chap. 4, can. 3; *Conc. Oec. Decr.*, p. 787; Dz-Sch. 3043.

19. See 1 Jn. 4:9 f.

20. See Vatican Council II, *Dogmatic Constitution on Divine Revelation*, n. 2.

21. See Paul VI, apost. exhortation *Quinque iam anni: AAS* 68 (1971), 99.

22. See 2 Tim. 4:1–5. See Paul VI, apost. exhortation *Quinque iam anni: AAS* 68 (1971), 103 f.

23. Paul VI, apost. exhortation *Quinque iam anni: AAS* 68 (1971), 103.

24. *Ibid.: AAS* 68 (1971), 100.

25. See Vatican Council II, *Dogmatic Constitution on the Church*, nn. 12, 15.

26. Vatican Council II, *Dogmatic Constitution on Divine Revelation*, n. 10.

105

DECLARATION IN DEFENCE OF THE CATHOLIC DOCTRINE ON THE CHURCH AGAINST SOME PRESENT-DAY ERRORS*

S.C.D.F., *Mysterium ecclesiae*, 24 June, 1973

The mystery of the Church, upon which the Second Vatican Council shed fresh light, has been repeatedly dealt with in numerous writings of theologians. While not a few of these studies have served to make this mystery more understandable, others, through the use of ambiguous or even erroneous language, have obscured Catholic doctrine, and at times have gone so far as to be opposed to Catholic faith even in fundamental matters.

To meet this situation, the bishops of several nations, conscious both of their duty of 'keeping pure and intact the deposit of faith' and of their task of 'proclaiming the gospel unceasingly',[1] have, through concurring declarations, sought to protect the faithful entrusted to their care from the danger of error. In addition, the second General Assembly of the Synod of Bishops, in dealing with the ministerial priesthood, expounded a number of important points of doctrine regarding the constitution of the Church.

Likewise, the Sacred Congregation for the Doctrine of the Faith, whose task it is to 'preserve the doctrine of faith and morals in the whole Catholic world',[2] intends to gather together and explain a number of truths concerning the mystery of the Church which at the present time are being either denied or endangered. In this it will follow above all the lines laid down by the two Vatican Councils.

The Oneness of Christ's Church

One is the Church, which 'after his Resurrection our Saviour handed over to Peter as Shepherd' (cf. John 21:17), commissioning him and the other Apostles to propagate and govern her (cf. Matt. 18:18 ff.) and which he erected for all ages as 'the pillar and mainstay of the truth' (cf. 1 Tim. 3:15). And this Church of Christ, 'constituted and organised in this world as a society, subsists in the Catholic Church, which is governed by the Successor of Peter and the bishops in union with that Successor'.[3]

This declaration of the Second Vatican Council is illustrated by the same Council's statement that 'it is through Christ's Catholic Church alone, which is the general means of salvation, that the fullness of the means of salvation can be obtained',[4] and that same Catholic Church 'has been endowed with all divinely revealed truth and with all the means of grace'[5] with which Christ wished to enhance his messianic community. This is no obstacle to the fact that during her earthly pilgrimage the Church, 'embracing sinners in her bosom, is at the same time holy and always in need of being purified',[6] nor to the fact that 'outside her visible structure', namely in Churches and ecclesial communities which are joined to the Catholic Church by an imperfect communion, there are to be found 'many elements of sanctification and truth (which), as gifts properly belonging to the Church of Christ, possess an inner dynamism towards Catholic unity'.[7]

For these reasons, 'Catholics must joyfully acknowledge and esteem the truly Christian endowments derived from our common heritage, which are to be found among our separated brethren',[8] and they must strive for the re-establishment of unity among all Christians, by making a 'common effort of purification and renewal'[9] so that the will of Christ may be fulfilled and the division of Christians may cease to be an obstacle to the proclamation of the Gospel throughout the world.[10] But at the same time Catholics are bound to profess that through the gift of God's mercy they belong to that Church which Christ founded and which is governed by the successors of Peter and the other Apostles, who are the depositories of the original Apostolic tradition, living and intact, which is the permanent heritage of doctrine and holiness of that same Church.[11] The followers of Christ are therefore not permitted to imagine that Christ's Church is nothing more than a collection (divided, but still possessing a certain unity) of Churches and ecclesial communities. Nor are they free to hold that Christ's Church nowhere really exists today and that it is to be considered only as an end which all Churches and ecclesial communities must strive to reach.

'In his gracious goodness, God has seen to it that what he had revealed for the salvation of all nations would abide perpetually in its full integrity'.[12] For this reason he entrusted to the Church the treasury of God's Word, so that the pastors and the holy people might strive together to preserve it, study it and apply it to life'.[13]

God, who is absolutely infallible, thus deigned to bestow upon his new people, which is the Church, a certain shared infallibility, which is restricted to matters of faith and morals, which is present when the whole People of God unhesitatingly holds a point of doctrine pertaining to these matters, and finally which always depends upon the wise providence and anointing of the grace of the Holy Spirit, who leads the Church into all truth until the glorious coming of her Lord.[14] Concerning this infallibility of the People of God the Second Vatican Council speaks as follows: 'The body of the faithful as a whole, anointed as they are by the Holy One (cf. 1 Jn 2:20, 27), cannot err in matters of belief. Thanks to a supernatural instinct of faith which characterizes the people as a whole, it manifests this unerring quality when, "from the bishops down to the last member of the laity" (St. Augustine, De. Praed. Sanct., 14, 27), it shows universal agreement in matters of faith and morals'.[15]

The Holy Spirit enlightens and assists the People of God inasmuch as it is the Body of Christ united in a hierarchical communion. The Second Vatican Council indicates this fact by adding to the words quoted above: 'For, by this instinct of faith which is aroused and sustained by the Spirit of truth, God's People accepts not the word of men but the very Word of God (cf. 1 Thess 2:13). It clings without fail to the faith once delivered to the saints (cf. Jude 3), penetrates it more deeply by accurate insights, and applies it more thoroughly to life. All this it does under the lead of a sacred teaching authority to which it loyally defers.'[16]

Without doubt the faithful, who in their own manner share in Christ's prophetic office,[17] in many ways contribute towards increasing the understanding of faith in the Church. 'For', as the Second Vatican Council says, 'there is a growth in the understanding of the realities and the words which have been handed down. This happens through the contemplation and study made by believers, who treasure these things in their hearts (cf. Lk 2:19, 51), through the intimate understanding of spiritual things they experience, and through the preaching of those who have received through episcopal succession the sure charism of truth'.[18] And the Supreme Pontiff Paul VI observes that the witness the pastors of the Church offer is 'rooted in Sacred Tradition and Holy Scripture and nourished by the ecclesial life of the whole People of God'.[19] But by divine institution it is the exclusive task of these pastors alone, the successors of Peter and the other Apostles, to teach the faithful authentically, that is with the authority of Christ shared in different ways; so that the faithful, who may not simply listen to them as experts in Catholic doctrine, must accept their teaching given in Christ's name, with an assent that is proportionate to the authority that they possess and that they mean to exercise.[20] For this reason the Second Vatican Council, in harmony with the First Vatican Council, teaches that Christ made Peter 'a perpetual and visible principle and foundation of the unity of faith and of communion';[21] and the Supreme Pontiff Paul VI has declared: 'The teaching office of the bishop is for the believer the sign and channel which enable him to receive and recognise the Word of God'.[22] Thus however much the Sacred Magisterium avails itself of the contemplation, life and study of the faithful, its office is not reduced merely to ratifying the assent already expressed by the latter; indeed, in the interpretation and explanation of the written or transmitted Word of God, the Magisterium can anticipate or demand their assent.[23] The People of God has particular need of the intervention and assistance of the Magisterium when internal disagreements arise and spread concerning a doctrine that must be believed or held, lest it lose the communion of the one faith in the one Body of the Lord (cf. Eph 4:45).

The Infallibility of the Church's Magisterium

Jesus Christ from whom derives the task prope. to the pastors of teaching the Gospel to all his people and to the entire human family, wished to endow the pastors' Magisterium with a fitting charism of infallibility in matters regarding faith and morals. Since this charism does not come from new revelations enjoyed by the Successor of Peter and the College of Bishops,[24] it does not dispense them from studying with appropriate means the treasure of divine Revelation contained both in Sacred Scripture which teaches us intact the truth that God willed to be written down for our salvation[25] and in living Tradition that comes from the Apostles.[26] In carrying out their task, the pastors of the Church enjoy the assistance of the Holy Spirit, this assistance reaches its highest point when they teach the People of God in such a manner that, through the promises of Christ made to Peter and the other Apostles, the doctrine they propose is necessarily immune from error.[27]

This occurs when the bishops scattered throughout the world but teaching in communion with the Successor of Peter present a doctrine to be held irrevocably. It occurs even more clearly both when the bishops by a collegial act (as in Ecumenical Councils), together with their visible Head, define a doctrine to be held,[28] and when the Roman Pontiff 'speaks ex cathedra, that is when, exercising the office of Pastor and Teacher of all Christians, through his supreme apostolic authority he defines a doctrine concerning faith or morals to be held by the universal Church'.[29]

According to Catholic doctrine, the infallibility of the Church's Magisterium extends not only to the deposit of faith but also to those matters without which that deposit cannot be rightly preserved and expounded.[30] The extension however of this infallibility to the deposit of faith itself is a truth that the Church has from the beginning held as having been certainly revealed in Christ's promises. The First Vatican Council, basing itself upon this truth, defined as follows the matter of Catholic faith: 'All those things are to be believed by divine and Catholic faith which are contained in the written or transmitted Word of God and which are proposed by the Church, either by a solemn judgment or by the ordinary and universal magisterium, to be believed as having been divinely revealed'.[31] Therefore the objects of Catholic faith—which are called dogmas—necessarily are and always have been the unalterable norm both for faith and for theological science.

The Church's Gift of Infallibility Not to be Diminished

From what has been said about the extent of and conditions governing the infallibility of the People of God and of the Church's Magisterium, it follows that the faithful are in no way permitted to see in the Church merely a fundamental permanence in truth which, as some assert, could be reconciled with errors contained here and there in the propositions that the Church's Magisterium teaches to be held irrevocably, as also in the unhesitating assent of the People of God concerning matters of faith and morals.

It is of course true that through the faith that leads to salvation men are converted to God,[32] who reveals himself in his Son Jesus Christ; but it would be wrong to deduce from this that the Church's dogmas can be belittled or even denied. Indeed the conversion to God which we should realise through faith is a form of obedience (cf. Rom. 16:26), which should correspond to the nature of divine Revelation and its demands. Now this Revelation, in the whole plan of salvation, reveals the mystery of God who sent his Son into the world (cf. 1 Jn 4:14) and teaches its application to Christian conduct. Moreover it demands that, in full obedience of the intellect and will to God who reveals,[33] we accept the proclamation of the good news of salvation as it is infallibly taught by the pastors of the Church. The faithful, therefore, through faith are converted as they should to God, who reveals himself in Christ, when they adhere to him in the integral doctrine of the Catholic faith.

It is true that there exists an order and as it were a hierarchy of the Church's dogmas, as a result of their varying relationship to the foundation of the faith.[34] This hierarchy means that some dogmas are founded on other dogmas which are the principal ones, and are illuminated by these latter. But all dogmas, since they are revealed, must be believed with the same divine faith.[35]

The Notion of the Church's Infallibility Not to be Falsified

The transmission of divine Revelation by the Church encounters difficulties of various kinds. These arise from the fact that the hidden mysteries of God 'by their nature so far transcend the human intellect that even if they are revealed to us and accepted by faith, they remain concealed by the veil of faith itself and are as it were wrapped in darkness'.[36] Difficulties arise also from the historical condition that affects the expression of Revelation.

With regard to this historical condition, it must first be observed that the meaning of the pronouncements of faith depend partly upon the expressive power of the language used at a certain point in time and in particular circumstances. Moreover, it sometimes happens that some dogmatic truth is first expressed incompletely (but not falsely), and at a later date, when considered in a broader context of faith or human knowledge, it receives a fuller and more perfect expression. In addition, when the Church makes new pronouncements she intends to confirm or clarify what is in some way contained in Sacred Scripture or in previous expressions of Tradition; but at the same time she usually has the intention of solving certain questions or removing certain errors. All these things have to be taken into account in order that these pronouncements may be properly interpreted. Finally, even though the truths which the Church intends to teach through her dogmatic formulas are distinct from the changeable conceptions of a given epoch and can be expressed without them, nevertheless it can sometimes happen that these truths may be enunciated by the Sacred Magisterium in terms that bear traces of such conceptions.

In view of the above, it must be stated that the dogmatic formulas of the Church's Magisterium were from the very beginning suitable for communicating revealed truth, and that as they are they remain for ever suitable for communicating this truth to those who interpret them correctly.[37] It does not however follow that every one of the formulas has always been or will always be so to the same extent. For this reason theologians seek to define exactly the intention of teaching proper to the various formulas, and in carrying out this work they are of considerable assistance to the living Magisterium of the Church, to which they remain subordinated. For this reason also it often happens that ancient dogmatic formulas and others closely connected with them remain living and fruitful in the habitual usage of the Church, but with suitable expository and explanatory additions that maintain and clarify their original meaning. In addition, it has sometimes happened that in this habitual usage of the Church certain of these formulas gave way to new expressions which, proposed and approved by the Sacred Magisterium, presented more clearly or more completely the same meaning.

As for the *meaning* of dogmatic formulas, this remains ever true and constant in the Church, even when it is expressed with greater clarity or more developed. The faithful therefore must shun the opinion, first, that dogmatic formulas (or some category of them) cannot signify truth in a determinate way, but can only offer changeable approximations to it, which to a certain extent distort or alter it; secondly, that these formulas signify the truth only in an indeterminate way, this truth being like a goal that is constantly being sought by means of such approximations. Those who hold such an opinion do not avoid dogmatic relativism and they corrupt the concept of the Church's infallibility relative to the truth to be taught or held in a determinate way.

Such an opinion clearly is in disagreement with the declarations of the First Vatican Council, which while fully aware of the progress of the Church in her knowledge of revealed truth,[38] nevertheless taught as follows: 'That meaning of sacred dogmas ...must always be maintained which Holy Mother Church declared once and for all, nor should one ever depart from that meaning under the guise of or in the name of a more advanced understanding'.[39] The Council moreover condemned the opinion that 'dogmas once proposed by the Church must with the progress of science be given a meaning other than that which was understood by the Church, or which she understands'.[40] There is no doubt that, according to these texts of the Council, the meaning of dogmas which is declared by the Church is determinate and unalterable.

Such an opinion is likewise in contrast with Pope John's assertion regarding Christian doctrine at the opening of the Second Vatican Council: 'This certain and unchangeable doctrine, to which faithful obedience is due, has to be explored and presented in a way that is demanded by our times. One thing is the deposit of faith, which consists of the truths contained in sacred doctrine, another thing is the manner of presentation, always however with the same meaning and signification'.[41] Since the Successor of Peter is here speaking about certain and unchangeable Christian doctrine, about the deposit of faith which is the same as the truths contained in that doctrine and about the truths which have to be preserved with the same meaning, it is clear that he admits that we can know the true and unchanging meaning of dogmas. What is new and what he recommends in view of the needs of the times pertains only to the modes of studying, expounding and presenting that doctrine while keeping its permanent meaning. In a similar way the Supreme Pontiff Paul VI exhorted the Pastors of the Church in the following words: 'Nowadays a serious effort is required of us to ensure that the teaching of the faith should keep the fullness of its meaning and force, while expressing itself in a form which allows it to reach the spirit and heart of the people to whom it is addressed'.[42]

The Church Associated With the Priesthood of Christ

Christ the Lord, the High Priest of the new and everlasting covenant, wished to associate with his perfect priesthood and to form in its likeness the people he had bought with his own blood (cf. Heb 7:20–22, 26–28; 10:14, 21). He therefore granted his Church a share in his priesthood, which consists of the common priesthood of the faithful and the ministerial or hierarchical priesthood. These differ from each other not only in degree but also in essence; yet they are mutually complementary within the communion of the Church.[43]

The common priesthood of the laity, which is also rightly called a royal priesthood (cf. 1 Peter 2:9; Rev 1:6; 5:9 ff.) since through it the faithful are united as members of the messianic people with their heavenly King, is conferred by the sacrament of Baptism. By this sacrament 'the faithful are incorporated into the Church and are empowered to take part in the worship of the Christian religion' in virtue of a permanent sign known as a character: 'reborn as children of God they are obliged to profess before men the faith which they have received from God through the Church'.[44] Thus those who are reborn in Baptism 'join in the offering of the Eucharist by virtue of their royal priesthood. They likewise exercise that priesthood by receiving the sacraments, by prayer and thanksgiving, by the witness of a holy life, and by self-denial and active charity.'[45]

Moreover, Christ, the Head of the Church, which is his Mystical Body, appointed as ministers of his priesthood his apostles and through them their successors the bishops, that they might act in his person within the Church[46] and also in turn legitimately hand over to priests in a subordinate degree the sacred ministry which they had received.[47] Thus there arose in the Church the apostolic succession of the ministerial priesthood for the glory of God and for the service of his people and of the entire human family, which must be converted to God.

By means of this priesthood bishops and priests are 'indeed set apart in a certain sense in the midst of God's people. But this is so, not that they may be separated from this people or from any man, but that they may be totally dedicated to the work for which the Lord has raised them up:'[48] namely, the work of sanctifying, teaching and ruling, the actual execution of which is more precisely specified by the hierarchical communion.[49] This manysided work has as its basis and foundation the continuous preaching of the Gospel,[50] and as the summit and source of the entire Christian life the Eucharistic Sacrifice.[51] Priests, acting in the person of Christ the Head, offer this Sacrifice in the Holy Spirit to God the Father in the name of Christ and in the name of the members of his Mystical Body.[52] This sacrifice is completed in the holy supper by which the faithful, partaking of the one body of Christ, are all made into one body (cf. 1 Cor 10:16 ff.).

The Church has ever more closely examined the nature of the ministerial priesthood, which can be shown to have been invariably conferred from apostolic times by a sacred rite (cf. 1 Tim 4:15; 2 Tim 1:6). By the assistance of the Holy Spirit, she recognized more clearly as time went on that God wished her to understand that this rite conferred upon priests not only an increase of grace for carrying out ecclesiastical duties in a holy way, but also a permanent designation by Christ, or character, by virtue of which they are equipped for their work and endowed with the necessary power that is derived from the supreme power of Christ. The permanent existence of this character, the nature of which is explained in different ways by theologians, is taught by the Council of Florence[53] and reaffirmed by two decrees of the Council of Trent.[54] In recent times the Second Vatican Council more than once mentioned it,[55] and the second General Assembly of the Synod of Bishops rightly considered the enduring nature of the priestly character throughout life as pertaining to the teaching of faith.[56] This stable existence of a priestly character must be recognised by the faithful and has to be taken into account in order to judge properly about the nature of the priestly ministry and the appropriate ways of exercising it.

Faithful to Sacred Tradition and to many documents of the Magisterium, the Second Vatican Council taught the following concerning the power belonging to the ministerial priesthood: 'Though everyone can baptise the faithful, the priest alone can complete the building up of the Body in the Eucharistic Sacrifice'.[57] And again: 'The same Lord, in order that the faithful might form one body in which "all the members have not the same function" (Rom 12:4), appointed some ministers within the society of believers who by the power of Orders would be capable of offering the Sacrifice and of forgiving sins.'[58]

In the same way the second General Assembly of the Synod of Bishops rightly affirmed that only the priest can act in the person of Christ and preside over and perform the sacrificial banquet in which the People of God are united with the oblation of Christ.[59] Passing over at this point questions regarding the ministers of the various sacraments, the evidence of Sacred Tradition and of the Sacred Magisterium make it clear that the faithful who have not received priestly ordination and who take upon themselves the office of performing the Eucharist attempt to do so not only in a completely illicit way but also invalidly. Such an abuse, wherever it may occur, must clearly be eliminated by the pastors of the Church.

* * *

It was not the intention of this Declaration, nor was it within its scope, to prove by way of a study of the foundations of our faith that divine revelation was entrusted to the Church so that she might thereafter preserve it unaltered in the world. But this dogma, from which the Catholic faith takes its beginning, has been recalled, together with other truths related to the mystery of the Church so that in the uncertainty of the present day the faith and doctrine the faithful must hold might clearly emerge.

The Sacred Congregation for the Doctrine of the Faith rejoices that theologians are by intense study exploring more and more the mystery of the Church. It recognises also that in their work they touch on many questions which can only be clarified by complementary studies and by various efforts and conjectures. However, the due freedom of theologians must always be limited by the Word of God as it is faithfully preserved and expounded in the Church and taught and explained by the living Magisterium of the Pastors and especially of the Pastor of the entire People of God.

The Sacred Congregation entrusts this Declaration to the diligent attention of the bishops and of all those who in any way share the task of guarding the patrimony of truth which Christ and his Apostles committed to the Church. It also confidently addresses the Declaration to the faithful and particularly, in view of the important office which they hold in the Church, to priests and theologians, so that all may be of one mind in the faith and may be in sincere harmony with the Church.

* Translation by Vatican Press Office. Latin original in AAS 65 (1973), 396–408.

1. Paul VI, Apostolic Exhortation, *Quinque iam Anni, AAS* 63 (1971), p. 99.

2. Paul VI, Apostolic Constitution, *Regiminis Ecclesiae Universae, AAS* 59 (1967), p. 897.

3. Second Vatican Council: Dogmatic Constitution on the Church *Lumen Gentium*, 8; *Constitutiones, Decreta, Declarationes*, editio Secretariae Generalis. Typis Polyglottis Vaticanis, 1966, p. 104 ff.

4. Second Vatican Council: Decree on Ecumenism *Unitatis Redintegratio*, 3; *Const. Decr. Decl.*, p. 250.

5. *Ibid.*, 4; *Const. Decr. Decl.*, p. 252.

6. Second Vatican Council: Dogmatic Constitution on the Church *Lumen Gentium*, 8; *Const. Decr. Decl.*, p. 106.

7. *Ibid.*, *Const. Decr. Decl.*, p. 105.

8. Second Vatican Council: Decree on Ecumenism *Unitatis Redintegratio* 4; *Const. Decr. Decl.*, p. 253.

9. Cf. *ibid.*, 6–8; *Const. Decr. Decl.*, pp. 255–258.

10. Cf. *ibid.*, 1; *Const. Decr. Decl.*, p. 243.

11. Cf. Paul VI, Encyclical Letter *Ecclesiam Suam, AAS* 56 (1964), p. 629.

12. Second Vatican Council: Dogmatic Constitution on Divine Revelation *Dei Verbum* 7; *Const. Decr. Decl.*, p. 428.

13. Cf. *ibid.*, 10; *Const. Decr. Decl.*, p. 431.

14. Cf. *ibid.*, 8; *Const. Decr. Decl.*, p. 430.

15. Second Vatican Council: Dogmatic Constitution on the Church *Lumen Gentium*, 12; *Const. Decr. Decl.*, pp. 113 ff.

16. *Ibid.*, *Const. Decr. Decl.*, p. 114.

17. Cf. *ibid.*, 35; *Const. Decr. Decl.*, p. 157.

18. Second Vatican Council: Dogmatic Constitution on Divine Revelation *Dei Verbum* 8; *Const. Decr. Decl.*, p. 430.

19. Paul VI, Apostolic Exhortation *Quinque iam Anni, AAS* 63 (1971), p. 99.

20. Cf. Second Vatican Council: Dogmatic Constitution on the Church *Lumen Gentium* 25; *Const. Decr. Decl.*, p. 138 ff.

21. Second Vatican Council: *ibid.*, 18; *Const. Decr. Decl.*, p. 124 ff. Cf. First Vatican Council: Dogmatic Constitution *Pastor Aeternus,* Prologue; *Conciliorum ecumenicorum Decreta*, ed. Istituto per le Scienze Religiose di Bolgona, Herder 1973, p. 812 (DS 3051).

22. Paul VI, Apostolic Exhortation *Quinque iam Anni, AAS* 63 (1971), p. 100.

23. Decree of the Holy Office *Lamentabili*, 6, *AAS* 40 (1907), p. 471 (DS 3406). Cf. First Vatican Council: Dogmatic Constitution *Pastor Aeternus*, ch. 4; Conc. *Oec. Decr.*, 3, p. 815 ff. (DS 3069, 3074).

24. First Vatican Council: Dogmatic Constitution *Pastor Aeternus*, ch. 4; *Conc. Oec. Decr.* 3, p. 816 (DS 3070).

25. Cf. Second Vatican Council: Dogmatic Constitution on Divine Revelation *Dei Verbum*, 11; *Const. Decr. Decl.*, p. 434.

26. Cf. *ibid.*, 9 ff.: *Const. Decr. Decl.*, pp. 430–432.

27. Cf. Second Vatican Council: Dogmatic Constitution on the Church *Lumen Gentium* 25; *Const. Decr. Decl.*, p. 139.

28. Cf. *ibid.*, 25 and 22; *Const. Decr. Decl.*, pp. 139 and 133.

29. First Vatican Council: Dogmatic Constitution *Pastor Aeternus*, ch. 4; *Conc. Oec. Decr.*, 3, p. 816 (DS 3074). Cf. Second Vatican Council: *ibid.*, 25, *Const. Oec. Decr.*, 3, pp. 139–141.

30. Cf. Second Vatican Council: Dogmatic Constitution on the Church *Lumen Gentium*, 25; *Const. Decr. Decl.*, p. 139.

31. First Vatican Council: Dogmatic Constitution *Dei Filius*, ch. 3; *Conc. Oec. Decr.*, 3, p. 807 (DS 3011). Cf. C.I.C. can. 1323, S 1 and can. 1325, S 2.

32. Cf. Council of Trent, Sess. 6; Decree on Justification, ch. 6; *Conc. Oec. Decr.*, 3, p. 672 (DS 1526).

33. Cf. First Vatican Council: Constitution on the Catholic Faith *Dei Filius*, ch. 3; *Conc. Oec. Decr.*, 3, p. 807 (DS 3008); cf. also Second Vatican Council: Dogmatic Constitution on Divine Revelation *Dei Verbum*, 5, *Const. Decr. Decl.*, p. 426.

34. Cf. Second Vatican Council: Decree on Ecumenism *Unitatis Redintegratio*, 11; *Const. Decr. Decl.*, p. 260.

35. 'Reflections and Suggestions Concerning Ecumenical Dialogue,' IV, 4b, in *The Secretariat for Promoting Christian Unity: Information Service*, n. 12 (December 1970, IV), p. 8.

36. First Vatican Council: Dogmatic Constitution *Dei Filius*, ch. 4; *Conc. Oec. Decr.*, 3, p. 808 (DS 3016).

37. Cf. Pius IX, Brief *Eximiam Tuam, AAS* 8 (1874–75), p. 447 (DS 2831); Paul VI, Encyclical Letter *Mysterium Fidei, AAS* 57 (1965), pp. 757 ff. and L'Oriente cristiano nella luce i immortali Concili' in *Insegnamenti di Paolo VI*, vol. 5, Vatican Polyglot Press, pp. 412 ff.

38. Cf. First Vatican Council: Dogmatic Constitution *Dei Filius*, ch. 4; *Conc. Oec. Decr.*, 3, 809 (DS 3020).

39. *Ibid.*

40. *Ibid.*, can 3; *Conc. Oec. Decr.*, 3, p. 811 (DS 3043).

41. John XXIII, 'Alloc. in Concilii Vaticani inauguratione', *AAS* 54 (1962), p. 792. Cf. Second Vatican Council: Pastoral Constitution on the Church in the Modern World *Gaudium et Spes*, 62; *Const. Decr. Decl.*, p. 780.

42. Paul VI, Apostolic Exhortation *Quinque iam Anni, AAS* 63 (1971), pp. 100 ff.

43. Cf. Second Vatican Council: Dogmatic Constitution on the Church *Lumen Gentium*, 10; *Const. Decr. Decl.*, p. 110.

44. *Ibid.*, 11; *Const. Decr. Decl.*, p. 111.

45. *Ibid.*, 10; *Const. Decr. Decl.*, p. 111.

46. Cf. Pius XI, Encyclical Letter *Ad Catholici Sacerdotii, AAS* 28 (1936), p. 10 (DS 3735).

47. Cf. Second Vatican Council: Dogmatic Constitution on the Church *Lumen Gentium*, 28; *Const. Decr. Decl.*, p. 625.

48. Second Vatican Council: Decree on the Priestly Life and Ministry *Presbyterorum Ordinis*, 3; *Const. Decr. Decl.*, p. 625.

49. Cf. Second Vatican Council: Dogmatic Constitution *Lumen Gentium*, 24, 27 ff.; *Const. Decr. Decl.*, pp. 137, 143–149.

50. Second Vatican Council: Decree on the Priestly Life and Ministry *Presbyterorum Ordinis*, 4; *Const. Decr. Decl.*, p. 627.

51. Cf. Dogmatic Constitution on the Church *Lumen Gentium*, 11; *Const. Decr. Decl.*, pp. 111 ff., also Council of Trent, Sess. 22; Doctrina

de Missae Sacrificio, ch. 1 and 2; *Conc. Oec. Decr.*, pp. 732–734 (DS 1739–1743).

52. Cf. Paul VI, 'Sollemnis Professio Fidei,' 24, *AAS* 60 (1968), p. 442.

53. Council of Florence 'Bulla unionis Armenorum, Exsultate Deo', *Conc. Oec. Decr.*, p. 546 (DS 1313).

54. Council of Trent: Decree on the Sacraments, can. 9 and Decree on the Sacrament of Order, ch. 4 and can. 4; *Conc. Oec. Decr.*, pp. 685, 742, 744 (DS 1609, 1767, 1774). ·

55. Cf. Second Vatican Council: Dogmatic Constitution on the Church *Lumen Gentium*, 21, and Decree on the Priestly Life and Ministry *Presbyterorum Ordinis*, 2; *Const. Decr. Decl.*, pp. 133, 622 ff.

56. Cf. Documents of the Synod of Bishops: 1 The Ministerial Priesthood, part one 5, *AAS* 63 (1971), p. 907.

57. Second Vatican Concil: Dogmatic Constitution on the Church *Lumen Gentium*, 17; *Const. Decr. Decl.*, p. 123.

58. Second Vatican Council: Decree on the Priestly Life and Ministry *Presbyterorum Ordinis*, 2; *Const. Decr. Decl.*, pp. 621 ff.

59. Documents of the Synod of Bishops: 1 The Ministerial Priesthood, part one 4. *AAS* 63 (1971), p. 906.

106

DECLARATION ON PROCURED ABORTION*

S.C.D.F., *Quaestio de abortu*, 18 November, 1974

INTRODUCTION

1. The problem of procured abortion and of its possible legal liberalization has become almost everywhere the subject of impassioned discussions. These debates would be less important were it not a question of human life, a primordial value, which must be protected and promoted. Everyone understands this, although many argue, even against all the evidence, for increased recourse to abortion. One cannot but be astonished to see an increase of unqualified protests against the death penalty and every form of war and simultaneously the vindication of the liberalization of abortion, either on demand or with—progressively diminishing—restrictions. The Church is too conscious of the fact that it belongs to her vocation to defend man against everything that could destroy or diminish his dignity to remain silent on such a topic. Because the Son of God became man, there is no man who is not his brother in humanity and who is not called to become a Christian in order to receive salvation from him.

2. In many countries the public authorities which resist the liberalization of abortion laws are the object of powerful pressures aimed at leading them to this goal. This, it is said, would violate no one's conscience, for each individual would be left free to follow his own opinion, while being prevented from imposing it on others. Ethical pluralism is claimed to be a normal consequence of ideological pluralism. There is, however, a great difference between the one and the other, for action affects the interests of others more quickly than does mere opinion. Moreover, one can never claim freedom of opinion as a pretext for attacking the rights of others, most especially the right to life.

3. Numerous Christian lay people, especially doctors, but also parents' associations, statesmen, or leading figures in posts of responsibility have vigorously reacted against this propaganda campaign. Above all, many episcopal conferences and many bishops acting in their own name have judged it opportune to

441

recall very strongly the traditional doctrine of the Church.[1] With a striking convergence these documents admirably emphasize an attitude of respect for life which is at the same time human and Christian. Nevertheless, it has happened that several of these documents have not been fully accepted or have been rejected.

4. Charged with the promotion and the defence of faith and morals in the universal Church,[2] the Sacred Congregation for the Doctrine of the Faith proposes to recall this teaching in its essential aspects to all the faithful. Thus, in showing the unity of the Church, it will confirm by the authority proper to the Holy See what the bishops have opportunely undertaken. It hopes that all the faithful, including those who might have been unsettled by the controversies and new opinions, will understand that it is not a question of opposing one opinion to another, but of transmitting to the faithful a constant teaching of the supreme magisterium, which teaches moral principles in the light of faith.[3] It is therefore clear that this declaration necessarily entails a grave obligation for Christian consciences.[4] May God deign to enlighten also all men who strive with their whole heart to 'act in truth' (John 3:21).

IN THE LIGHT OF FAITH

5. 'Death was not God's doing, he takes no pleasure in the extinction of the living' (Wis. 1:13). Certainly God has created beings who have only one lifetime and physical death cannot be absent from the world of those with a bodily existence. But what is immediately willed is life, and in the visible universe everything has been made for man, who is the image of God and the world's crowning glory (cf. Gen. 1:26-28). On the human level, 'it was the devil's envy that brought death into the world' (Wis. 2:24). Introduced by sin, death remains bound up with it: death is the sign and fruit of sin. But there is no final triumph for death. Confirming faith in the resurrection, the Lord proclaims in the gospel: 'God is God, not of the dead, but of the living' (Mt. 22:32). And death like sin will be definitively defeated by resurrection in Christ (cf. 1 Cor. 15:20-27). Thus we understand that human life, even on this earth, is precious. Infused by the creator,[5] life is again taken back by him (cf. Gen. 2:7; Wis. 15:11). It remains under his protection: man's blood cries out to him (cf. Gen. 4:10) and he will demand an account of it, 'for in the image of God man was made' (Gen. 9:5-6). The commandment of God is formal: 'You shall not kill' (Ex. 20:13). Life is at the same time a gift and a responsibility. It is received as a

'talent' (cf. Mt. 25:14-30); it must be put to proper use. In order that life may bring forth fruit, many tasks are offered to man in this world and he must not shirk them. More important still, the Christian knows that eternal life depends on what, with the grace of God, he does with his life on earth.

6. The tradition of the Church has always held that human life must be protected and cherished from the beginning, just as at the various stages of its development. Opposing the morals of the Greco-Roman world, the Church of the first centuries insisted on the difference that exists on this point between those morals and Christian morals. In the *Didaché* it is clearly said: 'You shall not kill by abortion the fruit of the womb and you shall not murder the infant already born.'[6] Athenagoras emphasizes that Christians consider as murderers those women who take medicines to procure an abortion; he condemns the killers of children, including those still living in their mother's womb, 'where they are already the object of the care of divine providence.'[7] Tertullian did not always perhaps use the same language; he nevertheless clearly affirms the essential principle: 'To prevent birth is anticipated murder; it makes little difference whether one destroys a life already born or does away with it in its nascent stage. The one who will be a man is already one.'[8]

7. In the course of history, the Fathers of the Church, her Pastors and her Doctors have taught the same doctrine—the various opinions on the infusion of the spiritual soul did not cast doubt on the illicitness of abortion. It is true that in the Middle Ages, when the opinion was generally held that the spiritual soul was not present until after the first few weeks, a distinction was made in the evaluation of the sin and the gravity of penal sanctions. In resolving cases, approved authors were more lenient with regard to that early stage than with regard to later stages. But it was never denied at that time that procured abortion, even during the first days, was objectively a grave sin. This condemnation was in fact unanimous. It is enough to cite some from among the many documents. The First Council of Mainz in 847 reconsiders the penalties against abortion which had been established by preceding Councils. It decided that the most rigorous penance would be imposed 'on women who procure the elimination of the fruit conceived in their womb.'[9] The Decree of Gratian reports the following words of Pope Stephen V.: 'That person is a murderer who causes to perish by abortion what has been conceived.'[10] St Thomas, the Common Doctor of the Church, teaches that abortion is a grave sin against the natural law.[11] At the time of the Renaissance Pope Sixtus V con-

demned abortion with the greatest severity.[12] A century later, Innocent XI rejected the propositions of certain lax canonists who sought to excuse an abortion procured before the moment accepted by some as the moment of the spiritual animation of the new being.[13] In our days the recent Roman Pontiffs have proclaimed the same doctrine with the greatest clarity. Pius XI explicitly answered the most serious objections.[14] Pius XII clearly excluded all direct abortion, that is, abortion which is either an end or a means.[15] John XXIII recalled the teaching of the Fathers on the sacred character of life 'which from its beginning demands the action of God the creator.'[16] Most recently, the Second Vatican Council, presided over by Paul VI, has most severely condemned abortion: 'Life must be safeguarded with extreme care from conception; abortion and infanticide are abominable crimes.'[17] The same Paul VI, speaking on this subject on many occasions, has not hesitated to declare that this teaching of the Church 'has not changed and is unchangeable.'[18]

IN THE ADDITIONAL LIGHT OF REASON

8. Respect for human life is not just a Christian obligation. Human reason is sufficient to impose it on the basis of the analysis of what a human person is and should be. Constituted by a rational nature, man is a person, a subject capable of reflecting on himself and of determining his acts and hence his own destiny: he is free. He is consequently master of himself, or rather, because self-mastery takes time, he has the means of becoming so: this is his task. Created immediately by God, man's soul is spiritual and therefore immortal. Hence man is open to God; he finds his fulfilment only in him. But he spends his life in the company of his own kind. He is nourished, as it were, by interpersonal relationships in society. And society is indispensable to him. While society and other men must be taken into account, each human person possesses himself, he possesses life and goods; he has these as a right. It is this that strict justice demands from all in his regard.

9. Nevertheless, temporal life lived in this world does not exhaust all that pertains to the person, for he has a higher and indeed everlasting life of his own. Bodily life is a fundamental good; here below it is the condition for all other goods. But there are higher values for which it could be legitimate or even necessary to be willing to expose oneself to the risk of losing bodily life. In a society of persons the common good is for each individual an end which he must serve and to which he must subordinate his particular interest. But it is not his last end and, from

this point of view, it is society which is at the service of the person, because the person will not fulfil his destiny except in God. The person can be definitively subordinated only to God. Man can never be treated simply as a means to be disposed of in order to obtain a higher end.

10. In regard to the mutual rights and duties of the person and of society, it belongs to moral teaching to enlighten consciences, it belongs to the law to specify and organize external behaviour. There is a definite number of rights which society is not in a position to grant since these rights precede society; but it is society's function to preserve and to enforce them. These comprise most of what today we call 'human rights' and which our age boasts of having formulated.

11. The first right of the human person is his life. He has other goods and some are more precious, but this one is fundamental—the condition of all the others. It does not belong to society, nor does it belong to public authority in any form to recognize this right for some and not for others: all discrimination is evil, whether it be founded on race, sex, colour or religion. It is not recognition by another that constitutes this right. This right is antecedent to its recognition; it demands recognition and it is strictly unjust to refuse it.

12. Any discrimination based on the various stages of life is no more justified than any other discrimination. The right to life remains complete in an old person, even one greatly weakened, it is not lost by one who is incurably sick. The right to life is no less to be respected in the small infant just born than in the mature person. In reality, respect for human life is called for from the time that the process of generation begins. From the time that the ovum is fertilized, a life is begun which is neither that of the father nor of the mother; it is rather the life of a new human being with his own growth. It would never be made human if it were not human already.

13. This has always been clear, and discussions about the moment of animation have no bearing on it.[19] Modern genetic science offers clear confirmation. It has demonstrated that from the first instant there is established the programme of what this living being will be: a man, this individual man with his characteristic aspects already well determined. Right from fertilization the adventure of a human life begins, and each of its capacities requires time—a rather lengthy time—to find its place and to be in a position to act. The least that can be said is that present science, in its most evolved state, does not give any substantial support to those who defend abortion. Moreover, it is not up to biological sciences to make a definitive judgment on questions

which are properly philosophical and moral, such as the moment when a human person is constituted or the legitimacy of abortion. From a moral point of view this is certain: even if a doubt existed concerning whether the fruit of conception is already a human person, it is objectively a grave sin to dare to risk murder. 'The one who will be a man is already one.'[20]

REPLY TO SOME OBJECTIONS

14. Divine law and natural reason, therefore, exclude all right to the direct killing of an innocent man. However, if the reasons given to justify an abortion were always manifestly evil and valueless the problem would not be so dramatic. The gravity of the problem comes from the fact that in certain cases, perhaps in quite a considerable number of cases, by denying abortion one endangers important values which men normally hold in great esteem and which may sometimes even seem to have priority. We do not deny these very great difficulties. It may be a serious question of health, sometimes of life or death, for the mother; it may be the burden represented by an additional child, especially if there are good reasons to fear that the child will be abnormal or retarded; it may be the importance attributed in different classes of society to considerations of honour or dishonour, of loss of social standing, and so forth. We proclaim only that none of these reasons can ever objectively confer the right to dispose of another's life, even when that life is only beginning. With regard to the future unhappiness of the child, no one, not even the father or mother, can act as its substitute, even if it is still in the embryonic stage, to choose in the child's name, life or death. The child itself, when grown up, will never have the right to choose suicide; no more may his parents choose death for the child while it is not of an age to decide for itself. Life is too fundamental a value to be weighed against even very serious disadvantages.[21]

15. The movement for the emancipation of women, in so far as it seeks essentially to free them from all unjust discrimination, is perfectly justified.[22] In many areas of society much remains to be done in this respect. But one cannot change nature. Nor can one exempt women, any more than men, from what nature demands of them. Furthermore, all publicly recognized freedom is always limited by the certain rights of others.

16. The same must be said of the claim to sexual freedom. If by this expression one is to understand the mastery progressively acquired by reason and by authentic love over instinctive impulse, without diminishing pleasure but keeping it in its proper

place—and in this sphere this is the only authentic freedom—then there is nothing to object to. But this kind of freedom will always be careful not to violate justice. If, on the contrary, one is to understand that men and women are 'free' to seek sexual pleasure to the point of satiety, without taking into account any law or the essential orientation of sexual life towards fertility,[23] then this idea has nothing Christian in it. It is even unworthy of man. In any case it does not confer any right to dispose of human life—even if embryonic—or to suppress it on the pretext that it is burdensome.

17. Scientific progress is opening to technology—and will open still more—the possibility of delicate interventions, the consequences of which can be very serious, for good as well as for evil. These are achievements of the human spirit which in themselves are admirable. But technology can never be independent of the criterion of morality, since technology exists for man and must respect his finality. Just as there is no right to use nuclear energy for every possible purpose, so there is no right to manipulate human life in every possible direction. Technology must be at the service of man, so as better to ensure the functioning of his normal abilities, to prevent or to cure his illnesses, to contribute to his better human development. It is true that the evolution of technology makes early abortion more and more easy, but the moral evaluation is in no way modified because of this.

18. We know what seriousness the problem of birth control can assume for some families and for some countries. That is why the last Council and subsequently the Encyclical *Humanae Vitae* of 25 July 1968, spoke of 'responsible parenthood.'[24] What we wish to say again with emphasis, as was pointed out in the conciliar Constitution *Gaudium et Spes,* in the Encyclical *Populorum Progressio* and in other papal documents, is that never, under any pretext, may abortion be resorted to, either by a family or by the political authority, as a legitimate means of regulating births.[25] The damage to moral values is always a greater evil for the common good than any disadvantage in the economic or demographic order.

MORALITY AND LAW

19. The moral discussion is being accompanied more or less everywhere by serious juridical debates. There is no country where legislation does not forbid and punish murder. Furthermore, many countries had specifically applied this condemnation and these penalties to the particular case of procured abor-

tion. In these days a vast body of opinion petitions the liberalization of this latter prohibition. There already exists a fairly general tendency which seeks to limit as far as possible all restrictive legislation, especially when it seems to touch upon private life. The argument of pluralism is also used. Although many citizens—the argument goes—in particular the Catholic faithful, condemn abortion, many others hold that it is licit at least as a lesser evil. Why force them to follow an opinion which is not theirs, especially in a country where they are in the majority? In addition it is apparent that, where they still exist, the laws condemning abortion appear difficult to apply. The crime has become too common for it to be punished every time, and the public authorities often find that it is wiser to close their eyes to it. But the preservation of a law which is not applied is always to the detriment of authority and of all the other laws. It must be added that clandestine abortion seriously endangers the fertility and even the lives of women who resort to it. Even if the legislator continues to regard abortion as an evil, may he not propose to restrict its damage?

20. These arguments and others in addition that are heard from varying quarters are not conclusive. It is true that civil law cannot expect to cover the whole field of morality or to punish all faults. No one expects it to do so. It must often tolerate what is in fact a lesser evil, in order to avoid a greater one. One must, however, be attentive to what a change in legislation can represent. Many will take as authorization what is perhaps only a refusal to punish. Even more, in the present case, this very refusal seems at the very least to admit that the legislator no longer considers abortion a crime against human life, since murder is still always severely punished. It is true that it is not the task of the law to choose between points of view or to impose one rather than another. But the life of the child takes precedence over all opinions. One cannot invoke freedom of thought to destroy life.

21. The role of law is not to record what is done, but to help in promoting improvement. It is at all times the task of the State to preserve each person's rights and to protect the weakest. In order to do so the State will have to right many wrongs. The law is not obliged to sanction everything, but it cannot act contrary to a law which is deeper and more majestic than any human law: the natural law engraved in men's hearts by the creator as a norm which reason clarifies and strives to formulate properly, and which one must always try to understand better, but which it is always wrong to contradict. Human law can abstain from

punishment, but it cannot declare to be right what would be opposed to the natural law, for this opposition suffices to give the assurance that a law is not a law at all.

22. It must in any case be clearly understood that a Christian can never conform to a law which is in itself immoral, and such is the case of a law which would admit in principle the liceity of abortion. Nor can a Christian take part in a propaganda campaign in favour of such a law, or vote for it. Moreover, he may not collaborate in its application. It is, for instance, inadmissible that doctors or nurses should find themselves obliged to cooperate closely in abortions and have to choose between the Christian law and their professional situation.

23. On the contrary it is the task of law to pursue a reform of society and of conditions of life in all milieux, starting with the most deprived, so that always and everywhere it may be possible to give every child coming into this world a welcome worthy of a person. Help for families and for unmarried mothers, assured grants for children, legislation for illegitimate children and reasonable arrangements for adoption—a whole positive policy must be put into force so that there will always be a concrete honourable and possible alternative to abortion.

CONCLUSION

24. Following one's conscience in obedience to the law of God is not always the easy way. One must not fail to recognize the weight of the sacrifices and the burdens which it can impose. Heroism is sometimes called for in order to remain faithful to the requirements of the divine law. Therefore we must emphasize that the path of true progress of the human person passes through this constant fidelity to a conscience maintained in uprightness and truth; and we must exhort all those who are able to do so to lighten the burdens still crushing so many men and women, families and children, who are placed in situations to which in human terms there is no solution.

25. A Christian's outlook cannot be limited to the horizon of life in this world. He knows that during the present life another one is being prepared, one of such importance that it is in its light that judgments must be made.[26] From this viewpoint there is no absolute misfortune here below, not even the terrible sorrow of bringing up a handicapped child. This is the contradiction proclaimed by the Lord: 'Happy those who mourn: they shall be comforted' (Mt. 5:5). To measure happiness by the absence of

sorrow and misery in this world is to turn one's back on the gospel.

26. But this does not mean that one can remain indifferent to these sorrows and miseries. Every man and woman with feeling, and certainly every Christian, must be ready to do what he can to remedy them. This is the law of charity, whose first pre-occupation must always be the establishment of justice. One can never approve of abortion; but it is above all necessary to combat its causes. This requires political action, which is the province of the law. But it is necessary at the same time to influence morality and to do everything possible to help families, mothers and children. Considerable progress in the service of life has been accomplished by medicine. One can hope that such progress will continue: it is not a doctor's vocation to take life, but to sustain it for as long as possible. It is also to be hoped that help will be more and more forthcoming, either institutionalized or by voluntary action rooted in Christian charity.

27. One cannot effectively safeguard morality unless one takes the fight on to the field of doctrine. A way of thinking or, rather, an emotional prejudice against large families—seeing them as an evil—cannot be allowed to go unchallenged. It is true that all forms of civilization are not equally favourable to large families. Industrialized and urbanized society pose much greater difficulties for them. This is why the Church in recent times has consistently invoked the principle of responsible parenthood, the exercise of true human and Christian prudence. Such prudence would not be authentic if it did not include generosity. It must preserve awareness of the grandeur of the task of co-operating with the Creator in the transmission of life, which gives new members to society and new children to the Church. A principal care and solicitude of the Church of Christ is to protect and foster life. This applies first and foremost to the life which Christ brought on earth: 'I have come so that they may have life and have it to the full' (John 10:10). But life at all its levels comes from God, and bodily life is for man the indispensable beginning. In this life on earth sin has introduced, multiplied and made harder to bear suffering and death. But in taking their burden upon himself Jesus Christ has transformed them: for whoever believes in him, suffering and death itself become instruments of resurrection. Hence St Paul can say: 'I think that what we suffer in this life can never be compared to the glory, as yet unrevealed, which is waiting for us' (Rom. 8:18). And, if we make this comparison we shall add with him: 'Yes, the troubles which are soon over, though they weigh little, train us for the

carrying of a weight of eternal glory which is out of all proportion to them' (2 Cor. 4:17).

*This translation is a corrected (by A. F.) version of that put out by the Vatican Press Office. Latin original in AAS 66 (1974) 730-747.
1. A certain number of bishop's documents are to be found in Gr. Caprile, *Non Uccidere. Il Magistero della Chiesa sull'aborto,* par. II, pp. 47-300, Rome, 1973.
2. *Regimini Ecclesiae Universae,* III, 1, 29. Cf. *ibid.,* 31 (*AAS* 59 (1967), p. 897). On the Sacred Congregation for the Doctrine of the Faith depend all the questions which are related to faith and morals or which are bound up with the faith.
3. *Lumen Gentium,* 12 (*AAS* 57 (1965), pp. 16-17). The present Declaration does not envisage all the questions which can arise in connection with abortion: it is for theologians to examine and discuss them. Only certain basic principles are here recalled which must be for the theologians themselves a guide and a rule, and confirm certain fundamental truths of Catholic doctrine for all Christians.
4. *Lumen Gentium,* 25 (*AAS* 57 (1965), pp. 29-31).
5. The authors of Scripture do not make any philosophical observations on when life begins but they speak of the period of life which precedes birth as being the object of God's attention: he creates and forms the human being, like that which is moulded by his hand (cf. Ps. 118:73). It would seem that this theme finds expression for the first time in Jr. 1:5. It appears later in many other texts. Cf. Is. 49:1, 5; 46:3; Jb. 10:8-12; Ps. 22:10, 71:6, 139:13. In the Gospels we read in Luke 1:44: 'For the moment your greeting reached my ears, the child in my womb leapt for joy.'
6. *Didaché Apostolorum,* edition Funk, *Patres Apostolici,* V, 2. *The Epistle of Barnabas,* XIX, 5, uses the same expressions (cf. Funk, *l.c.* 91-93).
7. Athenagoras, *A Plea on behalf of Christians,* 35 (cf. *PG* 6,970: *S.C.* 3, pp. 166-167). One may also consult the *Epistle to Diognetus,* V, 6 Funk, *o.c.,* 1,399: *S.C.* 33), where it says of Christians: 'They procreate children, but they do not reject the foetus.'
8. Tertullian, *Apologeticum,* IX, 8 *PL* 1,371-372: *Corp. Christ.* I, p. 103, 1.31-36).
9. Canon 21 (Mansi, 14, p. 909). Cf. Council of Elvira, canon 63 (Mansi, 2, p. 16) and the Council of Ancyra, canon 21 (*ibid,* 519). See also the decree of Gregory III regarding the penance to be imposed upon those who are guilty of this crime (Mansi 13,292, c. 17).
10. Gratian, *Concordantia Discordantium Canonum,* c. 20, C. 2, q. 2. During the Middle Ages appeal was often made to the authority of Saint Augustine who wrote as follows in regard to this matter in *De Nuptiis et Concupiscentiis,* c. 15: 'Sometimes this sexually indulgent cruelty or this cruel sexual indulgence goes so far as to procure potions which produce sterility. If the desired result is not achieved, the mother terminates the life and expels the foetus which was in her womb in such a way that the child dies before having lived or, if the baby was living already in its mother's womb, it is killed before being born' (*PL* 44,423-424: CSEL

33, 619. Cf. the *Decree of Gratian,* q. 2, C 32, c. 7).

11. *Commentary on the Sentences,* book IV, dist. 31, exposition of the text.

12. Constitutio *Effraenatum* in 1588 (*Bullarium Romanum,* V, 1, pp. 25-27; *Fontes Iuris Canonici,* I, no. 165, pp. 308-311).

13. Dz-Sch 1184. Cf. also the Constitution *Apostolicae Sedis* of Pius IX (Acta Pii IX, V, 55-72; *ASS* 5 (1869), pp. 305-331; *Fontes Iuris Canonici,* III, no. 552, pp. 24-31).

14. Encyclical *Casti Connubii, AAS* 22 (1930), pp. 562-565; Dz-Sch. 3719-21.

15. The statements of Pius XII are express, precise and numerous; they would require a whole study on their own. We quote only this one from the Discourse to the Saint Luke Union of Italian Doctors of 12 November 1944, because it formulates the principle in all its universality: 'As long as a man is not guilty, his life is untouchable, and therefore any act directly tending to destroy it is illicit, whether such destruction is intended as an end in itself or only as a means to an end, whether it is a question of life in the embryonic stage or in a stage of full development or already in its final stages' (Discourses and Radio-messages, VI, 183 ff.).

16. Encyclical *Mater et Magistra, AAS* 53 (1961), p. 447.

17. *Gaudium et Spes,* 51. Cf. 27 (*AAS* 58 (1966), p. 1072; cf. 1047).

18. The Speech: *Salutiamo con paterna effusione,* 9 December 1972, *AAS* 64 (1972), p. 737. Among the witnesses of this unchangeable doctrine one will recall the declaration of the Holy Office, condemning direct abortion (Denzinger 1890, *ASS* 17 (1884), p. 556; 22 (1888-1890), 748; Dz-Sch. 3258).

19. This declaration expressly leaves aside the question of the moment when the spiritual soul is infused. There is not a unanimous tradition on this point and authors are as yet in disagreement. For some it dates from the first instant, for others it could not at least precede nidation. It is not within the competence of science to decide between these views, because the existence of an immortal soul is not a question in its field. It is a philosophical problem from which our moral affirmation remains independent for two reasons: (i) supposing a later animation, there is still nothing less than a *human* life, preparing for and calling for a soul in which the nature received from parents is completed; (2) on the other hand it suffices that this presence of the soul be probable (and one can never prove the contrary) in order that the taking of life involve accepting the risk of killing a man, not only waiting for, but already in possession of his soul.

20. Tertullian, cited in footnote 8.

21. See Cardinal Villot, Secretary of State, on 10 October 1973 to Cardinal Döpfner, regarding the protection of human life (*L'Osservatore Romano,* German edition, 26 October 1973, p. 3).

22. Encyclical *Pacem in Terris, AAS* 55 (1963), p. 267. Constitution *Gaudium et Spes,* 29. Speech of Paul VI, *Salutiamo, AAS* 64 (1972) 779.

23. *Gaudium et Spes,* 48.

24. *Gaudium et Spes,* 50-51. Paul I, Encyclical *Humanae Vitae,* 10 (*AAS* 60 (1968), p. 487).

25. *Gaudium et Spes,* 87. Paul VI, Encyclical *Popolorum Progressio,* 31: Address to the United Nations, *AAS* 57 (1965), p. 883. John XXIII, *Mater et Magistra, AAS* 53 (1961), pp. 445-448. Responsible parenthood supposes the use of only morally licit methods of birth regulation. Cf. *Humanae Vitae,* 14 (*ibid.,* p. 490).

26. See Cardinal Villot, Secretary of State, to the World Congress of Catholic Doctors held in Barcelona, 26 May 1974 (*L'Osservatore Romano*, 29 May 1974).

107

STERILIZATION IN CATHOLIC HOSPITALS*

S.C.D.F., *Haec sacra congregatio*, 13 March, 1975

This sacred congregation has carefully examined the problem of therapeutic preventive sterilization and the various opinions put forward on how to solve it. It has also examined the problems posed by requests for collaboration in such sterilizations in Catholic hospitals. It offers the following replies to the questions asked of it:

1. Any sterilization whose sole, immediate effect, of itself, that is of its own nature and condition, is to render the generative faculty incapable of procreation is to be regarded as direct sterilization, as this is understood in statements of the pontifical magisterium, especially of Pius XII.[1] It is absolutely forbidden, therefore, according to the teaching of the Church, even when it is motivated by a subjectively right intention of curing or preventing a physical or psychological ill-effect which is foreseen or feared as a result of pregnancy. The sterilization of the faculty itself is even more strongly prohibited than is the sterilization of individual acts, since it is nearly always irreversible. Nor can any public authority justify the imposition of sterilization as being necessary for the common good, since it damages the dignity and inviolability of the human person.[2] Neither can one invoke the principle of totality in this case, the principle which would justify interference with organs for the greater good of the person. Sterility induced as such does not contribute to the person's integral good, properly understood, 'keeping things and values in proper perspective'.[3] Rather does it damage a person's ethical good, since it deprives subsequent freely-chosen sexual acts of an essential element. Hence article 20 of the ethical code published by the Conference held in 1971 faithfully reflects the correct teaching and its observance should be urged.

2. The congregation re-affirms this traditional Catholic teaching. It is aware that many theologians dissent from it, but it denies that this fact as such has any doctrinal significance, as

though it were a theological source which the faithful might invoke, forsaking the authentic magisterium for the private opinions of theologians who dissent from it.[4]

3. With regard to the administration of Catholic hospitals:

a. The following is absolutely forbidden: co-operation, officially approved or admitted, in actions which of themselves (that is of their own nature and condition) have a contraceptive purpose, the impeding of the natural effects of the deliberate sexual acts of the person sterilized. For the official approval of direct sterilization and, all the more so, its administration and execution according to hospital regulations is something of its nature—that is, intrinsically—objectively evil. Nothing can justify a Catholic hospital co-operating in it. Any such co-operation would accord ill with the mission confided to such an institution and would be contrary to the essential proclamation and defence of the moral order.

b. The traditional teaching on material co-operation, with its appropriate distinctions between necessary and freely-given co-operation, proximate and remote co-operation, remains valid, to be applied very prudently when the case demands it.

c. When applying the principle of material co-operation, as the case warrants it, scandal and the danger of creating misunderstanding must be carefully avoided with the help of suitable explanation of what is going on.

This sacred congregation hopes that the criteria outlined in this document will meet the expectations of this episcopate, so that having removed the doubts of the faithful they may the more easily perform their pastoral duty.

---

*Translated by A. F. Latin text in A.A.S. 68 (1976) 738-740.
1. See especially the two allocutions to the Catholic Union of Obstetricians and to the International Society of Hemathology; see also *Humanae Vitae.*
2. See Pius XI, *Casti Connubii.*
3. Paul VI, *Humanae Vitae.*
4. See Vatican Council II, *Lumen Gentium,* n. 25.

108

CHRISTIAN FAITH AND DEMONOLOGY*

S.C.D.W., *Les formes multiples de la superstition*,
26 June, 1975

I

INTRODUCTION

Over the centuries, the Church has repeatedly condemned superstition in its various forms, the obsessive preoccupation with Satan and demons, and any form of worship of, or morbid concentration on, such spirits.[1] It is, therefore, inaccurate to claim that Christianity ever forget the universal lordship of Christ and made Satan the preferred subject of preaching, thus transforming the Good News of the risen Lord into a message of terror. In his day, St. John Chrysostom told the Christians of Antioch: "I certainly find no pleasure in speaking to you of the devil but the teaching which the present passage suggests will nonetheless be of profit to you."[2] It would indeed be a fatal mistake to act as if history were already finished and redemption had achieved all its effects, so that it were no longer necessary to engage in the struggle of which the New Testament and the masters of the spiritual life speak.

CONTEMPORARY DISAFFECTION

Revision of New Testament Teaching?

It is possible even today to fall into the error just mentioned. In many quarters people are, in fact, asking whether we do not need to re-examine Catholic teaching on this matter and to begin the revision back in Scripture itself. Some think that no certain doctrinal position is possible (as if the problem could be left hanging!), on the grounds that the sacred books do not enable us either to affirm or to deny the existence of Satan and his demons. Most of the time, however, their existence is simply denied. Some critics claim they can identify the views of Jesus himself; they maintain that no statement of his guarantees the existence of the world of demons and that where the assertion of its existence does occur it reflects Jewish ideas or is based on New Testament traditions which do not stem from Christ. Therefore, the assertion of its existence is not a part of the central Gospel message and is not an obligatory part of our faith today; we are free to abandon it.

Eliminating Satan

Others are both more objective and more radical, for they accept the obvious meaning of Scriptural statements about demons but add straightway that such views are not acceptable in today's world, even to Christians. Thus, these people, too, end up dismissing his teachings. For others, finally, the idea of Satan, whatever its origin, is no longer important. If we insist on trying to justify it, the credibility of our teaching will suffer, and we will only distract attention from what we have to say about God, who alone is of real interest to us.

For all these groups, the very names "Satan" and "devil" are mythical personifications of functions and their only purpose is to emphasize in a dramatic way the influence of evil and sin on mankind. "Satan" and "devil" are simply words which our age must interpret in order to find a new way of bringing home to Christians the duty of struggling against all the forces of evil in the world.

Disturbance of the Faithful

These views, repeated with a display of erudition and broadcast in periodicals and some theological dictionaries, cannot but disturb many minds. The faithful, who are used to taking seriously the warnings of Christ and the apostolic writers, have the impression that writings of this kind are intended to effect a change of public opinion on the matter. Those of the faithful who have some acquaintance with the biblical and religious sciences are asking how far the process of demythologization is to go under the aegis of a certain type of hermeneutics.

* * *

Such, then, are the views being spread abroad, and such the mentality that produces them. In order to answer them, we must dwell briefly, first of all, on the New Testament, and document its authoritative testimony.

II
THE WORLD OF THE NEW TESTAMENT

Different Views on Demons

Even before we remind ourselves of the independence of mind Jesus always showed with regard to the opinions of his day, it is important to note that his contemporaries did not all share the common belief concerning angels and demons which some today seem to attribute to them and which (in their view) Jesus himself simply reflects. In the Book of Acts we read how a declaration of St. Paul caused a dispute among the members of the Sanhedrin. At this point, the writer of Acts comments that the Sadducees, unlike the Pharisees, admitted neither "resurrection... [nor] angels nor spirits." In other words (as the text is understood by competent exegetes), they did not believe in the resurrection and consequently did not believe in angels and demons either.[3] Contemporary opinion on Satan, demons, and angels thus followed two diametrically opposed lines. How, then, can it be claimed that when Jesus exorcised and later gave to others the power to expel demons, and when the New Testament writers in their turn accepted this, they were simply adopting, in a wholly uncritical way, the ideas and practices of their time?

There is no doubt, of course, that Christ and, much more, the apostles were men of their day and shared its culture. Jesus, however, by reason of his divine nature and the revelation he came to communicate, transcended his situation and his age and rose above the pressures these exerted. We need only read the Sermon on the Mount to be convinced that his intellectual freedom was no less than his respect for the past.[4] When, therefore, he revealed the meaning of his redemptive activity, he evidently had to take account not only of the Pharisees, who believed, as he did, in the future world, the soul, spirits, and resurrection, but also the Sadducees, who did not hold these beliefs. When the former accused him of expelling demons with the aid of the prince of demons, he could have countered by siding with the Sadducees but then he would have denied himself and his mission. Consequently, without repudiating the belief in spirits and the resurrection, which he shared with the Pharisees, he had to dissociate himself from this group while also opposing the Sadducees.

To maintain today, therefore, that Jesus' words about Satan express only a teaching borrowed from his culture and are unimportant for the faith of other believers is evidently to show little understanding either of the Master's character or of his age. If Jesus used this kind of language and, above all, if he translated it into practice during his ministry, it was because it expressed a doctrine that was to some extent essential to the idea and reality of the salvation he was bringing.

III
THE NEW TESTAMENT

A. The Personal Testimony of Jesus

Christ worked his major cures of possessed people at points which were decisive, according to the accounts of his ministry. The exorcisms he performed forced men to face the question of his person and mission, and also suggested the true answer, as the reactions these exorcisms elicited make sufficiently clear.[5] Without ever making Satan the focus of his Gospel, Jesus nevertheless spoke of him only at evidently crucial moments and in important statements.

Jesus and Satan

To begin with, Jesus started his public ministry by allowing the devil to tempt him in the wilderness; Mark's account, precisely because of its restraint, is as significant as those of Matthew and Luke.[6] Jesus warned his hearers against this enemy in the Sermon on the Mount and in the prayer he taught his disciples, the Our Father (as many exegetes admit today,[7] following the testimony of some liturgies[8]). In his parables he blamed Satan for the barriers set up against his preaching,[9] as in the parable of the weeds sown in the farmer's field.[10] He told Simon Peter that the "power of hell" would attempt to prevail over the Church[11] and that Satan would sift him and the other disciples.[12] As he left the supper room, he predicted the imminent coming of "the Prince of this world."[13] In Gethsemani, when the soldiers laid hands on him to arrest him, he declared that the hour of "the power of darkness"[14] had come; but he also knew, and had already said in the supper room, that "the prince of this world has been condemned."[15]

These facts and statements—circumstantial, repeated, and consistent among themselves—are not peripheral, nor can they be treated as novelistic intrusions which need to be demythologized. Otherwise, we would have to admit that at these critical moments the consciousness of Jesus, despite its evident lucidity and self-mastery in face of the Jews, was in fact, subject to delusions and that his words lacked all consistency. This would be in sharp contrast to the impression received by the first hearers and readers of the Gospel. The conclusion is therefore inescapable. Satan, whom Jesus attacked with his exorcisms and confronted in the wilderness and in his passion, cannot be simply a product of the human ability to tell stories and personify ideas nor a stray survival of a primitive culture and its language.

B. The Pauline Writings

It is true that in sketching with broad strokes the situation of mankind before Christ's coming, St. Paul in his Letter to the Romans personifies sin and death and shows the latter's fearful power. When viewed in the context of his teaching as a whole, this personification is clearly not a purely literary touch but springs from his acute awareness of the importance of the cross of Jesus and the necessity of the faith Jesus requires.

Satan Distinct from Sin

Moreover, Paul does not identify sin with Satan. He sees sin first and foremost for what it really is in its essence: a personal human act leading to that state of sin and blindness into which Satan desires to bring and keep men.[15] Paul thus clearly distinguishes Satan from sin. The same Apostle who admits that without grace he is helpless before "the law of sin in my members"[17] is also very decisive in his urging that we resist Satan,[18] not allow him to rule us and not give him any occasion or advantage,[19] but trample him underfoot.[20] The reason for this language is that in Paul's eyes Satan is a personal being, "the god of the present age,"[21] and a cunning adversary distinct both from us and from the sin which he urges on us.

The Activity of Satan

Like the evangelists, the Apostle sees Satan at work in the history of the world; in what he calls "the secret force of lawlessness"[22], in the unbelief which refuses to acknowledge Jesus as Lord[23] and in the aberration of idolatry[24]; in the seductive temptations which threaten the fidelity of the Church to Christ her Spouse[25]; and, finally, in the eschatological perversion which leads to the worship of the man who sets himself in God's place.[26] Satan assuredly leads men into sin but he is himself distinct from the evil he leads others to do.

C. The Apocalypse and the Gospel of John

The Apocalypse

The Apocalypse is, before all else, a splendid evocation of the power which the risen Christ exercises in those who bear witness to his Gospel. It proclaims the triumph of the Lamb who was slain but we would completely mistake the nature of this victory if we did not see it as the climax of a long struggle in which, through the mediation of the human powers that oppose the Lord Jesus, Satan and his angels play a significant role (all these spirits being distinct from one another as their agents on the scene of history). The Apocalypse emhasizes the various enigmatic names and symbols of Satan and unmasks them to show the one who lurks behind them.[27] Satan's action unfolds through all the centuries of history as man lives under God's eyes.

The Fourth Gospel

We will not be surprised, therefore, to find that in the Gospel of St. John Jesus speaks of the devil and calls him "the Prince of this world."[28] Satan's action on man is admittedly interior but it is impossible to regard him as therefore simply a personfication of sin and temptation. Jesus acknowledges that to sin is to be a "slave"[29] but he does not identify Satan either with this slavery or with the sin in which the slavery is manifested. The devil has only a moral influence on sinners, to the extent that they consent to the actions he suggests[30]; they freely follow his "wishes"[31] and do his "works."[32] Only in this sense, and to this extent, is Satan the "father" of sinners,[33] for between him and the conscience of the human person there always remains the spiritual distance separating the devil's "lies" and the consent we can give or refuse,[34] just as between Christ and us there will always be the distance which separates the "truth" he reveals and offers us, and the faith with which we accept it.

* * *

It was for all these reasons that the Fathers of the Church were convinced from Scripture that Satan and the demons are the enemies of man's redemption, and they did not fail to remind the faithful of their existence and action.

IV
GENERAL TEACHING OF THE FATHERS

As early as the second century of the Christian era Melito of Sardis wrote a work, *On the devil*[35]; it would be difficult to name a single Father who was completely silent on the subject. Those most concerned to shed light on the devil's action were, evidently, the writers who were trying to show the divine plan in history, especially St. Irenaeus and Tertullian, St. Victorinus of Pettau at a later date, and, finally, St. Augustine.

Important Patristic Views of Satan

St. Irenaeus held that the devil is an "apostate angel"[36] and that Christ, who focused on his own person the whole war this enemy was waging on us, had to confront him at the beginning of his ministry.[37] On a broader canvas, and with a more vigorous brush, St. Augustine showed Satan at work in the conflict between the "two cities," a conflict which began in heaven when God's first creatures, the angels, chose to be faithful or unfaithful to their Lord.[38] The society formed by sinners he regards as a mystical "body" of the devil.[39] St. Gregory the Great will speak of this "body" later on in his *Moralia in Job*.[40]

Pride and Malice of the Fallen Spirits

The majority of the Fathers rejected Origen's idea that the fallen angels had committed a fleshly sin and, instead, saw the angels' pride as the reason for their fall. The "pride" of the angels was manifested in their desire to exalt themselves above their condition, to maintain complete independence and to make themselves divine. Many Fathers, moreover, emphasized not only the pride of the angels but their malice towards men. For St. Irenaeus, the devil's apostasy began when he became jealous of man and sought to make him rebel against his Creator.[41] According to Tertullian, Satan tried to frustrate the Lord's plan by turning the pagan mysteries into caricatures of the Christian sacraments.[42] Patristic teaching was thus substantially faithful to the teaching and outlook of the New Testament.

V
THE FOURTH LATERAN COUNCIL (1215) AND ITS TEACHING ON DEMONS

A. The Dogmatic Statement

In the course of 20 centuries the teaching authority in the Church has made few dogmatic statements on the devil and the demons. The reason for this is that the occasions for such statements have been rare. In fact, there have been only two, the more important of them arising at the beginning of the 13th century when the Cathars or Albigensians revived Manichaean or Priscillianist dualism. Yet the dogmatic statement was placed in a doctrinal framework familiar to us; it is in tune with our present-day sensibilities, since it is set within the vision of the universe and its creation by God.

"We firmly believe and profess without qualification" that the Three Divine Persons "are the one and only principle of all things—Creator of all things visible and invisible, spiritual and corporeal, who, by his almighty power, from the very beginning of time has created both orders of creatures in the same way out of nothing, the spiritual or angelic world and the corporeal or visible universe. And afterward He formed the creature man, who in a way belongs to both orders, as he is composed of spirit and body. For the devil and the other demons were created by God good according to their nature, but they made themselves evil by their own doing. As for man, his sin was at the prompting of the devil."[43]

In this succinct exposition the Council says of the devil and the demons only that, being creatures of the one God, they are not evil by their very nature but became evil through the exercise of their free will. Nothing is said of the number of the demons or their precise sin or the extent of their power. Such questions, being irrelevant to the doctrinal issue then raised, were left to theological discussion. Yet, succinct though it is, the conciliar statement is highly significant inasmuch as it was made by the most important council of the 13th century and was part of its profession of faith. This profession was preceded, historically, by the professions required a short time before from the Cathars and the Waldensians,[44] and it links up with the condemnations of the Priscillianists some centuries earlier.[45]

Two Main Themes

The profession will repay careful study. It shows the structure usual in dogmatic creeds and readily fits into the series that began with the Council of Nicaea. According to the part of the text we have quoted, there are from our present viewpoint, two connected themes of equal importance for the faith: The statement about the devil, to which we will have to give special consideration, follows a statement about God as Creator of all things "visible and invisible," that is, of corporeal and incorporeal beings.

B. First Theme of the Council:
"God as Creator of Things
Visible and Invisible"

Scripture and the Fathers

This statement about the Creator and the way it is formulated are of special importance for our subject, since they are so old they have their roots in the teaching of St. Paul. In glorifying the risen Christ, the Apostle had said that Christ exercises dominion over all things "in the heavens, on the earth and under the earth,"[46] "in this age [and] in the age to come."[47] Moreover, in affirming the pre-existence of Christ, Paul taught that "in him everything in heaven and on earth was created, things visible and invisible."[48]

This doctrine of creation soon became very important in the Christian faith, because the Gnostics and the Marcionites tried for a long time to weaken it, in the period before Manichaeism and Priscillianism. The first creeds regularly stated that "things *visible and invisible* were all created by God." This teaching, put forth by the First Council of Nicaea and the First Council of Constantinople,[49] and then by the Council of Toledo,[50] was included in the creeds which the major Churches used in the rite of baptism.[51] It was also part of the great Eucharistic Prayers of St. James at Jerusalem,[52] of St. Basil in Asia Minor and at Alexandria,[53] and of the other Eastern Churches.[54] Among the Greek

Fathers it appears as early as St. Irenaeus[55] and the *Expositio fidei* of St. Athanasius.[56] In the West, we find it in St. Gregory of Elvira,[57] St. Augustine,[58] St. Fulgentius,[59] and so on.

At the time when the Cathars in the West, like the Bogomils in Eastern Europe, were reviving Manichaean dualism, Lateran IV could not do better in its profession of faith than to renew this declaration in its now traditional form. Henceforth, this dogmatic statement would be crucially important. It was soon repeated in the professions of faith issued by the Second Council of Lyons,[60] the Council of Florence[61] and the Council of Trent,[62] and reappeared, in the very terms of Lateran IV, in the Dogmatic Constitution on the Catholic Faith (*Dei Filius*) of Vatican I.[63]

We have here, then, a basic and constant affirmation of faith, which Lateran IV providentially emphasized in order to connect with it the conciliar statement on Satan and the demons. By so doing, the Council indicated that this subject, though important in its own right, belonged in the broader context of the teaching on creation in general and of faith in the existence of angelic beings.

C. Second Theme of the Council: The Devil

1. The Text

The statement on demons is far from being presented as a novelty called forth by circumstances and reached by way of doctrinal implication or theological deduction. On the contrary, it appears as a truth long since firmly established. The very formulation shows this, for, after affirming the creation of all things, the document does not pass to the devil and the demons as to a logical conclusion. It does not say: "*Therefore*, Satan and the demons were created naturally good," as it would have had to say if this statement were something new and deduced from what had just been affirmed. Instead, it presents Satan as a proof of the preceding statement and an argument against dualism. It says: "*For* the devil and the other demons were created by God good according to their nature." In other words, the proposition about Satan and the demons is offered as an undisputed statement of the Christian mind. This is an important aspect of the document and one that was inevitable, given the historical circumstances.

2. Preparation

a. Positive and Negative Formulations
(Fourth-Fifth Centuries)

The Traditional Teaching

Ever since the fourth century the Church had taken a position against the Manichaean thesis of two coeternal and opposed principles.[64] In both the East and the West it had taught unhesitatingly that Satan and the demons were not only created but created naturally good. To the newly baptized St. Gregory Nazianzus says: "You must believe that there exists nothing that is evil by essence, nor any kingdom [of evil], whether without a beginning or subsisting of itself or created by God."[65]

The devil was looked upon as a creature of God; he was originally good and filled with light but, unfortunately, did not persevere in the truth in which he had been created[65a] but rebelled against the Lord.[66] The evil, therefore, came not from his nature but from a contingent act of his free will.[67] Statements to this effect—which can be found in St. Basil,[68] St. Gregory Nazianzus,[69] St. John Chrysostom,[70] and Didymus of Alexandria[71] in the East, and in Tertullian,[72] St. Eusebius of Vercelli,[73] St. Ambrose,[74] and St. Augustine[75] in the West—could readily be put into firm dogmatic form when needed.

In the Form of Anathemas

The *De Trinitate* attributed to St. Eusebius of Vercelli expresses the doctrine unhesitatingly in a series of anathemas: "If anyone maintains that the fallen angels were not in their original nature created by God but are self-subsistent so as to be their own principle of existence, let him be anathema. If anyone maintains that God created the fallen angels evil, and does not assert that they became evil through the exercise of their own free will, let him be anathema. If anyone maintains—far be it from us! that an angel of Satan made the world, and does not affirm that all sin came through Satan, let him be anathema."[76]

The anathema form of this passage was not wholly unique at this period; we find it used again in the *Commonitorium* which was attributed to St. Augustine and written for use in the abjuration of Manichaeism. This instruction anathemizes "anyone who maintains there are two natures, originating from two disparate principles: one nature being good (the one coming from God) and the other evil and not created by him.'"[77]

In Positive Form

Writers generally preferred, however, to express this same teaching in the direct and positive form of a statement to be accepted in faith. At the beginning of his *De Genesi ad literam liber imperfectus* St. Augustine writes: "Catholic teaching bids us believe that the Trinity is one God who has made and created all things that exist, insofar as they do exist. Consequently, no creature, intellectual or corporeal (or, to use the succinct language of the divine Scriptures: invisible or visible), is part of the divine nature, but has been made, and made by none other than God."[78]

In Spain, the First Council of Toledo likewise professed that God is the Creator of "all [things] visible and invisible" and that apart from him "there exists no divine nature, angel, spirit or power that can be regarded as God."[79]

Thus, from the fourth century on, Christ faith, as taught and lived, found expression in this area in two dogmatic formulations, one positive and one negative. We will come upon them again, eight centuries later, in the time of Innocent III and the Fourth Lateran Council.

b. St. Leo the Great

St. Leo's Reply to Bishop Turibius

In the interval, however, the dogmatic expressions we have been examining did not fall into disuse. On the contrary: in the fifth century, Pope St. Leo, in his Letter to Bishop Turibius of Astorga (the authenticity of which is now beyond doubt), spoke with the same tone and the same clarity. Among the Priscillianist errors he condemned, the following were to be found: "As your sixth point shows,[80] they maintain that the devil was never good, nor was his nature God's handiwork; that he came forth from the abyss of darkness, since no one created him, but rather he is both the source and substance of all evil. The true Catholic faith, on the contrary, professes that the being of all creatures, be they spiritual or corporeal, is good, and that no being is by nature evil, since God, Creator of all things, made nothing that is not good. The devil, therefore, would be good in every sense if he had continued as God made him. When, however, he abused the excellence that was his by origin and 'did not abide in the truth' (*Jn* 8, 44), he did not indeed change his nature but he did rebel against the supreme Good to which he should have adhered."[8]

Influence of this Letter

This doctrinal statement (from the words, "The true Catholic faith...professes," to the end) was regarded as so important that it was repeated verbatim among the additions made in the sixth century to the *De ecclesiasticis dogmatibus* of Gennadius of Marseilles.[82] The same doctrine would be authoritatively taught in St. Fulgentius' *Regula fidei ad Petrum*. The Saint there says we must "maintain before all else," and "maintain unwaveringly," that whatever is not God is God's creature; that this is true of all things "visible and invisible"; that "some of the angels deliberately turned away from God their Creator who was the sole source of their happiness"; and that "evil does not have substance or nature."[83]

Given this historical background, we are not at all surprised that the *Statuta Ecclesiae antiqua,* a canonical collection of the fifth century, should include the following question among those to be asked concerning the Catholic faith of candidates for the episcopate: "Was the devil evil by nature or did he become evil through the misuse of his free will?"[84] The same formula will recur in the profession of faith which Innocent III required of the Waldensians.[85]

c. First Council of Braga (6th Century)

The teaching was, therefore, common and firmly held. The many documents which give expression to it (we have pointed out the main ones) provided the doctrinal background for the First Council of Braga in the middle of the sixth century. Against this background the seventh canon issued by the Synod is seen to be not an isolated text but a summation of fourth and fifth century teaching on the subject, and especially of the teaching of Pope St. Leo the Great: "If anyone maintains that the devil was not originally a good angel created by God and that his nature did not come from God's hand, but claims instead, as Mani and Priscillian do, that he emerged from the abyss of darkness and was not brought into being by anyone, but is himself the source of substance of evil, let him be anathema."[86]

3. The Coming of the Cathars
(12th and 13th Centuries)

The belief that the devil is a creature and that he turned away from God by a free act had thus long been explicit elements in the faith of the Church. At the Fourth Lateran Council, therefore, these statements had simply to be introduced into the conciliar profession of faith; there was no need to document them, because they represented beliefs which evidently were held by the Church. The insertion of these statements into a creed, which from a dogmatic viewpoint could have been done at an earlier time, had by now become a necessity, since the Cathars were making certain ancient Manichaean errors a part of their own heresy. In the 12th and 13th centuries numerous professions of faith had had to reassert that God is the Creator of all things "visible and invisible," as well as the author of the two Testaments, and, specifically, that the devil was not evil by nature but had become evil as the result of a free choice.[87]

The Contemporary Scene

The old dualist views, as part of a broad doctrinal and spiritual movement, were doing real harm to the faith in Southern France and Northern Italy. Ermengaud of Béziers had had to write a treatise against those heretics "who maintain and believe that our world and all visible things were created not by God but by the devil," and that there exist both a good and omnipotent God and an evil god, namely the devil.[88] In Northern Italy, Bonacursus, a convert from Catharism, had already sounded the alarm and described the various schools within the sect.[89] The *Summa contra haereticos* which appeared shortly afterward and for a long time was attributed to Prepositinus of Cremona, is more to the point for us, since it tells of the impact the dualist heresy had on the teaching of the period.

The treatment of the Catharist position in the *Summa* begins as follows: "Almighty God—this heretic says—created only invisible, incorporeal beings. The devil—whom he calls the god of darkness—created visible and corporeal beings. After saying this, the heretic adds that there are two sources of existing things, the source of good (almighty God) and the source of evil (the devil). Moreover, two kinds of natures exist: One is good, belongs to incorporeal beings and was created by almighty God; the other is evil, belongs to corporeal beings and was created by the devil. The heretic who holds these views used to be called a Manichaean in earlier times; today he is called a Cathar."[90]

The Book of the Two Principles

This summary, brief as it is, is important for its very compactness. Nowadays, we are in a position to supplement it with the *Book of the Two Principles,* which was written by a Carthist theologian shortly after the Fourth Lateran Council.[91] This little handbook for the use of militants in the sect goes deeply into the details of the Catharist arguments and bases them on Sacred Scripture. Its aim is to refute the doctrine of a single Creator and to prove from the Bible the existence of two ultimate and contrary principles.[92] Alongside the good God, it says, "we must acknowledge the existence of another principle, which is the source of evil and maliciously opposes the true God and his creatures."[93]

D. Value of The Fourth Lateran Statement

A Statement of the Faith

At the beginning of the 13th century, these last assertions were far from being the views simply of intellectuals and specialists. They reflected a set of erroneous beliefs which inspired, and were spread by, a multitude of interconnected, well-organized and active secret groups. The Church was forced to intervene and to repeat as forcefully as possible the doctrinal statements of earlier centuries. This is what Pope Innocent III did when he inserted the two dogmatic propositions we have been examining into the profession of faith drawn up at the Fourth Lateran Council. The profession was officially read to the bishops and they approved it; they were asked orally, "Do you believe everything contained herein?" and all replied, "We do."[94] The conciliar document in its entirety, then, is a statement of the faith; by reason of its nature and form, which are those of a creed, each main point has dogmatic value.

Interpreting a Profession of Faith

It would clearly be erroneous to maintain that each section of a profession of faith must contain only one dogmatic statement. This would be to apply to a profession of faith a principle of interpretation that is valid in the case, for example, of a decree of the Council of Trent, in which each chapter usually concentrates on a single dogmatic theme: The necessity of preparing ourselves for justification,[95] the real presence of Christ in the Eucharist,[96] and so on.

The first section of Lateran IV's profession of faith, on the contrary, though equal in number of lines to the chapter of Trent on the "gift of perseverance,"[97] contains a number of affirmations of faith (most of them already defined) concerning the oneness of God, the Trinity and equality of the Persons, the simplicity of their nature, the "processions" of the Son and the Holy Spirit. It also contains the doctrine on creation and especially the two statements on the creation by God of all beings spiritual and corporeal as well as on the creation of the devil and on his sin. As we have already shown, these points had been part of the Church's express teaching in the fourth and fifth centuries. When the Council made them part of its own creed, it simply recognized the fact that they belonged to the universal rule of faith.

The assertion that demons exist and have power is not based solely on these more categorical documents. They find another, more general and less formal expression in conciliar statements every time the condition of man without Christ is described.

VI
TRADITIONAL TEACHING OF POPES AND COUNCILS

Pope St. Leo the Great

Toward the middle of the fifth century, on the eve of the Council of Chalcedon, the *Tome* which Pope St. Leo the Great addressed to Flavian specified one purpose of the economy of salvation by speaking of Christ's victory over death and over the devil who, according to the Letter to the Hebrews, was prince of death.[98]

Councils of Florence and Trent

Later, when the Council of Florence spoke of the redemption, it portrayed it in biblical terms as a liberation from the domination of Satan.[99] The Council of Trent, summing up the teaching of St. Paul, asserted that sinful man is "under the power of the devil and of death."[100] In saving us, God "has rescued us from the power of darkness and transferred us into the kingdom of his beloved Son, in whom we have redemption and remission of sins,"[101] while those who sin after baptism "have given themselves over to...the power of the devil."[102]

This is, in fact, the primitive and universal faith of the Church as attested from the first centuries in the liturgy of Christian initiation. Here, just before the baptism, the catechumens renounce Satan, profess their faith in the Blessed Trinity and dedicate themselves to Christ their Saviour.[103]

It was with this traditional teaching in mind that the Second Vatican Council, being more concerned with the present life of the Church than with the doctrine of creation, did not fail to warn us against the activity of Satan and the demons. Vatican II, like the Councils of Florence and Trent before it, has once again proclaimed with the Apostle that Christ came to "rescue" us "from the power of darkness."[104] Using the Scriptural language of St. Paul and the Apocalypse, the conciliar Constitution on the Church in the World of Today says that "a monumental struggle against the powers of darkness pervades the whole history of man. The battle was joined in the very beginning of the world and will continue until the last day, as the Lord has said."[105]

Elsewhere Vatican II renews the warning issued by the Letter to the Ephesians that we must "put on the armor of God so that you may be able to stand firm against the tactics of the devil."[106] For, as this same document reminds the laity, "our battle is not against human forces but against the principalities and powers, the rulers of this world of darkness, the evil spirits in regions above."[107]

We are not surprised, finally, to see that when the Council wishes to present the Church as God's kingdom that has already begun, it appeals to the miracles of Jesus and specifically to his exorcisms.[108] For, it was precisely with reference to exorcisms that Jesus made the well-known statement: "The reign of God is upon you."[109]

The liturgy, to which we have already had occasion to refer, offers an especially valuable witness, since the liturgy is the concrete expression of the faith as it is actually lived. We should not ask the liturgy, however, to satisfy our curiosity about the nature, categories and names of the demons. The function of the liturgy in this area is simply to emphasize the existence of demons and the danger they represent for Christians. The liturgy directly echoes New Testament teaching when it reminds us that the life of the baptized is a struggle, carried on with the grace of Christ and the strength of his Spirit, against the world, the flesh and the demonic beings.[110]

We must be careful today in using the argument from the liturgy. On the one hand, the sacramental rites of the Eastern Churches, with their accumulated wealth of detail and complicated demonology, are likely to mislead us. On the other, the documents of the Latin liturgy have often been revised in the course of the centuries. This very fact should cause us to be prudent in the conclusions we draw.

Liturgical Rites of the Past

The ancient Latin rite of public penance gave forceful expression to the action of the devil in sinners; unfortunately, these texts, though still preserved in the *Roman Pontifical,*[111] have long since fallen into disuse. Until 1972 we could also have cited the prayer in the *Recommendation of the Departing Soul to God,* which evoked the horrors of hell and the final assaults of the devil[112] but these expressive texts have now disappeared from use.

The special ministry of the exorcist, though not totally abolished, has in our time been reduced to a remotely possible service which may be rendered only at the request of the bishop[113]; in fact, there is now no rite for the conferring of this ministry. Such an attitude to exorcism evidently does not mean that priests no longer have the power to exorcize or that they may no longer use it. Since, however, the Church no longer makes exorcism a special ministry, it no longer attributes to exorcisms the important role they had in the early centuries of its life. This development must certainly be taken into account.

We must not conclude from these changes in the rites that the liturgy now shows a lessening or revision of the traditional faith. The *Roman Missal* of 1970 still bears witness to the Church's convictions regarding the activity of demons.

a) The Gospels

Now, as in the past, the liturgy for the first Sunday of Lent reminds the faithful of how the Lord Jesus overcame the tempter; the three Synoptic accounts of the incident appear successively in the Mass readings of the three-year cycle. The "Proto-Evangel" (Genesis 3, 15), with its promise of victory for the seed of the woman over the seed of the serpent, is read on the 10th Sunday of Year B and on Saturday of the Fifth Week. On the feast of the Assumption and in the Common of the Blessed Virgin we read Apocalypse 12, 1-6, on the dragon's threat to the woman who is giving birth. Mark 3, 20-35, which relates the exchange between Jesus and the Pharisees concerning Beelzebul, is another of the readings for the 10th Sunday of Year B.

The parable of the wheat and the weeds (Matthew 13, 23-43) is read on the 15th Sunday of the Year A, and the explanation of the parable (Matthew 13, 36-46) on Wednesday of the 13th Week. The promise that the prince of this world will be defeated (John 12, 20-33) is read on the Fifth Sunday of Lent (Year B), and John 14, 30 during the following week.

b) The Apostolic Letters

Among readings from the Apostles, Ephesians 2, 1-10, is assigned to Monday of the 29th Week; Ephesians 6, 10-20, to the Common of the Saints and to Thursday of the 13th Week. 1 John 3, 7-10, is read on January 4, while the feast of St. Mark has the passage from the First Letter of Peter which speaks of the devil circling his prey as he prepares to devour it.

Many more passages would have to be cited if we wanted a complete list but the examples given show that the most important Scriptural texts on the devil are still part of the Church's official lectionary.

The Sacramental Rites

a) Rite of Christian Initiation of Adults

It is true enough that the rite of Christian initiation of adults has been altered and no longer addresses commands to the devil. It achieves the same purpose, however, by turning to God in prayer.[114] The language is now less striking but it is nonetheless expressive and effective. Consequently, it is an error to claim that exorcisms have been eliminated from the new ritual for Baptism. The error is, in fact, perfectly obvious, since the new rite for the catechumenate has even introduced hitherto unknown "minor" exorcisms throughout the period of the catechumenate, before the "major" exorcisms.[115]

b) Exorcisms in the Baptismal Rite

The exorcisms remain, then. Now, as in the past, they ask for victory over "Satan," "the devil," "the prince of this world" and "the power of darkness," while the three traditional "scrutinies," during which the exorcisms take place, as in the past, have the negative and positive aims they always had: To free the catechumens from sin and the devil, and, at the same time, to strengthen them in Christ.[116] The rite of infant Baptism, too, whatever people may think, still has an exorcism.[117] This does not mean that the Church considers these children to be possessed by Satan: the Church does, however, believe that they, too, need all the effects of the redemption wrought by Christ. Before baptism, every man, child or adult, bears the mark of sin and Satan's action.

c) Liturgy of Penance

The liturgy of private Penance has less to say of the devil today than in the past. On the other hand, communal penance services have brought back an old prayer which mentions the influence of Satan on sinners.[118]

d) Liturgy of the Sick

In the ritual of the sick, as we have already pointed out, the prayer in the *Recommendation of the Departing Soul to God* no longer emphasizes the disquieting presence of Satan. In the course of the anointing, however, the celebrant prays that the sick person "be freed from sin and every temptation."[119] The sacred oil is regarded as a "protection for body, soul, and spirit,"[120] and the prayer *Commendo te,* without mentioning hell and the devil, indirectly refers to their existence and action when it asks Christ to save the dying person and number him or her among "his" sheep and "his" chosen ones. The language used is evidently intended to avoid upsetting the sick person and his family but it derives nevertheless from faith in the mystery of evil.

VII
CONCLUSION

The Existence of Satan Is a Matter of Faith

To sum up: The position of the Catholic Church on demons is clear and firm. The existence of Satan and the demons has indeed never been the object of an explicit affirmation by the magisterium but this is because the question was never put in those terms. Heretics and faithful alike, on the basis of Scripture, were in agreement on the existence and chief misdeeds of Satan and his demons.

For this reason, when doubt is thrown these days on the reality of the devil we must, as we observed earlier, look to the constant and universal faith of the Church and to its chief source, the teaching of Christ. It is in the teaching of the Gospel and in the heart of the faith as lived that the existence of the world of demons is revealed as a dogma. The contemporary disaffection which we criticized at the beginning of this essay is, therefore, not simply a challenge to a secondary element of Christian thought but a direct denial of the constant faith of the Church, its way of conceiving redemption, and (at the source of both of these) the very consciousness of Jesus himself.

Therefore, when speaking recently of evil as this "terrible reality, mysterious and frightening," His Holiness Paul VI could assert with authority: "It is a departure from the picture provided by biblical and Church teaching to refuse to acknowledge the Devil's existence; to regard him as a self-sustaining principle who, unlike other creatures, does not owe his origin to God; or to explain the Devil as a pseudo-reality, a conceptual and fanciful personification of the unknown causes of our misfortunes."[121] Exegetes and theologians should not be deaf to this warning.

Neither Dualism nor Rationalist Reduction

We repeat, therefore that, though still emphasizing in our day the real existence of the demonic, the Church has no intention either of taking us back to the dualist and Manichaean speculations of the past or of proposing an alternative explanation more acceptable to reason. Its desire is simply to remain faithful to the Gospel and its requirements.

Men Are Responsible for the Evil They Do

The Church has evidently never allowed men to shrug off their own responsibility by blaming their sins on the devil. It has not hesitated to speak out against such an evasion when it appears; with Chrysostom it has said: "It is not the devil but men's own carelessness that is responsible for all their falls and for all the misfortunes they lament."[122]

In this area, Christian teaching with its energetic defence of man's liberty and dignity and its emphasis on the omnipotence and goodness of the Creator refuses to yield ground. It has condemned in the past, and will always condemn, any excessive readiness of man to excuse himself on the grounds that the devil tempted him. It has proscribed both superstition and magic; it has rejected every doctrinal capitulation to fatalism and every abdication of liberty in the face of violence.

Critical Attitude to Claims of Diabolical Intervention

In speaking, moreover, of a possible diabolical intervention, the Church always takes a critical stance, as it does in speaking of a possible miracle. In all these matters the Church asks for reserve and prudence. And, in fact, it is easy to fall victim to imagination and to let oneself be led astray by reports that are inaccurate, poorly transmitted or tendentiously interpreted. In these, as in other cases, discernment must be exercised and room left for investigation and its results.

Yet the Devil Is Real and to be Feared

All these considerations notwithstanding, the Church is simply being faithful to the example of Christ when it asserts that the warning of St. Peter to be "sober" and alert is always relevant.[123] In our day, we must indeed defend ourselves against a new "intoxication" with Satan. But technical knowledge and power, too, can intoxicate! Man today is proud of his discoveries, and often with good reason. But, in the area we are here discussing, is it certain that man's penetrating analyses have explained all the phenomena that characteristically manifest the presence of the devil? Is there nothing problematic left in this area? Have exegesis and the study of the Fathers solved all the difficulties that lurk in the texts? Nothing is less certain!

Modern Man Can be Naive

In other periods of history, men were certainly somewhat naive in expecting to meet one or other demon at the crossroads of their minds. But would it not be just as naive today to assume that our methods have enabled us to say the last word about those deep places of the mind where the relations between soul and body, between the supernatural, the preternatural and the human, and between revelation and reason all intertwine? These matters have always been regarded as vast and complicated. Our contemporary methods, like those of earlier generations, have insurmountable limitations. Modesty, which, after all, is a characteristic of true intelligence, must always have a place and help us keep to the right path. This virtue takes account of the future and enables the Christian to make room for the contribution of revelation, or, to put it in a single word, for faith.

The Importance of Faith

It is, in fact, to faith that St. Peter the Apostle appeals when he urges us to resist the devil as men "solid in your faith." Faith tells us that evil is "a living, spiritual being that is perverted and perverts others."[124] Faith is also a source of confidence, for it assures us that the devil's power must stop at boundaries set for him by God. It assures us, in addition, that while the devil is able to tempt, he cannot extort our consent. Most of all, faith opens the heart to prayer, wherein it finds its triumph and crown, for prayer wins for us the victory over evil, thanks to God's grace.

Evil Is a Mystery

It is certain that the reality of the devil, as concretely attested by what we call the mystery of evil, is today, as always, an enigma surrounding the Christian's life. We are little wiser than the Apostles as to why the Lord permits it and how he makes it serve his purposes. Yet, it may be that in our civilization, which is so secularized and so focused on the horizontal plane of man's life, unexpected manifestations of this mystery have a meaning not impossible to ascertain. For, such manifestations oblige us to look further and higher, beyond immediate evidences. The insolent threats with which evil darkens our path enable us to glimpse the existence of a beyond which challenges us to understand it and then turn to Christ so that we may hear from him the Good News of the salvation he graciously offers us.

---

*The Sacred Congregation for the Doctrine of the Faith commissioned an unnamed expert to prepare this French-language study, which it strongly recommends as a sure basis for grasping the teaching of the magisterium on "Christian Faith and Demonology." Italian text in L'Osservatore Romano, June 26, 1975. Translation courtesy of The Pope Speaks.
1. The firm stand of the Church with regard to superstition can be explained in part by the severity of the Mosaic Law, even if the latter was not formally motivated by the link between superstition and demons. *Ex 22*, 17, for example, without any explanation, decrees the death penalty for the practice of sorcery. *Lv 19*, 26 and 31 prohibits soothsaying, astrology, necromancy, and divination, and *Lv 20*, 27 adds the

conjuring up of spirits. *Dt* 18, 10 proscribes diviners, fortune-tellers, soothsayers, charmers, spell-casters, those who consult ghosts and spirits, and those who seek oracles from the dead. — In Europe during the early Middle Ages many pagan superstitions were still alive, as is clear from the sermons of St. Caesarius of Arles and St. Eligius, Martin of Braga's *De correctione rusticorum,* the contemporary lists of superstitions (see, e.g., the Concilium Leptinense of 743 in *PL* 89, 810-818), and the penitential books. The Council of Toledo (in Denzinger-Schönmetzer, *Enchiridion symbolorum, definitonum et declarationnum de rebus fidei et morum,* 32nd ed. [Rome, 1963], no. 205; henceforth *DS*) and later the Council of Braga (*DS*, no. 459) condemned astrology, as did Pope St. Leo the Great in his letter to Bishop Turibius of Astorga (*DS*, no. 483). The Council of Trent's Ninth Rule on the prohibition of books banned works on cheiromancy, necromancy, etc. (*DS*, no. 1859). Magic and sorcery have been the occasion for a few papal Bulls (Innocent VIII, Leo X, Hadrian VI, Gregory XV, Urban VIII) and many decrees of regional councils. On magnetism and spiritism, see especially the Letter of the Holy Office. August 4, 1856 (*DS*, nos. 283-285).

2. St. John Chrysostom, *De diabolo tentatore homilia,* 1: *Pg* 49, 257-258.

3. *Acts* 23, 8. Given the Jewish beliefs in angels and evil spirits, nothing obliges us to limit the generic term "spirits" in *Acts* 23, 8 to the spirits of the dead; it also refers to evil spirits, or demons. This is the view of two Jewish writers (G. F. Moore, *Judaism in the First Centuries of the Christian Era* [Cambridge, 1927], 1:68; M. Simon, *Les sectes juives au temps de Jesus* [Paris, 1960], p. 25), and a Protestant (R. Meyer, "Saddoukaios," *Theological Directory of the New Testament* 7:54).

4. When Jesus said, "Do not think that I have come to abolish the law and the prophets. I have come, not to abolish them, but to fulfill them" (*Mt* 5, 17), he clearly showed his respect for the past; the next verses (18-19) confirm this interpretation. On the other hand, his condemnation of divorce (*Mt* 5, 31), the law of retaliation (5, 38), etc., illustrate his complete independence as opposed to any desire simply to take over and complete the past. The same can be said, with even greater reason, of his condemnation of the Pharisees' exaggerated attachment to ancestral tradition (*Mk* 7, 1-22).

5. *Mt* 8, 28-34; 12, 22-45. Even if we admit variations in the meaning each Synoptic writer assigns to the exorcisms, we must also recognize the extensive convergence between them.

6. *Mk* 1, 12-13.

7. See *Mt* 5, 37; 6, 13; and Jean Carmagnac, *Recherches sur le "Notre Pere"* (Paris, 1969), pp. 305-319. This is also the interpretation of the Greek Fathers generally and of some Western writers (Tertullian, St. Ambrose, Cassian). But St. Augustine and the *Libera nos* prayer of the Roman Mass led to an impersonal interpretation of the phrase.

8. See E. Renaudot, *Liturgiarum Orientalium collectio 2* (Paris, 1716); H. Denzinger, *Ritus Orientalium* (2nd ed., 1961), 2:436. This also seems to be the interpretation followed by Pope Paul VI in an address to a general audience November 15, 1972, since he speaks there of "evil" as a living, spiritual principle; cf. *Osservatore Romano,* November 16, 1972 [*TPS* XVII, 316].

9. See *Mt* 13, 19.

10. See *Mt* 13, 39.

11. *Mt* 16, 18 as understood by J. Jöuon, M.-J. Lagrange, A. Médebielle, D. Buzy, M. Meinertz, W. Trilling, J. Jeremias, and others, It is incomprehensible, then, that anyone today should neglect *Mt* 16, 18 and concentrate solely on 16, 23.

12. See *Lk* 22, 31.

13. *Jn* 14, 30.

14. *Lk* 22, 53; see *Lk* 22, 3. The latter verse suggests, as the exegetes have recognized, that the evangelist understands this "power of darkness" to be a personal being.

15. *Jn* 16, 11.

16. See *Eph* 2, 1-2: *2 Thes* 2, 11; *2 Cor* 4, 4.

17. *Rom* 7, 23; see *Gal* 5, 17.

18. See *Eph* 6, 11-16.

19. See *Eph* 4, 27; *1 Cor* 7, 5.

20. See *Rom* 16, 20.

21. *2 Cor* 4, 4.

22. *2 Thes* 2, 7. [The words are translated "mystery of iniquity" in older versions of the New Testament.]

23. See *2 Cor* 4, 4, a passage invoked by Paul VI in the allocution already mentioned in note 8, above [*TPS* SVII, 317].

24. See *1 Cor* 10, 19-20; *Rom* 1, 21-22. This is the interpretation of the passage that is adopted in Vatican II's *Dogmatic Constitution on the Church*, no. 16: "But quite often men, deluded by the evil one, have become vain in their reasonings; they have exchanged God's truth for a lie, serving creature instead of Creator (cf. *Rom* 1, 21-25)" [*TPS* X, 370].

25. See *2 Cor* 11, 3.

26. See *2 Thes* 2, 3-4, 9-11.

27. See *Apoc* 12, 9.

28. *Jn* 12, 31; 14, 30; 16, 11.

29. *Jn* 8, 34.

30. See *Jn* 8, 38, 44.

31. *Jn* 8, 44.

32. *Jn* 8, 41.

33. *Ibid.*

34. *Jn* 8, 38-44.

35. See Johannes Quasten, *Patrology* 1 (Westminster, Md., 1951), p. 246.

36. *Adversus Haereses* V, 24, 3: *PG* 7, 1188A.

37. *Adversus Haereses* V, 21, 2: *PG* 7, 1179C-1180A.

38. *De civitate Dei* XI, 9: *PL* 41, 323-325.

39. *De Genesi ad litteram* XI, 24, 31: *PL* 34, 441-442.

40. *Moralia in Job* XXIII, 17, 33: *PL* 76, 694; XXIII, 28, 49: col. 705; XXIV, 4, 8: col. 722.

41. *Adversus haereses* IV, 11, 3: *PG* 7, 113C.

42. *De praescriptionibus,* 40; *PL* 2, 54; *De ieiuniis,* 16: *PL* 2, 977.

43. The Latin text is given in *Conciliorum Oecumenicorum Decreta* [henceforth, *COD*], edited by Joseph Alberigo *et al.* (3rd ed.; Bologna, 1973), p. 230, and in *DS,* no. 800. The translation is from *The Church Teaches,* translated by John F. Clarkson *et al.* (St. Louis, 1955), no. 306, p. 132. The Latin text is as follows: "Firmiter credimus et simpliciter confitemur . . . unum universorum principium, creator omnium invisibilium et visibilium, spiritualium et corporalium, qui sua omnipotenti virtute simul ab initio temporis, utramque de nihilo condidit creaturam, spiritualem et corporalem, angelicam scilicet et mundanam,

ac deinde humanam quasi communem ex spiritu et corpore constitutam. Diabolus enim et daemones alii a Deo quidem natura creati sunt boni, sed ipse per se facti sunt mali. Homo vero diaboli suggestione peccavit."

44. The first profession, chronlogically, was that formulated by the Synod of Lyons (1179-1181) and pronounced by Waldo (edited by A. Dondaine in *Archivum Fratum Praedicatorum* 16 [1946] 231 ff.); then came the profession required of Durandus of Huesca before the bishop of Tarragona in 1208 (*PL* 215, 1510–1513); finally, there was the profession made by Bernadus Primus in 1210 (*PL* 216, 289-292). The three professions are collated in *DS*, nos. 790-797.

45. At the Council of Braga, Portugal, in 560-563 (*DS*, nos. 451-464).

46. *Phil* 2, 10.

47. *Eph* 1, 21.

48. *Col* 1, 16.

49. *COD*, pp. 5 and 24; *DS*, nos. 125 and 150.

50. *DS*, no. 188.

51. For Jerusalem, see *DS*, no. 41; for Cyprus (testimony of St. Epiphanius of Salamis), see *DS*, no. 44; for Alexandria, *DS*, no. 46; for Antioch, *DS*, no. 50; for Armenia, *DS*, no. 48; etc.

52. See *Prex Eucharistica* [henceforth *PE*], edited by A. Hänggi and I. Pahl (Fribourg, 1968), p. 244.

53. See *PE*, pp. 232 and 348.

54. See *PE*, pp. 327, 332, 382.

55. *Adversus haereses* II, 30, 6; *PG* 7, 818B.

56. *PG* 25, 199-200.

57. *De fide orthodoxa adversus Arianos,* among the works attributed to St. Ambrose (*PL* 17, 549) and to St. Phoebadius (*PL* 20, 49).

58. *De Genesi ad litteram liber imperfectus,* 1, 1-2: *PL* 34, 221.

59. *De fide liber unus,* 3, 25: *PL* 65, 683.

60. This profession of faith subscribed to by Emperor Michael Paleologus and preserved by Hardouin and Mansi in the Acts of this Council, is readily accessible in *DS*, no. 851. *COD* omits it without giving a reason (at Vatican I the official expositor invoked it; see Mansi, *Sacrorum conciliorum nova et amplissima collectio* [reprint and continuation; Paris, 1899-1927], 52:1113B).

61. Session IX: *Bulla unionis Coptorum Aethiopumque* (*COD*, p. 571; *DS*, no. 1333).

62. *DS*, no. 1862 (not in *COD*).

63. Session III: *Constitutio dogmatica de fide catholica, (Dei Filius),* chapter 1 (*COD*, pp. 805-806; *DS*, no. 3002).

64. Mani, founder of the sect, lived in the third century of the Christian era. Beginning in the next century, the Fathers opposed Manichaeism: St. Epiphanius gave a lengthy exposition and refutation (*Haereses,* 66: *PG* 42, 29-172); St. Athanasius spoke of it in passing (*Oratio contra gentes,* 2: *PG* 25, 66); St. Basil wrote a little treatise entitled *Quod Deus non sit autor malorum* (*PG* 31, 330-354); Didymus of Alexandria composed a *Contra haereticos* (*PG* 39, 1085-1110). In the West, St. Augustine, who in his youth had accepted Manichaeism, fought it systematically after his conversion (cf. *PL* 42).

65. *Oratio* 40: *In sanctum Baptisma,* 45: *PG* 36, 424A.

65a. See *Jn* 8, 44.

66. The Fathers thus interpreted *Is* 14, 14, and *Ez* 28, 2, where the prophets were condemning the pride of the pagan kings of Babylon and Tyre.

67. "Do not tell me the devil was always evil! No, in the beginning he was without evil; evil is a supervenient qualification of his being, and was incurred at a later point" (St. John Chrysostom, *De diabolo tentatore homilia*, 2: *PG* 49, 260).

68. *Quod Deus non sit auctor malorum*, 8: *PG* 31, 345CD.

69. *Oratio* 38: *In Theophania*, 10: *PG* 36, 320A; *Oratio* 45: *In sanctum Pascha*: *PG* 36, 629B.

70. See above, note 67.

71. *Contra Manichaeos*, 16: *PG* 39, 1105C, where he thus interprets *Jn* 8, 44 ("in veritate non stetis"); see *Enarratio in Epistolam B. Judae*, on verse 9: *PG* 39, 1814C-1815B.

72. *Adversus Marcionem* II, 22: *PL* 2, 269-298.

73. See, in the next paragraph of the text, the first canon of Eusebius in his *De Trinitate*.

74. *Apologia phropetae David* I, 4: *PL* 14, 853CD; *In Psalmum 118, Sermo* 12, 10: *PL* 15, 1363D.

75. *De Genesi ad litteram* XI, 20-21, 27-28: *PL* 34, 439-440.

76. "Si quis confitetus angelum apostaticum in natura, qua factus est, non a Deo factum fuisse, sed ab se esse, ut de se illi principium habere adsignet, anathema sit.

"Si quis confitetus angelum apostaticum in mala natura a Deo factum fuisse et non dixerit eum per voluntatem suam malum concepisse, anathema illi.

"Si quis confitetur angelum Satanae mundum fecisse, quod absit, et non indicaverit [iudicaverit] omne peccatum per ipsum adinventum fuisse" (*De Trinitate* VI, 17, 1-3, edited by V. Bulhart; *CCL* 9, 89-90; *PL* 62, 280-281).

77. *Commonitorium de recipiendis Manichaeis qui convertuntur:* *CSEL* 25/2, 977-982; *PL* 42, 1153-1156.

78. *De Genesi ad litteram liber imperfectus*, 1, 1-2: *PL* 34, 221.

79. *DS*, no. 188.

80. That is, the sixth point in the memorial sent to the Pope by his correspondent, the bishop of Astorga.

81. "Sexta annotatio indicat eos dicere quod diabolus numquam fuerit bonus, nec natura eius opificium Dei sit, sed eum ex chao et tenebris emersisse: quia scilicet nullum sui habeat auctorem, sed omnis mali ipse sit principium atque substantia: cum fides vera, quae est catholica, omnium creaturarum sive spiritualium, sive corporalium bonam confiteatur substantiam, et mali nullam esse naturam: quia Deus, qui universitatis est conditor, nihil non bonum fecisse. Unde et diabolus bonus esset, si in eo quod factus est permaneret. Sed quia naturali excellentia male usus est, et in veritate non stetit (Ioan. VIII, 44), non in contrariam transiit substantiam, sed a summo bono, cui debuit adhaerere, descivit" (*Epist*. 15, 6: *PL* 54, 683; the critical text edited by B. Vollman, O.S.B., varies only in punctuation).

82. "Cap. IX: Fides vera, quae est catholica, omnium creaturarum sive spiritualium, sive corporalium bonam confiteatur substantiam, et mali nullam esse naturam: quia Deus, qui universitatis est conditor, nihil non bonum fecit. Unde et diabolus bonus esset, si in eo quod factus est permaneret. Sed quia naturali excellantia male usus est, et in veritate non stetit, non in contrariam substantiam transiit, sed a summo bono, cui debuit adhaerere, discessit" (*De ecclesiasticis dogmatibus*: *PL* 58, 995CD). But the original recension of this work, published in the appendix to the works of St. Augustine, lacks this chapter (see *PL* 42, 1213-1222).

83. *De fide seu de regula fidei ad Petrum liber unus: PL* 65, 671-706. See "Principaliter tene," 3, 25 (col. 683A); "Firmissime tene," 4, 45 (col. 694C); "Pars itaque angelorum quae a suo creatore Deo, quo solo bono beata fuit, voluntaria prorsus aversione discessit," 3, 31 (col. 687A); "nullamque esse mali naturam." 21, 62 (col. 689D-700A).

84. Edited by Charles Munier, in *Concilia Gallica [314-506],* in *CCL* 148, p. 165, lines 25-26; also in Appendix to *Ordo Romanus XXXIV,* in M. Andrieu, *Ordines Romani* 3 (Louvain, 1961), p. 616.

85. *PL* 215, 1512D; also edited by A. Dondaine, in *Archivum Fratrum Praedicatorum* 16 (1946) 232; *DS,* no. 797.

86. *DS,* no. 457.

87. See above, note 44.

88. *PL* 204, 1235-1272. See E. Delaruelle, "Ermengaud de Béziers," *Dictionnaire d'Histoire et de Géographie Ecclésiastiques,* 15, 754-757.

89. *PL* 204, 775-792. The historical situation in Northern Italy is well described by P. Ilarino da Milano. *Le eresie medioevali (sec. XI-XV),* in *Grande Antologia Filosofica* 4 (Milan 1954), pp. 1599-1689. Ilarino da Milano has studied Bonacursus' works in his article, "La *Manifestatio heresis Catarorum quam fecit Bonacursus* secondo il cod. Ottob. lat. 136 della Biblioteca Vaticana." *Aevum* 12 (1958) 281-333.

90. "Sed primo de fide. Contra quam proponit sententiam falsitatis et iniquitatis, dicens Deum omnipotentem sola invisibilia et incorporalia creasse; diabolum vero, quem deum tenebrarum appellat, dicit visibilia et corporalia creasse. Quibis predictis addit hereticus duo esse principia rerum: unum boni, scilicet Deum omnipotentem; alterum mali, scilicet diabolum. Addit etiam duas esse naturas: unam bonam, incorporalium, a Deo omnipotente creatam; alteram malam, corporalium, a diabolo creatam. Hereticus autem qui hoc dicit antiquitas Manicheus, nunc vero Catharus appellatur" (*Summa contra haereticos,* edited by Joseph N. Garvin and James A. Corbett [Notre Dame, 1958], p. 4).

91. This treatise, first discovered and edited by Antoine Dondaine, O.P., has recently been re-edited by Christine Thouzellier, *Livre des deux principes,* with introduction, critical text, translation, notes, and indexes (*Sources chrétiennes* 198; Paris, 1973).

92. *Op. cit.,* no. 1: Thouzellier, pp. 160-161.

93. *Op. cit.,* no. 12: Thouzellier, pp. 190-191.

94. "Dominus papa, summo mane missa celebrata et omnibus episcopis per sedes suas dispositis, in eminentiorem locum cum suis kardinalibus et ministries ascendens, sancte Trinitatis fidem et singulos fidei articulos recitari fecit. Quibus recitatis quesitum est ab universis alta voce: 'Creditis haec per omnia?' Responderunt omnes: 'Credimus.' Postmodum damnati sunt omnes heretici et reprobate quorumdam sententie, Ioachim scilicet et Emelrici Parisiensis. Quibus recitatis iterum quesitum est: 'An reprobatis sententias Ioachim et Emelrici?' At illi magis invalescebant clamando: 'Reprobamus'" ("A New Eyewitness Account of the Fourth Lateran Council," edited by Stephan Kuttner and Antonio Garcia y Garcia, in *Traditio* 20 [1964] 115-178, at pp. 127-128).

95. Session VI: *Decree on Justification,* chapter 5, in *COD,* p. 672; *DS,* no. 1525.

96. Session XIII: *Decree on the Holy Eucharist,* chapter 1, in *COD,* p. 693; *DS,* nos. 1636-1637.

97. Session VI, chapter 13, in *COD,* p. 676; *DS,* no. 1541. [The reference to the number of lines is to the two texts as printed in *DS.*]

98. *DS,* no. 291. The formula "prince of death" from *Heb.* 2, 14 is used

again in Session V: *Decree on Original Sin*, chapter 1, of the Council of Trent (*COD*, p. 666; *DS*, no. 1511).

99. Session XI; *Bulla Unionis Coptorum Aethiopumque*, in *COD*, pp. 575-576; *DS*, nos. 1347-1349.

100. Session VI, chapter 1, in *COD*, p. 671; *DS*, no. 1521 (translated in *The Church Teaches*, no. 557, p. 230).

101. Session VI, chapter 3, in *COD*, p. 672; *DS*, no. 1523 (*The Church Teaches*, no. 559, p. 231).

102. Session XIV: *Decree on the Sacrament of Penance*, chapter 1, in *COD*, p. 703; *DS*, no. 1668 (*The Church Teaches*, no. 788, p. 305).

103. This part of the rite was in use as early as the third century, according to the *Tradition Apostolica* of St. Hippolytus, chapter 21 (edited by B. Botte [Münster, 1963], pp. 46-51), and in the fourth century in the liturgy described in the *Constitutions Apostolorum*, VII, 41 (edited by F. X. Funk, *Didascalia et Constitutiones Apostolorum* 1 [Tübingen, 1905]).

104. *Decree on the Missionary Activity of the Church*, nos. 3 [*TPS* XI, 411] and 14 [*TPS* XI, 421]. Note the citation, in both passages, of *Col.* 1, 13, as well as the citations from Scripture in note 33 to no. 14.

105. *Pastoral Constitution on the Church in the World of Today*, no. 37 [*TPS* XI, 281].

106. *Eph* 6, 11, cited in the *Dogmatic Constitution on the Church*, no. 48 [*TPS* X, 392].

107. *Eph* 6, 12, cited in the *Dogmatic Constitution on the Church*, no. 35 [*TPS* X 382-383].

108. *Dogmatic Constitution on the Church*, no. 5 [*TPS* X, 361].

109. *Lk* 11, 20; see *Mt* 12, 28.

110. See C. Vagaggini, O.S.B., *Il senso teologico della liturgia: Saggio di liturgia teologica generale* (4th ed.: Rome, 1965), chapter 13: "Le due città, la liturgia e la lotta contra Santana" (pp. 346-427). See also Egon von Petersdorff, "De daemonibus in liturgia memoratis" *Angelicum* 19 (1942) 324-349; *Damonologie* 1: *Dämonen im Weltplan*, and 2: *Dämonen am Werk* (Munich, 1956-1957).

111. See the *Ordo excommunicandi et absolvendi*, and especially the lengthy exhortation that begins: "Quai N. diabolo suadente," in the *Pontificale Romanum* (2nd ed; Regensburg, 1908), pp. 392-398.

112. Cf. the prayer *Commendo te*: "May you be safe from the horror of darkness, the crackling flames, the agony and torment. May Satan, the hideous one, and his cohorts flee before you."

113. This was determined in the fourth norm set down in the Motu Proprio *Ministeria quaedam* of August 15, 1972: "Two ministries adapted to the present-day needs are to be preserved in the whole Latin Church, namely, those of lector and acolyte. The functions heretofore committed to the subdeacon are entrusted to the lector and the acolyte; consequently, the major order of the subdiaconate no longer exists in the Latin Church. There is nothing, however, to prevent the acolyte being also called a subdeacon in some places, if the episcopal conference so decides" (*AAS* 64 [1972] 532 [*TPS* SVII, 260]). The office of exorcist is thus suppressed, and there is no provision that the power now associated with this office can be exercised by the lector or the acolyte. The document simply says that the episcopal conferences may ask the Apostolic See to permit the establishment in their regions of the offices of porter, exorcist, and catechist (*AAS*, p. 531 [*TPS*, p. 259]).

114. The shift to the deprecative form was made only after "ex-

periments," which were followed by reflection and discussion within the *Concilium*.

115. *Rite of Christian Initiation of Adults* (Washington, D.C., 1974), nos. 101, 109-118 (pp. 28-32).

116. *Op. cit.,* no. 25 (p. 26) and nos. 154-157 (pp. 43-44).

117. This has been true since the first edition: *Ordo Baptismi Parvulorum (editio typica:* Rome, 1969*),* no. 49 (p. 27) and no. 221 (p. 85). The only thing new is the deprecative form (*oratio exorcismi*) and the fact that it is immediately followed by the prebaptismal anointing (no. 50). The two rites, of exorcism and anointing, each have their own conclusion.

118. The new *Ordo Paenitentiae (editio typica;* Rome, 1974*)* in its second Appendix, has the prayer *Deus humani generis benignissime conditor* (pp. 85-86); apart from some slight modifications it is the same as the prayer with the the same opening words in the *Ordo Reconciliationis Poenitentium* for Holy Thursday (*Pontificale Romanum,* p. 350*)*.

119. *Ordo Unctionis Infirmorum Eorumque Pastoralis Curae* (*editio typica:* Rome, 1972), no. 73 (p. 33).

120. *Op. cit.,* no. 75 (p. 34).

121. Pope Paul VI, Address *Quali sono* (cf. note 8, above) [*TPS* SVII, 316]. The Holy Father had expressed the same uneasiness in his homily on June 29, 1872 (*Essere forti nella fede*), in *Osservatore Romano,* June 30—July 1, 1972, pp. 1-2.

122. *De diabolo tentatore homilia,* 2: *PG* 49, 259.

123. 1 *Pt* 5, 8.

124. Pope Paul VI, *ibid.*

109

DECLARATION ON CERTAIN PROBLEMS OF SEXUAL ETHICS*

S.C.D.F., *Personae humanae*, 29 December, 1975

1. The human person, present-day scientists maintain, is so profoundly affected by sexuality that it must be considered one of the principal formative influences on the life of a man or woman. In fact, sex is the source of the biological, psychological and spiritual characteristics which make a person male or female and which thus considerably influence each individual's progress towards maturity and membership of society. Sex, as everyone is aware, is a topic which nowadays is frequently and frankly discussed in books, magazines, newspapers and other media.

In the meantime, morals are becoming increasingly corrupt. One of the most ominous signs of this is the unrestrained glorification of sex. The media and the entertainment world have spread the corruption to the field of education and the mentality of the age has become infected.

In this matter, some educators and moralists have contributed to an improved understanding of the values proper to each of the sexes and thus have helped people give expression to these values in their lives. On the other hand, others have proposed opinions and patterns of behaviour which are contrary to the true moral needs of the human person. Indeed they have been paving the way for hedonism.

All this has led, in the space of a few years, to the vigorous challenging, even by Christians, of doctrines, moral criteria and patterns of behaviour which had gone unquestioned hitherto. Many people, confronted with so many opinions contrary to what the Church had taught them, nowadays wonder what truths they must still cling to.

2. The Church cannot remain indifferent to this confusion of minds and corruption of morals. It is a matter of the utmost importance both for the personal lives of Christians and for the life of society today.[1]

Bishops know from daily experience that it is becoming increasingly difficult for the faithful to obtain sound moral instruction, especially in sexual matters, and that pastors are finding it increasingly difficult to expound moral doctrine effectively. Bishops know well that their pastoral office obliges them to meet the needs of the faithful in this important regard. Some of them have published important documents on the matter and so have episcopal conferences. However, false opinions and the immoral conduct to which they lead have continued to spread. Consequently, the Sacred Congregation for the Doctrine of the Faith judged it necessary to publish this declaration, in view of its function in the universal Church[2] and at the behest of the Supreme Pontiff.

3. Nowadays people are increasingly convinced that man's dignity and destiny, and indeed his development, demand that they should apply their intelligence to the discovery and constant development of the values inherent in human nature and should give practical effect to them in their lives.

However, man may not make moral judgments arbitrarily: 'Deep within his conscience man discovers a law which he has not laid upon himself, but which he must obey. . .For man has in his heart a law inscribed by God. His dignity lies in observing this law and by it he will be judged.'[3]

Moreover, God has revealed his plan of salvation to us Christians and has held up to us the teaching and example of Christ, the Saviour and Sanctifier, as the supreme and unchangeable law of life. Christ said: 'I am the light of the world. No follower of mine shall wander in the dark; he shall have the light of life.'[4]

Therefore, man's true dignity cannot be achieved unless the essential order of his nature be observed. It must, of course, be recognized that in the course of history civilization has taken many forms, that the requirements for human living have changed considerably and that many changes are still to come. But limits must be set to the evolution of mores and life-styles, limits set by the unchangeable principles based on the elements that go to make up the human person and on his essential relationships. Such things transcend historical circumstances.

These fundamental principles, which can be perceived by human reason, are contained in 'the divine law itself—eternal, objective and universal, by which God orders, directs and governs the whole world and the ways of the human community according to a plan conceived in his wisdom and love. God has enabled man to participate in this law of his so that, under the gentle disposition of his divine providence, many may be able to arrive at a deeper and deeper knowledge of the unchanging truth.'⁵ This divine law is accessible to our minds.

4. Consequently, it is wrong to assert as many do today that neither human nature nor revealed law provide any absolute and unchangeable norms as a guide for individual actions, that all they offer is the general law of charity and respect for the human person. Proponents of this view allege in its support that the norms of the natural law, as they are called, and the precepts of sacred scripture are to be seen rather as patterns of behaviour found in particular cultures at given moments of history.

Since revelation and, in its own sphere, philosophy have to do with the deepest needs of mankind, they inevitably at the same time reveal the unchangeable laws inscribed in man's nature and which are identical in all rational beings.

The Church was founded by Christ as 'the pillar and bulwark of the truth.'⁶ It preserves without ceasing and transmits without error the truths of the moral order. It interprets authentically both revealed positive law and 'the principles of the moral order which spring from human nature itself'⁷ and which relate to man's full development and sanctification. Throughout its history the Church has always held a certain number of precepts of the natural law to be absolute and unchangeable and in its eyes to disobey them is to go against the teaching and spirit of the gospel.

5. Since sexual ethics have to do with certain fundamental values of human and Christian life, this general teaching applies equally to sexual ethics. There are principles and norms in sexual ethics which the Church has always proclaimed as part of her teaching and has never had any doubt about it, however much the opinions and mores of the world opposed them. These principles and norms in no way owe their origin to a particular culture, but rather to knowledge of the divine law and of human nature. They do not therefore cease to oblige or become doubtful because cultural changes take place.

These are the principles on which the Second Council of the Vatican based its suggestions and directives for the establishment and the organization of a social order in which due account would be taken of the equal dignity of men and women, while respecting the difference between them.⁸

In speaking of 'man's sexuality and the faculty of reproduction,' the Council noted that they 'wondrously surpassed the endowments of lower forms of life'.⁹ It then dealt one by one with the principles and rules which relate to human sexuality in marriage and which are based on the specific purpose of sexuality.

With regard to the matter in hand, the Council declares that when assessing the propriety of conjugal acts, determining if they accord with true human dignity, 'it is not enough to take only the good intention and the evaluation of motives into account. Objective criteria must be used, criteria based on the nature of the human person and of human action, criteria which respect the total meaning of mutual self-giving and human procreation in the context of true love.'[10]

This last quotation summarizes the Council's teaching on the finality of the sexual act and on the principal criterion of its morality: when the finality of the act is respected the moral goodness of the act is ensured. This teaching is explained in greater detail in the same Constitution.[11]

This same principle, which the Church derives from divine revelation and from its authentic interpretation of the natural law, is at the core of its traditional teaching that only in legitimate marriage does the use of the sexual faculty find its true meaning and its probity.[12]

6. It is not the intention of this declaration to deal with all abuses of sex, nor with all that is involved in the cultivation of chastity. Its object is rather to re-state the Church's norms with regard to certain points of doctrine. It would seem that it has become a matter of urgent necessity to oppose the grave errors and depraved conduct which are now widespread.

7. Nowadays many claim the right to sexual intercourse before marriage, at least for those who have a firm intention of marrying and whose love for one another, already conjugal as it were, is deemed to demand this as its natural outcome. This argument is put with particular insistence when the celebration of marriage is impeded by external circumstances or when this intimate relationship is judged necessary for the preservation of love.

This opinion is contrary to Christian teaching, which asserts that sexual intercourse may take place only within marriage. No matter how definite the intention of those who indulge in pre-marital sex, the fact is that such liaisons can scarcely ensure mutual sincerity and fidelity in a relationship between a man and a woman, nor, especially, can they protect it from inconstancy of desires or whim. Jesus willed that such a union be stable and he restored it to its original condition, based on the difference between the sexes: 'Have you not read that the creator from the beginning made them male and female and that he said: "This is why a man must leave father and mother, and cling to his wife, and the two become one body. They are no longer two, therefore, but one body. So then, what God has united, man must not divide".[13] St Paul was more explicit, when he taught that if the unmarried or widows are unable to remain continent they have no alternative but to marry: 'Better be married than burn with vain desire.'[14] In marriage the love of a couple for each other becomes part of Christ's unfailing love for the Church.[15] An incontinent union of bodies defiles the temple of the Holy Spirit which the Christian himself has become.[16] Sexual intercourse is not lawful, therefore, save between a man and a woman who have embarked upon a permanent, life-long partnership.

The Church has always understood this and taught it[17] and has found the fullest confirmation of its teaching in natural philosophy and the testimony of history.

Experience teaches that love must be protected by the stability of marriage if sexual intercourse is really to meet the demands of its own finality and of human dignity. For this to be achieved there is need of a contract sanctioned and protected by society. The marriage contract inaugurates a state of life which is of the greatest importance. It makes possible a union between husband and wife that is exclusive and it promotes the good of their family and of the whole of human society. In fact, pre-marital liaisons very often exclude the expectation of a family. The love which, wrongly, is portrayed as conjugal will not be able to develop into paternal and maternal love, as it certainly should. Or, if children are born to partners in such a union it will be to their detriment. They will be deprived of a stable family-life in which to grow up properly and through which to find their place in the community.

Those who wish to be united in matrimony should, therefore, manifest their consent externally and in a manner which the community accepts as valid. The faithful, for their part, should declare their consent to marry in the way prescribed by the laws of the Church. This makes their marriage one of Christ's sacraments.

8. In our day there are those who, relying on the findings of psychology, have begun to judge homosexual relationships indulgently and even to excuse them completely. This goes against the constant teaching of the Magisterium and the moral sense of the Christian people.

They draw a distinction, not without reason, between two kinds of homosexuals. The first kind consists of homosexuals whose condition is temporary or at least is not incurable. It can be due to a faulty education, a lack of normal sexual development, to habit or bad example or other similar causes. The second type consists of homosexuals whose condition is permanent and who are such because of some kind of innate impulse or because of a constitutional defect presumed to be incurable.

Many argue that the condition of the second type of homosexuals is so natural that it justifies homosexual relations for them, in the context of a genuine partnership in life and love analogous to marriage, and granted that they feel quite incapable of leading solitary lives.

Certainly, pastoral care of such homosexuals should be considerate and kind. The hope should be instilled in them of one day overcoming their difficulties and their alienation from society. Their culpability will be judged prudently. However, it is not permissible to employ any pastoral method or theory to provide moral justification for their actions, on the grounds that they are in keeping with their condition. Sexual relations between persons of the same sex are necessarily and essentially disordered according to the objective moral order. Sacred scripture condemns them as gravely depraved and even portrays them as the tragic consequence of rejecting God.[18] Of course, the judgment of sacred scripture does not imply that all who suffer from this deformity are by that very fact guilty of personal fault. But it does show that homosexual acts are intrinsically disordered and may never be approved in any way whatever.

9. The traditional teaching of the Catholic Church that masturbation is gravely sinful is frequently doubted nowadays if not expressly denied. It is claimed that psychology and sociology show that, especially in adolescents, it is a normal concomitant of growth towards sexual maturity and that for this reason no grave fault is involved. The only exception is when a person deliberately indulges in solitary pleasure focussed exclusively on self (*ipsatio*), since such an action would be totally opposed to that loving partnership between persons of opposite sexes which, indeed, they claim to be the principal object of sexual activity.

The opinion, however, is contrary to both the teaching and the pastoral practice of the Church. Whatever force there may be in certain biological and philosophical arguments put forward from time to time by theologians, the fact remains that both the magisterium of the Church, in the course of a constant tradition, and the moral sense of the faithful have been in no doubt and have firmly maintained that masturbation is an intrinsically and gravely disordered action.[19] The principal argument in support of this truth is that the deliberate use of the sexual faculty, for whatever reason, outside of marriage is essentially contrary to its purpose. For it lacks that sexual relationship demanded by the moral order and in which 'the total meaning of mutual self-giving and human procreation in the context of true love'[20] is achieved. All deliberate sexual activity must therefore be referred to the married state. Although it cannot be established that sacred scripture condemned masturbation by name, the tradition of the Church has rightly taken it to have been condemned by the New Testament when it speaks of 'uncleanness' and 'unchastity' and other vices contrary to chastity and continence.

Sociological investigations can disclose the incidence of masturbation in this or that region, among this or that people, in any circumstances of time or place that are chosen for investigation. That is how facts are collected. But facts do not furnish a rule for judging the morality of human acts.[21] The incidence is linked, it is true, with the weakness implanted in man by original sin. But it is also linked with the loss of the sense of God, with the corruption of morals caused by the commercialization of vice, with the unrestrained licence of so many public entertainments and publications, with the neglect of modesty, which is the guardian of chastity.

Modern psychology has much that is valid and useful to offer on the subject of masturbation. It is helpful for gauging moral responsibility more accurately and for directing pastoral activity along the right lines. It can enable one to understand how adolescent immaturity, which sometimes outlasts adolescence, the lack of psychological balance and ingrained habit can influence a person's behaviour, diminishing his responsibility for his actions, with the result that he is not always guilty of subjectively grave fault. But the absence of grave responsibility must not always be presumed. If it were it would scarcely be a recognition of men's ability to behave morally.

In the pastoral ministry itself, when there is a question of reaching a sound judgment on an individual case, the habitual general conduct of the person concerned should be taken into account, not only the practice of justice and charity but also the care given to the observance of the special precept of chastity. In particular, one should ascertain whether necessary natural and supernatural helps are being used which age-long Christian ascetical experience recommends for curbing passion and making progress in virtue.

10. There is nowadays a considerable threat to the observance of the moral law on sexual matters and to the practice of chastity, especially among less fervent Christians. The threat is posed by the current tendency to minimise the reality of grave sin as much

as possible, at least in the concrete, and even at times to deny its existence altogether. Some have gone on to assert that mortal sin, which separated man from God, is to be found only in the direct and formal refusal of God's call, or when a person deliberately chooses self-love, to the total exclusion of the neighbour. They say that only then is there question of a 'fundamental option'—that is, a decision of the will which involves the person totally and without which there is no mortal sin. For it is by this option that from the depths of his personality a man adopts or ratifies a fundamental attitude towards God or people. On the contrary, they say, actions which are termed 'peripheral' (in which, they say, the choice is often not definitive) do not succeed in changing a person's fundamental option. Indeed, since they are often done out of habit, there is then even less chance of their doing so. Therefore, while such actions can indeed weaken a person's fundamental option, they cannot change it completely. Now, according to these authors, it is more difficult to change a fundamental option for God in sexual matters, where normally it is not by fully deliberate and responsible actions that a person violates the moral order, but rather under the influence of passion or because of weakness or immaturity; sometimes it happens because a person wrongly thinks he can thus express love for his neighbour. Social pressures are often a further cause.

It is true that it is a person's fundamental option which ultimately defines adequately his moral stance. But it can be radically altered by individual actions, especially when, as often happens, they have already been prepared for by previous less deliberate actions. However that may be, it is scarcely correct to say that individual actions are not sufficient to constitute mortal sin (*mortale peccatum*).

According to the Church's teaching, mortal sin, which is opposed to God, is not found solely in the formal and direct refusal to obey the precept of charity. It is also found in that opposition to true love which is involved in every deliberate transgression of the moral law in a grave matter (*in re gravi*).

Christ designated the double law of charity as the foundation of moral life. 'Everything in the law and the prophets hangs on these two commandments.'[22] They include therefore the other individual commandments. To the young man who asked him: 'What good must I do to gain eternal life?' Jesus replied: '. . .if you wish to enter into life, keep the commandments. . .Do not murder; do not commit adultery; do not steal; do not give false evidence; honour your father and your mother; and love your neighbour as yourself.'[23]

A person commits mortal sin, therefore, not only when his actions stem from direct contempt for God and his neighbour, but also when knowingly and willingly, for whatever reason, he makes a choice which is gravely at variance with right order (*aliquid graviter inordinatum*). For in that choice, as has been said, contempt for the divine precept is already implied: it involves turning away from God and losing charity. According to Christian and the Church's teaching, and as right reason acknowledges, sexual morality encompasses such important human values that every violation of it is objectively grave (*objective. . . gravis*).[24]

It must be acknowledged that, granted their nature and causes, totally free consent may easily be lacking in sins of sex. Prudence and caution are needed therefore in passing any judgment on a person's responsibility. The words of scripture are relevant here: 'Man looks at appearances, but God looks at the heart.'[25] However, while prudence is recommended in judging the subjective gravity of an individual sinful action (*actus pravi*), it in no way follows that there are no mortal sins in matters of sex.

Pastors of souls must therefore be patient and kind. However, they may not set God's commandments at naught nor diminish men's obligations more than is right. 'It is a great charity to souls to refuse to minimize any of the saving teaching of Christ, but this attitude must always go hand in hand with tolerance and charity. The Redeemer himself gave an example of it when talking to people and when dealing with them. He came not to judge but to save the world. He was unsparing in his condemnation of sin, but was patient and merciful towards sinners.'[26]

11. As has already been said, the purpose of this declaration is to put the faithful on their guard against certain current errors and patterns of behaviour. The virtue of chastity, however, does not at all consist solely in avoiding these faults. It demands something more as well: achievement of higher goals. It is a virtue which affects the whole person, both inwardly and in external behaviour.

People should cultivate this virtue in a way that is suited to their state of life. Some profess virginity or consecrated celibacy which enables them to give themselves to God alone with undivided heart in a remarkable manner.[27] Others live in the way prescribed for all by the moral law, whether they are married or single. However, in every state of life, chastity is not confined to an external bodily quality. It must purify the heart, as Christ said: 'You have learned that they were told, "Do not commit adultery." But what I tell you is this: If a man looks on a woman with a lustful eye, he has already committed adultery with her in his heart.'[28]

Chastity is part of that continence which St Paul numbers among the gifts of the Holy Spirit. Impurity, however, he condemns as a vice particularly unworthy of a Christian and as one which merits exclusion from the kingdom.[29] 'This is the will of God, that you should be holy: you must abstain from fornication; each one of you must learn to gain mastery over his body, to hallow and honour it, not giving way to lust like the pagans who are ignorant of God; and no man must do his brother wrong in this matter. . . For God called us to holiness, not to impurity. Anyone therefore who flouts these rules is flouting, not man, but God who bestows upon you his Holy Spirit.'[30] 'Fornication and indecency of any kind, or ruthless greed, must not be as much as mentioned among you, as befits the people of God. No coarse, stupid, or flippant talk; these things are out of place; you should rather be thanking God. For be very sure of this: no one given to fornication or indecency, or the greed which makes an idol of gain, has any share in the kingdom of Christ and of God. Do not let anyone deceive you with shallow arguments; it is for all these things that God's dreadful judgment is coming upon his rebel subjects. Have no part or lot with them. For though you were once all darkness, now as Christians you are light. Live like men who are at home in daylight, for where light is, there all goodness springs up, all justice and truth.'[31]

Further, St Paul indicates a specifically Christian motive for practising chastity. He condemns the sin of fornication, but not merely because the action injures a person's neighbours or the social order. He condemns it because the fornicator offends Christ, by whose blood he was saved and whose member he is, and he offends the Holy Spirit, whose temple he is: 'Do you know that your bodies are limbs and organs of Christ? . . . Every other sin that a man can commit is outside his own body; but the fornicator sins against his own body. Do you know that your body is a shrine of the indwelling Holy Spirit, and the Spirit is God's gift to you? You do not belong to yourselves, you were bought at a price. Then honour God in your body.'[32]

The more the faithful appreciate the importance of chastity and its necessary role in their lives, the more clearly will they perceive, by a kind of spiritual instinct, its directives and counsels. It will also be easier for them, in obedience to the magisterium of the Church, to accept and comply with the dictates of a right conscience in individual instances.

12. The apostle Paul has a vivid description of the bitter in-

terior struggle, experienced by a man enslaved to sin, between 'the law that. . .(his) reason approves' and another law, which is in his 'bodily members' and which holds him captive.[33] Man, however, can be liberated from 'this body doomed to death' through the grace of Jesus Christ.[34] This grace is given to men. They are justified through it and in Christ Jesus the life-giving law of the Spirit has set them free from the law of sin and death.[35] St Paul therefore implores them: 'So sin must no longer reign in your mortal body, exacting obedience to the body's desires.'[36]

However, while it is true that this liberation fits us for the service of God in a new life, it does not remove the concupiscence which comes from original sin, nor does it remove the inducements to evil provided by this world which lies wholly 'in the power of the evil one.'[37] Thus St Paul encourages the faithful to overcome temptations by the power of God,[38] to 'stand firm against the devices of the devil,'[39] by faith, watchful prayer[40] and austerity of life, by which the body is brought into subjection to the Spirit.[41]

The Christian life, which consists in following in the footsteps of Christ, requires of every one that 'he must leave self behind; day after day must take up his cross,'[42] sustained by the hope of reward, for 'if we died with him, we shall live with him; if we endure, we shall reign with him.'[43]

Granted the forcefulness of these admonitions, Christians of today—indeed, today more than ever before—should use the means which the Church has always recommended for living a chaste life. They are: discipline of the senses and of the mind, vigilance and prudence in avoiding occasions of sin, modesty, moderation in amusements, wholesome pursuits, constant prayer, frequent recourse to the sacraments of Penance and the Eucharist. Young people especially should diligently develop devotion to the Immaculate Mother of God and should take as models the lives of the saints and of other Christians, especially young Christians, who excelled in the practice of chastity.

It is particularly important that everyone should hold the virtue of chastity in high esteem, its beauty and its radiant splendour. This virtue emphasizes man's dignity and opens man to a love which is true, magnanimous, unselfish and respectful of others.

13. It is for the bishops to instruct the faithful in sexual morality, however difficult this may be today because of the thinking and behaviour-patterns which are everywhere prevalent. The traditional teaching must be studied more deeply. It must be

communicated in a way that will enlighten the consciences of people confronted with new situations. Lastly, it must be wisely enriched with whatever can truly and usefully be adduced about the meaning and power of human sexuality. The bishops must faithfully hold and teach the principles and norms on the moral life which have been reaffirmed in this declaration. In particular, it will be necessary to convince the faithful that the Church holds these principles not as old and unchangeable objects of superstition, nor, as is often alleged, as a Manichaean prejudice; that the Church, rather, knows for certain that these principles are in complete harmony with the divine order of creation and with the spirit of Christ, and therefore with human dignity also.

It will also be for the bishops to ensure that in theological faculties and in seminaries sound doctrine is expounded, in the light of faith and under the guidance of the magisterium of the Church. They must also ensure that confessors enlighten people's consciences and that catechetical instruction be imparted in perfect fidelity to Catholic doctrine.

It is for the bishops, priests and their collaborators to warn the faithful against erroneous opinions in books, reviews and public meetings.

Parents, first of all, and then teachers must try to lead their charges—their children or their pupils—by means of a complete education, to proper mental, affective and moral maturity. Thus, they will teach them about sex prudently and in a manner suited to their age. They will form their wills in accordance with Christian behaviour, not only by giving them advice but also by the powerful example of their own lives, supported by God's help, obtained through prayer. They will protect them from the many dangers whose existence the young do not suspect.

Artists, writers and all in whose hands are the means of social communication should use their skills in ways that are in keeping with their Christian faith and with a clear awareness of the great power that is theirs to exercise over men. They should bear in mind that 'all must accept the absolute primacy of the objective moral order'[44] and that it is wrong to give priority to what are known as[45] aesthetic considerations, to material advantage or success. Whether it be question of art or literature, entertainment or communication, each person in his or her province must be circumspect, prudent and moderate and must display sound judgment. In this way, far from increasing the growing permissiveness, each will help control it and make the moral climate of society more wholesome.

498 SECTION 5: CURRENT PROBLEMS

All lay people should do likewise, because of their rights and duties in the apostolate.

Finally, it will be helpful to remind everyone of the following statement of the Second Council of the Vatican: 'Similarly, the sacred Synod affirms that children and young people have the right to be stimulated to make sound moral judgments based on a well-formed conscience and to put them into practice with a sense of personal commitment, and to know and love God more perfectly. Accordingly, it earnestly entreats all who are in charge of civil administration or in control of education to make it their care to ensure that young people are never deprived of this sacred right.'[46]

* Translated from the Latin, *Osservatore Romano,* 16 January 1976, by Austin Flannery, O. P.

1. See Second Vatican Council, Constitution on the Church in the Modern World, *Gaudium et Spes,* 47.

2. See Apostolic Constitution, *Regimini Ecclesiae Universae,* 29 (15 August 1967).

3. *Gaudium et Spes,* 16.

4. John 8:12.

5. Second Vatican Council, Declaration on Religious Liberty, *Dignitatis Humanae,* 3.

6. 1 Tim. 3:15.

7. *Dignitatis Humanae,* 14; See Pius XII, *Casti Connubii,* AAS 1930, pp. 579-580; Allocution of 2 November 1954, AAS 1954, pp. 671-672; John XXIII, *Mater et Magistra,* AAS 1961, p. 457; Paul VI, *Humanae Vitae,* 4, AAS 1968, p. 483.

8. See Second Vatican Council, Declaration on Christian Education, *Gravissimum Educationis,* 1, 8; 726-727, 732-733; *Gaudium et Spes,* 29, 60, 67: ibid., pp. 929-930, 964-965, 972-973.

9. *Gaudium et Spes,* 51: ibid., p. 955.

10. *Gaudium et Spes,* 51; see also 49: ibid., pp. 955, 952-953.

11. *Gaudium et Spes,* 49, 50: ibid., pp. 952-954.

12. The present declaration does not go into further detail regarding the norms of sexual life within marriage; these have been clearly taught in the encyclical letters *Casti Connubii* and *Humanae Vitae.*

13. See Matt. 19:4-6.

14. 1 Cor. 7:9.

15. See Eph. 5:25-32.

16. Sexual intercourse outside marriage is formally condemned: 1 Cor. 5:1; 6:9; 7:2; 10:8; Eph. 5:5; 1 Tim. 1:10; Heb. 14:4; and with explicit reasons: 1 Cor. 6:12-20.

17. See Innocent IV, Letter *Sub catholica professione,* 6 March 1254, Denz. Schon., 835; Pius II, *Propos. damn. in Ep. Cum sicut accepimus,* 14 Nov. 1459, Denz. Schon., 1367; Decrees of the Holy Office, 24 Sept. 1665, Denz. Schon., 2045; 2 March 1679, Denz. Schon., 2148; Pius XI, *Casti Connubii,* 31 Dec. 1940, AAS 1930, pp. 558-559.

18. Rom. 1:24-27, 'for this reason God has given them up to the vile-

ness of their own desires, and the consequent degradation of their bodies, because they have bartered away the true God for a false one, and have offered reverence and worship to created things instead of to the creator, who is blessed for ever; amen. In consequence, I say, God has given them up to shameful passions. Their women have exchanged natural intercourse for unnatural, and their men in turn, giving up natural relations with women, burn with lust for one another; males behave indecently with males, and are paid in their own persons the fitting wage of such perversion.' See also that St Paul says of those 'guilty of homosexual perversion' in 1 Cor. 6:10; 1 Tim. 1:10.

19. See Leo IX, Letter *Ad splendidum nitentis*, in 1054, Denz. Schon. 587-688; Decree of the Holy Office, 2 March 1679, Denz. Schon., 2149; Pius XII, Allocution, 9 Oct. 1953, AAS 1953, pp. 677-678: AAS 1956, pp. 472-473.

20. *Gaudium et Spes.*

21. '. . . sociological surveys help disclose the thought patterns of a particular people, the anxieties and needs of those to whom we proclaim the word of God, and also the opposition of modern thought to it, based on the widespread notion that no legitimate knowledge exists outside of science. However, the conclusions drawn from such surveys could not of themselves provide criteria for determining truth.' Paul VI, Apostolic Exhortation, *Quinque jam anni,* 8 Dec. 1970, AAS 1971, p. 102.

22. Matt. 22:38, 40.

23. Matt. 19:16-19.

24. See notes 17 and 19 above: Decree of the Holy Office, 18 March 1666, Denz. Schon., 2060; Paul VI, Encyclical Letter *Humanae Vitae,* 13, 14.

25. 1 Sam. 16:7.

26. Paul VI, Encyclical Letter *Humanae Vitae,* 29: AAS 1968, p. 501.

27. See 1 Cor. 7:7, 34. Council of Trent, Session 24, can. 10: Denz. Schon. 1810; Second Vatican Council, Constitution *Lumen Gentium;* Synod of Bishops, *De Sacerdotio Ministeriali,* Part II, 4, b: AAS, 1971, pp. 915-916.

28. Matt. 5:28.

29. See Gal. 5:19-23; 1 Cor. 6:9-11.

30. 1 Thess. 4:3-8; see Col. 3:5-7.

31. Eph. 5:3-8; see 4:18-19.

32. 1 Cor. 6:15, 18-20.

33. See Rom. 7:23.

34. See Rom. 7:24-25.

35. See Rom. 8:2.

36. Rom. 6:12.

37. 1 John 5:11.

38. See 1 Cor. 10:13.

39. Eph. 6:11.

40. See Eph. 6:16, 18.

41. See 1 Cor. 9:27.

42. Luke 9:23.

43. 2 Tim. 2:11-12.

44. Second Council of the Vatican, Decree *Inter Mirifica,* 6: Flannery, p. 286.

45. Vatican Press Office version, 'so-called'.

46. Second Council of the Vatican, Declaration *Gravissimum Educationis,* 1: Flannery, p. 727.

110

THE REALITY OF LIFE AFTER DEATH*

S.C.D.F., *Recentiores episcoporum synodi*, 11 May, 1979

The recent Synods of Bishops dealing with evangelization and catechesis have created increasing awareness of the need for perfect fidelity to the fundamental truths of faith, especially at the present time, when profound changes in human society and the concern to integrate the Christian faith into the various cultures require that a greater effort be made than in the past to make that faith accessible and communicable. This latter need, so urgent at present, requires that greater care than ever be given to safeguarding the true meaning and the integrity of the faith.

Hence, those responsible in this matter must be extremely attentive to anything that might introduce into the general attitude of the faithful a gradual debasement or progressive extinction of any element of the baptismal creed necessary for the coherence of the faith and inseparably connected with important practices in the life of the Church.

We think it urgently necessary to call one of these elements to the attention of those to whom God has entrusted the function of advancing and protecting the faith, in order that they may forestall the dangers that could threaten this faith in the minds of the faithful.

The element in question is the article of the Creed concerning life everlasting and so everything in general after death. When setting forth this teaching, it is not permissible to remove any point, nor can a defective or uncertain outlook be adopted without endangering the faith and salvation of Christians.

The importance of this final article of the baptismal Creed is obvious: it expresses the goal and purpose of God's plan, the unfolding of which is described in the Creed. If there is no resurrection, the whole structure of faith collapses, as Saint Paul states so forcefully (cf. 1 Cor. 15). If the content of the words 'life everlasting' is uncertain for Christians, the promises contained in the Gospel and the meaning of creation and redemption disappear, and even earthly life itself must be said to be deprived of all hope (cf. Heb. 11:1).

But one cannot ignore the unease and disquiet troubling many with regard to this question. It is obvious that doubt is gradually insinuating itself deeply into people's minds. Even though, generally speaking, the Christian is fortunately not yet at the point of positive doubt, he often refrains from thinking about his destiny after death, because he is beginning to encounter questions in his mind to which he is afraid of having to reply, questions such as: Is there really anything after death? Does anything remain of us after we die? Is it nothingness that is before us?

Part of the cause of this is the unintentional effect on people's minds of theological controversies given wide publicity today, the precise subject and the significance of which is beyond the discernment of the majority of the faithful. One encounters discussions about the existence of the soul and the meaning of life after death, and the question is put of what happens between the death of the Christian and the general resurrection. All this disturbs the faithful, since they no longer find the vocabulary they are used to and their familiar ideas.

There is no question here of restricting or preventing the theological research that the faith of the Church needs and from which it should profit. But this does not permit any omission of the duty to safeguard promptly the faith of Christians on points called into doubt.

In the present serious situation, it is our intention to recall briefly the nature and various features of this difficult twofold duty.

To begin with, those who act as teachers must clearly discern what the Church considers to pertain to the essence of the faith; theological research cannot have any other aim in view than to investigate this more deeply and develop it.

The Sacred Congregation, whose task is to advance and protect the doctrine of the faith, here wishes to recall what the Church teaches in the name of Christ, especially concerning what happens between the death of the Christian and the general resurrection.

(1) The Church believes (cf. the Creed) in the resurrection of the dead.

(2) The Church understands this resurrection as referring to *the whole person*; for the elect it is nothing other than the extension to human beings of the Resurrection of Christ itself.

(3) The Church affirms that a spiritual element survives and subsists after death, an element endowed with consciousness and will, so that the 'human self' subsists. To designate this element, the Church uses the word 'soul', the accepted term in the usage of Scripture and Tradition. Although not unaware that this term has various meanings in the Bible, the Church thinks that there is no valid reason for rejecting it; moreover, she considers that the use of some word as a vehicle is absolutely indispensable in order to support the faith of Christians.

(4) The Church excludes every way of thinking or speaking that would render meaningless or unintelligible her prayers, her funeral rites and the religious acts offered for the dead. All these are, in their substance, *loci theologici*.

(5) In accordance with the Scriptures, the Church looks for 'the glorious manifestation of our Lord, Jesus Christ' (*Dei Verbum*, I, 4), believing it to be distinct and deferred with respect to the situation of people immediately after death.

(6) In teaching her doctrine about man's destiny after death, the Church excludes any explanation that would deprive the Assumption of the Virgin Mary of its unique meaning, namely the fact that the bodily glorification of the Virgin is an anticipation of the glorification that is the destiny of all the other elect.

(7) In fidelity to the New Testament and Tradition, the Church believes in the happiness of the just who will one day be with Christ. She believes that there will be eternal punishment for the sinner, who will be deprived of the sight of God, and that this punishment will have a repercussion on the whole being of the sinner. She believes in the possibility of a purification for the elect before they see God, a purification altogether different from the punishment of the damned. This is what the Church means when speaking of Hell and Purgatory.

When dealing with man's situation after death, one must especially beware of arbitrary imaginative representations: excess of this kind is a major cause of the difficulties that Christian faith often encounters. Respect must however be given to the images employed in the Scriptures. Their profound meaning must be discerned, while avoiding the risk of overattenuating them, since this often empties of substance the realities designated by the images.

Neither Scripture nor theology provides sufficient light for a proper picture of life after death. Christians must firmly hold the two following essential points: on the one hand they must believe in the fundamental continuity, thanks to the power of the Holy Spirit, between our present life in Christ and the future life (charity is the law of the Kingdom of God and our charity on earth will be the measure of our sharing God's glory in heaven); on the other hand they must be clearly aware of the radical break between the present life and the future one, due to the fact that the economy of faith will be replaced by the economy of fullness of life: we shall be with Christ and 'we shall see God' (cf. 1 John 3:2), and it is in these promises and marvellous mysteries that our hope essentially consists. Our imagination may be incapable of reaching these heights, but our heart does so instinctively and completely.

Having recalled these points of doctrine, we would now like to clarify the principal features of the pastoral responsibility to be exercised in the present circumstances in accordance with Christian prudence.

The difficulties connected with this questions impose serious obligations on theologians, whose function is indispensable. Accordingly they have every right to encouragement from us and to the margin of freedom lawfully demanded by their methodology. We must however unceasingly remind Christians of the Church's teaching, which is the basis both of Christian life and of scholarly research. Efforts must also be made to ensure that theologians share in our pastoral concern, so that their studies and research may not be thoughtlessly set before the faithful, who today more than ever are exposed to dangers to their faith.

The last Synod highlighted the attention given by the Bishops to the essential points of catechesis with a view to the good of the faithful. All who are commissioned to transmit these points must have a clear idea of them. We must therefore provide them with the means to be firm with regard to the essence of the doctrine and at the same time careful not to allow childish or arbitrary images to be considered truths of faith.

A Diocesan or National Doctrinal Commission should exercise constant and painstaking vigilance with regard to publications, not only to give timely warning to the faithful about writings that are unreliable in doctrine but also and especially to acquaint them with works that can nourish and support their faith. This is a difficult and important task, but it is made urgent both by the wide circulation of printed publications and by the decentralization of responsibilities demanded by circumstances and desired by the Ecumenical Council.

---

*Translation by Vatican Press Office. Latin original in *A.A.S.* 71 (1979), 939–943. The Latin title of the document, translated literally, is: "On certain questions pertaining to eschatology."

111

HUMAN SEXUALITY*

S.C.D.F., *The Book "Human Sexuality"*, 13 July, 1979

The book *Human Sexuality: New Directions in American Catholic Thought,* a study commissioned by the Catholic Theological Society of America and edited by the Reverend Anthony Kosnik, has been given wide publicity through its distribution not only in the United States but elsewhere, both in the English version and in various translations.

The Sacred Congregation for the Doctrine of the Faith wishes to commend the actions of the American bishops, who exercised their pastoral ministry as authentic teachers of the faith by calling to the attention of their priests and people the errors contained in this book, particularly in regard to the unacceptability of its "pastoral guidelines" as suitable norms for the formation of Christian consciences in matters of sexual morality.

The Congregation particularly wishes to commend the National Conference of Catholic Bishops' Committee on Doctrine for its statement of November, 1977, which gives an evaluation of the book that can serve the bishops and the Catholic community at large not only in the United States but wherever this book has made its appearance. The enclosed *Observations* of this Congregation may also be useful to the bishops for their continued prudent guidance of their people on this delicate pastoral question.

At the same time, the Congregation cannot fail to note its concern that a distinguished society of Catholic theologians would have arranged for the publication of this report in such a way as to give broad distribution to the erroneous principles and conclusions of this book and in this way provide a source of confusion among the people of God.

I would be grateful to Your Excellency for bringing this letter to the attention of the members of the Episcopal Conference. With kind regards and personal best wishes for you.

OBSERVATIONS

The book *Human Sexuality* has already received substantial criticism on the part of theologians, of numerous American bishops, and of the Doctrinal Commission of the American Episcopal Conference. It would seem clear that the authors of this book, who speak of "encouraging others to join us in the continuing search for more satisfying answers to the mystery of human sexuality" (p. XV), will have to give rigorous reconsideration to the position they have assumed in the light of such criticism. This is all the more important, since the topic of the book—human sexuality—and the attempt to offer "helpful practical guidelines to beleaguered pastors, priests, counsellors and teachers", charge the authors with an enormous responsibility for the erroneous conclusions and the potentially harmful impact these ideas can have on the correct formation of the Christian consciences of so many people.

This Sacred Congregation, considering the fact that this book and its opinions have been given wide distribution within the U.S.A. throughout the English-speaking world, and elsewhere through various translations, considers it a duty to intervene by calling attention to the errors contained in this book and by inviting the authors to correct these errors. Here we limit our considerations to some of these errors which seem to be the most fundamental and to touch the heart of the matter; this limitation should not lead to the inference that other errors of a historical, scriptural, and theological nature are not to be found in this book as well.

1. A most pervasive mistake in this book is the manipulation of the concept or definition of human sexuality. "Sexuality then is the mode or manner by which humans experience and express both the incompleteness of their individualities as well as their relatedness to each other as male and female. . . This definition broadens the meaning of sexuality beyond the merely genital and generative and is so to be understood in all that follows" (p. 82). This definition refers to what may be called *generic* sexuality, in which "sex is seen as a force that permeates, influences, and affects every act of a person's being at every moment of existence". In this generic sense the book quotes the Vatican *Declaration on Certain Questions concerning Sexual Ethics*, which acknowledged this basic human differentiation saying "it is from sex that the human person receives the characteristics which, on the biological, psychological and spiritual levels, make that person a man or a woman, and thereby largely condi-

tion his or her progress towards maturity and insertion into society" (*Persona Humana,* 1).

It is not, however, in this area of generic sexuality that the moral problematic of chastity is engaged. This occurs rather within the more specific field of sexual being and behaviour called *genital* sexuality, which, while existing within the field of generic sexuality, has its specific rules corresponding to its proper structure and finality. These do not simply coincide with those of generic sexuality. Hence while *Human Sexuality* cites the first paragraph of *Persona humana,* as noted above, it fails to refer to the rest of this document's teaching on human sexuality, especially n. 5, which clearly states that "the use of the sexual function has its true meaning and moral rectitude only in true marriage".

It is equally evident that Vatican II, in n. 51 of *Gaudium et spes,* speaks clearly of genital rather than generic sexuality when it indicates that the moral character of sexual conduct "does not depend solely on sincere intentions or on an evaluation of motives. It must be determined by objective standards. These, based on the nature of the human person and his acts, preserve the full sense of mutual self-giving and human procreation in the context of true love. Such a goal cannot be achieved unless the virtue of conjugal chastity is sincerely practised". While the first part of this quotation is often cited in *Human Sexuality,* the last part is regularly omitted, an omission extended also to the following sentence in GS 51, which states, "Relying on these principles, sons of the Church may not undertake methods of regulating procreation which are found blameworthy by the teaching authority of the Church in its unfolding of the divine law". While this book speaks in fact exclusively about genital sexuality, it sets aside the specific norms for genital sexuality and instead attempts to resolve questions by the criteria of generic sexuality (cf. n.2 below).

Furthermore, in regard to the teaching of Vatican II, we note here another mistaken notion. This book repeatedly states that the Council deliberately refused to retain the traditional hierarchy of primary and secondary ends of marriage, opening "the Church to a new and deeper understanding of the meaning and value of conjugal love" (p. 125 and passim). On the contrary, the Commission of the Modi declared explicitly, replying to a proposal brought forward by many Fathers to put this hierarchical distinction into the text of n. 48, "In a pastoral text which intends to institute a dialogue with the world, juridical elements are not required. . .In any case, the primordial importance of procreation and education is shown at least ten times in the text" (cf. nn. 48 and 50).

2. In the view of sexuality described in *Human Sexuality,* the formulation of its purpose undergoes a substantial change with respect to the classical formulation: the traditional "procreative and unitive purpose" of sexuality, consistently developed in all the magisterial documents through Vatican II and *Humanae Vitae,* is substituted by a "creative and integrative purpose", also called "creative growth towards integration", which describes a broad and vague purpose applicable to any generic sexuality (and practically to any human action). Admitting that procreation is only one possible form of creativity, but not essential to sexuality (cf. p. 83 sq.), is a gratuitous change in the accepted terms without any substantial argument, a change which contradicts the formulation used in Vatican II and assumed in *Persona humana.* This change of purpose and consequently of the criteria for morality in human sexuality evidently changes all the traditional conclusions about sexual behaviour; it even precludes the possibility of fruitful theological discussion by removing the common terminology.

3. The authors of this book try to give more concrete content to the formal criterion "creative growth towards integration" (p. 92 sq.), but hardly anything in this development seems to refer specifically to genital sexual activity. It is true that they intend to give only some "particularly significant" values (cf. p. 92); nevertheless, those cited (e.g. honest, joyous, socially responsible) may be postulated equally well of most human activity.

The authors pretend that these are not purely subjective criteria, though in fact they are: the personal judgments about these factors are so different, determined by personal sentiments, feelings, customs, etc., that it would be next to impossible to single out definite criteria of what exactly integrates a particular person or contributes to his or her creative growth in any specific sexual activity.

Thus in chapter five, the criteria for discerning "creative growth towards integration", when applied to specific areas of sexual activity, yield no manageable or helpful rules for serious conscience formation in matters of sexuality. In the book, moreover, they are called "guidelines" which can never be regarded as "absolute and universal moral norms" (p.97).

4. The practical applications proposed in chapter five show clearly the consequences of this theory of human sexuality. These conclusions either dissociate themselves from or directly contradict Catholic teaching as consistently proposed by moral

theologians and as taught by the Church's magisterium. The intention expressed in the preface—"The fifth chapter. . .attempts to provide information and assistance for leaders in pastoral ministry to help them form and guide consciences in this area according to the mind of Jesus"—is sadly unfulfilled, indeed even reversed.

The authors nearly always find a way to allow for integrative growth through the neglect or destruction of some intrinsic element of sexual morality, particularly its procreative ordination. And if some forms of sexual conduct are disapproved, it is only because of the supposed absence, generally expressed in the form of a doubt, of "human integration" (as in swinging, mate-swapping, bestiality), and not because these actions are opposed to the nature of human sexuality. When some action is considered completely immoral, it is never for intrinsic reasons, on the basis of objective finality, but only because the authors happen not to see, for their part, any way of making it serve for some human integration. This subjection of theological and scientific arguments to evaluation by criteria primarily derived from one's present experience of what is human or less than human gives rise to a relativism in human conduct which recognizes no absolute values.

Given these criteria, it is small wonder that this book pays such scant attention to the documents of the Church's magisterium, whose clear teaching and helpful norms of morality in the area of human sexuality it often openly contradicts.

*English text in *E.V.*, 6, nn. 1705–1721.

112

DECLARATION ON EUTHANASIA*

S.C.D.F., *Jura et bona*, 5 May, 1980

INTRODUCTION

The rights and values pertaining to the human person occupy an important place among the questions discussed today. In this regard, the Second Vatican Ecumenical Council solemnly reaffirmed the lofty dignity of the human person, and in a special way his or her right to life. The Council therefore condemned crimes against life "such as any type of murder, genocide, abortion, euthanasia, or wilful suicide" (Pastoral Constitution *Gaudium et Spes,* 27).

More recently, the Sacred Congregation for the Doctrine of the Faith has reminded all the faithful of Catholic teaching on procured abortion.[1] The Congregation now considers it opportune to set forth the Church's teaching on euthanasia.

It is indeed true that, in this sphere of teaching, the recent Popes have explained the principles, and these retain their full force;[2] but the progress of medical science in recent years has brought to the fore new aspects of the question of euthanasia, and these aspects call for further elucidation on the ethical level.

In modern society, in which even the fundamental values of human life are often called into question, cultural change exercises an influence upon the way of looking at suffering and death; moreover, medicine has increased its capacity to cure and to prolong life in particular circumstances, which sometimes give rise to moral problems. Thus people living in this situation experience no little anxiety about the meaning of advanced old age and death. They also begin to wonder whether they have the right to obtain for themselves or their fellowmen an "easy death", which would shorten suffering and which seems to them more in harmony with human dignity.

A number of Episcopal Conferences have raised questions on this subject with the Sacred Congregation for the Doctrine of the Faith. The Congregation, having sought the opinion of experts on the various aspects of euthanasia, now wishes to respond to the Bishops' questions with the present Declaration, in order to help them to give correct teaching to the faithful entrusted to their care, and to offer them elements for reflection that they can present to the civil authorities with regard to this very serious matter.

The considerations set forth in the present document concern in the first place all those who place their faith and hope in Christ, who, through his life, death and Resurrection, has given a new meaning to existence and especially to the death of the Christian, as Saint Paul says: "If we live, we live to the Lord, and if we die, we die to the Lord" (*Rom* 14:8; cf. *Phil* 1:20).

As for those who profess other religions, many will agree with us that faith in God the Creator, Provider and Lord of life—if they share this belief—confers a lofty dignity upon every human person and guarantees respect for him or her.

It is hoped that this Declaration will meet with the approval of many people of good will, who, philosophical or ideological differences notwithstanding, have nevertheless a lively awareness of the rights of the human person. These rights have often in fact been proclaimed in recent years through declarations issued by International Congresses;[3] and since it is a question here of fundamental rights inherent in every human person, it is obviously wrong to have recourse to arguments from political pluralism or religious freedom in order to deny the universal value of those rights.

THE VALUE OF HUMAN LIFE

Human life is the basis of all goods, and is the necessary source and condition of every human activity and of all society. Most people regard life as something sacred and hold that no one may dispose of it at will, but believers see in life something greater, namely a gift of God's love, which they are called upon to preserve and make fruitful. And it is this latter consideration that gives rise to the following consequences:

1. No one can make an attempt on the life of an innocent person without opposing God's love for that person, without violating a fundamental right, and therefore without committing a crime of the utmost gravity.[4]

2. Everyone has the duty to lead his or her life in accordance with God's plan. That life is entrusted to the individual as a good that must bear fruit already here on earth, but that finds its full perfection only in eternal life.

3. Intentionally causing one's own death, or suicide, is therefore equally as wrong as murder; such an action on the part of a person is to be considered as a rejection of God's sovereignty and loving plan. Furthermore, suicide is also often a refusal of love for self, the denial of the natural instinct to live, a flight from the duties of justice and charity owed to one's neighbour, to various communities or to the whole of society—although, as is generally recognized, at times there are psychological factors present that can diminish responsibility or even completely remove it.

However, one must clearly distinguish suicide from that sacrifice of one's life whereby for a higher cause, such as God's glory, the salvation of souls or the service of one's brethren, a person offers his or her own life or puts it in danger (cf. *Jn* 15:14).

EUTHANASIA

In order that the question of euthanasia can be properly dealt with, it is first necessary to define the words used.

Etymologically speaking, in ancient times *euthanasia* meant an *easy death* without severe suffering. Today one no longer thinks of this original meaning of the word, but rather of some intervention of medicine whereby the sufferings of sickness or of the final agony are reduced, sometimes also with the danger of suppressing life prematurely. Ultimately, the word *euthanasia* is used in a more particular sense to mean "mercy killing", for the purpose of putting an end to extreme suffering, or saving abnormal babies, the mentally ill or the incurably sick from the prolongation, perhaps for many years, of a miserable life, which could impose too heavy a burden on their families or on society.

It is therefore necessary to state clearly in what sense the word is used in the present document.

By euthanasia is understood an action or an omission which of itself or by intention causes death, in order that all suffering may in this way be eliminated. Euthanasia's terms of reference, therefore, are to be found in the intention of the will and in the methods used.

It is necessary to state firmly once more that nothing and no one can in any way permit the killing of an innocent human being, whether a foetus or an embryo, an infant or an adult, an old person, or one suffering from an incurable disease, or a person who is dying. Furthermore, no one is permitted to ask for this act of killing, either for himself or herself or for another person entrusted to his or her care, nor can he or she consent to it, either explicitly or implicitly. Nor can any authority legitimately recommend or permit such an action. For it is a question of the violation of the divine law, an offence against the dignity of the human person, a crime against life, and an attack on humanity.

It may happen that, by reason of prolonged and barely tolerable pain, for deeply personal or other reasons, people may be led to believe that they can legitimately ask for death or obtain it for others. Although in these cases the guilt of the individual may be reduced or completely absent, nevertheless the error of judgment into which the conscience falls, perhaps in good faith, does not change the nature of this act of killing, which will always be in itself something to be rejected. The pleas of gravely ill people who sometimes ask for death are not to be understood as implying a true desire for euthanasia; in fact it is almost always a case of an anguished plea for help and love. What a sick person needs, besides medical care, is love, the human and supernatural warmth with which the sick person can and ought to be surrounded by all those close to him or her, parents and children, doctors and nurses.

THE MEANING OF SUFFERING FOR CHRISTIANS AND THE USE OF PAINKILLERS

Death does not always come in dramatic circumstances after barely tolerable sufferings. Nor do we have to think only of extreme cases. Numerous testimonies which confirm one another lead one to the conclusion that nature itself has made provision to render more bearable at the moment of death separations that would be terribly painful to a person in full health. Hence it is that a prolonged illness, advanced old age, or a state of loneliness or neglect can bring about psychological conditions that facilitate the acceptance of death.

Nevertheless the fact remains that death, often preceded or accompanied by severe and prolonged suffering, is something which naturally causes people anguish.

Physical suffering is certainly an unavoidable element of the human condition; on the biological level, it constitutes a warning of which no one denies the usefulness; but, since it affects the human psychological makeup, it often exceeds its own biological usefulness and so can become so severe as to cause the desire to remove it at any cost.

According to Christian teaching, however, suffering, especially suffering during the last moments of life, has a special place in God's saving plan; it is in fact a sharing in Christ's Passion and a union with the redeeming sacrifice which he offered in obedience to the Father's will. Therefore one must not be surprised if some Christians prefer to moderate their use of pain-killers, in order to accept voluntarily at least a part of their sufferings and thus associate themselves in a conscious way with the sufferings of Christ crucified (cf. *Mt* 27:34). Nevertheless it would be imprudent to impose a heroic way of acting as a general rule. On the contrary, human and Christian prudence suggest for the majority of sick people the use of medicines capable of alleviating or suppressing pain, even though these may cause as a secondary effect semiconsciousness and reduced lucidity. As for those who are not in a state to express themselves, one can reasonably presume that they wish to take these painkillers, and have them administered according to the doctor's advice.

But the intensive use of painkillers is not without difficulties, because the phenomenon of habituation generally makes it necessary to increase their dosage in order to maintain their efficacy. At this point it is fitting to recall a declaration by Pius XII, which retains its full force; in answer to a group of doctors who had put the question: "Is the suppression of pain and consciousness by the use of narcotics . . . permitted by religion and morality to the doctor and the patient (even at the approach of death and if one foresees that the use of narcotics will shorten life)?", the Pope said: "If no other means exist, and if, in the given circumstances, this does not prevent the carrying out of other religious and moral duties: Yes".[5] In this case, of course, death is in no way intended or sought, even if the risk of it is reasonably taken; the intention is simply to relieve pain effectively, using for this purpose painkillers available to medicine.

However, painkillers that cause unconsciousness need special consideration. For a person not only has to be able to satisfy his or her moral duties and family obligations; he or she also has to prepare himself or herself with full consciousness for meeting Christ. Thus Pius XII warns: "It is not right to deprive the dying person of consciousness without a serious reason".[6]

DUE PROPORTION IN THE USE OF REMEDIES

Today it is very important to protect, at the moment of death, both the dignity of the human person and the Christian concept of life, against a technological attitude that threatens to become an abuse. Thus, some people speak of a "right to die", which is an expression that does not mean the right to procure death either by one's own hand or by means of someone else, as one pleases, but rather the right to die peacefully with human and Christian dignity. From this point of view, the use of therapeutic means can sometimes pose problems.

In numerous cases, the complexity of the situation can be such as to cause doubts about the way ethical principles should be applied. In the final analysis, it pertains to the conscience either of the sick person, or of those qualified to speak in the sick person's name, or of the doctors, to decide, in the light of moral obligations and of the various aspects of the case.

Everyone has the duty to care for his or her own health or to seek such care from others. Those whose task it is to care for the sick must do so conscientiously and administer the remedies that seem necessary or useful.

However, is it necessary in all circumstances to have recourse to all possible remedies?

In the past, moralists replied that one is never obliged to use "extraordinary" means. This reply, which as a principle still holds good, is perhaps less clear today, by reason of the imprecision of the term and the rapid progress made in the treatment of sickness. Thus some people prefer to speak of "proportionate" and "disproportionate" means. In any case, it will be possible to make a correct judgment as to the means by studying the type of treatment to be used, its degree of complexity or risk, its cost and the possibilities of using it, and comparing these elements with the result that can be expected, taking into account the state of the sick person and his or her physical and moral resources.

In order to facilitate the application of these general principles, the following clarifications can be added:

—If there are no other sufficient remedies, it is permitted, with the patient's consent, to have recourse to the means provided by the most advanced medical techniques, even if these means are still at the experimental stage and are not without a certain risk. By accepting them, the patient can even show generosity in the service of humanity.

—It is also permitted, with the patient's consent, to interrupt these means, where the results fall short of expectations. But for such a decision to be made, account will have to be taken of the reasonable wishes of the patient and the patient's family, as also of the advice of the doctors who are specially competent in the matter. The latter may in particular judge that the investment in instruments and personnel is disproportionate to the results foreseen; they may also judge that the techniques applied impose on the patient strain or suffering out of proportion with the benefits which he or she may gain from such techniques.

—It is also permissible to make do with the normal means that medicine can offer. Therefore one cannot impose on anyone the obligation to have recourse to a technique which is already in use but which carries a risk or is burdensome. Such a refusal is not the equivalent of suicide; on the contrary, it should be considered as an acceptance of the human condition, or a wish to avoid the application of a medical procedure disproportionate to the results that can be expected, or a desire not to impose excessive expense on the family or the community.

—When inevitable death is imminent in spite of the means used, it is permitted in conscience to take the decision to refuse forms of treatment that would only secure a precarious and burdensome prolongation of life, so long as the normal care due to the sick person in similar cases is not interrupted. In such circumstances the doctor has no reason to reproach himself with failing to help the person in danger.

CONCLUSION

The norms contained in the present Declaration are inspired by a profound desire to serve people in accordance with the plan of the Creator. Life is a gift of God, and on the other hand death is unavoidable; it is necessary therefore that we, without in any way hastening the hour of death, should be able to accept it with full responsibility and dignity. It is true that death marks the end of our earthly existence, but at the same time it opens the door to immortal life. Therefore all must prepare themselves for this event in the light of human values, and Christians even more so in the light of faith.

As for those who work in the medical profession, they ought to neglect no means of making all their skill available to the sick and the dying; but they should also remember how much more necessary it is to provide them with the comfort of boundless kindness and heartfelt charity. Such service to people is also service to Christ the Lord, who said: "As you did it to one of the least of these my brethren, you did it to me" (*Mt* 25:40).

* Translation by Vatican Press Office.
1. *Declaration on Procured Abortion,* 18 November 1974: *AAS* 66 (1974), pp. 730-747.
2. Pius XII, *Address to those attending the Congress of the International Union of Catholic Women's Leagues,* 11 September 1947: *AAS* 39 (1947), p. 483; *Address to the Italian Catholic Union of Midwives,* 29 October 1951: *AAS* 43 (1951), pp. 835-854; *Speech to the members of the International Office of military medicine documentation,* 19 October 1953: *AAS* 45 (1953), pp. 744-754; *Address to those taking part in the IXth Congress of the Italian Anaesthesiological Society,* 24 February 1957: *AAS* 49 (1957), p. 146; cf. also *Address on "reanima-*

tion" 24 November 1957: *AAS* 49 (1957), pp. 1027-1033; Paul VI, *Address to the members of the United Nations Special Committee on Apartheid,* 22 May 1974: *AAS* 66 (1974), p. 346; John Paul II: *Address to the Bishops of the United States of America,* 5 October 1979: *AAS* 71 (1979), p. 1225.

3. One thinks especially of Recommendation 779 (1976) on the rights of the sick and dying, of the Parliamentary Assembly of the Council of Europe at is XXVIIth Ordinary Session; cf. Sipeca, No. 1, March 1977, pp. 14-15.

4. We leave aside completely the problems of the death penalty and of war, which involve specific considerations that do not concern the present subject.

5. Pius XII, *Address* of 24 February 1957: *AAS* 49 (1957), p. 147.

6. Pius XII, *ibid.,* p. 145; cf. *Address* of 9 September 1958: *AAS* 50 (1958), p. 694.

113

THE INTERNATIONAL YEAR OF DISABLED PERSONS*

The Holy See, 4 March, 1981

From the very beginning the Holy See received favorably the United Nations' initiative of proclaiming 1981 the International Year of Disabled Persons. These persons deserve the practical concern of the world community, both by reason of their numbers (it is calculated that they exceed 400 million) and especially for their particular human and social condition. Therefore, in this noble enterprise, the church could not fail to show her caring and watchful solicitude, for by her very nature, vocation and mission she has particularly at heart the lives of the weakest and most sorely tried brothers and sisters.

For this reason, the church has followed with close attention everything that has been done up to the present time on behalf of the disabled on the legislative level, both national and international. Worthy of note in this regard are the U.N. Declaration of the Rights of the Disabled and the declaration concerning the rights of the mentally retarded, as also the progress and future prospects of scientific and social research, plus the new proposals and initiatives of various efforts now being developed in this area. These initiatives show a renewed awareness of the duty of solidarity in this specific field of human suffering. Also to be borne in mind is the fact that in the Third World countries the lot of the disabled is even more grave, and calls for closer attention and more careful consideration.

The church fully associates herself with the initiatives and praiseworthy efforts being made in order to improve the situation of the disabled and she intends to make her own specific contribution thereto. She does so, in the first place, through fidelity to the example and teaching of her founder. For Jesus Christ showed special care for the suffering in all the wide spectrum of human pain. During his ministry he embraced them with his merciful love and he showed forth in them the saving power of the redemption that embraces man in his individuality and

518

totality. The neglected, the disadvantaged, the poor, the suffering and sick were the ones to whom he specially brought, in words and actions, the proclamation of the good news of God's kingdom breaking into human history.

The community of Christ's disciples, following his example, has down the centuries caused to flourish works of extraordinary generosity, works that bear witness not only to faith and hope in god but also unshakable love and faith in the dignity of man, in the unrepeatable value of each individual human life and in the transcendent dignity of those who are called into existence.

In their view of faith and in their concept of man Christians know that in the disabled person there is reflected in a mysterious way the image and likeness which God himself impressed upon the lives of his sons and daughters. And as they remember that Christ himself mystically identified himself with the suffering neighbor and took as done to himself everything done for the least of his brethren (cf. Mt. 25:31-46), Christians feel a call to serve in him those whom physical accidents have affected and disabled; and they are resolved not to omit any of the things that must be done even at the cost of personal sacrifice in order to alleviate their disadvantaged condition.

At this moment one cannot fail to think with lively gratitude of all the communities and associations, all the men and women religious and all the lay volunteers who spend themselves in work for the disabled, thus manifesting the perennial vitality of that love that knows no barriers.

It is in this spirit that the Holy See, while expressing its gratitude and encouragement for what has been done by those responsible for the common good, by the international organizations and by all those who work for the handicapped, considers it useful to recall briefly a few principles that may be useful guides in dealing with the disabled and also to suggest some practical points.

I. Basic Principles

1. The first principle, which is one that must be stated clearly and firmly, is that the disabled person (whether the disability be the result of a congenital handicap, chronic illness or accident, or from mental or physical deficiency, and whatever the severity of the disability) is a fully human subject with the corresponding innate, sacred and inviolable rights. This statement is based upon the firm recognition of the fact that a human being

possesses a unique dignity and an independent value from the moment of conception and in every stage of development, whatever his or her physical condition. This principle, which stems from the upright conscience of humanity, must be made the inviolable basis of legislation and society.

Indeed, on reflection one may say that a disabled person, with the limitations and sufferings that he or she suffers in body and faculties, emphasizes the mystery of the human being with all its dignity and nobility. When we are faced with a disabled person we are shown the hidden frontiers of human existence, and we are impelled to approach this mystery with respect and love.

2. Since the person suffering from handicaps is a subject with full rights, he or she must be helped to take his or her place in society in all aspects and at all levels as far as is compatible with his or her capabilities. The recognition of these rights and the duty of human solidarity are a commitment and task to be carried out, and they will create psychological, social, family, educational and legislative conditions and structures that will favor the proper acceptance and complete development of the disabled individual.

The Declaration of the Rights of the Disabled states in Section 3 that "disabled persons have the right to respect for their human dignity. Disabled persons, whatever the origin, nature and seriousness of their handicaps and disabilities, have the same fundamental rights as their fellow citizens of the same age, which implies first and foremost the right to enjoy a decent life as normal and full as possible."

3. The quality of a society and a civilization is measured by the respect shown to the weakest of its members. A perfect technological society which only allowed fully functional members and which neglected, institutionalized or, what is worse, eliminated those who did not measure up to this standard or who were unable to carry out a useful role, would have to be considered as radically unworthy of man however economically successful it might be. Such a society would in fact be tainted by a sort of discrimination no less worthy of condemnation than racial discrimination; it would be discrimination by the strong and "healthy" against the weak and the sick. It must be clearly affirmed that a disabled person is one of us, a sharer in the same humanity. By recognizing and promoting that person's dignity and rights we are recognizing and promoting our own dignity and our rights.

4. The fundamental approach to the problems connected with the sharing by the disabled in the life of society must be inspired

by the principles of integration, normalization and personalization. The principle of integration opposes the tendency to isolate, segregate and neglect the disabled, but it also goes further than an attitude of mere tolerance. It includes a commitment to make the disabled person a subject in the fullest sense, in accordance with his or her capacities, in the spheres of family life, the school, employment, and, more generally, in the social, political and religious communities.

As a natural consequence there derives from this principle that of normalization, which signifies and involves an effort to ensure the complete rehabilitation of the disabled person, using all means and techniques now available and, in cases where this proves impossible, the achievement of a living and working environment that resembles the normal one as much as possible.

Third, the principle of personalization emphasizes the fact that in the various forms of treatment, as also in the various educational and social means employed to eliminate handicaps, it is always the dignity, welfare and total development of the handicapped person in all his or her dimensions and physical, moral and spiritual faculties that must be primarily considered, protected and promoted. This principle also signifies and involves the elimination of collectivized and anonymous institutions to which the disabled are sometimes relegated.

II. Operative Lines

1. One cannot but hope that such statements as those of the declaration cited wil be given full recognition in the international and national communities, avoiding limiting interpretations and arbitrary exceptions and perhaps even unethical applications which end by emptying the statements of meaning and import.

Developments in science and medicine have enabled us today to discover in the fetus some defects which can give rise to future malformations and deficiencies. The impossibility at present of providing a remedy for them by medical means has led some to propose and even to practice the suppression of the fetus. This conduct springs from an attitude of pseudohumanism, which compromises the ethical order of objective values and must be rejected by upright consciences. It is a form of behavior which if it were applied at a different age would be considered gravely antihuman. Furthermore, the deliberate failure to provide assistance or any act which leads to the suppression of the newborn disabled person represents a breach not only of medical ethics but also of the fundamental and inalienable right to life.

One cannot at whim dispose of human life by claiming an arbitrary power over it. Medicine loses its title of nobility when instead of attacking disease, it attacks life; in fact prevention should be against the illness, not against life. One can never claim that one wishes to bring comfort to a family by suppressing one of its members. The respect, the dedication, the time and means required for the care of handicapped persons, even those whose mental faculties are gravely affected, is the price that a society should generously pay in order to remain truly human.

2. A consequence of clear affirmation of this point is the duty to undertake more extensive and thorough research in order to overcome the causes of disabilities. Certainly much has been done in recent years in this field, but much more remains to be done. Scientists have the noble task of placing their skill and their studies at the service of bettering the quality and defense of human life. Present developments in the fields of genetics, fetology, perinatology, biochemistry and neurology, to mention only some disciplines, permit us to foster the hope of noticeable progress. A unified effort of research will not fail, it is hoped, to achieve encouraging results in the not too distant future.

These initiatives of fundamental research and of application of acquired knowledge deserve therefore more decisive encouragement and more concrete support. It is the hope of the Holy See that international institutions, the public powers in individual nations, research agencies, non-governmental organizations and private foundations will more and more foster research and allot the necessary funds for it.

3. The priority to be given the prevention of disabilities should also make us reflect on the distressing phenomenon of the many persons who undergo stress and shock that disturb their psychic and interior life. Preventing these disabilities and fostering the health of the spirit signifies and implies unified and creative effort in favor of integral education and an environment, human relations and means of communication in which the person is not damaged in his more profound needs and aspirations—in the first place moral and spiritual ones—and in which the person is not submitted to violence, which can end by compromising his interior balance and dynamism. Spiritual ecology is needed as much as natural ecology.

4. When, notwithstanding the responsible and rigorous application of all the techniques and cures possible today, the dis-

ability cannot be remedied or reversed, it is necessary to seek and bring about all the remaining possibilities of human growth and of social integration which remain open for the person affected. Apart from the right to appropriate medical treatment, the U.N. declaration enumerates other rights, which have as their objective the most complete possible integration or reintegration into society. Such rights have very wide repercussions on the whole of the services which exist at present or which must be developed, among which might be mentioned the organization of an adequate educational system, responsible professional training, counseling services and appropriate work.

5. One point seems to merit particular attention. The U.N. Declaration on the Rights of Disabled Persons affirms: "Disabled persons have the right to live with their families or with foster parents" (n. 9). It is extremely important that this right be put into effect. It is in the home, surrounded by loved ones, that a handicapped person finds the surroundings which are most natural and conducive to his development. Taking account of this primordial importance of the family for the development of the handicapped person and his integration into society, those responsible for socio-medical and orthopedagogical structures should make the family the starting point in planning their programs and make it the principal dynamic force in the process of social care and integration.

6. From this viewpoint it is necessary to take into account the decisive importance which lies in the help to be offered at the moment that parents make the painful discovery that one of their children is handicapped. The trauma which derives from this can be so profound and can cause such a strong crisis that it shakes their whole system of values.

The lack of early assistance of adequate support in this phase can have very unfortunate consequences for both the parents and the disabled person. For this reason one should not rest content with only making the diagnosis and then leaving the parents abandoned. Isolation and rejection by society could lead them to refuse to accept or, God forbid, to reject their disabled child. It is necessary therefore for families to be given great understanding and sympathy by the community and to receive from associations and public powers adequate assistance from the beginning of the discovery of the disability of one of their members.

The Holy See, conscious of the heroic strength of mind required of those families that have generously and courageously agreed to take care of and even adopt disabled children wants to assure them of its appreciation and gratitude. The witness which these families render to the dignity, values and sacredness of the human person deserves to be openly recognized and supported by the whole community.

7. When particular circumstances and special requirements for the rehabilitation of the disabled person necessitate a temporary stay or even a permanent one away from the family, the homes and institutions which take the family's place should be planned and should function in a way as near to the family model as is possible and should avoid segregation and anonymity. It must be arranged that, during their stay in these centers, the bonds linking the disabled persons with their families and friends should be cultivated with frequency and spontaneity. Apart from their professional competence, loving care and dedication of the parents, relatives and educators have obtained, as many have testified, results of unexpected effectiveness for the human and professional development of disabled persons. Experience has demonstrated—and this is an important point for reflection—that in a favorable and human family setting full of deep respect and sincere affection disabled persons can develop in surprising ways their human, moral and spiritual qualities and even, in their turn, bring others peace and joy.

8. The affective life of the disabled will have to receive particular attention. Above all when their handicaps prevent them from contracting marriage, it is important not only that they be adequately protected from promiscuity and exploitation, but that they also be able to find a community full of human warmth in which their need for friendship and love may be respected and satisfied in conformity with their inalienable moral dignity.

9. Handicapped children and young people obviously have the right to instruction. This will be assured them to the extent possible either through an ordinary school or a specialized school for people with their handicap. Where home schooling is required, it is hoped that the competent authorities will supply the family with the necessary means. Access to higher learning and opportune post-school assistance ought to be made possible and aid should be given for this purpose.

10. A particularly delicate moment in the life of the disabled person is the passage from school to placement in society or professional life. In this phase the person needs particular understanding and encouragement from various sectors of the community. Public authorities should guarantee and foster with effective measures the right of disabled persons to professional training and work so that they can be inserted into a professional

activity for which they are qualified. Much attention should be focused on working conditions, such as the assignment of jobs in accordance with the handicap, just wages and the possibility of promotion. Highly recommended is advance information for employers regarding the employment, the situation and the psychology of the disabled. These encounter various hindrances in the professional sector, for example, a sense of inferiority about their appearance or possible productiveness, worry about having accidents at work, etc.

11. Obviously the disabled person possesses all the civil and political rights that other citizens have and it should as a general rule be made possible for him or her to exercise them. However, certain forms of disability—for instance the numerically important category of those who have mental handicaps—constitute an obstacle to the responsible exercise of these rights. Even in these cases action should be taken not in an arbitrary manner or by applying repressive measures, but on the basis of rigorous and objective ethical and juridical criteria.

12. On the other hand, the disabled person must be urged not to be content with being only the subject of rights, accustomed to receiving care and solidarity from others with a merely passive attitude. He is not only a receiver, he must be helped to be a giver to the full extent of his capabilities. An important and decisive moment in his formation will be reached when he becomes aware of his dignity and worth and recognizes that something is expected from him and that he too can and should contribute to the progress and well-being of his family and community. The idea that he has of himself should of course be realistic, but also positive, allowing him to see himself as a person capable of responsibility, able to exercise his own will and to collaborate with others.

13. Many individuals, associations and institutions are today dedicated by professional and often by a genuine humanitarian and religious calling to helping the disabled. In many cases they have demonstrated a preference for "voluntary" personnel and educators, because they see in them a particular sense of unselfishness and solidarity. This observation makes clear that although technical and professional competence is certainly necessary and ought indeed to be cultivated and improved, by itself it is not sufficient. A rich human sensitivity must be added to competence.

Those who commendably dedicate themselves to the service of the disabled should have scientific knowledge of their disabilities, but they should also comprehend with their hearts the person who bears the handicap. They should learn to become sensitive to the special signs with which the disabled express themselves and communicate. They should acquire the art of making the proper gesture and saying the right word. They should know how to accept with calmness possible reactions or forms of emotion and learn to dialogue with the parents and families of the disabled. This competence will not be fully human unless it is interiorly sustained by suitable moral and spiritual dispositions: attentivenes, sensitivity and particular respect for everything in the human person that is a source of weakness and dependence. Care and help for disabled persons then become a school also for parents, educators and service personnel, a school of genuine humanity, a demanding school, a noble school, an uplifting school.

14. It is very important and even necessary that professional services receive material and moral support from the public authorities with a view to being organized in the most adequate way possible and to having the specialized interventions function effectively. Many countries have already provided or are in the process of providing exemplary legislation that defines and protects the legal status of the disabled person. Where such legislation does not yet exist it is the duty of the government to provide an effective guarantee and to promote the rights of the disabled. To this end it would be advantageous for families and voluntary organizations to be associated in drawing up juridical and social norms in this matter.

15. Even the best legislation, however, risks having no effect on the social context and not producing full results if it is not accepted into the personal conscience of the citizens and the collective consciousness of the community.

Handicapped persons, their families and relatives are part of the whole human family. However large their number may unfortunately be, they form a minority group within the whole community. This is enough to entail the danger that they may not be given sufficient general interest. Add to that the often spontaneous reaction of a community that rejects and psychologically represses that which does not fit into its habits. People do not want to be faced with forms of existence which visibly reflect the negative aspects of life. This gives rise to the phenomenon of exclusion and discrimination as a kind of mechanism of defense and rejection. Since, however, man and society are truly human when they enter into a conscious and willing process of accepting even weakness, of solidarity and of sharing in others' sufferings, the tendency referred to must be countered by education.

The celebration of the International Year of Disabled Persons therefore offers a favorable opportunity for a more precise overall reconsideration of the situation, of the problems and of the requirements of millions of those who make up the human family, particularly in the Third World. It is important that this occasion not be allowed to pass by in vain. With the contribution of science and of all levels of society, it should lead to a better understanding of the disabled person and of his dignity and rights. And above all it should foster sincere and active love for every human being in his or her uniqueness and concrete situation.

16. Christians have an irreplaceable mission to carry out in this regard. Recalling their responsibility as witnesses to Christ, they must adopt as their own the Savior's sentiments toward the suffering and stimulate an attitude of charity and examples of it in the world, so that there is never any lack of interest in our brothers and sisters who are less endowed.

The Second Vatican Council identified in that charitable presence the essential core of the apostolate of lay people. It recalled that Christ made love of one's neighbor his personal commandment "and enriched it with a new meaning when he identified himself with his brothers as the object of charity. . . . For in assuming human nature, he united all of humanity to himself as his family and he made charity the distinguishing mark of his disciples in the words: 'By this all men will know that you are my disciples, if you have love for one another.' (Jn. 13:35) In the early days the church linked 'agape' to the eucharistic supper and by so doing showed herself entirely united around Christ. So too at all times she is recognized by the distinguishing sign of love and, while rejoicing at initiatives taken elsewhere, she claims charitable works as her own inalienable duty and right. That is why mercy to the poor and the sick, and works of charity and mutual aid for the alleviation of all kinds of human needs, are held in special honor by the church" *(Apostolicam Actuositatem, 8)*.

In this International Year of Disabled Persons Christians will therefore stand side by side with their brothers and sisters of all organizations in order to foster, support and increase initiatives suitable for alleviating the situation of the suffering and for inserting them harmoniously into the context of normal civil life to the extent that this is possible. Christians will make their contribution in personnel and resources, especially through the deserving institutions that—in the name of Christ and of his love and with the marvelous example of people wholly consecrated to the Lord—devote themselves especially to giving education, professional training and post-school assistance to young disabled persons and to caring generously for the worse cases.

Parishes and youth groups of various kinds will give special care to families in which one of these children marked by sorrow is born and grows to maturity. They will also study, continually apply and, if necessary, revise suitable methods of catechesis to the disabled, and they will pay attention to their insertion into cultural and religious activities so as to ensure that they will be full members of their Christian community, in accordance with their clear right to appropriate spiritual and moral education.

17. Celebrating the day of peace at the beginning of this year, the Holy Father mentioned publicly in the Vatican basilica the initiatives of the International Year of Disabled Persons and called for special attention to solving their serious problems. He now renews his call to show concern for the lot of these brothers and sisters of ours. He repeats what he said then: "If only a minimum part of the budget for the arms race were assigned for this purpose, important successes could be achieved and the fate of many suffering persons alleviated" (Homily Jan. 1, 1981).

His Holiness applauds the various initiatives that will be undertaken on the international level and also those that will be attempted in other fields, and he urges especially the sons and daughters of the Catholic Church to give an example of total generosity. Entrusting the dear disabled persons throughout the world to the motherly protection of the holy Virgin, as he did on that occasion, he repeats his hopeful trust that "under Mary's maternal gaze, experiences of human and Christian solidarity will be multiplied in a renewed brotherhood that will unite the weak and the strong in the common path of the divine vocation of the human person" (*Ibid.*).

*English text in *Origins*, 7 May, 1981, 747–750.

114

GENERAL CATECHETICAL DIRECTORY*

S.C.C., *Ad norman decreti*, 11 April, 1971

INTRODUCTION

This 'General Catechetical Directory' is being published in conformity with the Decree, *Christus Dominus*, n. 44. Its preparation took some considerable time, not only because of the difficulty inherent in such a task, but also because of the method employed.

A special international commission of catechetical experts was set up, its members having been chosen in consultation with a number of episcopal conferences, and as a first step suggestions and proposals were invited from the various episcopal conferences.

A first summary draft was drawn up on the basis of those proposals and suggestions and was submitted to a special plenary assembly of the sacred congregation for the clergy. A fuller draft was then drawn up and the episcopal conferences were invited to offer their comments on it. The definitive draft of the directory was prepared in the light of this second consultation and before its publication it was examined by a special theological commission and was approved by the sacred congregation for the doctrine of the faith. The purpose of this directory is to present the fundamental theological-pastoral principles, taken from the magisterium of the Church and especially the Second Vatican Council, for the guidance and better co-ordination of the ministry of the word. Hence the emphasis on theory, though the practical aspect is not neglected. The main reason for this procedure is that the only way to avoid the mistaken approaches to catechesis which are common nowadays is to begin with a proper understanding of the nature and purpose of catechesis and of the truth which it transmits, taking into account the recipients of catechesis and their social conditions. It will be for the various episcopal conferences to see to the concrete application of the principles and pronouncements of this directory, by means of regional and national directories, catechisms and other means calculated to promote an effective ministry of the word.

It is obvious that not all parts of the directory are of equal importance. The parts which deal with divine revelation, with the nature of catechetics, with the criteria governing the imparting of the Christian message and with its main elements have universal value. What is said about the present situation, about the methodology and the kinds of catechesis for the different age-groups is drawn mainly from theoretical and practical human sciences, which can change and develop, and must therefore be seen more as indications and suggestions.

The directory is intended principally for bishops, episcopal conferences and, in general, for those who under their guidance have a responsibility in the field of catechetics. The immediate purpose of the directory is to assist the preparation of catechetical directories and of catechisms. With this in mind, a basic outline of the present situation is offered, in order to encourage throughout the Church a careful study of the various concrete situations and pastoral needs. Some general principles of methodology and of catechesis for the different age-groups are also offered, to emphasize the importance of acquiring the art and the wisdom of the educator. Particular care was taken with the third part, which offers criteria for the exposition of the contents of catechesis and also an over-view of the essential elements of the Christian faith, thus setting clearly in relief the never-to-be-relinquished goal of catechesis: the integral proclamation of the Christian message.

Since the directory is intended for countries of vastly varying concrete situations and pastoral needs, it is obvious that it could take into account only the general or average conditions. The directory must therefore be seen and judged in the light of its special character and structure. The same is true of the sixth part, with its description of pastoral work. What is in question is a plan for pastoral action described in the broadest terms. It may well appear inadequate in those parts where catechetics has made notable advances and, perhaps, excessive where catechetics is in its infancy.

The publication of this document is further evidence of the Church's concern for a ministry so vital for its mission to the world and it is to be hoped that it will be accepted and carefully studied in the light of the pastoral needs of each ecclesial community. It is to be hoped, too, that it will succeed in encouraging more thorough research, in keeping with the needs of the ministry of the word and with the norms of the ecclesiastical magisterium.

PART 1:
THE ACTUAL PROBLEM

Nature and scope of this section

1. It is the Church's fundamental concern to proclaim and to promote the faith among contemporary men and women, who live in a society subject to profound socio-cultural change. For this reason it is useful to outline some special characteristics of the present situation, bearing in mind what Vatican II had to say, and to point out their implications for the life of the spirit and the new challenges which they offer to the Church. This is not intended as an exhaustive treatment of the problem, which differs, sometimes profoundly, from one part of the Church to another. It will be for national directories to provide more detailed descriptions and to adapt the outlines to their own national or regional needs.

THE WORLD

The modern world in constant transformation

2. 'Ours is a new age of history with critical and swift upheavals spreading gradually to all corners of the earth.... We are entitled then to speak of a real social and cultural transformation whose repercussions are felt too on the religious level.' (GS 4)

By way of example, one can cite two such repercussions on the life of faith and which are of considerable moment for catechesis:

(a) In the past, the cultural tradition was more favourable to the transmission of the faith than is today's. The tradition has been greatly changed and less and less can one place one's reliance on cultural continuity. A renewed evangelization is therefore necessary to transmit the faith to the new generations.

(b) It must be borne in mind that if the Christian faith is to take root in successive cultures it must needs develop and must find new forms of expression. While the aspirations and profound desires which are part and parcel of the human nature and condition remain fundamentally the same, modern men and women are posing new problems about the importance and the meaning of life.

Today's believer is not in all respects like the believer of yesterday. Hence the need to ensure the continuity of the faith and at the same time proclaim the message of salvation in a new way.

One must also bear in mind today the enormous diffusion of the means of social communication. Their power transcends national boundaries, making the individual almost a citizen of the world. (See IM 22)

The media have enormous influence on the lives of the faithful, both in what they teach and in the attitudes and behaviour to which they expose the faithful. They must therefore be the object of careful consideration.

Pluralism today

3. 'As a result, the traditional structures of local communities—family, clan, tribe, village, various groupings and social relationships—are subjected to ever more sweeping changes.' (GS 6)

In Christian antiquity, religion was considered as it were the major unifying principle among people. Things are much different today. The phenomenon of democratization has resulted in people forming a cohesive whole, a fact which favours harmony among the different spiritual families. Pluralism is no longer regarded as an evil to be combatted, but as a fact that has to be taken into account. Each individual can make his own decisions without thereby becoming an outcast from society.

Those therefore who are engaged in the ministry of the word should never forget that faith is the human person's free response to the grace of God which is revealed. More than in the past, they should proclaim the good news of Christ in its marvellous reality as both mysterious key to an understanding of the entire human condition and as free gift of God imparted by heavenly grace while one confesses one's unworthiness. (See GS 10)

The dynamism of our age

4. The energies of the people of our time are mobilised in the building of human society and in the progress and execution of human projects. (See GS 4) The faith ought not to be a stranger to this human progress, which goes hand in hand with

serious aberrations. Such developments should, therefore, be judged in the light of the evangelical message and their significance explained.

The ministry of the word involves the acquisition of an increasingly profound understanding of people's human and divine calling in order to allow the gospel to sow its seeds of authentic liberty and progress (see AG 8 & 12), to bring forth the desire for the advancement of the human person and for combatting fatalistic ways of acting and thinking.

These remarks are intended merely to show how the ministry can direct its attention to the contemporary world: '...the Church is asked today to inject into the veins of the human community the perennial, vital and divine power of the Gospel.' (John XXIII, Apost. Const. *Humanae salutis*, AAS 54, 6)

The religious sense

5. Our scientific, technical, industrial and urban civilization in many cases turns people's minds away from the divine and makes an interior concern about religious matters more difficult. For many, God is perceived to be less present, less necessary, less capable of providing a valid explanation of personal and social life. A religious crisis can easily occur in such a situation (see GS 5 & 7).

The Christian faith, like the other religious confessions, is experiencing such a crisis among its members. Faced with a culture which is secularised and de-sacralised, the faith has the urgent duty of manifesting its true nature, which transcends all cultural progress, and of showing its originality.

It is for the ministry of the word to reveal and develop, freed of aberrations, the authentic values which are to be found in the spiritual patrimony of those cultures in which the religious sense remains still alive and active, deeply permeating all of human existence.

There was a time when offbeat and erroneous opinions about the faith and the Christian way of life were usually confined to a smaller number of people—to intellectual circles, in fact, more than is the case today. Nowadays, human progress and the mass media accelerate the spread of such opinions and increase their influence on the faithful, especially young people, who go through grave crises and are not infrequently driven to adopt ways of thinking and acting which are contrary to religion. Such a situation needs appropriate pastoral remedies.

THE CHURCH

These characteristics of the spiritual condition of the world today are important to the life of the Church itself.

'Traditional' faith

6.   The Christian faith of many is in grave danger, especially in places where religion was deemed to favour over-much the privileges of certain social classes, or where it relied too much on ancient customs and on regional unanimity of religious profession.

Very many people gradually fall into religious indifference or run the risk of preserving a faith which lacks the necessary dynamism and real influence on their lives. Rather than merely preserving traditional religious customs, there is also need today for people's re-evangelization, for their re-conversion, giving them a more profound and more mature education in the faith.

This is not to imply, however, that one should neglect the genuine faith preserved among people of traditionally Christian culture or that one should belittle the popular religious sense. The religious sense continues to flourish in many parts of the Church, in spite of the increase of secularization. Nobody can afford to neglect it since it finds expression, for the most part sincere and authentic expression, in the lives of very many people. Indeed, the popular religious sense offers an opportunity or starting point for the proclamation of the faith. It is obviously merely a question of purifying it and of correctly appraising what is valid in it, lest anybody be content with forms of pastoral action which nowadays are inadequate, totally unsuitable and perhaps even obsolete.

Religious indifference and atheism

7.   Many baptised people have become so distanced from religion that they profess religious indifference or, almost, atheism: 'Many of our contemporaries either do not at all perceive, or else explicitly reject, this intimate and vital bond of man to God. Atheism must therefore be regarded as one of the most serious problems of our time, and one that deserves more thorough treatment' (GS 19)

The Second Vatican Council considered the matter carefully (see GS, 19-20) and dealt expressly with the remedies to be applied: 'Atheism must be countered both by presenting true teaching in a fitting manner and by the full and complete life of the Church and of her members. For it is the function of the Church to render God the Father and his incarnate Son present and as it were visible, while ceaselessly renewing and purifying herself under the guidance of the Holy Spirit. This is brought about chiefly by the witness of a living and mature faith, one namely that is so well formed that it can see difficulties clearly and overcome them.' (GS 21)

It can also happen that the Christian faith can become contaminated by a new form of paganism, even if a certain religious sense still remains and a certain belief in a supreme Being. A religious sense can be far removed from the influence of the word of God and from the sacramental life, being nourished by superstitious practices and magic; the moral life can recede to a pre-Christian ethic. Sometimes, elements of nature worship, animism and divination are introduced into the Christian religion, thus inducing in some places a lapse into syncretism. It happens too that religious sects are propagated which mingle elements of the fables of antiquity with the Christian mysteries.

In such cases, what is needed most of all is the renewal of the ministry of the word, especially evangelization and catechesis, in accordance with the decree on *The Church's Missionary Activity*, nn 13, 14, 21, 22.

Faith and different cultures

8.   There are some Christians, of more advanced Christian education, for whom the language in which the faith is expressed poses a problem. They believe it to be too tied to ancient and obsolete formulae or too closely linked with Western culture. They seek a new language for religious truths, one in keeping with the modern human condition and which would enable the faith to cast light on the realities which cause concern to people today and would enable the gospel to become incarnate in different cultures. It is certainly the duty of the Church to give the greatest possible consideration to this aspiration.

The statement made in the decree *On the Church's Missionary Activity*, n. 22, concerning the young churches is valid for all who are engaged in the ministry of the word: 'They borrow from the customs, traditions, wisdom, teaching, arts and sciences of their people everything which could be used to praise the glory of the Creator, manifest the grace of the Saviour, or contribute to the right ordering of the Christian life.'

For this reason, 'the ministry of the word, renewed and proclaiming the gospel message, has the task of making manifest the unity of God's plan. It should not present a confused picture nor indulge in facile harmonisation, but should manifest the profound harmony that exists between God's salvific plan, realised in Christ, and people's aspirations, between the history of salvation and human history, between the Church, the people of God, and human experience, between the supernatural gifts and charisms and human values.' (Comm. 5-s/comm. 2 General Conference of Latin American Bishops, 1968)

The work of renewal

9.   It might be thought that in this new situation the apostolic zeal which the Church is endeavouring to foster is being hampered. Not indeed that one can fault the zeal of the pastors of souls or the faithful, which is truly considerable. What stands in the way of more effective action is either a lack of adequate preparation for the new and difficult tasks facing the ministry of the word, or insufficiently developed reflection, finding expression at times in theories which hinder rather than help evangelization. It was in view of these matters that the Second Vatican Council appealed again and again for a profound renewal of the ministry of the word in the Church. This renewal would appear to be endangered today, however, by:

those who are unable to appreciate how profound is the proposed renewal, as if it were merely a matter of eliminating ignorance of doctrine. For them, the remedy is more catechetical instruction. But this would be inadequate. In fact, the entire catechetical enterprise has to be renewed, and this applies to an ongoing formation in the faith not only for children but also for adults;

those who tend to reduce the gospel message to its effects on people's temporal lives. The gospel and its law of love certainly demand that Christians combine to the best of their ability— fulfilling their secular responsibilities—increasingly to restore justice and fraternity in the world. This however would not suffice as proper witness to Jesus Christ, Son of God and our Saviour, whose mystery, revealing God's ineffable love (see John 4:9), must be proclaimed openly and fully to those who are to be evangelised and must be acknowledged by them.

The Pastoral Constitution on the Church in the Modern World and the *Declaration on Religious Liberty* do not at all adopt a minimalist approach to the explanation of direct service of the faith through the ministry of the word. Both documents show their concern to remedy the state of affairs described above. However, the renewal of the ministry of the word, especially of catechesis, cannot be separated from universal pastoral renewal.

Difficult and very important undertakings must be brought to a successful conclusion: the promotion and the development of the traditional forms of the ministry of the word and the encouragement of new initiatives; the evangelization and catechising of the less well educated; establishing contact with the educated classes and meeting their needs; the improvement of the traditional modes of Christian presence and the discovery of new ones; the combining of all the present resources of the Church, avoiding what is less in conformity with the gospel.

The Church relies on all the members of God's people for the execution of this task. All—bishops, priests, religious men and women, laity—should play their part, in keeping with their responsibility. They should perform their task with full awareness of conditions in the world, for these profoundly affect the life of faith.

The catechetical renewal, in order to be able effectively to help these gospel workers, should avail itself of the help provided by the sacred sciences, theology, biblical study, pastoral theology, the human sciences and all the communications media.

PART 2:
THE MINISTRY OF THE WORD

Chapter 1:
The Ministry of the Word and Revelation

Revelation: gift of God

10. In the *Dogmatic Constitution on Divine Revelation*, the ecumenical council considered revelation as an act whereby God enters into personal communion with us: 'It pleased God, in his goodness and wisdom, to reveal himself and to make known the mystery of his will...in order to invite and receive them into his company.' (DV 2) God appears there as he who wishes to communicate himself, doing it under the inspiration of love.

Catechesis ought therefore to start from this gift of divine love. Faith is the acceptance and the coming to fruition of the divine gift in us. The fact that faith is a gift has implications for the entire subject-matter of the ministry of the word.

Revelation: facts and words

11.   God uses the events of the history of salvation and divinely-inspired words, which accompany and explain them, to give people knowledge of his plan:

'This economy of salvation is realised by deeds and words, which are intrinsically bound up with each other. As a result, the works performed by God in the history of salvation show forth and bear out the doctrine and realities signified by the words; the words for their part proclaim the works, and bring to light the mystery they contain.' (DV 2)

Revelation therefore is a combination of events and words, the words illuminating the events and the events the words. It is for the ministry of the word to proclaim them in a way that will make more clear and will communicate the profound mysteries which they contain. In this way the ministry of the word recalls the revelation of the wonders of God accomplished in time and perfected in Christ, but it also interprets, in the light of revelation, contemporary human existence, the signs of the times and world affairs, for the divine plan operates in them for the salvation of man.

Jesus Christ, mediator and fullness of all revelation

12.   'The most intimate truth which this revelation gives... shines forth in Christ, who is himself both the mediator and the sum total of revelation.' (DV 2) Christ is not merely the greatest of the prophets, he who has completed with his teaching what God had done and said previously. He is the eternal Son of God, become man, and thus the last event, focus of all the events of the history of salvation, the completion and the manifestation of God's final plans: 'As a result, he himself...completed and perfected revelation....'(DV 4)

The ministry of the word should set in relief this wonderful characteristic of the economy of revelation. The Son of God enters human history, assumes human life and death, and brings to completion in that history the covenant he had planned.

The ministry of the word ought, like Luke the Evangelist, first to describe the Jesus-event for believers, explaining its meaning, penetrating more and more into this unique and irreversible event: 'Many writers have undertaken to draw up an account of the events that have happened among us...and so I...as one who has gone over the whole course of these events in detail, have decided to write a connected narrative for you.' (Luke 1:1-3)

Therefore, the ministry of the word should be based on the divinely-inspired account of the redemptive incarnation given to us by Jesus himself, by the first disciples, especially the apostles, who were witnesses of the events: 'It is common knowledge that...the Gospels have a special place, and rightly so, because they are our principal source for the life and teaching of the incarnate Word, our Saviour.' (DV 18)

It must be borne in mind, further, that Jesus, Messiah and Lord, is always present in his Church through his Spirit. (See John 14:26; 16:13; Apoc. 2:7.) The ministry of the word should therefore present him not merely as its object, but as him who opens listeners' hearts to the reception and the understanding of the divine proclamation. (See Acts 16:14)

Ministry of the word or preaching the word of God: act of living tradition

13. 'What was handed on by the apostles comprises everything that serves to make the people of God live their lives in holiness and increase their faith. In this way the Church in her doctrine, life and worship, perpetuates and transmits to every generation all that she herself is, all that she believes.' (DV 8)

This tradition involves statements, but it is at once wider in scope and more profound than statements. It is a living tradition, since by its means God continues his conversation: 'Thus God, who spoke in the past, continues to converse with the spouse of his beloved Son. And the Holy Spirit, through whom the living voice of the gospel rings out in the Church —and through her to the world....' (DV 8)

For this reason, the ministry of the word can be seen as giving voice to this living tradition, within the context of the entire tradition: 'The tradition which comes from the apostles makes progress in the Church, with the help of the Holy Spirit. There is a growth in insight into the realities and words that are being passed on. This comes about in various ways. It comes through the contemplation and study of believers who ponder these things in their hearts (see Luke 2:19 and 51). It comes from the intimate sense of spiritual realities which they experience. And it comes from the preaching of those who have received, along with their right of succession in the episcopate, the sure charism of truth.' (DV 8)

On the one hand, divine revelation, object of Catholic belief, completed in apostolic times, must be clearly distinguished from the grace of the Holy Spirit, without whose inspiration and illumination nobody can believe. On the other hand, God, unseen, still directs his Bride the Church and speaks to her through the Holy Spirit, in the sacred tradition and in the light and the sense of the faith, so that God's people may, under the guidance of the magisterium, acquire a more profound knowledge of revelation; this same God who once spoke to the human race, revealing himself, through divine happenings and the message of the prophets, Christ and the apostles.

The pastors of the Church have the task not only of proclaiming and explaining to the people, directly, the deposit of faith committed to them. They must also judge correctly the formulations and explanations sought and offered by the faithful: '...in maintaining, practising and professing the faith that has been handed on there should be a remarkable harmony between the bishops and the faithful.' (EV 10)

Hence the need for the ministry of the word to present divine revelation as it is taught by the magisterium and as it is expressed in the living awareness and faith of God's people, under the surveillance of the magisterium. In this way, the ministry of the word is not mere repetition of ancient doctrine, but its faithful reproduction, adapted to new problems and better understood.

Sacred scripture

14.   Divine revelation has also been committed to writing, under the special inspiration of the Holy Spirit. It is to be found in the holy books of the Old and New Testaments, which contain and present divinely-revealed truth. (see DV 11)

The Church, custodian and interpreter of the sacred scriptures, is taught by them, assiduously meditating on them and penetrating their meaning more and more. Faithful to tradition, the ministry of the word finds in sacred scripture nourishment and norm. (See DV 21, 24, 25.) For, in the sacred books, the heavenly Father comes lovingly to meet his children and speaks to them. (See DV 21)

But while the sacred scriptures are normative for the Church's thinking, the Church in turn, animated by the Spirit, is their interpreter: '...the holy scriptures themselves are more thoroughly and constantly actualised in the Church.' (DV 8)

The ministry of the word, therefore, has its point of departure in the sacred scripture and in the preaching of the apostles, as these are understood by the Church, explained and applied to concrete situations.

Faith: response to the word of God

15. It is by faith that a person accepts revelation and through it becomes consciously a sharer in God's gift.

The response that is owed to the revealing God is the obedience of faith, by which a person freely assents to the gospel of the grace of God (see Acts 20:24), offering the homage of mind and will. Under the tutelage of the faith, a person will, by the gift of the Spirit, reach the stage of contemplating and savouring the God of love, who has made known the riches of his glory in Christ (see Col. 1:26). Indeed, a living faith is the commencement of eternal life in us, when the deep mysteries of God will at last be seen by us, unveiled (see 1 Cor. 2:10). Faith, which knows God's saving plan, leads people to a full understanding of God's will for us in this world and to co-operation with his grace. 'For faith throws a new light on all things and makes known the full ideal which God has set for the human person, thus guiding the mind towards solutions that are fully human.' (GS 11)

Role of the ministry of the word

16. In short, the minister of the word should be fully conversant with the nature of his task, which is to arouse a living faith, capable of turning the mind towards God, to urge conformity with his actions, to lead to a vivid understanding of the contents of tradition, to propound and manifest the true meaning of the world and of human existence.

The ministry of the word is the communication of the message of salvation: it brings the gospel to people. The mystery which has been proclaimed and handed on touches profoundly that will to live, that deep-seated desire for fulfilment and that expectation of future happiness which God has implanted in everybody's heart and which by his grace he elevates to the supernatural.

One of the truths to be believed is that of the love of God, who created all things for the sake of Christ and restored us to life in Christ Jesus. In expounding the various aspects of the mystery, one should ensure that primary importance is placed on the central fact of Jesus, God's greatest gift to mankind.

All other truths of Catholic teaching take their place in order after that truth and, from the point of view of pedagogy, their place in the hierarchy of truths.

Chapter 2:
Catechesis in the Pastoral Mission of the Church
(Nature, Purpose, Efficacy)

The ministry of the word in the church

17.   The ministry of the word takes many forms, catechesis being one of them; the forms vary because conditions for the exercise of the ministry vary or because different objectives are envisaged. Thus, there is evangelization, or missionary preaching, whose objective is to implant the faith for the first time (see CD 11, 13; AG 6, 13), thereby securing the acceptance of the word of God.

There follows catechesis: 'Its function is to develop in man a living, explicit and active faith, enlightened by doctrine.' (CD 14)

Next comes liturgy, in the context of a liturgical celebration, especially a eucharistic celebration (e.g. the homily) (see SC 33, 52; *Inter oecumenici*, 54)

Lastly, there is theology, the systematic treatment and scientific investigation of the truths of faith.

The distinction between these different forms of catechesis is important for our purposes, each of them being subject to its own laws. In the concrete reality of pastoral ministry, however, they are closely connected.

All that has been said up to now, therefore, about the ministry of the word in general applies also to catechesis.

Catechesis and evangelization

18.   Catechesis as such presupposes a total acceptance of the gospel of Christ, put forward by the Church. Often, however, it is directed towards people who, though belonging to the Church, have never given true personal commitment to the message of revelation.

This shows that in certain circumstances evangelization can precede or accompany catechesis as such. In all cases, however, it must be borne in mind that conversion is always part of the dynamism of faith and that every form of catechesis must involve evangelization.

Forms of catechesis

19.   Catechetical activity takes various forms to meet varying circumstances and multiple needs.

In the older Christian countries, catechesis often takes the form of religious instruction imparted to children or adolescents in school or outside of school. These countries also have many types of catechetical programmes for adults. There are also catechumenate programmes for candidates for baptism or for people who, though baptised, have not had a proper Christian initiation. Very often the reality is such that great masses of the faithful need evangelization as a pre-requisite to catechesis.

In younger churches, evangelization as such takes on particular importance and thus one has the classical form of the catechumenate for those who are being initiated into the faith in preparation for baptism. (AG 4)

In short, catechesis can take many different forms: systematic or for a specific occasion, individual or common, organised or spontaneous, etc.

20.   Pastors of souls should always be mindful of their duty to ensure that God's word continues to shed light on Christian existence for all age groups and in all historical circumstances, and indeed to promote it (see CD 14), so that it will be possible to encounter all, whether as individuals or as communities, in the spiritual state which is actually theirs.

They should bear in mind too that the catechesis of adults, since it has to do with people who are capable of fully responsible commitment, must be accepted as the principal kind of catechesis, towards which all other forms, while always needed, are directed. They should take great care, in obedience to the regulations of Vatican II, 'to re-establish or to modernise the adult catechumenate.' (CD 14; see AG 14)

Functions of catechesis

21.   In the realm of pastoral activity, catechesis is that ecclesial activity which leads the community and individual Christians to maturity of faith.

With the help of catechesis, Christian communities acquire a more profound knowledge of God and of his salvation, centred on Christ, Word of God incarnate; they develop by endeavouring to make their faith mature and enlightened and they share this mature faith with those who wish it.

For all who are open to the message of the gospel, catechesis is an especially suitable means for understanding God's plan as it relates to their own lives and for seeking the ultimate meaning of existence and of history, so that the lives of every individual and of society may be illuminated by the light of the Kingdom of God and responsive to its demands and so that the mystery of the Church may be understood as the community of believers in the gospel.

All of these determine the functions of catechesis.

Catechesis and the grace of faith

22.   Faith is a gift of God, calling people to conversion: 'Before this faith can be exercised, people must have the grace of God to move and assist them; they must have the interior helps of the Holy Spirit, who moves the heart and converts it to God, who opens the eyes of the mind and "makes it easy for all to accept and believe the truth".' (DV 5)

A Christian community of mature faith lives in religious attention to the word of God, is constantly in pursuit of conversion and renewal and listens carefully to what the Holy Spirit says to the Church.

Catechesis exercises the function (through the word, together with the witness of life and prayer) of preparing people to be receptive to the action of the Holy Spirit and to be more thoroughly converted.

Catechesis and performance of the duties of faith

23.   A person of mature faith accepts totally the invitation of the gospel message to communion with God and with brothers and sisters and lives up to the obligations which flow from the invitation. (See AG 12)

Catechesis helps people really to achieve this communion with God, to proclaim the Christian message in a way that makes clear that the highest human values are safeguarded by it. All of which requires that catechesis keep before its eyes people's legitimate aspirations and the progress and full development of the values contained in them.

Communion with God and commitment to him necessarily involve the exercise of human responsibilities and the duty of solidarity, because this is the will of God the Saviour (see GS 5).

Therefore catechesis must promote and guide the development of theological charity in individual believers and in the ecclesial community and must encourage individuals and community to behave charitably in fulfilling their obligations.

Catechesis and knowledge of the faith

24.   A person of mature faith knows the mystery of salvation revealed in Christ, as well as the divine signs and works which testify to its realisation in human history. Therefore it is not enough for catechesis merely to arouse a religious feeling, however true; it must lead the faithful gradually towards a full understanding of the divine plan, initiating them into the reading of the scriptures and into knowledge of tradition.

Catechesis and the life of liturgical and of private prayer

25.   'Every liturgical celebration, because it is an action of Christ the Priest and of his Body, which is the Church, is a sacred action surpassing all others. No other action of the Church can equal its efficacy by the same title and to the same degree.' (SC 7) The more mature in faith the Christian community becomes, the more it lives its worship in spirit and in truth in liturgical celebrations, especially eucharistic celebrations (see John 4:23).

Catechesis should therefore be at the service of active, conscious and genuine participation in the Church's liturgy, not only by explaining the meaning of the rites, but also by training the faithful for prayer, for thanksgiving, for penance, for confident prayer of petition, for a sense of community, giving them a proper understanding of the symbols—all of which are necessary for a proper liturgical life.

'The spiritual life, however, is not limited solely to participation in the liturgy. The Christian is indeed called to pray with others, but he must also enter into his bedroom to pray to his Father in secret; furthermore, according to the teaching of the apostle, he must pray without ceasing.' (SC 12)

Catechesis must therefore train the faithful to meditate on the word of God and to pray in private.

Catechesis and Christian light on human existence

26.   People of mature faith are able to see, in every situation and in every encounter with their neighbours, God's invitation, calling them to fulfil his saving plan.

It is for catechesis, therefore, to emphasize this task, teaching the faithful a Christian interpretation of human affairs, especially the signs of the times, so that all 'will succeed in evaluating and interpreting everything with an authentically Christian sense of values.' (GS 62)

Catechesis and Christian unity

27.   Christian communities, in their own situation, should take part in the ecumenical dialogue and the other enterprises aimed at the restoration of Christian unity (see UR 5).

Catechesis should therefore collaborate in this matter (see UR 6), explaining clearly the full teaching of the Catholic Church (see UR 11), developing a good understanding of other religions, both where they agree and where they disagree with the Catholic faith, avoiding expressions or explanations that 'might by word or deed lead the separated brethren or any others whatever into error about the true doctrine of the Church.' (LG 67) The order or hierarchy of the truths of Catholic teaching should be observed (see UR 11; AG 15; *Ad Ecclesiam totam*, 14 May 1967 AAS 59 (1967) 574-592). The arguments in favour of Catholic teaching must be proposed with charity as well as with due firmness.

Catechesis and the church's mission in the world

28.   The Church is in Christ as a sacrament or sign and instrument of salvation and of the unity of the human race (see LG 1). This will be more obvious, however, the more mature in faith the individual Christian communities become. Catechesis should assist these communities in propagating the light of the gospel and in setting up fruitful dialogue with non-Christian people and cultures, providing religious liberty, properly understood, is safeguarded (see DH; AG 22).

Catechesis and eschatological hope

29.   People of mature faith direct their thoughts towards the total completion of the Kingdom in eternal life.

Catechesis therefore has the task of channelling people's hopes towards the future benefits in the heavenly Jerusalem, inviting them at the same time to involve themselves with all men and women in the construction of a better society (GS 39, 40-43).

Catechesis and the progress of the life of faith

30.   The one faith is found in the faithful, varying in intensity according to the measure of the grace of the Holy Spirit given to each one, and to be constantly prayed for (see Mark 9:23), and according to each one's response to this grace. Further, the life of faith changes as people's existence evolves, as

they reach maturity and take on life's responsibilities. Consequently, the life of faith, both in the over-all acceptance of the word of God, and in its development and application to life's responsibilities, can admit of varying degrees, depending on each person's maturity and the differences between individuals. (See n. 38) In other words, the acceptance of the faith, its development and application to people's lives vary from smaller to older children, from adolescents to adults. Catechesis has the task of assisting the rise and development of this life of faith through a person's entire life until the full manifestation of revealed truth and its impact on the person's life has been achieved.

The richness of catechetical work

31.   Catechesis is concerned with the community, but it does not ignore individual believers. It is linked with other pastoral duties in the Church, but it does not lose its specific character. It is involved simultaneously in initiation, education and formation.

It is very important that catechesis retain this rich variety of aspects, not allowing any one of them to become separated from the others, to their detriment.

Effectiveness of the word of God in catechesis

32.   The verse of scripture which says 'the word of God is alive and active' (Heb. 4:12) applies to catechesis too.

The divine word is made present in catechesis by the human word. Catechesis must faithfully expound the word of God and present it properly if it is to bear fruit in people, inducing in them the interior sentiments which remove indifference or uncertainty and leading them to embrace the faith. Further, the effectiveness of catechesis is greatly strengthened by the life-witness of the catechist and of the ecclesial community (see n. 35).

Catechesis, therefore, must convey the word of God, as expounded by the Church, in the language of the people for whom it is intended (see DV 13; OT 16). When God revealed himself to the human race, he entrusted his word to human words, giving it expression in the language of a particular culture (see DV 12). The Church, to which Christ committed the deposit of revelation, tries to convey it until the end of time in living language[1] to people of every culture and condition and to explain and interpret it.

God's pedagogy in revealing and the Church's in catechising

33.   The pedagogy employed by God in the unfolding of revelation was to announce his plan of salvation through prophecy and signs in the old covenant, thus preparing for the coming of his Son, the author of the new covenant and the perfecter of belief (see Heb., 12:2).

Now that revelation has been concluded, the Church must communicate the entire mystery of our salvation in Christ to those who are to be catechised. Because God employed pedagogy, the Church does too, but a new pedagogy, suited to the new needs of the message. She sees to it, that is to say, that it is adapted to the capacity of those to be catechised, without adulteration or mutilation.

On the one hand, therefore, for those of limited ability, she expounds the doctrine simply and briefly, using also suitable summaries which will be further developed later. On the other hand, for those with more lively and capable minds, she tries to meet their needs by providing more profound explanations.

Being faithful to God and concerned for people

34.   The Church discharges this task through catechesis, principally (see DV 24). Catechesis derives the truth from the word of God, totally committed to its security when it is given expression, and it endeavours to teach this word of God in total fidelity. However, the task cannot be merely a matter of repeating traditional formulas. The formulas must be understood and, where necessary, faithfully re-formulated in language suited to the capacity of the audience. The language will be different for different age groups, social conditions, cultures and civilisations. (DV 8; CD 14)

The need for ecclesial witness

35.   Catechesis, lastly, requires from catechists and the entire ecclesial community the witness of faith, allied to the example of an authentic Christian life and willingness to make sacrifices (see LG 12, 17; NA 2).

For Christ encounters men and women not just through the sacred ministry, but also through individual believers and their communities (see LG 35), which therefore places on them the duty to bear witness. If such witness is lacking, an obstacle is placed in the way of the acceptance of God's word by the listeners.

Catechesis needs to be supported by the witness of the ecclesial community. For catechesis is more effective when speaking about what actually exists visibly in the community. The catechist is, as it were, the interpreter of the Church for those who are to be catechised. He reads the signs of the faith, of which the Church is the chief one, and teaches how they should be read. (See First Vatican Council, Dogmatic Constitution, *Dei Filius*: DS 3014)

Hence it is clear how necessary it is that, according to the mind of the Church and following the lead of its pastors, the ecclesial community should remove or correct whatever disfigures the face of the Church and places an obstacle to people's acceptance of the faith (see GS 19).

Catechists therefore have the duty not only to teach catechesis directly, but also to help animate the ecclesial community so that it will give a genuinely Christian witness.

Catechetical activity, therefore, is part of that general pastoral activity in which all the elements of the life of the Church are properly arranged and linked together (see GS 4, 7, 43).

PART 3:
THE CHRISTIAN MESSAGE

Significance and scope of this section

36. Faith, whose maturity is to be developed by catechesis, can be regarded in two ways: either as a person's total commitment, under the influence of grace, to God revealing himself (faith by which one believes, *fides qua*), or as the content of revelation and of the Christian message (the faith which one believes, *fides quae*).[2]

These two aspects of their very nature are inseparable and normal maturing in the faith presupposes that they would both grow in unison. However, they can be distinguished for methodological purposes.

This third part treats of the content of the faith, in the following manner. The first chapter describes the norms or criteria which catechesis must observe in the discovery and exposition of its content. The second chapter treats of the content itself. Not that it in any way sets out to expound every single Christian truth which comes within the ambit of faith and catechesis, nor to enumerate the principal errors of our time or those truths of faith which nowadays are being more strongly denied or neglected. The ordinary and extraordinary magisterium of the Church provides for this authoritatively in its public pronouncements.

Much less is there any intention in this chapter of showing how the truths of faith can be set out in an organic synthesis which takes account of their objective relative importance or of what is most needed for the people of today, either according to their ages or their socio-cultural situation. This is a task for theology or for the various forms of exposition of Christian doctrine.

It was deemed useful, rather, to describe in the second chapter—using formulations broad enough to include later refinements—some of the more fundamental elements of the saving message, organically linked together, certainly, especially under those aspects which must emerge more clearly in a renewed catechesis, in faithful pursuit of its goal.

Chapter 1:
Norms or Criteria

The content of catechesis in relation to various forms of ecclesial life, to different cultures and different languages

37.   Revelation is the manifestation in history of the mystery of God and of his saving action, by means of a personal communication of God to humankind, the contents of which comprise the message of salvation to be preached to all peoples.

It is the fundamental and inescapable task of the prophetic ministry of the Church to make the contents of this message intelligible to people of every age, so that they may be converted to God through Christ, may interpret their entire lives by the light of faith, whatever the time and place in which they live and may live as befits the dignity which the message of salvation has brought and faith revealed to them.

To achieve this aim catechesis—and here is an excellent opportunity for the prophetic ministry of the Church—should not only develop a close and constant contact with the various ways of life in the ecclesial community and should endeavour to bring the various formulations of the divine message into line with different cultures and languages.

The aim of catechesis is to present the entire content

38.   The parts of the message of salvation are closely inter-

connected, even though its revelation by God was a gradual process, first by the prophets, last of all in his Son (see Heb., 1:1). Since the aim of catechesis, as has been said, is to lead both individual Christians and communities to mature faith, it should take great care to proclaim the treasure of the Christian message faithfully in its entirety. This must certainly be done after the example of the divine pedagogy (see n. 33), but taking into account the fullness of the divine revelation which has been communicated, so that the people of God may be nourished by it and live by it.

Catechesis begins therefore with a more simple presentation of the whole structure of the Christian message (using also summary or general formulations), and propounds it in a manner suited to the varying cultural and spiritual conditions of those to be catechised. There can be no question of catechesis ceasing after this initial presentation. It is well to bear in mind the need for a fuller and more detailed treatment, so that the individual believers and the Christian community may arrive at an increasingly profound and vital acceptance of the Christian message and may resolve the concrete problems of the human condition in the light of revelation.

Catechesis must perform this difficult task under the guidance of the Church's magisterium, whose task it is to safeguard always the truth of the divine message and, further, to ensure that the ministry of the word employs appropriate terms and takes prudently into account the assistance afforded by theological research and the human sciences.

The content of catechesis comprises an organic, vital whole

39.   The object of faith is a complex matter: God in his mystery and his saving intervention in history; all of which are known from what God revealed about himself and his works. Christ is of central importance both in God's saving intervention and in his manifestation to people. The objects therefore of catechesis are the mysteries of God and the works of God, that is works which God did, does and will do for us men and for our salvation. All of these form a coherent whole and comprise the economy of salvation.

A catechesis which would neglect such a synthesis and harmony would be totally ineffective.

Catechesis is Christo-centric

40.   Since Christ Jesus, Word of God Incarnate, is the ulti-

mate reason why God intervened in the world and showed himself to people, he is the centre of the gospel message in salvation history.

He is 'the image of the invisible God; his is the primacy over all created things. In him everything in heaven and on earth was created'. (Col 1:15) He is in fact the one valid mediator through whom God encounters man and woman and through whom they are led to God (see 1 Tim 2:5). The Church is founded on him. In him all things are renewed. (See Eph. 1:10) Created things, therefore, the human conscience, the genuine values to be found in other religions, the various signs of the times: all of these are to be considered paths and steps—though not all to the same degree—by which one can approach God, under the influence of divine grace and oriented towards the Church of Christ.

For this reason, catechesis must necessarily be Christocentric.

Trinitarian theocentrism of catechesis

41.   Just as Christ is the centre of salvation history, so the mystery of God is the centre from which this mystery originated and towards which it is ordained as to its final end. The crucified and risen Christ leads people to the Father by sending the Spirit to God's people. For this reason, the structure of the entire content of catechesis must be theocentric-trinitarian: through Christ, to the Father, in the Spirit.

Through Christ: The entire economy of salvation is given meaning by the Word Incarnate, whose coming it prepared, whose kingdom on earth it manifests and extends after his death and resurrection until his second glorious coming, which will complete God's work. The mystery of Christ thus throws light on the entire content of catechesis. The different elements —biblical, evangelical, ecclesial, human and even cosmic— which catechesis has to take up and expound are to be seen in relation to the Son of God Incarnate.

To the Father: The ultimate purpose of the Incarnation of the Word and of the entire economy of salvation is to lead all men and women to the Father. Catechesis, therefore, since it falls to it to help make this loving plan of the heavenly Father increasingly understood, must be at pains to show that the ultimate meaning of human life consists in this: to know God and to glorify him by doing his will, as Christ taught us by his words and by the example of his life, and thus to attain eternal life.

In the Spirit: Knowledge of the mystery of Christ and making one's way to the Father are achieved in the Holy Spirit. When catechesis is expounding the content of the Christian mystery, therefore, it should always emphasise this presence of the Holy Spirit, by which people are constantly led to communion with God and people and to do their duty.

If catechesis lacks these three elements or ignores the close relationship between them, the Christian message can really cease to be itself.

For us men and women and for our salvation

42. The theocentric-trinitarian purpose of the economy of salvation cannot be separated from its objective, which is to free people from sin and its consequences and to make them as much like Christ as possible (see LG 39). Every revealed truth, like the incarnation of the Word, is for us people and for our salvation. One of the conditions for a most fruitful understanding of the various Christian truths is that one sees them from the perspective of people's last end (see First Vatican Council, Const. *Dei Filius,* DS 3016).

Catechesis therefore must show clearly the intimate connection between the mystery of God, Christ, human existence and the last end. This is by no means to disparage earthly aims, to whose achievement people are called by God as individuals or as communities, but rather to teach clearly that the ultimate destiny of human beings is not to be found in temporal goals, but rather that it surpasses them beyond all expectations, to an extent that only God's love for humankind could have devised.

Hierarchy of truths to be observed in catechesis

43. There is a certain hierarchy of truths in the message of salvation (see UR 10), which the Church has always acknowledged in composing creeds or summaries of the truths of faith. The fact that there is a hierarchy does not imply that some truths have less connection with the faith than others, but that some truths are based on more important truths which clarify their meaning.

Catechesis must, at every level, take this hierarchy of truths into account.

These truths can be grouped under four basic headings: the mystery of God, Father, Son and Holy Spirit, creator of all things; the mystery of Christ, Word incarnate, who was born of the Virgin Mary, suffered, died and rose again for our salvation; the mystery of the Holy Spirit, present in the Church and sanctifying and guiding it until the coming of Christ, our Saviour and Judge, in glory; the mystery of the Church, the mystical Body of Christ, in which the Virgin Mary has the highest place.

Historical character of the mystery of salvation

44. The economy of salvation is being perfected in the temporal order. It began in the past, progressed towards its apex in Christ, unfolds its meaning in the present time and awaits its completion in the future. It is therefore entirely appropriate that memory of the past, awareness of the present and hope of the future life should figure in the exposition of the content of catechesis.

Catechesis recalls the greatest event in all of salvation history, the event with which Christians are united by faith, the incarnation, passion, death and resurrection of Christ.

Catechesis, moreover, enables Christians to perceive how the saving mystery of Christ operates through the Holy Spirit and the ministry of the Church today and through the ages and it helps them to understand what their duties are towards God, towards themselves and towards their neighbour.

Catechesis, lastly, opens people's hearts to hope of the future life, the fulfillment of the entire history of salvation, towards which Christians have to travel with filial trust, but not without a holy fear of the divine judgment. Because of this hope, the Christian community is pervaded by a deep eschatological expectation which gives it a sound understanding of human and earthly values, reducing them to their proper proportions without at the same time despising them as valueless.

Constant and effective account must be taken of these three aspects in the exposition of the content of catechesis.

Sources of catechesis

45. The content of catechesis is to be found in the word of God in scripture and tradition[3]; its meaning is more deeply penetrated and developed by the community of believers under the guidance of the magisterium, the sole authentic teacher; it is celebrated in the liturgy; it shines out in the life of the Church, especially in holy people and in saints; and to some extent it appears in the genuine moral values which by God's providence exist in society.

All these are the sources of catechesis, whether principal or subsidiary sources. They must by no means be all accorded the same level of acceptance. In employing them, the catechist will firstly and always take account of the undoubted pre-eminence of the revelation in scripture and tradition and of the authority of the magisterium of the Church in matters connected with the faith.

Further, in expounding any portion of the content of the faith, the catechist should mark well how the mystery of Christ is its centre; how the Church interprets that part and defines it, how she celebrates it, puts it into effect and makes it part of the liturgy and of Christian practice. Lastly, the catechist should examine closely the problem of how God's plan can be carried out today with the help of the Holy Spirit.

General principle of the methodology of catechesis

46. The above norms, which pertain to the exposition of the content of catechesis, should be applied in the different types of catechesis: in biblical and liturgical catechesis, in a doctrinal synthesis, in interpreting the conditions of human existence, etc.

However, one cannot deduce from them the order to be observed in expounding the material. It is permissible to begin with God to arrive at Christ, and vice versa; similarly, it is permissible to begin with humanity to arrive at God, and vice versa. A method of pedagogy must be chosen in the light of the situation of the ecclesial community or the individual believers to be catechised. Hence the necessity of being at pains to discover the method best suited to each situation.

It will be for episcopal conferences to issue more precise directives and to apply them in catechetical directories, catechisms geared to the different age-groups and cultural levels, and other aids that seem appropriate.

Chapter 2:
The More Important Elements of the Christian Message

The mystery of the one God: Father, Son and Holy Spirit

47. The history of salvation is the story of how the one, true God, Father, Son and Holy Spirit, revealed himself to the human race, reconciled and joined to himself those who had turned away from their sins.

The Old Testament, while clearly affirming the unity of God in a polytheistic world, already foreshadows to some extent the mystery of the Trinity, which is fully unfolded in the person and in the words of Jesus Christ. For when he reveals himself as Son of God, he also reveals the Father and the Holy Spirit. An intimate knowledge of the true God pervades the entire soul of the divine Master. He communicates it to his followers, inviting them to become sons of God through the gift of his filial Spirit which he bestowed on them (see John 1:12).

In catechesis therefore the encounter with God one and triune occurs first and principally when the Father, Son and Holy Spirit are recognised as the authors of that plan of salvation which culminated in the death and resurrection of Jesus. (See St. Ireneus, *The Proof of the Apostolic Preaching*, n. 6) In this way, the revelation of the mystery transmitted in the Church is met by the growing awareness of the faithful that from baptism their lives consist in achieving more intimate familiarity with the three divine persons, called as they are to share their divine nature. Lastly, Christians are able, with the eyes of faith, through the gift of the Holy Spirit, to contemplate now and to approach in filial love the most holy Trinity of Persons, as it exists from eternity in God's intimate life.

Genuine worship of God in a secularized world

48. 'The God and Father of our Lord Jesus Christ' (Eph. 1:3) is 'the living God' (Matt. 16:16). He is holy, just, merciful, he is God the author of the covenant with men, God who sees, frees, saves, God who loves as a father, as a bridegroom. Catechesis joyfully announces this God, the source of all our hope (see 1 Pet., 1:3-4).

Catechesis cannot ignore the fact that many people of our time have an acute sense of a remoteness, even an absence, of God. This is part of the process of secularization and it is a danger to the faith, but it also urges us to have a purer faith and to become more humble before the mystery of God, as is right: 'Truly you are a hidden God, the God of Israel, our saviour.' (Is. 45:15) From this viewpoint it is possible to understand more easily the true nature of worship which God requires and which glorifies him: a worship, that is, which goes hand in hand with the resolve to fulfil his will in all spheres of activity and faithfully to multiply in charity the talents bestowed by the Lord (see Matt 25:14 ff). In the liturgy, the faithful bring the fruits of all their acts of charity, justice and peace and offer them humbly to God. From the liturgy they receive the words of life and grace, which they need to speak the truth in charity (see Eph. 4:15) in the world, in communion with Christ, who offers his body and blood for the human race.

Knowledge of God and the witness of charity

49. The greatest contribution that Christians can make towards bringing the atheistic world to God is the witness of a life in conformity with Christ's message of love and of a living and mature faith which is expressed in works of justice and charity (see GS 21).

The right use of human reason should not be neglected, however, for as the Church holds and teaches (see Vatican Council 1, Const. *Dei Filius:* DS 3004-3005, 3026) God the beginning and end of all things can be known from created things. Not only does this knowlege of God not diminish human dignity, it gives it foundation and stability.

The eternal salvation of the human race is indeed the Church's objective, but at the same time belief in God carries with it a serious obligation to collaborate in solving human problems (see 1 John 4:20-21). Christians must bear witness to the worth of the Lord's message by their actions in this field.

Jesus Christ, Son of God, first-born of all creation, Saviour

50. God's greatest work is the incarnation of his Son, Jesus Christ. The first-born of all creation, he takes precedence over all and all things are held together in him (Col. 1:15-17). In him, through him and for him all things have been created (Col. 1:15, ff).

Having become obedient unto death, he was exalted as Lord of all and was made manifest to us through the resurrection as Son of God by a mighty act (see Rom. 1:4). First-born from the dead, he gave life to all (1 Cor. 15:22). In him we have been made a new creation (see Eph 2:10). Through him all of creation will be freed from the slavery of corruption (see Rom. 8:19-21). 'There is no salvation in anyone else at all.' (Acts 4:12)

Creation the beginning of the economy of salvation

51. The world created out of nothing is in fact the world in which salvation and redemption are effected in Jesus Christ.

Already in the Old Testament, the truth of God's creative activity is not put forward as an abstract philosophical principle, but gains entry into the minds of the Israelites with the help of the notion of the unity of God, as a proclamation of Yahweh's power and victory, as demonstration that God always stands by his people (see Is., 40:27-28). The omnipotence of God the creator is most clearly manifested in Christ's resurrection, in which is revealed 'how vast are the resources of his power.' (Eph 1:19)

Consequently, the truth of creation is not to be put forward simply as a truth standing on its own, artificially separated from the rest, but as something which is in fact related to the salvation won by Jesus Christ. The creation of things visible and things invisible, of the world and of angels, is the commencement of the history of salvation (see DV 3); the creation of man (see Pius XII, Enc. *Humani generis;* GS 12, 14) is to be regarded as the first gift and the first call that leads to glorification in Christ (see Rom 8:29-30).

When they hear the exposition of the teaching on creation, Christians ought not to stop short at thinking about that first act when God 'created heaven and earth' (Gen. 1:1), they should turn their minds also to all of God's salvific enterprises. They are always present in human and world history; they are especially visible in the history of Israel and they lead towards the supreme event, the resurrection of Christ and they will at last be fulfilled at the end of time, when there will be a new heaven and a new earth (see 2 Pet. 3:13).

Jesus Christ, centre of the entire economy of salvation

52. The faithful recognize in Jesus Christ their solidarity with history and with the entire human race. The history of salvation is inserted into the history of the world and through it God puts into effect his plan to perfect 'the whole Christ' in time. Christians acknowledge simply and sincerely that they have a part in this work, whose object is that, through the power of Jesus the Saviour, creation should fully glorify God (see 1 Cor. 15:28).

Jesus Christ, true God and true man, in the unity of the divine person

53. This great mystery, that Christ is Head and Lord of all things, has been 'manifested in the body' to men and women. The man Jesus Christ, who lived among men and women labouring with his hands, thinking with a human mind, acting with a human will, loving with a human heart, is truly the Word and Son of God, who in a sense joined himself to every man and woman through his incarnation (see GS 22).

Catechesis must preach Jesus in his concrete existence and in his message: it must, that is to say, give people such access to the wonderful perfection of his humanity that they will be able to acknowledge the mystery of his divinity. In fact, even though Christ Jesus was joined to the Father in an assiduous and unique habit of prayer, he lived in closest contact with men and women. His goodness embraced all, the just and sinners, the poor and the rich, fellow-citizens and foreigners. If he loved any people more than the rest, it was the sick, the poor and the lowly. He showed a reverence and a solicitude for the human person which nobody had ever shown before.

Catechesis must constantly defend and strengthen belief in the divinity of Jesus Christ, so that he may be accepted not only for his admirable human life, but will be acknowledged from his words and signs as God's only Son (see John 1:18): 'God from God, light from light, true God from true God, begotten not made, consubstantial with the Father' (DS 150) The right understanding of the mystery of the incarnation has developed in Christian tradition: Fathers and councils directed their efforts, by constant study of the faith, towards refining the concepts, towards explaining more deeply the exact nature of the mystery of Christ, towards investigating the mysterious links between him and the heavenly Father and the human race. There is the witness to this truth which the Church has provided through the ages, the witness of the Christian life: the communion between God and human beings which is given in Christ is a source of joy and unbounded hope. The fullness of divinity is in Christ, God's love for the human race is made manifest in him.

Saint Ignatius of Antioch has written: 'There is but one physician, bodily and spiritual, born and unborn, God in flesh, true life in death, from Mary and from God, at first incapable of suffering and then capable of suffering, Jesus Christ our Lord.' (*Enchiridion patristicum,* 39)

Jesus Christ Saviour and Redeemer of the world

54. The mystery of Christ appears in human and world history, subject as it is to sin, as the mystery not merely of the incarnation but of salvation and redemption.

God so loved sinful humanity as to give his Son to reconcile the world with himself (see 2 Cor. 5:19). Jesus therefore, the first born of many brothers (see Rom. 8:29), holy, innocent, immaculate (see Heb. 7:26), freely obedient to his Father out of filial love (see Phil 2:8), accepted death for the sake of his brothers and sisters as their Mediator, death being for them the wages of sin (see Rom 6:23; GS 18). He redeemed the human race from slavery to sin and to the devil by his holy death and he poured out the spirit of adoption on it, establishing a new humanity in himself.

The Sacraments are the actions of Christ in the church, the primordial sacrament

55. The Church always enjoys Christ's presence and ministers to him; the mystery of Christ continues in the Church, specifically through those signs instituted by Christ which signify and produce the gift of grace and which are known as sacraments (see Council of Trent, Decree on the Sacraments, DS 1601).

Since the Church is not merely the people of God but also, as it were, in Christ 'a sign and instrument...of communion with God and of unity among all men' (LG 1) it should be regarded as the primordial sacrament.

The sacraments are the primary and fundamental actions by which Jesus Christ constantly bestows his Spirit on the faithful, making them a holy people who, in him and with him, offer themselves as an acceptable offering to the Father. The sacraments are surely to be regarded as being of inestimable value to the Church, to which belongs the power to administer them. They must always however be referred to Christ, from whom their effectiveness derives. In fact, it is Christ who baptizes. It is not so much a man who celebrates the Eucharist, as Christ himself: he offers himself by the ministry of priests in the sacrifice of the Mass, DS 1743). The sacramental action is, first and foremost, Christ's action and the Church's ministers are, as it were, his instruments.

The full significance of the sacraments

56. It will be for catechesis to present the seven sacraments in a way that brings out their full meaning.

First, they must be presented as sacraments of faith. Of themselves they certainly express the effective will of Christ the Saviour; for their part, men and women must manifest a sincere willingness to respond to God's love and mercy. Therefore catechesis must take care to evoke the proper dispositions and to stimulate sincerity and generosity so as to ensure worthy reception of the sacraments.

Second, the sacraments should be presented—each of them, of course, in keeping with its nature and purpose—not only as remedies for sin and for its consequences, but especially as sources of grace for individuals and for communities, in such wise that the entire dispensation of grace in the lives of the faithful would be seen to be linked to the sacramental economy.

Catechesis on the sacraments

57. By baptism men and women are cleansed from original sin and from all personal sins, they are born again as children of God, are made part of the Church and are made holy by the gifts of the Holy Spirit. By an indelible character impressed on their souls, they are given an initial share in Christ's priestly, prophetic and kingly power (see 1 Pet., 2:9).

By confirmation Christians are more closely linked to the Church and are especially strengthened by the Holy Spirit to enable them to live in the world as Christ's witnesses.

The life of Christians on earth is a battle, exposed to temptation and sin. For this reason, the way of the sacrament of penance is open to them, enabling them to obtain pardon from the God of mercy and to be reconciled with the Church.

Orders impart to some of God's people a special likeness to Christ the Mediator, giving them the sacred power to care for the Church, to nourish the faithful with God's word and to sanctify them and, above all, acting for Christ, to offer the sacrifice of the Mass and to preside at the eucharistic banquet.

'By the sacred anointing of the sick and the prayer of the priests the whole Church commends those who are ill to the suffering and glorified Lord that he may raise up and save them' (see James 5:14-16) (LG 11).

The eucharist, centre of the entire sacramental life

58. The primacy of the eucharist over all the sacraments is beyond question, as is its supreme effectiveness in building up the Church (see LG 11, 17; 'Instruction on the Worship of the Eucharist', 5-15).

In the eucharist, when the words of consecration have been pronounced, the profound reality (but not the appearance) of bread and wine is changed into the body and blood of Christ. This wonderful change has been given the name 'transubstantiation' in the Church. Thus it is that under the appearance (that is, the phenomenal reality) of bread and wine, the very humanity of Christ—not just its power, but itself, that is the substance—is hidden in a totally unfathomable way, together with his divine person (see Paul VI, Encyc., *Mysterium fidei: AAS* 57 (1965), 766).

This sacrifice is not merely a rite commemorating a past sacrifice. Over the centuries Christ perpetuates in it in an unbloody manner the sacrifice of the cross (see SC 47) and gives himself, the bread of life, as food to believers so that they may be filled with love of God and of their neighbour and thus increasingly become a people acceptable to God.

When they have been to the table of the sacrificial victim, the faithful must by their genuine and active love give the lie to the accusation sometimes levelled against them, that their worship is sterile, cutting them off from human collaboration and fraternity. The eucharistic banquet is intended to enable the faithful by frequent prayer to join their hearts increasingly to God and thus acknowledge and love other men and women as brothers and sisters and children.

The sacrament of matrimony

59. Without denying the superiority which Christian witness accords to virginity (see 1 Cor. 7:38; Counc. of Trent, Canons on Sacr. of Matrimony, DS 1810), considerable emphasis must be placed nowadays on catechetical instruction on marriage, which was instituted by the creator himself and equipped with various benefits, purposes and laws (see GS 48).

Catechesis on marriage should be based on the words of the faith and on natural law, should be guided by the magisterium of the Church, the authentic interpreter of moral and natural law (see *Humanae Vitae* 4) and should take proper account of present-day progress in the science of anthropology. It should make matrimony the foundation of family life, in its values and in the divine law of unity and indissolubility, in its obligation to love, which of its very nature is ordered to the procreation and education of children. In the regulation of births, conjugal chastity according to the teaching of the Church must be observed (see *Humanae Vitae,* 14).

Christ raised marriage to the dignity of a sacrament for Christians. The spouses administer the sacrament to each other when they exchange personal and irrevocable consent. Living in the grace of Christ, they imitate and in a sense represent the love of Christ himself for his Church (see Eph. 5:25). Christian couples are given strength by this special sacrament to fulfill the duties of their state and to uphold its dignity and, as it were, they are consecrated (see GS 48).

Lastly, it is part of the vocation of a family to be a community open also to the Church and the world.

The new man

60. When people receive the Spirit of Christ, they establish a way of life with God which is totally new and free.

The Holy Spirit, present in Christians' souls, makes them sharers in the divine nature, intimately united with the Father and with Christ in a shared life, which not even death can destroy (see John 14:23). The Holy Spirit cures people of their spiritual weaknesses and maladies; frees them from slavery to their passions and immoderate love of self, giving them strength to obey the divine law; equips them with hope and courage; enlightens them in their pursuit of the good; gives them the fruits of charity, joy, peace, patience, kindness, goodness, magnanimity, gentleness, fidelity, modesty, continence, chastity (see Gal. 5:22-23). This is why the Holy Spirit is invoked as the guest of the soul.

Justification from sin and God's indwelling in the soul are called grace. When sinners are said to be justified by God, to be enlivened by the Spirit of God, to possess the life of Christ in themselves, or to have grace, we are using expressions which say the same thing in different words—that is, that they die to sin, they become sharers in the Son's divine nature through the spirit of adoption and that they enter into an intimate shared life with the Most Holy Trinity.

Men and women in the history of salvation are people called to the grace of being adopted sons and daughters and to eternal life. Christian anthropology finds its proper character in the grace of Christ the Saviour.

Human and Christian liberty

61. God's call to men and women requires of them a free response in Jesus Christ.

Men and women cannot be unfree. Their dignity and their role very definitely demand that, in control of their own activity, they should obey the moral natural and supernatural law and thus come close to God who revealed himself in Christ. Because of original sin, human liberty has become so limited that men and women are incapable, without the help of God's grace, of observing the obligations of even the natural law for very long. With the advent of grace, however, their liberty is elevated and strengthened and it is made possible for them to live earthly lives of holiness in the faith of Jesus Christ (see Gal 2:20).

It is for the Church to defend and promote a true understanding of freedom and its proper use, against every sort of unjust restriction. The Church should also protect freedom against those who deny its existence, maintaining that human activity is psychologically determined or is determined by economic, social and cultural conditions, etc.

The Church however is by no means unaware that freedom, even when helped by divine grace, can be affected by grave psychological difficulties and by a person's environment to such an extent that human responsibility is often diminished, in some cases the person being only barely responsible, or not at all. The Church also takes cognizance of research into the use and limits of human freedom and of modern progress in the anthropological sciences in this field. Therefore she concerns herself with teaching and promoting genuine liberty and with procuring the proper psychological, social, economic, political and religious conditions for the true and just exercise of freedom. Christians therefore should work unremittingly and sincerely in the temporal order for the establishment, as far as possible, of the optimum conditions for the right exercise of liberty. This is a duty they share with all people of good will, but they know that they have a more valid and more urgent reason. What is in question, in fact, is not just the promotion of an earthly value, rather is it a matter of a duty which in the ultimate analysis will lead to the acquisition of the inestimable benefits of grace and of eternal salvation.

Sin

62. The principal obstacle to human liberty, however, does not come from people's history and environment. The greatest obstacle to the work of salvation is sin.

'Although set up by God in a state of rectitude, man, enticed by the evil one, abused his freedom at the very start of history. He lifted himself up against God, and sought to attain his goal apart from him.' (GS 13) 'Through one man sin entered the world, and with sin death, death thus coming to all men inasmuch as all sinned.' (Rom. 5:12) 'It is human nature thus fallen, deprived of the gift of grace with which it had previously been endowed, wounded in its natural powers and subject to the dominion of death, which is given to all men and women, for which reason they are all born in sin.' (Paul VI, *Profession of Faith*, n. 16) Consequently, the multiplication of sins has become the sad experience of humanity and has become the cause of sorrows of all kinds and of ruin. Nor should one fail to mention the doctrine of the nature and effects of personal sin, by which a person knowingly and deliberately transgresses the moral law and offends God gravely in a grave manner.

The history of salvation is also the history of liberation from sin. The purpose of all of God's interventions, whether in the Old Testament or in the New Testament, has been to guide people in their struggle against the forces of sin. Christ's role in the history of salvation is the destruction of sin and he accomplished this in the mystery of the cross. Saint Paul's profound reflections on the reality of sin and on Christ's consequent 'work of justice' (see Rom. 5) are among the principal elements of the Christian faith and must be included in catechesis.

At the same time, the salvation effected by Christ is much more important than redemption from sin, since it marks the completion of God's plan to communicate himself in Jesus in a way that is totally beyond human comprehension. What is in question is a plan which has not been shelved because of human transgressions but confers grace in superabundance in comparison with the death caused by sin (see Rom. 5:15-17). This plan, the product of love, by which people are invited to share the divine life itself through the Holy Spirit, is always in force and applies to every age. Even though men and women are sinners, they belong always in the only order of things willed by God, that in which God mercifully communicates himself to us in Jesus Christ. They can therefore, under the impulse of grace, attain salvation through repentance.

The moral life of Christians

63. Christ commissioned his apostles to teach the observance of all that he had commanded (see Matt. 28:20). Catechesis, therefore, must be concerned not only with what has to be believed, but with what has to be done.

The moral life of Christians, which is behaviour befitting men and women adopted by God as his sons and daughters, is in conformity with the obligation to live and grow, under the guidance of the Holy Spirit, in the new life communicated by Jesus Christ.

The moral life of Christians is guided by grace and by the gifts of the Holy Spirit: 'The love of God has been poured out in our hearts through the Holy Spirit which has been given to us.' (Rom 5:5)

Docility to the Holy Spirit implies also the faithful observance of God's commandments, of the laws of the Church and of just civil laws.

Christian liberty needs, further, to be regulated and guided in the everyday conditions of human life. For this reason, the consciences of the faithful must be guided by the virtue of prudence, but must also be subject to the Church's magisterium, whose task it is to expound authoritatively the entire moral law so that it will be a right and true expression of the objective moral order.

Christian consciences must also be taught that there are absolute norms, which are binding in every instance and on all peoples. For this reason, the saints gave witness to Christ by the exercise of heroic virtues and the martyrs suffered torture and death rather than deny Christ.

The perfection of charity

64. To single out what is characteristic of Christian moral teaching is to show clearly the meaning of the action of the Spirit of Christ, for all the precepts and counsels of Christian moral teaching can be reduced, as to its soul, to faith working through charity (see Gal 5:6).

Men and women are called to obey the will of God freely in all things. This is 'the obedience of faith by which people freely commit their entire selves to God' (DV 5). God is love and his design is to communicate his love in Jesus Christ and to call people together in love of one another. It follows that to commit oneself freely and perfectly to God and to his design amounts to taking on a way of life that is ruled by love in the observance of the commandments. In other words, it is the same as accepting the precept of charity as a new commandment and putting it into practice.

Men and women therefore are called to take on in faith a life of love of God and neighbour. Here is their greatest responsibility and their high moral dignity. For men and women, whatever their vocation and state in life, holiness is simply the perfection of charity (see LG 39-42).

The church, people of God and saving institution

65. The Church, instituted by Christ, began from his death and resurrection. It is the new people of God, prepared through Israel's history, a people to which Christ gives life and growth by the outpouring of the Spirit and which he perpetually renews and directs with hierarchical and charismatic gifts: 'a people brought into unity from the unity of the Father, the Son and the Holy Spirit.' (LG 4)

The Church, therefore, as people of God, society of the faithful, communion of people in Christ, is the work of God's saving love in Christ.

For the elements which make Christians what they are, which form them and make them a community—that is, the deposit of faith, the sacraments, apostolic ministries—are found in the Catholic Church, entrusted to it, and they are the source of ecclesial activities. In other words, in the Church are all the means that are needed to gather it together and to bring it to maturity as the communion of men and women in Christ. This work is the product not only of the transcendental action of God, not only of the invisible activity of Christ and of his Spirit. It is also the product of the institutions, offices and saving actions of the Church. The Church therefore is not only the society of believers, it is also, thanks to its ministerial and saving work, the mother of believers.

The Church, the holy people of God, shares in Christ's prophetic office (see LG 12). Gathered together by the word of God, it accepts it and bears witness to it in all the world. It is a priestly people: 'Christ the Lord, high priest taken from among men, made the new people "a kingdom of priests to God his Father" (Apod. 1:6). The baptized, by regeneration and the anointing of the Holy Spirit, are consecrated to be a spiritual house and a holy priesthood, that through all the works of Christian men and women they may offer spiritual sacrifices and proclaim the perfection of him who called them out of darkness into his marvellous light.' (LG 10) The Church, however, is essentially an hierarchical society: a people led by its pastors united with the Supreme Pontiff, the Vicar of Christ, and under his guidance (see LG 22). The faithful look to them with filial love and obedient respect. It is a people on pilgrimage towards the fullness of the mystery of Christ.

On the one hand, the presence of the Holy Spirit in the Church is an unfailing guarantee of the objective conditions for its saving encounter with Christ. On the other hand, it ensures that in its members, and for its members, and in such of its structures as are changeable, it strives for continual purification and renewal.

The church as communion

66. The Church is a communion: it itself acquired a fuller understanding of that truth at the Second Vatican Council.

It is the people gathered together by God and united by close spiritual bonds. Its structure requires diversity of gifts and duties. This distinction, while it can be one not merely of grade but of essence, as for example between the ministerial priesthood and the common priesthood of the faithful, by no means removes the radical and constitutive equality of persons in the Church: 'There is, therefore, one chosen people of God: "one Lord, one faith, one baptism" (Eph. 4:5); there is a common dignity of members deriving from their rebirth in Christ, a common grace as sons, a common vocation to perfection, one salvation, one hope and undivided charity. . . . Although by Christ's will some are established as teachers, dispensers of the mysteries and pastors for the others, there remains, nevertheless, a true equality between all with regard to the dignity and to the activity which is common to all the faithful in the building up of the Body of Christ.' (LG 32)

Every vocation in the Church, therefore, is deserving of respect and is a call to the fullness of love, which is holiness. Every person has his or her outstanding supernatural quality, to which respect is due; all offices and charisms, even though some are more important than others, work together for the good of all the members in a wide-ranging multiplicity of ways which the apostolic office must judge and coordinate (see LG 12). This is also true of individual local churches; in each one, even if it be small and poor and existing in diaspora, 'Christ is present through whose power and influence the one, holy, Catholic and apostolic Church is constituted.' (LG 26)

The Catholic faithful ought to be concerned for separated Christians, who do not live in full communion with the Catholic Church, praying for them, discussing Church affairs with them, taking the first steps towards them. In the first place, all should, as their situation warrants, examine carefully and sincerely whatever needs to be renewed and accomplished in the Catholic family, so that their lives will bear a more faithful and a clearer witness to the teaching and institutions handed down by Christ through the apostles (see UR 4, 5).

The church as saving institution

67. The Church is not only a communion between brothers and sisters, with Christ at its head, it is also an institution to which the universal mission of salvation has been entrusted. The people of God is 'established by Christ as a communion of life, love and truth, it is taken up by him also as the instrument for the salvation of all; as the light of the world and the salt of the earth it is sent forth into the whole world.' (LG 9)

For this reason, the Church was presented by the Second

Vatican Council as a reality embracing all of history, accepting its various cultures and directing them towards God, established as 'the universal sacrament of salvation' through the action of the Holy Spirit. It is also presented as a Church in dialogue with the world; observing the signs of the times, it discovers what matters are of importance to men and women and where it is in agreement with them. Further, it takes care to be understood and recognized by the world, endeavouring to rid itself of external forms which are less in keeping with the Gospel and which are too clearly marked by the traces of past ages.

The Church indeed is not of this world, it 'is not motivated by an earthly ambition' (GS 3) and will attain perfection only in heaven, towards which it looks and travels. At the same time, it is involved with the world and with its history. However, 'the deep concern of the Church for people's needs—their joys and hopes, sorrows and labours—is but its compelling desire to be with them in order to bestow Christ's light on them, gathering all of them together and uniting them with him, their sole saviour. Such concern, however, can never mean that the Church would conform to the world or would expect less eagerly the Lord and his eternal kingdom.' (Paul VI, Profession of Faith, n. 27)

Mary Mother of God, mother and model of the church

68. Mary is united with the Lord in a way that is beyond description. She is his ever-virgin Mother, who 'occupies a place in the Church which is the highest after Christ and also closest to us.' (LG 54)

The gift of the Spirit of Christ is manifested in her in an altogether special way, because Mary is 'full of grace' (Luke 1:28) and is 'the model of the Church' (LG 63). The Holy Spirit has already fully manifested his role in her, for she was preserved from all stain of original sin, was freely and fully faithful to the Lord and was assumed body and soul into heavenly glory. She was fully conformed 'to her Son, the Lord of Lords and conqueror of sin and death' (LG 59). Since she is Mother of God and 'mother to us in the order of grace' (LG 61), the model of virginity and motherhood for the entire Church (see LG 63-65), the sign of certain hope and consolation for the pilgrim people of God (see LG 69), Mary 'in a way unites in her person and re-echoes the most important doctrines of the faith' and 'she prompts the faithful to come to her Son, to his sacrifice, and to love for the Father' (LG 65). For this reason the Church, which honours the faithful and the saints who are already with the Lord and intercede for us, venerates in a very special way her who is Mother of Christ and Mother of the Church.

Final Communion with God

69. The faithful, through Jesus Christ and through his mystery, already in this earthly life await in hope 'our Lord Jesus Christ, who will give a new form to this lowly body of ours and remake it according to the pattern of his glorified body' (Phil. 3:21; see 1 Cor. 15). The ultimate realities [of the story of salvation] will become manifest and perfect only when Christ will come with power, as Judge of the living and the dead, to bring history to an end and to hand over his people to the Father so that 'God may be all in all' (1 Cor., 15:24-28). Until 'the lord will come in glory, and all his angels with him, [when] death will be no more and all things will be subject to him. But at the present time some of his disciples are pilgrims on earth. Others have died and are being purified and still others are in glory, contemplating in full light God himself triune and one, exactly as he is.' (LG 49)

The entire Church will reach its perfection on the day of the Lord's coming and will enter into the fullness of God: this is the fundamental objective of Christian hope and prayer ('thy kingdom come'). When treating of the last things, catechesis should on the one hand emphasise consolation, hope and salutary feat (see Thess. 4:18), for modern men and women very much need this approach. On the other hand it should ensure that the full truth is imparted. It is not right to minimise the grave responsibility which all people have for their future destiny. Catechesis cannot be silent about the particular judgment which faces each person after death, nor the expiatory punishment of Purgatory, nor the sad and lamentable reality of eternal death, nor the last judgment. On that day all will fully achieve their destiny because all of us will appear 'before the tribunal of Christ, so that each one may receive the recompense, good or bad, according to his life in the body' (2 Cor. 5:10) and 'those who have done right shall rise to live; the evildoers shall rise to be damned.' (John 5:29; see LG 48)

PART 4:
PRINCIPLES OF METHODOLOGY

Nature and scope of this section

70. In this century, catechists have thoroughly examined

methodological problems posed by the psychological, educational and pedagogical sciences. Studies have been undertaken of the method of teaching catechism; the scope for active methods in teaching catechesis has been demonstrated; catechising itself in all its ramifications has been analysed in the light of the laws of learning (experience, imagination, memory, intelligence); lastly, a varying methodology has been elaborated, changing according to the age, social condition and maturity of the students.

Not all such problems are discussed here but we discuss a number of points which are of considerable importance today. Special directories and other work tools will be needed for suitable specific treatment of these problems in the various conditions.

Role of the catechist

71. No method, however well proven by experience, exempts the catechist from the task of personally weighing and judging the concrete situation and adjusting to it. Excellent human and Christian qualities in catechists are a greater guarantee of success than the methods chosen.

The work of the catechist must be considered of greater importance than the choice of texts and of other work tools (see AG 17).

The importance and the magnitude of the task of catechists, however, does not preclude the setting of limits to their role. It is their responsibility to choose and create the appropriate conditions for the quest of the Christian message, for its acceptance and for deeper study of it. The activity of catechists goes that far and stops there. For, ultimately, commitment by the recipients of catechesis is the fruit of grace and liberty and does not depend on the catechist. Catechetical activity, therefore, should be accompanied by prayer. It is useful to recall this nowadays, even if it is self-evident, because great demands are being made on the ability and genuine Christian spirit of catechists and at the same time they are being urged to have the greatest possible respect for the liberty and creativity of those being catechized.

Inductive and deductive methods

72. The inductive method has considerable advantages.

It consists of the presentation of facts (such as biblical events, liturgical actions, the life of the Church and everyday life) and of their consideration and examination so as to discern their

significance in the Christian mystery. This method is in conformity with the economy of revelation and, among other things,
with that fundamental process by which the human spirit progresses from the visible to the invisible. It is also in harmony with
the knowledge which comes with faith, which is knowledge
through signs.

The inductive method does not exclude the deductive, in fact
it needs to be complemented by it. The deductive method explains and describes facts from their causes. But deductive synthesis is at its best when it is preceded by the inductive process.

Formulas

73. The main advantages of the inductive method are that it
involves the exercise of the spiritual faculties and constant
reference to the concrete in the explanation of intellectual concepts. These however must not lead to forgetfulness of the need
and the usefulness of formulas.

Formulas permit the accurate expression of thoughts, are
suitable for correct exposition of the faith and, committed to
memory, facilitate the firm possession of the truth. Lastly, they
provide a common language for believers.

Formulas are usually proposed and explained when the lesson
or investigation has reached the point of synthesis.

Preference should be given to formulas which are within the
listeners' capacity while faithfully expressing the truths of faith.
It must not be forgotten that dogmatic formulas are a true expression of Catholic dogma and, as such, must be accepted by
believers in the sense in which the Church understands them.
The traditional formulas used for professing the faith and for
praying, such as the Apostles' Creed, the Lord's Prayer, the
Hail Mary and other similar prayers are to be carefully taught.

Experience

74. (a) Experience gives rise to concern and questioning,
hope and anxiety, reflection and judgment, all of which merge
together in the desire to regulate human existence.

Catechesis should be at pains to make people aware of their
more important experiences, both personal and social. It is also
its task to throw the light of the gospel on the questions to which
these give rise, thus stimulating in people themselves a right
desire of transforming their way of life.

In this way, experience enables people to respond actively to
God's gift.

(b) Experience can help make the Christian message intelligible.

Christ himself preached the kingdom of God, explaining its nature with the aid of parables drawn from human experience. He recalled certain human situations (the successful businessman, the servants putting their talents to good or bad use) in order to explain eschatological and transcendental realities and thus inculcate the way of life that these realities postulate from us.

In this way experience is of assistance in the examination and the assimilation of the truths which are contained in the deposit of revelation.

(c) Experience as such needs to be illuminated by the light of revelation. Catechesis, by recalling what God did in effecting salvation, should help people to examine, interpret and judge their experiences and to give a Christian meaning to their own existence. This task, though difficult, should not be shirked.

Stimulating the activity or creativity of those to be catechised

75. The first thing that is expected of all human education and true communication is that they facilitate and stimulate interior activity in the recipients. Catechesis, therefore, must evoke the act of believing (and also of hoping and loving); for accurate and firm judgment, the fruit of active education, here assist the acceptance of God's word. The confidence which marks active education should not allow one to forget that the act of faith necessarily involves a person's conversion. This said, it is clear that active education is in complete harmony with the economy of revelation and salvation. The pedagogy which requires an active response from the recipients is in accord with the Christian life in general. For Christians respond actively to the gift of God by prayer, by participation in the sacraments and the sacred liturgy, by taking on tasks in the Church and in civil life and by the practice of charity.

The recipients of catechesis, especially if they are adults, can contribute actively to the development of catechesis. Thus, they should be asked how they understand the Christian message and how they would express it in their own words. Their answers should be compared with the teaching of the magisterium and only what is in accord with the faith accepted. This method will be found particularly helpful in expounding the one true Christian message.

Groups

76. The group is becoming increasingly important in catechesis.

To catechise children in groups helps to educate them for life in society, both children attending catechism classes and children in small groups formed in view of some activity.

The group must be regarded as vitally necessary for adolescents and young adults. Adolescents and young adults discover themselves, are supported and stimulated in groups.

The group must nowadays be considered necessary for adult catechesis aimed at fostering a sense of Christian responsibility.

In a group comprising adolescents or adults, catechesis takes on the character of a quest in common.

The object of this common quest is to explore the mutual relations and links between the content of the Christian message, which is always the norm for belief and action, and the experience of the group.

Catechists should take part in the common quest, but should have a special place in the group. They are witnesses to the Christian message in the name of the Church, ministering to others, sharing with them the fruits of their mature faith, expertly guiding the common quest towards its objective.

The fact that catechists are witnesses to the message does not necessarily imply that they should be put in charge of groups as directors.

A group which functions with a high degree of success can offer its members not merely an opportunity for religious education but also an excellent experience of ecclesial life.

When catechesis is done in this way, it can show young people that the Church is by no means something extrinsic to their lives, but rather a reality for which everybody, as calling and function direct, is responsible.

PART 5:
CATECHESIS BY AGE LEVEL

Nature and scope of this part

77. There are many ways of adjusting the Christian message to different human situations.

In a missionary situation one employs evangelization and initiation of catechumens.

Catechesis adapted to varying age levels enables one to adjust to the physical and psychological levels of the recipients.

Catechesis adapted to different mentalities (catechesis for workers, technicians, etc.) makes it possible to adjust to different sociological and cultural environments.

Lastly, if one takes into account the varying degrees of familiarity with the faith among baptised people, one can provide catechesis both for believers who wish to acquire a fuller and deeper knowledge of the truths of faith and for those who still lack the very fundamentals of the faith.

All of these methods are interconnected and interdependent and obviously have each their own value and importance.

It will be for national or regional catechetical directories to furnish specific and detailed norms in this matter, to meet local conditions and needs.

Here, by way of example, only a number of general elements are proposed to show the worth and importance of catechesis adapted to age levels.

Infancy and its importance

78. Religious and moral life makes its first appearance at the commencement of human life. The first months and years are of the greatest importance for a person's future equilibrium and in a believing family they can provide the outlines of a Christian personality. The baptism of the children makes complete sense when the Christian lives of the parents—of the mother especially, but not exclusively—enable the grace of the sacrament to bear fruit. The infant assimilates by a sort of osmosis the behaviour patterns and attitudes of the members of its family. The consequent accumulation of experiences will provide the foundation for the life of faith which will gradually develop and find expression.

What inclines an infant towards belief is; first, a good relationship between it and its mother and, subsequently, between it and its father: the inclination is fostered by pleasure shared and by the experience of loving authority. The unimpeded development of the theological virtues depends partly on this initial inclination, while at the same time they tend to strengthen it. At this time the affirmation of personality, or autonomy, commences. This is needed for the acquisition of the moral virtues and for life in society. It itself needs a balance between inflexibility and permissiveness. Then, the capacity for autonomous activity develops and this will be most necessary for entry into social life and for increasing and consolidating the person's service of God and of the Church.

This development must be accompanied by formation in prayer, so that the infant will learn to pray to God who loves and protects us; to Jesus Christ, Son of God and our Brother, who leads us to the Father; to the Holy Spirit, who dwells in our hearts; so that, also, the infant will address confident prayers to Mary, the Mother of Jesus and our Mother.

If these foundations have not been laid, catechesis must determine whatever is lacking as a result, if anything, and how it can be remedied. The efforts of Christian parents to help in this matter should be supported by educational back-up which, even if simple and adjusted to their cultural level, must be given by competent teachers. Nor is this a work of supererogation for pastors, for the Church is being built when parents are helped to perform their duty. It also provides an excellent opportunity for adult catechesis.

Childhood and its importance

79. When they go to school, children become part of a society wider than their families and they are initiated into the company of adults, very intensively, in a way which absorbs much of their energies and interests. They have their first experience of work at school (see GE 5).

Before this, the family mediated between children and the people of God. Now they are capable of beginning to share directly in the Church's life and they may be admitted to the sacraments.

Children's intelligence evolves gradually and catechesis must adjust to this mental development. Children try to understand the religious life of adults. For this reason, a genuinely Christian life in the adult community is an excellent contribution towards providing in-depth formation of children; indeed, instruction will be added if the religious life of the adults and the activities of the people of God are explained in the light of the history of salvation.

The first experience of work should not be regarded as outside the scope of catechesis. The pleasure derived from doing things and doing them properly, collaboration with others, the manifest and reasonable discipline arising out of this: here are many experiences which are offered and which assist not merely involvement in society, but also active participation in the Church's life.

With this in mind, catechetical pedagogy, whatever method it follows, should stimulate the children's activity. If it fails in this, catechesis will not be able to perform its function of teaching the believer to give an increasingly personal response to the word and the gift of God. Such active pedagogy is not limited to external expressions, however useful, but endeavours to evoke a response from the heart and a taste for prayer. This interior education is very difficult, but is all the more necessary because of the frenetic character of contemporary civilization.

Collaboration between catechists and parents (exchange of opinions about programmes, methods and difficulties which occur) is necessary if the children's education is to develop properly and harmoniously. Such collaboration is useful to both sides, helping them in the performance of their respective tasks.

Children who do not attend school

80. There are places, both vast areas and densely populated areas, where there are not enough schools. Where this is so, the families themselves should be the object of intense pastoral activity. Where possible, different associations for the care of children should be established, so organised that they will be in tune with local conditions and will meet the children's spiritual needs.

Children whose families are affected by religious indifference

81. There is increasing awareness of the difficulty of catechising children who live in areas or in families where religion is not practised or is totally inadequately practised. Sometimes doubt is expressed about the very possibility and appropriateness of such catechesis.

Catechesis of such children must not, of course, be abandoned, but it must rather be conceived and imparted in a way that takes account of their circumstances and conditions. Contact should be established with the families in such cases, their attitudes and life-styles examined so as to pave the way towards discussion. The content of catechesis must be presented in a manner really adapted to the children's capacity.

Adolescence and early adulthood and their importance

82. The period of adolescence and, more generally, the 'youth phenomenon' as it is called, are of the greatest importance (see AA 12). In pre-industrial societies, where the number of schools is small, the transition from childhood to the community of adults is almost immediate. In our time the custom of extending the length of time devoted to the education of adolescents has become increasingly common. This has created in our society a generation not directly involved in productive work. Though they have the physical and intellectual capability, they engage in no activity apart from study and the acquisition of a profession. This social class exercises a considerable influence

on adult society, thereby creating no small problem.

The problem is also to be found in the Church. It takes different forms, but is not any the less serious. Adolescents and young adults are less in danger of positively opposing the Church than of being tempted to leave it. This is a very serious problem in catechesis, not least because it is often difficult for adults to see what worthwhile contribution adolescents and young adults can make.

The more catechists show themselves capable of understanding and accepting their role, the less distrustful will the young people be.

Pre-adolescence, adolescence, early adulthood and their importance

83. National directories ought to distinguish between pre-adolescence, adolescence and early adulthood.

Here it can only be noted that in developed countries, where the matter arises, the difficulties proper to pre-adolescence are not always acknowledged in practice, or are insufficiently acknowledged. Educators can succumb to the temptation to look upon pre-adolescents as children and thus it is to be feared that they will not win their attention. Or they can look upon them as adolescents, in which case they will assign them themes and methods of work which presuppose a maturity of personality and experience which they have not attained.

Pre-adolescence is characterized by the laborious birth of self-awareness [*subjectivitas*]. Therefore at this age the simple and objective instruction which is appropriate for children should not be continued. But one must also avoid proposing problems and themes which are suitable for adolescents.

Worthwhile pabulum for pupils of this age group could be supplied by concrete illustrations from the lives and achievements of the saints and of people of worth, as well as from the current life of the Church.

The period of young adulthood, understood strictly, which comes after adolescence, is also a period of life little investigated up to now and its characteristic marks are insufficiently known.

Some believe that theological education should commence at this age. Others think that human and social problems should be examined, adding simple theological explanations and a certain amount of exhortation to Christian living. The preferable method would seem to be to discuss the typical basic problems of concern to this age group in the context of careful theological and human documentation and in group discussions.

Searching for life's meaning

84. Adolescents are aware of profound physical and psychological changes in themselves. They are searching for their roles in society. They are no longer satisfied with the religious attitudes of their childhood. However, they have not yet attained the maturity of faith of adults. They seek a fundamental orientation which would enable them to unify their lives once more. But this search often leads to religious crisis.

The principal task of catechesis for adolescents will be to promote a genuinely Christian understanding of life. It must shed the light of the Christian message on the realities which mean most to adolescents, such as the meaning of bodily existence, love and the family, standards for their lives, work and leisure, justice and peace, etc.

Paying attention to genuine values

85. Adolescents try to set out their vision of their lives and the course of their existence in accordance with certain principal and primary values. Today, however, adolescents feel that they are immersed in mutually opposing values. For adolescents, this sharpens the conflict among the different values which they are seeking and they decide to reject the values which do not find expression in the way of life of adults.

Catechesis should help them increasingly to discover genuine values and to establish priority among them.

Personal autonomy

86. In their efforts to attain the autonomy they desire, adolescents often exaggerate their self-affirmation and find fault with the pattern of life received from adults.

Adults should bear in mind that for adolescents commitment to the faith and their confirmation in it come not from identifying with adults but as a result of personal conviction gradually arrived at.

This autonomy gives rise to what can be termed a 'temptation to naturalism' because of which adolescents tend to act and to seek salvation by their own powers. The stronger the personality, the more marked will be this tendency.

It will be for catechesis, therefore, to lead adolescents to that personal maturity which will permit them to set aside concern with self and to discover a new hope in the strength and the wisdom of God.

Groups of adolescents

87. In their search for their own autonomy, adolescents like to form associations in order to facilitate the search for their own ideas and identity and in order to protect their autonomy from adult groupings. In the ambience of these groups, adolescents are attracted by the various life values and are moved to live in accordance with them. In ordinary daily life, adolescents communicate more easily with young people of the same age than with adults.

Catechesis has the task of working with these groups of adolescents, which can mediate between young people and the over-all community of the Church (see AA 12).

Adolescent groups do not always hold positive values. Hence the need to foster relations between them and Christian communities so that the human and Christian view of the Christian communities may be duly recognized and appreciated by the adolescents (see AA 12).

Intellectual needs

88. Adolescents, essentially, are capable of a 'formal' use of reason. They are learning how to use their intelligence properly and are discovering that the culture being proposed to them needs to be thought about and applied in their lives.

Catechesis, if it is to be capable of awakening an experience of the life of faith, must on no account neglect to inculcate a religious way of thinking. This demonstrates the link between the mysteries themselves and between them and humankind's final end (see First Vatican Council, Const. *Dei Filius,* c. iv, DS 3015-3020). To ensure the internal coherence of this kind of religious thinking, witness is not enough. Nowadays, scientific rigour is demanded everywhere. Catechesis must take every care to provide rational justification for the faith.

The structuring of the intellectual faith of adolescents must in no way be regarded as an optional extra, but as essential for the life of faith. The method of teaching is particularly important. The catechist must stimulate the adolescents' minds, in dialogue with them.

Action

89. Activity is needed for the development of the adoles-

cents' personalities. They need contact with reality, with success or failure, if they are to be freed from self-centredness and subjectivism.

Catechesis should encourage personal faith experience and disciplined reflection on religious matters. It will have achieved its purpose when it has led to the fulfillment of Christian obligations. Christian catechesis should educate adolescents to assume the responsibilities of the faith and should gradually make them fit for the open profession of their Christianity.

Adolescents who do not attend school

90. Young people in trades or professions, and their number is enormous, undergo an accelerated development of their personalities, with fortunate or unfortunate, perfect or imperfect results.

There is therefore need for special catechesis for these adolescents. It will have to examine the immediate day-to-day problems, to support the young people when they commence working, helping them to engage in activity commensurate with their ability in collaboration with Catholic movements.

Further, to the extent that the young workers still retain adolescent characteristics and needs, catechesis should not merely throw light on their concrete activity, it should also guide them towards acceptance of God's over-all plan.

Handicapped children and adolescents

91. This task may not be relegated to a secondary or subsidiary place. Handicapped children and adolescents constitute no small proportion of our citizens. Present-day conditions in society make it difficult, very often, for young people to develop properly and to adjust properly to society.

Catechesis must offer these the possibility of living the life of faith in keeping with their state. This is an eminently evangelical task and a most important witness, a constant in the tradition of the Church.

The education of these young people in the faith is of great pastoral value and is of the greatest importance in that it offers the possibility of reaching many families.

Finally, the special difficulty presented by this task and the necessity of having to impart only the essentials to these young people can prove beneficial to catechesis in general, making available to it the methodology developed in the course of pedagogical research undertaken for the sake of the handicapped.

Adulthood

92. This general directory categorically asserts the need for adult catechesis, for the following reasons:

(a) Before undertaking responsibilities in social and family life, in professional, civil and political life, adults should embark on a special and appropriate completion of their Christian formation in the light of God's word (see AA, 29-32). There is need for collaboration between those involved in adult catechesis and those involved in the lay apostolate.

(b) Aptitudes and capacities which reach full development in adult life—such as experience of life, maturity of personality, etc.—need to be cultivated and illuminated by the word of God.

(c) Moreover, adults have to cope with moments of crisis in their lives. These may be less obvious than those experienced by adolescents, but they are no less profound or less dangerous. At such times, the faith of adults must be constantly illuminated, developed and protected.

Dynamic characteristics of adulthood: community and solitude

93. When people become adults, they are ordinarily more capable of being part of a community and of establishing relationships with others.

This capacity and need for community are exercised within the context of family duties and of the relationships of social life. All of which are sometimes both instrument and obstacle to community.

In truth, people sometimes experience overmuch solitude, especially nowadays.

Catechesis must show that God, who is love, is the author of the community of faith, which is the Church, and at the same time enkindles a desire for establishing fellowship with everybody. It reminds married couples that, in virtue of the sacrament of matrimony, their intimate union signifies and shares in the mystery of unity and the fruitful love of Christ and the Church (see Eph 5:32).

In the context of small groups of the faithful, catechesis will help adults to live Christian charity to the full. This charity, as the sign of a shared experience, enables them to help each other in the faith.

The perfection of the personality

94. Adulthood is characterized principally by awareness of a fully developed personality.

People who have passed successfully through the various stages of their development, have been able to establish relationships and to exercise creative ability, when they become adults endeavour to unify their experiences of their personal, social and spiritual lives. The danger here is that the adults, especially if they live in industrialized society, may think that they can achieve this unity merely by conforming to the society in which they live. However, perfect maturity does not consist in a merely extrinsic balance between personal life and social ambience, in particular, it aims at the attainment of Christian wisdom.

Consequently, catechesis should endeavour to persuade people to observe the order among ends, which means becoming more fully aware of the true meaning of life and death, in the light of the death and resurrection of Christ.

Old age

95. The importance of old age in the pastoral ministry is not yet sufficiently recognised.

In our times, the number of old people continues to increase. They are often neglected in modern society and this must be carefully noted for its implications for pastoral activity.

In fact, old people can make a considerable contribution to the community, both through their industry, which is not always properly appreciated, and through what their experience can teach.

Further, there is a duty in justice to help the aged by catechesis to prepare for death. Biologically, death is near at hand and socially it is already present, in a certain sense, since almost nothing is expected any more from their activity.

Catechesis should teach the aged supernatural hope, which enables them to see death as the passage to true life and encounter with the divine Saviour. In this way, old age can become the sign of the presence of God, of everlasting life and of the coming resurrection. The aged will thus be able to bear an eschatological witness by their patience with their lot and towards others, by their benevolence and by their prayers in praise of God, by their spirit of poverty and their trust in God.

Without doubt, it would be a serious loss for the Church if the multitude of the aged baptised did not show that their Christian faith became more resplendent with the approach of death.

Special types of catechesis for adults

96. There are situations and circumstances which demand special kinds of catechesis.

(a) There is the catechesis for Christian initiation, or catechumenate of adults.

(b) There is catechesis for those who are specially involved in the apostolate of the laity. It is obvious that in such cases catechesis must provide a deeper study of the Christian message.

(c) There is a catechesis suited to the principal events of life, such as marriage, the baptism of children, first communion and confirmation, critical periods in the education of the children, an illness, etc. These are the occasions on which people are especially impelled to look for the true meaning of life.

(d) There is a catechesis to be given on the occasion of a change in a person's life, such as when a person commences work, joins the army, emigrates, changes profession or social status. These changes may indeed be a source of interior enrichment, but they can also be a source of worry and discouragement. It is for the Christian community to provide the necessary support in a spirit of brotherly or sisterly love. The word of God, which sometimes meets a readier acceptance on such occasions, ought to provide light and help.

(e) There is a catechesis which is concerned with the Christian use of leisure and one for people undertaking journeys for recreation (see General Directory for Pastoral Ministry to Tourism, nn. 19, 25).

(f) There is a catechesis to suit events of particular importance in the life of the Church or of society.

These special types of catechesis do not lessen the need for establishing catechetical courses for the systematic study of the entire Christian message. This systematic and planned arrangement is certainly not to be reduced to a simple series of conferences and sermons.

Special tasks for adult catechesis

97. If adult catechesis is to be always ready to respond to the more urgent problems of our time, it must:

(a) *Educate for the proper understanding, in the light of faith, of sociological and cultural changes in today's world*. The Christian people is becoming increasingly aware of the need to ask where the present progress of society could be leading and of discerning the real benefits and the dangers of human civilisation at present. It looks for help in examining the constant changes and wants advice on the courses of action which it can and ought to adopt.

(b) *Explain contemporary religious and moral problems*. Catechesis ought to make its own the new questions which people ask nowadays. For example, nowadays great importance attaches to social questions. People want to give a new shape to the society in which they live. This attempt at renewal, in which people's responsibilities and limitations emerge clearly (see encyclical, *Populorum progressio:* AAS 59, 257-399), cannot escape the attention of catechesis.

(c) *Clarify the relationship between temporal action and ecclesial action*. It is for catechesis to teach Christians to understand the reciprocal relationships between temporal and ecclesial duties. It must show that the performance of temporal duty can have a beneficial effect in the ecclesial community, in that it makes the ecclesial community more conscious of its transcendent goal and of its mission in the world; that, further, the performance of ecclesial duties brings benefits to the human society (see GS 40-45).

(d) *Develop the rational foundations of faith*. The Church has always upheld the rational foundations of faith against fideism. Catechesis must increasingly develop a proper understanding of faith, demonstrating that the act of believing and the truths of faith are in harmony with the demands of human reason. Catechesis must show that the gospel is always real and relevant. Pastoral action on Christian teaching and culture must therefore be promoted.

PART 6:
PASTORAL ACTION,
THE MINISTRY OF THE WORD

Pastoral action

98. A plan for pastoral action can be devised from what has been said about catechising and the contents of catechesis and its main outlines are discussed in this part.

Pastoral action requires that episcopal conferences set up, at the national level, appropriate organs for planning, research and administration. In general, such organs comprise (a) an episcopal commission on catechesis, composed of selected *ex officio* members and experts; and (b) a permanent executive structure (office, centre, etc.)

Effective and co-ordinated pastoral action in the ministry of the word requires that:

(1) a report be drawn up on the local situation and on what can be achieved by the ministry of the word in such conditions;

(2) a plan of action be published;

(3) care be taken with the formation and instruction of those involved;

(4) suitable aids for the work be properly designed and prepared;

(5) the catechesis be properly structured;

(6) pastoral action in catechesis be coordinated with other forms of pastoral activity;

(7) research be done;

(8) international cooperation be encouraged.

The guidelines and suggestions set out here cannot always be all implemented simultaneously in all parts of the Church. For countries or regions where catechetical action is not yet sufficiently advanced, their purpose is to indicate goals to be achieved gradually.

Chapter 1:
Analysis of the Situation

Purpose

99. It is necessary that within the [episcopal] conference there be a clear understanding of the situation where the ministry of the word is exercised.

The object of the analysis is to discover how successful the Church's evangelization has been in achieving the objective set for it. The way in which the ministry of the word has been exercised must be carefully examined, as must the results—in so far as these can be humanly ascertained—achieved by catechesis and by other means of presenting the Christian message. The Church's initiatives must be examined, as must the way they were received—where, by whom, with what effect, etc.

Object

100. The object of this investigation is manifold. It involves an examination of pastoral activity, an analysis of the religious situation and of the sociological, cultural and economic conditions, since these collective processes can have profound repercussions on evangelization.

Methods

101. This work is quite difficult and there are two dangers to be avoided. One must avoid (a) accepting data and indications

as certain when they have not been sufficiently analysed or verified; (b) setting unattainable standards of scientific perfection.

It should be clearly understood that technical investigations by means of questionnaires or consultations are of little use unless they have been preceded by careful consideration of the different options in pastoral activity. What episcopal conferences need, therefore, is a complete picture of the situation. This can be acquired by consulting experts who are really well versed in the examination of documentary evidence and in drawing conclusions from pastoral action already under way. Monographs can be very helpful here.

The entire Christian community should be involved in the study of the situation so that they will be aware of the problems and prepared for action.

Effects

102. An investigation of this sort is not an end in itself. It ought rather to highlight the more effective courses of action and pave the way for their adoption, both by giving more scope to undertakings whose effectiveness has been proved and by promoting others. What is involved is foreseeing and preparing for what will have to be done in the future.

Such an investigation should also persuade those engaged in the ministry of the word that human situations are changeable as far as pastoral action is concerned. For this reason, gospel workers should learn to uncover the possibilities open to their ministry in a new and different situation. There is the danger that awareness of the difficulties might lead people to conclude that pastoral action is impossible. Each one should, on the contrary, be convinced that cultural realities are not inert, unchangeable, identical data, capable of reducing grace and pastoral action to impotence, as it were. A process of transformation, opening the way to faith, is always possible.

Chapter 2:
Program of Action

Program of action

103. When the situation has been carefully examined, the next step is to publish a program of action, especially in the form of a catechetical directory. This program determines the objectives, the means to be used in catechetical pastoral activity and

the norms for directing it. The norms must be in harmony with
the objectives and norms of the objective Church and must also
meet the local needs.

In proposing a program of action, one should bear in mind the
tasks that the strictly ecclesial institutions can perform, institutions such as the parish, special communities of the faithful,[4]
apostolic associations, the family, educational establishments,
both Christian and non-denominational, and every other kind
of social grouping.

Such a program of action should be seen as hinging on the
goals to be attained and the means to be employed.

Goals to be attained

104. The pastoral goals to be achieved can vary, as place and
needs vary, in degree and measure.[5] All however should have to
do with the progress of faith and morals among the faithful and
with the development of their relationships with God and neighbour. For example, they should have to do with adults achieving
a mature faith, with Christian doctrine reaching scientific and
technical circles, with the family doing its Christian duty, with
the Christian presence contributing to social transformation.

Since, generally speaking, the goals are numerous, it is particularly advisable that they be selected in good time and having
regard to the order of priority among the objectives to be achieved.

It is also useful to compare the pastoral goals set up in one
region with those set up by episcopal conferences closest to it
geographically or culturally.

Means to be used

105. The chief means to be employed are: catechetical institutions which are to be promoted or supported, programs, texts
(see chapter 5 of this part), working tools, instructions about
methods (see part 4). In practice, one cannot assign limits to research on means. At the same time, one must always take care
that the means proposed are capable of achieving the spiritual
objectives intended.

Norms

106. There are a number of norms which can be given with
regard to catechesis; they vary with the ends to be achieved. The
more important of them are those which have to do with
catechesis in preparation for the sacraments, such as the norms
with regard to the adult catechumenate, the sacramental initia-

tion of children, the preparation of families for the baptism of infants.

If such norms are to be effective they must be few in number and simple, using external rather than internal criteria.

As is obvious, no particular norm may derogate from the Church's general laws and from common practice, except with the permission of the Holy See.

Distribution and promotion of responsibilities

107. First, one must ensure that one has a clear and effective distribution of responsibilities. It is very important, for example, that the responsibilities of Christian families, of ecclesial communities, of the clergy and of catechists be clarified and set in relief. However, it is not enough to rest content with the distribution of existing resources; it is necessary increasingly to stimulate and promote the involvement of all of the faithful. One should ensure that the Christian community becomes increasingly conscious of its role, which is to be a sign of the wisdom and love of God manifested to us in Christ. To this end, both the entire community and every individual believer should, as far as possible, always be made aware at the appropriate time of what has to be done and all should be invited to take part in taking on projects, in making decisions and in carrying out what has been decided.

In preparing programs of catechetical action, it should be remembered that some undertaking can at times cause trouble and disagreement. Difficulties can arise, for example, from changes in language and from new opinions on the educative and apostolic relationship. In all such cases, every effort should be made to avoid whatever might disturb people unduly.

Lastly, it is necessary that all catechetical activities be provided with proper financial support.

Chapter 3:
Catechetical Formation

Catechetical formation

108. Any pastoral activity will come to nothing if there is nobody at hand, properly formed and prepared, to carry it out. The working tools themselves are useless except in the hands of properly formed catechists. For this reason, the proper formation of catechists should precede the renewal of textbooks and the strengthening of catechetical organization.

The first thing is to ensure the formation of those in charge of catechetical activities at the national level. This is the task of the episcopal conference. Hand in hand with the formation of those involved in catechetics at the national level should go, as its natural complement and continuation, the formation of catechists with regional or diocesan responsibility. This is the task of regional episcopal conferences and of individual bishops.

Higher institutes and catechetical schools

109. Higher institutes of catechetics should be further developed or founded, so that suitable catechists may be trained to take charge of catechetics at diocesan level or in religious congregations. Such higher institutes can be national or international. They should set university standards with regard to the curriculum, length of courses and conditions for admission.

Schools of catechetics should also be established by individual dioceses or at least by regional episcopal conferences. These would offer a less advanced but equally valid course for the training of full-time catechists.

Ongoing formation

110. There are different kinds and degrees of ongoing formation. It must continue throughout the entire period of involvement in catechesis. It applies therefore both to those in charge of catechetics and to ordinary catechists.

Ongoing formation cannot be entrusted solely to the central offices. Lesser Christian communities should also accept responsibility for it, since the conditions and needs of catechesis vary from place to place. The clergy and all who have charge of catechesis have the obligation to ensure the ongoing formation of their collaborators in catechesis.

Objective of catechetical formation

111. The summit and centre of catechetical formation consists in the aptitude and the ability to communicate the gospel message. It requires an exact theological-doctrinal, anthropological and methodological formation, to the level of knowledge aimed at. The formation does not end, however, with the acquisition of knowledge of doctrine. It is complete when the catechist is able to choose the best way of communicating the gospel message to groups and individuals in situations which are different and singular.

112. (a) *Doctrine*. The need to acquire a valid doctrinal patrimony is obvious. It should always include an adequate knowledge of Catholic teaching and in the higher institutes of catechetics should reach the level of scientific theology. Sacred scripture should be the soul of this formation, so to speak.

In any event, the doctrine should be so assimilated that the catechist will be able not only to impart the gospel message accurately, but also to evoke an active reception of the message on the part of those to be catechized and will be able to discern whatever is in harmony with the faith in their spiritual odysseys.

(b) *The human sciences*. Our age is characterized by an enormous development of the human sciences. They are no longer the preserve of the specialist. They penetrate the awareness that modern men and women have of themselves. They influence social relations and form a kind of cultural texture for modern humanity, even for the less developed.

The teaching of the human sciences gives rise to difficult problems concerning their selection and the way of teaching them, because of their great number and diversity. Since what is in question here is the education not of experts in psychology, but of catechists, the norm to be observed is this: choose whatever will directly help them to acquire the capacity to communicate.

(c) *Methodological formation*. Methodology is nothing other than careful consideration of methods which have stood the test of experience. Therefore, greater store must be set by practical exercises than by instruction in pedagogical theory. Nevertheless, theoretical instruction is needed in order to help catechists to cope properly in differing situations, to avoid empirical methods of teaching, to keep abreast of changes in educational rapport and to plan future work properly.

It must be borne in mind that as far as the formation of ordinary catechists goes (those, that is, who teach rudimentary catechesis) the knowledge described above is more easily acquired if it is imparted while they are working (for example, during sessions devoted to the preparation and criticism of catechism lessons).

Learning the art of catechesis

113. Catechists need a preparation that will fit them to interpret accurately the reactions of a group or of an individual, to discern their spiritual aptitude and to choose the method that will enable the gospel message to be heard fruitfully and effectively. Many methods are available: practical exercises, group

work, analysis of cases, etc. The whole question hinges on grasping the communicative potential of the Christian message. Catechesis, which is a Church activity, is not learned in a merely theoretical way. The art of imparting catechesis is acquired from experience, from the guidance of competent teachers and from practice. The art is a synthesis of apostolic aptitude and knowledge of the faith, of people and of the laws which regulate the progress of individuals and of communities.

The spiritual life of catechists

114. The catechists' task demands an intense sacramental and spiritual life, a habit of prayer, a profound sense of the pre-eminence of the Christian message and of its ability to transform people's lives. It also requires the cultivation of charity, humility and prudence, which permit the Holy Spirit to complete his fruitful labours in those being catechised.

Formation of catechists

115. Ecclesiastical authorities must needs be persuaded that the formation of catechists is a matter of the greatest importance.

This information is intended for all catechists (see AG 17, 26), lay and religious, for Christian parents, who will find it very helpful when involved in the preliminary and occasional cate-chesis that falls to them. It is intended for deacons and especially for priests. For 'in virtue of the sacrament of orders, after the image of Christ, the supreme and eternal priest (see Heb. 5:1-10; 7:24; 9:11-28), they are consecrated in order to preach the gospel and shepherd the faithful as well as to celebrate divine worship as true priests of the New Testament.' (LG 28) In fact, in every parish it is to the priests that the preaching of the word of God is principally entrusted. They are obliged to open the treasures of sacred scripture to the faithful and, through the liturgical year, to expound the mysteries of faith and the norms of the Christian life in homilies (see SC 51, 52). Hence it is of the greatest impor-tance that students in seminaries and scholasticates be given a sound grounding in catechetics and that this be completed later by the ongoing formation mentioned above (see n. 110).

Lastly, it is intended for teachers of religion in Church and State schools. Only those who are distinguished by ability, learn-ing and spiritual life are to be chosen for so important a task (see GE 5).

It is much to be hoped that in formation there would be real co-operation between catechesis and the various other apostolic activities. They share a common task, if under different aspects: that of communicating the Christian message.

Chapter 4:
Aids

Aids

116. Among the principal working tools of catechesis, the following are discussed here: directories published by episcopal conferences, programs, catechisms, textbooks and audiovisual aids.

Catechetical directories

117. The purpose of directories is to promote and co-ordinate catechetical activity in a regional or national territory, or in several nations which belong to the same socio-cultural area. Before they are promulgated, every local ordinary should be consulted and they should be submitted to the Holy See (see n. 134).

Programs

118. Programs establish the educational objectives to be achieved, according to age, place or time, the methodological criteria to be used and the contents to be conveyed. The mysteries of faith proposed for the belief of the adult faithful must certainly be included in catechetical programs intended for children and adolescents, in a manner suited to their ages (see n. 134).

Catechisms

119. The greatest importance must be attributed to catechisms published by ecclesiastical authority. Their object is to convey in summary and practical form the documents of revelation and of Christian tradition, as well as the main elements which must be of service for catechetical activity, that is, for personal education in the faith. The documents of tradition ought therefore to be held in proper esteem and the greatest care is to be taken lest particular interpretations, which are only private opinions or the opinions of some theological school, be presented as the teachings of faith. The teaching of the Church must be faithfully presented. The norms outlined in the first chapter, part one, are to be applied here.

On account of the great editorial difficulties and the special importance of these documents, it will be very useful if: (a) there be collaboration between a number of experts in catechetics and in theology; (b) experts in other religious and human disciplines be consulted, as well as other pastoral organizations; (c) individual local ordinaries be consulted and their opinions carefully considered; (d) special experiments precede the definitive publication; (e) these books be duly revised after a certain elapse of time.

These catechisms must be submitted to the Apostolic See for examination and approval, before promulgation (see n. 134).

Textbooks

120. Textbooks are aids for the Christian community embarking on catechesis. No text can substitute for the live communication of the Christian message. At the same time, texts are of great importance because they provide for a fuller exposition of the documents of Christian tradition and of the elements which foster catechetical activity. The compilation of these texts requires the collaboration of many experts in catechetics and the consultation of other experts.

Books for the use of catechists

121. Such books should contain: an explanation of the message of salvation (there should be constant reference to the sources and there must be a clear distinction between what is of faith and doctrine and what is merely a theological opinion); psychological and pedagogical advice; methodological suggestions.

Books or other written materials should be provided for study and activity by those being taught. These written materials can be inserted in the books for the use of those being catechised, or they can be published separately.

In the case of the catechesis of children, books for parents should also be published.

Audiovisual aids

122. Audiovisual aids are used mainly: (a) by way of documenting the teaching of catechetics with factual elements, in which case they should be wholly accurate, should be carefully chosen and clearly presented; (b) by way of visual education of the sensibility and of the imagination, in which case they should

be things of beauty and should have emotive power.

The following needs to be done with regard to these aids: the promotion of the study of the criteria which should guide the creation and selection of these aids, taking into account the particular aspects of the Christian message which are to be presented and the particular groups of people for whom they are intended; the instruction of catechists in their proper use (it often happens that catechists do not understand the nature of visual language; it happens even more frequently that incorrect use of audiovisual aids induces a passive rather than an active reception; etc.).

The mass media

123. Among other things, the mass media impart an air of reality and actuality to the facts, institutions and opinions on which they report and on the other hand they diminish the popular estimation of whatever they pass over in silence.

The proclamation of salvation must therefore have a place among the media of social communication (see IM, 3). For this reason, it is not sufficient to perfect the Church's own media. Co-operation should be promoted between producers, writers and artists engaged in this task. Such co-operation presupposes the establishment at national and international level of groups of experts who would be of real service if consulted about programs of activities concerned with religion.

Further, it is the task of catechesis to educate the faithful to discern the nature and value of what is presented by the mass media. It is obvious however that this presupposes a technical knowledge of the language of these media.

Programmed instruction

124. Catechesis should not neglect the new and increasingly popular method in the field of audiovisual aids which it can and should employ in furtherance of its aims. This method is known in educational circles as 'programmed instruction.'

In this matter, granted the difficulties presented by the truths to be imparted and by the purpose of catechesis, improvised explanations are to be avoided. Rather, both in the preparation of the programs and in the visual presentation of truth, recourse should be had to the collaboration of experts in theology, in catechesis and in the art of audiovisual education.

Chapter 5:
Organization of Catechesis

Organization of catechesis

125. The organization of catechesis in the territory of each episcopal conference consists mainly of diocesan, regional and national structures.

The main purpose of these structures is: (a) to promote catechetical activities and (b) to co-operate in other apostolic undertakings and works (with the liturgical commission, for example, with organizations involved in the lay apostolate, with the ecumenical commission, etc.), because all of these Church activities are involved, in different ways, in the ministry of the word.

Diocesan structures

126. The decree *Provido sane* (see AAS, 1935, 151 ff) established the Diocesan Catechetical Office and its function is to regulate the entire organization of catechesis. . . The diocesan office ought to consist of a group of people competent in this matter. The extent and the diversity of the problems involved demand that the responsibilities be divided among a number of really competent people.

The diocesan office should also promote and direct the work of these organizations (such as the parochial catechetical centre, the Confraternity of Christian Doctrine, etc.) which are basic cells of catechetical activity.

Permanent centres for training catechists should be established by local communities. In this way, it will be clear to the Christian people that the work of evangelization and the teaching of the message of salvation are the concern of all.

The catechetical office, therefore, which is part of the diocesan curia, is the means by which the bishop, head of the community and teacher of doctrine, directs and regulates all catechetical activity in the diocese.

No diocese should be without its own catechetical office.

Regional structures

127. Individual dioceses can, usefully, to their common benefit, combine forces, pooling experiments and initiatives, functions and resources. Better endowed dioceses can help others and a common program of action can be prepared for the entire region.

National structures

128. It is essential that the episcopal conference or, more immediately, the episcopal catechetical commission, be provided with a permanent structure.

This national catechetical office or centre has a twofold task:

—to meet the catechetical needs of the country as a whole. This involves publications relevant to the entire country, national congresses, relations with the mass media and, in general, activities and undertakings which are outside the capacity of individual dioceses or regions.

—to serve dioceses and regions by seeing to the dissemination of information and of catechetical enterprises, to the co-ordination of activities and to the provision of help for dioceses less advanced in catechetics.

Further, it is the task of the national office or centre to collaborate with other national pastoral institutes and with the international catechetical movement.

Chapter 6:
Co-ordination of Pastoral Catechetical Activity With All of Pastoral Activity

Catechesis and pastoral activity

129. Since every important Church activity shares in the ministry of the word and since catechesis is always related to universal ecclesial life, it follows that catechetical activity necessarily demands to be co-ordinated with pastoral activity in general. The purpose of this co-operation is the harmonious and orderly growth and development of the Christian community which, while it is distinguished by different functions, yet has the same fundamental goal.

It is necessary therefore that catechesis be associated with other pastoral activities (see Motu proprio, *Ecclesiae sanctae,* 17), that is, with the biblical, liturgical and ecumenical movements, with the lay apostolate and social action, etc. Further, it must be remembered that this co-operation is needed from the beginning, that is from the commencement of studies and plans for pastoral actions.

Catechumenate for adults

130. The catechumenate for adults is at one and the same

time catechesis, participation in the liturgy and life in community. It is thus a clear example of an institution born of collaboration between different pastoral activities. Its purpose is to direct the spiritual journey of people who are preparing for baptism and to direct their change of mentality and mores. It is a preparatory school of the Christian life, an introduction to the religious, liturgical, charitable and apostolic life of the people of God (see AG 13-14; SC 65; CD 14). The entire Christian community, through godparents acting in its name, is involved in this work, and not only the priests and catechists.

Chapter 7:
The Need to Promote Scientific Research

Scientific research

131. The catechetical movement will be totally incapable of making progress without scientific research, granted the rapid cultural evolution of today.

The national organs of episcopal conferences must therefore promote joint research projects. What is required is that a program of problems to be investigated be established; that it be determined which problems are already being investigated and that appropriate contact be established with the experts involved; that a study of the problems not yet investigated be set in train and that the necessary finances be provided.

There are subjects for research which are of universal importance: for example, the relationship between catechesis and modern exegesis, catechesis and anthropology, catechesis and the mass media. The nature and difficulty of such research is frequently such as to suggest international co-operation.

Chapter 8:
International Co-operation and Relations With the Holy See

International co-operation

132. The apostolic college is an example of solidarity in the way it performs its task (see LG 22-23; AG 38; CD 2,4). Several times in this part of the directory, consequences of this solidarity in the matter of catechesis have been discussed (for example, chapter 2, the harmonization of pastoral goals among neighbouring countries; chapter 3, the establishment of higher insti-

tutes; chapter 4, the elaboration of common aids; chapter 7, scientific research).

International co-operation is required also among those involved in the ministry of the word to emigrants.

The task is two-fold. On the one hand, the word of God has to be preached to the migrants. Since there are differences of language, culture and customs, there is need for an exchange of information and of personnel between the churches in the countries from which the migrants have come and the churches of the host countries. On the other hand, the ministry of the word must make Christians in the host countries aware of the pressing problems which migrants face and must persuade them to receive them in a spirit of brotherly and sisterly love.

International co-operation is required also for the catechesis of tourists. It is clear that tourism is becoming increasingly international (see General Directory for Pastoral Ministry to Tourists, *passim*.).

International co-operation must take into account the responsibilities and conditions of the local churches. Countries therefore which are more advanced with regard to personnel, economic means and scientific research should help the less progressive countries, without imposing their own ways of thinking or acting.

The Holy See

133. Just as Peter was constituted head of the apostolic college and foundation of the Church, so his successor, the Roman Pontiff (see LG 22) is the visible head of the college of bishops and of the entire people of God. He fulfills his universal role of teaching and governing as Vicar of Christ and pastor of the entire Church (see LG 22) and always for the benefit and spiritual progress of the people of God. He can however exercise his office freely, as the needs of the Church demand, either in a personal manner or in a properly collegial manner—together with the bishops of the universal Church, that is. He exercises his office in a personal manner either by acting on his own or through the acts of his ministers, principally the offices of the Roman curia.

Sacred Congregation for the Clergy

134. The Sacred Congregation for the Clergy (Second Office) is entrusted with the central responsibility for catechesis in territories of the common law, as they are called. Its task of

elaborating, co-ordinating and regulating is exercised in promoting what pertains to the preaching of the word and the works of the apostolate; it is also exercised in disseminating information and in promoting where possible co-operation between various countries.

It assists in the development of offices in charge of catechesis and it gives direction to them.

It reviews and approves catechetical directives, catechisms and programs for preaching the word of God prepared by episcopal conferences. It encourages national catechetical congresses and approves or summons international congresses (see Apostolic Constitution, *Regimini Ecclesiae universae,* n. 69, Letter of the Secretariat of State, 20 August 1969).

APPENDIX
THE FIRST RECEPTION OF THE SACRAMENTS OF PENANCE AND THE EUCHARIST

The preparation of children for the sacraments of penance and the eucharist is a very important function of catechesis. In this connection it is appropriate to recall certain principles and to comment on some experiments which have been taking place recently in certain parts of the Church.

The age of discretion

1. The appropriate age for the first reception of these sacraments is reckoned to be what in Church documents is called the age of reason or of discretion. This, 'for both confession and communion is [the age] at which a child begins to reason, which is at about the seventh year, give or take something. The precepts of confession and communion begin to oblige from that time.' (Decree, *Quam singulari,* 1, AAS 2 (1910), 682). It is good to study and describe this age from the standpoint of pastoral psychology, for what is in question is a gradual process, variously conditioned and with different characteristics in every child. At the same time, however, one should be careful not to extend beyond the above limits, which certainly are not rigid, the time at which the precept of confession and communion begins to oblige *per se*.

Formation and growth of the moral conscience of children

2. Children's moral consciences develop as their capacity to

reason gradually evolves. Moral conscience is the faculty of judging their actions by moral standards. Various elements and circumstances combine to form this moral conscience in children: the family, with its character and discipline, the most important educational influence in the first years of children's lives; interpersonal relationships and the activities and witness of the ecclesial community. Catechesis, as it instructs and forms in the Christian faith, co-ordinates these various educational influences, encourages them and collaborates with them. Only thus will catechesis be able appropriately to direct children's steps towards the heavenly Father and to correct possible deviations or wrong orientations in life. At this age, children should certainly be told in the simplest terms about God as our Lord and Father and of his love for us, about Jesus, who became man, died and rose again for us. By thinking of the love of God, children will be able gradually to see the malice of sin, which is always offensive to God the Father and to Jesus and which is contrary to the love we should have for our neighbour and for ourselves.

On explaining the importance of the sacrament of penance to children

3. Children who commence to offend God by sinning begin also to desire pardon, not only from parents or relatives, but from God. Catechesis helps by a salutary stimulation of this desire, instilling in them a holy aversion from sin, the need for amendment and, especially, for love of God. The special task of catechesis in this context is to explain properly that sacramental confession is offered to the Church's children as a means of receiving pardon and indeed as a necessary means for anybody who has fallen into mortal sin. Certainly, Christian parents and religious educators ought so to train children that they will endeavour before all else to advance in more intimate love of God and in genuine love of neighbour. The doctrine of the sacrament of penance should be expounded in the broad context of achieving purification and spiritual growth, with great trust in God's love and mercy. In this way, not only will children be able gradually to acquire delicate consciences, they will also not be discouraged when they do something not quite right.

The eucharist is the apex and centre of the entire Christian life. Great purity of soul is clearly appropriate in one receiving holy communion, apart from the requisite state of grace. One must however avoid giving children the impression that confession is essential before the reception of the eucharist even when a person sincerely loves God and has not seriously transgressed the commandments of God.

Certain new experiments

4. Very recently, doubt and confusion have been occasioned in some parts of the Church by experiments with regard to the first reception of penance and the eucharist.

Some people think that children should be admitted to first communion without having received the sacrament of penance. Their object is to facilitate the early reception of communion, to avoid possible future psychological disturbances in the Christian life as a result of too early recourse to confession and to foster a better formation in the spirit of penance and a more solid catechetical preparation for confession.

In fact, however, recourse to the sacrament of penance from the commencement of the age of discretion does not of itself cause psychological damage to children, provided it is preceded, as is right, by a humane and prudent catechetical preparation. The spirit of penance can be further developed by catechetical formation after first communion; likewise, awareness and appreciation of the great gift which Christ gave to sinful men and women can increase—the gift, that is, of the sacrament of pardon to be accepted by them and of reconciliation with the Church (see LG 11).

In spite of all this, in some places the practice has been introduced of allowing several years to elapse between first communion and first confession. In other places, greater caution has prevailed, with the result that first confession has not been postponed for so long a time or the parents' wishes that the children go to first confession before first communion have been acceded to.

Value of the common practice

5. The Supreme Pontiff Pius X declared: 'The custom of not admitting to confession children who have attained the use of reason, or of never giving them absolution, is to be totally condemned.' (Decree, *Quam singulari*, VII, AAS 1910, p. 583) One can scarcely acknowledge the right of baptised children to confess their sins if when they reach the age of discretion they are not prepared for the sacrament of penance and gently persuaded to receive it.

One ought also to bear in mind the usefulness of confession. It is still effective even when only venial sins are in question, it gives an increase of grace and charity, improves the children's good dispositions for the reception of the eucharist and helps to perfect the Christian life. It would seem therefore that one cannot disregard the usefulness of confession for the sake of those penitential services or those forms of the ministry of the word which cultivate the virtue of penance in children, but which can fruitfully go hand in hand with the sacrament of penance, preceded by a suitable catechesis. The pastoral experience of the Church, confirmed by ample evidence, including evidence from the present day, teaches it how very well qualified is the age of discretion, as it is called, to ensure that children's baptismal grace will, thanks to the well-prepared reception of the sacraments of penance and the eucharist, bear first fruits, which of course will later have to be augmented with the help of a continued catechesis.

All things considered and bearing in mind the common and general practice which cannot be derogated, per se, without the approval of the Holy See, having consulted episcopal conferences, this same Holy See judges it proper that the current custom of putting confession before first communion be retained; which by no means precludes the present custom being perfected in various ways—with the help of communal penitential celebration, for example, before or after the administration of the sacrament of penance.

The Holy See does not ignore the special characteristics and conditions that obtain in different regions, but it urges bishops not to depart from the current usage in this important matter without having first consulted it in a spirit of hierarchical communion. Nor should they by any means allow parishes, teachers or religious institutes to begin or to continue to depart from the current usage.

In regions where new practices differing notably from earlier practices have already been introduced, the episcopal conferences should re-examine these experiments. If they should then decide that they wish to prolong them further, they should first consult the Holy See, which will willingly listen, and should be of one mind with it.[6]

Translator's note: In view of the approval given by the Sacred Congregation for the Clergy to the English version of this directory copyrighted by the United States Catholic Conference, readers may welcome the indication of where this version differs *in meaning* from theirs. The following is a list of the principal instances, none of them in fact of major importance. Except where there is no point in doing it, we give first the Latin original of the word or phrase, followed by our version and, between brackets, the U.S.C.C. version:

2 (b) *enodationes:* develop[ments], (explanations).

Introduction to n. 6: *Ecclesiae vitae intersunt:* are important in the life of the Church (are also found in the life of the Church)

16 *probe conscius:* fully conversant (honestly aware)

25 *symbolorum:* of the symbols, (of the creeds)

44 *suam vim explicat:* unfolds its meaning (displays its force)

45 *vel:* and (or), but see footnote 4.

53 *primum impassibilis et tunc passibilis:* first incapable of suffering and then capable of suffering (first capable of suffering and then incapable of suffering).

56 *in debitis dispositionibus procurandis:* to evoke the proper dispositions, (the acquisition of proper dispositions)

60 *vitae rationem cum Deo:* a way of life with God (a way of life)

66 *quaelibet munera et quaelibet charisma:* all offices and charisms (all gifts and charisms)

68 *munus suum jam manifestavit:* manifested his role (manifested his gift)

70 *artem discendi:* the art of learning (the art of teaching)

75 In the last sentence, *expositione* not translated.

77 *psychica:* psychological (spiritual)

78 *animi fidentis dispositio:* what inclines . . .towards belief (the right orientation of a trusting spirit)

87 *suamque indolem:* [their] identity, (their . . .talents)

89 *christiana munera:* Christian obligations (religious duties)

112 (c) *et gradum theologiae scientificae attingere debet apud instituta scholastica superiora:* and in the higher institutes of catechetics should reach the level of scientific theology (together with a degree of scientific theology obtained at higher catechetical institutes). The Italian of EV is *'e negli istituti superiori di catechetica deve raggiungere il livello della teologia scientifica.*

112 (c) *in relationibus educativis:* in educational rapport (in educational reports)

119 *documenta:* documents (witnesses)—throughout.

Appendix, n. 5, par. 3 *perficiatur:* perfected (carried out)

*Translated from the Latin by Austin Flannery, O.P., who compared his version with the Italian version given in *Enchiridion Vaticanum,* vol. 4, pp 225–399 and with the English version published by the United States Catholic Conference. To avoid sexist language and also to avoid the awkward 'he or she', he has changed singular to plural on a number of occasions where this made no difference whatever to the sense. The Latin original is in *Enchiridion Vaticanum,* vol. 3, pp. 224–398 and in AAS 64 (1972), pp. 97–176. In a number of instances, this version gives a different meaning from that given in the U.S.C.C. version. The differences are not major. A list of them is appended at the end, together with the Latin original of the word or phrase in question.

1. Literally, 'in a living manner', *modo vivo.* (Translator)

2. In other words, 'faith' as the act of believing and 'faith' as what one believes. (Translator)

3. The Latin here has *in verbo Dei scripto vel tradito.* I have translated *vel* as 'and' here and in the next paragraph, as does the Italian transla-

tion already referred to. The Latin *vel* is closer to the English 'and' than to 'or'. The Latin *aut*, 'or', is much stronger and is described by *Cassell's New Latin Dictionary* as 'generally (unlike *vel*) introducing a second alternative which positively excludes the first.' The use of the word 'and', instead of 'or', avoids giving the impression of scripture and tradition as two mutually exclusive, or even independent, sources of revelation. See DV 9, 10 (Translator).

4. The Italian translation in Enchiridion Vaticanum renders this *le communità di base*, basic communities. (Translator).

5. The Latin is *gradus et modos* and the U.S.C.C. version renders it 'degree and style'. However, ecclesiastical Latin is tolerant of words that do not always add greatly to the sense and perhaps the words are not of very great importance. Italian translators are usually regarded as being on an inside track—sometimes the Italian version is produced before the Latin—and the E.V. Italian version does not translate the words at all (Translator).

6. On 24 May, 1973, the Congregations for the Discipline of the Sacraments and for the Clergy issued a joint declaration on the question of first confession and first communion, the last paragraph of which reads as follows: 'After mature declaration and having taken account of the views of the bishops, the Sacred Congregations for the Discipline of the Sacraments and for the Clergy declare by this present document, with the approval of the Sovereign Pontiff, Paul VI, that these experiments, which have lasted for two years up to the end of the school year 1972-73, should cease and that everybody everywhere should conform to the decree, *Quam singulari.*' (Full text in *Vatican Council II,* The Conciliar and Postconciliar Documents, p. 241. Latin Text in AAS, 65, p. 410) Similarly, on 28 May, 1977, the same congregations answered a 'dubium' as to whether 'it is still permitted to administer first communion, as a general rule, before the sacrament of penance, in the parishes where this practice has been introduced in recent years?' The reply: 'The Sacred Congregations for the Sacraments and Divine Worship, and for the Clergy, with the approval of the Supreme Pontiff, reply in the negative, in accordance with the sense of that declaration. The sense of the declaration is that, within one year of its promulgation, there should be an end to all experiments whereby first communion is administered without previous reception of the sacrament of penance, so that the Church's discipline should be in conformity with the decree, *Quam singulari.*' (Latin text in AAS 69, p. 427)

115

CATHOLIC SCHOOLS*

S.C.C.E., *Malgré les déclarations*, 24 June, 1977

I
INTRODUCTION

1. Catholic schools are receiving more and more attention in the Church since the Second Vatican Council, especially with the emphasis now being placed on the Church as portrayed in the constitutions *Lumen Gentium* and *Gaudium et Spes*. In the Council's declaration *Gravissimum Educationis* they are discussed in the wider sphere of Christian education. The present document develops the thinking of this declaration, limiting itself to a deeper reflection on the Catholic school.

2. The Sacred Congregation for Catholic Education is aware of the serious problems which are inseparable from Christian education in a pluralistic society. It regards as a prime duty, therefore, to focus attention on the nature and distinctive characteristics of a school which would present itself as Catholic. Yet the diverse situations and legal systems in which the Catholic school has to function in Christian and non-Christian countries demand that local problems be faced and solved by each Church within its own social-cultural context.

3. While acknowledging this duty of the local Churches, the Sacred Congregation believes that now is the opportune moment to offer its own contribution by re-emphasizing clearly the educational value of the Catholic school. It is in this value that the Catholic school's fundamental reason for existing and the basis of its genuine apostolate is to be found. This document does not pretend to be an exhaustive treatment of the subject; it merely proposes to state the premises that will lead to further fruitful study and development.

4. To episcopal conferences, pastorally concerned for all young Catholics whatever school they attend, the Sacred Congregation for Catholic Education entrusts this present docu-

ment in order that they may seek to achieve an effective system of education at all levels which corresponds to the total educational needs of young people today in Catholic schools. The Sacred Congregation also addresses itself to all who are responsible for education—parents, teachers, young people and school authorities—and urges them to pool all their resources and the means at their disposal to enable Catholic schools to provide a service which is truly civic and apostolic.

II

THE CATHOLIC SCHOOL AND THE SALVIFIC MISSION OF THE CHURCH

THE SALVIFIC MISSION OF THE CHURCH

5. In the fullness of time, in his mysterious plan of love, God the Father sent his only son to begin the kingdom of God on earth and bring about the spiritual rebirth of mankind. To continue his work of salvation, Jesus Christ founded the Church as a visible organism, living by the power of the Spirit.

6. Moved by the same Spirit, the Church is constantly deepening her awareness of herself and meditating on the mystery of her being and mission. Thus she is ever rediscovering her living relationship with Christ 'in order to discover greater light, energy, and joy in fulfilling her mission and determining the best way to ensure that her relationship with humanity is closer and more efficacious'—that humanity of which she is a part and yet from which she is so undeniably distinct. Her destiny is to serve humanity until it reaches its fullness in Christ.

7. Evangelization is, therefore, the mission of the Church; that is, she must proclaim the good news of salvation to all, generate new creatures in Christ through baptism, and train them to live in the awareness that they are children of God.

MEANS AVAILABLE FOR THE MISSION OF THE CHURCH

8. To carry out her saving mission, the Church uses, above all, the means which Jesus Christ has given her. She also uses other means which at different times and in different cultures have proved effective in achieving and promoting the development of the human person. The Church adapts these means to

the changing conditions and emerging needs of mankind. In her encounter with differing cultures and with man's progressive achievements, the Church proclaims the faith and reveals 'to all ages the transcendent goal which alone gives life its full meaning'. She establishes her own schools because she considers them as a privileged means of promoting the formation of the whole man, since the school is a centre in which a specific concept of the world, of man, and of history is developed and conveyed.

CONTRIBUTION OF THE CATHOLIC SCHOOLS TOWARDS THE CHURCH'S SALVIFIC MISSION

9. The Catholic school forms part of the saving mission of the Church, especially for education in the faith. Remembering that 'the simultaneous development of man's psychological and moral consciousness is demanded by Christ almost as a precondition for the reception of the appropriate divine gifts of truth and grace', the Church fulfills her obligation to foster in her children a full awareness of their rebirth to a new life. It is precisely in the Gospel of Christ, taking root in the minds and lives of the faithful, that the Catholic school finds its definition as it comes to terms with the cultural conditions of the times.

THE CHURCH'S EDUCATIONAL INVOLVEMENT AND CULTURAL PLURALISM

10. In the course of the centuries 'while constantly holding to the fullness of divine truth' the Church has progressively used secular culture as a source and a means for deepening her understanding of revelation and for promoting constructive dialogue with the world. Impelled by her belief that she is led by the Spirit of the Lord, the Church seeks to discern in the events, needs and hopes of our era what is most urgently demanded of her if she is to carry out God's plan.

11. One pressing need is to ensure the presence of a Christian mentality in the society of the present day, marked, among other things, by cultural pluralism. For it is Christian thought which constitutes a sound criterion of judgement in the midst of conflicting concepts and behaviour: 'Reference to Jesus Christ teaches man to differentiate between the values which ennoble man and those which degrade him.'

12. Cultural pluralism, therefore, leads the Church to reaffirm her mission to educate, to ensure strong character forma-

tion. Her children, then, will be capable both of resisting the debilitating influence of relativism and of living up to the demands made on them by their baptism. It also stimulates her to foster truly Christian living and apostolic communities, equipped to make their own positive contribution, in a spirit of co-operation, to the building up of the secular society. For this reason the Church is prompted to mobilize her educational resources in the face of the materialism, pragmatism and technocracy of contemporary society.

13. The Church upholds the principle of a plurality of school systems in order to safeguard her objectives in the face of cultural pluralism. In other words, she encourages the coexistence and, if possible, the co-operation of diverse educational institutions which will allow young people to be formed by value-judgements based on a specific view of the world and to be trained to take an active part in the construction of a community through which the building of society is promoted.

14. Thus, while policies and opportunities differ from place to place, the Catholic school has its place in any national school system. By offering such an alternative the Church wishes to respond to the obvious need for co-operation in a society characterized by cultural pluralism. Moreover, in this way she helps to promote that freedom of teaching which champions and guarantees freedom of conscience and the parental right to choose the school best suited to parents' educational objectives.

15. Finally, the Church is absolutely convinced that Catholic schools, with their educational objectives, perform a vital service for the Church herself in today's world. She participates in cultural dialogue through schools, making her own positive contribution to the cause of the total formation of man. The absence of the Catholic school would be a great loss for civilization and for the natural and supernatural destiny of man.

II

PRESENT DIFFICULTIES OVER CATHOLIC SCHOOLS

16. In the light of her mission of salvation, the Church considers that the Catholic school provides a privileged environment for the complete formation of her members, and that it also provides a highly important service to mankind.

Nevertheless, she is aware of the many problems that exist and objections that are made against Catholic schools sometimes regarding the very validity of their existence and their functions. The issue is really part of a much wider problem which faces all institutions as such in a society such as the present, characterized by rapid and profound change.

OBJECTIONS TO CATHOLIC SCHOOLS

17. In the debate about Catholic schools there are some easily identifiable central objections and difficulties. These need to be borne in mind if discussion is to be relevant to the actual situation and if teachers are to make a serious attempt to adapt their work to the needs of the contemporary world.

18. In the first place many people, both inside and outside the Church, motivated by a mistaken sense of the lay role in secular society, attack Catholic schools as institutions. They do not admit that, apart from the individual witness of her members, the Church also may offer witness by means of her institutions, e.g., those dedicated to the search for truth or to works of charity.

19. Others claim that Catholic schools make use of a human institution for religious and confessional purposes. Christian education can sometimes run into the danger of a so-called proselytism, of imparting a one-sided outlook. This can happen only when Christian educators misunderstand the nature and methods of Christian education. Complete education necessarily includes a religious dimension. Religion is an effective contribution to the development of other aspects of a personality in the measure in which it is integrated into general education.

20. According to others, Catholic schools have outlived their time—as institutions they were a necessary substitute in the past but have no place at a time when civil authority assumes responsibility for education. In fact, as the State increasingly takes control of education and establishes its own so-called neutral and monolithic system, the survival of those natural communities, based on a shared concept of life, is threatened. Faced with this situation, the Catholic school offers an alternative which is in conformity with the wishes of the members of the community of the Church.

21. In some countries Catholic schools have been obliged to restrict their educational activities to wealthier social classes, thus giving an impression of social and economic discrimina-

tion in education. But this occurs only where the State has not weighed the advantages of an alternative presence in their pluralistic society. From such nearsightedness considerable difficulties have arisen for Catholic schools.

22. Allied to these points, objections are raised concerning the educational effectiveness of Catholic schools. They are sometimes accused of not knowing how to form convinced articulate Christians ready to take their place in social and political life. Every educational enterprise, however, involves the risk of failure and one must not be too discouraged by apparent or even real failures, since there are very many formative influences on young people and results often have to be calculated on a long-term basis.

23. Before concluding these comments on the objections raised against Catholic schools, one must remember the context in which contemporary work in the field of education is undertaken, and especially in the Church. The school problem in our rapidly changing society is serious for everyone. The second Vatican Council has encouraged a more openminded approach which has sometimes been misrepresented in theory and practice. There are difficulties in the provision of adequate staff and finance. In such a situation should the Church perhaps give up her apostolic mission in Catholic schools, as some people would like her to do, and direct her energy to a more direct work of evangelization in sectors considered to be of higher priority or more suited to her spiritual mission, or should she make State schools the sole object of her pastoral activity? Such a solution would not only be contrary to the directives of the Vatican Council, but would also be opposed to the Church's mission and to what is expected of her by Christian people. What follows emphasizes this fact.

SOME ASPECTS OF SCHOOLS TODAY

24. To understand the real nature of the Catholic school one cannot divorce it from wider modern problems concerning schools in general. Apart from the ideas advanced by the promoters of deschooling—a theory which now seems of minor significance—contemporary society tends to place greater importance than ever on the specific function of the school: its social significance (parental participation, increased democratization, equality of opportunity); its tendency to coordinate and eventually include the educational work of other institutions; the extension of the statutory duration of attendance at school.

III

THE SCHOOL AS A CENTRE
OF HUMAN FORMATION

25. To understand fully the specific mission of the Catholic school it is essential to keep in mind the basic concept of what a school is; that which does not reproduce the characteristic features of a school cannot be a Catholic school.

THE GENERAL PURPOSE OF A SCHOOL

26. A close examination of the various definitions of a school and of new educational trends at every level, leads one to formulate the concept of a school as a place of integral formation by means of a systematic and critical assimilation of culture. A school is, therefore, a privileged place in which, through a living encounter with a cultural inheritance, integral formation occurs.

27. This vital process takes place in the school through personal contacts and commitments which consider absolute values in a life-context and seek to insert them into a life-framework. Indeed, culture is only educational when young people can relate their study to real-life situations with which they are familiar. The school must stimulate the pupil to exercise his intelligence through the dynamics of understanding to attain clarity and inventiveness. It must help him spell out the meaning of his experiences and their truths. Any school which neglects this duty and which offers merely pre-cast conclusions hinders the personal development of its pupils.

SCHOOL AND ATTITUDES OF LIFE

28. From this it is clear that the school has to prepare its entire programme of formation, both its content and the methods used, in the light of that vision of the reality from which it draws its inspiration and on which it depends.

29. Either implicit or explicit reference to a determined attitude to life (*Weltanschauung*) is unavoidable in education because it comes into every decision that is made. It is, therefore, essential, if for no other reason than a unity in teaching, that each member of the school community, albeit with differing degrees of awareness, adopts a common vision, a common outlook on life, based on adherence to a scale of values in which he believes. This is what gives teachers and adults authority to educate. It must never be forgotten that the purpose of instruction at school is education, that is, the development of man from within, freeing him from that conditioning which would prevent

him from becoming a fully-integrated human being. The school must begin from the principle that its educational program is intentionally directed to the growth of the whole person.

30. It is one of the formal tasks of a school, as an institution for education, to draw out the ethical dimension for the precise purpose of arousing the individual's inner spiritual dynamism and to aid his achieving that moral freedom which complements the psychological. Behind this moral freedom, however, stand those absolute values which alone give meaning and value to human life. This has to be said because the tendency to adopt present-day values as a yardstick is not absent even in the educational world. The danger is always to react to passing superficial ideas and to lose sight of the much-deeper needs of the contemporary world.

THE SCHOOL IN TODAY'S SOCIETY

31. Precisely because the school endeavours to answer the needs of a society characterized by depersonalization and a mass production mentality which so easily result from scientific technological developments, it must develop into an authentically formational school, reducing such risks to a minimum. It must develop persons who are responsible and innerdirected, capable of choosing freely in conformity with their conscience. This is simply another way of saying that the school is an institution where young people gradually learn to open themselves up to life as it is, and to create in themselves a definite attitude of life as it should be.

32. When seen in this light, a school is not only a place where one is given a choice of intellectual values, but a place where one has presented an array of values which are actively lived. The school must be a community whose values are communicated through the interpersonal and sincere relationships of its members and through both individual and corporate adherence to the outlook on life that permeates the school.

IV

THE EDUCATIONAL WORK OF THE CATHOLIC SCHOOL

SPECIFIC CHARACTER OF THE CATHOLIC SCHOOL

33. Having stated the characteristics of the Catholic school

from the point of view of 'school', we can now examine its Catholic quality, namely its reference to a Christian concept of life centered on Jesus Christ.

34. Christ is the foundation of the whole educational enterprise in a Catholic school. His revelation gives new meaning to life and helps man to direct his thought, action and will according to the Gospel, making the beatitudes his norm of life. The fact that in their own individual ways all members of the school community share this Christian vision, makes the school 'Catholic'; principles of the Gospel in this manner become the educational norms since the school then has them as its internal motivation and final goal.

35. The Catholic school is committed thus to the development of the whole man, since in Christ, the perfect man, all human values find their fulfilment and unity. Herein lies the specifically Catholic character of the school. Its duty to cultivate human values in their own legitimate right in accordance with its particular mission to serve all men has its origin in the figure of Christ. He is the one who ennobles man, gives meaning to human life, and is the model which the Catholic school offers to its pupils.

36. If, like every other school, the Catholic school has as its aim the critical communication of human culture and the total formation of the individual, it works towards this goal guided by its Christian vision of reality 'through which our cultural heritage acquires its special place in the total vocational life of man'. Mindful of the fact that man has been redeemed by Christ, the Catholic school aims at forming in the Christian those particular virtues which will enable him to live a new life in Christ and help him to play faithfully his part in building up the kingdom of God.

37. These premises indicate the duties and the content of the Catholic school. Its task is fundamentally a synthesis of culture and faith, and a synthesis of faith and life: the first is reached by integrating all the different aspects of human knowledge through the subjects taught, in the light of the Gospel; the second in the growth of the virtues characteristic of the Christian.

INTEGRATION OF FAITH AND CULTURE

38. In helping pupils to achieve through the medium of its teaching an integration of faith and culture, the Catholic school sets out with a deep awareness of the value of knowledge as such. Under no circumstances does it wish to divert the imparting of knowledge from its rightful objective.

39. Individual subjects must be taught according to their own particular methods. It would be wrong to consider subjects as mere adjuncts to faith or as a useful means of teaching apologetics. They enable the pupil to assimilate skills, knowledge, intellectual methods and moral and social attitudes, all of which help to develop his personality and lead him to take his place as an active member of the community of man. Their aim is not merely the attainment of knowledge but the acquisition of values and the discovery of truth.

40. Since the educative mission of the Catholic school is so wide, the teacher is in an excellent position to guide the pupil to a deepening of his faith and to enrich and enlighten his human knowledge with the data of the faith. While there are many occasions in teaching when pupils can be stimulated by insights of faith, a Christian education acknowledges the valid contribution which can be made by academic subjects towards the development of a mature Christian. The teacher can form the mind and heart of his pupils and guide them to develop a total commitment to Christ, with their whole personality enriched by human culture.

41. The school considers human knowledge as a truth to be discovered. In the measure in which subjects are taught by someone who knowingly and without restraint seeks the truth, they are to that extent Christian. Discovery and awareness of truth leads man to the discovery of truth itself. A teacher who is full of Christian wisdom, well prepared in his own subject, does more than convey the sense of what he is teaching to his pupils. Over and above what he says, he guides his pupils beyond his mere words to the heart of total truth.

42. The cultural heritage of mankind includes other values apart from the specific ambience of truth. When the Christian teacher helps a pupil to grasp, appreciate and assimilate these values, he is guiding him towards eternal realities. This movement towards the uncreated source of all knowledge highlights the importance of teaching for the growth of faith.

43. The achievement of this specific aim of the Catholic school depends not so much on subject matter or methodology as on the people who work there. The extent to which the Christian message is transmitted through education depends to a very great extent on the teachers. The integration of culture and faith is mediated by the other integration of faith and life in the person of the teacher. The nobility of the task to which teachers are called demands that, in imitation of Christ, the only teacher, they reveal the Christian message not only by word but also by every facet of their behaviour. This is what

makes the difference between a school whose education is permeated by the Christian spirit and one in which religion is only regarded as an academic subject like any other.

INTEGRATION OF FAITH AND LIFE

44. The fundamental aim of teaching is the assimilation of objective values, and, when this is undertaken for an apostolic purpose, it does not stop at an integration of faith and culture but leads the pupil on to a personal integration of faith and life.

45. The Catholic school has as its specific duty the complete Christian formation of its pupils, and this task is of special significance today because of defects in family life and in society. It knows that this integration of faith and life is part of a life-long process of conversion until the pupil becomes what God wishes him to be. Young people have to be taught to share their personal lives with God. They are to overcome their individualism and discover, in the light of faith, their specific vocation to live responsibly in a community with others. The very pattern of the Christian life draws them to commit themselves to serve God in their brethren and to make the world a better place for man to live in.

46. The Catholic school should teach its pupils to discern in the sound of the universe the creator whom it reveals and, in the achievements of science, to know God and man better. In the daily life of the school, the pupil should learn that he is called to be a living witness to God's love for men by the way he acts, and that he is part of that salvation history which has Christ, the saviour of the world, as its goal.

47. Being aware that baptism by itself does not make a Christian—living and acting in conformity with the Gospel is necessary—the Catholic school tries to create within its walls a climate in which the pupil's faith will gradually mature and enable him to assume the responsibility placed on him by baptism. It will give pride of place in the education it provides through Christian doctrine to the gradual formation of conscience in fundamental, permanent virtues—above all the theological virtues, and charity in particular, which is, so to speak, the life-giving spirit which transforms a man of virtue into a man of Christ. Christ, therefore, is the teaching-centre, the model on whom the Christian shapes his life. In him the Catholic school differs from all others which limit themselves to forming men. Its task is to form Christian men, and, by its teaching and witness, show non-Christians something of the mystery of Christ who surpasses all human understanding.

48. The Catholic school will work closely with other Christian bodies (the family, the parish and Christian community, youth associations, and so on). But one must not overlook many other spheres of activity in society which are sources of information and in their various ways have an educational influence. Alongside this so-called 'parallel school', the school proper is an active force through the systematic formation of the pupils' critical faculties to bring them to a measure of self-control and the ability to choose freely and conscientiously in the face of what is offered by the organs of social communication. They must be taught to subject these things to a critical and personal analysis, take what is good, and integrate it into their Christian human culture.

RELIGIOUS TEACHING

49. The specific mission of the school, then, is a critical, systematic transmission of culture in the light of faith and the bringing forth of the power of Christian virtue by the integration of culture with faith and of faith with living. Consequently, the Catholic school is aware of the importance of the Gospel-teaching as transmitted through the Catholic Church. It is, indeed, the fundamental element in the educative process as it helps the pupil towards his conscious choice of living a responsible and coherent way of life.

50. Without entering into the whole problem of teaching religion in schools, it must be emphasized that, while such teaching is not merely confined to 'religious classes' within the school curriculum, it must, nevertheless, also be imparted explicitly and in a systematic manner to prevent a distortion in the child's mind between general and religious culture. The fundamental difference between religious and other forms of education is that its aim is not simply intellectual assent to religious truths but also a total commitment of one's whole being to the person of Christ.

51. It is recognized that the proper place for catechesis is the family helped by other Christian communities, especially the local parish. But the importance and need for catechetical instruction in Catholic schools cannot be sufficiently emphasized. Here young people are helped to grow towards maturity in faith.

52. The Catholic school must be alert at all times to developments in the fields of child psychology, pedagogy and particularly catechesis, and should especially keep abreast of directives from competent ecclesiastical authorities. The school

must do everything in its power to aid the Church to fulfil its catechetical mission and so must have the best possible qualified teachers of religion.

THE CATHOLIC SCHOOL AS THE CENTRE OF THE EDUCATIVE CHRISTIAN COMMUNITY

53. For all these reasons, Catholic schools must be seen as 'meeting places for those who wish to express Christian values in education'. The Catholic school, far more than any other, must be a community whose aim is the transmission of values for living. Its work is seen as promoting a faith-relationship with Christ in whom all values find fulfilment. But faith is principally assimilated through contact with people whose daily life bears witness to it. Christian faith, in fact, is born and grows inside a community.

54. The community aspect of the Catholic school is necessary because of the nature of man and the nature of the educational process which is common to every school. No Catholic school can adequately fulfil its educational role on its own. It must continually be fed and stimulated by its source of life, the saving word of Christ as it is expressed in Sacred Scripture, in Tradition, especially liturgical and sacramental tradition, and in the lives of people, past and present, who bear witness to that word.

55. The Catholic school loses its purpose without constant reference to the Gospel and a frequent encounter with Christ. It derives all the energy necessary for its educational work from him and thus 'creates in the school community an atmosphere permeated with the Gospel spirit of freedom and love.' In this setting the pupil experiences his dignity as a person before he knows its definition. Faithful, therefore, to the claims of man and of God, the Catholic school makes its own contribution towards man's liberation, making him, in other words, what his destiny implies, one who talks consciously with God, one who is there for God to love.

56. 'This simple religious doctrine is the corner-stone of the existential, Christian metaphysic.' This is the basis of a Catholic school's educational work. Education is not given for the purpose of gaining power but as an aid towards a fuller understanding of, and communion with man, events and things. Knowledge is not to be considered as a means of material prosperity and success, but as a call to serve and to be responsible for others.

OTHER ASPECTS OF THE EDUCATIONAL PROCESS IN CATHOLIC SCHOOLS

57. Whether or not the Catholic community forms its young people in the faith by means of a Catholic school, a Catholic school in itself is far from being divisive or overbearing. It does not exacerbate differences, but rather aids co-operation and contact with others. It opens itself to others and respects their way of thinking and of living. It wants to share their anxieties and their hopes as it, indeed, shares their present and future lot in this world.

58. Since it is motivated by the Christian ideal, the Catholic school is particularly sensitive to the call from every part of the world for a more just society, and it tries to make its own contribution towards it. It does not stop at the courageous teaching of the demands of justice even in the face of local opposition, but tries to put these demands into practice in its own community in the daily life of the school. In some countries, because of local laws and economic conditions, the Catholic school runs the risk of giving counter-witness by admitting a majority of children from wealthier families. Schools may have done this because of their need to be financially self-supporting. This situation is of great concern to those responsible for Catholic education, because first and foremost the Church offers its educational service to 'the poor or those who are deprived of family help and affection or those who are far from the faith.' Since education is an important means of improving the social and economic condition of the individual and of peoples, if the Catholic school were to turn its attention exclusively or predominantly to those from the wealthier social classes, it could be contributing towards their privileged position, and could thereby continue to favour a society which is unjust.

59. It is obvious that in such a demanding educational policy all participants must be committed to it freely. It cannot be imposed, but is offered as a possibility, as good news, and as such can be refused. However, in order to bring it into being and to maintain it, the school must be able to count on the unity of purpose and conviction of all its members.

THE PARTICIPATION OF THE CHRISTIAN COMMUNITY IN THE CATHOLIC SCHOOL'S WORK

60. From the outset the Catholic school declares its program and its determination to uphold it. It is a genuine community

bent on imparting, over and above an academic education, all the help it can to its members to adopt a Christian way of life. For the Catholic school mutual respect means service to the person of Christ. Co-operation is between brothers and sisters in Christ. A policy of working for the common good is undertaken seriously as working for the building up of the kingdom of God.

61. The co-operation required for the realization of this aim is a duty in conscience for all members of the community—teachers, parents, pupils, administrative personnel. Each has his or her own part to play. Co-operation of all, given in the spirit of the Gospel, is by its very nature a witness not only to Christ as the corner-stone of the community, but also as the light which shines far beyond it.

THE CATHOLIC SCHOOL AS A SERVICE TO THE CHURCH AND TO SOCIETY

62. The Catholic school community, therefore, is an irreplaceable source of service, not only to the pupils and its other members, but also to society. Today especially one sees a world which clamours for solidarity and yet experiences the rise of new forms of individualism. Society can take note from the Catholic school that it is possible to create true communities out of a common effort for the common good. In the pluralistic society of today the Catholic school, moreover, by maintaining an institutional Christian presence in the academic world, proclaims by its very existence the enriching power of the faith as the answer to the enormous problems which afflict mankind. Above all, it is called to render a humble loving service to the Church by ensuring that she is present in the scholastic field for the benefit of the human family.

63. In this way the Catholic school performs "an authentic apostolate." To work, therefore, in this apostolate "means performing a unique and invaluable work for the Church."

V

THE RESPONSIBILITY OF THE CATHOLIC SCHOOL TODAY

64. The real problem facing the Catholic school is to identify and lay down the conditions necessary for it to fulfil its mission. It is, therefore, a problem requiring clear and positive thinking, courage, perseverance and co-operation to tackle the necessary measures without being overawed by the size of the difficulties from within and without, nor 'by persistent and

outdated slogans', which in the last analysis aim to abolish Catholic schools. To give in to them would be suicidal. To favour in a more or less radical form a merely non-institutional presence of the Church in the scholastic field is a dangerous illusion.

65. At great cost and sacrifice our forebears were inspired by the teaching of the Church to establish schools which enriched mankind and responded to the needs of time and place. While it recognizes its own inadequacies, the Catholic school is conscious of its responsibility to continue this service. Today, as in the past, some scholastic institutions which bear the name Catholic do not appear to correspond fully to the principles of education which should be their distinguishing feature and, therefore, do not fulfil the duties which the Church and society has every right to expect of them. Without pretending to make an exhaustive enquiry into the factors which may explain the difficulties under which the Catholic school labours, here are a few points in the hope of encouraging some thought as a stimulus to courageous reform.

66. Often what is perhaps fundamentally lacking among Catholics who work in a school is a clear realization of the identity of a Catholic school and the courage to follow all the consequences of its uniqueness. One must recognize that, more than ever before, a Catholic school's job is infinitely more difficult, more complex, since this is a time when Christianity demands to be clothed in fresh garments, when all manner of changes have been introduced in the Church and in secular life, and, particularly, when a pluralist mentality dominates and the Christian Gospel is increasingly pushed to the sidelines.

67. It is because of this that loyalty to the educational aims of the Catholic school demands constant self-criticism and return to basic principles, to the motives which inspire the Church's involvement in education. They do not provide a quick answer to contemporary problems, but they give a direction which can begin to solve them. Account has to be taken of new pedagogical insights and collaboration with others, irrespective of religious allegiance, who work honestly for the true development of mankind—first and foremost with schools of other Christians—in the interests, even in this field, of Christian unity but also with State schools. In addition to meetings of teachers and shared research, this collaboration can be extended to the pupils themselves and their families.

68. In conclusion it is only right to repeat what has been said above about the considerable difficulties arising from legal and economic systems operating in different countries which

hinder the activities of the Catholic school, difficulties which prevent them from extending their service to all social and economic classes and compel them to give the false impression of providing schools simply for the rich.

VI
PRACTICAL DIRECTIVES

69. After reflecting on the difficulties which the Catholic school encounters, we turn now to the practical possibilities open to those who work in, or are responsible for, these schools. The following more serious questions have been selected for special comment: organization and planning, ensuring the distinctive Catholic character of the school, the involvement of religious in the school apostolate, the Catholic school in mission countries, pastoral care of teachers, professional associations, the economic question.

THE ORGANIZATION AND PLANNING OF THE CATHOLIC SCHOOL

70. Catholic education is inspired by the general principles enunciated by the Second Vatican Council concerning collaboration between the hierarchy and those who work in the apostolate. In consequence of the principle of participation and coresponsibility, the various groupings which constitute the educational community are, according to their several competencies, to be associated in decision-making concerning the Catholic school and in the application of decisions once taken. It is first and foremost at the stage of planning and of putting into operation an educational project that this principle of the Council is to be applied. The assigning of various responsibilities is governed by the principle of subsidiarity, and, with reference to this principle, ecclesiastical authority respects the competence of the professionals in teaching and education. Indeed, 'the right and duty of exercising the apostolate is common to all the faithful, clerical and lay, and laypeople have their own proper competence in the building up of the Church.'

71. This principle enunciated by the Second Vatican Council is particularly applicable to the apostolate of the Catholic school which so closely unites teaching and religious education to a well-defined professional activity. It is here, above all,

that the particular mission of the lay person is put into effect, a mission which has become 'all the more imperative in view of the fact that many areas of human life have become very largely autonomous. This is as it should be, but it sometimes involves a certain withdrawal from ethical and religious influences and thereby creates a serious danger to Christian life.' Moreover, lay involvement in Catholic schools is an invitation 'to co-operate more closely with the apostolate of the bishops', both in the field of religious instruction and in more general religious education which they endeavour to promote by assisting the pupils to a personal integration of culture and faith and of faith and living. The Catholic school in this sense, therefore, receives from the bishops in some manner the 'mandate' of an apostolic undertaking.

72. The essential element of such a mandate is 'union with those whom the Holy Spirit has assigned to rule God's Church' and this link is expressed especially in overall pastoral strategy. 'In the whole diocese or in given areas of it the co-ordination and close interconnection of all apostolic works should be fostered under the direction of the bishop. In this way all undertakings and organization, whether catechetical, missionary, charitable, social, family, educational, or any other programme serving a pastoral goal will be co-ordinated. Moreover, the unity of the diocese will thereby be made more evident.' This is something which is obviously indispensable for the Catholic school, inasmuch as it involves 'apostolic co-operation on the part of both branches of the clergy, as well as of the religious and the laity.'

ENSURING THE DISTINCTIVE CATHOLIC CHARACTER OF THE SCHOOL

73. This is the framework which guarantees the distinctive Catholic character of the school. While the bishop's authority is to watch over the orthodoxy of religious instruction and the observance of Christian morals in the Catholic schools, it is the task of the whole educative community to ensure that a distinctive Christian educational environment is maintained in practice. This responsibility applies chiefly to Christian parents who confide their children to the school. Having chosen it does not relieve them of a personal duty to give their children a Christian upbringing. They are bound to co-operate actively with the school—which means supporting the educational efforts of the school and utilizing the structures offered

for parental involvement, in order to make certain that the school remains faithful to Christian principles of education. An equally important role belongs to the teachers in safeguarding and developing the distinctive mission of the Catholic school, particularly with regard to the Christian atmosphere which should characterize its life and teaching. Where difficulties and conflicts arise about the authentic Christian character of the Catholic school, hierarchical authority can and must intervene.

INVOLVEMENT OF RELIGIOUS IN THE SCHOOL APOSTOLATE

74. Some problems arise from the fact that certain religious institutes, founded for the school apostolate, have subsequently abandoned school work because of social or political changes and have involved themselves in other activities. In some cases they have given up their schools as a result of their efforts to adapt their lives and mission to the recommendations of the Second Vatican Council and to the spirit of their original foundation.

75. It is necessary, however, to reassess certain arguments adopted against the teaching apostolate. Some would say they have chosen a 'more direct' apostolate, forgetting the excellence and the apostolic value of educational work in the school. Others would appeal to the greater importance of individual over community involvement, of personal over institutional work. The advantages, however, of a community apostolate in the educational field are self-evident. Sometimes the abandonment of Catholic schools is justified on the grounds of an apparent failure to gain perceptible results in pursuing certain objectives. If this were true, it would surely be an invitation to undertake a fundamental revision of the whole conduct of the school, reminding everyone who ventures into education of the need for humility and hope and the conviction that his work cannot be assessed by the same rationalistic criteria which apply to other professions.

76. It is the responsibility of competent local ecclesiastical authority to evaluate the advisability and necessity of any change to other forms of apostolic work whenever particular circumstances dictate the need for a reassessment of the school apostolate, keeping in mind the observations above on overall pastoral strategy.

THE CATHOLIC SCHOOL IN MISSION COUNTRIES

77. The importance of the Catholic school apostolate is much greater when it is a question of the foreign missions. Where the young Churches still rely on the presence of foreign missionaries, the effectiveness of the Catholic school will largely depend on its ability to adapt to local needs. It must ensure that it is a true expression of the local and national Catholic community and that it contributes to the community's willingness to co-operate. In countries where the Christian community is still at its beginning and incapable of assuming responsibility for its own schools, the bishops will have to undertake this responsibility themselves for the time being, but must endeavour little by little to fulfil the aims outlined above in connection with the organization of the Catholic schools.

PASTORAL CARE OF TEACHERS

78. The witness and conduct of teachers are of primary importance in imparting a distinctive character to Catholic schools. It is, therefore, indispensable to ensure their continuing formation through some form of suitable pastoral provision. This must aim to animate them as witnesses of Christ in the classroom and tackle the problems of their particular apostolate, especially regarding a Christian vision of the world and of education, problems also connected with the art of teaching in accordance with the principles of the Gospel. A huge field is thus opened up for national and international organizations which bring together Catholic teachers and educational institutions at all levels.

79. Professional organizations whose aim is to protect the interests of those who work in the educational field cannot themselves be divorced from the specific mission of the Catholic school. The rights of the people who are involved in the school must be safeguarded in strict justice. But, no matter what material interests may be at stake, or what social and moral conditions affect their professional development, the principle of the Second Vatican Council has a special application in this context: 'The faithful should learn how to distinguish carefully between those rights and duties which are theirs as members of the Church, and those which they have as members of society. Let them strive to harmonize the two, remembering that in every temporal affair they must be guided by a Christian conscience.' Moreover, 'even when preoccupied

with temporal cares, the laity can and must perform valuable work for the evangelization of the world.' Therefore, the special organizations set up to protect the rights of teachers, parents and pupils must not forget the special mission of the Catholic school to be of service in the Christian education of youth. 'The layman is at the same time a believer and a citizen and should be constantly led by Christian conscience alone.'

80. In the light of what has been said, these associations, while being concerned for the rights of their members, must also be alive to the responsibilities which are part and parcel of the specific apostolate of the Catholic school. Catholic teachers who freely accept posts in schools, which have a distinctive character, are obliged to respect that character and give their active support to it under the direction of those responsible.

ECONOMIC SITUATION OF CATHOLIC SCHOOLS

81. From the economic point of view the position of very many Catholic schools has improved and in some countries is perfectly acceptable. This is the case where governments have appreciated the advantages and the necessity of a plurality of school systems which offer alternatives to a single State system. While at first Catholic schools received various public grants, often as a concession, they later began to enter into agreements, conventions, contracts, etc. which guarantee both the preservation of the special status of the Catholic school and its ability to perform its function adequately. Catholic schools are thereby more or less closely associated with the national system and are assured of an economic and juridical status similar to State schools.

82. Such agreements have been reached through the good offices of the respective governments, which have recognized the public service provided by Catholic schools, and through the determination of the bishops and the Catholic community at the national level. These solutions are an encouragement to those responsible for Catholic schools in countries where the Catholic community must still shoulder a very heavy burden of cost to maintain an often highly important network of Catholic schools. These Catholics need to be assured, as they strive to regularize the frequent injustices in their school situation, that they are not only helping to provide every child with an education that respects his complete development, but they are also defending freedom of teaching and the right of parents to

choose an education for their children which conforms to their legitimate requirements.

VII

COURAGEOUS AND UNIFIED COMMITMENT

83. To commit oneself to working in accordance with the aims of a Catholic school is to make a great act of faith in the necessity and influence of this apostolate. Only one who has this conviction and accepts Christ's message, who has a love for and understands today's young people, who appreciates what people's real problems and difficulties are, will be led to contribute with courage and even audacity to the progress of this apostolate in building up a Catholic school, which puts its theory into practice, which renews itself according to its ideals and to present needs.

84. The validity of the educational results of a Catholic school, however, cannot be measured by immediate efficiency. In the field of Christian education, not only is the freedom-factor of teacher and pupil relationship with each other to be considered, but also the factor of grace. Freedom and grace come to fruition in the spiritual order which defies any merely temporal assessment. When grace infuses human liberty, it makes freedom of the spirit. It is when the Catholic school adds its weight, consciously and overtly, to the liberating power of grace, that it becomes the Christian leaven in the world.

85. In the certainty that the Spirit is at work in every person, the Catholic school offers itself to all, non-Christians included, with all its distinctive aims and means, acknowledging, preserving and promoting the spiritual and moral qualities, the social and cultural values, which characterize different civilizations.

86. Such an outlook overrides any question of the disproportion between resources available and the number of children reached directly by the Catholic school; nothing can stop it from continuing to render its service. The only condition it would make, as is its right, for its continued existence would be remaining faithful to the educational aims of the Catholic school. Loyalty to these aims is, moreover, the basic

motive which must inspire any needed reorganization of the Catholic school institution.

87. If all who are responsible for the Catholic school would never lose sight of their mission and the apostolic value of their teaching, the school would enjoy better conditions in which to function in the present and would faithfully hand on its mission to future generations. They themselves, moreover, would most surely be filled with a deep conviction, joy and spirit of sacrifice in the knowledge that they are offering innumerable young people the opportunity of growing in faith, of accepting and living its precious principles of truth, charity and hope.

88. The Sacred Congregation for Catholic Education, to foster the full realization of the aims of the Catholic school, extends once more its warmest and heartfelt encouragement to all who work in these schools. There can be no doubt whatever of the importance of the apostolate of teaching in the total saving mission of the Church.

89. The Church herself in particular looks with confidence and trust to religious institutes which have received a special charism of the Holy Spirit and have been most active in the education of the young. May they be faithful to the inspiration of their founders and give their wholehearted support to the apostolic work of education in Catholic schools and not allow themselves to be diverted from this by attractive invitations to undertake other, often seemingly more effective, apostolates.

90. A little more than ten years after the end of the Second Vatican Council the Sacred Congregation for Catholic Education repeats the final exhortation of the *Declaration on Christian Education* to the priests, religious and lay people who fulfil their mission in the Catholic school. It reads: 'They are urged to persevere generously in their chosen duty, continuing to instil in their pupils the spirit of Christ; let them endeavour to excel in the art of teaching and in the advancement of knowledge. Thus they will not only foster the internal renewal of the Church, but will safeguard and intensify her beneficial presence in the modern world, and above all, in the world of the intellect.'

CONCLUSION

91. This document in no way wishes to minimize the value of the witness and work of the many Catholics who teach in State schools throughout the world. In describing the task confided to the Catholic school it is intended to encourage every effort

to promote the cause of Catholic education, since in the pluralistic world in which we live, the Catholic school is in a unique position to offer, more than ever before, a most valuable and necessary service. With the principles of the Gospel as its abiding point of reference, it offers its collaboration to those who are building a new world—one which is freed from a hedonistic mentality and from the efficiency syndrome of modern consumer society.

92. We appeal to each episcopal conference to consider and to develop these principles which should inspire the Catholic school and to translate them into concrete programs which will meet the real needs of the educational systems operating in their countries.

93. Realizing that the problems are both delicate and highly complex, the Sacred Congregation for Catholic Education also addresses itself to the whole people of God. In the economy of salvation we poor humans must confront problems, suffer their consequences and work might and main to solve them. We are certain that in the last analysis success in any venture does not come from trust in our own solutions but from trust in Jesus who allowed himself to be called teacher. May he inspire, guide, support and bring to a safe conclusion all that is undertaken in his name.

*Translation put out by Vatican Press Office. French original in Documentation Catholique, Aug., 1977, 7-21.

116

LAY CATHOLICS IN SCHOOLS: WITNESSES TO FAITH*

S.C.C.E., *Les laics Catholiques*, 15 October, 1982

INTRODUCTION

1. Lay Catholic men and women who teach in primary and secondary schools have become increasingly and deservedly important in recent years,[1] both in schools in general and in Catholic schools. For it is on them especially, as on other lay people, whether believers or not, that a school's success in achieving its aims depends.[2] At the Second Vatican Council the Church, in the Declaration on Christian Education, acknowledged the role and responsibility which this implied for lay Catholics working in schools as teachers, principals, administrators or auxiliary staff. The Declaration encouraged further reflection on the matter. To say all this, however, is not to imply that one wishes to underestimate the achievements of other Christians or non-Christians in education.

2. The most basic reason for the newly-acquired importance of the Catholic laity, an importance which the Church sees as positive and enriching, is theological. In the course of the last century, especially, the true role of the laity within the People of God has become increasingly clear, finding expression in two documents in the Second Vatican Council which describe in depth the richness and the characteristics of the lay vocation: the Dogmatic Constitution on the Church and the Decree on the Apostolate of the Laity.

3. Social, economic and political developments of recent times have not been unconnected with this development. Increasing progress, closely linked with scientific and technological developments, has meant that more intensive preparation is needed in every profession. To this must be added a more general acceptance of every person's right to a full education, one meeting all the needs of the human person. These two human advances have required, and in part have achieved, an extensive development of school systems everywhere in the

world, together with an extraordinary increase in the number of people who are professionally trained in education, with a corresponding growth in the number of Catholic laity involved.

This process has coincided with a notable decrease in recent years in the number of priest and religious teachers. The decrease is due to a lack of vocations, to the urgency of other apostolic needs, and at times to the erroneous opinion that a school is no longer an appropriate place for the Church's pastoral activity.[3] Granted the praiseworthy work, highly esteemed by the Church, which religious families have traditionally done in education, the Church cannot but regret the decline in the numbers of religious personnel which has had such a profound effect on Catholic schools, especially in some countries. The Church believes that, for an integral education of children and young people, both religious and lay Catholics are needed in schools.

4. This Sacred Congregation sees a genuine "sign of the times" for schools in the facts and their causes described above; it is an invitation to pay special attention to the role of lay Catholics, as witnesses to the faith in what can only be described as a privileged environment for human formation. Without claiming to be exhaustive, but after serious and prolonged reflection on the importance of the theme, it desires to offer some reflections which will complete what has already been said in the document "The Catholic School", and which will be of help to all those interested in the problem, encouraging them to embark on a more extended consideration of it.

I.
THE IDENTITY OF THE LAY CATHOLIC IN A SCHOOL

5. One should begin by attempting to describe the identity of lay Catholics who work in schools. How they bear witness to the faith will depend on how they perceive their identity in the Church and in their work. The Congregation sincerely hopes that its contribution to this discussion will be of help both to the lay Catholics who teach in schools and who need to have a clear understanding of their vocation, and to the rest of the People of God who on their part need to understand those lay persons [teachers] who belong to the People of God and who perform a very important task for the Church.

The Laity in the Church

6. The lay Catholic who works in a school is, along with every Christian, a member of the People of God. As such, united to Christ through Baptism, he or she shares in the basic dignity that is common to all members. For, "they share a common dignity from their rebirth in Christ. They have the same filial grace and the same vocation to perfection. They possess in common one salvation, one hope, and one undivided charity".[4] Although it is true that, in the Church, "by the will of Christ, some are made teachers, dispensers of mysteries and shepherds on behalf of others, yet all share a true equality with regard to the dignity and to the activity common to all the faithful for the building up of the Body of Christ".[5]

Every Christian, and therefore also every lay person, has been made a sharer in "the priestly, prophetic, and kingly functions of Christ",[6] and their apostolate "is a participation in the saving mission of the Church itself...All are commissioned to that apostolate by the Lord Himself".[7]

7. This call to personal holiness and to apostolic mission is common to all believers; but there are many cases in which the life of a lay person takes on specific characteristics which transform this life into a specific and "admirable" vocation within the Church. The laity "seeks the kingdom of God by engaging in temporal affairs and by ordering them according to the plan of God".[8] They live in the midst of the world's activities and professions, and in the ordinary circumstances of family and social life; and there they are called by God to exercise their proper function so that being led by the spirit of the Gospel they can work for the sanctification of the world as a leaven from within. In this way they can make Christ known to others, especially by the testimony of a life marked by faith, hope, and charity.[9]

8. The renewal and the Christian animation of the temporal order is the special role of the laity and should encourage them to heal "the institutions and conditions of the world"[10] when it is seen that these can be inducements to sin. In this way, these realities are elevated to the greatest possible conformity to the Gospel; and "the world is permeated by the Spirit of Christ, and more effectively achieves its purpose in justice, charity, and peace".[11] "Therefore, by their competence in secular fields, and by their grace-elevated behaviour let them labour vigorously so that, by human labour, technical skill, and civic culture, created goods may be perfected for the benefit of every last person... and be more suitably distributed among them".[12]

9. The evangelization of the world takes place in such a variety and complexity of situations that frequently it is only the laity who can be effective witnesses to the Gospel in many instances and for many people. Therefore, "the laity are called in a special way to make the Church present and active in those places and circumstances where only through them can she become the salt of the earth".[13] In order to achieve this presence of the whole Church, and of the Saviour whom she proclaims, lay people must be ready to proclaim the message through their words, and witness to it by their deeds.

10. Lay people's experience and their involvement in all domains of human activity make them especially capable of discerning the signs of the times in which God's people live today.

Therefore, since it is properly part of their vocation, they should by their initiative and creativity, their competent, conscientious and ungrudging contribution help ensure that the People of God will be able to distinguish clearly between evangelical and counter-evangelical values.

Lay Catholics in Schools

11. The characteristics of the lay vocation in the Church apply also, obviously, to lay people who live that vocation in schools. If, however, the specific vocations of lay people carry them to different sectors of human endeavour, it follows that their common vocation will take on different characteristics from one sector to another.

If, then, we are to have a better understanding of the vocation of the lay Catholic in schools, we must first look more closely at the school.

The School

12. While it is true that parents are the first and principal educators of their children[14] and that their rights and duties in this regard are "original and primary with respect to the educational role of others",[15] it is also true that the school enjoys a fundamental value and importance among the means which assist and complement the exercise of the educational rights and duties of the family. In virtue of its mission, then, the school must give constant and careful attention to cultivating in students the intellectual, creative, and aesthetic faculties of the human person; to develop in them sound judgement and the correct application of will and affectivity; to promote in them a sense of values; to

encourage just attitudes and prudent behaviour; to introduce them to the cultural patrimony handed down from previous generations; to prepare them for professional life, and to encourage the friendly interchange among students who differ in character and social background that will lead to mutual understanding.[16] For all of these reasons, the school enters into the specific mission of the Church.

13. The school has an irreplaceable function in our society, for it is society's most important institutional response to date to the right of each individual to an education and, therefore, to full personal development; it is one of the decisive elements in the structuring and the life of society itself. The school is becoming increasingly indispensable in view of the growing importance of the social environment and of the mass media, which wield a countervailing and sometimes harmful influence, in view too of the continuing expansion of the cultural milieu, and of the increasing complexity, variety and specialisation of the preparation for professional life. The family is less and less capable of facing these serious problems on its own.

14. Granted the importance of the role of the school in education, it follows that the pupils have the right to choose the system of education—and therefore the type of school—that they prefer.[17] If the pupils are not yet capable of choosing, it is for the parents to choose, for their rights are primary in this matter.[18] From this it clearly follows that, in principle, a State monopoly of education is not acceptable,[19] and that only a pluralism of school systems will respect the fundamental right and the freedom of individuals—although the exercise of this right may be subject to many factors, varying from one country to another. The Church offers the Catholic school as a specific and enriching contribution to this variety of school systems. The lay Catholic, however, can exercise an evangelizing role in any, not just a Catholic, school to the extent that this is possible in today's diverse socio-political contexts.

The Lay Catholic as an Educator

15. The Second Vatican Council gives attention to the vocation of an educator, a vocation which belongs both to the laity[20] and to those who follow other states of life in the Church.

If all who contribute to integral human formation are educators, teachers, who have made it their very profession, deserve special consideration when schools are under discussion, because of their number, but also because of the institutional purpose of schools. But all who are involved in this formation are also to be included in the discussion: especially those who are responsible for the direction of schools, or are counsellors, tutors or coordinators; also those who complement and complete the educational activities of the teacher or help in administrative and auxiliary positions. While this analysis of lay Catholics as educators will concentrate on their teaching role, it can throw light on the other roles and can provide matter for deep personal reflection.

16. The teacher under discussion here is not simply a professional person whose contribution is limited to the systematic transmission of knowledge in a school; "teacher" is to be understood as "educator"—one who helps to form human persons. The task of a teacher goes well beyond mere teaching, though it includes it. Therefore, like teaching, but more so than teaching, *educating* requires adequate professional preparation to fulfil its task. It is an indispensable human formation and without it it would be foolish to undertake any educational work.

One specific characteristic of the educational profession assumes its most profound significance in the Catholic educator: the communication of truth. For the Catholic educator, every truth is a participation in Him who is the Truth; the communication of truth, therefore, as a professional activity, is thus fundamentally transformed into a particular participation in the prophetic mission of Christ, carried on through teaching.

17. The integral formation of the human person, which is the purpose of education, includes the development of all the human faculties of the students, their preparation for professional life, the formation of ethical and social sense in them, imparting an awareness of the transcendental, and giving them a religious education. Every school, and every educator in the school, ought to be endeavouring "to form strong and responsible individuals, who are capable of making free and correct choices", thus preparing young people "to open themselves more and more to reality, and to form in themselves a clear idea of the meaning of life".[21]

18. All education is influenced by a particular concept of what it means to be a human person. In today's pluralistic world, the Catholic educator is called consciously to inspire his or her activity with the Christian concept of the person, in communion with the Magisterium of the Church. It is a concept which includes a defence of human rights, but as something befitting the dignity of a child of God; it attributes the fullest liberty, freed from sin itself by Christ, the most exalted destiny,

which is the definitive and total possession of God Himself, through love. It establishes the strictest possible relationship of solidarity among all persons, through mutual love and in an ecclesial community. It calls for the fullest development of all that is human, because we have been made masters of the world by its Creator. Finally, it proposes Christ, Incarnate Son of God and perfect Man, as both model and means; to imitate Him is, for all men and women, the inexhaustible source of personal and communal perfection. Thus, Catholic educators can be certain that they make human beings more human.[22] Moreover, the special task of those educators who are lay persons is to offer to their students a concrete example of the fact that people deeply immersed in the world, living fully the same secular life as the vast majority of the human family, possess this same exalted dignity.

19. The vocation of every Catholic educator includes the work of ongoing social development: to form men and women who will be ready to take their place in society, preparing them for the social commitment to work for the improvement of social structures, bringing them more into conformity with the Gospel. Thus, they will form human beings who will make human society more peaceful, fraternal, and communitarian. Today's world has terrible problems: hunger, illiteracy and human exploitation; sharp contrasts in the standard of living of individuals and of countries; aggression and violence, a growing drug problem, legalization of abortion, along with many other examples of the degradation of human life. All of this demands that Catholic educators develop in themselves, and cultivate in their students, a keen social awareness and a profound civic and political responsibility. The Catholic educator, in other words, must be committed to the task of forming men and women who will make the "civilization of love"[23] a reality.

But lay educators must enrich, out of their own experience and life-style, this social development and social awareness, so that students can be prepared to take their place in society with an appreciation of the specific role of the lay person—for this is the life that nearly all of the students will be called to live.

20. A school uses its own specific means for the integral formation of the human person: the communication of culture. It is extremely important, then, that the Catholic educator reflect on the profound relationship that exists between culture and the Church. For the Church influences culture and is, in turn, conditioned by culture. It also embraces everything in human culture which is compatible with Revelation and which it needs

in order to proclaim the message of Christ and to express it more adequately according to the cultural characteristics of each people and each age. The close relationship between culture and the life of the Church is an especially clear manifestation of the unity that exists between creation and redemption.

For this reason, if the communication of culture is to be termed educative, it must not only be organic, but also critical and evaluative, historical and dynamic. Faith will provide Catholic educators with essential principles of critique and evaluation; it will help them to see all of human history as a history of salvation which culminates in the fulness of the Kingdom. This puts culture into a creative context, open to perfection and to the future.

In the communication of culture lay educators, as authors of and sharers in its more secular aspects, have the task of helping students to understand, from a lay point of view the global character of culture, the synthesis to be achieved between its religious and non-religious aspects and the personal contribution which the students can be expected to make.

21. The communication of culture as an educative process in school involves a methodology, whose principles and techniques form together a consistent pedagogy. A variety of pedagogical theories exist; the choice of the Catholic educator, based on a Christian concept of the human person, should be the practice of a pedagogy which gives special emphasis to direct and personal contact with the students. If the teacher undertakes this contact with the conviction that students have a fundamental active role in their own education, this will lead to a dialogue which will pave the way for a witness of faith offered by the teacher's personal life.

22. All of the Catholic educator's work in school takes place within the framework of the educational community, composed of various categories of people—students, parents, teachers, directors, non-teaching staff—who work together and make of the school an institution of integral education. Although it is not exhaustive, this concept of the scholarly institution as an educational community, together with a more widespread awareness of this concept, is one of the most enriching developments for the contemporary school. The Catholic educator exercises his or her profession as a member of one of the constitutive elements of this community. The professional structure itself offers an excellent opportunity to live—and bring to life in the students—the communitarian dimension of the human person. Every human being is called to live in a community, as a social being,

and as a member of the People of God.

Therefore, the educational community is itself a school which teaches how to be a member of the wider social communities; and when the educational community is also a Christian community—which a Catholic school is called to be—then it offers a great opportunity for the teachers to provide the students with a living example of what it means to be a member of that great community which is the Church.

23. The communitarian structure of the school brings the Catholic educator into contact with a wide and rich assortment of people; not only the students, who are the reason why the school and the teaching profession exist, but also with colleagues in education, with parents, with other personnel in the school, with the school governing body. The Catholic educator must be a source of spiritual inspiration for each of these groups, as well as for each of the scholastic and cultural organizations that the school comes in contact with, for the local and parish Church, for the entire human ambience in which he or she is inserted and should influence in various ways. In this way, the Catholic educator is called to display that kind of spiritual animation which can range from what is called preevangelization to evangelization as such.

24. To summarize: The Lay Catholic educator is a person who exercises a specific mission within the Church by living, in faith, a secular vocation in the communitarian structure of the school; with the best possible professional qualifications, with an apostolic intention inspired by faith, for the integral formation of the human person, in a communication of culture, in an exercise of that pedagogy which will give emphasis to direct and personal contact with students, giving spiritual inspiration to the educational community of which he or she is a member, as well as to all the different persons related to the educational community. To this lay person, as a member of this community, the family and the Church entrust the school's educational endeavour. Lay teachers must be profoundly convinced that they share in the sanctifying, and therefore educational mission of the Church; they cannot regard themselves as cut off from the ecclesial complex.

II.
HOW TO LIVE ONE'S PERSONAL IDENTITY

25. The human person is called to be a worker; work is one of the characteristics which distinguish human beings from the rest

of creatures.[24] From this it is evident that it is not enough to possess a vocational identity, an identity which involves the whole person, if it is not lived. More concretely, if, through their work, human beings must contribute "above all to elevating unceasingly the cultural and moral level of society",[25] then the educator who does not educate can no longer truly be called an educator. Nor can educators lay claim to be such if there is no trace of their Catholic identity in their teaching. Some of the aspects of this living out of one's identity are common and essential; they must be present no matter what the school is in which the lay educator exercises his or her vocation. Others will differ according to the nature of the school.

Common Elements of an Identity

Realism Combined with Hope

26. The identity of the lay Catholic educator is, of necessity, an ideal; innumerable obstacles stand in the way of its accomplishment. Some are due to personal circumstances; others are due to deficiencies in schools and in society; all of them have their strongest effect on children and young people. Identity crisis, loss of trust in social structures, the resulting insecurity and loss of any personal convictions, the contagion of a progressive secularization of society, loss of the proper concept of authority and lack of a proper use of freedom—these are only a few of the multitude of difficulties which, varying in degree with different cultures and countries, the adolescents and young people of today bring to the Catholic educator. Moreover, the teacher, as a lay person, can face serious family and labour problems.

These difficulties should be faced realistically. But they should, at the same time, be viewed and confronted with a healthy optimism, and with the courage that Christian hope and a sharing in the mystery of the Cross demand of all believers. Therefore, the first indispensable necessity in one who is going to be a lay Catholic educator is sincerely to share in, and make one's own, the statements that the Church, enlightened by Divine Revelation, has made about the identity of an educator. The strength needed to do this should be found through a personal identification with Christ.

Professionalism. A Christian Concept of Humanity and of Life

27. If professionalism is one of the most important charac-

teristics in the identity of every lay Catholic, the first requirement for a lay educator who wishes to follow his or her ecclesial
vocation is the acquisition of a solid professional formation. In
the case of an educator, this includes competency in a wide range
of cultural, psychological, and pedagogical areas.[26] However, it
is not enough to attain a good level initially, it must be maintained and deepened, always bringing it up to date. This can be
very difficult for a lay teacher, and to ignore this fact is to ignore
reality: salaries are often inadequate, and supplementary employment is often a necessity. Such a situation is incompatible
with professional development, either because of the time required for other work, or because of the fatigue that results. In
many countries, especially in those less developed, the problem
is insoluble at the present time.

Even so, educators must realize that poor teaching, resulting
from insufficient preparation of classes or outdated pedagogical
methods, is going to hinder them severely as they attempt to contribute to an integral formation of the students; it will also
obscure the life witness that they must present.

28. The entire thrust of Catholic teaching is aimed at the integral formation of each student. New horizons will be opened
to students through the responses that Christian revelation brings
to questions about the ultimate meaning of the human person,
of human life, of history, and of the world. These must be offered to the students as responses which flow out of the profound faith of the educator, but at the same time with the most
sensitive respect for the conscience of each student. Students
will surely have many different levels of faith response; the
Christian vision of existence must be presented in such a way
that it meets all of these levels, ranging from the most elementary
evangelization all the way to communion in the same faith. And
whatever the situation, the presentation must always be in the
nature of a gift: however warmly and insistently offered, it cannot be imposed.

On the other hand, the gift cannot be offered with indifference. It must be seen as a vital reality, one which deserves the
commitment of the entire person, something which is to become
a part of one's own life.

Synthesis of Faith, Culture and Life

29. For the accomplishment of this vast undertaking, many
different educational elements must converge; in each of them,
the lay Catholic must appear as a witness to faith. An organic,

critical, and value-oriented communication of culture[27] clearly includes the communication of truth and knowledge; while doing this, a Catholic teacher should always be alert for opportunities to initiate the appropriate dialogue between culture and faith—two things which are intimately related—in order to bring the interior synthesis of the student to this deeper level. It is, of course, a synthesis which should already exist in the teacher.

30. Critical transmission also involves the presentation of a set of values and counter-values. These must be judged within the context of an appropriate concept of life and of the human person. The Catholic teacher, therefore, cannot be content simply to present Christian values as a set of abstract objectives to be admired, even if this be done positively and with imagination; they must be presented as values which generate human attitudes, and these attitudes must be encouraged in the students. Examples of such attitudes would be these: a freedom which includes respect for others; conscientious responsibility; a sincere and constant search for truth; a calm and peaceful critical spirit; a spirit of solidarity with and service toward all other persons; a sensitivity for justice; a special awareness of being called to be positive agents of change in a society that is undergoing continuous transformation.

Since Catholic teachers frequently have to exercise their mission within a general atmosphere of secularization and unbelief, it is important that they go beyond a mentality that is merely experimental and critical and are able to bring the students to an awareness of the transcendental, disposing them to welcome revealed truth.

31. In the process of developing attitudes such as these, the teacher can more easily show the positive nature of the behaviour that flows from them. It should be his highest aspiration to ensure that such attitudes and behaviour will gradually be motivated by, and flow out of, the interior faith of the individual student, thus achieving their greatest richness and extending to such things as filial prayer, sacramental life, love for one another, and the following of Jesus Christ—all of the elements that form a part of the specific heritage of the faithful. Knowledge, values, attitudes, and behaviour fully integrated with faith will result in the student's personal synthesis of life and faith. Very few Catholics, then, have the opportunity that the educator has to accomplish the very purpose of evangelization: the incarnation of the Christian message in the lives of men and women.

Personal Life Witness.
Direct and Personal Contact With Students

32. Conduct is always much more important than speech for students in their period of formation. The more completely an educator conforms to the ideal that is being presented to the students, the more this ideal will be believed and imitated. For it will then be seen as something reasonable and worthy of being lived, something concrete and realizable. It is in this context that the faith witness of the lay teacher becomes especially important. Students should see in their teachers the Christian attitude and behaviour that is often so conspicuously absent from the secular atmosphere in which they live. Without this witness, living in such an atmosphere, they may begin to regard Christian behaviour as an impossible ideal. It must never be forgotten that, in the crises "which have their greatest effect on the younger generations", the most important element in the educational endeavour is "always the individual person: the person, and the moral dignity of that person which is the result of his or her principles, and the conformity of actions with those principles".[28]

33. In this context, what was said above about direct and personal contact between teachers and students[29] becomes especially significant: it is a privileged opportunity for giving witness. A personal relationship is always a dialogue rather than a monologue, and the teacher must be convinced that the enrichment in the relationship is mutual. But the mission must never be lost sight of: the educator can never forget that students need a companion and guide during their period of growth; they need help from others in order to overcome doubts and disorientation. Also, rapport with the students ought to be a prudent combination of familiarity and distance; and this must be adapted to the need of each individual student. Familiarity will make a personal relationship easier, but a certain distance is also needed: students need to learn how to express their own personality gradually; they need to be freed from inhibitions in the responsible exercise of their freedom.

It is good to remember here that a responsible use of freedom also involves the choice of one's own state of life. In contacts with students who are believers, Catholic teachers should not hesitate to discuss their personal vocation in the Church. This involves as much discerning and encouraging vocations to the priesthood or religious life, to a personal commitment in a secular institute or Catholic apostolic organization, areas often neglected, as it does helping students discover a vocation to marriage or to consecrated celibacy within the lay state.

This direct and personal contact is not just a method of helping in the formation of the students; it is also the means by which teachers learn what they need to know about the students in order to guide them adequately. The difference in generation is deeper, and the time between generations is shorter, today more than ever before; direct contact, then, is more necessary than ever.

Communitarian Aspects

34. Along with a proper development of their individual personalities, and as an integral part of this process, students should be guided by their Catholic teachers toward the development of a sense of community: toward others in the educational community, in the other communities that they may belong to, and with the entire human community. Lay Catholic educators are also members of the educational community; they influence, and are influenced by, the social ambience of the school. Therefore, close relationship should be established between colleagues; they should work together as a team. And teachers should establish close relationships with the other groups that make up the educational community, and be willing to contribute their share to all of the diverse activities that make up the common educational endeavour of a scholastic institution.

Since the family is "the first and fundamental school of social living",[30] there is a special duty to welcome and even to encourage opportunities for contact with the parents of students. These contacts are very necessary, because the educational task of the family and that of the school complement one another in many concrete areas; and they will facilitate the "serious duty" that parents have "to commit themselves totally to a cordial and active relationship with the teachers and the school authorities".[31] Finally, such contacts will offer to many families the assistance they need in order to educate their own children properly, and thus fulfill the "irreplaceable and inalienable"[32] function that is theirs.

35. A teacher must also be constantly attentive to the sociocultural, economic, and political environment of the school: the immediate locality, the wider region and the nation. Given today's means of communication, the national scene exerts a great influence on the local situation. Only close attention to the global reality—local, national, and international—will provide the data needed to give the kind of formation that students need

now, and to prepare them for the likely future.

36. While it is only natural to expect lay Catholic educators to give preference to Catholic professional associations, it is not foreign to their educational role to participate in and collaborate with all educational groups and associations, along with other groups that are connected with education. They should also lend support to the struggle for an adequate national educational policy, in whatever ways such support is possible. Their involvement may also include Trade Union activity, though they should be always mindful of human rights and Christian educational principles.[33] Lay teachers should be reminded that professional life can sometimes be very remote from the activities of associations; they should realize that if they are never involved in or even aware of these activities, this absence could be seriously harmful to important educational issues.

It is true that there is often no reward for such activities; success or failure depends on the generosity of those who participate. But when there are issues at stake so vital that the Catholic teacher cannot ignore them, then generosity is called for.

A Vocation, Rather than a Profession

37. The work of a lay educator has an undeniably professional aspect; but it is not to be limited to it. Professionalism is marked by, and raised to, a supernatural Christian vocation. The life of the Catholic teacher must be marked by the exercise of a personal vocation in the Church, and not simply by the exercise of a profession. In a lay vocation, detachment and generosity are joined to legitimate defence of personal rights; but it is still a vocation, with the fulness of life and the personal commitment that the word implies. It offers ample opportunity for a life filled with enthusiasm.

It is, therefore, very desirable that every lay Catholic educator become fully aware of the importance, the richness, and the responsibility of this vocation. They should fully respond to all of its demands, secure in the knowledge that their response is vital for the construction and ongoing renewal of the earthly city, and for the evangelization of the world.

Elements of the Catholic Educational Vocation Which Are Specific to Different Types of Schools

In the Catholic School

38. What distinguishes the Catholic school is that it attempts

"to create for the school community an atmosphere enlivened by the gospel spirit of freedom and charity. It aims to help the adolescent in such a way that the development of his or her own personality will be matched by the growth of that new creation which he or she becomes by baptism. It strives to relate all human culture eventually to the news of salvation, so that the light of faith will illumine the knowledge which students gradually gain of the world, of life and of the human race".[34] From all this, it is obvious that the Catholic school "fully enters into the salvific mission of the Church, especially in the need for education in the faith",[35] and involves a sincere adherence to the Magisterium of the Church, a presentation of Christ as the supreme model of the human person, and a special care for the quality of religious education in the school.

The lay Catholic who works in a Catholic school should be aware of the ideals and specific objectives which constitute the general educational philosophy of the institution, and realize that it is because of this educational philosophy that it is in a Catholic school that the vocation of the lay Catholic teacher can be lived most freely and most completely. It is the model for the apostolic activity of lay Catholics in all other schools, according to the possibilities that each one of them offers. This realization will inspire lay Catholics in Catholic schools to commit themselves sincerely and personally to share in the responsibility for the attainment of these ideals and objectives. This is not to deny that difficulties exist; among them we mention, because of the great consequences that it has, the great heterogeneity of both students and teachers within the Catholic schools of many countries today.

39. Certain elements will be characteristic of all Catholic schools. But these can be expressed in a variety of ways; often enough, the concrete expression will correspond to the specific charism of the religious institute that founded the school and continues to direct it. Whatever be its origin—diocesan, religious, or lay—each Catholic school can preserve its own specific character, spelled out in an educational philosophy, rationale, or in its own pedagogy. Lay Catholics should try to understand the special characteristics of the school they are working in, and the reasons that have inspired them. They should try to so identify themselves with these characteristics that their own work will help toward realizing the specific nature of the school.

40. As a visible manifestation of the faith they profess and the life witness they are expected to give,[36] it is important that lay Catholics who work in a Catholic school participate in the liturgical and sacramental life of the school. Students will share

in this life more readily when they are given good example, when they see the importance that this life has for believers. In today's secularized world, students will see many lay people who call themselves Catholics, but who never take part in worship. It is very important that they also have the example of lay adults who take such things seriously, who find in them a source and nourishment for Christian living.

41. The educational community of a Catholic school should endeavour to become a Christian community: a genuine community of faith. This will not take place, it will not even begin to happen, unless there is a sharing of the Christian commitment among at least a portion of each of the principal groups that make up the educational community: parents, teachers, and students. It is highly desirable that every lay Catholic, especially the educator, be ready to participate actively in groups of pastoral inspiration, or in other groups capable of nourishing a life lived according to the Gospel.

42. At times there are students in Catholic schools who do not profess the Catholic faith, or perhaps are without any religious faith at all. Faith does not admit of violence; it is a free response of the human person to God as he reveals himself. Therefore, while Catholic educators will teach doctrine in conformity with their own religious convictions and in accord with the identity of the school, they must at the same time have the greatest respect for those students who are not Catholics. They should be open at all times to authentic dialogue, convinced that in these circumstances the best testimony that they can give of their own faith is a warm and sincere appreciation for anyone who is honestly seeking God according to his or her own conscience.[37]

43. Since education in the faith is a part of the purpose of a Catholic school, the more fully the educational community represents the richness of the ecclesial community, the more capable it will be of fulfilling this mission. When priests, men and women religious and lay people are all present together in a school, they will present students with a living image of this richness, which can lead to a better understanding of the reality of the Church. Lay Catholics should reflect on the importance of their presence, from this point of view, alongside the priests and religious. For each of these types of ecclesial vocation presents to the students its own distinct incarnational model: lay Catholics, the intimate dependence of earthly realities on God in Christ, the lay professional as one who disposes the world toward God; the priest, the multiple sources of grace offered by Christ to all believers through the sacraments, the revealing light

of the Word, and the character of service which clothes the hierarchical structure of the Church; religious, the radical spirit of the Beatitudes, the continuous call of the Kingdom as the single definitive reality, the love of Christ, and the love of all men and women in Christ.

44. If each vocation has its own distinct characteristics, then all should be aware of the fact that a mutual and complementary presence will be a great help in ensuring the character of the Catholic school. This means that each one should be dedicated to the search for unity and coordination. Furthermore, the attitude of the lay people should be one which will help to insert the Catholic school into pastoral activities, in union with the local Church—a perspective which must never be forgotten—in ways that are complementary to the activities of parish ministry. The initiatives and experiences of lay people should also help to bring about more effective relationships and closer collaboration among Catholic schools, as well as between Catholic schools and other schools—especially those which share a Christian orientation—and with society as a whole.

45. Lay Catholic educators must be very aware of the real impoverishment which will result if priests and religious disappear from the Catholic schools, or noticeably decline in number. This is to be avoided as far as is possible; and yet, the laity must prepare themselves in such a way that they will be able to maintain Catholic schools on their own whenever this becomes necessary or at least more desirable, in the present or in the future. Historical forces at work in the schools of today lead to the conclusion that, at least for the immediate future, the continued existence of Catholic schools in many traditionally Catholic countries is going to depend largely on the laity, just as it has depended and does depend, to good effect, on lay people in so many of the young Churches. This responsibility cannot be assumed with passive attitudes of fear and regret; it is a responsibility that offers a challenge to firm and effective action. And this action means even now looking to and planning for the future with the help of the religious institutes who see their possibilities diminishing in the days immediately ahead.

46. There are times in which the Bishops will take advantage of the availability of competent lay persons who wish to give clear Christian witness in the field of education, and will entrust them with complete direction of Catholic schools, thus incorporating them more closely into the apostolic mission of the Church.[38]

Given the ever greater expansion of the field of education, the

Church needs to take advantage of every available resource for the Christian education of youth. To increase the participation of lay Catholic educators is not meant to diminish the importance of those schools directed by religious congregations in any way. The unique kind of witness that men and women Religious give in their own teaching centres, whether as individuals or as a community, surely implies that these schools are more necessary than ever in a secularized world.

Few situations offer more scope to members of a religious community for this kind of witness than do their own schools. For in the schools, religious men and women establish an immediate and lasting contact with young people, in a context in which the truths of faith frequently come up spontaneously as a means to illuminate the varied dimensions of existence. This contact has a special importance at a time of life in which ideas and experiences leave such a lasting impression on the personality of the students.

However, the call of the Church to lay Catholic educators to commit themselves to an active apostolate in education is not a call limited to the Church's own schools. It is a call that extends to the entire vast teaching field, to the extent in which it may be possible to give Christian witness in teaching.

In Schools That Have Different Educational Philosophies

47. We now consider all those schools, public or private, whose educational philosophy is different from that of the Catholic school, but is not essentially incompatible with the Christian concept of the human person and of life. Schools of this type form the vast majority of the schools that exist in the world. Their educational philosophy may be developed by means of a well-defined concept of the human person and of life; more simply and narrowly, they may have a determined ideology;[39] or the school may admit the coexistence of a variety of philosophies and ideologies among the teachers, within the framework of some general principles. "Coexistence" should be understood here as a manifestation of pluralism: in such schools, each of the educators takes classes, explains principles, and promotes values according to his or her own concept of the human person, and specific ideology. We do not speak here about what is termed the neutral school because, in practice, such a school does not exist.

48. In today's pluralistic and secularized world, it will frequently happen that the presence of lay Catholics in these

schools is the only way in which the Church is present. This is a concrete example of what was said above: that the Church can only reach out to certain situations or institutions through the laity.[40] A clear awareness of this fact will be a great help to encourage lay Catholics to assume the responsibility that is theirs.

49. Lay Catholic teachers should be influenced by a Christian faith vision in the way they teach their course, to the extent that this is consistent with the subject matter, and the circumstances of the student body and the school. In doing this, they will help students to discover true human values; and even though they must work within the limitations proper to a school that makes no attempt to educate in the faith, in which many factors will actually work directly against faith education, they will still be able to contribute to the beginnings of a dialogue between faith and culture. It is a dialogue which may, one day, lead to the students' genuine synthesis of the two. This effort can be especially fruitful for those students who are Catholics; it can be a form of evangelization for those who are not.

50. In a pluralistic school, living according to one's faith must be joined to careful respect for the ideological convictions and the work of the other educators, assuming always that they do not violate the human rights of the students. Mutual respect should lead to constructive dialogue, especially with other Christians, but also with all men and women of good will. In this way it can become clearly evident that religious and human freedom, the logical fruit of a pluralistic society, is not only defended in theory by Christian faith, but also put into practice.

51. Active participation in the activities of colleagues, contacts with other members of the educational community, and especially contacts with parents of the students, are extremely important. In this way the objectives, programmes, and teaching methods of the school in which the lay Catholic is working can be gradually impregnated with the spirit of the Gospel.

52. A lay Catholic in a pluralist school will be seen by colleagues and students to be an image[40a] of an evangelical person if her or she brings to the task professional commitment, concern for truth, justice and freedom, breadth of vision, an habitual spirit of service, personal commitment to the students, fraternal solidarity with all and total moral integrity.

In Other Schools

53. Here we consider more specifically the situation in

schools of what are called mission countries, or countries where the practice of Christianity has almost totally disappeared. The lay Catholic's may be the only presence of the Church, not only in the school, but also in the place in which he or she is living. The call of faith makes this situation especially compelling: the lay Catholic teacher may be the only voice that proclaims the message of the Gospel to students, to other members of the educational community, to everyone that he or she comes in contact with, as an educator or simply as a person.[41] Everything that has been said above about awareness of responsibility, a Christian perspective in teaching (and in education more generally), respect for the convictions of others, constructive dialogue with other Christians as well as with those who do not believe in Christianity, active participation in various school groups, and, most important of all, personal life witness—all of these things become crucially important in this type of school.

54. Finally, we cannot forget those lay Catholics who work in schools in countries where the Church is persecuted, where one who is known to be a Christian is forbidden to function as an educator. The orientation of the schools is atheist; laity who work in them must conceal the fact that they are believers. In this difficult situation simple presence, if it is the silent but vital presence of a person inspired by the Gospel, is already an effective proclamation of the message of Christ. It is a counterbalance to the pernicious intentions of those who promote an atheistic education in these schools. And this witness, when joined to personal contact with the students, can, in spite of the difficulties, lead to opportunities for more explicit evangelization. Although forced to live his or her Catholicism anonymously, the lay educator can still offer (because of regrettable human and religious motives) the only way that many of the young people in these countries can come to some genuine knowledge of the Gospel and of the Church, which are distorted and attacked in the school.

55. In every kind of school, Catholic educators will not infrequently come in contact with non-Catholic students, especially in some countries. Their attitude should not only be one of respect, but also welcoming, and open to dialogue—motivated by a universal Christian love. Furthermore, they should always remember that true education is not limited to the imparting of knowledge; it promotes human dignity and genuine human relationships, and prepares the way for opening oneself to the Truth that is Christ.

The Lay Catholic Educator as a Teacher of Religion

56. Religious instruction is appropriate in every school, for the purpose of the school is human formation in all of its fundamental dimensions, and the religious dimension is an integral part of this formation. Religious education is actually a right—with the corresponding duties—of the student and of the parents. It is also, at least in the case of the Catholic religion, an extremely important instrument for attaining the adequate synthesis of faith and culture that has been insisted on so often.

Therefore, the teaching of the Catholic religion, distinct from and at the same time complementary to catechesis properly so called,[42] ought to form a part of the curriculum of every school.

57. The teaching of religion is, along with catechesis, "an eminent form of the lay apostolate".[43] Because of this, and because of the number of religion teachers needed for today's vast school systems, lay people will have the responsibility for religious education in the majority of cases, especially at the level of basic education.

58. Lay Catholics, therefore, in different places and according to different circumstances, should become aware of the great role that is offered to them in this field of religious education. Without their generous collaboration, the number of religion teachers will not be adequate to meet the need that exists; this is already the situation in some countries. In this respect, as in so many others, the Church depends on lay collaboration. The need can be especially urgent in young Churches.

59. The role of the religion teacher is of first importance; for "what is asked for is not that one impart one's own doctrine, or that of some other teacher, but the teaching of Jesus Christ Himself".[44] In their teaching, therefore, taking into account the nature of the group being taught, teachers of religion (and also catechists) "should take advantage of every opportunity to profit from the fruits of theological research, which can shed light on their own reflections and also on their teaching, always taking care...to be faithful to the genuine sources, and to the light of the Magisterium", on which they depend for the proper fulfillment of their role; and "they should refrain from upsetting the minds of children and young people...with outlandish theories".[45] The norms of the local bishop should be faithfully followed in everything that has to do with their own theological and pedagogical formation, and also in the course syllabi; and they should remember that, in this area above all, life witness and

an intensely lived spirituality have an especially great importance.

III.
THE FORMATION THAT IS NEEDED FOR LAY CATHOLICS TO WITNESS TO THE FAITH IN A SCHOOL

60. To live a vocation as rich and profound as that of the lay Catholic in a school requires an appropriate formation, both on the professional plane and on the religious plane. In particular, the educator should have a mature spiritual personality, expressed in a profound Christian life. "This calling," says the Second Vatican Council, speaking about educators, requires "the most careful preparation".[46] "(Teachers) should therefore be trained with particular care, so that they may be enriched with both secular and religious knowledge, appropriately certified, and may be equipped with an educational skill which reflects modern day findings".[47] The need for an adequate formation is often felt most acutely in religious and spiritual areas; all too frequently, lay Catholics have not had a religious formation that is equal to their general, cultural, and, most especially, professional formation.

Awareness and Stimulation

61. Generally speaking, lay Catholics preparing themselves for work in a school have a genuine human vocation; they are very aware of the good professional formation that they need in order to become educators. But an awareness that is limited only to the professional level is not what ought to characterize a lay Catholic attempting to make his educational work the fundamental means of his personal sanctification and of his apostolate. What is being asked of lay Catholics who work in schools is an awareness that this is precisely how they are to live their vocation. To what extent they actually do have such an awareness is something that these lay people should be asking themselves.

62. The need for religious formation is related to this specific awareness that is being asked of lay Catholics; religious formation must be broadened and be kept up to date, on the same level as, and in harmony with, human formation as a whole. Lay Catholics need to be keenly aware of the need for this kind of religious formation; it is not only the exercise of an apostolate that depends on it, but even an appropriate professional compe-

tence, especially when the competence is in the field of education.

63. The purpose of these reflections is to help awaken such a consciousness, and to help each individual to consider his or her own personal situation in an area which is so fundamental for the full exercise of the lay vocation of a Catholic educator. What is at stake is so essential that simply to become aware of it should be a major stimulus toward putting forth the effort needed to acquire whatever may have been lacking in formation, and to maintain at an adequate level all that has been already acquired. Lay Catholic educators also have a right to expect that, within the ecclesial community, bishops, priests, and religious, especially those dedicated to the apostolate of education, and also various groups and associations of lay Catholic educators, will help to awaken them to their personal needs in the area of formation, and will find the means to stimulate them so that they can give themselves more totally to the social commitment that such a formation requires.

Professional and Religious Formation

64. It may be worth noting that centres of teacher formation will differ in their ability to provide the kind of professional training that will best help Catholic educators to fulfill their educational mission. The reason for this is the close relationship that exists between the way a discipline (especially in the humanities) is taught, and the teacher's basic concept of the human person, of life, and of the world. If the ideological orientation of a centre for teacher formation is pluralist, it can easily happen that the future Catholic educator will have to do supplementary work in order to make a personal synthesis of faith and culture in the different disciplines that are being studied. It must never be forgotten, during the days of formation, that the role of a teacher is to present subject matter to the students in a way that will first facilitate dialogue and subsequently a personal synthesis between faith and culture. If we take all of this into account, it follows that it would be better to attend a centre for teacher formation under the direction of the Church where one exists, and to create such centres, if possible, where they do not yet exist.

65. For the Catholic educator, religious formation does not come to an end with the completion of basic education; it must be a part of and a complement to one's professional formation, and so be proportionate to adult faith, human culture, and the specific lay vocation. This means that religious formation must

be directed toward both personal sanctification and apostolic mission, for these are two inseparable elements in a Christian vocation. "Formation for apostolic mission means a certain human and well-rounded formation, adapted to the natural abilities and circumstances of each person" and requires "in addition to spiritual formation, . . . solid doctrinal instruction . . . in theology, ethics and philosophy".[48] Nor can we forget, in the case of an educator, adequate formation in the social teachings of the Church, which are "an integral part of the Christian concept of life",[49] and help to keep intensely alive the kind of social sensitivity that is needed.[50]

With regard to the doctrinal plane, and speaking more specifically of teachers, it may be worth recalling that the Second Vatican Council speaks of the need for religious knowledge guaranteed by appropriate certification.[51] It is highly recommended, therefore, that all Catholics who work in schools, and most especially those who are educators, obtain the necessary qualifications by pursuing programmes of religious formation in Ecclesiastical Faculties or in Institutes of Religious Science that are suitable for this purpose, wherever this is possible.

66. With appropriate degrees, and with an adequate preparation in religious pedagogy, they will have the basic training needed for the teaching of religion. Bishops will promote and provide for the necessary training, both for teachers of religion and for catechists; at the same time, they will not neglect the kind of dialogue with the corps of teachers being formed that can be mutually enlightening.

Updating. Permanent Formation

67. The extraordinary advance of science and technology and the unrelenting critical analysis of every object, situation and value in our time have resulted in continuous and accelerating change affecting people and society under every aspect. Change makes knowledge and structures obsolete rapidly and creates a demand for new knowledge and methods.

68. Faced with this reality, which lay people are the first to experience, the Catholic educator has an obvious and constant need for updating: in personal attitudes, in the content of the subjects that are taught, in the pedagogical methods that are used. Let educators recall that their vocation requires "a constant readiness to begin anew and to adapt".[52] If the need for updating is constant, then the formation must be permanent. This

need is not limited to professional formation; it includes religious formation and, in general, the enrichment of the whole person. In this way, the Church will constantly adapt its pastoral mission to the circumstances of the men and women of each age, so that the message of Jesus Christ can be brought to them in a way that is intelligible and suited to their condition.

69. Permanent formation involves a wide variety of different elements; a constant search for ways to achieve it is therefore required of both individuals and the community. Among the variety of means for permanent formation, some have become ordinary and virtually indispensable instruments: reading periodicals and pertinent books, attending conferences and seminars, participating in workshops, assemblies and congresses, making appropriate use of periods of free time for formation. All lay Catholics who work in schools should make these a habitual part of their own human, professional, and religious life.

70. No one can deny that permanent formation, as the name itself suggests, is a difficult task; not everyone can achieve it. This becomes especially true in the face of the growing complexity of contemporary life and the difficult nature of the educational mission, combined with the economic insecurity that so often accompanies it. But in spite of all these factors, no lay Catholic who works in a school can ignore this present-day need. To do so would be to remain locked up in outdated knowledge, criteria, and attitudes. To reject a formation that is permanent and that involves the whole person—human, professional, and religious—is to isolate oneself from that very world that has to be brought closer to the Gospel.

IV
THE CHURCH'S SUPPORT
FOR LAY CATHOLICS IN SCHOOLS

71. The different circumstances in which lay Catholics have to work in schools can often create feelings of isolation or of being misunderstood, and as a result lead to depression, or even to abandonment of their responsibilities. In order to find help in overcoming such difficulties; in order, more generally, to be helped to fulfill the vocation to which they are called, lay Catholics who work in schools should always be able to count on the support and aid of the entire Church.

Support in the Faith, in the Word, and in Sacramental Life

72. Above all else, lay Catholics will find support in their own faith. Faith is the unfailing source of the humility, the hope, and the charity needed for perseverance in their vocation.[53] For all educators need humility in order to recognize their limitations, their mistakes, along with the need for constant growth, and the realization that the ideal being pursued is always beyond their grasp. Every educator needs a firm hope, because the teacher is never the one who truly reaps the fruits of the labour expended on the students. And, finally, every educator is in need of a permanent and growing charity, in order to love each of the students as an individual created in the image and likeness of God, raised to the status of a child of God by the redemption of Jesus Christ.

This humble faith, hope, and charity are supported by the Church through the Word, the life of the sacraments, and the prayer of the entire People of God. For the Word will speak to educators, and remind them of the immense grandeur of their identity and of their task; sacramental life will give them the strength they need to live this career, and will give support when they fail; the prayer of the whole Church will present to God, with them and for them, with the assured response that Jesus Christ has promised, all that the human heart desires and pleads for, and even the things that it does not dare to desire or plead for.

Community Support

73. The work of education is arduous, and very important; for that reason, its realization is delicate and complex. It requires calm, interior peace, a reasonable, not excessive workload, continuous cultural and religious enrichment. In today's society, it is seldom that these conditions can all be met simultaneously. The nature of the educational vocation of lay Catholics should be publicized more frequently and more profoundly among the People of God by those in the Church most capable of doing it. The theme of education, with all that is implied in this term, should be developed more insistently; for education is one of the great opportunities for the salvific mission of the Church.

74. From this knowledge will logically flow understanding and proper esteem. All of the faithful should be conscious of the

fact that, without lay Catholics as educators, the Church's education in the faith would lack one of its important basic elements. As far as they can, therefore, all believers should actively collaborate in the work of helping educators to reach the social status and the economic level that is their due, together with the stability and the security that they must have if they are to accomplish their task. No members of the Church can be considered exempt from the struggle to ensure that, in the countries in which they live, both the legislation on educational policy and the practical implementation of this legislation reflect, as far as possible, Christian educational principles.

75. Contemporary world conditions should be an inducement for hierarchies, along with those religious institutes that have a commitment to education, to support existing groups, movements, and Catholic Associations of lay believers engaged in education; and also to create other, new groups, always searching for the type of association that will best respond to the needs of the times and the differing situations in different countries. The vocation of the lay Catholic educator requires the fulfillment of many educational objectives, along with the social and religious objectives that flow from them. These will be virtually impossible to achieve without the united strength of strong associations.

The Support of the Educational Institutions Themselves. The Catholic School and the Laity

76. The importance of the Catholic school suggests that we reflect specifically on it; it can serve as a concrete example of how other Catholic institutions should support the lay people who work in them. In speaking about lay people, this Sacred Congregation has declared without hesitation that "by their witness and behaviour, teachers are of the first importance in imparting a distinctive character to Catholic schools".[54]

77. Before all else, lay people should find in a Catholic school an atmosphere of sincere respect and cordiality; it should be a place in which authentic human relationships can be formed among all of the educators. Priests, men and women religious, and lay persons, each preserving their specific vocational identity,[55] should be integrated fully into one educational community; and each one should be treated as a fully equal member of that community.

78. If the directors of the school and the lay people who work

in the school are to live according to the same ideals, two things are essential. First, lay people must receive an adequate salary, guaranteed by a well defined contract, for the work they do in the school: a salary that will permit them to live in dignity, without excessive work or a need for additional employment that will interfere with the duties of an educator. This may not be immediately possible without putting an enormous financial burden on the families, or making the school so expensive that it becomes a school for a small elite group; but so long as a truly adequate salary is not being paid, the laity should be able to expect and understand a veritable preoccupation on the part of the school authorities to find the resources necessary to achieve this end. Secondly, the laity should have a genuine share of responsibility for the school; this assumes that they have the ability that is needed in all areas, and are sincerely committed to the educational objectives of a Catholic school. And the school should use every means possible to encourage this kind of commitment; without it, the objectives of the school can never be fully realized. It must never be forgotten that the school itself is always in the process of being created, due to the labour brought to fruition by all those who have a role to play in it, and most especially by those who are teachers.⁵⁶ To achieve the kind of participation that is desirable, several conditions are indispensable: genuine esteem of the lay vocation, sharing the information that is necessary, deep confidence, and, finally, when it should become necessary, turning over the different responsibilities for teaching, administration, and government of the school, to the laity.

79. As a part of its mission, an element proper to the school is solicitous care for the permanent professional and religious formation of its lay members. Lay people should be able to look to the school for the orientation and the assistance that they need, including the willingness to make time available when this is needed. Formation is indispensable; without it, the school will wander further and further away from its objectives. Often enough, if it will join forces with other educational centres and with Catholic professional organizations, a Catholic school will not find it too difficult to organize conferences, seminars, and other meetings which will provide the required formation. According to circumstances, these could be expanded to include other lay Catholic educators who do not work in Catholic schools; these people would thus be offered an opportunity they are frequently in need of, and do not easily find elsewhere.

80. The ongoing improvement of the Catholic school, and the assistance which the school, joined to other educational in-

stitutions of the Church, can offer to lay Catholic educators, depend heavily on the support that Catholic families offer to the school—families in general, and most especially those that send their children to these schools. Families should recognize the level of their responsibility for a support that extends to all aspects of the school: interest, esteem, collaboration, and economic assistance. Not everyone can collaborate to the same degree or in the same way; nonetheless, each one should be ready to be as generous as possible, according to the resources that are available. Collaboration of the families should extend to a share in accomplishing the objectives of the school, and also sharing in responsibility for the school. And the school should keep the families informed about the ways in which the educational philosophy is being applied or improved on, about formation, about administration, and, in certain cases, about the management.

CONCLUSION

81. Lay Catholic educators in schools, whether teachers, principals, administrators, or auxiliary staff, must never have any doubts about the fact that they constitute an element of great hope for the Church. The Church has confidence in them, entrusting to them with the task of gradually bringing about an integration of temporal reality with the Gospel, so that the Gospel can thus reach into the lives of all men and women. More particularly, it has entrusted to them the integral human formation and the faith education of young people. These young people are the ones who will determine whether the world of tomorrow is more closely or more loosely bound to Christ.

82. This Sacred Congregation for Catholic Education echoes the same hope. When it considers the tremendous evangelical resource embodied in the millions of lay Catholics who devote their lives to schools, it recalls the words with which the Second Vatican Council ended its Decree on the Apostolate of the Laity, and "earnestly entreats in the Lord that all lay persons give a glad, generous, and prompt response to the voice of Christ, who is giving them an especially urgent invitation at this moment; . . . they should respond to it eagerly and magnanimously. . . and, recognizing that what is his is also their own (*Phil* 2, 5), to associate themselves with him in his saving mission . . . Thus they can show that they are his co-workers in the various forms and methods of the Church's one apostolate, which must be constantly adapted to the new needs of the times. May they always

abound in the works of God, knowing that they will not labour in vain when their labour is for Him (Cf *1 Cor* 15, 58)".[57]

* Translation from the French, by Austin Flannery, O.P.; *Documentation Catholique*, 7 November, 1982, but utilising to a considerable extent the English version put out by the Vatican press office. There are now several hundred thousand Catholics teaching in state schools while in Catholic schools there are many more lay teachers than religious. The Congregation for Christian Education convened a meeting of laity, priests and religious men and women to discuss the matter in June 1980. Their recommendations were discussed by the Congregation in March 1981 and it was decided to produce the present document, a draft of which was sent to episcopal conferences and education commissions.[Editor]

1. Vatican II: Const. *Lumen Gentium*, n. 31.
2. See Vatican II: Decl. *Gravissimum educationis*, n. 8.
3. See *The Catholic School*, S.C.C.E., nn. 18–22. Included in this volume.
4. Vatican II: Const. *Lumen Gentium*, n. 32.
5. Ibid.
6. Ibid., n. 31.
7. Ibid., n. 33.
8. Ibid., n. 31.
9. Ibid.
10. Vatican II: Const. *Lumen Gentium*, n. 36; Cf. Decl. *Apostolicam actuositatem*, n. 7.
11. Vatican II: Const. *Lumen Gentium*, n. 36.
12. Ibid.
13. Ibid., n. 33.
14. Cf. Vatican II: Decl. *Gravissimum educationis*, n. 3.
15. John Paul II, Apostolic Exhortation *Familiaris consortio*, Nov. 22, 1981, n. 36. Included in this volume.
16. Cf. Vatican II: Decl. *Gravissimum educationis*, n. 5.
17. Ibid., n. 3.
18. Ibid., n. 3; Universal Declaration on Human Rights, art. 26, 3.
19. Cf. Vatican II: Decl. *Gravissimum educationis*, n. 6.
20. Ibid., n. 5; Cf. Paul VI, Apostolic Exhortation *Evangelii nuntiandi*, December 8, 1975, n. 70. Included in this volume.
21. Sacred Congregation for Catholic Education: "*The Catholic School*", n. 31.
22. Cf. Paul VI, Encyclical Letter *Populorum progressio*; March 26, 1967, AAS 59 (1967), n. 19, pp. 267–268; cf. John Paul II, *Discourse to UNESCO*, June 2, 1980, AAS 72 (1980) n. 11, p. 742.
23. Paul VI, *Discourse on Christmas Night*, December 25, 1976, AAS 68 (1976) p. 145.
24. Cf. John Paul II, Encyclical Letter *Laborem exercens*, 14. Sept. 1981, AAS 73 (1981), Foreword, p. 578.
25. John Paul II, Encyclical Letter *Laborem exercens,* ibid. p. 577.
26. Cf. above, n. 16.
27. Cf. above, n. 20.
28. John Paul II, *Discourse to* UNESCO, June 2, 1980, AAS 72 (1980) n. 11, p. 742.
29. Cf. above, n. 21.

30. John Paul II, Apostolic Exhortation *Familiaris consortio*, AAS, 74 (1982) n. 37, p. 127.

31. Ibid., n. 40.

32. Ibid., n. 36.

33. Cf. John Paul II, Encyclical Letter*Laborem exercens*, September 14, 1981, AAS 73 (1981) n. 20, pp. 629–632.

34. Vatican II: Decl. *Gravissimum educationis*, n. 8; cf. Sacred Congregation for Catholic Education: "*The Catholic School*", n. 34.

35. Sacred Congregation for Catholic Education: "*The Catholic School*", n. 9.

36. Cf. above, n. 29 and n. 32.

37. Cf. Vatican II: Decl. *Dignitatis humanae*, n. 3.

38. Cf. *Apostolicam actuositatem*, n. 2.

39. The concept here is a more ample one: a system of ideas joined to social, economic, and/or political structures.

40. Cf. above n. 9.

40a. I took the liberty of changing the metaphor from 'mirror in which they will see an image reflected', since when one looks in a mirror all one sees is oneself. [Editor]

41. Cf. Vatican II: Decl. *Ad Gentes*, n. 21.

42. Cf. John Paul II, *Discourse to the Clerics of Rome Concerning the Teaching of Religion and Catechesis*, March 5, 1981, *Insegnamenti di Giovanni Palo II*, 1981, IV, 1, n. 3, p. 630.

43. John Paul II, Apostolic Exhortation *Catechesi tradendae*. October 16, 1979, AAS 71 (1979) n. 66, p. 1331. Included in this volume.

44. Ibid., n. 6.

45. Ibid., n. 61.

46. Vatican II: Decl. *Gravissimum educationis*, n. 5.

47. Ibid., n. 8.

48. Vatican II: Decree *Apostolicam actuositatem*, n. 29.

49. John Paul II, *Discourse on the Occasion of the 90th Anniversary of "Rerum Novarum"*, May 13, 1981 (not delivered), L'Osservatore Romano, May 15, 1981.

50. Cf. Ibid.

51. Cf. Vatican II: Decl. *Gravissimum educationis*, n. 8.

52. Vatican II: Decl. *Gravissimum educationis*, n. 5.

53. Cf. Sacred Congregation for Catholic Education, "*The Catholic School*", n. 75.

54. Sacred Congregation for Catholic Education, "*The Catholic School*", n. 78.

55. Cf. above, n. 43.

56. Cf. John Paul II, Encyclical Letter *Laborem Exercens*, AAS, 73, (1981) n. 14, p. 614.

57. Vatican II: Decree *Apostolicam actuositatem*, n. 33.

117

ON DANGEROUS OPINIONS
AND ON ATHEISM*

Synod of Bishops, *Ratione habita*, 28 October, 1967

INTRODUCTION

In accordance with the instructions of the Cardinal Presidents, this Synodal Commission has endeavoured to prepare, in the short time given, a true and accurate summary of what the Fathers said in the Synod Hall. It has taken account of the interventions of the Fathers regarding the document of the Sacred Congregation for the Doctrine of the Faith, and the report of His Eminence Cardinal Browne.

The Commission particularly noted that the Fathers spoke especially of the difficulties regarding the integrity of the Faith of the Church and its presentation in modern circumstances, and that not many of them treated explicitly of the problem of atheism, although all were conscious of a certain atheistic mentality, and its influence on the modern world.

Leaving aside particular observations, in the present report we intend to submit to the venerable Fathers of the Synod three points:

First, there will be a brief report of what was said by the Fathers about the crisis in which the People of God find themselves today in what pertains to preserving unimpaired and setting forth their faith.

Second, principles will be proposed which in this crisis should inspire the manner of acting, especially of pastors of the Church and of theologians.

Third, proposals will be presented which seem to us, in accordance with the thinking of the Fathers, more likely to meet the present difficulties.

1. THE CURRENT CRISIS CONCERNING CATHOLIC FAITH AND DOCTRINE

Very many Fathers spoke of the difficulties which today are disturbing, or can disturb, the faith of the People of God. They also mentioned that these difficulties arise in great part from the modern crises of civilisation and of human culture themselves.

The Second Vatican Council expressly treated of this crisis, especially in the Pastoral Constitution on the Church in the modern world, which the Fathers often cited in detail.

For example, some noted that in secular life there is an evolution of structures and of the very way of thinking, and doubt is being cast on the traditional image of man and of the world.

This happens partly, at least, because of the remarkable progress of science and of secular civilisation, by reason of which men are often completely caught up in the demands of their work; partly, also, because of an ever-increasing awareness of the evolution of the universe and of man's own life and history.

All this is reflected in a kind of anthropology, which is expressed also in philosophical systems, by which man so exalts himself and his earthly responsibilities, that the "vertical dimension," by which he is related to God and to supernatural salvation, becomes obscure, and so man is easily led to atheism, either practical or theoretical.

And so it happens that not a few men, imbued with this mentality, reject the Church or religion itself, at least in practice, as an institution which impedes rather than promotes human progress.

1. Dangers

Therefore, some Fathers, citing the words of John XXIII, stated that the Church cannot remain silent in these circumstances, and must express, in new formulations, the revealed truth which she has always handed down; formulations adapted to a new view of conditions, keeping, of course, the same meaning and the same thought.

This work is altogether necessary, although it is difficult and brings with it dangers which are not to be minimised. The pastors of the Church, however, from the very beginning of the Council, under the leadership of the Holy See, have earnestly entered on this work.

In order that the Council might bear its fruit, many theologians have already been working vigorously and successfully. They have carefully studied the great themes of the Council and illustrated their riches, especially in the fields of biblical, dogmatic and moral theology, as well as in the fields of ecumenism and liturgy. All the Fathers agreed that this work is greatly to be commended.

Also, a large number of priests, dedicated to the care of souls, have made great efforts to communicate a sound understanding of the Council to the faithful, and to foster the renewal of the liturgy and the whole life of the Church consistently with the Council.

There is reason for joy, also, as the Fathers remarked, in the diligence manifested by many faithful laymen who earnestly seek to increase knowledge of the Christian message as it is contained in the Sacred Scriptures and shines forth in the liturgy of the Church and her activity in the world.

It does not seem surprising, it may be noted, that the opportune and fruitful renewal which the Second Vatican Council brought to the Church, changing as it did many seemingly permanent customs and ways of thinking, and giving a strong impulse to new thought and to the beginning of a new manner of Christian life and liturgy, has aroused difficulty and even uncertainty.

Nevertheless—and this is greatly to be deplored and was noted by a large number of the Fathers—in some places matters have reached such a point that it is no longer a question of sound and fruitful investigation, or legitimate efforts to adapt the expression of traditional doctrine to new needs and to the ways of modern human culture, but rather of unwarranted innovations, false opinions, and even errors in the Faith.

For truths of the Faith are falsely understood or explained, and in the developing process of understanding doctrine its essential continuity is neglected.

In a special way the Fathers deplored the fact that some actually call into doubt some truths of the faith, among others those concerning the knowledge we have of God, the Person of Christ and His Resurrection, the Eucharist, the mystery of the Original Sin, the enduring objectivity of the Moral Law and the perpetual virginity of the Blessed Virgin Mary.

For this reason, there is noted a state of unrest and anxiety in the Church, both among the faithful and among pastors, and therefore the spiritual life of the People of God suffers no little harm.

This, indeed, is not felt in the same way everywhere, nor in equal measure among all groups of the People of God. It is more apparent, as may be easily understood, among men of more advanced education, because of their special difficulties in reconciling faith with reason.

Even among the working classes there are some difficulties and problems about the faith and the Church, which are felt in a similar way in all parts of the world.

In missionary lands and in certain other regions, where the first and greatest problem is the proclaiming of the faith and an adequate catechetical instruction of the people, the difficulties seem to be restricted to a few groups of priests and laymen.

But the Fathers noted that it is to be feared that false opinions may soon spread and develop even in these parts of the world, with greater harm both to the apostolate of the Church and to the faithful themselves.

2. Causes and Remedies

Of this unfortunate state of affairs, the Fathers listed causes which must be carefully considered so that suitable remedies may be provided.

Among the principal ones should be numbered: A certain decrease in the sense of supernatural faith among men conscious of their own natural powers; and, among many, a neglect of personal prayer to God.

Sometimes, according to the opinion of some, insufficient pastoral ministry in teaching the truth or preventing errors; an ignoring or a disrespect for the teaching and the authority of the Church, whether of the bishops or of the Roman Pontiff himself.

A certain arbitrary and false interpretation of the spirit of the Council; and not always a well understood distinction between those matters which belong to Catholic doctrine and those which are left to the free and legitimate discussion of theologians.

A problem special to our times arises from the fact that publications and other means of communication immediately spread any news of a religious nature to the whole world.

And such news gives an easy occasion for scandal, whether because of the deforming simplicity with which it is sometimes reported or because of different circumstances of religious life in different parts of the world; or, finally, because the meaning of the traditional doctrine is not sufficiently taken into account.

Sometimes these matters are imprudently spread about even

by priests, religious, theologians, educators and others, without sufficient regard for the way in which the Faith is taught.

After faithfully noting the above, there is no reason why, in this brief report, we should dwell on particular deviations from the Faith, and the Fathers did not do this either.

Rather we shall immediately set forth, according to what they said in an ordered way, the pastoral principles to be observed in these circumstances.

2. PRINCIPLES

1. The Necessity for the Unceasing Proclamation of the Faith

By Catholic Faith we embrace the good news of God who reveals Himself in His Son. This we do in keeping with the nature of this message which was entrusted to the Church for safe-keeping and is proposed by Her living teaching authority for our belief (Cf. Dog. Const. Dei Verbum, Par. 10).

This faith of ours is a divine gift by which we who believe are drawn to God by a movement of reverence and commitment, a movement which is the beginning of salvation, but which also depends on the preaching of men, according to the words of the Apostle: "Faith comes from hearing" (Rom. 10:17).

It is necessary, therefore—especially in today's circumstances—that the faith with which man makes his response to God, who speaks through Christ in the Church, be constantly cultivated and strengthened.

This task of cultivating the faith belongs first of all to the bishops along with their collaborators in the priesthood, and among the religious who help the bishops.

But it also belongs to those laymen who are engaged in teaching the faith. It belongs, in fact, to all the faithful and, in a special way, to parents with regard to their children.

All the sons of the Church therefore, each according to his charisms, must feel responsible for passing on the sacred gift of faith to the men of our time.

This is something the Synod most gladly calls to mind during this "Year of Faith," which the Supreme Pontiff has decreed as he pursues his untiring, zealous dedication to the duty of preaching the faith.

2. The Individual and the Collegial Exercise of the Authentic Magisterium

According to the teaching of the Church, the office of

teaching on questions of faith and morals authentically, that is, with the authority of Christ has been entrusted to all successors of the Apostles.

It belongs to the Roman Pontiff personally and to the Episcopal College gathered in Ecumenical Council to meet the needs of the Christian people by the conscientious exercise of the magisterium.

But it is not limited to them, since every pastor of the Church, each in his own see or region, is by the reason of his office bound by the same heavy responsibility. Today this sacred work is done more fittingly when it is done collegiately through the episcopal conferences.

In accomplishing its mission, each of the conferences should be mindful of the communion in teaching that is to be maintained with the College of Bishops throughout the entire world, but especially with the Apostolic See.

This will result in support that comes from mutual help in the avoidance of turmoil, and in the strengthening of unity, while account is taken of the needs of all the churches.

All the faithful, in any case, are to be taught clearly, and in ways adapted to the contemporary mentality, about the filial obedience and sincere adherence owed to the declarations of the teaching authority in the Church, all according to the different nature of different pronouncements, as is taught by the Second Vatican Council (Cf. Const. Lumen Gentium, II, Par. 25).

3. Pastoral Approach in Exercising the Magisterium

In fulfilling their office of teaching, the bishops must be concerned both with faithfully preserving the deposit of faith and with protecting their flocks from the dangers that threaten them.

But a positive way of setting forth the truth will usually be more fitting than a mere negative condemnation of error. Insistence should always be placed on those things which present revealed mystery as a true message of salvation, meeting the problems and aspirations of modern man.

Above all, pastors should be aware of how legitimate, and even necessary, it is for preserving the deposit of faith that there be progress in the understanding that takes into account the progress of the sciences and culture and the ever new questions that face mankind.

Therefore, before they teach the faithful concerning new and difficult matters, they should consult attentively theologians and other experts and seek the prudent advice of their priests and of the laity (Cf. Lumen Gentium, IV, Par.37).

Indeed, "since it is the mission of the Church to enter into dialogue with the human society in which she lives, bishops especially are called upon to approach men, seeking and fostering dialogue with them" (Decr. Christus Dominus, II, Par. 15).

This way of acting must not prevent the firm exercise of authority in directing the Church of God, according to the mind of the Second Vatican Council, to the exclusion of abuses and deviations either in doctrinal matters or in pastoral or liturgical questions.

Those who are rash or imprudent should be warned in all charity; those who are pertinacious should be removed from office.

The Apostle himself gives a warning about the firmness to be shown, "with all patience and teaching," towards those who do not hold sound doctrine (Cf. 2 Tim. 4:2f).

4. The Activity and Responsibility of Theologians

Although the office of teaching authentically does not belong to theologians, nevertheless their office in the Church is an outstanding one, and the service they render to the Church is indispensable.

It is their duty in the expression of the Divine Mystery to do all they can to provide an answer to the new questions which continually arise, and which are often very important even for the existence of Christianity.

For them to be able to accomplish this task adequately, it is beyond doubt that they must be given the necessary freedom to investigate new questions and to further the study of old ones.

However, they must put themselves humbly and faithfully at the service of the Word of God, and they must never make use of it to favour their own opinions.

True freedom must always be contained within the limitations set by the Word of God as it has been constantly preserved and as it is taught and explained by the living magisterium of the Church and especially of the Vicar of Christ.

Let theologians be aware of their responsibility, which is indeed great, in seeking the truth with scientific honesty and in communicating their conclusions in such a way as to imbue their brethren with a spirit of love and reverence toward the Word of God and the teaching Church.

The bishops should encourage the cooperation of theologians among themselves and, particularly, they should favour the establishment of contacts between the theologians and the magisterium, especially by means of episcopal commissions on doctrine.

5. The Diffusion of Doctrine

All who, in any way, diffuse theological teachings, should be persons of special pastoral prudence, above all, because the instruments of social communications reach so many persons so rapidly.

If this diffusion of theological teachings is to have positive and not negative results, sound pedagogical principles must be respected.

First of all, let what is certain and fundamental be proposed as the unshaken basis of the faith and of Christian life; then what is new should be presented in such a way that a fitting explanation will manifest the continuity in the Faith of the Church.

Finally, hypotheses should be put forth with that grade of probability which they in fact enjoy and with attention to the ways in which it is foreseen they will be understood.

Account must also be taken of the difficulty which arises from the fact that some persons incline to give an exaggerated interpretation to every word which, at first sight, seems to be different from the accepted way of conceiving or expressing the truth.

As a result of this inclination, it happens that even theologians who are always careful to think with the Church, sometimes can unjustly be considered in the estimation of the faithful, to be imprudent revolutionaries.

Bishops should see to it that in a world which is every day becoming more united, the faithful are prepared to acquire more mature faith. But they must also see to it, with prudent and vigilant charity, that, especially in the matter of publications, the faith of the whole community does not suffer harm from lack of qualifications or lack of prudence on the part of a few.

Let all those, then, who teach, write or preach be aware of the duty which obliges them to act in communion with the magisterium and according to its directions.

6. The Witness of Teaching Joined to the Witness of Life

Bishops, with the collaboration of all the faithful and especially of priests and religious, must give witness to their faith not only with their words, but also in their actions, most of all with authentic charity, in imitation of Christ Who loved us.

In this regard, it must be stated emphatically how necessary it is that the Church, thanks to the united efforts and activity of her pastors and her faithful alike, and especially of those who hold more responsible posts in civil society, be seen as effectively concerned with justice and charity, not only in private matters but also on social and international levels.

Indeed this important witness to justice and charity, a witness adapted to the conditions of our times and in keeping with the teachings of the Second Vatican Council and the encyclicals "Mater et Magistra," "Pacem in Terris," and "Populorum Progressio," is essential if the Church is to be truly recognised as the sign raised up among the nations (Is. 11:12) by the multitudes who throughout the world, are victims of widespread poverty, social injustice or various kinds of discrimination.

3. PROPOSALS

In addition to these pastoral principles, the Synodal Commission has brought together statements from the Fathers to formulate two proposals to be offered to the Supreme Pontiff.

First Proposal—The setting up of a Theological Commission.
(a) Does it meet with the approval of the Fathers that a Commission be set up composed of theologians of diverse schools, to be appointed for a definite term, all men of intellectual ability, recognised as scholars, who reside in various parts of both the Western and the Eastern Church, whose duty it will be, acting with all lawful academic freedom, to assist the Holy See and especially the Sacred Congregation for the Doctrine of the Faith, principally in connection with questions of greater importance?
(b) Does it meet with their approval that the names of these theologians be proposed to the Supreme Pontiff—leaving the final selection to his discretion—by the Episcopal Conferences themselves, whose members, having duly consulted universities and theological faculties in their territories, believe that they are in a position to recommend the names of competent theologians?

Second proposal: The drawing up of a declaration concerning questions of Faith.

Does it meet with the approval of the Fathers that, having heard the views of the Episcopal Conferences, the Holy See draw up a positive pastoral declaration concerning questions involved in the doctrinal "crisis" of today, so that the faith of the People of God may be given secure direction?

---

* Translation by the Vatican Press Office. Latin original in the *Osservatore Romano*, 30–31 October, 1967.

On 14 October, 1968, the secretary general of the Roman synod, Ladislaus Rubin, wrote a circular letter to the presidents of episcopal conferences (text in E.V., 3, 663–667) about the execution of the synod's proposals, pointing out that Pope Paul VI had promulgated a profession of the faith of the Church on 30 June of that year (text in this volume, number 101). He added that the pope had decreed the establishment of a theological commission by the Sacred Congregation of the Doctrine of the Faith, which had already begun asking episcopal conferences for the names of suitable candidates for submission to the pope. The statutes of the theological commission were promulgated on 12 July, 1969, text in AAS 61 (1969), 540–541. Archbishop Rubin also referred to other proposals made by the synod, stating that the commission for the revision of the code of canon law followed the lines desired by the synod (the new code of canon law was promulgated on 26 January, 1983); that a 'ratio studiorum' for seminaries would be drawn up: the constitution *Sapientia Christiana* was promulgated on 29 April, 1979, text in AAS 71 (1979), 469–499; that a new instruction on mixed marriages would be drawn: *Matrimonia mixta* was promulgated on 7 January, 1970, English text in Flannery, vol. 1, number 39.

118

THE MINISTERIAL PRIESTHOOD*

Synod of Bishops, *Ultimis temporibus*,
30 November, 1967 71

INTRODUCTION

In recent times, especially since the close of the Second Vatican Council, the Church is experiencing a profound movement of renewal, which all Christians should follow with great joy and with fidelity to the Gospel. The power of the Holy Spirit is present to illumine, strengthen and perfect our mission.

Every true renewal brings the Church undoubted benefits of great value. We well know that through the recent Council priests have been fired with new zeal and that they have contributed much to fostering this renewal by their daily solicitude. We have before our minds our many heroic brothers who, in fidelity to their ministry, live lives dedicated to God with joy, either among the peoples where the Church is subjected to a harsh yoke or in mission lands. At the same time, however, the renewal also entails difficulties, which are especially felt by all in the priesthood, whether bishops or priests.

We should all scrutinize the signs of the times in this age of renewal and interpret them in the light of the Gospel (cf. GS 4), in order that we may work together in distinguishing between spirits, to see if they come from God, lest ambiguity cloud the unity of the Church's mission or excessive uniformity hinder needed adaptation. Thus by testing everything and holding fast to what is good, the present crisis can give occasion for an increase of faith.

In accordance with its importance, the Holy Father put forward the ministerial priesthood for discussion by this year's Synod. Before the Synod many episcopal conferences examined this theme together with priests and quite frequently with lay people. Some priests were also called to the Synod as *auditores*, to assist the bishops in dealing with important questions.

We wish to fulfill our duty with the evangelical simplicity which befits pastors who are serving the Church. Considering our responsibility before the fraternal community of the

Church, we desire to strengthen the faith, uplift the hope and stimulate the love both of our brothers in the ministerial priesthood and of all the faithful. May our words bring solace to the People of God and the priests dedicated to their service and renew their joy!

Description of the Situation

1. The extent of the Church's mission was illustrated at length by the Second Vatican Council.

Indeed, the Church's relationship with the world was the subject especially of the pastoral constitution *Gaudium et Spes.* Many good results followed from a closer consideration of this matter: it is more clearly seen that salvation is not an abstract category outside, as it were, of history and time, but that it comes from God and ought to permeate the whole of man and the whole history of men and lead them freely to the Kingdom of God, so that at last "God may be all in all" (*1 Cor* 15:28).

However, as is understandable, difficulties have also arisen: some priests feel themselves estranged from the movements which permeate society and unable to solve the problems which touch men deeply. Often too the problems and troubles of priests derive from their having, in their pastoral and missionary care, to use methods which are now perhaps obsolete to meet the modern mentality. Serious problems and several questions then arise, especially from real difficulties which they experience in exercising their function and not—although this is sometimes the case—from an exasperated spirit of protest or from selfish personal concerns. Is it possible to exhort the laity as if from the outside? Is the Church sufficiently present to certain groups without the active presence of the priest? If the situation characteristic of a priest consists in segregation from secular life, is not the situation of the layman better? What is to be thought of the celibacy of Latin-rite priests in present-day circumstances, and of the personal spiritual life of the priest immersed in the world?

2. Many priests, experiencing within themselves the questionings that have arisen with the secularization of the world, feel the need to sanctify worldly activities by exercising them directly and bring the leaven of the Gospel into the midst of events. Similarly, the desire is developing of cooperating with the joint efforts of men to build up a more just and fraternal society. In a world in which almost all problems have political aspects, participation in politics and even in revolutionary activity is by some considered indispensable.

3. The Council emphasized the pre-eminence of the proclamation of the Gospel, which should lead through faith to the fullness of the celebration of the sacraments. But current thinking about the religious phenomenon fosters doubts in many minds concerning the sense of a sacramental and cultic ministry. Many priests not suffering from a personal identity crisis ask themselves another question: What methods should be used so that sacramental practice may be an expression of faith really affecting the whole of personal and social life, in order that Christian worship should not be wrongly reduced to a mere external ritualism?

Since priests are very concerned with the image of herself that the Church seems to present to the world, and at the same time are deeply conscious of the singular dignity of the human person, they desire to bring about a change within the Church herself in inter-personal relationships, in relations between persons and institutions, and in the very structures of authority.

4. And still, relationships between bishops and priests and between priests themselves are growing more difficult by the very fact that the exercise of the ministry is becoming more diversified. Present-day society is divided into many groups with different disciplines, which call for differing skills and forms of apostolate. This gives rise to problems concerning brotherhood, union and consistency in the priestly ministry.

Happily the recent Council recalled the traditional and fruitful teaching on the common priesthood of the faithful (cf. *LG* 10). That, however, gives rise, as by a swing of the pendulum, to certain questions which seem to obscure the position of the priestly ministry in the Church and which deeply trouble the minds of some priests and faithful. Many activities which in the past were reserved to priests—for instance, catechetical work, administrative activity in the communities, and even liturgical activities—are today quite frequently carried out by lay people, while on the other hand many priests, for reasons already mentioned, are trying to involve themselves in the condition of life of lay persons. Hence a number of questions are being asked: Does the priestly ministry have any specific nature? Is this ministry necessary? Is the priesthood incapable of being lost? What does being a priest mean today? Would it not be enough to have for the service of the Christian communities presidents designated for the preservation of the common good, without sacramental ordination, and exercising their office for a fixed period?

5. Still more serious questions are posed, some of them as a result of exegetical and historical research, which show a crisis

of confidence in the Church: Is the present-day Church too far removed from its origins to be able to proclaim the ancient Gospel credibly to modern man? Is it still possible to reach the reality of Christ after so many critical investigations? Are the essential structures of the early Church well enough known to us that they can and must be considered an invariable scheme for every age, including our own?

6. The above-mentioned questions, some of them new, others already long familiar but appearing in new forms today, cannot be understood outside of the whole context of modern culture, which has strong doubts about its meaning and value. New means of technology have stirred up a hope based excessively on enthusiasm and at the same time they have aroused profound anxiety. One rightly asks whether man will be capable of being master of his work and directing it towards progress.

Some, especially the young, despair of the meaning of this world and look for salvation in purely meditative systems and in artificial marginal paradises, abandoning the common striving of mankind.

Others dedicate themselves with ardent utopian hope devoid of reference to God to the attainment of some state of total liberation, and transfer the meaning of their whole personal lives from the present to the future.

There is therefore a profound cleavage between action and contemplation, work and recreation, culture and religion, and between the immanent and the transcendent aspects of human life.

Thus the world itself is obscurely awaiting a solution to this dilemma and is paving a way whereby the Church may go forward proclaiming the Gospel. Certainly, the only complete salvation offered to men is Christ himself, Son of God and Son of Man, who makes himself present in history through the Church. He joins inseparably together love for God and the love which God has until the end for men as they seek their way amid the shadows, and the value of human love whereby a man gives his life for his friends. In Christ, and only in him, do all of these become one whole, and in this synthesis the meaning of human life, both individual and social, shines forth. The mission of the Church, Christ's Body, far from being obsolete, is therefore rather of the highest relevance for the present and the future: the whole Church is the witness and effective sign of this union, especially through the priestly ministry. The minister's proper task in the Church's midst is to render present, by the word and sacrament, the love of God in Christ for us, and at the same time to promote the fellowship of men with God and with each other. All this of course demands that we should all, especially those who perform the sacred office, strive to renew ourselves daily in accordance with the Gospel.

7.   We know that there are some parts of the world in which that profound cultural change has hitherto been less felt, and that the questions raised above are not being asked everywhere, nor by all priests, nor in the same way. But since communications between men and peoples have today become more frequent and more speedy, we judge it good and opportune to examine these questions in the light of faith and to give humbly but in the strength of the Holy Spirit some principles for finding more concrete answers to them. Although this response must be applied differently according to the circumstances of each region, it will have the force of truth for all those faithful and priests who live in situations of greater tranquility. Therefore, ardently desiring to strengthen the witness of faith, we fraternally urge all the faithful to strive to contemplate the Lord Jesus living in his Church and to realize that he wishes to work in a special way through his ministers; they will thus be convinced that the Christian community cannot fulfil its complete mission without the ministerial priesthood. Let priests be aware that their anxieties are truly shared by the bishops, and that the bishops desire to share them still more.

Moved by this desire, the Synod Fathers, in the spirit of the Gospel, following closely the teaching of the Second Vatican Council, and considering also the documents and addresses of the Supreme Pontiff Paul VI, intend to set forth briefly some principles of the Church's teaching on the ministerial priesthood which are at present more urgent, together with some guidelines for pastoral practice.

Part I
PRINCIPLES OF DOCTRINE

1. Christ, Alpha and Omega

Jesus Christ, the Son of God and the Word, "whom the Father sanctified and sent into the world" (*Jn* 10:36), and who was marked with the seal of the fullness of the Holy Spirit (cf. *Lk* 4:1, 18-21; *Ac* 10:38), proclaimed to the world the Good News of reconciliation between God and Men. His preaching as a prophet, confirmed by signs, reaches its summit in the paschal mystery, the supreme word of the divine love with which the Father addressed us. On the cross Jesus showed himself to the greatest possible extent to be the Good Shepherd who laid down his life for his sheep in order to gather them into that unity which depends on himself (cf. *Jn* 10:1ff.; 11:52). Exercising a supreme and unique priesthood by the offering of himself, he surpassed, by fulfilling them, all the ritual priesthoods and holocausts of the Old Testament and indeed of the pagans. In his sacrifice he took on himself the miseries and sacrifices of men of every age and also the efforts of those who suffer for the cause of justice or who are daily oppressed by misfortune. He took on himself the endeavours of those who abandon the world and attempt to reach God by asceticism and contemplation as well as the labours of those who sincerely devote their lives to a better present and future society. He bore the sins of us all on the cross; rising from the dead and being made Lord (cf. *Phil* 2:9-11), he reconciled us to God; and he laid the foundation of the people of the New Covenant, which is the Church.

He is the "one mediator between God and men, the man Christ Jesus" (*1 Tim.* 2:5), "for in him were created all things" *Col* 1:16; cf. *Jn* 1:3ff.) and everything is brought together under him, as head (cf. *Eph* 1:10). Since he is the image of the Father and manifestation of the unseen God (cf. *Col* 1:15), by emptying himself and by being raised up he brought us into the fellowship of the Holy Spirit in which he lives with the Father.

When therefore we speak of the priesthood of Christ, we should have before our eyes a unique, incomparable reality, which includes the prophetic and royal office of the Incarnate Word of God.

So Jesus Christ signifies and manifests in many ways the presence and effectiveness of the anticipatory love of God. The Lord himself, constantly influencing the Church by his Spirit, stirs up and fosters the response of all those who offer themselves to this freely given love.

2. Coming to Christ, in the Church

The way to the person and mystery of Christ lies ever open in the Holy Spirit through the Scriptures understood in the living tradition of the Church. All the Scriptures, especially those of the New Testament, must be interpreted as intimately interlinked and inter-related by their single inspiration. The books of the New Testament are not of such differing value that some of them can be reduced to mere late inventions.

A personal and immediate relationship with Christ in the Church should still for the faithful of today sustain their whole spiritual lives.

3. The Church from Christ Through the Apostles

The Church which he had declared would be built on Peter, Christ founded on the Apostles (cf. *LG* 18). In them are already manifested two aspects of the Church: in the Group of the Twelve Apostles there are already both fellowship in the Spirit and the origin of the hierarchical ministry (cf. *AG* 5). For that reason, the New Testament writings speak of the Church as founded on the Apostles (cf. *Rev* 21:14; *Mt* 16:18). This was concisely expressed by ancient tradition: "The Church from the Apostles, the Apostles from the Christ, Christ from God" (1).

The Church, which was founded on the Apostles and sent into the world and is a pilgrim there, was established to be a sacrament of the salvation which came to us from God in Christ. In her, Christ is present and operative for the world as a saviour, so that the love offered by God to men and their response meet. The Holy Spirit stirs up in and through the Church impulses of generous free will by which man participates in the very work of creation and redemption.

4. The Origin and Nature of Hierarchical Ministry

The Church, which through the gift of the Spirit is made up organically, participates in different ways in the functions of Christ as Priest, Prophet and King, in order to carry out her mission of salvation in his name and by his power, as a priestly people (cf. *LG* 10).

It is clear from the New Testament writings that an Apostle and a community of faithful united with one another by a mutual link under Christ as head and the influence of his Spirit belong to the original inalienable structure of the Church. The Twelve Apostles exercised their mission and functions, and "they not only had helpers in their ministry (cf. *Ac* 6:2-6; 11:30; 13:1; 14:23; 24:17; *1 Th* 5:12-13; *Phil* 1:1; *Col* 4:11 and passim), but also, in order that the mission assigned to them might continue after their death, they passed on to their immediate co-operators, as a kind of testament, the duty of perfecting and consolidating the work begun by themselves (*Ac* 20:5-27; *2 Tim* 4:6 taken together with *1 Tim* 5:22; *2 Tim* 2:2; *Tit* 1:5; Saint Clement of Rome to the Corinthians 44:3), charging them to attend to the whole flock in which the Holy Spirit placed them to shepherd the Church of God (cf. *Ac* 20:28). They appointed such men, and made provision that, when these men should die, other approved men would take up their ministry (cf. Saint Clement of Rome to the Corinthians 44:2)" (*LG* 20).

The letters of Saint Paul show that he was conscious of acting by Christ's mission and mandate (cf. *2 Cor* 5:18ff.). The powers entrusted to the Apostle for the Churches were handed on to others insofar as they were communicable (cf. *2 Tim* 1:16), and these others were obliged to hand them on to yet others (cf. *Tit* 1:5).

This essential structure of the Church—consisting of a flock and of pastors appointed for this purpose (cf. *1 Pt* 5:1-4)—according to the Tradition of the Church herself was always and remains the norm. Precisely as a result of this structure, the Church can never remain closed in on herself and is always subject to Christ as her origin and head.

Among the various charisms and services, the priestly ministry of the New Testament, which continues Christ's function as mediator, and which in essence and not merely in degree is distinct from the common priesthood of all the faithful (cf. *LG* 10), alone perpetuates the essential work of the Apostles: by effectively proclaiming the Gospel, by gathering together and leading the community, by remitting sins, and especially by celebrating the Eucharist, it makes Christ, the head of the community, present in the exercise of his work of redeeming mankind and glorifying God perfectly.

Bishops and, on a subordinate level, priests, by virtue of the sacrament of Orders, which confers an anointing of the Holy Spirit and configures to Christ (cf. *PO* 2), become sharers in the functions of sanctifying, teaching and governing. and the exercise of these functions is determined more precisely by hierarchichal communion (cf. *LG* 24-27-28).

The priestly ministry reaches its summit in the celebration of the Eucharist, which is the source and centre of the Church's unity. Only a priest is able to act in the person of Christ in presiding over and effecting the sacrificial banquet wherein the People of God are associated with Christ's offering (cf. *LG* 28).

The priest is a sign of the divine anticipatory plan proclaimed and effective today in the Church. He makes Christ, the Saviour of all men, sacramentally present among his brothers and sisters, in both their personal and social lives. He is a guarantor both of the first proclamation of the Gospel for the gathering together of the Church and of the ceaseless renewal of the Church which has already been gathered together. If the Church lacks the presence and activity of the ministry which is received by the laying on of hands with prayer, she cannot have full certainty of her fidelity and of her visible continuity.

5. Permanence of the Priesthood

By the laying on of hands there is communicated a gift of the Holy Spirit which cannot be lost (cf. *2 Tim* 1:6). This reality configures the ordained minister to Christ the Priest, consecrates him (cf. *PO* 2) and makes him a sharer in Christ's mission under its two aspects of authority and service.

That authority does not belong to the Minister as his own: it is a manifestation of the *exousia* (i.e. the power) of the Lord, by which the priest is an ambassador of Christ in the eschatological work of reconciliation (cf. *2 Cor* 5:18-20). He also assists the conversion of human freedom to God for the building up of the Christian community.

The lifelong permanence of this reality, which is a sign, and which is a teaching of the faith and is referred to in the Church's tradition as the priestly character, expresses the fact that Christ associated the Church with himself in an irrevocable way for the salvation of the world, and that the Church dedicates herself to Christ in a definitive way for the carrying out of his work. The minister whose life bears the seal of the gift received through the sacrament of Orders reminds the Church that the gift of God is irrevocable. In the midst of the Christian community which, in spite of its defects, lives by the Spirit, he is a pledge of the salvific presence of Christ.

This special participation in Christ's priesthood does not disappear even if a priest for ecclesial or personal reasons is dispensed or removed from the exercise of his ministry.

6. For the Service of Fellowship

Even if he exercises his ministry in a determined community the priest nevertheless cannot be exclusively devoted to a particular group of faithful. His ministry always tends towards the unity of the whole Church and to the gathering together in her of all men. Each individual community of faithful needs fellowship with the bishop and the universal Church. In this way the priestly ministry too is essentially communitarian within the presbyterium and with the bishop who, preserving communion with the Successor of Peter, is a part of the body of bishops. This holds also for priests who are not in the immediate service of any community or who work in remote and isolated territories. Religious priests also, within the context of the special purpose and structure of their institute, are indissolubly part of a mission which is ecclesially ordered.

Let the whole life and activity of the priest be imbued with a spirit of catholicity, that is, with a sense of the universal mission of the Church, so that he will willingly recognize all the gifts of the Spirit, give them freedom and direct them towards the common good.

Let priests follow Christ's example and cultivate with the bishop and with each other that brotherhood which is founded on their ordination and the oneness of their mission so that priestly witness may be more credible.

7. The Priest and Temporal Matters

All truly Christian undertakings are related to the salvation of mankind, which, while it is of an eschatological nature, also embraces temporal matters. Every reality of this world must be subjected to the lordship of Christ. This however does not mean that the Church claims technical competence in the secular order, with disregard for the latter's autonomy.

The proper mission entrusted by Christ to the priest, as to the Church, is not of the political, economic or social order, but of the religious order (cf. GS 42); yet, in the pursuit of his ministry, the priest can contribute greatly to the establishment of a more just secular order, especially in places where the human problems of injustice and oppression are more serious. He must always, however, preserve ecclesial communion and reject violence in words or deeds as not being in accordance with the Gospel.

In fact, the word of the Gospel which he proclaims in the name of Christ and the Church, and the effective grace of sacramental life which he administers should free man from his personal and social egoism and foster among men conditions of justice, which would be a sign of the love of Christ present among us (cf. GS 58).

Part II
GUIDELINES FOR THE PRIESTLY LIFE AND MINISTRY

Considering the priestly mission in the light of the ministry of Christ and the communion of the Church, the Fathers of this

Synod, united with the Roman Pontiff and conscious of the anxieties which bishops and priests are expressing in the fulfilment of their common role today, present the following guidelines to clarify certain questions and to give encouragement.

I. PRIESTS IN THE MISSION OF CHRIST AND THE CHURCH

1. Mission: Evangelization and Sacramental Life

a) "By their vocation and ordination, the priests of the New Testament are indeed set apart in a certain sense within the midst of God's people. But this is so, not that they may be made distant from this people or from any man, but that they be totally dedicated to the work for which the Lord has raised them up" (*PO* 3). Priests thus find their identity to the extent that they fully live the mission of the Church and exercise it in different ways in communion with the entire People of God, as pastors and ministers of the Lord in the Spirit, in order to fulfil by their work the plan of salvation in history. "By means of their own ministry, which deals principally with the Eucharist as the source of perfecting the Church, priests are in communion with Christ the Head and are leading others to this communion. Hence they cannot help realizing how much is yet wanting to the fullness of that Body, and how much therefore must be done if it is to grow from day to day" (*AG* 39).

b) Priests are sent to all men and their mission must begin with the preaching of God's Word. "Priests have as their duty the proclamation of the Gospel of Christ to all. . . For through the saving Word the spark of faith is struck in the hearts of unbelievers and fed in the hearts of the faithful" (*PO* 4). The goal of evangelization is "that all who are made sons of God by faith and baptism should come together to praise God in the midst of his Church, to take part in her sacrifice and to eat the Lord's supper" (*SC* 10). The ministry of the Word, if rightly understood, leads to the sacraments and to the Christian life, as it is practised in the visible community of the Church and in the world.

The sacraments are celebrated in conjunction with the proclamation of the Word of God and thus develop faith by strengthening it with grace. They cannot be considered of slight importance, since through them the word is brought to fuller effect, namely communion in the mystery of Christ.

Let priests then perform their ministry in such a way that the faithful will "have recourse with great eagerness to the

sacraments which were instituted to nourish the Christian life"
(SC 59).

An enduring evangelization and a well-ordered sacramental
life of the community demand, by their nature, a *diaconia* of
authority, that is, a serving of unity and a presiding over charity.
Thus the mutual relationship between evangelization and the
celebration of the sacraments is clearly seen in the mission of the
Church. A separation between the two would divide the heart of
the Church to the point of imperilling the faith, and the priest,
who is dedicated to the service of unity in the community, would
be gravely distorting his ministry.

Unity between evangelization and sacramental life is always
proper to the ministerial priesthood and must carefully be kept
in mind by every priest. And yet the application of this principle
to the life and ministry of individual priests must be made with
discretion, for the exercise of the priestly ministry often in practice needs to take different forms in order better to meet special
or new situations in which the Gospel is to be proclaimed.

c) Although the pedagogy of faith demands that man be
gradually initiated into the Christian life, the Church must
nevertheless always proclaim to the world the Gospel in its entirety. Each priest shares in the special responsibility of
preaching the whole of the Word of God and of interpreting it
according to the faith of the Church.

The proclamation of the Word of God is the announcement in
the power of the Spirit of the wonders performed by God and
the calling of men to share the paschal mystery and to introduce
it as a leaven into a concrete human history. It is the action of
God in which the power of the Holy Spirit brings the Church
together interiorly and exteriorly. The minister of the word by
evangelization prepares the ways of the Lord with great patience
and faith, conforming himself to the various conditions of individuals' and people's lives, which are evolving more or less
rapidly.

Impelled by the need to keep in view both the personal and
social aspects of the announcement of the Gospel, so that in it an
answer may be given to all the more fundamental questions of
men (cf. *CD* 13), the Church not only preaches conversion to
God to individual men, but also, to the best of her ability, as the
conscience of humanity, she addresses society itself and performs a prophetic function in society's regard, always taking
pains to effect her own renewal.

As regards the experiences of life, whether of men in general
or of priests, which must be kept in mind and always interpreted
in the light of the Gospel, these experiences cannot be either the

sole or the principal norm of preaching.

d) Salvation, which is effected through the sacraments, does not come from us but from God; this demonstrates the primacy of action of Christ, the one priest and mediator, in his body, which is the Church.

Since the sacraments are truly sacraments of faith (cf. *SC* 59), they require conscious and free participation by every Christian who has the use of reason. This makes clear the great importance of preparation and of a disposition of faith on the part of the person who receives the sacraments; it also makes clear the necessity for a witness of faith on the part of the minister in his entire life and especially in the way he values and celebrates the sacraments themselves.

To bishops and, in the cases foreseen by law, to episcopal conferences is committed the role of authentically promoting, in accordance with the norms given by the Holy See, pastoral activity and liturgical renewal better adapted to each region, and also of determining the criteria for admission to the sacraments. These criteria, which must be applied by priests, are likewise to be explained to the faithful, so that a person who asks for a sacrament may become more aware of his own responsibility.

Let priests, with consciousness of their office of reconciling all men in the love of Christ and with attention to the dangers of divisions, strive with great prudence and pastoral charity to form communities which are imbued with apostolic zeal and which will make the Church's missionary spirit present everywhere. Small communities, which are not opposed to the parish or diocesan structure, ought to be inserted into the parochial or diocesan community in such a way that they may serve it as a leaven of missionary spirit. The need to find apt forms of effectively bringing the Gospel message to all men, who live in differing circumstances, furnishes a place for the multiple exercise of ministries lower than the priesthood.

2. Secular and Political Activity

a) The priestly ministry, even if compared with other activities, not only is to be considered as a fully valid human activity but indeed as more excellent than other activities, though this great value can be fully understood only in the light of faith. Thus, as a general rule, the priestly ministry shall be a full-time occupation. Sharing in the secular activities of men is by no means to be considered the principal end nor can such participation suffice to give expression to priests' specific responsibility. Priests, without being of the world and without taking it as their model, must nevertheless live in the world (cf. *PO* 3, 17; *Jn* 17:14-16), as witness and stewards of another life (cf. *PO* 3).

In order to determine in concrete circumstances whether secular activity is in accord with the priestly ministry, inquiry should be made whether and in what way those duties and activities serve the mission of the Church, those who have not yet received the Gospel message and finally the Christian community. This is to be judged by the local bishop with his presbyterium, and if necessary in consultation with the episcopal conference.

When activities of this sort, which ordinarily pertain to the laity, are as it were demanded by the priest's very mission to evangelize, they must be harmonized with his other ministerial activities, in those circumstances where they can be considered as necessary forms of true ministry (cf. *PO* 8).

b) Together with the entire Church, priests are obliged, to the utmost of their ability, to select a definite pattern of action, when it is a question of the defence of fundamental human rights, the promotion of the full development of persons and the pursuit of the cause of peace and justice; the means must indeed always be consonant with the Gospel. These principles are all valid not only in the individual sphere, but also in the social field; in this regard priests should help the laity to devote themselves to forming their consciences rightly.

In circumstances in which there legitimately exist different political, social and economic options, priests like all citizens have a right to select their personal options. But since political options are by nature contingent and never in an entirely adequate and perennial way interpret the Gospel, the priest, who is the witness of things to come, must keep a certain distance away from any political office or involvement.

In order that he may remain a valid sign of unity and be able to preach the Gospel in its entirety, the priest can sometimes be obliged to abstain from the exercise of his own right in this matter. Moreover, care must be taken lest his option appear to Christians to be the only legitimate one or become a cause of division among the faithful. Let priests be mindful of the laity's maturity, which is to be valued highly when it is a question of their specific role.

Leadership or active militancy on behalf of any political party is to be excluded by every priest unless, in concrete and exceptional circumstances, this is truly required by the good of the community, and receives the consent of the bishop after consultation with the priest's council and, if circumstances call for it, with the episcopal conference.

The priority of the specific mission which pervades the entire priestly existence must therefore always be kept in mind so that, with great confidence, and having a renewed experience of the things of God, priests may be able to announce these things efficaciously and with joy to the men who await them.

3. The Spiritual Life of Priests

Every priest will find in his very vocation and ministry the deep motivation for living his entire life in oneness and strength of spirit. Called like the rest of those who have been baptized to become a true image of Christ (cf. *Rom* 8:29), the priest, like the Apostles, shares besides in a special way companionship with Christ and his mission as the Supreme Pastor: "And he appointed twelve; they were to be his companions and to be sent out to preach" (*Mk* 3:14). Therefore in the priestly life there can be no dichotomy between love for Christ and zeal for souls.

Just as Christ, anointed by the Holy Spirit, was impelled by his deep love for his Father to give his life for men, so the priest, consecrated by the Holy Spirit, and in a special way made like to Christ the Priest, dedicates himself to the work of the Father performed through the Son. Thus the whole rule for the priest's life is expressed in the words of Jesus: "And for their sake I consecrate myself, that they also may be consecrated in truth" (*Jn* 17:19).

Following the example of Christ who was continually in prayer, and led by the Holy Spirit in whom we cry, "Abba, Father", priests should give themselves to the contemplation of the Word of God and daily take the opportunity to examine the events of life in the light of the Gospel, so that having become faithful and attentive hearers of the Word they may become true ministers of the Word. Let them be assiduous in personal prayer, in the Liturgy of the Hours, in frequent reception of the sacrament of penance and especially in devotion to the mystery of the Eucharist. Even if the Eucharist should be celebrated without participation by the faithful, it nevertheless remains the centre of the life of the entire Church and the heart of priestly existence.

With his mind raised to heaven and sharing in the communion of saints, the priest should very often turn to Mary the Mother of God, who received the Word of God with perfect faith, and daily ask her for the grace of conforming himself to her Son.

The activities of the apostolate for their part furnish an indispensable nourishment for fostering the spiritual life of the priest: "By assuming the role of the Good Shepherd, they will find precisely in the pastoral exercise of love the bond of priestly perfection which will unify their lives and activities" (*PO* 14). In the exercise of his ministry the priest is enlightened and strengthened by the action of the Church and the example of the faithful. The renunciations imposed by the pastoral life itself help him to acquire an ever greater sharing in Christ's Cross and hence a purer pastoral charity.

This same charity of priests will also cause them to adapt their spiritual lives to the modes and forms of sanctification which are more suitable and fitting for the men of their own times and culture. Desiring to be all things to all men, to save all (cf. *1 Cor* 9:22), the priest should be attentive to the inspiration of the Holy Spirit in these days. Thus he will announce the Word of God not only by human means but he will be taken as a valid instrument by the Word himself, whose message is "living and active and sharper than any two-edged sword" (*Heb* 4:12).

4. Celibacy

a) The basis for celibacy.

Celibacy for priests is in full harmony with the vocation to the apostolic following of Christ and also with the unconditional response of the person who is called and who undertakes pastoral service. Through celibacy, the priest, following his Lord, shows in a fuller way his availability, and embarking upon the way of the Cross with paschal joy he ardently desires to be consumed in an offering which can be compared to the Eucharist.

If celibacy is lived in the spirit of the Gospel, in prayer and vigilance, with poverty, joy, contempt of honours, and brotherly love, it is a sign which cannot long be hidden, but which effectively proclaims Christ to modern men also. For words today are scarcely heeded, but the witness of a life which displays the radical character of the Gospel has the power of exercising a strong attraction.

b) Convergence of motives.

Celibacy, as a personal option for some more important good, even a merely natural one, can promote the full maturity and integration of the human personality. This is all the more true in regard to celibacy undertaken for the Kingdom of heaven, as is evident in the lives of so many saints and of the faithful who, living the celibate life, dedicated themselves totally to promoting human and Christian progress for the sake of God and men.

Within modern culture, in which spiritual values are to a great extent obscured, the celibate priest indicates the presence of the Absolute God, who invites us to be renewed in his image. Where the value of sexuality is so exaggerated that genuine love is forgotten, celibacy for the sake of the Kingdom of Christ calls men back to the sublimity of faithful love and reveals the ultimate meaning of life.

Furthermore, one rightly speaks of the value of celibacy as an eschatological sign. By transcending every contingent human value, the celibate priest associates himself in a special way with Christ as the final and absolute good and shows forth, in anticipation, the freedom of the children of God. While the value of the sign and holiness of Christian marriage is fully recognized, celibacy for the sake of the Kingdom nevertheless more clearly displays that spiritual fruitfulness or generative power of the New Law by which the apostle knows that in Christ he is the father and mother of his communities.

From this special way of following Christ, the priest draws greater strength and power for the building up of the Church; and this power can be preserved and increased only by an intimate and permanent union with Christ's Spirit. The faithful people of God wish to see in their pastors this union with Christ, and they are able to recognize it.

Through celibacy, priests are more easily able to serve God with undivided heart and spend themselves for their sheep, and as a result they are able more fully to be promoters of evangelization and of the Church's unity. For this reason, priests, even if they are fewer in number, but are resplendent with this outstanding witness of life, will enjoy greater apostolic fruitfulness.

Priestly celibacy, furthermore, is not just the witness of one person alone, but by reason of the special fellowship linking members of the presbyterium it also takes on a social character as the witness of the whole priestly order enriching the People of God.

c) Celibacy to be kept in the Latin Church.

The traditions of the Eastern Churches shall remain unchanged, as they are now in force in the various territories.

The Church has the right and duty to determine the concrete form of the priestly ministry and therefore to select more suitable candidates, endowed with certain human and supernatural qualities. When the Latin Church demands celibacy as a necessary condition for the priesthood (cf. *PO* 16), she does not do so out of a belief that this way of life is the only path to attaining sanctification. She does so while carefully considering the concrete form of exercising the ministry in the community for the building up of the Church.

Because of the intimate and multiple coherence between the pastoral function and a celibate life, the existing law is upheld:

one who freely wills total availability, the distinctive characteristic of this function, also freely undertakes a celibate life. The
candidate should feel this form of living not as having been imposed from outside, but rather as a manifestation of his free self-
giving, which is accepted and ratified by the Church through the
bishop. In this way the law becomes a protection and safeguard
of the freedom wherewith the priest gives himself to Christ, and
it becomes "an easy yoke".

d) Conditions favouring celibacy.

We know well that in the world of today particular difficulties
threaten celibacy from all sides; priests have indeed already
repeatedly experienced them in the course of the centuries. But
they can overcome these difficulties if suitable conditions are
fostered, namely: growth of the interior life through prayer, renunciation and fervent love for God and one's neighbour and by
other aids to the spiritual life; human balance through well-
ordered integration into the fabric of social relationships; fraternal association and companionship with other priests and
with the bishop, through pastoral structures better suited to this
purpose and with the assistance also of the community of the
faithful.

It must be admitted that celibacy, as a gift of God, cannot be
preserved unless the candidate is adequately prepared for it.
From the beginning, candidates should give attention to the positive reasons for choosing celibacy, without letting themselves be
disturbed by objections, the accumulation and continual
pressure of which are rather a sign that the original value of
celibacy itself has been called in question. Let them also
remember that the power with which God strengthens us is
always available for those who strive to serve him faithfully and
entirely.

A priest who leaves the ministry should receive just and fraternal treatment; even though he can give assistance in the service
of the Church, he is not however to be admitted to the exercise of
priestly activities.

e) The Law of Celibacy.

The law of priestly celibacy existing in the Latin Church is to
be kept in its entirety (2).

f) The ordination of married men.

Two formulas were proposed to the vote of the Fathers: (3)

Formula A: Excepting always the right of the Supreme Pontiff, the priestly ordination of married men is not permitted,
even in particular cases.

Formula B: It belongs solely to the Supreme Pontiff, in

particular cases, by reason of pastoral needs and the good of the universal Church to allow the priestly ordination of married men, who are of mature age and proven life.

II. PRIESTS IN THE COMMUNION OF THE CHURCH

1. Relations Between Priests and Bishop

Priests will adhere more faithfully to their mission the more they know and show themselves to be faithful to ecclesial communion. Thus the pastoral ministry, which is exercised by bishops, priests and deacons, is an eminent sign of this ecclesial communion, in that they have received a special mandate to serve this communion.

But in order that this ministry may really become a sign of communion, the actual conditions in which it is exercised must be considered to be of the greatest importance.

The guiding principle expressed by the Second Vatican Council in the decree *Presbyterorum Ordinis,* namely that the very unity of consecration and mission requires the hierarchical communion of priests with the order of bishops, is considered fundamental to a practical restoration or renewal, with full confidence, of the mutual relationship between the bishop and the presbyterium over which the bishop presides. This principle is more concretely to be put into practice especially by the diligence of the bishops.

The service of authority on the one hand and the exercise of not merely passive obedience on the other should be carried out in a spirit of faith, mutual charity, filial and friendly confidence and constant and patient dialogue. Thus the collaboration and responsible cooperation of priests with the bishop will be sincere, human and at the same time supernatural (cf. *LG* 28; *CD* 15; *PO* 7).

Personal freedom, responding to the individual vocation and to the charism received from God, and also the ordered solidarity of all for the service of the community and the good of the mission to be fulfilled are two conditions which should shape the Church's proper mode of pastoral action (cf. *PO* 7). The guarantee of these conditions is the bishop's authority, to be exercised in a spirit of service.

The Council of Priests, which is of its nature something diocesan, is an institutional manifestation of the brotherhod among priests which has its basis in the sacrament of Orders.

The activity of this council cannot be fully shaped by law. Its effectiveness depends especially on a repeated effort to listen to the opinions of all in order to reach a consensus with the bishop, to whom it belongs to make the final decision.

If this is done with the greatest sincerity and humility, and if all onesidedness is overcome, it will be easier to provide properly for the common good.

The Priest's Council is an institution in which priests recognize, at a time when variety in the exercise of their ministry increases every day, that they are mutually complementary in serving one and the same mission of the Church.

It is the task of this Council, among other things, to seek out clear and distinctly defined aims, to suggest priorities, to indicate methods of acting, to assist whatever the Spirit frequently stirs up through individuals or groups, and to foster the spiritual life, whence the necessary unity may more easily be attained.

New forms of hierarchical communion between bishops and priests (cf. *PO* 7) must be found, to facilitate contacts between local Churches. A search must be made for ways whereby priests may collaborate with bishops in supra-diocesan bodies and enterprises.

The collaboration of religious priests with the bishop in the presbyterium is necessary, though their work is of valuable assistance to the universal Church.

2. Relations of Priests With Each Other

Since priests are bound together by an intimate sacramental brotherhood and by their mission, and since they work and plan together for the same task, some community of life or a certain association of life shall be encouraged among them and can take various forms, including non-institutional ones. This shall be allowed for by the law itself through opportune norms and by renewed or newly-discovered pastoral structures.

Priestly associations should also be fostered which in a spirit of ecclesial communion and being recognized by the competent ecclesiastical authority, "through an apt and properly approved rule of life and through brotherly assistance" (*PO* 8), seek to advance the aims which belong to their function and "holiness in the exercise of the ministry" *(ibid)*.

It is desirable that, as far as possible, ways be sought, even if they prove rather difficult, whereby associations which perhaps divide the clergy into factions may be brought back to communion and to the ecclesial structure.

There should be greater communication between religious

priests and diocesan priests, so that true priestly fraternity may exist between them and that they may provide one another with mutual help, especially in spiritual matters.

3. Relations Between Priests and Laity

Let priests remember "confidently to entrust to the laity duties in the service of the Church, allowing them freedom and room for action. In fact, on suitable occasions, they should invite them to undertake works on their own initiative" (PO 9). The Laity, "likewise sharing their cares, should help their priests by prayer and work to the extent possible, so that their priests can more readily overcome difficulties and be able to fulfil their duties more fruitfully" (ibid).

It is necessary to keep always in mind the special character of the Church's communion in order that personal freedom, in accordance with the recognized duties and charisms of each person, and the unity of life and activity of the People of God may be fittingly combined.

The pastoral council, in which specially chosen clergy, religious and lay people take part (cf. CD 27), furnishes by its study and reflection elements necessary for enabling the diocesan community to arrange its pastoral programme organically and to fulfil it effectively.

In proportion as the co-responsibility of bishops and priests daily increases (especially through priests' councils), the more desirable it becomes that a pastoral council be established in each diocese.

4. Economic Affairs

The economic questions of the Church cannot be adequately solved unless they are carefully examined within the context of the communion and mission of the People of God. All the faithful have the duty of assisting the Church's needs.

In treating these questions account must be taken not only of solidarity within the local Church, diocese or religious institute, but also of the condition of dioceses of the same region or nation, indeed of the whole world, especially of the Churches in the so-called mission territories, and of other poor regions.

The remuneration of priests, to be determined certainly in a spirit of evangelical poverty, but as far as possible equitable and sufficient, is a duty of justice and ought to include social security. Excessive differences in this matter must be removed, especially among priests of the same diocese or jurisdiction, account also being taken of the average condition of the people of the region.

It seems greatly to be desired that the Christian people be gradually instructed in such a way that priests' incomes may be separated from the acts of their ministry, especially sacramental ones.

CONCLUSION

To priests exercising the ministry of the Spirit (cf. *2 Cor* 3:4-12) in the midst of the communion of the entire Church, new ways are open for giving a profoundly renewed witness in today's world.

It is necessary therefore to look to the future with Christian confidence and to ask the Holy Spirit that by his guidance and inspiration doors may be opened to the Gospel, in spite of the dangers which the Church cannot overcome by merely human means.

Having always before our eyes the Apostles, especially Peter and Paul, as the examples for the renewal of the priesthood, we should give thanks to God the Father that he has given us all the opportunity of manifesting more faithfully the countenance of Christ.

Already there are true signs of a rebirth of spiritual life, while men everywhere, amid the uncertainties of modern times, look forward to fullness of life. This renewal certainly cannot take place without a sharing in the Lord's Cross, because the servant is not greater than his master (cf. *Jn* 13:16). Forgetting the past let us strive for what is still to come (cf. *Phil* 3:13).

With real daring we must show the world the fullness of the mystery hidden through all ages in God so that men through their sharing in it may be able to enter into the fullness of God (cf. *Eph* 3:19).

"We proclaim to you the eternal life which was with the Father and was made manifest to us—that which we have seen and heard we proclaim also to you, so that you may have fellowship with us; and our fellowship is with the Father and with his Son Jesus Christ" (*1Jn* 1:2-3).

---

*Translation by Vatican Press Office. Latin original in AAS 63 (1971), 898–942.

1. Tertulian, *De Praescr. Haer* XXI, 4; cf. also I Letter of Clement *Ad Cor.* XLII, 1-4; Ignatius of Antioch *Ad Magn.* VI and passim; Irenaeus *Adv. Haer.* 4, 21, 3; Origen *De Princip.* IV, 2, 1; Serapion,

Bishop of Antioch, in Eusebius *Hist. Eccl.* VI, 12.

2. Result of the vote on this proposition: *Placet* 168. *Non placet* 10. *Placet iuxta modum* 21. Abstentions 3.

3. According to the directives of the Presidents the vote was taken not by *Placet* or *Non placet,* but by the choice of the first or second formula. The first formula, *A,* obtained 107 votes; the second, *B,* obtained 87. There were 2 abstentions and also 2 null votes.

119

JUSTICE IN THE WORLD*

Synod of Bishops, *Convenientes ex universo*,
30 November, 1971

INTRODUCTION

Gathered from the whole world, in communion with all who believe in Christ and with the entire human family, and opening our hearts to the Spirit who is making the whole of creation new, we have questioned ourselves about the mission of the People of God to further justice in the world.

Scrutinizing the "signs of the times" and seeking to detect the meaning of emerging history, while at the same time sharing the aspirations and questionings of all those who want to build a more human world, we have listened to the Word of God that we might be converted to the fulfilling of the divine plan for the salvation of the world.

Even though it is not for us to elaborate a very profound analysis of the situation of the world, we have nevertheless been able to perceive the serious injustices which are building around the world of men a network of domination, oppression and abuses which stifle freedom and which keep the greater part of humanity from sharing in the building up and enjoyment of a more just and more fraternal world.

At the same time we have noted the inmost stirring moving the world in its depths. There are facts constituting a contribution to the furthering of justice. In associations of men and among peoples themselves there is arising a new awareness which shakes them out of any fatalistic resignation and which spurs them on to liberate themselves and to be responsible for their own destiny. Movements among men are seen which express hope in a better world and a will to change whatever has become intolerable.

Listening to the cry of those who suffer violence and are oppressed by unjust systems and structures, and hearing the appeal of a world that by its perversity contradicts the plan of its Creator, we have shared our awareness of the Church's vocation to be present in the heart of the world by proclaiming the Good News to the poor, freedom to the oppressed, and joy to the afflicted. The hopes and forces which are moving the world in its very foundations are not foreign to the dynamism of the Gospel, which through the power of the Holy Spirit frees men from personal sin and from its consequences in social life.

The uncertainty of history and the painful convergences in the ascending path of the human community direct us to sacred history; there God has revealed himself to us, and made known to us, as it is brought progressively to realization, his plan of liberation and salvation which is once and for all fulfilled in the Paschal Mystery of Christ. Action on behalf of justice and participation in the transformation of the world fully appear to us as a constitutive dimension of the preaching of the Gospel, or, in other words, of the Church's mission for the redemption of the human race and its liberation from every oppressive situation.

I. JUSTICE AND WORLD SOCIETY

The world in which the Church lives and acts is held captive by a tremendous paradox. Never before have the forces working for bringing about a unified world society appeared so powerful and dynamic; they are rooted in the awareness of the full basic equality as well as of the human dignity of all. Since men are members of the same human family, they are indissolubly linked with one another in the one destiny of the whole world, in the responsibility for which they all share.

The new technological possibilities are based upon the unity of science, on the global and simultaneous character of communications and on the birth of an absolutely interdependent economic world. Moreover, men are beginning to grasp a new and more radical dimension of unity; for they perceive that their resources, as well as the precious treasures of air and water—without which there cannot be life—and the small delicate biosphere of the whole complex of all life on earth, are not infinite, but on the contrary must be saved and preserved as a unique patrimony belonging to all mankind.

The paradox lies in the fact that within this perspective of unity the forces of division and antagonism seem today to be increasing in strength. Ancient divisions between nations and empires, between races and classes, today possess new technological instruments of destruction. The arms race is a threat to man's highest good, which is life; it makes poor peoples and individuals yet more miserable, while making richer those already powerful; it creates a continuous danger of conflagration, and in the case of nuclear arms, it threatens to destroy all life from the face of the earth. At the same time new divisions are being born to separate man from his neighbour. Unless combatted and overcome by social and political action, the influence of the new industrial and technological order favours the concentration of wealth, power and decision-making in the hands of a small public or private controlling group. Economic injustice and lack of social participation keep a man from attaining his basic human and civil rights.

In the last twenty-five years a hope has spread through the human race that economic growth would bring about such a quantity of goods that it would be possible to feed the hungry at least with the crumbs falling from the table, but this has proved a vain hope in underdeveloped areas and in pockets of poverty in wealthier areas, because of the rapid growth of population and of the labour force, because of rural stagnation and the lack of agrarian reform, and because of the massive migratory flow to the cities, where the industries, even though endowed with huge sums of money, nevertheless provide so few jobs that not infrequently one worker in four is left unemployed. These stifling oppressions constantly give rise to great numbers of "marginal" persons, ill-fed, inhumanly housed, illiterate and deprived of political power as well as of the suitable means of acquiring responsibility and moral dignity.

Furthermore, such is the demand for resources and energy by the richer nations, whether capitalist or socialist, and such are the effects of dumping by them in the atmosphere and the sea that irreparable damage would be done to the essential elements of life on earth, such as air and water, if their high rates of consumption and pollution, which are constantly on the increase, were extended to the whole of mankind.

The strong drive towards global unity, the unequal distribution which places decisions concerning three quarters of income, investment and trade in the hands of one third of the human race, namely the more highly developed part, the insufficiency of a merely economic progress, and the new recognition of the material limits of the biosphere—all this makes us aware of the fact that in today's world new modes of understanding human dignity are arising.

In the face of international systems of domination, the bringing about of justice depends more and more on the determined will for development.

In the developing nations and in the so-called socialist world, that determined will asserts itself especially in a struggle for forms of claiming one's rights and self-expression, a struggle caused by the evolution of the economic system itself.

This aspiring to justice asserts itself in advancing beyond the threshold at which begins a consciousness of enhancement of personal worth (cf. *Populorum Progressio* 15; *A.A.S.* 59, 1967, p. 265) with regard both to the whole man and the whole of mankind. This is expressed in an awareness of the right to development. The right to development must be seen as a dynamic interpenetration of all those fundamental human rights upon which the aspiration of individuals and nations are based.

This desire however will not satisfy the expectations of our time if it ignores the objective obstacles which social structures place in the way of conversion of hearts, or even of the realization of the ideal of charity. It demands on the contrary that the general condition of being marginal in society be overcome, so that an end will be put to the systematic barriers and vicious circles which oppose the collective advance towards enjoyment of adequate remuneration of the factors of production, and which strengthen the situation of discrimination with regard to access to opportunities and collective services from which a great part of the people are now excluded. If the developing nations and regions do not attain liberation through development, there is a real danger that the conditions of life created especially by colonial domination may evolve into a new form of colonialism in which the developing nations will be the victims of the interplay of international economic forces. That right to development is above all a right to hope according to the concrete measure of contemporary humanity. To respond to such a hope, the concept of evolution must be purified of those myths and false convictions which have up to now gone with a thought-pattern subject to a kind of deterministic and automatic notion of progress.

By taking their future into their own hands through a determined will for progress, the developing peoples—even if they do not achieve the final goal—will authentically manifest their own personalization. And in order that they may cope with the unequal relationships within the present world complex, a certain responsible nationalism gives them the impetus needed to acquire an identity of their own. From this basic self-determination can come attempts at putting together new political groupings allowing full development to these peoples; there can also come measures necessary for overcoming the inertia which could render fruitless such an effort—as in some cases population pressure; there can also come new sacrifices which the growth of planning demands of a generation which wants to build its own future.

On the other hand, it is impossible to conceive true progress without recognizing the necessity—within the political system chosen—of a development composed both of economic growth and participation; and the necessity too of an increase in wealth implying as well social progress by the entire community as it overcomes regional imbalance and islands of prosperity. Participation constitutes a right which is to be applied both in the economic and in the social and political field.

While we again affirm the right of people to keep their own identity, we see ever more clearly that the fight against a modernization destructive of the proper characteristics of nations remains quite ineffective as long as it appeals only to sacred historical customs and venerable ways of life. If modernization is accepted with the intention that it serve the good of the nation, men will be able to create a culture which will constitute a true heritage of their own in the manner of a true social memory, one which is active and formative of authentic creative personality in the assembly of nations.

We see in the world a set of injustices which constitute the nucleus of today's problems and whose solution requires the undertaking of tasks and functions in every sector of society, and even on the level of the global society towards which we are speeding in this last quarter of the twentieth century. Therefore we must be prepared to take on new functions and new duties in every sector of human activity and especially in the sector of world society, if justice is really to be put into practice. Our action is to be directed above all at those men and nations which because of various forms of oppression and because of the present character of our society are silent, indeed voiceless, victims of injustice.

Take, for example, the case of migrants. They are often forced to leave their own country to find work, but frequently find the doors closed in their faces because of discriminatory attitudes, or, if they can enter, they are often obliged to lead an insecure life or are treated in an inhuman manner. The same is true of groups that are less well off on the social ladder such as workers and especially farm workers who play a very great part in the process of development.

To be especially lamented is the condition of so many millions of refugees, and of every group of people suffering persecution—sometimes in institutionalized form—for racial or ethnic origin or on tribal grounds. This persecution on tribal grounds can at times take on the characteristics of genocide.

In many areas justice is seriously injured with regard to people who are suffering persecution for their faith, or who are in many ways being ceaselessly subjected by political parties and public authorities to an action of oppressive atheization, or who are deprived of religious liberty either by being kept from honouring God in public worship, or by being prevented from publicly teaching and spreading their faith, or by being prohibited from conducting their temporal affairs according to the principles of their religion.

Justice is also being violated by forms of oppression, both old and new, springing from restriction of the rights of individuals. This is occurring both in the form of repression by the political power and of violence on the part of private reaction, and can reach the extreme of affecting the basic conditions of personal integrity. There are well known cases of torture, especially of political prisoners, who besides are frequently denied due process or who are subjected to arbitrary procedures in their trial. Nor can we pass over the prisoners of war who even after the Geneva Convention are being treated in an inhuman manner.

The fight against legalized abortion and against the imposition of contraceptives and the pressures exerted against war are significant forms of defending the right to life.

Furthermore, contemporary consciousness demands truth in the communications systems, including the right to the image offered by the media and the opportunity to correct its manipulation. It must be stressed that the right, especially that of children and the young, to education and to morally correct conditions of life and communications media is once again being threatened in our days. The activity of families in social life is rarely and insufficiently recognized by State institutions. Nor should we forget the growing number of persons who are often abandoned by their families and by the community: the old, orphans, the sick and all kinds of people who are rejected.

To obtain true unity of purpose, as is demanded by the world society of men, a mediatory role is essential to overcome day by day the opposition, obstacles and ingrained privileges which are to be met with in the advance towards a more human society.

But effective mediation involves the creation of a lasting atmosphere of dialogue. A contribution to the progressive realization of this can be made by men unhampered by geo-political, ideological or socioeconomic conditions or by the generation gap. To restore the meaning of life by adherence to authentic values, the participation and witness of the rising generation of youth is as necessary as communication among peoples.

II. THE GOSPEL MESSAGE AND THE MISSION OF THE CHURCH

In the face of the present-day situation of the world, marked as it is by the grave sin of injustice, we recognize both our responsibility and our inability to overcome it by our own strength. Such a situation urges us to listen with a humble and open heart to the word of God, as he shows us new paths towards action in the cause of justice in the world.

In the Old Testament God reveals himself to us as the liberator of the oppressed and the defender of the poor, demanding from man faith in him and justice towards man's neighbour. It is only in the observance of the duties of justice that God is truly recognized as the liberator of the oppressed.

By his action and teaching Christ united in an indivisible way the relationship of man to God and the relationship of man to other men. Christ lived his life in the world as a total giving of himself to God for the salvation and liberation of men. In his preaching he proclaimed the fatherhood of God towards all men and the intervention of God's justice on behalf of the needy and the oppressed (*Lk.* 6:21-23). In this way he identified himself with his "least brethren," as he stated: "As you did it to one of the least of these my brethren, you did it to me" (*Mt.* 25:40).

From the beginning the Church has lived and understood the Death and Resurrection of Christ as a call by God to conversion in the faith of Christ and in fraternal love, perfected in mutual help even to the point of a voluntary sharing of material goods.

Faith in Christ, the Son of God and the Redeemer, and love of neighbour constitute a fundamental theme of the writers of the New Testament. According to St. Paul, the whole of the Christian life is summed up in faith effecting that love and service of neighbour which involve the fulfillment of the demands of justice. The Christian lives under the interior law of liberty, which is a permanent call to man to turn away from self-sufficiency to confidence in God and from concern for self to sincere love of neighbour. Thus takes place his genuine liberation and the gift of himself for the freedom of others.

According to the Christian message, therefore, man's relationship to his neighbour is bound up with his relationship to God; his response to the love of God, saving us through Christ, is shown to be effective in his love and service of men. Christian love implies an absolute demand for justice, namely a recognition of the dignity and rights of one's neighbour. Justice attains its inner fullness only in love. Because every man is truly a visible image of the invisible God and a brother of Christ, the Christian finds in every man God himself and God's absolute demand for justice and love.

The present situation of the world, seen in the light of faith, calls us back to the very essence of the Christian message, creating in us a deep awareness of its true meaning and of its urgent demands. The mission of preaching the Gospel dictates at the present time that we should dedicate ourselves to the liberation of man even in his present existence in this world. For unless the Christian message of love and justice shows its effectiveness through action in the cause of justice in the world, it will only with difficulty gain credibility with the men of our times.

The Church has received from Christ the mission of preaching the Gospel message, which contains a call to man to turn away from sin to the love of the Fathers, universal brotherhood and a consequent demand for justice in the world. This is the reason why the Church has the right, indeed the duty, to proclaim justice on the social, national and international level, and to denounce instances of injustice, when the fundamental rights of man and his very salvation demand it. The Church, indeed, is not alone responsible for justice in the world; however, she has a proper and specific responsibility which is identified with her mission of giving witness before the world of the need for love and justice contained in the Gospel message, a witness to be carried out in Church institutions themselves and in the lives of Christians.

Of itself it does not belong to the Church, insofar as she is a religious and hierarchical community, to offer concrete solutions in the social, economic and political spheres for justice in the world. Her mission involves defending and promoting the dignity and fundamental rights of the human person.

The members of the Church, as members of society, have the same right and duty to promote the common good as do other citizens. Christians ought to fulfill their temporal obligations with fidelity and competence. They should act as a leaven in the world, in their family, professional, social, cultural and political life. They must accept their responsibilities in this entire area under the influence of the Gospel and the teaching of the Church. In this way they testify to the power of the Holy Spirit through their action in the service of men in those things which are decisive for the existence and the future of humanity. While in such activities they generally act on their own initiative without involving the responsibility of the ecclesiastical hierarchy, in a sense they do involve the responsibility of the Church whose members they are.

III. THE PRACTICE OF JUSTICE

Many Christians are drawn to give authentic witness on behalf of justice by various modes of action for justice, action inspired by love in accordance with the grace which they have received from God. For some of them, this action finds its place in the sphere of social and political conflicts in which Christians bear witness to the Gospel by pointing out that in history there are sources of progress other than conflict, namely love and right. This priority of love in history draws other Christians to prefer the way of non-violent action and work in the area of public opinion.

While the Church is bound to give witness to justice, she recognizes that anyone who ventures to speak to people about justice must first be just in their eyes. Hence we must undertake an examination of the modes of acting and of the possessions and life style found within the Church herself.

Within the Church rights must be preserved. No one should be deprived of his ordinary rights because he is associated with the Church in one way or another. Those who serve the Church by their labour, including priests and religious, should receive a sufficient livelihood and enjoy that social security which is customary in their region. Lay people should be given fair wages and a system for promotion. We reiterate the recommendations that lay people should exercise more important functions with regard to Church property and should share in its administration.

We also urge that women should have their own share of responsibility and participation in the community life of society and likewise of the Church.

We propose that this matter be subjected to a serious study employing adequate means: for instance, a mixed commission of men and women, religious and lay people, of differing situations and competence.

The Church recognizes everyone's right to suitable freedom

of expression and thought. This includes the right of everyone to be heard in a spirit of dialogue which preserves a legitimate diversity within the Church.

The form of judicial procedure should give the accused the right to know his accusers and also the right to a proper defence. To be complete, justice should include speed in its procedure. This is especially necessary in marriage cases.

Finally, the members of the Church should have some share in the drawing up of decisions, in accordance with the rules given by the Second Vatican Ecumenical Council and the Holy See, for instance with regard to the setting up of councils at all levels.

In regard to temporal possessions, whatever be their use, it must never happen that the evangelical witness which the Church is required to give becomes ambiguous. The preservation of certain positions of privilege must constantly be submitted to the test of principle. Although in general it is difficult to draw a line between what is needed for right use and what is demanded by prophetic witness, we must certainly keep firmly to this principle: our faith demands of us a certain sparingness in use, and the Church is obliged to live and administers its own goods in such a way that the Gospel is proclaimed to the poor. If instead the Church appears to be among the rich and the powerful of this world its credibility is diminished.

Our examination of conscience now comes to the life style of all: bishops, priests, religious and lay people. In the case of needy peoples it must be asked whether belonging to the Church places people on a rich island within an ambient of poverty. In societies enjoying a higher level of consumer spending, it must be asked whether our life style exemplifies that sparingness with regard to consumption which we preach to others as necessary in order that so many millions of hungry people throughout the world may be fed.

Christians' specific contribution to justice is the day-to-day life of the individual believer acting like the leaven of the Gospel in his family, his school, his work and his social and civic life. Included with this are the perspectives and meaning which the faithful can give to human effort. Accordingly, educational method must be such as to teach men to live their lives in its entire reality and in accord with the evangelical principles of personal and social morality which are expressed in the vital Christian witness of one's life.

The obstacles to the progress which we wish for ourselves and for mankind are obvious. The method of education very frequently still in use today encourages narrow individualism. Part of the human family lives immersed in a mentality which exalts possessions. The school and the communications media, which are often obstructed by the established order, allow the formation only of the man desired by that order, that is to say, man in its image, not a new man but a copy of man as he is.

But education demands a renewal of heart, a renewal based on the recognition of sin in its individual and social manifestations. It will also inculcate a truly and entirely human way of life in justice, love and simplicity. It will likewise awaken a critical sense, which will lead us to reflect on the society in which we live and on its values; it will make men ready to renounce these values when they cease to promote justice for all men. In the developing countries, the principal aim of this education for justice consists in an attempt to awaken consciences to a knowledge of the concrete situation and in a call to secure a total improvement; by these means the transformation of the world has already begun.

Since this education makes men decidedly more human, it will help them to be no longer the object of manipulation by communications media or political forces. It will instead enable them to take in hand their own destinies and bring about communities which are truly human.

Accordingly, this education is deservedly called a continuing education, for it concerns every person and every age. It is also a practical education: it comes through action, participation and vital contact with the reality of injustice.

Education for justice is imparted first in the family. We are well aware that not only Church institutions but also other schools, trade unions and political parties are collaborating in this.

The content of this education necessarily involves respect for the person and for his dignity. Since it is world justice which is in question here, the unity of the human family within which, according to God's plan, a human being is born must first of all be seriously affirmed. Christians find a sign of this solidarity in the fact that all human beings are destined to become in Christ sharers in the divine nature.

The basic principles whereby the influence of the Gospel has made itself felt in contemporary social life are to be found in the body of teaching set out in a gradual and timely way from the encyclical *Rerum novarum* to the letter *Octogesima Adveniens*. As never before, the Church has, through the Second Vatican Council's constitution *Gaudium et Spes,* better understood the situation in the modern world, in which the Christian works out his salvation by deeds of justice. *Pacem in Terris* gave us an authentic charter of human rights. In *Mater et Magistra* international justice begins to take first place; it finds more elaborate expression in *Populorum Progressio,* in the form of a true and suitable treatise on the right to development, and in *Octogesima Adveniens* is found a summary of guidelines for political action.

Like the apostle Paul, we insist, welcome or unwelcome, that the Word of God should be present in the centre of human situations. Our interventions are intended to be an expression of that faith which is today binding on our lives and on the lives of the faithful. We all desire that these interventions should always be in conformity with circumstances of place and time. Our mission demands that we should courageously denounce injustice, with charity, prudence and firmness, in sincere dialogue with all parties concerned. We know that our denunciations can secure assent to the extent that they are an expression of our lives and are manifested in continuous action.

The liturgy, which we preside over and which is the heart of the Church's life, can greatly serve education for justice. For it is a thanksgiving to the Father in Christ, which through its communitarian form places before our eyes the bonds of our brotherhood and again and again reminds us of the Church's mission. The liturgy of the world, catechesis and the celebration of the sacraments have the power to help us to discover the teaching of the prophets, the Lord and the Apostles on the subject of justice. The preparation for baptism is the beginning of the formation of the Christian conscience. The practice of penance should emphasize the social dimension of sin and of the sacrament. Finally, the Eucharist forms the community and places it at the service of men.

That the Church may really be the sign of that solidarity which the family of nations desires, it should show in its own life greater cooperation between the Churches of rich and poor regions through spiritual communion and division of human and material resources. The present generous arrangements for assistance between Churches could be made more effective by real coordination (Sacred Congregation for the Evangelization of Peoples and the Pontifical Council "*Cor Unum*"), through their overall view in regard to the common administration of the gifts of God, and through fraternal solidarity, which would always encourage autonomy and responsibility on the part of the beneficiaries in the determination of criteria and the choice of concrete programmes and their realization.

This planning must in no way be restricted to economic programmes; it should instead stimulate activities capable of developing that human and spiritual formation which will serve as the leaven needed for the integral development of the human being.

Well aware of what has already been done in this field, together with the Second Vatican Ecumenical Council we very highly commend cooperation with our separated Christian brethren for the promotion of justice in the world, for bringing about development of peoples and for establishing peace. This cooperation concerns first and foremost activities for securing human dignity and man's fundamental rights, especially the right to religious liberty. This is the source of our common efforts against discrimination on the grounds of differences of religion, race and colour, culture and the like. Collaboration extends also to the study of the teaching of the Gospel insofar as it is the source of inspiration for all Christian activity. Let the Secretariat for Promoting Christian Unity and the Pontifical Commission for Justice and Peace devote themselves in common counsel to developing effectively this ecumenical collaboration.

In the same spirit we likewise commend collaboration with all believers in God in the fostering of social justice, peace and freedom; indeed we commend collaboration also with those who, even though they do not recognize the Author of the world, nevertheless, in their esteem for human values, seek justice sincerely and by honourable means.

Since the Synod is of a universal character, it is dealing with those questions of justice which directly concern the entire human family. Hence, recognizing the importance of international cooperation for social and economic development, we praise above all else the inestimable work which has been done among the poorer peoples by the local Churches, the missionaries and the organizations supporting them; and we intend to foster those initiatives and institutions which are working for peace, international justice and the development of man. We therefore urge Catholics to consider well the following propositions:

1. Let recognition be given to the fact that international order is rooted in the inalienable rights and dignity of the human being. Let the United Nations Declaration of Human Rights be ratified by all Governments who have not yet adhered to it, and let it be fully observed by all.

2. Let the United Nations—which because of its unique purpose should promote participation by all nations—and international organizations be supported insofar as they are the beginning of a system capable of restraining the armaments

race, discouraging trade in weapons, securing disarmament and settling conflicts by peaceful methods of legal action, arbitration and international police action. It is absolutely necessary that international conflicts should not be settled by war, but that other methods better befitting human nature should be found. Let a strategy of non-violence be fostered also, and let conscientious objection be recognized and regulated by law in each nation.

3. Let the aims of the Second Development Decade be fostered. These include the transfer of a precise percentage of the annual income of the richer countries to the developing nations, fairer prices for raw materials, the opening of the markets of the richer nations and, in some fields, preferential treatment for exports of manufactured goods from the developing nations. These aims represent first guidelines for a graduated taxation of income as well as for an economic and social plan for the entire world. We grieve whenever richer nations turn their backs on this ideal goal of worldwide sharing and responsibility. We hope that no such weakening of international solidarity will take away their force from the trade discussions being prepared by the United Nations Conference on Trade and Development (UNCTAD).

4. The concentration of power which consists in almost total domination of economics, research, investment, freight charges, sea transport and securities should be progressively balanced by institutional arrangements for strengthening power and opportunities with regard to responsible decision by the developing nations and by full and equal participation in international organizations concerned with development. Their recent *de facto* exclusion from discussions on world trade and also the monetary arrangements which vitally affect their destiny are an example of lack of power which is inadmissible in a just and responsible world order.

5. Although we recognize that international agencies can be perfected and strengthened, as can any human instrument, we stress also the importance of the specialized agencies of the United Nations, in particular those directly concerned with the immediate and more acute questions of world poverty in the field of agrarian reform and agricultural development, health, education, employment, housing, and rapidly increasing urbanization. We feel we must point out in a special way the need for some fund to provide sufficient food and protein for the real mental and physical development of children. In the face of the population explosion we repeat the words by which Pope Paul VI defined the functions of public authority in his encyclical

Populorum Progressio: "There is no doubt that public authorities can intervene, within the limit of their competence, by favouring the availability of appropriate information and by adopting suitable measures, provided that these can be in conformity with the moral law and that they absolutely respect the rightful freedom of married couples" (37; *A.A.S.* 59, 1967, p. 276).

6. Let the governments continue with their individual contributions to a development fund, but let them also look for a way whereby most of their endeavours may follow multilateral channels, fully preserving the responsibility of the developing nations, which must be associated in decision-making concerning priorities and investments.

7. We consider that we must also stress the new worldwide preoccupation which will be dealt with for the first time in the conference on the human environment to be held in Stockholm in June 1972. It is impossible to see what right the richer nations have to keep up their claim to increase their own material demands, if the consequence is either that others remain in misery or that the danger of destroying the very physical foundations of life on earth is precipitated. Those who are already rich are bound to accept a less material way of life, with less waste, in order to avoid the destruction of the heritage which they are obliged by absolute justice to share with all other members of the human race.

8. In order that the right to development may be fulfilled by action:

a) people should not be hindered from attaining development in accordance with their own culture;

b) through mutual cooperation, all peoples should be able to become the principal architects of their own economic and social development;

c) every people, as active and responsible members of human society, should be able to cooperate for the attainment of the common good on an equal footing with other peoples.

The examination of conscience which we have made together, regarding the Church's involvement in action for justice, will remain ineffective if it is not given flesh in the life of our local Churches at all their levels. We also ask the episcopal conferences to continue to pursue the perspectives which we have had in view during the days of this meeting and to put our recommendations into practice, for instance by setting up centres of social and theological research.

We also ask that there be recommended to the Pontifical Commission for Justice and Peace, the Council of the Secretariat of the Synod and to competent authorities, the description, consideration and deeper study of the wishes and desires of our assembly, and that these bodies should bring to a successful conclusion what we have begun.

IV. A WORD OF HOPE

The power of the Spirit, who raised Christ from the dead, is continuously at work in the world. Through the generous sons and daughters of the Church likewise, the People of God is present in the midst of the poor and of those who suffer oppression and persecution; it lives in its own flesh and its own heart the Passion of Christ and bears witness to his resurrection.

The entire creation has been groaning till now in an act of giving birth, as it waits for the glory of the children of God to be revealed (cf. *Rom.* 8:22). Let Christians therefore be convinced that they will yet find the fruits of their own nature and effort cleansed of all impurities in the new earth which God is now preparing for them, and in which there will be the kingdom of justice and love, a kingdom which will be fully perfected when the Lord will come himself.

Hope in the coming kingdom is already beginning to take root in the hearts of men. The radical transformation of the world in the Paschal Mystery of the Lord gives full meaning to the efforts of men, and in particular of the young, to lessen injustice, violence and hatred and to advance all together in justice, freedom, brotherhood and love.

At the same time as it proclaims the Gospel of the Lord, its Redeemer and Saviour, the Church calls on all, especially the poor, the oppressed and the afflicted, to cooperate with God to bring about liberation from every sin and to build a world which will reach the fullness of creation only when it becomes the work of man for man.

*Translation by Vatican Press Office. Latin text in *E.V.* 4, nn. 1238–1308.

120

EVANGELIZATION IN THE MODERN WORLD*

Paul VI, *Evangelii nuntiandi*, 8 December, 1975

1. The preaching of the gospel to the men of our times, full as they are of hope, but harassed by fear and anxiety, must undoubtedly be regarded as a duty which will redound to the benefit, not only of the Christian community, but of the whole human race.

The duty of giving encouragement to the brethren has been entrusted to us by Christ Our Lord as appertaining to the function of the successor of Peter[1] and we regard it as a part of 'the daily pressure of my anxiety'[2] as the motive of our life and activity and as a primary duty of our pontificate. This duty seems to us to assume a special urgency and importance when we are encouraging our brethren in the work of evangelization so that in these uncertain and disturbed times they may apply themselves to this activity with ever increasing love, zeal and joy.

2. This is what we wish to do now at the close of the Holy Year in the course of which the church, striving to proclaim the gospel to all men[3] has sought to fulfil its function as the herald of the good news brought to us by Christ and promulgated through her by virtue of these two fundamental exhortations: 'Put on the new nature'[4] and 'Be reconciled to God'.[5] Furthermore, the tenth anniversary of the closing of the second Vatican Council seems a fitting occasion for this exhortation. Its teaching can be summed up in this single objective: to ensure that the church of the twentieth century may emerge ever better equipped to proclaim the gospel to the people of this century. We are undertaking this task one year after the assembly of the third general synod of bishops, whose deliberations, as is well known, were devoted to the question of evangelization, and we undertake it all the more readily because we have been asked to do so by the fathers of that synod.

In fact, when the synod had concluded its meetings, the fathers decided to place the results of their deliberations in the hands of the Pastor of the Universal Church in a spirit of simplicity and confidence, saying that they looked to the Roman Pontiff to provide a new stimulus which would introduce the church, now more thoroughly imbued with the strength and power of Pentecost, into a new and more fruitful era of evangelization.[6]

3. We have repeatedly stressed the importance of this question of evangelization long before the holding of the synod. Speaking to the College of Cardinals on 22 June 1973 we said: 'The conditions of society today require us all to revise our methods and to seek out with all our energy new ways and means by which the Christian message may be brought to the men of our times, for it is only in this message that they can find the answer to their doubts and the inspiration to carry out the obligations arising from their mutual dependency'.[7] And we added that in order to respond to the demands of the Council, as was our duty, it was absolutely necessary to keep before our minds the heritage of the faith which the church must transmit whole and entire, and at the same time seek to present this heritage to the men of our time in a form which is at once clear and convincing.

4. The whole problem of evangelization depends on our fidelity to the message of which we are servants, and to mankind to whom it is our duty to transmit that vital, universal message. This raises three difficult questions to which the fathers of the synod of 1974 gave the gravest consideration:

What is the effectiveness today of that innate force of the gospel message which can penetrate to the depth of man's conscience? To what extent and in what manner is the power of the gospel able to transform the minds of the men of this century? What methods and approaches should we employ in preaching the gospel to ensure that it will achieve its full effect?

These queries go to the root of the question which the church is asking herself today. It may be expressed in these words: whether, after the Council and thanks to the Council, which may be described as the hour of God in the annals of recent history, the church does or does not find herself better equipped to announce the gospel message and to implant it with conviction, effectively and in liberty of spirit in the hearts of men?

5. We all appreciate the necessity of giving a sincere, humble and courageous answer to this question and of basing our course of action on the reply. 'In our anxiety for all the churches'[8] we

wish to offer our help to our brethren and to our sons in answering these questions. May these words of ours regarding the problem of evangelization, based as they are on the rich fruits of the synod, be an encouragement to the whole people of God united in the church to undertake similar reflections. May they arouse a new zeal in all and especially in those 'who labour in preaching and teaching'⁹ so that each one of them may make himself one who 'rightly handles the word of truth'¹⁰ and acquits himself perfectly of his ministry in carrying out the work of evangelization.

It has seemed to us of vital importance to make an exhortation of this kind because the promulgation of the gospel message is not something which the church may undertake or neglect at her discretion; it is rather the function and duty imposed on her by Our Lord Jesus Christ so that all may believe and achieve salvation. The gospel message is, therefore, necessary; it is unique; it is irreplaceable. It does not admit of any indifference, of any accommodation to the principles of other religious beliefs or of any compromise, for on it depends the whole issue of man's salvation and in it are contained all the splendours of divine revelation. It expresses a wisdom not of this world and by virtue of its content evokes the spirit of faith—a faith which rests on the power of God.¹¹ It is truth itself and it is fitting, therefore, that the herald of that truth should consecrate to its cause all his time, all his strength and, if the occasion arises, his very life.

1. FROM CHRIST THE EVANGELIZER TO THE EVANGELIZING CHURCH

6. The testimony which Christ Our Lord has given of himself and which St. Luke has recorded in his gospel: 'I must preach the good news of the kingdom of God'¹² is of the utmost importance because it sums up in a word the whole mission and mandate of Jesus: 'I was sent for this purpose'.¹³ These words assume their full significance in the context of the preceding verses of the gospel in which Christ applies to himself the words of the prophet Isaiah: 'The Spirit of the Lord is upon me because he has anointed me; he has sent me to preach the good news to the poor'.¹⁴ To bring the good news from city to city and especially to the poor, who are often better disposed to receive it, so that it might be proclaimed that the promises of the New Covenant made by God had been fulfilled, this was the special mission for the accomplishment of which Jesus declared that he had been sent by the Father. All the elements of the mystery of Christ: the Incarnation itself, his miracles, his teaching, his call-

ing of the disciples, the sending forth of the apostles, the Cross and the Resurrection, his enduring presence among his own, all were predetermined in view of the activity of preaching the gospel.

7.   During the meetings of the synod the bishops repeatedly stressed the fact that Jesus himself, the Revelation of God,[15] was the first and principal herald of the gospel. This he was until the end, until the consummation in the sacrifice of his human life.

To proclaim the gospel. What meaning did Christ attach to this mandate which had been given to him? It is not possible to state in brief and precise terms what exactly this evangelization is, what elements it comprises, by what means it may be accomplished, how Christ understood it and how he put it into effect. It is not possible to achieve an adequate synthesis; it must suffice for us to record some essential aspects.

8.   Christ, as the herald of the gospel, announces first of all the kingdom, that is the kingdom of God, and to this he attributes such essential importance that all else becomes 'those other things which shall be yours without the asking'.[16] The kingdom of God is to be considered, therefore, as the absolute good so that everything else is subordinate to it. It is the pleasure of Christ to describe in many ways the joy of belonging to this kingdom and this happiness comprises many things which the world rejects.[17] He elaborates the requirements of this kingdom and its Magna Charta,[18] its heralds,[19] its mysteries,[20] the status of little children in it[21] and the vigilance and fidelity required of all who assist its coming.[22]

9.   Christ proclaims salvation as the outstanding element and, as it were, the central point of his good news. This is the great gift of God which is to be considered as comprising not merely liberation from all those things by which man is oppressed but especially liberation from sin and from the domination of the evil one, a liberation which incorporates that gladness enjoyed by every man who knows God and is known by him, who sees God and who surrenders himself trustingly to him. All this is inaugurated in the course of the life of Christ and established definitively by his death and resurrection, but it must be patiently promoted in the course of history until it is fully realized on the day of the final coming of Christ, a day the time of which is known to no one but the Father.[23]

10. This kingdom and this salvation—these words may be regarded as the key to a full understanding of the evangelization of Jesus Christ—may be received by all men as the fruits of grace and mercy, but at the same time each man must achieve them by

force: 'men of violence take them by force'[24] as the Lord says. They must achieve them by labour and sorrows, by a life lived according to the standards of the gospel, by self-denial and the cross in the spirit of the beatitudes of the gospel. But above all each individual can achieve them by a total spiritual renewal of himself which the gospel calls *metanoia*, that is by a conversion of the whole man by virtue of which there is a radical change of mind and heart.[25]

11. This proclamation of the kingdom of God by Christ is achieved by the assiduous preaching of the word—a word which is peerless:'Here is a teaching that is new and with authority behind it.'[26] 'And all spoke well of him and wondered at the gracious words which came from his lips'.[27] 'No man ever spoke like this man'.[28] For the words of Christ reveal the secrets of God, his plan and his promises and thereby change the heart of man and his destiny.

12. Christ also proclaims his message by means of innumerable signs which arouse the wonder of the multitudes and at the same time draw them to him in their desire to see him, to hear him and to be transformed by his works. These include the curing of the sick, the changing of water into wine, the multiplication of the loaves, the raising of the dead to life. One sign in particular stands out among all those to which he attributes a special importance: the weak and the poor are evangelized; they become his disciples, come together 'in his name' and form the great community of those who believe in him. For this same Jesus who declared: 'I must preach the good news of the kingdom of God'[29] is he of whom John the evangelist affirmed that he had come and was destined to die in order 'to gather into one the children of God who are scattered abroad'.[30] In this way he accomplishes his revelation, completing and confirming it by the complete manifestation of himself which he achieves by his words and his works, by signs and miracles, and above all by his death and resurrection and by the sending of the Spirit of Truth.[31]

13. Those who sincerely accept the good news, by virtue of it and the faith which it generates, are united in the name of Jesus so that they may together seek the kingdom, built it up and implement it in their own lives. In this way they establish a community which becomes itself a herald of the gospel. The command which was given to the twelve: 'Go preach the gospel' applies to all Christians though in different ways. This is why Peter calls them a 'chosen race—to declare the wonderful deeds of him who called you out of darkness into his marvellous light',[32] that

is those mighty works of God which the faithful were able to hear each in his own native language.[33]

Moreover, the gospel of the kingdom which is coming and has already begun concerns all men of all times. All those, therefore, who have received this message and by virtue of it have been united in the community of salvation have the power and the obligation to hand it on and disseminate it.

14. The church is keenly aware of this: she realizes that the words of the Saviour: 'I must preach the good news of the kingdom of God'[34] have a direct application to herself. And with St. Paul she freely declares: 'If I preach the gospel, that gives me no cause for boasting. For necessity is laid upon me. Woe to me if I do not preach the gospel'.[35] It was accordingly for us a great joy and consolation at the close of the great assembly of bishops in the month of October 1974 to hear those inspiring words: 'We wish to affirm once more that the essential mission of the church is to evangelize all men.'[36] It is a task and mission which the great and fundamental changes of contemporary society make all the more urgent. Evangelization is the special grace and vocation of the church. It is her essential function. The church exists to preach the gospel, that is to preach and teach the word of God so that through her the gift of grace may be given to us, sinners may be reconciled to God, and the sacrifice of the Mass, the memorial of his glorious death and resurrection, may be perpetuated.

15. Anyone who reads through the pages of the New Testament and reflects on the beginnings of the church, considering her amazing development and the nature of her life and activity, cannot fail to realize that evangelization is inherent in the very nature of the church.

The church takes its origin from the work of evangelization by Christ and the twelve apostles. Of this work she is the natural fruition. She is the end to which this work was directed, its immediate and most striking achievement: 'Go, therefore, and make disciples of all nations'.[37] And further: 'Those who received the word were baptized and there were added that day about three thousand souls. . .and the Lord added to their numbers day by day those who were being saved'.[38]

Drawing its origin from this mission, the church in her turn is sent forth by Jesus himself. She remains in the world while the Lord of Glory returns to the Father. She stands out as the sign at once mysterious and clear of the new presence of Jesus, of his setting out and of his abiding. She protracts and perpetuates his presence. And it is above all his mission and his work of evangelization which the church must constantly maintain.[39] For the Christian community can never be confined within itself, because its intimate life, that is its zeal for prayer, its hearing of the word and the teaching of the apostles, its exercise of fraternal charity, the breaking of bread,[40] cannot achieve its full force and value unless it becomes a witness and evokes admiration and conversion of souls. It must preach the gospel and announce the good news. In this way the mission of evangelization is undertaken by the whole church and the work of each individual redounds to the good of all.

Accordingly the church begins her work of evangelization by evangelizing herself. As a community sharing a common faith and a common hope which she proclaims and communicates to others by her life, and sharing likewise a common fraternal love, it is essential that she should constantly hear the truths in which she believes, the grounds on which her hope is based and the new command of mutual love. As the people of God which has been placed in the world and is often tempted by its idols, she needs to hear constantly the proclamation of 'the mighty works of God'[41] by which she has been converted to the Lord so that she may hear his call anew and be confirmed in unity. To put the matter briefly, if the church is to preserve the freshness, the ardour and the strength of her own work of preaching the gospel she must herself be continuously evangelized. The second ecumenical Vatican council declared, and the synod of bishops of 1974 repeated it, that the church must evangelize herself by a constant conversion and renewal if she is convincingly to evangelize the world.[42]

The proclamation of the good news to men has been entrusted to the church. The promises of the new covenant fulfilled in Jesus Christ, the teaching of Our Lord and the apostles, the word of life, the sources of grace and the bounty of God, the way of salvation: all these have been confided to her. All these good things which are contained in the gospel, and are therefore the subject matter of evangelization, are preserved by her as a precious living heritage and must not be kept hidden but proclaimed to man. The church, having been herself sent forth and evangelized, sends out evangelizers in her turn. She teaches them, putting on their lips, as it were, the word of salvation. She communicates to them the message which has been confided to her. She hands on to them the mandate which she has herself received and sends them out to preach, not to preach themselves or their personal ideas,[43] but rather the gospel of which neither they nor the church herself are the absolute masters, free to dispose of as they wish, but rather the ministers charged to hand it on with complete fidelity.

16. There is, therefore, a very close connection between Christ, the church and evangelization. During this 'era of the church' the task of evangelization is entrusted to her. This task cannot be carried out without her, and much less in opposition to her. It is expedient to recall this truth because in these days we hear, not without grief, of men, in good faith, as we like to believe, but certainly misguided, who frequently declare that they are willing to love Christ but not the church. The absurdity of this distinction appears clearly from those words of the gospel: 'He who rejects you rejects me'.[44] How can anyone claim to love Christ without loving his church in face of that most striking testimony given by St. Paul:'Christ loved the church and gave himself up for her'.[45]

2. WHAT IS EVANGELIZATION?

17. In the church's work of evangelization there are undoubtedly certain elements and aspects which are deserving of special attention. Some of these are indeed of such inportance that they may at times be regarded as constituting in themselves the whole of evangelization. Thus, for example, evangelization has been defined as consisting in the proclamation of Christ Our Lord to those who do not know him, in preaching, catechetics, baptism and the administration of the other sacraments. But no such defective and incomplete definition can be accepted for that complex, rich and dynamic reality which is called evangelization without the risk of weakening or even distorting its real meaning. It cannot be fully understood unless all its necessary elements are taken into account. Those elements on which particular stress was laid in the 1974 synod of bishops in the course of its discussions are the subject of profound study nowadays. We are propounded by the second Vatican council, and especially with the constitutions *Lumen Gentium, Gaudium et Spes* and with the decree *Ad Gentes*.

18. The church appreciates that evangelization means the carrying forth of the good news to every sector of the human race so that by its strength it may enter into the hearts of men and renew the human race. 'Behold, I make all things new'.[46] But there cannot be a new human race unless there are first of all new men, men renewed by baptism[47] and by a life lived in accordance with the gospel.[48] It is the aim of evangelization, therefore, to effect this interior transformation. In a word, the church may be truly said to evangelize when, solely in virtue of that news which

she proclaims,[49] she seeks to convert both the individual consciences of men and their collective conscience, all the activities in which they are engaged and, finally, their lives and the whole environment which surrounds them.

19. We speak of sectors of the human race which must be transformed, for the purpose of the church is not confined to preaching the gospel in ever extending territories and proclaiming it to ever increasing multitudes of men. She seeks by virtue of the gospel to affect and, as it were, recast the criteria of judgment, the standard of values, the incentives and life standards of the human race which are inconsistent with the word of God and the plan of salvation.

20. All this may be summarized thus: evangelization is to be achieved, not from without as though by adding some decoration or applying a coat of colour, but in depth, going to the very centre and roots of life. The gospel must impregnate the culture and the whole way of life of man, taking these words in the widest and fullest sense which they are given in the constitution *Gaudium et Spes*.[50] This work must always take the human person as its starting point, coming back to the interrelationships between persons and their relation with God.

The gospel and, therefore, evangelization cannot be put in the same category with any culture. They are above all cultures. Nevertheless, the kingdom of God which is proclaimed by the gospel is put into practice by men who are imbued with their own particular culture, and in the building up of the kingdom it is inevitable that some elements of these human cultures must be introduced. The gospel and evangelization are not specially related to any culture but they are not necessarily incompatible with them. On the contrary, they can penetrate any culture while being subservient to none.

The rift between the gospel and culture is undoubtedly an unhappy circumstance of our times just as it has been in other eras. Accordingly we must devote all our resources and all our efforts to the sedulous evangelization of human culture, or rather of the various human cultures. They must be regenerated through contact with the gospel. But this contact cannot be effected unless the good news is proclaimed.

21. This proclamation must be made above all else by witness. We envisage, therefore, a Christian or a group of Christians as people who, in the midst of the community in which they live, will show that they are capable of understanding and accepting others and of cooperating with all those who are seeking to protect what is noble and good.

We envisage them radiating simply and spontaneously their

faith in values which transcend common values and their hope in things which are not seen and of which even the boldest mind cannot form an image. By bearing such silent witness these Christians will inevitably arouse a spirit of enquiry in those who see their way of life. Why are they like this? Why do they live in this way? Why are they among us? Witness of this kind constitutes in itself a proclamation of the good news, silent, but strong and effective.

This constitutes a first step in the work of evangelization. In this way the first question may be aroused in the minds of many non-Christians, whether they be men to whom Christ has never been preached or those who, although baptized, are not practicing their religion, or those who are living in a Christian community but whose own lives are in no way Christian, or, finally, men who are painfully seeking something or 'someone' whose existence they divine but whom they cannot identify. Other questions, deeper and more important, will arise which will be evoked by this witness, but it must involve actual presence, social intercourse and cooperation. This witness is an essential element and often the initial element in the work of evangelization.[51]

All Christians are called to bear this witness and in this way they can be true evangelizers. We are thinking especially of the duty and responsibility of migrants to those countries which receive them.

22. But this will never be enough, for witness, no matter how excellent, will ultimately prove ineffective unless its meaning is clarified and corroborated—what St Peter used to call accounting 'for the hope that is in you'.[52] The meaning of a person's witness will be clarified by preaching, clearly and unambiguously, the Lord Jesus. The good news proclaimed by witness of life sooner or later has to be proclaimed by the word of life. There is no true evangelization if the name, the teaching, the life, the promises, the kingdom and the mystery of Jesus of Nazareth, the Son of God, are not proclaimed.

The whole history of the church, beginning with the sermon of Peter on the day of Pentecost, is interwoven and united with the history of this proclamation. In every age of human history the church, inspired by this zeal and desire to evangelize, has been preoccupied with this one anxiety: who is to be sent to proclaim the mystery of Jesus? How can it be assured that it will be understood and that it will reach all those who ought to hear it? This proclamation of the news, *kerygma*—that is preaching or catechetics—has such importance in the work of evangelization that it is often called by that name. In fact, however, it constitutes only a part of the whole.

23. For evangelization will never achieve its full force and significance unless it is received, accepted and adopted, and unless it evokes the wholehearted allegiance of those who hear it. A man may assent to the truths which a merciful God has revealed, but he will give a much deeper and fuller assent to the spirit and way of life—that is a life now transformed—which these truths propose to him. In a word, a man gives his allegiance to the kingdom, that is to 'a new world', a new state of things, a new manner of existence, a new way of life, of communal life, which the gospel inaugurates. This allegiance, which cannot abstract from the external circumstances of life, is expressed by the visible and objective entry of a man into the community of the faithful. Therefore those who have experienced this conversion enter into a community which by its very nature is a sign of transformation and of a new life: that community is the church, the visible sacrament of salvation.[53]

But this entry into the community of the church will in turn be manifested by many other signs which extend and explain the symbolism of the church. In accordance with the dynamic force of evangelization the man who accepts the church as the word of salvation generally gives expression to this acceptance by these sacramental signs: his fidelity to the church and his frequentation of the sacraments which manifest and maintain this allegiance by the grace which they confer.

24. Finally, the man who has been evangelized becomes himself an evangelizer. This is the proof, the test of the genuineness of his own conversion. It is inconceivable that a man who has received the word and surrendered himself to the kingdom should not himself become a witness and proclaimer of the truth.

Having made these observations about the meaning of evangelization, we must now add something which we think will help to clarify the following considerations.

As we have already said, evangelization is a complex process involving many elements as, for example, a renewal of human nature, witness, public proclamation, wholehearted acceptance of, and entrance into, the community of the church, the adoption of the outward signs and of apostolic works. These elements may appear to be inconsistent and even mutually exclusive, but in fact they are complementary and perfect each other. Accordingly it is essential to consider each element in relation to the others. The recent synod of bishops made a valuable contribution to the problem in urging everyone to consider these elements, not in contrast to each other but rather as interrelated, in order to arrive at a complete understanding of the work of evangelization on which the church is engaged. It is our aim now to expound this universal view by investigating what elements are comprised in evangelization as well as the aids to evangelization, and by establishing to whom the message of evangelization is directed and on whom the responsibility for the work devolves.

3. THE MESSAGE OF EVANGELIZATION

25. The message which is disseminated by the church includes certainly many secondary elements, the presentation of which depends on changing circumstances. They may certainly vary but they do contain certain essential features, a vital substance, which cannot be changed or ignored without endangering the very idea of evangelization.[54]

26. It may be useful at this stage to make it clear that evangelizing means above all else bearing witness simply and clearly to God as he is revealed by Our Lord Jesus Christ, proclaiming that he has loved the world in his Son and that in the Incarnate Word he has given existence to all creatures and has called men to eternal life. This witness concerning God will perhaps to many be the announcement of an unknown God,[55] a being whom they adore although they are unable to identify him or whom they are impelled to seek by some secret instinct of their hearts when they have realized the futility of all their idols. But this witness achieves its full effectiveness only when it has made men see that God is not a remote power without a name but rather the Father. 'We are called children of god and so we are'[56] and for this reason we are brothers one to another in God.

27. Evangelization will always contain, as the foundation, the centre and the apex of its whole dynamic power, this explicit declaration: in Jesus Christ who became man, died and rose again from the dead salvation is offered to every man as the gift of the grace and mercy of God himself.[57]

And this is not an immediate salvation corresponding to the measure of man's material or even spiritual needs. It is not a salvation confined within the limits of life on this earth and which is coterminous with the desires, the hopes, the occupations and the stresses of this life, rather is it a salvation which far exceeds all these limits, finding its consummation in a union with the one Absolute, that is with God. It is a transcendent, eschatological salvation which has its beginning certainly in this life but which achieves its consummation in eternity.

28. Accordingly, evangelization will include a prophetic proclamation of another life, that is of man's sublime and eternal vocation. This vocation is at once connected with and

distinct from his present state; it is the vocation of a life to come which transcends time and history and all the transient circumstances of this world of which the hidden significance will one day be revealed. It transcends man himself whose true destiny is not confined to this temporal life but will be revealed in the life to come.[58]

Evangelization, therefore, includes the preaching of the promises made by God in the new covenant through Jesus Christ, the preaching of the love of God for us and of our love for God. It includes the preaching of fraternal love for all men, that is the capacity to bestow gifts and pardon, to practise self denial and to come to the aid of our brethren. This, inspired by the love of God, is the kernel of the gospel. Evangelization includes the preaching of the mystery of evil and of the active pursuit of good. It must likewise include, and this is always of primary importance, the preaching of the search for God first through prayer, prayer primarily of adoration and thanksgiving, but also through membership of that visible sign of our union with God which is the church of Jesus Christ. This membership is itself attested by the reception of those other signs of Christ who is living and operating in his church, that is, the sacraments.

To accept the sacraments as constituting the true fulness of the Christian life does not mean, as some have falsely asserted, erecting an obstacle to evangelization or permitting a deviation from its true purpose. It is rather to set the seal on the work. For the consummation of evangelization, in addition to the preaching of the message, consists in the building up of the church which has no real existence without that spirit which is the sacramental life culminating in the blessed Eucharist.[59]

29. But evangelization will not be complete unless it constantly relates the gospel to men's actual lives, personal and social. Accordingly, evangelization must include an explicit message, adapted to the various conditions of life and constantly updated, concerning the rights and duties of the individual person and concerning family life, without which progress in the life of the individual is hardly possible.[60] It must deal with community life in society, with the life of all nations, with peace, justice and progress. It must deliver a message, especially relevant and important in our age, about liberation.

30. It is well known on what terms the bishops from all parts of the world have spoken about this matter in the recent synod, and especially the bishops from what is known as the third world. They spoke with the vigour and accent of pastors echoing the voice of millions of the children of the church who make up these peoples.

These peoples, as we all know, are striving with all their power and energy to overcome all those circumstances which compel them to live on the border line of existence: hunger, chronic epidemics, illiteracy, poverty, injustice between nations and especially in the commercial sphere, economic and cultural neo-colonialism which are often as bad as the old political colonialism. The church is in duty bound—as her bishops have insisted—to proclaim the liberation of these hundreds of millions of people since very many of them are her children. She has the duty of helping this liberation, of bearing witness on its behalf and of assuring its full development. All this is in no way irrelevant to evangelization.

31. In fact there are close links between evangelization and human advancement, that is development and liberation. There is a connection in the anthropological order because the man who is to be evangelized is not an abstract being but a person subject to social and economic factors. There is also a connection in the theological sphere because the plan of creation cannot be isolated from the plan of redemption which extends to the very practical question of eradicating injustice and establishing justice. There is, finally, a connection in the evangelical order, that is the order of charity: for how can the new law be proclaimed unless it promotes a true practical advancement of man in a spirit of justice and peace? This is what we intended to assert when we pointed out that in the work of evangelization 'we cannot and must not disregard the immense importance of those questions which are so much at issue today: questions concerning justice, liberation, progress and world peace. If we disregard these we are likewise disregarding the teaching of the gospel about the love of our neighbour who is suffering and in want'.[61]

The wise and forceful contributions made in the synod furnished, to our great joy, clear principles from which can be deduced the significance and the full meaning of liberation as Jesus of Nazareth proclaimed it and achieved it and as the church now preaches it.

32. We must recognize the fact that many generous Christians who are preoccupied with the burning problems of liberation are so anxious to see the church involved in liberation, that they would reduce her role to temporal activity, merely. They would assign her a purely anthropocentric function, would reduce the salvation of which she is the herald to material prosperity, her activity to intiatives in the political or social order. If this were to be accepted the church would be deprived of all her true significance. The message of liberations which she proclaims would

lose its true value and could easily be influenced and distorted by ideological groups and political parties. The church would then lose its authority to proclaim the cause of liberation in the name of God. For this reason at the beginning of the third meeting of the synod we thought it wise to emphasize in the same address the necessity of asserting 'the essentially religious purpose of evangelization. For it would lose all its true significance if it were divorced from the religious basis by which it is sustained which is the kingdom of God in its full theological sense'.[62]

33. In considering that liberation which evangelization proclaims and seeks to achieve the following points should be recognized:

It cannot be confined to any restricted sphere whether it be economic, political, social or doctrinal. It must rather embrace the whole man in all his aspects and components, extending to his relation to the absolute, even to the Absolute which is God.

It is based therefore on a clear concept of man, on a definite anthropology which can never be sacrificed for any reasons of strategy or custom or to achieve some transient success.

34. The church proclaims liberation and cooperates with all those who are working and suffering on its behalf. She does not assert that her function is strictly confined to the religious sphere without regard for the temporal problems of men. But she reaffirms the primacy of her spiritual function and refuses to substitute for the preaching of the kingdom of God a proclamation of liberation of the merely human order. She declares that her advocacy of liberation would not be complete or perfect if she failed to preach salvation in Jesus Christ.

35. While recognizing the connection between them, the church never identifies human liberation with salvation in Jesus Christ. She knows from divine revelation, from the experience of history and from the principles of faith that not every idea of liberation is necessarily compatible or consistent with the evangelical understanding of man, of things and of events. She knows that the achievement of liberation, the development of prosperity and progress are not of themselves sufficient to assure the coming of the kingdom of God. The church is indeed firmly convinced that every form of temporal and political liberation contains within itself the seeds of its own frustration and deviates from its noble purpose if it is no part of its fundamental aim to establish justice in charity, if the burning ardour and zeal

which inspires it lack a spiritual foundation and are directed towards salvation and eternal happiness in God as the ultimate goal. And this is true even if it seeks to justify itself by this or that passage in the Old or New Testament, even if it adduces the authority of theological principles and conclusions for its ideology and norms of action, even if it claims to be itself the new contemporary theology.

36. The church certainly attaches great importance to the establishment of a system which will be more humane, more just, more solicitous for the rights of the individual, and which will be less oriented towards oppression and subjection. However, she realizes that the best structures, the most carefully planned systems can easily become inhuman unless the inhuman tendencies of the heart of man are reformed, unless there is a conversion of those who live under these systems or control them.

37. The church cannot accept any form of violence, and especially of armed violence—for this cannot be restrained when once it is unleashed—nor the death of any man as a method of liberation. She knows that violence always provokes violence and inevitably gives rise to new forms of oppression, new forms of servitude even more grievous than those from which men were supposed to be emancipated. We stated this clearly during our recent visit to Colombia: 'We urge you not to put your trust in violence or revolution; this attitude is repugnant to the Christian spirit, and so far from helping, it may well hinder the social progress to which you rightly aspire'.[63] 'We feel bound to affirm and to re-affirm that violence is neither Christian nor evangelical, and sudden or violent structural changes are chimerical and of their very nature ineffective and beyond all doubt unworthy of human dignity'.[64]

38. Having said this, we rejoice that the church is coming increasingly to understand the manner of working for the liberation of man that is appropriate for her, a way that is of its very nature evangelical. And what is she in fact doing? She is trying with ever increasing zeal to encourage many Christians to dedicate themselves to the liberation of others. She is giving these Christian liberators the spirit and guidance of faith, the motive of fraternal love and a creed of social teaching which no true Christian can ignore, which should form the basis of his wisdom and experience and constitute the pattern of his activity, of his cooperation and his commitment. All these things, which are not to be reduced to the level of mere tactics nor put at the service of some political faction, must be the inspiration of the ardent

Catholic. It is the church's constant endeavour to incorporate the Christians' effort for liberation into the universal plan of salvation which she preaches.

All these matters which we have just discussed were frequently raised in the synodal debates and we thought it well besides to add a few words for the sake of explicitness in our address to the fathers at the close of the synod.[65]

It is our confident hope that these considerations will remove these ambiguities which are too often associated with the word 'liberation' in ideologies, movements and political groups. The liberation which evangelization proclaims and works for is that liberation which Christ himself announced and gave to man by his sacrifice.

39. This legitimate liberation, which is closely connected with evangelization, seeking as it does to establish systems which will defend human liberty, cannot be dissociated from the protection of the fundamental rights of man amongst which religious liberty holds pride of place. We have spoken recently of this most urgent question, recalling: 'How many Christians, even now, just because they are Christians and Catholics are overwhelmed by deliberate oppression. The tribulations of fidelity to Christ and of religious liberty continue even to this day although they are often cloaked by passionate declarations in favour of the rights of man and of human society'.[66]

4. THE MEANS OF EVANGELIZATION

40. The manifest importance of the contents of evangelization must not prejudice our appreciation of the importance of the ways and means by which this work is to be carried out. This question remains constantly relevant because the methods of evangelization change according to the times, the places, and the prevailing cultures, and accordingly they present, as it were, a challenge to our ability to discern them and adapt them.

It is our special responsibility as pastors of the church, while maintaining a scrupulous fidelity to the content of evangelization, to review with courage and wisdom the most suitable and effective methods of bringing the evangelical message to the men of our day. Bearing this in mind let it suffice for us to recall certain methods which for one reason or another are clearly of primary importance.

41. And first, while we do not wish to repeat what we have already said, it may be useful to stress the point: that in the church the witness given by a life truly and essentially Christian

which is dedicated to God in an indissoluble union and which is likewise dedicated with the utmost fervour of soul to our neighbour is the primary organ of evangelization. As we said recently in an address to a group of laymen: 'the men of our day are more impressed by witness than by teachers, and if they listen to these it is because they also bear witness'[67]. This has been admirably expressed by the apostle Paul when he propounded the admirable example of a reverent and chaste life by which some though they do not obey the word may be won without a word.[68] It is therefore by her own conduct, by her own manner of life, that the church can most effectively evangelize the world, that is by the witness given by her own life which clearly proclaims her fidelity to God, her poverty and asceticism, her independence in face of all the powers of this world, in a word, her sanctity.

42. It will not be irrelevant, however, at this point to emphasise the importance and necessity of preaching. 'How are they to believe in him of whom they have never heard? And how are they to hear without a preacher—so faith comes from what is heard and what is heard comes by the preaching of Christ'.[69] This principle, enunciated of old by the apostle Paul, retains its full force and value today.

Preaching, that is the verbal proclamation of the message, is always essential. We know that there are today many men who are wearied of talk, who often seem to be tired of listening and, which is more serious, to have closed their minds to the spoken word. We are familiar with the view of many psychologists and sociologists who hold that men have outgrown the culture evoked by words which is now ineffective and useless, and that they respond now to a new visual culture. These circumstances constitute a cogent argument for employing these more recent instruments which this new culture has introduced for the transmission of the evangelical message. Valuable experiments have been made in this sphere of which we fully approve and it is our earnest wish that they should be pursued. Nevertheless, the weariness which is caused in these days by the spate of useless words, and the greater importance attached to various other forms of communication must not lead us to lose our confidence in the word. The spoken word has always its own excellence and efficacy and this is especially true when it proclaims the power of God.[70] For this reason the words of St Paul are still true in our time: 'Faith comes from what is heard'[71]. It is the word which is heard which leads to belief.

43. This preaching by which the gospel is proclaimed may assume many forms and zeal for souls will suggest an almost in-

finite variety. There are in fact innumerable events in life and circumstances in which men find themselves which furnish the occasion for preaching, prudently but clearly, those truths which the Lord would wish to impart, given the suitable opportunity. It suffices for each man to have that spiritual sense which can detect the expression of God's message in the course of events. But since, in the revised liturgy great importance is attached to the 'liturgy of the word', it would be a serious error to deny that the homily is a powerful and most suitable instrument of evangelization. It is necessary to understand thoroughly the exigencies and the possibilities of the homily if it is to achieve its full pastoral effect. Each individual must be conscious of its value and implement it with loving zeal. This form of preaching, which is specifically included in the celebration of the Eucharist from which it derives an especial strength and force, undoubtedly plays a primary role in evangelization, impregnated as it is with love and expressing the intimate faith of the minister. From it the faithful, assembled to form the paschal church as it celebrates the feast of the Lord present in their midst, anticipates and receives abundant fruits. It will bear these fruits provided it is simple, clear, straightforward, well adapted to the hearers and firmly rooted in the teaching of the gospel. It must faithfully follow the magisterium and should be inspired and guided by that apostolic zeal which is inherent in it. It must be full of salutary hope and foster peace and unity. When it possesses these qualities the Sunday homily is a source of life and strength to many parish and other communities.

Furthermore, on account of the liturgical renewal, the celebration of the Eucharist is not the only suitable occasion for the homily. The homily has a place and should not be neglected in the celebration of all the sacraments and on the occasion of paraliturgical ceremonies when the faithful are assembled together. All these will furnish an admirable opportunity to proclaim the word of God.

44. Catechetical instruction is another instrument of evangelization which must on no account be neglected. A systematic course of religious instruction should lead the minds of all and especially those of children and adolescents to an understanding of the principal components of that living treasure of truth which God has been pleased to communicate to us and which the church in the course of her long history has always been zealous to enunciate ever more comprehensively. No one will deny that this doctrine is to be imparted, not as a mere intellectual exercise, but in order to inculcate the Christian way of life. There can

be no doubt that the whole work of evangelization will be materially helped if the catechetical teachers can avail themselves of suitable books, wisely and competently prepared under the direction of the bishops. This applies to educational instruction given by the church, to instruction in the schools where this is possible, and always to instruction in Christian homes. It is essential that the form of teaching be adapted to the age, the educational level and the intellectual capacity of the individuals and that care be taken to implant the necessary truths firmly in the memory, mind and heart so that they may exercise a profound influence on the whole life of their hearers. Above all it is essential that skilled teachers of catechetics be trained, whether these be the parochial catechists or school teachers or parents. It is for them to educate themselves and perfect themselves in this art of religious instruction which is of such value, is so necessary, and so demanding. On the other hand, while the teaching of children must on no account be neglected, it is evident that the circumstances of our times make it ever more urgent to provide catechetical instruction under some form of catechumenate for the many adolescents who, under the influence of grace, are gradually discerning the countenance of Christ and are beginning to appreciate the necessity of surrendering themselves to him.

45. In our age which is characterized by the mass media we must not fail, as we have already pointed out, to avail of the media for the first proclamation of the message, for catechetical instruction and for a deeper study of the faith.

These, when they are employed in the service of the gospel, can disseminate the word of God over a vast area and carry the message of salvation to millions of men. The church would feel herself guilty before God if she did not avail of those powerful instruments which human skill is constantly developing and perfecting. With their aid she may preach 'upon the housetops'[72] the message which has been entrusted to her. In them she finds in a new and more effective form a platform or pulpit from which she can address the multitudes. However, the use of these means of communication in the service of evangelization presents a certain challenge. Through them the evangelical message will certainly reach a vast multitude of men, but it must also have the power to penetrate the mind of each individual with all his particular and personal characteristic as though he alone were being addressed; it must be capable of evoking a personal acceptance and commitment.

46. Accordingly, in addition to this public and general proclamation of the gospel the other form of individual communication of the gospel from person to person must be encouraged

and esteemed. This is the method which Our Lord himself constantly employed—as we see in his discussions with Nicodemus, with Zaccheus, with the Samaritan woman and with Simon the Pharisee—it is the method employed by the apostles. It may indeed be said that the only true form of evangelization is that by which the individual communicates to another those truths of which he is personally convinced by faith. We must not allow the necessity of proclaiming the good news to the multitude to make us neglect this method by which the personal conscience of the individual is touched by some inspiring words which he hears from another. We cannot sufficiently extol the outstanding merit of those priests who, in the sacrament of penance or in their pastoral interviews, exercise their zeal in leading souls in the ways of the gospel, in encouraging those who are striving to advance, in bringing back those who have fallen and in helping all with discernment and generosity.

47. We must, however, always remember that the work of evangelization cannot be fully accomplished by sermons alone or by any communication of doctrine. It must extend to life itself: to the natural life which it enriches with a new meaning based on the hope and expectation revealed in the words of the gospel message; it must extend to the supernatural life, which does not reject the natural life but rather purifies it and ennobles it. The seven sacraments and the wonderful radiation of grace and sanctity which flows from them are the vital expression of the nature and value of this supernatural life. This evangelization is revealed in all its richness when it establishes the closest link, or rather an unbroken connection, between the word and the sacraments. There is a certain ambiguity if, as sometimes happens, the proclamation of the gospel and the administration of the sacraments are, as it were, divorced from each other. To administer the sacraments without any firm basis of catechesis, on the sacraments are, as it were, divorced from each other. To administer the sacraments without any firm basis of catechesis on the For the true purpose of the evangelist is to lead people to the faith so that by virtue of it individual Christians may be brought to live the sacraments as true sacraments of faith and not merely to receive them passively.

48. And now we must introduce another aspect of evangelization which cannot be ignored and which it is therefore opportune to consider. This is the practice of what is commonly known as popular religiosity. Both in those regions where the church has been established for many centuries and also where it is still in the process of being organized we find among the people particular customs expressive of their search for God and

their faith. These customs have long been regarded as unhealthy and have sometimes been the object of contempt but in these days they are almost everywhere being reviewed and reconsidered. At the recent meeting of the synod the bishops, moved by an admirable zeal and a practical appreciation of pastoral realities, have endeavoured to discern their full significance.

It must be admitted that popular religiosity has but a strictly limited value. It not infrequently opens the way to many false forms of religion and may verge on superstition. It is often confined to the lower forms of religious worship which do not lead souls to a generous adherence to the faith. It may lead to the establishment of sects and factions endangering the well-being of the ecclesial community.

But on the other hand, if it is prudently directed and especially when it is directed along the path and according to the methods of evangelization, it may be productive of great good. For it does indicate a certain thirst for God such as only those who are simple and poor in spirit can experience. It can arouse in men a capacity for self dedication and for the exercise of heroism when there is question of professing the faith. It gives men a keen sensitivity by virtue of which they can appreciate the ineffable attributes of God: his fatherly compassion, his providence, his benevolence and loving presence. It can develop in the inmost depths of man habits of virtue rarely to be found otherwise in the same degree, such as patience, acceptance of the Cross in daily life, detachment, openness to other men and a spirit of ready service. It is on account of these qualities that we prefer to call it *popular piety* or the religion of the people rather than *religiosity*. It is a matter of pastoral charity for all those whom God has put in charge of ecclesial communities to establish principles for directing in the right channels this sentiment which can bear such excellent fruits and yet is fraught with danger. Above all we must be sympathetic in our approach, quick to appreciate its inherent nature and its desirable qualities and zealous to direct it so that the dangers arising out of its errors may be avoided. When it is wisely directed popular piety of this kind can make a constantly increasing contribution towards bringing the masses of our people into contact with God in Jesus Christ.

5. THE UNIVERSALITY OF EVANGELIZATION

49. In the closing words of the gospel according to Mark, Jesus invests the evangelization which he enjoins on the apostles with a universality which knows no frontiers: 'Go into all the world and preach the gospel to the whole creation'.[73]

The twelve apostles and the first generations of Christians fully appreciated the teaching of this and other similar texts and they developed from it a programme of action. The persecution by which the apostles were dispersed played its part in the dissemination of the gospel and the constant extension of the church to distant regions. The admission of Paul into the number of the apostles and his special mission to preach to the Gentiles rather than the Jews the coming of Jesus Christ gave further emphasis to this universality.

50. Generations of Christians in the course of twenty centuries have overcome a variety of obstacles to this universal mission. For on the one hand the preachers themselves tended on various pretexts to restrict the field of their missionary activity and on the other hand those to whom they preached put up a resistance which could not be overcome by merely human resources. Moreover, sad to relate, the evangelical efforts of the church have been subject to virulent opposition, not to say actual obstruction, at the hands of governments. Even today the heralds of the divine word are deprived of their rights, harassed by persecution, threatened and even killed for no other reason than that they are preaching Jesus Christ and his gospel. It is our confident hope that, in spite of these trials, the zeal of these apostolic men will not fail in any part of the world.

Although she labours under these difficulties the church constantly renews that noble inspiration which comes to her directly from the divine Master as she recalls those words: 'into all the world', 'to the whole creation', 'to the furthest ends of the earth'. And she has reiterated this in the recent synod of bishops when they insisted that the evangelical message must not be restricted either to one section of the human family or to one social class or one form of human culture. Some examples may help to clarify this point.

51. From the day of Pentecost the church has recognized that her primary function, entrusted to her by her founder, was to reveal Jesus Christ and his gospel to those who did not know him. The whole of the New Testament and especially the Acts of the Apostles show us that this time was ideally suited to evangelization and in a certain sense offers us a prototype for the accomplishment of this work, a work of which the whole history of the church furnishes a splendid counterpart.

This first proclamation of Jesus Christ was introduced by many and varied activities which are sometimes described as pre-evangelization but which in fact are already evangelization although in its initial stages and not yet in a comprehensive form. In order to attain the desired end an almost interminable series of intermediate steps must be taken: public preaching certainly, as far as it is possible, but it may also be desirable to bring into service the arts, a scientific approach, philosophical enquiry and a legitimate appeal to men's emotions.

52. While this first proclamation will be directed primarily towards those who have never heard the good news of Jesus, or to children, it will always be needed nevertheless on account of the extent of dechristianization today. Many people who have been baptized live lives entirely divorced from Christianity. It must be directed also to those simple people who have a certain measure of faith but know little even of its fundamental principles. It must extend to intellectuals who feel that they need to approach Jesus Christ from a different standpoint from that which was taught them in their childhood days. And there are many others for whom it is no less necessary.

53. This proclamation is relevant also for immense sections of the human race who profess non-Christian religions in which the spiritual life of innumerable human communities finds valid expression. In these we hear re-echoed, as it were, the voices of those who for a thousand years have sought God in a manner which, while imperfect, has always been sincere and upright. These religions, possessing as they do, a splendid patrimony of religious writings, have taught generations of men how to pray. They are adorned by innumerable 'seeds of the Word'[74] and therefore truly constitute a genuine 'preparation for the gospel',[75] to adopt the excellent expression of the second Vatican council inspired by the work of Eusebius of Caesarea. But this consideration gives rise to many very complex questions which call for the greatest prudence. Theologians have still to study these important and difficult questions in the light of Christian tradition and the magisterium of the church so that new paths may be opened to missionaries both now and in the future which they may follow in their approach to non-Christian religions.

Neither our respect for these religions nor the high esteem in which we hold them nor the complexity of the questions involved should deter the church from proclaiming the message of Jesus Christ to these non-Christians. On the contrary she holds that these multitudes of men have the right to know the riches of the mystery of Christ.[76] It is in these, we believe, that the whole human family can find in the most comprehensive form and beyond all their expectations everything for which they have been groping, as it were, about God, about man and his ultimate destiny, about life and death and about truth itself. Accordingly, even in the face of the most admirable forms of natural religion, the church judges that it is her special function, by virtue of the religion of Jesus Christ which she proclaims in her evangelization, to bring men into contact with God's plan, with his living presence, with his solicitude. In this way she presents to men the mystery of the divine paternity which extends to the human race; in other words, by virtue of our religion a true and living relationship with God is established which other religions cannot achieve even though they seem, as it were, to have their arms raised up towards heaven. The church therefore seeks to foster and maintain her missionary zeal: it is, in fact, her aim to increase it in these present times. She feels bound by a duty to all peoples in the discharge of which she will spare no pains in her efforts to spread the good news of Jesus Our Saviour. She is constantly training new generations of missionaries for this purpose. This is a fact to which we are glad to advert in these days when there are some who think and say that all eagerness and zeal for the apostolate is extinguished and that the age of missionary work is past. In reply to this assertion the synod of bishops has declared that the missionary proclamation has lost none of its vigour and that the church will always strive to fulfil its function in this regard.

54. But the church recognizes that she has an equally grave duty to care for those who have accepted the faith, many of them having inherited the gospel message over several generations. She makes every effort therefore to cultivate, consolidate and foster the faith of those who already profess belief so that it may grow increasingly stronger and their loyalty to the faith ever more fervent. The faith in these days has often to contend with *secularism* or even atheism. It is challenged and threatened. Indeed it is often assailed and actively opposed. There is a danger therefore that it may either be overwhelmed by these attacks or starved for want of spiritual nourishment unless it is constantly fed and supported. Evangelization therefore requires that the faithful be constantly provided with this nourishment and support for their faith and this will be done mainly by catechetical instruction which must be impregnated with the spirit of the gospel and imparted in language adapted to the times and to the hearers.

The catholic church is also assiduous in her solicitude for those Christians who are not in full communion with her: she seeks to establish with them that unity which Christ desired and it is her aim to achieve this unity in truth. She appreciates that she would be failing gravely in her duty if she did not bear witness to them of the fulness of revelation of which she is the depository.

55. The synod of bishops was gravely concerned about two matters relating to the condition of men and of affairs, matters very diverse in themselves but closely connected in that both of them, each in its own way, present a challenge to evangelization.

The first of these may be described as the increasing measure of unbelief in the world today. The synod sought to analyse this modern world: how many values, real and fictitious, how many latent aspirations or seeds of destruction, how many traditional views disappearing and new views imposing themselves on the minds of men are comprised under this heading if we take 'modern world' in its widest sense? From the spiritual point of view the world of today seems to be buffeted in what a contemporary writer has described as 'the drama of atheistic humanism'.[77] We must recognize that there is one element established in the very heart of the world of today, constituting, as it were, its characteristic feature: this is secularism.

We do not mean by this secularization which is the effort, in itself quite proper and legitimate and in no way inconsistent with faith or religion, to discern in creation, in every thing and in every event in the whole world, universal laws by which they are controlled in what may be described as an autonomous manner. This is legitimate provided we accept without question the fact that these laws have been established by God. In recent times the council has asserted in this sense the legitimate autonomy of human culture and especially the autonomy of the sciences.[78] We are speaking here of secularism strictly so-called, that is the conception of the world according to which it is entirely self-explanatory without any reference to God, who thus becomes unnecessary and is, as it were, an embarrassment. Secularism of this kind in seeking to assert the power of man, leads to a situation in which God is ignored or even denied.

From this a new form of atheism seems to evolve, a man-centered atheism which is not abstract or metaphysical but pragmatic, based on a pre-ordained plan and militant. Daily and under diverse forms a new consumer society, which is closely connected with this secularist atheism, reveals itself. Pleasure is proclaimed as the supreme good; the desire for power and domination; discrimination of every kind. Such are the inhuman propensities of this humanism.

In this modern world, strange as it may seem, and many find it incredible, there is undoubtedly a certain connection between the Christian religion and at least the initial elements of evangelization on the one hand and the feeling of emptiness and dissatisfaction which preoccupies the minds of men. It would not be too much to say that we have here an urgent and moving plea for the evangelization of the world.

56. Another problem is presented by those who do not practise their religion. There are great numbers of people who have been baptized and, while they have not formally renounced their membership of the church, are, as it were, on the fringe of it and do not live according to her teaching. In the history of Christianity the problem of the non-practising Christian is of long standing: it arises from a certain natural weakness and inherent inconstancy which, alas, is deeply rooted in the minds of men. But in our days it presents certain new features and this may often be explained by the fact, which is characteristic of our time, that men are, so to speak, without roots. As a result of this, Christians associate a great deal with non-believers and are constantly being influenced by those who have no religion. Furthermore, our contemporaries who do not practice any religion are much more eager than in other days to explain their attitude and to justify it as a form of internal religion based on their own laws and standards of authenticity.

Therefore on the one hand the atheists and the non-believers and on the other hand the non-practising Christians offer no small resistance to evangelization. The first group resist because they more or less reject the faith. They are incapable of accepting a new order of things and a new significance of the world, of life, of history; it is impossible to accept this unless one begins from the Absolute which is God. The others resist from inertia, from that vaguely hostile attitude peculiar to those who feel that they are getting on very well on their own, who claim that they know all about the faith: they have experienced it all and no longer believe in it.

This atheistic secularism and non-practice of religion is to be found among adults and among young people, among the elite and the masses. It is to be met with at every level of society, in churches which are long established and in those recently founded. The evangelical activity of the church cannot neglect either group or admit defeat but must seek constantly the right approach and suitable language to expound to the one group and revive in the other the divine revelation and faith in Jesus Christ.

57. Just as Christ did when he was preaching, as the apostles did on the morning of Pentecost, so the church sees before her an immense multitude of men who hunger for the gospel and claim it as their right because God 'desires all men to be saved and to come to the knowlege of truth'.[79]

As the church is sensible of her duty to preach salvation to all men, knowing that the gospel message is intended, not for the few initiated, for the privileged or for some chosen ones, but for all, she is moved by the same solicitude which Christ felt when he looked on the crowd harassed and helpless like 'sheep without a shepherd' and she constantly makes her own his words: 'I have compassion on the crowds'.[80] But she realizes that, if her preaching is to be effective, she must direct her message to the multitudes, to communities of the faithful whose reaction can, and in fact must, affect others.

58. The recent synod devoted a great deal of attention to small groups, or basic communities as they are called, because there is much discussion about them in the church of today. What are these groups and how is it that they are the object of evangelization and at the same time are themselves evangelizers?

While, according to various reports which we heard in the synod they are flourishing more or less everywhere in the church, they differ a great deal even in the same region and differ much more from one region to another. In some regions they arise and develop, with a few exceptions, within the church. They participate in her life, are nourished by her teaching and are loyal to their pastors. When they are of this kind they arise because men want to live the life of the church with greater fervour or because they desire and seek a more human way of life which the larger ecclesial communities cannot easily provide, especially in the larger towns of today where life tends to be crowded and impersonal. These communities can be extensions, after their own fashion, at the spiritual and religious levels—worship, deeper understanding of the faith, fraternal charity, communion with pastors—of small local communities, such as villages and whatever. Or groups may come together to read or study the Bible, for the reception of the sacraments or to foster community: people linked by age, common interests, or social position—such as married couples, young people, or members of the different professions or trades, etc. Or they may be comprised of men with a similar outlook on life who want to promote justice, want to give fraternal help to the poor, or to further social progress. Finally they may serve to bring together Christians when the scarcity of clergy makes it difficult to organize the normal community life of the parish. All this can take place within the community constituted by the church and especially in particular churches or parishes.

In other districts, however, these groups come together animated by a spirit of bitter criticism of the church which they do not hesitate to describe as 'institutional'. They set themselves up in opposition to her as charismatic communities independent of her structures and inspired solely by the gospel. Their special purpose is to attack and reject the hierarchy and all those signs which represent the church. Their attitude is one of fundamental opposition to the church. Thus the considerations by which they are motivated may be described in a word as ideological and not infrequently they fall victim to some political group, some sect or organization or faction with every danger of becoming their tool.

There is a great difference between these two types. Those groups which estrange themselves from the church by their spirit of opposition and impair her unity may certainly be called basic communities but only in the strictly sociological sense. They cannot in the true sense of the word be called ecclesial basic communities even though they claim that they remain within the unity of the church, but yet in opposition to the hierarchy.

This title belongs properly to those other groups which come together within the church so that they may be closely united with her and contribute to her development. These latter groups will be nurseries of evangelization and will be of great service to larger communities, especially to individual churches. As we said at the close of the synod, they will be a source of hope for the universal church in so far as:

They draw their nourishment from the word of God and do not allow themselves to become the prisoners of extreme political factions or of popular ideologies which are always eager to exploit their immense human potential.

They resist the ever present temptation of offering a systematic challenge to the established order and of subjecting it to unbridled criticism under the pretext of serving truth and seeking to be helpful.

They are firm in their loyalty to the church of the district in which they are established and to the universal church. In this way they are preserved from the danger which can only too easily arise of becoming introspective and of thinking that they represent the only true church of Christ, rejecting the other ecclesial communities.

They maintain close and sincere relations with the pastors to whom the Lord has confided the church and with the magisterium which the Spirit of Jesus has entrusted to them.

They never entertain the illusion that the gospel has been announced to them alone, that they alone have the task of proclaiming it or are its sole custodians. On the contrary, realizing that the church has a much wider extension and is much more diversified, they accept the fact that she must find expression in other forms and not solely through them.

They make constant progress in their sense of responsibility, in their religious ardour and in their solicitude and missionary zeal for others.

They adopt an open attitude to all men, in no way favoring any special categories of people.

Given these conditions, which are certainly demanding but are a powerful source of inspiration for souls, these basic ecclesial groups will achieve their primary object: hearing the gospel which is proclaimed to them and accepting wholeheartedly the evangelization of which they are the object, they will become forthwith heralds of the gospel themselves.

6. THE EVANGELIZERS

59. If there be men who preach the gospel of salvation in the world, they do so by the command of Christ Our Saviour, in his name and by virtue of his grace. 'How can men preach unless they be sent?'[81] These are the words of a man who was undoubtedly one of the greatest preachers of the gospel. No one, therefore, may undertake this work unless he has been sent.

To whom has this mission of evangelization been entrusted? The second Vatican council has given an unambiguous reply to this question: 'The church has the duty by divine mandate of going out into the whole world and preaching the gospel to all men'.[82] And in another statement it declares that the whole church is missionary and that the word of evangelization is a fundamental duty of the people of God.[83]

We have already spoken of the close connection existing between the church and evangelization. As the church proclaims and builds up the kingdom of God she takes her place in the very midst of the world as the sign and the instrument of that kingdom which already is and is to come. In reference to this the council quoted those trenchant words of St. Augustine when he spoke of the missionary activity of the apostles: 'They preached the word of truth and procreated churches'.[84]

60. From the fact that the church has been given a mission and that the work of evangelization has been specially entrusted to her we may draw two conclusions. First, the work of evangelization is not an individual activity; it is essentially ecclesial. Accordingly, when the humblest preacher, catechist or pastor is preaching the gospel, assembling his little flock or administering the sacraments, he is acting on behalf of the church and his work

is united with the evangelical activity of the whole church. And this is not merely an institutional connection; there are invisible bonds and hidden roots in the order of grace. From which it follows that he is working not at a task which he has assumed on his own initiative or under the impulse of his own personal inclination but rather in conjunction with the mission of the church and in her name. Another conclusion follows from this: if anyone is evangelizing in the name of the church, a work which she carries out by virtue of a mandate from the Lord, he cannot be the final arbiter of his activity, exercising his own independent discretion and carrying it out according to his own ideas and inclinations. He must exercise his function in the closest communion with the church and her pastors.

It is, as we have already said, the whole church which evangelizes. Therefore, both for the whole world and for every part of it, it is the church which has the responsibility of spreading the gospel.

61. Having discussed these questions, we must now pause to consider with you another matter which is of particular importance nowadays. The early Christians, in their liturgy, in their witness before the judges and the executioners and in their apologetic writings constantly asserted their firm belief in the church, which they described as being spread over the whole earth. They were keenly conscious of belonging to an immense community with no limits of time or space: 'from Abel the just to the last of the chosen ones',[85] 'to the end of the earth',[86] 'to the close of the age'.[87]

This was what the Lord wished his church to be: universal, a great tree in the branches of which the birds of the air come and make their nests,[88] a net gathering fish of every kind[89] or the net which Peter drew in with one hundred and fifty-three great fish,[90] the flock that is cared for by one shepherd.[91] He willed that it should be a universal church knowing no bounds or limits except those, alas, which are to be found in the minds and hearts of sinful men.

62. However, this universal church is closely involved in the particular churches which comprise this or that part of the human race, speaking this or that language. Each will have its own cultural heritage, its own outlook on the world, its own historical memories, its own human foundations, and these features will give a certain unity to each. It is in accordance with the tendencies of our times to appreciate the special qualities of the individual churches.

We must be careful, however, not to regard the church as a collection or, so to speak, a federated association of more or less heterogeneous individual churches, essentially different from each other. It is in accordance with the will of God that his church, which is universal in her vocation and her mission, when she establishes herself in differing circumstances, civil, social and human, in any part of the world should assume different outward appearances and characteristics.

Therefore, if any individual church of its own volition cuts itself off from the universal church, it breaks its connection with God's plan and its ecclesial status is impoverished. Moreover, the church spread throughout the world would become a mere abstraction unless it assumed body and life in the individual churches. It is only if we bear constantly in mind this, as it were, balance between the two that we can appreciate the full significance of the relations between the universal church and the individual churches.

63. The individual churches—which are involved not only with men but also with their aspirations, their wealth and their poverty, with their manner of praying and living and their outlook on the world—must make their own the substance of the evangelical message. Without any sacrifice of the essential truths they must transpose this message into an idiom which will be understood by the people they serve and thus proclaim it.

The churches must make this transposition with all the judgment, care, reverence and competence which the nature of the task demands in fields relating to the sacred liturgy,[92] to catechetics, to the formulation of theological principles, to the secondary ecclesial structures and to the ministry. When we speak of idiom we must be understood to mean not so much an explanation of the words or a literary style as an anthropological and cultural adaptation.

This is a question which calls for no small measure of prudence, because evangelization will lose much of its power and efficacy if it does not take into consideration the people to whom it is addressed, if it does not make use of their language, their signs and their symbols, if it does not offer an answer to the questions which are relevant to them, if, in word, it does not reach and influence their way of life. On the other hand there is the danger that evangelization may lose its very nature and its savour if on the pretext of transposing its content into another language that content is rendered meaningless or is corrupted, or if in the effort to adapt the universal truth to some particular region this truth is in fact rejected and unity destroyed. For without unity there cannot be universality. In fact it is only a church which is conscious of her universal mission and which in practice always shows herself to be universal that can have a message to deliver which can be understood by all and knows no territorial boundaries.

When there is due consideration for the needs of the particular church the universal church will certainly be invigorated and this must be regarded as important and urgent because it is in accordance with the inherent desire of peoples and communities for an ever increasing recognition of their own natural predispositions.

64. If this invigoration is to be achieved it is essential that the individual churches should be wholeheartedly receptive to the universal church. It is especially worthy of note that those Christians who are most simple and faithful to the gospel are keenly conscious of the true significance of the gospel and have a spontaneous appreciation of this universal dimension. They have an instinctive and eager desire for it. They see themselves as a part of it, are in the fullest harmony with it and are really troubled when, on account of some ideology which they do not understand, they find themselves confined within the bounds of a church lacking this universality, circumscribed by local boundaries and restricted in her horizons.

Furthermore, it is a clear lesson of history that if any individual church, even when acting with the best of intentions and relying on arguments based on theology, social theory or pastoral considerations, or moved by the desire for a certain liberty of action, cuts herself off from the universal church and the visible centre of her life, she can rarely if ever avoid two equally grave dangers. There is on the one hand the danger of an arid isolation and on the other hand the danger of a rapid disintegration as each of her constituent parts separates from her just as she has separated from the principal centre. From this arises the danger of losing her liberty since, being separated from her and from the other churches which gave her strength and vigour, she can easily become the prey of various forces which may seek to reduce her to servitude and exploit her.

The individual churches should be united to the universal church by enduring bonds, bonds of charity and loyalty, of ready obedience to the magisterium of Peter, of unity in the law of prayer: *lex orandi* which is also the law of belief: *lex credendi* and finally by solicitude for the preservation of that unity which constitutes universality. The stronger these bonds are, the better fitted she will be to transpose the treasure of the faith into a legitimate variety of ways of communicating her message, whether it be the profession of faith, forms of prayer or worship, Christian life and conduct or the spiritual vigour of the people to whom it is addressed. And her evangelization will be all the more authentic since she will be able to draw from the universal patrimony all that is profitable for her people and will be able to give the universal church the experience and the life of her people to the advantage of all.

65. It was in view of this that we thought it fitting towards the end of the assembly of the third synod to stress in a few clear words full of paternal affection the role of the successor of Peter as the visible, living and dynamic foundation of the unity between the churches and therefore of the universality of the one church.[93] We insisted again and again on the grave duty which is incumbent on us, but which we share with our brothers in the episcopacy, to preserve inviolate the immutable deposit of faith which was entrusted to the apostles by Our Lord. This deposit, though it may be translated into all languages, may never be violated or curtailed. Although it be clothed in symbols suited to different peoples and expressed in theological terms adapted to different cultural, social and even racial environments, it must always remain the exposition of the same Catholic faith as the ecclesial magisterium has received it and transmits it.

66. The universal church has been called to preach the gospel. This task involves various activities, differing one from another. The variety of ministry exercised under one and the same mandate constitutes the richness and the beauty of evangelization. It is fitting therefore to call attention to the following points.

First we may recall with what earnestness the Lord enjoined on the apostles the task of proclaiming the message. He chose them.[94] For some years he trained them as his close companions.[95] He appointed them[96] and sent them forth[97] as witnesses and teachers of the message of salvation, clothed with authority. And the twelve in their turn sent forth their successors who, following in the footsteps of the apostles, continued to preach the gospel.

67. It is therefore by the will of Christ that the successor of Peter is endowed with the pre-eminent responsibility of teaching revealed truth. How often does the New Testament represent Peter as being filled with the Holy Spirit when he spoke in the name of all.[98] So also St Leo the Great says of him that he merited the primacy of the apostles.[99] It is for this reason likewise that the solemn declaration of the church has affirmed that the Supreme Pontiff is the supreme head—*in apice in specula*—of the apostolate.[100] The second Vatican council has declared that 'Christ's mandate to preach the gospel to the whole creation (cf. Mk 16, 15) is directed primarily to the bishops with Peter and in subordination to Peter'.[101]

Accordingly the full, supreme and universal authority which Christ entrusted to his vicar for the pastoral government of his church is vested primarily in him. The Supreme Pontiff himself discharges the duty of preaching and entrusts the same task to others so that the good news of salvation may be proclaimed.[102]

68. In union with the successor of Peter, the bishops, as the successors of the apostles, by virtue of their episcopal ordination are endowed with authority to teach the revealed truths in the church. They are constituted teachers of the faith.

Associated with the bishops in the ministry of evangelization and sharing in their power by a special title are those who by their priestly ordination 'act in the person of Christ'[103] as educators of the people of God in the faith, as heralds of the divine Word and as ministers of the Eucharist and the other sacraments. It is therefore incumbent on all of us pastors, more than on any other section of the church, to enkindle in ourselves a full appreciation of this duty. It is this purpose behind all our actions—'to preach the gospel of God'[104]—which distinguishes our priestly ministry, which gives a unity to those innumerable tasks which occupy our attention throughout our lives and which finally gives a special character to all our work.

This then is our genuine image which we must allow no doubts to weaken, no objections to obscure. Unworthy though we are we have been chosen as pastors in the merciful plan of the Supreme Pastor to preach the word of God with authority, to bring together the scattered people of God, to nourish that people with the sacraments which are the signs of Christ's activity. We have been chosen, at various levels, to lead them to him on the way of salvation and to preserve them in that unity of which we have been constituted the active and living instruments. We have been chosen finally to lead and inspire this community gathered around Christ in line with its essential vocation. If we carry out all this to the best of our human ability and according to the measure of God's grace, then certainly we shall be carrying out the task of evangelization. We fulfil for our part that duty as pastor of the universal church, our brothers in the episcopate in the individual churches under their charge, and the priests and deacons in union with the bishops whose cooperators they are by virtue of that communion which derives from the sacrament of Holy Orders and the charity of the church.[105]

69. Religious for their part find in their own lives consecrated to God an instrument of special excellence for effective evangelization.

By the very nature of their religious life they are involved in the dynamic action of the church which, aspiring ardently towards the 'Absolute' which is God, is called to sanctity. They themselves are witnesses to this sanctity since they are the living expression of the church's aspiration to respond to the more exigent demands of the beatitudes. By their manner of life they constitute a symbol of total dedication to the service of God, of the church and of their fellow men. Accordingly, religious have a special importance in regard to that form of witness which, as we have already said, is a primary element of evangelization. This silent witness of poverty, of detachment from the things of this world, of chastity, pure innocence of life and voluntary obedience, as well as offering a challenge to the world and to the church herself, constitutes an excellent form of preaching which can influence even non-Christians who are of good will and appreciative of certain spiritual values.

In this perspective it is easy to appreciate the role played in the work of evangelization by religious men and women dedicated to prayer, silence and works of penance. Some, indeed very many, religious devote themselves directly to the proclamation of Christ. Their missionary activity will naturally be dependent on the hierarchy and must be coordinated with the whole pastoral organization to the effectiveness of which they seek to contribute. They have made and do make an inestimable contribution to the work of evangelization. By virtue of their religious consecration they are particularly free and willing to leave all things and go to the ends of the earth to preach the gospel. They are always full of courage in their work and their apostolate is often outstanding in its admirable resourcefulness and initiative. They are generous and are often to be found in the most remote mission stations where they may have to endure great dangers to health and even to life. The church is undoubtedly greatly indebted to them.

70. Laymen, whose vocation commits them to the world and to various temporal enterprises, should exercise a special form of evangelization.

Their principal and primary function is not to establish or promote ecclesial communities, which is the special function of pastors, but to develop and make effective all those latent Christian and evangelical possibilities which already exist and operate in the world.

The special field for their evangelical zeal is the wide and complex arena of politics, sociology and economics. They can be effective also in the spheres of culture, the sciences, the arts, international relations and the communications media. There are certain other fields which are especially appropriate for evangelization such as human love, the family, the education of children and adolescents, the practice of the various professions and the relief of human suffering. If laymen who are actively involved in these spheres are inspired with the evangelical spirit, if they are competent and determined to bring into play all those Christian powers in themselves which so often lie hidden and dormant, then all these activities will be all the more helpful in the building up of the kingdom of God and in bringing salvation in Jesus Christ. And in this their effectiveness in the temporal sphere will be in no way diminished; on the contrary new fields of higher achievement will be opened up to them.

71. We must not fail to draw attention to the role played by the family in the sphere of the apostolate which is proper to the laity. It has rightly been called the *domestic* church and this title has been confirmed by the second Vatican council.[106] It declares that in every Christian family the various features and characteristics of the universal church should be found. And accordingly the family, just like the church, must always be regarded as a centre to which the gospel must be brought and from which it must be proclaimed.

Therefore in a family which is conscious of this role all the members of the family are evangelizers and are themselves evangelized. Not only will the parents impart the gospel to their children's lives. Such a family will bring the gospel to many other families and to the whole social circle to which it belongs. Families of mixed marriages must teach Christ to their children, stressing the significance and efficacy of a common baptism. There is also incumbent on them the difficult task of making themselves the architects of unity.

72. Existing circumstances suggest to us that we should devote our attention in particular to young people. Their increasing numbers, the fact that increasingly they are making their presence felt in society, the questions which trouble them should arouse in everyone the desire to offer them zealously and wisely, the evangelical ideal as something to be known and lived. But it is essential that young people themselves, well versed in the faith and in prayer, should be ever more zealous in their apostolate to their contemporaries. The church relies greatly on such help from young people and we ourselves have repeatedly expressed our full confidence in them.

73. It follows that the active presence of the laity in temporal affairs is of the greatest importance. We must not, however, overlook or neglect another aspect: the laity must realize that

they have been called, or are being called, to cooperate with their pastors in the service of the ecclesial community, to extend and invigorate it by the exercise of different kinds of ministries according to the grace and charisms which the Lord has been pleased to bestow on them.

It is with the greatest joy that we see a multitude of pastors, religious and laymen who, in their zeal for the task of preaching Christ, are seeking constantly to improve the proclamation of the gospel. We fully approve the open approach which the church of our time has adopted in pursuance of this objective. There is an openness to reflection, first of all, and then an openness to ecclesial ministries capable of renewing and strengthening the vigour of our evangelization.

There can be no doubt that, side by side with the ministry conferred by the sacrament of Holy Orders, by virtue of which men are constituted pastors and dedicate themselves in a special way to the service of the community, the church recognizes other ministries which, although not related to Holy Orders, are capable of rendering special service to the church. A consideration of the development of the primitive church is very revealing and enables us to avail of her age-long experience in relation to the ministry. This experience is all the more valuable as it enabled the primitive church to grow, to develop its strength and to expand. This investigation of the beginnings of the church must be complemented by a consideration of the needs of mankind and of the church in our day. To avail of these sources, so full of wisdom, sacrificing none of the good which they contain, and adapting them prudently to the demands and requirements of our times: these are the essentials which will allow us to search out and bring to light the forms of ministry which the church needs and which many of the faithful will gladly embrace in order to develop an ever-increasing vitality in the ecclesial community. These ministries will have a true practical value in the measure that they preserve the unity and the norms prescribed by the pastors who have been constituted the protectors and the architects of the unity of the church. Ministries of this kind, which seem to be new but which are in fact closely linked with the experience of the church during the long centuries of her existence—the ministry, for example, of the catechist, of directors of prayer and chant, of Christians dedicated to preaching the Word of God or to caring for their brethren in need, the ministry of directors of small communities, of the heads of apostolic movements and of others of this kind—can be of the greatest value for establishing, vitalizing and extending the church and can help her to cast a more extended radiance so that she may reach those who are far distant from her. We wish to express our deep appreciation of those laymen who are willing to give some of their time and energy—some indeed devote their whole lives—to the service of the missions.

Careful preparation is essential for all workers in the field of evangelization and it is especially necessary for those who devote themselves to the ministry of the Word. Inspired by an ever deeper appreciation of the nobility and richness of the word of God, they whose function it is to proclaim the Word must exercise every care to ensure that their words are dignified, well-chosen and adapted to their audience. Everyone knows the vital importance of the art of speaking in these days. Surely, therefore, preachers and catechists cannot neglect it. It is our earnest desire that in every church the bishops provide suitable instruction for all the ministers of the Word. If this education is undertaken seriously it will not only develop their self-confidence but will also serve to increase their zeal to preach Jesus Christ in our times.

7. THE SPIRIT OF EVANGELIZATION

74. We feel that we should not close this discussion with our dearly beloved brothers and sons without adding one other consideration regarding the spirit and judgment which must guide those who undertake the work of spreading the gospel.

In the name of our Lord Jesus Christ and of the holy apostles Peter and Paul, we urge all those who, under the inspiration of the Holy Spirit and the mandate of the church, are true heralds of the gospel, to be worthy of the vocation to which they have been called, to yield to no fear or hesitation in carrying it out and to omit nothing which can prepare the way for evangelization or make it effective and fruitful. With this end in view it may be useful to suggest the following primary requirements.

75. There can be no evangelization without the cooperation of the Holy Spirit. He descended on Jesus of Nazareth when he was being baptized and at that moment the voice of the Father saying: 'This is my beloved Son in whom I am well pleased'[107] clearly affirmed the election of Jesus and his mission. Furthermore, Jesus being 'led by the Spirit' went into the wilderness and undertook the decisive contest and the supreme test before beginning his mission.[108] 'In the power of the Spirit'[109] he returned to Galilee to preach in his own city of Nazareth and there he applied to himself the words of Isaiah: 'The Spirit of the Lord is upon me' and added: 'Today this scripture has been fulfilled'.[110] Furthermore, when he was about to send forth his disciples,

breathing on them, he said: 'Receive the Holy Spirit'.[111]

In fact, it was only after the coming of the Holy Spirit on the day of Pentecost that the apostles set out to all parts of the earth to undertake the great work of evangelization entrusted to the church. And Peter explained their mission to the people as a fulfilment of the prophecy of Joel when he said: 'I will pour out my spirit on all flesh'.[112] Peter himself is filled with the Holy Spirit when he speaks to the people about the Son of God.[113] And Paul is filled with the Holy Spirit[114] before undertaking his apostolic mission. Similarly Stephen is full of the Holy Spirit when he is chosen as a deacon and later achieves martyrdom by the shedding of his blood.[115] This Spirit, who caused Peter, Paul and the twelve to speak, inspiring the words that they should say, descends likewise 'on those who hear the Word of God'.[116]

The Holy Spirit is the soul of the church and it is by the help of the Holy Spirit that she is multiplied.[117] It is through him, as we have said, that the faithful have a true understanding of the doctrine and mystery of Christ. It is he, as in the first days of the church, who acts through every preacher of the gospel who submits himself to his guidance. He suggests to them the right words which he alone could provide and at the same time predisposes the minds of the hearers to a full acceptance of the gospel and of the kingdom which it proclaims. The techniques of evangelization are valuable, but even though they be perfect, they cannot dispense with the secret action of the Holy Spirit. The most careful preparation by a preacher will be of no avail without him and no discourse will be capable of moving men's hearts unless it is inspired by him. Without him the most skilful plans of sociologists will prove valueless. We see the church today in an age dominated, as it were, by the Holy Spirit. The faithful are striving everywhere, not merely to know and understand him better as he is revealed in holy scripture, but also to surrender themselves to him with joyous hearts, opening their minds to his inspiration. They assemble in great numbers in his honour. They are eager to be guided by him. If the Holy Spirit is of great importance in the life of the church, it is certainly in the work of evangelization that his action is most significant. We must not think it was simply by chance that the first steps in evangelization were initiated on the day of Pentecost under the influence of the Holy Spirit.

We may readily conclude that the Holy Spirit plays a primary part in the propagation of the gospel. It is he who moves the preacher to preach and prepares the souls of men to receive and understand the word of salvation.[118] It may likewise be said that he is the end and the goal of all evangelization. It is he alone who produces that new creation, that is the new human nature towards which evangelization is striving through that unity in variety which evangelization must necessarily evoke in the Christian community. It is through the Holy Spirit that the gospel is disseminated throughout the world as it is he alone who reveals the signs of the times—that is God's—which evangelization receives and elucidates in the life of men.

The synod of bishops which was held in 1974, after it had duly stressed the action of the Holy Spirit in the work of evangelization, declared that the pastors of souls and theologians—and we may include also the faithful who have received the seal of the Holy Spirit in baptism—should study in greater depth the nature and the manner of the action of the Holy Spirit in evangelization in these times. This is also our desire and we urge all the heralds of the gospel, whatever be their order or rank, to pray unceasingly to the divine Spirit with faith and ardour and to submit themselves prudently to his guidance as the principal author of their plans, of their initiatives and their work in the field of evangelization.

76. Let us now consider the preachers of the gospel themselves. It is often said that our age is thirsting for sincerity and honesty. Young people in particular are said to have a horror of falsity and hypocrisy and to seek above all truth and clarity.

These 'signs of the times' should convince us of the necessity for the utmost vigilance. We are continuously being questioned, sometimes tacitly, sometimes openly: Do you believe yourselves what you are saying to us? Is your life in accord with your beliefs? Is your preaching in accord with your life? More than ever before the witness of our life has become an essential requirement if our preaching is to be fully effective. Accordingly, the development and the effectiveness of our preaching of the gospel depends in a large measure on ourselves who are preaching it.

How does the church stand ten years after the council? This is the question which we asked at the beginning of this discourse. Is she firmly established in the midst of the world and yet sufficiently free and independent to challenge the world? Does she bear witness to solidarity with men and at the same time with the 'Absolute' which is God? Are her contemplation and adoration more vital? Is she increasingly zealous in her efforts to maintain the initiatives to restore that full unity of Christians which will give a greater efficacy to our united testimony 'so that the world may believe'?[119] These are questions which we must all face.

We exhort, therefore, our Venerable Brothers whom the Holy

Spirit has appointed to feed the Church of God.[120] We exhort the priests and deacons who are the assistants of the bishops and the promoters of spiritual zeal in assemblies of the people of God and in local communities. We exhort religious, witnesses as they are to the church which is called to sanctity, who have been inspired to adopt a form of life that bears testimony to the gospel beatitudes. We exhort the laity: Christian families, the young and the adults, all those who practise a trade or profession, managers, nor can we omit the poor who so often excel in faith and hope; we exhort all those lay people who are conscious of their role in evangelization, whether it be in the service of the church or in the midst of society and the world. To all of these we say that it is essential that our eager zeal for evangelization should have its source in a true sanctity of life which will be fed by prayer and especially by a love for the blessed eucharist and, as the second Vatican council tells us, preaching will of itself make the preacher more holy.[121]

The world, in spite of the general opinion to the contrary, and although it gives every outward sign of denying God, is in fact seeking God by strange ways and is in desperate need of God. This world is looking for preachers of the gospel to speak to it of God whom they know as being close to them, as though seeing him who is invisible.[122] The world expects of us, and demands of us, a life of simplicity, the habit of prayer, charity towards all and especially towards children and the poor. It expects obedience and humility, forgetfulness of self and abnegation. If these signs of sanctity are wanting, our words will not reach the hearts of men of our time. There is a grave danger that they will be vain and sterile.

77. The effectiveness of evangelization will be gravely diminished if the preachers of the gospel are divided among themselves in various ways. Is not this one of the great obstacles to evangelization at the present time? If the gospel which we preach appears to be rent by doctrinal disputes, by opposing opinions or even by mutual recriminations between Christians—according to each individual's views about Christ and the church and according to differing opinions about society and human institutions—is it not inevitable that those to whom our preaching is directed will be troubled, led into error, and, indeed, scandalized.

The Lord's spiritual testament teaches us that unity among Christians is not only the proof of our enrolment in the number of his elect but also the proof of his mission from the Father. It is the outstanding testimony to the credence due to Christians and to Christ himself.

Since we are preachers of the gospel we must appear before the faithful, not as men disputing and disagreeing about controversies which can give no edification, but rather as men strong in the faith who are able to come together, in spite of differences which may now and then arise, united in a sincere, disinterested search for the truth. Thus it is clear that the success of evangelization is undoubtedly dependent on the witness of unity given by the church. This imposes on us a heavy responsibility but it is also a source of consolation.

Here we would like to stress the fact that the sign of unity among Christians is the aim and the instrument of all evangelization. The division now existing among Christians is a very grave state of affairs which is impeding the very work of Christ. The second Vatican council has stated clearly and emphatically: 'The division among Christians is prejudicing the sacred cause of preaching the gospel to all creation and is for many an obstacle to their approach to the faith'.[123] For this reason, when we were inaugurating the jubilee year, we thought it necessary to address this admonition to all the faithful of the Catholic world: 'Before all men can be brought back and restored in the grace of God our Father it is essential that unity be re-established between all those who acknowledge and accept Jesus Christ in the spirit of faith as the God of mercy who frees men and unites them in the Spirit of love and truth'.[124] It is, therefore, with great hope that we observe those efforts which Christians are now making for a complete restoration of that unity which Christ desires. St Paul tells us in this connection that 'hope does not disappoint us'.[125] While we are still making every effort to obtain from God the grace of this perfect unity we wish to see an intensification of prayer for this intention. Moreover, we endorse the desire expressed by the Fathers of the third general assembly of the synod of bishops for unceasing collaboration with our Christian brethren with whom we are not yet united in perfect unity and, likewise, their desire that this collaboration be based on our common baptism and our common heritage of the faith so that, in the very work of evangelizaton, we may offer to the world a broader common witness to Christ.

The command of Christ prescribes this and the duty of preaching and giving witness to the gospel requires it.

78. The gospel which has been entrusted to us is also the word of truth. This truth confers liberty on men and it is it alone which can bring peace to the soul. When we approach them proclaiming the good news it is this truth which men desire: truth about God, truth about man and his hidden destiny, truth about the world,

that difficult truth which we discover in the Word of God and of which we are—let us repeat it—neither the masters not the authors but the guardians, the heralds and the ministers.[126]

It is required of the preacher of the gospel that he be a disciple of truth and this all the more because the truth which he accepts and communicates is revealed truth and, above all, part of that primary truth which is God himself. The preacher of the gospel is, therefore, a man who, forgetful of himself, and even at the cost of great personal sacrifice, is always seeking out the truth to hand it on to others. He must never falsify it, never conceal it in the desire to please men, to astonish or shock, to show originality or to attract attention. He must never reject the truth nor allow it to be obscured by his lethargy in seeking it out neither for his own advantage nor from motives of fear. He will not fail to devote himself to its study. He will serve it generously but will never attempt to make it serve him.

As we are the pastors of the faithful our ministry makes it incumbent on us to protect, defend and communicate the truth without regard for any loss or suffering it may involve. Many excellent and holy pastors have given us an example of this love for truth; not infrequently they have exhibited heroic virtue in its service. The God of truth expects us also to be vigilant defenders and dedicated preachers of this truth.

To those of you who are scholars, whether it be of theology, of exegesis or of history, we say: the work of evangelization needs the fruits of your tireless studies, of your diligence and wisdom in transmitting that truth with which your studies make you familiar, but which always transcends the hearts of men because it is the very truth of God.

To parents and teachers we say: your responsibility—and present-day tensions make it more difficult—is to help your children and pupils to discern all truth, including religious and spiritual truth.

79. The ministry of evangelization requires of the evangelizer fraternal and ever increasing love for those whom he is evangelizing. The apostle Paul, the model for every preacher, wrote these words to the Thessalonians which may serve as our plan of action: 'So, being affectionately desirous of you, we were ready to share with you, not only the gospel of God but also our own selves because you had become very dear to us'.[127] What is this love? It is the love, not so much of a teacher as of a father, or rather of a mother. It is the Lord's wish that every preacher of the gospel, every builder up of the church, should have this love.

The sign of this love is our concern to communicate the truth and to bring all those to whom we preach into the fold of unity. A further sign of this love is to devote oneself without any reserve or hesitation to the task of preaching Jesus Christ.[128]

We may be permitted to mention some other signs of this love. The first is that we show respect for those whom we are evangelizing. We must not fail to show consideration for their religious beliefs, for their dispositions and their way of life which we must not try to force unduly. We must show consideration for their conscience and their opinions.[129]

Another sign of this love is that we are careful lest anyone, and especially anyone whose faith is weak, be offended by what we say. Words which may be clear to the educated can wound the souls of the simple faithful and be a source of trouble and scandal.

Finally, it will be a sign of love if we strive to communicate to Christians, not doubts and hesitations arising from an ill-digested learning, but a firm certainty so that they may lead a Christian life. They claim it as of right, as children of God to whom they submit themselves in all things which love requires of them.

80. At this point our exhortation is inspired by the example of those great preachers and evangelists whose lives were dedicated to the apostolate. It gives us special pleasure to signalize among them those whom we have proposed in this holy year for the veneration of the faithful. They overcame many obstacles to evangelization.

We too have many obstacles to contend with in our own times. We shall mention one which is complex and all the more serious because it arises from within: that is the apathy and especially the lack of joy and hope in many of our evangelizers. We earnestly exhort, therefore, all those who in any capacity are engaged in the work of evangelization to nourish and increase their fervour.[130]

This fervour requires above all that we reject all excuses which might deflect us from evangelization. The most insidious of these are those which are allegedly based on this or that teaching of the council.

So it is that only too often we hear it asserted in various forms that to insist on a truth, even though it be a truth of the gospel, to prescribe a way of life, even though it be the way of salvation, is to do violence to religious liberty. And, they will add, why should the gospel be preached if all men can attain salvation by their own uprightness of heart? Furthermore, they say, the world and its history are full of the 'seeds of the word'; it is therefore a mere illusion to seek to bring the gospel to places where it is already present in the seeds which the Lord himself has sown.

Anyone who studies these questions more deeply in the documents of the Council will find that they express a view entirely different from that which the propounders of these ideas have drawn from a superficial reading.

It is certainly wrong to force anything on the conscience of our brothers. But it is quite another matter to present to their conscience the gospel truth and salvation in Jesus Christ clearly, while fully respecting their freedom of choice and election—'excluding every form of action which appears to savour of coercion or dishonest or undue persuasion'.[131] So far from this being a violation of liberty of conscience, it is a mark of respect for that liberty when we give the opportunity of choosing a way of life which seems noble and praiseworthy even to those who do not believe in God. Can it be regarded as a crime against the liberty of another to proclaim in the spirit of joy the gospel which we have received from the all-merciful God?[132] Why should it be only errors and falsehood, the unworthy and obscene, which may be proposed? Can it be right that these should be inculcated as, alas, they frequently are, through the persuasive and pernicious propaganda of the mass media or as a result of the undue tolerance of legislation, or of the cowardice of good men and the audacity of the evil?

To proclaim Christ and his kingdom with all due respect for others is not merely the right of the evangelizer: it is his duty. It is likewise the right of men as the brothers of the evangelizer to hear the message of salvation proclaimed to them by him. God can indeed effect the salvation of whomsoever he wishes by extraordinary means known to him alone.[133] But his son came into the world in order to open up to us by his teaching and his life the ordinary way of salvation. He has commissioned us and invested us with his authority to transmit this revelation. It would be a useful exercise for every member of the faithful and every evangelizer to meditate prayerfully on this consideration: men may attain salvation, even though the gospel is not preached to them, by other ways through the mercy of God; if, however, through lack of zeal or lack of courage, or 'being ashamed of the gospel' as St Paul has put it,[134] or in deference to false theories, we fail to proclaim the gospel, can we ourselves be saved? This is simply to ignore the call of God who wants the good seed to fructify by virtue of the voice of the ministers of the gospel; it depends on us whether the seed will develop into a tree and bear its due fruit.

Let us maintain, therefore, our fervour of spirit. Let us preserve the sweet and heartfelt joy of evangelizing, even when we have to sow in tears. We must be possessed of the same eagerness of spirit that inspired John the Baptist, Peter and Paul, the other apostles and all the multitude of admirable evangelizers down through the ages—a spirit which neither men nor circumstances can ever extinguish. May it be a great source of joy to us who have dedicated our lives to the task. And may the world of our time which is searching, now in anguish and now in hope, receive the gospel not from evangelizers who are dejected or dispirited, not from those who are impatient or anxious; let them hear it from ministers of the gospel whose lives are aglow with fervour, from those who, having received the joy of Christ into their own hearts, are ready to risk their lives so that the kingdom may be proclaimed and the church established throughout the world.

81. This, then, my brothers, is the appeal which we make to you from the depths of our heart. It echoes the words of our brothers who met in the third general assembly of the synod of bishops. This is the course of action that we have prescribed at the close of the holy year which has given us a much deeper appreciation of the needs and the appeals of so many of our fellow men who, whether they be Christians or non-Christians, are looking to the church for the word of salvation.

May this light of the holy year, which has shone for such an immense number of souls who have been reconciled to God both in their own churches and here in Rome, continue to give its light after the jubilee by virtue of a programme of pastoral activity in which evangelization will play the primary part. May it illuminate our age which is the prelude to a new century and to the third millenium of Christianity.

82. It is with joy that we confide our desires to the Blessed Virgin Mary on this day specially consecrated to her Immaculate Conception and the tenth anniversary of the close of the second Vatican council. On the morning of Pentecost she presided in prayer at the beginning of evangelization under the guidance of the Holy Spirit. May she shine forth as the star of that constantly renewed evangelization which the church, in obedience to the command of the Lord, must promote and accomplish especially in these days, so difficult but so full of hope.

In the name of Christ we impart to you all, to your communities, your families and all those who are dear to you our paternal benediction in the words of St Paul to the Philippians: 'I thank my God in all my remembrance of you, always in every prayer of mine for you all making my prayer with joy, thankful for your participation in the gospel. . . It is right for me to feel thus about you all because I hold you in my heart, for you are all partakers with me of grace in the defence and confirmation of the gospel. For God is my witness how I yearn for you with the affection of Christ Jesus'.[135]

* Translated by Dom Matthew Dillon, O.S.B., from the Latin original in the *Acta Apostolicae Sedis*, LXVIII (1976), pages 1 to 96.
1. Cfr. Lk. 22, 32.
2. 2 Cor. 11, 28.
3. Cfr. Decree on the church's missionary activity, n. 1, *Vatican Council II: Conciliar and post-conciliar documents,* edited by Austin Flannery, O.P., p. 813. (Hereafter referred to as Flannery).
4. Cfr. Eph. 4, 24; 2, 15; Col. 3, 10; Gal. 3, 27; Rom. 13, 14; 2 Cor. 5, 17.
5. 2 Cor. 5, 20
6. See Paul VI, Address to Synod of Bishops, 26 Oct. 1974.
7. Paul IV, Address to College of Cardinals, 22 June, 1973.
8. 2 Cor. 11, 28.
9. 1 Tim. 5, 17.
10. 2 Tim. 5, 15.
11. Cfr. 1 Cor. 2, 5.
12. Lk. 4, 43.
13. Ibidem.
14. Lk. 4, 18; Cfr. Is. 61, 1.
15. Cfr. Mk. 1, 1; Rom. 1, 1-3.
16. Cfr. Mt. 6, 33.
17. Cfr. Mt. 5, 3-12.
18. Cfr. Mt. 5-7.
19. Cfr. Mt. 10.
20. Cfr. Mt. 13.
21. Cfr. Mt. 18.
22. Cfr. Mt. 24-25.
23. Cfr. Mt. 24, 36; Act 1, 7; 1 Th. 5, 1-2.
24. Cfr. Mt. 11, 12; Lk. 16, 16.
25. Cfr. Mt. 4, 17.
26. Mk. 1, 27.
27. Lk. 4, 22.
28. Jn. 7, 46.
29. Lk. 4, 43.
30. Jn. 11, 52.
31. Cfr. Dogmatic constitution on divine revelation, n. 4, Flannery, p. 750.
32. Cfr. 1 Pt. 2, 9.
33. Cfr. Act 2, 11.
34. Lk. 4, 43.
35. 1 Cor. 9, 16.
36. See Declaration by the Synod Fathers, n. 4, *Doctrine and Life,* Jan. 1975, pp. 53-54.
37. Mt. 28, 19.

38. Act 2, 41, 47.
39. Cfr. Dogmatic constitution on the church, n. 8, Flannery, p. 357; decree on the church's missionary activity, n. 5, op. cit., p. 817.
40. Cfr. Act 2, 42-46, 4, 32-35, 5, 12-16.
41. Cfr. Act 2, 11; 1 Pt. 2, 9.
42. Cfr. Decree on the church's missionary activity, nn. 5, 11, 12, Flannery, pp. 803, 807, 809.
43. Cfr. 2 Cor. 4, 5; St Augustine, *Sermo XLVI, De Pastoribus:* C.C.L., XLI, pp. 529-530.
44. Lk. 10, 16; cfr. St Cyprian, *De Unitate Ecclesiae, 14:* PL 4, 527; St Augustine, *Ennarat. 88, sermo 2, 14:* PL 37, 1140; St John Chrysostom, *Hom de capto Eutropio, 6:* PG 52, 402.
45. Eph. 5, 25.
46. Ap. 21, 5; cfr. 2 Cor. 5, 17; Gal. 6, 15.
47. Cfr. Rom. 6, 4.
48. Cfr. Eph. 4, 23-24; Col. 3, 9-10.
49. Cfr. Rom. 1, 16; 1 Cor. 1, 18; 2, 4.
50. Cfr. n. 53: A.A.S. 58 (1966), p. 1075.
51. Cfr. Tertullian, *Apologeticum.*
52. 1 Pt. 3, 15.
53. Cfr. Dogmatic constitution on the church, nn. 1, 9, 48, Flannery, pp. 350, 359, 407; Pastoral constitution on the church in the modern world, nn. 42, 45, op. cit., pp. 942, 947; decree on the church's missionary activity, nn. 1, 5, op, cit., 813, 817.
54. Cfr. Rom. 1, 16; 1 Cor. 1, 18.
55. Cfr. Act 17, 22-23.
56. 1 Jn. 3, 1; cfr. Rom. 8, 14-17.
57. Cfr. Eph. 2, 8; Tom. 1, 16 and 'Declaration on safeguarding belief in the Incarnation and the Trinity from recent errors', Sacr. Cong. for Doctrine of the Faith.
58. Cfr. 1 Jn. 3, 2; Rom. 8, 29; Phil. 3, 20-21 and Dogmatic Constitution on the church, nn. 48-51, Flannery, pp. 407-413.
59. Cfr. 'Declaration in Defence of the Catholic Doctrine on the Church', Sacr. Cong. for the Doctrine of the Faith, 24 June, 1973, *Doctrine and Life,* August, 1973, pp. 447-457.
60. Cfr. Pastoral constitution on the church in the modern world, nn. 47-52, Flannery, pp. 949-957; *Humanae vitae, Doctrine and Life,* Sept. 1968, pp. 519-538.
61. Paul VI, Address during third synod of bishops, 27 Sept., 1974.
62. Paul VI, Address during third synod of bishops, 27 Sept., 1974.
63. Paul VI, Address to the people of Colombia, 23 August, 1968.
64. Paul VI, Address for the 'Day of Progress'. Bogota, 23 Aug. 1968; see Augustine, Letter 229 PL 33, 1020.
65. Paul VI, Address to the third synod of bishops, 26 Oct. 1964.
66. Paul VI, Address on 15 Oct. 1975.
67. Paul VI, Address to members of the 'Consilium de Laicis', 2 Oct. 1974.
68. Cfr. 1 Pt. 3, 1.
69. Rom. 10, 14, 17.
70. Cfr. 1 Cor. 2, 1-5.
71. Rom. 10, 17.
72. Cfr. Mt. 10, 27; Lk. 12, 3.
73. Mk. 16, 15.
74. Cfr. St Justin, *I Apologia,* 46, 1-4; *II Apologia,* 7, 1-4; 10, 1-3; 3-4.
75. Eusebius of Caesaria, *praeparatio Evangelics,* 1, 1; PG 21, 26-28.

76. Cfr. Eph. 3, 8.

77. Henri de Lubac, *Le drame de l'humanisme athée,* Ed. Spes, Paris 1945.

78. Cfr. Pastoral constitution on the church in the modern world, n. 59, Flannery, p. 963.

79. 1 Tim. 2, 4.

80. Mt. 9, 36; 15, 32.

81. Rom. 10, 15.

82. Declaration on religious liberty, n. 13, Flannery, p. 809; Dogmatic constitution on the church, n. 5, op. cit., p. 352; Decree on the church's missionary activity, n. 1, op. cit., p. 813.

83. Cfr. Decree on the church's missionary activity, n. 35, Flannery, p. 849.

84. St Augustine, *Ennarat.* in Ps. 44, 23; C.C.L. XXXVIII, p. 510; cfr. Decree on the church's missionary activity, n. 1, Flannery, p. 813.

85. St Gregory the Great, *Homil. in Evangelia,* 19, 1: PL 76, 1154.

86. Act 1, 8; cfr. *Didache,* 9, 1; Funk, *Patres Apostolici,* 1, 22.

87. Mt. 28, 20.

88. Cfr. Mt. 13, 32.

89. Cfr. Mt. 13, 47.

90. Cfr. Jn. 21, 11.

91. Cfr. Jn. 10, 1-16.

92. Cfr. Constitution on the Sacred liturgy, nn. 37-38 and liturgical books and other documents following on the reformation of the liturgy.

93. Paul VI, Address to the third synod of bishops, 24 Oct. 1974.

94. Cfr. Jn. 15, 16; Mk. 3, 13-19, Lk. 6, 13-16.

95. Cfr. Act 1, 21-22.

96. Cfr. Mk. 3, 14.

97. Cfr. Mk. 3, 15; Lk. 9, 2.

98. Act 4, 8; cfr. Act 2, 14; 3, 12.

99. Cfr. St. Leo the Great, *Sermo 69,* 3; *Sermo 70,* 1-3; *Sermo 94,* 3; *Sermo 95,* 2; S. Ch. 200, pp. 50-52; 58-66; 258-260; 268.

100. Cfr. 1st Council of Lyons, Const. *Ad apostolicae dignitatis;* Council of Vienna, Const. *Ad Providam Christi.*

101. Decree on the church's missionary activity, n. 38, Flannery, p. 851.

102. Cfr. Dogmatic constitution on the church, n. 22, Flannery, p. 374.

103. Cfr. Dogmatic constitution on the church, nn. 10, 37, Flannery, pp. 30, 394; on the church's missionary activity, n. 39, Flannery, p.853, on the ministry and life of priests, n. 2, 12, 13, op. cit., pp. 864, 885, 887.

104. Cfr. 1 Th. 2, 9.

105. Cfr. 1 Pt. 5, 4.

106. Dogmatic constitution on the church, n. 11, Flannery, p. 361; decree on the apostolate of lay people, n. 11, op. cit., p. 778; St John Chrysostom, *In Genesim Serm.* VI, 2; VII, 1; PG 54, 607-608.

107. Mt. 3, 17.

108. Mt. 4, 1.

109. Lk. 4, 14.

110. Lk. 4, 18, 21; cfr. Is. 61, 1.

111. Jn. 20, 22.

112. Act 2, 27.

113. Cfr. Act 4, 8.

114. Cfr. Act 9, 17.

115. Cfr. Act 6, 5, 10; 7, 55.

116. Cfr. Act 10, 44.

117. Cfr. Act 9, 31.

118. Cfr. Decree on the church's missionary activity, n. 4, Flannery, p. 816.

119. Jn. 17, 21.

120. Cfr. Act 20, 28.

121. Cfr. Decree on the ministry and life of priests, n. 13, Flannery, p. 887.

122. Cfr. Heb. 11, 27.

123. Decree on the church's missionary activity, n. 6, Flannery, p. 818; Decree on ecumenism, n. 1, op. cit, p. 452.

124. Bulla *Apostolorum limina,* VII; A.A.S. 66 (1974), p. 305.

125. Rom. 5, 5.

126. Cfr. Jn. 8, 32.

127. 1 Th. 2, 8; cfr. Phil. 1, 8.

128. Cfr. 1 Th. 2, 7, 11; 1 Cor. 4, 15; Gal. 4, 19.

129. Cfr. 1 Cor. 8, 9-13, Rom. 14, 15.

130. Cfr. Rom. 12, 11.

131. Cfr. Declaration on religious liberty, n. 4, Flannery, p. 802.

132. Ibidem, nn. 9-14, op. cit., pp. 806-811.

133. Cfr. Decree on the church's missionary activity, n. 7, Flannery, p. 821.

134. Cfr. Rom. 1, 16.

135. Phil. 1, 3-4, 7-8.

121

CATECHESIS IN OUR TIME*

John Paul II, *Catechesi tradendae*, 16 October, 1979

INTRODUCTION

Christ's Final Command

1. The Church has always considered catechesis one of her primary tasks, for, before Christ ascended to his Father after his Resurrection, he gave the Apostles a final command—to make disciples of all nations and to teach them to observe all that he had commanded.[1] He thus entrusted them with the mission and power to proclaim to humanity what they had heard, what they had seen with their eyes, what they had looked upon and touched with their hands, concerning the Word of Life.[2] He also entrusted them with the mission and power to explain with authority what he had taught them, his words and actions, his signs and commandments. And he gave them the Spirit to fulfil this mission.

Very soon the name of catechesis was given to the whole of the efforts within the Church to make disciples, to help people to believe that Jesus is the Son of God, so that believing they might have life in his name,[3] and to educate and instruct them in this life and thus build up the Body of Christ. The Church has not ceased to devote her energy to this task.

Paul VI's Solicitude

2. The most recent Popes gave catechesis a place of eminence in their pastoral solicitude. Through his gestures, his preaching, his authoritative interpretation of the Second Vatican Council (considered by him the great catechism of modern times), and through the whole of his life, my venerated predecessor Paul VI served the Church's catechesis in a particularly exemplary fashion. On March 18, 1971 he approved the General Catechetical Directory prepared by the Sacred Congregation for the Clergy, a directory that is still the basic document for encouraging and guiding catechetical renewal throughout the

Church. He set up the International Council for Catechesis in 1975. He defined in masterly fashion the role and significance of catechesis in the life and mission of the Church when he addressed the participants in the First International Catechetical Congress on September 25, 1971,[4] and he returned explicitly to the subject in his Apostolic Exhortation *Evangelii Nuntiandi*.[5] He decided that catechesis, especially that meant for children and young people, should be the theme of the Fourth General Assembly of the Synod of Bishops,[6] which was held in October 1977 and which I myself had the joy of taking part in.

A Fruitful Synod

3.   At the end of that Synod the Fathers presented the Pope with a very rich documentation, consisting of the various interventions during the Assembly, the conclusions of the working groups, the Message that they had with his consent sent to the people of God,[7] and especially the imposing list of "Propositions" in which they expressed their views on a very large number of aspects of present-day catechesis.

The Synod worked in an exceptional atmosphere of thanksgiving and hope. It saw in catechetical renewal a precious gift from the Holy Spirit to the Church of today, a gift to which the Christian communities at all levels throughout the world are responding with a generosity and inventive dedication that win admiration. The requisite discernment could then be brought to bear on a reality that is very much alive and it could benefit from great openness among the people of God to the grace of the Lord and the directives of the Magisterium.

Purpose of This Exhortation

4.   It is in the same climate of faith and hope that I am today addressing this Apostolic Exhortation to you, Venerable Brothers and dear sons and daughters. The theme is extremely vast and the Exhortation will keep to a few only of the most topical and decisive aspects of it, as an affirmation of the happy results of the Synod. In essence, the Exhortation takes up again the reflections that were prepared by Pope Paul VI, making abundant use of the documents left by the Synod. Pope John Paul I, whose zeal and gifts as a catechist amazed us all, had taken them in hand and was preparing to publish them when he was suddenly called to God. To all of us he gave an example of catechesis at once popular and concentrated on the essential, one made up of simple words and actions that were able to touch

the heart. I am therefore taking up the inheritance of these two Popes in response to the request which was expressly formulated by the Bishops at the end of the Fourth General Assembly of the Synod and which was welcomed by Pope Paul VI in his closing speech.[8] I am also doing so in order to fulfil one of the chief duties of my apostolic charge. Catechesis has always been a central care in my ministry as a priest and as a bishop.

I ardently desire that this Apostolic Exhortation to the whole Church should strengthen the solidity of the faith and of Christian living, should give fresh vigour to the initiatives in hand, should stimulate creativity—with the required vigilance—and should help to spread among the communities the joy of bringing the mystery of Christ to the world.

I
WE HAVE BUT ONE TEACHER, JESUS CHRIST

Putting Into Communion With the Person of Christ

5. The Fourth General Assembly of the Synod of Bishops often stressed the Christocentricity of all authentic catechesis. We can here use the word "Christocentricity" in both its meanings, which are not opposed to each other or mutually exclusive, but each of which rather demands and completes the other.

In the first place, it is intended to stress that at the heart of catechesis we find, in essence, a Person, the Person of Jesus of Nazareth, "the only Son from the Father. . .full of grace and truth",[9] who suffered and died for us and who now, after rising, is living with us forever. It is Jesus who is "the way, and the truth, and the life",[10] and Christian living consists in following Christ, the *sequela Christi*.

The primary and essential object of catechesis is, to use an expression dear to Saint Paul and also to contemporary theology, "the mystery of Christ". Catechizing is in a way to lead a person to study this Mystery in all its dimensions: "To make all men see what is the plan of the mystery. . .comprehend with all the saints what is the breadth and length and height and depth. . . know the love of Christ which surpasses knowledge. . .(and be filled) with all the fullness of God".[11] It is therefore to reveal in the Person of Christ the whole of God's eternal design reaching fulfilment in that Person. It is to seek to understand the meaning of Christ's actions and words and of the signs worked by him, for they simultaneously hide and reveal his mystery. Accordingly, the definitive aim of catechesis is to put people not only in touch but in communion, in intimacy, with Jesus Christ: only he can lead us to the love of the Father in the Spirit and make us share in the life of the Holy Trinity.

Transmitting Christ's Teaching

6. Christocentricity in catechesis also means the intention to transmit not one's own teaching or that of some other master, but the teaching of Jesus Christ, the Truth that he communicates or, to put it more precisely, the Truth that he is.[12] We must therefore say that in catechesis it is Christ, the Incarnate Word and Son of God, who is taught—everything else is taught with reference to him—and it is Christ alone who teaches—anyone else teaches to the extent that he is Christ's spokesman, enabling Christ to teach with his lips. Whatever be the level of his responsibility in the Church, every catechist must constantly endeavour to transmit by his teaching and behaviour the teaching and life of Jesus. He will not seek to keep directed towards himself and his personal opinions and attitudes the attention and the consent of the mind and heart of the person he is catechizing. Above all, he will not try to inculcate his personal opinions and options as if they expressed Christ's teaching and the lessons of his life. Every catechist should be able to apply to himself the mysterious words of Jesus: "My teaching is not mine, but his who sent me".[13] Saint Paul did this when he was dealing with a question of prime importance: "I received from the Lord what I also delivered to you".[14] What assiduous study of the word of God transmitted by the Church's Magisterium, what profound familiarity with Christ and with the Father, what a spirit of prayer, what detachment from self must a catechist have in order that he can say: "My teaching is not mine"!

Christ the Teacher

7. This teaching is not a body of abstract truths. It is the communication of the living mystery of God. The person teaching it in the Gospel is altogether superior in excellence to the "masters" in Israel, and the nature of his doctrine surpasses theirs in every way because of the unique link between what he says, what he does and what he is. Nevertheless, the Gospels clearly relate occasions when Jesus "taught". "Jesus began to do and teach"[15]—with these two verbs, placed at the beginning of the book of the Acts, Saint Luke links and at the same time distinguishes two poles in Christ's mission.

Jesus taught. It is the witness that he gives of himself: "Day after day I sat in the Temple teaching".[16] It is the admiring observation of the evangelists, surprised to see him teaching everywhere and at all times, teaching in a manner and with an authority previously unknown: "Crowds gathered to him again; and again, as his custom was, he taught them";[17] "and they were astonished at his teaching, for he taught them as one who had authority".[18] It is also what his enemies note for the purpose of drawing from it grounds for accusation and condemnation: "He stirs up the people, teaching throughout all Judaea, from Galilee even to this place".[19]

The One "Teacher"

8.   One who teaches in this way has a unique title to the name of "Teacher". Throughout the New Testament, especially in the Gospels, how many times is he given this title of Teacher![20] Of course the Twelve, the other disciples, and the crowds of listeners call him "Teacher" in tones of admiration, trust and tenderness.[21] Even the Pharisees and the Sadducees, the Doctors of the Law, and the Jews in general do not refuse him the title: "Teacher, we wish to see a sign from you";[22] "Teacher, what shall I do to inherit eternal life"?[23] But above all, Jesus himself at particularly solemn and highly significant moments calls himself Teacher: "You call me Teacher and Lord; and you are right, for so I am";[24] and he proclaims the singularity, the uniqueness of his character as Teacher: "You have one teacher",[25] the Christ. One can understand why people of every kind, race and nation have for two thousand years in all the languages of the earth given him this title with veneration, repeating in their own ways the exclamation of Nicodemus: "We know that you are a teacher come from God".[26]

This image of Christ the Teacher is at once majestic and familiar, impressive and reassuring. It comes from the pen of the evangelists and it has often been evoked subsequently in iconography since earliest Christian times,[27] so captivating is it. And I am pleased to evoke it in my turn at the beginning of these considerations on catechesis in the modern world.

Teaching Through His Life as a Whole

9.   In doing so, I am not forgetful that the majesty of Christ the Teacher and the unique consistency and persuasiveness of his teaching can only be explained by the fact that his words, his parables and his arguments are never separable from his life and his very being. Accordingly, the whole of Christ's life was a con-

tinual teaching: his silences, his miracles, his gestures, his prayer, his love for people, his special affection for the little and the poor, his acceptance of the total sacrifice on the Cross for the redemption of the world, and his Resurrection are the actualization of his word and the fulfilment of revelation. Hence for Christians the crucifix is one of the most sublime and popular images of Christ the Teacher.

These considerations follow in the wake of the great traditions of the Church and they all strengthen our fervour with regard to Christ, the Teacher who reveals God to man and man to himself, the Teacher who saves, sanctifies and guides, who lives, who speaks, rouses, moves, redresses, judges, forgives, and goes with us day by day on the path of history, the Teacher who comes and will come in glory.

Only in deep communion with him will catechists find light and strength for an authentic, desirable renewal of catechesis.

II

AN EXPERIENCE AS OLD AS THE CHURCH

The Mission of the Apostles

10. The image of Christ the Teacher was stamped on the spirit of the Twelve and of the first disciples, and the command "Go. . .and make disciples of all nations"[28] set the course for the whole of their lives. Saint John bears witness to this in his Gospel when he reports the words of Jesus: "No longer do I call you servants, for the servant does not know what his master is doing; but I have called you friends, for all that I have heard from my Father I have made known to you".[29] It was not they who chose to follow Jesus; it was Jesus who chose them, kept them with him, and appointed them even before his Passover, that they should go and bear fruit and that their fruit should remain.[30] For this reason he formally conferred on them after the Resurrection the mission of making disciples of all nations.

The whole of the book of the Acts of the Apostles is a witness that they were faithful to their vocation and to the mission they had received. The members of the first Christian community are seen in it as "devoted to the apostles' teaching and fellowship, to the breaking of bread and the prayers".[31] Without any doubt we find in that a lasting image of the Church being born of and continually nourished by the word of the Lord, thanks to the teaching of the Apostles, celebrating that word in the Eucharistic Sacrifice and bearing witness to it before the world in the sign of charity.

When those who opposed the Apostles took offence at their activity, it was because they were "annoyed because (the Apostles) were teaching the people"[32] and the order they gave them was not to teach at all in the name of Jesus.[33] But we know that the Apostles considered it right to listen to God rather than to men on this very matter.[34]

Catechesis in the Apostolic Age

11. The Apostles were not slow to share with others the ministry of apostleship.[35] They transmitted to their successors the task of teaching. They entrusted it also to the deacons from the moment of their institution: Stephen, "full of grace and power", taught unceasingly, moved by the wisdom of the Spirit.[36] The Apostles associated "many others" with themselves in the task of teaching,[37] and even simple Christians scattered by persecution "went about preaching the word".[38] Saint Paul was in a pre-eminent way the herald of this preaching, from Antioch to Rome, where the last picture of him that we have in Acts is that of a person "teaching about the Lord Jesus Christ quite openly".[39] His numerous letters continue and give greater depth to his teaching. The letters of Peter, John, James and Jude are also, in every case, evidence of catechesis in the apostolic age.

Before being written down, the Gospels were the expression of an oral teaching passed on to the Christian communities, and they display with varying degrees of clarity a catechetical structure. Saint Matthew's account has indeed been called the catechist's gospel, and Saint Mark's the catechumen's gospel.

The Fathers of the Church

12. This mission of teaching that belonged to the Apostles and their first fellow workers was continued by the Church. Making herself day after day a disciple of the Lord, she earned the title of "Mother and Teacher".[40] From Clement of Rome to Origen,[41] the post-apostolic age saw the birth of remarkable works. Next we see a striking fact: some of the most impressive Bishops and pastors, especially in the third and fourth centuries, considered it an important part of their episcopal ministry to deliver catechetical instructions and write treatises. It was the age of Cyril of Jerusalem and John Chrysostom, of Ambrose

and Augustine, the age that saw the flowering, from the pen of numerous Fathers of the Church, of works that are still models for us.

It would be impossible here to recall, even very briefly, the catechesis that gave support to the spread and advance of the Church in the various periods of history, in every continent, and in the widest variety of social and cultural contexts. There was indeed no lack of difficulties. But the word of the Lord completed its course down the centuries; it sped on and triumphed, to use the words of the Apostle Paul.[42]

Councils and Missionary Activity

13. The ministry of catechesis draws ever fresh energy from the Councils. The Council of Trent is a noteworthy example of this. It gave catechesis priority in its constitutions and decrees. It lies at the origin of the Roman Catechism, which is also known by the name of that Council and which is a work of the first rank as a summary of Christian teaching and traditional theology for use by priests. It gave rise to a remarkable organization of catechesis in the Church. It aroused the clergy to their duty of giving catechetical instruction. Thanks to the work of holy theologians such as Saint Charles Borromeo, Saint Robert Bellarmine and Saint Peter Canisius, it involved the publication of catechisms that were real models for that period. May the Second Vatican Council stir up in our time a like enthusiasm and similar activity.

The missions are also a special area for the application of catechesis. The people of God have thus continued for almost two thousand years to educate themselves in the faith in ways adapted to the various situations of believers and the many different circumstances in which the Church finds herself.

Catechesis is intimately bound up with the whole of the Church's life. Not only her geographical extension and numerical increase but even more her inner growth and correspondence with God's plan depend essentially on catechesis. It is worthwhile pointing out some of the many lessons to be drawn from the experiences in Church history that we have just recalled.

Catechesis as the Church's Right and Duty

14. To begin with, it is clear that the Church has always looked on catechesis as a sacred duty and an inalienable right. On the one hand, it is certainly a duty springing from a com-

mand given by the Lord and resting above all on those who in the New Covenant receive the call to the ministry of being pastors. On the other hand, one can likewise speak of a right: from the theological point of view every baptized person, precisely by reason of being baptized, has the right to receive from the Church instruction and education enabling him or her to enter on a truly Christian life; and from the viewpoint of human rights, every human being has the right to seek religious truth and adhere to it freely, that is to say "without coercion on the part of individuals or of social groups and any human power", in such a way that in this matter of religion, "no one is to be forced to act against his or her conscience or prevented from acting in conformity to it".[43]

That is why catechetical activity should be able to be carried out in favourable circumstances of time and place, and should have access to the mass media and suitable equipment, without discrimination against parents, those receiving catechesis or those imparting it. At present this right is admittedly being given growing recognition, at least on the level of its main principles, as is shown by international declarations and conventions in which, whatever their limitations, one can recognize the desires of the consciences of many people today.[44] But the right is being violated by many States, even to the point that imparting catechesis, having it imparted, and receiving it become punishable offences. I vigorously raise my voice in union with the Synod Fathers against all discrimination in the field of catechesis, and at the same time I again make a pressing appeal to those in authority to put a complete end to these constraints on human freedom in general and on religious freedom in particular.

Priority of This Task

15. The second lesson concerns the place of catechesis in the Church's pastoral programmes. The more the Church, whether on the local or the universal level, gives catechesis priority over other works and undertakings the results of which would be more spectacular, the more she finds in catechesis a strengthening of her internal life as a community of believers and of her external activity as a missionary Church. As the twentieth century draws to a close, the Church is bidden by God and by events— each of them a call from him—to renew her trust in catechetical activity as a prime aspect of her mission. She is bidden to offer catechesis her best resources in people and energy, without sparing effort, toil or material means, in order to organize it better and

to train qualified personnel. This is no mere human calculation; it is an attitude of faith. And an attitude of faith always has reference to the faithfulness of God, who never fails to respond.

Shared but Differentiated Responsibility

16. The third lesson is that catechesis always has been and always will be a work for which the whole Church must feel responsible and must wish to be responsible. But the Church's members have different responsibilities, derived from each one's mission. Because of their charge, pastors have, at differing levels, the chief responsibility for fostering, guiding and coordinating catechesis. For his part, the Pope has a lively awareness of the primary responsibility that rests on him in this field: in this he finds reasons for pastoral concern but principally a source of joy and hope. Priests and religious have in catechesis a preeminent field for their apostolate. On another level, parents have a unique responsibility. Teachers, the various ministers of the Church, catechists, and also organizers of social communications, all have in various degrees very precise responsibilities in this education of the believing conscience, an education that is important for the life of the Church and affects the life of society as such. It would be one of the best results of the General Assembly of the Synod that was entirely devoted to catechesis if it stirred up in the Church as a whole and in each sector of the Church a lively and active awareness of this differentiated but shared responsibility.

Continual Balanced Renewal

17. Finally, catechesis needs to be continually renewed by a certain broadening of its concept, by the revision of its methods, by the search for suitable language, and by the utilization of a new means of transmitting the message. Renewal is sometimes unequal in value; the Synod Fathers realistically recognized not only an undeniable advance in the vitality of catechetical activity and promising initiatives but also the limitations or even "deficiencies" in what has been achieved to date.[45] These limitations are particularly serious when they endanger integrity of content. The Message to the People of God rightly stressed that "routine, with its refusal to accept any change, and improvisation, with its readiness for any venture, are equally dangerous" for catechesis.[46] Routine leads to stagnation, lethargy and eventual paralysis. Improvisation begets confusion on the part of those being given catechesis and, when these are children, on the part of

their parents; it also begets all kinds of deviations, and the fracturing and eventually the complete destruction of unity. It is important for the Church to give proof today, as she has done at other periods of her history, of evangelical wisdom, courage and fidelity in seeking out and putting into operation new methods and new prospects for catechetical instruction.

III

CATECHESIS IN THE CHURCH'S PASTORAL AND MISSIONARY ACTIVITY

Catechesis as a Stage in Evangelization

18. Catechesis cannot be dissociated from the Church's pastoral and missionary activity as a whole. Nevertheless it has a specific character which was repeatedly the object of inquiry during the preparatory work and throughout the course of the Fourth General Assembly of the Synod of Bishops. The question also interests the public both within and outside the Church.

This is not the place for giving a rigorous formal definition of catechesis, which has been sufficiently explained in the General Catechetical Directory.[47] It is for specialists to clarify more and more its concept and divisions.

In view of uncertainties in practice, let us simply recall the essential landmarks—they are already solidly established in Church documents—that are essential for an exact understanding of catechesis and without which there is a risk of failing to grasp its full meaning and import.

All in all, it can be taken here that catechesis is an education of children, young people and adults in the faith, which includes especially the teaching of Christian doctrine imparted, generally speaking, in an organic and systematic way, with a view to initiating the hearers into the fullness of Christian life. Accordingly, while not being formally identified with them, catechesis is built on a certain number of elements of the Church's pastoral mission that have a catechetical aspect, that prepare for catechesis, or that spring from it. These elements are: the initial proclamation of the Gospel or missionary preaching through the kerygma to arouse faith, apologetics or examination of the reasons for belief, experience of Christian living, celebration of the sacraments, integration into the ecclesial community, and apostolic and missionary witness.

Let us first of all recall that there is no separation or opposition between catechesis and evangelization. Nor can the two be simply identified with each other. Instead, they have close links whereby they integrate and complement each other.

The Apostolic Exhortation *Evangelii Nuntiandi* of December 8, 1975, on evangelization in the modern world, rightly stressed that evangelization—which has the aim of bringing the Good News to the whole of humanity, so that all may live by it—is a rich, complex and dynamic reality, made up of elements, or one could say moments, that are essential and different from each other, and that must all be kept in view simultaneously.[48] Catechesis is one of these moments—a very remarkable one—in the whole process of evangelization.

Catechesis and the Initial Proclamation of the Gospel

19. The specific character of catechesis, as distinct from the initial conversion-bringing proclamation of the Gospel, has the twofold objective of maturing the initial faith and of educating the true disciple of Christ by means of a deeper and more systematic knowledge of the person and the message of our Lord Jesus Christ.[49]

But in catechetical practice, this model order must allow for the fact that the initial evangelization has often not taken place. A certain number of children baptized in infancy come for catechesis in the parish without receiving any other initiation into the faith and still without any explicit personal attachment to Jesus Christ; they only have the capacity to believe placed within them by baptism and the presence of the Holy Spirit; and opposition is quickly created by the prejudices of their non-Christian family background or of the positivist spirit of their education. In addition, there are other children who have not been baptized and whose parents agree only at a later date to religious education: for practical reasons, the catechumenal stage of these children will often be carried out largely in the course of the ordinary catechesis. Again, many pre-adolescents and adolescents who have been baptized and been given a systematic catechesis and the sacraments still remain hesitant for a long time about committing their whole lives to Jesus Christ, even though they do not actually try to avoid religious instruction in the name of their freedom. Finally, even adults are not safe from temptations to doubt or to abandon their faith, especially as a result of their unbelieving surroundings. This means that "catechesis" must often concern itself not only with nourishing and teaching the faith but also with arousing it unceasingly with the help of grace, with opening the heart, with converting, and with preparing total adherence to Jesus Christ on the part of those who are still on the threshold of faith. This concern will in part decide the tone, the language and the method of catechesis.

Specific Aim of Catechesis

20. Nevertheless, the specific aim of catechesis is to develop, with God's help, an as yet initial faith, and to advance in fullness and to nourish day by day the Christian life of the faithful, young and old. It is in fact a matter of giving growth, at the level of knowledge and in life, to the seed of faith sown by the Holy Spirit with the initial proclamation and effectively transmitted by baptism.

Catechesis aims therefore at developing understanding of the mystery of Christ in the light of God's word, so that the whole of a person's humanity is impregnated by that word. Changed by the working of grace into a new creature, the Christian thus sets himself to follow Christ and learns more and more within the Church to think like him, to judge like him, to act in conformity with his commandments, and to hope as he invites us to.

To put it more precisely: within the whole process of evangelization, the aim of catechesis is to be the teaching and maturation stage, that is to say, the period in which the Christian, having accepted by faith the person of Jesus Christ as the one Lord and having given him complete adherence by sincere conversion of heart, endeavours to know better this Jesus to whom he has entrusted himself: to know his "mystery", the Kingdom of God proclaimed by him, the requirements and promises contained in his Gospel message, and the paths that he has laid down for any one who wishes to follow him.

It is true that being a Christian means saying "yes" to Jesus Christ, but let us remember that this "yes" has two levels: it consists in surrendering to the word of God and relying on it, but it also means, at a later stage, endeavouring to know better and better the profound meaning of this word.

Need for Systematic Catechesis

21. In his closing speech at the Fourth General Assembly of the Synod, Pope Paul VI rejoiced "to see how everyone drew attention to the absolute need for systematic catechesis, precisely because it is this reflective study of the Christian mystery that fundamentally distinguishes catechesis from all other ways of presenting the word of God".[50]

In view of practical difficulties, attention must be drawn to some of the characteristics of this instruction:

—it must be systematic, not improvised but programmed to reach a precise goal;

—it must deal with essentials, without any claim to tackle all disputed questions or to transform itself into theological research or scientific exegesis;

—it must nevertheless be sufficiently complete, not stopping short at the initial proclamation of the Christian mystery such as we have in the kerygma;

—it must be an integral Christian initiation, open to all the other factors of Christian life.

I am not forgetting the interest of the many different occasions for catechesis connected with personal, family, social and ecclesial life—these occasions must be utilized and I shall return to them in Chapter VI—but I am stressing the need for organic and systematic Christian instruction, because of the tendency in various quarters to minimize its importance.

Catechesis and Life Experience

22. It is useless to play off orthopraxis against orthodoxy: Christianity is inseparably both. Firm and well-thought-out convictions lead to courageous and upright action; the endeavour to educate the faithful to live as disciples of Christ today calls for and facilitates a discovery in depth of the mystery of Christ in the history of salvation.

It is also quite useless to campaign for the abandonment of serious and orderly study of the message of Christ in the name of a method concentrating on life experience. "No one can arrive at the whole truth on the basis solely of some simple private experience, that is to say without an adequate explanation of the message of Christ, who is 'the way, the truth, and the life'" (*Jn* 14:6).[51]

Nor is any opposition to be set up between a catechesis taking life as its point of departure and a traditional, doctrinal and systematic catechesis.[52] Authentic catechesis is always an orderly and systematic initiation into the revelation that God has given of himself to humanity in Christ Jesus, a revelation stored in the depths of the Church's memory and in Sacred Scripture, and constantly communicated from one generation to the next by a living active *traditio*. This revelation is not however isolated from life or artificially juxtaposed to it. It is concerned with the ultimate meaning of life and it illumines the whole of life with the light of the Gospel, to inspire it or to question it.

That is why we can apply to catechists an expression used by the Second Vatican Council with special reference to priests: "instructors (of the human being and his life) in the faith".[53]

Catechesis and Sacraments

23. Catechesis is intrinsically linked with the whole of liturgical and sacramental activity, for it is in the sacraments, especially in the Eucharist, that Christ Jesus works in fullness for the transformation of human beings.

In the early Church, the catechumenate and preparation for the sacraments of baptism and the Eucharist were the same thing. Although in the countries that have long been Christian the Church has changed her practice in this field, the catechumenate has never been abolished; on the contrary, it is experiencing a renewal in those countries[54] and is abundantly practised in the young missionary Churches. In any case, catechesis always has reference to the sacraments. On the one hand, the catechesis that prepares for the sacraments is an eminent kind, and every form of catechesis necessarily leads to the sacraments of faith. On the other hand, authentic practice of the sacraments is bound to have a catechetical aspect. In other words, sacramental life is impoverished and very soon turns into hollow ritualism if it is not based on serious knowledge of the meaning of the sacraments, and catechesis becomes intellectualized if it fails to come alive in sacramental practice.

Catechesis and Ecclesial Community

24. Finally, catechesis is closely linked with the responsible activity of the Church and of Christians in the world. A person who has given adherence to Jesus Christ by faith and is endeavouring to consolidate that faith by catechesis needs to live in communion with those who have taken the same step. Catechesis runs the risk of becoming barren if no community of faith and Christian life takes the catechumen in at a certain stage of his catechesis. That is why the ecclesial community at all levels has a twofold responsibility with regard to catechesis: it has the responsibility of providing for the training of its members, but it also has the responsibility of welcoming them into an environment where they can live as fully as possible what they have learned.

Catechesis is likewise open to missionary dynamism. If catechesis is done well, Christians will be eager to bear witness to their faith, to hand it on to their children, to make it known to others, and to serve the human community in every way.

Catechesis in the Wide Sense Necessary for Maturity and Strength of Faith

25. Thus through catechesis the Gospel kerygma (the initial ardent proclamation by which a person is one day overwhelmed and brought to the decision to entrust himself to Jesus Christ by faith) is gradually deepened, developed in its implicit consequences, explained in language that includes an appeal to reason, and channelled towards Christian practice in the Church and the world. All this is no less evangelical than the kerygma, in spite of what is said by certain people who consider that catechesis necessarily rationalizes, dries up and eventually kills all that is living, spontaneous and vibrant in the kerygma. The truths studied in catechesis are the same truths that touched the person's heart when he heard them for the first time. Far from blunting or exhausting them, the fact of knowing them better should make them even more challenging and decisive for one's life.

In the understanding expounded here, catechesis keeps the entirely pastoral perspective with which the Synod viewed it. This broad meaning of catechesis in no way contradicts but rather includes and goes beyond a narrow meaning which was once commonly given to catechesis in didactic expositions, namely the simple teaching of the formulas that express faith.

In the final analysis, catechesis is necessary both for the maturation of the faith of Christians and for their witness in the world: it is aimed at bringing Christians to "attain to the unity of the faith and of the knowledge of the Son of God, to mature manhood, to the measure of the stature of the fullness of Christ";[55] it is also aimed at making them prepared to make a defence to anyone who calls them to account for the hope that is in them.[56]

IV

THE WHOLE OF THE GOOD NEWS DRAWN FROM ITS SOURCE

Content of the Message

26. Since catechesis is a moment or aspect of evangelization, its content cannot be anything else but the content of evangelization as a whole. The one message—the Good News of salvation—that has been heard once or hundreds of times and has been accepted with the heart, is in catechesis probed unceasingly by re-

flection and systematic study, by awareness of its repercussions
on one's personal life—an awareness calling for ever greater
commitment—and by inserting it into an organic and harmonious whole, namely Christian living in society and the world.

The Source

27. Catechesis will always draw its content from the living
source of the word of God transmitted in Tradition and the
Scriptures, for "sacred Tradition and sacred Scripture make up
a single sacred deposit of the word of God, which is entrusted to
the Church", as was recalled by the Second Vatican Council,
which desired that "the ministry of the word—pastoral
preaching, catechetics and all forms of Christian instruction. . .
—(should be) healthily nourished and (should) thrive in holiness
through the word of Scripture",[57]

To speak of Tradition and Scripture as the source of catec he-
sis is to draw attention to the fact that catechesis must be impregnated and penetrated by the thought, the spirit and the outlook
of the Bible and the Gospels through assiduous contact with the
texts themselves; but it is also a reminder that catechesis will be
all the richer and more effective for reading the texts with the intelligence and the heart of the Church and for drawing inspiration from the two thousand years of the Church's reflection and
life.

The Church's teaching, liturgy and life spring from this
source and lead back to it, under the guidance of the pastors
and, in particular, of the doctrinal Magisterium entrusted to
them by the Lord.

The Creed an Exceptionally Important Expression of Doctrine

28. An exceptionally important expression of the living heritage placed in the custody of the pastors is found in the Creed
or, to put it more concretely, in the Creeds that at crucial moments have summed up the Church's faith in felicitous syn-
theses. In the course of the centuries an important element of
catechesis was constituted by the *traditio Symboli* (transmission
of the summary of the faith), followed by the transmission of the
Lord's Prayer. This expressive rite has in our time been reintro-
duced into the initiation of catechumens.[58] Should not greater
use be made of an adapted form of it to mark that most important stage at which a new disciple of Jesus Christ accepts with
full awareness and courage the content of what will from then on
be the object of his earnest study?

In the Creed of the People of God, proclaimed at the close of the nineteenth centenary of the martyrdom of the Apostles Peter and Paul, my predecessor Paul VI decided to bring together the essential elements of the Catholic faith, especially those that presented greater difficulty or risked being ignored.[59] This is a sure point of reference for the content of catechesis.

Factors that Must Not Be Neglected

29. In the third chapter of his Apostolic Exhortation *Evangelii Nuntiandi*, the same Pope recalled "the essential content, the living substance" of evangelization.[60] Catechesis too must keep in mind each of these factors and also the living synthesis of which they are part.[61]

I shall therefore limit myself here simply to recalling one or two points.[62] Anyone can see, for instance, how important it is to make the child, the adolescent, the person advancing in faith understand "what can be known about God";[63] to be able in a way to tell them: "What you worship as unknown, this I proclaim to you";[64] to set forth briefly for them[65] the mystery of the Word of God become man and accomplishing man's salvation by his Passover, that is to say through his death and Resurrection, but also by his preaching, by the signs worked by him, and by the sacraments of his permanent presence in our midst. The Synod Fathers were indeed inspired when they asked that care should be taken not to reduce Christ to his humanity alone or his message to a no more than earthly dimension, but that he should be recognized as the Son of God, the mediator giving us in the Spirit free access to the Father.[66]

It is important to display before the eyes of the intelligence and of the heart, in the light of faith, the sacrament of Christ's presence constituted by the mystery of the Church, which is an assembly of human beings who are sinners and yet have at the same time been sanctified and who make up the family of God gathered together by the Lord under the guidance of those whom "the Holy Spirit has made. . .guardians, to feed the Church of God".[67]

It is important to explain that the history of the human race, marked as it is by grace and sin, greatness and misery, is taken up by God in his Son Jesus, "foreshadowing in some way the age which is to come".[68]

Finally, it is important to reveal frankly the demands—demands that involve self-denial but also joy—made by what the Apostle Paul liked to call "newness of life",[69] "a new creation",[70] being in Christ,[71] and "eternal life in Christ

Jesus",[72] which is the same thing as life in the world but lived in accordance with the beatitudes and called to an extension and transfiguration hereafter.

Hence the importance in catechesis of personal moral commitments in keeping with the Gospel and of Christian attitudes, whether heroic or very simple, to life and the world—what we call the Christian or evangelical virtues. Hence also, in its endeavour to educate faith, the concern of catechesis not to omit but to clarify properly realities such as man's activity for his integral liberation,[73] the search for a society with greater solidarity and fraternity, the fight for justice and the building of peace.

Besides, it is not to be thought that this dimension of catechesis is altogether new. As early as the patristic age, Saint Ambrose and Saint John Chrysostom—to quote only them—gave prominence to the social consequences of the demands made by the Gospel. Close to our own time, the catechism of Saint Pius X explicitly listed oppressing the poor and depriving workers of their just wages among the sins that cry to God for vengeance.[74] Since *Rerum Novarum* especially, social concern has been actively present in the catechetical teaching of the Popes and the bishops. Many Synod Fathers rightly insisted that the rich heritage of the Church's social teaching should, in appropriate forms, find a place in the general catechetical education of the faithful.

Integrity of Content

30. With regard to the content of catechesis, three important points deserve special attention today.

The first point concerns the integrity of the content. In order that the sacrificial offering of his or her faith[75] should be perfect, the person who becomes a disciple of Christ has the right to receive "the word of faith"[76] not in mutilated, falsified or diminished form but whole and entire, in all its rigour and vigour. Unfaithfulness on some point to the integrity of the message means a dangerous weakening of catechesis and putting at risk the results that Christ and the ecclesial community have a right to expect from it. It is certainly not by chance that the final command of Jesus in Matthew's Gospel bears the mark of a certain entireness: "All authority. . .has been given to me. . . make disciples of all nations. . .teaching them to observe all. . . I am with you always". This is why, when a person first becomes aware of "the surpassing worth of knowing Christ Jesus",[77] whom he has encountered by faith, and has the perhaps unconscious desire to know him more extensively and better, "hearing about him and being taught in him, as the truth is in Jesus",[78] there is no valid pretext for refusing him any part whatever of that knowledge. What kind of catechesis would it be that failed to give their full place to man's creation and sin, to God's plan of redemption and its long, loving preparation and realization, to the Incarnation of the Son of God, to Mary, the Immaculate One, the Mother of God, ever Virgin, raised body and soul to the glory of heaven, and to her role in the mystery of salvation, to the mystery of lawlessness at work in our lives[79] and the power of God freeing us from it, to the need for penance and asceticism, to the sacramental and liturgical actions, to the reality of the Eucharistic presence, to participation in divine life here and hereafter, and so on? Thus, no true catechist can lawfully, on his own initiative, make a selection of what he considers important in the deposit of faith as opposed to what he considers unimportant, so as to teach the one and reject the other.

By Means of Suitable Pedagogical Methods

31. This gives rise to a second remark. It can happen that in the present situation of catechesis reasons of method or pedagogy suggest that the communication of the riches of the content of catechesis should be organized in one way rather than another. Besides, integrity does not dispense from balance and from the organic hierarchical character through which the truths to be taught, the norms to be transmitted, and the ways of Christian life to be indicated will be given the proper importance due to each. It can also happen that a particular sort of language proves preferable for transmitting this content to a particular individual or group. The choice made will be a valid one to the extent that, far from being dictated by more or less subjective theories or prejudices stamped with a certain ideology, it is inspired by the humble concern to stay closer to a content that must remain intact. The method and language used must truly be means for communicating the whole and not just a part of "the words of eternal life"[80] and "the ways of life".[81]

Ecumenical Dimension of Catechesis

32. The great movement, one certainly inspired by the Spirit of Jesus, that has for some years been causing the Catholic Church to seek with other Christian Churches or confessions the restoration of the perfect unity willed by the Lord, brings me to the question of the ecumenical character of catechesis. This movement reached its full prominence in the Second Vatican

Council[82] and since then has taken on a new extension within the Church, as is shown concretely by the impressive series of events and initiatives with which everyone is now familiar.

Catechesis cannot remain aloof from this ecumenical dimension, since all the faithful are called to share, according to their capacity and place in the Church, in the movement towards unity.[83]

Catechesis will have an ecumenical dimension if, while not ceasing to teach that the fullness of the revealed truths and of the means of salvation instituted by Christ is found in the Catholic Church,[84] it does so with sincere respect, in words and in deeds, for the ecclesial communities that are not in perfect communion with this Church.

In this context, it is extremely important to give a correct and fair presentation of the other Churches and ecclesial communities that the Spirit of Christ does not refrain from using as means of salvation; "moreover, some, even very many, of the outstanding elements and endowments which together go to build up and give life to the Church herself, can exist outside the visible boundaries of the Catholic Church".[85] Among other things, this presentation will help Catholics to have both a deeper understanding of their own faith and a better acquaintance with and esteem for their other Christian brethren, thus facilitating the shared search for the way towards full unity in the whole truth. It should also help non-Catholics to have a better knowledge and appreciation of the Catholic Church and her conviction of being the "universal help towards salvation".

Catechesis will have an ecumenical dimension if, in addition, it creates and fosters a true desire for unity. This will be true all the more if it inspires serious efforts—including the effort of self-purification in the humility and the fervour of the Spirit in order to clear the ways—with a view not to facile irenics made up of omissions and concessions on the level of doctrine, but to perfect unity, when and by what means the Lord will wish.

Finally, catechesis will have an ecumenical dimension if it tries to prepare Catholic children and young people, as well as adults, for living in contact with non-Catholics, affirming their Catholic identity while respecting the faith of others.

Ecumenical Collaboration in the Field of Catechesis

33. In situations of religious plurality, the Bishops can consider it opportune or even necessary to have certain experiences of collaboration in the field of catechesis between Catholics and

other Christians, complementing the normal catechesis that must in any case be given to Catholics. Such experiences have a theological foundation in the elements shared by all Christians.[86] But the communion of faith between Catholics and other Christians is not complete and perfect; in certain cases there are even profound divergences. Consequently, this ecumenical collaboration is by its very nature limited; it must never mean a "reduction" to a common minimum. Furthermore, catechesis does not consist merely in the teaching of doctrine: it also means initiating into the whole of Christian life, bringing full participation in the sacraments of the Church. Therefore, where there is an experience of ecumenical collaboration in the field of catechesis, care must be taken that the education of Catholics in the Catholic Church should be well ensured in matters of doctrine and of Christian living.

During the Synod, a certain number of Bishops drew attention to what they referred to as the increasingly frequent cases in which the civil authority or other circumstances impose on the schools in some countries a common instruction in the Christian religion, with common textbooks, class periods, etc., for Catholics and non-Catholics alike. Needless to say, this is not true catechesis. But this teaching also has ecumenical importance when it presents Christian doctrine fairly and honestly. In cases where circumstances impose it, it is important that in addition a specifically Catholic catechesis should be ensured with all the greater care.

The Question of Textbooks Dealing With the Various Religions

34. At this point another observation must be made on the same lines but from a different point of view. State schools sometimes provide their pupils with books that for cultural reasons (history, morals or literature) present the various religions, including the Catholic religion. An objective presentation of historical events, of the different religions and of the various Christian confessions can make a contribution here to better mutual understanding. Care will then be taken that every effort is made to ensure that the presentation is truly objective and free from the distorting influence of ideological and political systems or of prejudices with claims to be scientific. In any case, such schoolbooks can obviously not be considered catechetical works: they lack both the witness of believers stating their faith to other believers and an understanding of the Christian mysteries and of what is specific about Catholicism, as

these are understood within the faith.

V

EVERYBODY NEEDS TO BE CATECHIZED

The Importance of Children and the Young

35. The theme designated by my predecessor Paul VI for the Fourth General Assembly of the Synod of Bishops was: "Catechesis in our time, with special reference to the catechesis of children and young people". The increase in the number of young people is without doubt a fact charged with hope and at the same time with anxiety for a large part of the contemporary world. In certain countries, especially those of the Third World, more than half of the population is under twenty-five or thirty years of age. This means millions and millions of children and young people preparing for their adult future. And there is more than just the factor of numbers: recent events, as well as the daily news, tell us that, although this countless multitude of young people is here and there dominated by uncertainty and fear, seduced by the escapism of indifference or drugs, or tempted by nihilism and violence, nevertheless it constitutes in its major part the great force that amid many hazards is set on building the civilization of the future.

In our pastoral care we ask ourselves: How are we to reveal Jesus Christ, God made man, to this multitude of children and young people, reveal him not just in the fascination of a first fleeting encounter but through an acquaintance, growing deeper and clearer daily, with him, his message, the plan of God that he has revealed, the call he addresses to each person, and the Kingdom that he wishes to establish in this world with the "little flock"[87] of those who believe in him, a Kingdom that will be complete only in eternity? How are we to enable them to know the meaning, the import, the fundamental requirements, the law of love, the promises and the hopes of this Kingdom?

There are many observations that could be made about the special characteristics that catechesis assumes at the different stages of life.

Infants

36. One moment that is often decisive is the one at which the very young child receives the first elements of catechesis from its parents and the family surroundings. These elements

will perhaps be no more than a simple revelation of a good and provident Father in heaven to whom the child learns to turn its heart. The very short prayers that the child learns to lisp will be the start of a loving dialogue with this hidden God whose word it will then begin to hear. I cannot insist too strongly on this early initiation by Christian parents in which the child's faculties are integrated into a living relationship with God. It is a work of prime importance. It demands great love and profound respect for the child who has a right to a simple and true presentation of the Christian faith.

Children

37. For the child there comes soon, at school and in church, in institutions connected with the parish or with the spiritual care of the Catholic or State school not only an introduction into a wider social circle, but also the moment for a catechesis aimed at inserting him or her organically into the life of the Church, a moment that includes an immediate preparation for the celebration of the sacraments. This catechesis is didactic in character, but is directed towards the giving of witness in the faith. It is an initial catechesis but not a fragmentary one, since it will have to reveal, although in an elementary way, all the principal mysteries of faith and their effects on the child's moral and religious life. It is a catechesis that gives meaning to the sacraments, but at the same time it receives from the experience of the sacraments a living dimension that keeps it from remaining merely doctrinal, and it communicates to the child the joy of being a witness to Christ in ordinary life.

Adolescents

38. Next comes puberty and adolescence, with all the greatness and dangers which that age brings. It is the time of discovering oneself and one's own inner world, the time of generous plans, the time when the feeling of love awakens, with the biological impulses of sexuality, the time of the desire to be together, the time of a particularly intense joy connected with the exhilarating discovery of life. But often it is also the age of deeper questioning, of anguished or even frustrating searching, of a certain mistrust of others and dangerous introspection, and the age sometimes of the first experiences of setbacks and of disappointments. Catechesis cannot ignore these changeable aspects of this delicate period of life. A catechesis capable of leading the adolescent to reexamine his or her life and to engage in dialogue, a catechesis that does not ignore the adolescent's

great questions—self-giving, belief, love and the means of expressing it constituted by sexuality—such a catechesis can be decisive. The revelation of Jesus Christ as a friend, guide and model, capable of being admired but also imitated; the revelation of his message which provides an answer to the fundamental questions; the revelation of the loving plan of Christ the Saviour as the incarnation of the only authentic love and as the possibility of uniting the human race—all this can provide the basis for genuine education in faith. Above all, the mysteries of the Passion and death of Jesus, through which, according to Saint Paul, he merited his glorious Resurrection, can speak eloquently to the adolescent's conscience and heart and cast light on his first sufferings and on the sufferings of the world that he is discovering.

The Young

39. With youth comes the moment of the first great decisions. Although the young may enjoy the support of the members of their family and their friends, they have to rely on themselves and their own conscience and must ever more frequently and decisively assume responsibility for their destiny. Good and evil, grace and sin, life and death will more and more confront one another within them, not just as moral categories but chiefly as fundamental options which they must accept or reject lucidly, conscious of their own responsibility. It is obvious that a catechesis which denounces selfishness in the name of generosity, and which without any illusory over-simplification presents the Christian meaning of work, of the common good, of justice and charity, a catechesis on international peace and on the advancement of human dignity, on development, and on liberation, as these are presented in recent documents of the Church,[88] fittingly completes in the minds of the young the good catechesis on strictly religious realities which is never to be neglected. Catechesis then takes on considerable importance, since it is the time when the Gospel can be presented, understood and accepted as capable of giving meaning to life and thus of inspiring attitudes that would have no other explanation, such as self-sacrifice, detachment, forbearance, justice, commitment, reconciliation, a sense of the Absolute and the unseen. All these are traits that distinguish a young person from his or her companions as a disciple of Jesus Christ.

Catechesis thus prepares for the important Christian commitments of adult life. For example, it is certain that many vocations to the priesthood and religious life have their origin during a well imparted catechesis in infancy and adolescence.

From infancy until the threshold of maturity, catechesis is thus a permanent school of faith and follows the major stages of life, like a beacon lighting the path of the child, the adolescent and the young person.

The Adaptation of Catechesis for Young People

40. It is reassuring to note that, during the Fourth General Assembly of the Synod and the following years, the Church has widely shared in concern about how to impart catechesis to children and young people. God grant that the attention thus aroused will long endure in the Church's consciousness. In this way the Synod has been valuable for the whole Church by seeking to trace with the greatest possible precision the complex characteristics of present-day youth; by showing that these young persons speak a language into which the message of Jesus must be translated with patience and wisdom and without betrayal; by demonstrating that, in spite of appearances, these young people have within them, even though often in a confused way, not just a readiness or openness, but rather a real desire to know "Jesus... who is called Christ";[89] and by indicating that if the work of catechesis is to be carried out rigorously and seriously, it is today more difficult and tiring than ever before, because of the obstacles and difficulties of all kinds that it meets; but it is also more consoling, because of the depth of the response it receives from children and young people. This is a treasure which the Church can and should count on in the years ahead.

Some categories of young people to whom catechesis is directed call for special attention because of their particular situation.

The Handicapped

41. Children and young people who are physically or mentally handicapped come first to mind. They have a right, like others of their age, to know "the mystery of faith". The greater difficulties they encounter give greater merit to their efforts and to those of their teachers. It is pleasant to see that Catholic organizations especially dedicated to young handicapped people contributed to the Synod their experience in this matter, and drew from the Synod a renewed desire to deal better with this important problem. They deserve to be given warm encouragement in this endeavour.

Young People Without Religious Support

42. My thoughts turn next to the ever increasing number of

children and young people born and brought up in a non-Christian or at least non-practising home but who wish to know the Christian faith. They must be ensured a catechesis attuned to them, so that they will be able to grow in faith and live by it more and more, in spite of the lack of support or even the opposition they meet in their surroundings.

Adults

43. To continue the series of receivers of catechesis, I cannot fail to emphasize now one of the most constant concerns of the Synod Fathers, a concern imposed with vigour and urgency by present experiences throughout the world: I am referring to the central problem of the catechesis of adults. This is the principal form of catechesis, because it is addressed to persons who have the greatest responsibilities and the capacity to live the Christian message in its fully developed form.[90] The Christian community cannot carry out a permanent catechesis without the direct and skilled participation of adults, whether as receivers or as promoters of catechetical activity. The world in which the young are called to live and give witness to the faith which catechesis seeks to deepen and strengthen is governed by adults: the faith of these adults too should continually be enlightened, stimulated and renewed, so that it may pervade the temporal realities in their charge. Thus, for catechesis to be effective, it must be permanent, and it would be quite useless if it stopped short just at the threshold of maturity, since catechesis, admittedly under another form, proves no less necessary for adults.

Quasi-catechumens

44. Among the adults who need catechesis, our pastoral missionary concern is directed to those who were born and reared in areas not yet Christianized, and who have never been able to study deeply the Christian teaching that the circumstances of life have at a certain moment caused them to come across. It is also directed to those who in childhood received a catechesis suited to their age but who later drifted away from all religious practice and as adults find themselves with religious knowledge of a rather childish kind. It is likewise directed to those who feel the effects of a catechesis received early in life but badly imparted or badly assimilated. It is directed to those who, although they were born in a Christian country or in sociologically Christian surroundings, have never been educated in their faith and, as adults, are really catechumens.

Diversified and Complementary Forms of Catechesis

45. Catechesis is therefore for adults of every age, including the elderly—persons who deserve particular attention in view of their experience and their problems—no less than for children, adolescents and the young. We should also mention migrants, those who are by-passed by modern developments, those who live in areas of large cities which are often without churches, buildings and suitable organization, and other such groups. It is desirable that initiatives meant to give all these groups a Christian formation, with appropriate means (audio-visual aids, booklets, discussions, lectures), should increase in number, enabling many adults to fill the gap left by an insufficient or deficient catechesis, to complete harmoniously at a higher level their childhood catechesis, or even to prepare themselves enough in this field to be able to help others in a more serious way.

It is important also that the catechesis of children and young people, permanent catechesis, and the catechesis of adults should not be separate watertight compartments. It is even more important that there should be no break between them. On the contrary, their perfect complementarity must be fostered: adults have much to give to young people and children in the field of catechesis, but they can also receive much from them for the growth of their own Christian lives.

It must be restated that nobody in the Church of Jesus Christ should feel excused from receiving catechesis. This is true even of young seminarians and young religious, and of all those called to the task of being pastors and catechists. They will fulfil this task all the better if they are humble pupils of the Church, the great giver as well as the great receiver of catechesis.

VI

SOME WAYS AND MEANS OF CATECHESIS

Communications Media

46. From the oral teaching by the Apostles and the letters circulating among the Churches down to the most modern ways and means, catechesis has not ceased to look for the most suitable ways and means for its mission, with the active participation of the communities and at the urging of the pastors. This effort must continue.

I think immediately of the great possibilities offered by the means of social communication and the means of group communication: television, radio, the press, records, tape-recordings—the whole series of audio-visual means. The achievements in these spheres are such as to encourage the greatest hope. Experience shows, for example, the effect had by instruction given on radio or television, when it combines a high aesthetic level and rigorous fidelity to the Magisterium. The Church now has many opportunities for considering these questions—as, for instance, on Social Communications Days—and it is not necessary to speak of them at length here, in spite of their prime importance.

Utilization of Various Places, Occasions and Gatherings

47. I am also thinking of various occasions of special value which are exactly suitable for catechesis: for example, diocesan, regional or national pilgrimages, which gain from being centred on some judiciously chosen theme based on the life of Christ, of the Blessed Virgin or of the Saints. Then there are the traditional missions, often too hastily dropped but irreplaceable for the periodic and vigorous renewal of Christian life—they should be revived and brought up to date. Again, there are Bible-study groups, which ought to go beyond exegesis and lead their members to live by the word of God. Yet other instances are the meetings of ecclesial basic communities, insofar as they correspond to the criteria laid down in the Apostolic Exhortation *Evangelii Nuntiandi*.[91] I may also mention the youth groups that, under varying names and forms but always with the purpose of making Jesus Christ known and of living by the Gospel, are in some areas multiplying and flourishing in a sort of springtime that is very comforting for the Church: these include Catholic Action groups, charitable groups, prayer groups and Christian meditation groups. These groups are a source of great hope for the Church of tomorrow. But, in the name of Jesus, I exhort the young people who belong to them, their leaders, and the priests who devote the best part of their ministry to them: No matter what it costs, do not allow these groups—which are exceptional occasions for meeting others, and which are blessed with such riches of friendship and solidarity among the young, of joy and enthusiasm, of reflection on events and facts—do not allow them to lack serious study of Christian doctrine. If they do, they will be in danger—a danger that has unfortunately proved only too real—of disappointing their members and also the Church.

The catechetical endeavour that is possible in these various surroundings, and in many others besides, will have all the greater chance of being accepted and bearing fruit if it respects their individual nature. By becoming part of them in the right way, it will achieve the diversity and complementarity of approach that will enable it to develop all the riches of its concept, with its three dimensions of word, memorial and witness—doctrine, celebration and commitment in living—which the Synod message to the People of God emphasized.[92]

The Homily

48. This remark is even more valid for the catechesis given in the setting of the liturgy, especially at the Eucharistic assembly. Respecting the specific nature and proper cadence of this setting, the homily takes up again the journey of faith put forward by catechesis, and brings it to its natural fulfilment. At the same time it encourages the Lord's disciples to begin anew each day their spiritual journey in truth, adoration and thanksgiving. Accordingly, one can say that catechetical teaching too finds its source and its fulfilment in the Eucharist, within the whole circle of the liturgical year. Preaching, centered upon the Bible texts, must then in its own way make it possible to familiarize the faithful with the whole of the mysteries of the faith and with the norms of Christian living. Much attention must be given to the homily: it should be neither too long nor too short; it should always be carefully prepared, rich in substance and adapted to the hearers, and reserved to ordained ministers. The homily should have its place not only in every Sunday and feast-day Eucharist, but also in the celebration of baptisms, penitential liturgies, marriages and funerals. This is one of the benefits of the liturgical renewal.

Catechetical Literature

49. Among these various ways and means—all the Church's activities have a catechetical dimension—catechetical works, far from losing their essential importance, acquire fresh significance. One of the major features of the renewal of catechetics today is the rewriting and multiplication of catechetical books taking place in many parts of the Church. Numerous very successful works have been produced and are a real treasure in the service of catechetical instruction. But it must be humbly and honestly recognized that this rich flowering has brought with it articles and publications which are ambiguous and harmful to young people and to the life of the Church. In certain places, the

desire to find the best forms of expression or to keep up with fashions in pedagogical methods has often enough resulted in certain catechetical works which bewilder the young and even adults, either by deliberately or unconsciously omitting elements essential to the Church's faith, or by attributing excessive importance to certain themes at the expense of others, or, chiefly, by a rather horizontalist overall view out of keeping with the teaching of the Church's Magisterium.

Therefore, it is not enough to multiply catechetical works. In order that these works may correspond with their aim, several conditions are essential:

a)   they must be linked with the real life of the generation to which they are addressed, showing close acquaintance with its anxieties and questionings, struggles and hopes;

b)   they must try to speak a language comprehensible to the generation in question;

c)   they must make a point of giving the whole message of Christ and his Church, without neglecting or distorting anything, and in expounding it they will follow a line and structure that highlights what is essential;

d)   they must really aim to give to those who use them a better knowledge of the mysteries of Christ, aimed at true conversion and a life more in conformity with God's will.

Catechisms

50. All those who take on the heavy task of preparing these catechetical tools, especially catechism texts, can do so only with the approval of the pastors who have the authority to give it, and taking their inspiration as closely as possible from the General Catechetical Directory, which remains the standard of reference.[93]

In this regard, I must warmly encourage the Episcopal Conferences of the whole world to undertake, patiently but resolutely, the considerable work to be accomplished in agreement with the Apostolic See in order to prepare genuine catechisms which will be faithful to the essential content of Revelation and up to date in method, and which will be capable of educating the Christian generations of the future to a sturdy faith.

This brief mention of ways and means of modern catechetics does not exhaust the wealth of suggestions worked out by the Synod Fathers. It is comforting to think that at the present time every country is seeking valuable collaboration for a more organic and more secure renewal of these aspects of catechetics.

There can be no doubt that the Church will find the experts and the right means for responding, with God's grace, to the complex requirements of communicating with the people of today.

VII

HOW TO IMPART CATECHESIS

Diversity of Methods

51. The age and the intellectual development of Christians, their degree of ecclesial and spiritual maturity and many other personal circumstances demand that catechesis should adopt widely differing methods for the attainment of its specific aim: education in the faith. On a more general level, this variety is also demanded by the social and cultural surroundings in which the Church carries out her catechetical work.

The variety in the methods used is a sign of life and a resource. That is how it was considered by the Fathers of the Fourth General Assembly of the Synod, although they also drew attention to the conditions necessary for that variety to be useful and not harmful to the unity of the teaching of the one faith.

At the Service of Revelation and Conversion

52. The first question of a general kind that presents itself here concerns the danger and the temptation to mix catechetical teaching unduly with overt or masked ideological views, especially political and social ones, or with personal political options. When such views get the better of the central message to be transmitted, to the point of obscuring it and putting it in second place or even using it to further their own ends, catechesis then becomes radically distorted. The Synod rightly insisted on the need for catechesis to remain above one-sided divergent trends—to avoid "dichotomies"—even in the field of theological interpretation of such questions. It is on the basis of Revelation that catechesis will try to set its course, Revelation as transmitted by the universal Magisterium of the Church, in its solemn or ordinary form. This Revelation tells of a creating and redeeming God, whose Son has come among us in our flesh and enters not only into each individual's personal history but into human history itself, becoming its centre. Accordingly, this Revelation tells of the radical change of man and the universe, of all that makes up the web of human life under the influence of the Good

News of Jesus Christ. If conceived in this way, catechesis goes beyond every form of formalistic moralism, although it will include true Christian moral teaching. Chiefly, it goes beyond any kind of temporal, social or political "messianism". It seeks to arrive at man's innermost being.

The Message Embodied in Cultures

53. Now a second question. As I said recently to the members of the Biblical Commission: "The term 'acculturation' or 'inculturation' may be a neologism, but it expresses very well one factor of the great mystery of the Incarnation".[94] We can say of catechesis, as well as of evangelization in general, that it is called to bring the power of the Gospel into the very heart of culture and cultures. For this purpose, catechesis will seek to know these cultures and their essential components; it will learn their most significant expressions; it will respect their particular values and riches. In this manner it will be able to offer these cultures the knowledge of the hidden mystery[95] and help them to bring forth from their own living tradition original expressions of Christian life, celebration and thought. Two things must however be kept in mind.

On the one hand the Gospel message cannot be purely and simply isolated from the culture in which it was first inserted (the Biblical world or, more concretely, the cultural milieu in which Jesus of Nazareth lived), nor, without serious loss, from the cultures in which it has already been expressed down the centuries; it does not spring spontaneously from any cultural soil; it has always been transmitted by means of an apostolic dialogue which inevitably becomes part of a certain dialogue of cultures.

On the other hand, the power of the Gospel everywhere transforms and regenerates. When that power enters into a culture, it is no surprise that it rectifies many of its elements. There would be no catechesis if it were the Gospel that had to change when it came into contact with the cultures.

To forget this would simply amount to what Saint Paul very forcefully calls "emptying the cross of Christ of its power".[96]

It is a different matter to take, with wise discernment, certain elements, religious or otherwise, that form part of the cultural heritage of a human group and use them to help its members to understand better the whole of the Christian mystery. Genuine catechists know that catechesis "takes flesh" in the various cultures and milieux: one has only to think of the peoples with their great differences, of modern youth, of the great variety of circumstances in which people find themselves today. But they refuse to accept an impoverishment of catechesis through a renunciation or obscuring of its message, by adaptations, even in language, that would endanger the "precious deposit" of the faith,[97] or by concessions in matters of faith or morals. They are convinced that true catechesis eventually enriches these cultures by helping them to go beyond the defective or even inhuman features in them, and by communicating to their legitimate values the fullness of Christ.[98]

The Contribution of Popular Devotion

54. Another question of method concerns the utilization in catechetical instruction of valid elements in popular piety. I have in mind devotions practised by the faithful in certain regions with moving fervour and purity of intention, even if the faith underlying them needs to be purified or rectified in many aspects. I have in mind certain easily understood prayers that many simple people are fond of repeating. I have in mind certain acts of piety practised with a sincere desire to do penance or to please the Lord. Underlying most of these prayers and practices, besides elements that should be discarded, there are other elements which, if they were properly used, could serve very well to help people advance towards knowledge of the mystery of Christ and of his message: the love and mercy of God, the Incarnation of Christ, his redeeming Cross and Resurrection, the activity of the Spirit in each Christian and in the Church, the mystery of the hereafter, the evangelical virtues to be practised, the presence of the Christian in the world, etc. And why should we appeal to non-Christian or even anti-Christian elements, refusing to build on elements which, even if they need to be revised and improved, have something Christian at their root?

Memorization

55. The final methodological quesion the importance of which should at least be referred to—one that was debated several times in the Synod—is that of memorization. In the beginnings of Christian catechesis, which coincided with a civilization that was mainly oral, recourse was had very freely to memorization. Catechesis has since then known a long tradition of learning the principal truths by memorizing. We are all aware that this method can present certain disadvantages, not the least of which is that it lends itself to insufficient or at times almost non-existent assimilation, reducing all knowledge to formulas that are repeated without being properly understood. These

disadvantages and the different characteristics of our own civilization have in some places led to the almost complete suppression—according to some, alas, the definitive suppression—of memorization in catechesis. And yet certain very authoritative voices made themselves heard on the occasion of the Fourth General Assembly of the Synod, calling for the restoration of a judicious balance between reflection and spontaneity, between dialogue and silence, between written work and memory work. Moreover certain cultures still set great value on memorization.

At a time when, in non-religious teaching in certain countries, more and more complaints are being made about the unfortunate consequences of disregarding the human faculty of memory, should we not attempt to put this faculty back into use in an intelligent and even an original way in catechesis, all the more since the celebration or "memorial" of the great events of the history of salvation require a precise knowledge of them? A certain memorization of the words of Jesus, of important Bible passages, of the Ten Commandments, of the formulas of profession of the faith, of the liturgical texts, of the essential prayers, of key doctrinal ideas, etc., far from being opposed to the dignity of young Christians, or constituting an obstacle to personal dialogue with the Lord, is a real need, as the Synod Fathers forcefully recalled. We must be realists. The blossoms, if we may call them that, of faith and piety do not grow in the desert places of a memory-less catechesis. What is essential is that the texts that are memorized must at the same time be taken in and gradually understood in depth, in order to become a source of Christian life on the personal level and the community level.

The plurality of methods in contemporary catechesis can be a sign of vitality and ingenuity. In any case, the method chosen must ultimately be referred to a law that is fundamental for the whole of the Church's life: the law of fidelity to God and of fidelity to man in a single loving attitude.

VIII

THE JOY OF FAITH IN A TROUBLED WORLD

Affirming Christian Identity

56. We live in a difficult world in which the anguish of seeing the best creations of man slip away from him and turn against him creates a climate of uncertainty.[99] In this world catechesis

should help Christians to be, for their own joy and the service of all, "light" and "salt".[100] Undoubtedly this demands that catechesis should strengthen them in their identity and that it should continually separate itself from the surrounding atmosphere of hesitation, uncertainty and insipidity. Among the many difficulties, each of them a challenge for faith, I shall indicate a few in order to assist catechesis in overcoming them.

In an Indifferent World

57. A few years ago, there was much talk of the secularized world, the post-Christian era. Fashion changes, but a profound reality remains. Christians today must be formed to live in a world which largely ignores God or which, in religious matters, in place of an exacting and fraternal dialogue, stimulating for all, too often flounders in a debasing indifferentism, if it does not remain in a scornful attitude of "suspicion" in the name of the progress it has made in the field of scientific "explanations". To "hold on" in this world, to offer to all a "dialogue of salvation"[101] in which each person feels respected in his or her most basic dignity, the dignity of one who is seeking God, we need a catechesis which trains the young people and adults of our communities to remain clear and consistent in their faith, to affirm serenely their Christian and Catholic identity, to "see him who is invisible"[102] and to adhere so firmly to the absoluteness of God that they can be witnesses to him in a materialistic civilization that denies him.

With the Original Pedagogy of the Faith

58. The irreducible originality of Christian identity has for corollary and condition no less original a pedagogy of the faith. Among the many prestigious sciences of man that are nowadays making immense advances, pedagogy is certainly one of the most important. The attainments of the other sciences— biology, psychology, sociology—are providing it with valuable elements. The science of education and the art of teaching are continually being subjected to review, with a view to making them better adapted or more effective, with varying degrees of success.

There is also a pedagogy of faith, and the good that it can do for catechesis cannot be overstated. In fact, it is natural that techniques perfected and tested for education in general should be adapted for the service of education in the faith. However, account must always be taken of the absolute originality of faith. Pedagogy of faith is not a question of transmitting human knowledge, even of the highest kind; it is a question of communicating God's Revelation in its entirety. Throughout sacred history, especially in the Gospel, God himself used a pedagogy that must continue to be a model for the pedagogy of faith. A technique is of value in catechesis only to the extent that it serves the faith that is to be transmitted and learned; otherwise it is of no value.

Language Suited to the Service of the Credo

59. A problem very close to the preceding one is that of language. This is obviously a burning question today. It is paradoxical to see that, while modern studies, for instance in the field of communication, semantics and symbology, attribute extraordinary importance to language, nevertheless language is being misused today for ideological mystification, for mass conformity in thought and for reducing man to the level of an object.

All this has extensive influence in the field of catechesis. For catechesis has a pressing obligation to speak a language suited to today's children and young people in general and to many other categories of people—the language of students, intellectuals and scientists; the language of the illiterate or of people of simple culture; the language of the handicapped, and so on. Saint Augustine encountered this same problem and contributed to its solution for his own time with his well-known work *De Catechizandis Rudibus*. In catechesis as in theology, there is no doubt that the question of language is of the first order. But there is good reason for recalling here that catechesis cannot admit any language that would result in altering the substance of the content of the Creed, under any pretext whatever, even a pretended scientific one. Deceitful or beguiling language is no better. On the contrary, the supreme rule is that the great advances in the science of language must be capable of being placed at the service of catechesis so as to enable it really to "tell" or "communicate" to the child, the adolescent, the young people and adults of today the whole content of doctrine without distortion.

Research and Certainty of Faith

60. A more subtle challenge occasionally comes from the very way of conceiving faith. Certain contemporary philosophical schools, which seem to be exercising a strong influence on some theological currents and, through them, on pastoral practice, like to emphasize that the fundamental human attitude is that of seeking the infinite, a seeking that never attains its ob-

ject. In theology, this view of things will state very categorically that faith is not certainty but questioning, not clarity but a leap in the dark.

These currents of thought certainly have the advantage of reminding us that faith concerns things not yet in our possession, since they are hoped for; that as yet we see only "in a mirror dimly";[103] and that God dwells always in inaccessible light.[104] They help us to make the Christian faith not the attitude of one who has already arrived, but a journey forward as with Abraham. For all the more reason one must avoid presenting as certain things which are not.

However, we must not fall into the opposite extreme, as too often happens. The Letter to the Hebrews says that "faith is the assurance of things hoped for, the conviction of things not seen".[105] Although we are not in full possession, we do have an assurance and a conviction. When educating children, adolescents and young people, let us not give them too negative an idea of faith—as if it were absolute non-knowing, a kind of blindness, a world of darkness—but let us show them that the humble yet courageous seeking of the believer, far from having its starting point in nothingness, in plain self-deception, in fallible opinions or in uncertainty, is based on the word of God who cannot deceive or be deceived, and is unceasingly built on the immovable rock of this word. It is the search of the Magi under the guidance of a star,[106] the search of which Pascal, taking up a phrase of Saint Augustine, wrote so profoundly: "You would not be searching for me, if you had not found me".[107]

It is also one of the aims of catechesis to give young catechumens the simple but solid certainties that will help them to seek to know the Lord more and better.

Catechesis and Theology

61. In this context, it seems important to me that the connection between catechesis and theology should be well understood.

Obviously this connection is profound and vital for those who understand the irreplaceable mission of theology in the service of faith. Thus it is no surprise that every stirring in the field of theology also has repercussions in that of catechesis. In this period immediately after the Council, the Church is living through an important but hazardous time of theological research. The same must be said of hermeneutics with respect to exegesis.

Synod Fathers from all continents dealt with this question in very frank terms: they spoke of the danger of an "unstable balance" passing from theology to catechesis and they stressed the need to do something about this difficulty. Pope Paul VI himself had dealt with the problem in no less frank terms in the introduction to his Solemn Profession of Faith[108] and in the Apostolic Exhortation marking the fifth anniversary of the close of the Second Vatican Council.[109]

This point must again be insisted on. Aware of the influence that their research and their statements have on catechetical instruction, theologians and exegetes have a duty to take great care that people do not take for certainty what on the contrary belongs to the area of questions of opinion or of discussion among experts. Catechists for their part must have the wisdom to pick from the field of theological research those points that can provide light for their own reflection and their teaching, drawing, like the theologians, from the true sources, in the light of the Magisterium. They must refuse to trouble the minds of children and young people, at this stage of their catechesis, with outlandish theories, useless questions and unproductive discussions, things that Saint Paul often condemned in his pastoral letters.[110]

The most valuable gift that the Church can offer to the bewildered and restless world of our time is to form within it Christians who are confirmed in what is essential and who are humbly joyful in their faith. Catechesis will teach this to them, and it will itself be the first to benefit from it: "The man who wishes to understand himself thoroughly—and not just in accordance with immediate, partial, often superficial, and even illusory standards and measures of his being—must come to Christ with his unrest and uncertainty, and even his weakness and sinfulness, his life and death. He must, so to speak, enter into Christ with all his own self, he must 'appropriate' Christ and assimilate the whole of the reality of the Incarnation and Redemption in order to find himself".[111]

IX

THE TASK CONCERNS US ALL

Encouragement to All Responsible for Catechesis

62. Now, beloved Brothers and sons and daughters, I would like my words, which are intended as a serious and heartfelt exhortation from me in my ministry as pastor of the universal

Church, to set your hearts aflame, like the letters of Saint Paul to his companions in the Gospel, Titus and Timothy, or like Saint Augustine writing for the deacon Deogratias, when the latter lost heart before his task as a catechist, a real little treatise on the joy of catechizing.[112] Yes, I wish to sow courage, hope and enthusiasm abundantly in the hearts of all those many diverse people who are in charge of religious instruction and training for life in keeping with the Gospel.

Bishops

63. To begin with, I turn to my brother Bishops: The Second Vatican Council has already explicitly reminded you of your task in the catechetical area,[113] and the Fathers of the Fourth General Assembly of the Synod have also strongly underlined it.

Dearly beloved Brothers, you have here a special mission within your Churches: you are beyond all others the ones primarily responsible for catechesis, the catechists par excellence. Together with the Pope, in the spirit of episcopal collegiality, you too have charge of catechesis throughout the Church. Accept therefore what I say to you from my heart.

I know that your ministry as Bishops is growing daily more complex and overwhelming. A thousand duties call you: from the training of new priests to being actively present within the lay communities, from the living, worthy celebration of the sacraments and acts of worship to concern for human advancement and the defence of human rights. But let the concern to foster active and effective catechesis yield to no other care whatever in any way. This concern will lead you to transmit personally to your faithful the doctrine of life. But it should also lead you to take on in your diocese, in accordance with the plans of the Episcopal Conference to which you belong, the chief management of catechesis, while at the same time surrounding yourselves with competent and trustworthy assistants. Your principal role will be to bring about and maintain in your Churches a real passion for catechesis, a passion embodied in a pertinent and effective organization, putting into operation the necessary personnel, means and equipment, and also financial resources. You can be sure that if catechesis is done well in your local Churches, everything else will be easier to do. And needless to say, although your zeal must sometimes impose upon you the thankless task of denouncing deviations and correcting errors, it will much more often win for you the joy and consolation of seeing your Churches flourishing because catechesis is given in them as the Lord wishes.

Priests

64. For your part, priests, here you have a field in which you are the immediate assistants of your Bishops. The Council has called you "instructors in the faith";[114] there is no better way for you to be such instructors than by devoting your best efforts to the growth of your communities in the faith. Whether you are in charge of a parish, or are chaplains to primary or secondary schools or universities, or have responsibility for pastoral activity at any level, or are leaders of large or small communities, especially youth groups, the Church expects you to neglect nothing with a view to a well-organized and well-oriented catechetical effort. The deacons and other ministers that you may have the good fortune to have with you are your natural assistants in this. All believers have a right to catechesis; all pastors have the duty to provide it. I shall always ask civil leaders to respect the freedom of catechetical teaching; but with all my strength I beg you, ministers of Jesus Christ: Do not, for lack of zeal or because of some unfortunate pre-conceived idea, leave the faithful without catechesis. Let it not be said that "the children beg for food, but no one gives to them".[115]

Men and Women Religious

65. Many religious institutes for men and women came into being for the purpose of giving Christian education to children and young people, especially the most abandoned. Throughout history, men and women religious have been deeply committed to the Church's catechetical activity, doing particularly apposite and effective work. At a time when it is desired that the links between religious and pastors should be accentuated and consequently the active presence of religious communities and their members in the pastoral projects of the local Churches, I wholeheartedly exhort you whose religious consecration should make you even more readily available for the Church's service to prepare as well as possible for the task of catechesis according to the differing vocations of your institutes and the missions entrusted to you, and to carry this concern everywhere. Let the communities dedicate as much as possible of what ability and means they have to the specific work of catechesis.

Lay Catechists

66. I am anxious to give thanks in the Church's name to all of you, lay teachers of catechesis in the parishes, the men and the still more numerous women throughout the world, who are de-

voting yourselves to the religious education of many generations. Your work is often lowly and hidden but it is carried out with ardent and generous zeal, and it is an eminent form of the lay apostolate, a form that is particularly important where for various reasons children and young people do not receive suitable religious training in the home. How many of us have received from people like you our first notions of catechism and our preparation for the sacrament of penance, for our first communion and confirmation! The Fourth General Assembly of the Synod did not forget you. I join with it in encouraging you to continue your collaboration for the life of the Church.

But the term "catechists" belongs above all to the catechists in mission lands. Born of families that are already Christian or converted at some time to Christianity and instructed by missionaries or by another catechist, they then consecrate their lives, year after year, to catechizing children and adults in their own country. Churches that are flourishing today would not have been built up without them. I rejoice at the efforts made by the Sacred Congregation for the Evangelization of Peoples to improve more and more the training of these catechists. I gratefully recall the memory of those whom the Lord has already called to himself. I beg the intercession of those whom my predecessors have raised to the glory of the altars. I wholeheartedly encourage those engaged in the work. I express the wish that many others may succeed them and that they may increase in numbers for a task so necessary for the missions.

In the Parish

67. I now wish to speak of the actual setting in which all these catechists normally work. I am returning this time, taking a more overall view, to the "places" for catechesis, some of which have already been mentioned in Chapter VI: the parish, the family, the school, organizations.

It is true that catechesis can be given anywhere, but I wish to stress, in accordance with the desire of very many Bishops, that the parish community must continue to be the prime mover and pre-eminent place for catechesis. Admittedly, in many countries the parish has been as it were shaken by the phenomenon of urbanization. Perhaps some have too easily accepted that the parish should be considered old-fashioned, if not doomed to disappear, in favour of more pertinent and effective small communities. Whatever one may think, the parish is still a major point of reference for the Christian people, even for the non-practising. Accordingly, realism and wisdom demand that we continue along the path aiming to restore to the parish, as needed, more adequate structures and, above all, a new impetus through the increasing integration into it of qualified, responsible and generous members. This being said, and taking into account the necessary diversity of places for catechesis (the parish as such, families taking in children and adolescents, chaplaincies for State schools, Catholic educational establishments, apostolic movements that give periods of catechesis, clubs open to youth in general, spiritual formation weekends, etc.), it is supremely important that all these catechetical channels should really converge on the same confession of faith, on the same membership of the Church, and on commitments in society lived in the same Gospel spirit: "one Lord, one faith, one baptism, one God and Father".[116] That is why every big parish or every group of parishes with small numbers has the serious duty to train people completely dedicated to providing catechetical leadership (priests, men and women religious, and lay people), to provide the equipment needed for catechesis under all aspects, to increase and adapt the places for catechesis to the extent that it is possible and useful to do so, and to be watchful about the quality of the religious formation of the various groups and their integration into the ecclesial community.

In short, without monopolizing or enforcing uniformity, the parish remains, as I have said, the pre-eminent place for catechesis. It must rediscover its vocation, which is to be a fraternal and welcoming family home, where those who have been baptized and confirmed become aware of forming the People of God. In that home, the bread of good doctrine and the Eucharistic Bread are broken for them in abundance, in the setting of the one act of worship;[117] from that home they are sent out day by day to their apostolic mission in all the centres of activity of the life of the world.

In the Family

68. The family's catechetical activity has a special character, which is in a sense irreplaceable. This special character has been rightly stressed by the Church, particularly by the Second Vatican Council.[118] Education in the faith by parents, which should begin from the children's tenderest age,[119] is already being given when the members of a family help each other to grow in faith through the witness of their Christian lives, a witness that is often without words but which perseveres throughout a day-to-day life lived in accordance with the Gospel. This catechesis is more incisive when, in the course of family events (such as the re-

ception of the sacraments, the celebration of great liturgical feasts, the birth of a child, a bereavement) care is taken to explain in the home the Christian or religious content of these events. But that is not enough: Christian parents must strive to follow and repeat, within the setting of family life, the more methodical teaching received elsewhere. The fact that these truths about the main questions of faith and Christian living are thus repeated within a family setting impregnated with love and respect will often make it possible to influence the children in a decisive way for life. The parents themselves profit from the effort that this demands of them, for in a catechetical dialogue of this sort each individual both receives and gives.

Family catechesis therefore precedes, accompanies and enriches all other forms of catechesis. Furthermore, in places where anti-religious legislation endeavours even to prevent education in the faith, and in places where widespread unbelief or invasive secularism makes real religious growth practically impossible, "the Church of the home"[120] remains the one place where children and young people can receive an authentic catechesis. Thus there cannot be too great an effort on the part of Christian parents to prepare for this ministry of being their own children's catechists and to carry it out with tireless zeal. Encouragement must also be given to the individuals or institutions that, through person-to-person contacts, through meetings, and through all kinds of pedagogical means, help parents to perform their task: the service they are doing to catechesis is beyond price.

At School

69. Together with and in connection with the family, the school provides catechesis with possibilities that are not to be neglected. In the unfortunately decreasing number of countries in which it is possible to give education in the faith within the school framework, the Church has the duty to do so as well as possible. This of course concerns first and foremost the Catholic school: it would no longer deserve this title if, no matter how much it shone for its high level of teaching in non-religious matters, there were justification for reproaching it for negligence or deviation in strictly religious education. Let it not be said that such education will always be given implicitly and indirectly. The special character of the Catholic school, the underlying reason for it, the reason why Catholic parents should prefer it, is precisely the quality of the religious instruction integrated into the education of the pupils. While Catholic establishments

should respect freedom of conscience, that is to say avoid burdening consciences from without by exerting physical or moral pressure, especially in the case of the religious activity of adolescents, they still have a grave duty to make them understand that, although God's call to serve him in spirit and truth, in accordance with the commandments of God and the precepts of the Church, does not apply constraint, it is nevertheless binding in conscience.

But I am also thinking of non-confessional and public schools. I express the fervent wish that, in response to a very clear right of the human person and of the family, and out of respect for everyone's religious freedom, all Catholic pupils may be enabled to advance in their spiritual formation with the aid of a religious instruction dependent on the Church, but which, according to the circumstances of different countries, can be offered either by the school or in the setting of the school, or again within the framework of an agreement with the public authorities regarding school timetables, if catechesis takes place only in the parish or in another pastoral centre. In fact, even in places where objective difficulties exist, it should be possible to arrange school timetables in such a way as to enable the Catholics to deepen their faith and religious experience, with qualified teachers, whether priests or lay people.

Admittedly, apart from the school, many other elements of life help in influencing the mentality of the young, for instance, recreation, social background and work surroundings. But those who study are bound to bear the stamp of their studies, to be introduced to cultural or moral values within the atmosphere of the establishment in which they are taught, and to be faced with many ideas met with in school. It is important for catechesis to take full account of this effect of the school on the pupils, if it is to keep in touch with the other elements of the pupils' knowledge and education; thus the Gospel will impregnate the mentality of the pupils in the field of their learning, and the harmonization of their culture will be achieved in the light of faith. Accordingly I give encouragement to the priests, religious and lay people who are devoting themselves to sustaining these pupils' faith. This is moreover an occasion for me to reaffirm my firm conviction that to show respect for the Catholic faith of the young to the extent of facilitating its education, its implantation, its consolidation, its free profession and practice would certainly be to the honour of any Government, whatever be the system on which it is based or the ideology from which it draws its inspiration.

Within Organizations

70. Lastly, encouragement must be given to the lay associations, movements and groups, whether their aim is the practice of piety, the direct apostolate, charity and relief work, or a Christian presence in temporal matters. They will all accomplish their objectives better, and serve the Church better, if they give an important place in their internal organization and their method of action to the serious religious training of their members. In this way every association of the faithful in the Church has by definition the duty to educate in the faith.

This makes more evident the role given to the laity in catechesis today, always under the pastoral direction of their Bishops, as the Propositions left by the Synod stressed several times.

Training Institutes

71. We must be grateful to the Lord for this contribution by the laity, but it is also a challenge to our responsibility as Pastors, since these lay catechists must be carefully prepared for what is, if not a formally instituted ministry, at the very least a function of great importance in the Church. Their preparation calls on us to organize special Centres and Institutes, which are to be given assiduous attention by the Bishops. This is a field in which diocesan, interdiocesan or national cooperation proves fertile and fruitful. Here also the material aid provided by the richer Churches to their poorer sisters can show the greatest effectiveness, for what better assistance can one Church give to another than to help it to grow as a Church with its own strength?

I would like to recall to all those who are working generously in the service of the Gospel, and to whom I have expressed here my lively encouragement, the instruction given by my venerated predecessor Paul VI: "As evangelizers, we must offer. . .the image of people who are mature in faith and capable of finding a meeting-point beyond the real tensions, thanks to a shared, sincere and disinterested search for truth. Yes, the destiny of evangelization is certainly bound up with the witness of unity given by the Church. This is a source of responsibility and also of comfort".[121]

CONCLUSION

The Holy Spirit, the Teacher Within

72. At the end of this Apostolic Exhortation, the gaze of my

heart turns to him who is the principle inspiring all catechetical work and all who do this work—the Spirit of the Father and of the Son, the Holy Spirit.

In describing the mission that this Spirit would have in the Church, Christ used the significant words: "He will teach you all things, and bring to your remembrance all that I have said to you".[122] And he added: "When the Spirit of truth comes, he will guide you into all the truth. . .he will declare to you the things that are to come".[123]

The Spirit is thus promised to the Church and to each Christian as a Teacher within, who, in the secret of the conscience and the heart, makes one understand what one has heard but was not capable of grasping: "Even now the Holy Spirit teaches the faithful", said Saint Augustine in this regard, "in accordance with each one's spiritual capacity. And he sets their hearts aflame with greater desire according as each one progresses in the charity that makes him love what he already knows and desire what he has yet to know".[124]

Furthermore, the Spirit's mission is also to transform the disciples into witnesses to Christ: "He will bear witness to me; and you also are witnesses".[125]

But this is not all. For Saint Paul, who on this matter synthesizes a theology that is latent throughout the New Testament, it is the whole of one's "being a Christian", the whole of the Christian life, the new life of the children of God, that constitutes a life in accordance with the Spirit.[126] Only the Spirit enables us to say to God: "Abba, Father".[127] Without the Spirit we cannot say: "Jesus is Lord".[128] From the Spirit come all the charisms that build up the Church, the community of Christians.[129] In keeping with this, Saint Paul gives each disciple of Christ the instruction: "Be filled with the Spirit".[130] Saint Augustine is very explicit: "Both (our believing and our doing good) are ours because of the choice of our will, and yet both are gifts from the Spirit of faith and charity".[131]

Catechesis, which is growth in faith and the maturing of Christian life towards its fullness, is consequently a work of the Holy Spirit, a work that he alone can initiate and sustain in the Church.

This realization, based on the text quoted above and on many other passages of the New Testament, convinces us of two things.

To begin with, it is clear that, when carrying out her mission of giving catechesis, the Church—and also every individual Christian devoting himself to that mission within the Church and in her name—must be very much aware of acting as a living pliant instrument of the Holy Spirit. To invoke this Spirit constantly, to be in communion with him, to endeavour to know his authentic inspirations must be the attitude of the teaching Church and of every catechist.

Secondly, the deep desire to understand better the Spirit's action and to entrust oneself to him more fully—at a time when "in the Church we are living an exceptionally favourable season of the Spirit", as my predecessor Paul VI remarked in his Apostolic Exhortation *Evangelii Nuntiandi*[132]—must bring about a catechetical awakening. For "renewal in the Spirit" will be authentic and will have real fruitfulness in the Church, not so much according as it gives rise to extraordinary charisms, but according as it leads the greatest possible number of the faithful, as they travel their daily paths, to make a humble, patient and persevering effort to know the mystery of Christ better and better, and to bear witness to it.

I invoke on the catechizing Church this Spirit of the Father and the Son, and I beg him to renew catechetical dynamism in the Church.

Mary, Mother and Model of the Disciple

73. May the Virgin of Pentecost obtain this for us through her intercession. By a unique vocation, she saw her Son Jesus "increase in wisdom and in stature, and in favour".[133] As he sat on her lap and later as he listened to her throughout the hidden life at Nazareth, this Son, who was "the only Son from the Father", "full of grace and truth", was formed by her in human knowledge of the Scriptures and of the history of God's plan for his people, and in adoration of the Father.[134] She in turn was the first of his disciples. She was the first in time, because even when she found her adolescent son in the Temple she received from him lessons that she kept in her heart.[135] She was the first disciple above all else because no one has been "taught by God"[136] to such depth. She was "both mother and disciple", as Saint Augustine said of her, venturing to add that her discipleship was more important for her than her motherhood.[137] There are good grounds for the statement made in the Synod Hall that Mary is "a living catechism" and "the mother and model of catechists".

May the presence of the Holy Spirit, through the prayers of Mary, grant the Church unprecedented enthusiasm in the catechetical work that is essential for her. Thus will she effectively carry out, at this moment of grace, her inalienable and universal mission, the mission given her by her Teacher: "Go therefore and make disciples of all nations".[138]

* Translation by Vatican Press Office. Latin text in *AAS* 71, (1979), 1277–1340.

1. Cf. *Mt* 28: 19-20.
2. Cf. *1 Jn* 1:1.
3. Cf. *Jn* 20:31.
4. Cf. *AAS* 63 (1971), pp. 758-764.
5. Cf. 44; cf. also 45-48 and 54: *AAS* 68 (1976), pp. 34-35; 35-38; 43.
6. According to the Motu Proprio *Apostolica Sollicitudo* of 15 September 1965, the Synod of Bishops can come together in General Assembly, in Extraordinary Assembly or in Special Assembly. In the present Apostolic Exhortation the words "Synod", "Synod Fathers" and "Synod Hall" always refer, unless otherwise indicated, to the Fourth General Assembly of the Synod of Bishops on catechesis, held in Rome in October 1977.
7. Cf. *Synodus Episcoporum, De catechesi hoc nostro tempore tradenda praesertim pueris atque invenibus, Ad Populum Dei Nuntius*, e Civitate Vaticana, 28-X-1977; cf. "L'Osservatore Romano", 30 October 1977, pp. 3-4.
8. Cf. *AAS* 69 (1977), p. 633.
9. *Jn* 1:14.
10. *Jn* 14:6.
11. *Eph* 3:9, 18-19.
12. *Jn* 14:6.
13. *Jn* 7:16. This is a theme dear to the Fourth Gospel: cf. *Jn* 3:34; 8:28; 12: 49-50; 14:24; 17:8, 14.
14. *1 Cor* 11:23: the word "deliver" employed here by St. Paul was frequently repeated in the Apostolic Exhortation *Evangelii Nuntiandi* to describe the evangelizing activity of the Church, for example 4, 15, 78, 79.
15. *Acts* 1:1.
16. *Mt* 26:55, cf. *Jn* 18:20.
17. *Mk* 10:1.
18. *Mk* 1:22; cf. also *Mt* 5:2; 11:1; 13:54; 22:16; *Mk* 2:13; 4:1; 6:2, 6; *Lk* 5:3, 17; *Jn* 7:14; 8:2, etc.
19. *Lk* 23:5.
20. In nearly fifty places in the four Gospels, this title, inherited from the whole Jewish tradition but here given a new meaning that Christ himself often seeks to emphasize, is attributed to Jesus.
21. Cf., among others, *Mt* 8:19; *Mk* 4:38; 9:38; 10:35; 13:1; *Jn* 11:28.
22. *Mt* 12:38.
23. *Lk* 10:25; cf. *Mt* 22:16.
24. *Jn* 13:13-14; cf. also *Mt* 10:25; 26:18 and parallel passages.
25. *Mt* 23:8. Saint Ignatius of Antioch takes up this affirmation and comments as follows: "We have received the faith; this is why we hold fast, in order to be recognized as disciples of Jesus Christ, our only Teacher" (*Epistola ad Magnesios*, IX, 2, Funk 1, 198).
26. *Jn* 3:2.
27. The portrayal of Christ as Teacher goes back as far as the Roman Catacombs. It is frequently used in the mosaics of Romano-Byzantine art of the third and fourth centuries. It was to form a predominant artistic motif in the sculptures of the great Romanesque and Gothic cathedrals of the Middle Ages.
28. *Mt* 28:19.
29. *Jn* 15:15.

30. Cf. *Jn* 15:16.
31. *Acts* 2:42.
32. *Acts* 4:2.
33. Cf. *Acts* 4:18; 5:28.
34. Cf. *Acts* 4:19.
35. Cf. *Acts* 1:25.
36. Cf. *Acts* 6:8ff; cf. also Philip catechizing the minister of the Queen of the Ethiopians: *Acts* 8:26ff.
37. Cf. *Acts* 15:35.
38. *Acts* 8:4.
39. *Acts* 28:31.
40. Cf. Pope John XXIII, Encyclical *Mater et Magistra (AAS* 53 [1961], p. 401): the Church is "mother" because by baptism she unceasingly begets new children and increases God's family; she is "teacher" because she makes her children grow in the grace of their baptism by nourishing their *sensus fidei* through instruction in the truths of faith.
41. Cf., for example, the letter of Clement of Rome to the Church of Corinth, the *Didache,* the *Epistola Apostolorum,* the writings of Irenaeus of Lyons (*Demonstratio Apostolicae Praedicationis* and *Adversus Haereses),* of Tertullian (*De Baptismo),* of Clement of Alexandria (*Paedagogus),* of Cyprian (*Testimonia ad Quirinum*), of Origen (*Contra Celsum*), etc.
42. Cf. *2 Thess* 3:1.
43. Second Vatican Council, Declaration on Religious Liberty *Dignitatis Humanae,* 2: *AAS* 58 (1966), p. 930.
44. Cf. The Universal Declaration of Human Rights (UNO), 10 December 1948, art. 18; The International Pact on Civil and Political Rights (UNO), 16 December 1966, art. 4; Final Act of the Conference on European Security and Cooperation, para. VII.
45. Cf. *Synodus Episcoporum, De catechesi hoc nostro tempore tradenda praesertim pueris iuvenibus, Ad Populum Dei Nuntius,* 1: *loc. cit.,* pp. 3-4; cf. "L'Osservatore Romano", 30 October 1977, p.3.
46. *Ibid,* 6: *loc. cit.* pp. 7-8.
47. Sacred Congregation for the Clergy, *Directorium Catechisticum Generale,* 17-35: *AAS* 64 (1972), pp. 110-118.
48. Cf. 17-24: *AAS* 68 (1976), pp. 17-22.
49. Cf. *Synodus Episcoporum, De catechesi hoc nostro tempore tradenda praesertim pueris atque iuvenibus, Ad Populum Dei Nuntius,* 1: *loc. cit.,* pp. 3-4; cf. "L'Osservatore Romano", 30 October 1977, p.3.
50. Concluding Address to the Synod, 29 October 1977: *AAS* 69 (1977), p. 634.
51. *Ibid.*
52. *Directorium Catechisticum Generale,* 40 and 46: *AAS* 64 (1972), pp. 121 and 124-125.
53. Decree on the Ministry and Life of Priests *Presbyterorum Ordinis,* 6: *AAS* 58 (1966), p. 999.
54. Cf. *Ordo Initiationis Christianae Adultorum.*
55. *Eph* 4:13.
56. Cf. *1 Pt* 3:15.
57. Dogmatic Constitution on Divine Revelation *Dei Verbum,* 10 and 24: *AAS* 58 (1966), pp. 822 and 828-829; cf. also Sacred Congregation for the Clergy, *Directorium Catechisticum Generale,* 45 (*AAS* 64 [1972], p. 124), where the principal and complementary sources of catechesis are well set out.
58. Cf. *Ordo Initiationis Christianae Adultorum,* 25-26; 183-187.

59. Cf. *AAS* 60 (1968), pp. 436-445. Besides these great professions of faith of the Magisterium, note also the popular professions of faith, rooted in the traditional Christian culture of certain countries; cf. what I said to the young people at Gniezno, 3 June 1979, regarding the Bogurodzica song-message: "This is not only a song: it is also a profession of faith, a symbol of the Polish Credo, it is a catechesis and also a document of Christian education. The principal truths of faith and the principles of morality are contained here. This is not only a historical object. It is a document of life. (It has even been called) 'the Polish catechism'" (AAS 71 [1979], p. 754).

60. 25: *AAS* 68 (1976), p. 23.

61. *Ibid.*, especially 26-39: *l.c.*, pp. 23-25; the "principal elements of the Christian message" are presented in a more systematic fashion in the *Directorium Catechisticum Generale*, 47-69 (*AAS* 64 [1972], pp. 125-141), where one also finds the norm for the essential doctrinal content of catechesis.

62. Consult also on this point the *Directorium Catechisticum Generale*, 37-46 (*l.c.*, pp. 120-125).

63. *Rom* 1:19.

64. *Acts* 17:23.

65. Cf. *Eph* 3:3.

66. Cf. *Eph* 2:18.

67. *Acts* 20:28.

68. Second Vatican Council, Pastoral Constitution on the Church in the Modern World *Gaudium et Spes*, 39: *AAS* 58 (1966), pp. 1056-1057.

69. *Rom* 6:4.

70. *2 Cor* 5:17.

71. Cf. *ibid.*

72. *Rom* 6:23.

73. Cf. Pope Paul VI, Apostolic Exhortation *Evangelii Nuntiandi*, 30-38: *AAS* 68 (1976), pp. 25-30.

74. Cf. *Catechismo maggiore*, Fifth part, chap. 6, 965-966.

75. Cf. *Phil* 2:17.

76. *Rom* 10:8.

77. *Phil* 3:8.

78. Cf. *Eph* 4:20-21.

79. Cf. *2 Thess* 2:7.

80. *Jn* 6:69; cf. *Acts* 5:20; 7:38.

81. *Acts* 2:28, quoting *Ps* 16:11.

82. Cf. the entire Decree on Ecumenism *Unitatis Redintegratio: AAS* 57 (1965), pp. 90-112.

83. Cf. *ibid.*, 5: *l.c.*, p. 96; cf. also Second Vatican Council, Decree on the Missionary Activity of the Church *Ad Gentes*, 15: *AAS* 58 (1966), pp. 963-965; Sacred Congregation of the Clergy, *Directorium Catechisticum Generale*, 27: *AAS* 64 (1972), p. 115.

84. Cf. Second Vatican Council, Decree on Ecumenism *Unitatis Redintegratio*, 3-4: *AAS* 57 (1965), pp. 92-96.

85. *Ibid.*, 3: *l.c.*, pp. 93.

86. Cf. *ibid.*; cf. also Dogmatic Constitution on the Church *Lumen Gentium*, 15: *AAS* 57 (1965), p. 19.

87. *Lk* 12:32.

88. Cf., for example, Second Vatican Council, Pastoral Constitution on the Church in the Modern World *Gaudium et Spes: AAS* 58 (1966), pp. 1025-1120; Pope Paul VI, Encyclical *Populorum Progressio: AAS* 59 (1967), pp. 257-299; Apostolic Letter *Octogesina Adveniens: AAS*

63 (1971), pp. 401-441; Apostolic Exhortation *Evangelii Nuntiandi:*
AAS 68 (1976), pp. 5-76.
89. *Mt* 1:16.
90. Cf. Second Vatican Council, Decree on the Bishop's Pastoral Office in the Church *Christus Dominus,* 14: *AAS* 58 (1966), p. 679; Decree on the Missionary Activity of the Church *Ad Gentes,* 14: *AAS* 58
(1966), pp. 962-963; Sacred Congregation for the Clergy, *Directorium
Catechisticum Generale,* 20: *AAS* 64 (1972), p.112; cf. also *Ordo Initiationis Christianae Adultorum.*
91. Cf. 58: *AAS* 68 (1976), pp. 46-49.
92. Cf. *Synodus Episcoporum, De catechesi hoc nostro tempore tradenda praesertim pueris atque iuvenibus, Ad Populorum Dei Nuntius,*
7-10: *loc. cit.,* pp. 9-12; cf. "L'Osservatore Romano", 30 October
1977, p.3.
93. Cf. Sacred Congregation for the Clergy, *Directorium Catechisticum Generale,* 119-121; 134: *AAS* 64 (1972), pp. 166-167; 172.
94. Cf. *AAS* 71 (1979), p. 607.
95. Cf. *Rom* 16:25; *Eph* 3:5.
96. *1 Cor* 1:17.
97. Cf. *2 Tim* 1:14.
98. Cf. *Jn* 1:16; *Eph* 1:10.
99. Cf. Encyclical *Redemptor Hominis,* 15-16: *AAS* 71 (1979), pp.
286-295.
100. Cf. *Mt* 5: 13-16.
101. Cf. Pope Paul VI, Encyclical *Ecclesiam Suam,* Part Three, *AAS*
56 (1964), pp. 637-659.
102. Cf. *Heb* 11:27.
103. *1 Cor* 13:12.
104. Cf. *1 Tim* 6:16.
105. *Heb* 11:1.
106. Cf. *Mt* 2:1ff.
107. Blaise Pascal, *Le Mystère de Jésus: Pensées,* 553.
108. Pope Paul VI, *Sollemnis Professio Fidei,* 4: *AAS* 60 (1968),
p. 434.
109. Pope Paul VI, Apostolic Exhortation *Quinque Iam Anni: AAS*
63 (1971), p. 99.
110. Cf. *1 Tim* 1:3ff.; 4:1ff.; *2 Tim* 2:14ff.; 4: 1-5; *Tit* 1: 10-12; cf.
also Apostolic Exhortation *Evangelii Nuntiandi,* 78: *AAS* 68 (1976),
p. 70.
111. Encyclical *Redemptor Hominis,* 10: *AAS* 71 (1979), p. 274.
112. *De Catechizandis Rudibus, PL* 40, 310-347.
113. Cf. Decree on the Bishop's Pastoral Office in the Church *Christus Dominus,* 14: *AAS* 58 (1966), p. 679.
114. Decree on the Ministry and Life of Priests *Presbyterorum Ordinis,* 6: *AAS* 58 (1966), p. 999.
115. *Lam* 4:4.
116. *Eph* 4: 5-6.
117. Cf. Second Vatican Council, Constitution on the Sacred Liturgy *Sacrosanctum Concilium,* 35, 52: *AAS* 56 (1964), pp. 109, 114;
cf. also *Institutio Generalis Missalis Romani,* promulgated by a
Decree of the Sacred Congregation of Rites on 6 April 1969, 33, and
what has been said above in Chapter VI concerning the homily.
118. Since the High Middle Ages, provincial councils have insisted on
the responsibility of parents in regard to education in the faith: cf.
Sixth Council of Arles (813), Canon 19; Council of Mainz (813),

Canons 45, 47; Sixth Council of Paris (829), Book 1, Chapter 7: Mansi, *Sacrorum Conciliorum Nova et Amplissima Collectio,* XIV, 62, 74, 542. Among the more recent documents of the Magisterium, note the Encyclical *Divini Illius Magistri* of Pius XI, 31 December 1929: *AAS* 22 (1930), pp. 49-86; the many discourses and messages of Pius XII; and above all the texts of the Second Vatican Council: the Dogmatice Constitution on the Church *Lumen Gentium,* 11, 35: *AAS* 57 (1965), pp. 15, 40; the Decree on the Apostolate of the Laity *Apostolicam Actuositatem,* 11, 30: *AAS* 58 (1966), pp. 847, 860; the Pastoral Constitution on the Church in the Modern World *Gaudium et Spes,* n. 52: *AAS* 58 (1966), p. 1073; and especially the Declaration on Christian Education *Gravissimum Educationis,* 3: *AAS* 58 (1966), p. 731.

119. Cf. Second Vatican Council, Declaration on Christian Education *Gravissimum Educationis,* 3: *AAS* 58 (1966), p. 731.

120. Second Vatican Council, Dogmatic Constitution on the Church *Lumen Gentium,* 11: *AAS* 57 (1965), p. 16; cf. Decree on the Apostolate of the Laity *Apostolicam Actuositatem,* 11: *AAS* 58 (1966), p. 848.

121. Apostolic Exhortation *Evangelii Nuntiandi,* 77: *AAS* 68 (1976), p. 69.

122. *Jn* 14: 26.

123. *Jn* 16:13.

124. *Jn Ioannis Evangelium Tractatus,* 97, 1: *PL* 35, 1877.

125. *Jn* 15: 26-27.

126. Cf. *Rom* 8: 14-17; *Gal* 4:6.

127. *Rom* 8:15.

128. *1 Cor* 12:3.

129. Cf. *1 Cor* 12: 4-11.

130. *Eph* 5: 18.

131. *Retractationum Liber 1,* 23, 2: *PL* 32, 621.

132. 75: *AAS* 68 (1976), p. 66.

133. Cf. *Lk* 2:52.

134. Cf. *Jn* 1:14; *Heb* 10:5; *S. Th. lll.* Q. 12, a. 2; a. 3, ad 3.

135. Cf. *Lk* 2:51.

136. Cf. *Jn* 6:45.

137. Cf. *Sermo* 25, 7: *PL* 46, 937-938.

138. *Mt* 28: 19.

122

THE CHRISTIAN FAMILY
IN THE MODERN WORLD

John Paul II, *Familiaris consortio*, 22 November, 1981

INTRODUCTION

1. The family in the modern world, as much as and perhaps more than any other institution, has been beset by the many profound and rapid changes that have affected society and culture. Many families are living this situation in fidelity to those values that constitute the foundation of the institution of the family. Others have become uncertain and bewildered over their role or even doubtful and almost unaware of the ultimate meaning and truth of conjugal and family life. Finally, there are others who are hindered by various situations of injustice in the realization of their fundamental rights.

Knowing that marriage and the family constitute one of the most precious of human values, the Church wishes to speak and offer her help to those who are already aware of the value of marriage and the family and seek to live it faithfully, to those who are uncertain and anxious and searching for the truth, and to those who are unjustly impeded from living freely their family lives. Supporting the first, illuminating the second and assisting the others, the Church offers her services to every person who wonders about the destiny of marriage and the family.[1]

In a particular way the Church addresses the young, who are beginning their journey towards marriage and family life, for the purpose of presenting them with new horizons, helping them to discover the beauty and grandeur of the vocation to love and the service of life.

2. A sign of this profound interest of the Church in the family was the last Synod of Bishops, held in Rome from 26 September to 25 October 1980. This was a natural continuation of the two preceding Synods:[2] the Christian family, in fact, is the first community called to announce the Gospel to the human person during growth and to bring him or her, through a progressive education and catechesis, to full human and Christian maturity.

Furthermore, the recent Synod is logically connected in some way as well with that on the ministerial priesthood and on justice in the modern world. In fact, as an educating community, the family must help man to discern his own vocation and to accept responsibility in the search for greater justice, educating him from the beginning in interpersonal relationships, rich in justice and in love.

At the close of their assembly, the Synod Fathers presented me with a long list of proposals in which they had gathered the fruits of their reflections, which had matured over intense days of work, and they asked me unanimously to be a spokesman before humanity of the Church's lively care for the family and to give suitable indications for renewed pastoral effort in this fundamental sector of the life of man and of the Church.

As I fulfil that mission with this Exhortation, thus actuating in a particular matter the apostolic ministry with which I am entrusted, I wish to thank all the members of the Synod for the very valuable contribution of teaching and experience that they made, especially through the *Propositiones*, the text of which I am entrusting to the Pontifical Council for the Family with instructions to study it so as to bring out every aspect of its rich content.

3. Illuminated by the faith that gives her an understanding of all the truth concerning the great value of marriage and the family and their deepest meaning, the Church once again feels the pressing need to proclaim the Gospel, that is the "good news", to all people without exception, in particular to all those who are called to marriage and are preparing for it, to all married couples and parents in the world.

The Church is deeply convinced that only by the acceptance of the Gospel are the hopes that man legitimately places in marriage and in the family capable of being fulfilled.

Willed by God in the very act of creation,[3] marriage and the family are interiorly ordained to fulfillment in Christ[4] and have need of his graces in order to be healed from the wounds of sin[5] and restored to their "beginning",[6] that is, to full understanding and the full realization of God's plan.

At a moment of history in which the family is the object of numerous forces that seek to destroy it or in some way to deform it, and aware that the well-being of society and her own good are intimately tied to the good of the family,[7] the Church perceives in a more urgent and compelling way her mission of proclaiming to all people the plan of God for marriage and the family, ensuring their full vitality and human and Christian development, and thus contributing to the renewal of society and of the People of God.

PART ONE
BRIGHT SPOTS AND SHADOWS
FOR THE FAMILY TODAY

4. Since God's plan for marriage and the family touches men and women in the concreteness of their daily existence in specific social and cultural situations, the Church ought to apply herself to understanding the situations within which marriage and the family are lived today, in order to fulfil her task of serving.[8]

This understanding is, therefore, an inescapable requirement of the work of evangelization. It is, in fact, to the families of our times that the Church must bring the unchangeable and ever new Gospel of Jesus Christ, just as it is the families involved in the present conditions of the world that are called to accept and to live the plan of God that pertains to them. Moreover, the call and demands of the Spirit resound in the very events of history, and so the Church can also be guided to a more profound understanding of the inexhaustible mystery of marriage and the family by the circumstances, the questions and the anxieties and hopes of the young people, married couples and parents of today.[9]

To this ought to be added a further reflection of particular importance at the present time. Not infrequently ideas and solutions which are very appealing, but which obscure in varying degrees the truth and the dignity of the human person, are offered to the men and women of today, in their sincere and deep search for a response to the important daily problems that affect their married and family life. These views are often supported by the powerful and pervasive organization of the means of social communication, which subtly endanger freedom and the capacity for objective judgment.

Many are already aware of this danger to the human person and are working for the truth. The Church, with her evangelical discernment, joins with them, offering her own service to the truth, to freedom and to the dignity of every man and every woman.

5. The discernment effected by the Church becomes the offering of an orientation in order that the entire truth and the full dignity of marriage and the family may be preserved and realized.

This discernment is accomplished through the sense of faith,[10] which is a gift that the Spirit gives to all the faithful,[11] and is therefore the work of the whole Church according to the diversity of the various gifts and charisms that, together with and according to the responsibility proper to each one, work together for a more profound understanding and activation of the word of God. The Church, therefore, does not accomplish this discernment only through the Pastors, who teach in the name and with the power of Christ, but also through the laity: Christ "made them his witnesses and gave them understanding of the faith and the grace of speech (cf. *Acts* 2:17–18; *Rev* 19:10), so that the power of the Gospel might shine forth in their daily social and family life".[12] The laity, moreover, by reason of their particular vocation have the specific role of interpreting the history of the world in the light of Christ, in as much as they are called to illuminate and organize temporal realities according to the plan of God, Creator and Redeemer.

The "supernatural sense of faith"[13] however does not consist solely or necessarily in the consensus of the faithful. Following Christ, the Church seeks the truth, which is not always the same as the majority opinion. She listens to conscience and not to power, and in this way she defends the poor and the downtrodden. The Church values sociological and statistical research, when it proves helpful in understanding the historical context in which pastoral action has to be developed and when it leads to a better understanding of the truth. Such research alone, however, is not to be considered in itself an expression of the sense of faith.

Because it is the task of the apostolic ministry to ensure that the Church remains in the truth of Christ and to lead her ever more deeply into that truth, the Pastors must promote the sense of the faith in all the faithful, examine and authoritatively judge the genuineness of its expressions, and educate the faithful in an ever more mature evangelical discernment.[14]

Christian spouses and parents can and should offer their unique and irreplaceable contribution to the elaboration of an authentic evangelical discernment in the various situations and cultures in which men and women live their marriage and their family life. They are qualified for this role by their charism or specific gift, the gift of the sacrament of matrimony.[15]

6.   The situation in which the family finds itself presents positive and negative aspects: the first are a sign of the salvation of Christ operating in the world; the second, a sign of the refusal that man gives to the love of God.

On the one hand, in fact, there is a more lively awareness of personal freedom and greater attention to the quality of interpersonal relationships in marriage, to promoting the dignity of women, to responsible procreation, to the education of children. There is also an awareness of the need for the development of interfamily relationships, for reciprocal spiritual and material assistance, the rediscovery of the ecclesial mission proper to the family and its responsibility for the building of a more just society. On the other hand, however, signs are not lacking of a disturbing degradation of some fundamental values: a mistaken theoretical and practical concept of the independence of the spouses in relation to each other; serious misconceptions regarding the relationship of authority between parents and children; the concrete difficulties that the family itself experiences in the transmission of values; the growing number of divorces; the scourge of abortion; the ever more frequent recourse to sterilization; the appearance of a truly contraceptive mentality.

At the root of these negative phenomena there frequently lies a corruption of the idea and the experience of freedom, conceived not as a capacity for realizing the truth of God's plan for marriage and the family, but as an autonomous power of self-affirmation, often against others, for one's own selfish well-being.

Worthy of our attention also is the fact that, in the countries of the so-called Third World, families often lack both the means necessary for survival, such as food, work, housing, and medicine, and the most elementary freedoms. In the richer countries, on the contrary, excessive prosperity and the consumer mentality, paradoxically joined to a certain anguish and uncertainty about the future, deprive married couples of the generosity and courage needed for raising up new human life: thus life is often perceived not as a blessing, but as a danger from which to defend oneself.

The historical situation in which the family lives therefore appears as an interplay of light and darkness.

This shows that history is not simply a fixed progression towards what is better, but rather an event of freedom, and even a struggle between freedoms that are in mutual conflict, that is, according to the well-known expression of Saint Augustine, a conflict between two loves: the love of God to the point of disregarding self, and the love of self to the point of disregarding God.[16]

It follows that only an education for love rooted in faith can lead to the capacity of interpreting "the signs of the times", which are the historical expression of this twofold love.

7. Living in such a world, under the pressures coming above all from the mass media, the faithful do not always remain im-

mune from the obscuring of certain fundamental values, nor set themselves up as the critical conscience of family culture and as active agents in the building of an authentic family humanism.

Among the more troubling signs of this phenomenon, the Synod Fathers stressed the following, in particular: the spread of divorce and of recourse to a new union, even on the part of the faithful; the acceptance of purely civil marriage in contradiction to the vocation of the baptized to "be married in the Lord"; the celebration of the marriage sacrament without living faith, but for other motives; the rejection of the moral norms that guide and promote the human and Christian exercise of sexuality in marriage.

8. The whole Church is obliged to a deep reflection and commitment, so that the new culture now emerging may be evangelized in depth, true values acknowledged, the rights of men and women defended, and justice promoted in the very structures of society. In this way the "new humanism" will not distract people from their relationship with God, but will lead them to it more fully.

Science and its technical applications offer new and immense possibilities in the construction of such a humanism. Still, as a consequence of political choices that decide the direction of research and its applications, science is often used against its original purpose, which is the advancement of the human person.

It becomes necessary, therefore, on the part of all, to recover an awareness of the primacy of moral values, which are the values of the human person as such. The great task that has to be faced today for the renewal of society is that of recapturing the ultimate meaning of life and its fundamental values. Only an awareness of the primacy of these values enables man to use the immense possibilities given him by science in such a way as to bring about the true advancement of the human person in his or her whole truth, in his or her freedom and dignity. Science is called to ally itself with wisdom.

The following words of the Second Vatican Council can therefore be applied to the problems of the family: "Our era needs such wisdom more than bygone ages if the discoveries made by man are to be further humanized. For the future of the world stands in peril unless wiser people are forthcoming".[17]

The education of the moral conscience, which makes every human being capable of judging and of discerning the proper ways to achieve self-realization according to his or her original truth, thus becomes a pressing requirement that cannot be renounced.

Modern culture must be led to a more profoundly restored covenant with divine Wisdom. Every man is given a share of such Wisdom through the creating action of God. And it is only in faithfulness to this covenant that the families of today will be in a position to influence positively the building of a more just and fraternal world.

9. To the injustice originating from sin—which has profoundly penetrated the structures of today's world—and often hindering the family's full realization of itself and of its fundamental rights, we must all set ourselves in opposition through a conversion of mind and heart, following Christ Crucified by denying our own selfishness: such a conversion cannot fail to have a beneficial and renewing influence even on the structures of society.

What is needed is a continuous, permanent conversion which, while requiring an interior detachment from every evil and an adherence to good in its fullness, is brought about concretely in steps which lead us ever forward. Thus a dynamic process develops, one which advances gradually with the progressive integration of the gifts of God and the demands of his definitive and absolute love in the entire personal and social life of man. Therefore an educational growth process is necessary, in order that individual believers, families and peoples, even civilization itself, by beginning from what they have already received of the mystery of Christ, may patiently be led forward, arriving at a richer understanding and a fuller integration of this mystery in their lives.

10. In conformity with her constant tradition, the Church receives from the various cultures everything that is able to express better the unsearchable riches of Christ.[18] Only with the help of all the cultures will it be possible for these riches to be manifested ever more clearly, and for the Church to progress towards a daily more complete and profound awareness of the truth, which has already been given to her in its entirety by the Lord.

Holding fast to the two principles of the compatibility with the Gospel of the various cultures to be taken up and of communion with the universal Church, there must be further study, particularly by the Episcopal Conferences and the appropriate departments of the Roman Curia, and greater pastoral diligence so that this "inculturation" of the Christian faith may come about ever more extensively, in the context of marriage and the family as well as in other fields.

It is by means of "inculturation" that one proceeds towards the full restoration of the covenant with the Wisdom of God, which is Christ himself. The whole Church will be enriched also by the cultures which, though lacking technology, abound in human wisdom and are enlivened by profound moral values.

So that the goal of this journey might be clear and consequently the way plainly indicated, the Synod was right to begin by considering in depth the original design of God for marriage and the family: it "went back to the beginning", in deference to the teaching of Christ.[19]

PART TWO
THE PLAN OF GOD FOR MARRIAGE AND THE FAMILY

11. God created man in his own image and likeness:[20] calling him to existence *through love*, he called him at the same time *for love*.

God is love[21] and in himself he lives a mystery of personal loving communion. Creating the human race in his own image and continually keeping it in being, God inscribed in the humanity of man and woman the vocation, and thus the capacity and responsibility, of love and communion.[22] Love is therefore the fundamental and innate vocation of every human being.

As an incarnate spirit, that is a soul which expresses itself in a body and a body informed by an immortal spirit, man is called to love in his unified totality. Love includes the human body, and the body is made a sharer in spiritual love.

Christian revelation recognizes two specific ways of realizing the vocation of the human person, in its entirety, to love: marriage and virginity or celibacy. Either one is, in its own proper form, an actuation of the most profound truth of man, of his being "created in the image of God".

Consequently, sexuality, by means of which man and woman give themselves to one another through the acts which are proper and exclusive to spouses, is by no means something purely biological, but concerns the innermost being of the human person as such. It is realized in a truly human way only if it is an integral part of the love by which a man and a woman commit themselves totally to one another until death. The total physical self-giving would be a lie if it were not the sign and fruit of a total personal self-giving, in which the whole person, including the temporal dimension, is present: if the person were to withhold something or reserve the possibility of deciding otherwise in the future, by this very fact he or she would not be giving totally.

This totality which is required by conjugal love also corresponds to the demands of responsible fertility. This fertility is directed to the generation of a human being, and so by its nature it surpasses the purely biological order and involves a whole series of personal values. For the harmonious growth of these values a persevering and unified contribution by both parents is necessary.

The only "place" in which this self-giving in its whole truth is made possible is marriage, the covenant of conjugal love freely and consciously chosen, whereby man and woman accept the intimate community of life and love willed by God himself,[23] which only in this light manifests its true meaning. The institution of marriage is not an undue interference by society or authority, nor the extrinsic imposition of a form. Rather it is an interior requirement of the covenant of conjugal love which is publicly affirmed as unique and exclusive, in order to live in complete fidelity to the plan of God, the Creator. A person's freedom, far from being restricted by this fidelity, is secured against every form of subjectivism or relativism and is made a sharer in creative Wisdom.

12. The communion of love between God and people, a fundamental part of the Revelation and faith experience of Israel, finds a meaningful expression in the marriage covenant which is established between a man and a woman.

For this reason the central word of Revelation, "God loves his people", is likewise proclaimed through the living and concrete word whereby a man and a woman express their conjugal love. Their bond of love becomes the image and the symbol of the covenant which unites God and his people.[24] And the same sin which can harm the conjugal covenant becomes an image of the infidelity of the people to their God: idolatry is prostitution,[25] infidelity is adultery, disobedience to the law is abandonment of the spousal love of the Lord. But the infidelity of Israel does not destroy the eternal fidelity of the Lord, and therefore the ever faithful love of God is put forward as the model of the relations of faithful love which should exist between spouses.[26]

13. The communion between God and his people finds its definitive fulfilment in Jesus Christ, the Bridegroom who loves and gives himself as the Saviour of humanity, uniting it to himself as his body.

He reveals the original truth of marriage, the truth of the "beginning",[27] and, freeing man from his hardness of heart, he makes man capable of realizing this truth in its entirety.

This revelation reaches its definitive fullness in the gift of love which the Word of God makes to humanity in assuming a human nature, and in the sacrifice which Jesus Christ makes of himself on the Cross for his bride, the Church. In this sacrifice there is entirely revealed that plan which God has imprinted on the humanity of man and woman since their creation;[28] the marriage of baptized persons thus becomes a real symbol of that new and eternal covenant sanctioned in the blood of Christ. The Spirit which the Lord pours forth gives a new heart, and renders man and woman capable of loving one another as Christ has loved us. Conjugal love reaches that fullness to which it is interiorly ordained, conjugal charity, which is the proper and specific way in which the spouses participate in and are called to live the very charity of Christ who gave himself on the Cross.

In a deservedly famous page, Tertullian has well expressed the greatness of this conjugal life in Christ and its beauty: "How can I ever express the happiness of the marriage that is joined together by the Church, strengthened by an offering, sealed by a blessing, announced by angels and ratified by the Father?... How wonderful the bond between two believers, with a single hope, a single desire, a single observance, a single service! They are both brethren and both fellow-servants; there is no separation between them in spirit or flesh; in fact they are truly two in one flesh, and where the flesh is one, one is the spirit".[29]

Receiving and meditating faithfully on the word of God, the Church has solemnly taught and continues to teach that the marriage of the baptized is one of the seven sacraments of the New Covenant.[30]

Indeed, by means of baptism, man and woman are definitively placed within the new and eternal covenant, in the spousal covenant of Christ with the Church. And it is because of this indestructible insertion that the intimate community of conjugal life and love, founded by the Creator,[31] is elevated and assumed into the spousal charity of Christ, sustained and enriched by his redeeming power.

By virtue of the sacramentality of their marriage, spouses are bound to one another in the most profoundly indissoluble manner. Their belonging to each other is the real representation, by means of the sacramental sign, of the very relationship of Christ with the Church.

Spouses are therefore the permanent reminder to the Church of what happened on the Cross; they are for one another and for the children witnesses to the salvation in which the sacrament makes them sharers. Of this salvation event marriage, like every sacrament, is a memorial, actuation and prophecy: "As a memorial, the sacrament gives them the grace and duty of commemorating the great works of God and of bearing witness to them before their children. As actuation, it gives them the grace and duty of putting into practice in the present, towards each other and their children, the demands of a love which forgives and redeems. As prophecy, it gives them the grace and duty of living and bearing witness to the hope of the future encounter with Christ".[32]

Like each of the seven sacraments, so also marriage is a real symbol of the event of salvation, but in its own way. "The spouses participate in it as spouses, together, as a couple, so that the first and immediate effect of marriage (*res et sacramentum*) is not supernatural grace itself, but the Christian conjugal bond, a typically Christian communion of two persons because it represents the mystery of Christ's incarnation and the mystery of his covenant. The content of participation in Christ's life is also specific: conjugal love involves a totality, in which all the elements of the person enter—appeal of the body and instinct, power of feeling and affectivity, aspiration of the spirit and of will. It aims at a deeply personal unity, the unity that, beyond union in one flesh, leads to forming one heart and soul; it demands indissolubility and faithfulness in definitive mutual giving; and it is open to fertility (cf. *Humanae Vitae, 9*). In a word it is a question of the normal characteristics of all natural conjugal love, but with a new significance which not only purifies and strengthens them, but raises them to the extent of making them the expression of specifically Christian values".[33]

14. According to the plan of God, marriage is the foundation of the wider community of the family, since the very institution of marriage and conjugal love are ordained to the procreation and education of children, in whom they find their crowning.[34]

In its most profound reality, love is essentially a gift; and conjugal love, while leading the spouses to the reciprocal "knowledge" which makes them "one flesh",[35] does not end with the couple, because it makes them capable of the greatest possible gift, the gift by which they become cooperators with God for giving life to a new human person. Thus the couple, while giving themselves to one another, give not just themselves but also the reality of children, who are a living reflection of their love, a permanent sign of conjugal unity and a living and inseparable synthesis of their being a father and a mother.

When they become parents, spouses receive from God the gift of a new responsibility. Their parental love is called to become for the children the visible sign of the very love of God, "from whom every family in heaven and on earth is named".[36]

It must not be forgotten however that, even when procreation is not possible, conjugal life does not for this reason lose its value. Physical sterility in fact can be for spouses the occasion for other important services to the life of the human person, for example, adoption, various forms of educational work, and assistance to other families and to poor or handicapped children.

15. In matrimony and in the family a complex of interpersonal relationships is set up—married life, fatherhood and motherhood, filiation and fraternity—through which each human person is introduced into the "human family" and into the "family of God", which is the Church.

Christian marriage and the Christian family build up the Church: for in the family the human person is not only brought into being and progressively introduced by means of education into the human community, but by means of the rebirth of baptism and education in the faith the child is also introduced into God's family, which is the church.

The human family, disunited by sin, is reconstituted in its unity by the redemptive power of the death and Resurrection of Christ.[37] Christian marriage, by participating in the salvific efficacy of this event, constitutes the natural setting in which the human person is introduced into the great family of the Church.

The commandment to grow and multiply, given to man and woman in the beginning, in this way reaches its whole truth and full realization.

The Church thus finds in the family, born from the sacrament, the cradle and the setting in which she can enter the human generations, and where these in their turn can enter the Church.

16. Virginity or celibacy for the sake of the Kingdom of God not only does not contradict the dignity of marriage but presupposes it and confirms it. Marriage and virginity or celibacy are two ways of expressing and living the one mystery of the covenant of God with his people. When marriage is not esteemed, neither can consecrated virginity or celibacy exist; when human sexuality is not regarded as a great value given by the Creator, the renunciation of it for the sake of the Kingdom of Heaven loses its meaning.

Rightly indeed does Saint John Chrysostom say: "Whoever denigrates marriage also diminishes the glory of virginity. Whoever praises it makes virginity more admirable and resplendent. What appears good only in comparison with evil would not be particularly good. It is something better than what is admitted to be good that is the most excellent good".[38]

In virginity or celibacy, the human being is awaiting, also in a bodily way, the eschatological marriage of Christ with the Church, giving himself or herself completely to the Church in the hope that Christ may give himself to the Church in the full truth of eternal life. The celibate person thus anticipates in his or her flesh the new world of the future resurrection.[39]

By virtue of this witness, virginity or celibacy keeps alive in the Church a consciousness of the mystery of marriage and defends it from any reduction and impoverishment.

Virginity or celibacy, by liberating the human heart in a unique way,[40] "so as to make it burn with greater love for God and all humanity",[41] bears witness that the Kingdom of God and his justice is that pearl of great price which is preferred to every other value no matter how great, and hence must be sought as the only definitive value. It is for this reason that the Church, throughout her history, has always defended the superiority of this charism to that of marriage, by reason of the wholly singular link which it has with the Kingdom of God.[42]

In spite of having renounced physical fecundity, the celibate person becomes spiritually fruitful, the father and mother of many, cooperating in the realization of the family according to God's plan.

Christian couples therefore have the right to expect from celibate persons a good example and a witness of fidelity to their vocation until death. Just as fidelity at times becomes difficult for married people and requires sacrifice, mortification and self-denial, the same can happen to celibate persons, and their fidelity, even in the trials that may occur, should strengthen the fidelity of married couples.[43]

These reflections on virginity or celibacy can enlighten and help those who, for reasons independent of their own will, have been unable to marry and have then accepted their situation in a spirit of service.

PART THREE
THE ROLE OF THE CHRISTIAN FAMILY

17. The family finds in the plan of God the Creator and Redeemer not only its *identity*, what it *is*, but also its *mission*, what it can and should *do*. The role that God calls the family to perform in history derives from what the family is; its role represents the dynamic and existential development of what it is. Each family finds within itself a summons that cannot be ignored, and

that specifies both its dignity and its responsibility: family, *become* what you *are*.

Accordingly, the family must go back to the "beginning" of God's creative act, if it is to attain self-knowledge and self-realization in accordance with the inner truth not only of what it is but also of what it does in history. And since in God's plan it has been established as an "intimate community of life and love",[44] the family has the mission to become more and more what it is, that is to say, a community of life and love, in an effort that will find fulfilment, as will everything created and redeemed, in the Kingdom of God. Looking at it in such a way as to reach its very roots, we must say that the essence and role of the family are in the final analysis specified by love. Hence the family has *the mission to guard, reveal and communicate love*, and this is a living reflection of and a real sharing in God's love for humanity and the love of Christ the Lord for the Church his bride.

Every particular task of the family is an expression and concrete actuation of that fundamental mission. We must therefore go deeper into the unique riches of the family's mission and probe its contents, which are both manifold and unified.

Thus, with love as its point of departure and making constant reference to it, the recent Synod emphasized four general tasks for the family: 1) forming a community of persons; 2) serving life; 3) participating in the development of society; 4) sharing in the life and mission of the church.

I—FORMING A COMMUNITY OF PERSONS

18. The family, which is founded and given life by love, is a community of persons: of husband and wife, of parents and children, of relatives. Its first task is to live with fidelity the reality of communion in a constant effort to develop an authentic community of persons.

The inner principle of that task, its permanent power and its final goal is love: without love the family is not a community of persons and, in the same way, *without love the family cannot live, grow and perfect itself as a community of persons*. What I wrote in the Encyclical *Redemptor Hominis* applies primarily and especially within the family as such: "Man cannot live without love. He remains a being that is incomprehensible for himself, his life is senseless, if love is not revealed to him, if he does not encounter love, if he does not experience it and make it his own, if he does not participate intimately in it".[45]

The love between husband and wife and, in a derivatory and

broader way, the love between members of the same family—between parents and children, brothers and sisters and relatives and members of the household—is given life and sustenance by an unceasing inner dynamism leading the family to ever deeper and more intense *communion*, which is the foundation and soul of the *community* of marriage and the family.

19. The first communion is the one which is established and which develops between husband and wife: by virtue of the covenant of married life, the man and woman "are no longer two but one flesh"[46] and they are called to grow continually in their communion through day-to-day fidelity to their marriage promise of total mutual self-giving.

This conjugal communion sinks its roots in the natural complementarity that exists between man and woman, and is nurtured through the personal willingness of the spouses to share their entire life-project, what they have and what they are: for this reason such communion is the fruit and the sign of a profoundly human need. But in the Lord Christ God takes up this human need, confirms it, purifies it and elevates it, leading it to perfection through the sacrament of Matrimony: the Holy Spirit who is poured out in the sacramental celebration offers Christian couples the gift of a new communion of love that is the living and real image of that unique unity which makes of the Church the indivisible Mystical Body of the Lord Jesus.

The gift of the Spirit is a commandment of life for Christian spouses and at the same time a stimulating impulse so that every day they may progress towards an ever richer union with each other on all levels—of the body, of the character, of the heart, of the intelligence and will, of the soul[47]—revealing in this way to the Church and to the world the new communion of love, given by the grace of Christ.

Such a communion is radically contradicted by polygamy: this, in fact, directly negates the plan of God which was revealed from the beginning, because it is contrary to the equal personal dignity of men and women who in matrimony give themselves with a love that is total and therefore unique and exclusive. As the Second Vatican Council writes: "Firmly established by the Lord, the unity of marriage will radiate from the equal personal dignity of husband and wife, a dignity acknowledged by mutual and total love".[48]

20. Conjugal communion is characterized not only by its unity but also by its indissolubility: "As a mutual gift of two persons, this intimate union, as well as the good of children, imposes total fidelity on the spouses and argues for an unbreakable oneness between them"[49].

It is a fundamental duty of the Church to reaffirm strongly, as the Synod Fathers did, the doctrine of the indissolubility of marriage. To all those who, in our times, consider it too difficult, or indeed impossible, to be bound to one person for the whole of life, and to those caught up in a culture that rejects the indissolubility of marriage and openly mocks the commitment of spouses to fidelity, it is necessary to reconfirm the good news of the definitive nature of that conjugal love that has in Christ its foundation and strength.[50]

Being rooted in the personal and total self-giving of the couple, and being required by the good of the children, the indissolubility of marriage finds its ultimate truth in the plan that God has manifested in his revelation: he wills and he communicates the indissolubility of marriage as a fruit, a sign and a requirement of the absolutely faithful love that God has for man and that the Lord Jesus has for the Church.

Christ renews the first plan that the Creator inscribed in the hearts of man and woman, and in the celebration of the sacrament of matrimony offers "a new heart": thus the couples are not only able to overcome "hardness of heart",[51] but also and above all they are able to share the full and definitive love of Christ, the new and eternal Covenant made flesh. Just as the Lord Jesus is the "faithful witness",[52] the "yes" of the promises of God[53] and thus the supreme realization of the unconditional faithfulness with which God loves his people, so Christian couples are called to participate truly in the irrevocable indissolubility that binds Christ to the Church his bride, loved by him to the end.[54]

The gift of the sacrament is at the same time a vocation and commandment for the Christian spouses, that they may remain faithful to each other forever, beyond every trial and difficulty, in generous obedience to the holy will of the Lord: "What therefore God has joined together, let not man put asunder".[55]

To bear witness to the inestimable value of the indissolubility and fidelity of marriage is one of the most precious and most urgent tasks of Christian couples in our time. So, with all my Brothers who participated in the Synod of Bishops, I praise and encourage those numerous couples who, though encountering no small difficulty, preserve and develop the value of indissolubility: thus, in a humble and courageous manner, they perform the role committed to them of being in the world a "sign"—a small and precious sign, sometimes also subjected to temptation, but always renewed—of the unfailing fidelity with which God and Jesus Christ love each and every human being. But it is also proper to recognize the value of the witness of those spouses who, even when abandoned by their partner, with the strength of faith and of Christian hope have not entered a new union: these spouses too give an authentic witness to fidelity, of which the world today has a great need. For this reason they must be encouraged and helped by the pastors and the faithful of the Church.

21. Conjugal communion constitutes the foundation on which is built the broader communion of the family, of parents and children, of brothers and sisters with each other, of relatives and other members of the household.

This communion is rooted in the natural bonds of flesh and blood, and grows to its specifically human perfection with the establishment and maturing of the still deeper and richer bonds of the spirit: the love that animates the interpersonal relationships of the different members of the family constitutes the interior strength that shapes and animates the family communion and community.

The Christian family is also called to experience a new and original communion which confirms and perfects natural and human communion. In fact the grace of Jesus Christ, "the first-born among many brethren",[56] is by its nature and interior dynamism "a grace of brotherhood", as Saint Thomas Aquinas calls it.[57] The Holy Spirit, who is poured forth in the celebration of the sacraments, is the living source and inexhaustible sustenance of the supernatural communion that gathers believers and links them with Christ and with each other in the unity of the Church of God. The Christian family constitutes a specific revelation and realization of ecclesial communion, and for this reason too it can and should be called "the domestic Church".[58]

All members of the family, each according to his or her own gift, have the grace and responsibility of building, day by day, the communion of persons, making the family "a school of deeper humanity":[59] this happens where there is care and love for the little ones, the sick, the aged; where there is mutual service every day; when there is a sharing of goods, of joys and of sorrows.

A fundamental opportunity for building such a communion is constituted by the educational exchange between parents and children,[60] in which each gives and receives. By means of love, respect and obedience towards their parents, children offer their specific and irreplaceable contribution to the construction of an authentically human and Christian family.[61] They will be aided in this if parents exercise their unrenounceable authority as a true and proper "ministry", that is, as a service to the human and Christian well-being of their children, and in particular as a service aimed at helping them acquire a truly responsible freedom, and if parents maintain a living awareness of the "gift" they continually receive from their children.

Family communion can only be preserved and perfected through a great spirit of sacrifice. It requires, in fact, a ready and generous openness of each and all to understanding, to forbearance, to pardon, to reconciliation. There is no family that does not know how selfishness, discord, tension and conflict violently attack and at times mortally wound its own communion: hence there arise the many and varied forms of division in family life. But, at the same time, every family is called by the God of peace to have the joyous and renewing experience of "reconciliation", that is, communion reestablished, unity restored. In particular, participation in the sacrament of reconciliation and in the banquet of the one Body of Christ offers to the Christian family the grace and the responsibility of overcoming every division and of moving towards the fullness of communion willed by God, responding in this way to the ardent desire of the Lord: "that they may be one".[62]

22. In that it is, and ought always to become, a communion and community of persons, the family finds in love the source and the constant impetus for welcoming, respecting and promoting each one of its members in his or her lofty dignity as a person, that is, as a living image of God. As the Synod Fathers rightly stated, the moral criterion for the authenticity of conjugal and family relationships consists in fostering the dignity and vocation of the individual persons, who achieve their fullness by sincere self-giving.[63]

In this perspective the Synod devoted special attention to women, to their rights and role within the family and society. In the same perspective are also to be considered men as husbands and fathers, and likewise children and the elderly.

Above all it is important to underline the equal dignity and responsibility of women with men. This equality is realized in a unique manner in that reciprocal self-giving by each one to the other and by both to the children which is proper to marriage and the family. What human reason intuitively perceives and acknowledges is fully revealed by the word of God: the history of salvation, in fact, is a continuous and luminous testimony to the dignity of women.

In creating the human race "male and female",[64] God gives man and woman an equal personal dignity, endowing them with the inalienable rights and responsibilities proper to the human person. God then manifests the dignity of women in the highest form possible, by assuming human flesh from the Virgin Mary, whom the Church honours as the Mother of God, calling her the new Eve and presenting her as the model of redeemed woman. The sensitive respect of Jesus towards the women that he called to his following and his friendship, his appearing on Easter morning to a woman before the other disciples, the mission entrusted to women to carry the good news of the Resurrection to the Apostles—these are all signs that confirm the special esteem of the Lord Jesus for women. The Apostle Paul will say: "In Christ Jesus you are all children of God through faith... There is neither Jew nor Greek, there is neither slave nor free, there is neither male nor female; for you are all one in Christ Jesus".[65]

23. Without intending to deal with all the various aspects of the vast and complex theme of the relationships between women and society, and limiting these remarks to a few essential points, one cannot but observe that in the specific area of family life a widespread social and cultural tradition has considered women's role to be exclusively that of wife and mother, without adequate access to public functions, which have generally been reserved for men.

There is no doubt that the equal dignity and responsibility of men and women fully justifies women's access to public functions. On the other hand the true advancement of women requires that clear recognition be given to the value of their maternal and family role, by comparison with all other public roles and all other professions. Furthermore, these roles and professions should be harmoniously combined, if we wish the evolution of society and culture to be truly and fully human.

This will come about more easily if, in accordance with the wishes expressed by the Synod, a renewed "theology of work" can shed light upon and study in depth the meaning of work in the Christian life and determine the fundamental bond between work and the family, and therefore the original and irreplaceable meaning of work in the home and in rearing children.[66] Therefore the Church can and should help modern society by tirelessly insisting that the work of women in the home be recognized and respected by all in its irreplaceable value. This is of particular importance in education: for possible discrimination between the different types of work and professions is eliminated at its very root once it is clear that all people, in every area, are working with equal rights and equal responsibilities. The image of God in man and in woman will thus be seen with added lustre.

While it must be recognized that women have the same right as men to perform various public functions, society must be structured in such a way that wives and mothers are *not in practice compelled* to work outside the home, and that their families can live and prosper in a dignified way even when they themselves devote their full time to their own family.

Furthermore, the mentality which honours women more for their work outside the home than for their work within the family must be overcome. This requires that men should truly esteem and love women with total respect for their personal dignity, and that society should create and develop conditions favouring work in the home.

With due respect to the different vocations of men and women, the Church must in her own life promote as far as possible their equality of rights and dignity: and this for the good of all, the family, the Church and society.

But clearly all of this does not mean for women a renunciation of their femininity or an imitation of the male role, but the fullness of true feminine humanity which should be expressed in their activity, whether in the family or outside of it, without disregarding the differences of customs and cultures in this sphere.

24.   Unfortunately the Christian message about the dignity of women is contradicted by that persistent mentality which considers the human being not as a person but as a thing, as an object of trade, at the service of selfish interest and mere pleasure: the first victims of this mentality are women.

This mentality produces very bitter fruits, such as contempt for men and for women, slavery, oppression of the weak, pornography, prostitution—especially in an organized form—and all those various forms of discrimination that exist in the fields of education, employment, wages, etc.

Besides, many forms of degrading discrimination still persist today in a great part of our society that affect and seriously harm particular categories of women, as for example childless wives, widows, separated or divorced women, and unmarried mothers.

The Synod Fathers deplored these and other forms of discriminations as strongly as possible. I therefore ask that vigorous and incisive pastoral action be taken by all to overcome them definitively so that the image of God that shines in all human beings without exception may be fully respected.

25.   Within the conjugal and family communion-community, the man is called upon to live his gift and role as husband and father.

In his wife he sees the fulfilment of God's intention: "It is not good that the man should be alone; I will make him a helper fit for him",[67] and he makes his own the cry of Adam, the first husband: "This at last is bone of my bones and flesh of my flesh".[68]

Authentic conjugal love presupposes and requires that a man have a profound respect for the equal dignity of his wife: "You are not her master", writes Saint Ambrose, "but her husband; she was not given to you to be your slave, but your wife...Reciprocate her attentiveness to you and be grateful to her for her love".[69] With his wife a man should live "a very special form of personal friendship".[70] As for the Christian, he is called upon to develop a new attitude of love, manifesting towards his wife a charity that is both gentle and strong like that which Christ has for the Church.[71]

Love for his wife as mother of their children and love for the children themselves are for the man the natural way of understanding and fulfilling his own fatherhood. Above all where social and cultural conditions so easily encourage a father to be less concerned with his family or at any rate less involved in the work of education, efforts must be made to restore socially the conviction that the place and task of the father in and for the family is of unique and irreplaceable importance.[72] As experience teaches, the absence of a father causes psychological and moral imbalance and notable difficulties in family relationships, as does, in contrary circumstances, the oppressive presence of a father, especially where there still prevails the phenomenon of "machismo", or a wrong superiority of male prerogatives which humiliates women and inhibits the development of healthy family relationships.

In revealing and in reliving on earth the very fatherhood of God,[73] a man is called upon to ensure the harmonious and united development of all the members of the family: he will perform this task by exercising generous responsibility for the life conceived under the heart of the mother, by a more solicitous commitment to education, a task he shares with his wife,[74] by work which is never a cause of division in the family but promotes its unity and stability, and by means of the witness he gives of an adult Christian life which effectively introduces the children into the living experience of Christ and the Church.

26. In the family, which is a community of persons, special attention must be devoted to the children, by developing a profound esteem for their personal dignity, and a great respect and generous concern for their rights. This is true for every child, but it becomes all the more urgent the smaller the child is and the more it is in need of everything, when it is sick, suffering or handicapped.

By fostering and exercising a tender and strong concern for every child that comes into this world, the Church fulfils a fundamental mission: for she is called upon to reveal and put forward anew in history the example and the commandment of Christ the Lord, who placed the child at the heart of the Kingdom of God: "Let the children come to me, and do not hinder them; for to such belongs the kingdom of heaven".[75]

I repeat once again what I said to the General Assembly of the United Nations on 2 October 1979: "I wish to express the joy that we all find in children, the springtime of life, the anticipation of the future history of each of our present earthly homelands. No country on earth, no political system can think of its own future otherwise than through the image of these new generations that will receive from their parents the manifold heritage of values, duties and aspirations of the nation to which they belong and of the whole human family. Concern for the child, even before birth, from the first moment of conception and then throughout the years of infancy and youth, is the primary and fundamental test of the relationship of one human being to another. And so, what better wish can I express for every nation and for the whole of mankind, and for all the children of the world than a better future in which respect for human rights will become a complete reality throughout the third millennium, which is drawing near".[76]

Acceptance, love, esteem, manysided and united material, emotional, educational and spiritual concern for every child that comes into this world should always constitute a distinctive, essential characteristic of all Christians, in particular of the Christian family: thus children, while they are able to grow "in wisdom and in stature, and in favour with God and man",[77] offer their own precious contribution to building up the family community and even to the sanctification of their parents.[78]

27. There are cultures which manifest a unique veneration and great love for the elderly: far from being outcasts from the family or merely tolerated as a useless burden, they continue to be present and to take an active and responsible part in family life, though having to respect the autonomy of the new family; above all they carry out the important mission of being a witness to the past and a source of wisdom for the young and for the future.

Other cultures, however, especially in the wake of disordered industrial and urban development, have both in the past and in the present set the elderly aside in unacceptable ways. This causes acute suffering to them and spiritually impoverishes many families.

The pastoral activity of the Church must help everyone to discover and to make good use of the role of the elderly within the civil and ecclesial community, in particular within the family. In fact, "the life of the aging helps to clarify a scale of human values; it shows the continuity of generations and marvellously demonstrates the interdependence of God's people. The elderly often have the charism to bridge generation gaps before they are made: how many children have found understanding and love in the eyes and words and caresses of the aging! And how many old people have willingly subscribed to the inspired word that the 'crown of the aged is their children's children' (*Prov* 17:6)!"[79]

II—SERVING LIFE

1) *The transmission of life*

28. With the creation of man and woman in his own image and likeness, God crowns and brings to perfection the work of his hands: he calls them to a special sharing in his love and in his power as Creator and Father, through their free and responsible cooperation in transmitting the gift of human life: "God blessed them, and God said to them, 'Be fruitful and multiply, and fill the earth and subdue it'".[80]

Thus the fundamental task of the family is to serve life, to actualize in history the original blessing of the Creator—that of transmitting by procreation the divine image from person to person.[81]

Fecundity is the fruit and the sign of conjugal love, the living testimony of the full reciprocal self-giving of the spouses: "While not making the other purposes of matrimony of less account, the true practice of conjugal love, and the whole meaning of the family life which results from it, have this aim: that the couple be ready with stout hearts to cooperate with the love of the Creator and the Saviour, who through them will enlarge and enrich his own family day by day".[82]

However, the fruitfulness of conjugal love is not restricted solely to the procreation of children, even understood in its specifically human dimension: it is enlarged and enriched by all those fruits of moral, spiritual and supernatural life which the father and mother are called to hand on to their children, and through the children to the Church and to the world.

29. Precisely because the love of husband and wife is a unique participation in the mystery of life and of the love of God himself, the Church knows that she has received the special mission of guarding and protecting the lofty dignity of marriage and the most serious responsibility of the transmission of human life.

Thus, in continuity with the living tradition of the ecclesial community throughout history, the recent Second Vatican Council and the magisterium of my predecessor Paul VI, expressed above all in the Encyclical *Humanae Vitae*, have handed on to our times a truly prophetic proclamation, which reaffirms and reproposes with clarity the Church's teaching and norm, always old yet always new, regarding marriage and regarding the transmission of human life.

For this reason the Synod Fathers made the following declaration at their last assemby: "This Sacred Synod, gathered together with the Successor of Peter in the unity of faith, firmly holds what has been set forth in the Second Vatican Council (cf. *Gaudium et Spes,* 50) and afterwards in the Encyclical *Humanae Vitae,* particularly that love between husband and wife must be fully human, exclusive and open to new life (*Humanae Vitae,* 11; cf. 9, 12)".[83]

30. The teaching of the Church in our day is placed in a social and cultural context which renders it more difficult to understand and yet more urgent and irreplaceable for promoting the true good of men and women.

Scientific and technical progress, which contemporary man is continually expanding in his dominion over nature, not only offers the hope of creating a new and better humanity, but also causes ever greater anxiety regarding the future. Some ask themselves if it is a good thing to be alive or if it would be better never to have been born; they doubt therefore if it is right to bring others into life when perhaps they will curse their existence in a cruel world with unforeseeable terrors. Others consider themselves to be the only ones for whom the advantages of technology are intended and they exclude others by imposing on them contraceptives or even worse means. Still others, imprisoned in a consumer mentality and whose sole concern is to bring about a continual growth of material goods, finish by ceasing to understand, and thus by refusing, the spiritual riches of a new human life. The ultimate reason for these mentalities is the absence in people's hearts of God, whose love alone is stronger than all the world's fears and can conquer them.

Thus an anti-life mentality is born, as can be seen in many current issues: one thinks, for example, of a certain panic deriving from the studies of ecologists and futurologists on population growth, which sometimes exaggerate the danger of demographic increase to the quality of life.

But the Church firmly believes that human life, even if weak and suffering, is always a splendid gift of God's goodness. Against the pessimism and selfishness which cast a shadow over the world, the Church stands for life: in each human life she sees the splendour of that "Yes", that "Amen", who is Christ himself.[84] To the "No" which assails and afflicts the world, she replies with this living "Yes", thus defending the human person and the world from all who plot against and harm life.

The Church is called upon to manifest anew to everyone, with clear and stronger conviction, her will to promote human life by every means and to defend it against all attacks, in whatever condition or state of development it is found.

Thus the Church condemns as a grave offence against human dignity and justice all those activities of governments or other public authorities which attempt to limit in any way the freedom of couples in deciding about children. Consequently any violence applied by such authorities in favour of contraception or, still worse, of sterilization and procured abortion, must be altogether condemned and forcefully rejected. Likewise to be denounced as gravely unjust are cases where, in international relations, economic help given for the advancement of peoples is made conditional on programmes of contraception, sterilization and procured abortion.[85]

31. The Church is certainly aware of the many complex problems which couples in many countries face today in their task of transmitting life in a responsible way. She also recognizes the serious problem of population growth in the form it has taken in many parts of the world and its moral implications.

However, she holds that consideration in depth of all the aspects of these problems offers a new and stronger confirmation of the importance of the authentic teaching on birth regulation reproposed in the Second Vatican Council and in the Encyclical *Humanae Vitae*.

For this reason, together with the Synod Father I feel it is my duty to extend a pressing invitation to theologians, asking them to unite their efforts in order to collaborate with the hierarchical Magisterium and to commit themselves to the task of illustrating ever more clearly the biblical foundations, the ethical grounds and the personalistic reasons behind this doctrine. Thus it will be possible, in the context of an organic exposition, to render the teaching of the Church on this fundamental question truly accessible to all people of good will, fostering a daily more enlightened and profound understanding of it: in this way God's plan will be ever more completely fulfilled for the salvation of humanity and for the glory of the Creator.

A united effort by theologians in this regard, inspired by a convinced adherence to the Magisterium, which is the one authentic guide for the People of God, is particularly urgent for reasons that include the close link between Catholic teaching on this matter and the view of the human person that the Church proposes: doubt or error in the field of marriage or the family involves obscuring to a serious extent the integral truth about the human person, in a cultural situation that is already so often confused and contradictory. In fulfilment of their specific role, theologians are called upon to provide enlightenment and a deeper understanding, and their contribution is of incomparable value and represents a unique and highly meritorious service to the family and humanity.

32. In the context of a culture which seriously distorts or entirely misinterprets the true meaning of human sexuality, because it separates it from its essential reference to the person, the Church more urgently feels how irreplaceable is her mission of presenting sexuality as a value and task of the whole person, created male and female in the image of God.

In this perspective the Second Vatican Council clearly affirmed that "when there is a question of harmonizing conjugal love with the responsible transmission of life, the moral aspect of any procedure does not depend solely on sincere intentions or on an evaluation of motives. It must be determined by *objective standards*. These, *based on the nature of the human person and his or her acts*, preserve the full sense of mutual self-giving and human procreation in the context of true love. Such a goal cannot be achieved unless the virtue of conjugal chastity is sincerely practised".[86]

It is precisely by moving from "an integral vision of man and of his vocation, not only his natural and earthly, but also his supernatural and eternal vocation",[87] that Paul VI affirmed that the teaching of the Church "is founded upon the inseparable connection, willed by God and unable to be broken by man on his own initiative, between the two meanings of the conjugal act: the unitive meaning and the procreative meaning"[88]. And he concluded by re-emphasizing that there must be excluded as intrinsically immoral "every action which, either in anticipation of the conjugal act, or in its accomplishment, or in the development of its natural consequences, proposes, whether as an end or as a means, to render procreation impossible".[89]

When couples, by means of recourse to contraception, separate these two meanings that God the Creator has inscribed in the being of man and woman and in the dynamism of their sexual communion, they act as "arbiters" of the divine plan and they "manipulate" and degrade human sexuality—and with it themselves and their married partner—by altering its value of "total" self-giving. Thus the innate language that expresses the total reciprocal self-giving of husband and wife is overlaid, through contraception, by an objectively contradictory language, namely, that of not giving oneself totally to the other. This leads not only to a positive refusal to be open to life but also to a falsification of the inner truth of conjugal love, which is called upon to give itself in personal totality.

When, instead, by means of recourse to periods of infertility, the couple respect the inseparable connection between the unitive and procreative meanings of human sexuality, they are acting as "ministers" of God's plan and they "benefit from" their sexuality according to the original dynamism of "total" self-giving, without manipulation or altercation.[90]

In the light of the experience of many couples and of the data provided by the different human sciences, theological reflection is able to perceive and is called to study further *the difference, both anthropological and moral*, between contraception and recourse to the rhythm of the cycle: it is a difference which is much wider and deeper than is usually thought, one which involves in the final analysis two irreconcilable concepts of the human person and of human sexuality. The choice of the natural rhythms involves accepting the cycle of the person, that is, the woman, and thereby accepting dialogue, reciprocal respect, shared responsibility and self-control. To accept the cycle and to enter into dialogue means to recognize both the spiritual and corporal character of conjugal communion, and to live personal love with its requirement of fidelity. In this context the couple comes to experience how conjugal communion is enriched with those values of tenderness and affection which constitute the inner soul of human sexuality, in its physical dimension also. In this way sexuality is respected and promoted in its truly and fully human dimension, and is never "used" as an "object" that, by breaking the personal unity of soul and body, strikes at God's creation itself at the level of the deepest interaction of nature and person.

33. In the field of conjugal morality the Church is Teacher and Mother and acts as such.

As Teacher, she never tires of proclaiming the moral norm

that must guide the responsible transmission of life. The Church is in no way the author or the arbiter of this norm. In obedience to the truth which is Christ, whose image is reflected in the nature and dignity of the human person, the Church interprets the moral norm and proposes it to all people of good will, without concealing its demands of radicalness and perfection.

As Mother, the Church is close to the many married couples who find themselves in difficulty over this important point of the moral life: she knows well their situation, which is often very arduous and at times truly tormented by difficulties of every kind, not only individual difficulties but social ones as well; she knows that many couples encounter difficulties not only in the concrete fulfilment of the moral norm but even in understanding its inherent values.

But it is one and the same Church that is both Teacher and Mother. And so the Church never ceases to exhort and encourage all to resolve whatever conjugal difficulties may arise without ever falsifying or compromising the truth: she is convinced that there can be no true contradiction between the divine law on transmitting life and that on fostering authentic married love.[91] Accordingly, the concrete pedagogy of the Church must always remain linked with her doctrine and never be separated from it. With the same conviction as my predecessor, I therefore repeat: "To diminish in no way the saving teaching of Christ constitutes an eminent form of charity for souls".[92]

On the other hand, authentic ecclesial pedagogy displays its realism and wisdom only by making a tenacious and courageous effort to create and uphold all the human conditions—psychological, moral and spiritual—indispensable for understanding and living the moral value and norm.

There is no doubt that these conditions must include persistence and patience, humility and strength of mind, filial trust in God and in his grace, and frequent recourse to prayer and to the sacraments of the Eucharist and of Reconciliation.[93] Thus strengthened, Christian husbands and wives will be able to keep alive their awareness of the unique influence that the grace of the sacrament of marriage has on every aspect of married life, including therefore their sexuality: the gift of the Spirit, accepted and responded to by husband and wife, helps them to live their human sexuality in accordance with God's plan and as a sign of the unitive and fruitful love of Christ for his Church.

But the necessary conditions also include knowledge of the bodily aspect and the body's rhythms of fertility. Accordingly, every effort must be made to render such knowledge accessible to all married people and also to young adults before marriage, through clear, timely and serious instruction and education given by married couples, doctors and experts. Knowledge must then lead to education in self-control: hence the absolute necessity for the virtue of chastity and for permanent education in it. In the Christian view, chastity by no means signifies rejection of human sexuality or lack of esteem for it: rather it signifies spiritual energy capable of defending love from the perils of selfishness and aggressiveness, and able to advance it towards its full realization.

With deeply wise and loving intuition, Paul VI was only voicing the experience of many married couples when he wrote in his Encyclical: "To dominate instinct by means of one's reason and free will undoubtedly requires ascetical practices, so that the affective manifestations of conjugal life may observe the correct order, in particular with regard to the observance of periodic continence. Yet this discipline which is proper to the purity of married couples, far from harming conjugal love, rather confers on it a higher human value. It demands continual effort, yet, thanks to its beneficent influence, husband and wife fully develop their personalities, being enriched with spiritual values. Such discipline bestows upon family life fruits of serenity and peace, and facilitates the solution of other problems; it favours attention for one's partner, helps both parties to drive out selfishness, the enemy of true love, and deepens their sense of responsibility. By its means, parents acquire the capacity of having a deeper and more efficacious influence in the education of their offspring".[94]

34. It is always very important to have a right notion of the moral order, its values and its norms; and the importance is all the greater when the difficulties in the way or respecting them become more numerous and serious.

Since the moral order reveals and sets forth the plan of God the Creator, for this very reason it cannot be something that harms man, something impersonal. On the contrary, by responding to the deepest demands of the human being created by God, it places itself at the service of that person's full humanity with the delicate and binding love whereby God himself inspires, sustains and guides every creature towards its happiness.

But man, who has been called to live God's wise and loving design in a responsible manner, is an historical being who day by day builds himself up through his many free decisions; and so he knows, loves and accomplishes moral good by stages of growth.

Married people too are called upon to progress unceasingly in their moral life, with the support of a sincere and active desire to gain every better knowledge of the values enshrined in and fostered by the law of God. They must also be supported by an upright and generous willingness to embody these values in their concrete decisions. They cannot however look on the law as merely an ideal to be achieved in the future: they must consider it as a command of Christ the Lord to overcome difficulties with constancy. "And so what is known as 'the law of gradualness' or step-by-step advance cannot be identified with 'gradualness of the law', as if there were different degrees or forms of precept in God's law for different individuals and situations. In God's plan, all husbands and wives are called in marriage to holiness, and this lofty vocation is fulfilled to the extent that the human person is able to respond to God's command with serene confidence in God's grace and in his or her own will".[95] On the same lines, it is part of the Church's pedagogy that husbands and wives should first of all recognize clearly the teaching of *Humanae Vitae* as indicating the norm for the exercise of their sexuality, and that they should endeavour to establish the conditions necessary for observing that norm.

As the Synod noted, this pedagogy embraces the whole of married life. Accordingly, the function of transmitting life must be integrated into the overall mission of Christian life as a whole, which without the Cross cannot reach the Resurrection. In such a context it is understandable that sacrifice cannot be removed from family life, but must in fact be wholeheartedly accepted if the love between husband and wife is to be deepened and become a source of intimate joy.

This shared progress demands reflection, instruction and suitable education on the part of the priests, religious and lay people engaged in family pastoral work: they will all be able to assist married people in their human and spiritual progress, a progress that demands awareness of sin, a sincere commitment to observe the moral law, and the ministry of reconciliation. It must also be kept in mind that conjugal intimacy involves the wills of two persons, who are however called to harmonize their mentality and behaviour: this requires much patience, understanding and time. Uniquely important in this field is unity of moral and pastoral judgment by priests, a unity that must be carefully sought and ensured, in order that the faithful may not have to suffer anxiety of conscience.[96]

It will be easier for married people to make progress if, with respect for the Church's teaching and with trust in the grace of Christ, and with the help and support of the pastors of souls and the entire ecclesial community, they are able to discover and experience the liberating and inspiring value of the authentic love that is offered by the Gospel and set before us by the Lord's commandment.

35. With regard to the question of lawful birth regulation, the ecclesial community at the present time must take on the task of instilling conviction and offering practical help to those who wish to live out their parenthood in a truly responsible way.

In this matter, while the Church notes with satisfaction the results achieved by scientific research aimed at a more precise knowledge of the rhythms of women's fertility, and while it encourages a more decisive and wide-ranging extension of that research, it cannot fail to call with renewed vigour on the responsibility of all—doctors, experts, marriage counsellors, teachers and married couples—who can actually help married people to live their love with respect for the structure and finalities of the conjugal act which expresses that love. This implies a broader, more decisive and more systematic effort to make the natural methods of regulating fertility known, respected and applied.[97]

A very valuable witness can and should be given by those husbands and wives who through the joint exercise of periodic continence have reached a more mature personal responsibility with regard to love and life. As Paul VI wrote: "To them the Lord entrusts the task of making visible to people the holiness and sweetness of the law which unites the mutual love of husband and wife with their cooperation with the love of God the author of human life".[98]

2) Education

36. The task of giving education is rooted in the primary vocation of married couples to participate in God's creative activity: by begetting in love and for love a new person who has within himself or herself the vocation to growth and development, parents by that very fact take on the task of helping that person effectively to live a fully human life. As the Second Vatican Council recalled, "since parents have conferred life on their children, they have a most solemn obligation to educate their offspring. Hence, parents must be acknowledged as the first and foremost educators of their children. Their role as educators is so decisive that scarcely anything can compensate for their failure in it. For it devolves on parents to create a family atmosphere so animated with love and reverence for God and others that a well-rounded personal and social development will be fostered

among the children. Hence, the family is the first school of those social virtues which every society needs".[99]

The right and duty of parents to give education is *essential*, since it is connected with the transmission of human life; it is *original and primary* with regard to the educational role of others, on account of the uniqueness of the loving relationship between parents and children; and it is *irreplaceable and inalienable*, and therefore incapable of being entirely delegated to others or usurped by others.

In addition to these characteristics, it cannot be forgotten that the most basic element, so basic that it qualifies the educational role of parents, is *parental love*, which finds fulfilment in the task of education as it completes and perfects its service of life: as well as being a *source*, the parents' love is also the *animating principle* and therefore the *norm* inspiring and guiding all concrete educational activity, enriching it with the values of kindness, constancy, goodness, service, disinterestedness and self-sacrifice that are the most precious fruit of love.

37. Even amid the difficulties of the work of education, difficulties which are often greater today, parents must trustingly and courageously train their children in the essential values of human life. Children must grow up with a correct attitude of freedom with regard to material goods, by adopting a simple and austere life style and being fully convinced that "man is more precious for what he is than for what he has".[100]

In a society shaken and split by tensions and conflicts caused by the violent clash of various kinds of individualism and selfishness, children must be enriched not only with a sense of true justice, which alone leads to respect for the personal dignity of each individual, but also and more powerfully by a sense of true love, understood as sincere solicitude and disinterested service with regard to others, especially the poorest and those in most need. The family is the first and fundamental school of social living: as a community of love, it finds in self-giving the law that guides it and makes it grow. The self-giving that inspires the love of husband and wife for each other is the model and norm for the self-giving that must be practised in the relationships between brothers and sisters and the different generations living together in the family. And the communion and sharing that are part of everyday life in the home at times of joy and at times of difficulty are the most concrete and effective pedagogy for the active, responsible and fruitful inclusion of the children in the wider horizon of society.

Education in love as self-giving is also the indispensable

premise for parents called to give their children a clear and delicate *sex education*. Faced with a culture that largely reduces human sexuality to the level of something commonplace, since it interprets and lives it in a reductive and impoverished way by linking it solely with the body and with selfish pleasure, the educational service of parents must aim firmly at a training in the area of sex that is truly and fully personal: for sexuality is an enrichment of the whole person—body, emotions and soul—and it manifests its inmost meaning in leading the person to the gift of self in love.

Sex education, which is a basic right and duty of parents, must always be carried out under their attentive guidance, whether at home or in educational centres chosen and controlled by them. In this regard, the Church reaffirms the law of subsidiarity, which the school is bound to observe when it cooperates in sex education, by entering into the same spirit that animates the parents.

In this context *education for chastity* is absolutely essential, for it is a virtue that develops a person's authentic maturity and makes him or her capable of respecting and fostering the "nuptial meaning" of the body. Indeed Christian parents, discerning the signs of God's call, will devote special attention and care to education in virginity or celibacy as the supreme form of that self-giving that constitutes the very meaning of human sexuality.

In view of the close links between the sexual dimension of the person and his or her ethical values, education must bring the children to a knowledge of and respect for the moral norms as the necessary and highly valuable guarantee for responsible personal growth in human sexuality.

For this reason the Church is firmly opposed to an often widespread form of imparting sex information dissociated from moral principles. That would merely be an introduction to the experience of pleasure and a stimulus leading to the loss of serenity—while still in the years of innocence—by opening the way to vice.

38. For Christian parents the mission to educate, a mission rooted, as we have said, in their participation in God's creating activity, has a new specific source in the sacrament of marriage, which consecrates them for the strictly Christian education of their children: that is to say, it calls upon them to share in the very authority and love of God the Father and Christ the Shepherd, and in the motherly love of the Church, and it enriches them with wisdom, counsel, fortitude and all the other gifts of the Holy Spirit in order to help the children in their growth as

human beings and as Christians.

The sacrament of marriage gives to the educational role the dignity and vocation of being really and truly a "ministry" of the Church at the service of the building up of her members. So great and splendid is the educational ministry of Christian parents that Saint Thomas has no hesitation in comparing it with the ministry of priests: "Some only propagate and guard spiritual life by a spiritual ministry: this is the role of the sacrament of Orders; others do this for both corporal and spiritual life, and this is brought about by the sacrament of marriage, by which a man and a woman join in order to beget offspring and bring them up to worship God".[101]

A vivid and attentive awareness of the mission that they have received with the sacrament of marriage will help Christian parents to place themselves at the service of their children's education with great serenity and trustfulness, and also with a sense of responsibility before God, who calls them and gives them the mission of building up the Church in their children. Thus in the case of baptized people, the family, called together by word and sacrament as the Church of the home, is both teacher and mother, the same as the worldwide Church.

39. The mission to educate demands that Christian parents should present to their children all the topics that are necessary for the gradual maturing of their personality from a Christian and ecclesial point of view. They will therefore follow the educational lines mentioned above, taking care to show their children the depths of significance to which the faith and love of Jesus Christ can lead. Furthermore, their awareness that the Lord is entrusting to them the growth of a child of God, a brother or sister of Christ, a temple of the Holy Spirit, a member of the Church, will support Christian parents in their task of strengthening the gift of divine grace in their children's souls.

The Second Vatican Council describes the content of Christian education as follows: "Such an education does not merely strive to foster maturity . . . in the human person. Rather, its principal aims are these: that as baptized persons are gradually introduced into a knowledge of the mystery of salvation, they may daily grow more conscious of the gift of faith which they have received; that they may learn to adore God the Father in spirit and in truth (cf. *Jn* 4:23), especially through liturgical worship; that they may be trained to conduct their personal life in true righteousness and holiness, according to their new nature (*Eph* 4:22–24), and thus grow to maturity, to the stature of the fullness of Christ (cf. *Eph* 4:13), and devote themselves to the upbuilding of the Mystical Body. Moreover, aware of their calling, they should grow accustomed to giving witness to the hope that is in them (cf. *1 Pt* 3:15), and to promoting the Christian transformation of the world".[102]

The Synod too, taking up and developing the indications of the Council, presented the educational mission of the Christian family as a true ministry through which the Gospel is transmitted and radiated, so that family life itself becomes an itinerary of faith and in some way a Christian initiation and a school of following Christ. Within a family that is aware of this gift, as Paul VI wrote, "all the members evangelize and are evangelized".[103]

By virtue of their ministry of educating, parents are, through the witness of their lives, the first heralds of the Gospel for their children. Furthermore, by praying with their children, by reading the word of God with them and by introducing them deeply through Christian initiation into the Body of Christ—both the Eucharistic and the ecclesial Body—they become fully parents, in that they are begetters not only of bodily life but also of the life that through the Spirit's renewal flows from the Cross and Resurrection of Christ.

In order that Christian parents may worthily carry out their ministry of educating, the Synod Fathers expressed the hope that a suitable *catechism for families* would be prepared, one that would be clear, brief and easily assimilated by all. The Episcopal Conferences were warmly invited to contribute to producing this catechism.

40. The family is the primary but not the only and exclusive educating community. Man's community aspect itself—both civil and ecclesial—demands and leads to a broader and more articulated activity resulting from well-ordered collaboration between the various agents of education. All these agents are necessary, even though each can and should play its part in accordance with the special competence and contribution proper to itself.[104]

The educational role of the Christian family therefore has a very important place in organic pastoral work. This involves a new form of cooperation between parents and Christian communities, and between the various educational groups and pastors. In this sense, the renewal of the Catholic school must give special attention both to the parents of the pupils and to the formation of a perfect educating community.

The right of parents to choose an education in conformity with their religious faith must be absolutely guaranteed.

The State and the Church have the obligation to give families all possible aid to enable them to perform their educational role properly. Therefore both the Church and the State must create and foster the institutions and activities that families justly demand, and the aid must be in proportion to the families' needs. However, those in society who are in charge of schools must never forget that the parents have been appointed by God himself as the first and principal educators of their children and that their right is completely inalienable.

But corresponding to their right, parents have a serious duty to commit themselves totally to a cordial and active relationship with the teachers and the school authorities.

If ideologies opposed to the Christian faith are taught in the schools, the family must join with other families, if possible through family associations, and with all its strength and with wisdom help the young not to depart from the faith. In this case the family needs special assistance from pastors of souls, who must never forget that parents have the inviolable right to entrust their children to the ecclesial community.

41. Fruitful married love expresses itself in serving life in many ways. Of these ways, begetting and educating children are the most immediate, specific and irreplaceable. In fact, every act of true love towards a human being bears witness to and perfects the spiritual fecundity of the family, since it is an act of obedience to the deep inner dynamism of love as self-giving to others.

For everyone this perspective is full of value and commitment, and it can be an inspiration in particular for couples who experience physical sterility.

Christian families, recognizing with faith all human beings as children of the same heavenly Father, will respond generously to the children of other families, giving them support and love not as outsiders but as members of the one family of God's children. Christian parents will thus be able to spread their love beyond the bonds of flesh and blood, nourishing the links that are rooted in the spirit and that develop through concrete service to the children of other families, who are often without even the barest necessities.

Christian families will be able to show greater readiness to adopt and foster children who have lost their parents or have been abandoned by them. Rediscovering the warmth of affection of a family, these children will be able to experience God's loving and provident fatherhood witnessed to by Christian parents, and they will thus be able to grow up with serenity and confidence in life. At the same time the whole family will be enriched with the spiritual values of a wider fraternity.

Family fecundity must have an unceasing "creativity", a marvelous fruit of the Spirit of God, who opens the eyes of the heart to discover the new needs and sufferings of our society and gives courage for accepting them and responding to them. A vast field of activity lies open to families: today, even more preoccupying than child abandonment is the phenomenon of social and cultural exclusion, which seriously affects the elderly, the sick, the disabled, drug addicts, ex-prisoners, etc.

This broadens enormously the horizons of the parenthood of Christian families: these and many other urgent needs of our time are a challenge to their spiritually fruitful love. With families and through them, the Lord Jesus continues to "have compassion" on the multitudes.

III—PARTICIPATING IN THE DEVELOPMENT OF SOCIETY

42. "Since the Creator of all things has established the conjugal partnership as the beginning and basis of human society", the family is "the first and vital cell of society".[105]

The family has vital and organic links with society, since it is its foundation and nourishes it continually through its role of service to life: it is from the family that citizens come to birth and it is within the family that they find the first school of the social virtues that are the animating principle of the existence and development of society itself.

Thus, far from being closed in on itself, the family is by nature and vocation open to other families and to society, and undertakes its social role.

43. The very experience of communion and sharing that should characterize the family's daily life represents its first and fundamental contribution to society.

The relationships between the members of the family community are inspired and guided by the law of "free giving". By respecting and fostering personal dignity in each and every one as the only basis for value, this free giving takes the form of heartfelt acceptance, encounter and dialogue, disinterested availability, generous service and deep solidarity.

Thus the fostering of authentic and mature communion between persons within the family is the first and irreplaceable school of social life, an example and stimulus for the broader community relationships marked by respect, justice, dialogue and love.

The family is thus, as the Synod Fathers recalled, the place of origin and the most effective means for humanizing and personalizing society: it makes an original contribution in depth to building up the world, by making possible a life that is properly speaking human, in particular by guarding and transmitting virtues and "values". As the Second Vatican Council states, in the family "the various generations come together and help one another to grow wiser and to harmonize personal rights with the other requirements of social living".[106]

Consequently, faced with a society that is running the risk of becoming more and more depersonalized and standardized and therefore inhuman and dehumanizing, with the negative results of many forms of escapism—such as alcoholism, drugs and even terrorism—the family possesses and continues still to release formidable energies capable of taking man out of his anonymity, keeping him conscious of his personal dignity, enriching him with deep humanity and actively placing him, in his uniqueness and unrepeatability, within the fabric of society.

44. The social role of the family certainly cannot stop short at procreation and education, even if this constitutes its primary and irreplaceable form of expression.

Families therefore, either singly or in association, can and should devote themselves to manifold social service activities, especially in favour of the poor, or at any rate for the benefit of all people and situations that cannot be reached by the public authorities' welfare organization.

The social contribution of the family has an original character of its own, one that should be given greater recognition and more decisive encouragement, especially as the children grow up, and actually involving all its members as much as possible.[107]

In particular, note must be taken of the ever greater importance in our society of hospitality in all its forms, from opening the door of one's home and still more of one's heart to the pleas of one's brothers and sisters, to concrete efforts to ensure that every family has its own home, as the natural environment that preserves it and makes it grow. In a special way the Christian family is called upon to listen to the Apostle's recommendation: "Practise hospitality",[108] and therefore, imitating Christ's example and sharing in his love, to welcome the brother or sister in need: "Whoever gives to one of these little ones even a cup of cold water because he is a disciple, truly, I say to you, he shall not lose his reward".[109]

The social role of families is called upon to find expression also in the form of *political intervention*: families should be the first to take steps to see that the laws and institutions of the State not only do not offend but support and positively defend the rights and duties of the family. Along these lines, families should grow in awareness of being "protagonists" of what is known as "family politics" and assume responsibility for transforming society; otherwise families will be the first victims of the evils that they have done no more than note with indifference. The Second Vatican Council's appeal to go beyond an individualistic ethic therefore also holds good for the family as such.[110]

45. Just as the intimate connection between the family and society demands that the family be open to and participate in society and its development, so also it requires that society should never fail in its fundamental task of respecting and fostering the family.

The family and society have complementary functions in defending and fostering the good of each and every human being. But society—more specifically the State—must recognize that "the family is a society in its own original right"[111] and so society is under a grave obligation in its relations with the family to adhere to the principle of subsidiarity.

By virtue of this principle, the State cannot and must not take away from families the functions that they can just as well perform on their own or in free associations; instead it must positively favour and encourage as far as possible responsible initiative by families. In the conviction that the good of the family is an indispensable and essential value of the civil community, the public authorities must do everything possible to ensure that families have all those aids—economic, social, educational, political and cultural assistance—that they need in order to face all their responsibilities in a human way.

46. The ideal of mutual support and development between the family and society is often very seriously in conflict with the reality of their separation and even opposition.

In fact, as was repeatedly denounced by the Synod, the situation experienced by many families in various countries is highly problematical, if not entirely negative: institutions and laws unjustly ignore the inviolable rights of the family and of the human person; and society, far from putting itself at the service of the family, attacks it violently in its values and fundamental requirements. Thus the family, which in God's plan is the basic cell of society and a subject of rights and duties before the State or any other community, finds itself the victim of society, of the delays and slowness with which it acts, and even of its blatant injustice.

For this reason, the Church openly and strongly defends the

rights of the family against the intolerable usurpations of society and the State. In particular, the Synod Fathers mentioned the following rights of the family:

—the right to exist and progress as a family, that is to say, the right of every human being, even if he or she is poor, to found a family and to have adequate means to support it;

—the right to exercise its responsibility regarding the transmission of life and to educate children;

—the right to the intimacy of conjugal and family life;

—the right to the stability of the bond and of the institution of marriage;

—the right to believe in and profess one's faith and to propagate it;

—the right to bring up children in accordance with the family's own traditions and religious and cultural values, with the necessary instruments, means and institutions;

—the right, especially of the poor and the sick, to obtain physical, social, political and economic security;

—the right to housing suitable for living family life in a proper way;

—the right to expression and to representation, either directly or through associations, before the economic, social and cultural public authorities and lower authorities;

—the right to form associations with other families and institutions, in order to fulfil the family's role suitably and expeditiously;

—the right to protect minors by adequate institutions and legislation from harmful drugs, pornography, alcoholism, etc;

—the right to wholesome recreation of a kind that also fosters family values;

—the right of the elderly to a worthy life and a worthy death;

—the right to emigrate as a family in search of a better life.[112]

Acceding to the Synod's explicit request, the Holy See will give prompt attention to studying these suggestions in depth and to the preparation of a Charter of Rights of the Family, to be presented to the quarters and authorities concerned.

47. The social role that belongs to every family pertains by a new and original right to the Christian family, which is based on the sacrament of marriage. By taking up the human reality of the love between husband and wife in all its implications, the sacrament gives to Christian couples and parents a power and a commitment to live their vocation as lay people and therefore to "seek the kingdom of God by engaging in temporal affairs and by ordering them according to the plan of God".[113]

The social and political role is included in the kingly mission of service in which Christian couples share by virtue of the sacrament of marriage, and they receive both a command which they cannot ignore and a grace which sustains and stimulates them.

The Christian family is thus called upon to offer everyone a witness of generous and disinterested dedication to social matters, through a "preferential option" for the poor and disadvantaged. Therefore, advancing in its following of the Lord by special love for all the poor, it must have special concern for the hungry, the poor, the old, the sick, drug victims and those who have no family.

48. In view of the worldwide dimension of various social questions nowadays, the family has seen its role with regard to the development of society extended in a completely new way: it now also involves cooperating for a new international order, since it is only in worldwide solidarity that the enormous and dramatic issues of world justice, the freedom of peoples and the peace of humanity can be dealt with and solved.

The spiritual communion between Christian families, rooted in a common faith and hope and given life by love, constitutes an inner energy that generates, spreads and develops justice, reconciliation, fraternity and peace among human beings. In so far as it is a "small-scale Church", the Christian family is called upon, like the "large-scale Church", to be a sign of unity for the world and in this way to exercise its prophetic role by bearing witness to the Kingdom and peace of Christ, towards which the whole world is journeying.

Christian families can do this through their educational activity—that is to say by presenting to their children a model of life based on the values of truth, freedom, justice and love—both through active and responsible involvement in the authentically human growth of society and its institutions, and by supporting in various ways the associations specifically devoted to international issues.

IV—SHARING IN THE LIFE AND MISSION OF THE CHURCH

49. Among the fundamental tasks of the Christian family is its ecclesial task: the family is placed at the service of the building up of the Kingdom of God in history by participating in the life and mission of the Church.

In order to understand better the foundations, the contents

and the characteristics of this participation, we must examine the many profound bonds linking the Church and the Christian family and establishing the family as a "Church in miniature" (*Ecclesia domestica*),[114] in such a way that in its own way the family is a living image and historical representation of the mystery of the Church.

It is, above all, the Church as Mother that gives birth to, educates and builds up the Christian family, by putting into effect in its regard the saving mission which she has received from her Lord. By proclaiming the word of God, the Church reveals to the Christian family its true identity, what it is and should be according to the Lord's plan; by celebrating the sacraments, the Church enriches and strengthens the Christian family with the grace of Christ for its sanctification to the glory of the Father; by the continuous proclamation of the new commandment of love, the Church encourages and guides the Christian family to the service of love, so that it may imitate and relive the same self-giving and sacrificial love that the Lord Jesus has for the entire human race.

In turn, the Christian family is grafted into the mystery of the Church to such a degree as to become a sharer, in its own way, in the saving mission proper to the Church: by virtue of the sacrament, Christian married couples and parents "in their state and way of life have their own special gift among the People of God".[115] For this reason they not only *receive* the love of Christ and become a *saved* community, but they are also called upon to *communicate* Christ's love to their brethren, thus becoming a *saving* community. In this way, while the Christian family is a fruit and sign of the supernatural fecundity of the Church, it stands also as a symbol, witness and participant of the Church's motherhood.[116]

50. The Christian family is called upon to take part actively and responsibly in the mission of the Church in a way that is original and specific, by placing itself, in what it is and what it does as an "intimate community of life and love", at the service of the Church and of society.

Since the Christian family is a community in which the relationships are renewed by Christ through faith and the sacraments, the family's sharing in the Church's mission should follow *a community pattern*: the spouses together *as a couple*, the parents and children *as a family*, must live their service to the Church and to the world. They must be "of one heart and soul"[117] in faith, through the shared apostolic zeal that animates them, and through their shared commitment to works of service in the ecclesial and civil communities.

The Christian family also builds up the Kingdom of God in history through the everyday realities that concern and distinguish its *state of life*. It is thus in *the love between husband and wife and between the members of the family*—a love lived out in all its extraordinary richness of values and demands: totality, oneness, fidelity and fruitfulness[118]—that the Christian family's participation in the prophetic, priestly and kingly mission of Jesus Christ and of his Church finds expression and realization. Therefore, love and life constitute the nucleus of the saving mission of the Christian family in the Church and for the Church.

The Second Vatican Council recalls this fact when it writes: "Families will share their spiritual riches generously with other families too. Thus the Christian family, which springs from marriage as a reflection of the loving covenant uniting Christ with the Church, and as a participation in that covenant will manifest to all people the Saviour's living presence in the world, and the genuine nature of the Church. This the family will do by the mutual love of the spouses, by their generous fruitfulness, their solidarity and faithfulness, and by the loving way in which all the members of the family work together".[119]

Having laid the *foundation* of the participation of the Christian family in the Church's mission, it is now time to illustrate its *substance in reference to Jesus Christ as Prophet, Priest and King*—three aspects of a single reality—by presenting the Christian family as 1) a believing and evangelizing community, 2) a community in dialogue with God, and 3) a community at the service of man.

1) The Christian family as a believing and evangelizing community

51. As a sharer in the life and mission of the Church, which listens to the word of God with reverence and proclaims it confidently, [120] *the Christian family fulfils its prophetic role by welcoming and announcing the word of God*: it thus becomes more and more each day a believing and evangelizing community.

Christian spouses and parents are required to offer "the obedience of faith".[121] They are called upon to welcome the word of the Lord which reveals to them the marvellous news—the Good News—of their conjugal and family life sanctified and made a source of sanctity by Christ himself. Only in faith can they discover and admire with joyful gratitude the dignity to which God has deigned to raise marriage and the family, making them a sign and meeting-place of the loving covenant between God and man, between Jesus Christ and his bride, the Church.

The very preparation for Christian marriage is itself a journey of faith. It is a special opportunity for the engaged to rediscover and deepen the faith received in Baptism and nourished by their Christian upbringing. In this way they come to recognize and freely accept their vocation to follow Christ and to serve the Kingdom of God in the married state.

The celebration of the sacrament of marriage is the basic moment of the faith of the couple. This sacrament, in essence, is the proclamation in the Church of the Good News concerning married love. It is the word of God that "reveals" and "fulfils" the wise and loving plan of God for the married couple, giving them a mysterious and real share in the very love with which God himself loves humanity. Since the sacramental celebration of marriage is itself a proclamation of the word of God, it must also be a "profession of faith" within and with the Church, as a community of believers, on the part of all those who in different ways participate in its celebration.

This profession of faith demands that it be prolonged in the life of the married couple and of the family. God, who called the couple *to* marriage, continues to call them *in* marriage.[122] In and through the events, problems, difficulties and circumstances of everyday life, God comes to them, revealing and presenting the concrete "demands" of their sharing in the love of Christ for his Church in the particular family, social and ecclesial situation in which they find themselves.

The discovery of and obedience to the plan of God on the part of the conjugal and family community must take place in "togetherness", through the human experience of love between husband and wife, between parents and children, lived in the Spirit of Christ.

Thus the little domestic Church, like the greater Church, needs to be constantly and intensely evangelized: hence its duty regarding permanent education in the faith.

52. To the extent in which the Christian family accepts the Gospel and matures in faith, it becomes an evangelizing community. Let us listen again to Paul VI: "The family, like the Church, ought to be a place where the Gospel is transmitted and from which the Gospel radiates. In a family which is conscious of this mission, all the members evangelize and are evangelized. The parents not only communicate the Gospel to their children, but from their children they can themselves receive the same Gospel as deeply lived by them. And such a family becomes the evangelizer of many other families, and of the neighborhood of which it forms part".[123]

As the Synod repeated, taking up the appeal which I launched at Puebla, the future of evangelization depends in great part on the Church of the home.[124] This apostolic mission of the family is rooted in Baptism and receives from the grace of the sacrament of marriage new strength to transmit the faith, to sanctify and transform our present society according to God's plan.

Particularly today, the Christian family has a special vocation to witness to the paschal covenant of Christ by constantly radiating the joy of love and the certainty of the hope for which it must give an account: "The Christian family loudly proclaims both the present virtues of the Kingdom of God and the hope of a blessed life to come".[125]

The absolute need for family catechesis emerges with particular force in certain situations that the Church unfortunately experiences in some places: "In places where anti-religious legislation endeavours even to prevent education in the faith, and in places where widespread unbelief or invasive secularism makes real religious growth practically impossible, 'the Church of the home' remains the one place where children and young people can receive an authentic catechesis".[126]

53. The ministry of evangelization carried out by Christian parents is original and irreplaceable. It assumes the characteristics typical of family life itself, which should be interwoven with love, simplicity, practicality and daily witness.[127]

The family must educate the children for life in such a way that each one may fully perform his or her role according to the vocation received from God. Indeed, the family that is open to transcendent values, that serves its brothers and sisters with joy, that fulfils its duties with generous fidelity, and is aware of its daily sharing in the mystery of the glorious Cross of Christ, becomes the primary and most excellent seedbed of vocations to a life of consecration to the Kingdom of God.

The parents' ministry of evangelization and catechesis ought to play a part in their children's lives also during adolescence and youth, when the children, as often happens, challenge or even reject the Christian faith received in earlier years. Just as in the Church the work of evangelization can never be separated from the sufferings of the apostle, so in the Christian family parents must face with courage and great interior serenity the difficulties that their ministry of evangelization sometimes encounters in their own children.

It should not be forgotten that the service rendered by Christian spouses and parents to the Gospel is essentially an ecclesial service. It has its place within the context of the whole Church as an evangelized and evangelizing community. In so far as the ministry of evangelization and catechesis of the Church of the home is rooted in and derives from the one mission of the Church and is ordained to the upbuilding of the one Body of Christ,[128] it must remain in intimate communion and collaborate responsibly with all the other evangelizing and catechetical activities present and at work in the ecclesial community at the diocesan and parochial levels.

54. Evangelization, urged on within by irrepressible missionary zeal, is characterized by a universality without boundaries. It is the response to Christ's explicit and unequivocal command: "Go into all the world and preach the Gospel to the whole creation".[129]

The Christian family's faith and evangelizing mission also posesses this catholic missionary inspiration. The sacrament of marriage takes up and reproposes the task of defending and spreading the faith, a task that has its roots in Baptism and Confirmation,[130] and makes Christian married couples and parents witnesses of Christ "to the end of the earth",[131] missionaries, in the true and proper sense, of love and life.

A form of missionary activity can be exercised even within the family. This happens when some member of the family does not have the faith or does not practise it with consistency. In such a case the other members must give him or her a living witness of their own faith in order to encourage and support him or her along the path towards full acceptance of Christ the Saviour.[132]

Animated in its own inner life by missionary zeal, the Church of the home is also called to be a luminous sign of the presence of Christ and of his love for those who are "far away", for families who do not yet believe, and for those Christian families who no longer live in accordance with the faith that they once received. The Christian family is called to enlighten "by its example and its witness . . . those who seek the truth".[133]

Just as at the dawn of Christianity Aquila and Priscilla were presented as a missionary couple,[134] so today the Church shows forth her perennial newness and fruitfulness by the presence of Christian couples and families who dedicate at least a part of their lives to working in missionary territories, proclaiming the Gospel and doing service to their fellowman in the love of Jesus Christ.

Christian families offer a special contribution to the missionary cause of the Church by fostering missionary vocations among their sons and daughters[135] and, more generally, "by training their children from childhood to recognize God's love for all people".[136]

2) The Christian family
as a community in dialogue with God

55. The proclamation of the Gospel and its acceptance in faith reach their fullness in the celebration of the sacraments. The Church which is a believing and evangelizing community is also a priestly people invested with the dignity and sharing in the power of Christ the High Priest of the New and Eternal Covenant.[137]

The Christian family too is part of this priestly people which is the Church. By means of the sacrament of marriage, in which it is rooted and from which it draws its nourishment, the Christian family is continuously vivified by the Lord Jesus and called and engaged by him in a dialogue with God through the sacraments, through the offering of one's life, and through prayer.

This is the *priestly role* which the Christian family can and ought to exercise in intimate communion with the whole Church, through the daily realities of married and family life. In this way the Christian family *is called to be sanctified and to sanctify the ecclesial community and the world*.

56. The sacrament of marriage is the specific source and original means of sanctification for Christian married couples and families. It takes up again and makes specific the sanctifying grace of Baptism. By virtue of the mystery of the death and Resurrection of Christ, of which the spouses are made part in a new way by marriage, conjugal love is purified and made holy: "this love the Lord has judged worthy of special gifts, healing, perfecting and exalting gifts of grace and of charity".[138]

The gift of Jesus Christ is not exhausted in the actual celebration of the sacrament of marriage, but rather accompanies the married couple throughout their lives. This fact is explicitly recalled by the Second Vatican Council when it says that Jesus Christ "abides with them so that, just as he loved the Church and handed himself over on her behalf, the spouses may love each other with perpetual fidelity through mutual self-bestowal ... For this reason, Christian spouses have a special sacrament by which they are fortified and receive a kind of consecration in the duties and dignity of their state. By virtue of this sacrament, as spouses fulfil their conjugal and family obligations, they are penetrated with the Spirit of Christ, who fills their whole lives with faith, hope and charity. Thus they increasingly advance towards their own perfection, as well as towards their mutual sanctification, and hence contribute jointly to the glory of God".[139]

Christian spouses and parents are included in the universal call to sanctity. For them this call is specified by the sacrament they have celebrated and is carried out concretely in the realities proper to their conjugal and family life.[140] This gives rise to the grace and requirement of an authentic and profound *conjugal and family spirituality* that draws its inspiration from the themes of creation, covenant, cross, resurrection, and sign, which were stressed more than once by the Synod.

Christian marriage, like the other sacraments, "whose purpose is to sanctify people, to build up the body of Christ, and finally, to give worship to God",[141] is in itself a liturgical action glorifying God in Jesus Christ and in the Church. By celebrating it, Christian spouses profess their gratitude to God for the sublime gift bestowed on them of being able to live in their married and family lives the very love of God for people and that of the Lord Jesus for the Church, his bride.

Just as husbands and wives receive from the sacrament the gift and responsibility of translating into daily living the sanctification bestowed on them, so the same sacrament confers on them the grace and moral obligation of transforming their whole lives into a "spiritual sacrifice".[142] What the Council says of the laity applies also to Christian spouses and parents, especially with regard to the earthly and temporal realities that characterize their lives: "As worshippers leading holy lives in every place, the laity consecrate the world itself to God".[143]

57. The Christian family's sanctifying role is grounded in Baptism and has its highest expression in the Eucharist, to which Christian marriage is intimately connected. The Second Vatican Council drew attention to the unique relationship between the Eucharist and marriage by requesting that "marriage normally be celebrated within the Mass".[144] To understand better and live more intensely the graces and responsibilities of Christian marriage and family life, it is altogether necessary to rediscover and strengthen this relationship.

The Eucharist is the very source of Christian marriage. The Eucharistic Sacrifice, in fact, represents Christ's covenant of love with the Church, sealed with his blood on the Cross.[145] In this sacrifice of the New and Eternal Covenant, Christian spouses encounter the source from which their own marriage covenant flows, is interiorly structured and continuously renewed. As a representation of Christ's sacrifice of love for the Church, the Eucharist is a fountain of charity. In the Eucharistic gift of charity the Christian family finds the foundation and soul of its "communion" and its "mission": by partaking in the Eucharistic bread, the different members of the Christian family become one body, which reveals and shares in the wider unity of the Church. Their sharing in the Body of Christ that is "given up" and in his Blood that is "shed" becomes a never-ending source of missionary and apostolic dynamism for the Christian family.

58. An essential and permanent part of the Christian family's sanctifying role consists in accepting the call to conversion that the Gospel addresses to all Christians, who do not always remain faithful to the "newness" of the Baptism that constitutes them "saints". The Christian family too is sometimes unfaithful to the law of baptismal grace and holiness proclaimed anew in the sacrament of marriage.

Repentance and mutual pardon within the bosom of the Christian family, so much a part of daily life, receive their specific sacramental expression in Christian Penance. In the Encyclical *Humanae Vitae*, Paul VI wrote of married couples: "And if sin should still keep its hold over them, let them not be discouraged, but rather have recourse with humble perseverance to the mercy of God, which is abundantly poured forth in the sacrament of Penance".[146]

The celebration of this sacrament acquires special significance for family life. While they discover in faith that sin contradicts not only the covenant with God, but also the covenant between husband and wife and the communion of the family, the married couple and the other members of the family are led to an encounter with God, who is "rich in mercy",[147] who bestows on them his love which is more powerful than sin,[148] and who reconstructs and brings to perfection the marriage covenant and the family communion.

59. The Church prays for the Christian family and educates the family to live in generous accord with the priestly gift and role received from Christ the High Priest. In effect, the baptismal priesthood of the faithful, exercised in the sacrament of marriage, constitutes the basis of a priestly vocation and mission for the spouses and family by which their daily lives are transformed into "spiritual sacrifices acceptable to God through Jesus Christ".[149] This transformation is achieved not only by celebrating the Eucharist and the other sacraments and through offering themselves to the glory of God, but also through a life of prayer, through prayerful dialogue with the Father, through Jesus Christ, in the Holy Spirit.

Family prayer has its own characteristic qualities. It is prayer offered *in common*, husband and wife together, parents and children together. Communion in prayer is both a consequence of and a requirement for the communion bestowed by the sacraments of Baptism and Matrimony. The words with which the Lord Jesus promises his presence can be applied to the members of the Christian family in a special way: "Again I say to you, if two of you agree on earth about anything they ask it will be done for them by my Father in heaven. For where two or three are gathered in my name, there am I in the midst of them".[150]

Family prayer has for its very own object *family life itself*, which in all its varying circumstances is seen as a call from God and lived as a filial response to his call. Joys and sorrows, hopes and disappointments, births and birthday celebrations, wedding anniversaries of the parents, departures, separations and home-comings, important and far-reaching decisions, the death of those who are dear, etc.—all of these mark God's loving intervention in the family's history. They should be seen as suitable moments for thanksgiving, for petition, for trusting abandonment of the family into the hands of their common Father in heaven. The dignity and responsibility of the Christian family as the domestic Church can be achieved only with God's unceasing aid, which will surely be granted if it is humbly and trustingly petitioned in prayer.

60. By reason of their dignity and mission, Christian parents have the specific responsibility of educating their children in prayer, introducing them to gradual discovery of the mystery of God and to personal dialogue with him: "It is particularly in the Christian family, enriched by the grace and the office of the sacrament of Matrimony, that from the earliest years children should be taught, according to the faith received in Baptism, to have a knowledge of God, to worship him and to love their neighbour".[151]

The concrete example and living witness of parents is fundamental and irreplaceable in educating their children to pray. Only by praying together with their children can a father and mother —exercising their royal priesthood—penetrate the innermost depths of their children's hearts and leave an impression that the future events in their lives will not be able to efface. Let us again listen to the appeal made by Paul VI to parents: "Mothers, do you teach your children the Christian prayers? Do you prepare them, in conjunction with the priests, for the sacraments that they receive when they are young: Confession, Communion and Confirmation? Do you encourage them when they are sick to think of Christ suffering, to invoke the aid of the Blessed Virgin and the saints? Do you say the family Rosary together? And you, fathers, do you pray with your children, with the whole domestic community, at least sometimes? Your example of

paid to the image of God in which our neighbour has b
created, and also to Christ the Lord to whom is really offe
whatever is given to a needy person".[163]

While building up the Church in love, the Christian fa[
places itself at the service of the human person and the wo
really bringing about the "human advancement" whose s
stance was given in summary form in the Synod's Messag
families: "Another task for the family is to form persons in l
and also to practise love in all its relationships, so that it does
live closed in on itself, but remains open to the community, mo
by a sense of justice and concern for others, as well as by a c
sciousness of its responsibility towards the whole of society"

PART FOUR

PASTORAL CARE OF THE FAMILY: STAGES, STRUCTURES, AGENTS AND SITUATIONS

I—STAGES OF PASTORAL CARE OF THE FAMILY

65. Like every other living reality, the family too is ca
upon to develop and grow. After the preparation of engagem
and the sacramental celebration of marriage, the couple b
their daily journey towards the progressive actuation of
values and duties of marriage itself.

In the light of faith and by virtue of hope, the Christian fa[
oo shares, in communion with the Church, in the experienc
he earthly pilgrimage towards the full revelation and manife
on of the Kingdom of God.

Therefore, it must be emphasized once more that the past
ervention of the Church in support of the family is a matt
gency. Every effort should be made to strengthen and dev
storal care for the family, which should be treated as a
tter of priority, in the certainty that future evangelization
ds largely on the domestic Church.[165]

he Church's pastoral concern will not be limited only to
istian families closest at hand; it will extend its horizon
mony with the Heart of Christ, and will show itself to be e
lively for families in general and for those families in [
r which are in difficult or irregular situations. For al
the Church will have a word of truth, goodness, und
ng, hope and deep sympathy with their sometimes tra
ulties. To all of them she will offer her disinterested hel[

honesty in thought and action, joined to some common prayer,
is a lesson for life, an act of worship of singular value. In this way
you bring peace to your homes: *Pax huic domui*. Remember, it is
thus that you build up the Church".[152]

61. There exists a deep and vital bond between the prayer of
the Church and the prayer of the individual faithful, as has been
clearly reaffirmed by the Second Vatican Council.[153] An important purpose of the prayer of the domestic Church is to serve as
the natural introduction for the children to the liturgical prayer
of the whole Church, both in the sense of preparing for it and of
extending it into personal, family and social life. Hence the need
for gradual participation by all the members of the Christian
family in the celebration of the Eucharist, especially on Sundays
and feast days, and of the other sacraments, particularly the
sacraments of Christian initiation of the children. The directives
of the Council opened up a new possibility for the Christian
family when it listed the family among those groups to whom it
recommends the recitation of the Divine Office in common.[154]
Likewise, the Christian family will strive to celebrate at home,
and in a way suited to the members, the times and feasts of the
liturgical year.

As preparation for the worship celebrated in church, and as its
prolongation in the home, the Christian family makes use of
private prayer, which presents a great variety of forms. While
this variety testifies to the extraordinary richness with which the
Spirit vivifies Christian prayer, it serves also to meet the various
needs and life situations of those who turn to the Lord in prayer.
Apart from morning and evening prayers, certain forms of
prayer are to be expressly encouraged, following the indications
of the Synod Fathers, such as reading and meditating on the
word of God, preparation for the reception of the sacraments,
devotion and consecration to the Sacred Heart of Jesus, the
various forms of veneration of the Blessed Virgin Mary, grace
before and after meals, and observance of popular devotions.

While respecting the freedom of the children of God, the
Church has always proposed certain practices of piety to the
faithful with particular solicitude and insistence. Among these
should be mentioned the recitation of the Rosary: "We now desire, as a continuation of the thought of our predecessors, to
recommend strongly the recitation of the family Rosary...
There is no doubt that...the Rosary should be considered as
one of the best and most efficacious prayers in common that the
Christian family is invited to recite. We like to think, and sincerely hope, that when the family gathering becomes a time of

prayer the Rosary is a frequent and favoured manner of praying".[155] In this way authentic devotion to Mary, which finds expression in sincere love and generous imitation of the Blessed Virgin's interior spiritual attitude, constitutes a special instrument for nourishing loving communion in the family and for developing conjugal and family spirituality. For she who is the Mother of Christ and of the Church is in a special way the Mother of Christian families, of domestic Churches.

62. It should never be forgotten that prayer constitutes an essential part of Christian life, understood in its fullness and centrality. Indeed, prayer is an important part of our very humanity: it is "the first expression of man's inner truth, the first condition for authentic freedom of spirit".[156]

Far from being a form of escapism from everyday commitments, prayer constitutes the strongest incentive for the Christian family to assume and comply fully with all its responsibilities as the primary and fundamental cell of human society. Thus the Christian family's actual participation in the Church's life and mission is in direct proportion to the fidelity and intensity of the prayer with which it is united with the fruitful vine that is Christ the Lord.[157]

The fruitfulness of the Christian family in its specific service to human advancement, which of itself cannot but lead to the transformation of the world, derives from its living union with Christ, nourished by the Liturgy, by self-oblation and by prayer.[158]

3) The Christian family as a community at the service of man

63. The Church, a prophetic, priestly and kingly people, is endowed with the mission of bringing all human beings to accept the word of God in faith, to celebrate and profess it in the sacraments and in prayer, and to give expression to it in the concrete realities of life in accordance with the gift and new commandment of love.

The law of Christian life is to be found not in a written code, but in the personal action of the Holy Spirit who inspires and guides the Christian. It is the "law of the Spirit of life in Christ Jesus":[159] "God's love has been poured into our hearts through the Holy Spirit who has been given to us".[160]

This is true also for the Christian couple and family. Their guide and rule of life is the Spirit of Jesus poured into their hearts in the celebration of the sacrament of Matrimony. In continuity with Baptism in water and the Spirit, marriage sets forth anew the evangelical law of love, and with the gift of the Spirit engraves it more profoundly on the hearts of Christian hus-

bands and wives. Their love, purified and saved, is a fruit of the Spirit acting in the hearts of believers and constituting, at the same time, the fundamental commandment of their moral life to be lived in responsible freedom.

Thus the Christian family is inspired and guided by the new law of the Spirit and, in intimate communion with the Church, the kingly people, it is called to exercise its "service" of love towards God and towards its fellow human beings. Just as Christ exercises his royal power by serving us,[161] so also the Christian finds the authentic meaning of his participation in the kingship of his Lord in sharing his spirit and practice of service to man. "Christ has communicated this power to his disciples that they might be established in royal freedom and that by self-denial and a holy life they might conquer the reign of sin in themselves (cf. *Rom* 6:12). Further, he has shared this power so that by serving him in their fellow human beings they might through humility and patience lead their brothers and sisters to that King whom to serve is to reign. For the Lord wishes to spread his kingdom by means of the laity also, a kingdom of truth and life, a kingdom of holiness and grace, a kingdom of justice, love and peace. In this kingdom, creation itself will be delivered out of slavery to corruption and into the freedom of the glory of children of God (cf. *Rom* 8:21)".[162]

64. Inspired and sustained by the new commandment of the Christian family welcomes, respects and serves every being, considering each one in his or her dignity as a person as a child of God.

It should be so especially between husband and wife and in the family, through a daily effort to promote a truly community, initiated and fostered by an inner comm love. This way of life should then be extended to the wid of the ecclesial community of which the Christian part. Thanks to love within the family, the Chur ought to take on a more homelike or family dimensi ing a more human and fraternal style of relationsh

Love, too, goes beyond our brothers and sister faith since "everybody is my brother or sister". In ual, especially in the poor, the weak, and those wh unjustly treated, love knows how to discover the and discover a fellow human being to be loved

In order that the family may serve man in a way, the instructions of the Second Vatican carefully put into practice: "That the exerci may rise above any deficiencies in fact and ev certain fundamentals must be observed. Th

that they can come closer to that model of a family which the Creator intended from "the beginning" and which Christ has renewed with his redeeming grace.

The Church's pastoral action must be progressive, also in the sense that it must follow the family, accompanying it step by step in the different stages of its formation and development.

66. More than ever necessary in our times is preparation of young people for marriage and family life. In some countries it is still the families themselves that, according to ancient customs, ensure the passing on to young people of the values concerning married and family life, and they do this through a gradual process of education or initiation. But the changes that have taken place within almost all modern societies demand that not only the family but also society and the Church should be involved in the effort of properly preparing young people for their future responsibilities. Many negative phenomena which are today noted with regret in family life derive from the fact that, in the new situations, young people not only lose sight of the correct hierarchy of values but, since they no longer have certain criteria of behaviour, they do not know how to face and deal with the new difficulties. But experience teaches that young people who have been well prepared for family life generally succeed better than others.

This is even more applicable to Christian marriage, which influences the holiness of large numbers of men and women. The Church must therefore promote better and more intensive programmes of marriage preparation, in order to eliminate as far as possible the difficulties that many married couples find themselves in, and even more in order to favour positively the establishing and maturing of successful marriages.

Marriage preparation has to be seen and put into practice as a gradual and continuous process. It includes three main stages: remote, proximate and immediate preparation.

Remote preparation begins in early childhood, in that wise family training which leads children to discover themselves as beings endowed with a rich and complex psychology and with a particular personality with its own strengths and weaknesses. It is the period when esteem for all authentic human values is instilled, both in interpersonal and in social relationships, with all that this signifies for the formation of character, for the control and right use of one's inclinations, for thee manner of regarding and meeting people of the opposite sex, and so on. Also necessary, especially for Christians, is solid spiritual and catechetical formation that will show that marriage is a true vocation and mission, without excluding the possibility of the total gift of self to God in the vocation to the priestly or religious life.

Upon this basis there will subsequently and gradually be built up the *proximate preparation*, which—from the suitable age and with adequate catechesis, as in a catechumenal process—involves a more specific preparation for the sacraments, as it were a rediscovery of them. This renewed catechesis of young people and others preparing for Christian marriage is absolutely necessary in order that the sacrament may be celebrated and lived with the right moral and spiritual dispositions. The religious formation of young people should be integrated, at the right moment and in accordance with the various concrete requirements, with a preparation for life as a couple. This preparation will present marriage as an interpersonal relationship of a man and a woman that has to be continually developed, and it will encourage those concerned to study the nature of conjugal sexuality and responsible parenthood, with the essential medical and biological knowledge connected with it. It will also acquaint those concerned with correct methods for the education of children, and will assist them in gaining the basic requisites for well-ordered family life, such as stable work, sufficient financial resources, sensible administration, notions of housekeeping.

Finally, one must not overlook preparation for the family apostolate, for fraternal solidarity and collaboration with other families, for active membership in groups, associations, movements and undertakings set up for the human and Christian benefit of the family.

The *immediate preparation* for the celebration of the sacrament of Matrimony should take place in the months and weeks immediately preceding the wedding, so as to give a new meaning, content and form to the so-called premarital enquiry required by Canon Law. This preparation is not only necessary in every case, but is also more urgently needed for engaged couples that still manifest shortcomings or difficulties in Christian doctrine and practice.

Among the elements to be instilled in this journey of faith, which is similar to the catechumenate, there must also be a deeper knowledge of the mystery of Christ and the Church, of the meaning of grace and of the responsibility of Christian marriage, as well as preparation for taking an active and conscious part in the rites of the marriage liturgy.

The Christian family and the whole of the ecclesial community should feel involved in the different phases of the preparation for marriage, which have been described only in their broad outlines. It is to be hoped that the Episcopal Conferences, just as they are concerned with appropriate initiatives to help engaged couples to be more aware of the seriousness of their choice and also to help pastors of souls to make sure of the couples' proper dispositions, so they will also take steps to see that there is issued a *Directory for the Pastoral Care of the Family*. In this they should lay down, in the first place, the minimum content, duration and method of the "Preparation Courses", balancing the different aspects—doctrinal, pedagogical, legal and medical—concerning marriage, and structuring them in such a way that those preparing for marriage will not only receive an intellectual training but will also feel a desire to enter actively into the ecclesial community.

Although one must not underestimate the necessity and obligation of the immediate preparation for marriage—which would happen if dispensations from it were easily given—nevertheless such preparation must always be set forth and put into practice in such a way that omitting it is not an impediment to the celebration of marriage.

67. Christian marriage normally requires a liturgical celebration expressing in social and community form the essentially ecclesial and sacramental nature of the conjugal covenant between baptized persons.

Inasmuch as it is a *sacramental action of sanctification*, the celebration of marriage—inserted into the liturgy, which is the summit of the Church's action and the source of her sanctifying power[166]—must be *per se* valid, worthy and fruitful. This opens a wide field for pastoral solicitude, in order that the needs deriving from the nature of the conjugal covenant, elevated into a sacrament, may be fully met, and also in order that the Church's discipline regarding free consent, impediments, the canonical form and the actual rite of the celebration may be faithfully observed. The celebration should be simple and dignified, according to the norms of the competent authorities of the Church. It is also for them—in accordance with concrete circumstances of time and place and in conformity with the norms issued by the Apostolic See[167]—to include in the liturgical celebration such elements proper to each culture which serve to express more clearly the profound human and religious significance of the marriage contract, provided that such elements contain nothing that is not in harmony with Christian faith and morality.

Inasmuch as it is a *sign*, the liturgical celebration should be conducted in such a way as to constitute, also in its external reality, a proclamation of the word of God and a profession of faith on the part of the community of believers. Pastoral commitment will be expressed here through the intelligent and careful preparation of the Liturgy of the Word and through the education to faith of those participating in the celebration and in the first place the couple being married.

Inasmuch as it is a *sacramental action of the Church*, the liturgical celebration of marriage should involve the Christian community, with the full, active and responsible participation of all those present, according to the place and task of each individual: the bride and bridegroom, the priest, the witnesses, the relatives, the friends, the other members of the faithful, all of them members of an assembly that manifests and lives the mystery of Christ and his Church. For the celebration of Christian marriage in the sphere of ancestral cultures or traditions, the principles laid down above should be followed.

68. Precisely because in the celebration of the sacrament very special attention must be devoted to the moral and spiritual dispositions of those being married, in particular to their faith, we must here deal with a not infrequent difficulty in which the pastors of the Church can find themselves in the context of our secularized society.

In fact, the faith of the person asking the Church for marriage can exist in different degrees, and it is the primary duty of pastors to bring about a rediscovery of this faith and to nourish it and bring it to maturity. But pastors must also understand the reasons that lead the Church also to admit to the celebration of marriage those who are imperfectly disposed.

The sacrament of Matrimony has this specific element that distinguishes it from all the other sacraments: it is the sacrament of something that was part of the very economy of creation; it is the very conjugal covenant instituted by the Creator "in the beginning". Therefore the decision of a man and a woman to marry in accordance with this divine plan, that is to say, the decision to commit by their irrevocable conjugal consent their whole lives in indissoluble love and unconditional fidelity, really involves, even if not in a fully conscious way, an attitude of profound obedience to the will of God, an attitude which cannot exist without God's grace. They have thus already begun what is in a true and proper sense a journey towards salvation, a journey which the celebration of the sacrament and the immediate preparation for it can complement and bring to completion, given the uprightness of their intention.

On the other hand it is true that in some places engaged couples ask to be married in church for motives which are social rather than genuinely religious. This is not surprising. Marriage, in fact, is not an event that concerns only the persons actually getting married. By its very nature it is also a social matter, committing the couple being married in the eyes of society. And its celebration has always been an occasion of rejoicing that brings together families and friends. It therefore goes without saying that social as well as personal motives enter into the request to be married in church.

Nevertheless, it must not be forgotten that these engaged couples, by virtue of their Baptism, are already really sharers in Christ's marriage Covenant with the Church, and that, by their right intention, they have accepted God's plan regarding marriage and therefore at least implicitly consent to what the Church intends to do when she celebrates marriage. Thus, the fact that motives of a social nature also enter into the request is not enough to justify refusal on the part of pastors. Moreover, as the Second Vatican Council teaches, the sacraments by words and ritual elements nourish and strengthen faith:[168] that faith towards which the married couple are already journeying by reason of the uprightness of their intention, which Christ's grace certainly does not fail to favour and support.

As for wishing to lay down further criteria for admission to the ecclesial celebration of marriage, criteria that would concern the level of faith of those to be married, this would above all involve grave risks. In the first place, the risk of making unfounded and discriminatory judgments; secondly, the risk of causing doubts about the validity of marriages already celebrated, with grave harm to Christian communities, and new and unjustified anxieties to the consciences of married couples; one would also fall into the danger of calling into question the sacramental nature of many marriages of brethren separated from full communion with the Catholic Church, thus contradicting ecclesial tradition.

However, when in spite of all efforts engaged couples show that they reject explicitly and formally what the Church intends to do when the marriage of baptized persons is celebrated, the pastor of souls cannot admit them to the celebration of marriage. In spite of his reluctance to do so, he has the duty to take note of the situation and to make it clear to those concerned that, in these circumstances, it is not the Church that is placing an obstacle in the way of the celebration that they are asking for, but themselves.

Once more there appears in all its urgency the need for evangelization and catechesis before and after marriage, effected by the whole Christian community, so that every man and woman that gets married celebrates the sacrament of Matrimony not only validly but also fruitfully.

69. The pastoral care of the regularly established family signifies, in practice, the commitment of all the members of the local ecclesial community to helping the couple to discover and live their new vocation and mission. In order that the family may be ever more a true community of love, it is necessary that all its members should be helped and trained in their responsibilities as they face the new problems that arise, in mutual service, and in active sharing in family life.

This holds true especially for young families, which, finding themselves in a context of new values and responsibilities, are more vulnerable, especially in the first years of marriage, to possible difficulties, such as those created by adaptation to life together or by the birth of children. Young married couples should learn to accept willingly, and make good use of, the discreet, tactful and generous help offered by other couples that already have more experience of married and family life. Thus, within the ecclesial community—the great family made up of Christian families—there will take place a mutual exchange of presence and help among all the families, each one putting at the service of the others its own experience of life, as well as the gifts of faith and grace. Animated by a true apostolic spirit, this assistance from family to family will constitute one of the simplest, most effective and most accessible means for transmitting from one to another those Christian values which are both the starting-point and goal of all pastoral care. Thus young families will not limit themselves merely to receiving, but in their turn, having been helped in this way, will become a source of enrichment for other longer established families, through their witness of life and practical contribution.

In her pastoral care of young families, the Church must also pay special attention to helping them to live married love responsibly in relationship with its demands of communion and service to life. She must likewise help them to harmonize the intimacy of home life with the generous shared work of building up the Church and society. When children are born and the married couple becomes a family in the full and specific sense, the Church will still remain close to the parents in order that they may accept their children and love them as a gift received from the Lord of life, and joyfully accept the task of serving them in their human and Christian growth.

II—STRUCTURES OF FAMILY PASTORAL CARE

Pastoral activity is always the dynamic expression of the reality of the Church, committed to her mission of salvation. Family pastoral care too—which is a particular and specific form of pastoral activity—has as its operative principle and responsible agent the Church herself, through her structures and workers.

70. The Church, which is at the same time a saved and a saving community, has to be considered here under two aspects: as universal and particular. The second aspect is expressed and actuated in the diocesan community, which is pastorally divided up into lesser communities, of which the parish is of special importance.

Communion with the universal Church does not hinder but rather guarantees and promotes the substance and originality of the various particular Churches. These latter remain the more immediate and more effective subjects of operation for putting the pastoral care of the family into practice. In this sense every local Church and, in more particular terms, every parochial community, must become more vividly aware of the grace and responsibility that it receives from the Lord in order that it may promote the pastoral care of the family. No plan for organized pastoral work, at any level, must ever fail to take into consideration the pastoral care of the family.

Also to be seen in the light of this responsibility is the importance of the proper preparation of all those who will be more specifically engaged in this kind of apostolate. Priests and men and women religious, from the time of their formation, should be oriented and trained progressively and thoroughly for the various tasks. Among the various initiatives I am pleased to emphasize the recent establishment in Rome, at the Pontifical Lateran University, of a Higher Institute for the study of the problems of the family. Institutes of this kind have also been set up in some dioceses. Bishops should see to it that as many priests as possible attend specialized courses there before taking on parish responsibilities. Elsewhere, formation courses are periodically held at Higher Institutes of theological and pastoral studies. Such initiatives should be encouraged, sustained, increased in number, and of course are also open to lay people who intend to use their professional skills (medical, legal, psychological, social or educational) to help the family.

71. But it is especially necessary to recognize the unique place that, in this field, belongs to the mission of married couples and Christian families, by virtue of the grace received in the sacra-

ment. This mission must be placed at the service of the building up of the Church, the establishing of the Kingdom of God in history. This is demanded as an act of docile obedience to Christ the Lord. For it is he who, by virtue of the fact that marriage of baptized persons has been raised to a sacrament, confers upon Christian married couples a special mission as apostles, sending them as workers into his vineyard, and, in a very special way, into this field of the family.

In this activity, married couples act in communion and collaboration with the other members of the Church, who also work for the family, contributing their own gifts and ministries. This apostolate will be exercised in the first place within the families of those concerned, through the witness of a life lived in conformity with the divine law in all its aspects. through the Christian formation of the children, through helping them to mature in faith, through education to chastity, through preparation for life, through vigilance in protecting them from the ideological and moral dangers with which they are often threatened, through their gradual and responsible inclusion in the ecclesial community and the civil community, through help and advice in choosing a vocation, through mutual help among family members for human and Christian growth together, and so on. The apostolate of the family will also become wider through works of spiritual and material charity towards other families, especially those most in need of help and support, towards the poor, the sick, the old, the handicapped, orphans, widows, spouses that have been abandoned, unmarried mothers and mothers-to-be in difficult situations who are tempted to have recourse to abortion, and so on.

72. Still within the Church, which is the subject responsible for the pastoral care of the family, mention should be made of the various groupings of members of the faithful in which the mystery of Christ's Church is in some measure manifested and lived. One should therefore recognize and make good use of— each one in relationship to its own characteristics, purposes, effectiveness and methods—the different ecclesial communities, the various groups and the numerous movements engaged in various ways, for different reasons and at different levels, in the pastoral care of the family.

For this reason the Synod expressly recognized the useful contribution made by such associations of spirituality, formation and apostolate. It will be their task to foster among the faithful a lively sense of solidarity, to favour a manner of living inspired by the Gospel and by the faith of the Church, to form consciences according to Christian values and not according to the standards of public opinion; to stimulate people to perform works of charity for one another and for others with a spirit of openness which will make Christian families into a true source of light and a wholesome leaven for other families.

It is similarly desirable that, with a lively sense of the common good, Christian families should become actively engaged, at every level, in other non-ecclesial associations as well. Some of these associations work for the preservation, transmission and protection of the wholesome ethical and cultural values of each people, the development of the human person, the medical, juridical and social protection of mothers and young children, the just advancement of women and the struggle against all that is detrimental to their dignity, the increase of mutual solidarity, knowledge of the problems connected with the responsible regulation of fertility in accordance with natural methods that are in conformity with human dignity and the teaching of the Church. Other associations work for the building of a more just and human world; for the promotion of just laws favouring the right social order with full respect for the dignity and every legitimate freedom of the individual and the family, on both the national and the international level; for collaboration with the school and with the other institutions that complete the education of children, and so forth.

III—AGENTS OF THE PASTORAL CARE OF THE FAMILY

As well as the family, which is the object but above all the subject of pastoral care of the family, one must also mention the other main agents in this particular sector.

73. The person principally responsible in the diocese for the pastoral care of the family is the Bishop. As father and pastor, he must exercise particular solicitude in this clearly priority sector of pastoral care. He must devote it to personal interest, care, time, personnel and resources, but above all personal support for the families and for all those who, in the various diocesan structures, assist him in the pastoral care of the family. It will be his particular care to make the diocese ever more truly a "diocesan family", a model and source of hope for the many families that belong to it. The setting up of the Pontifical Council for the Family is to be seen in this light: to be a sign of the importance that I attribute to pastoral care for the family in the world, and at

the same time to be an effective instrument for aiding and promoting it at every level.

The Bishops avail themselves especially of the priests, whose task—as the Synod expressly emphasized—constitutes an essential part of the Church's ministry regarding marriage and the family. The same is true of deacons to whose care this sector of pastoral work may be entrusted.

Their responsibility extends not only to moral and liturgical matters but to personal and social matters as well. They must support the family in its difficulties and sufferings, caring for its members and helping them to see their lives in the light of the Gospel. It is not superfluous to note that from this mission, if it is exercised with due discernment and with a truly apostolic spirit, the minister of the Church draws fresh encouragement and spiritual energy for his own vocation too and for the exercise of his ministry.

Priests and deacons, when they have received timely and serious preparation for this apostolate, must unceasingly act towards families as fathers, brothers, pastors and teachers, assisting them with the means of grace and enlightening them with the light of truth. Their teaching and advice must therefore always be in full harmony with the authentic Magisterium of the Church, in such a way as to help the People of God to gain a correct sense of the faith, to be subsequently applied to practical life. Such fidelity to the Magisterium will also enable priests to make every effort to be united in their judgments, in order to avoid troubling the consciences of the faithful.

In the Church, the pastors and the laity share in the prophetic mission of Christ: the laity do so by witnessing to the faith by their words and by their Christian lives; the pastors do so by distinguishing in that witness what is the expression of genuine faith from what is less in harmony with the light of faith; the family, as a Christian community, does so through its special sharing and witness of faith. Thus there begins a dialogue also between pastors and families. Theologians and experts in family matters can be of great help in this dialogue, by explaining exactly the content of the Church's Magisterium and the content of the experience of family life. In this way the teaching of the Magisterium becomes better understood and the way is opened to its progressive development. But it is useful to recall that the proximate and obligatory norm in the teaching of the faith— also concerning family matters—belongs to the hierarchical Magisterium. Clearly defined relationships between theologians, experts in family matters and the Magisterium are of no little assistance for the correct understanding of the faith and for promoting —within the boundaries of the faith—legitimate pluralism.

74. The contribution that can be made to the apostolate of the family by men and women religious and consecrated persons in general finds its primary, fundamental and original expression precisely in their consecration to God. By reason of this consecration, "for all Christ's faithful religious recall that wonderful marriage made by God, which will be fully manifested in the future age, and in which the Church has Christ for her only spouse",[169] and they are witnesses to that universal charity which, through chastity embraced for the Kingdom of heaven, makes them ever more available to dedicate themselves generously to the service of God and to the works of the apostolate.

Hence the possibility for men and women religious, and members of Secular Institutes and other institutes of perfection, either individually or in groups, to develop their service to families, with particular solicitude for children, especially if they are abandoned, unwanted, orphaned, poor or handicapped. They can also visit families and look after the sick; they can foster relationships of respect and charity towards one-parent families or families that are in difficulties or are separated; they can offer their own work of teaching and counselling in the preparation of young people for marriage, and in helping couples towards truly responsible parenthood; they can open their own houses for simple and cordial hospitality, so that families can find there the sense of God's presence and gain a taste for prayer and recollection, and see the practical examples of lives lived in charity and fraternal joy as members of the larger family of God.

I would like to add a most pressing exhortation to the heads of institutes of consecrated life to consider—always with substantial respect for the proper and original charism of each one—the apostolate of the family as one of the priority tasks, rendered even more urgent by the present state of the world.

75. Considerable help can be given to families by lay specialists (doctors, lawyers, psychologists, social workers, consultants, etc.) who either as individuals or as members of various associations and undertakings offer their contribution of enlightenment, advice, orientation and support. To these people one can well apply the exhortations that I had the occasion to address to the Confederation of Family Advisory Bureaux of Christian Inspiration: "Yours is a commitment that well deserves the title of mission, so noble are the aims that it pursues, and so determining, for the good of society and the Christian community itself, are the results that derive from it...All that

you succeed in doing to support the family is destined to have an effectiveness that goes beyond its own sphere and reaches other people too and has an effect on society. The future of the world and of the Church passes through the family".[170]

76. This very important category in modern life deserves a word of its own. It is well known that the means of social communication "affect, and often profoundly, the minds of those who use them, under the affective and intellectual aspect and also under the moral and religious aspect", especially in the case of young people.[171] They can thus exercise a beneficial influence on the life and habits of the family and on the education of children, but at the same time they also conceal "snares and dangers that cannot be ignored".[172] They could also become a vehicle—sometimes cleverly and systematically manipulated, as unfortunately happens in various countries of the world—for divisive ideologies and distorted ways of looking at life, the family, religion and morality, attitudes that lack respect for man's true dignity and destiny.

This danger is all the more real inasmuch as "the modern life style—especially in the more industrialized nations—all too often causes families to abandon their responsibility to educate their children. Evasion of this duty is made easy for them by the presence of television and certain publications in the home, and in this way they keep their children's time and energies occupied."[173] Hence "the duty. . . to protect the young from the forms of aggression they are subjected to by the mass media", and to ensure that the use of the media in the family is carefully regulated. Families should also take care to seek for their children other forms of entertainment that are more wholesome, useful and physically, morally and spiritually formative, "to develop and use to advantage the free time of the young and direct their energies".[174]

Furthermore, because the means of social communication, like the school and the environment, often have a notable influence on the formation of children, parents as recipients must actively ensure the moderate, critical, watchful and prudent use of the media, by discovering what effect they have on their children and by controlling the use of the media in such a way as to "train the conscience of their children to express calm and objective judgments, which will then guide them in the choice or rejection of programmes available".[175]

With equal commitment parents will endeavour to influence the selection and the preparation of the programmes themselves, by keeping in contact—through suitable initiatives—

with those in charge of the various phases of production and transmission. In this way they will ensure that the fundamental human values that form part of the true good of society are not ignored or deliberately attacked. Rather they will ensure the broadcasting of programmes that present in the right light family problems and their proper solution. In this regard my venerated predecessor Paul VI wrote: "Producers must know and respect the needs of the family, and this sometimes presupposes in them true courage, and always a high sense of responsibility. In fact they are expected to avoid anything that could harm the family in its existence, its stability, its balance and its happiness. Every attack on the fundamental value of the family—meaning eroticism or violence, the defence of divorce or of antisocial attitudes among young people—is an attack on the true good of man".[176]

I myself, on a similar occasion, pointed out that families "to a considerable extent need to be able to count on the good will, integrity and sense of responsibility of the media professionals—publishers, writers, producers, directors, playwrights, newsmen, commentators and actors".[177] It is therefore also the duty of the Church to continue to devote every care to these categories, at the same time encouraging and supporting Catholics who feel the call and have the necessary talents, to take up this sensitive type of work.

77. An even more generous, intelligent and prudent pastoral commitment, modelled on the Good Shepherd, is called for in the case of families which, often independently of their own wishes and through pressures of various other kinds, find themselves faced by situations which are objectively difficult.

In this regard it is necessary to call special attention to certain particular groups which are more in need not only of assistance but also of more incisive action upon public opinion and especially upon cultural, economic and juridical structures, in order that the profound causes of their needs may be eliminated as far as possible.

Such for example are the families of migrant workers; the families of those obliged to be away for long periods, such as members of the armed forces, sailors and all kinds of itinerant people; the families of those in prison, of refugees and exiles; the families in big cities living practically speaking as outcasts; families with no home; incomplete or single-parent families; families with children that are handicapped or addicted to drugs; the families of alcoholics; families that have been uprooted from their cultural and social environment or are in danger of losing it; families discriminated against for political or other reasons; families that are ideologically divided; families that are unable to make ready contact with the parish; families experiencing violence or unjust treatment because of their faith; teenage married couples; the elderly, who are often obliged to live alone with inadequate means of subsistence.

The families of migrants, especially in the cases of manual workers and farm workers, should be able to find a homeland everywhere in the Church. This is a task stemming from the nature of the Church, as being the sign of unity in diversity. As far as possible these people should be looked after by priests of their own rite, culture and language. It is also the Church's task to appeal to the public conscience and to all those in authority in social, economic and political life, in order that workers may find employment in their own regions and homelands, that they may receive just wages, that their families may be reunited as soon as possible, be respected in their cultural identity and treated on an equal footing with others, and that their children may be given the chance to learn a trade and exercise it, as also the chance to own the land needed for working and living.

A difficult problem is that of the family which is *ideologically divided*. In these cases particular pastoral care is needed. In the first place it is necessary to maintain tactful personal contact with such families. The believing members must be strengthened in their faith and supported in their Christian lives. Although the party faithful to Catholicism cannot give way, dialogue with the other party must always be kept alive. Love and respect must be freely shown, in the firm hope that unity will be maintained. Much also depends on the relationship between parents and children. Moreover, ideologies which are alien to the faith can stimulate the believing members of the family to grow in faith and in the witness of love.

Other difficult circumstances in which the family needs the help of the ecclesial community and its pastors are: the children's adolescence, which can be disturbed, rebellious and sometimes stormy; the children's marriage, which takes them away from their family; lack of understanding or lack of love on the part of those held most dear; abandonment by one of the spouses, or his or her death, which brings the painful experience of widowhood, or the death of a family member, which breaks up and deeply transforms the original family nucleus.

Similarly, the Church cannot ignore the time of old age, with all its positive and negative aspects. In old age married love, which has been increasingly purified and ennobled by long and unbroken fidelity, can be deepened. There is the opportunity of offering to others, in a new form, the kindness and the wisdom gathered over the years, and what energies remain. But there is also the burden of loneliness, more often psychological and emotional rather than physical, which results from abandonment or neglect on the part of children and relations. There is also suffering caused by ill-health, by the gradual loss of strength, by the humiliation of having to depend on others, by the sorrow of feeling that one is perhaps a burden to one's loved ones, and by the approach of the end of life. These are the circumstances in which, as the Synod Fathers suggested, it is easier to help people understand and live the lofty aspects of the spirituality of marriage and the family, aspects which take their inspiration from the value of Christ's Cross and Resurrection, the source of sanctification and profound happiness in daily life, in the light of the great eschatological realities of eternal life.

In all these different situations let prayer, the source of light and strength and the nourishment of Christian hope, never be neglected.

78. The growing number of mixed marriages between Catholics and other baptized persons also calls for special pastoral attention in the light of the directives and norms contained in the most recent documents of the Holy See and in those drawn up by the Episcopal Conferences, in order to permit their practical application to the various situations.

Couples living in a mixed marriage have special needs, which can be put under three main headings.

In the first place, attention must be paid to the obligations that faith imposes on the Catholic party with regard to the free exercise of the faith and the consequent obligation to ensure, as far as is possible, the Baptism and upbringing of the children in the Catholic faith.[178]

There must be borne in mind the particular difficulties inherent in the relationships between husband and wife with regard to respect for religious freedom: this freedom could be violated either by undue pressure to make the partner change his or her beliefs, or by placing obstacles in the way of the free manifestations of these beliefs by religious practice.

With regard to the liturgical and canonical form of marriage, Ordinaries can make wide use of their faculties to meet various necessities.

In dealing with these special needs, the following points should be kept in mind:

—In the appropriate preparation for this type of marriage, every reasonable effort must be made to ensure a proper understanding of Catholic teaching on the qualities and obligations of marriage, and also to ensure that the pressures and obstacles mentioned above will not occur.

—It is of the greatest importance that, through the support of the community, the Catholic party should be strengthened in faith and positively helped to mature in understanding and practising that faith, so as to become a credible witness within the family through his or her own life and through the quality of love shown to the other spouse and the children.

Marriages between Catholics and other baptized persons have their own particular nature, but they contain numerous elements that could well be made good use of and developed, both for their intrinsic value and for the contribution that they can make to the ecumenical movement. This is particularly true when both parties are faithful to their religious duties. Their common Baptism and the dynamism of grace provide the spouses in these marriages with the basis and motivation for expressing their unity in the sphere of moral and spiritual values.

For this purpose, and also in order to highlight the ecumenical importance of mixed marriages which are fully lived in the faith of the two Christian spouses, an effort should be made to establish cordial cooperation between the Catholic and the non-Catholic ministers from the time that preparations begin for the marriage and the wedding ceremony, even though this does not always prove easy.

With regard to the sharing of the non-Catholic party in Eucharistic Communion, the norms issued by the Secretariat for Promoting Christian Unity should be followed.[179]

Today in many parts of the world marriages between Catholics and non-baptized persons are growing in numbers. In many such marriages the non-baptized partner professes another religion, and his beliefs are to be treated with respect, in accordance with the principles set out in the Second Vatican Council's Declaration *Nostra Aetate* on relations with non-Christian religions. But in many other such marriages, particularly in secularized societies, the non-baptized person professes no religion at all. In these marriages there is a need for Episcopal Conferences and for individual Bishops to ensure that there are proper pastoral safeguards for the faith of the Catholic partner and for the free exercise of his faith, above all in regard to his duty to do all in his power to ensure the Catholic baptism and education of the children of the marriage. Likewise the Catholic must be assisted in every possible way to offer within his family a genuine witness to the Catholic faith and to Catholic life.

79. In its solicitude to protect the family in all its dimensions, not only the religious one, the Synod of Bishops did not fail to take into careful consideration certain situations which are irregular in a religious sense and often in the civil sense too. Such situations, as a result of today's rapid cultural changes, are unfortunately becoming widespread also among Catholics, with no little damage to the very institution of the family and to society, of which the family constitutes the basic cell.

a) *Trial marriages*

80. A first example of an irregular situation is provided by what are called "trial marriages", which many people today would like to justify by attributing a certain value to them. But human reason leads one to see that they are unacceptable, by showing the unconvincing nature of carrying out an "experiment" with human beings, whose dignity demands that they should be always and solely the term of a self-giving love without limitations of time or of any other circumstance.

The Church, for her part, cannot admit such a kind of union, for further and original reasons which derive from faith. For, in the first place, the gift of the body in the sexual relationship is a real symbol of the giving of the whole person: such a giving, moreover, in the present state of things cannot take place with full truth without the concourse of the love of charity, given by Christ. In the second place, marriage between two baptized persons is a real symbol of the union of Christ and the Church, which is not a temporary or "trial" union but one which is eternally faithful. Therefore between two baptized persons there can exist only an indissoluble marriage.

Such a situation cannot usually be overcome unless the human person, from childhood, with the help of Christ's grace and without fear, has been trained to dominate concupiscence from the beginning and to establish relationships of genuine love with other people. This cannot be secured without a true education in genuine love and in the right use of sexuality, such as to introduce the human person in every aspect, and therefore the bodily aspect too, into the fullness of the mystery of Christ.

It will be very useful to investigate the causes of this phenomenon, including its psychological and sociological aspect, in order to find the proper remedy.

b) *De facto free unions*

81. This means unions without any publicly recognized insti-

tutional bond, either civil or religious. This phenomenon, which is becoming ever more frequent, cannot fail to concern pastors of souls, also because it may be based on widely varying factors, the consequences of which may perhaps be containable by suitable action.

Some people consider themselves almost forced into a free union by difficult economic, cultural or religious situations, on the grounds that, if they contracted a regular marriage, they would be exposed to some form of harm, would lose economic advantages, would be discriminated against, etc. In other cases, however, one encounters people who scorn, rebel against or reject society, the institution of the family and the social and political order, or who are solely seeking pleasure. Then there are those who are driven to such situations by extreme ignorance or poverty, sometimes by a conditioning due to situations of real injustice, or by a certain psychological immaturity that makes them uncertain or afraid to enter into a stable and definitive union. In some countries, traditional customs presume that the true and proper marriage will take place only after a period of cohabitation and the birth of the first child.

Each of these elements presents the Church with arduous pastoral problems, by reason of the serious consequences deriving from them, both religious and moral (the loss of the religious sense of marriage seen in the light of the Covenant of God with his people; deprivation of the grace of the sacrament; grave scandal), and also social consequences (the destruction of the concept of the family; the weakening of the sense of fidelity, also towards society; possible psychological damage to the children; the strengthening of selfishness).

The pastors and the ecclesial community should take care to become acquainted with such situations and their actual causes, case by case. They should make tactful and respectful contact with the couples concerned, and enlighten them patiently, correct them charitably and show them the witness of Christian family life, in such a way as to smooth the path for them to regularize their situation. But above all there must be a campaign of prevention, by fostering the sense of fidelity in the whole moral and religious training of the young, instructing them concerning the conditions and structures that favour such fidelity, without which there is no true freedom; they must be helped to reach spiritual maturity and enabled to understand the rich human and supernatural reality of marriage as a sacrament.

The People of God should also make approaches to the public authorities, in order that the latter may resist these tendencies which divide society and are harmful to the dignity, security and welfare of the citizens as individuals, and they must try to ensure that public opinion is not led to undervalue the institutional importance of marriage and the family. And since in many regions young people are unable to get married properly because of extreme poverty deriving from unjust or inadequate social and economic structures, society and the public authorities should favour legitimate marriage by means of a series of social and political actions which will guarantee a family wage, by issuing directives ensuring housing fitting for family life and by creating opportunities for work and life.

c) Catholics in civil marriages

82. There are increasing cases of Catholics who, for ideological or practical reasons, prefer to contract a merely civil marriage, and who reject or at least defer religious marriage. Their situation cannot of course be likened to that of people simply living together without any bond at all, because in the present case there is at least a certain commitment to a properly-defined and probably stable state of life, even though the possibility of a future divorce is often present in the minds of those entering a civil marriage. By seeking public recognition of their bond on the part of the State, such couples show that they are ready to accept not only its advantages but also its obligations. Nevertheless, not even this situation is acceptable to the Church.

The aim of pastoral action will be to make these people understand the need for consistency between their choice of life and the faith that they profess, and to try to do everything possible to induce them to regularize their situation in the light of Christian principles. While treating them with great charity and bringing them into the life of the respective communities, the pastors of the Church will regrettably not be able to admit them to the sacraments.

d) Separated or divorced persons who have not remarried

83. Various reasons can unfortunately lead to the often irreparable breakdown of valid marriages. These include mutual lack of understanding and the inability to enter into interpersonal relationships. Obviously, separation must be considered as a last resort, after all other reasonable attempts at reconciliation have proved vain.

Loneliness and other difficulties are often the lot of separated spouses, especially when they are the innocent parties. The ecclesial community must support such people more than ever. It must give them much respect, solidarity, understanding and practical help, so that they can preserve their fidelity even in their difficult situation; and it must help them to cultivate the need to forgive which is inherent in Christian love, and to be ready perhaps to return to their former married life.

The situation is similar for people who have undergone divorce, but, being well aware that the valid marriage bond is indissoluble, refrain from becoming involved in a new union and devote themselves solely to carrying out their family duties and the responsibilities of Christian life. In such cases their example of fidelity and Christian consistency takes on particular value as a witness before the world and the Church. Here it is even more necessary for the Church to offer continual love and assistance, without there being any obstacle to admission to the sacraments.

e) Divorced persons who have remarried

84. Daily experience unfortunately shows that people who have obtained a divorce usually intend to enter into a new union, obviously not with a Catholic religious ceremony. Since this is an evil that, like the others, is affecting more and more Catholics as well, the problem must be faced with resolution and without delay. The Synod Fathers studied it expressly. The Church, which was set up to lead to salvation all people and especially the baptized, cannot abandon to their own devices those who have been previously bound by sacramental marriage and who have attempted a second marriage. The Church will therefore make untiring efforts to put at their disposal her means of salvation.

Pastors must know that, for the sake of truth, they are obliged to exercise careful discernment of situations. There is in fact a difference between those who have sincerely tried to save their first marriage and have been unjustly abandoned, and those who through their own grave fault have destroyed a canonically valid marriage. Finally, there are those who have entered into a second union for the sake of the children's upbringing, and who are sometimes subjectively certain in conscience that their previous and irreparably destroyed marriage had never been valid.

Together with the Synod, I earnestly call upon pastors and the whole community of the faithful to help the divorced, and with solicitous care to make sure that they do not consider themselves as separated from the Church, for as baptized persons they can, and indeed must, share in her life. They should be encouraged to listen to the word of God, to attend the Sacrifice of the Mass, to persevere in prayer, to contribute to works of charity and to community efforts in favour of justice, to bring up their children in the Christian faith, to cultivate the spirit and practice of penance and thus implore, day by day, God's grace. Let the Church pray for them, encourage them and show herself a merciful mother, and thus sustain them in faith and hope.

However, the Church reaffirms her practice, which is based upon Sacred Scripture, of not admitting to Eucharistic Communion divorced persons who have remarried. They are unable to be admitted thereto from the fact that their state and condition of life objectively contradict that union of love between Christ and the Church which is signified and effected by the Eucharist. Besides this, there is another special pastoral reason: if these people were admitted to the Eucharist, the faithful would be led into error and confusion regarding the Church's teaching about the indissolubility of marriage.

Reconciliation in the sacrament of Penance, which would open the way to the Eucharist, can only be granted to those who, repenting of having broken the sign of the Covenant and of fidelity to Christ, are sincerely ready to undertake a way of life that is no longer in contradiction to the indissolubility of marriage. This means, in practice, that when, for serious reasons such as for example the children's upbringing, a man and a woman cannot satisfy the obligation to separate, they "take on themselves the duty to live in complete continence, that is, by abstinence from the acts proper to married couples".[180]

Similarly, the respect due to the sacrament of Matrimony, to the couples themselves and their families, and also to the community of the faithful, forbids any pastor, for whatever reason or pretext even of a pastoral nature, to perform ceremonies of any kind for divorced people who remarry. Such ceremonies would give the impression of the celebration of a new sacramentally valid marriage, and would thus lead people into error concerning the indissolubility of a validly contracted marriage.

By acting in this way, the Church professes her own fidelity to Christ and to his truth. At the same time she shows motherly concern for these children of hers, especially those who, through no fault of their own, have been abandoned by their legitimate partner.

With firm confidence she believes that those who have rejected the Lord's command and are still living in this state will be able to obtain from God the grace of conversion and salvation, provided that they have persevered in prayer, penance and charity.

85. I wish to add a further word for a category of people

whom, as a result of the actual circumstances in which they are living, and this often not through their own deliberate wish, I consider particularly close to the Heart of Christ and deserving of the affection and active solicitude of the Church and of pastors.

There exist in the world countless people who unfortunately cannot in any sense claim membership of what could be called in the proper sense a family. Large sections of humanity live in conditions of extreme poverty, in which promiscuity, lack of housing, the irregular nature and instability of relationships and the extreme lack of education make it possible in practice to speak of a true family. There are others who, for various reasons, have been left alone in the world. And yet for all of these people there exists a "good news of the family".

On behalf of those living in extreme poverty, I have already spoken of the urgent need to work courageously in order to find solutions, also at the political level, which will make it possible to help them and to overcome this inhuman condition of degradation.

It is a task that faces the whole of society but in a special way the authorities, by reason of their position and the responsibilities flowing therefrom, and also families, which must show great understanding and willingness to help.

For those who have no natural family the doors of the great family which is the Church—the Church which finds concrete expression in the diocesan and the parish family, in ecclesial basic communities and in movements of the apostolate—must be opened even wider. No one is without a family in this world: the Church is a home and family for everyone, especially those who "labour and are heavy laden".[181]

CONCLUSION

86. At the end of this Apostolic Exhortation my thoughts turn with earnest solicitude:

to you, married couples, to you, fathers and mothers of families;

to you, young men and women, the future and the hope of the Church and the world, destined to be the dynamic central nucleus of the family in the approaching third millennium;

to you, venerable and dear Brothers in the Episcopate and in the priesthood, beloved sons and daughters in the religious life, souls consecrated to the Lord, who bear witness before married couples to the ultimate reality of the love of God;

to you, upright men and women, who for any reason whatever give thought to the fate of the family.

The future of humanity passes by way of the family.

It is therefore indispensable and urgent that every person of good will should endeavour to save and foster the values and requirements of the family.

I feel that I must ask for a particular effort in this field from the sons and daughters of the Church. Faith gives them full knowledge of God's wonderful plan: they therefore have an extra reason for caring for the reality that is the family in this time of trial and grace.

They must *show the family special love*. This is an injunction that calls for concrete action.

Loving the family means being able to appreciate its values and capabilities, fostering them always. Loving the family means identifying the dangers and the evils that menace it, in order to overcome them. Loving the family means endeavouring to create for it an environment favourable for its development. The modern Christian family is often tempted to be discouraged and is distressed at the growth of its difficulties; it is an eminent form of love to give it back its reasons for confidence in itself, in the riches that it possesses by nature and grace, and in the mission that God has entrusted to it. "Yes indeed, the families of today must be called back to their original position. They must follow Christ".[182]

Christians also have the mission of *proclaiming with joy and conviction the Good News about the family*, for the family absolutely needs to hear ever anew and to understand ever more deeply the authentic words that reveal its identity, its inner resources and the importance of its mission in the City of God and in that of man.

The Church knows the path by which the family can reach the heart of the deepest truth about itself. The Church has learned this path at the school of Christ and the school of history interpreted in the light of the Spirit. She does not impose it but she feels an urgent need to propose it to everyone without fear and indeed with great confidence and hope, although she knows that the Good News includes the subject of the Cross. But it is through the Cross that the family can attain the fullness of its being and the perfection of its love.

Finally, I wish to call on all Christians to *collaborate cordially and courageously* with all people of good will who are serving the family in accordance with their responsibilities. The individuals and groups, movements and associations in the Church which devote themselves to the family's welfare, acting in the

Church's name and under her inspiration, often find themselves side by side with other individuals and institutions working for the same ideal. With faithfulness to the values of the Gospel and of the human person and with respect for lawful pluralism in initiatives this collaboration can favour a more rapid and integral advancement of the family.

And now, at the end of my pastoral message, which is intended to draw everyone's attention to the demanding yet fascinating roles of the Christian family, I wish to invoke the protection of the Holy Family of Nazareth.

Through God's mysterious design, it was in that family that the Son of God spent long years of a hidden life. It is therefore the prototype and example for all Christian families. It was unique in the world. Its life was passed in anonymity and silence in a little town in Palestine. It underwent trials of poverty, persecution and exile. It glorified God in an incomparably exalted and pure way. And it will not fail to help Christian families—indeed, all the families in the world—to be faithful to their day-to-day duties, to bear the cares and tribulations of life, to be open and generous to the needs of others, and to fulfil with joy the plan of God in their regard.

Saint Joseph was "a just man", a tireless worker, the upright guardian of those entrusted to his care. May he always guard, protect and enlighten families.

May the Virgin Mary, who is the Mother of the Church, also be the Mother of "the Church of the home". Thanks to her motherly aid, may each Christian family really become a "little Church" in which the mystery of the Church of Christ is mirrored and given a new life. May she, the Handmaid of the Lord, be an example of humble and generous acceptance of the will of God. May she, the Sorrowful Mother at the foot of the Cross, comfort the sufferings and dry the tears of those in distress because of the difficulties of their families.

May Christ the Lord, the Universal King, the King of Families, be present in every Christian home as he was at Cana, bestowing light, joy, serenity and strength. On the solemn day dedicated to his Kingship I beg of him that every family may generously make its own contribution to the coming of his Kingdom in the world —"a kingdom of truth and life, a kingdom of holiness and grace, a kingdom of justice, love, and peace",[183] towards which history is journeying.

I entrust each family to him, to Mary, and to Joseph. To their hands and their hearts I offer this Exhortation: may it be they who present it to you, venerable Brothers and beloved sons and daughters, and may it be they who open your hearts to the light that the Gospel sheds on every family.

I assure you all of my constant prayers and I cordially impart the Apostolic Blessing to each and every one of you, in the name of the Father, and of the Son, and of the Holy Spirit.

*Translation by Vatican Press Office.

1. Cf. Second Vatican Ecumenical Council, Pastoral Constitution on the Church in the Modern World *Gaudium et Spes*, 52.
2. Cf. John Paul II, Homily for the Opening of the Sixth Synod of Bishops (26 September 1980), 2: *AAS* 72 (1980), 1008.
3. Cf. *Gen* 1–2.
4. Cf. *Eph* 5.
5. Cf. Second Vatican Ecumenical Council, Pastoral Constitution on the Church in the Modern World *Gaudium et Spes*, 47; Pope John Paul II, Letter *Appropinquat Iam* (15 August 1980), 1: *AAS* 72 (1980), 791.
6. Cf. *Mt* 19:4.
7. Cf. Second Vatican Ecumenical Council, Pastoral Constitution on the Church in the Modern World *Gaudium et Spes*, 47.
8. Cf. John Paul II, Address to the Council of the General Secretariat of the Synod of Bishops (23 February 1980): *Insegnamenti di Giovanni Paolo II*, III, 1 (1980), 472–476.
9. Cf. Second Vatican Ecumenical Council, Pastoral Constitution on the Church in the Modern World *Gaudium et Spes*, 4.
10. Cf. Second Vatican Ecumenical Council, Dogmatic Constitution on the Church *Lumen Gentium*, 12.
11. Cf. *1 Jn* 2:20.
12. Second Vatican Ecumenical Council, Dogmatic Constitution on the Church *Lumen Gentium*, 35.
13. Cf. Second Vatican Ecumenical Council, Dogmatic Constitution on the Church *Lumen Gentium*, 12; Sacred Congregation for the Doctrine of the Faith, Declaration *Mysterium Ecclesiae*, 2: *AAS* 65 (1973), 398–400.
14. Cf. Second Vatican Ecumenical Council, Dogmatic Constitution on the Church *Lumen Gentium* 12; Dogmatic Constitution on Divine Revelation *Dei Verbum*, 10.
15. Cf. John Paul II, Homily for the opening of the Sixth Synod of Bishops (26 September 1980), 3: *AAS* 72 (1980), 1008.
16. Cf. Saint Augustine, *De Civitate Dei*, XIV, 28: *CSEL* 40, II, 56–57.
17. Pastoral Constitution on the Church in the Modern World *Gaudium et Spes*, 15.
18. Cf. *Eph* 3:8; Second Vatican Ecumenical Council, *Gaudium et Spes*, 44; Decree on the Church's Missionary Activity *Ad Gentes*, 15, 22.
19. Cf. *Mt* 19:4–6.
20. Cf. *Gen* 1:26–27.
21. *1 Jn* 4:8.
22. Cf. Second Vatican Ecumenical Council, Pastoral Constitution on the Church in the Modern World *Gaudium et Spes*, 12.
23. Cf. *ibid.*, 48.
24. Cf. e.g. *Hos* 2:21; *Jer* 3:6–13; *Is* 54.
25. Cf. *Ezek* 16:25.
26. Cf. *Hos* 3.
27. Cf. *Gen* 2:24; *Mt* 19:5.

28. Cf. *Eph* 5:32-33.

29. Tertullian, *Ad Uxorem*, II, VIII, 6-8: *CCL* I, 393.

30. Cf. Ecumenical Council of Trent, Session XXIV, canon 1: I. D. Mansi, *Sacrorum Conciliorum Nova et Amplissima Collectio*, 33, 149-150.

31. Cf. Second Vatican Ecumenical Council, Pastoral Constitution on the Church in the Modern World *Gaudium et Spes*, 48.

32. John Paul II, Address to the Delegates of the Centre de Liaison des Equipes de Recherche (3 November 1979), 3: *Insegnamenti di Giovanni Paolo II*, II, 2 (1979), 1038.

33. *Ibid.*, 4: *loc cit.*, 1032.

34. Cf. Second Vatican Ecumenical Council, Pastoral Constitution on the Church in the Modern World *Gaudium et Spes*, 50.

35. Cf. *Gen* 2:24.

36. *Eph* 3:15.

37. Cf. Second Vatican Ecumenical Council, Pastoral Constitution on the Church in the Modern World *Gaudium et Spes*, 78.

38. Saint John Chrysostom, *Virginity*, X: *PG* 48:540.

39. Cf. *Mt* 22:30.

40. Cf. *1 Cor* 7:32-35.

41. Second Vatican Ecumenical Council, Decree on Renewal of Religious Life *Perfectae Caritatis*, 12.

42. Cf. Pius XII, Encyclical *Sacra Virginitas*, II: *AAS* 46 (1954), 174 ff.

43. Cf. John Paul II, Letter *Novo Incipiente* (8 April 1979), 9: *AAS* 71 (1979), 410-411.

44. Second Vatican Ecumenical Council, Pastoral Constitution on the Church in the Modern World *Gaudium et Spes*, 48.

45. Encyclical *Redemptor Hominis*, 10: *AAS* 71 (1979), 274.

46. *Mt* 19:6; cf. *Gen* 2:24.

47. Cf. John Paul II, Address to Married People at Kinshasa (3 May 1980), 4: *AAS* 72 (1980), 426-427.

48. Pastoral Constitution on the Church in the Modern World *Gaudium et Spes*, 49; cf. John Paul II, Address to Married People at Kinshasa (3 May 1980), 4: *loc. cit.*

49. Second Vatican Ecumenical Council, Pastoral Constitution on the Church in the Modern World *Gaudium et Spes*, 48.

50. Cf. *Eph* 5:25.

51. *Mt* 19:8.

52. *Rev* 3:14.

53. Cf. *2 Cor* 1:20.

54. Cf. *Jn* 13:1.

55. *Mt* 19:6.

56. *Rom* 8:29.

57. Saint Thomas Aquinas, *Summa Theologiae*, II-II, q. 14, art. 2, ad 4.

58. Second Vatican Ecumenical Council, Dogmatic Constitution on the Church *Lumen Gentium*, 11; cf. Decree on the Apostolate of the Laity *Apostolicam Actuositatem*, 11.

59. Second Vatican Ecumenical Council, Pastoral Constitution on the Church in the Modern World *Gaudium et Spes*, 52.

60. Cf. *Eph* 6:1-4; *Col* 3:20-21.

61. Cf. Second Vatican Ecumenical Council, Pastoral Constitution on the Church in the Modern World *Gaudium et Spes*, 48.

62. *Jn* 17:21.

63. Cf. Second Vatican Ecumenical Council, Pastoral Constitution on the Church in the Modern World *Gaudium et Spes*, 24.

64. *Gen* 1:27.
65. *Gal* 3:26, 28.
66. Cf. John Paul II Encyclical *Laborem Exercens*, 19: *AAS* 73 (1981), 625.
67. *Gen* 2:18.
68. *Gen* 2:23.
69. Saint Ambrose, *Exameron*, V, 7, 19: *CSEL* 32, I, 154.
70. Paul VI, Encyclical *Humanae Vitae* 9: *AAS* 60 (1968), 486.
71. Cf. *Eph* 5:25.
72. Cf. John Paul II, Homily to the faithful of Terni (19 March 1981), 3–5: *AAS* 73 (1981), 268–271.
73. Cf. *Eph* 3:15.
74. Cf. Second Vatican Ecumenical Council, Pastoral Constitution on the Church in the Modern World *Gaudium et Spes*, 52.
75. *Lk* 18:16; cf. *Mt* 19:14; *Mk* 18:16.
76. John Paul II, Address to the General Assembly of the United Nations (2 October 1979), 21; *AAS* 71 (1979), 1159.
77. *Lk* 2:52.
78. Cf. Second Vatican Ecumenical Council, Pastoral Constitution on the Church in the Modern World *Gaudium et Spes*, 48.
79. John Paul II, Address to the participants in the International Forum on Active Aging (5 September 1980), 5: *Insegnamenti di Giovanni Paolo II*, III, 2 (1980), 539.
80. *Gen* 1:28.
81. Cf. *Gen* 5:1–3.
82. Second Vatican Ecumenical Council, Pastoral Constitution on the Church in the Modern World *Gaudium et Spes*, 50.
83. *Propositio* 21. Section 11 of the Encyclical *Humanae Vitae* ends with the statement: "The Church, calling people back to the observance of the norms of the natural law, as interpreted by her constant doctrine, teaches that each and every marriage act must remain open to the transmission of life (*ut quilibet matrimonii usus ad vitam humanam procreandam per se destinatus permaneat*)": *AAS* 60 (1968), 488.
84. Cf. *2 Cor* 1:19; *Rev* 3:14.
85. Cf. the Sixth Synod of Bishops' Message to Christian Families in the Modern World (24 October 1980), 5.
86. Pastoral Constitution on the Church in the Modern World *Gaudium et Spes*, 51.
87. Encyclical *Humanae Vitae*, 7: *AAS* 60 (1968), 485.
88. *Ibid.*, 12: *loc. cit.*, 488–489.
89. *Ibid.*, 14: *loc. cit.*, 490.
90. *Ibid.*, 13: *loc. cit.*, 489.
91. Cf. Second Vatican Ecumenical Council, Pastoral Constitution on the Church in the Modern World *Gaudium et Spes*, 51.
92. Encyclical *Humanae Vitae*, 29: *AAS* 60 (1968), 501.
93. Cf. *ibid.*, 25: *loc. cit.* 498–499.
94. *Ibid.*, 21: *loc. cit.*, 496.
95. John Paul II, Homily at the close of the Sixth Synod of Bishops (25 October 1980), 8: *AAS* 72 (1980), 1083.
96. Cf. Paul VI, Encyclical *Humanae Vitae*, 28: *AAS* 60 (1968), 501.
97. Cf. John Paul II, Address to the Delegates of the Centre de Liaison des Equipes de Recherche (3 November 1979), 9: *Insegnamenti de Giovanni Paolo II*, II, 2 (1979), 1035; and cf. Address to the participants in the First Congress for the Family of Africa and Europe (15 January 1981): *L'Osservatore Romano*, 16 January 1981.

98. Encyclical *Humanae Vitae*, 25: *AAS* 60 (1968), 499.

99. Declaration on Christian Education *Gravissimum Educationis*, 3.

100. Second Vatican Ecumenical Council, Pastoral Constitution on the Church in the Modern World *Gaudium et Spes*, 35.

101. Saint Thomas Aquinas, *Summa contra Gentiles*, IV, 58.

102. Declaration on Christian Education *Gravissimum Educationis*, 2.

103. Apostolic Exhortation *Evangelii Nuntiandi*, 71: *AAS* 68 (1976), 60–61.

104. Cf. Second Vatican Ecumenical Council, Declaration on Christian Education *Gravissimum Educationis*, 3.

105. Second Vatican Ecumenical Council, Decree on the Apostolate of the Laity *Apostolicam Actuositatem*, 11.

106. Pastoral Constitution on the Church in the Modern World *Gaudium et Spes*, 52.

107. Cf. Second Vatican Ecumenical Council, Decree on the Apostolate of the Laity *Apostolicam Actuositatem*, 11.

108. *Rom* 12:13.

109. *Mt* 10:42.

110. Cf. Pastoral Constitution on the Church in the Modern World *Gaudium et Spes*, 30.

111. Second Vatican Ecumenical Council, Declaration on Religious Freedom *Dignitatis Humanae*, 5.

112. Cf. *Propositio* 42.

113. Second Vatican Ecumenical Council, Dogmatic Constitution on the Church *Lumen Gentium*, 31.

114. Cf. Second Vatican Ecumenical Council, Dogmatic Constitution on the Church *Lumen Gentium*, 11; Decree on the Apostolate of the Laity *Apostolicam Actuositatem*, 11; Pope John Paul II, Homily for the opening of the Sixth Synod of Bishops (26 September 1980), 3: *AAS* 72 (1980), 1008.

115. Second Vatican Ecumenical Council, Dogmatic Constitution on the Church *Lumen Gentium*, 11.

116. Cf. *ibid.*, 41.

117. *Acts* 4:32.

118. Cf. Paul VI, Encyclical *Humanae Vitae*, 9: *AAS* 60 (1968), 486–487.

119. Pastoral Constitution on the Church in the Modern World *Gaudium et Spes*, 48.

120. Cf. Second Vatican Council, Dogmatic Constitution on Divine Revelation *Dei Verbum*, 1.

121. *Rom* 16:26.

122. Cf. Paul VI, Encyclical *Humanae Vitae*, 25: *AAS* 60 (1968), 498.

123. Apostolic Exhortation *Evangelii Nuntiandi*, 71: *AAS* 68 (1976), 60–61.

124. Cf. Address to the Third General Assembly of the Bishops of Latin America (28 January 1979), IV a: *AAS* 71 (1979), 204.

125. Second Vatican Ecumenical Council, Dogmatic Constitution on the Church *Lumen Gentium*, 35.

126. John Paul II, Apostolic Exhortation *Catechesi Tradendae*, 68: *AAS* 71 (1979), 1334.

127. Cf. *ibid.*, 36: *loc. cit.* 1308.

128. Cf. *1 Cor* 12:4–6; *Eph* 4:12–13.

129. *Mk* 16:15.

130. Cf. Second Vatican Ecumenical Council, Dogmatic Constitution on the Church *Lumen Gentium*, 11.

131. *Acts* 1:8.

132. Cf. *1 Pt* 3:1-2.
133. Second Vatican Ecumenical Council, Dogmatic Constitution on the Church *Lumen Gentium*, 35; cf. Decree on the Apostolate of the Laity *Apostolicam Actuositatem*, 11.
134. Cf. *Acts* 18; *Rom* 16:3-4.
135. Cf. Second Vatican Ecumenical Council, Decree on the Church's Missionary Activity *Ad Gentes*, 39.
136. Second Vatican Ecumenical Council, Decree on the Apostolate of the Laity *Apostolicam Actuositatem*, 30.
137. Cf. Second Vatican Ecumenical Council, Dogmatic Constitution on the Church *Lumen Gentium*, 10.
138. Second Vatican Ecumenical Council, Pastoral Constitution on the Church in the Modern World *Gaudium et Spes*, 49.
139. *Ibid.*, 48.
140. Cf. Second Vatican Ecumenical Council, Dogmatic Constitution on the Church *Lumen Gentium*, 41.
141. Second Vatican Ecumenical Council, Constitution on the Sacred Liturgy *Sacrosanctum Concilium*, 59.
142. Cf. *1 Pt* 2:5; Second Vatican Ecumenical Council, Dogmatic Constitution on the Church *Lumen Gentium*, 34.
143. Second Vatican Ecumenical Council, Dogmatic Constitution on the Church *Lumen Gentium*, 34.
144. Constitution on the Sacred Liturgy *Sacrosanctum Concilium*, 78.
145. Cf. *Jn* 19:34.
146. Section 25: *AAS* 60 (1968), 499.
147. *Eph* 2:4.
148. Cf. John Paul II, Encyclical *Dives in Misericordia*, 13: *AAS* 72 (1980), 1218-1219.
149. *1 Pt* 2:5.
150. *Mt* 18:19-20.
151. Second Vatican Ecumenical Council, Declaration on Christian Education *Gravissimum Educationis*, 3; cf. Pope John Paul II, Apostolic Exhortation *Catechesi Tradendae*, 36: *AAS* 71 (1979), 1308.
152. General Audience Address, 11 August 1976: *Insegnamenti di Paolo VI*, XIV (1976), 640.
153. Cf. Constitution on the Sacred Liturgy *Sacrosanctum Concilium*, 12.
154. Cf. *Institutio Generalis de Liturgia Honorum*, 27.
155. Paul VI, Apostolic Exhortation *Marialis Cultus*, 52, 54: *AAS* 66 (1974), 160-161.
156. John Paul II, Address at the Mentorella Shrine (29 October 1978): *Insegnamenti di Giovanni Paolo II*, I (1978), 78-79.
157. Cf. Second Vatican Ecumenical Council, Decree on the Apostolate of the Laity *Apostolicam Actuositatem*, 4.
158. Cf. John Paul I, Address to the Bishops of the Twelfth Pastoral Region of the United States of America (21 September 1978): *AAS* 70 (1978), 767.
159. *Rom* 8:2.
160. *Rom* 5:5.
161. Cf. *Mk* 10:45.
162. Second Vatican Ecumenical Council, Dogmatic Constitution on the Church *Lumen Gentium* 36.
163. Decree on the Apostolate of the Laity *Apostolicam Actuositatem*, 8.
164. Cf. the Sixth Synod of Bishops' Message to Christian Families in the Modern World (24 October 1980), 12.

165. Cf. John Paul II, Address to the Third General Assembly of the Bishops of Latin America (28 January 1979), IV a: *AAS* 71 (1979), 204.

166. Cf. Second Vatican Ecumenical Council, Constitution on the Sacred Liturgy *Sacrosanctum Concilium*, 10.

167. Cf. *Ordo Celebrandi Matrimonium*, 17.

168. Cf. Second Vatican Ecumenical Council, Constitution on the Sacred Liturgy *Sacrosanctum Concilium*, 59.

169. Second Vatican Ecumenical Council, Decree on Renewal of Religious Life *Perfectae Caritatis*, 12.

170. John Paul II, Address to the Confederation of Family Advisory Bureaux of Christian Inspiration (29 November 1980), 3–4: *Insegnamenti di Giovanni Paolo II*, III, 2 (1980), 1453–1454.

171. Paul VI, Message for the Third Social Communications Day (7 April 1969): *AAS* 61 (1969), 455.

172. John Paul II, Message for the 1980 World Social Communications Day (1 May 1980): *Insegnamenti di Giovanni Paolo II*, III, 1 (1980), 1042.

173. John Paul II, Message for the 1981 World Social Communications Day (10 May 1981), 5: *L'Osservatore Romano*, 22 May 1981.

174. *Ibid*.

175. Paul VI, Message for the Third Social Communications Day: *AAS* 61 (1969), 456.

176. *Ibid*.

177. John Paul II, Message for the 1980 World Social Communications Day: *Insegnamenti di Giovanni Paolo II*, III, 1 (1980), 1044.

178. Cf. Paul VI, Motu Proprio *Matrimonia Mixta*, 4–5: *AAS* 62 (1970), 257–259; John Paul II, Address to the participants in the plenary meeting of the Secretariat for Promoting Christian Unity (13 November 1981): *L'Osservatore Romano*, 14 November 1981.

179. Instruction *In Quibus Rerum Circumstantiis* (15 June 1972): *AAS* 64 (1972), 518–525; Note of 17 October 1973: *AAS* 65 (1973), 616–619.

180. John Paul II, Homily at the close of the Sixth Synod of Bishops, 7 (25 October 1980): *AAS* 72 (1980), 1082.

181. *Mt* 11:28.

182. John Paul II, Letter *Appropinquat Iam* (15 August 1980), 1: *AAS* 72 (1980), 791.

183. The Roman Missal, Preface of Christ the King.

INDEX

Abandoned families, 882
Abnormalities, congenital, 519
   abortion and, 446, 449, 521-22
   euthanasia and, 512
Abortion, 404, 441-53, 510, 512,
   700, 819, 839
   abnormal fetuses, 521-22
   feminist movement and,
     446-47
   legal considerations, 447-49
Absolution, 38
   general, 20, 62-63
Abstinence, 5, 6-7
   defined, 8
Accidents, disability after,
     See Disabled persons
Acclamations
   children's Masses, 53, 54, 55,
     56, 57
   Eucharistic, 77, 95
Active life, contemplation and,
     246-47, 248
Acts of the Apostles, 138
   Paschal time readings from,
     146
   Pentecost account, 146, 147
Adam's Fall, 5
Adaptability, 322
Administrative work, women in,
   324
Adolescents, 859
   autonomy and, 579-80
   catechesis for, 574, 577-81,
     730, 785-86
   meaning of life and, 579
   values and, 579
Adoption, 826
Adultery, 823
Adults, catechesis for, 574,
     582-85, 730, 788
Advent readings, 143
Africa, evangelization in, 368
Age, catechesis varied by, 578
Aged, *see* Elderly
Albigensians, 463, 465, 469, 470
Alleluia, 125-26
Almsgiving, 2, 5, 6-7
Altar servers, 98, 99
Ambo (Pulpit), 128

Ambrose, St., 104, 466, 768,
   780, 835
Amen, 97
   after Eucharistic Prayer, 95
Anabaptists, 105
Anamnesis, 76
Angels, 389
   existence of, 458, 462, 463
   fall of, 462, 463
Animation of foetus, 444-45
Animism, 535
Anna (prophetess), 3
Announcements, 127
Anointing, baptismal, 23, 33
Anointing of the Sick, 13-19,
   475, 561
   Paul VI on, 13-14
   scriptural bases, 13
Anthropology
   doctrine and, 663
   evangelization and, 724-25
Anti-war activities, 700, 707-8
Apologetics, 772
Apostles, 678-79
   forgiveness of sins allowed to,
     36
   male exclusively, 334
   marital status of, 286, 291
Apostolic college, 598-99
Apostolic Tradition, 104
Aquinas, St. Thomas, 107, 339,
   443, 831, 848
Armed forces chaplains, 161
Arms race, 696-97
Ascension Thursday readings,
   146
Asceticism, 251-52
   priesthood and, 304, 307
Ash Wednesday liturgy, 41
Assumption of Mary, 391
Athanagoras, 443
Athanasius, St., 465
Atheism, 534-35, 735, 736, 737
   schools oriented to, 650
Audiovisual materials for
   catechesis, 593, 594-95
Augustine, St., 346, 819
   on baptism, 104, 105, 106-7

899